Oddball
Sports Yearbook
2001

Editor **Peter Nichols**

Deputy Editor **Michael Hughes**

PUBLISHING

Published in Great Britain by Oddball Publishing Ltd, Brighton, East Sussex
Phone: 01273 722824   Fax: 01273 722824
e-mail: oddball@mistral.co.uk

Text design and layout by Oddball Publishing Ltd
using QuarkXpress on Apple Mac computers
Printed and bound in Great Britain by Biddles Ltd, Guildford and Kings Lynn

A catalogue record for this book is available from the British Library

ISBN 0-9524044-8-6

Introduction

Our apologies to the hundreds of readers who phoned when this edition didn't appear in the spring, all of whom (remarkably without exception) had nothing but kind comments to make about the book. It made us all the more determined to try to get the yearbook back on course for the next edition. That this edition is late is due, as they say in the business, to production problems. More specifically, over the past 12 months Oddball has has enjoyed an increasing demand for its sports research services, which left us with too little time for the book. We would have had to have commissioned work out, but we chose not to. The yearbook is a complex operation and keeping it in house (even if it's dreadfully late) ensures that we keep the quality as we would like it. For next year's (2002) edition we have put in place a structure that will allow us to get back to normal and bring the book out in spring.

Completely unconnected with the lateness of this edition is the fact that the book has changed its name. This is not because we fell out of love with Radio 5 Live, but because we thought it about time that we marketed the book with our own company's name.

As with every edition, our prime thanks to Penny Dain, Betty Maitland, Pat Molyneux, Chris Sainty, Brian Smith, David Smith, Iain Smith, Anna Wallace and Hugh Wallace are the mainstays and without whom there just wouldn't be a book. To Michael Hughes and Andrew Haslam, who are experts in every sport from octopush to orienteering. To Michael Butcher, Stephen Hughes and our associate editor Andy Edwards for their invaluable contributions.

Finally, good reader, our thanks to you.

Peter Nichols
Editor

• CONTENTS •

• GENERAL REVIEW •

REVIEW OF THE YEAR **1**
HEADLINES **7**
OLYMPIC GAMES **23**

• SPORT BY SPORT •

AMERICAN FOOTBALL **43**   ANGLING **47**   ARCHERY **48**
ASSOCIATION FOOTBALL **51**   ATHLETICS **90**   BADMINTON **106**
BASEBALL **110**   BASKETBALL **113**   BILLIARDS **118**   BOBSLEIGH/LUGE **120**
BOWLS **122**   BOXING **125**   CANOEING **131**   CRICKET **134**   CURLING **174**
CYCLING **175**   DARTS **182**   EQUESTRIANISM **183**   FENCING **185**   GOLF **186**
GYMNASTICS **209**   HOCKEY **213**   HORSE RACING **219**   ICE HOCKEY **239**   ICE SKATING **243**
JUDO **245**   MODERN PENTATHLON **248**   MOTOR CYCLING **251**   MOTOR RACING **261**
NETBALL **271**   ORIENTEERING **272**   ROWING **273**   RUGBY LEAGUE **279**
RUGBY UNION **286**   SAILING **298**   SKIING **302**   SNOOKER **305**
SPEED SKATING **309**   SQUASH **311**   SWIMMING **315**
TABLE TENNIS **323**   TENNIS **327**   TRIATHLON **349**
VOLLEYBALL **353**   WEIGHTLIFTING **354**
WRESTLING **355**   EXTRAS **357**

• ARCHIVE •

PAST CHAMPIONS BY SPORT **359**

• OBITUARY •

SPORTING OBITUARIES **464**

• PREVIEW •

CALENDAR OF EVENTS **471**

• GENERAL REFERENCE •

FEDERATIONS **489**
BRITISH WORLD CHAMPIONS **493**
SPORTS INTERNET DIRECTORY **495**
ABBREVIATIONS **505**

Review of the Year

Those who had endured Atlanta were reluctant to make early judgments in Sydney, but by the close of the first week, there were few who were not won over. At the end of the fortnight, the almost universal acclamation was that the Australians had given sport the best Olympic Games in history. Even the memories of balmy nights in Barcelona eight years before, of cava and calamares in the Barri Gotic, found their equal in Sydney.

It helped, too, that hardly a day passed without a British medal, and when we sat back in the Royal Oak at Paddington (Sydney, not west London), the cold midis downed with alarming ease, and counted up the score, Britain had won 28 medals in total, of which 11 were gold, more titles than at any Games since Antwerp in 1920, and even that comparison is a false one, for in Antwerp only 29 nations took part. In Sydney, it was almost 200.

The centre of attention was inevitably Steve Redgrave, latterly to become Sir Steven, who duly won his fifth successive Olympic title *(See Olympic and Rowing sections)*. You know you've made it when Princess Anne carries the cushion with your medal on and the president of the International Olympic Committee, plain old Mr Samaranch, presents it.

Redgrave retired after the Games, although he waited until November before he formally announced it. Redgrave's reputation is secure, but don't bet against Matthew Pinsent matching it. He collected his third Olympic title at Sydney, an achievement only surpassed by Redgrave and only matched by the two water polo players, Charles Smith and Paul Radmilovic (1908-1912-1920). For those of a statistical bent, we should add that Radmilovic also won a swimming relay gold in the London Olympics.

Redgrave may stand alone in British Olympic history, but his achievements were matched in Sydney by the unsung Birgit Fischer. The kayak canoeist won her first gold medal in the individual 500m at Moscow in 1980, when competing for East Germany. Fischer missed the following Games, when the Soviet states boycotted, but returned to win gold medals in the K2 and the K4, and a silver in the individual races at Seoul. Four years later, in Barcelona, she took her fourth Olympic title, when she won the individual for the second time, and added a silver in the K4. Her fifth title came in Atlanta in the K4 race, another silver coming in the K2. In Sydney, Fischer went one better than Redgrave winning two titles, the K2 and the K4 to bring her career tally to seven Olympic titles.

Fischer's world championship record is even more imperious; she has won 27 world canoeing titles, which could almost be a record for any sport, six silver medals and two bronze medals. After 23 years competing at the top level, Fischer retired after Sydney. There was no fabulous send-off, no honours, not even a drum roll.

The Athens organisers, who were in Sydney to learn, must have left the city stony-faced realising the act they had to follow. Throughout the year, the doubts re-surfaced at regular intervals about Athens' capability to mount the Games successfully. They'll manage it all right, but how they must have wished they could have followed Atlanta, not Sydney.

The warm glow left by the Olympic Games was rather different to national feelings in the aftermath of Euro 2000. England beat Germany in their second match, but it was a worthless win for the Romanians immediately despatched England from the competition. Three months later, after losing to Germany in a world cup qualifier (and thereby negating the only slight positive in the year) the architect of England's downfall resigned. Kevin Keegan was far too honest for his own good, when he announced to all and sundry that he had technical shortcomings as a manager. As Keegan's attributes (and failings) were clear to the FA when he was appointed, it leaves one wondering why he was left so exposed. Whatever, tactical defeciencies notwithstanding, he was still good enough for Manchester City, who would snap him up nine months later.

Euro 2000 was also the international swansong for Alan Shearer, who gave up playing for England before England gave up picking him. In all, he won 63 caps and scored 30 goals, including the one that beat Germany. His strike rate doesn't compare with Jimmy Greaves (44 goals from 57 games), but he did make a habit of scoring when it was needed.

England cricketers, by contrast, had a happy old time. Four series, four successes; you have to go back a few years to find anything comparable. Zimbabwe are not the strong men of world cricket, and given the circumstances back home, where the farming community was under siege from Robert Mugabe's land reform programme, players must have found it immensely difficult to focus on cricket. But a win's a win as far as English cricket goes, and it proved the basis for a change in fortune.

Not so long ago, the West Indies really were the strong men of world cricket, but only three legends were left in the team that lined up against England. Two of them - Curtley Ambrose and Courtney Walsh - were closing on retirement and the third, Brian Lara, was going through a whimsical phase. Even so, England's first series victory over the West Indies since 1969 came with surprising ease. At Lord's the West Indians were bowled out for 54, at Headingley for 61, their second and third worst totals ever.

The Pakistan series promised to go nowhere, and after two Tests and four days of the Third Test, it appeared to be keeping its promise. However, what happened on the final day will ensure that the series has its place in the folklore of the sport. A run chase in the evening darkness, when half of the Pakistan team in the field could not see the ball, secured a famous win.

Though England's mini-revival was big news at home, the cricket story of the year (almost of any year) was a much murkier tale. Hansie Cronje's confession to the King Commission in June that he had supplied information for money astounded his friends, fellow cricketers and fans alike. It was pure chance that Cronje was caught, a police investigation in India into illegal bookmaking chanced upon a Cronje call.

> ``Even when we increased the size of the picture, after being tipped off today, we couldn't be certain that we had seen what we thought we had seen"
>
> Matthew Engel, editor of Wisden Cricket Almanack 2000, after Leicestershire spinner Matthew Brimson exposed himself in a team photograph.

The story unravelled around the world, with implications for every Test nation. In the Indian investigation (the Madhavan Report), bookmaker M K Gupta made allegations against a string of international players, including Australia's Mark Waugh and Shane Warne, and England's Alex Stewart. In his native country, Gupta could tell his story without legally incriminating himself. Away from India, it would be different and Gupta would later refuse to substantiate any of the allegations, and Australia and England found that the players had no case to answer. Stung into action, the ICC set up its own worldwide investigation under the ex-policeman Sir Paul Condon, which began work in September.

England's rugby union team matched England's cricketers with a succession of victories, two of them against the very best. Scotland lost its way, though its single victory of substance at least came against England, and the Welsh revival, under Graham Henry, faltered. Italy was welcomed to the fold, for the first Six Nations and amazed the rugby world by winning a match. But perhaps, the most seminal moment of the year came when Jason Robinson signed up for Sale. Robinson was one of the few British stars in rugby league, and his desertion of league could well be a portent. League's very survival as a professional sport is now being questioned. Amalgamation could be closer than we think.

Tim Henman won two tournaments, but neither qualifies as major title, let alone a Grand Slam. One was in Brighton, where he probably earned more to turn up than to win, and the other was in Vienna. It remains a truly British phenomenon how Henman can continue to excite such hopes when he has never once realised them. The law of diminishing returns just doesn't apply to him. Greg Rusedski had a disastrous year, barely fit enough to jump a net most of the time. He didn't have to, though, because he didn't win a single tournament.

Venus Williams broke her Grand Slam duck in a serious fashion, winning Wimbledon and the US Open, the Olympic title, a month later, the icing on the cake. Pete Sampras won Wimbledon for the seventh time and passed Roy Emerson record of 12 Grand Slam wins. Sampras, you feel, may never win another. He's done enough.

Tiger Woods has only just begun, but his sequence of success genuinely qualifies as awesome, a word we are not inclined to use. Three Majors, six straight tournament wins at the end of the year, and a new contract with Nike. What more could a man desire before his 25th birthday? Woods won £6m ($9m) in prize money, which is vastly more than any other golfer has earned in a year, but was dwarfed by the income from his Nike deal. His salary for the year would amount to a figure in the region of £35m. *Forbes Magazine*, in its wisdom, estimates that Woods comes second to Michael Schumacher in sports' big money league, but we would rate Schumacher's earnings as lower than Woods.

As ever, the only British sports stars who rate a mention in the worldwide figures are boxers and generally the biggest earning boxers are the heavyweights. Lennox Lewis, who ended the year as the undisputed world champion (though this would change) was easily the highest earning Briton for the second year running. Lewis was paid £15.5m, mostly in fight fees. He generated about the same total for three fights in 2000 as he was for two fights in 1999, the difference being the quality of his opponents. In 1999, the two fights were against Evander Holyfield, who was, and remains, considerably more of a draw than Michael Grant, Frans Botha or David Tua.

Naseem Hamed continued to collect serious money from his deal with HBO, but his fight career is imploding. He lost his only title - the WBO crown - when he refused to fight the mandatory challenger.

Eddie Irvine knows how he feels, the Ulsterman signing away his career for a mess of pottage (well, five million quid actually). Had he stayed at Ferrari, Irvine could have been counting championship points instead of money, but if you can't have one you might as well have the other. Irvine is not in the first flush of youth at 35, so it could be that - with Jaguar struggling to find its feet - he really has sacrificed any chance of a future championship.

David Coulthard continues to chugg along at McLaren, still earning nicely and nurturing hopes of one day realising the talent that was ascribed to him. Coulthard probably has a more philosopical attitude these days, having come perilously close to saying goodbye to money, points and life itself in a plane crash in May.

Four footballers make our top 10 this year, but despite the vast amount of money in the sport and the extraordinary rise and rise of transfer fees (fuelled by Real Madrid, who paid £37m to Barcelona for Luis Figo despite the club being bankrupt! It helps when the government bails you out) no footballer has ever topped the list. David Beckham is currently the highest paid, which is no surprise, but the figure will be. Time and again we see earnings for Beckham that have no basis in reality - people citing £1m-a-year deals with Brylcreem when he's just cut all his hair off is a good example. Beckham certainly has the potential to earn more - and will do so when his next contract with Manchester United is resolved - but for 2000, the only people who paid Beckham more than £1m were the club and adidas.

Steve McMananam, Michael Owen and Alan Shearer were predictable inclusions in the list, though it may be the last such occasion for Shearer whose marketability will drop now that he no longer plays for his country. McManaman is the subject of constant transfer speculation and another move would certainly help to line his pockets. Chris Sutton is one player who has made a very comfortable living for the past two seasons with his two major moves - from Blackburn to Chelsea for £10m, and from Chelsea to Celtic for £6m. Sutton, who cost Blackburn £5m from Norwich, may currently be the costliest British player with a total of £21m in fees paid.

It's not quite as much as the fees accumulated by David Platt - his career total was £22m - but it's not bad for a footballer who has played only once for his country, and then he came on as a substitute.

> **"Football has become a religion and, to be up to date, we have to share the feelings of people who admire Beckham"**
> Chan Theerapany, a Buddhist monk, who unveiled a gold statue of Beckham in his temple in Thailand.
>
> **"Sir Shane has got a good ring to it, but I don't think that will ever happen"**
> Shane Warne, Australian leg-break bowler who was the only one of Wisden's five Cricketers of the Century without a knighthood.

Britain's Highest Earners

1 Lennox Lewis   Boxing   £15.5m

Lewis makes it eight straight years in the top 10 and the second successive year at number one. But Lewis knows that the fight with Tyson would fetch him more in one payday than he's made in the last six.

2 Naseem Hamed   Boxing   £7.5m

HBO television were not too happy when Hamed lined up the lowly-rated Augie Sanchez as the third match in his six-fight deal. Hamed won, but the titles were lost outside the ring.

3 Eddie Irvine   Motor Racing   £5.8m

Irvine parted with Ferrari for a deal with Jaguar estimated to be worth £15m over three years.

4 David Beckham   Football   £3.6m

With a new contract at Man Utd about to be signed and a new deal with adidas starting in 2001, Beckham's star is still rising.

5 Michael Owen   Football   £3.5m

Owen, Beckham and Shearer are all managed by the SFX Group which puts them in a powerful position. Owen's current Liverpool contract was negotiated after the last World Cup, the next one could go through the roof.

6 David Coulthard   Motor Racing   £3.4m

Coulthard negotiated a new deal from the 2001 season which, with win bonuses, will see him top £4m. For 2000, though, even third in the title race will not have taken him that high.

7 Lee Westwood   Golf   £3.1m

After a dodgy start to the season, Westwood came good in style topping the European lists with almost £2m in prize money. Endorsements are plentiful and the Worksop player replaces Montgomerie at the top of the pile.

8 Steve McManaman   Football   £3.0m

His Real Madrid career was stop-start for a while, but he was in the team which won the European Cup.

9 Alan Shearer   Football   £2.9m

Retirement from international football will affect Shearer's future earnings, but 2000 was yet another profitable year for football's Mr Endorsement.

10 Tim Henman   Tennis   £2.8m

Seven straight ATP final defeats before Henman pulled it round at Vienna and Brighton in 2000. There is a very serious contribution from adidas, but the heavens would open and it would rain money if Henman won a slam.

Figures for 2000 calendar year, dollars converted at $1.50 to £1 sterling.

British golf had a subdued year, reflected in the earnings of the top players, none of whom broke the £3m barrier. Colin Montgomerie has, for seven years, topped the European money list, but everything passes and Montgomerie, who was 37 in June 2000, is not only watching his hopes of a Major fade, but his wage packet shrink. Lee Westwood, after a dreadful start to the summer, and Darren Clarke, dominated the Order of Merit.

The most intriguing money story of the year concerns basketball player John Amaechi, from Stockport. Amaechi signed a two-year contract with Orlando Magic in August 1999 for a modest fee of around $600,000 a year, turning down an offer from LA Lakers worth $17m over six years. With the Orlando contract due to expire in August, Amaechi's new deal, either with Orlando or elsewhere, could make him one of the highest paid British sports stars in next year's list.

No woman broke the million-pound barrier in 2000, though Laura Davies came close. The Surrey player won almost $600,000 prize money in the USA, but there was not much money to add on from the European tour and her sponsor deal with Maruman ended. You have to drop down substantially to find the second highest earning British woman. Denise Lewis may have won the Olympic title, but that success has not yet been reflected in her earnings. For 2000, her earnings will be around £400,000. Lewis immediately signed a new deal with Nike after the Games, and she is in considerable demand for promotional work. Lewis may find her hardest task is finding the motivation for the training, when so much else is happening in her life.

January

1   **Henry Cooper** and Stirling Moss are knighted in the New Year honours.

4   **Phil Taylor** won his 6th Skol World Darts title in a row and 8th in all.
    Sammy McIlroy named Northern Ireland boss.

5   **England** lost the series in South Africa after slumping to an innings defeat in the Cape Town Test.

6   **Man United** started their Club World Championship campaign with a 1-1 draw against Necaxa. David Beckham was sent off.

8   **Man United** were eliminated from the Club World Championship after losing 3-1 to Vasco Da Gama.

10 **Naseem Hamed** was stripped of his WBC featherweight title, by the governing body.

14 **Corinthians** beat Vasco Da Gama to win the Club World Championship.
    Sheffield MPs Joe Ashton and David Blunkett led calls for the sacking of Sheffield Wednesday's manager, Danny Wilson.

15 **Ted 'The Count' Hankey** won the World Darts title, beating Ronnie Baxter 6-0 in the final and finishing with a maximum checkout of 170.

17 **Mike Tyson** was allowed to enter Britain to fight Julius Francis despite his rape conviction.

18 **England** won the 5th Test against South Africa after the captains fixed a target and forfeited an innings apiece. South Africa won the series 2-1.

22 **Tim Henman** lost in the 4th round of the Australian Open, beaten in five sets by American Chris Woodruff.
    Melbourne beat St Helens 44-6 in the World Club Challenge at Wigan.

22 **Tommi Makinen** won the Monte Carlo Rally.

23 **Robert Weale** won the World Indoor Bowls Championships.
    England thrashed South Africa by nine wickets in the first one-day tournament match.

24 **Jenson Button**, aged 20, with a driving test failure to his name, signed a contract to drive F1 with Williams.
    Rivaldo was named World Player of the Year, ahead of David Beckham and Gabriel Batistuta.

26 **England** were beaten by one run in the second one-day international against South Africa.

28 **Ian McGeechan** stepped down as coach of the Lions rugby team.
    Glenn Hoddle took over as manager of Southampton whilst Dave Jones stood down to concentrate on his pending court case.

29 **Lindsay Davenport** won the Australian Open, defeating Martina Hingis in the final. Hingis had won the title for the past three years.
    Mike Tyson took four minutes and three seconds to beat Julius Francis in Manchester. Joe Calzaghe defended his world title successfully.
    Gillingham beat Sheffield Wednesday 3-1 in the FA Cup their second successive 3-1 victory over a Premiership side.

30 **Andre Agassi** won the Australian Open men's singles. It was his fourth Grand Slam final in succession.
    Mark Ealham took 5-15 as England beat Zimbabwe. His five LBWs were the most ever in a one-day international.
    St Louis Rams won the Superbowl, beating Tennessee Titans 23-16.

February

4 **Martin Pipe** became the all-time leader in the trainers table overtaking Arthur Stephenson.

5 **Ben Cohen**, nephew of 1966 World Cup winner George, scored two tries as England beat Ireland in the Six Nations opener. Italy won their first game at home to Scotland and France won in Wales.

6 **Czech Republic** beat Great Britain 4-1 in the Davis Cup first round.

8 **Tiger Woods** won his 6th PGA tour title in a row, to equal Ben Hogan's sequence.

Inverness Caledonian Thistle beat Celtic 3-1 at Parkhead in a Scottish Cup upset. Celtic boss John Barnes was dismissed shortly after.

Mark Richardson was suspended after testing positive for nandrolone.

13 **Matthew Stevens** won the Masters Snooker at Wembley. His defeated opponent in the final, Ken Doherty made a break of 140, only missing the final black.

An 11 year old boy was killed whilst spectating at a local rally event in Northumberland.

England lost by 38 runs in the one-day final, despite having bowled South Africa out for just 150.

14 **Leeds**, Chelsea, Wimbledon and Tottenham were all charged with disrepute after a series of ugly scenes at Premiership games.

16 **Linford Christie** was banned by the New South Wales government from using their training facilities.

Geoff Miller was chosen as the fourth selector for the England cricket team.

19 **England** won their second Six Nations match in France. Ireland and Wales won home games.

20 **David Beckham** was dropped from the Man United team after a training ground spat with Alex Ferguson, but United still beat Leeds to go six points clear at the top of the Premiership.

Chelsea beat Gillingham 5-0 in the FA Cup quarter-final. Newcastle, Bolton and Aston Villa also won.

Cedric Pioline beat Tim Henman in the final of the Rotterdam ATP tour event.

23 **Sir Stanley Matthews** died, aged 85.

England drew 0-0 with Argentina, Wales beat Qatar 1-0, Northern Ireland won 3-1 in Luxembourg and Republic of Ireland beat Czech Republic 3-2, in friendly matches.

26 **Alan Shearer** announced his intention to retire from international football after Euro 2000.

27 **Darren Clarke** beat Tiger Woods 4&3 to win the World Matchplay Championship. Paul Lawrie had lost to Woods in the quarter-final.

Jason Gardener and Christian Malcolm won gold medals at the European Indoor Championships.

Leicester beat Tranmere 2-1 at Wembley to win the Worthington Cup.

Richard Burns won the Safari Rally in Kenya.

Mark Rosset beat Yevgeny Kafelnikov to win the AXA Cup in London.

28 **David Lloyd** was sacked as Davis Cup coach and replaced by Roger Taylor.

March

1 **The English and Wales Cricket Board** put 12 players under contract for the England team. The biggest surprise was the inclusion of Craig White.

2 **New Zealand** retained the Americas Cup, becoming the only nation other than America to do so. NZL-60 beat the Italian boat Prada 5-0.
Newcastle fans lost their court case against their removal from "guaranteed" seats.

4 **England** beat Wales to stay top of the Six Nations table. Ireland gained their second win in a row after beating Italy and Scotland remained bottom after losing to France.

7 **Clydebank** mustered their first win in the Scottish League First Division at the 27th attempt.
South Africa beat India 2-0 to inflict the home side's first series defeat on their own soil for 13 years.

11 **Naseem Hamed** successfully defended his WBO Featherweight title for the 14th time against the South African Vuyani Bungu.

12 **Michael Schumacher** won the first GP of the season in Australia.
Tim Henman lost to Lleyton Hewitt in the final of the ATP event in Scottsdale, Arizona.
Brett Sinkinson and Shane Howarth were exposed as being ineligible to play for Wales at Rugby Union. The players were dropped.

13 **Dan Marino**, the Miami Dolphins quarterback, retired aged 38.

14 **Istabraq** won the Champion Hurdle for the third succesive year, only the fifth horse to do so.

14 **Lee Bowyer** and Jonathan Woodgate were charged by police after an Asian student was beaten up in Leeds.
Chelsea qualified for the Champions League quarter-finals.

15 **Manchester United** joined Chelsea in the Champions League last eight.

16 **Looks Like Trouble** won the Cheltenham Gold Cup.
The British women's 4x200 metres freestyle team won gold, and broke the world record, at the World Short Course Championships in Athens.

17 **Mark Foster** won gold in the 50m freestyle.

18 **Great Britain** men's hockey team qualified for the Olympics with a 3-1 play-off victory against Argentina. The women later followed suit.
James Hickman won Britain's third gold medal in Athens in the 200m Fly.
England came from behind to beat Italy in the Six nations, whilst Wales beat Scotland in Cardiff.

19 **Ireland** won in Paris against France 27-25, with Brian O'Driscoll scoring three tries.
Paula Radcliffe came fourth in the short race at the World Cross-Country Championships, after coming 5th the previous day in the long race.
Celtic beat Aberdeen to win the CIS Insurance Cup.
Richard Burns won the Portuguese Rally.
Mark Foster won his second gold medal to bring Great Britain's final tally at Athens to four.

20 **West Indies** bowled Zimbabwe out for 63 to win the first-ever Test between the two sides.

21 **Bernie Ecclestone** sold half of his F1 empire to a German company.

23 **Freddy Fletcher** stepped down as Newcastle chief for a second time.
Walter Swinburn returned to race riding at Wolverhampton.
The International Rugby Board threatened to take action against Wales and Scotland for playing ineligible players. It had emerged that Dave Hilton was not eligible for Scotland.

25 **Oxford** won the Boat Race for the first time in eight years.
Dubai Millenium, appropriately, won racing's Dubai World Cup.

26 **Hull fans** rioted on the pitch after losing the Challenge Cup semi-final to Leeds at Huddersfield.
Roger Chapman won his first Golf event in 18 years as a professional.

27 **Courtney Walsh** became the all-time leading wicket taker in Test Matches, overtaking Kapil Dev.

28 **Seven Leicester City** players and officials were fined amounts of up to £20,000 after ticket irregularities regarding the 1999 Worthington Cup Final.

29 **Ryan Giggs** played his first-ever friendly for Wales. The team lost 2-1 to Finland.

April

1 **England** clinched the Six Nations title without playing after Wales beat Ireland in Dublin. A Welsh fan died 10 days after the match. He had been involved in a street brawl and did not recover. In Paris, France beat Italy. The Italians, in their first tournament, picked up the wooden spoon.

2 **Scotland** yet again denied England the chance of a Grand Slam when they won a rain-soaked Calcutta Cup match at Murrayfield.
Colin McRae won the latest round of the World Rally Championship. Richard Burns' second place kept him at the top of the drivers standings.

3 **Pembrey** and East London were announced as the sites for the two new Horse Racing courses.
London was awarded the 2005 World Athletics championships.

4 **Ashia Hansen** was reported to be the subject of a race-hate campaign.

5 **Two Leeds** fans were stabbed to death in Istanbul prior to Leeds United's UEFA Cup semi-final against Galatasaray. The game went ahead and Leeds lost 2-0.

7 **Hansie Cronje** was reported on match fixing charges. It was a blow to ICC's Week of Cricket.

8 **Papillon** won the Grand National. Backed from 40-1 on the eve of the race, the horse won at 10-1. There was a remarkable similarity to the 1999 race; the horse was Irish, a 10-1 winner and was trained and ridden by a father/son combination exactly the same circumstances as the previous year.

8 **Johnny Nelson** retained his WBO Cruiserweight Title.
Will Carling announced his retirement.

9 **Jean Tigana** was announced as the new Fulham manager from July 1
Michael Schumacher won his third Grand Prix in a row. His victory in San Marino took him 21 points clear in the Drivers' Championship.
Vijay Singh of Fiji won the US Masters, his second Major title.

11 **Hansie Cronje** was sacked after he admitted dishonesty in his role as South African captain. Cronje admitted only to match forecasting.

12 **Lennox Lewis** was stripped of his WBA title for not defending against a Don King boxer.
Ronaldo's career was plunged into doubt after he collapsed cluching his right knee, whilst playing for Inter Milan in the Italian cup final.
Shaun Edwards called time on his 17-year Rugby League career.

14 **UEFA** decided that no away fans were to be allowed into Elland Road for the second leg of the Leeds-Galatasaray UEFA Cup tie.

15 **Stephen Hendry** lost in the first round of the Embassy World Snooker Championship to Stuart Bingham.

16 **Europe** won the inaugural Seve Ballesteros trophy, beating Britain and Ireland by a single point.
Antonio Pinto set a course record as he won his third London Marathon. Tegla Loroupe won the women's race

18 **Chelsea** lost 5-1 in Barcelona to go out of the Champions League quarter-final, 6-4 on aggregate.

19 **Manchester United** were stunned at home 3-2 by Real Madrid, and went out of the Champions League.

20 **Leeds** lost their emotional game with Galatasaray 4-2 on aggregate after a 2-2 draw at Elland Road. Arsenal beat Lens to become England's last representative in Europe.
Hamilton had 15 points deducted for failing to fulfil a fixture against Stenhousemuir, when the players went on strike.
Fulham announced that their women's side would be the first in Britain to have professional players.

21 **Manchester United** 'signed' Ruud van Nistelrooy from PSV Eindhoven for £19m. However the move was thrown into doubt just days later when the player failed a medical.

22 **Man United and Rangers** clinched the respective league titles.

24 **David Coulthard** won the British Grand Prix at Silverstone. The race was overshadowed by the state of the parking facilities which meant that people had to abandon their cars.
Carl Fogarty crashed at the World Superbike event in Australia, breaking his arm. It would be his last race.
Walter Swinburn retired.

26 **Scotland** drew 0-0 with Holland in a Euro 2000 warm-up for the Dutch.

29 **Bradford Bulls** won the Challenge Cup beating Leeds 24-18.
Jemima Johnson became the sixth person to be killed at a British horse trials meeting in 12 months.
Lennox Lewis beat Michael Grant in New York, while Paul Ingle retained his IBF featherweight title against Junior Jones on the undercard.

30 **Roy Keane** won the Football Writers' footballer of the year award.
Jo Goode and Donna Kellogg won the European Badminton title.

May

1 **Egil Olsen** parted company with Wimbledon after a disastrous season which would see the London club relegated.
  Mark Williams won the World Snooker title, beating fellow Welshman Matthew Stevens in the final

2 **David Coulthard** and his fiancée were injured in a plane crash in Lyon which killed the pilots, David Saunders and Daniel Worley.

3 **Dorchester Gladiators** 3rd XV rugby team were mistaken for a top English side and against Romanian side Steaua Bucharest, in front of a big crowd, lost 61-17.

5 **Venus Williams** lost a 2nd round match to Irina Spirlea in Hamburg. It was only her second match in six months.

6 **Burnley** earned promotion from the second division, whilst Chester City lost their league status.
  Glenn Catley won the WBC super-middleweight title, after he defeated the German, Markus Beyer in Frankfurt.

7 **Mika Hakkinen** won the Spanish Grand Prix. David Coulthard was second, just days after his plane crash.
  Manchester City sealed their return to the Premiership with a comfortable 4-1 win at Blackburn. Walsall went back to the Second Division after one season.

9 **Sheffield Wednesday** were relegated from the Premiership.

14 **Barnsley** beat Birmingham 4-0 at St Andrews in the play-offs, first leg.

14 **Wasps** won the Tetley Bitter Cup Final, beating Northampton.
  Bradford sent Wimbledon down to the Nationwide League after the Valley Parade club beat Liverpool and Wimbledon lost at Southampton. Rodney Marsh had to have his head shaved as a result. Leeds claimed the third Champions League spot.
  Coventry lost to Watford and ended up with no away victories all season.
  Padraig Harrington was disqualified from the International Open tournament for failing to sign his 1st round card. The mistake was only spotted later when the player was leading after the third day.
  Lazio won Serie A on the final day. They beat Reggiana while Juventus lost at Perugia in a match where rain extended half time to over an hour.
  Neil Hodgson finished third and first in the World Superbike event at Donington Park.
  Leicester retained the Rugby Union Premiership title.

17 **Arsenal** lost to Galatasaray on penalties in the UEFA Cup Final.
  Jonathan Lewis of Gloucestershire took a hat-trick and Paul Franks of Nottinghamshire took 3-9 in 13 overs as bowlers dominated an early season county match at Trent Bridge.
  Susie O'Neill broke the oldest swimming record in the book at the Australian Olympic trials. Mary T Meagher's 200m butterfly mark had stood since 1981.
  Hull were fined £50,000 with £30,000 suspended after crowd trouble at the Challenge Cup semi-final.

20 **Chelsea** won the last FA Cup Final at Wembley, 1-0 against Aston Villa.

21 **England** beat Zimbabwe at Lord's by an innings and 209 runs.

23 **Martina Navratilova** made a winning return to competitive tennis. With partner Marian de Swaart she won a doubles match at the Madrid Open.

Brazil played Wales in an 'indoor' game under the Millenium Stadium roof. The Brazilians won 3-0

24 **Real Madrid** won the Champions League. Steve McManaman scored in a 3-0 win over Valencia

Former Pakistan cricketer Salim Malik was charged with match-fixing.

27 **Brazil** drew 1-1 with England at Wembley. Michael Owen scored England's goal.

Northampton won the European Cup after beating Munster 9-8.

Jim Leighton's final game as a professional ended after three minutes when he collided with Rangers' Rod Wallace. Rangers won the Scottish Cup Final 4-0 after forward Robbie Winters stood in for Leighton.

28 **Jeremy McWilliams** became the first British rider to finish on the podium in a 500cc Grand Prix for seven years. McWilliams was third in Italy

29 **Greg Rusedski**, who wasted 22 break points, lost to Slava Dosedel in the first round of the French Open.

Colin Montgomerie won his third Volvo PGA tournament in a row.

Ipswich were promoted to the Premiership after beating Barnsley at Wembley.

30 **Curtly Ambrose** announced that he would retire after the Test series in England.

31 **England** beat Ukraine 2-0 in a Euro 2000 warm-up match.

June

1 **Andre Agassi** lost his French Open title after losing to Karol Kucera

Frankie Dettori and Ray Cochrane were involved in a plane crash in Newmarket. The pilot, Patrick Mackey, was killed.

2 **Portugal** beat Wales 3-0 in a Euro 2000 warm-up.

Tim Henman lost in five sets to Fernando Vicente of Spain in the 3rd round of the French Open.

Chelsea signed striker Jimmy Floyd Hasselbaink for a British record equalling £15m.

3 **England** beat Malta 2-1 in a Euro 2000 warm-up.

4 **David Coulthard** won the Monaco Grand Prix.

5 **England** drew the 2nd Test with Zimbabwe, but won the series 1-0.

7 **Ken Buchanan** was inducted to the boxing Hall of Fame.

Andy Robinson was brought in to the England coaching set-up, with Clive Woodward now the manager.

Ian Wright announced his retirement from football.

9 **Herschelle Gibbs** was dropped from the South African Test team after he and Henry Williams admitted receiving $15,000 from Hansie Cronje in the bribes scandal.

Shoaib Akhtar was released from his Nottinghamshire contract without playing a game.

Derbyshire beat Surrey in the County Championship, but had eight points docked for a sub-standard pitch.

Love Divine won the Oaks

10 **Sindaar** won the Derby at Epsom for owner the Aga Khan.

Mary Pierce beat Conchita Martinez in the final of the French Open

Belgium kicked off Euro 2000 with a 2-1 win against Sweden.

Gloucestershire won the Super Cup, their third consecutive one-day cup title win coming against Glamorgan.

Hansie Cronje was offered criminal immunity if he spilled the beans on match-fixing.

11 **Gustavo Kuerten** won the French Open, the Brazilian beating Swede Magnus Norman in the final.

12 **England** lost 3-2 to Portugal in Euro 2000 after leading 2-0.

13 **The BBC** lost the rights to Premier League highlights to ITV, signalling the end of Match of the Day. Sky retained the majority of coverage.

16 **Wasim Akram** reached 400 Test wickets, the fourth bowler to do so.

17 **England** finally beat Germany. Alan Shearer scored the only goal.

   West Indies won the First Test at Edgbaston. They beat England by an innings and 93 runs.

   South Africa beat England 18-13 in a Rugby Union Test.

18 **Tiger Woods** won the US Open by a mind-blowing 15 shots.

   Michael Schumacher won the Canadian Grand Prix.

19 **Hosts Belgium** went out of Euro 2000 at the group stage.

20 **England** crashed out of Euro 2000 after losing their final group game to Romania 3-2. Phil Neville conceded a late penalty to seal England's fate.

21 **Gloucestershire** finally lost a one-day match, but the NatWest tie had to be replayed as their opponents, Worcestershire, fielded an ineligible player. Gloucestershire won the replay.

22 **Chris Hutchings** was appointed manager of Bradford City.

24 **Italy** qualified for the semi-finals of Euro 2000 after a comfortable 2-0 win over Romania. Gheorghe Hagi was sent off for diving.

   England beat South Africa 27-22 in Bloemfontein. Scotland lost 69-20 to New Zealand.

   Mike Tyson beat Lou Savarese in 38 seconds at Hampden Park. Tyson floored referee John Coyle while trying to fight on after the match had been stopped.

25 **Albert Costa** and Alex Corretja pulled out of Wimbledon in a protest over the seedings.

   Holland beat Yugoslavia 6-1 and France beat Spain 2-1 in Euro 2000 quarter-finals.

   Nasser Hussain broke his thumb fielding for Essex.

26 **Sir Paul Condon** was appointed to head the ICC's anti-corruption investigation.

   Greg Rusedski lost to Vince Spadea in the 1st round at Wimbledon. Spadea had lost his previous 22 matches on the ATP tour.

28 **France** reached the Euro 2000 final, beating Portugal on a Golden Goal penalty scored by Zinedine Zidane. The Portugese players, objecting to the handball decision which cost them the match manhandled the referee and his assistants.

29 **Damir Dokic** was thrown out of Wimbledon for causing a disturbance.

   Hosts Holland lost to Italy on penalties in the second semi-final of Euro 2000.

30 **The West Indies** were all out for 54 in the Second Test at Lord's.

July

1 **Portugese players** were banned for a total of 23 months as a result of incidents at the end of their Euro 2000 semi-final.

England completed a two-wicket victory over the West indies at Lord's.

David Millar became the fourth Britain to wear the yellow jersey after winning the Tour de France prologue.

2 **France** won the final of Euro 2000 after coming from behind to beat Italy 2-1, David Trezeguet scoring the Golden Goal winner.

David Coulthard won the French GP after an angry mid-race exchange with Michael Schumacher.

Motorcycle legend Joey Dunlop was killed in a racing accident in Estonia. The 48-year old was the most successful rider in the history of the Isle of Man TT races.

Sinndar earned a $1m bonus for adding the Irish Derby to its Epsom victory.

3 **Brazil** withdrew their 2006 World Cup bid. They agreed to vote for South Africa in return for that country's support for a 2010 bid.

Tim Henman was eliminated from Wimbledon by Mark Philippoussis.

5 **Vladimir Voltchkov** from Belarus became the first qualifier since John McEnroe in 1977 to reach the Wimbledon men's semi-finals.

6 **Venus Williams** beat her sister Serena to reach the Wimbledon final.

Germany won the vote to host the 2006 World Cup after New Zealand delegate Charles Dempsey abstained. England was eliminated in the second ballot.

6 **Zimbabwe** beat West Indies by six wickets in Bristol. The match was the first-ever floodlit international in Britain.

8 **Venus Williams** beat Lindsay Davenport to win the Wimbledon singles title.

9 **Pete Sampras** won his seventh Wimbledon title and his 13th Grand Slam overall, overtaking Roy Emerson's record of 12.

Twelve people were crushed to death at a football international between Zimbabwe and South Africa.

Andrew Flintoff was dropped from the England team for being overweight.

10 **The Williams sisters** won the women's doubles title which was held over until the third Monday.

12 **Edu,** an Arsenal transfer target was refused entry to Britain when his passport was found to be forged.

13 **Greg Rusedski** split with his coach Sven Groenveld.

15 **Lennox Lewis** beat Frans Botha in round two at the London Arena.

New Zealand beat Australia in Rugby Union's Tri-nations, 39-35 in front of a 109,874 crowd in Stadium Australia.

16 **Great Britain** were relegated from the Davis Cup world group after losing to Ecuador at Wimbledon.

Britain's men's team won the European Cup athletics crown by half a point, despite a long list of withdrawals.

Mika Hakkinen won the Austrian Grand Prix.

17 **Paul Gascoigne** joined Everton from Middlesbrough on a free transfer.

18 **Richard Lewis** left the LTA, with Frenchman Patrice Hagelauer replacing him as tennis chief.

21 **Jack Nicklaus** bowed out of the Open for the final time after missing the cut at St Andrews.
Bernard Murray the ground controller at the Hillsborough disaster was cleared of manslaughter in a private prosecution.
Martin Bicknell took 9-47 for Surrey against Middlesex. His figures of 16-119 were the finest in this country since the famous Jim Laker Test in 1956, where Laker took all but one of the Australian wickets.

22 **England** won the NatWest triangular series final against Zimbabwe.

23 **Tiger Woods** won the Open by eight shots to become the youngest person to win all four majors.
Lance Armstrong retained the Tour de France title.

24 **The jury** failed to reach a verdict on the manslaughter charge against David Duckenfield, who was match commander on the day of the Hillsborough disaster.
Luis Figo joined Real Madrid from Barcelona for a world record £37m.

25 **Mark Richardson** was cleared of doping by UK Athletics, but the IAAF refused to recognise the decision.

26 **Johnny Herbert** announced that he was leaving Formula 1 to join the USA Cart series in 2001.
John Regis retired from competitive athletics.

28 **Barcelona** paid a combined fee of £32m for the Arsenal pair of Marc Overmars and Emmanuel Petit.

29 **Robbie Keane** joined Inter Milan from Coventry.

30 **Rubens Barrichello** won the German Grand Prix from 18th on the grid.

August

2 **Mark James** resigned as vice-captain of the European Ryder Cup team after the controversy stirred up by his autobiography.

3 **Aston Villa** and Bradford both crashed out of the Inter Toto Cup.

4 **Alec Stewart** scored a century on his 100th Test appearance.

5 **Frankie Dettori** rode a winner on his return to riding after a plane crash emulating Ray Cochrane. However, the victory was soured by an injury to Dubai Millenium.

6 **England** and the West Indies drew the Third Test.

10 **Tim Henman** finally beat Pete Sampras - in the Masters Series in Cincinnati - but then lost to Thomas Enqvist in the final.

12 **Evander Holyfield** beat John Ruiz to capture the vacant WBA heavyweight title. Joe Calzaghe retained his WBO super-middleweight title after stopping Omar Sheika.

13 **Kevin Pressman** was sent off after only 13 seconds of Sheffield Wednesday's opening league game of the season at Wolves.

14 **Mark Lewis-Francis** opted not to go to the Olympics and instead concentrate on the World Junior championships. Iwan Thomas was a controversial non-selection in the 400m.

17 **Curtly Ambrose** became only the fifth bowler to reach 400 wickets in Test matches.

18 **England** won the Fourth Test at Headingley inside two days. They bowled West Indies out for 61 to clinch an innings victory.

19 **Naseem Hamed** beat Augie Sanchez to retain his WBO featherweight crown.

20 **Tiger Woods** won the US PGA after a play-off and became only the second man, after Ben Hogan in 1953, to win three majors in one year.

21 **Patrick Vieira** was sent off for the second game running as Arsenal beat Liverpool 2-0.

Linford Christie, Dougie Walker and Gary Cadogan had two-year bans enforced by the IAAF for nandrolone offences.

27 **Celtic** beat Rangers 6-2 at Celtic Park in Martin O'Neill's first Old Firm derby.

Bunny Austin died aged 94.

Gloucestershire completed an unprecedented four-in-a-row, after taking the final NatWest Trophy, by beating Warwickshire by the Duckworth/Lewis method.

Mika Hakkinen won the Belgian Grand Prix

28 **Herschelle Gibbs** and Henry Williams were banned for six months from international cricket after being found guilty of conspiring with Hansie Cronje.

September

1 **Greg Rusedski** lost to Cedric Pioline in the US Open after winning the first two sets.

Glenn Catley was knocked out by Dingaan Thobelajust of South Africa just seven seconds from the end of the first defence of his WBC super-middleweight title in Johannesburg.

2 **The home nations** had mixed results in the opening World Cup qualifiers. Scotland won in Latvia, while Northern Ireland beat Malta at home, both scores 1-0. Republic of Ireland threw away a 2-0 lead to draw against a weak Holland side, while Wales lost 2-1 in Belarus. England drew a friendly with France 1-1.

4 **England** won the Fifth Test against the West Indies and secured a 3-1 series win, the first against the West Indies for 31 years.

6 **Twenty-seven Chinese** athletes were withdrawn from their Olympic team after internal drug tests.

Gloucestershire won the National League, their third title of the year, when Lancashire beat Somerset.

9 **Mark Richardson** pulled out of the Olympics in order to gain more time to prepare his appeal.

Venus Williams added the US Open to her Wimbledon triumph. Williams again beat Lindsay Davenport in the final.

10 **Michael Schumacher** won the Italian Grand Prix, but his success was marred by the death of a marshall.

Marit Safin beat Pete Sampras in straight sets to win the US Open.

12 **Gianluca Vialli** was sacked as manager of Chelsea.

13 **Matthew Pinsent** was selected to carry the flag at the opening ceremony of the Olympics.

15 **Cathy Freeman** lit the Olympic flame to begin the Sydney games.
Claudio Ranieri was named as the new Chelsea coach.

16 **Jason Queally** won Britain's first gold medal at the Olympics in the 1km cycling time trial.
Ian Thorpe won the 400m gold medal and anchored Australia to an historic win in the 4x100m freestyle relay. It was the first time the USA had failed to win the event.

17 **Jason Queally** won a second medal, taking silver with Craig MacLean and Chris Hoy in the Olympic sprint. Ian Peel won a trap shooting silver medal.

18 **Yvonne McGregor** won a bronze medal in the cycling pursuit at the age of 39.
Kenny Dalglish announced that he would sue Celtic for wrongful dismissal.

19 **Leeds** beat AC Milan 1-0 at home in the Champions League
Ivan Ivanov lost his weightlifting silver medal after a positive drugs test. Ivanov was the first of many drug positives during the games, the most notable of which was Andreea Raducan, the Romanian gymnast who lost the all-around gold medal after she had tested positive. Raducan claimed that she had taken a cold remedy but an appeal was later rejected.

20 **Richard Faulds** won Britain's second Olympic gold medal in double trap shooting. Canoeist Paul Ratcliffe and judo player Kate Howey won silver medals.

21 **Simon Archer and Jo Goode** won a bronze medal for the mixed doubles in badminton.
Carl Fogarty announced his retirement after failing to recover from a crash earlier in the year.
Juan Pablo Montoya signed for Williams as a replacement for Jenson Button who was loaned to Benetton.

23 **Steve Redgrave** secured his fifth consecutive Olympic gold medal after the coxless four won a close race with the Italians.
Marion Jones and Maurice Greene won the 100m titles whilst Steve Backley had to settle for silver in the javelin at Sydney.

24 **Denise Lewis** won gold in the Heptathlon. **Britain** won another men's rowing gold after the eight were victorious. The women's quad sculls team won silver.
Michael Schumacher won the US Grand Prix.

25 **Cathy Freeman** took centre stage at the Sydney Olympics, the Australian winning the 400m title. Katharine Merry took bronze . Kelly Holmes also won bronze in the 800m, but Jonathan Edwards took the British honours, winning gold in the triple jump. Sailors Ian Barker and Simon Hiscocks won a surprise silver medal in the 49er class.

28 **Darren Campbell** won a 200m silver medal, finishing behind unheralded Greek winner Konstantinos Kenderis. Dean Macey narrowly missed a medal, finishing fourth in the decathlon. The winner, Erki Nool, was initially disqualified in the discus, but despite a clear foul, he was reinstated on appeal.

28 **Hearts**, Leicester and Chelsea all crashed out of the UEFA Cup.

29 **Ben Ainslie** and Shirley Robertson both won sailing golds at the Olympics.

Robert Korzeniowski achieved the remarkable feat of winning both 20km and 50km walks at the same games. The Pole's 17-year old countrywoman Kamila Skolimowska also won a remarkable hammer event. The favourite Mihaela Melinte was escorted from the track before the qualifying event having failed a pre-Games drug test.

30 **Iain Percy** won Britain's third sailing gold of the games. Also on the water Ian Walker and Mark Covell won sailing silver and Tim Brabants a canoeing bronze.

October

1 **Audley Harrison** and Stephanie Cook won gold medals on the final day of Olympic competition to take Britain's gold medal tally to 11, the highest since 1920. Juan Antonio Samaranch pronounced the Games the best ever.

2 **Silverstone** secured a return to a July Grand Prix date after the 2000 event in April was beset by problems.

Claudio Caniggia, a World Cup player with Argentina agreed to sign for Dundee.

5 **England** beat Bangladesh in the ICC knockout trophy.

Mark Richardson, Darren Campbell and Jonathan Edwards all earned victories in the IAAF Grand Prix final.

7 **Johnny Nelson** defended his WBO cruiserweight title against Australia's Adam Watt.

England lost to Germany 1-0 in the last-ever Wembley game, prompting Kevin Keegan to resign. Northern Ireland and Wales had home draws, while Republic of Ireland held Portugal to a draw. Scotland beat San Marino 2-0.

8 **Europe** won the Solheim Cup beating the USA at Loch Lomond.

Michael Schumacher won the drivers' title after taking the Japanese Grand Prix. It was Ferrari's first drivers' title since 1979.

10 **Naseem Hamed** vacated his last title, the WBO featherweight belt, after refusing to box the mandatory challenger.

Arsene Wenger was given a 12-match touchline ban. It was later thrown out on appeal.

England lost tamely to South Africa in the ICC knockout trophy.

Greg Rusedski beat Olympic champion Yevgeny Kafelikov as he tried to defend his CA Trophy title in Vienna. However, the Briton lost in the next round.

11 **England**, Scotland and Wales all drew World Cup qualifiers, but Northern Ireland lost to a last-minute goal in Iceland. The Republic of Ireland beat Estonia.

Hansie Cronje was banned for life by the South African cricket board.

14 **St Helens** won the rugby league Grand Final against Wigan at Old Trafford.

15 **Tim Henman** won the CA Trophy in Vienna, his first ATP victory for almost two years.

15 **New Zealand** were the surprise winners of the ICC Knockout Trophy.

18 **The race-fixing enquiry**, which had been running for three years, collapsed when Judge Elwen decided the defendants had no case to answer.

NTL pulled out of a £328m deal to show pay-per-view Premiership games.

21 **Andrew Golota** quit at the end of the second round of his fight with Mike Tyson. Golota was booed out of the building but was later found to have damaged vertebrae.

24 **England** scored 306 batting second to beat Pakistan in the first of three one-day internationals.

27 **Chris Boardman** retired after breaking the world one-hour record in Manchester.

28 **Yvonne McGregor** won the world pursuit title in Manchester to add to her Olympic bronze.

Australia beat England 22-2 to win the opening match of the Rugby League World Cup at Twickenham.

29 **Tony Cascarino** claimed in his book that he was not eligible to win any of his 88 Republic of Ireland caps.

Britain finished the Paralympics in fourth place, with the best-ever tally of 41 gold medals.

Muttiah Muralitharan took a world record 7-30 against India in the one-day Sharjah Cup.

30 **Swede Sven-Goran Eriksson** was announced as the new England manager, to start at the end of the current season.

31 **Steve Redgrave** announced his retirement from rowing after his wonderful career.

November

1 **Alec Stewart** was accused of taking £5000 from a bookmaker for information during England's 1992-93 tour to India.

3 **Nike** signed a £302m deal to carry their logo on Manchester United's kit.

4 **Kalanisi** won the Breeders' Cup Turf race for Michael Stoute and Johnny Murtagh.

7 **Rangers** were eliminated from the Champions League after the opening group stage. Leeds, Manchester United and Arsenal all progressed.

11 **Lennox Lewis** beat David Tua to retain his world heavyweight title.

Ireland beat Japan, Wales beat Samoa and Scotland lost to Australia in Rugby Union internationals.

12 **Paula Radcliffe** won the World Half-marathon championships in Mexico.

Lee Westwood ended Colin Montgomerie's seven-year reign as European Order of Merit winner.

15 **England**, under temporary manager Peter Taylor, lost 1-0 to Italy. Scotland lost 2-0 at home to Australia, while the Republic of Ireland beat Finland 3-0.

High Jumper Steve Smith retired from athletics because of injuries.

18 **New Zealand** defeated England to reach the final of the Rugby League World Cup.

England beat Australia at Twickenham, Dan Luger scoring a late try. Scotland beat Samoa.

19 **South Africa** narrowly beat Ireland at Lansdowne Road.

Australia beat Wales to reach the final of the Rugby League World Cup.

19 **England** drew the First Test in Pakistan.

20 **Ron Noades** sacked himself as the manager of Brentford.

21 **England** Rugby Union players threatened a strike before the international against Argentina. The dispute was over win bonuses.

Arsenal and Leeds lost in the second phase of the Champions League.

Emil Zatopek, triple gold medallist at the 1952 Helsinki Olympics, died.

24 **Iran** beat Guam 19-0 in a World Cup qualifier.

Carl Myerscough, the British shot putter, admitted taking banned substances.

25 **Australia** beat New Zealand to retain the World Cup.

England beat Argentina 19-0 at Twickenham, after the players had called off their strike.

Rio Ferdinand signed for Leeds from West Ham for £18m, a British transfer record.

Australia beat West Indies to win their 11th Test match in a row.

26 **Richard Burns** won the Network Q Rally of Great Britain but Finland's Marcus Gronhölm took the world title.

Tim Henman won the Samsung Open in Brighton, beating Dominik Hrbaty 6-2 6-2 in the final.

South Africa beat Wales 23-13 at the Milennium Stadium in Cardiff.

27 **Mohammad Azharuddin** was found guilty of match-fixing by the Board of Control for Cricket in India.

29 **Andy Flower** hit an unbeaten 232 as Zimbabwe drew with India. India won the series, but Flower scored 540 runs at an average of 270.

December

1 **Glenn McGrath** took a hat-trick in the 2nd Test against West Indies. The second wicket of the three, that of Brian Lara, was McGrath's 300th Test wicket. Australia duly completed a record twelfth win in a row

2 **England** beat South Africa 25-17 to complete a clean sweep in the Autumn internationals.

Bristol beat Bath for the first time since the English League began in 1987.

3 **Australia** completed a record 12 Test wins in a row after beating West Indies who had held the previous record with 11 straight wins.

England drew the 2nd Test with Pakistan.

Gustavo Kuerten beat Andre Agassi in the Masters Cup final to finish the year as world number one.

4 **Terry Venables** accepted a coaching role with struggling Middlesbrough.

5 **Lord Cowdrey** died aged 67.

Mohammad Azharuddin and Ajay Sharma were banned for life by the Indian Cricket Board.

7 **Rangers** crashed out of Europe for the second time this season.

10 **Steve Redgrave** was named the BBC Sports Personality of the Year.

Spain beat Australia to win the Davis Cup.

11 **Murray Walker** announced his retirement at the end of the 2001 season.

England beat Pakistan in almost total darkness to clinch a 1-0 series win.

14 **England** crashed out of the Women's Cricket World Cup.

16 **Joe Calzaghe** beat Ritchie Woodhall to retain his WBO super-middleweight crown but his victory was overshadowed by the injury to Paul Ingle, who was taken to hospital with brain damage after his IBF featherweight title loss to South African Mbulelo Botilo.

17 **Liverpool** inflicted Manchester United's first home league defeat for almost two years. Danny Murphy scored the only goal.
Mark Foster and Joanna Fargus won gold medals in the European Short Course Championships in Valencia.

23 **New Zealand** upset Australia to win the women's cricket world cup.

26 **Francois Doumen** won his fifth King George VI Chase at Kempton when First Gold cruised to victory.

28 **Martin Johnson**, the England Rugby Union captain, was banned for 35 days.

30 **Steve Redgrave** was knighted in the New Year's honours list.

Olympic Games

Y ou can watch the toaster for hours, but only when you turn away to do something else does the toast pop up. The Olympics can be like that. In Sydney, on the opening day the focus was on Penrith, where Steve Redgrave was launching the latest episode in his extraordinary adventure, and, with half an eye on the next's day's triathlon, where Simon Lessing looked the second-best bet for a British gold, it was easy to overlook events in the modest Sydney suburb of Bankstown.

On Saturday night, while we were still purring over the coxless four's easy victory in their morning heat, Jason Queally, exceeding even his own expectations, won a gold medal. It wasn't quite as bad as 1988, when the Ben Johnson drugs story broke in the early hours of the rest day, and every poor tired and emotional journalist (without a mobile phone between them) almost caused the telecommunications system to seize up, but there was a distinct sense of panic in Sydney. Not only was Queally an almost-unknown in the great wide world of sport, it was also the first time that Britain had won an Olympic title on the first full day of competition since (and it took us a while to dig this one out) the Games went from a one-week to a two-week circus in 1932. It was stunning.

The Frenchman, Arnaud Tournand, had started favourite for the one kilometre time trial and had it been a greco-roman wrestling contest instead would have won easily. However, muscularity only counts if you gear the bike properly and Tournant was beating his chest afterwards because he hadn't. Queally's demeanour was one of gentle bewilderment. "I thought I had an outside chance of bronze," he said, but he'd cut 1.4 seconds off his best and broken the Olympic record so it was hardly a fluke. The British cyclists, managed astutely by Peter Keen, would continue to confound, earning a silver and two bronzes and laying claim to be Britain's most successful sport in Sydney - but that didn't last for long

The second gold was no certainty either. On all known form, the Australian Russell Mark was favourite for the double trap. He had, however, been practising with Britain's Richard Faulds in Melbourne, and that certainly did the farmer's son from Hampshire no harm. Faulds, who had been fifth in the Atlanta Games, had also prepared by working with psychologist Paul Terry, who had given him the image of the ice-man to identify with. Terry's methods were meticulous, including playing Whitney Houston's 'One Moment in Time' on the car stereo every day as they approached the Cecil Park venue. Faulds was an unlikely ice-man, but bought into the idea and it worked wonderfully well. When Mark faltered in the shoot-off, Faulds stayed cool. "You get bought just as many beers for a silver," said the generous loser, though it's easier to be generous when there's already a gold medal on the mantlepiece. Faulds became Britain's first gold medallist in a shotgun event since Bob Braithwaite in 1968.

Five days into the Games, the British team had doubled the Atlanta tally and the stone-cold certainty was yet to play his cards. When Redgrave won gold in Los Angeles in the coxed four, he was one of five British title winners; in Seoul there were five again; in Barcelona five again; but in Atlanta only he and Pinsent stood atop a podium, and brought a measure of respect to the British performance. At least Queally and Faulds, by their early successes had allowed Redgrave the option of failure - not that he would ever have seen it like that. Saturday at Penrith was unsettling; a surreal mist lay across the lake, just a few metres above the water level. It was the kind of day when kings draw swords from stones. Redgrave had not been his usual self, which had been a cause for concern. The intensity which usually leads him to introspection when the highest prizes are on offer was absent. The hair shirt had been left out of the kitbag. This was the all-singing, all-dancing Redgrave. He was enjoying himself. Saturday morning, September 23rd, came and went and grown men had lumps in their throat. The four of Redgrave, James Cracknell, Matthew Pinsent and Tim Foster just held off the challenge of the Italian quartet, who would blame the draw for their defeat, as on their outside lane the wind had been stronger. No one was listening, except other Italians. Pinsent scrambled across the boat to cuddle Redgrave, and fell in the water after doing so. The four rowed across the to main tribunes, jammed with British supporters and drunk in the adulation. Juan Antonio Samaranch and the Princess Royal awarded the celebrated fifth gold medal, plus a third to Pinsent and firsts for Foster and Cracknell. At the press conference, Redgrave thanked the journalists for helping make it such a special day, and the journalists were wide-eyed for they had never heard anyone say such a thing before. "Was he being ironic?" said one, but nobody knew. The News of the World paid Redgrave £30,000 so they could fly in the other four medals; for the next day's front page. And the next morning, with the party still in full swing, the eights embellished the occasion with a second rowing gold. "I wished I had done it with their panache," said Redgrave, who had turned away with almost a quarter of the race still left, saying to his family and friends that it was all over, they had won. There was a third medal, too, the first for a British women's crew when the quad sculls team of Miriam and Guin Batten, Gillian Lindsay and Kath Grainger chased home the German boat. It was a weekend when the women had finally come good; when the men's rowers confirmed themselves as the best sweep squad in the world; when Redgrave, so long an unsung hero, drew his last sword (and his hardest) from the stone, and wrote himself into legend.

British Medals

Gold (11)

Jonathan Edwards	Athletics	Triple Jump
Denise Lewis	Athletics	Heptathlon
Audley Harrison	Boxing	+91kg
Jason Queally	Cycling	1km TT
Stephanie Cook	Modern Pentathlon	
Men's Coxless Four	Rowing	
James Cracknell/Steve Redgrave/Tim Foster/Matthew Pinsent		
Men's Eight	Rowing	
Andrew Lindsay/Ben Hunt-Davis/Simon Dennis/Luka Grubor/Louis Atrill/Kieran West/Fred Scarlett/Steve Trapmore/Rowley Douglas		
Ben Ainslie	Sailing	Laser
Iain Percy	Sailing	Finn
Shirley Robertson	Sailing	Europe
Richard Faulds	Shooting	Double Trap

Silver (10)

Steve Backley	Athletics	Javelin
Darren Campbell	Athletics	200m
Paul Ratcliffe	Canoeing	C1 Slalom
Olympic Sprint	Cycling	
Craig MacLean/Chris Hoy/Jason Queally		
Eventing Team	Equestrianism	
Jeanette Bracewell/Leslie Law/Pippa Funnell/Ian Stark		
Kate Howey	Judo	under-70kg
Women's Quad Sculls	Rowing	
Guin Batten/Gillian Lindsay/Kath Grainger/Miriam Batten		
49er Class	Sailing	
Simon Barker/Ian Hiscocks		
Star Class	Sailing	
Ian Walker/Mark Covell		
Ian Peel	Shooting	Trap

Bronze (7)

Kelly Holmes	Athletics	800m
Katharine Merry	Athletics	400m
Mixed Doubles	Badminton	
Simon Archer/Jo Goode		
Tim Brabants	Canoeing	K1 1000m
Yvonne McGregor	Cycling	Pursuit
Men's Team Pursuit	Cycling	
Paul Manning/Bradley Wiggins/Chris Newton/Bryan Steel		
Kate Allenby	Modern Pentathlon	

Record Olympians

Nine Gold Medals

CARL LEWIS
(USA-Athletics)
100m-1984 & 1988; 200m-1984
Long Jump-1984, 1988, 1992 & 1996; 4x100m-1984 & 1992

MARK SPITZ
(USA-Swimming)
100m Free-1972; 200m Free-1972; 100m Fly-1972; 200m Fly-1972
4x100m Free-1968 &1972; 4x200m Free-1968 & 1972; 4x100m Medley-1972

LARYSA LATYNINA
(Soviet Union/Ukraine-Gymnastics)
All Around-1956 & 1960; Vault-1956; Floor-1956, 1960 & 1964
Team-1956, 1960 & 1964

PAAVO NURMI
(Finland-Athletics)
1500m-1924; 5000m-1924; 10,000m-1920 & 1928; 3000m Team-1924
Cross-country Individual-1920 & 1924; Cross-country Team-1920 & 1924

Gold Medals in Successive Games

6
ALADAR GEREVICH
(Hungary-Fencing)
1932-Sabre Team; 1936-Sabre Team; 1948-Sabre Individual & Sabre Team
1952-Sabre Team; 1956-Sabre Team; 1960-Sabre Team

5
STEVE REDGRAVE
(Great Britain-Rowing)
1984-Coxed Four; 1988-Coxless Pair; 1992-Coxless Pair
1996-Coxless Pair; 2000-Coxless Four

BIRGIT FISCHER*
(Germany/German Democratic Republic-Canoeing)
1980-K1 500m; 1988-K2 500m & K4 500m; 1992-K1 500m
1996-K4 500m; 2000-K2 500m & K4 500m

Fischer was unable to compete at the 1984 Olympic Games due to the East German participation in the Soviet-led boycott. A strict five-in-a-row for Fischer was therefore an impossiblity, but her achievement in winning five titles over six Olympic Games matches, if not surpasses, that of Redgrave.

On the same day the eight wrapped up gold, Denise Lewis held injury at bay to take her first Olympic heptathlon title. Damaged ankle ligaments almost prevented her from starting in the final event, the 800m. Lewis had fortune favour her, though; Ghada Shouaa was never fit enough (physically) to defend her title, and Eunice Barber, the French world champion was never fit enough (mentally) to put together a serious challenge. The competition was still close, Lewis not knowing when she crossed the line in the 800m that she had won by 53 points from the Russian, Yelena Prokhorova. Lewis thus became only the sixth British woman ever to win an athletics gold medal; the others being Sally Gunnell, Tessa Sanderson, Mary Rand, Ann Packer and Mary Peters, who won this equivalent title when it was a pentathlon.

Jonathan Edwards was the enigma, so far ahead of the opposition since his boundless leaps in Gothenburg in 1995 that not to win in Atlanta was a calamity. This time, failure did not seem to alarm him as much and he settled into his rhythm and duly won. Kelly Holmes won a bronze in the 800m when the odds were long that she would never reach Sydney such was the catalogue of injuries, and Katharine Merry took the same medal in the 400m, Donna Fraser close enough in fourth to undo her shoelaces. Steve Backley announced he would be back, after failing to beat Jan Zelezny yet again. Backley cherished his silver, but no one deserves a gold more than the Cambridge Harrier.

Marion Jones won only three of the five titles she was chasing (put off no doubt by the string of positive drug tests that were attributed to her husband C J Hunter). Heike Drechsler won the long jump ahead of Jones, the 35-year-old having won her first global long jump title back in 1983, when she won the world title as an 18-year-old.

Michael Johnson bowed out of major events with a facile win in the 400, but Cathy Freeman, in the women's 400m, had the hardest task, having to live up to the alarming hype generated by the home nation media. It could not have been helped by her selection as the candle lighter at the opening ceremony. Our statistics are not rock-solid here, but we can't find any previous occasion when the lighter of the Olympic flame went on to win an Olympic title. Ron Clarke, who lit the flame at Melbourne in 1956, had the opportunity. But though he broke 14 world records he never did win an Olympic title.

Over the nine competition days, not a single world record was broken. Primo Nebiolo, were he still with us, would have been horrified. Yet the atmostphere was electric and the competition was sensational. You do not need records to have great athletics.

Midway through the second week, British competitiors had accumulated six gold medals, the best tally since the last occasion the Games were in Australia, at Melbourne in 1956. Amazingly, the best was yet to come. On the periphery for the first week was super-heavyweight Audley Harrison and the sailors, who came to Sydney without a single global champion, yet would end the Olympics with three.

Ian Barker and Simon Hiscocks set the tone, winning silver in the newest Olympic class, the 49er. Barker took the ensuing celebrations so seriously that he probably has no knowledge to this day what happened in the next three days. Several team members were surprised to see him standing, and on his own feet, to receive his medal. Their silver would be matched by the Star class crew of Ian Walker and Mark Covell, who were only in their second season in the class. For Walker it matched the medal he won in Atlanta with the late John Merricks. Covell's partner Glyn Charles had also died, lost overboard in the tumultuous seas of the 1998 Sydney-Hobart race. The medal was sweet, but the memories were sad.

"Even when he is throwing rubbish in the bin, he has to be the best"
Jürgen Gröbler, the British men's rowing coach, on Redgrave.

"You will remember this six minutes for the rest of your life"
Tim Foster, recounting Steve Redgrave's words to him after the race.

"I can navigate through a crowded room, though I wouldn't be able to recognise people around me. I can run by myself on the track, on roads and on wood-chip trails, but sometimes I can't see my coach standing 10 feet away"
Marla Runyan, the US athlete who has been registered blind since the age of 11. Runyan was eighth in the 1500m final.

"My dream is to see posters of female weightlifters on the walls of guys' locker rooms, like you do pin-ups"
Cheryl Haworth, 17-year-old US female weightlifter.

"The image is the ice-man. You walk like an ice-man and think like an ice-man"
Peter Terry, sports psychologist, explaining how he had helped Richard Faulds to win double trap gold.

"I guess what comes around goes around"
Ben Ainslie, after tactically out-playing Robert Scheidt to win the Olympic laser class title. Scheidt had teased Ainslie into a false start in Atlanta to ensure he took the title that day.

"He's a lazy bugger. He doesn't want to work too hard"
Joe Bugner, on Audley Harrison.

"No matter how much I shower with soap, I always smell of chlorine"
Lenny Krayzelburg, US gold medallist in the 100m and 200m backstroke.

"I had never been in a pool that big before, I was scared"
Eric Moussambani, or Eric the Eel, as he was better known.

"We wouldn't have even qualified if it hadn't been for them and all they taught us. There's never a day gone by when we don't think of their families and we dedicate this to their memory"
Ian Walker who won silver in the Star class with Mark Covell. Each of their previous partners had died tragically, John Merricks in a car crash, Glyn Charles in the Sydney-Hobart race.

Shirley Robertson was the first to strike gold, the first British female sailor ever. The red-hot favourite was the Dutchwoman Margriet Matthijsse whose coach accused her of throwing the Olympic title away. "You are too arrogant. You always go right when everyone else goes left," he said. That gives no credit to Robertson who grasped the tactical requirements of the harbour course. The wind abided by its own rules during this competition, so the secret was to play the percentage game. The 32-year-old Scot did it to perfection. Matthijsse won the last three races, but it was too late. A relaxed and confident Robertson, so often a medallist and so seldom a champion, had finally made it.

Ben Ainslie's victory was comfortably the most cerebral moment of the Olympic Games. When he set out on the 11th and final race of the series to steal Robert Scheidt's wind, even weather-beaten stalwarts of the team management weren't quite sure what was happening. Including the two discards, Ainslie started the final race seven points behind the Brazilian and calculated, quite sensibly, that however well he sailed it was unlikely that Scheidt would finish eight places lower.

The answer lay in the second discard; Ainslie's was an 11th place, Scheidt's was a 20th place. Ainslie's stratagem was to keep Scheidt at the back of the fleet for the last race, their lowly placings therefore becoming discards. This would bring into play the 11th and the 20th, the nine points difference sufficient for Ainslie to overhaul the world champion. The plan worked a treat, Ainslie so frustrating the Brazilian that he resorted to bulldozing the British boat aside and was subsequently disqualified. "I didn't believe he would do this," said Scheidt, whose memory must have been failing him. In Atlanta, he teased Ainslie into a false start to secure his Olympic title. He who wins by the rules can lose by them too.

Iain Percy's victory was, by comparison, utterly uneventful. He would probably have sewed it up on Friday - to make it a three-gold day for Briton - but the wind had no respect for such statistics and abated. Percy's 20-point margin was never threatened on the Saturday and he did not even need to sail the last race to guarantee the title.

So to Sunday, with nine medals down and two to play for. Audley Harrison had only to win four fights to become an Olympic champion and he did. Moreover, not once was the Brunel graduate seriously threatened. He coasted it. No sooner was that title posted on the medal board than another came in the women's pentathlon where Stephanie Cook proved that you can be a dodgy fencer and still win an Olympic title. As the press gathered for Cook's conference, the television in the press room was relaying the marathon. It showed Jon Brown with the leading pack and the joy was mingled with panic amongst the writers most of whom were athletics correspondents doubling up on the modern pentathlon. Brown didn't win, but he just could have. It was that kind of day; that kind of Olympics.

For Australia, the Games was an immeasurable success, defined by attitude. They passionately wanted it to work, and so it did, magnificently. Australians were also responsible for the greatest race of the Games. No, not Freeman, but the men's 4x100m freestyle relay. It helped that the Americans had never lost the event, that gave the moment its edge. When Gary Hall jr sounded off about "smashing them like guitars (Weird man, weird quote) it sharpened the edge. Ian Thorpe supplied the rebuke with a mesmeric final leg that took Australia to the gold medal. Even the rest of the swimming (as wonderful as it was) paled in comparison to that.

See also individual Sports sections for more Olympic reports

Medal Table

1	USA	39	25	33	97	41	Uzbekistan	1	1	2	4
2	Russia	32	28	28	88	42	Yugoslavia	1	1	1	3
3	China	28	16	15	59		Latvia	1	1	1	3
4	Australia	16	25	17	58	44	Bahamas	1	1	0	2
5	Germany	14	17	26	57	45	New Zealand	1	0	3	4
6	France	13	14	11	38	46	Thailand	1	0	2	3
7	Italy	13	8	13	34		Estonia	1	0	2	3
8	Netherlands	12	9	4	25	48	Croatia	1	0	1	2
9	Cuba	11	11	7	29	49	Mozambique	1	0	0	1
10	Great Britain	11	10	7	28		Cameroon	1	0	0	1
11	Romania	11	6	9	26		Colombia	1	0	0	1
12	Korea	8	9	11	28	52	Brazil	0	6	6	12
13	Hungary	8	6	3	17	53	Jamaica	0	4	3	7
14	Poland	6	5	3	14	54	Nigeria	0	3	0	3
15	Japan	5	8	5	18	55	South Africa	0	2	3	5
16	Bulgaria	5	6	2	13		Belgium	0	2	3	5
17	Greece	4	6	3	13	57	Argentina	0	2	2	4
18	Sweden	4	5	3	12	58	Chinese Taipei	0	1	4	5
19	Norway	4	3	3	10		Morocco	0	1	4	5
20	Ethiopia	4	1	3	8	60	North Korea	0	1	3	4
21	Ukraine	3	10	10	23	61	Moldova	0	1	1	2
22	Kazakhstan	3	4	0	7		Trinidad & Tobago	0	1	1	2
23	Belarus	3	3	11	17		Saudi Arabia	0	1	1	2
24	Canada	3	3	8	14	64	Ireland	0	1	0	1
25	Spain	3	3	5	11		Vietnam	0	1	0	1
26	Iran	3	0	1	4		Uruguay	0	1	0	1
	Turkey	3	0	1	4	67	Georgia	0	0	6	6
28	Czech Republic	2	3	3	8	68	Costa Rica	0	0	2	2
29	Kenya	2	3	2	7		Portugal	0	0	2	2
30	Denmark	2	3	1	6	70	Armenia	0	0	1	1
31	Finland	2	1	1	4		Barbados	0	0	1	1
32	Austria	2	1	0	3		Chile	0	0	1	1
33	Lithuania	2	0	3	5		Iceland	0	0	1	1
34	Azerbaijan	2	0	1	3		India	0	0	1	1
35	Slovenia	2	0	0	2		Israel	0	0	1	1
36	Switzerland	1	6	2	9		Kuwait	0	0	1	1
37	Indonesia	1	3	2	6		Kyrgyzstan	0	0	1	1
38	Slovakia	1	3	1	5		Macedonia	0	0	1	1
39	Mexico	1	2	3	6		Qatar	0	0	1	1
40	Algeria	1	1	3	5		Sri Lanka	0	0	1	1

Archery

Sydney International Archery Park
Sep 16-22

Men
1 Simon Fairweather AUS
2 Victor Wunderle USA
3 Wietse van Altan NED
17 Simon Needham GBR
Needham's details...
Ranking rd: 9th
bt Ken Uprichard NZL 160-155
lost to Ismely Arias CUB
164-164 (on shoot-off)

Men's Team
1 South Korea
2 Italy
3 United States
No British team

Women
1 Jun Mi-jin KOR
2 Kim Nam-soon KOR
3 Kim Soo-nyung KOR
9 Alison Williamson GBR
39 Vladlena Priestman GBR
Williamson's details...
Ranking rd: 20th
bt Kristina Nordlander SWE 156-145
bt Elif Altinkaynaf TUR 157-154
lost to Jun Mi-jin KOR 164-173
Priestman's details...
Ranking rd: 46th
lost to Cornelia Pfohl GER 155-159

Women's Team
1 South Korea
2 Ukraine
3 Germany
No British team

Athletics

Sydney Olympic Stadium
Sep 22-Oct 1

Men

100m
1 Maurice Greene USA	9.87
2 Ato Bolden TRI	9.99
3 Obadele Thompson BAR	10.04
4 Dwain Chambers GBR	10.08
6 Darren Campbell GBR	10.13

200m
1 Konstantinos Kenteris GRE	20.09
2 Darren Campbell GBR	20.14
3 Ato Bolden TRI	20.20
5 Christian Malcolm GBR	20.23

Elim q-f: Marlon Devonish GBR

400m
1 Michael Johnson USA	43.84
2 Alvin Harrison USA	44.40
3 Gregory Haughton JAM	44.70

Elim s-f: Daniel Caines GBR
Elim rd 1: Sean Baldock GBR

800m
1 Nils Schumann GER	1:45.08
2 Wilson Kipketer DEN	1:45.14
3 Aissa Said-Guerni ALG	1:45.16

Elim s-f: James McIlroy GBR

1500m
1 Noah Ngeny KEN	3:32.07
2 Hicham El Guerrouj MAR	3:32.32
3 Bernard Lagat KEN	3:32.44
9 John Mayock ENG	3:39.41

Elim s-f: Andrew Graffin GBR

5000m
1 Millon Wolde ETH	13:35.49
2 Ali Saidi-Sief ALG	13:36.20
3 Brahim Lahlafi MAR	13:36.47

Elim rd 1: Kristen Bowditch GBR

10,000m
1 Haile Gebrselassie ETH	27:18.20
2 Paul Tergat KEN	27:18.29
3 Assefa Mezegebu ETH	27:19.75
8 Karl Keska GBR	27:44.09

Elim rd 1: Rob Denmark GBR

Marathon
1 Gezaghne Abera ETH	2:10:11
2 Eric Wainaina KEN	2:10:31
3 Tesfaye Tola ETH	2:11:10
4 Jon Brown GBR	2:11:17
56 Mark Steinle GBR	2:24:42

3000m Steeplechase
1 Reuben Koskei KEN	8:21.43
2 Wilson Boit Kipketer KEN	8:21.77
3 Ali Ezzine MAR	8:22.15

Eim rd 1: Justin Chaston GBR,
Christian Stephenson GBR

110m Hurdles
1 Anier Garcia CUB	13.16
2 Mark Crear USA	13.23
3 Terrance Trammell USA	13.32
5 Colin Jackson GBR	13.34

Elim 2nd rd: Damien Greaves GBR

400m Hurdles
1 Angelo Taylor USA	47.50
2 Hadi Souan Somayli KSA	47.53
3 Llewellyn Herbert RSA	47.81

Elim s-f: Chris Rawlinson GBR

Pole Vault
1 Nick Hysong USA	5.90m
2 Lawrence Johnson USA	5.90m
3 Maksim Tarasov RUS	5.90m

Elim qual: Kevin Hughes GBR

High Jump
1 Sergey Klyugin RUS	2.35m
2 Javier Sotomayor CUB	2.32m
3 A Hammad ALG	2.32m

Elim qual: Ben Challenger GBR

Long Jump
1 Ivan Pedroso CUB	8.55m
2 Jai Taurima AUS	8.49m
3 Roman Shchurenko UKR	8.31m

Elim qual: Nathan Morgan GBR

Triple Jump
1 Jonathan Edwards GBR	17.71m
2 Yoel Garcia CUB	17.47m
3 Denis Kapustin RUS	17.46m
5 Larry Achike GBR	17.29m
6 Phillips Idowu GBR	17.08m

Shot
1 Arsi Harju FIN	21.29m
2 Adam Nelson USA	21.21m
3 John Godina USA	21.20m

Elim qual: Mark Proctor GBR

Discus
1 Virgilius Alekna LTU	69.30m
2 Lars Riedel GER	68.50m
3 Frantz Kruger RSA	68.19m

Elilm qual: Robert Weir GBR,
Glen Smith GBR

Hammer
1 Szymon Ziolkowski POL	80.02m
2 Nicola Vizzoni ITA	79.64m
3 Igor Astapkovich BLR	79.17m

Javelin
1 Jan Zelezny CZE	90.17m
2 Steve Backley GBR	89.85m
3 Sergey Makarov RUS	88.67m
11 Mick Hill GBR	81.00m

Elim qual: Nick Nieland GBR

Decathlon
1 Erki Nool EST	8641

(10.68/7.76m/15.11m/2.00m/46.71/
14.48/43.66m/5.00m/65.82m/4:29.48)

2 Roman Sebrle CZE	8606
3 Chris Huffins USA	8595
4 Dean Macey GBR	8567

(10.81/7.77m/14.62m/2.09m/46.41/
14.53/43.37m/4.80m/60.38m/4:23.45)

20km Walk
1 Robert Korzeniowski POL	1:18:59
2 Noe Hernandez MEX	1:19:03
3 Vladimir Andreyev RUS	1:19:27

50km Walk
1 Robert Korzeniowski POL	3:42:22
2 Aigars Fadejevs LAT	3:43:40
3 Joel Sanchez MEX	3:44:36
39 Chris Maddocks GBR	4:52:12

4x100m Relay
1 USA	37.61

(Drummond/Williams/Lewis/Greene)

2 Brazil	37.90
3 Cuba	38.04

Great Britain (Condon/Gardner/
Devonish/Chambers)disqualified in rd 1
for faulty changeover

4x400m Relay
1 USA	2:56.35

(A Harrison/Pettigrew/C Harrison/
Johnson)

2 Nigeria	2:58.68
3 Jamaica	2:58.78
6 Great Britain	3:01.22

(Deacon/Caines/Thomas/Baulch)

Women

100m
1	Marion Jones USA	10.75
2	Ekaterini Thanou GRE	11.12
3	Tanya Lawrence JAM	11.18

Elim rd1: Joice Maduaka GBR, Shani Anderson GBR, Marcia Richardson GBR

200m
1	Marion Jones USA	21.84
2	Pauline Davis-Thompson BAH	22.27
3	Susanthika Jayasinghe SRI	22.28

Elim rd 2: Samantha Davies GBR, Joice Maduaka GBR

400m
1	Cathy Freeman AUS	49.11
2	Lorraine Graham JAM	49.58
3	Katharine Merry GBR	49.72
4	Donna Fraser GBR	49.79

Elim rd 2: Allison Curbishley GBR

800m
1	Maria Mutola MOZ	1:56.16
2	Stephanie Graf AUT	1:56.64
3	Kelly Holmes GBR	1:56.80

Elim rd 1: Diane Modahl GBR

1500m
1	Nouria Merah-Benida ALG	4:05.10
2	Violeta Szekely ROM	4:05.15
3	Gabriela Szabo ROM	4:05.27
7	Kelly Holmes GBR	4:08.02
11	Hayley Tullett GBR	4:22.29

Elim s-f: Helen Pattinson GBR

5000m
1	Gabriela Szabo ROM	14:40.79
2	Sonia O'Sullivan IRL	14:41.02
3	Gete Wami ETH	14:42.23
12	Jo Pavey GBR	14:58.27

Elim qual: Andrea Whitcombe GBR

10,000m
1	Derartu Tulu ETH	30:17.49
2	Gete Wami ETH	30:22.48
3	Fernando Ribeiro POR	30:22.88
4	Paula Radcliffe GBR	30:26.97

Marathon
1	Naoko Takahashi JPN	2:23:14
2	Lidia Simon ROM	2:23:22
3	Joyce Chepchumba KEN	2:24:45
26	Marian Sutton GBR	2:34:33

110m Hurdles
1	Olga Shishigina KZK	12.65
2	Glory Alozie NGR	12.68
3	Melissa Morrison USA	12.76

Elim rd 2: Diane Allahgreen GBR

400m Hurdles
1	Irina Privalova RUS	53.02
2	Deon Hemmings JAM	53.45
3	Nezha Bidouane MAR	53.57
8	Natasha Danvers GBR	55.00

Elim rd 1: Keri Maddox GBR, Sinead Dudgeon GBR

Pole Vault
1	Stacy Dragila USA	4.60m
2	Tatiana Grigorieva AUS	4.55m
3	Vala Flosadottir ISL	4.50m

Elim qual: Janine Whitlock GBR

High Jump
1	Yelena Yelesina RUS	2.01m
2	Hestrie Cloete RSA	2.01m
3	Kajsa Bergqvist SWE	1.99m

Long Jump
1	Heike Drechsler GER	6.99m
2	Fiona May ITA	6.92m
3	Marion Jones USA	6.92m

Elim qual: Jo Wise GBR

Triple Jump
1	Tereza Marinova BUL	15.20m
2	Tatyana Lebedeva RUS	15.00m
3	Olena Hovorova UKR	14.96m
11	Ashia Hansen GBR	13.44m

Shot
1	Yanina Korolchik BLR	20.56m
2	Larisa Peleshenko RUS	19.92m
3	Astrid Kumbernuss GER	19.62m

Elim qual: Judy Oakes GBR

Discus
1	Ellina Zvereva BLR	68.40m
2	Anastasia Kelesidou GRE	65.71m
3	Irina Yatchenko BLR	65.20m

Hammer
1	Kamila Skolimowska POL	71.16m
2	Olga Kuzenkova RUS	69.77m
3	Kirsten Münchow GER	69.28m
9	Lorraine Shaw GBR	64.27m

Javelin
1	Trine Hattestad NOR	68.91m
2	Mirella Maniani-Tzelili GRE	67.51m
3	Osleidys Menendez CUB	66.18m

Pentathlon
1	Denise Lewis GBR	6584

(13.23/1.75m/15.55m/24.34/6.48m/ 50.19m/2:16.83)

2	Yelena Prokhorova RUS	6531
3	Natalya Sazanovich BLR	6527

20km Walk
1	Wang Liping CHN	1:29:05
2	Kjersti Plaetzer NOR	1:29:33
3	Mario Vasco ESP	1:30:23
33	Lisa Kehler GBR	1:37:47

4x100m Relay
1	Bahamas	41.95
2	Jamaica	42.13
3	USA	42.20

Elim s-f: Great Britain

4x400m Relay
1	USA	3:22.62
2	Jamaica	3:23.25
3	Russia	3:23.46
6	Great Britain	3:25.67

(Danvers/Fraser/Curbishley/Merry)

Badminton

Pavilion 3, Olympic Park
Sep 16-23

Men's Singles
1	Ji Xinpeng CHN
2	Hendrawan INA
3	Xia Xuanze CHN

Richard Vaughan GBR
bt Boonsak Ponsana THA 15-8 15-12
bt Rasmus Wengberg SWE 15-8 15-4
lost to Sun Jun CHN 10-15 8-15
Peter Knowles GBR
lost to Ewe Hock Ong MAS 15-3 12-15 5-15

Men's Doubles
1	Gunawan/Wijawa INA
2	Lee/Yoo CHN
3	Ha/Kim KOR

Simon Archer/Nathan Robertson GBR
bt Logosz/Mateusiak POL 15-1 15-10
lost to Gunawan/Wijawa INA 15-13 15-11
Peter Knowles/Julian Robertson GBR
bt Clarisse/Constantin MRI 15-6 15-10
lost to Hiam/Limpele INA 15-4 15-8

Women's Singles
1	Gong Zhichao CHN
2	Camilla Martin DEN
3	Ye Zhaoying CHN

Kelly Morgan GBR...
bt Aparna Popat IND 5-11 11-7 11-2
bt Wai Koon HKG 8-11 11-3 11-1
lost to Camila Martin DEN 7-11 3-11
Julia Mann GBR...
bt Amrita Sawaram MRI 11-0 11-0
bt Maja Pohar SLO 11-4 11-7
lost to Yasuko Mizui JPN 9-11 5-11

Women's Doubles
1	Ge/Gu CHN
2	Huang/Yang CHN
3	Gao/Qin CHN

Joanne Goode/Donna Kellogg GBR
bt Cloutier/Hermitage CAN 15-4 15-10
lost to Gao/Qin CHN 2-15 7-15
Joanne Davies/Sarah Hardaker GBR
bt Elysa/Lomban INA 15-13 15-11
lost to Chung/Ra 6-15 1-15

Mixed Doubles
1	Zhang/Gao CHN
2	Kusharyanto/Timur INA
3	Archer/Goode GBR

Simon Archer/Jo Goode...
bt Olynyk/Hermitage CAN 15-9 15-9
bt Holst-Christensen/Jorgensen DEN 15-17 15-11 15-7
bt Bruil/Heuvel NED 15-12 15-12
lost to Kusharyanto/Timur INA 15-2 15-17 11-15
bt Sogaard/Olsen DEN 15-4 12-15 17-14
Chris Hunt/Donna Kellogg GBR...
lost to Suprianto/Resiana INA 15-0 15-10

Baseball

Baseball Centre & Aquilina Reserve
Sep 17-27

Men
1 USA
2 Cuba
3 South Korea
USA bt Cuba 4-0 in final
South Korea bt Japan 3-1 in bronze match

Basketball

The Dome/SuperDome
Sep 16-Oct 1

Men
1 USA
2 France
3 Lithuania
USA bt France 85-75 in final
Lithuania bt Australia 89-71 in bronze match

Women
1 USA
2 Australia
3 Brazil
USA bt Australia 76-54 in final
Brazil bt South Korea 84-73 in bronze match

Boxing

Sydney Exhibition Centre
Sep 16-Oct 1

51kg (Flyweight)
1 Wijan Ponlid THA
2 Bulat Jumadilov KZK
3 Jerome Thomas FRA

54kg (Bantamweight)
1 Ortiz Rigondeaux CUB
2 Raimkoul Malakhbekov RUS
3 Sergey Daniltchenko UKR

57kg (Featherweight)
1 Bekhat Sattarkhanov KZK
2 Ricardo Juarez USA
3 Tahar Tamsamani MAR

60kg (Lightweight)
1 Mario Kindelin CUB
2 Andrey Kotelnyk UKR
3 Cristian Bejarano MEX

63.5kg (Light-welterweight)
1 Mahamadkadyz Abdullaev UZB
2 Ricardo Williams USA
3 Mohamed Allalou ALG

67kg (Welterweight)
1 Oleg Saitov RUS
2 Sergey Dotsenko UKR
3 Vitaly Grusac MDA

71kg (Light-middleweight)
1 Yermakhan Ibraimov KZK
2 Marin Simion CUB
3 Pornchai Thongburan THA

75kg (Middleweight)
1 Jorge Gutierrez CUB
2 Gaidarbek Gaidarbekov RUS
3 Vugar Alekperov AZE

81kg (Light-heavyweight)
1 Alexander Lebziak RUS
2 Rudolf Kraj CZE
3 Andri Fedtchouk UKR
Courtney Fry GBR...
lost to Charles Adamu GHA 16-3

91kg (Heavyweight)
1 Felix Savon CUB
2 Sultanahmed Ibzagimov RUS
3 Vladimir Tchantouria GEO

+91kg (Super-heavyweight)
1 Audley Harrison GBR
2 Mukhtarkham Dildabekov KZK
3 Paolo Vidoz ITA
Harrison... bt Alexey Lezin RUS
Ref stopped contest - head injury
bt Oleksi Mazikin UKR 19-5
bt Vidoz 32-16
bt Dildabekov 30-16

Canoeing,Slalom

Whitewater Stadium, Penrith
Sep 17-20

Men

K1 Slalom
1 Thomas Schmidt GER	217.25	
(108.64/108.61)		
2 Paul Ratcliffe GBR	223.71	
(112.22/109.49)		
3 Pierpaolo Ferrazzi ITA	225.03	
(111.79/113.24)		

C1 Slalom
1 Tony Estanguet FRA	231.87
(115.25/114.62)	
2 Michal Martikan SVK	233.76
(119.17/114.59)	
3 Juraj Mincik SVK	234.22
(117.55/116.67)	
8 Stuart McIntosh GBR	243.61
(121.23/118.38)	

C2 Slalom
1 Pavol & Peter Hornschorner CZE	
(121.01/116.73)	237.74
2 Kolomanski/Staniszweski POL	
(124.19/119.62)	243.81
3 Jiras/Mader CZE	
(123.43/126.02)	249.45
4 Stuart Bowman/Nick Smith GBR	
(123.85/126.08)	249.93

Women

K1 Slalom
1 Stepanka Hilgertova CZE	247.04
(125.21/121.83)	
2 Brigitte Guibal FRA	251.88
(124.98/126.90)	
3 Anne-Lise Bardet FRA	254.77
(125.77/129.00)	
12 Laura Blakeman GBR	273.71
(136.91/136.80)	

Canoeing, Sprint

Regatta Centre, Penrith
Sep 27-Oct 1

Men

K1 500m
1 Knut Holmann NOR	1:57.847
2 Petar Merkov BUL	1:58.393
3 Michael Kolganov ISR	1:59.563

Elim s-f: Ian Wynne GBR

K1 1000m
1 Knut Holmann NOR	3:33.269
2 Petar Merkov BUL	3:34.649
3 Tim Brabants GBR	3:35.057

K2 500m
1 Kammerer/Storcz HUN	1:47.055
2 Collins/Trim AUS	1:47.895
3 Rauhe/Wieskötter GER	1:48.771

Elim s-f: Ross Sabberton/Paul Darby-Dowman GBR

K2 1000m
1 Bonomi/Rossi ITA	3:14.461
2 Oscarsson/Nilsson SWE	3:16.075
3 Bartfai/Vereb HUN	3:16.357

Elim s-f: Sabberton/Darby-Dowman

K4 1000m
1 Hungary	2:55.188

(Verecki/Horvath/Kammerer/Storcz)
2 Germany	2:55.704
3 Poland	2:57.192

C1 500m
1 Gyorgy Kolonics HUN	2:24.813
2 Maxim Opalev RUS	2:25.809
3 Andreas Dittmer GER	2:27.591

C1 1000m
1 Andreas Dittmer GER	3:54.379
2 Ledys Balciero CUB	3:56.071
3 Steve Giles CAN	3:56.437

C2 500m
1 Novak/Pulai HUN	1:51.284
2 Jedraszko/Baraszkiewicz POL	
	1:51.536
3 Popescu/Pricop ROM	1:54.260

Elim s-f: Stephen & Andrew Train GBR

C2 1000m
1 Popescu/Pricop ROM	3:37.355
2 Rojas/Pereira CUB	3:38.753
3 Kober/Utess GER	3:41.129

Elim s-f: Stephen & Andrew Train GBR

Women

K1 500m
1 Josepha Idem ITA	2:13.848
2 Caroline Brunet CAN	2:14.646
3 Katrin Borchert AUS	2:15.138

Elim s-f: Anna Hemmings GBR

K2 500m
1 Fischer/Wagner GER	1:56.996
2 Kovacs/Szabo HUN	1:58.580
3 Pastuszka/Sokolowska POL	
	1:58.784

K4 500m
1 Germany	1:34.532

(Fischer/Schuk/Mucke/Wagner)
2 Hungary	1:34.946
3 Romania	1:37.010

Cycling, Mountain Bikes

Fairfield   Sep 23-24

Men's Cross-country

1	Miguel Martinez FRA	2:09:02.50
2	Filip Meirhaeghe BEL	+1:03.01
3	Christoph Sauser SUI	+2:18.50
23	Oliver Beckinsale GBR	+9:14.51
25	Nick Craig GBR	+10:57.77

Women's Cross-country

1	Paola Pezzo ITA	1:49:24.38
2	Barbara Blatter SUI	+27.04
3	Margarita Fullana ESP	+33.01
12	Caroline Alexander GBR	+7:11.33
15	Louise Robinson GBR	+8:33.68

Cycling, Road

Centennial Park
Sep 11, 12 & 15

Men

Individual Time Trial

1	Viacheslav Ekimov RUS	57:40
2	Jan Ullrich GER	+8
3	Lance Armstrong USA	+34
11	Chris Boardman GBR	+1:52
16	David Millar GBR	+2:37

Road Race

1	Jan Ullrich GER	5:29.08
2	Alexandre Vinokourov KZK	+9
3	Andreas Klöden GER	+12
35	Max Sciandri GBR	+1:28
38	John Tanner GBR	+1:38

DNF: Rob Hayles, Nick Craig, Jeremy Hunt, all GBR

Women

Individual Time Trial

1	Leontien Zijlaard NED	42:00
2	Mari Holden USA	+37
3	Jeannie Longo-Ciprelli FRA	+52
14	Ceris Gilfillan GBR	+1:21
17	Yvonne McGregor GBR	+2:37

Road Race

1	Leontien Zijlaard NED	3:06:31
2	Hanka Kupfernagel GER	st
3	Diane Ziliute LTU	st
10	Sara Symington GBR	st
24	Yvonne McGregor GBR	st
27	Ceris Gilfillan GBR	+6

Cycling, Track

Dunc Gray Velodrome, Bankstown
Sep 16-21

Men

Sprint

1	Marty Northstein USA	10.874
2	Florian Rousseau FRA	11.066
3	Jens Fieldler GER	

Elim q-f: Craig MacLean GBR

Individual Pursuit

1	Robert Bartko GER	4:18.515
2	Jens Lehmann GER	4:23.824
3	Brad McGee AUS	
4	Rob Hayles GBR	

1km Time Trial

1	Jason Queally GBR	1:01.609
2	Stefan Nimke GER	1:02.487
3	Shane Kelly AUS	1:02.818

Points Race

1	Juan Llaneras ESP	14
2	Milton Wynants URU	18 (-1 lp)
3	Alexey Markov RUS	16 (-1 lp)
13	Jonny Clay GBR	10 (-2 lps)

Keirin

1	Florian Rousseau FRA	11.020
2	Gary Neiwand AUS	
3	Jens Fieldler GER	

Elim rd 1: Chris Hoy GBR

Olympic Sprint

1	France	44.233
(Gane/Tournant/Rousseau)		
2	Great Britain	44.680
(MacLean/Hoy/Queally)		
3	Australia	

Team Pursuit

1	Germany	3:59.710
(Bartko/Fulst/Lehmann/Becke)		
2	Ukraine	4:04.520
3	Great Britain	
(Manning/Wiggins/Newton/Steel)		

Madison

1	Aitken/McGrory AUS	26pts
2	De Wilde/Gilmore BEL	22pts
3	Villa/Martinello ITA	15pts
4	Wiggins/Hayles GBR	13pts

Women

Sprint

1	Felicia Ballanger FRA	11.810
2	Oxana Grichina RUS	12.533
3	Iryna Yanovych UKR	

Individual Pursuit

1	Leontien Zijlaard NED	3:33.360
2	Marion Clignet FRA	3:38.751
3	Yvonne McGregor GBR	

500m Time Trial

1	Felicia Ballanger FRA	34.140
2	Michelle Ferris AUS	34.696
3	Jiang Cuihua CHN	34.768

Points Race

1	Antonella Bellutti ITA	19
2	Leontien Zijlaard NED	16
3	Olga Slioussareva RUS	15
14	Emma Davies GBR	-

Diving

Olympic Pool, Ryde Leisure Centre
Sep 22-30

Men

3m Springboard

1	Xiong Ni CHN	708.72
2	Fernando Platas MEX	708.42
3	Dmitri Sautin RUS	703.20
12	Tony Ally GBR	583.80
46	Mark Shipman GBR	

10m Platform

1	Tian Liang CHN	724.53
2	Hu Jia CHN	713.55
3	Dmitri Sautin RUS	679.26
13	Leon Taylor GBR	
33	Peter Waterfield GBR	

3m Synchro

1	Xiao/Xiong CHN	365.58
2	Dobroskok/Sautin RUS	329.97
3	Newbery/Pullar AUS	322.86
7	Ally/Shipman GBR	296.64

10m Synchro

1	Loukachine/Sautin RUS	365.04
2	Hu/Tian CHN	358.74
3	Hempel/Meyer GER	338.88
4	Taylor/Waterfield GBR	335.34

Women

3m Springboard

1	Fu Mingxia CHN	609.42
2	Guo Jingjing CHN	597.81
3	Dörte Lindner GER	574.35
16	Jane Smith GBR	
31	Karen Smith GBR	

10m Platform

1	Laura Wilkinson USA	543.75
2	Li Na CHN	542.01
3	Anne Montminy CAN	540.15
25	Sally Freeman GBR	
28	Lesley Ward GBR	

3m Synchro

1	Ilina/Pakhalina RUS	332.64
2	Fu/Guo CHN	321.60
3	Sorokina/Zhupina UKR	290.34

10m Synchro

1	Li/Sang CHN	345.12
2	Heymans/Montminy CAN	312.03
3	Gilmore/Tourky AUS	301.50

Equestrianism

Horsley Park
Three-day Events: Sep 16-Oct 1

Dressage

Individual

1 Anky van Grunsven NED	239.18
(Bonfire)	
2 Isabell Werth GER	234.19
(Gigolo)	
3 Ulla Salzgeber GER	230.57
(Rusty)	

Elim: Emil Faurie (Rascher Hopes)
Carl Hester (Argentile Gullit)
Richard Davidson (Askari)
Kirsty Mepham (Dikkiloo), all GBR

Team

1 Germany	5632
2 Netherlands	5579
3 USA	5166
8 Great Britain	4898

Showjumping

Individual

1 Jeroen Dubbeldam NED	4.00
(Sjiem)	
2 Albert Voorn NED	4.00
(Lando)	
3 Khaled Al Eid KSA	4.00
(Khasm Al Aan)	
24 Geoff Billington GBR	24.00
(It's Otto)	

Elim: Carl Edwards (Bit More Candy)
Michael Whitaker (Prince of Wales)
John Whitaker (Calvaro)

Team

1 France	8.00
2 Germany	8.00
3 Switzerland	8.00
9 Great Britain	20.50

(Billington/M Whitaker/J Whitaker/
Edwards - mounts as above)

Three-day Event

Individual

1 David O'Connor AUS	34.00
(Custom Made)	
2 Andrew Hoy AUS	39.80
(Swizzle In)	
3 Mark Todd NZL	42.00
(Eyespy II)	
7 Mary King GBR	52.00
(Star Appeal)	
10 Ian Stark GBR	56.00
(Arakai)	
11 Karen Dixon GBR	60.40
(Too Smart)	

Team

1 Australia	112.60
(Hoy/Dutton/Tinney/Ryan)	
2 Great Britain	115.20
(Jeanette Breakwell/Leslie Law/	
Pippa Funnell/Ian Stark)	
3 USA	125.40

(D O'Connor/Fout/Wiesman/K O'Connor)

Fencing

Sydney Convention Centre
Sep 16-24

Men

Individual Foil

1 Kim Youn-ho KOR
2 Ralf Bissdorf GER
3 Dmitri Chevtchenko RUS
28 James Beevers GBR
Beevers...
bt Marco Martins BRA 15-7
lost to Sergey Golubytsky RUS 1-15

Team Foil

1 France
2 China
3 Italy

Individual Epée

1 Pavel Kolobkov RUS
2 Hugues Obry FRA
3 Lee Sang-ki KOR

Team Epée

1 Italy
2 France
3 Cuba

Individual Sabre

1 Mihau Claudiu Covaliu ROM
2 Mathieu Gourdain FRA
3 Wiradech Kothny GER
16 James Williams GBR
Williams...
bt Diego Drajer ARG 15-13
bt Zsolt Nemcsik HUN 15-10
lost to Alexei Frossine RUS 8-15

Team Sabre

1 Russia
2 France
3 Germany

Women

Individual Foil

1 Valentina Vezzali ITA
2 Rita König GER
3 Giovanni Trillini ITA
28 Eloise Smith GBR
Smith...
bt Jo Halls AUS 15-8
lost to Giovanni Trillini ITA 2-15

Team Foil

1 Italy
2 Poland
3 Germany

Individual Epée

1 Timea Nagy HUN
2 Gianna Hablützel-Bürki SUI
3 Laura Flessel-Colovic FRA

Team Epée

1 Russia
2 Switzerland
3 China

Football

Brisbane Cricket Ground
Bruce Stadium, Canberra
Hindmarsh Stadium, Adelaide
Melbourne Cricket Ground
Sydney Football Stadium
Sep 13-30

Men

1 Cameroon
2 Spain
3 China
Final: Cameroon 2 Spain 2
(Cameroon win 5-3 on penalties)
Bronze Match: Chile 2 USA 0

Women

1 Norway
2 USA
3 Germany
Final: Norway 3 USA 2
(golden goal in extra time)
Bronze Match: Germany 2 Brazil 0

Gymnastics, Artistic

Sydney SuperDome
Sep 16-26

Men

Team

1 China	231.919
2 Ukraine	230.306
3 Russia	230.019

All-around

1 Alexey Nemov RUS	58.474
2 Yang Wei CHN	58.361
3 Oleksandr Beresh UKR	58.212
32 Craig Heap GBR	55.348

Floor

1 Igors Vihrovs LAT	9.812
2 Alexei Nemov RUS	9.800
3 Iordan Iovtchev BUL	9.787

Pommel Horse

1 Marius Urzica ROM	9.862
2 Eric Poujade FRA	9.825
3 Alexey Nemov RUS	9.800

Rings

1 Szilveszter Csollany HUN	9.850
2 Dimos Tampakos GRE	9.762
3 Iordan Iovtchev BUL	9.737

Vault

1 Gervasio Deferr ESP	9.712
2 Alexey Bondarenko RUS	9.587
3 Leszek Blanik POL	9.475

Parallel Bars

1 Li Xiaopeng CHN	9.825
2 Lee Joo-hyung KOR	9.812
3 Alexey Nemov RUS	9.800

Horizontal Bars

1 Alexey Nemov RUS	9.787
2 Benjamin Varonian FRA	9.787
3 Lee Joo-hyung KOR	9.775

Women
Team

1 Romania	154.608
2 Russia	154.403
3 China	154.008
10 Great Britain	149.483

All-around

1 Simona Amanar ROM	38.642
2 Maria Olaru ROM	38.581
3 Liu Xuan CHN	38.418
23 Lisa Mason GBR	37.167
32 Emma Williams GBR	36.443
35 Annika Reeder GBR	16.536

Vault

1 E Zamolodtchikova RUS	9.731
2 Andreea Raducan ROM	9.693
3 Ekaterina Lobazniouk RUS	9.674

Uneven Bars

1 Svetlana Khorkina RUS	9.862
2 Ling Jie CHN	9.837
3 Yang Yun CHN	9.787

Beam

1 Liu Xuan CHN	9.825
2 Ekaterina Lobazniouk RUS	9.787
3 Elena Prodounova RUS	9.775

Floor

1 E Zamolodtchikova RUS	9.850
2 Svetlana Khorkina RUS	9.812
3 Simona Amanar ROM	9.712

Gymnastics, Rhythmic

Sydney SuperDome
Sep 28-Oct 1
Team

1 Russia	39.500
2 Belarus	39.500
3 Greece	39.283

All-around

1 Yulia Barsukova RUS	39.632
2 Yulia Raskina BLR	39.548
3 Alina Kabaeva RUS	39.466

Gymnastics, Trampoline

Sydney SuperDome
Sep 22-23
Men

1 Alexandre Moskalenko RUS	41.70
2 Ji Wallace AUS	39.30
3 Mathieu Turgeon CAN	39.10
6 Lee Brearley GBR	37.90

Women

1 Irina Karavaeva RUS	38.90
2 Oxana Tsyhuleva UKR	37.70
3 Karen Cockburn CAN	37.40

Elim qual: Jaime Moore GBR (12th)

Handball

Sydney SuperDome
Sep 16-Oct 1
Men
1 Russia
2 Sweden
3 Spain
Final: Russia 28 Sweden 26
Bronze Match: Spain 26 Yugoslavia 22
Women
1 Denmark
2 Hungary
3 Norway
Final: Denmark 31 Hungary 27
Bronze Match: Norway 22 S Korea 21

Hockey

State Hockey Centre, Olympic Park
Sep 16-30
Men
1 Netherlands
2 South Korea
3 Australia
6 Great Britain
Final: Netherlands 3 Korea 3
(Netherlands won 5-4 on pens)
Bronze Match: Australia 6 Pakistan 3
Great Britain...
Pool A: Netherlands 4 G Britain 2
Pakistan 8 Great Britain 1
Malaysia 2 Great Britain 2
Canada 1 Great Britain 1
Great Britain 2 Germany 1
Classification: G Britain 2 India 1
5th/6th Play-off: Germany 4 Britain 0
Women
1 Australia
2 Argentina
3 Netherlands
6 Great Britain
Final: Australia 3 Argentina 1
Bronze Match: Netherlands 2 Spain 0
Great Britain...
Pool C: Australia 2 Great Britain 1
Argentina 1 Great Britain 0
Great Britain 2 South Korea 2
Great Britain 2 Spain 0
Classification: G Britain 3 S Africa 2
7/8th Play-off: Germany 2 G Britain 0

Judo

Sydney Convention Centre
Sep 16-22
Men
-60kg
1 Tadahiro Nomura JPN
2 Jung Bu-kyung KOR
3 Manolo Poulot CUB
3 Aidyn Smagulov KGZ
John Buchanan GBR...
lost to Oscar Penas ESP

-66kg
1 Huseyin Ozkan TUR
2 Larbi Benboudaoud FRA
3 Girolami Giovanazzo ITA
3 Giorgi Vazagashvili GEO
David Somerville GBR...
bt Miguel Angel Moreno ESA
lost to Larbi Benboudaoud FRA
-73kg
1 Giuseppe Maddaloni ITA
2 Tiago Camilo BRA
3 Anatoly Laryukov BLR
3 Vsevolods Zelonijs LAT
-81kg
1 Makoto Takimoto JPN
2 Cho In-chul KOR
3 Nuno Delgado POR
3 Aleksai Budolin EST
Graeme Randall GBR...
bt Abdessalem Arous TUN
lost to Kazem Sarikhani IRI
-90kg
1 Mark Huizinga NED
2 Carlos Honorato BRA
3 Frederic Demontfaucon FRA
3 Ruslan Mashurenko UKR
-100kg
1 Kosei Inoue JPN
2 Nicolas Gill CAN
3 Iouri Stepkine RUS
3 Stephane Traineau FRA
+100kg
1 David Douillet FRA
2 Shinichi Shinohara JPN
3 Indrek Pertelson EST
3 Tamerlan Tmenov RUS

Women
-48kg
1 Ryoko Tamura JPN
2 Liubov Brouletova RUS
3 Anna-Marie Gradante GER
3 Ann Simons BEL
Victoria Dunn GBR...
bt Natalya Kuligina KGZ
lost to Liubov Brouletova RUS
lost to Amarilys Savon CUB
-52kg
1 Legna Verdecia CUB
2 Noriko Narazaki JPN
3 Kye Sun Hui PRK
3 Liu Yuxiang CHN
Disq: Debbie Allan GBR
Allen failed to make the weight
-57kg
1 Isabel Fernandez ESP
2 Driulys Gonzalez CUB
3 Kie Kusakabe JPN
3 Maria Pekli AUS
Cheryl Peel GBR...
lost to Kie Kusakabe JPN

-63kg
1 Severine Vandenhende FRA
2 Li Shufang CHN
3 Gella Vandecaveye BEL
3 Jung Sung-sook KOR
Karen Roberts GBR...
bt Kenia Rodriguez CUB
lost to Anja von Rekowski GER
lost to Saida Dhahri TUN
-70kg
1 Sibelius Veranis CUB
2 Kate Howey GBR
3 Cho Min-sun KOR
3 Ylenia Scapin ITA
Howey...
bt Daniela Yael Krukower ARG
bt Edith Bosch NED
bt Ursula Martin ESP
lost to Sibelius Veranis CUB
-78kg
1 Tang Lin CHN
2 Celine Lebrun FRA
3 Simona Richter ROM
3 Emanuela Pierantozzi ITA
Chloe Cowen GBR...
bt Laisa Laveti FIJ
lost to Simona Richter ROM
+78kg
1 Yuan Hua CHN
2 Daima Mayelis Beltran CUB
3 Kim Seon-young KOR
3 Mayumi Yamashita JPN
Karina Bryant GBR...
bt Adja Diop SEN
lost to Christine Cicot FRA

Modern Pentathlon

Sydney SuperDome
Sep 16-Oct 1
Men
1 Dmitri Svatkovski RUS   5,376
(1048/880/1224/1070/1154)
2 Gabor Balogh HUN   5,338
(1108/920/1221/980/1124)
3 Pavel Dovgal BLR   5,338
(1168/760/1254/1070/1086)
Women
1 Stephanie Cook GBR   5,318
1072/760/1138/1040/1308)
2 Emily deRiel USA   5,310
(1156/800/1182/1070/1102)
3 Kate Allenby GBR   5,273
(1036/920/1191/1040/1086)

Rowing

Regatta Centre, Penrith
Sep 16-Oct 1
Men
Single Sculls
1 Rob Waddell NZL   6:48.90
2 Xeno Müller SUI   6:50.55
3 Marcel Hacker GER   6:50.83
Matthew Wells GBR; 3rd in B Final
Double Sculls
1 Spik/Cop SLO   6:16.63
2 Tufte/Bekken NOR   6:17.98
3 Calabrese/Sartori ITA   6:20.49
Quad Sculls
1 Italy   5:45.56
(Abagnali/Sartori/Galtarossa/Raineri)
2 Netherlands   5:47.91
(Verberne/Lippits/Simon/Bartman)
3 Germany   5:48.64
(Geisler/Hajek/Volkert/Willms)
Coxless Pair
1 Andrieux/Rolland FRA   6:32.97
2 Murphy/Lea USA   6:33.80
3 Long/Tompkins AUS   6:34.26
4 Coode/Searle GBR   6:34.38
Coxless Four
1 Great Britain   5:56.24
(Cracknell/Redgrave/Foster/Pinsent)
2 Italy   5:56.62
(Molea/Rossi/Carboncini/Mornati)
3 Australia   5:57.61
(Stewart/Dodwell/Stewart/Hanson)
Eight
1 Great Britain   5:33.08
(Lindsay/Hunt-Davis/Dennis/Attrill/
Grubor/West/Scarlett/Trapmore/Douglas)
2 Australia   5:33.88
(Ryan/Gordon/Porzig/Jahrling/McKay/
Welch/Bruke/Fernandez/Hayman)
3 Croatia   5:34.85
(Francetic/Frankovic/Smoljanovic/
Skelin/Skelin/Culjak/Boraska/Vujevic/
Petrisko)
Lightweight Double Sculls
1 Kucharski/Sycz POL   6:21.75
2 Luini/Pettinari ITA   6:23.47
3 Touron/Chapelle FRA   6:24.85
Tom Kay/Tom Middleton GBR; 2nd in
C Final
Lightweight Coxless Four
1 France   6:01.68
(Porchier/Bette/Hocde/Dorfman)
2 Australia   6:02.09
(Burgess/Edwards/Balmforth/Richards)
3 Denmark   6:03.51
(Madsen/Ebert/Ebbesen/Feddersen)

Women
Single Sculls
1 Ekaterina Karsten BLR   7:28.14
2 Rumyana Neykova BUL   7:28.15
3 Katrin Stomporowski GER 7:28.99
Alison Mowbray GBR; 4th in B Final

Double Sculls
1 Thieme/Boron GER   6:55.44
2 Dishoeck/Van Nes NED   7:00.36
3 Sakickiene/Poplavskaja LTU   7:01.71
Houghton/Winckless GBR; 3rd in B
Final
Quad Sculls
1 Germany   6:19.58
(Kowalski/Evers/Lutze/Kowalski)
2 Great Britain   6:21.64
(G Batten/Lindsay/Grainger/M Batten)
3 Russia   6:21.65
(Dorodnova/Fedotova/Levina/Merk)
Coxless Pair
1 Damian/Ignat ROM   7:11.00
2 Taylor/Slatter AUS   7:12.56
3 Ryan/Kraft USA   7:13.00
Dot Blackie/Cath Bishop GBR; 3rd in
B Final
Eight
1 Romania   6:06.44
(Damian/Susanu/Olteanu/Cochela/
Dumitrache/Lipa/Gafencu/Ignat/
Georgescu)
2 Netherlands   6:09.39
(Venema/Beekter/Penninx/Dishoeck/
Nes/Appeldoorn/Westerhof/Meijer/
Quik)
3 Canada   6:11.58
(McDermid/Davis/Urbaniak/Luke/
Robinson/Korn/Biesenthal/
Alexander/Thompson)
Elim qual: Great Britain (Sanders/
Carroll/Laverisk/Zino/Trickey/Beever/
Mackenzie/Eyre/Miller)
Lightweight Double Sculls
1 Burcica/Alupei ROM   7:02.64
2 Viehoff/Blasberg GER   7:02.95
3 Collins/Garner USA   7:06.37

Sailing

Rushcutter's Bay
Sep 16-30
Men's Mistral
1 Christoph Sieber AUT   38
2 Carlos Espinola ARG   43
3 Aaron McIntosh NZL   48
16 Nick Dempsey GBR   125
Women's Mistral
1 Alessandra Sensini ITA*   15
2 Amelie Lux GER   15
3 Barbara Kendall NZL   19
18 Christine Johnstone GBR   146
* Sensini won more races
Men's 470
1 King/Turnbull AUS   38
2 Foerster/Merrick USA   42
3 Conte/De la Fuente ARG   57
4 Rogers/Glanfield GBR   58
Women's 470
1 Armstrong/Stowell AUS   33
2 Isler/Glaser USA   47
3 Taran/Pakholchyk UKR   48

Europe (women)
1 Shirley Robertson GBR 37
2 Margriet Matthysse NED 39
3 Serena Amato ARG 51
Finn (men)
1 Iain Percy GBR 35
2 Luca Devotti ITA 46
3 Fredrik Loof SWE 47
49er (open)
1 Johanson/Jarvi FIN 55
2 Barker/Hiscocks GBR 60
3 McKee/McKee USA 64
Laser (open)
1 Ben Ainslie GBR 42
2 Robert Scheidt BRA 44
3 Michael Blackburn AUS 60
Soling (open)
1 Denmark
(Bank/Blakskjaer/Jacobsen)
2 Germany
(Schümann/Bahr/Borkowski)
3 Norway
(Johanessen/Davis/Stokkeland)
Elim Rd Robin: Great Britain
(Beadsworth/Sydenham/Parkin)
Star
1 Reynolds/Liljedahl USA 34
2 Walker/Covell GBR 35
3 Grael/Ferreira BRA 39
Tornado (open)
1 Hagara/Steinacher AUT 16
2 Bundock/Forbes AUS 25
3 Gaebler/Schwall GER 38
6 Styles/May 53

Shooting

Cecil Park   *Sep 16-23*
Score carried forward from qualifying
+ score in final = competition total

Men

10m Running Target
1 Yang Ling CHN 681.1
(581/100.1)
2 Oleg Moldovan MDA 681
(580/101)
3 Niu Zhiyuan CHN 677.4
(578/99.4)
10m Air Pistol
1 Franck Dumoulin FRA 688.9
(590/98.9)
2 Wang Yifu CHN 686.9
(590/96.9)
3 Ihar Basinski BLR 682.7
(583/99.3)
25m Rapid Fire Pistol
1 Sergey Alifirenko RUS 687.6
(587/100.6)
2 Michel Ansermet SUI 686.1
(587/99.1)
3 Iulian Raicea ROM 684.6
(587/97.6)
50m Air Pistol
1 Tanu Kiriakov BUL 666
(570/96)

2 Ihar Basinski BLR 663.3
(569/94.3)
3 Martin Tenk CZE 662.5
(566/96.5)
10m Air Rifle
1 Cai Yalin CHN 696.4
(594/102.4)
2 Artem Khadjibekov 693.8
(592/101.8)
3 Eugeni Aleinikov RUS 693.8
(592/101.8)
50m Rifle, Prone
1 Jonas Edman SWE 701.3
(599/102.3)
2 Torben Grimmel DEN 700.4
(597/103.4)
3 Siarhei Martynau BLR 700.3
(598/102.3)
25 Michael Babb 592
Babb did not qualify for final
50m Rifle, Three Positions
1 Rajmond Debevec SLO 1275.1
(1177/98.1)
2 Juha Hirvi FIN 1270.5
(1171/99.5)
3 Harald Stenvaag NOR 1268.6
(1175/93.6)
Trap
1 Michael Diamond AUS 147
(122/25)
2 Ian Peel GBR 142
(118/24)
3 Giovanni Pellielo ITA 140
(116/24)
26 Peter Boden GBR 108
Boden did not qualify for final
Double Trap
1 Richard Faulds GBR 187
(141/46)
2 Russell Mark AUS 187
(143/44)
3 Fehaid Aldeehani KUW 186
(141/45)
Skeet
1 Mikola Milchev UKR 150
(125/25)
2 Petr Malek CZE 148
(124/24)
3 James Graves USA 147
(123/24)
19 John Davidson GBR 120
39 Drew Harvey GBR 116
Davidson & Harvey did not qualify for final

Women

10m Air Pistol
1 Tao Luna CHN 488.2
(390/98.2)
2 Jasna Sekaric YUG 486.5
(388/98.5)
3 Anne-Marie Forder AUS 484
(385/99)

25m Pistol
1 Maria Grozdeva BUL 690.3
(589/101.3)
2 Tao Luna CHN 689.8
(590/99.8)
3 Lalita Yauhleuskaya BLR 686
(583/103)
10m Air Rifle
1 Nancy Johnson USA 497.7
(395/102.7)
2 Kang Cho-hyun KOR 497.5
(397/100.5)
3 Gao Jing CHN 497.2
(394/103.2)
50m Rifle, Three Positions
1 Renata Mauer POL 684.6
(585/99.6)
2 Tatiana Goldobina RUS 680.9
(585/95.9)
3 Maria Feklistova RUS 679.9
(582/97.9)
Trap
1 Daina Gudzineviciiute LTU 93
(71/22)
2 Delphine Racinet FRA 92
(67/25)
3 Gao E CHN 90
(68/22)
Double Trap
1 Pia Hansen SWE 148
(112/36)
2 Deborah Gelisio ITA 144
(107/37)
3 Kimberly Rhode USA 139
(103/36)
Skeet
1 Zemfira Meftakhetdinova AZE 98
(73/25)
2 Svetlana Demina RUS 95
(70/25)
3 Diana Igaly HUN 93
(71/22)

Softball

Aquillina Reserve   *Sep 17-26*
1 USA
2 Japan
3 Australia
Final: USA 2 Japan 1

Swimming

Olympic Pool   *Sep 16-23*
World Records in bold

Men

50m Free
1	Anthony Ervin USA	21.98
1	Gary Hall Jr USA	21.98
3	Pieter vd Hoogenband NED	22.03
7	Mark Foster GBR	22.41

100m Free
1	Pieter vd Hoogenband NED	48.30
2	Alexander Popov RUS	48.69
3	Gary Hall Jr USA	48.73

Hoogenband 47.84WR in semi-final

200m Free
1	P vd Hoogenband NED	**1:45.35**
2	Ian Thorpe AUS	1:45.83
3	Masso Rosolino ITA	1:46.65
5	Paul Palmer GBR	1:47.95
6	James Salter GBR	1:48.74

Hoogenband 1:45.35 for WR in semi-final; equalled record in final

400m Free
1	Ian Thorpe AUS	**3:40.59**
2	Masso Rosolino ITA	3:43.40
3	Klete Keller USA	3:47.00

Elim hts: Paul Palmer, James Salter

1500m Free
1	Grant Hackett AUS	14:48.33
2	Kieren Perkins AUS	14:53.59
3	Chris Thompson USA	14:56.81

Elim hts: Paul Palmer, Adam Faulkner GBR

100m Back
1	Lenny Krayzelburg USA	53.72
2	Matthew Welsh AUS	54.07
3	Stev Theloke GER	54.82

Elim s-f: Adam Ruckwood GBR

200m Back
1	Lenny Krayzelburg USA	1:56.76
2	Aaron Peirsol USA	1:57.35
3	Matthew Welsh AUS	1:57.59

Elim hts: Ruckwood, Simon Militis

100m Breast
1	Domenico Fioravanti ITA	1:00.46
2	Ed Moses USA	1:00.73
3	Roman Sloudnov RUS	1:00.91

Elim ht: Adam Whitehead GBR
Elim s-f: Darren Mew GBR

200m Breast
1	Domenico Fioravanti ITA	2:10.87
2	Terence Parkin RSA	2:12.50
3	Davide Rummolo ITA	2:12.73

Elim ht: Adam Whitehead

100m Fly
1	Lars Frölander SWE	52.00
2	Michael Klim AUS	52.18
3	Geoff Huegill AUS	52.22

Elim s-f: James Hickman GBR

200m Fly
1	Tom Malchow USA	1:55.35
2	Denys Silantiev UKR	1:55.76
3	Justin Norris AUS	1:56.17
6	Stephen Parry GBR	1:57.01

Elim s-f: James Hickman

200 IM
1	Masso Rosolino ITA	1:58.98
2	Tom Dolan USA	1:59.77
3	Tom Wilkens USA	2:00.87

400 IM
1	Tom Dolan USA	**4:11.76**
2	Erik Vendt USA	4:14.23
3	Curtis Myden CAN	4:15.33

Elim ht: Simon Militis

4x100m Free
1	Australia	**3:13.67**

*(Klim-**48.18**/Fydler-48.48/Callus-48.71/Thorpe-48.30)*

2	USA	3:13.86

(Ervin-48.89/Walker-48.31/Lezak-48.42/Hall Jr-48.24)

3	Brazil	3:17.40

(Scherer-49.79/Borges-48.61/Jayme-49.88/Silva Filho-49.12)
Klim's 1st leg time for AUS was WR
Elim ht: Great Britain
(Belk/Brinn/Howard/Stevens)

4x200m Free
1	Australia	**7:07.05**

(Thorpe-1:46.03/Klim-1:46.40/Pearson-1:47.36/Kirby-1:47.26)

2	USA	7:12.64

(Goldblatt-1:49.66/Davis-1:46.49/Rauch-1:48.74/Keller-1:47.75)

3	Netherlands	7:12.70

(Zuijdweg-1:49.89/Kenkhuis-1:49.37/Wouda-1:48.56/Hoogenband-1:44.88)

5	Great Britain	7:12.98

(Sinclair-1:49.61/Palmer-1:47.15/Spackman-1:48.85/Salter-1:47.37)

4x100m Medley
1	USA	**3:33.73**

(Krayzelburg-53.87/Moses-59.84/Crocker-52.10/Hall Jr-47.92)

2	Australia	3:35.27

(Welsh-54.29/Harrison-1:01.48/Huegill-51.33/Klim-48.17)

3	Germany	3:35.88

(Theloke-55.05/Kruppa-1:00.52/Rupprath-52.14/Spanneberg-48.15)

8	Great Britain	3:40.19

(Willey-56.49/Mew-1:01.76/Hickman-52.53/Brinn-49.41)
In the Dutch team which finished 4th Hoogenband swam a freestyle leg of 47.24

Women

50m Free
1	Inge de Bruijn NED	24.32
2	Therese Alshammar SWE	24.51
3	Dara Torres USA	24.63
6	Alison Sheppard GBR	25.45

*De Bruijn **24.13** WR in semi-final*
Elim ht: Sue Rolph GBR

100m Free
1	Inge de Bruijn NED	53.83
2	Therese Alshammar SWE	54.33
3	Dara Torres USA	54.43

*De Bruijn **53.77** WR in semi-final*
Elim s-f: Karen Pickering, Sue Rolph

200m Free
1	Susie O'Neill AUS	1:58.24
2	Martina Moravcova SVK	1:58.32
3	Claudia Poll CRC	1:58.81

Elim ht: Karen Pickering GBR

400m Free
1	Brooke Bennett USA	4:05.80
2	Diana Munz USA	4:07.07
3	Claudia Poll CRC	4:07.83

800m Free
1	Brooke Bennett USA	8:19.67
2	Yana Klochkova UKR	8:22.66
3	Kaitlin Sandeno USA	8:24.29

Elim ht: Rebecca Cooke GBR

100m Back
1	Diana Mocanu ROM	·1:00.21
2	Mai Nakamura JPN	1:00.55
3	Nina Zhivaneskaya ESP	1:00.89

Elim s-f: Katy Sexton GBR
Elim ht: Sarah Price GBR

200m Back
1	Diana Mocanu ROM	2:08.16
2	Roxana Maracineanu FRA	2:10.25
3	Miki Nakao JPN	2:11.05

Elim s-f: Helen Don-Duncan, Joanna Fargus GBR

100m Breast
1	Megan Quann USA	1:07.05
2	Leisel Jones AUS	1:07.49
3	Penny Heyns RSA	1:07.55

Elim ht: Heidi Earp GBR

200m Breast
1	Agnes Kovacs HUN	2:24.35
2	Kristy Kowal USA	2:24.56
3	Amanda Beard USA	2:25.35

Elim ht: Jaime King GBR

100m Fly
1	Inge de Bruijn NED	**56.61**
2	Martina Moravcova SVK	57.97
3	Dara Torres USA	58.20

Elim ht: Margaretha Pedder GBR

200m Fly
1	Misty Hyman USA	2:05.88
2	Susie O'Neill AUS	2:06.58
3	Petria Thomas AUS	2:07.12

Elim s-f: Georgina Lee, Margaretha Pedder GBR

200 IM
1	Yana Klochkova UKR	2:10.68
2	Beatrice Caslaru ROM	2:12.57
3	Cristina Teuscher USA	2:13.32

Elim s-f: Sue Rolph
Elim ht: Kathryn Evans GBR

400m IM
1	Yana Klochkova UKR	**4:33.59**
2	Yasuko Tajima JPN	4:35.96
3	Beatrice Caslaru ROM	4:37.18

4x100m Free
1 USA **3:36.61**
(Van Dyken-55.08/Torres-53.51/
Shealy-54.40/Thompson-53.62)
2 Netherlands 3:39.83
(Van Rooijen-56.35/Van Rijn-55.19/
Henneken-54.88/De Bruijn-53.41)
3 Sweden 3:40.30
(Joehncke-55.93/Alshammar-53.78/
Sjoeberg-55.06/Kammerling-55.53)
5 Great Britain 3:40.58
(Pickering-56.01/Sheppard-54.95/
Brett-54.92/Rolph-54.66)
4x200m Free
1 USA 7:57.80
(Arsenault-1:59.92/Munz-1:59.19/
Benko-1:59.34/Thompson-1:59.35)
2 Australia 7:58.52
(O'Neill-1:58.70/Rooney-1:59.37/
Thomson-2:00.13/Thomas-2:00.32)
3 Germany 7:58.64
(Almsick-1:59.51/Buschschulte-2:00.35/
Harstick-2:00.88/Kielglass-1:57.90)
6 Great Britain 8:03.69
(Jackson-2:00.56/Legg-2:01.55/
Belton-2:00.79/Pickering-2:00.79)
4x100 Medley
1 USA 3:58.30
(Bedford-1:01.39/Quann-1:06.29/
Thompson-57.25/Torres-53.37)
2 Australia 4:01.59
(Calub-1:01.83/Jones-1:08.08/
Thomas-57.39/O'Neill-54.29)
3 Japan 4:04.16
(Nakamura-1:02.08/Tanaka-1:08.65/
Onishi-58.72/Minamoto-54.71)
7 Great Britain 4:07.61
(Sexton-1:02.05/Earp-1:10.25/
Rolph-1:00.05/Pickering-55.26)

Synchronised Swimming
Olympic Pool   *Sep 24-29*
Duet
1 Brusnikina/Kisseleva RUS 99.580
2 Tachibana/Takeda JPN 99.000
3 Dedieu/Lignot FRA 97.600
Team
1 Russia 99.146
2 Japan 98.860
3 Canada 97.357

Table Tennis
State Sports Centre   *Sep 16-25*
Men's Singles
1 Kong Linghui CHN
2 Jan-Ove Waldner SWE
3 Liu Guoliang CHN
Final: 21-16 21-19
Matthew Syed...
bt J Sahajasein MRI 21-3 21-8 21-9
lost to P Franz GER 8-21 4-21 21-23

Men's Doubles
1 Wang/Yan CHN
2 Kong/Liu CHN
3 Chila/Gatien FRA
Final: 22-20 17-21 21-19 21-18
Women's Singles
1 Wang Nan CHN
2 Li Ju CHN
3 Chen Jing TPE
Final: 21-12 12-21 19-21 21-17 21-18
Women's Doubles
1 Li/Wang CHN
2 Sun/Yang CHN
3 Kim/Ryu KOR
Final: 21-18 21-11 21-11

Taekwondo
State Sports Centre
Sep 27-30
Men
-59kg
1 Michail Mouroursos GRE
2 Gabriel Esparza ESP
3 Huang Chih-Hsiung TPE
-68kg
1 Steven Lopez USA
2 Sin Joon-sik KOR
3 Hadi Saeibonehkohal IRI
-80kg
1 Angel Malodia Matos CUB
2 Faissal Ebnoutalib GER
3 Victor Manuel Estrada MEX
+80kg
1 Kim Kyong-hun KOR
2 Daniel Trenton AUS
3 Pascal Gentil FRA
Colin Daley GBR...
lost to Trenton
bt Marcus Thoren SWE
lost to Gentil

Women
-49kg
1 Lauren Burns AUS
2 Urbia Melendez CUB
3 Chi Shu-ju TPE
-57kg
1 Jung Jae-eun KOR
2 Tran Hieu Ngan VIE
3 Hamide Bikcin TUR
-67kg
1 Lee Sun-hee KOR
2 Trude Gundersen NOR
3 Yoriko Okamoto JPN
Sarah Stevenson GBR...
bt Monica del Real Jaime MEX
bt He Lumin CHN
lost to Gundersen
bt Kirsimarja Koskinen FIN
lost to Okamoto
+67kg
1 Chen Zhong CHN
2 Natalia Ivanova RUS
3 Dominique Bosshart CAN

Tennis
NSW Tennis Centre
Sep 19-28
Men's Singles
1 Yevgeny Kafelnikov RUS
2 Tommy Haas USA
3 Arnaud di Pasquale FRA
Final: 7-6 3-6 6-2 4-6 6-3
Tim Henman GBR...
lost to Karol Kucera SVK 6-3 6-2
Greg Rusedski GBR...
lost to Arnaud Clement FRA 6-2 6-3
Barry Cowan GBR...
lost to Daniel Nestor CAN 5-7 6-1 6-4
Men's Doubles
1 Lareau/Nestor CAN
2 Woodbridge/Woodforde AUS
3 Corretja/Costa ESP
Final: 5-7 6-3 6-4 7-6
Cowan/Kyle Spencer GBR...
lost to Kafelnikov/Safin RUS 7-6 6-4
Women's Singles
1 Venus Williams USA
2 Elena Dementieva RUS
3 Monica Seles USA
Final: 6-2 6-4
Women's Doubles
1 Williams/Williams USA
2 Boogert/Oremans NED
3 Callens/Van Roost BEL
Final: 4-6 6-4 6-1
Julie Pullin/Lorna Woodroffe GBR...
lost to Boogert/Oremans 6-2 6-1

All British entrants lost in the first round.

Triathlon
Sydney Centre/Harbour
Sep 16-17
Men
1 Simon Whitfield CAN 1:48:24.02
2 Stephan Vukovic GER 1:48:37.58
3 Jan Rehula CZE 1:48:46.64
9 Simon Lessing GBR 1:49:24.32
10 Tim Don GBR 1:49:28.85
DNF: Andrew Johns GBR
Women
1 Brigitte McMahon SUI 2:00:40.52
2 Michellie Jones AUS 2:00:42.55
3 Magali Messmer SUI 2:01:08.83
15 Stephanie Forrester GBR
2:03:56.11
DNF: Sian Brice, Michelle Dillon GBR

OLYMPIC GAMES

Volleyball, Beach
Bondi Beach
Sep 16-26
Men
1 Blanton/Fonoimoana USA
2 Ze Marco/Ricardo BRA
3 Ahmann/Hager GER
Final: 12-11 12-9
Women
1 Cook/Pottharst AUS
2 Adriana Behar/Shelda BRA
3 Sandra/Adriana BRA
Final: 12-11 12-10

Volleyball, Indoor
Darling Harbour/Pavilion 4
Sep 16-Oct 1
Men
1 Yugoslavia
2 Russia
3 Italy
Final: 25-22 25-22 25-20
Women
1 Cuba
2 Russia
3 Brazil
Final: 25-27 32-24 25-19 25-18 15-7

Water Polo
Olympic Pool/Ryde Leisure Centre
Sep 16-Oct 1
Men
1 Hungary
2 Russia
3 Yugoslavia
Final: 13-6
Women
1 Australia
2 USA
3 Russia
Final: 4-3

"I'm just a normal Aussie guy who likes a smoke and a drink. I wish they'd had the final between 2am and 4am. I might have won"
Jai Taurima, Australia's long jump silver medallist.

"Gold Medal Specialists. Sprints! Relays! Marathons! Hot and Raring to Go"
A Sydney brothel, advertising its services.

"Today I lifted not only weights but my country as well"
Martinho De Araujo the East Timor weightlifter who became the first from his country to compete at an Olympic Games

"She made it clear that if I carry on in a boat we won't have a marriage. I'll give it some thought"
Steve Redgrave, on his wife Anne's thoughts on his future rowing career.

"Mademoiselle La Chicken"
Headline from a Sydney tabloid after Marie-Jose Perec left the Games.

"She didn't like the idea of her little girl doing judo. She wanted me to play the piano, or maybe take tennis lessons. Something more girl-like"
Ryoko Tamura, the gold medallist in the 48kg judo class, recalling her mother's disappointment when she took up jud.

"For the first time in my life, I felt like we are the same people who share the same emotion and the same blood. Blood is thicker than anything else"
Pak Jung Chul, who carried the North Korean flag as his country marched with South Korean at the opening ceremony.

Weightlifting

Sydney Convention Centre
Sep 16-26
(Bodyweight/Snatch/Clean & Jerk)

Men

-56kg
1 Halil Mutlu TUR   **305.0**
*(55.62/137.5/**167.5**)*
2 Wu Wenxiong CHN   287.5
(55.48/125.0/162.5)
3 Zhang Xiangxiang CHN   287.5
(55.94/125.0/287.5)

-62kg
1 Nicolay Pechalov CRO   325.0
(61.56/150.0/175.0)
2 Leonidas Sabanis GRE   317.5
(61.30/147.5/170.0)
3 Gennady Oleshchuk BLR   317.5
(61.68/142.5/175.0))

-69kg
1 Galabin Boevski BUL   357.5
(68.78/162.5/195.0)
2 Georgi Markov BUL   352.5
*(68.92/**165.0**/187.5)*
3 Sergey Lavrenov BLR   340.0
(68.42/157.5/182.5)

-77kg
1 Zhan Xugang CHN   367.5
(76.20/160.0/207.5)
2 Viktor Mitrou GRE   367.5
(76.48/165.0/202.5)
3 Arsen Melikyan ARM   365.0
(76.68/167.5/197.5)

-85kg
1 Pyrros Dimas GRE   390.0
(84.06/175.0/215.0)
2 Marc Huster GER   390.0
(84.22/177.5/212.5)
3 George Asanidze GEO   390.0
(84.70/180.0/210.0)

-94kg
1 Akakios Kakiasvilis GRE   405.0
(92.06/185.0/220.0)
2 Szymon Kolecki POL   405.0
(93.58/182.5/222.5)
3 Alexey Petrov RUS   402.5
(93.30/180.0/222.5)

-105kg
1 Hossein Tavakoli IRI   425.0
(104.70/190.0/235.0)
2 Alan Tsagaev BUL   422.5
(104.48/187.5/235.0)
3 Said Asaad QAT   420.0
(104.12/190.0/230.0)
No Lift: Tommy Yule GBR

+105kg
1 Hossein Rezazadeh IRI   **472.5**
*(147.48/**212.5**/260.0)*
2 Ronny Weller GER   467.5
(146.88/210.0/257.5)
3 Ashot Danielyan ARM   465.0
(160.62/207.5/257.5)

Women

-48kg
1 Tara Nott USA   185.0
(47.48/82.5/102.5)
2 Raema Rumbewas INA   185.0
(47.98/80.00/105.00)
3 Sri Indriyani INA   182.5
(47.28/82.5/100.00)

-53kg
1 Yang Xia CHN   225.0
(52.46100.0/125.0)
2 Li Feng-ying TPE   212.5
(52.42/98.0/115.0)
3 Winarni Slamet INA   202.5
(52.44/90.0/112.5)

-58kg
1 Soraya Jimenez MEX   222.5
(56.92/95.0/127.5)
2 Ri Song Hui PRK   220.0
(53.90/97.5/122.5)
3 Khassaraporn Suta THA   210.0
(56.84/92.5/117.5)

-63kg
1 Chen Xiaomin CHN   242.5
(62.82/112.5/130.0)
2 Valentina Popova RUS   235.0
(62.08/107.5/127.5)
3 Ioanna Chatziioannou GRE   222.5
(61.82/97.5/125.0)

-69kg
1 Lin Weinging CHN   242.5
(66.74/110.0/132.5)
2 Erzsebet Markus HUN   242.5
(68.52/112.5/130.0)
3 Karnam Malleswari IND   240.0
(67.90/110.0/130.0)

-75kg
1 Maria Isabel Urrutia ESP   245.0
(73.28/110.0/135.0)
2 Ruth Ogbeifo NGR   245.0
(74.20/105.0/140.0)
3 Kuo Yi-hang TPE   245.0
(74.52/107.5/137.5)

+75kg
1 Ding Miyuan CHN   300.0
(103.56/135.0/165.0)
2 Agata Wrobel POL   295.0
(119.42/132.5/162.5)
3 Cheryl Haworth USA   270.0
(139.38/125.0/145.0)

Wrestling

Sydney Convention Centre
Sep 24-Oct 1

Freestyle

54kg
1 Namik Abdullaev AZE
2 Samuel Henson USA
3 Amiran Kartanov GRE

58kg
1 Ali Reza Dabier IRI
2 Evgeni Buslovich UKR
3 Terry Brands USA

63kg
1 Mourat Umakhanov RUS
2 Serafim Barzakov BUL
3 Jae Sung Jang KOR

69kg
1 Daniel Igali CAN
2 Arsen Gitinow RUS
3 Lincoln McIlravy USA

76kg
1 Brandon Slay USA
2 Eui-Jae Moon KOR
3 Adem Bereket TUR

85kg
1 Adam Saitiev RUS
2 Yoel Romero Palacio CUB
3 Magomed Ibragimov MKD

97kg
1 Sagid Murtasaliev RUS
2 Islam Bairamukov KAZ
3 Eldari Kurtanidze GEO

130kg
1 David Musulbes RUS
2 Artur Taimazov UZB
3 Alexis Rodriguez Valera CUB

Greco-Roman

54kg
1 Sim Kwon-ho KOR
2 Lazaro Rivas CUB
3 Kang Yong Gyun PRK

58kg
1 Armen Nazarian BUL
2 Kim In-sub KOR
3 Sheng Zetian CHN

63kg
1 Samourgachev RUS
2 Juan Luis Maren CUB
3 Akaki Chachua GEO

69kg
1 Filiberto Azcuy CUB
2 Katsuhito Nagata JPN
3 Alexey Glouchkov RUS

76kg
1 Mourat Kardanov RUS
2 Matt James Lindland USA
3 Marko Yli-Hannuksela FIN

85kg
1 Hamza Yerlikaya TUR
2 Sandor Istvan Bardosi HUN
3 Mukhran Vakhtangadze GEO

97kg
1 Mikael Ljungberg SWE
2 Davyd Saldadze UKR
3 Garrett Lowney USA

130kg
1 Rulon Gardner USA
2 Alexander Karelin RUS
3 Dmitri Debelka BLR

First defeat for Karelin since 1987

American Football

They say that when Kurt Warner was stacking shelves at the Hy-Vee store in Cedar Falls, Iowa, he just stood at one end of the shop and every single product landed on the right shelf. Maybe he missed a few now and then, after all they were only paying the wannabe footballer $5 an hour. Four years on and St Louis Rams weren't overpaying the quarterback either at an annual salary of just $225,000, but Warner only got the job when first choice quarterback Tom Green was ruled out for the season. In the Superbowl that no one predicted (900-1 were the pre-season odds on it happening) between the teams who have never won anything, Warner didn't miss a trick. He set a Superbowl record by throwing 414 yards and was nominated the game's Most Valuable Player. Back at the Hy-Vee Store, they were glowing at the best publicity they've had for years.

Neither the Tennessee Titans nor the St Louis Rams had ever figured in a Superbowl. The Titans had struggled since their relocation from Houston three seasons earlier, and the Rams had just, well, struggled. Throughout the nineties, no team in the NFL had a worse record. No team worried if their next game was the Rams.

Yet the game they served up was a treat. St Louis held a 16-point lead in the third quarter, but the Titans clawed it back to level with less than two minutes of the game to go. Warner took control, winging a 73-yard pass to Isaac Brown, for a decisive touchdown. To their credit, Tennessee came straight back, with quarterback Steve McNair throwing to Kevin Dyson on the one-yard line, but a tackle from Mike Jones prevented the receiver from making the end zone and the clock counted them out.

Warner, who only two years ago was playing for Amsterdam Admirals in the NFL Europe, ran sobbing to his wife, Brenda, and the American media ran sobbing to their laptops; the Warner story took over. Brenda, had a visually-impaired son, Zachary, from a previous marriage. Warner had adopted the child and wore special glasses himself to try and understand how Zachary saw the world. Four years earlier his wife's parents had been killed in a tornado. Warner, a committed Christian from that day, gives part of his endorsement money to charity. Middle America took him to their hearts.

"I've probably surprised a lot of people today, but not myself. I knew what I could do," said the object of everyone's affection. Certainly his coach Dick Vermeil was blinking in disbelief. "I've never seen a player mature so quickly. I don't know if it's ever been done before. Heck, he has the third best quarterback ratings of all time," said Vermeil, who then went off to do some crying of his own.

Georgia Frontiere, a former Las Vegas chorus-girl, was left 70% of the Rams by one of her seven husbands (we don't know which one). Frontiere, who is the only woman owner in the NFL, maintains she is just 34, though received wisdom doubles that and some. The Rams' owner claims that when she met the Queen (our Queen, that is) she agreed with her that women should never divulge their age. So there.

Super Bowl XXXIV

St Louis Rams 23
Tennessee Oilers 16

Georgia Dome, Atlanta
Jan 30
Attendance: 72,625

TEAMS

St Louis	*Offense*	Tennessee
T Holt	WR	K Dyson
O Pace	LT	B Hopkins
T Nutten	LG	B Matthews
M Gruttadauria	C	K Long
A Timmerman	RG	B Olson
F Miller	RT	J Runyan
R Williams	TE	F Wycheck
I Bruce	WR	I Byrd
K Warner	QB	S McNair
R Holcombe	RB	E George
M Faulk	FB	J Harris
	Defense	
K Carter	LE	J Kearse
R Agnew	LT	J Evans
D Farr	RT	J Fisk
G Winstrom	RE	K Holmes
M Jones	LLB-WLB	E Robinson
L Fletcher	HLB	B Wortham
T Collins	RLB-SLB	J Bowden
T Lyght	LCB	D Walker
D McCleon	RCB	S Rolle
B Jenkins	SS	B Bishop
K Lyle	FS	A Dorsett

SUBSTITUTIONS
St Louis
P-M Horan, K-J Wilkins, S-D Bush, RB-A Lee,
CB-B Bly, S-R Coady, RB-J Hodgins, TE-J Robinson,
C-R Tucker, LB-L Styles, LB-C Clemens, LB-L Little,
LB-M Morton, G-A McCollum, WR-A Hakim,
WR-T Horne, TE-E Conwelll, WR-R Proehl,
DT-J Zgonina, DT-N Hobgood-Chittick, DE-J Williams

Tennessee
K-A Del Greco, P-C Henrith, RB-R Thomas,
S-S Jackson, CB-D Mitchell, S-P Phenix, CB-D Sidney,
CB-G McCullough, FB-L Neal, LB-T Killens,
LB-G Favors, LB-D Coleman, G-J Layman,
DT-J Thornton, WR-C Sanders, TE-L Brown,
WR-D Mason, WR-J Kent, DT-H Ford, DT-J Salave'a

Most Valuable Player
Kurt Warner (St Louis, QB)

Scoring

ST LOUIS (AFC)	3	6	7	7	23
TENNESSEE (NFC)	0	0	6	10	16

First Quarter
STL: FG, Wilkins 27yd (12:00)
Second Quarter
STL: FG, Wilkins 29yd (10:44)
STL: FG, Wilkins 28yd (14:45)
Third Quarter
STL: TD, Holt, 9yd pass - Warner, Wilkins Kick (7:40)
TEN: TD, George, 1yd run, pass failed (14:45)
Fourth Quarter
TEN: TD, George, 2yd run, Del Greco Kick (7:39)
TEN: FG, Del Greco 43yd (12:45)
STL: TD, Bruce, 73yd pass - Warner, Wilkins Kick (13:06)

Team Statistics

	St Louis	Tennessee
Total First Downs	23	27
Total Net Yardage	436	367
Total Offensive Plays	59	73
- Average Gain	7.4	5.0
Rushes	13	36
- Yards Gained	29	159
Passes Attempted	45	36
- Passes Completed	24	22
- Yards Gained	407	208
Punts	2	3
- Average Distance	38.5	43.0
Punt Returns	2	1
- Return Yardage	8	(-1)
Kickoff Returns	4	5
- Return Yardage	55	122
Penalties	8	7
- Yards Penalised	60	45
Touchdowns	2	2
- Rushing	0	2
- Passing	2	0

Individual Statistics

Passing

St Louis	Att	Comp	Yds	TD	LG	IN
K Warner	45	24	414	2	73	0
Tennessee						
S McNair	36	22	214	0	32	0

Rushing

St Louis	No	Yds	Ave	LG	TD
M Faulk	10	17	1.7	4	0
Tennessee					
E George	28	95	3.4	13	2

Receiving

St Louis	No	Yds	TD	Longest	TD
T Holt	7	109	15.6	32	1
Tennessee					
J Harris	7	64	9.1	21	0

NFL Final League Standings 1999

NATIONAL FOOTBALL CONFERENCE

Eastern Division

	W	L	T	Pct	Pts	PA
Washington Reds*	10	6	0	.625	443	377
Dallas Cowboys*	8	8	0	.500	352	276
New York Giants	7	9	0	.438	299	358
Arizona Cardinals	6	10	0	.375	245	382
Philadelphia Eagles	5	11	0	.313	272	357

Central Division

	W	L	T	Pct	Pts	OP
Tampa Bay Buccs	**11**	**5**	**0**	**.688**	**270**	**235**
Minnesota Vikings*	10	6	0	.625	399	335
Detroit Lions*	8	8	0	.500	322	323
Green Bay Packers	8	8	0	.500	357	341
Chicago Bears	6	10	0	.375	272	341

Western Division

	W	L	T	Pct	Pts	OP
St. Louis Rams	**13**	**3**	**0**	**.813**	**526**	**242**
Carolina Panthers	8	8	0	.500	421	381
Atlanta Falcons	5	11	0	.313	285	380
San Fransisco 49ers	4	12	0	.250	295	453
New Orleans Saints	3	13	0	.188	260	434

AMERICAN FOOTBALL CONFERENCE

Eastern Division

	W	L	T	Pct	PF	PA
Indianapolis Colts	**13**	**3**	**0**	**.813**	**423**	**333**
Buffalo Bills*	11	5	0	.688	320	229
Miami Dolphins*	9	7	0	.563	326	336
New England Patriots	8	8	0	.500	299	284
New York Jets	8	8	0	.500	308	309

Central Division

	W	L	T	Pct	PF	PA
Jacksonville Jags	**14**	**2**	**0**	**.875**	**396**	**217**
Tennessee Oilers*	13	3	0	.813	392	324
Baltimore Ravens	8	8	0	.500	324	277
Cincinatti Bengals	4	12	0	.250	283	460
Cleveland Browns	2	14	0	.125	217	437

Western Division

	W	L	T	Pct	Pts	OP
Seattle Seahawks	9	7	0	.563	338	298*
Kansas City Chiefs	9	7	0	.563	390	322
Oakland Raiders	8	8	0	.500	390	329
San Diego Chargers	8	8	0	.500	390	329
Denver Broncos	6	10	0	.375	314	318

*Wild card qualifier for play-offs; teams in bold go straight through to Divisional play-offs.

NFL Play-off Games

NATIONAL FOOTBALL CONFERENCE
Wild Card Play-off Games

Minnesota Vikings 27	Dallas Cowboys 10
Washington Reds 27	Detroit Lions 13

Divisional Play-off Games

Tampa Bay Buccs 14	Washington Redskins 13
St Louis Rams 49	Minnesota Vikings 41

NFC Championship Game

St Louis Rams 11	Tampa Bay Buccaneers 6

AMERICAN FOOTBALL CONFERENCE
Wild Card Play-off Games

Tennessee Oilers 22	Buffalo Bills 16
Miami Dolphins 20	Seattle Seahawks 17

Divisional Play-off Games

Jacksonville Jaguars 62	Miami Dolphins 7
Tennessee Oilers 19	Indianapolis Colts 6

AFC Championship Game

Tennessee Oilers 19	Jacksonville Jaguars 14

Football Briefing

Subscriptions:

Trevor Kendall, 2 Drury Close, Waltham, Grimsby DN37 0XP

World League

Apr 15

Frankfurt Galaxy 32	Berlin Thunder 7
Barcelona Dragons 17	Rhein Fire 28

Apr 16

Amsterdam Admirals 9	Scottish Claymores 28

Apr 22

Rhein Fire 20	Amsterdam Admirals 23
Scottish Claymores 17	Frankfurt Galaxy 14

Apr 24

Berlin Thunder 28	Barcelona Dragons 21

Apr 29

Rhein Fire 34	Frankfurt Galaxy 27
Berlin Thunder 24	Scottish Claymores 20

Apr 30

Amsterdam Admirals 20	Barcelona Dragons 27

May 6

Amsterdam Admirals 20	Frankfurt Galaxy 17
Rhein Fire 18	Barcelona Dragons 7

May 7

Berlin Thunder 3	Scottish Claymores 42

May 13

Barcelona Dragons 42	Frankfurt Galaxy 26
Berlin Thunder 21	Amsterdam Admirals 24
Scottish Claymores 10	Rhein Fire 22

May 20

Amsterdam Admirals 16	Barcelona Dragons 22

May 21

Frankfurt Galaxy 31	Scottish Claymores 30
Rhein Fire 21	Berlin Thunder 25

May 27

Berlin Thunder 27	Rhein Fire 28

May 28

Barcelona Dragons 0	Scottish Claymores 28
Frankfurt Galaxy 7	Amsterdam Admirals 41

June 3

Barcelona Dragons 22	Berlin Thunder 9
Scottish Claymores 42	Amsterdam Admirals 10

June 4

Rhein Fire 53	Frankfurt Galaxy 14

June 10

Rhein Fire 24	Scottish Claymores 31
Amsterdam Admirals 15	Berlin Thunder 28

June 11

Frankfurt Galaxy 14	Barcelona Dragons 8

June 17

Berlin Thunder 17	Frankfurt Galaxy 24
Scottish Claymores 25	Barcelona Dragons 28

June 18

Amsterdam Admirals 28	Rhein Fire 31

Final Table	*W*	*L*	*T*	*PF*	*PA*
Rhein Fire	7	3	0	279	209
Scottish Claymores	6	4	0	237	165
Barcelona Dragons	5	5	0	194	212
Amsterdam Admirals	4	6	0	206	243
Frankfurt Galaxy	4	6	0	206	269
Berlin Thunder	4	6	0	189	249

World Bowl 2000

Waldstadion   June 25

Rhein Fire 13
Scottish Claymores 10

SCORING

Rhein Fire	3	3	0	7	13
Scottish Claymores	7	3	0	0	10

Most Valuable Player

Aaron Stecker (Scottish Claymores)

Angling

Fly Fishing

World Championships

Blagdon & Chew Valley Lake, River Test, Hampshire
May 14-21
Individual

		Pts
1	Pascal Cognard FRA	13
2	Jean Michel Lauret FRA	16
3	Gareth Jones WAL	18
10	Hywel Morgan WAL	28
16	Maurice Willis IRL	36
19	John Horsey ENG	39

Team (5-person)

1	France	135
2	Wales	203
3	Australia	214
4	Italy	217
5	Norway	250
6	Czech Republic	265
10	Scotland	273
12	England	276
17	Ireland	306

Coarse Fishing

World Championships
MEN
River Arno, Florence   Sept 9-10

Individual		pts	kgs
1	Jacopo Falsini ITA	2	31.92
2	William Raison ENG	2	28.36
3	Jean-P Fougeat FRA	4	23.30
4	Alan Scotthorne ENG	4	22.70

Team		pts	kgs
1	Italy	37.0	114.70
2	England	59.5	98.46
3	Hungary	89.5	75.66
4	Wales	95.5	64.98

WOMEN

Individual		pts	kgs
1	Franca Tagliaferri ITA	3	29.14
2	Simona Pollastri ITA	4	27.34
3	Stefania Conforto ITA	4	20.06
6	Gillian Foy ENG	5	22.86

Team		pts	kgs
1	Italy	37	106.08
2	Portugal	43	85.66
3	England	50	99.56

National Championships

DIVISION 1, MEN
Leeds & Liverpool Canal, Wigan
July 1
Team
1 Daiwa Gordon League
2 Liverpool DAA
3 Browning Hotrods
4 Starlets AS
5 Browing Scunthorpe
Individual
1 Terry Flannery (Newton-Le-Willows)
2 Keith Wilson (Pilkington AA)

Archery

Target Archery

European Championships

Antalya, Turkey   June 14-17
Only British placings given in early rounds

Men's Recurve
18 Simon Needham 635; 36 Ian Crowther 624
42 Jonathan Shales 621; 68 James Bingham 602
2nd round
Jari Lipponen FIN 162 bt Ian Crowther 153
Mattias Eriksson SWE 152 bt Jonathan Shales 145
Simon Needham 157 bt Alexander Froese GER 155
3rd round
Matteo Bisiani ITA 146 bt Simon Needham 144
Semi-final
Balzinima Tsirempilov RUS 115 bt Jocelyn De Grandis
FRA 107
Ilario Di Buo ITA 116 bt Bair Badenov RUS 109
Bronze Medal Match
Jocelyn De Grandis FRA 110 bt Bair Badenov RUS
(shoot-off)
Final
Baljinma Tsirempilov 114 bt Ilario Di Buo 110
Final British Rankings
30 Simon Needham; 46 Ian Crowther; 63 J Shales

Men's Recurve Team
Qualification round
8 Great Britain 1880
(Simon Needham/Ian Crowther/Jonathan Shales)
2nd round
Netherlands bt Great Britain
Semi-finals
Netherlands 251 bt France 238
Turkey 239 bt Ukraine 238
Bronze Medal Match
France 241 bt Ukraine 237
Final
Turkey bt Netherlands

Men's Compound
Qualification Round
2 Simon Tarplee GBR 688; 3 Michael Peart GBR 687
20 Steven Gooden GBR 673; 36 Chris White GBR 663
2nd round
Maurice Vandenhoek BEL 164 bt Steven Gooden 160
Michael Peart 172 bt Jean Claude Denis BEL 159
Simon Tarplee 170 bt Massimo Van Der Leeuw NED 160
3rd round
Michael Peart 172 bt Dejan Sitar SLO 170
Simon Tarplee 173 bt Morten Boee NOR 168
Quarter-final
Michael Peart 115 bt Antonio Gonzalez ESP 110
Simon Tarplee 115 bt Rini Donders NED 113
Semi-final
Simon Tarplee bt Michael Peart

Bronze Medal Match
Michael Peart 113 bt Stefan Osep SLO 113 (shoot-out)
Final
Simon Tarplee bt Tibor Ondrik HUN
Final British Rankings
1 Simon Tarplee; 3 Michael Peart; 29 Steven Gooden

Men's Compound Team
Qualification round
1 Great Britain 2048
(Simon Tarplee/Michael Peart/Steven Gooden
2nd round
Great Britain 254 bt France 249
Semi-final
Slovenia bt Great Britain
Bronze Medal Match
Great Britain bt Italy
Final
Slovenia 256 bt Hungary 256 (shoot-out)

World Rankings

As at March 1, 2001
Recurve (Olympic) only

Men

1	Michele Frangilli	ITA	240.000
2	Wietse van Alten	NED	172.000
3	Ilario Di Buo	ITA	164.000
4	Balzinima Tsyrempilov	RUS	163.000
5	Victor Wunderle	USA	152.000
6	Simon Fairweather	AUS	149.000
7	Yuri Leontiev	RUS	140.000
8	Matteo Bisiani	ITA	134.000
9	Lionel Torres	FRA	132.000
10	Jari Lipponen	FIN	122.000
29	Simon Needham	GBR	71.500
84	Ian Crowther	GBR	25.500

Women

1	He Ying	CHN	167.750
2	Alison Williamson	GBR	153.900
3	Kim Soo-nyung	KOR	142.000
4	Natalya Bolotova	RUS	139.300
5	Yun Mi-jin	KOR	136.000
6	Almudena Gallardo	ESP	129.800
7	Natalya Valeeva	ITA	128.200
8	Wiebke Nulle	GER	125.600
9	Natalya Nasaridze	TUR	124.000
10	Kim Nam-soon	KOR	119.200
51	Vladlena Priestman	GBR	42.200
61	Susan McGrath	GBR	36.850

Women's Recurve

Qualification round
10 Vladlena Priestman 609; 14 Sue McGrath 604
21 Alison Williamson 593; 58 Lindsay Smeeton 532
2nd round
Elif Altinkaynak TUR 144 bt Alison Williamson 134
Cristina Ioriatti ITA 156 bt Sue McGrath 133
Vladlena Priestman 149 bt Kaisa Suutari FIN 141
3rd round
Vladlena Priestman 154 Natalia Valeeva ITA 151
Quarter-final
Natalia Nasaridze TUR 101 bt Vladlena Priestman 99
Semi-final
Natalie Bolotova RUS 104 bt Olga Moroz BLR 94
Natalia Nasaridze TUR 102 bt Anna Karaseva BLR 101
Bronze Medal Match
Anna Karaseva BLR 109 bt Olga Moroz BLR 106
Final
Natalia Nasaridze TUR 106 bt Nataliya Bolotova RUS 103
Final British Rankings
6 Vladlena Priestman; 31 Alison Williamson;
32 Sue McGrath

Women's Recurve Team

Qualification Round
4 Great Britain 1806
(Alison Williamson/Vladlena Priestman/Sue McGrath)
Quarter-final
Italy 227 bt Great Britain 213
Semi-final
Turkey bt Italy
Germany bt Ukraine
Bronze Medal Match
Italy bt Ukraine
Final
Turkey 227 bt Germany 222

Women's Compound

Qualification Round
2 Claire Trenaman GBR 666; 4 Linda Garner GBR 662
10 M Richardson GBR 652; 15 Katy Moir GBR 646
2nd round
Svenson NOR 161 bt Linda Garner 159
Maryann Richardson 159 bt Senserini ITA 156
Claire Trenaman 166 bt Panico 149
Katy Moir 159 bt Friedl AUT
3rd round
Maryann Richardson 166 bt Knoebel GER 155
Claire Trenaman 167 bt Moir 164
Quarter-final
Claire Trenaman 109 bt Maryann Richardson 104
Semi-final
Luyting NED 114 bt Fabre FRA 112
Agudo 115 bt Claire Trenaman 107
Bronze Medal Match
Claire Trenaman 115 bt Fabre 111
Final
Luyting 114 bt Agudo 111
Final Ranking
3 Claire Trenaman; 6 Maryann Richardson;
11 Katy Moir; 22 Linda Garner

Women's Compound Team

Qualification
1 Great Britain 1980
(Claire Trenaman/Linda Garner/Maryann Richardson)
Quarter-final
Great Britain 244 bt Turkey 228
Semi-final
Netherlands bt Great Britain
France bt Italy
Bronze Medal Match
Great Britain bt Italy
Final
Netherlands 245 bt France 245 (shoot-off)

UK Masters

Lilleshall   June 3-4
Final Standings
Men's Recurve

1	Ian Crowther	2596
2	Jonathan Shales	2588
3	Steve Hallard	2586

Men's Compound

1	Michael Peart	2771
2	Chris White	2757
3	Andrew Rose	2737

Women's Recurve

1	Lindsay Smeeton	2562
2	Jill Newlands	2536
3	Yvonne Murton	2535

Women's Compound

1	Lesley Gray	2641
2	Carol Morris-Lewis	2578
3	Maureen Cornish	256

Field Archery

World Championships

Cortina D'Ampezzo, Italy   July 9-16
Only British placings given in early rounds

Men's Recurve
Qualification Round
5 Jonathan Shales GBR 652
13 Nathan Bell GBR 637
17 Paul Kelly GBR 627
2nd round
7 Jonathan Shales 163
10 Nathan Bell 158
3rd round
4 Jonathan Shales 162
Semi-final
Michele Frangilli ITA 54 bt Jonathan Shales 50
Goran Bjerendal SWE 54 bt Gerard Koonigs NED 46
Bronze Medal Match
Jonathan Shales 52 bt Gerard Koonigs 46
Final
Michele Frangilli ITA 55 bt Goran Bjerendal SWE 46

Men's Compound
Qualification Round
6 Chris White 701
7 Gary Kinghorn GBR 701
2nd round
10 Chris White 174
11 Gary Kinghorn 174
Semi-finals
Morgan Lundin SWE 60 bt Peter Penner GER 56
Dave Cousins USA 56 bt Andre Grawinkel GER 55
Bronze Medal Match
Peter Penner GER 59 bt Andre Grawinkel GER 57
Final
Morgan Lundin SWE 58 bt Dave Cousins USA 57

Men's Barebow
Qualification Round (GB only - top 16 qualify)
15 Peter Mulligan 598
2nd round (top 8 qualify)
11 Peter Mulligan 148
Semi-final
Marjan Porzaj SLO 48 bt Erik Jonsson SWE 43
Mattias Larsson SWE 51 bt Zare Krajnc SLO 45
Bronze Medal Match
Erik Jonsson SWE 52 bt Zare Krajnc SLO 50
Final
Mattias Larsson SWE 50 bt Marjan Porzaj SLO 47

Men's Team
Qualification Round
5 Great Britain 1951
Jonathan Shales/Peter Mulligan/Chris White
Quarter-finals
France 102 bt Great Britain 101
Semi-finals
Sweden 53 bt France 49
Netherlands 106 bt USA 98
Bronze Medal Match
France 53 bt Italy 53 (shoot-off)
Final
Sweden 57 bt Netherlands 55

Women's Recurve
Semi-finals
Christel Van Berkel NED 52 bt Cristina Ioriatti ITA 47
Manuela Kaltenmark GER 49 bt Carole Ferriou FRA 48
Bronze Medal Match
Crisitina Loriatti 54 bt Carole Ferriou 45
Final
Christel Van Berkel 49 bt Manuela Kaltenmark 49 (shoot-off)

Women's Compound
Qualification Round
17 Sam Stretton 634
18 Maggie Squires 628
23 Jan Howells GBR 308
Semi-finals
Rosanna Spada ITA 58 bt Ulrika Sjowall SWE 53
Jahna Davis USA 55 bt Monika Blume GER 54
Bronze Medal Match
Monika Blume GER 56 bt Ulrika Sjowall SWE 55
Final
Jahna Davis USA 55 bt Rosanna Spada 54

Women's Barebow
Qualification Round
2 Patricia Lovell 580
2nd round
2 Patricia Lovell 142
3rd round
1 Patricia Lovell 135
Semi-finals
Patricia Lovell 45 bt Anne Viljanen FIN 35
Odile Boussiere 44 bt Reingild Linhart AUT 38
Bronze Medal Match
Anne Viljanen 46 bt Reingild Linhart 37
Final
Patricia Lovell GBR 49 bt Odile Boussiere 47

Women's Team
Semi-finals
Sweden 47 bt France 43
Italy 42 bt Slovenia 36
Bronze Medal Match
France 50 bt Slovenia 43
Final
Italy 50 bt Sweden 42

Association Football

F inally, after all the years of hurt, England beat Germany in a competitive fixture. Yes, we won, we won we, we won. The flags were out, the bunting was up and grown men openly wept in the streets. Well, the match was on Saturday, but the crying didn't actually start until the Tuesday. We'll come to that later.

The opening match in Euro 2000 had started well for England as they led Portugal 2-0, through Paul Scholes and Steve McManaman. That was as good as it got for Keegan's men for Portugal quickly worked out the mathematics and scored the requisite three times. It meant the German game was not just about tradition, but about survival too. Well, thanks to Alan Shearer, who had already announced his retirement from international football, England beat Germany by a single goal. All that tempered the jubilation was the almost universal acceptance that this was the worst German team since the 1934 World Cup in Italy when they lost a replay 4-2 to the might of Switzerland.

Thereafter, Romania stood between England and qualification. In goal, Nigel Martyn stepped in for David Seaman who picked up a late injury and, if the Leeds' keeper was not to blame for the first goal (and we'll be as fair as we can), he was for the second. With the score at 2-2, it was still enough for England, but nobody told Phil Neville, whose maths was evidently not as good as the Portuguese. In the 86th minute the younger Neville, who had in fact been one of England's better players, committed an unnecessary foul in the box; Ganea scored from the ensuing penalty and England were out of the championship. Still, we beat Germany, ay? Well, even that hollow victory was made hollower still when Keegan's crew - playing the first half in a holly bush formation, the second half as a spreading chestnut tree - lost the 2002 World Cup qualifier to Germany in the last match at Wembley. Keegan immediately sacked the arboriculturist who was advising him and then sacked himself. "It's a fair cop, Kev," he said, as his boot landed on his own arse.

Nobody missed England as the tournament, which was a huge success, progressed. The semi-finals saw Holland against Italy and France against Portugal. In a perfect world, the final would have been between Holland against Portugal (well, in our perfect world anyway), but the Italians outschemed the co-hosts and, against France, Portugal self-destructed. It took a golden goal penalty to settled that match, awarded when Abel Xavier allegedly handled a cross. Well, there are some replays that tell you nothing, the slow-mo more confusing than the realtime-mo, and this was the case here. In the instant, it looked a handball. As our colours were nailed to the Portuguese mast, it was a hard call to make. Still is. The referee and his assistants were jostled by Portugal's players, including Xavier, who were given post-tournament bans. They'll be back.

Italy, criticised for negative play in earlier rounds, were the better team in the final, but France played the golden goal joker, equalising in the third minute of injury time and then pinching the win from the dejected Italians, courtesy of David Trezeguet. France thus became the first team to hold the World Cup and European championship at the same time.

Domestically, Manchester United knew they had an impossible task trying to repeat the treble of European Cup, Premiership and FA Cup, so they didn't bother to try. Rather than entering the FA Cup, as they'd done for the past 108 years (as Newton Heath in the old days), United opted to play in the fabulous club world championship in Brazil (Sorry, we slipped into sarcasm there). Well, United went nowhere in Brazil and Sep Blatter's event disappeared without trace a year later. United had no worries, though, while they were screwing up in Brazil, the other Premiership sides were screwing up in England. They returned to find that no one had taken advantage of their absence, so they went on to win the title by 18 points.

Real Madrid were made of sterner stuff than the Premiership, however, and brushed them aside in the European Cup quarter-finals. with Steve McManaman playing an influential midfield role (and tackling like a demon) they went on to beat Valenica in the final.

In the UEFA Cup two English sides made the semi-finals; Leeds and Arsenal. However the achievements of a young Leeds team in reaching that stage was overtaken by events on their trip to Turkey for the semi-final first-leg with Galatasaray. Two Leeds supporters were murdered before the match. They did not turn a 2-0 deficit around in the second-leg, but football had became irrelevant anyway.

Galatasaray did the double over the English sides by beating Arsene Wengers' side in the final. It was the second time that Arsenal had lost a European final on penalties - the first coming against Valencia in the 1980 Cup Winners' Cup.

In the Manchester United free zone that was the FA Cup, Roberto Di Matteo had the distinction of scoring the last goal in an FA Cup final at Wembley. His was the only goal of the final between Chelsea and Aston Villa and stands alongside his goal in the 1997 final, which was the fastest ever in a Cup final.

Martin O'Neill's Leicester won the Worthington Cup, defeating First Division Tranmere Rovers, who also got to the FA Cup quarter-finals, but had an average League campaign. Manchester United were the only team in the League not to be beaten at home, Coventry City the only not to win away. The Sky Blues continued the miracle by not being relegated (at least this time), but as they cast their eyes down to Chester City, who fell off the bottom League, they may just have thought, "There but for fortune go you and I..."

FIFA RANKINGS

As at February 2001

1	Brazil	818
2	France	799
3	Argentina	769
4	Italy	740
5	Czech Republic	739
6	Portugal	736
7	Spain	732
8	Netherlands	706
9	Yugoslavia	705
10	Paraguay	704
11	Germany	703
12	Mexico	688
13	Romania	681
14	Norway	673
14	Colombia	673
16	United States	657
17	England	655
18	Croatia	654
19	South Africa	633
20	Russia	632
21	Slovakia	629
22	Chile	628
23	Denmark	624
24	Sweden	622
25	Scotland	610
26	Tunisia	609
27	Belgium	608
28	Morocco	606
29	Trinidad & Tobago	602
30	Turkey	597
Also		
31	Republic of Ireland	594
93	Northern Ireland	436
109	Wales	385

Euro 2000

Group A

Stade de Sclessin, Liege   June 12
GERMANY (1) 1   ROMANIA (1) 1
Scholl (28)   Moldovan (5)

Germany: Kahn, Babbel, Matthäus (Deisler 77), Linke (Rehmer 46), Nowotny, Hassler (Hamann 73), Jeremies, Ziege, Rink, Scholl, Bierhoff
Romania: Stelea, Petrescu (Contra 69), Filipescu, Popescu, Ciobotariu, Munteanu, Hagi (Mutu 73), Galca, Chivu, Ilie, Moldovan (Lupescu 85)

Referee: K Neilsen DEN
Attendance: 29,450

Philips Stadium, Eindhoven   June 12
ENGLAND (2) 2   PORTUGAL (2) 3
Scholes (2)   Figo (21)
McManaman (19)   Joao Pinto (37)
*   Nuno Gomes (58)*

England: Seaman, G Neville, Adams (Keown 82), Campbell, P Neville, Beckham, Ince, Scholes, McManaman (Wise 57), Owen (Heskey 46), Shearer
Portugal: Vitor Baia, Xavier, Vidigal, Couto, Dimas, Jorge Costa, Figo, Rui Costa (Beto 84), Joao Pinto (Conceicao 75), Bento, Nuno Gomes (Capucho 90)

Referee: A Frisk SWE
Attendance: 33,000

Gelredome, Arnhem   June 17
ROMANIA (0) 0   PORTUGAL (0) 1
*   Costinha (90)*

Romania: Stelea, Contra, Popescu, Filipescu,Chivu, Petrescu (Petre 64), Munteanu, Galca, Hagi, Ilie (Rosu 78), Moldovan (Ganea 69)
Portugal: Vitor Baia, Secretario,Couto, Jorge Costa, Dimas, Figo, Vidigal, Rui Costa (Costinha 87), Bento, Joao Pinto (Conceicao 57), Nuno Gomes (Sa Pinto 57)

Referee: G Veissiere FRA
Attendance: 18,000

Stade du Pays de Charleroi   June 17
ENGLAND (0) 1   GERMANY (0) 0
Shearer (52)

England: Seaman, G Neville, Keown, Campbell, P Neville, Beckham, Scholes (Barmby 71), Ince, Wise, Shearer, Owen (Gerrard 60)
Germany: Kahn, Babbel, Nowotny, Matthäus, Deisler (Ballack 71), Scholl, Jeremies (Bode 77), Hamann, Ziege, Jancker, Kirsten (Rink 69)

Referee: P Collina ITA
Attendance: 35,000

Stade du Pays de Charleroi   June 20
ENGLAND (2) 2   ROMANIA (1) 3
Sheaer (pen 40)   Chivu (22)
Owen (45)   Munteanu (47)
*   Ganea (pen 88)*

England: Martyn, G Neville, Keown, Campbell, P Neville, Beckham, Scholes (Southgate 80), Ince, Wise (Barmby 74), Shearer, Owen (Heskey 65)
Romania: Stelea, Contra, Popescu (Belodedici 31), Filipescu, Petrescu, Munteanu, Mutu, Galca (Rosu 67), Chivu, Ilie, (Ganea 73), Moldovan

Referee: U Meier SUI
Attendance: 33,000

De Kuip, Rotterdam   June 20
PORTUGAL (1) 3   GERMANY (0) 0
Conceicao (35, 54, 71)

Portugal: Espinha (Quim 90), Beto (Vidigal 72), Couto, Jorge Costa,Conceicao, Costinha,Paulo Sousa, Capucho, Rui Jorge, Pauleta (Gomes 67), Sa Pinto
Germany: Kahn, Rehmer, Matthäus, Linke, Deisler, Nowotny, Hamann, Scholl (Hassler 60), Ballack (Rink 46), Bode, Jancker (Kirsten 69)

Referee: D Jol NED
Attendance: 44,000

Group B

King Baudouin Stadium, Brussels   June 10
BELGIUM (1) 2   SWEDEN (0) 1
Goor (42)   Mjallby (52)
E Mpenza (46)
Belgium: De Wilde, Deflandre, Valgaeren, Staelens, Leonard (Van Kerckoven 73), Verheyen (Peeters 88), Wilmots, Vanmderhaeghe, Goor, E Mpenza, Strupar (Nilis 70)
Sweden: Hedman, Nilsson (Lucic 45), P Andersson, Bjorklund, Mellberg, Alexandersson, D Andersson (Osmanovski 71), Ljungberg, Mjallby, K Andersson, Pettersson (Larsson 50)

Referee: M Merk GER
Attendance: 50,000

Gelodrome, Arnhem   June 11
ITALY (0) 2   TURKEY (0) 1
Conte (51)   Okan (60)
Inzaghi pen (69)
Italy: Toldo, Cannavaro, Nesta, Maldini, Zambrotta, Conte, Albertini, Fiore (Del Piero 74), Pessotto (Iuliano 62), Inzaghi, Totti (Di Livio 83)
Turkey: Rustu, Fatih, Ogun, Alpay, Abdullah, Tayfur, Korkut, Okan (Ergun 89), Sergun (Arif 81), Sukur, Umit (Tugay 76)

Referee: H Dallas SCO
Attendance: 25,000

Brussels   June 14
ITALY (1) 2   BELGIUM (0) 0
Totti (6)
Fiore (66)

Italy: Toldo, Cannavaro, Nesta, Iuliano, Maldini, Conte, Albertini, Zambrotta, Totti (Del Piero 64), Fiore (Ambrosini 83), Inzaghi (Delvecchio 77)
Belgium: De Wilde, Deflandre, Valgaeren, Staelens, Van Kerckoven (Hendrikx 44), Verheyen (M Mpenza 67), Vanmderhaeghe, Wilmots, Goor, E Mpenza, Strupar (Nilis 58)

Referee: J M Garcia-Aranda ESP
Attendance: 50,000

Philips Stadium, Eindhoven   June 15
SWEDEN (0)   TURKEY (0) 0

Sweden: Hedman, Lucic, Bjorklund, Mellberg,Sundgren, Alexandersson (D Andersson 63), Ljungberg, Mjallby, Mild, K Andersson (Pettersson 46), Larsson (Svensson 78)
Turkey: Rustu, Fatih, Ogun, Alpay, Izzet (Sergen 58), Umit (Tayfur 49), Okan (Tugay 59), Suat, Unsal, Arif, Hakan Sukur

Referee: D Jol NED
Attendance: 28,000

King Baudouin Stadium, Brussels   June 19
BELGIUM (0) 0   TURKEY (1) 2
                    Hakan Sukur (45, 70)

Belgium: De Wilde, Deflandre, Staelens,Valgaeren, Van Kerckoven, Verheyen (Strupar 64), Vanmderhaeghe, Goor (Hendrikx 59), Wilmots, E Mpenza, Nilis (De Bilde 77)
Turkey: Rustu, Fatih, Ogun, Alpay, Tayfun, Okan (Ergun 77), Suat, Tugay (Tayfur 37), Abdullah, Hakan Sukur, Arif (Osman 84)

Referee: K Neilsen DEN; replaced by G Benko AUT
Attendance: 48,000

Philips Stadium, Eindhoven   June 19
SWEDEN (0) 1   ITALY (1) 2
Larsson (77)   Di Biagio (39)
                    Del Piero (88)

Sweden: Hedman, Gustafsson (K Andersson 75), Bjorklund, P Andersson, Mellberg,Svensson (Alexandersson 52), Ljungberg, Mild, Mjallby (D Andersson 63), Larsson, Osmanovski
Italy: Toldo, Ferrara, Negro, Iuliano (Cannavaro 46), Pessotto, Di Livio (Fiore 64), Di Biagio, Ambrosini, Maldini (Nesta 42), Montella, Del Piero

Referee: M Pereira POR
Attendance: 33,000

Group C

De Kuip, Rotterdam   June 13
SPAIN (0) 0   NORWAY (0) 1
                    Iversen (66)

Spain: Molina, Salgado, Paco, Hierro, Aranzabal, Fran (Mendieta 72), Guardiola, Valeron (Helguera 80), Etxeberria (Alfonso 72), Raul, Urzaiz
Norway: Myhre, Heggem, Berg (Eggen 59), Bragstad, Bergdolmo, Iversen (Riseth 91), Bakke, Skammelsrud, Mykland, Flo (Carew 71), Solskjaer

Referee: G El Ghandour EGY
Attendance: 43,000

Stade du Pays de Charleroi   June 13
SLOVENIA (1) 3   YUGOSLAVIA (0) 3
Zahovic (22, 56)   Milosevic (66, 72)
Pavlin (52)   Drulovic (69)

Slovenia: Dabanovic, Milanic, Galic, Milinovic, Karic (Osterc 77), Novak, Ceh, Pavlin (Pavlovic 73), Rudonja, Zahovic, Udovic (Acimovic 63)
Yugoslavia: Kralj, Dudic, Djukic, Mihajlovic, Nadj, Stankovic (Stojkovic 35), Jokanovic, Drulovic, Mijatovic (Kezman 81), Kovacevic (Milosevic 51)

Referee: V Melo Pereira POR
Attendance: 20,000

Amsterdam ArenA   June 18
SLOVENIA (0) 1   SPAIN (1) 2
Zahovic (59)   Raul (4)
                     Etxeberria (60)

Slovenia: Dabanovic, Milanic (Knavs 68), Galic, Milinovic, Novak, Udovic (Osterc 46), Ceh, Karic, Rudonja, Pavlin (Acimovic 82), Zahovic
Spain: Canizares, Salgado, Hierro, Abelardo, Aranzabal, Etxeberria, Guardiola (Helguera 81), Valeron (Engonga 89), Mendieta, Alfonso (Urzaiz 71), Raul

Referee: M Merk GER
Attendance: 45,000

Sclessin Stadium   June 18
NORWAY (0) 0   YUGOSLAVIA (1) 1
                    Milosevic (8)

Norway: Myhre, Heggem (Bjornebye 35), Eggen, Bragstad, Bergdolmo, Iversen (Carew 71), Mykland, Bakke (Strand 76), Skammelsrud, Solskjaer, Flo
Yugoslavia: Kralj, Komljenovic, Djukic, Savelic, Djorovic, Jokanovic (Govedaric 89), Stojkovic (Nadj 84), Jugovic, Drulovic, Milosevic, Mijatovic (Kezman 87)

Referee: H Dallas SCO
Attendance: 24,000

Bruges   *June 21*
YUGOSLAVIA (1) 3   **SPAIN (1) 4**
Milosevic (31)   *Alfonso (39, 90)*
Govedaric (51)   *Munitis (51)*
Komljenovic (75)   *Mendieta (pen 90)*

Yugoslavia: Kralj, Komljenovic, Mihajlovic, Djukic, Djorovic (J Stankovic 12), Stojkovic (Saveljic 68), Jugovic (Govedaric 46), Jokanovic, Drulovic, Milosevic, Mijatovic
Spain: Canizares, Salgado (Munitis 46),Abelardo, Paco (Urzaiz 64), Sergi,Mendieta, Helguera, Guardiola, Fran (Etxeberria 22), Raul, Alfonso

Referee: G Veissiere FRA
Attendance: 22,000

Gelredome, Arnhem   *June 21*
SLOVENIA (0) 0   **NORWAY (0) 0**

Slovenia: Dabanovic, Knavs, Galic (Acimovic 82), Milinovic, Novak, Ceh, Pavlin, Rudonja, Karic, Zahovic, Siljak (Osterc 86),
Norway: Myhre, Bergdolmo, Eggen, Bragstad, Bjornebye, Solbakken, Carew (Bakke 61; Strand 82), Iversen, Mykland, Skammelsrud, Solskjaer, Flo

Referee: G Poll ENG
Attendance: 21,000

Group D

Jan Breydal Stadium, Bruges   *June 11*
FRANCE (1) 3   **DENMARK (0) 0**
Blanc 16
Henry (64)
Wiltord (90)

France: Barthez, Thuram, Blanc, Desailly, Lizarazu, Deschamps, Zidane, Petit, Djorkaeff (Vieira 58), Henry, Anelka (Wiltord 81)
Denmark: Schmeichel, Colding, Schjonberg, Henriksen, Heintze, Bisgaard (Jorgensen 72), Tofting (Gravesen 72), A Nielsen, Gronkjaer, Sand, Tomasson (Beck 79)

Referee: G Benko AUT
Attendance: 29,000

Amsterdam ArenA   *June 11*
HOLLAND (0) 1   **CZECH REPUBLIC (0) 0**
F de Boer (pen 89)

Holland: Van Der Sar, Reiziger, Stam (Konterman 75), F De Boer, Van Bronckhorst, Seedorf (R De Boer 57), Cocu, Davids, Zenden (Overmars 78), Bergkamp, Kluivert
Czech Republic: Srnicek, Latal (Bejbl 70), Repka, Rada, Gabriel, Poborsky, Nemec, Rosicky, Nedved (Lokvenc 90), Smicer (Kuka 83), Koller

Referee: P Collina ITA
Attendance: 50,000

Jan Breydel Stadium, Bruges   *June 16*
FRANCE (1) 2   **CZECH REPUBLIC (1) 1**
Henry (8)   *Poborsky (pen 34)*
Djorkaeff (60)

France: Barthez, Thuram, Blanc, Desailly, Candela, Vieira, Deschamps, Zidane, Petit (Djorkaeff 46), Henry (Wiltord 90), Anelka (Dugarry 55)
Czech Republic: Srnicek, Repka, Rada, Gabriel (Fukal 46), Poborsky, Nemec, Bejbl (Lokvenc 49), Nedved, Rosicky (Jankulovski 62), Smicer, Koller

Referee: G Poll ENG
Attendance: 25,000

De Kuip, Feyernoord, Rotterdam   *June 16*
HOLLAND (0) 3   **DENMARK (0) 0**
Kluivert (57)
R de Boer (66)
Zenden (77)

Holland: Van Der Sar (Westerveld 90), Reiziger, Konterman, F De Boer, Van Bronckhorst, Zenden, Cocu, Davids, Overmars (R De Boer 62), Kluivert, Bergkamp (Winter 76)
Denmark: Schmeichel, Colding, Henriksen, Schjonberg (Helveg 82), Heintze, Bisgaard , A Nielsen (Tofting 61), Gravesen (B Nielsen 67), Gronkjaer, Sand, Tomasson

Referee: U Meier SUI
Attendance: 50,000

Stade du Standard de Liege   *June 21*
CZECH REPUBLIC (0) 2   **DENMARK (0) 0**
Smicer (64, 67)

Czech Republic: Srnicek, Repka, Rada, Fukal, Nedved, Nemec, Bejbl (Jankulovski 61), Poborsky, Berger, Koller (Kuka 74), Smicer (Lokvenc 79)
Denmark: Schmeichel, Heintze (Colding 69), Henriksen, Schjonberg, Helveg, Tofting, A Nielsen, Goldaek, Tomasson, Gronkjaer, Beck (Molnar 74)

Referee: G Al Ghandour EGY
Attendance: 25,000

Amsterdam ArenA   *June 21*
FRANCE (2) 2   **HOLLAND (1) 3**
Dugarry (8)   *Kluivert (14)*
Trezeguet (31)   *F De Boer (51)*
         Zenden (59)

France: Lama, Karembeu, Leboeuf, Desailly, Candela, Pires, Micoud, Vieira (Deschamps 90), Dugarry (Djorkaeff 68), Trezeguet, Wiltord (Anelka 80)
Holland: Westerveld, Bosvelt, Stam, F De Boer, Numan, Overmars (Van Vossen 89), Cocu, Davids, Zenden, Bergkamp (Winter 76) Kluivert (Makaay 60)

Referee: A Frisk SWE
Attendance: 50,000

Quarter-Finals

Amsterdam ArenA   *June 24*
PORTUGAL (1) 2   **TURKEY (0) 0**
Gomes (44, 56)

Portugal: Baia, Jorge Costa, Couto, Dimas, Figo, Rui
Costa (Capucho 86), Conceicao, Costinha (Sousa 46),
Bento, Joao Pinto, Gomes (Sa Pinto 75)
Turkey: Rustu, Fatih, Ergun, Ogun (Sergen 84), Alpay,
Hakan Unsal, Tayfun, Okan (Oktay 62), Tayfur, Arif
(Kaya 62), Hakan Sukur

Referee: D Jol NED
Attendance: 45,000

King Baudoiun Stadium, Brussels   *June 24*
ITALY (2) 2   **ROMANIA (0) 0**
Totti (33)
Inzaghi (42)

Italy: Toldo, Cannavaro, Nesta, Maldini
(Pessotto 46), Zambrotta, Albertini, Conte (Di Biagio 54),
Iuliano, Fiore, Totti (Del Piero 74), Inzaghi
Romania: Stelea, Filipescu, Belodedici, Ciobotariu,
Petre,Galca (Lupescu 67), Chivu, Mutu, Hagi, Munteanu,
Moldovan (Ganea 53)

Referee: V Pereira POR
Attendance: 40,000

De Kuip, Rotterdam   *June 25*
HOLLAND (2) 6   **YUGOSLAVIA (0) 1**
Kluivert (34, 38, 54)   *Milosevic (90)*
Govedarica o.g. (51)
Overmars (78, 88)

Holland: Van der Sar (Westerveld 65), Numan, Stam,
F. De Boer, Bosvelt, Cocu, Davids, Zenden
(R. de Boer 79), Overmars, Bergkamp, Kluivert
(Makaay 59)
Yugoslavia: Kralj, Komljenovic, Djukic, Mihajlovic,
Saveljic (J Stankovic 56), Stojkovic (D Stankovic 52) ,
Govedaric, Jugovic, Drulovic (Kovacevic 70), Mijatovic,
Milosevic

Referee: J M Garcia Aranda ESP
Attendance: 50,000

Bruges   *June 25*

FRANCE (2) 2   **SPAIN (1) 1**
Zidane (32)   *Mendieta (pen 36)*
Djorkaeff (43)

France: Barthez, Thuram, Desailly, Blanc, Lizarazu,
Vieira, Deschamps, Zidane, Dugarry, Djorkaeff, Henry
(Anelka 80)
Spain: Canizares, Salgado Abelardo, Paco, Helguera
(Gerard 76), Guardiola, Mendieta (Urzaiz 56), Aranzabal
Munitis (Etxeberria 72), Alfonso, Raul

Referee: P Collina ITA
Attendance: 33,000

Semi-Finals

King Baudouin Stadium, Brussels   *June 28*
FRANCE (0) 2   **PORTUGAL (1) 1**
Henry (51)   *Nuno Gomes (19)*
Zidane (pen 117)

France: Barthez, Thuram, Blanc, Desailly, Lizarazu,
Vieira, Deschamps, Zidane, Petit (Pires 87), Anelka
(Wiltord 71), Henry (Trezeguet 105)
Portugal: Baia, Xavier, Couto, Jorge Costa, Vidigal
(Bento 60), Dimas (Rui Jorge 91), Conceicao, Costinha,
Figo, Rui Costa (Joao Pinto 76), Gomes

Referee: G Benko AUT
Attendance: 50,000
After extra time; France won on golden goal

Amsterdam ArenA   *June 29*
ITALY (0) 0   **HOLLAND (0) 0**

Italy: Toldo, Cannavaro, Iuliano, Nesta, Zambrotta, Fiore
(Totti 82), Di Biagio, Albertini (Pessotto 78), Maldini
Del Piero, Inzaghi(Delvecchio 67)
Holland: Van der Sar, Bosvelt, Stam, F. De Boer, Van
Bronckhorst, Zenden (Van Vossen 77), Overmars,
Davids, Cocu (Winer 95), Bergkamp (Seedorf 86),
Kluivert

Referee: M Merk GER
Attendance: 50,000

After extra time; Italy won 3-1 on penalties
Di Biagio-goal (1-0), F. de Boer-saved (1-0), Pessotto-
goal (2-0), Stam-miss (2-0), Totti-goal (3-0), Kluivert-goal
(3-1), Maldini-saved (3-1), Bosvelt-saved (3-1)

FINAL

De Kuip Stadium, Rotterdam   *July 2*
FRANCE (0) 2   **ITALY (0) 1**
Wiltord (90)   *Delvecchio (53)*
Trezeguet (102)

France: Barthez, Thuram, Blanc, Desailly, Lizarazu
(Pires 86), Vieira, Deschamps, Zidane, Dugarry
(Wiltord 57), Djorkaeff (Trezeguet 76), Henry
Italy: Toldo, Cannavaro, Nesta, Iuliano, Pessotto,
Albertini, Di Biagio (Ambrosini 65), Totti, Maldini, Fiore
(Del Piero 53), Delvecchio (Montella 86)

Referee: A Frisk SWE
Attendance: 51,000
After extra time; France won on golden goal

European Championships Goalscorers
Alphabetically, by country

5 goals
Patrick Kluivert (Holland), Savo Milosevic (Yugoslavia)

4 goals
Nuno Gomes (Portugal)

3 goals
Thierry Henry (France), Sergio Conceicao (Portugal), Zlatko Zahovic (Slovenia)

2 goals
Vladimir Smicer (Czech Republic), Alan Shearer (England), Youri Djorkaeff (France), David Trezeguet (France), Sylvain Wiltord (France), Zinedine Zidane (France), Ronald De Boer (Holland), Marc Overmars (Holland), Boudewijn Zenden (Holland), Filippo Inzaghi (Italy), Francesco Totti (Italy), Gaizka Mendieta (Spain), Alfonso Perez (Spain), Hakan Sukur (Turkey)

1 goal
Bart Goor (Belgium), Emile Mpenza (Belgium), Karel Poborsky (Czech Republic), Steve McManaman (England), Michael Owen (England), Paul Scholes (England), Laurent Blanc (France), Christophe Dugarry (France), Mehmet Scholl (Germany), Frank De Boer (Holland), Antonio Conte (Italy), Alessandro Del Piero (Italy), Marco Delvecchio (Italy), Luigi Di Biagio (Italy), Stefano Fiore (Italy), Steffen Iversen (Norway), Costinha (Portugal), Luis Figo (Portugal), Joao Pinto (Portugal), Cristian Chivu (Romania), Ioan Ganea (Romania), Viorel Moldovan (Romania), Dorinel Munteanu (Romania), Miran Pavlin (Slovenia), Joseba Exteberria (Spain), Raul Gonzalez (Spain), Pedro Munitis (Spain), Henrik Larsson (Sweden), Johan Mjallby (Sweden), Buruk Okan (Turkey), Ljubinko Drulovic (Yugoslavia), Dejan Govedarica (Yugoslavia), Slobodan Komljenovic (Yugoslaa)

Own goals
Dejan Govedarica (Yugoslavia, against Holland)

"It was just such a relief to hear that final whistle and to know we had beaten the Germans. It's been a long time coming but for the lads and the staff, this is something that can live with you forever - that you've been part of the team who beat the Germans"
Paul Ince.

"No. Never's a hard call, isn't it? Never . . . ish"
Terry Venables when asked if he would ever take the England job again.

"I think it is a betrayal of our heritage, of our culture and of the structure of the game in this country"
Gordon Taylor, head of the PFA, on the appointment of Eriksson.

"He has an enormous knowledge of soccer, he's exactly the same person he was at his first club - even though he's bigger than the Pope now"
Borje Andersson, trainer of Norwegian club Raufoss and friend of Sven-Goran Eriksson.

English Football

FA Carling Premiership 1999-2000

		P	W	D	L	GF	GA	W	D	L	GF	GA	GD	Pts
1	Manchester United	38	15	4	0	59	16	13	3	3	38	29	+52	91
2	Arsenal	38	14	3	2	42	17	8	4	7	31	26	+30	73
3	Leeds United	38	12	2	5	29	18	9	4	6	29	25	+15	69
4	Liverpool	38	11	4	4	28	13	8	6	5	23	17	+21	67
5	Chelsea	38	12	5	2	35	12	6	6	7	18	22	+19	65
6	Aston Villa	38	8	8	3	23	12	7	5	7	23	23	+11	58
7	Sunderland	38	10	6	3	28	17	6	4	9	29	39	+1	58
8	Leicester City	38	10	3	6	31	24	6	4	9	24	31	0	55
9	West Ham United	38	11	5	3	32	23	4	5	10	20	30	-1	55
10	Tottenham Hotspur	38	10	3	6	40	26	5	5	9	17	23	+8	53
11	Newcastle United	38	10	5	4	42	20	4	5	10	21	34	+9	52
12	Middlesbrough	38	8	5	6	23	26	6	5	8	23	26	-6	52
13	Everton	38	7	9	3	36	21	5	5	9	23	28	+10	50
14	Coventry City	38	12	1	6	38	22	0	7	12	9	32	-7	44
15	Southampton	38	8	4	7	26	22	4	4	11	19	40	-17	44
16	Derby County	38	6	3	10	22	25	3	8	8	22	32	-13	38
17	Bradford City	38	6	8	5	26	29	3	1	15	12	39	-30	36
18	Wimbledon	38	6	7	6	30	28	1	5	13	16	46	-28	33
19	Sheffield Wednesday	38	6	3	10	21	23	2	4	13	17	47	-32	31
20	Watford	38	5	4	10	24	31	1	2	16	11	46	-42	24

AXA FA CHARITY SHIELD
Wembley, Aug 1, 1999

ARSENAL 2
(Kanu 67 (pen), Parlour)

MANCHESTER UNITED 1
(Yorke 36)

Arsenal: Manninger, Dixon, Winterburn, Vieira, Keown, Grimandi, Parlour (Luzhny), Kanu, Petit, Ljungberg, Silvinho (Boa Morte)

Manchester United: Bosnich, Neville P., Irwin, Berg, Scholes, Stam (May), Beckham, Butt (Sheringham), Cole, Yorke, Cruyff (Solskjaer)

Referee: Graham Barber

Attendance: 70,185

Goalscorers

	Lg	Cps	Euro	Total
Kevin Phillips (Sunderland)	30	0	0	30
Alan Shearer (Newcastle)	23	5	2	30
Thierry Henry (Arsenal)	17	1	8	26
Dwight Yorke (Manchester U)	20	0	4	24
Andy Cole (Manchester U)	19	0	3	22
Michael Bridges (Leeds)	19	0	2	21
Tore Andre Flo (Chelsea)	10	1	8	19
Gustavo Poyet (Chelsea)	10	6	2	18
Paolo Di Canio (West Ham)	16	0	1	17
Steffen Iversen (Tottenham)	14	2	1	17
Nwankwo Kanu (Arsenal)	12	1	4	17
Harry Kewell (Leeds)	10	2	5	17
Dion Dublin (Aston Villa)	12	3	0	15
O G Solskjaer (Manchester U)	12	0	3	15
Paolo Wanchope (West Ham)	12	0	3	15
Carl Cort (Wimbledon)	9	6	0	15
Chris Armstrong (Tottenham)	14	0	0	14
Niall Quinn (Sunderland)	14	0	0	14
Robbie Keane (Coventry)	14	0	0	14
(includes two goals for Wolverhampton)				
Hamilton Ricard (Middlesbrough)	12	2	0	14

	Arsenal	Aston Villa	Bradford	Chelsea	Coventry	Derby	Everton	Leeds	Leicester	Liverpool	Man U	Middlesbro'	Newcastle	Sheffield W	Soton	Sunderland	Tottenham	Watford	West Ham	Wimbledon
Arsenal	****	1-1	2-1	2-3	3-2	1-2	0-1	0-1	0-4	2-0	0-3	2-1	4-2	1-1	0-1	0-0	2-1	2-3	2-1	1-3
Aston Villa	3-1	****	1-0	1-0	2-1	0-1	0-2	1-2	0-0	3-1	3-0	0-0	0-1	0-1	2-0	2-0	2-4	0-1	1-1	2-2
Bradford C	2-0	1-0	****	1-0	4-0	0-1	4-0	2-1	3-0	2-0	4-0	0-1	2-0	0-1	1-0	1-0	1-1	1-0	5-4	3-2
Chelsea	2-1	0-0	1-0	****	2-1	2-2	1-1	0-2	3-1	2-2	0-1	1-0	0-1	2-0	1-2	4-1	0-1	0-1	0-0	0-1
Coventry C	3-0	1-0	1-0	1-1	****	2-0	4-0	0-0	1-1	3-0	2-0	2-0	2-0	0-0	0-0	1-1	1-1	3-2	1-0	1-1
Derby C	4-1	1-0	2-0	4-4	3-0	****	1-0	2-1	2-0	0-1	1-4	3-1	2-0	2-0	3-1	1-1	1-1	0-0	1-1	2-2
Everton	2-0	0-2	4-0	1-1	1-0	1-2	****	1-0	3-4	0-2	5-0	0-4	4-1	0-1	7-2	3-2	0-1	1-0	0-3	0-1
Leeds U	2-1	1-2	2-1	0-2	0-0	2-1	1-0	****	2-1	2-2	1-2	0-3	0-2	3-1	0-1	4-1	2-1	0-1	1-0	4-0
Leicester C	0-1	0-0	3-0	3-1	1-1	2-0	3-4	4-4	****	0-0	1-1	1-2	0-0	3-0	4-1	5-0	0-1	3-1	4-2	4-0
Liverpool	1-2	0-2	2-0	0-2	0-0	0-1	0-1	0-1	0-2	****	0-2	1-3	2-2	1-1	0-2	1-2	2-2	0-1	2-2	3-3
Manchester U	5-1	3-0	4-0	5-0	2-0	1-4	5-0	0-0	2-3	1-0	****	3-4	3-0	2-3	3-2	2-3	3-1	2-4	2-2	2-2
Middlesbrough	2-3	0-0	0-1	0-4	0-1	3-1	2-1	1-2	3-0	1-1	1-0	****	2-2	1-0	1-0	3-2	1-3	0-1	2-4	2-3
Newcastle U	0-0	0-1	2-0	0-4	1-0	3-2	3-0	3-1	0-2	2-0	5-1	2-2	****	2-1	5-1	2-1	1-2	4-1	4-2	2-0
Sheffield W	3-3	0-1	0-1	1-0	1-1	2-0	0-2	3-3	3-0	1-1	1-2	1-0	3-0	****	0-1	5-2	2-1	0-1	1-3	2-1
Southampton	3-1	2-0	1-0	1-2	4-0	1-1	1-0	2-1	1-0	1-0	2-1	2-0	3-0	1-0	****	2-1	1-0	4-1	1-0	1-3
Sunderland	4-1	2-2	3-2	0-0	2-1	4-0	0-1	2-0	4-2	0-1	4-0	1-1	0-5	4-2	2-0	****	2-2	3-1	1-0	1-0
Tottenham H	2-1	1-1	3-0	0-1	1-0	1-0	3-1	2-2	0-1	1-0	3-1	2-1	2-1	1-1	7-1	0-1	****	3-1	2-0	1-1
Watford	2-3	0-1	1-0	0-1	3-2	0-0	1-0	0-1	3-1	0-1	2-4	0-1	4-1	0-1	4-1	3-1	1-0	****	1-2	2-3
West Ham U	2-1	1-1	5-4	0-0	1-0	1-1	0-3	1-0	4-2	2-2	2-2	2-4	4-2	1-3	1-0	1-0	1-0	0-0	****	2-1
Wimbledon	1-3	2-2	3-2	0-1	1-1	2-2	0-1	4-0	4-0	3-3	2-2	2-3	2-0	2-1	3-1	1-0	1-1	2-3	2-1	****

Nationwide League 1999-2000

Division One

		P	W	D	L	GF	GA	W	D	L	GF	GA	GD	Pts
1	Charlton Athletic	46	15	3	5	37	18	12	7	4	42	27	+34	91
2	Manchester City	46	17	2	4	48	17	9	9	5	30	23	+38	89
3	Ipswich Town	46	16	3	4	39	17	8	8	5	32	25	+29	87
4	Barnsley	46	15	4	4	48	24	9	6	8	40	43	+21	82
5	Birmingham City	46	15	5	3	37	16	7	6	10	28	28	+21	77
6	Bolton Wanderers	46	14	5	4	43	26	7	8	8	26	24	+19	76
7	Wolverhampton Wand'rs	46	15	5	3	45	20	6	6	11	19	28	+16	74
8	Huddersfield Town	46	14	5	4	43	21	7	6	10	19	28	+13	74
9	Fulham	46	13	7	3	33	13	4	9	10	16	28	+8	67
10	Queen's Park Rangers	46	9	12	2	30	20	7	6	10	32	33	+9	66
11	Blackburn Rovers	46	10	9	4	33	20	5	8	10	22	31	+4	62
12	Norwich City	46	11	6	6	26	22	3	9	11	19	28	-5	57
13	Tranmere Rovers	46	10	8	5	35	27	5	4	14	22	41	-11	57
14	Nottingham Forest	46	9	10	4	29	18	5	4	14	24	37	-2	56
15	Crystal Palace	46	7	11	5	33	26	6	4	13	24	41	-10	54
16	Sheffield United	46	10	8	5	38	24	3	7	13	21	47	-12	54
17	Stockport County	46	8	8	7	33	31	5	7	11	22	36	-12	54
18	Portsmouth	46	9	6	8	36	27	4	6	13	19	39	-11	51
19	Crewe Alexandra	46	9	5	9	27	31	5	4	14	19	36	-21	51
20	Grimsby Town	46	10	8	5	27	25	3	4	16	14	42	-26	51
21	West Bromich Albion	46	6	11	6	25	26	4	8	11	18	34	-17	49
22	Walsall	46	7	6	10	26	34	4	7	12	26	43	-25	46
23	Port Vale	46	6	6	11	27	30	1	9	13	21	39	-21	36
24	Swindon Town	46	5	6	12	23	37	3	6	14	15	40	-39	36

Play-offs

Semi-finals *(over 2 legs)*

Birmingham City 0 — Barnsley 4
(Shipperley 12, Dyer 48, 60, Hignett 84)

Barnsley 1 — Birmingham City 2
(Dyer 54) — *(Rowett 33, Marcelo 75)*
Barnsley won 5-2 on aggregate

Bolton Wanderers 2 — Ipswich Town 2
(Holdsworth 5, Gudjohnsen 26) — *(Stewart 36, 65)*

Ipswich Town 5 — Bolton Wanderers 3
(Magilton 18 pen, 49, 90, Clapham 94 pen, Reuser 109) — *(Holdsworth 6, 39, Johnston 50)*
aet; Ipswich won 7-5 on aggregate

FINAL
Wembley — *May 29*
IPSWICH 4 — **BARNSLEY 2**
(Mowbray 28, Naylor 52, Stewart 58 Reuser 90) — *(Wright R. og 6, Hignett 78 pen)*
Ipswich: Wright R., Croft, Clapham, Venus, Mowbray, McGreal, Holland, Wright J. (Wilnis), Johnson (Naylor), Magilton, Stewart (Reuser)
Barnsley: Miller, Curtis (Eaden), Barnard, Morgan, Chettle, Brown, Appleby, Hignett, Shipperley, Dyer (Hristov), Tinkler (Thomas)
Attendance: 73,427

Goalscorers

	Lg	Cps	Total
Shaun Goater (Manchester C)	23	6	29
Andy Hunt (Charlton A)	24	1	25
David Johnson (Ipswich T)	22	1	23
Robert Taylor (Manchester C)	20	3	23
Total includes 18 goals for Gillingham			
Craig Hignett (Barnsley)	19	2	21
Eidur Gudjohnsen (Bolton W)	13	8	21
Marcus Stewart (Ipswich T)	16	4	20
Total includes 14 goals for Huddersfield Town			
Iwan Roberts (Norwich C)	17	2	19
Wayne Allison (Tranmere R)	16	3	19
Martin Smith (Huddersfield T)	14	5	19
Total includes 15 goals for Sheffield United			
Ade Akinbiyi (Wolverhampton W)	18	0	18
Total includes two goals for Bristol City			
Marcus Bent (Sheffield U)	16	1	17
Total includes one goal for Port Vale			
Clyde Wijnhard (Huddersfield T)	15	1	16
Ian Lawson (Stockport C)	15	1	16
Total includes 12 goals for Bury			
Lee Hughes (West Brom)	12	4	16
Darren Barnard (Barnsley)	13	2	15
Clinton Morrison (Crystal P)	13	2	15
James Scowcroft (Ipswich T)	13	2	15
Neil Shipperley (Barnsley)	13	2	15
Dean Holdsworth (Bolton W)	11	4	15

Cups include Play-off goals

	Barnsley	Birmingham	Blackburn R	Bolton W	Charlton A	Crewe A	Crystal P	Fulham	Grimsby	Huddersfield	Ipswich	Man C	Norwich C	Notts For	Portsmouth	Port Vale	QPR	Sheff Utd	Stockport	Swindon	Tranmere	Walsall	WBA	Wolves
Barnsley	****	2-1	1-1	1-1	1-1	0-2	2-3	1-0	3-0	4-2	0-2	2-1	2-1	1-0	6-0	3-1	1-0	2-0	1-0	1-1	3-0	3-2	0-2	2-0
Birmingham	3-1	****	5-1	1-0	1-0	5-1	2-0	2-2	2-1	1-0	1-1	1-4	2-0	1-0	1-0	0-0	2-0	2-0	2-1	2-0	3-0	3-2	2-2	2-1
Blackburn R	1-2	1-0	****	1-0	1-2	0-1	0-0	2-2	0-0	3-2	0-2	2-0	1-1	2-1	1-0	2-2	0-1	0-1	0-1	0-1	2-1	1-1	1-1	2-1
Bolton W	2-2	0-3	3-1	****	3-1	1-3	2-1	1-3	2-0	1-3	2-2	1-0	0-0	2-3	3-0	2-1	2-1	0-1	0-0	0-4	0-0	2-0	2-0	1-0
Charlton A	3-1	1-0	2-1	3-1	****	2-1	2-0	2-2	1-1	1-2	1-2	1-3	1-0	3-0	1-1	1-0	3-0	0-2	3-0	2-3	0-0	2-4	2-0	2-3
Crewe A	0-1	2-3	0-0	2-1	0-2	****	3-0	1-1	4-0	1-0	1-1	2-1	1-1	2-0	4-0	1-3	1-1	2-2	0-3	0-1	1-4	1-4	1-0	2-0
Crystal P	0-2	1-0	2-1	1-1	2-1	1-0	****	0-0	3-0	1-0	2-1	0-1	0-3	2-0	4-0	2-0	1-3	0-0	2-1	2-4	0-2	1-2	0-0	2-1
Fulham	0-1	2-1	2-1	0-0	1-1	2-2	0-0	****	0-1	1-3	1-1	0-1	1-0	2-1	1-3	2-0	0-2	2-2	0-1	1-0	1-0	1-2	0-0	3-0
Grimsby	1-3	0-2	2-2	0-3	1-0	0-1	2-0	0-1	****	0-0	0-1	1-0	1-0	2-0	1-1	2-0	1-0	2-1	1-0	2-1	0-0	2-1	0-1	3-0
Huddersfield	0-3	0-2	0-0	0-1	0-3	3-0	7-1	3-0	3-1	****	2-1	1-0	0-1	0-3	2-1	3-0	2-1	4-1	0-2	2-0	1-0	2-0	2-0	0-1
Ipswich	2-1	0-1	3-2	0-1	1-2	2-1	2-1	1-1	2-0	2-1	****	1-0	0-0	3-0	4-2	2-1	1-0	0-0	1-0	1-4	0-0	1-1	1-1	2-1
Man C	6-1	1-0	0-0	2-0	4-2	4-0	2-1	4-0	2-1	1-0	1-0	****	1-0	3-2	0-1	2-2	4-0	4-1	1-2	0-2	3-0	0-1	1-0	4-1
Norwich C	1-0	0-1	2-0	2-1	1-1	2-1	0-1	1-2	3-0	0-1	3-1	2-1	****	0-3	0-1	0-0	1-3	4-1	1-0	1-2	2-0	2-2	2-1	1-0
Notts For	2-2	1-0	0-0	0-0	0-3	1-0	1-0	4-0	2-1	1-0	2-1	1-1	3-1	****	2-0	0-0	1-4	1-0	2-0	0-0	1-0	0-2	0-2	3-0
Portsmouth	2-2	0-1	0-1	1-2	1-1	0-2	3-1	0-2	2-1	0-0	0-0	1-2	1-1	1-0	****	0-0	1-3	2-0	3-3	1-1	3-1	2-0	1-0	1-1
Port Vale	3-0	2-2	0-2	1-1	1-2	1-0	2-0	0-2	0-1	1-3	2-2	1-2	1-3	4-3	2-0	****	1-1	5-0	1-1	2-1	1-0	1-2	0-0	2-2
QPR	2-2	3-1	1-2	0-1	2-5	1-0	0-1	3-1	2-1	0-1	3-1	1-2	2-1	2-1	2-1	3-2	****	3-1	1-1	0-1	2-0	5-1	1-2	3-2
Sheff Utd	2-2	2-2	0-1	0-1	0-2	2-1	3-1	0-0	4-0	2-1	1-2	0-2	6-0	1-0	3-0	2-1	1-1	****	1-0	1-3	2-1	4-1	2-1	1-0
Stockport	3-3	1-2	0-1	0-0	2-2	2-1	3-1	2-0	0-0	0-2	1-1	2-2	0-0	0-0	2-4	0-0	1-3	1-0	****	1-1	2-3	1-1	2-0	2-2
Swindon	1-3	1-4	0-1	0-4	1-2	0-1	2-4	1-0	2-1	2-0	1-4	0-2	2-2	2-1	2-4	2-1	0-1	3-1	2-1	****	2-0	1-1	2-1	1-1
Tranmere	1-2	2-1	2-1	0-0	1-3	1-4	1-2	1-0	0-1	1-0	0-1	1-1	2-2	1-1	1-1	1-0	2-1	2-1	1-2	3-1	****	4-0	3-1	1-1
Walsall	2-2	1-0	1-1	2-0	2-4	1-4	2-2	1-3	1-0	2-0	0-1	0-1	1-1	0-2	2-4	2-1	2-3	2-1	2-0	0-2	3-1	****	2-1	4-0
WBA	0-2	0-3	2-2	4-4	2-0	1-0	0-0	0-0	2-1	0-1	1-1	0-2	1-1	1-1	1-0	0-0	0-1	2-2	1-2	1-2	2-0	1-2	****	1-1
Wolves	2-0	2-1	2-1	1-0	2-3	2-0	2-1	3-0	3-0	0-1	2-1	4-1	1-0	3-0	1-1	2-2	3-2	1-0	2-2	1-2	1-0	1-1	1-1	****

Nationwide League 1999-2000

Division Two

		P	W	D	L	GF	GA	W	D	L	GF	GA	GD	Pts
1	**Preston North End**	46	15	4	4	37	23	13	7	3	37	14	+37	95
2	**Burnley**	46	16	3	4	42	23	9	10	4	27	24	+22	88
3	**Gillingham**	46	16	3	4	46	21	9	7	7	33	27	+31	85
4	**Wigan Athletic**	46	15	3	5	37	14	7	14	2	35	24	+34	83
5	**Millwall**	46	14	7	2	41	18	9	6	8	35	32	+26	82
6	**Stoke City**	46	13	7	3	37	18	10	6	7	31	24	+26	82
7	**Bristol Rovers**	46	13	7	3	34	19	10	4	9	35	26	+24	80
8	**Notts County**	46	9	6	8	32	27	9	5	9	29	28	+6	65
9	**Bristol City**	46	7	14	2	31	18	8	5	10	28	39	+2	64
10	**Reading**	46	10	9	4	28	18	6	5	12	29	45	-6	62
11	**Wrexham**	46	9	6	8	23	24	8	5	10	29	37	-9	62
12	**Wycombe Wanderers**	46	11	4	8	32	24	5	9	9	24	29	+3	61
13	**Luton Town**	46	10	7	6	41	35	7	3	13	20	30	-4	61
14	**Oldham Athletic**	46	8	5	10	27	28	8	7	8	23	27	-5	60
15	**Bury**	46	8	10	5	38	33	5	8	10	23	31	-3	57
16	**Bournemouth**	46	11	6	6	37	19	5	3	15	22	43	-3	57
17	**Brentford**	46	8	6	9	27	31	5	7	11	20	30	-14	52
18	**Colchester United**	46	9	4	10	36	40	5	6	12	23	42	-23	52
19	**Cambridge United**	46	8	6	9	38	33	4	6	13	26	32	-1	48
20	**Oxford United**	46	6	5	12	24	38	6	4	13	19	35	-30	45
21	**Cardiff City**	46	5	10	8	23	34	4	7	12	22	33	-22	44
22	**Blackpool**	46	4	10	9	26	37	4	7	12	23	40	-28	41
23	**Scunthorpe United**	46	4	6	13	16	34	5	6	12	24	40	-28	39
24	**Chesterfield**	46	5	7	11	17	25	2	8	13	17	38	-29	36

Play-offs

Semi-finals *(over 2 legs)*

Millwall 0	Wigan Athletic 0

Wigan Athletic 1   Millwall 0
(Sheridan 61)
Wigan Athletic won 1-0 on aggregate

Stoke City 3   Gillingham 2
(Gunnlaugsson 1,   (Gooden 18, Hessenthaler 90)
Lightbourne 8,
Thorne 67)

Gillingham 3   Stoke City 0
(Ashby 55, Onuora
102, Smith 118)
aet; Gillingham won 5-3 on aggregate

FINAL
Wembley   May 28
Gillingham 3   Wigan Athletic 2
(McGibbon og 35   (Haworth 52, Barlow 99 pen)
Butler 114,
Thomson 118)
Gillingham: Bartram, Southall, Edge (Smith), Pennock, Butters, Ashby (Butler), Lewis, Hessenthaler, Asaba, Onuora (Thomson), Gooden
Wigan: Stillie, Green, Sharp, McGibbon, Balmer, De Zeeuw, Kilford, Sheridan, Haworth (Peron), Liddell, (Bradshaw), Redfearn (Barlow)
aet

Attendance: 53,764

Goalscorers

	Lg	Cps	Total
Peter Thorne (Stoke C)	24	6	30
Andy Payton (Burnley)	27	0	27
Neil Harris (Millwall)	25	0	25
Sean Devine (Wycombe W)	23	2	25
Jonathan Macken (Preston NE)	22	3	25
Jason Roberts (Bristol R)	22	3	25
Jamie Cureton (Bristol R)	22	2	24
Trevor Benjamin (Cambridge U)	20	3	23
Stuart Barlow (Wigan A)	18	5	23
Martin Butler (Reading)	18	5	23
Total includes 19 goals for Cambridge United			
Darren Caskey (Reading)	17	6	23
Simon Haworth (Wigan A)	13	7	20
Matt Murphy (Oxford U)	11	9	20
David Reeves (Chesterfield)	14	4	18
Tony Thorpe (Bristol C)	14	4	18
Total includes one goal for Luton Town			
Steve McGavin (Colchester U)	16	0	16
Liam George (Luton T)	13	2	15
Mark Stein (Bournemouth)	11	4	15

Cups include Auto Windscreens Shield & Play-offs

	Blackpool	Bournemouth	Brentford	Bristol City	Bristol Rovers	Burnley	Bury	Cambridge U	Cardiff City	Chesterfield	Colchester U	Gillingham	Luton Town	Millwall	Notts County	Oldham A	Oxford U	Preston NE	Reading	Scunthorpe U	Stoke City	Wigan Ath	Wrexham	Wycombe W
Blackpool	****	0-0	0-1	1-2	2-1	2-1	2-1	1-1	2-2	2-2	1-1	3-3	1-2	2-1	1-2	1-1	1-1	0-0	0-2	1-1	1-2	2-2	2-1	1-2
Bournem'th	2-0	****	4-1	2-3	1-0	0-1	0-1	3-1	0-0	0-1	3-1	4-1	1-2	3-1	5-1	1-0	1-0	1-0	3-0	3-1	1-0	3-1	1-0	2-1
Brentford	2-0	0-2	****	0-2	0-1	1-1	2-2	2-2	0-0	0-3	1-0	2-0	2-0	1-2	0-1	0-0	3-0	1-1	1-0	0-1	1-0	1-0	1-0	2-0
Bristol C	5-2	3-1	2-1	****	2-1	1-1	1-0	2-2	2-0	3-4	0-2	3-0	2-1	4-1	4-4	1-1	3-0	3-0	1-1	1-2	2-1	2-1	1-1	1-2
Bristol R	3-1	1-0	0-1	2-1	****	1-0	0-5	0-0	0-1	5-4	0-1	0-1	1-4	0-1	0-2	3-0	0-5	1-4	0-1	0-2	3-1	3-1	2-1	1-1
Burnley	1-0	2-3	1-1	1-2	1-0	****	1-0	4-2	1-1	1-2	2-1	2-2	2-2	1-2	0-0	1-1	0-1	2-0	0-0	2-2	1-2	1-1	0-1	1-1
Bury	3-2	2-2	2-2	1-0	0-5	1-0	****	3-0	2-1	0-2	3-0	2-1	1-0	1-3	2-0	3-0	1-0	1-1	1-1	2-0	3-0	1-1	1-0	3-0
CambridgeU	1-0	2-1	2-0	2-2	0-0	4-2	3-0	****	0-4	0-3	4-1	0-0	2-0	2-0	2-1	2-3	1-0	1-0	1-0	0-3	1-0	1-1	1-1	1-0
Cardiff C	1-1	0-2	2-2	2-0	0-1	0-0	0-0	0-2	****	1-1	0-3	4-1	2-1	3-1	1-1	2-2	1-0	1-0	3-1	3-0	3-0	1-3	3-0	0-0
Chesterfield	0-0	0-1	1-0	0-2	1-0	1-2	3-0	2-0	1-0	****	1-0	1-1	0-1	2-0	0-1	0-1	0-0	0-2	0-1	1-1	0-1	1-0	2-0	1-2
Colchester U	1-1	3-1	1-0	0-2	0-1	2-1	3-0	4-1	0-3	1-0	****	0-1	1-2	2-3	1-1	1-0	2-0	2-3	1-1	0-1	3-1	3-0	1-0	3-0
Gillingham	1-3	4-1	2-0	3-0	0-1	2-2	2-1	0-0	4-1	1-1	0-0	****	2-0	3-0	4-1	1-2	4-2	2-2	2-0	3-1	2-1	3-1	2-0	1-0
Luton T	3-2	1-2	1-2	2-1	1-4	2-2	1-0	2-1	1-1	0-1	1-2	2-1	****	2-0	2-0	1-1	1-0	0-2	0-2	3-1	0-1	1-4	3-1	1-1
Millwall	1-1	3-1	3-2	4-1	0-1	1-2	1-3	2-0	0-1	2-0	2-3	2-2	0-2	****	0-2	1-1	0-2	0-2	0-2	1-2	4-1	3-3	3-1	1-1
Notts C	2-1	5-1	0-1	4-4	0-2	0-0	2-0	2-1	1-1	0-0	1-1	0-1	0-0	1-1	****	1-0	0-1	1-1	2-2	5-0	3-1	0-0	5-1	2-2
Oldham	1-1	1-0	0-0	1-1	3-0	1-1	3-0	2-3	2-2	3-0	1-0	1-2	1-3	1-1	2-3	****	0-1	0-1	1-3	2-0	3-0	0-2	1-4	0-0
Oxford U	1-1	1-0	3-0	3-0	0-5	0-1	1-0	1-0	1-0	1-1	2-0	4-2	1-0	0-1	2-0	0-1	****	2-0	0-1	4-0	4-0	3-3	5-1	2-1
Preston NE	0-1	1-0	1-1	3-0	1-4	2-0	1-1	1-0	1-0	1-0	2-3	2-2	1-2	3-2	2-3	1-0	2-0	****	0-4	1-3	0-1	1-4	1-4	3-2
Reading	3-0	3-0	1-0	1-0	0-1	0-0	1-1	1-0	3-1	3-1	1-1	2-0	2-0	2-0	2-0	1-1	2-0	2-2	****	2-2	5-0	2-1	5-1	0-0
Scunthorpe	1-0	3-1	0-0	1-2	0-2	2-2	2-0	0-3	2-1	0-0	0-1	3-1	3-1	1-2	2-3	2-0	1-2	1-3	2-2	****	5-3	2-1	3-1	2-1
Stoke C	3-0	1-0	1-0	2-1	3-1	1-2	3-0	1-0	2-0	5-1	3-1	2-0	3-0	3-0	3-0	3-0	3-0	3-0	0-1	1-0	****	2-1	1-0	3-1
Wigan A	5-1	3-1	1-0	2-1	3-1	1-1	1-1	1-1	2-1	3-0	3-0	3-1	2-1	3-1	2-1	0-1	2-1	0-0	0-1	0-2	0-2	****	0-1	1-1
Wrexham	1-1	1-0	1-0	0-1	2-1	0-1	1-0	1-1	0-0	1-1	1-0	2-0	1-0	1-1	2-0	0-3	2-0	0-0	2-1	0-4	2-3	1-1	****	0-1
Wycombe W	0-2	2-1	2-0	1-2	1-1	1-1	3-0	1-0	3-1	3-0	3-0	1-0	0-1	1-2	2-0	0-0	0-1	1-1	1-1	2-1	1-2	2-1	1-3	****

Nationwide League 1999-2000

Division Three

		P	W	D	L	GF	GA	W	D	L	GF	GA	GD	Pts
1	Swansea City	46	15	6	2	32	11	9	7	7	19	19	+21	85
2	Rotherham United	46	13	5	5	43	17	11	7	5	29	19	+36	84
3	Northampton Town	46	16	2	5	36	18	9	5	9	27	27	+18	82
4	Darlington	46	13	9	1	43	15	8	7	8	23	21	+30	79
5	Peterborough United	46	14	4	5	39	30	8	8	7	24	24	+9	78
6	Barnet	46	12	6	5	36	24	9	6	8	23	29	+6	75
7	Hartlepool United	46	16	1	6	32	17	5	8	10	28	32	+11	72
8	Cheltenham Town	46	13	4	6	28	17	7	6	10	22	25	+8	70
9	Torquay United	46	12	6	5	35	20	7	6	10	27	32	+10	69
10	Rochdale	46	8	7	8	21	25	10	7	6	36	29	+3	68
11	Brighton & Hove Albion	46	10	7	6	38	25	7	9	7	26	21	+18	67
12	Plymouth Argyle	46	12	10	1	38	18	4	8	11	17	33	+4	66
13	Macclesfield Town	46	9	7	7	36	30	9	4	10	30	31	+5	65
14	Hull City	46	7	8	8	26	23	8	6	9	17	20	0	59
15	Lincoln City	46	11	6	6	38	23	4	8	11	29	46	-2	59
16	Southend United	46	11	5	7	37	31	4	6	13	16	30	-8	56
17	Mansfield Town	46	9	6	8	33	26	7	2	14	17	39	-15	56
18	Halifax Town	46	7	5	11	22	24	8	4	11	22	34	-14	54
19	Leyton Orient	46	7	7	9	22	22	6	6	11	25	30	-5	52
20	York City	46	7	10	6	21	21	5	6	12	18	32	-14	52
21	Exeter City	46	8	6	9	27	30	3	5	15	19	42	-26	44
22	Shrewsbury Town	46	5	6	12	20	27	4	7	12	20	40	-27	40
23	Carlisle United	46	6	8	9	23	27	3	4	16	19	48	-33	39
24	Chester City	46	5	5	13	20	36	5	4	14	24	43	-35	39

Play-offs

Semi-finals (over 2 legs)

Barnet 1   Peterborough U 2
(Arber 22)   *(Lee 5, Clarke 68)*

Peterborough U 3   Barnet 0
(Farrell 28, 70, 89)
Peterborough won 5-1 on aggregate

Hartlepool United 0   Darlington 2
    (Liddle 35, Gabbiadini 76 pen)

Darlington 1   Hartlepool United 0
(Strodder og 9)
Darlington won 3-0 on aggregate

FINAL
Wembley   *May 26*
PETERBOROUGH 1   DARLINGTON 0
(Clarke 25)

Peterborough: Tyler, Scott, Drury (Hanlon), Castle, Rea, Edwards, Farrell, Cullen, Clarke (Green), Oldfield, Jelleyman
Darlington:Collett, Liddle, Heckinbottom (Naylor), Gray, Tutill, Aspin, Heaney, Oliver, Duffield (Nogan), Gabbiadini, Atkinson (Holsgrove)

Attendance: 33,383

Goalscorers

	Lg	Cps	Total
Marco Gabbiadini (Darlington)	24	4	28
Martin Carruthers (Southend U)	19	0	19
Gary Alexander (Exeter C)	16	3	19
Luke Beckett (Chester C)	14	5	19
Andy Clarke (Peterborough U)	15	3	18
Leo Fortune-West (Rotherham U)	17	0	17
Richard Barker (Macclesfield U)	16	1	17
Tony Bedeau (Torquay U)	16	1	17
Lee Thorpe (Lincoln C)	16	1	17
Tommy Miller (Hartlepool U)	15	1	16
Paul McGregor (Plymouth A)	13	3	16
Carlo Corazzin (Northampton T)	14	1	15

Cups include Auto Windscreens Shield & Play-offs

Home \ Away	Barnet	Brighton	Carlisle	Cheltenham	Chester C	Darlington	Exeter	Halifax	Hartlepool	Hull	Leyton O	Lincoln	Macclesfield	Mansfield	Northampton	Peterboro	Plymouth	Rochdale	Rotherham	Shrewsbury	Southend	Swansea	Torquay	York
Barnet	****	0-1	3-0	3-2	2-0	1-0	2-2	0-1	1-1	0-0	2-2	5-3	2-1	2-1	0-1	0-2	1-0	0-2	1-0	1-1	2-1	0-1	1-2	1-0
Brighton	1-1	****	1-0	1-0	2-1	0-1	1-1	2-1	0-0	0-3	0-1	1-2	1-1	1-0	1-0	0-0	3-3	4-3	3-3	0-0	2-1	2-0	0-0	0-0
Carlisle	3-1	0-1	****	1-0	3-2	1-0	1-0	5-2	1-0	5-2	2-1	5-0	2-1	1-1	2-1	0-0	2-0	3-2	4-2	4-1	2-0	1-0	4-1	1-1
Cheltenham	1-2	1-0	1-0	****	1-1	1-1	0-1	1-1	1-2	0-1	0-1	1-0	1-0	0-1	3-2	0-2	1-0	0-0	0-0	0-2	2-1	2-0	1-1	1-2
Chester C	0-2	1-7	4-1	2-1	****	1-1	2-1	2-1	1-0	0-2	2-0	2-2	2-1	2-1	3-1	2-1	0-0	2-1	4-0	0-1	3-1	2-3	2-2	2-2
Darlington	4-0	1-1	0-1	1-0	1-0	****	2-0	0-1	2-0	0-1	0-1	0-1	0-2	2-3	0-3	1-2	0-0	4-2	0-3	2-1	0-0	1-0	1-0	0-0
Exeter	0-0	1-1	1-0	0-1	4-1	0-0	****	1-2	0-1	2-0	2-2	0-1	1-0	1-2	0-1	1-0	3-1	3-1	2-1	0-1	2-0	0-1	1-0	0-0
Halifax	3-0	2-1	5-2	0-1	2-1	0-1	1-0	****	1-0	0-2	0-1	0-1	0-2	2-1	2-3	2-1	1-0	2-1	0-1	4-1	3-1	1-2	1-0	2-1
Hartlepool	1-2	0-0	2-1	1-2	2-1	2-1	1-0	1-0	****	0-3	1-4	0-1	3-3	3-3	2-1	1-1	1-1	2-0	1-1	2-1	2-1	0-1	0-0	2-1
Hull	1-3	0-3	1-0	0-1	0-4	0-0	4-0	0-1	0-3	****	2-0	2-2	1-0	2-1	0-0	1-2	0-1	0-0	3-4	1-1	0-0	2-1	4-0	0-1
Leyton O	0-0	0-0	2-1	1-0	2-1	2-1	2-1	1-0	2-0	2-0	****	2-3	1-0	1-4	2-1	2-2	5-0	2-1	2-1	1-0	0-0	1-2	0-1	2-1
Lincoln	0-0	1-2	5-0	1-2	3-1	1-2	1-0	0-1	1-1	1-0	2-0	****	1-0	1-0	2-1	2-2	1-1	1-1	0-5	1-2	2-0	0-0	5-2	2-0
Macclesfield	2-0	1-1	2-1	1-2	1-1	2-1	1-1	0-2	2-3	0-2	1-0	1-1	****	0-0	2-0	1-0	1-0	2-0	1-0	3-2	1-0	2-1	3-2	0-2
Mansfield	0-1	1-0	1-1	0-1	2-1	1-0	1-0	0-1	3-3	2-1	0-1	5-2	1-1	****	2-1	1-0	1-0	2-1	2-3	0-1	3-1	1-0	0-1	0-1
Northampton	1-0	1-0	2-1	3-2	3-1	0-3	4-0	3-4	2-1	0-0	2-1	2-0	2-3	2-1	****	0-0	0-1	0-3	2-1	1-0	0-1	1-2	1-2	0-1
Peterboro	1-2	0-0	0-0	0-1	2-1	1-2	5-0	2-1	1-1	0-4	1-0	3-0	2-2	1-0	0-0	****	2-0	2-1	1-0	2-1	0-0	0-1	2-1	0-1
Plymouth	4-1	3-3	2-0	1-0	0-0	2-1	0-2	3-0	2-1	3-0	5-0	1-1	3-2	5-0	2-1	0-1	****	2-1	2-2	4-1	3-1	0-0	0-4	0-0
Rochdale	1-1	4-3	3-2	0-0	2-1	4-2	3-1	2-1	2-0	0-0	2-1	1-1	2-0	2-1	0-3	2-3	1-1	****	0-1	0-1	2-0	1-0	1-0	0-3
Rotherham	2-0	3-3	4-2	2-0	4-0	0-3	2-1	0-1	1-1	3-4	2-1	0-5	1-0	2-3	2-1	1-0	2-2	1-1	****	1-1	0-1	1-2	2-1	1-2
Shrewsbury	1-1	0-0	4-1	0-2	0-1	2-1	0-1	4-1	2-1	1-1	1-0	1-2	3-2	0-1	1-0	2-1	4-1	3-3	4-0	****	3-2	2-1	3-1	0-0
Southend	1-3	2-1	2-0	2-1	3-1	0-0	2-0	3-1	2-1	0-0	0-0	2-2	1-0	0-1	0-1	2-2	3-0	3-1	2-0	2-1	****	2-1	0-2	1-0
Swansea	1-2	2-0	1-0	0-0	2-1	1-2	1-2	2-1	1-0	2-0	1-0	2-1	1-0	0-1	2-2	2-0	1-1	1-0	2-3	1-1	3-1	****	1-0	1-0
Torquay	0-1	0-0	4-1	1-1	2-2	1-0	4-0	0-0	2-1	1-1	0-0	1-0	1-0	0-1	1-2	0-1	2-2	0-4	0-2	0-0	0-2	1-1	****	2-2
York	1-0	0-0	1-1	1-2	2-2	0-0	0-0	2-0	2-1	1-1	2-1	2-0	0-2	0-1	0-1	0-2	0-0	0-1	1-2	2-0	0-0	0-1	2-2	****

English Non-League Football

GM Vauxhall Conference

	P	W	D	L	F	A	Pts
Kidderminster Harriers	42	26	7	9	75	40	85
Rushden & Diamonds	42	21	13	8	71	42	76
Morecambe	42	18	16	8	70	48	70
Scarborough	42	19	12	11	60	35	69
Kingstonian	42	20	7	15	58	44	67
Dover Athletic	42	18	12	12	65	56	66
Yeovil Town	42	18	10	14	60	63	64
Hereford United	42	15	14	13	61	52	59
Southport	42	15	13	14	55	56	58
Stevenage Borough	42	16	9	17	60	54	57
Hayes	42	16	8	18	57	58	56
Doncaster Rovers	42	15	9	18	46	48	54
Kettering Town	42	12	16	14	44	50	52
Woking	42	13	13	16	45	53	52
Nuneaton Borough	42	12	15	15	49	53	51
Telford United	42	14	9	19	56	66	51
Hednesford United	42	15	6	21	45	68	51
Northwich Victoria	42	13	12	17	53	78	51
Forest Green Rovers	42	13	8	21	54	63	47
Welling United	42	13	8	21	54	66	47
Altrincham	42	9	19	14	51	60	46
Sutton United	42	8	10	24	39	75	34

Leading Scorers	Total
Justin Jackson (Morecambe)	31
Carl Alford (Stevenage Borough)	26

Unibond League

Premier Division

	P	W	D	L	F	A	Pts
Leigh RMI	44	28	8	8	91	45	92
Hyde United	44	24	13	7	77	44	85
Gateshead	44	23	13	8	79	41	82
Marine	44	21	16	7	78	46	79
Emley	44	20	12	12	54	41	72
Lancaster City	44	20	11	13	65	55	71
Stalybridge Celtic	44	18	12	14	64	54	66
Bishop Auckland	44	18	11	15	63	61	65
Runcorn	44	18	10	16	64	65	64
Worksop Town	44	19	6	19	78	65	63
Gainsborough Trinity	44	16	15	13	59	49	63
Whitby Town	44	15	13	16	66	66	58
Barrow	44	14	15	15	65	59	57
Blyth Spartans	44	15	9	20	62	67	54
Droylsden	44	14	12	18	53	60	54
Frickley Athletic	44	15	9	20	64	85	54
Bamber Bridge	44	14	11	19	70	67	53
Hucknall Town	44	14	11	19	55	61	53
Leek Town	44	14	10	20	58	79	52
Colwyn Bay	44	12	12	20	46	85	48
Spennymoor United*	44	10	13	21	41	71	42
Guiseley	44	8	17	19	52	72	41
Winsford United	44	3	7	34	40	119	16

*Deducted one point for breach of a rule

Leading Scorers	Total
Simon Yeo (Hyde United)	37
Simon Parke (Guiseley)	30

Dr Martens League

Premier Division

	P	W	D	L	F	A	Pts
Boston United	42	27	11	4	102	39	92
Burton Albion	42	23	9	10	73	43	78
Margate	42	23	8	11	64	43	77
Bath City	42	19	15	8	70	49	72
Kings Lynn	42	19	14	9	59	43	71
Tamworth	42	20	10	12	80	51	70
Newport County	42	16	18	8	67	50	66
Clevedon Town	42	18	9	15	52	52	63
Ilkeston Town	42	16	12	14	77	69	60
Weymouth	42	14	16	12	60	51	58
Halesowen Town	42	14	14	14	52	54	56
Crawley Town	42	15	8	19	68	82	53
Havant & Waterlooville	42	13	13	16	63	68	52
Cambridge City	42	14	10	18	52	66	52
Worcester City	42	13	11	18	60	66	50
Salisbury City	42	14	8	20	70	84	50
Merthyr Tydfil	42	13	9	20	51	63	48
Dorchester Town	42	10	17	15	56	65	47
Grantham Town	42	14	5	23	63	76	47
Gloucester City	42	8	14	20	40	82	38
Rothwell Town	42	5	14	23	48	85	29
Atherstone united	42	5	13	24	30	76	28

Leading Scorers	Total
M Hallam (Tamworth)	35
J Taylor (Havant & Waterlooville)	32
C Moore (Burton Albion)	29

Ryman League

Premier Division

	P	W	D	L	F	A	Pts
Dagenham & Redbridge	42	32	5	5	97	35	101
Aldershot Town	42	24	5	13	71	51	77
Chesham United	42	20	10	12	64	50	70
Purfleet	42	18	15	9	70	48	69
Canvey Island	42	21	6	15	70	53	69
St. Albans City	42	19	10	13	75	55	67
Billericay Town	42	18	12	12	62	62	66
Hendon	42	18	8	16	61	64	62
Slough Town	42	17	9	16	61	59	60
Dulwich Hamlet	42	17	5	20	62	68	56
Gravesend & Northfleet	42	15	10	17	66	67	55
Farnborough Town	42	14	11	17	52	55	53
Hampton & Richmond	42	13	13	16	49	57	52
Enfield	42	13	11	18	66	68	50
Heybridge Swifts	42	13	11	18	57	65	50
Hitchin Town	42	13	11	18	59	72	50
Carshalton Athletic	42	12	12	18	55	65	48
Basingstoke Town	42	13	9	20	56	71	48
Harrow Borough	42	14	6	22	54	70	48
Aylesbury United	42	13	9	20	64	81	48
Boreham Wood	42	11	10	21	44	71	43
Walton & Hersham	42	11	8	23	44	70	41

Leading Scorers	Total
Gary Abbott (Aldershot Town)	29
George Georgiou (Purfleet)	27
Steve Darlington (Farnborough Town)	25

FA Challenge Cup 1999-2000

First Round

Aldershot T 1 *(Abbott)*
Hednesford 1 *(Robinson)*

Hednesford T 1 *(Lake)*
Aldershot T 2 *(Chewins, Abbott)*

Barnet 0
Burnley 1 *(Cook)*

Bath City 0
Hendon 2 *(Gentle, Guentchev)*

Blackpool 2 *(Carlisle, Nowland)*
Stoke C 0

Brentford 2 *(Owusu, Marshall)*
Plymouth A 2 *(Stonebridge,*
McGregor)

Plymouth A 2 *(McGregor 2)*
Brentford 1 *(Quinn) aet*

Bristol C 3 *(Tinnion 2, Murray)*
Mansfield T 2 *(Lormor, Blake)*

Bristol R 0
Preston NE 1 *(McKenna)*

Burton A 0
Rochdale 0

Rochdale 3 *(Platt, Peake, Dowe)*
Burton A 0

Cambridge C 0
Wigan A 2 *(Barlow 2)*

Cambridge U 1 *(Taylor)*
Gateshead 0

Cheltenham 1 *(Brough)*
Gillingham 1 *(Southall)*

Gillingham 3 *(Thomson, Pennock,*
McGlinchey)
Cheltenham 2 *(Milton, Howarth)*

Chesterfield 1 *(Lomas)*
Enfield 2 *(Bunn, Brown)*

Darlington 2 *(Tutill, Gabbiadini pen)*
Southport 1 *(Bolland)*

Doncaster R 0
Halifax T 2 *(Tate, Paterson)*

Exeter C 2 *(Flack, Gale)*
Eastwood T 1 *(Smith)*

Forest Green R 6 *(Hunt 3,*
McGregor, Drysdale,
Sykes)
Guiseley 0

Hartlepool 1 *(Jones)*
Millwall 0

Hayes 2 *(Bunce, Charles)*
Runcorn 1 *(McDonald)*

Hereford U 1 *(May)*
York C 0

Ilkeston T 2 *(Moore, Raynor)*
Carlisle U 1 *(Harries)*

Leyton O 1 *(Ampadu)*
Cardiff C 1 *(Nugent pen)*

Cardiff C 3 *(Brazier, Perrett,*
Nugent)
Leyton O 1 *(Smith)*

Lincoln C 1 *(Smith)*
Welling U 0

Luton T 4 *(Gray, George, Spring,*
Taylor)
Kingstonian 2 *(Crossley, Leworthy)*

Macclesfield T 0
Hull C 0

Hull C 4 *(Eyre 2, Greaves, Brown)*
Macclesfield T 0

Merthyr T 2 *(Mitchell 2)*
Stalybridge C 2 *(Parr, Sullivan)*

Stalybridge C 3 *(Bauress pen,*
Pickford, Sullivan)
Merthyr T 1 *(Lima)*

Notts C 1 *(Rapley)*
Bournemouth 1 *(Warren)*

Bournemouth 4 *(Fletcher 2, Stein,*
Robinson pen)
Notts C 2 *(Redmile, Tierney)*

Oldham A 4 *(Dudley, Sheridan,*
Duxbury, Whitehall)
Chelmsford C 0

Oxford U 3 *(Lilley, Powell, Abbey)*
Morecambe 2 *(Wright, Jackson)*

Peterborough U 1 *(Clarke)*
Brighton & HA 1 *(Freeman)*

Brighton & HA 3 *(Rogers, Watson,*
Mayo)
Peterborough U 0

Reading 4 *(Bernal, Caskey pen,*
Hunter, M Williams)
Yeovil T 2 *(Foster, Eaton)*

Rotherham U 3 *(Thompson, Garner,*
Martindale pen)
Worthing 0

Rushden & D 2 *(Warburton,*
Hamsher pen)
Scunthorpe U 0

Shrewsbury T 2 *(Kerrigan, Wilding)*
Northampton T 1 *(Hendon)*

St Albans C 0
Bamber Bridge 2 *(Whittaker,*
Carroll)

Swansea C 2 *(Cusack, Watkin)*
Colchester U 1 *(Lua-Lua)*

Tamworth 2 *(Haughton, Hallam)*
Bury 2 *(Bullock, Littlejohn)*

Bury 2 *(Billy, James)*
Tamworth 1 *(Haughton)*

Torquay U 1 *(O'Brien)*
Southend U 0

Whyteleafe 0
Chester C 0

Chester C 3 *(Cross 2, Beckett)*
Whyteleafe 1 *(Lunn)*

Wrexham 1 *(Roberts pen)*
Kettering T 1 *(Brown)*

Kettering T 0
Wrexham 2 *(S Roberts, Williams)*

Wycombe W 1 *(Simpson)*
Oxford C 1 *(Pierson)*

Oxford C 1
Wycombe W 1
Abandoned after extra time; fire

Oxford C 0
Wycombe W 1 *(Brown)*

Second Round

Blackpool 2 *(Clarkson, Durnin)*
Hendon 0

Bournemouth 0
Bristol C 2 *(Murray 2)*

Burnley 2 *(Cook, Mullin)*
Rotherham U 0

Bury 0
Cardiff C 0

Cardiff C 1 *(Ford)*
Bury 0

Cambridge U 1 *(Butler pen)*
Bamber Bridge 0

Exeter C 2 *(Alexander, Flack)*
Aldershot T 0

Forest Green R 0
Torquay U 3 *(Brandon, Hill,
            Donaldson)*

Gillingham 3 *(Butters, Taylor 2)*
Darlington 1 *(Duffield)*

Hayes 2 *(Charles 2, 1 pen)*
Hull C 2 *(Roddis og, Edwards)*

Hull C 3 *(Brown, Edwards, Wood)*
Hayes 2 *(Gallen, Charles)*
aet

Hereford U 1 *(Elms)*
Hartlepool U 0

Ilkeston T 1 *(Eshelby)*
Rushden & D 1 *(De Souza)*

Rushden & D 3 *(Wooding, Town,
              Collins)*
Ilkeston T 0

Luton T 2 *(Doherty 2)*
Lincoln C 2 *(Gordon, D Barnett)*

Lincoln C 0
Luton T 1 *(Douglas)*

Oldham A 1 *(Whitehall)*
Swansea C 0

Plymouth A 0
Brighton & HA 0

Plymouth A 1 *(Cullip)*
Brighton & HA 2 *(Bastow,
                Hargreaves)*

Preston NE 0
Enfield 0

Enfield 0
Preston NE 3 *(Eyres, Alexander
              pen, Gunnlaugsson)*

Reading 1 *(Caskey pen)*
Halifax T 1 *(Mitchell)*

Haifax T 0
Reading 1 *(Caskey pen)*

Shrewsbury T 2 *(Kerrigan 2)*
Oxford U 2 *(Murphy, Folland)*

Oxford U 2 *(Murphy 2)*
Shrewsbury T 1 *(Jagielka)*
aet

Stalybridge C 1 *(Scott)*
Chester C 2 *(Cross, Beckett)*

Wrexham 2 *(Roberts N,
           Faulconbridge)*
Rochdale 1 *(Atkinson)*

Wycombe W 2 *(Devine, Ryan)*
Wigan A 2 *(Haworth 2)*

Wigan A 2 *(Liddell, Haworth)*
Wycombe W 1 *(Baird)*

Third Round

Arsenal 3 *(Grimandi, Adams,
           Overmars)*
Blackpool 1 *(Clarkson)*

Aston V 2 *(Carbone, Dublin)*
Darlington 1 *(Heckingbottom)*

Bolton W 1 *(Gudjohnsen)*
Cardiff C 0

Cambridge U 2 *(Benjamin,
              Wanless)*
Crystal P 0

Charlton A 2 *(Kinsella 2)*
Swindon T 1 *(Gooden)*

Chester C 1 *(Richardson)*
Manchester C 4 *(Goater 2, Bishop,
                Doughty og)*

Crewe A 1 *(Little)*
Bradford C 2 *(Blake, Saunders)*

Derby C 0
Burnley 1 *(Cooke)*

Exeter C 0
Everton 0

Everton 1 *(Barmby)*
Exeter C 0

Fulham 2 *(Horsfield, Davis)*
Luton T 2 *(George, Spring)*

Luton T 0
Fulham 3 *(Hayles 2, Hayward)*

Grimsby 3 *(Livingstone 2, Allen)*
Stockport C 2 *(Bailey, Moore)*

Hereford U 0
Leicester C 0

Leicester C 2 *(Elliott, Izzet)*
Hereford U 1 *(Fewings)*
aet

Huddersfield T 0
Liverpool 2 *(Camara, Matteo)*

Hull C 1 *(Brown)*
Chelsea 6 *(Poyet 3, Sutton,
           Di Matteo, Edwards og)*

Ipswich T 0
Southampton 1 *(Richards)*

Leeds U 2 *(Bakke 2)*
Port Vale 0

Norwich C 1 *(Llewellyn)*
Coventry C 3 *(Whelan, Roussel,
              Eustace)*

Nottingham F 1 *(Freedman)*
Oxford U 1 *(Powell)*

Oxford U 1 *(Powell)*
Nottingham F 3 *(Bart-Williams 2,
                1 pen, Rogers)*

Preston NE 2 *(Macken, Alexander)*
Oldham A 1 *(Adams)*

QPR 1 *(Wardley)*
Torquay U 1 *(O'Brien)*

Torquay U 2 *(Bedeau, Thomas)*
QPR 3 *(Wardley 2, Kiwomya)*

Reading 1 *(McIntyre)*
Plymouth A 1 *(Hargreaves)*

Plymouth A 1 *(Heathcote)*
Reading 0

Sheffield U 1 *(Bent)*
Rushden & D 1 *(Brady)*

Rushden & D 1 *(Warburton)*
Sheffield U 1 *(Derry)*
*aet; Sheffield U won 6-5 on
penalties*

Sheffield W 1 *(Booth)*
Bristol C 0

Sunderland 1 *(McCann)*
Portsmouth 0

Tottenham H 1 *(Iversen)*
Newcastle U 1 *(Speed)*

Newcastle U 6 *(Speed, Dabizas, Ferguson, Dyer, Shearer 2, 1 pen)*
Tottenham H 1 *(Ginola)*

Tranmere R 1 *(Henry)*
West Ham 0

Walsall 1 *(Robins pen)*
Gillingham 1 *(Southall)*

Gillingham 2 *(Barras og, Thomson)*
Walsall 1 *(Larusson)*
aet

Watford 0
Birmingham C 1 *(Rowett)*

WBA 2 *(Hughes, Evans)*
Blackburn R 2 *(Frandsen, Blake)*

Blackburn R 2 *(Duff, Carsley pen)*
WBA 0
aet

Wigan A 0
Wolverhampton W 1 *(Robinson)*

Wimbledon 1 *(Cort)*
Barnsley 0

Wrexham 2 *(Gibson, Ferguson)*
Middlesbrough 1 *(Deane)*

Fourth Round

Arsenal 0
Leicester C 0

Leicester C 0
Arsenal 0
aet; Leicester C won 6-5 on penalties

Aston V 1 *(Southgate)*
Southampton 0

Charlton A 1 *(MacDonald)*
QPR 0

Chelsea 2 *(Leboeuf, Wise)*
Nottingham F 0

Coventry C 3 *(Chippo 2, Whelan)*
Burnley 0

Everton 2 *(Unsworth 2 pens)*
Birmingham C 0

Fulham 3 *(Collins 2, Finnan)*
Wimbledon 0

Gillingham 3 *(Thomson, Ashby, Hodge)*
Bradford C 1 *(Saunders)*

Grimsby T 0
Bolton W 2 *(Gudjohnsen, Hansen)*

Liverpool 0
Blackburn R 1 *(Blake)*

Manchester C 2 *(Goater, Bishop)*
Leeds U 5 *(Bakke, Smith, Kewell 2, Bowyer)*

Newcastle U 4 *(Shearer, Dabizas, Ferguson, Gallacher)*
Sheffield U 1 *(Smith)*

Plymouth A 0
Preston NE 3 *(O'Sullivan og, Alexander pen, Beswetherick og)*

Sheffield W 1 *(Alexandersson)*
Wolverhampton W 1 *(Sedgley)*

Wolverhampton W 0
Sheffield W 0
aet; Sheffield W won 4-3 on penalties

Tranmere R 1 *(Allison)*
Sunderland 0

Wrexham 1 *(Connolly)*
Cambridge U 2 *(Benjamin, Butler)*

Fifth Round

Aston V 3 *(Carbone 3)*
Leeds U 2 *(Harte, Bakke)*

Blackburn 1 *(Jansen)*
Newcastle U 2 *(Shearer 2)*

Cambridge U 1 *(Benjamin)*
Bolton W 3 *(Taylor 2, Gudjohnsen)*

Chelsea 2 *(Poyet, Weah)*
Leicester C 2 *(Elliott)*

Coventry C 2 *(Roussel 2)*
Charlton A 3 *(Robinson, Newton, Hunt)*

Everton 2 *(Unsworth, Moore)*
Preston NE 0

Fulham 1 *(Coleman)*
Tranmere R 2 *(Allison, Kelly)*

Gillingham 3 *(Saunders, Thomson, Southall)*
Sheffield W 1 *(Sibon)*

Sixth Round

Bolton W 1 *(Gudjohnsen)*
Charlton A 0

Chelsea 5 *(Flo, Terry, Weah, Zola pen, Morris)*
Gillingham 0

Everton 1 *(Moore)*
Aston V 2 *(Stone, Carbone)*

Tranmere R 2 *(Allison, G Jones)*
Newcastle U 3 *(Speed, Domi, Ferguson)*

Semi-finals

Bolton W 0
Aston V 0
aet; Aston V won 4-1 on penalties

Newcastle U 1 *(Lee)*
Chelsea 2 *(Poyet 2)*

FINAL
Wembley, May 20

Aston Villa 0
Chelsea 1 *(Di Matteo 72)*

Aston Villa: James, Delaney, Wright (Hendrie), Southgate, Ehiogu, Barry, Taylor (Stone), Boateng, Dublin, Carbone (Joachim), Merson

Chelsea: De Goey, Melchiot, Babayaro, Deschamps, Leboeuf, Desailly, Poyet, Di Matteo, Weah (Flo), Zola (Morris), Wise

Referee: Graham Poll
Attendance: 78,217

Worthington Cup 1999-2000

First Round

Birmingham C 3 *(A Johnson, Richardson og, Adebola)*
Exeter C 0

Exeter C 1 *(McConnell pen)*
Birmingham C 2 *(Richardson og, O'Connor)*
Birmingham won 5-1 on aggregate

Blackpool 2 *(Hughes, Clarkson)*
Tranmere R 1 *(Thompson og)*

Tranmere R 3 *(S Taylor, Kelly 2)*
Blackpool 1 *(Clarkson)*
Tranmere won 4-3 on aggregate

Bournemouth 2 *(Hayter, Huck)*
Barnet 0

Barnet 3 *(McGleish 2, 1 pen, Hackett)*
Bournemouth 2 *(Stein 2)*
Bournemouth won 4-3 on aggregate

Brentford 0
Ipswich T 2 *(Johnson, Clapham)*

Ipswich T 2 *(Scowcroft, Clapham)*
Brentford 0
Ipswich won 4-0 on aggregate

Brighton & HA 0
Gillingham 2 *(Ormerod og, Hessenthaler)*

Gillingham 2 *(Taylor, Southall)*
Brighton & HA 0
Gillingham won 4-0 on aggregate

Bury 1 *(Lawson)*
Notts C 0

Notts C 2 *(Blackmore, Ramage pen)*
Bury 0
Notts C won 2-1 on aggregate

Cambridge U 2 *(Butler 2)*
Bristol C 2 *(Hutchings, Mortimer)*

Bristol C 2 *(Torpey, Thorpe)*
Cambridge U 1 *(Butler)*
Bristol C won 4-3 on aggregate

Cardiff C 1 *(Bowen)*
QPR 2 *(Langley, Fowler og)*

QPR 1 *(Peacock pen)*
Cardiff C 2 *(Brazier, Hughes)*
aet; Cardiff won 3-2 on penalties

Carlisle U 0
Grimsby T 0

Grimsby T 6 *(Lester 3, Groves, Coldicott, Donovan)*
Carlisle U 0
Grimsby won 6-0 on aggregate

Chester C 2 *(Richardson, Beckett pen)*
Port Vale 1 *(Rougier)*

Port Vale 4 *(Naylor 2, Minton pen, Griffiths)*
Chester C 4 *(Beckett 2 1 pen, Shelton, Jones)*
Chester won 6-5 on aggregate

Colchester U 2 *(Dozzell, Lua-Lua)*
Crystal P 2 *(Smith, Rodger)*

Crystal P 3 *(Smith, Morrison, Rizzo)*
Colchester U 1 *(Keith)*
Palace won 5-3 on aggregate

Darlington 1 *(Oliver)*
Bolton W 1 *(Frandsen)*

Bolton W 5 *(Reed og, Gardner, Taylor, Frandsen, Johansen pen)*
Darlington 3 *(Nogan 2 Gabbiadini)*
Bolton won 6-4 on aggregate

Halifax T 0
WBA 0

WBA 5 *(Kilbane 2, Hughes, De Freitas, Evans)*
Halifax T 1 *(Gaughan)*
WBA won 5-1 on aggregate

Hartlepool U 3 *(Miller, Di Lella, Stephenson)*
Crewe A 3 *(Little 2, Cramb)*

Crewe A 1 *(Little)*
Hartlepool U 0
Crewe Alex won 4-3 on aggregate

Lincoln C 2 *(Fleming, Thorpe)*
Barnsley 4 *(Shipperley, Van der Laan, Eaden)*

Barnsley 2 *(Sheron, Eaden)*
Lincoln C 2 *(Gordon, Peacock)*
Barnsley won 6-4 on aggregate

Luton T 0
Bristol R 2 *(Roberts 2)*

Bristol R 2 *(Roberts, Cureton)*
Luton T 2 *(Kandol, Doherty)*
Bristol R won 4-2 on aggregate

Macclesfield T 1 *(Priest)*
Stoke C 1 *(Keen)*

Stoke C 3 *(Conner, Thorpe, O'Connor)*
Macclesfield T 0
Stoke won 4-1 on agg

Manchester C 5 *(Goater, Kennedy 2, Horlock pen, G Taylor)*
Burnley 0

Burnley 0
Manchester C 1 *(Cooke)*
Manchester C won 6-0 on agg

Northampton T 1 *(Corazzin pen)*
Fulham 2 *(Davis, Horsfield)*

Fulham 3 *(Horsfield 3)*
Northampton T 1 *(Byfield)*
Crewe A won 4-3 on aggregate

Norwich C 2 *(Roberts 2)*
Cheltenham T 0

Cheltenham T 2 *(Grayson pen, Victory)*
Norwich C 1 *(L Marshall)*
aet; Norwich won 3-2 on aggregate

Nottingham F 3 *(Bart-Williams, Quashie, Allou)*
Mansfield T 0

Mansfield T 1 *(Peacock)*
Nottingham F 0
Forest won 3-1 on agregate

Preston NE 1 *(Appleton)*
Wrexham 0

Wrexham 0
Preston NE 2 *(Basham, Macken)*
Preston won 3-0 on aggregate

Reading 0
Peterborough U 0

Peterborough U 1 *(Shields)*
Reading 2 *(Caskey, Scott)*
Reading won 2-1 on aggregate

Rochdale 1 *(Lancashire)*
Chesterfield 2 *(Reeves, Hill og)*

Chesterfield 2 *(Bayliss og, Ebdon)*
Rochdale 1 *(Evans)*
Chesterfield won 4-2 on aggregate

Rotherham U 0
Hull C 1 *(Eyre)*

Hull C 2 *(Alcide, Brown)*
Rotherham U 0
Hull won 3-0 on agg

Scunthorpe U 0
Huddersfield T 2 *(Lucketti, Beech)*

Huddersfield T 0
Southend U 0
Huddersfield won 2-0 on aggregate

Sheffield U 3 *(Katchuro, Smith 2)*
Shrewsbury T 0

Shrewsbury T 0
Sheffield U 3 *(Marcelo 2, Smith)*
Sheffield U won 6-0 on aggregate

Southend U 0
Oxford U 2 *(Murphy, Beauchamp)*

Oxford U 1 *(Murphy)*
Southend U 0
Oxford won 3-0 on agg

Stockport C 2 *(Cooper, Angell)*
Oldham A 0

Oldham A 1 *(Allott)*
Stockport C 1 *(Woodthorpe)*
Stockportwon 3-1 on aggregate

Swansea C 2 *(Watkin, Price)*
Millwall 0

Millwall 1 *(Sadlier)*
Swansea C 1 *(Bird pen)*
Swansea won 3-1 on aggregate

Swindon T 0
Leyton O 1 *(Inglethorpe)*

Leyton O 1 *(Lockwood)*
Swindon T 1 *(Walters pen)*
Leyton Orient won 2-1on aggregate

Torquay U 0
Portsmouth 0

Portsmouth 3 *(Nightingale 2,*
Lovell)
Torquay U 0
Portsmouth won 3-0 on aggregate

Walsall 4 *(Bukran, Robins,*
Eyjolfsson 2)
Plymouth A 1 *(Stonebridge)*

Plymouth A 1 *(Gritton)*
Walsall 4 *(Keates, Barras, Bukran,*
Eyjolfsson)
Walsall won 8-2 on aggregate

Wycombe W 0
Wolverhampton W 1 *(Curle pen)*
Wolverhampton W 2 *(Larkin,*
Emblen)
Wycombe W 4 *(Muscat og,*
McSporran 2, Ryan)
Wycombe won 4-3 on aggregate

York C 0
Wigan A 1 *(Haworth)*

Wigan A 2 *(Barlow 2, 1 pen)*
York C 1 *(Rowe)*
Wigan won 3-1 on aggregate

Second Round

Barnsley 1 *(Barnard)*
Stockport C 1 *(Briggs)*

Stockport C 3 *(Wilbraham, D'Jaffo,*
Dinning pen)
Barnsley 3 *(Hristov 2, Jones)*
aet; Barnsley won on away goals

Birmingham C 2 *(O'Connor pen,*
Holdsworth)
Bristol R 0

Bristol R 0
Birmingham C 1 *(Rowett)*
Birmingham won 3-0 on aggregate

Bradford C 1 *(Blake pen)*
Reading 1 *(Caskey pen)*

Reading 2 *(Scott, Hunter,)*
Bradford C 2 *(Saunders, Wetherall)*
aet; Bradford C won on away goals

Cardiff C 1 *(Nugent pen)*
Wimbledon 1 *(M Hughes)*

Wimbledon 3 *(Cort, Earle 2)*
Cardiff C 1 *(Bowen)*
Wimbledon won 4-2 on aggregate

Charlton A 0
Bournemouth 0

Bournemouth 0
Charlton A 0
aet; Bournemouth won 3-1 on pens

Chester C 0
Aston V 1 *(Hendrie)*

Aston V 5 *(Boateng, Taylor,*
Hendrie 2, Thompson)
Chester C 0
Aston V won 6-0 on aggregate

Chesterfield 0
Middlesbrough 0

Middlesbrough 2 *(Ince, Vickers)*
Chesterfield 1 *(Reeves)*
Middlesbrough won 2-1 on agg

Crewe A 2 *(Rivers, Little)*
Ipswich T 1 *(Venus)*

Ipswich T 1 *(Scowcroft)*
Crewe A 4 *(Rivers)*
Crewe A won 3-2 on aggregate

Crystal P 3 *(Morrison, Zhiyi,*
Mullins)
Leicester C 3 *(Digby og, Lennon,*
Taggart)

Leicester C 4 *(Oakes 2, 1 pen,*
Marshall, Fenton)
Crystal P 2 *(Thomson, Bradbury)*
Leicester C won 7-5 on aggregate

Gillingham 1 *(Hessenthaler)*
Bolton W 4 *(Cox, Gudjohnsen 2,*
Bergsson)

Bolton W 2 *(Hansen, Holdsworth)*
Gillingham 0
Bolton W won 6-1 on aggregate

Grimsby T 4 *(D Smith, Gallimore,*
Ashcroft pen, Groves)
Leyton O 1 *(Lockwood pen)*

Leyton O 1 *(Watts)*
Grimsby T 0
Grimsby T won 4-2 on aggregate

Huddersfield T 2 *(Wijnhard,*
Stewart)
Notts C 1 *(Ramage)*

Notts C 2 *(Blackmore, Darby)*
Huddersfield T 2 *(Irons, Gorre)*
Huddersfield T won 4-3 on agg

Ipswich T 2 *(Scowcroft, Thetis)*
Luton T 1 *(Douglas)*

Luton T 4 *(Fotiadis, Douglas,*
Davis S, Johnson)
Ipswich T 2 *(Johnson, Davis S og)*
aet; Luton T won 5-4 on aggregate

Hull C 1 *(Brown)*
Liverpool 5 *(Murphy 2, Meijer 2,*
Staunton)

Liverpool 4 *(Murphy, Maxwell,*
Riedle 2)
Hull C 2 *(Eyre pen, Alcide)*
Liverpool won 9-3 on aggregate

Manchester C 0
Southampton 0

Southampton 4 *(Dodds pen,*
Oakley 2, Richards)
Manchester C 3 *(Dickov, Goater 2)*
aet; Southampton won 4-3 on
aggregate

Norwich C 0
Fulham 4 *(Peschisolido, Coote og, Clark, Collins)*

Fulham 2 *(Hayles, Davis)*
Norwich C 0
Fulham won 6-0 on agg

Nottingham F 2 *(Harewood, Rogers)*
Bristol C 1 *(Jordan)*

Bristol C 0
Nottingham F 0
Nottingham F won 2-1 on agg

Oxford U 1 *(Murphy)*
Everton 1 *(Cadamarteri)*

Everton 0
Oxford U 1 *(Beauchamp)*
Oxford U won 2-1 on agg

Portsmouth 0
Blackburn R 3 *(Cundy og, Jansen 2)*

Blackburn R 3 *(Duff, Dunn, Gallacher)*
Portsmouth 1 *(McLoughlin)*
Blackburn R won 6-1 on agg

Sheffield U 2 *(Smith, Katchuro)*
Preston NE 0

Preston NE 3 *(Alexander, Mathie 2)*
Sheffield U 0
Preston NE won 3-2 on agg

Stoke C 0
Sheffield W 0

Sheffield W 3 *(Alexandersson 2, De Bilde)*
Stoke C 1 *(G Kavanagh)*
Sheffield W won 3-1on aggregate

Sunderland 3 *(Dichio, Barras og, Williams)*
Walsall 2 *(Bukran, Brissett)*

Walsall 0
Sunderland 5 *(Dichio 2, Roy, Fredgaard 2)*
Sunderland won 8-2 on agg

Swansea C 0
Derby C 0

Derby C 3 *(Fuertes, Sturridge, Borbokis)*
Swansea C 1 *(Bound pen)*
Derby C won 3-1 on aggregate

Tranmere R 5 *(S Taylor 2, Kelly 3)*
Coventry C 1 *(McAllister)*

Coventry C 3 *(McAllister, Chippo 2)*
Tranmere R 1 *(P Taylor)*
Tranmere R won 6-4 on agg

Watford 2 *(Easton, Hyde)*
Wigan A 0

Wigan A 3 *(Haworth 2, Bradshaw pen)*
Watford 1 *(Kennedy)*
aet; Watford won on away goals

WBA 1 *(Flynn)*
Wycombe W 1 *(McCarthy)*

Wycombe W 3 *(Devine, Carroll, Brown pen)*
WBA 4 *(Raven, DeFreitas, Quinn, Hughes)*
aet; WBA won 5-4 on aggregate

Third Round

Arsenal 2 *(Kanu, Malz)*
Preston NE 1 *(Macken)*

Aston V 3 *(Joachim, Taylor, Stone)*
Manchester U 0

Birmingham C 2 *(O'connor pen, Purse)*
Newcastle U 0

Bradford 2 *(Mills, Wetherall)*
Barnsley 3 *(Sheron, Morgan, Barnard pen)*

Chelsea 0
Huddersfield T 1 *(Irons)*

Derby C 1 *(Beck)*
Bolton W 2 *(Fish, Johansen)*

Leeds U 1 *(Mills)*
Blackburn R 0

Leicester C 2 *(Izzet, Heskey)*
Grimsby T 0

Middlesbrough 1 *(Juninho)*
Watford 0

Sheffield W 4 *(Cresswell, Booth, Sonner, Rudi)*
Nottingham F 1 *(Freedman)*

Southampton 2 *(Richards, Soltvedt)*
Liverpool 1 *(Owen)*

Tottenham H 3 *(Leonhardsen, Ginola, Sherwood)*
Crewe A 1 *(S Smith pen)*

Tranmere R 2 *(Yates, Grant)*
Oxford U 0

WBA 1 *(Hughes)*
Fulham 2 *(Peschisolido, Collymore)*

West Ham U 2 *(Keller, Lampard)*
Bournemouth 0

Wimbledon 3 *(Cort 3)*
Sunderland 2 *(Dichio, Ball)*
aet

Fourth Round

Aston V 4 *(Watson, Joachim, Dublin 2)*
Southampton 0

Birmingham C 2 *(Hyde, Grainger)*
West Ham U 3 *(Lomas, Kitson, Cole)*

Bolton W 1 *(Elliott)*
Sheffield W 0

Fulham 3 *(Hayles, Collins, Horsfield)*
Tottenham H 1 *(Iversen)*

Huddersfield T 1 *(Sellars)*
Wimbledon 2 *(Kimble, Euell)*
aet

Leicester C 0
Leeds U 0
aet; Leicester C won 4-2 on penalties

Middlesbrough 2 *(Ricard 2, 1 pen)*
Arsenal 2 *(Henry, Suker)*
aet; Middlesbrough won 3-1 on penalties

Tranmere R 4 *(Parkinson, Morgan, Hill, Black)*
Barnsley 0

Fifth Round

Bolton W 2 *(Gudjohnsen, Johansen pen)*
Wimbledon 1 *(Cort)*

Leicester C 3 *(Marshall 2, Walsh)*
Fulham 3 *(Peschisolido, Horsfield, Coleman)*
aet; Leicester C won 3-0 on penalties

Tranmere R 2 *(Kelly, Parkinson)*
Middlesbrough 1 *(Ziege)*

West Ham U 2
Aston V 2
aet; West Ham U won 5-4 on penalties; match ordered to be replayed after West Ham U fielded an ineligible player

West Ham U 1 *(Lampard)*
Aston V 3 *(Taylor 2, Joachim)*
aet

Semi-finals

Aston V 0
Leicester C 0

Leicester C 1 *(Elliott)*
Aston V 0
Leicester C won 1-0 on aggregate

Bolton W 0
Tranmere R 1 *(Hill)*
Tranmere R 3 *(Henry, Mahon pen, Kelly)*
Bolton W 0
Tranmere R won 4-0 on aggregate

FINAL

Wembley, Feb 27

Leicester City 2 *(Elliott 29, 81)*
Tranmere Rovers 1
(Kelly 77)

Leicester: Flowers, Savage, Guppy, Elliott, Taggart, Sinclair, Lennon, Izzet, Cottee (Marshall), Oakes (Impey), Heskey

Tranmere: Murphy, Hazell, Roberts, Henry, Hill, Challinor, Mahon, Parkinson (Yates), Jones G, Kelly, Taylor S

Referee: Alan Wilkie; substitute P Richards

Attendance: 74,313

Auto Windscreens Shield 1999-2000

Second Round

North

Carlisle U 2 *(Pitts, Soley)*
Wigan Ath 1 *(Martinez)*

Hull City 2 *(Joyce, Morgan)*
Chester City 0

Lincoln City 1 *(Henry)*
Scunthorpe U 2 *(Hodges, Sheldon)*

Mansfield Town 0
Blackpool 1 *(Matthews)*

Oldham Ath 0
Stoke City 1
abandoned due to floodlight failure

Oldham Ath 0
Stoke City 1 *(O'Connor)*
aet

Preston NE 1 *(Gunnlaugsson)*
Hartlepool U 2 *(Midgley, Miller)*

Rochdale 3 *(Monington 2, Lancashire)*
Macclesfield T 2 *(Davies, Barker)*

Rotherham U 1 *(White)*
Chesterfield 4 *(Branston og, Wilsterman og, Wilkinson, Reeves)*

South

Barnet 1 *(Hackett)*
Reading 2 *(Caskey, Scott) aet*

Bournemouth 1 *(Hayter)*
Brighton & HA 0 *aet*

Bristol C 3 *(Holland, Goodridge, Beadle)*
Cheltenham T 1 *(McAuley)*

Exeter City 2 *(Alexander, Buckle)*
Swansea City 0

Northampton Town 0
Bristol R 0
aet; Bristol R won 5-3 on penalties

Oxford U 1 *(Powell pen)*
Wycombe W 1 *(McSporran)*
aet; Oxford U won 5-3 on penalties

Peterborough U 0
Brentford 1 *(Owusu)*

Plymouth A 0
Torquay U 1 *(Donaldson)*

Quarter-finals

North

Blackpool 1 *(Jaszczun)*
Stoke C 2*(Gunnarsson, Kavanagh)*

Carlisle U 2 *(Halliday, McKinnon)*
Hartlepool U 1 *(Lee)*

Rochdale 0
Hull City 0
aet; Rochdale won 5-4 on penalties

Scunthorpe U 1 *(Stamp)*
Chesterfield 2 *(Blatherwick,Reeves)*

South

Brentford 2 *(Bryan, Scott)*
Oxford U 0

Bristol C 1 *(Hewlett)*
Bournemouth 1 *(Stein)*
aet; Bristol C won 4-1 on penalties

Bristol R 1 *(Cureton pen)*
Reading 2 *(Nicholls 2)*

Exeter City 1 *(Speakman)*
Torquay U 0

Semi-finals

North

Carlisle U 0
Rochdale 1 *(Hill)*

Chesterfield 0
Stoke City 1 *(O'Connor)*

South

Bristol C 4 *(Beadle, Murray, Thorpe 2)*
Reading 0

Exeter C 3 *(Breslan, Alexander, Powell og)*
Brentford 2 *(Powell, Evans pen)*

Northern Final (2 legs)

Rochdale 1 *(Holt)*
Stoke C 3 *(Hansson, Thorne 2)*

Stoke C 1 *(Thorne)*
Rochdale 0
Stoke C won 4-1 on aggregate

Southern Final (2 legs)

Bristol C 4 *(Thorpe, Beadle, Murray, Burnell)*
Exeter C 0

Exeter C 1 *(Speakman)*
Bristol C 1 *(Beadle)*
Bristol C won 5-1 on aggregate

Final

Bristol City 1 *(Spencer 73)*

Stoke City 2 *(Kavanagh 31, Thorne 81)*

Bristol City: Mercer, Carey (Amankwaah), Bell, Jordan, Millen, Holland, Murray, Brown A (Spencer), Beadle, Thorpe, Tinnion

Stoke: Ward, Hansson, Clarke, Mohan, Gudjonsson, Gunnlaugsson (Dryden), Gunnarsson, Kavanagh, Lightbourne (Iwelumo), Thorne, O'Connor

Referee: K Lynch

Attendance: 75,057

Scottish Football

They told John Barnes it was too big a job to take on for his first in management and they - the Celtic fans, the Rangers fans and just about everybody else - were right. But nobody expected the relationship to end in quite as spectacular a way as it did. Inverness Caledonian Thistle have only existed since 1994, but they went to Parkhead in the third round of the Scottish Cup and unceremoniously dumped Celtic out. Deservedly so, the 3-1 scoreline did not flatter them one bit. For the Celtic fans it was enough and Barnes' days were numbered.

The argument for the defence was the absence from the team of Henrik Larsson. On Saturday, October 17th, Celtic had thumped Aberdeen 7-0 to move four points behind Rangers, with a game in hand. Henrik Larsson scored a hat-trick that day, taking his total to for the season to 12 from just 11 games. Four days later, on the Wednesday, Celtic travelled to Lyon for a second round UEFA Cup tie. After just 12 minutes, Larsson broke his leg. It was an horrific injury that finished his season (he returned as a substitute in the very last game) and Celtic's challenge. As is the way with these things, as soon as Barnes left the club, Celtic won a trophy. The CIS Insurance Cup, which they won by beating Aberdeen 2-0, is small potatoes, though, and no compensation at all for the fact that Rangers won the Scottish League by a monstrous 21 points. In a two-horse race, which it has been since Alex Ferguson's days at Aberdeen, a distant second is equivalent to a dismal failure. Dear John, said the directors, we think you'd better go now.

If Rangers retained their League title at a canter, it was the same old story in Europe. Rangers played in both European tournaments without getting a sniff of a quarter-final in either. Yet their performance, in comparative terms, was an encouraging one. They qualified for the first group stage of the Champions League after a splendid two-leg win over Parma. Taking a two-goal lead to Italy, Rangers limited the damage to a single-goal defeat. In Group F, two defeats at the hands of an unsung Valencia team would not look bad at all as the competition wore on. Rangers beat PSV Eindhoven both at home and away and, had they not conceded an 88th minute equaliser against Bayern Munich, they and not the Germans would have proceeded. As it was they fell through the skylight and into the third round of the UEFA Cup (thereby outlasting Celtic in that competition without even playing a match). Again Rangers could be considered a trifle unlucky. They had taken another two-goal lead in the first leg. As the second leg at Borussia Dortmund reached injury time, the looked set for a 1-0 defeat which would have secured qualification. But Dortmund scored and, maintaining a German tradition, won the tie on penalties.

Rangers completed the domestic double with a Scottish Cup final win over Aberdeen (two finals, two defeats). The game was Jim Leighton's swansong, but after four minutes, his jaw was shattered by a Rod Wallace challenge. Robbie Winters was forced to come off the bench, but being a striker, he let in four. Not a happy end to Leighton's career. A quick mention of the national team, who were not at Euro 2000 thanks to England. Paul Scholes's brace won the game and virtually the play-off at Hampden. Rarely can a Scotland win at Wembley - 1-0 thanks to Don Hutchison - have subsequently seemed so flat.

Bell's Scottish Premier League 1999-2000

		P	W	D	L	GF	GA	W	D	L	GF	GA	GD	Pts
1	**Rangers**	36	16	1	1	52	12	12	5	1	44	14	+70	**90**
2	**Celtic**	36	12	3	3	58	17	9	3	6	32	21	+52	**69**
3	**Heart of Midlothian**	36	7	6	5	25	18	8	3	7	22	22	+7	**54**
4	**Motherwell**	36	8	3	7	27	34	6	7	5	22	29	-14	**52**
5	**St. Johnstone**	36	5	7	6	16	18	5	5	7	20	26	-8	**42**
6	**Hibernian**	36	7	6	5	30	27	3	5	10	19	34	-12	**41**
7	**Dundee**	36	4	3	11	20	33	8	2	8	25	31	-19	**41**
8	**Dundee United**	36	6	4	8	16	22	5	2	10	18	35	-23	**39**
9	**Kilmarnock**	36	5	5	8	16	22	3	8	7	22	30	-14	**37**
10	**Aberdeen**	36	6	4	8	28	37	3	2	13	16	46	-39	**33**

There was no relegation in 1999-2000

	Aberdeen	Celtic	Dundee	Dundee U	Hearts	Hibernian	Kilmarnock	Motherwell	Rangers	St Johnstone
Aberdeen	**** ****	0-5 0-6	0-2 0-1	1-2 3-1	3-1 1-2	2-2 4-0	2-2 5-1	1-1 2-1	1-5 1-1	0-3 2-1
Celtic	7-0 5-1	**** ****	6-2 2-2	4-1 2-0	4-0 2-3	4-0 1-1	5-1 4-2	0-1 4-0	1-1 0-1	3-0 4-1
Dundee	1-3 0-2	1-2 0-3	**** ****	0-2 3-0	1-0 0-0	3-4 1-0	0-0 1-2	0-1 4-1	2-3 1-7	1-2 1-1
Dundee U	3-1 1-1	2-1 0-1	2-1 1-0	**** ****	0-2 0-1	3-1 0-0	0-0 2-2	0-2 1-2	0-4 0-2	1-0 0-1
Hearts	3-0 3-0	1-2 1-0	4-0 2-0	3-0 1-2	**** ****	0-3 2-1	2-2 0-0	1-1 0-0	0-4 1-2	1-1 0-0
Hibernian	2-0 1-0	0-2 2-1	5-2 1-2	3-2 1-0	1-1 3-1	**** ****	0-3 2-2	2-2 2-2	0-1 2-2	0-1 3-3
Kilmarnock	2-0 1-0	0-1 1-1	0-2 2-2	1-1 1-0	2-2 0-1	0-2 1-0	**** ****	0-1 0-2	1-1 0-2	1-2 3-2
Motherwell	5-6 1-0	3-2 1-1	0-2 0-3	2-2 1-3	2-1 0-2	2-2 2-0	0-4 2-0	**** ****	1-5 2-0	1-0 2-1
Rangers	3-0 5-0	4-2 4-0	1-2 3-0	4-1 3-0	1-0 1-0	2-0 5-2	2-1 1-0	4-1 6-2	**** ****	3-1 0-0
St Johnstone	1-1 2-1	1-2 0-0	0-1 2-1	0-1 2-0	1-4 0-1	1-1 1-0	2-0 0-0	1-1 1-1	1-1 0-2	**** ****

Goalscorers

	Lg	Cups	Total
Mark Viduka (Celtic)	25	2	27
Billy Dodds (Rangers)	19	6	25
Total includes 10 goals for Dundee United			
Jorg Albertz (Rangers)	17	3	20
Rodney Wallace (Rangers)	16	3	19
Willie Falconer (Dundee)	13	4	17
Gary McSwegan (Hearts)	13	2	15
Kenny Miller (Hibernian)	11	2	13
Michael Mols (Rangers)	9	4	13

	Lg	Cups	Total
Mark Burchill (Celtic)	11	1	12
Russell Latapy (Hibernian)	9	3	12
Lee McCulloch (Motherwell)	9	3	12
Henrik Larsson (Celtic)	7	5	12
Larsson played 13 games, one as a substitute, in the whole season			
John Spencer (Motherwell)	11	0	11
Arild Stavrum (Aberdeen)	9	2	11
Colin Cameron (Hearts)	8	3	11

First Division 1999-2000

		P	W	D	L	GF	GA	W	D	L	GF	GA	GD	Pts
1	St Mirren	36	12	3	3	42	19	11	4	3	33	20	+36	76
2	Dunfermline	36	10	7	1	34	13	10	4	4	32	20	+33	71
3	Falkirk	36	11	2	5	38	23	9	6	3	29	17	+27	68
4	Livingston	36	9	5	4	29	17	10	2	6	31	28	+15	64
5	Raith Rovers	36	11	3	4	35	21	6	5	7	20	19	+15	59
6	Inverness CT	36	7	6	5	34	25	6	4	8	26	30	+5	49
7	Ayr United	36	6	3	9	25	24	4	5	9	17	28	-10	38
8	Greenock Morton	36	7	3	8	22	23	3	3	12	23	38	-16	36
9	Airdrieonians	36	4	5	9	15	26	3	3	12	14	43	-40	29
10	Clydebank	36	1	3	14	11	40	0	4	14	6	42	-65	10

Second Division 1999-2000

		P	W	D	L	GF	GA	W	D	L	GF	GA	GD	Pts
1	Clyde	36	12	5	1	35	7	6	6	6	30	30	+28	65
2	Alloa Athletic	36	11	5	2	36	18	6	8	4	22	20	+20	64
3	Ross County	36	9	5	4	31	20	9	3	6	26	19	+18	62
4	Arbroath	36	6	7	5	28	26	5	7	6	24	29	-3	47
5	Partick Thistle	36	7	5	6	25	22	5	5	8	17	22	-2	46
6	Stranraer	36	6	8	4	25	22	3	10	5	22	24	+1	45
7	StirlingAlbion	36	7	4	7	34	33	4	3	11	26	39	-12	40
8	Stenhousemuir	36	6	4	8	24	26	4	4	10	20	33	-15	38
9	Queen of the South	36	5	6	7	24	32	3	3	12	21	43	-30	33
10	Hamilton Academicals*	36	5	7	6	18	23	5	7	6	21	21	-5	29

*Hamilton Academicals deducted 15 points for failing to field a team against Stenhousemuir

Third Division 1999-2000

		P	W	D	L	GF	GA	W	D	L	GF	GA	GD	Pts
1	Queen's Park	36	11	2	5	28	20	9	7	2	26	17	+17	69
2	Berwick Rangers	36	7	6	5	20	14	12	3	3	33	16	+23	66
3	Forfar Athletic	36	10	5	3	39	18	7	5	6	25	22	+24	61
4	East Fife	36	9	6	3	24	16	8	2	8	21	23	+6	59
5	Cowdenbeath	36	6	5	7	30	23	9	4	5	29	20	+16	54
6	Dumbarton	36	7	7	4	26	22	8	1	9	27	29	+2	53
7	East Stirlingshire	36	6	2	10	15	27	5	5	8	13	23	-22	40
8	Brechin City	36	6	3	9	25	25	4	5	9	17	26	-9	38
9	Montrose	36	5	2	11	19	31	5	5	8	20	23	-15	37
10	Albion Rovers	36	2	3	13	13	35	3	4	11	20	40	-42	22

Goalscorers

Division 1

	Lg	Cp	Ttl
Yardley (St Mirren)	19	0	19
Bingham (Livingston)	15	3	18
Crabbe (Falkirk)	14	4	18
Sheerin (Inverness CT)	11	6	17

4 players on 16 goals

Division 2

	Lg	Cp	Ttl
Carrigan (Clyde)	18	7	25
Cameron (Alloa Athletic)	15	7	22
Graham (Stirling A)	17	4	21
McGlashan (Arbroath)	16	3	19
Irvine (Alloa Athletic)	13	5	18
Shaw (Ross County)	13	5	18

Division 3

	Lg	Cp	Ttl
Milne (Forfar Athletic)	16	3	19
Flannery (Dumbarton)	14	2	16
Gallagher (Queen's Park)	13	2	15
Brown (Cowdenbeath)	12	2	14
McDowell (Cowdenbeath)	13	0	13
Taylor (Montrose)	12	1	13

Tennents Scottish Cup

First Round

Hamilton A 1 *(D Henderson)*
Clyde 2 *(Carrigan pen, Grant)*

Huntly 0
East Stirling 1 *(Higgins)*

Ross Co 2 *(Shaw, Irvine)*
Forfar A 2 *(Donaldson pen, Robson)*
Forfar A 0
Ross Co 0
aet; Forfar won 4-2 on penalties

Threave R 1 *(Smith)*
Stenhousemuir 7 *(Fisher 2,*
Graham 2, Mooney,
Fraser og, Forrester)

Second Round

Albion R 0
Dalbeattie Star 0

Dalbeattie Star 1 *(Parker)*
Albion R 5 *(Flannigan 3, McLees,*
McStay)

Arbroath 0
Fraserburgh 0

Fraserburgh 1 *(Florence og)*
Arbroath 3 *(McGlashan, Mercer,*
Devine)

Brechin C 2 *(Bailey, Smith)*
Annan Ath 2 *(McGuffie, Sloan)*

Annan Ath 2 *(Docherty, Thomson)*
Brechin C 3 *(Christie, Nairn, Black)*
aet

Cowdenbeath 2 *(Brown 2)*
Clyde 3 *(Carrigan 2 (1 pen),*
McLaughlin)

Dumbarton 0
Stenhousemuir 2 *(Fisher,*
Hamilton R)

Montrose 1 *(O'Driscoll)*
Queen OTS 3 *(Eadie, Hawke,*
Adams)

Partick T 2 *(Lennon, Brown og)*
East Stirling 1 *(Hay)*

Peterhead 2 *(Clark G, Cheyne)*
Forfar A 1 *(Milne)*

Queen's P 1 *(Carroll)*
Berwick R 2 *(Haddow pen, Findlay)*

Stirling A 2 *(Whiteford, Graham)*
East Fife 1 *(O'Hara)*

Stranraer 1 *(Blaikie)*
Clachnacuddin 0

Whitehill W 2 *(Bird, Samuel)*
Alloa A 2 *(Irvine, McKechnie)*

Alloa A 2 *(Donaghy, Cameron)*
Whitehill W 0

Third Round

Albion R 1 *(Duncan)*
Partick T 2 *(Dunn, Lennon)*

Arbroath 1 *(Bryce)*
Motherwell 1 *(Goodman)*

Motherwell 2 *(Goodman,*
McCulloch)
Arbroath 0

Celtic 1 *(Burchill)*
Inverness CT 3 *(Wilson,*
Moravcik og, Sheerin pen)

Clyde 3 *(Carrigan 2 (1 pen),*
Woods)
Raith R 1 *(Dargo)*

Clydebank 1 *(Wishart)*
Stirling A 0

Dundee 0
Ayr U 0

Ayr U 1 *(Duffy)*
Dundee 1 *(Rae)*
aet; Ayr U won 7-6 on penalties

Dundee U 4 *(Hannah 2, Mathie,*
Ferraz)
Ardrieonians 1 *(McCann pen)*

Falkirk 3 *(Nicholls, Crabbe, Hagen)*
Peterhead 1 *(Gibson)*

Hearts 3 *(Cameron pen,*
McSwegan 2)
Stenhousemuir 2 *(Hamilton R,*
Mooney)

Hibernian 4 *(Miller, Brebner,*
Murray, Collins)
Dunfermline A 1 *(Graham)*

Kilmarnock 0
Alloa A 0

Alloa A 1 *(Cameron)*
Kilmarnock 0

Morton 1 *(Anderson J)*
Brechin C 1 *(Black)*

Brechin C 0
Morton 0
aet; Morton won 4-2 on penalties
Queen OTS 0
Livingston 7 *(McKinnon 2, Keith 3,*
Bingham, McPhee)

St Johnstone 0
Rangers 2 *(Numan,*
Van Bronckhorst)

St Mirren 1 *(McGarry)*
Aberdeen 1 *(Zerouali)*

Aberdeen 2 *(Zerouali, Bernard)*
St Mirren 0

Stranraer 1 *(Ronald)*
Berwick R 2 *(Haddow pen, Findlay)*

Fourth Round

Alloa A 2 *(Beaton, Cameron)*
Dundee U 2 *(Hamilton 2)*

Dundee U 4 *(Preget, Hamilton,*
Thompson 2)
Alloa A 0

Berwick R 0
Falkirk 0

Falkirk 3 *(Crabbe, Hagen,*
McQuilken)
Berwick R 0

Clyde 0
Hearts 2 *(Jackson, Wales)*

Hibernian 1 *(Hartley)*
Clydebank 1 *(Gardner pen)*

Clydebank 0
Hibernian 3 *(Lovell, Lehmann,*
Sauzee)

Inverness CT 1 *(Mann)*
Aberdeen 1 *(Guntweit)*

Aberdeen 1 *(Stavrum)*
Inverness CT 0

Morton 0
Rangers 1 *(Moore)*

Motherwell 3 *(McCulloch,*
Goodman, Brannan pen)
Ayr U 4 *(Teale 2 (1 pen), Tarrant 2)*

Partick T 2 *(Craig, McLean)*
Livingston 1 *(Bingham)*

Quarter-finals

Ayr U 2 *(Campbell, Tarrant)*
Partick T 0

Hibernian 3 *(Latapy 2 (1 pen),*
McGinlay)
Falkirk 1 *(Lawrie)*

Dundee U 0
Aberdeen 1 *(Jess)*

Rangers 4 *(Ferguson B, Numan,*
Amoruso, Dodds pen)
Hearts 1 *(Cameron pen)*

Semi-finals

Ayr U 0
Rangers 7 *(Rozental 2,*
Kanchelskis, Wallace, Dodds 3)

Hibernian 1 *(Latapy)*
Aberdeen 2 *(Stavrum, Dow)*

FINAL
Hampden Park, May 27

Aberdeen 0

Rangers 4 *(Van Bronckhorst 36,*
Vidmar 47, Dodds 49, Albertz 51)

Aberdeen: Leighton (Winters),
Solberg, McAllister, Whyte,
Anderson (Belabed), Dow, Bernard,
Jess, Rowson, Guntweit, Stavrum
(Zerouali)

Rangers: Klos, Reyna, Moore
(Porrini), Vidmar, Numan,
Kanchelskis, Ferguson B, Albertz,
Van Bronckhorst (Kerimoglu),
Wallace (McCann), Dodds

Referee: Jim McCluskey

Attendance: 50,685

CIS Cup
From Second Round

Second Round
Aberdeen 1 *(Gillies)*
Livingston 0

Ayr U 2 *(Reynolds, Bone)*
Hamilton A 1 *(Henderson D)*

Clyde 2 *(Woods, Carrigan)*
Hibernian 2 *(McGinlay, Hartley)*
aet; Hibernian won 3-0 on pens

Dundee 4 *(Boyack 2, Falconer 2)*
Dumbarton 0

Dundee U 3 *(Ferraz, Thompson 2)*
Ross C 1 *(Escalon)*
aet

Dunfermlne A 4 *(Coyle 2, Petrie,*
Smith)
Queen's Park 0

East Fife 2 *(Logan, Robertson pen)*
Ardrieonians 2 *(McCormick 2)*
aet; East Fife won 5-4 on pens

East Stirling 0
Falkirk 2 *(Crabbe, Bowsher og)*
aet

Inverness CT 2 *(Sheerin pen,*
Byers)
St Mirren 0
aet

Morton 1 *(Curran)*
Alloa A 3 *(Irvine 2, Cameron)*

Queen OTS 1 *(Leslie)*
Hearts 3 *(Jackson 2, Severin)*

Raith R 2 *(Burns, Dargo)*
Motherwell 2 *(Browne og, Halliday)*
aet; Motherwell won 5-4 on pens

Third Round

Aberdeen 1 *(Lawrie og)*
Falkirk 1 *(Crabbe)*
aet; Aberdeen won 5-3 on pens

Alloa A 1 *(Cameron)*
Dundee 3 *(Falconer 2, Grady)*

Ayr U 0
Celtic 4 *(Viduka, Blinker, Mjallby,*
Petta)

East Fife 0
Hearts 2 *(Cameron, Holmes)*

Inverness CT 0
Motherwell 1 *(McCulloch)*

Kilmarnock 3 *(McCoist 2, Vareille)*
Hibernian 2 *(McGinlay, Miller)*

Rangers 1 *(Wallace)*
Dunfermline A 0

St Johnstone 1 *(Griffin)*
Dundee U 2 *(Davidson, Telesnikov)*

Quarter-finals
Aberdeen 1 *(Dow)*
Rangers 0

Celtic 1 *(Wieghorst)*
Dundee 0
Dundee U 3 *(Dodds, Easton,*
Thompson)
Motherwell 2 *(Townsley, Teale)*

Kilmarnock 1 *(Jeffrey)*
Hearts 0

Semi-finals

Aberdeen 1 *(Stavrum)*
Dundee U 0

Celtic 1 *(Moravcik)*
Kilmarnock 0

FINAL
Hampden Park Mar 19

Celtic 2
(Riseth 11, Johnson 58)
Aberdeen 0

Celtic: Gould, Boyd, Riseth,
Mjallby, Mahe, McNamara,
Wieghorst, Petrov, Moravcik
(Stubbs),Johnson (Berkovic),
Viduka

Aberdeen: Leighton, Perry,
McAllister, Solberg, Anderson, Dow,
Bernard, Jess (Mayer), Guntweit
(Belabed), Zerouali (Winters),
Stavrum

Referee: K Clark

Attendance: 50,073

BELL'S CHALLENGE CUP FINAL
Shyberry Excelsior Stadium, Ardrie
Nov 21

Alloa Athletic 4

(Clark G 19, Wilson 34,
Cameron 48, 103)

Inverness CT 4
(Wilson 28, Sheerin 46, 53, 110)

Alloa Ath: Cairns, Boyle, Clark D,
McAneny, Beaton, Valentine, Little,
Clark G (Christie), Cameron, Irvine,
Wilson (McKechnie)

Inverness CT: Fridge, Tokely,
Hastings, Teasdale, McCulloch,
Sheerin, Wilson, Xausa (Glancy),
Wyness (Bavidge), Christie,
Golabek (Byres)
aet; Alloa won 5-4 on penalties

Referee: Jim McCluskey

Attendance: 4047

Welsh Football
League of Wales 1999-2000

	P	W	D	L	GF	GA	Pts
TNS Llansantffraid	34	24	4	6	69	37	76
Barry Town	34	23	5	6	98	34	74
Cwmbran Town	34	21	6	7	71	37	69
Carmarthen Town	34	22	3	9	68	42	69
Llanelli	34	21	3	10	76	46	66
Aberystwyth Town	34	19	4	11	70	46	61
Connah's Quay Nomads	34	17	6	11	57	35	57
Newtown	34	14	6	14	49	41	48
Bangor City	34	15	3	16	56	61	48
Afan Lido	34	12	10	12	44	42	46
Rhyl	34	13	5	16	40	60	44
Caersws	34	11	8	15	49	50	41
Flexsys Cefn Druids	34	13	2	19	44	63	41
Rhayader Town	34	9	7	18	34	47	34
Haverfordwest County	34	6	6	20	30	62	30
Inter Cardiff*	34	6	11	17	37	65	28
Conwy United**	34	6	5	23	33	97	21
Caernarfon Town	34	1	8	25	21	81	11

*One point deducted for fielding ineligible player
**Two points deducted for failing to fulfil fixture

Welsh Cup Final
Racecourse, Wrexham May 7
Bangor City 1 Cwmbran Town 0

Northern Irish Football
Smirnoff Irish League 1999-2000

Premier Division	P	W	D	L	GF	GA	Pts
Linfield	36	24	7	5	67	30	79
Coleraine	36	18	7	11	64	42	61
Glenavon	36	17	10	9	55	34	61
Glentoran	36	18	7	11	59	51	61
Portadown	36	15	7	14	64	62	52
Newry Town	36	11	7	18	44	58	40
Crusaders	36	9	13	14	41	55	40
Ballymena United	36	6	16	14	45	62	34
Cliftonville	36	7	13	16	38	59	34
Lisburn Distillery	36	9	5	22	39	63	32

First Division	P	W	D	L	GF	GA	Pts
Omagh Town	36	20	10	6	65	35	70
Ards	36	16	16	4	65	36	64
Limavady United	36	17	9	10	54	42	60
Bangor	36	16	9	11	60	49	57
Larne	36	15	9	12	56	53	54
Institute	36	14	9	13	59	53	51
Armagh City	36	10	10	16	50	61	40
Dungannon Swifts	36	9	8	19	43	62	35
Carrick Rangers	36	8	10	18	45	64	34
Ballyclare Comrades	36	8	4	24	39	81	28

Bass Irish Cup Final
Glentoran 1 Portadown 0 *(at Windsor Park)*

"I get asked a lot why so many people take an instant dislike to Doug Ellis. My answer is that it saves time"
Ron Atkinson

"On top of everything you get footballing cretins like Ken Bates writing that we'd come along and play for penalties"
Martin O'Neill, on Ken Bates.

"It takes one to know one"
Ken Bates, on Martin O'Neill.

"If every player could give two per cent more in their performance then, in theory, the team will be better by 22% as well"
Ebbe Skovdahl, the Aberdeen manager, who later worked out if he included the reserve team as well would get a 44% improvement.

"If that is not a sending-off offence, what is? What do we need to see, a leg with blood dripping off the stump?'"
Peter Willis, president of the Referees' Association, outraged by Roy Keane's tackle in the Charity Shield game.

"I have a definite sense of spirituality. I want Brooklyn to be christened, but I don't know what religion yet"
David Beckham.

European Leagues 1999-2000

BELGIUM

	P	W	D	L	GF	GA	Pts
Anderlecht	**34**	**22**	**9**	**3**	**86**	**36**	**75**
Club Brugge	34	21	4	9	70	32	67
Gent	34	20	3	11	78	54	63
Mouscron	34	16	9	9	67	45	57
Standard Liege	34	18	2	14	67	51	56
Westerlo	34	16	8	10	73	66	56
Antwerp	34	16	7	11	56	45	55
Genk	34	16	6	12	63	59	54
Lierse	34	15	7	12	65	47	52
Lokeren	34	12	11	11	56	58	47
Mechelen	34	12	5	17	47	77	41
Aalst	34	11	4	19	52	73	37
St Truiden	34	10	7	17	41	65	37
Harelbeke	34	10	5	19	56	72	35
Beveren	34	9	8	17	51	69	35
Charleroi	34	7	10	17	42	62	31
Geel	34	5	13	16	32	60	28
Lommel	34	5	12	17	35	66	27

Cup Final: Anderlecht 2 Mouscron 2

aet; Anderlecht won 4-3 on penalties
Top Scorer: Ole-Martin Aarst (Gent), Toni Brogno
(Westerlo) 30

FRANCE

	P	W	D	L	GF	GA	Pts
Monaco	**34**	**20**	**5**	**9**	**69**	**38**	**65**
Paris St Germain	34	16	10	8	54	40	58
Lyon	34	16	8	10	45	42	56
Bordeaux	34	15	9	10	52	40	54
Lens	34	14	7	13	42	41	49
St Etienne	34	13	9	12	46	47	48
Sedan	34	13	9	12	43	44	48
Auxerre	34	13	8	13	37	39	47
Strasbourg	34	13	7	14	42	52	46
Bastia	34	11	12	11	43	39	45
Metz	34	9	17	8	38	33	44
Nantes	34	12	7	15	39	40	43
Rennes	34	12	7	15	44	48	43
Troyes	34	13	4	17	36	52	43
Marseille	34	9	15	10	45	45	42
Nancy	34	11	9	14	43	45	42
Le Havre	34	9	7	18	30	52	34
Montpellier	34	7	10	17	39	50	31

Cup Final: Nantes 2 Calais 1
Top scorer: Sonny Anderson (Lyon) 23

GERMANY

	P	W	D	L	GF	GA	Pts
Bayern Munich	**34**	**22**	**7**	**5**	**73**	**28**	**73**
Bayer Leverkusen	34	21	10	3	74	36	73
Hamburg	34	16	11	7	63	39	59
Munich 1860	34	14	11	9	55	48	53
Kaiserslautern	34	15	5	14	54	59	50
Hertha Berlin	34	13	11	10	39	46	50
Wolfsburg	34	12	13	9	51	58	49
Stuttgart	34	14	6	14	44	47	48
Werder Bremen	34	13	8	13	65	52	47
Unterhaching	34	12	8	14	40	42	44
Borussia Dortmund	34	9	13	12	41	38	40
Freiburg	34	10	10	14	45	50	40
Eintracht Frankfurt	34	12	5	17	42	44	39
Schalke	34	8	15	11	42	44	39
Hansa Rostock	34	8	14	12	44	60	38
Ulm	34	9	8	17	36	62	35
Bielefeld	34	7	9	18	40	61	30
Duisburg	34	4	10	20	37	71	22

Cup Final: Bayern Munich 3 Werder Bremen 0
Top scorer: Martin Max (Munich 1860) 19

IRELAND

	P	W	D	L	GF	GA	Pts
Shelbourne	**33**	**19**	**12**	**2**	**49**	**20**	**69**
Cork City	33	16	10	7	53	32	58
Bohemians	33	16	9	8	40	22	57
UCD	33	13	12	8	40	29	51
Shamrock Rovers	33	13	11	9	49	36	50
St. Patrick's Athletic	33	13	11	9	40	31	50
Derry City	33	12	10	11	32	38	46
Finn Harps	33	8	10	15	39	41	34
Galway United	33	8	10	15	32	49	34
Waterford United	33	7	12	14	24	38	33
Sligo Rovers	33	5	10	18	31	60	25
Drogheda United	33	4	11	18	20	53	23

Cup Final: Shelbourne 0 Bohemians 0

Replay: Shelbourne 1 Bohemians 0
Top scorer: Pat Morley (Cork City) 20

ITALY

	P	W	D	L	GF	GA	Pts
Lazio	**34**	**21**	**9**	**4**	**64**	**33**	**72**
Juventus	34	21	8	5	46	20	71
AC Milan	34	16	13	5	65	40	61
Internazionale	34	17	7	10	58	36	58
Parma	34	16	10	8	52	37	58
Roma	34	14	12	8	57	34	54
Fiorentina	34	13	12	9	48	38	51
Udinese	34	13	11	10	55	45	50
Verona	34	10	13	11	40	45	43
Perugia	34	12	6	16	36	52	42
Bologna	34	9	13	12	32	39	40
Reggina	34	9	13	12	31	42	40
Lecce	34	10	10	14	33	49	40
Bari	34	10	9	15	34	48	39
Torino	34	8	12	14	35	47	36
Venezia	34	6	8	20	30	60	26
Cagliari	34	3	13	18	29	54	22
Piacenza	34	4	9	21	19	45	21

Cup Final: Lazio 2 Internazionale1
           Internazionale 0 Lazio 0
Lazio won 2-1 on aggregate
Top scorer: Andrii Shevchenko (AC Milan) 24

NETHERLANDS

	P	W	D	L	GF	GA	Pts
PSV Eindhoven	34	27	3	4	105	24	84
Heerenveen	34	21	5	8	65	36	68
Feyenoord	34	18	10	6	66	42	64
Vitesse Arnhem	34	18	9	7	66	42	63
Ajax	34	18	7	9	72	51	51
Twente	34	16	12	6	57	37	60
AZ	34	17	4	13	69	59	55
Roda JC	34	16	7	11	62	53	55
Willem II	34	13	9	12	55	65	48
Utrecht	34	14	4	16	55	61	46
RKC Waalwijk	34	12	6	16	44	67	42
Fortuna Sittard	34	10	8	16	47	54	38
Sparta Rotterdam	34	11	4	19	48	75	37
De Graafschap	34	8	9	17	41	60	33
NEC Nijmegen	34	7	6	21	35	62	27
Maastricht	34	6	7	21	38	68	25
Cambuur	34	6	7	21	35	66	25
Den Bosch	34	4	11	19	36	74	23

Cup Final: Roda JC 2 NEC Nijmegen o
Top scorer: Ruud Van Nistelrooy (PSV Eindhoven) 29

PORTUGAL

	P	W	D	L	GF	GA	Pts
Sporting Lisbon	34	23	8	3	57	22	77
Porto	34	22	7	5	66	26	73
Benfica	34	21	6	7	58	33	69
Boavista	34	16	7	11	40	31	55
Gil Vicente	34	14	11	9	48	34	53
Maritimo	34	13	11	10	42	36	50
Vitoria Guimaraes	34	14	6	14	48	43	48
Estrela Amadora	34	10	15	9	40	35	45
Sporting Braga	34	12	7	15	44	45	43
Uniao Leiria	34	10	12	12	31	35	42
Alverca	34	11	8	15	39	48	41
Belenenses	34	9	13	12	36	38	40
Campomaiorense	34	10	6	18	31	51	36
Farense	34	8	11	15	35	60	35
Salgueiros	34	9	7	18	30	49	34
Rio Ave	34	8	9	17	34	54	33
Setubal	34	9	6	19	25	49	33
Santa Clara	34	7	10	17	35	50	31

Cup Final: Sporting Lisbon 1 Porto 1

Replay: Sporting Lisbon 0 Porto 2
Top scorer: Mario Jardel (Porto) 38

RUSSIA

	P	W	D	L	GF	GA	Pts
Spartak Moscow	30	22	6	2	75	24	72
Lokomotiv Moscow	30	20	5	5	62	30	65
CSKA Moscow	30	15	10	5	56	29	55
Torpedo Moscow	30	13	11	6	38	33	50
Dynamo Moscow	30	12	8	10	44	41	44
Alaniya Vladikavkaz	30	12	7	11	54	45	43
Rostov	30	11	8	11	32	37	41
Zenit St Petersburg	30	9	12	9	36	34	39
Uralan	34	10	6	14	27	34	36
Saturn	30	8	10	12	30	38	34

	P	W	D	L	GF	GA	Pts
Lokomotiv Nizhniy	30	9	6	15	33	48	33
Kryliya Sovekov	30	8	7	15	39	49	31
Rotor Volgograd	30	7	10	13	36	51	31
Chernomorets	30	7	8	15	30	49	29
Sotchi	30	5	11	14	29	55	26
Shinnik	30	5	9	16	21	45	24

Cup Final: Lokomotiv Moscow 3 CSKA Moscow 2 (aet)
Top scorer: Georgi Demetradze (Alaniya Vladikavkaz) 21

SPAIN

	P	W	D	L	GF	GA	Pts
Deportivo La Coruna	38	21	6	11	66	44	69
Barcelona	38	19	7	12	70	46	64
Valencia	38	18	10	10	59	39	64
Real Zaragoza	38	16	15	7	60	40	63
Real Madrid	38	16	14	8	58	48	62
Alaves	38	17	10	11	41	37	61
Celta Vigo	38	15	8	15	45	43	53
Vallodolid	38	14	11	13	36	44	53
Rayo Vallecano	38	15	7	16	51	53	52
Real Mallorca	38	14	9	15	52	45	51
Athletic Bilbao	38	12	14	12	47	57	50
Malaga	38	11	15	12	55	50	48
Espanyol	38	12	11	15	51	48	47
Real Sociedad	38	11	14	13	42	49	47
Racing Santander	38	10	16	12	52	50	46
Numancia	38	11	12	15	47	59	45
Real Oviedo	38	11	12	15	44	60	45
Real Betis	38	11	9	18	33	56	42
Athletico Madrid	38	9	11	18	48	64	38
Sevilla	38	5	13	20	42	67	28

Cup Final: Espanyol 2 Athletico Madrid 1
Top scorer: Salva (Racing Santander) 27

SWEDEN

	P	W	D	L	GF	GA	Pts
Helsingborgs	26	17	3	6	44	24	54
AIK	26	16	5	5	42	14	53
Halmstads	26	14	6	6	43	22	48
Orgryte	26	11	10	5	41	23	43
Norrköping	26	11	6	9	41	36	39
IFK Gothenburg	26	11	5	10	27	33	38
Västra Frölunda	26	9	7	10	30	33	34
Trelleborgs	26	9	6	11	39	47	33
Elfsborg	26	9	5	12	41	48	32
Hammarby	26	8	5	13	32	42	29
Kalmar	26	8	4	14	27	41	28
Orebro	26	8	3	15	24	36	27
Malmö	26	7	4	15	30	48	25
Djurgaarden	26	5	9	12	27	41	24

Kalmar relegated after play-off

Cup Final: Orgryte 0 AIK 1
AIK 0 Orgryte 2
Orgryte won 2-1 on aggregate
Top scorer: Marcus Allback (Orgryte) 15

European Cup Competitions

European Cup
Qualifying Round

Barry Town 0
Valletta 0

Valletta 3 *(Agius 2, Chetcuti)*
Barry Town 2 *(Sloan 2)*

HB Torshavn 1 *(Lakjuni)*
Haka 1 *(Popovic)*
Haka 6 *(Salli, Reynders,*
Nyyssonen, Wilson, Popovic,
Torkkeli)
HB Torshavn 0

IBV 1 *(Johannesson)*
SK Tirana 0

SK Tirana 1 *(Bulku)*
IBV 2 *(Johannesson, Sigurdsson)*

Jeunesse Esch 0
Skonto Riga 2 *(Astafyev, Miholap)*

Skonto Riga 8 *(Bleidelis 2,*
Miholap 5 (2 pens), Koleschenko)
Jeunesse Esch 0

Litets 3 *(Hadji, Bushi pen, Petrov)*
Glentoran 0

Glentoran 0
Litets 2 *(Haxhi, Bushi)*

Partizan Belgrade 6 *(Ilic, Pekovic 2,*
Ivic 2, Kezman)
Flora Tallinn 0

Flora Tallinn 1 *(Viikmae)*
Partizan Belgrade 4 *(Kezman 2,*
Ilic, Tomic)

Sloga 1 *(Memedi)*
Kapaz 0

Kapaz 2 *(Mamedov, Rzayev pen)*
Sloga 1 *(Arif)*

St. Patrick's Athletic 0
Zimbru Chisinau 5 *(Berco 2,*
Epureanu 2, Boret)

Zimbru Chisinau 5 *(Tropanet 2,*
Borets 2, Oprea pen)
St. Patrick's Athletic 0

Zalgiris 2 *(I Stesjko, A Stesjko)*
Tsement 0

Tsement 0
Zalgiris 3 *(Novikov, Jokshas,*
Vasilauskas)

Second Qualifying Round

Anorthosis 2 *(Obicu 2 (1 pen))*
Slovan Bratislava 1 *(Hrncar)*

Slovan Bratislava 1 *(Timko)*
Anorthosis 1 *(Obicu)*

Besiktas 1 *(Akhman)*
Hapoel Haifa 1 *(Rosso)*

Hapoel Haifa 0
Besiktas 0

CSKA Moscow 2 *(Siskin,*
Khomukha)
Molde 0

Molde 4 *(Tessem, Berg Hestad,*
Hoseth 2)
CSKA Moscow 0

Dnepr Mogilev 0
AIK Stockholm 1 *(Tjernstrom)*

AIK Stockholm 2 *(Corneliusson,*
Gustafsson)
Dnepr Mogilev 0

Dynamo Kiev 2 *(Shatskikh 2)*
Zalgiris 0

Zalgiris 0
Dynamo Kiev 1 *(Rebrov)*

Dynamo Tbilisi 2 *(Tsitaishvili,*
Khomeriki)
Zimbru Chisinau 1 *(Berko)*

Zimbru Chisinau 2 *(Dodul,*
Epureanu)
Dynamo Tbilisi 0

Haka 1 *(Niemi)*
Rangers 4 *(Amoruso, Mols 2,*
Johansson)

Rangers 3 *(Wallace, Johansson,*
Amato)
Haka 0

IBV 0
MTK Budapest 2 *(Halmai,*
Preisinger)

MTK Budapest 3 *(Illes 2, Kuttor)*
IBV 1 *(Moller)*

Litets 4 *(Todorov 2, Zivkovic pen,*
Dodrov)
Widzew Lodz 1 *(Wichniarek pen)*

Widzew Lodz 4 *(Gesior,*
Wichniarek 2, Michalski)
Litets 1 *(Todorov)*
aet; Widzew Lodz won 3-2 on pens

Maribor 5 *(Balajic, Galic, Karic pen,*
Simundza, Djuranovic)
Genk 1 *(Strupar)*

Genk 3 *(T Gudjonsson 2, Horvath)*
Maribor 0

Partizan Belgrade 3 *(Ilic, Krstajic 2)*
Rijeka 1 *(Stipanovic)*

Rijeka 0
Partizan Belgrade 3 *(Kezman 2,*
Ivic)

Rapid Bucharest 3 *(Barbu,*
Schumacher, Mutica)
Skonto Riga 3 *(Chaladze 2,*
Astafyev)

Skonto Riga 2 *(Laizans, Rubins)*
Rapid Bucharest 1 *(Raducanu)*

Rapid Vienna 3 *(Dawe, Savicevic,*
Penksa)
Valletta 0

Valletta 0
Rapid Vienna 2 *(Dawe,*
Lagonikakis)

Sloga 0
Brondby 1 *(Daugaard)*

Bronby 1 *(Daugaard pen)*
Sloga 0

Third Qualifying Round

Aalborg 1 *(Strandli)*
Dynamo Kiev 2 *(Rebrov, Shatskikh)*

Dynamo Kiev 2 *(Gusin, Shatskikh)*
Aalborg 2 *(Oper, Gaarde)*

AEK Athens 0
AIK Stockholm 0

AIK Stockholm 1 *(Novakovic)*
AEK Athens 0

Brondby 1 *(Smith)*
Boavista 2 *(Mario Silva, Moreira)*

Brondby 4 *(Litos, Ahinful 2,*
Rui Bento)
Boavista 2 *(Christensen, Bjur)*
aet

Chelsea 3 *(Babayaro, Poyet,*
Sutton)
Skonto Riga 0

Skonto Riga 0
Chelsea 0

Croatia Zagreb 0
MTK Budapest 0

MTK Budapest 0
Croatia Zagreb 2 *(Simic 2)*

Fiorentina 3 *(Adani, Cois, Rui Costa)*
Widzew Lodz 1 *(Adani og)*

Widzew Lodz 0
Fiorentina 2 *(Chiesa, Cois)*

Hapoel Haifa 0
Valencia 2 *(Lopez, Farinas)*

Valencia 2 *(Sanchez 2)*
Hapoel Haifa 0

Hertha Berlin 2 *(Daei, Preetz)*
Anorthosis 0

Anorthosis 0
Hertha Berlin 0

Lyon 0
Maribor 1 *(Filipovic)*

Maribor 2 *(Simundza, Balajic)*
Lyon 0

Molde 0
Mallorca 0

Mallorca 1 *(Stankovic pen)*
Molde 1 *(Lund pen)*

Rangers 2 *(Vidmar, Reyna)*
Parma 0

Parma 1 *(Walem)*
Rangers 0

Rapid Vienna 0
Galatasaray 3 *(Hakan Unsal, Fatih, Hagi)*

Galatasaray 1 *(Okan)*
Rapid Vienna 0

Spartak Moscow 2 *(Shirko, Tikhonov)*
Partizan Belgrade 0

Partizan Belgrade 1 *(Kezman)*
Spartak Moscow 3 *(Shirko 2, Titov pen)*

Sturm Graz 2 *(Vastic, Martens)*
Servette 1 *(Lonfat)*

Servette 2 *(Kocijan, Thurre)*
Sturm Graz 2 *(De Souza, Vastic)*

Teplice 0
Borussia Dortmund 1 *(Nerlinger)*

Borussia Dortmund 1 *(Herrlich)*
Teplice 0

Zimbru Chisinau 0
PSV Eindhoven 0

PSV Eindhoven 2 *(Nilis, Ooijer)*
Zimbru Chisinau 0

Champions League
First Group Stage
Group A

Dynamo Kiev 0
Maribor 1 *(Simunadza)*

Leverkusen 1 *(Neuville)*
Lazio 1 *(Mihajlovic)*

Lazio 2 *(Negro, Salas)*
Dynamo Kiev 1 *(Rebrov pen)*

Maribor 0
Leverkusen 2 *(Zivkovic, Kirsten)*

Leverkusen 1 *(Kirsten)*
Dynamo Kiev 1 *(Gusin)*

Lazio 4 *(Inzaghi, Conceicao, Salas 2)*
Maribor 0

Dynamo Kiev 4 *(Kossovski, Shatskikh, Golovko, Vashchuk)*
Leverkusen 2 *(Kirsten, Neuville)*

Maribor 0
Lazio 4 *(Mihajlovic, Inzaghi 2, Stankovic)*

Lazio 1 *(Nedved)*
Leverkusen 1 *(Kirsten)*

Maribor 1 *(Balajic)*
Dynamo Kiev 2 *(Rebrov 2 (1 pen))*

Leverkusen 0
Maribor 0

Dynamo Kiev 0
Lazio 1 *(Mamedov og)*

Final Table	P	W	D	L	F	A	Pts
Lazio	6	4	2	0	13	3	14
Dynamo Kiev	6	2	1	3	8	8	7
Leverkusen	6	1	4	1	7	7	7
Maribor	6	1	1	4	2	12	4

Group B

AIK Stockholm 1 *(Novakovic)*
Barcelona 2 *(Abelardo, Dani)*

Fiorentina 0
Arsenal 0

Arsenal 3 *(Ljungberg, Henry, Suker)*
AIK Stockholm 1 *(Nordin)*

Barcelona 4 *(Figo, Luis Enrique, Rivaldo 2 (1 pen))*
Fiorentina 2 *(Batistuta, Chiesa)*

AIK Stockholm 0
Fiorentina 0

Barcelona 1 *(Luis Enrique)*
Arsenal 1 *(Kanu)*

Arsenal 2 *(Bergkamp, Overmars)*
Barcelona 4 *(Rivaldo pen, Luis Enrique, Figo, Cocu)*

Fiorentina 3 *(Batistuta, Chiesa, Balbo)*
AIK Stockholm 0

Arsenal 0
Fiorentina 1 *(Batistuta)*

Barcelona 5 *(Kluivert 2, Zenden, Gabri, Dehu)*
AIK Stockholm 0

AIK Stockholm 2 *(A Andersson 2)*
Arsenal 3 *(Overmars 2, Suker)*

Fiorentina 3 *(Bressan, Balbo 2)*
Barcelona 3 *(Figo, Rivaldo 2)*

Final Table	P	W	D	L	F	A	Pts
Barcelona	6	4	2	0	19	9	14
Fiorentina	6	2	3	1	9	7	9
Arsenal	6	2	2	2	9	9	8
AIK Stockholm	6	0	1	5	4	16	1

Group C

Boavista 0
Rosenborg 3 *(Sorensen, Berg, Strand)*

Feyenoord 1 *(Van Wonderen)*
Borussia Dortmund 1 *(Bobic)*

Borussia Dortmund 3 *(Moller, Bobic 2)*
Boavista 1 *(Rui Bento)*

Rosenborg 2 *(Carew 2)*
Feyenoord 2 *(Tomasson, Kalou)*

Boavista 1 *(Mario Silva)*
Feyenoord 1 *(Bosvelt)*

Rosenborg 2 *(Sorensen, Carew)*
Borussia Dortmund 2 *(Babarez, Kohler)*

Borussia Dortmund 0
Ros'borg 3 *(Sorensen 2, Winsnes)*

Feyenoord 1 *(Tomasson)*
Boavista 1 *(Timofte pen)*

Borussia Dortmund 1 *(Addo)*
Feyenoord 1 *(Van Vossen)*

Rosenborg 2 *(Berg, Dahlum)*
Boavista 0

Boavista 1 *(Emanuel)*
Borussia Dortmund 0

Feyenoord 1 *(Somalia)*
Rosenborg 0

Final Table	P	W	D	L	F	A	Pts
Rosenborg	6	3	2	1	12	5	11
Feyenoord	6	1	5	0	7	6	8
B Dortmund	6	1	3	2	7	9	6
Boavista	6	1	2	3	4	10	5

Group D

Manchester United 0
Croatia Zagreb 0

Marseille 2 *(Pires, Ravanelli)*
Sturm Graz 0

Croatia Zagreb 1 *(Sokota)*
Marseille 2 *(Bakayoko, Perez)*

Sturm Graz 0
Manchester United 3 *(Keane, Yorke, Cole)*

Croatia Zagreb 3 *(Rukavina, Sokota 2 (1 pen))*
Sturm Graz 0

Manchester United 2 *(Cole, Scholes)*
Marseille 1 *(Bakayoko)*

Marseille 1 *(Gallas)*
Manchester United 0

Sturm Graz 1 *(Kocijan)*
Croatia Zagreb 0

Croatia Zagreb *(Prosinecki)*
Manchester United 2 *(Beckham, Keane)*

Sturm Graz 3 *(Mahlich, Kocijan 2)*
Marseille 2 *(Dugarry 2)*

Manchester United 2 *(Solskjaer, Keane)*
Sturm Graz 1 *(Vastic pen)*

Marseille 2 *(Bakayoko, Diawara)*
Croatia Zagreb 2 *(Mujcin, Mikic)*

Final Table	P	W	D	L	F	A	Pts
Manchester U	6	4	1	1	9	4	13
Marseille	6	3	1	2	10	8	10
Sturm Graz	6	2	0	4	5	12	6
Cr Zagreb	6	1	2	3	7	7	5

Group E

Molde 0
Porto 1 *(Deco)*

Olympiakos 3 *(Giovanni 2, Zahovic)*
Real Madrid 3 *(Savio, Roberto Carlos, Raul)*

Porto 2 *(Esquerdinha, Jardel)*
Olympiakos 0

Real Madrid 4 *(Morientes, Savio 2 (1 pen), Guti)*
Molde 1 *(Lindbaek)*

Olympiakos 3 *(Giovanni 2, Luciano)*
Molde 1 *(Lund)*

Real Madrid 3 *(Morientes, Helguera, Hierro pen)*
Porto 1 *(Jardel)*

Molde 3 *(Lund 3, Hestad)*
Olympiakos 2 *(Mavrogenidis, Zahovic)*

Porto 2 *(Jardel 2)*
Real Madrid 1 *(Peixe og)*

Porto 3 *(Deco 2, Jardel)*
Molde 1 *(Hestad)*

Real Madrid 3 *(Raul, Morientes, Roberto Carlos)*
Olympiakos 0

Molde 0
Real Madrid 1 *(Karembeu)*

Olympiakos 1 *(Giannkopoulos)*
Porto 0

Final Table	P	W	D	L	F	A	Pts
Real Madrid	6	4	1	1	15	7	13
Porto	6	4	0	2	9	6	12
Olympiakos	6	2	1	3	9	12	7
Molde	6	1	0	5	6	14	3

Group F

Bayern Munich 2 *(Paulo Sergio 2)*
PSV Eindhoven 1 *(Khokhlov)*

Valencia 2 *(Moore og, Gonzalez)*
Rangers 0

PSV Eindhoven 1 *(Van Nistelrooy pen)*
Valencia 1 *(Lopez)*

Rangers 1 *(Albertz)*
Bayern Munich 1 *(Tarnat)*

Bayern Munich 1 *(Elber)*
Valencia 1 *(Gerard)*

PSV Eindhoven 0
Rangers 1 *(Albertz)*

Rangers 4 *(Amoruso, Mols 2, McCann)*
PSV Eindhoven 1 *(Van Nistelrooy pen)*

Valencia 1 *(A Ilie)*
Bayern Munich 1 *(Effenberg pen)*

PSV Eindhoven 2 *(Van Nistelrooy, Nilis)*
Bayern Munich 1 *(Santa Cruz)*

Rangers 1 *(Moore)*
Valencia 2 *(Mendieta, Lopez)*

Bayern Munich 1 *(Strunz pen)*
Rangers 0

Valencia 1 *(Lopez)*
PSV Eindhoven 0

Final Table	P	W	D	L	F	A	Pts
Valencia	6	3	3	0	8	4	12
Bayern Munich	6	2	3	1	7	6	9
Rangers	6	2	1	3	7	7	7
PSV	6	1	1	4	5	10	4

Group G

Sparta Prague 0
Bordeaux 0

Willem II 1 *(Arts)*
Spartak Moscow 3 *(Tikhonov 3 (2 pens))*

Bordeaux 3 *(Victoria og, Laslandes, Feindouno)*
Willem II 2 *(Abdellaoui, Sanou)*

Spartak Moscow *(Bezrodny)*
Sparta Prague 1 *(Lokvenc)*

Bordeaux 2 *(Wiltord, Micoud)*
Saprtak Moscow 1 *(Bezrodny)*

Sparta Prague 4 *(Novotny, Prohaszka pen, Rosicky, Jarosik)*
Willem II 0

Spartak Moscow 1 *(Tikhonov pen)*
Bordeaux 2 *(Micoud, Wiltord)*

Willem II 3 *(Bombarda, Shoukov,*
Schenning)
Sparta Prague 4 *(Novotny,*
Labant 2 (2 pens), Baranek)

Bordeaux 0
Sparta Prague 0

Spartak Moscow 1 *(Bezrodny)*
Willem II 1 *(Sanou)*

Sparta Prague 5 *(Lokvenc 2,*
Rosicky, Fukal, Labant pen)
Spartak Moscow 2 *(Bulatov,*
Bezrodny)

Willem II 0
Bordeaux 0

Final Table	P	W	D	L	F	A	Pts
Sparta Prague	6	3	3	0	14	6	12
Bordeaux	6	3	3	0	7	4	12
S Moscow	6	1	2	3	9	12	5
Willem II	6	0	2	4	7	15	2

Group H

Chelsea 0
AC Milan 0

Galatasaray 2 *(Hakan Sukur,*
Hagi pen)
Hertha Berlin 2 *(Preetz, Wosz)*

Hertha Berlin 2 *(Daei 2)*
Chelsea 1 *(Leboeuf pen)*

AC Milan *(Leonardo, Shevchenko)*
Galatasaray 1 *(Umit)*

Chelsea 1 *(Petrescu)*
Galatasaray 0

AC Milan 1 *(Bierhoff)*
Hertha Berlin 1 *(Daei)*

Galatasaray 0
Chelsea 5 *(Flo 2, Zola, Wise,*
Ambrosetti)

Hertha Berlin 1 *(Wosz)*
AC Milan 0

AC Milan 1 *(Bierhoff)*
Chelsea 1 *(Wise)*

Hertha Berlin 1 *(Rekdal pen)*
Galatasaray 4 *(Hakan Sukur 2,*
Tugay, Okan)

Chelsea 2 *(Deschamps, Ferrer)*
Hertha Berlin 0

Galatasaray 3 *(Capone,*
Hakan Sukur, Umit pen)
AC Milan 2 *(Weah, Giunti)*

Final Table	P	W	D	L	F	A	Pts
Chelsea	6	3	2	1	10	3	11
Hertha Berlin	6	2	2	2	7	10	8
Galatasaray	6	2	1	3	10	13	7
AC Milan	6	1	3	2	6	7	6

Second Group Stage
Group A

Hertha Berlin 1 *(Michalke)*
Barcelona 1 *(Luis Enrique)*

Sparta Prague 0
Porto 2 *(Drulovic, Jardel)*

Barcelona 5 *(Kluivert 2, Luis*
Enrique 2, Guardiola)
Sparta Prague 0

Porto 1 *(Drulovic)*
Hertha Berlin 0

Barcelona 4 *(Rivaldo 2, F De Boer,*
Kluivert)
Porto 2 *(Jardel 2)*

Hertha Berlin 1 *(Veit)*
Sparta Prague 1 *(Siegl)*

Porto 0
Barcelona 2 *(Abelardo, Rivaldo)*

Sparta Prague 1 *(Fukal)*
Hertha Berlin 0

Barcelona 3 *(Xavi, Gabri, Kluivert)*
Hertha Berlin 1 *(Alves)*

Porto 2 *(George Costa, Capucho)*
Sparta Prague 2 *(Lokvenc, Fukal)*

Hertha Berlin 0
Porto 1 *(Clayton)*

Sparta Prague 1 *(Svoboda)*
Barcelona 2 *(Gabri 2)*

Final Table	P	W	D	L	F	A	Pts
Barcelona	6	5	1	0	17	5	16
Porto	6	3	1	2	8	8	10
Sparta Prague	6	1	2	3	5	12	5
Hertha Berlin	6	0	2	4	3	8	2

Group B

Fiorentina 2 *(Batistuta, Balbo)*
Manchester United 0

Valencia 3 *(Farinos, A Ilie,*
Gonzalez)
Bordeaux 0

Bordeaux 0
Fiorentina 0

Manchester United 3 *(Keane,*
Solskjaer, Scholes)
Valencia 0

Manchester United 2 *(Giggs,*
Sheringham)
Bordeaux 0

Fiorentina 1 *(Mijatovic pen)*
Valencia 0

Bordeaux 1 *(Pavon)*
Manchester United 2 *(Keane,*
Solskjaer)

Valencia 2 *(A Ilie, Mendieta pen)*
Fiorentina 0

Bordeaux 1 *(Wiltord)*
Valencia 4 *(Djukic, Mendieta pen,*
Kily Gonzalez, Sanchez)

Manchester United 3 *(Cole, Keane,*
Yorke)
Fiorentina 1 *(Batistuta)*

Fiorentina 3 *(Chiesa pen, Batistuta,*
Rui Costa)
Bordeaux 3 *(Wiltord, Zanotti,*
Battles)

Valencia 0
Manchester United 0

Final Table	P	W	D	L	F	A	Pts
Manchester U	6	4	1	1	10	4	13
Valencia	6	3	1	2	9	5	10
Fiorentina	6	2	2	2	7	8	8
Bordeaux	6	0	2	4	5	14	2

Group C

Dynamo Kiev 1 *(Rebrov pen)*
Real Madrid 2 *(Morientes, Raul)*

Rosenborg 1 *(Skammelsrud)*
Bayern Munich 1 *(Jancker)*

Bayern Munich 2 *(Jancker, Sergio)*
Dynamo Kiev 1 *(Rebrov)*

Real Madrid 3 *(Raul, Savio,*
Roberto Carlos)
Rosenborg 1 *(Carew)*

Real Madrid 2 *(Morientes, Raul)*
Bayern Munich 4 *(Scholl, Effenberg,*
Fink, Paulo Sergio)

Dynamo Kiev 2 *(Khatskevich,*
Rebrov)
Rosenborg 1 *(Jakobsen)*

Bayern Munich 4 *(Scholl, Elber,*
            Zickler 2)
Real Madrid 1 *(Helguera)*

Rosenborg 1 *(Berg)*
Dynamo Kiev 2 *(Rebrov 2)*

Bayern Munich 2 *(Scholl,*
          Paulo Sergio pen)
Rosenborg 1 *(Carew)*

Real Madrid 2 *(Raul pen,*
         Roberto Carlos)
Dynamo Kiev 2 *(Khatskevich,*
         Hierro og)

Dynamo Kiev 2 *(Kaladze,*
         Demetradze)
Bayern Munich 0

Rosenborg 0
Real Madrid 1 *(Raul*

Final Table	P	W	D	L	F	A	Pts
BayernMunich	6	4	1	1	13	8	13
Real Madrid	6	3	1	2	11	12	10
Dynamo Kiev	6	3	1	2	10	8	10
Rosenborg	6	0	1	5	5	11	1

Group D

Chelsea 3 *(Babayaro, Flo 2)*
Feyenoord 1 *(Cruz)*

Marseille 0
Lazio 2 *(Stankovic, Conceicao)*

Feyenoord 3 *(Cruz 2, Bosvelt)*
Marseille 0

Lazio 0
Chelsea 0

Lazio 1 *(Veron)*
Feyenoord 2 *(Tomasson 2)*

Marseille 1 *(Pires)*
Chelsea 0

Chelsea 1 *(Wise)*
Marseille 0

Feyenoord 0
Lazio 0

Feyenoord 1 *(Kalou)*
Chelsea 3 *(Zola, Wise, Flo)*

Lazio 5 *(Inzaghi 4, Boksic)*
Marseille 1 *(Leroy)*

Chelsea 1 *(Poyet)*
Lazio 2 *(Inzaghi, Mihajlovic)*

Marseille 0
Feyenoord 0

Final Table	P	W	D	L	F	A	Pts
Lazio	6	3	2	1	10	4	11
Chelsea	6	3	1	2	8	5	10
Feyenoord	6	2	2	2	7	7	8
Marseille	6	1	1	4	2	11	4

Quarter-finals

Chelsea 3 *(Zola, Flo 2)*
Barcelona 1 *(Figo)*

Barcelona 5 *(Rivaldo 2 (1 pen),*
         Figo, Dani, Kluivert)
Chelsea 1 *(Flo)*
aet; Barcelona won 6-4 on agg

Porto 1 *(Jardel)*
Bayern Munich 1 *(Sergio)*

Bayern Munich 2 *(Sergio, Linke)*
Porto 1 *(Jardel)*
Bayern Munich won 3-2 on
aggregate

Real Madrid 0
Manchester United 0

Manchester United 2 *(Beckham,*
         Scholes pen)
Real Madrid 3 *(Keane og, Raul 2)*
Real Madrid won 3-2 on aggregate

Valencia 5 *(Angulo, Gerard 3,*
         Lopez)
Lazio 2 *(Inzaghi, Salas)*

Lazio 1 *(Veron)*
Valencia 0
Valencia won 5-3 on aggregate

Semi-finals

Valencia 4 *(Angulo 2,*
         Mendieta pen, Lopez)
Barcelona 1 *(Pellégrino og)*

Barcelona 2 *(F De Boer, Cocu)*
Valencia 1 *(Mendieta)*
Valencia won 5-3 on agg

Real Madrid 2 *(Anelka,*
         Jeremies og)
Bayern Munich 0

Bayern Munich 2 *(Jancker, Elber)*
Real Madrid 1 *(Anelka)*
Real Madrid won 3-2 on aggregate

FINAL
Paris, May 24

Real Madrid 3
(Morientes 39, McManaman 67,
Raul 75)

Valencia 0

Real Madrid: Casillas, Michel
Salgado (Hierro), Roberto Carlos,
Campo, Helguera, Karanka,
McManaman, Anelka (Sanchis),
Raul, Morientes (Savio), Redondo

Valencia: Canizares, Angloma,
Gerardo, Mendieta, Djukic,
Pellegrino, Kily Gonzalez, Farinos,
Angulo, Lopez, Gerard (A Ilie)

Referee: Braschi
Attendance: 78, 759

UEFA Cup
British and Irish Clubs only

First Qualifying Round

Cwmbran Town 0
Celtic 6 *(Berkovic, Tebily, Larsson 2, Viduka, Brattbakk)*

Celtic 4 *(Brattbakk, Smith, Mjallby, Johnson)*
Cwmbran Town 0
Celtic won 10-0 on agg

Gorica 2 *(Mitrakovic pen, Zlogar)*
Inter Cardiff 0

Inter Cardiff 1 *(Mainwaring)*
Gorica 0
Gorica won 2-1 on agg

Grasshoppers 4 *(Chapuisat 2, Isabella 2)*
Bray Wanderers 0

Bray Wanderers 0
Grasshoppers 4 *(Tikva 2, De Napoli, Muff)*
Grasshoppers won 8-0 on agg

IFK Gothenberg 3 *(P Andersson, Karlsson 2)*
Cork City 0

Cork City 1 *(Morley)*
IFK Gothenberg 0
IFK won 3-1 on agg

KR Reykjavik 1 *(Hinriksson)*
Kilmarnock 0

Kilmarnock 2 *(Wright pen, Bagan)*
KR Reykjavik 0
aet; Kilmarnock won 2-1 on agg

Lokomotiv Tbilisi 1 *(Kebadze)*
Linfield 0

Linfield 1 *(Larmour)*
Lokomotiv Tbilisi 1 *(Kebadze)*
Lokomotiv won 2-1 on agg

Portadown 0
CSKA Sofia 3 *(Mantchev, Kovacevic, Boukarev)*

CSKA Sofia 5 *(Petkov pen, Litera 2, Hristov pen, Simeonov)*
Portadown 0
CSKA Sofia won 8-0 on agg

VPS Vaasa 1 *(Pohja)*
St Johnstone 1 *(Lowndes)*

St Johnstone 2 *(Simao 2)*
VPS Vaasa 0
St Johnstone won 3-1 on agg

First Round

Celtic 2 *(Larsson 2 (1 pen))*
Hapoel Tel Aviv 0

Hapoel Tel Aviv 0
Celtic 1 *(Larsson)*
Celtic won 3-0 on aggregate

CSKA Sofia 0
Newcastle United 2 *(Solano, Ketsbaia)*

Newcastle United 2 *(Shearer, Robinson)*
CSKA Sofia 2 *(Litera, Simeonov)*
Newcastle won 4-2 on aggregate

Kaiserslautern 3 *(Koch, Djorkaeff, Marschall)*
Kilmarnock 0

Kilmarnock 0
Kaiserslautern 2 *(Djorkaeff, Ramzy)*
Kaiserslautern won 5-0 on agg

Monaco 3 *(Simone 2, Trezeguet)*
St Johnstone 0

St Johnstone 3 *(Leonard og, Dasovic, O'Neil)*
Monaco 3 *(Prso, Riise, Legwinski)*
Monaco won 6-3 on aggregate

Partizan Belgrade 1 *(Tomic)*
Leeds United 3 *(Bowyer 2, Radebe)*

Leeds United 1 *(Huckerby)*
Partizan Belgrade 0
Leeds won 4-1 on agg

Tottenham Hotspur 3 *(Leonhardsen, Perry, Sherwood)*
Zimbru Chisinau 0

Zimbru Chisinau 0
Tottenham Hotspur 0
Tottenham won 3-0 on agg

West Ham United 3 *(Wanchope, Di Canio, Lampard)*
Osijek 0

Osijek 1 *(Bubalo)*
West Ham United 3 *(Kitson, Ruddock, Foe)*
West Ham United won 6-1 on agg

Second Round

Leeds United 4 *(Bowyer 2, Smith, Kewell)*
Lokomotic Moscow 1 *(Loskov)*

Lokomotiv Moscow 0
Leeds United 3 *(Harte pen, Bridges 2)*
Leeds won 7-1 on agg

Lyon 1 *(Blanc)*
Celtic 0

Celtic 0
Lyon 1 *(Vairelles)*
Lyon won 2-0 on agg

Steaua 2 *(Rosu, S Ilie)*
West Ham United 0

West Ham United 0
Steaua 0
Steaua won 2-0 on aggregate

Tottenham Hotspur 1 *(Iversen pen)*
Kaiserslautern 0

Kaiserslautern 2 *(Buck, Carr og)*
Tottenham Hotspur 0
Kaiserslautern won 2-1 on agg

Zurich 1 *(Castillo)*
Newcastle United 2 *(Maric, Shearer)*

Newcastle United 3 *(Maric, Ferguson, Speed)*
Zurich 1 *(Jamarauli)*
Newcastle won 5-2 on agg

Third Round

Arsenal 3 *(Overmars pen, Winterburn, Bergkamp)*
Nantes 0

Nantes 3 *(Sibierski 2, Vahirua)*
Arsenal 3 *(Grimandi, Henry, Overmars)*
Arsenal won 6-3 on aggregate

Rangers 2 *(Kohler og, Wallace)*
Borussia Dortmund 0

Borussia Dortmund 2 *(Ikpeba, Bobic)*
Rangers 0
aet; Dortmund won 3-1 on penalties

Roma 1 *(Totti pen)*
Newcastle United 0

Newcastle United 0
Roma 0
Roma won 1-0 on aggregate

Spartak Moscow 2 *(Shirko, Robson)*
Leeds United 1 *(Kewell)*

Leeds United 1 *(Radebe)*
Spartak Moscow 0
Leeds won on away goals

Fourth Round

Arsenal 5 *(Dixon, Henry 2, Kanu,*
Bergkamp)
La Coruna 1 *(Djalminha pen)*

La Coruna 2 *(Victor, Ivan)*
Arsenal 1 *(Henry)*
Arsenal won 6-3 on agg

Roma 0
Leeds United 0

Leeds United 1 *(Kewell)*
Roma 0
Leeds won 1-0 on agg

Quarter-finals

Arsenal 2 *(Henry, Ljungberg)*
Werder Bremen 0

Werder Bremen 2 *(Bode,*
Bogdanovic)
Arsenal 4 *(Parlour 3, Henry)*
Arsenal won 6-2 on agg

Leeds United 3 *(Wilcox, Kewell,*
Bowyer)
Slavia Prague 0

Slavia Prague 2 *(Ulich 2 (1 pen))*
Leeds United 1 *(Kewell)*
Leeds won 4-2 on aggregate

Semi-finals

Arsenal 1 *(Bergkamp)*
Lens 0

Lens 1 *(Nouma)*
Arsenal 2 *(Henry, Kanu)*
Arsenal won 3-1 on agg

Galatasaray 2 *(Hakan Sukur,*
Capone)
Leeds United 0

Leeds United 2 *(Bakke 2)*
Galatasaray 2 *(Hagi pen,*
Hakan Sukur
Galatasaray won 4-2 on aggregate

FINAL

Copenhagen, May 17

Galatasaray 0
Arsenal 0

*aet; Galatasaray won 4-1 on
penalties*

Galatasaray: Taffarel, Capone,
Ergun, Suat (Ahmet), Popescu,
Bulent, Okan (Hakan Unsal), Umit,
Arif (Hasan), Hagi, Hakan Sukur

Arsenal: Seaman, Dixon, Silvinho,
Vieira, Keown, Adams, Parlour,
Henry, Petit, Bergkamp (Kanu),
Overmars (Sukur)

Referee: Nieto
Attendance: 38,919

"I am a life-long Hull fan but the deal was too good to turn down"
Roary The Tiger, the Hull City mascot, explaining why he became the Exeter mascot Alexander the Greek instead.

"I just felt that I fell short of what was required in the job. It's a massive job. Lots of parts I was adequate with and some parts I did very well, but not in the key part of getting players to win football matches"
Not Roary The Tiger again, but Kevin Keegan after resigning as England coach.

"He's very experienced. He's done his time. He's managed Dover Athletic"
John Gregory on Peter Taylor, after Taylor appointment as caretaker manager of England.

"Canvey Island, your cup exploits end tonight"
Announcer at Port Vale before the FA Cup first round replay. Canvey won 2-1.

"Obviously there's a language barrier. The majority of the lads speak Italian but there are a few who don't"
Dennis Wise, when Chelsea captain.

Women's Football

European Championships

Qualifying Group 2

	P	W	D	L	GF	GA	Pts
Norway	5	5	0	0	24	0	15
England	6	3	1	2	8	13	10
Portugal	6	1	1	4	4	14	4
Switzerland	5	1	0	4	1	9	3

Play-offs

England beat Ukraine 4-1 on aggregate

Draw for the European Championships 2001

Group A

Germany, Sweden, Russia, England

Date	Venue	
June 23	*Erfurt*	*Germany v Sweden*
June 24	*Jena*	*Russia V England*
June 27	*Erfurt*	*Germany V Russia*
June 27	*Jena*	*Sweden V England*
June 30	*Jena*	*England V Germany*
June 30	*Erfurt*	*Sweden V Russia*

Group B

Norway, France, Italy, Denmark

Date	Venue	
June 25	*Ulm*	*Norway V France*
June 25	*Aalen*	*Italy V Denmark*
June 28	*Reutlingen*	*Norway V Italy*
June 28	*Reutlingen*	*France V Denmark*
July 1	*Aalem*	*Denmark V Norway*
July 1	*Ulm*	*France V Italy*
July 4	*Ulm*	*Semi-finals*
July 7	*Ulm*	*Final*

FA Women's Premier League

National Division

	P	W	D	L	GF	GA	Pts
Croydon	18	15	2	1	58	13	47
Doncaster Belles	18	15	1	2	66	14	46
Arsenal	18	13	2	3	73	13	41
Everton	18	10	3	5	62	31	33
Tranmere Rovers	18	9	1	8	43	36	28
Southampton Saints	18	5	3	10	23	32	18
Millwall Lionesses	18	5	3	10	19	43	18
Liverpool	18	4	4	10	15	38	16
Reading Royals	18	3	2	13	20	84	11
Aston Villa	18	0	1	17	6	81	1

Northern Division

	P	W	D	L	GF	GA	Pts
Blysh Spartans Kestrels	22	20	1	1	90	21	61
Bangor City	22	14	6	2	44	19	48
Wolverhampton W	22	13	3	6	64	34	48
Leeds United	22	12	3	7	48	30	39
Sheffield Wednesday	22	10	5	7	44	42	35
Garswood Saints	22	9	7	6	45	39	34
Ilkeston Town	22	7	4	11	33	40	25
Birmingham City	22	6	5	11	32	47	23
Coventry City	22	5	4	13	24	48	19
Huddersfield Town	22	5	4	13	28	56	19
Bradford City	22	5	2	15	40	69	17
Arnold Town	22	3	2	17	14	61	11

Southern Division

	P	W	D	L	GF	GA	Pts
Barry Town	22	16	1	5	73	25	49
Brighton & Hove Albion	22	15	4	3	59	22	49
Wembley Mill HIll	22	14	2	6	56	20	44
Ipswich Town	22	14	0	8	54	41	42
Langford	22	11	4	7	46	29	37
Berkhamsted Town	22	9	5	8	41	46	32
Wimbledon	22	9	3	10	58	44	30
Barnet	22	7	7	8	40	50	28
Barking	22	8	3	11	67	57	27
Cardiff City	22	6	3	13	31	63	21
Three Bridges	22	4	6	12	30	48	18
Whitehawk	22	0	0	22	15	125	0

AXA FA Women's Cup

Final

Bramell Lane   *May 1*

Croydon 2   **Doncaster Belles 1**

Women's League Cup

Final

Arsenal 4   **Croydon 1**

Athletics

It would be nice to think that the wheel has turned. In 1992, Britain returned from Barcelona with two Olympic champions and the sport was riding high. Four years later, there were no titles in Atlanta and the sport was under the wave, not on it. Financial problems, drug scandals and the suicide of the much-loved journalist from the Sunday Times, Cliff Temple, took its toll on the sport. The bankruptcy of the British Athletics Federation in the autumn of 1997 became the defining moment. It shouldn't have happened. Amateur officials had failed to recognise the impending crisis, but ironically it took terrified professionals to bury the governing body. Sometimes, though, and this is no mitigation for their actions, you have to put the past behind you. You just have to.

Sydney was a beaut; a Games so sweet that even those of us who were still lingering over the aromas of Barcelona were eventually won over. There were no records in Sydney either. Imagine that, no absolutes. Indeed, throughout the whole year not a single men's world record was broken. We like this. We applaud this. Though the graph may incline upwards over decades, quite naturally, there must be years when performances regress to the norm, when there are no quantum leaps. If you don't get years like that, there is only one reason why. The drugs do work. Another year with men's distances records being re-written and we could all feel embarrassed, and ashamed.

Sadly, the IOC did not exorcise the demons in Sydney. They had the technology to detect EPO use within a period of four weeks of use, but chose not to apply the test during the Games, using a method that would only detect EPO within a couple of days of use. It would have been more effective if they had asked the athletes to stick out their tongues and say 'Aaah'. Nobody takes EPO two days before a race. You do not need to ask why they adopted that policy. The Olympics, the IAAF, the sport has its sacred cows. They don't want another Ben Johnson. They don't want it to happen on the biggest stage of all.

Elsewhere is another matter and the nandrolone controversy rolled on and on, with Linford Christie, Merlene Ottey, Dieter Baumann, Doug Walker and Mark Richardson - to name but a few - still embroiled in it. It is difficult to feel much sympathy with Christie who is deliberately parsimonious with information. He took no supplements - until the suggestion that supplements might be responsible.It is difficult to feel much sympathy for Ottey, who got off a ban because the officials of the IAAF couldn't operate a calculator properly - the sign for percentages confused them. Nor even Walker, who also denied taking any supplements when his positive test was announced, upon the advice of his lawyer presumably.

You can, though, feel some sympathy for Richardson, who acknowledged from the outset that he had taken additives, and named them, and who has not hidden behind legal obfuscation. Research being undertaken in Scotland, headed by Ron Maugham at Aberdeen University may yet make some sense of the plethora of nandrolone positives. Such research is as important as the tests which detect EPO, growth hormone, PBOCs and (heaven forbid) genetic manipulation. Research must detect and protect; it must cut both ways.

How did we get into all that? Well, probably because of the lingering uncertainty about the condition of the sport. On the track, there can be no argument that the wheel has turned. In July, with the European Cup the last thing on anyone's mind, Britain men's won it for the third time in the history of the competition. Even with 16 withdrawals they still won it. Even with the Duke of Edinburgh, restless spirit that he is, finding the extended wait for the final result too much to bear (previous engagement - must rush), they still won it. It is only a modest trophy, but in individual sports team trophies sometimes count even more.

There had already been decent wins at the World Indoors in March; Jason Gardner and Christian Malcolm re-confirming, yet again, that we are now a nation of sprinters. There was Richardson, later, winning a Grand Prix final to earn the money from the IAAF to sustain the fight against the IAAF, but gusting through it all, came the rawest, freshest talent of the lot - Mark Lewis-Francis. Chambers was something as a junior, his world junior record of 10.06 quicker than thought, but Lewis-Francis will leave that record standing; third in the Olympic trials, the 18-year-old opted to run at the world juniors instead and duly won the 100m in 10.12 and anchored the relay team to the title and to within five one-hundredths of the world junior relay record. Lewis-Francis is the business.

All this, plus two golds, two silvers and two bronzes in Sydney (see Olympic Games section), so why the anxiety? Well, it comes back to off-the-track business like the daring new venture of British athletics, a purpose-built stadium at Picketts Lock in north London which will act as the venue for the 2005 World Athletics Championships. What does it have going for it? Well,the fragrant aroma of nearby sewage is a big plus, and the accessibility (nowhere near any international airport) is another huge advantage. Also, it has absolutely no role in any future Olympic bid, so this is purely an athletics only stadium, designed so that international athletes will rush to London to take part in Picketts Lock events. Wow, you can feel the clamour already. Picketts Lock is the last option, which is why the sport has adopted it. And the last option, as we all know, is no option at all. Go back to the drawing board UK Athletics and come up with something that reflects the magnificence of the sport.

WORLD OUTDOOR RECORDS 2000

Men
no world records broken

Women

20km	1:05:26.6	**Tegla Loroupe**	KEN	Borgholzhausen	September 3
3000m Steeplechase	9:40.20	**Cristina Iloo-Casandra**	ROM	Reims	August 30
Pole Vault	4.60m*	**Stacey Dragila**	USA	Modesto	May 13
	4.62m	**Stacey Dragila**	USA	Phoenix	May 26
	4.63m	**Stacey Dragila**	USA	Sacramento	July 23
Javelin	69.48m	**Trine Solberg-Hatteshad**	NOR	Oslo	July 28
20km Walk	1:35:23.7	**Kristina Saltanovic**	LTU	Kaunas	August 3
4x200m	1:27.46	**USA team**		Philadelphia	April 29

* Equalled world record

European Cup

Super League

Gateshead July 15-16

Men

100m	1	Darren Campbell	GBR	10.09
(+2.3)	2	Roland Nemeth	HUN	10.19
	3	Andrea Colombo	ITA	10.23
200m	1	Christian Malcolm	GBR	20.45
(0.0)	2	Alessandro Cavallaro	ITA	20.48
	3	Kostas Kenteris	GRE	20.48
400m	1	Jamie Baulch	GBR	46.64
	2	Alessandro Attene	ITA	46.71
	3	Jimisola Laursen	SWE	46.93
800m	1	Mehdi Baala	FRA	1:47.90
	2	Nils Schumann	GER	1:47.94
	3	Balazs Koranyi	CZE	1:48.52
	7	Alasdair Donaldson	GBR	1:49.17
1500m	1	Mehdi Baala	FRA	3:41.75
	2	John Mayock	GBR	3:42.32
	3	Vyacheslav Shabunin	RUS	3:42.44
3000m	1	Driss Maazouzi	FRA	7:58.70
	2	Vyacheslav Shabunin	RUS	7:59.00
	3	Anthony Whiteman	GBR	8:01.00
5000m	1	Mustapha Essaid	FRA	13:47.44
	2	Dmitry Makisov	RUS	13:48.43
	3	Sebastian Hallmann	GER	13:49.95
	6	Kris Bowditch	GBR	14:03.10
3000sc	1	Panvabdevah Tahri	FRA	8:27.28
	2	Damian Kallabis	GER	8:29.16
	3	Guiseppe Maffei	ITA	8:34.47
	6	Stuart Stokes	GBR	8:53.90
110mh	1	Falk Balzer	GER	13.52
(+1.4)	2	Emiliano Pizzoli	ITA	13.54
	3	Robert Kronberg	SWE	13.67
	4	Damien Greaves	GBR	13.80
400mh	1	Chris Rawlinson	GBR	48.84
	2	Rustan Mashchenko	RUS	49.19
	3	Fabrizio Mori	ITA	49.98
HJ	1	Stefan Holm	SWE	2.28m
	2	Wolfgang Kreissig	GER	2.25m
	3	Lambros Papakostas	GRE	2.20m
	4	Ben Challenger	GBR	2.15m
PV	1	Yevgeny Smiryagin	RUS	5.85m
	2	Tim Lobinger	GER	5.75m
	3	Patrik Kristiansson	SWE	5.70m
	6	Timothy Thomas	GBR	5.40m
LJ	1	Vitaly Shkurlatov	RUS	8.22m
	2	Kofi Amoah Prah	GER	8.15m
	3	Peter Haggström	SWE	8.08m
	5	Nathan Morgan	GBR	7.57m
TJ	1	Larry Achike	GBR	17.31m
	2	Fabrizio Donato	ITA	17.17m
	3	Stamatis Lenis	GRE	17.01m
SP	1	Paolo Dal Soglio	ITA	19.99m
	2	Michael Mertens	GER	19.71m
	3	Jimmy Nordin	SWE	19.46m
	8	Mark Edwards	GBR	17.59m
DT	1	Lars Riedel	GER	63.30m
	2	Robert Fazekas	HUN	62.15m
	3	Vitaliy Sidorov	RUS	60.91m
	4	Robert Weir	GBR	60.78m
HT	1	Christophe Epalle	FRA	78.51m
	2	Alexandros Papadimitriou	GRE	77.64m
	3	Karsten Kobs	GER	77.55m
	7	Paul Head	GBR	67.75m
JT	1	Sergey Makarov	RUS	89.92m
	2	Kostas Gatsioudis	GRE	84.56m
	3	Boris Henry	GER	82.83m
	5	Mick Hill	GBR	80.24m
4x100	1	Great Britain		38.41
		(Campbell/Malcolm/Devonish/Chambers)		
	2	Greece		38.67
	3	Italy		39.17
4x400	1	France		3:04.50
	2	Great Britain		3:05.24
		(Knowles/Baldock/Rawlinson/Baulch)		
	3	Hungary		3:05.88

FINAL POSITIONS
1. Great Britain 101.5; 2. Germany 101; 3. France 97;
4. Italy 96.5; 5. Russia 88.5; 6. Greece 88.5;
7. Sweden 75; 8. Hungary 62
Sweden and Hungary relegated

Women

100m	1	Ekaterini Thanou	GRE	10.84
(+2.9)	2	Christine Arron	FRA	11.02
	3	Manuela Levorato	ITA	11.13
	7	Marcia Richardson	GBR	11.47
200m	1	Muriel Hurtis	FRA	22.70
(-0.3)	2	Natalya Voronova	RUS	22.81
	3	Andrea Philipp	GER	22.88
	6	Donna Fraser	GBR	23.14
400m	1	Svetlana Pospelova	RUS	50.63
	2	Donna Fraser	GBR	51.78
	3	Uta Rohlander	GER	52.17
800m	1	Irina Mistyukevich	RUS	2:02.52
	2	Linda Kisabaka	GER	2:03.88
	3	Patricia Djate	FRA	2:04.44
	4	Tanya Blake	GBR	2:04.71
1500m	1	Helen Pattinson	GBR	4:12.05
	2	Yelena Zadorozhnaya	RUS	4:12.20
	3	Kristina da Fonseca	GER	4:13.11
3000m	1	Gabriela Szabo	ROM	8:43.33
	2	Yalina Bogomolova	RUS	8:43.45
	3	Hayley Tullett	GBR	8:45.39

5000m	1	Tatyana Tomashova	RUS	14:53.00
	2	Irina Mikitenko	GER	14:54.30
	3	Yamna Belkacem	FRA	14:57.05
	6	Hayley Yellling	GBR	15:36.27

100mh	1	Linda Ferga	FRA	12.93
(+0.2)	2	Mayya Shemchishina	UKR	12.95
	3	Yulia Graudyn	RUS	13.08
	4	Keri Maddox	GBR	13.15

400mh	1	Tetyana Tereshchuk	UKR	54.68
	2	Ulrike Urbansky	GER	56.10
	3	Monika Niedestatter	ITA	56.33
	4	Keri Maddox	GBR	56.36

HJ	1	Monica Dinescu	ROM	1.93m
	2	Yulia Lyakhova	RUS	1.91m
	3	Jo Jennings	GBR	1.86m

PV	1	Svetlana Foefanova	RUS	4.35m
	2	Yvonne Buschbaum	GER	4.30m
	3	Francesca Dolcini	ITA	4.20m
	4	Janine Whitlock	GBR	4.10m

LJ	1	Olga Rublyova	RUS	6.87m
	2	Olena Shekhovtsova	UKR	6.79m
	3	Fiona May	ITA	6.74m
	7	Jade Johnson	GBR	6.15m

TJ	1	Tatyana Lebedeva	RUS	14.98m
	2	Olena Govorova	UKR	14.31m
	3	Barbara Lah	ITA	13.86m
	7	Michelle Griffith	GBR	13.50m

SP	1	Astrid Kumbernuss	GER	18.94m
	2	Kaliopi Ouzouni	GRE	18.16m
	3	Judy Oakes	GBR	18.08m

DT	1	Nicoleta Grasu	ROM	63.35m
	2	Ilke Wyludda	GER	62.45m
	3	Anastasia Kelesidou	GRE	62.30m
	8	Shelley Drew	GBR	52.74m

HT	1	Mihaela Melinte	ROM	70.20m
	2	Olga Kuzenkova	RUS	70.20m
	3	Kirsten Münchow	GER	68.31m
	5	Lorraine Shaw	GBR	67.44m

JT	1	Ana Mirela Termure	ROM	63.23m
	2	Tatyana Shikolenko	RUS	60.41m
	3	Mirela Tzelili	GRE	57.84m
	8	Karen Martin	GBR	51.08m

4x100	1	France		42.97
	2	Russia		43.38
	3	Germany		43.51
		disq: Great Britain		

4x400	1	Russia		3:25.50
	2	Germany		3:27.70
	3	Great Britain		3:28.12

FINAL POSITIONS
1. Russia 123; 2. Germany 110; 3. France 86; Romania 80; Italy 78; Great Britain 77; Ukraine 70; Greece 55
Ukraine and Greece relegated

First League
Group A
Oslo, Norway   July 8-9
Men
1. Spain 116; 2, Finland 101; 3. Norway 98;
4. Czech Republic 93; 5. Portugal 87; 6. Switzerland 85;
7. Belgium 82; 8. Denmark 54
Spain promoted, Belgium and Denmark relegated
Women
1. Czech Republic 108; 2. Sweden 106; 3. Spain 96; 4. Finland 89; 5. Hungary 83; 6. Portugal 72;
7 Norway 71; 8. Switzerland 59
Czech Rep promoted, Norway and Switzerland relegated

Group B
Bydgoszcz, Poland   July 8-9
Men
1. Poland 134; 2. Ukraine 111; 3. Netherlands 108;
4. Bulgaria 86; 5. Slovenia 79; 6. Romania 78;
7. Austria 64; 8. Croatia 60
Poland promoted, Austria and Croatia relegated
Women
1. Belarus 112; 2. Bulgaria 108; 3. Poland 101;
4.Slovenia 92; 5. Netherlands 68; 6. Ireland 62;
7. Austria 62; 8. Croatia 40
Belarus promoted, Austria and Croatia relegated

Combined Events
Super League
Oulu, Finland
Decathlon Team
1. France 23,495; 2. Ukraine 23,164; 3. Russia 23,144; 4. Germany 23,006; 5.Finland 22,615; 6. Hungary 22,523; 7 Czech Republic 22,350; 8. Spain 22,229
Decathlon Individual
1. Alexander Yurkov RUS 8192

Heptathlon Team
1. Russia 18,637; 2. Poland 17,759; 3. France 17,710; 4. Finland 17,621; 5. Germany 17,304; 6. Czech Rep 17,196; 7. Ukraine 16,750; 8. Netherlands 16,347
Heptathlon Individual
1. Natalya Rachhupkina RUS 6377

First League
Schwyz-Ibach, Switzerland
Decathlon Team 1. Switzerland 23,419; 2. Greece 23,093; 3. Estonia 22,917; 4. Netherlands 22,487; 5. Italy 22,007; 6. Sweden 21,926; 7. Poland 21,748; 8. Norway 21,538
Decathlon Individual
1. Prodromos Korkizoglou GRE 8069

Heptathlon Team 1. Belarus 18,248; 2. Italy 17,324; 3. Hungary 17,255; 4. Great Britain 16,553; 5. Switzerland 16,059; 6. Sweden 15,914; 7. Spain 15,856; 8. Estonia 15,309
Heptathlon Individual 1. Natalia Sazanovich BLR 6288

Second League
Esbjer, Denmark
Decathlon Team 1. Austria 22,366; 4 Great Britain 20,793

Heptathlon Team 1. Lithuania 16,221

IAAF Golden League and GP Final

Meeting de Paris
St Denis   June 23
Men *GP*100m: Brian Lewis USA 10.10; 800m: Djabir Said-Guerni ALG 1:45.99; 1500m: Hicham El Guerroj MAR 3:30.75; 3000m: Ali Säidi-Sief ALG 7:27.67; 3000msc: Ali Ezzine MAR 8:03.57; *GP*400mh: Llewellyn Herbert RSA 48.41; *GP*HJ: Sergei Klyugin RUS 2.31m; *GP*PV: Maksim Tarasov RUS 5.65m; *GP*SP: John Godina USA 21.25m
Women *GP*100m: Zhanna Pintusevich-Block UKR 11.09; 200m: Cathy Freeman AUS 22.62; 800m: Sandra Stals BEL 2:00.53; *GP*1500m: Kutre Dulecha ETH 4:03.73; *GP*3000m: Lidia Chojecka POL 8:33.35; *GP*100mh: Olga Shishigina KZK 12.76; 400mh: Deon Hemmings JAM 54.56; *GP*LJ: Tatyana Kotova RUS 7.04m; JT: Tatyana Shikolenko RUS 64.50m

Golden Gala
Rome   June 30
Men *GP*100m(+0.7): Maurice Greene USA 9.97; 200m: Maurice Greene USA 20.02; 800m: Djabir Säid-Guerni ALG 1:44.32; *GP*1500m: Noah Ngeny KEN 3:29.99; *GP*5000m: Ali Säidi-Sief ALG 12:50.86; 3000msc: Brahim Boulami MAR 8:03.82; 110mh(+0.7): Allen Johnson 13.19; *GP* 400mh: Eric Taylor USA 47.94; *GP*HJ: Vyacheslav Voronin 2.35m; *GP*PV: Maksim Tarasov 5.80m; *GP*TJ: R Dimitrov BUL 17.25m; *GP*SP: C J Hunter USA 21.34m
Women *GP*100m(+0.1): Marion Jones USA 10.91; *GP*1500m: Kutre Dulecha ETH 4:02.92; 100mh(+0.5): Gail Devers USA 12.47; 400mh: Nezha Bidouane MAR 53.53; HJ: Inga Babakova UKR 1.97m; *GP*LJ: Tatyana Kotova RUS 6.89m; *GP*JT: Trine Solberg-Hatteshad 68.22**WR**

Exxon Mobil Bislett Games
Oslo   July 28
Men *GP*100m: (+0.2) Ato Boldon TRI 10.00; 200m: Ato Boldon TRI 20.26; 800m: Noah Ngeny 1:44.49; *GP*Dream Mile: Hicham El Guerrouj MAR 3:46.24; GP 5000m: Sammy Kipketer KEN 12:55.03; *GP*400mh: Eric Thomas USA 48.66; *GP*HJ: Vyacheslav Voronin RUS 2.31m; *GP*PV: Jean Galfione FRA 5.80m; *GP*SP: Adam Nelson USA 21.43m; JT: Jan Zelezny CZE 90.56m
Women *GP*100m: (+0.3) Zhanna Pintusevich-Block UKR 10.93; *GP*400m: Cathy Freeman AUS 50.74; GP 1500m: Suzy Hamilton-Favor USA 3:57.40; *GP*100mh: (0.0) Gail Devers USA 12.56; *GP*LJ: Tatyana Kotova RUS 7.00m; *GP*JT: Trine Hattestad NOR 69.84m **WR**

Welklasse Zurich
Zurich   Aug 11
Men *GP*100m: (-1.0) Maurice Greene USA 9.94; *GP*400m: Hendrik Mokganyetsi RSA 44.83; 880m: Andre Bucher SUI 1:43.72; *GP*1500m: Hicham El Guerrouj MAR 3:27.21; *GP*5000m: Haile Gebrselassie ETH 12:57.95; 3000msc; Wilson Boit Kipketer KEN 8:11.19; 110mh: (-0.6) Allen Johnson USA 13.17; *GP*400mh: Angelo Taylor USA 47.90; *GP*HJ: Charles Austin USA 2.32m; *GP*PV: Danny Ecker GER 5.85m; *GP*TJ: Jonathan Edwards GBR 17.36m; *GP*SP: Adam Nelson USA 21.64m; DT: Virgilijus Alekna LTU 71.12m

Women
*GP*100m; Marion Jones USA 10.95; 800m: Maria Mutola MOZ 1:56.90; *GP*1500m: Lidia Chojecka POL 4:00.37; *GP*3000m: Gabriela Szabo ROM 8:26.35; *GP*100mh: Gail Devers USA 12.39; *GP*LJ; Marion Jones USA 6.93m; *GP*JT: Trine Solberg-Hattestad NOR 66.50m

Herculis Zepter
Monaco   Aug 18
Men *GP*100m: Maurice Greene USA 10.01; 800m: Djabir Said Guerni ALG 1:43.79; *GP*1500m: William Chirchir KEN 3:31.02; *GP*3000m: Ali Saidi-Sief ALG 7:25.02; 3000msc: Bernard Barmasai KEN 8:02.76; 110mh: Anier Garcia CUB 13.18; *GP*400mh: Llewellyn Herbert RSA 48.18; *GP*HJ: J Sotomayor CUB 2.30m; *GP*PV: Michael Stolle GER 5.95m; *GP*SP: Yuriy Belonog UKR 21.02m
Women *GP*100m: Inger Miller USA 10.91m; *GP*400m: Cathy Freeman AUS 49.48; *GP*1500m: Violeta Beclea-Szekely ROM 3:58.29; *GP*3000m: Lydia Cheromei KEN · 8:30.80; *GP*100mh: Gail Devers USA 12.54; 400mh: Irina Privalova RUS 54.06; *GP*LJ: Erica Johansson SWE 6.81m

Ivo Van Damme Memorial
Brussels   Aug 25
Men *GP*100m: Maurice Greene USA 9.88; 200m: Ato Boldon TRI 20.19; *GP*400m: Michael Johnson USA 44.07; 800m: Djabir Said Guerni ALG 1:43.25; *GP*Mile: Hicham El Gerrouj MAR 3:47.91; *GP*5000m: Brahim Lahlafi MAR 12:49.28; 10,000m: Paul Tergat KEN 27:03.87; 110mh: Dominique Arnold USA 13.15; *GP*400mH: Llewellyn Herbert RSA 48.30; *GP*HJ Charles Austin USA 2.31m; *GP*PV: Danny Ecker GER 5.90m; *GP*SP: Adam Nelson USA 21.58m; DT: Virgilijus Alekna LTU 68.06m
Women *GP*100m: Marion Jones USA 10.83; *GP*400m: Cathy Freeman AUS 49.78; 800m: Maria Mutola MOZ 1:58.06; *GP*1500m: Carla Sacramento POR 4:00.35; *GP*110mh: Gail Devers USA 12.53; *GP*LJ: Tatyana Kotova RUS 6.96m; *GP*JT: Trine Solberg-Hattestad NOR 67.76m

ISTAF 2000
Berlin   Sep 1
Men 100m(-0.2): Maurice Greene USA 9.86 *GP*400m: Michael Johnson USA 45.00 *GP*1500m: Hicham El Guerrouj MAR 3:30.90; *GP*3000m: Ali Säidi-Sief ALG 7:30.76; 110mh(-0.4): Terrance Trammell USA 13.28; *GP*400mh: Angelo Taylor USA 48.26; *GP*HJ: Mark Boswell CAN 2.32m; *GP*PV: Jeff Hartwig USA 5.71m; *GP*TJ: Charles Michael Friedek GER 17.20m; *GP*SP: Adam Nelson USA 20.89m; DT: Lars Riedel GER 69.72m: 4x100m: USA1 37.45
Women *GP*100m(+0.1): Marion Jones USA 10.78; *GP*1500m: Violeta Beclea-Szekely ROM 4:02.80; *GP*5000m: Leah Malot KEN 14:39.83; *GP*100mh(-0.2): Glory Alozie NGR 12.66; *GP*LJ: Tatyana Kotova RUS 6.96m; *GP*JT: Trine Solberg-Hattestad NOR 68.32m; 4x100m: USA 42.95

Grand Prix Final
Doha, Qatar   Oct 5

Men *GP*100m(+0.5): Darren Campbell GBR 10.25; *GP*400m: Mark Richardson GBR 45.20; *GP*1500m: Noah Ngeny KEN 3:36.62; *GP*3000m: Luke Kipkosgei KEN 7:46.21; *GP*400mh: Angelo Taylor USA 48.14; *GP*HJ: Vuacheslav Voronin *GP*PV: Tim Lobinger USA 5.70m; *GP*TJ: Jonathan Edwards GBR 17.12m; *GP*SP: Andy Bloom USA 21.82m; *GP*HT: Andrey Skvaruk UKR 81.43m

Women *GP*100m(+1.6): Marion Jones USA 11.00; *GP*400m: Lorraine Graham JAM 50.21; *GP*1500m: Violeta Beclea-Szekely ROM 4:15.63; *GP*3000m: Sonia O'Sullivan IRL 8:52.01; *GP*100mh(+1.2): Gail Devers USA 12.85; *GP*LJ: Heike Daute-Drechsler GER 7.07m; *GP*DT: Franka Dietzsch GER 65.41m; *GP*JT: Sonia Bisset CUB 65.87m

Overall Grand Prix Ratings
GP Overall Standings (placings and points)
Men

1 Angelo Taylor USA 101
2 Yuriy Belonog UKR 94
3 Adam Nelson USA 93
4 Nick Hysong USA 86.5
5 Bernard Lagat KEN 78
6 Tim Lobinger GER 77.5
7 Maurice Greene USA 77
7 Eric Thomas USA 77
9 Luke Kipkosgei KEN 75
9 Samuel Matete ZAM 75
24 Darren Campbell GBR 66
37 Jonathan Edwards GBR 57
44 Mark Richardson GBR 54
47 Larry Achike GBR 52
51 Chris Rawlinson GBR 51
88 John Mayock GBR 27
153 Jamie Baulch GBR 11
153 Dwain Chambers GBR 11
170 Jason Gardener GBR 9
170 Julian Golley GBR 9

Women
1 Trine Solberg-Hattestad NOR 110
2 Gail Devers USA 104
2 Marion Jones USA 104
4 Violeta Beclea-Szekely ROM 94
5 Glory Alozie NGR 91
6 Osleidys Menéndez CUB 90
7 Tatyana Shikolenko RUS 88
8 Fiona May ITA 83
9 Kutre Dulecha ETH 81
9 Delloreen Ennis-London JAM 81
71 Katharine Merry GBR 21
81 Hayley Parry-Tullett GBR 19
83 Paula Radcliffe GBR 18
111 Donna Fraser GBR 12
172 Helen Pattinson GBR 6

IAAF Grand Prix 1

IAAF Grand Prix in Osaka 2000
Osaka   May 8

Men *GP*100m(-0.4): Maurice Greene USA 9.91; *GP*400m: Antonio Pettigrew USA 45.21; *GP*1500m: Japheth Kimutai KEN 3:34.14; *GP*5000m: Simon Maina Munyi KEN 13:19.6; 110m(+0.2): Dudley Dorival HAI 13.55; *GP*400mh: Angelo Taylor USA 49.06; *GP*HJ: Steffan Strand SWE 2.28m; *GP*SP: C. J. Hunter USA 21.33m; *GP*HT: Koji Murofushi JPN 80.23m

Women *GP*100m(-0.7): Marion Jones USA 10.84; *GP*400m: Falilat Ogunkoya NGR 50.04; *GP*5000m: Yimenashu Taye ETH 15:20.32; *GP*100mh(-0.1): Michelle Freeman JAM 12.84; HJ: Monica Jagar ROM 1.96m; PV: Andrea Muller GER 4.10m; *GP* LJ: Yingnan Guan CHN 6.70m; *GP*DT: Ellina Zvereva BLR 65.51m

Grand Prix Brasil
Rio de Janeiro   May 14

Men *GP*100m(+0.4): Andre Da Silva BRA 10.35; 200m(+0.4): Claudinei Da Silva BRA 20.39; *GP*400M: Sanderlei Parrela BRA 45.00; *GP*1500m: Hudson De Souza BRA 3:36.34; 110mh(+0.7): Anier Garcia CUB 13.48; *GP*400mh: Eric Thomas USA 49.17; *GP*PV: Okkert Brits RSA 5.80m; *GP*TJ: Ketill Hanstveit NOR 16.48m; *GP*SP: Kevin Toth USA 20.76m

Women *GP*100m(+1.7): Nanceen Perry USA 11.36; 200m(+1.3): Rosemar Maria Coelho Neto BRA 23.54; *GP*400m: Sandie Richards JAM 51.44; *GP*100mh(+1.0): Sharon Jewell USA 12.91; *GP*LJ: Fiona May ITA 7.09m; *GP*DT: Yelena Antonova UKR 66.67m

Pontiac Grand Prix
Raleigh, USA   June 17

Men *GP*100m(+0.2): Michael Marsh USA 10.0; *GP*400m: Antonio Pettigrew USA 44.65; 800m: William Chirchir KEN 1:44.63; *GP*1500m: Mark Carroll IRL 3:34.91; 110mh:(+0.0): Allen Johnson USA 13.34; *GP*HJ: Kwaku Boateng CAN 2.28; *GP*SP: C J Hunter USA 21.86

Women *GP*100m(+0.0): Chandra Sturrup BAH 11.09; GP 400 m: 1 Lorraine Graham JAM 50.47; GP 1500m: 1 Regina Jacobs USA 4:11.24; 9 Kathy Butler GBR 4:19.78; *GP*100mh(+0.0): Michelle Freeman JAM 12.75; 400mh: Tonja Buford-Bailey USA 55.76; PV: Kellie Suttle USA 4.43m; *GP*LJ: Chandra Sturrup BAH 6.70m; *GP*DT: Lisa-MarieVizaniari AUS 63.68

Prefontaine Classic
Eugene, USA   June 24

Men *GP*100m(+1.9): Coby Miller USA 10.00; 200m(+2.1): Maurice Greene USA 19.93; *GP*400m: Michael Johnson USA 43.92; 800: Khadevis Robinson USA 1:45.90; *GP*1 mile: William Chirchir KEN 3:51.84; *GP*5000m: Luke Kipkosgei KEN 13:21.59; 110mh(+3.4): Allen Johnson USA 13.28; *GP*PV: Nick Hysong USA 5.75m; *GP*SP: C J Hunter USA 21.38m; *GP*HT: Lance Deal USA 80.14m

Women *GP*100m(+2.6): Marion Jones USA 10.93; *GP*400m: Latasha Colander-Richardson USA 50.86; 800m: Maria Mutola MOZ 1:57.65; 1500m: Gabriela Szabo ROM 4:00.73; 100mh(+1.3): Gail Devers USA 12.64; *GP*LJ: Marion Jones USA 6.97m; *GP*GP: Lisa-Marie Vizaniari AUS 65.34m

Tsiklitiria Meeting
Athens   June 28
Men GP100m(-0.8): Gregory Saddler USA 10.08; 200m (-0.1): Kevin Little USA 20.80; 400m: Stilianos Dimotsios GRE 46.28; 1000m: Noah Ngeny KEN 2:15.53; GP3000m: Daniel Komen KEN 7:31.96; GP400mh: Eronilde Nunes de Araujo BRA 48.25; GPPV: Maksim Tarasov RUS 5.80m; GPSP: John Godina USA 20.82m; JT: Kostas Gatsouidis GRE 88.46m
Women GP100m(+1.7): Chryste Gaines USA 10.97; GP400m: Natalya Nazarova RUS 51.57; 800m: Hasna Benhassi MAR 1:59.24; GP3000m: Dong Yanmei CHN 8:33.07; PV: Svetlana Feofanova RUS 4.50m; TJ: Tatyana Lebedeva RUS 14.78m; GPJT: Osleidys Menendez CUB 66.35m

Athletissima 2000
Lausanne   July 5
Men GP100m(+1.0): Ato Boldon TRI 9.95; 200m(+0.3): Ato Boldon TRI 19.97; 800m: Andre Bucher SUI 1:43.12; GP1500m: Noah Ngeny KEN 3:31.61; GP5000m: Sammy Kipketer KEN 13:01.93; 110mh(+0.6): Allen Johnson USA 13.06; GP400mh: Llewellyn Herbert RSA 47.98; GPPole Vault: Dmitry Markov AUS 5.85m; GPSP: Yury Belonog UKR 20.46m; JT: Jan Zelezny CZE 87.66m
Women GP100m(+0.9): Ekaterini Thanou GRE 10.91 200m(+1.0): Debbie Ferguson BAH 22.43; GP400m: Cathy Freeman AUS 49.56; 800m: Ludmila Formanova CZE 1:59.94; GP1500m: Kutre Dulecha ETH 4:03.34; GP100mh(+0.8): Gail Devers USA 12.50; 400m: Deon Hemmings JAM 54.18; HJ: Hestrie Storbeck-Cloete RSA 1.97m; GPLJ: Erica Johansson SWE 7.04m

Nikaia
Nice   July 8
GP100m(-0.1): Francis Obikwelu NGR 10.06; GP400m: Anthuan Maybank USA 44.80; 1000m: Noah Ngeny KEN 2:14.78; GP1500m: William Chirchir KEN 3:32.75; GP3000m: Benjamin Limo KEN 7:37.73; 3000msc: Brahim Boulami MAR 8:03.30; GP400mh: 1 Eric Thomas USA 48.20; GPHJ: Staffan Strand SWE 2.32m; GPPV: M Tarasov RUS 5.82m; HT: Lance Deal USA 80.99m
Women GP100m(-0.1); Chandra Sturrup BAH 11.18; GP400m: Katharine Merry GBR 50.05; 1000m: Violeta Beclea-Szekely ROM 2:37.22; GP1500m: Olga Kuznetsova RUS 4:03.50; GP3000m: Tatyana Tomashova RUS 8:36.37; GP100mh(-1.4): Olga Shishigina KZK 12.75; 400mh: Tetyana Tereshchuk-Antipov UKR 54.52; PV: Svetlana Feofanova RUS 4.46m; GPDT: Irina Yatchenko BLR 65.42

DN Galan
Stockholm   Aug 2
Men GP100m(+0.4): Ato Boldon TRI 10.01; GP400m: Alejandro Cardenas MEX 45.31; 1000m: Japheth Kimutai KEN 2:14.28; GP1500m: Andres Diaz ESP 3:32.75; GP5000m: Richard Limo KEN 13:04.79; 3000msc: Reuben Kosgei KEN 8:06.58; 110mh(+1.5): Allen Johnson USA 13.15; GPHJ: Vyacheslav Voronin RUS 2.32m; GPTJ; Rostislav Dimitrov BUL 17.30m; JT: Sergey Makarov RUS 83.42m
Women GP100m: Marion Jones USA 10.68; 800m: Maria Mutola MOZ 1:56.98; GP5000m: Olga Yegorova RUS 14:42.91; GP100mh(+1.3): Delloreen Ennis-London JAM 12.74; HJ: Kajsa Bergqvist SWE 1.96m; PV: Anzhela Balakhonova UKR 4.50m; GPLJ: Dawn Burrell USA 6.98m; JT: Trine Solberg-Hattestad NOR 67.92m

Norwich Union British Grand Prix
London   Aug 5
Men GP100m(-0.1): Bruny Surin CAN 10.16; 200m: Bernard Williams USA 20.45; GP400m: Greg Haughton JAM 44.91; 800m: Anthony Whiteman GBR 1:45.81; GPMile: Hicham El Guerrouj MAR 3:45.96; GP5000m: Haile Gebrselassie ETH 13:06.23; 110mh(+0.2): Allen Johnson USA 13.35; GP400mh: Angelo Taylor USA 48.66; GPHJ: Vyacheslav Voronin RUS 2.40m; GPPV: Nick Hysong USA 5.80m; GPTJ: Jonathan Edwards GBR 17.34m; JT: Aki Parviainen FIN 87.81m
Women GP100m(+1.1): Marion Jones USA 10.78; GP400m: Ana Guevara MEX 50.12; GP1500m: Violeta Beclea-Szekely ROM 4:05.01; GP5000m: Ayelech Worku ETH 14:41.23; 400mh: Sandra Glover-Cummins USA 53.92; GPLJ: Inessa Kravets UKR 6.92m

IAAF Grand Prix 2

Grand Prix Meeting
Melbourne   Mar 2
Men 100m(+1.6): Patrick Johnson AUS 10.10; GP200m(+1.1): Darryl Wohlsen AUS 20.57; 400m: Patrick Dwyer AUS 45.57; 800m: David Lelei KEN 1:43.97; 1500m: William Chirchir KEN 3:32.55; 3000m: Luke Kipkosgei KEN 7:45.20; 10,000m: Joseph Kimani KEN 28:30.32; 3000msc: John Kosgei KEN 8:19.47; 110mh(+1.7): Joseph-Berlioz Randrianmihaja MAD 13.94; 400mh: Rohan Robinson AUS 49.41; HJ: Konstantin Matusevich ISR 2.30m; GPPV: Paul Burgess AUS 5.60m; LJ: Peter Burge AUS 8.30m; GPTJ: Larry Achike GBR 16.76m; SP: Miroslav Menc CZE 19.11m; GPHT: Chris Harmse RSA 73.72m
Women 100m (+2.8): Melinda Gainsford-Taylor AUS 11.16; GP400m: Cathy Freeman AUS 50.31; 800m: Tamsyn Lewis AUS 1:59.42; GP1500m: Toni Hodgkinson NZL 4:06.23; 100mh(+1.8): Mame Tacko Diaf SEN 13.14; 400mh: Lauren Poetschka AUS 55.37; HJ: Yelena Yelesina RUS 1.85m; PV: Emma George AUS 4.45m; LJ: Bronwyn Thompson AUS 6.19m; GPDT: Lisa-Marie Vizaniari AUS 63.84m

Engen Grand Prix
Pretoria, South Africa   March 24
Men GP100m(0.0): Patrick van Balkom NED 10.24; 200m: Patrick van Balkom NED 20.43; 300m: Michael Johnson USA 30.85; GP400m: Patrick Dwyer AUS 44.73; 800m: Mbuireni Mulaudzi 1:45.99; 3000m: Aaron Gabonewe RSA 8:04.72; 110mh: Chris Phillips USA 13.52; 400mh: Llewellyn Herbert RSA 48.37; HJ: Jacques Freitag RSA 2.25m; PV: Lawrence Johnson USA 5.90m; LJ: Hassan Al Sabaa KSA 7.92m; GPSP: Burger Lambrechts RSA 20.16m; DT: Franz Kruger RSA 63.40m; GPHT Olli-Pekka Karjalainen FIN 79.63m; JT: Jan Zelezny CZE 90.59m
Women 100m(0.0): Wendy Hartman RSA 11.36; 200m(-0.4): Dikeledi Moropane RSA 23.07; GP400m: Falilat Ogunkoya NGR 50.84; 800: Tina Paulino MOZ 2:01.08; 400mh: Surita Febbraio RSA 55.41; HJ: Hestrie Storbeck-Cloete RSA 1.90m; LJ: Zita Ajkler HUN 6.57m; SP: Veronica Abrahamse RSA 16.54m; GPDT: Beatrice Faumuina NZL 61.50m; JT: Karen Martin GBR 53.68m

Adriaan Paulen Memorial
Hengelo   May 28
Men *GP*HT: Igor Astapkovic h BLR 80.90m
Rest of the meeting abandoned

Grand Prix Meeting
Seville   May 28
Men 100 m(+0.7): Tim Montgomery USA 10.20; 200m
(0.0): Michael Johnson USA 19.91; 400m: Jerome Davis
USA 45.95; 1500m: Hicham El Guerrouj MAR 3:33.48;
3000m: Noah Ngeny KEN 7:35.46; 3000mSC: Wilson
Boit-Kipketer KEN 8:21.90; GP 400mH: William Porter
USA 50.10; PV: Grigoriy Yegorov KZK 5.60m; LJ: Iván
Pedroso CUB 8.08m; SP: Kevin Toth USA 20.90m; HT:
Heinz Weiss GER 79.30m; 4 x 100 metres: Cuba 39.23
Women 200m (-0.4): Nanceen Perry USA 22.97; 400m:
Lisette Ferri ESP 54.22; 800m: Hasna Benhassi MAR
2:00.11; 1500 metres: Yulia Kosenkova RUS 4:12.79;
5000 metres: Berhane Adere ETH 15:08.39; LJ: Lyudmila
Galkina RUS 6.76m; SP: Nadine Kleinert GER 19.20m

Ericsson GP Helsinki
Helsinki   June 15
Men *GP*100m (+0.4): Brian Lewis USA 10.06; 800m:
Wilson Kipketer DEN 1:44.27; 3000m: Abiyote Abate
ETH 7:42.58;110mH (+0.9): Anier Garcia CUB 13.19;
*GP*400 mH: Llewellyn Herbert RSA 49.42; LJ: Aleksey
Lukashevich UKR 8.06m; *GP*SP: Mika Halvari FIN 21.04;
JT: Kostas Gatsioudis GRE 88.74;
Women
*GP*100m (+1.4): Torri Edwards USA 11.16; 400m:
Katharine Merry GBR 50.72; 800m:Zulia Calatayud CUB
2:01.67; 3000m: Sonia O'Sullivan IRL 8:45.85;
400mH: Ulrike Urbansky GER 55.92; PV: Svetlana
Feofanova RUS 4.50m; *GP*LJ: Erica Johansson SWE
6.71m; *GP* JT: Osleidys Menendez CUB 62.97

Slovak Gold
Bratislava   June 22
Men 100m: Roland Nemeth HUN 10.30; 200m: Marian
Vanderka SVK 20.76; *GP*400m: Alejandro Cardenas
MEX 44.92; 800m: James McIlroy GBR 1:47.01; 5000m:
John Cheruiyot Korir KEN 13:11.04; *GP*400mH: James
Carter USA 49.08; *GP*SP: Mikulas Konopka SVK 19.81m
Women100m: Pavla Andriskova CZE 12.06; 200:
Barbara Petrahn HUN 23.73; *GP*400m: Svetlana
Goncharenko RUS 51.08; 800m: Irina Krakoviak LTU
2:01.82; *GP*100mH: Yulia Graudyn RUS 12.88; HJ:
Zuzana Hlavonova CZE 1.97m; PV: Anzhela
Balakhonova UKR 4.42m; TJ: Tatyana Lebedeva RUS
14.89m; *GP*DT: Franka Dietzsch GER 64.20m;

IAAF Meeting
Zagreb, Croatia   July 3
Men100m (-1.0): Obadele Thompson BAR 10.17; 200m
(-0.4): Thompson 20.16; 400m: Greg Haughton JAM
44.99; 1500m: Benson Koech KEN 3:35.32; 3000mSC:
Julius Chelule KEN 8:21.41; 110mH (0.0): Allen Johnson
USA 13.10; *GP*400mH: Eric Thomas USA 48.60; HJ:
Kwaku Boateng CAN 2.34m; *GP*TJ: Larry Achike GBR
17.16m; *GP*HT: Vasiliy Sidorenko RUS 79.90m
Women 100m (-0.9): Chandra Sturrup BAH 11.38; 200m
(-1.0): Alenka Bikar 22.94; *GP*400m: Svetlana Pospelova
RUS 50.66; 800m: Letitia Vriesde SUR 2:00.02;
*GP*100mH (-0.0): Delloreen Ennis-London JAM 12.78;
400mH: Daimi Pernia CUB 54.14; HJ: Inga Babakova
UKR 2.00m; *GP*JT: Osleidys Menendez CUB 65.20m

Gugl Grand Prix
Gugl, Austria   Aug 8
Men 100m: (+0.7) Coby Miller USA 10.05; 200m(+0.5):
Obadele Thompson BAR 20.11; *GP*400m: Alvin Harrison
USA 45.19; 1500m: Paul Mwangi KEN 3:34.29;
3000mSC: Gunther Weidlinger AUT 8:20.37; 110mH
(+0.7): Allen Johnson USA 13.14; LJ: Kareem Streete-
Thompson CAY 8.26m; *GP*SP: Mikulas Konopka SVK
19.19m; JT: Eriks Rags LAT 80.47m
Women 100m(-0.2): Zhanna Pintusevich-Block UKR
11.10; 200m (+0.7): Beverly McDonald JAM 22.66;
800m: Stephanie Graf AUT 1:59.75; *GP*3000m:
Yimenashu Taye ETH 8:45.12; *GP*100mH: Michelle
Freeman JAM 12.72; 400m: Sandra Cummings-Glover
USA 54.08; HJ: Monica Iagar-Dinescu ROM 1.94m; PV:
Anzhela Balakhonova UKR 4.56m; *GP* LJ; Dawn Burrell
USA 6.81m; *GP*DT: Franka Dietzsch GER 66.11m

"I didn't have much in common with girls...I've never had a doll in my life"
Marion Jones, reflecting on her schooldays.

"Dean's going to do well here..."
Daley Thompson, before the Olympics. It was Thompson's advice to Erki Nool that caused the Estonian to appeal against his clear foul in the discus. The mark was reinstated and Nool became Olympic champion. Had the foul stood, Nool would have finished outside the medals and Macey would have won bronze.

"I have been completely cheated. I feel lied to"
Iwan Thomas, after the British selectors allocated all three 400m places after the trials. Thomas maintained that they told him a place would be kept open for him to prove his fitness.

CGU Classic
Gateshead   Aug 28
Men 100m: Dwain Chambers GBR 10.11; 200m: Christian Malcolm GBR 20.45; *GP*400m: Angelo Taylor USA 45.05; 800m: Andre Bucher SUI 1:44.62; *GP*1500m: Ali Saidi-Sief ALG 3:30.82; 110mH: Dominique Arnold USA 13.23; *GP*TJ: Jonathan Edwards GBR 17.48m; JT: Steve Backley GBR 82.13m
Women *GP*100m: Myriam Mani CMR 11.23; 200m: Cathy Freeman AUS 22.57; 300m: Donna Fraser GBR 35.71; 800m: Hasna Benhassi MAR 1:59.86; *GP*3000m: Sonia O'Sullivan IRL 8:33.00; 400mH: Deon Hemmings JAM 54.64; PV: Anzhela Balakhonova UKR 4.21m; TJ: Sheila Hudson USA 13.42; *GP*DT: Franka Dietzsch GER 65.30m

Rieti 2000
Rieti   Sept 3
Men 100m (+0.1): Aziz Zakari GHA 10.13; 200m (+0.3): Francis Obikwelu NGR 20.21; 400m: Michael Johnson USA 44.46; 800m:Andrea Longo ITA 1:43.74; *GP*1500m: Noah Ngeny KEN 3:30.42; 5000m: Daniel Komen KEN 13:04.43; *GP*HJ: Konstantin Matusevich ISR 2.30m; PV: Vadim Strogalyov RUS 5.60m; JT: Yoel Garcia CUB 17.00m; *GP*SP: Paolo Dal Soglio ITA 20.75m
Women 100m (+1.1): Mercy Nku NGR 11.20; 200m (+0.6): Nku NGR 22.96; 400m: Ana Guevara MEX 50.58; 800m: Letitia Vriesde SUR 2:01.42; *GP*1500m: Olga Komyagina RUS 4:04.02; *GP*110mH: Melissa Morrison USA 12.81; PV: Doris Auer AUT 4.20m; *GP*J: Osleidys Menendez CUB 63.48

World Junior Championships
Santiago, Chile   Oct 17-22
Men 100m(+0.1): Mark Lewis-Francis GBR 10.12; 200m (+1.3): Paul Gorries RSA 20.64, 3 Tim Benjamin GBR 20.94; 400m: Hamdan Al-Bishi KSA 44.66; 800m: Nicholas Wachira KEN 1:47.16; 1500m: Cornelius Chirchir KEN 3:38.80; 5000m: Gordon Mugi KEN 13:44.93; 10000m: Robert Kipchumba KEN 28:54.37; 110mH: Yuniel Hernandez CUB 13.60; 400mH: Marek Plawgo POL 49.23; 3000mSC: Raymond Yator KEN 8:16.34; HJ: Jacques Freitag RSA 2.24m; PV: Aleksey Khanafin RUS 5.30m; LJ: Cai Peng CHN 7.88m; TJ: Marian Oprea ROM 16.41m; SP: Rutger Smith NED 19.48m; DT: Hannes Hopley RSA 59.51; HT: Esref Apak TUR 69.97m; JT: Gerhardus Pienaar RSA 78.11m; 4x100m: Great Britain (Tyrone Edgar/Dwayne Grant/Tim Benjamin/Mark Lewis-Francis) 39.05; 4x400m: Jamaica 3:06.06; Dec: Dennis Leyckes GER 7897; 10kmW: David Berdeja MEX 40:56.47
Women 100m(+2.0): Veronica Campbell JAM 11.12; 200m(+0.7): Campbell 22.87; 400m: Jana Pittman AUS 52.45; 800m: Jebet Langat KEN 2:01.51; 1500m: Abebech Negussie ETH 4:19.93; 3000m: Beatrice Jepchumba KEN 9:08.80; 5000m: Dorcus Inzikuru UGA 16:21.32; 100mH: Susanna Kallur SWE 13.02; 400mH: Jana Pittman AUS 56.27; HJ: Blanka Vlasic CRO 1.91m; PV: Yelena Isinbayeva RUS 4.20m; LJ: Concepcion Montaner ESP 6.47m; TJ: Anastasiya Ilyina RUS 14.24m; SP: Kathleen Kluge 17.37m; DT: Seema Antil IND 55.27; HT: Ivana Brkljacic CRO 62.22m; JT: Jarmila Klimesova CZE 54.82; 4x100m: Germany 43.91; 4x400m: Great Britain (Kim Wall/Jennifer Meadows/Helen Thieme/Lisa Miller) 3:33.82; Hept: Carolina Klüft SWE 6056; 10kmW: Lyudmila Yefmkina RUS 44:07.74

Domestic Events

Olympic Trials

Birmingham   Aug 11-13

Men

100m	1	Dwain Chambers	Belgrave	10.11
(-0.8)	2	Darren Campbell	Belgrave	10.12
	3	Mark Lewis-Francis	Birchfield	10.24
200m	1	Darren Campbell	Belgrave	20.20
(-0.8)	2	Christian Malcolm	Cardiff	20.59
	3	Marlon Devonish	Coventry	20.55
400m	1	Mark Richardson	WSE	45.55
	2	Sean Baldock	Belgrave	45.71
	3	Jamie Baulch	Cardiff	46.07
800m	1	James McIlroy	Ballymena	1:50.08
	2	Andy Hart	Coventry	1:50.09
	3	Alasdair Donaldson	NEB	1:50.57
1500m	1	John Mayock	Barnsley	3:45.29
	2	Tony Whiteman	Shaftesbury	3:45.57
	3	John McCallum	Croydon	3:46.14
5000m	1	Andres Jones	Cardiff	13:45.86
	2	Michael Openshaw	C-le-Street	13:49.34
	3	Mark Hudspith	Morpeth	13:52.74
3000sc	1	Chris Stephenson	Cardiff	8:28.21
	2	Justin Chaston	Belgrave	8:32.21
	3	Craig Wheeler	Trafford	8:39.72
110mh	1	Colin Jackson	Brecon	13.24
(-2.3)	2	Tony Jarrett	Enf'ld/Haringay	13.78
	3	Damien Greaves	NEB	13.85
400mh	1	Chris Rawlinson	Belgrave	48.95
	2	Anthony Borsumato	Sale	49.71
	3	Matthew Douglas	Belgrave	49.89
HJ	1	Ben Challenger	Belgrave	2.22m
	2	Brendan Reilly	Belgrave/IRL	2.22m
	3	Stuart Ohrland	NEB	2.17m
PV	1	Kevin Hughes	Enf'ld/Haringey	5.50m
	2	Paul Williamson	Puma TVH	5.40m
	3	Ben Flint	Belgrave	5.30m
LJ	1	George Audu	Puma TVH	7.89m
	2	Darren Ritchie	Sale	7.84m
	3	Darren Thompson	Belgrave	7.48m
TJ	1	Phillips Idowu	Belgrave	16.87m
	2	Larry Achike	Belgrave	16.83m
	3	Francis Ageypong	Shaftesbury	16.40m
SP	1	Steph Hayward	Sale	18.24m
	2	Emeka Udechuku	Blackheath	17.47m
	3	Mark Proctor	RAF	17.21m
DT	1	Bob Weir	Birchfield	62.13m
	2	Glen Smith	Birchfield	60.84m
	3	Emeka Udechuku	Blackheath	59.58m
HT	1	Mick Jones	Belgrave	71.51m
	2	Paul Head	NEB	69.63m
	3	John Pearson	Charnwood	67.22m
JT	1	Steve Backley	Cambridge	85.09m
	2	Nick Nieland	Shaftesbury	81.83m
	3	Mick Hill	Leeds	80.28m
10kw	1	Matthew Hales	Steyning	43:12.85
	2	Steve Partington	Manx	43:30.50
	3	Jamie O'Rawe	Leicester	43:54.49

Women

100m	1	Marcia Richardson	WSE	11.49
(-2.2)	2	Joice Maduaka	Wood/Essex	11.47
	3	Sam Davies	Birchfield	11.47
200m	1	Sarah Wilhelmy	Southend	23.39
(+1.0)	2	Sam Davies	Birchfield	23.42
	3	Shani Anderson	Shaftesbury	23.53
400m	1	Donna Fraser	Croydon	50.94
	2	Allison Curbishley	Edinburgh	51.50
	3	Helen Frost	Birchfield	53.33
800m	1	Kelly Holmes	Ealing	2:02.08
	2	Claire Raven	Coventry	2:05.12
	3	Jo Fenn	Wood/Essex	2:05.48
1500m	1	Hayley Tullett	Swansea	4:06.44
	2	Helen Pattinson	Preston	4:11.40
	3	Kelly Caffel	Oxford	4:15.29
5000m	1	Paula Radcliffe	Bedford	15:05.48
	2	Joanne Pavey	Bristol	15:21.15
	3	Hayley Yelling	Hounslow	15:50.41
100mh	1	Diane Allahgreen	Liverpool	13.24
(-2.1)	2	Melanie Wilkins	WSE	13.35
	3	Julie Pratt	Wood/Essex	13.57
400mh	1	Keri Maddox	Sale	55.22
	2	Natasha Danvers	Shaftesbury	55.34
	3	Sinead Dudgeon	Edinburgh	55.74
HJ	1	Jo Jennings-Steele	Rugby	1.89m
	2	Michelle Dunkley	Wood/Essex	1.89m
	3	Lee McConnell	Shaftesbury	1.86m
PV	1	Janine Whitlock	Trafford	4.10m
	2	Irie Hill	WSE	4.00m
	3	Alison Davies	WSE	4.00m
LJ	1	Jo Wise	Coventry	6.44m
	2	Jade Johnson	HHH	6.34m
	3	Donita Benjamin	WSE	6.28m
TJ	1	Michelle Griffith	WSE	13.67m
	2	Liz Patrick	Birchfield	12.79m
	3	Connie Henry	Shaftesbury	12.75m
SP	1	Judy Oakes	Croydon	17.91m
	2	Julie Dunkley	Shaftesbury	16.40m
	3	Joanne Duncan	Wood/Essex	16.00m
DT	1	Shelley Drew	Sutton	59.03m
	2	Pippa Roles	Sale	54.73m
	3	Emma Merry	Rugby	53.00m
HT	1	Lorraine Shaw	Sale	66.85m
	2	Lynn Sprules	Shaftesbury	62.48m
	3	Liz Pidgeon	Wood/Essex	59.95m
JT	1	Kelly Morgan	WSE	58.45m
	2	Karen Martin	RAF	57.75m
	3	Shelley Holroyd	Wood/Essex	51.96m
10kw	1	Lisa Kehler	Wolves	45:09.57
	2	Nicola Huckerby	Birchield	54:53.35
	3	Kath Horwill	Dash	55:59.54

Indoor Athletics

European Championships

Ghent, Belgium   Feb 25-27

Men

60m	1	Jason Gardener	GBR	6.49
	2	Georgios Theodoridis	GRE	6.51
	3	Angelos Pavlakakis	GRE	6.54
		Jamie Henthorn GBR elim 1st rd		
200m	1	Christian Malcolm	GBR	20.54
	2	Patrick Stevens	BEL	20.70
	3	Julian Golding	GBR	21.05
		Tim Benjamin GBR elim s-f		
400m	1	Ilya Tsevontov	BUL	46.63
	2	David Canal	ESP	46.85
	3	Marc Raquil	FRA	47.28
	6	Daniel Caines	GBR	48.36
800m	1	Yuriy Borzakovskiy	RUS	1:47.92
	2	Nils Schumann	GER	1:48.41
	3	Balazs Koranyi	HUN	1:48.42
1500m	1	Jose Redolat	ESP	3:40.51
	2	James Nolan	IRE	3:41.59
	3	Mehdi Baala	FRA	3:42.27
		Eddie King GBR elim s-f		
3000m	1	Mark Carroll	IRE	7:49.24
	2	Rui Silva	POR	7:49.70
	3	John Mayock	GBR	7:49.97
		Rob Whalley GBR elim s-f		
60mh	1	Stanislavs Olijars	LAT	7.50
	2	Tony Jarrett	GBR	7.53
	3	Tomasz Scigaczewski	POL	7.56
		Damien Greaves GBR elim s-f		
HJ	1	Vyacheslav Voronin	RUS	2.34m
	2	Martin Buss	GER	2.34m
	3	Dragotin Topic	YUG	2.34m
		Ben Challenger GBR elim qual		
PV	1	Alex Averbukh	ISR	5.75m
	2	Martin Eriksson	SWE	5.70m
	3	Rens Blom	NED	5.60m
		Paul Williamson GBR elim qual		
LJ	1	Petar Dachev	BUL	8.26m
	2	Bogdan Tarus	ROM	8.20m
	3	Vitaly Shkurlatov	RUS	8.10m
TJ	1	Charles Friedek	GER	17.28m
	2	Rostislav Dimitrov	BUL	17.22m
	3	Paolo Camossi	ITA	17.05m
	8	Julian Golley	GBR	16.16m
SP	1	Aleksandr Bagach	UKR	21.18m
	2	Timo Aaltonen	FIN	20.62m
	3	Manuel Martinez	ESP	20.38m
		Mark Proctor GBR elim qual		
Hep	1	Tomas Dvorak	CZE	6424pts
	2	Roman Serble	CZE	6271pts
	3	Erki Nool	EST	6200pts
4 x 400	1	Czech Republic		3:06.10
	2	Germany		3:06.64
	3	Hungary		3:09.35
	4	Great Britain		3:09.79
		(White/Naismith/Slythe/Knowles)		

Women

60m	1	Ekaterini Thanou	GRE	7.05
	2	Petya Pendereva	BUL	7.11
	3	Irina Pukha	UKR	7.11
	8	Marcia Richardson	GBR	7.27
		Joice Maduaka GBR elim s-f		
200m	1	Muriel Hurtis	FRA	23.06
	2	Alekna Bikar	SLO	23.16
	3	Yekaterina Leschchova	RUS	23.21
		Joyce Maduaka elim s-f		
		Catherine Murphy GBR elim s-f		
		Christine Bloomfield GBR elim 1st rd		
400m	1	Svetlana Pospelova	RUS	51.68
	2	Natalya Nazarova	RUS	51.69
	3	Helena Fuchsova	CZE	52.32
800m	1	Stephanie Graf	AUT	1:59.70
	2	Natalya Tsyganova	RUS	2:00.17
	3	Sandra Stals	BEL	2:01.34
1500m	1	Violeta Szekely-Beclea	ROM	4:12.82
	2	Olga Kuznetsova	RUS	4:13.45
	3	Yulia Kosenkova	RUS	4:13.60
3000m	1	Gabriela Szabo	ROM	8:42.06
	2	Lidia Chojecka	POL	8:42.42
	3	Marta Dominguez	ESP	8:44.08
	7	Hayley Tullett	GBR	8:55.31
60mh	1	Linda Ferga	FRA	7.88
	2	Patricia Girard	FRA	7.98
	3	Yelena Krasovska	UKR	8.03
	5	Diane Allahgreen	GBR	8.04
		(7.99 British rec in s-f)		
HJ	1	Kajsa Bergqvist	SWE	2.00m
	2	Zuzana Hlavonova	CZE	1.98m
	3	Olga Kaliturina	RUS	1.96m
PV	1	Pavla Hamackova	CZE	4.40m
	2	Yelena Belyakova	RUS	4.35m
	3	Christine Adams	GER	4.35m
	5	Janine Whitlock	GBR	4.30m
LJ	1	Erica Johansson	SWE	6.89m
	2	Heike Dreschler	GER	6.86m
	3	Iva Prandzheva	BUL	6.80m
		Jade Johnson GBR elim qual		
TJ	1	Tatyana Lebedeva	RUS	14.68m
	2	Cristina Nicolau	ROM	14.63m
	3	Iva Prandzheva	BUL	14.63m
SP	1	Larisa Peleshenko	RUS	20.15m
	2	Nadine Kleinert-Schmitt	GER	19.23m
	3	Astrid Kumbernuss	GER	19.12m
		Judy Oakes GBR elim qual		
Pen	1	Karin Ertl	GER	4671pts
	2	Irina Vostrikova	RUS	4615pts
	3	Ursula Wlodarczyk	POL	4590pts
4 x 400	1	Russia		3:32.53WIR
	2	Italy		3:35.01
	3	Romania		3:36.28

European Indoor Championships Medal Table

	G	S	B	Total
Russia	6	5	4	15
Czech Republic	3	2	1	6
Germany	2	5	2	9
Bulgaria	2	2	2	6
Romania	2	2	1	5
France	2	1	2	5
Great Britain	2	1	2	5
Spain	1	1	2	4
Greece	1	1	1	3
Ireland	1	1	0	2
Ukraine	1	0	2	3
Austria	1	0	0	1
Israel	1	0	0	1
Latvia	1	0	0	1
Poland	0	1	2	3
Belgium	0	1	1	2
Italy	0	1	1	2
Finland	0	1	0	1
Portugal	0	1	0	1
Slovenia	0	1	0	1
Hungary	0	0	2	2
Estonia	0	0	1	1
Netherlands	0	0	1	1
Yugoslavia	0	0	1	1

AAA Indoor Championships

Birmingham   Jan 29-30

Men 60m: Jason Gardener 6.53; 200m: Christian Malcolm 20.74; 400m: Daniel Caines 46.89; 800m: Luke Kipkoech KEN 1:51.72; 1500m Gareth Turnbull IRE 3:44.06; 3000m: Rob Whalley 8:02.40; 60mH: Tony Jarrett 7.65; HJ:Stuart Ohrland 2.19m; PV: Benjamin Flint 5.35m; LJ: Chris Tomlinson 7.57m; TJ: Julian Golley 16.56m; SP:Steph Hayward 17.67m; 3000W Robert Hefferan IRL 11:38.20
Women 60m: Marcia Richardson 7.25; 200m: Christine Bloomfield 23.31; 400m: Michelle Thomas 55.26; 800m: Emma Davies 2:07.34; 1500m: Shirley Griffiths 4:25.69; 60mH: Diane Allahgreen 8.24; HJ: Wanita May CAN 1.84m; PV: Janine Whitlock 4.20m; LJ: Jade Johnson 6.46m; TJ: Deborah Rowe 12.47m; SP: Judy Oakes 18.06m; 3000W: Gillian O'Sullivan IRL 12:33.11

Air Force Millrose Games

New York   Feb 4

Men 60m: Maurice Greene USA 6.45; 500m: Mark Everett USA 62.59; 800m: Johnny Gray USA 1:49.88; Mile: Mark Carroll IRL 3:58.19; 3000m: Paul Bitok KEN 7:48.89; 60mH: Dominique Arnold USA 7.51; HJ: Lavy USA 2.23m; PV: Jeff Hartwig USA 5.70m; SP: Andy Bloom USA 20.74m
Women 60m: Carlotte Guidry USA 7.14; 400m: Suziann Reid USA 53.61; 800m: Joetta Clark-Diggs USA 2:04.79; Mile: Regina Jacobs USA 4:24.04; 60mH: Melissa Morrison USA 7.94; HJ: Tisha Waller 1.89m; PV: Stacy Dragila USA 4.42m; SP: Jesseca Cross USA 18.48m

Ricoh Indoor Tour

Ghent   Feb 11

Men 60m: Greg Saddler USA 6.51; 200m: Marlon Devonish GBR 21.01; 400m: Mark Hylton GBR 47.14; 800m: Jean-Jimmy Joseph FRA 1:49.24; 1000m: Kenneth Kimwetich KEN 2:20.05; 2000m: John Mayock GBR 5:02.53; 60mH: Anier Garcia CUB 7.45; HJ: Vyatcheslav Voronin RUS 2.30m; PV: Tribaut Duval BEL 5.50m
Women 60m: Philomena Mensah CAN 7.02; 200m: Nanceen Perry USA 22.96; 800m Stephanie Graf AUT 1:59.13; 3000m: Helena Javornik SLO 8:52.57; 60mH: Kim Carson USA 7.92; LJ: Olga Rublyova RUS 6.61m;
Liévin   Feb 13
Men 60m: Leonard Myles-Mills GHA 6.53; 200m: Petko Yankov BUL 20.66; Mile: Haylu Mekonnen ETH 3:54.78; 60mh: Anier Garcia CUB 7.43; HJ: Vyatcheslav Voronin RUS 2.18m; PV: Maxim Tarasov RUS 5.80m
Women 60m: Sevatheda Fynes BAH 7.03; 200m: Nanceen Perry USA 22.52; 1000m: Maria Mutola MOZ 2:35.68; 2000m: Gabriela Szabo ROM 5:38.76; 60mh: Michelle Freeman JAM 7.78; LJ: Iva Prandzheva BUL 6.80m
Stockholm   Feb 17
Men 60m: Leonard Myles-Mills GHA 6.57; 400m: Alejandro Cardenas MEX 45.93; 800m: Roman Oravec CZE 1:47.46; 1000m: Wilson Kipketer DEN 2:16.47; 1500m: Rui Silva POR 3:36.46; 3000m: Ali Saidi-Sief ALG 7:40.39; 60mh: Robert Kronberg SWE 7.72; HJ: Vyatcheslav Voronin RUS 2.32m; PV: Evgeny Smiryagin RUS 5.75m
Women 60m: Philomena Mensah CAN 7.20m; 800m Stephanie Graf AUT 1:58.43; HJ: Kajsa Bergqvist SWE 1.95m; PV:Anzhela Balakhonova UKR 4.37m; LJ: Erica Johansson SWE 6.69m
Birmingham   Feb 20
Men 60m: Maurice Greene USA 6.47; 200m: Christian Malcolm GBR 20.68; 400m: Alejandro Cardenas MEX 46.54; 1000m: Wilson Kipketer DEN 2:14.96 **WR**; 2Miles: Hailu Mekonnen ETH 8:09.66 **WR**; 50mH: Anier Garcia CUB 6.39; 60mh: Anier Garcia CUB 7.41; HJ: Sergey Klyugin RUS 2.31m; LJ: James Beckford JAM 8.06m
Women 60m: Philomena Mensah CAN 7.11; 200m: Juliet Campbell JAM 22.70; 800m: Stephanie Graf AUT 1:57.80; 3000m: Gabriela Szabo ROM 8:35.42; 60mH: Michelle Freeman JAM 7.96; PV: Elmarie Gerryts RSA 4.41m; LJ: Heike Drechsler GER

Ricoh Tour final points standings:
Men: 1 Anier Garcia CUB 24
Women: 1= Stephanie Graf AUT & Philomena Mensah CAN 24

Cross-Country

IAAF World Championships

Vilamoura, Portugal   *Mar 18-19*

Senior Men 4km
1	John Kibowen	KEN	11:11
2	Sammy Kipketer	KEN	11:12
3	Paul Kosgei	ETH	11:15

GBR
38. David Heath 11:57; 64. Robert Whalley 12:08;
65. Phil Mowbray 12:08; 78. Andrew Graffin 12:17;
89. Spencer Barden 12:27; 97. Matthew Smith 12:34

Teams: 1. Kenya 10; 2. Ethiopia 46; 3. Morocco 68;
4. Algeria 88; 5. Portugal 100; 6. Spain 130;
7. Tanzania 136; 8. Germany 166; 9. Italy 178;
10. Great Britain 245

Senior Men 12km
1	Mohammed Mourhit	BEL	35:00
2	Assefa Mezegebu	ETH	35:01
3	Paul Tergat	KEN	35:02

GBR
13. Karl Keska 36:13; 34. Glynn Tromans 37:03;
47. Matthew O'Dowd 38:45; 62. Jonathan Wild 37:43;
88. Nick Comerford 43:05; 107. Rob Denmark 39:43

Teams: 1. Kenya 18; 2. Ethiopia 68; 3. Portugal 69; 4.
Spain 86; 5. Tanzania 94; 6. Great Britain 156; 7 Italy
163; 8. Algeria 167; 9. Morocco 167; 10. Zambia 183

Junior Men 8km
1	Robert Kipchumba	KEN	22:49
2	Duncan Kipkorir Lebo	KEN	22:52
3	John Cheruiyot Korir	KEN	22:55

GBR
25. Mohammed Farah 24:37; 41. Christopher Thompson
25:14; 49. Robert Maycock 25:25; 101. Paul Shaw 26:29;
111. Andrew Sherman 26:42; 107. Nick McCormick 26:54

Teams: 1. Kenya 10; 2. Ethiopia 47; 3. Uganda 68;
4. Tanzania 84; 5. Qatar 98; 6. Morocco 105;
7. Japan 125; 8.South Africa 151; 9. United States 171;
10. Algeria 176

Senior Women 4km
1	Kutre Dulecha	ETH	13:00
2	Zahra Ouaziz	MAR	13:00
3	Margaret Ngotho	KEN	13:00

GBR
4. Paula Radcliffe 13:01; 34. Helen Pattison 13:40;
40. Hayley Tullett 13:40; 61. Angela Newport 13:54;
76. Lucy Wright 14:09; 94. Caroline Walsh 14:34

Teams: 1. Portugal 46; 2. Ethiopia 55; 3.France 57;
4. Kenya 59; 5. Morocco 81; 6. Romania 122;
7. Great Britain 138; 8. Germany 149; 9. Norway 188;
10. Spain 217

Senior Women 8km
1	Derartu Tulu	ETH	25:42
2	Gete Wami	ETH	25:48
3	Susan Chepkemei	KEN	25:50

Other GBR
5. Paula Radcliffe 26:03; 34. Hayley Yelling 27:43;
44 Liz Yelling 28:02; 54 Sharon Morris 28:27;
56. Hayley Haining 28:37; 59 Tara Kryzwicki 28:39

Teams: 1. Ethiopia 20; 2. Kenya 23; 3. USA 98;
4. Ireland 101; 5. Spain 137; 6. Great Britain 137;
7. Japan 148; 8. Italt 164; 9. Portugal 167;
10. Tanzania 188

Junior Women 6km
1	Vivian Cheruiyot	KEN	20:34
2	Alice Timbilili	KEN	20:35
3	Viola Kibiwot	KEN	20:36

GBR
55. Henrietta Freeman 22:56; 63. Emma Ward 23:09;
66. Collette Fagan 23:14; 75. Kate Reed 23:24;
84. Jane Potter 23:44; 95. Zoe Jelbert 24:19

Teams: 1. Kenya 12; 2. Ethiopia 24; 3. Japan 78; 4.
South Africa 105; 5. Uganda 131; 6. United States 146; 7.
Algeria 155; 8. Canada 184; 9. Russia 184; 10. Great
Britain 259

IAAF World Cross Challenge

Date	Venue (Distance M/W)	Men's Winner	Time	Women's Winner	Time
Dec 19	Brussels (10.5km/6km)	Eduardo Henriques POR	32:37	Lydia Cheromei KEN	20:30
Jan 16	Sevilla (10km/6.6km)	Charles Kamathi KEN	30:20	Gete Wami ETH	21:15
Jan 22	Durham (9km/6.5km)	Sergey Lebed UKR	26:37	Gete Wami ETH	21:21
Feb 6	Vilamoura (10m/6km)	Charles Kamathi KEN	29:34	Gete Wami ETH	19:46
Feb 19	Nairobi (12km/8km)	Paul Tergat KEN	35:53	Lydia Cheromei KEN	27:44
Feb 20	Chiba (12km/8km)	Sergey Lebed UKR	35:38	Yoshiko Ichikawa JPN	26:53

Final Standings - Men

			Score
1	Paul Tergat	KEN	107
2	Patrick Ivuti	KEN	104
3	Assefa Mezegbu	ETH	102
4	Charles Kamathi	KEN	102
5	Sergey Lebed	UKR	86
6	Eduardo Henriques	POR	75
7	Phaustin Baha Sulle	TAN	52
8	Mohammed Mourhit	BEL	50
9	Paul Koech	KEN	45
10	Abraham Cherono	KEN	42
12	Keith Cullen	GBR	33

Final Standings - Women

			Score
1	Lydia Cheromei	KEN	122
2	Gete Wami	ETH	119
3	Ayelech Worku	ETH	94
4	Susan Chepkemei	KEN	92
5	Jackline Maranga	KEN	79
6	Paula Radcliffe	GBR	68
7	Constantina Dita	ROM	60
8	Leah Malot	KEN	58
9	Derartu Tulu	ETH	50
10	Joseph Restituta	TAN	50

Final classification is calculated on a maximum of four events: the winner of a race receives 25 points, second place 22, third 19 down to one point for 20th place. Double points were awarded for the World Championships in Vilamoura.

Mountain Running World Trophy
Bergen, Germany   Sept 9-10

Men
Individual

1	Jonathan Wyatt	NZL	47:29
2	Hans Kogler	AUT	49:48
3	Alexis Gex-Fabry	SUI	50:16
4	Thomas Gregor	GER	50:31
5	Sergio Chiesa	ITA	50:39
6	Raymond Fontaine	FRA	50:47
7	Billy Burns	ENG	50:50
8	Martin Cox	ENG	50:59
9	Helmut Schmuck	AUT	51:18
10	Massimo Galliano	ITA	51:25
19	Richard Findlow	ENG	52:23
25	Chris Robison	SCO	52:59
45	Jon Duncan	ENG	54:44

Junior Men

1	Nebai Habtegiorgis	ERI	44:08
2	Florian Heinzle	AUT	44:48
3	Tomasz Klisz	POL	46:31
4	Alessandro Tonazzini	ITA	46:45
5	Matteo Massi	ITA	47:10
18	James Mason	ENG	49:20
19	Andrew Lemoncello	SCO	49:22
24	Jonathan Parker	ENG	50:00
29	Andrew Symonds	ENG	51:06

Women

1	Angela Mudge	SCO	49:24
2	Birgit Sonntag	GER	49:43
3	Izabela Zatorska	POL	50:11
4	Melissa Moon	NZL	50:52
5	Matilde Ravizza	ITA	51:22
6	Alessandra Olarte	COL	51:32
7	Anna Pichrtova	CZE	51:37
8	Meagan Edhouse	NZL	51:49
9	Elisabeth Rust	AUT	51:54
10	Angela Baronchelli	ITA	51:58
21	Ruth Pickvance	ENG	54:21
28	Claire Tomkinson	ENG	55:32
35	Megan Clark	ENG	56:00
38	Helen Diamantides	SCO	56:24

Junior Women

1	Elise Marcot	FRA	29:05
2	Chris Tye	NZL	29:20
3	Lean Vetsch	SUI	29:18*
4	Adele Montonati	ITA	29:45
5	Agnieszka Stafa	POL	30:40
7	Kate Bailey	ENG	31:23
24	Marbeth Shiell	SCO	33:31
26	Emily Crowley	WAL	33:44

* The timing beam was 10m beyond the finish line

Road Racing/Walking

OSAKA MARATHON
Jan 30
Women
1 Lidia Simon	ROM	2:22:54
2 Harumi Hiroyama	JPN	2:22:56
3 Esther Wanjiru	KEN	2:23:31

LAKE BIWA MARATHON
Mar 5
Men
1 Martin Fiz	ESP	2:08:14
2 S Kawashima	JPN	2:09:04
3 Takei	JPN	2:09:23

PARIS MARATHON
Apr 9
Men
1 Mohamed Ouaadi	FRA	2:08:49
2 Samuel Otieno	KEN	2:09:09
3 Abdellah Behar	FRA	2:09:13

Women
1 Marleen Renders	BEL	2:23:43
2 Alina Tecuta	ROM	2:28:18
3 Irina Timofeyeva	RUS	2:30:02

ROTTERDAM MARATHON
Apr 16
Men
1 Kenneth Cheruiyot	KEN	2:08:22
2 Francisco Cortes	ESP	2:08:30
3 Vanderlei de Lima	BRA	2:08:34

Women
1 Ana Isabel Alonso	ESP	2:30:21
2 Mineko Yamanouchi	JPN	2:31:30
3 Sue Reinsford	GBR	2:33:41

BOSTON MARATHON
Apr 17
Men
1 Elijah Lagat	KEN	2:09:47
2 Gezaghne Abera	ETH	2:09:47
3 Moses Tanui	KEN	2:09:50

Women
1 Catherine Ndereba	KEN	2:26:11
2 Irina Bogacheva	KGZ	2:26:27
3 Fatuma Roba	ETH	2:26:27

BERLIN MARATHON
Sept 10
Men
1 Simon Biwott	KEN	2:07:42
2 Antonio Pena	ESP	2:07:47
3 Jackson Kabiga	KEN	2:09:52

Women
1 Kazumi Matsuo	JPN	2:26:15
2 Franca Fiacconi	ITA	2:26:42
3 Zhang Shujing	CHN	2:27:14

WORLD HALF-MARATHON CHAMPIONSHIPS
Veracruz, Mexico   Nov 12
Men
1 Paul Tergat	KEN	1:03:47
2 Phaustin Baha Sulle	TAN	1:03:48
3 Tesfaye Jifar	ETH	1:03:50

Teams
1 Kenya	3:11:38
2 Ethiopia	3:14:45
3 Belgium	3:18:35
17 Great Britain	3:35:43

Women
1 Paula Radcliffe	GBR	1:09:07
2 Susan Chepkemei	KEN	1:09:40
3 Lidia Simon	ROM	1:10:24

Teams
1 Romania	3:34:22
2 Japan	3:36:25
3 Russia	3:45:41
6 Great Britain	3:49:55

GREAT NORTH RUN
Oct 22
Men
1 Phaustin Baha Sulle	TAN	1:01:57
2 Andy Coleman	GBR	1:02:28
3 John Mutai	KEN	1:02:34

Women
1 Paula Radcliffe	GBR	1:07:07
2 Tegla Loroupe	KEN	1:10:07
3 Jelena Prokopcuka	LAT	1:13:56

AMSTERDAM MARATHON
Oct 17
Men
1 Francisco Cortes	ESP	2:08:57
2 Abraham Limo	ETH	2:09:17
3 David KiptumBusinel	KEN	2:10:38

Women
1 Abebe Tola	ETH	2:29:54

CHICAGO MARATHON
Oct 22
Men
1 Khalid Khannouchi	USA	2:07:01
2 Josephat Kiprono	KEN	2:07:29
3 Moses Tanui	KEN	2:07:47

Women
1 Catherine Ndereba	KEN	2:21:33
2 Margaret Okayo	KEN	2:26:00
3 Irina Timofeyeva	RUS	2:29:13

NEW YORK MARATHON
Nov 5
Men
1 Abdel El Mouaziz	MAR	2:10:09
2 Japhet Kosgei	KEN	2:12:30
3 Shem Kororia	KEN	2:12:33

Women
1 Ludmila Petrova	RUS	2:25:45
2 Franca Fiacconi	ITA	2:26:03
3 Margaret Okayo	KEN	2:26:36

TOKYO MARATHON
Nov 19
Women
1 Joyce Chepchumba	KEN	2:24:02
2 Reiko Tosa	JPN	2:24:47
3 Derartu Tulu	ETH	2:26:38

EUROPEAN WALKING CUP
Eisenhüttenstadt, GER   June 17-18

Men's 20km
1 Robert Korzeniowski	POL	1:18:29
2 Andreas Erm	GER	1:18:42
3 Francisco Fernandez	ESP	1:18:56

Also
50 Chris Maddocks	GBR	1:31:39
51 Andy Penn	GBR	1:33:10

Disqualified
Darrell Stone GBR
Andrew Drake GBR

Teams
1.Spain 32; 2.Poland 35;
3. Germany 43

Men's 50km
1 Jesus Angel Garcia	ESP	3:42:51
2 Yevgeniy Shmaliuk	RUS	3:44:33
3 Denis Langlois	FRA	3:47:38

Also
28 Steven Hollier	GBR	4:07:18
43 Chris Cheeseman	GBR	4:23.19
74 Don Bearman	GBR	4:36:15

Tim Watt DNF

Teams
1. France 12; 2. Spain 15; 3.
Germany 30; 12. Great Britain 200

Women's 20km
1 Olimpiada Ivanova	RUS	1:26:48
2 Elisabetta Perrone	ITA	1:27:42
3 Kjersti Platzer	NOR	1:27:53

Also
23 Lisa Kehler	GBR	1:33:57
46 Niobe Menendez	GBR	1:43:18
77 Kimberley Braznell	GBR	1:46:24

Sara Jane Cattermole GBR DNF

Teams
1. Italy 11; 2. Romania 29; 3.
Ukraine 38 54; 11. Great Britain 119

Flora London Marathon

It was Antonio Pinto's ability as a 5000m runner that first caused the London Marathon to sign him up in 1992. In the Portuguese runner's sixth visit to London (and yet to finish outside the top three) he ran the last 5000m of the race almost as fast as the one in Jerez which had first awakened the original interest. The only difference was that in Jerez he hadn't run 37km first. Pinto has always look tough; he used to run his races like a boxer on a training run. Over the years, the extra leanness has accentuated the stride rather than the shoulders, but if ever a man found his metier in 1992, it was Pinto. The international race director of the time just happens to be the editor of this book and he reckons it was easily the most perceptive signing he made.

The men's race in London has had its share of famous winners, but never quite hit the top tier as far as times go. The wind is usually the problem, invariably at its most capricious in April. Pinto's run changed everything, his final time of two hours six minutes and 36 seconds was not just a course record by miles, but a European record and the fifth fastest time ever.

Pinto's strongest challenge came from the Moroccan winner in 1999, Abdelkader El Mouaziz, but his effort waned when, in the 20th mile of the race, Pinto covered the distance in four minutes 32 seconds. If Pinto slowed thereafter, it wasn't by much. The last 10km took less than 30 minutes and the 34-year-old positively bounded up The Mall to cross the line over a minute clear of Mouaziz. In third place was Khalid Khannouchi who is one of the four men to have run faster. Six months earlier, in Chicago, he had set a new world record. "Sometimes it's your day, sometimes it's not," he said, after running three minutes slower than that in London.

Tecla Loroupe won the women's race, but could match neither her world best, set in Berlin, nor London's world best, set (would you believe) in London - believing as they do that times in mixed races do not count as world records. Incidentally, one of the most surprising aspects of the day was that London laid no claim for Pinto's time to be accepted as a world record. Though they probably will.

But back to Loroupe, who patters rather than bounds through her races.The German-based Kenyan was worried about a hip injury which may explain why she ran the most extraordinary negative split covering the first half of the race in 74 minutes and 12 seconds, and the second half almost four minutes quicker.

Blackheath-The Mall
Apr 18

	Men				Women		
1	Antonio Pinto	POR	2:06:36	1	Tegla Loroupe	KEN	2:24:33
2	Abdel El Mouaziz	MAR	2:07.33	2	Lidia Simon	ROM	2:24.56
3	Khalid Khannouchi	MAR	2:08:36	3	Joyce Chepchumba	KEN	2:24:57
4	William Kiplagat	KEN	2:09.06	4	Adriana Fernandez	MEX	2:25.42
5	Hendrick Ramaala	RSA	2:09.43	5	Kerryn McCann	AUS	2:25:59
6	Stefano Baldini	ITA	2:09.45	6	Derartu Tulu	ETH	2:26:09
7	Mathias Ntawulikura	BUR	2:09.55	7	Maria Guida	ITA	2:26:12
8	Josiah Thugwane	RSA	2:10.29	8	Lyubox Morgunova	RUS	2:26:33
9	Mohammed Nazipov	RUS	2:10.35	9	Manuela Machado	POR	2:26:41
10	Danilo Goffi	ITA	2:10:54	10	Svetlana Zakharova	RUS	2:28:11
11	Mark Steinle	GBR	2:11:18	20	Lynne McDougal	GBR	2:38:32

Badminton

They give nothing away in badminton; if you want an Olympic bronze medal, you have to play for it. Rikke Olsen didn't want to, Michael Sogaard, her partner, was indignant that they had to. Even Simon Archer felt the same. And that was after he had won. "We had two sets of bronze medals for semi-final losers in Barcelona. We lost that in Atlanta and it should be brought back. They do it for boxers because they get beaten up. Well, we get beaten up out there," he said, offering in evidence an inflamed patella tendon, a blackened toenail that meant a bigger boot on one foot than the other (and a different colour) and a pulled pectoral muscle that had to be massaged during the breaks.

It was the pectoral muscle, not the boots nor the tendon, which affected play, and could have cost Archer and Jo Goode their Olympic medal, Britain's first-ever. It meant that constantly, when the shuttlecock hung there waiting to be walloped, Archer could only dink it over the net. For Archer to contain his aggressive instincts is a rare day indeed, which proved, if nothing else, that it really hurt. Nor could he leave the smashes to his partner for Goode never does play that way. She has soft hands, teasing the shuttle over the net and beguiling her opponents into errors. It worked a treat in the quarter-final against the Dutch couple Erica van den Heuvel and Chris Bruil, who had beaten them in the European championships in April, though it didn't quite work against the Indonesians Tri Kusharyanto and Minarti Timur in the semi-finals, where the utter dominance of the opening set, which Archer and Goode won 15-2, suddenly evaporated as the Indonesians recovered their poise.

It was old and lost causes that still played on their minds as they lined up for the bronze medal match and the Danes felt the same. They had led the Chinese Zhang Jun and Gao Ling by 14-7 in the third game in their semi-final. They were mentally dusting down their tuxedos when it all went horribly awry. The Chinese won the last set 17-16.

So, all four entered a match without commitment, argued against being there, bristling against the rules. And what did they do then? Served up a match that was an absolute belter. If they ever believed that the IBF might one day revert to two sets of bronze medals for the Olympic Games, rest assured they won't now. This wonderfully entertaining match was the best possible argument against.

Archer and Goode rode the waves in the first game, Sogaard stormed through the second, leaving his partner Olsen mostly watching in admiration. The third game went Archer and Goode's way 17-14, but only after such see-saw activity that most British supporters with any sense were in the bar before it ended. "We play a lot of games like that," said Goode casually.

Zhang and Gao won the mixed doubles title, and the Chinese completely dominated the tournament winning four of the five titles on offer in Sydney (Ji Xinpeng - men's singles, Gong Zhichao - women's singles, Ge/Gu - women's doubles) and nine of the 15 medals. It almost ranked with their efforts at ping pong. We don't care though. We won a bronze medal and from little acorns huge badminton trees grow.

European Championships
Glasgow   Apr 22-29
All results from second round onwards

Men's Singles
2nd Round
Richard Vaughan WAL bt A Kvedarauskas LTU 15-2 15-6
Tjitte Weistra NED bt Robert Blair SCO 7-15 15-6 15-8
Quarter-finals
Vaughan bt Martin Hagberg SWE 15-13 15-13
Semi-finals
Peter Gade Christensen DEN bt Vaughan 15-3 15-4
Poul-Erik Hoyer-Larsen DEN bt
Kenneth Jonassen DEN 15-8 5-15 15-8
Final
Gade Christensen bt Hoyer-Larsen 15-5 15-11

Women's Singles
2nd Round
Petra Overzier GER bt Fiona Sneddon SCO 11-8 11-8
Kelly Morgan WAL bt Susan Hughes SCO 11-0 11-3
Rebecca Pantaney ENG bt Corinne Jorg SUI 11-6 11-1
Karina De Wit NED bt Julia Mann ENG 9-11 11-9 11-9
3rd Round
Morgan bt Neli Nedialkova BUL 11-8 11-2
Marina Andrievskaia SWE bt Pantaney 11-4 11-5
Quarter-finals
Morgan bt Judith Meulendijks NED 11-1 11-1
Semi-finals
Camilla Martin DEN bt Morgan 4-11 11-6 11-1
Andrievskaia bt Mette Sorensen DEN 11-7 11-4
Final
Martin bt Andrievskaia 13-10 11-3

Men's Doubles
2nd Round
Mohr/Tesche GER bt Hunt/J Robertson ENG 15-12 4-15 15-8
Archer/N Robertson ENG bt Kritjansson/Solvason ISL 15-4 15-5
Quarter-finals
Archer/Robertson bt Lens/Van Dalm NED 15-2 15-3
Semi-finals
Eriksen/Larsen DEN bt Archer/Robertson 15-13 7-15 15-3
Axelsson/Jonsson SWE bt
Mateusiak/Logosz POL 15-6 10-15 15-11
Final
Eriksen/Larsen bt Axelsson/Jonsson 15-7 15-6

Women's Doubles
2nd Round
Joanne Davies/Sarah Hardaker ENG bt
Sandra Watt/Kirsteen McEwan SCO 15-5 15-6
Joanne Goode/Donna Kellogg ENG bt
Krasowska/Augustyn POL 15-7 15-10
Quarter-final
Goode/Kellogg bt
Grether/Stechmann GER 14-17 15-3 15-9
Van Hooren/Jonathans NED bt
Davies/Hardaker 17-14 15-10
Semi-finals
Goode/Kellogg bt
Yakusheva/Rusljakova RUS 15-13 15-13
Olsen/Kirkegaard DEN 15-6 15-1 bt
Van/Hooren/Jonathans 15-6 15-1

Final
Goode/Kellogg bt Olsen/Kirkegaard 7-15 15-10 15-8

Mixed Doubles
2nd Round
Sogaard/Olsen DEN bt
Chris Davies/Robyn Ashworth WAL 15-2 15-3
Chris Hunt/Donna Kellogg ENG bt
Kenny Middlemiss/Kirsteen McEwan SCO bt
Strelcov/Golovkina UKR 15-10 15-8
Ian Sullivan/Gail Emms ENG bt Keck/Pitro GER w/o
Bruil/Van den·Heuvel NED bt
Martyn Lewis/Kate Ridler WAL 15-8 15-7
Simon Archer/Joanne Goode ENG bt
Koch/Lengauer AUT 15-3 15-2
James Anderson/Sara Sankey ENG bt
Aydogmus/Dogan TUR 15-0 15-4
3rd Round
Hunt/Kellogg bt Miznikov/Esipenko UKR 15-3 15-7
Holst-Christensen/Jorgensen DEN bt
Middlemiss/McEwan SCO 15-2 15-9
Sullivan/Emms bt Dubrulle/Eymard FRA 15-7 15-4
Archer/Goode bt Pohar/Pohar SLO 15-2 15-5
Eriksen/Schjoldager DEN bt Anderson/Sankey 15-2 15-0
Quarter-finals
Sogaard/Olsen bt Hunt/Kellogg 12-15 15-6 15-8
Holst-Christensen/Jorgensen bt Sullivan/Emms 15-3 15-9
Bruil/Van den Heuvel bt Archer/Goode 15-5 15-12
Semi-finals
Sogaard/Olsen bt
Holst-Christensen/Jorgensen 15-5 13-15 15-3
Eriksen/Schjoldager bt
Bruil/Van den Heuvel 15-8 15-9
Final
Sogaard/Olsen bt Eriksen/Schjoldager 15-7 15-12

Team
The team event is played over all the five disciplines. Sixteen teams took part, eight in the main competition and a further eight in the second tier. The eight were split into two round robin groups with the winners of group A playing the winner of group B with runner-up v runner-up and so on.

Final
Denmark bt England 4-1
Men's Singles: Peter Gade Christensen bt Peter Knowles 15-4 15-3
Women's Singles: Camilla Martin bt Rebecca Pantaney 11-1 11-0
Men's Doubles: Lars Paaske/Martin Lundgaard lost to Simon Archer/Nathan Robertson 15-4 15-2
Women's Doubles: Rikke Olsen/Helene Kirkegaard beat Jo Goode/Donna Kellogg 15-1 15-12
Mixed Doubles: Jens Eriksen/Mette Schjoldager beat Simon Archer/Jo Goode 15-11 8-15 15-6

Final Standings
Division 1
1. Denmark; 2. England; 3. Netherlands; 4. Sweden;
5. Germany; 6. Ukraine; 7. Russia; 8. Bulgaria
Division 2
9. Finland; 10. France; 11. Wales; 12. Poland;
13. Scotland; 14. Iceland; 15. Switzerland; 16. Portugal

IBF WORLD RANKINGS
As at Feb 8, 2001

Men's Singles

1	Peter Gade Christensen	DEN	278.48
2	Xia Xuanze	CHN	272.30
3	Ji Xinpeng	CHN	256.86
4	Hendrawan	INA	251.34
5	Taufik Hidayat	INA	249.26
6	Pulella Gopichand	IND	204.81
7	Roslin Hashim	MAS	183.32
8	Marleve Mainaky	INA	178.82
9	Kenneth Jonassen	DEN	171.77
10	Richard Vaughan	WAL	169.35
28	Colin Haughton	ENG	112.90
38	Mark Constable	ENG	99.03
51	Darren Hall	ENG	82.73
56	Robert Nock	ENG	78.07
60	Michael Edge	ENG	77.42
61	Robert Blair	SCO	76.81

Women's Singles

1	Camilla Martin	DEN	308.31
2	Gong Zhichao	CHN	266.03
3	Dai Yun	CHN	234.70
4	Kim Ji-hyun	KOR	219.19
5	Gong Ruina	CHN	211.91
6	Wang Chen	HKG	190.46
7	Ye Zhaoying	CHN	176.23
8	Lidya Djaelawijaya	INA	174.08
9	Yasuko Mizui	JPN	173.02
10	Kelly Morgan	WAL	168.56
33	Julia Mann	ENG	111.95
43	Tracy Hallam	ENG	90.33
47	Rebecca Pantaney	ENG	86.28
54	Fiona Sneddon	SCO	79.08
55	Susan Hughes	SCO	77.48

Men's Doubles

1	Lee/Yoo	KOR	292.05
2	Limpele/Hian	INA	262.67
3	Ha/Kim	KOR	262.00
4	Eriksen/Larsen	DEN	236.22
5	Choong/Lee	MAS	216.47
8	Archer/Robertson	ENG	199.27

Women's Doubles

1	Huang/Yang	CHN	324.19
2	Ge Fei/Gu Jun	CHN	262.02
3	Yim/Lee	KOR	235.15
4	Goode/Kellogg	ENG	228.41
5	Olsen/Kirkegaard	DEN	207.84
15	Davies/Hardaker	ENG	130.35

Mixed Doubles

1	Sogaard/Olsen	DEN	280.95
2	Zhang/Gao	CHN	276.49
3	Kim/Ra	KOR	238.38
4	Eriksen/Schjoldager	DEN	231.15
5	Archer/Goode	ENG	228.83
8	Sullivan/Emms	ENG	156.83

Thomas Cup, men
Kuala Lumpur, Malaysia May 11-21

Group A

	W	L	MW	ML
Korea	3	0	10	5
Denmark	2	1	11	4
Malaysia	1	2	7	8
India	0	3	2	13

Group B

	W	L	MW	ML
Indonesia	3	0	14	1
China	2	1	10	5
England	1	2	5	10
Sweden	0	3	1	14

Semi-Finals
China 3   Korea 1
Indonesia 3   Denmark 2

Finals
China 0   Indonesia 3

Uber Cup, women
Kuala Lumpur, Malaysia May 11-21

Group A

	W	L	MW	ML
Denmark	3	0	11	4
Indonesia	2	1	9	6
Japan	1	2	7	8
Malaysia	0	3	3	12

Group B

	W	L	MW	ML
China	3	0	15	0
Korea	2	1	5	10
Netherlands	1	2	3	12
Sweden	0	3	2	13

Semi-Finals
Denmark 3   Korea 0
Indonesia 0   China 3

Finals
Denmark 0   China 3

England finished fourth in the qualifying round at Sofia. The top three qualified.

All England Open
Birmingham   *Mar 7-12*
Men's Singles
XIa Xuanze CHN bt Taufik Hidayat INA 15-6 15-13
Women's Singles
Gong Zhichao CHN bt Dai Yun CHN 11-5 8-11 11-5
Men's Doubles
Ha/Kim KOR bt Lee/Yoo KOR 15-4 13-15 17-15
Women's Doubles
Ge/Gu CHN bt Chung/Ra KOR 15-5 15-3
Mixed Doubles
Kim/Ra KOR bt Liu/Ge CHN 15-10 15-2

Korea Open
Cheju Island   *Jan 11-16*
Men's Singles
Peter Gade Christensen DEN bt Rashid Sidek MAS
Women's Singles
Camilla Martin DEN bt Kanako Yonekura JPN
Men's Doubles
Lee/Yoo KOR bt Subagja/Mainaky INA
Women's Doubles
Chung/Ra KOR bt Huang/Yang CHN
Mixed Doubles
Kim/Ra KOR bt Kusharyanto/Timur INA

Chinese Taipei Open
Taipei   *Jan 19-23*
Men's Singles
PeterGade Christensen DEN bt
Wong Choong Hann MAS
Women's Singles
Mia Audina Tjiptawan NED bt
Sujitra Ekmongkolpaisarn THA
Men's Doubles
Gunawan/Wijaya INA bt Cheah/Yap MAS
Women's Doubles
Ra/Chung KOR bt Huang/Yang CHN
Mixed Doubles
Sogaard/Olsen DEN bt Eriksen/Schjoldager DEN

Yonex Open Japan
Tokyo   *April 5-9*
Men's Singles
Ji Xinpeng CHN bt Hendrawan INA
Women's Singles
Gong Zhichao CHN bt Ye Zhaoying CHN
Men's Doubles
Gunawan/Wijaya INA bt Lee/Yoo KOR
Women's Doubles
Huang/Yang CHN bt Ge/Gu CHN
Mixed Doubles
Liu/Ge CHN bt Kusharyanto/Timur INA

Sanyo Indonesia Open
Senayan   *July 19-23*
Men's Singles
Taufik Hidayat INA bt Ong Ewe Hock MAS
Women's Singles
Camilla Martin DEN bt Wang Chen HKG
Men's Doubles
Gunawan/Wijaya INA bt Limpele/Hian INA
Women's Doubles
Goode/Kellogg ENG bt Jonathans/Van Hooren NED
Mixed Doubles
Archer/Goode ENG bt Sogaard/Olsen DEN

Proton-Eon Malaysia Open
Shah Alam   *Aug 16-23*
Men's Singles
Taufix Hidayat INA bt Xia Xuanze CHN
Women's Singles
Gong Zhichao CHN bt Dai Yun CHN
Men's Doubles
Limpele/Hian INA bt Lee/Yoo KOR
Women's Doubles
Ge/Gu CHN bt Huang/Yang CHN
Mixed Doubles
Kim/Ra KOR bt Kusharyanto/Timur INA

Holland Plaza Dutch Open
's Hertogenbosch   *Oct 25-30*
Men's Singles
Chen Hong CHN bt Roslin Hashim MAS
Women's Singles
Zhou Mi CHN bt Gong Ruina CHN
Men's Doubles
Budiarto/Haryanto INA bt Sogaard/Laugesen DEN
Women's Doubles
Olsen/Kirkegaard DEN bt Chen/Jiang CHN
Mixed Doubles
Chen/CHen CHN bt Archer/Van den Heuvel ENG/NED

Danish Open
Farum   *Oct 25-30*
Men's Singles
Peter Gade Christensen DEN bt George Rimarcdi INA
Women's Singles
Zhou Mi CHN bt Camilla Martin DEN
Men's Doubles
Limpele/Hian INA bt Eriksen/Larsen DEN
Women's Doubles
Chen/Jiamg CHN bt Wei/Zhang CHN
Mixed Doubles
Sogaard/Olsen DEN bt Eriksen/Schjoldager DEN

Baseball

This was the 14th Subway Series, but the first for 44 years. New York was naturally self-obsessed for the 10 days from Championship-winning pennant to World Series win, but when Yankee pitcher Roger Clemens slung a broken bat-end in the direction of Mike Piazza, the $13m-a-year Mets hitter, in the second game of the series, the rest of America sat up and took a bit of notice too.

The Yankees were always red-hot favourites. With 25 pennants already in the trophy cabinet at the Bronx, and three in the last four years, nobody expected the Mets to win their first series since 1986. To say it started slowly is an understatement. The first game took four hours and 51 minutes to complete, making it the longest World Series game in four years. The 101st batter of the evening, Jose Vizcaino, finally settled it 4-3 in the Yankees favour at a little past one in the morning. The pace was upped in the second game.

Back in July, Roger Clemens had struck batter Mike Piazza in the head in an interleague game. This was the rematch, 106 days later. The first two balls to Piazza were strikes, the third was out of the zone and the fourth struck and split Piazza's bat. The barrel rolled towards Clemens who picked it up and threw it towards Piazza. As acts of hostility go, it ranked some way below Prime Minister's question time, but it caused a right old stir nevertheless. The Mets were off the bench, rushing to the mound. Piazza, to his credit, seemed to be calming them down. Some of his team members were not so placid. "If I was hitting and someone would have thrown the bat at me, I would have fought. I don't care if Mike Tyson was pitching. I would have had to go out there and take a whipping," said Mike Hampton. Clemens later maintained that he had no idea that Piazza was running and that the throw had not been aimed at him at all. Clemens, though, is not a naturally warm, cuddly human being, and that inclines people not to believe him even when he is telling the truth.

It was Clemens, nevertheless, who gave Yankees control of the second game which they led 6-0 going into the last inning, and while the Mets clawed back to 6-5, it was still two down and five to play. Mets won the third, perhaps aided by the fact they started from the moral high ground. The fourth though went to form and the subway train halted at the Yankee Stadium in the fifth game for the home team's fourth World Series win in five years. They say the Yankees are an old team, but age doesn't appear to be wearying them.

That Clinking-Clanking Sound

The top contracts in US Sport

All baseball

Player, Club (Date contract signed)	Annual Pay
Ken Griffey Jr, Mariners (Jan 1996)	$8.50m
Albert Belle, White Sox (Nov 1996)	$11m
Barry Bonds, Giants (Feb 1997)	$11.45m
Greg Maddux, Braves (Aug 1997)	$11.5m
Pedro Martínez, Red Sox (Dec 1997)	$12.5m
Mike Piazza, Mets (Oct 1998)	$13m
Mo Vaughn, Angels (Nov 1998)	$13.33m
Kevin Brown, Dodgers (Nov 1998)	$15m
Roger Clemens, Yankees (Aug 2000)	$15.45m
Carlos Delgado, Blue Jays (Oct 2000)	$17m
Alex Rodriguez, Rangers (Dec 2000)	$25.2m

2000 World Series

New York Yankees v New York Mets
October

GAME 1
Yankee Stadium, Oct 21

	1	2	3	4	5	6	7	8	9	10	11	12	R
Mets	0	0	0	0	0	0	3	0	0	0	0	0	**3**
Yankees	0	0	0	0	0	2	0	0	1	0	0	1	**4**

GAME 2
Yankee Stadium, Oct 22

	1	2	3	4	5	6	7	8	9	R
Mets	0	0	0	0	0	0	0	0	5	**5**
Yankees	2	1	0	0	1	0	1	1	X	**6**

GAME 3
Shea Stadium, Oct 24

	1	2	3	4	5	6	7	8	9	R
Yankees	0	0	1	1	0	0	0	0	0	**2**
Mets	0	1	0	0	0	1	0	2	X	**4**

GAME 4
Shea Stadium, Oct 25

	1	2	3	4	5	6	7	8	9	R
Yankees	1	1	1	0	0	0	0	0	0	**3**
Mets	0	0	2	0	0	0	0	0	0	**2**

GAME 5
Shea Stadium, Oct 27

	1	2	3	4	5	6	7	8	9	R
Yankees	0	1	0	0	0	1	0	0	2	**4**
Mets	0	2	0	0	0	0	0	0	0	**2**

New York Yankees won the series 4-1

Championship Series

American League

NEW YORK YANKEES V SEATTLE MARINERS

Seattle Mariners 2	New York Yankees 0
New York Yankees 7	Seattle Mariners 1
New York Yankees 8	Seattle Mariners 2
New York Yankees 5	Seattle Mariners 0
Seattle Mariners 6	New York Yankees 2
New York Yankees 9	Seattle Mariners 7

New York Yankees won series 4-2

National League

ST LOUIS CARDINALS V NEW YORK METS

New York Mets 6	St Louis Cardinals 2
New York Mets 6	St Louis Cardinals 5
St Louis Cardinals 8	New York Mets 2
New York Mets 10	St Louis Cardinals 6
New York Mets 7	St Louis Cardinals 0

New York Mets won series 4-1

Division Series

American League

Oakland Athletics 5	New York Yankees 3
New York Yankees 4	Oakland Athletics 0
New York Yankees 4	Oakland Athletics 2
Oakland Athletics 11	New York Yankees 1
New York Yankees 7	Oakland Athletics 5

New York Yankees won series 3-2

Seattle Mariners 7	Chicago White Sox 4 (10 inns)
Seattle Mariners 5	Chicago White Sox 2
Seattle Mariners 2	Chicago White Sox 1

Seattle Mariners won series 3-0

National League

San Francisco Giants 5	New York Mets 1
New York Mets 5	San Francisco Giants 4
New York Mets 3	San Francisco Giants 2 (13 inns)
New York Mets 4	San Francisco Giants 0

New York Mets won series 3-1

St Louis Cardinals 7	Atlanta Braves 5
St Louis Cardinals 10	Atlanta Braves 4
St Louis Cardinals 7	Atlanta Braves 1

St Louis Cardinals won series 3-0

Baseball Briefing

Subscriptions:

Trevor Kendall, 2 Drury Close, Waltham, Grimsby DN37 0XP

American League standings

EAST

	Won	Lost	PCT	GB	Home	Road	Runs F	Runs A	Streak
X-New York Yankees	87	74	.540	-	44-36	43-38	871	814	Lost 7
Boston Red Sox	85	77	.525	2.5	42-39	43-38	792	745	Lost 1
Toronto Blue Jays	83	79	.512	4.5	45-36	38-43	861	908	Lost 4
Baltimore Orioles	74	88	.457	13.5	44-37	30-51	794	913	Won 4
Tampa Bay Devil Rays	69	92	.429	18	36-44	33-48	733	842	Won 1

CENTRAL

	Won	Lost	PCT	GB	Home	Road	Runs F	Runs A	Streak
X-Chicago White Sox	95	67	.586	-	46-25	49-32	978	839	Lost 1
Cleveland Indians	90	72	.556	5	48-33	42-39	950	816	Won 3
Detroit Tigers	79	83	.488	16	43-38	36-45	823	827	Won 3
Kansas City Royals	77	85	.475	18	42-39	35-46	879	930	Won 1
Minnesota Twins	69	93	.426	26	36-45	33-48	748	880	Lost 3

WEST

	Won	Lost	PCT	GB	Home	Road	Runs F	Runs A	Streak
X-Oakland Athletics	91	70	.565	-	47-34	44-36	947	813	Won 3
Y-Seattle Mariners	91	71	.562	0.5	47-34	44-37	907	780	Won 2
Anaheim Angels	82	80	.506	9.5	46-35	36-45	864	869	Lost 2
Texas Rangers	71	91	.438	20.5	42-39	29-52	848	974	Lost 3

National League standings

EAST

	Won	Lost	PCT	GB	Home	Road	Runs F	Runs A	Streak
X-Atlanta Braves	95	67	.586	-	51-30	44-37	810	714	Lost 1
Y-New York Mets	94	68	.580	1	55-26	39-42	807	738	Won 5
Florida Marlins	79	82	.491	15.5	43-38	36-44	731	797	Won 6
Montreal Expos	67	95	.414	28	37-44	30-51	738	902	Lost 9
Philadelphia Phillies	65	97	.401	30	34-47	31-59	708	830	Lost 3

CENTRAL

	Won	Lost	PCT	GB	Home	Road	Runs F	Runs A	Streak
X-St Louis Cardinals	95	67	.586	-	50-31	45-36	887	771	Won 1
Cincinatti Reds	85	77	.525	10	43-38	42-39	822	762	Lost 1
Milwaukee Brewers	73	89	.451	22	42-39	31-50	737	823	Lost 2
Houston Astros	72	90	.444	23	39-42	33-48	938	944	Won 2
Pittsburgh Pirates	69	93	.426	26	37-44	32-49	793	888	Lost 1
Chicago Cubs	65	97	.401	30	38-43	27-54	764	904	Won 1

WEST

	Won	Lost	PCT	GB	Home	Road	Runs F	Runs A	Streak
X-San Francisco Giants	97	65	.599	-	55-26	42-39	925	747	Won 1
Los Angeles Dodgers	86	76	.531	11	44-37	42-39	798	729	Lost 1
Arizona Diamondbacks	85	77	.525	12	47-34	38-43	792	754	Lost 1
Colorado Rockies	82	80	.506	15	48-33	34-47	968	897	Won 1
San Diego Padres	76	86	.469	21	41-40	35-46	752	815	Won 1

X - Division Title   Y - Wild Card

Basketball

If the players can command sky-high salaries, then what on earth is Phil Jackson worth. While the Lakers languished for a decade, nurturing fading memories of Kareem Abdul-Jabeer and Magic Johnson, coach Jackson was up on the great lake collecting rings like Liberace. Six times he won the NBA title with the Chicago Bulls in eight sweet seasons. Then it was time to move on and the Bulls were left to lament the pausing of not only Michael Jordan but the man who pulled the great man's strings.

In 1999 San Antonio Spurs set about the Knicks and ran away with their first NBA crown. The Bulls languished beneath the also rans. Twelve months later, with the Bulls now so low that the oxygen levels are worrying, it was Knight time again. Jackson proving that you don't have to have a Jordan to win a title. You can do it with any old superhuman.

"This is what I came to the NBA for. I withheld the emotions for 11 years. It just came out," said Shaquille O'Neal, whose tears flowed as Lakers closed the series in the sixth game with a 116-111 victory. O'Neal was Jordanesque, the seven-footer hitting a 38-point average over the series. When he didn't manage a virtuoso performance, which wasn't often, there was Kobe Bryant, comfortably the best support act in the NBA. Pacers coach Larry Bird, who won a few rings in his time, had no excuses. "It gets to the point you know that you are not the best team," he said.

In the European championship semi-final round, the England team lost when they should have won and won when they should have lost and finished in the middle of the Group A pack leaving them neither winners nor losers. The defeat by Latvia, at Coventry in November, was the worst of times, a win then could have put them in the final at Turkey. They will now start the next championship qualifying round in the late autumn in exactly the same position as they started the last - in the semi-final round.

The win over the Hungarians in the final 2001 qualifier could, though, be a watershed. It was the last occasion on which Roger Huggins or Steve Buckley slipped on an England singlet, and the coach Laszlo Nemeth is also undecided about his future.

Manchester Giants, currently dwelling on a move from the MEN Arena, were the champions. The real story in the BBL, though, was its failure to land a title sponsor for the

> **"Why would I want to fit into the stereotype of what a normal NBA player is supposed to be anyway. I don't see any reason why I would want to fall into that: listen to loud music, drive fast cars, have a large house, very little substance to my personality, a woman in every town. Why would I want to be in that stereotype. It's so shallow."**
>
> Manchester's John Amaechi, enjoying considerable success at Orlando Magic. Amaechi is a graduate in child psychology, and continuing his studies for a Ph D.

Play-offs

EASTERN CONFERENCE

Miami Heat v Detroit Pistons
Miami 95 Detroit 85; Miami 84 Detroit 82;
Detroit 72 Miami 91
Miami won series 3-0

Philadelphia 76ers v Charlotte Hornets
Charlotte 82 Philadelphia 92; Charlotte 108
Philadelphia 98; Philadelphia 81 Charlotte 76;
Philadelphia 105 Charlotte 99
Philadelphia won series 3-1

New York Knicks v Toronto Raptors
New York 92 Toronto 88; New York 84 Toronto 83;
Toronto 80 New York 87
New York won series 3-0

Indiana Pacers v Milwaukee Bucks
Indiana 88 Milwaukee 85; Indiana 91 Milwaukee 104;
Milwaukee 96 Indiana 109; Milwaukee 100 Indiana 87;
Indiana 96 Milwaukee 95
Indiana won series 3-2

WESTERN CONFERENCE

Phoenix Suns v San Antonio Spurs
San Antonio 70 Phoenix 72; San Antonio 85 Phoenix 70;
Phoenix 101 San Antonio 94; Phoenix 89 San Antonio 78
Phoenix won series 3-1

Utah Jazz v Seattle Supersonics
Utah 104 Seattle 93; Utah 107 Seattle 87;Seattle 89
Utah 78; Seattle 104 Utah 93; Utah 96 Seattle 93
Utah won series 3-2

Portland Trailblazers v Minnesota Timberwolves
Portland 91 Minnesota 88; Portland 86 Minnesota 82;
Minnesota 94 Portland 87; Minnesota 77 Portland 85
Portland won series 3-1

LA Lakers v Sacramento Kings
Lakers 117 Sacramento 107; Lakers 113 Sacramento 89;
Sacramento 99 Lakers 91; Sacramento 101 Lakers 88;
Lakers 113 Sacramento 86
Lakers won series 3-2

Conference Semi-finals

EASTERN CONFERENCE

Indiana Pacers v Philadelphia 76ers
Indiana 108 Philadelphia 91; Indiana 103 Philadelphia 97;
Philadelphia 89 Indiana 97;Philadelphia 92 Indiana 90;
Indiana 86 Philadelphia 107;Philadelphia 90 Indiana 106;
Indiana won series 4-2

Miami Heat v New York Knicks
Miami 87 New York 83; Miami 76 New York 82;
New York 76 Miami 77; New York 91 Miami 83;
Miami 87 New York 71; New York 72 Miami 70;
Miami 82 New York 83
New York won series 4-3

WESTERN CONFERENCE

Portland Trailblazers v Utah Jazz
Portland 94 Utah 75; Portland 103 Utah 85;
Utah 84 Portland 103; Utah 88 Portland 85;
Portland 81 Utah 79
Portland won series 4-1

LA Lakers v Phoenix Suns
LA Lakers 105 Phoenix 77; LA Lakers 97 Phoenix 76;
Phoenix 99 LA Lakers 105; Phoenix 117 LA Lakers 98;
LA Lakers 87 Phoenix 65
Lakers won series 4-1

Conference Finals

EASTERN CONFERENCE

New York Nicks v Indiana Pacers
Game 1: Indiana 102 New York 88
Game 2: Indiana 88 New York 84
Game 3: New York 98 Indiana 95
Game 4: New York 91 Indiana 89
Game 5: Indiana 88 New York 79
Game 6: New York 80 Indiana 93
Indiana won series 4-2

WESTERN CONFERENCE

LA Lakers v Portland Trailblazers
Game 1: LA Lakers 109 Portland 94
Game 2: LA Lakers 77 Portland 106
Game 3: Portland 91 LA Lakers 93
Game 4: Portland 91 LA Lakers 103
Game 5: LA Lakers 88 Portland 96
Game 6: Portland 103 LA Lakers 93
Game 7: LA Lakers 89 Portland 84
LA Lakers won series 4-3

NBA Finals

LA Lakers v Indiana Pacers

Game 1: *Los Angeles, June 7*
LA Lakers 104 Indiana Pacers 87
*Shaquille O'Neal was totally dominant scoring 43
points to take Lakers to a cosy win.*

Game 2: *Los Angeles, June 9*
LA Lakers 111 Indiana Pacers 104
*Kobe Bryant retired injured so O'Neal had to go it
alone and he did, with another 39 points.*

Game 3: *Indiana, June 11*
Indiana Pacers 100 LA Lakers 91
*With Bryant still out injured and O'Neal missing 10
free throws, Pacers had a chance to fight back
and took it.*

Game 4: *Indiana, June 14*
Indiana Pacers 118 LA Lakers 120 (OT)
*The lead changed 17 times after halftime,
Bryant's basket with six seconds left finally
settling it.*

Game 5: *Indiana, June 16*
Indiana Pacers 118 LA Lakers 120 (OT)
*The Pacers finest hour, spurred on by the fact that
they didn't want to concede the title at home, they
were all over the Knicks.*

Game 6: *Los Angeles, June 19*
LA Lakers 116 Indiana Pacers 111
*As ever, O'Neal was imposing, ending the Finals
with a 38-point average to bring the Lakers their
12th NBA title.*

LA LAKERS WON SERIES 4-2
**MVP: Shaquille O'Neal/Kobe Bryant (both
Lakers)**

National Basketball Association

Final Tables

EASTERN CONFERENCE

Atlantic Division

	W	L	Pct	GB	Home	Road
Miami Heat*	52	30	.634	0	36-5	20-21
New York Nicks†	50	32	.610	2	33-8	17-24
Philadelphia 76ers†	49	33	.598	3	29-12	20-21
Orlando Magic	41	41	.500	11	26-15	15-26
Boston Celtics	35	47	.427	17	26-15	9-32
New Jersey Nets	31	51	.378	21	22-19	9-32
Washington Wizards	29	53	.354	23	17-24	12-29

Central Division

	W	L	Pct	GB	Home	Road
Indiana Pacers	56	26	.683	0	36-5	20-21
Charlotte Hornets†	49	33	.598	7	30-11	19-22
Toronto Raptors†	45	37	.549	11	26-15	19-22
Detroit Pistons†	42	40	.512	14	27-14	15-26
Milwaukee Bucks†	42	40	.512	14	23-18	19-22
Cleveland Cavaliers	32	50	.390	24	22-19	10-31
Atlanta Hawks	28	54	.341	28	21-10	7-34
Chicago Bulls	17	65	.207	39	12-29	5-36

WESTERN CONFERENCE

Midwest Division

	W	L	Pct	GB	Home	Road
Utah Jazz*	55	27	.671	0	31-10	24-17
San Antonio Spurs†	53	29	.646	2	31-10	22-19
Minnesota TW†	50	32	.610	5	26-15	24-17
Dallas Mavericks	40	42	.488	15	22-19	18-23
Denver Nuggets	35	47	.427	20	25-16	10-31
Houston Rockets	34	48	.415	21	22-19	12-29
Vancouver Grizzlies	22	60	.268	33	12-29	10-31

Pacific Division

	W	L	Pct	GB	Home	Road
L A Lakers*	67	15	.817	0	36-5	31-10
Portland Trailblazers†	59	23	.720	8	30-11	29-12
Phoenix Suns†	53	29	.646	14	32-9	21-20
Seattle Supersonics†	45	37	.549	22	24-17	21-20
Sacramento Kings†	44	38	.537	23	30-11	14-27
Golden State Warriors	19	63	.232	48	12-29	7-34
L.A. Clippers	15	67	.183	52	10-31	5-36

Regular Season Statistics

Leading Scorers

	P	FG	FT	Pts	PPG
1 Shaquille O'Neal (LA-L)	79	956	432	2344	29.7
2 Allen Iverson (Phi)	70	729	442	1989	28.4
3 Grant Hill (Detroit)	74	696	478	1904	25.8
4 Vince Carter (Toronto)	82	788	436	2107	25.7
5 Karl Malone (Utah)	82	752	589	2095	25.5
6 Chris Webber (Sacra)	75	748	311	1834	24.5
7 Gary Payton (Seattle)	82	747	311	1982	24.2
8 Jerry Stackhouse (Detroit)	82	619	618	1939	23.6
9 Tim Duncan (San Ant)	74	628	459	1718	23.2
10 Kevin Garnett (Minnesota)	81	759	309	1857	22.9

Rebounds

	P	Off	Def	Total	Ave
1 Dikembe Mutombo (Atl)	82	304	853	1157	14.1
2 Shaquille O'Neal (LA-L)	79	336	742	1078	13.6
3 Tim Duncan (San Antonio)	74	262	656	918	12.4
4 Kevin Garnett (Minnesota)	81	223	733	956	11.8
5 Chris Webber (Sacra)	75	189	598	787	10.5

Field Goal Percentage

	P	FG	Att	FG%
1 Shaquille O'Neal (L.A. Lakers)	79	956	1665	.574
2 Dikembe Mutombo (Atlanta)	82	322	573	.562
3 Alonzo Mourning (Miami)	79	652	1184	.551
4 Ruben Patterson (Seattle)	81	354	661	.536
5 Rasheed Wallace (Portland)	81	542	1045	.519

3-Pt Field Goal Percentage

	P	3FG	Att	%
1 Hubert Davis (Dallas)	79	82	167	.491
2 Jeff Hornacek (Utah)	77	66	.138	.478
3 Matt Bullard (Houston)	56	79	.177	.446
4 Rodney Rogers (Phoenix)	82	115	.262	.439
5 Allan Houston (New York)	82	106	.243	436

Free Throw Percentage

	P	FT	Att	%
1 Jeff Hornacek (Utah)	77	171	180	.950
2 Reggie Miller (Indiana)	81	373	406	.919
3 Darrell Armstrong (Orlando)	82	225	247	.911
4 Terrell Brandon (Minnesota)	71	187	208	.889
5 Ray Allen (Milwaukee)	82	353	398	.887

Assists

	P	Ass	Ave
1 Jason Kidd (Phoenix)	67	678	10.1
2 Sam Cassell (Milwaukee)	81	729	9.0
2 Nick Van Exel (Denver)	79	714	9.0
4 Terrell Brandon (Minnesota)	71	629	8.9
4 Gary Payton (Seattle)	82	732	8.9

Steals

	P	Stl	Ave
1 Eddie Jones (Charlotte)	72	192	2.67
2 Paul Pierce (Boston)	73	152	2.08
3 Darrell Armstrong (Orlando)	82	169	2.06
4 Allen Iverson (Phi)	70	144	2.06
5 Mookie Blaylock (GS)	73	146	2.00

Blocked Shots

	P	Blk	Ave
1 Alonzo Mourning (Miami)	79	294	3.72
2 Dikembe Mutombo (Atlanta)	82	269	3.28
3 Shaquille O'Neal (LA-L)	79	239	3.03
4 Theo Ratliff (Phi)	57	171	3.00
5 Shawn Bradley (Phi)	77	190	2.47

Minutes

	P	MIN	MPG
1 Allen Iverson (Philadelphia)	48	1990	41.5
2 Jason Kidd (Phoenix)	50	2060	41.2
3 Michael Finley (Dallas)	50	2051	41.0
4 Chris Webber (Sacramento)	42	1719	40.9
5 Shareef Abdur-Rahim (Vancouver)	50	2021	40.4

Money Talks
NBA 2000-2001

Individual Salaries

1	Kevin Garnett (Minn)	$19,606,300
2	Shaquille O'Neal (LA-L)	19,285,715
3	Alonzo Mourning (Miami)	16,879,800
4	Juwan Howard (Wash)	16,875,000
5	Hakeem Olajuwon (Houston)	16,700,000
6	Karl Malone, Utah	15,750,000
7	David Robinson (San Antonio)	14,700,000
8	Dikembe Mutombo (Atlanta)	14,442,780
9	Patrick Ewin (Seattle)	14,000,000
10	Scottie Pippen (Portland)	13,750,000

Team Payrolls

1	Portland	$86.5M
2	Miami	$73.8M
3	New York	$73.6M
4	New Jersey	$69.0M
5	Washington	$59.1M
6	L.A. Lakers	$58.8M
7	Milwaukee	$57.3M
8	San Antonio	$57.2M
9	Indiana	$55.2M
10	Utah	$53.5M
11	Phoenix	$53.5M
12	Denver	$51.8M
13	Boston	$51.7M
14	Dallas	$50.9M
15	Seattle	$50.6M
16	Philadelphia	$50.6M
17	Cleveland	$49.4M
18	Houston	$49.3M
19	Vancouver	$48.2M
20	Minnesota	$47.1M
21	Charlotte	$46.5M
22	Sacramento	$46.3M
23	Golden State	$41.8M
24	Detroit	$40.5M
25	Atlanta	$39.2M
26	Toronto	$37.9M
27	Orlando	$37.3M
28	Chicago	$29.7M
29	L.A. Clippers	$29.6M

European Championship 2001
Semi-final Round
In the semi-final round, there are four groups with six teams in each group. England results and Group A standings only below.

Sheffield   Nov 24, 1999
England 60   Switzerland 73

Bratislava Nov 27, 1999
Slovak Rep 73   England 81

Riga Dec 1, 1999
Latvia 90   England 97

Birmingham Feb 23, 2000
England 77   Croatia 81

Budapest Feb 26, 2000
Hungary 96   England 89

Porrentruy Nov 22, 2000
Switzerland 53   England 61

Coventry Nov 25, 2000
England 74   Slovak Rep 62

Coventry Nov 29, 2000
England 69   Latvia 74

Dubrovnik Jan 24, 2001
Croatia 82   England 72

Coventry Jan 27, 2001
England 59   Hungary 52

Group A
Final Standings

Croatia	10	10	0	856	693	20
Latvia	10	6	4	843	774	12
England	10	5	5	739	736	10
Hungary	10	5	5	698	704	10
Switzerland	10	4	6	678	738	8
Slovak Rep	10	0	10	630	799	0

England failed to qualify for the finals tournament in Turkey. However, their third place keeps them in the semi-final round for the 2003 championships.

European Club Competitions
Men
EuroLeague
Final
Thessaloniki Apr 20
Panathinaikos 73   Maccabi Tel Aviv 67

Saporta Cup
Final
Lausanne   Apr 11
AEK Athens 83   Kinder Bologna 76

Korac Cup
Winner: Limoges

Women
EuroLeague
Final
Ruzomborek, Cze   Apr 6
Bourges Basket 64   SCP OT 67

Ronchetti Cup
Winner: Lavezzini Basket

Domestic Results
Men
Dairylea Dunkers League
Northern Conference

		P	W	L	Pts
1	Manchester Giants	36	31	5	62
2	Sheffield Sharks	36	29	7	58
3	Edinburgh Rocks	36	19	17	38
4	Chester Jets	36	17	19	34
5	Derby Storm	36	17	19	34
6	Newcastle Eagles	36	10	26	18
7	Leicester Riders	36	10	26	18

Southern Conference

		P	W	L	Pts
1	London Towers	34	23	11	46
2	Thames Valley Tigers	34	18	16	36
3	Birmingham Bullets	34	17	17	34
4	Milton Keynes Lions	34	15	19	30
5	London Leopards	34	11	23	22
6	Brighton Bears	34	11	23	22

Championship Play-off Final
Wembley May 6
Manchester 74   Birmingham 65

National Basketball League

Division One

		P	W	L	Pts
1	Teeside Mohawks	24	22	2	44
2	Worthing Thunder	24	21	3	42
3	Solent Stars	24	18	6	36
4	Plymouth Raiders	24	16	8	32
5	Sutton Pumas	24	12	12	24
6	Islington White Heat	24	12	12	24
7	Coventry Crusaders	24	11	13	22
8	Taunton Tigers	24	9	15	18
9	Birmingham Bullets	24	8	16	16
10	Westminster Warriors	24	7	17	14
11	Cardiff Clippers	24	7	17	14
12	Oxford Devils	24	7	17	14
13	Mid-Sussex Magic	24	6	18	12

Championship Play-off Final
Teeside 80   Solent 63

Division Two

		P	W	L	Pts
1	Manchester Attitude	24	20	4	40
2	Liverpool	24	18	6	36
3	Kingston Wildcats	24	17	7	34
4	Brixton Topcats	24	17	7	34
5	Reading Rockets	24	17	7	34
6	North London Lords	24	16	8	32
7	Hull Icebergs	24	11	13	22
8	Northampton 89'ers	24	11	13	22
9	Flintshire Flyers	24	10	14	20
10	Portsmouth Pirates	24	7	17	14
11	Wandsworth Hurricanes	24	5	19	10
12	Bournemouth Blitz	24	4	20	8
13	Swindon Sonics	24	3	21	6

Championship Play-off Final
Kingston 68   Manchester 62

Division Three

		P	W	L	Pts
1	Doncaster Eagles	24	23	1	46
2	Mansfield Express	24	20	4	40
3	Ealing Tornadoes	24	19	5	38
4	Ware Fire	24	16	8	32
5	Univ of Birmingham	24	15	9	30
6	Bristol Bombers	24	11	13	22
7	NW London Wolves	24	9	15	18
8	Barking & Dagenham	24	9	15	18
9	Thames Valley Tigers	24	9	15	18
10	Hanley Hornets	24	7	17	14
11	Brighton Cougars	24	7	17	14
12	Croydon Pumas	24	6	18	12
13	Derbyshire Arrows	24	5	19	10

Sainsbury's Classic Cola Cup
Sheffield 89   Manchester 80

Uniball Trophy
London Towers 74   Manchester 73

Women
National Basketball League
Division One

		P	W	L	Pts
1	Sheffield Hatters	22	21	1	42
2	Spelthorne Acers	22	17	5	32
3	Nottingham Wildcats	22	15	7	30
4	Rhondda Rebels	22	15	7	30
5	Thames Valley	22	15	7	30
6	Wandsworth	22	14	8	28
7	Northampton 76'ers	22	11	11	22
8	Ipswich Bobcats	22	9	13	18
9	NW London Amazons	22	6	16	12
10	Birmingham QC	22	4	18	8
11	London Towers	22	3	19	6
12	Plymouth Racers	22	3	19	6

Division One Play-off Final
Sheffield 64   Spelthorne 52

Division Two
Northern Conference

		P	W	L	Pts
1	Stockport Lapwings	20	19	1	38
2	Tyneside	20	13	7	26
3	Doncaster Panthers	20	10	10	20
4	Derby Storm	20	8	12	16
5	Leicester Ladies	20	6	14	12
6	Loughborough Uni	20	4	16	8

Southern Conference

		P	W	L	Pts
1	St Albans Saints	16	13	3	26
2	Cardiff Clippers	16	11	5	22
3	Spelthorne Acers B	16	8	8	16
4	Brighton Magic	16	7	9	14
5	Chelmsford Swifts	16	1	15	2

NW London (0-7) withdrew

Championship Play-off final
St Albans 59   Doncaster 56

Billiards

Strachan World Matchplay Championship

Centurion Hotel, Radstock, Somerset   *Feb 29-Mar 3*

First Round
Ian Williamson ENG bt Andrew Sage ENG 750-259; Manoj Kothari IND bt B Morgan ENG 751-115; Mukesh Rehani IND bt Eugene Hughes IRE 752-418; Bob Close ENG bt Paul Bennett ENG 750-644; Mark Hirst ENG bt Michael Ferreira IND 750-469; Clive Everton ENG bt Brian Dix ENG 751-476

Round 2 onwards

Peter Gilchrist ENG Peter Sheehan ENG	Peter Gilchrist 1001-169	Peter Gilchrist 1250-48	Peter Gilchrist 1250-1014	
Robbie Foldvari AUS Manoj Kothari IND	Robbie Foldvari 1000-809			
Geet Sethi IND Mark Hirst ENG	Geet Sethi 1001-761	Geet Sethi 1252-673		Peter Gilchrist 1500-1200
Nalin Patel IND Devendra Joshi IND	Nalin Patel 1000-611			
David Causier ENG Ian Williamson ENG	David Causier 1001-611	David Causier 1250-766		
Roxton Chapman ENG Bob Close ENG	Roxton Chapman 1000-811		Mike Russell 1251-786	
Chris Shutt ENG Mukesh Rehani IND	Chris Shutt 1000-392	Mike Russell 1252-362		
Clive Everton ENG Mike Russell ENG	Mike Russell 1002-193			

UK Championship

Harrogate Spa Hotel *Nov 23-26, 1999*

First Round

Brian Dix ENG bt Martin Spoormans BEL 454-412; Paul Bennett ENG bt Joe Grech MLT walkover; Rom Surin THA bt Ashok Potikyan ARM 715-215

Second Round

Arun Agrawal IND bt Mark Hirst ENG 479-462; Bob Close ENG bt Brian Dix ENG 586-251; Paul Bennett ENG bt Manoj Kothari IND 688-322; Devendra Joshi IND bt Michael Ferreira IND walkover; Ian Williamson ENG bt Andrew Sage ENG 473-184; Peter Sheehan ENG bt Mark Wildman ENG 1172-255; Rom Surin THA bt Rex Williams ENG 716-226; Ashok Shandilya IND bt Balachandra Bhaskar IND 616-396

Round 3 onwards

Mike Russell ENG Arun Agrawal IND	Mike Russell 1111-293	Mike Russell 676-511		
Peter Gilchrist ENG Bob Close ENG	Peter Gilchrist 783-459		Roxton Chapman 911-751	
Paul Bennett ENG Roxton Chapman ENG	Roxton Chapman 738-337	Roxton Chapman 814-177		
Devendra Joshi IND Robbie Foldvari AUS	Robbie Foldvari 458-328			Roxton Chapman 1382-1277
Ian Williamson ENG David Causier ENG	David Causier 690-391	David Causier 843-586		
Peter Sheehan ENG Nalin Patel IND	Peter Sheehan 758-387		David Causier 1165-990	
Chris Shutt ENG Rom Surin THA	Chris Shutt 712-548	Geet Sethi 885-533		
Geet Sethi IND Ashok Shandilya IND	Geet Sethi 611-562			

Women's World Championship

FINAL

Emma Bonney bt Caroline Walch 218-50 retired

Bobsleigh/Luge

Bobsleigh

World Championships
Altenberg, Germany   Feb 5-13

Two Man

1 Christoph Langen/Markus Zimmermann GER	3:48.66
2 Andre Lange/Rene Hoppe GER	3:48.73
3 Christian Reich/Urs Aeberhard SUI	3:49.47
19 Lee Johnston/Eric Sekwalor GBR	3:54.87
21 Neil Scarisbrick/Justin Dixon GBR	3:57.12

Four Man

1 Germany	3:40.31
Lange/Hoppe/Behrendt/Embach	
2 Germany	3:40.93
Langen/Zimmerman/Platzer/Rühr	
3 Switzerland	3:42.38
Reich/Aeberhard B./Aeberhard U./Keller	
13 Sean Olsson GBR	3:44.04
Olsson/Lewis/Goedluck/Attwood	
19 Lee Johnston GBR	3:46.52
Johnston/Grey/St. Hillaire/Sekwalor	

World Cup
Final Standings (Drivers only)

Two Man

1	Christian Reich SUI	224
2	Reto Götschi SUI	209
3	Marcel Rohner SUI	205
4	Pierre Lueders CAN	199
5	Fabrizio Tosini ITA	154
18	Sean Olsson GBR	96
32	Lee Johnston GBR	28
41	Neil Scarisbrick GBR	8

Four Man

1	Marcel Röhner SUI	224
2	Sandis Prousis LAT	192
3	Pierre Leiders CAN	181
4	Christian Reich SUI	175
5	Christoph Langen GER	168
13	Sean Olsson GBR	125
27	Lee Johnston GBR	44
37	Neil Scarisbrick GBR	11

Overall Standings (two and four-man)

1	Marcel Röhner SUI	429
2	Christian Reich SUI	399
3	Pierre Lueders CAN	380
4	Sandis Prousis LAT	342
5	Bruno Mingeon FRA	307
12	Sean Olsson GBR	221
29	Lee Johnston GBR	72
41	Neil Scarisbrick GBR	19

European Championships
Cortina d'Ampezzo, Italy   Jan 15-16
The European event was part of the World Cup programme, but we have only included the European entrants in the ranking. We have done the same for the European Luge Championships.

Two Man

1 Andre Lange/Rene Hoppe GER	1:46.52
2 Günther Huber/Ubaldo Ranzi ITA	1:46.66
3 Christoph Langen/Markus Zimmermann GER	1:46.73
13 Sean Olsson/Eric Sekwalor GBR	1:47.94
23 Neil Scarisbrick/Wilson St Hilaire GBR	1:49.36

Four Man

1 France	1:44.38
Mingeon/Hostache/Fouquet/Robert	
2 Latvia	1:44.67
Prousis/Rullis/Zacmanis/Ozols	
3 Germany	1:44.75
Langen/Rühr/Platzer/Treffer	
17 Sean Olsson GBR	1:46.65
Olsson/Lewis/Goedluck/Attwood	
19 Neil Scarisbrick GBR	1:47.64
Scarisbrick/Gray/St. Hillaire/Sekwalor	

Women
World Championships
Winterburg   Feb 5

1 Gabi Kohlisch/Kathleen Hering GER	1:58.09
2 Jean Racine/Jennifer Davidson USA	1:58.20
3 Francine Burdet/Katharina Sutter SUI	1:58.39
7 Michelle Coy/Emma Merry GBR	1:58.66
21 Cheryl Done/Paula Wilson GBR	1:59.37

Women's World Cup
Two Woman
Final Standings (Drivers only)

1	Jean Racine USA	149
2	Jill Bakken USA	145
3	Francine Burdet SUI	139
5	Michelle Coy GBR	100
7	Cheyl Done GBR	89

Luge

World Championships
St Moritz, Switzerland   Feb 3-6

Men's Singles

1	Jens Müller GER	2:04.146
2	Armin Zoeggeler ITA	2:04.481
3	Georg Hackl GER	2:04.605
38	Andrew Croucher GBR	2:11.214
40	Mark Hatton GBR	2:27.521

Men's Doubles

1	Leitner/Resch GER	1:54.303
2	Skel/WoellerGER	1:54.703
3	Grimmette/Martin USA	1:54.978

Women's Singles

1	Sylke Otto GER	1:55.128
2	Barbara Niedernhuber GER	1:55.359
3	Sonja Wiedemann GER	1:55.397

Team

1. Germany II 2:56.682; 2. Germany 2:56.523;
3. Austria 2:57.217

World Cup

Men's Singles

1	Armin Zoeggeler ITA	589
2	Jens Müller GER	585
3	Georg Hackl GER	445
41	Mark Hatton GBR	20
46	Andrew Croucher GBR	17

Men's Doubles

1	Leitner/Resch GER	585
2	Skel/WoellerGER	575
3	Grimmette/Martin USA	485

Women's Singles

1	Sylke Otto GER	625
2	Silke Kraushaar GER	570
3	Barbara Niedernhuber GER	490
39	Rachel Keen GBR	32

European Championships
Winterburg, Germany   Jan 10-16

Men's Singles

1	Jens Müller GER	1:50.273
2	Georg Hackl GER	1:50.570
3	Armin Zoeggeler ITA	1:50.613
26	Mark Hatton GBR	1:54.740
30	Andrew Croucher GBR	1:56.382

Men's Doubles

1	Leitner/Resch GER	1:28.478
2	Skel/WoellerGER	1:28.920
3	Schiegl/Schiegl AUT	1:29.019

Women's Singles

1	Sylke Otto GER	1:29.008
2	Silke Kraushaar GER	1:29.499
3	Barbara Niedernhuber GER	1:29.534
23	Rachel Keen GBR	1:34.816
24	Laura James GBR	1:36.177

Team

1	Germany	2:23.705

Skeleton

World Championships
Igls, Austria   Feb 12

Men

1	Gregor Staehli SUI	1:48.23
2	Willi Schneider GER	1:48.41
3	Alex Mueller AUT	1:48.52
10	Kristan Bromley GBR	1:49.43
16	Adrian Collins GBR	1:50.07
20	Steve Anson GBR	1:50.62

Men

1	Steffi Hanzlik GER	1:51.96
2	Alex Hamilton GBR	1:52.76
3	Melissa Hollingsworth CAN	1:52.84
16	Donna Nevens GBR	1:57.93

World Cup
Final Standings

Men

1	Andy Böhme GER	153
2	Chris Soule USA	145
3	Kristan Bromley GBR	144
9	Adrian Collins GBR	97
14	Steve Anson GBR	80
38	Mike Maddock GBR	3

Women

1	Alex Hamilton GBR	113
2	Michelle Kelly CAN	88
	Maya Bieri SUI	88
17	Donna Nevens GBR	14

No doubting who is the best British hope for a Winter Olympic title since Torvill and Dean. Alex Hamilton started favourite for the world championships at Igls, but just missed out to the German Steffi Hanzlik. Hamilton (now Comber) compensated with the World Cup title and though the margins will get tighter as the Games approaches, the RAF officer has real chances.

Bowls

Margaret Johnston would have started favourite for the pairs title at the world championships in Moama, New South Wales, had she been able to convince the Irish selectors that she was the best partner for Phyllis Nolan. Apparently, she couldn't. Winning the title with Nolan at the past three world championships, was not considered evidence enough and Nolan was paired with Barbara Cameron, that partnership finishing an undistinguished ninth in their group.

Johnston was, at least, left with other fish to fry, but three singles defeats had threatened her chancesof reaching the final when she came up against Scotland's Margaret Letham, who was beginning to shape up like a championship favourite. The Scot won their encounter 21-16, and was set fair for the gold medal match, but that wasn't the end of the affair. Johnston filed an appeal, claiming her opponent's bowls did not have the correct bias. "I just queried the bowls out of curiosity. I don't need a medal that much," she said. But the offending bowls were ferried off to the measuring station at Bendigo, in the neighbouring state of Victoria, and the measurers concurred.

Letham suffered the indignity of having the result overturned. It left Johnston having only to win her final match, against the unfancied American Katy Stone, and she was in the final. The Ballymoney bowler managed that comfortably and followed up with a victory over Wales' Rita Jones to take the title. Letham fumed, opting out of her ranking match to leave England's Jean Baker ranked fifth, herself sixth. The Scot had a pairs title as compensation, but that didn't alter the fact that the blue riband had been lost, defeated by a dodgy set of bowls that travelled too straight to be true.

Johnston's victory made it an Irish double, for just a month earlier in South Africa, the 27-year-old Ulsterman, Jeremy Henry, had taken the men's title, beating Israel's Jeff Rabkin 21-13 in the final to become the youngest bowler in the 34-year history of the event to take the singles crown. Henry had already proved his mettle at the highest level winning the pairs title in 1996 at Adelaide, with Sammy Allen, when a mere stripling of 23.

Henry hails from Portrush, no more than a dozen miles north-west of Ballymoney on the Northern Ireland coast, so we can now justifiably call that corner of Ireland the hotbed of world bowls.

On a good day, the USA pairs team of Barry Pickup and Ian Ho would have been struggling for top 10 status in the world championships. However, when lead Pickup was ruled out with high blood pressure and his place was taken by South Africa's Dave Kempthorne, the new pairing won three straight matches and needed only to win the last game to qualify for the bronze-medal match. It was the sight of Pickup, pint in hand, cheering from the stands, that caused the other nations to question whether a South African should be carrying the Americans to a medal. Kempthorne was ruled ineligible, the Americans lost the last match and Pickup went off for another pint - medicinal purposes naturally.

Outdoor, Men

World Championships

Marks Park, Johannesburg   *Apr 1-15*
SINGLES
Semi-finals
Steve Glasson AUS bt Tony Allcock ENG 21-16
Jeremy Henry IRL bt Jeff Rabkin ISR 21-13
Final
Jeremy Henry bt Steve Glasson 21-14.

PAIRS
Semi-finals
George Sneddon/Alex Marshall SCO bt Brett
Duprez/Mark Jacobsen AUS 24-14
Shaun Addinall/Gerry Baker RSA bt Russell Meyer/Paul
Girdler (New Zealand) 22-17
Final
Sneddon/Marshall bt Addinall/Baker 24-14

TRIPLES
Semi-finals
New Zealand (Andrew Curtain/Rowan Brassey/Peter
Belliss) bt Ireland (Martin McHugh/Ian McClure/Gary
McCloy) 16-13
Australia (Adam Jeffery/Steve Glasson/Rex Johnston) bt
Scotland (Robert Marshall/Jim McIntyre/Willie Wood) 20-13
Final
New Zealand bt Australia 23-13

FOURS
Semi-finals
Wales (Mark Williams, Steve Rees, Robert Weale, Will
Thomas) bt New Zealand (Russell Meyer, Paul Girdler,
Rowan Brassey, Peter Belliss) 23-19
South Africa (Bruce Makkink, Shaun Addinall, Bobby
Donnelly, Neil Burkett) bt Scotland (George Sneddon,
Jim McIntyre, Robert Marshall, Willie Wood) 20-8
Final
Wales bt South Africa 21-12

EBA Championships
Worthing   Aug 20-Sep 2
Singles Final
John Ottaway (Wymondham) bt
Andy Wise (Marlow) 21-9

Pairs Final
Paul Barlow/Stephen Farish (Wigton) bt
John Rednall/Clive Webb (Felixstowe) 24-13

Triples Final
Northern Electric (Ging/Birdsey/Lant) bt
Portsmouth CS (Marchant/Bailey/Bishop) 15-12

Fours Final
Norfolk (Ottaway/Harlow/Barr/King) bt
Worcester (Wilde/Parker/Stanley/Burgess) 22-19

Champion of Champions Final
T Humpries (Durham) bt I Wones (Norfolk) 21-19

Middleton Cup Final
Durham 123   Norfolk 117

Home International Series/ British Isles Championships
Rock Park, Llandrindod Wells   July 3-7
HOME INTERNATIONAL
Final Standing
1. Scotland 62pts (+64); 2. Ireland 59pts (+59);
3. England 49pts (+45); 4 Wales 46pts (+5);
5 Channel Islands 4 (-173)

INDIVIDUAL EVENTS
Singles Final
Neil Rees (Wales) bt Barry McKay (Scotland) 21-14
Pairs Final
Peter Jenkins/Malcolm Bishop (Wales) bt
Barrie Fokerd/Paul Broderick (England) 20-16
Triples Final
Penhill, Wales (Davies/Wason/Letman) bt
Ballymoney, Ireland (Smith/McCaw/Milliken) 24-9
Fours Final
Tenby, Wales (Day/Diment/Muskett/Currie) bt
CYM, Ireland (Kelly/Garvey/Farren/Vaughan) 23-17

Outdoor, Women

World Championships
Moama Bowling Club, NSW   Mar 8-25

SINGLES
Final
Margaret Johnston IRL bt Rita Jones WAL 21-14
3rd /4th Place Playoff
Karen Murphy AUS bt Karina Horman JER 21-4

PAIRS
Final
Margaret Letham/Joyce Lindores SCO bt
Arrienne Wynen/Karen Murphy AUS 17-13
3rd/4th Place Play-off
Jean Baker/Mary Price ENG bt
Lalu Kisekol/Maggie Worri PNG 21-17

TRIPLES
Final
New Zealand (Patsy Jorgensen/Sharon Sims/Anne
Lomas) bt England (Kath Hawes/Norma May/Norma
Shaw) 18-10
3rd /4th Place Playoff
Australia (Roma Dunn/Margaret Sumner/Willow Fong) bt
S Africa (Trish Steyn/Hester Bekker/Lorna Trigwell) 28-11

FOURS
Final
New Zealand (Patsy Jorgensen/Jan Khan/Sharon
Sims/Anne Lomas) bt Scotland (Julie Forrest/Betty
Forsyth/Sarah Gourlay/Joyce Lindores) 18-17
3rd /4th Place Playoff
Australia (Roma Dunn/Arrienne Wynen/Margaret Sumner/
Willow Fong) bt Jersey (Liz Cole/Gean O'Neill/Sue Dingle/
Sheila Syvret) 33-10

EWBA Championships
Leamington Aug 9-19
Singles Final
Ann Anderson (Woodlands, Darlington) bt
Janet Green (Dorset) 21-12

Pairs Final
Pauline Morgan/Sue Langdon (Minehead) bt
Mary Taylor/Kay Kerley (Oakley) 19-17

Triples Final
Magdalen Park (Lawrence/Maylin/Duarte) bt
Kingscroft Earl Shilton (Latimer/Fudger/Sutton) 15-8

Fours Final
Baldock (Haywood/Castle/Calver/Page) bt
Oxford (Mainwaring/Storer/Penson/Molyneux) 22-15

Champion of Champions Final
Sue Gurr (Kent) bt
Claire Edmundson (Cumbria) 21-16

Home International Series/ British Isles Championships

Leamington Spa   June 16-19

HOME INTERNATIONAL
Final Standing
1. Wales; 2. England; 3. Scotland; 4. Ireland

INDIVIDUAL EVENTS
Singles Final
Hazel Wilson (Wales) bt Margaret Letham (Scotland) 21-16
Pairs Final
Jean Morris/Jill Edson (England) bt
Maureen Leishman/Vikki Leishman (Scotland) 24-14
Triples Final
Leinster, Ireland (Tormey/McCann/Day) bt
Jersey (Andrews/Syvret/Lowery) 15-14
Fours Final
CYM, Ireland (Culligan/Elliott/McCulloch/Hoey) bt
Clevedon (Sellars/Rowsell/Bisset/Dyer) 26-11

Indoor, Men

World Championships
Hopton-on-sea, Norfolk   Jan 20-23
Quarter-finals
Alex Marshall SCO bt Noel Kennedy HKG 4-7, 7-0, 7-4, 7-3
Robert Weale WAL bt Tony Allcock ENG 7-6, 7-5, 7-4
John Price WAL bt Richard Corsie SCO 7-3, 7-4, 7-2
Les Gillett ENG bt David Gourlay SCO 0-7, 7-2, 4-7, 7-6, 7-6
Semi-finals
Robert Weale bt Alex Marshall 7-3, 0-7, 7-5, 2-7, 7-1
John Price bt Les Gillett 1-7, 7-6, 7-6, 7-4
Final
Robert Weale bt John Price 7-6, 4-7, 7-1, 7-3

World Pairs Championship
Hopton-on-sea, Norfolk   Jan 20-23
Quarter-finals
Steve Rees/John Price WAL bt Graham
Robertson/Richard Corsie SCO 3-7, 7-1, 7-6, 1-7, 7-6
Gary Smith/Andy Thomson ENG bt David Lockhart/David
Holt ENG 7-4, 7-4, 7-1
Hugh Duff/Paul Foster SCO bt Robert Weale/Jason
Greenslade WAL 7-3, 7-6, 6-7, 2-7, 7-4
David Gourlay/Alex Marshall SCO bt Les Gillett/Robert
Newman ENG 0-7, 7-4, 7-5, 1-7, 7-3
Semi-finals
Gary Smith/Andy Thomson bt Steve Rees/John Price
6-7, 7-2, 7-6, 7-4
David Gourlay/Alex Marshall bt Hugh Duff/Paul Foster
7-3, 7-0, 4-7, 7-0
Final
David Gourlay/Alex Marshall bt Gary Smith/Andy
Thomson 4-7, 7-5, 7-6, 6-7, 7-2

BUPA Care Homes International
Sheffield   Nov 12-19
Quarter-finals
David Gourlay SCO bt Paul Foster SCO 4-7, 7-3, 3-7, 7-3, 7-5
Noel Kennedy HKG bt Mark Sandford CAN 7-0, 1-7, 4-7, 7-5, 7-0
Mark Royal ENG bt Richard Corsie SCO 2-7, 7-4, 7-3, 7-4
John Price WAL bt Jason Greenslade WAL 7-3, 7-3, 7-3
Semi-finals
David Gourlay bt Noel Kennedy 7-5, 7-5, 1-7, 7-1
John Price bt Mark Royal 3-7, 7-4, 4-7, 7-6, 7-2
Final
David Gourlay bt John Price 7-2, 7-2, 0-7, 5-7, 7-3

Boxing

H ow beguiling it was; at the end of 2000, Britain could not only lay claim to being home to the best professional heavyweight in the world (well, we use the world home loosely), but the best amateur too. Nobody had regarded Audley Harrison as a serious Olympic contender, unless we count Harrison himself, but for four bouts and 32 minutes in Sydney, he was barely threatened. Having questioned his ability to win the Olympic title, it is possibly not our place to question his ability to win the world professional title, but we will. Harrison is far too nice, for starters. When his opponent goes down, his instinct will be to lean forward and ask if he's okay.

Lennox Lewis is not a natural fighter either, but he is huge and strong and, for the most part, has conquered any of his better instincts. Lewis started and finished the year as undisputed world heavyweight champion and though he did manage to lose a belt along the way, it made no impact on his standing. The WBA crown was the one that went astray, as Lewis demurred from fights against their leading contenders. It was hardly surprising, for the first contender was Henry Akinwande who had once previously shared a ring with Lewis. On that occasion in 1997, after five rounds of leaning, Akinwande was disqualified for not throwing a punch. Not one.

When Akinwande was ruled out through hepatitis, the WBA wheeled out John Ruiz, who would eventually fight Evander Holyfield for the title when Lewis rejected him too. Holyfield would win the title and lose it back (in 2001), but the over-riding question was why a man who owns half of Georgia was still boxing anyway. Does he not want a brain?

The fights Lewis did have were against Michael Grant, Frans Botha and David Tua. Grant was knocked out in the second round, Frans Botha, went in the same round, but 14 seconds, while Tua went the distance, though offering little threat. Yes, Lewis was clearly the top heavyweight around, but this wasn't vintage stuff.

At Tyson was where the Lewis camp was looking, though he hardly looked a worthier contender than Akinwande. In January he demolished the hapless Julius Francis in a fight that just about lasted into the second round at Manchester. In fact Tyson had more trouble getting in the country than he did in beating Francis, a significant lobby wanting the boxer's entry barred because of his rape conviction. Francis was knocked down five times in four minutes by Tyson, which was good news for the Daily Mirror, which had branded the soles of his shoes, but not for Francis. Two months later Francis would lose his British title to Michael Holden, but at least he went the distance that day.

Tyson continued his love affair with the British at Hampden Park in June, where Lou Savarese made Julius Francis look good. Maybe Tyson realised that he'd been sold a pup, for he started looking for a fight elsewhere and tonked the referee instead. Well, that's unfair on Tyson, for once. Tyson also started looking for a fight with his promoter, Frank Warren, something to do with the cost of some jewellery. Frank said everything was fine and we all believed him, but it was evident that the love affair was over. Thank God.

Tyson's next bout was in another country and against Andrew Golota. Thirty-five times in his 39-fight career, Golota has been competitive. However when he steps up to the highest level, his mind has let him down. He lost twice to Riddick Bowe, disqualified on both occasions, was dispatched in the first round by Lennox Lewis and in October came the Tyson bout in Michigan. After two competitive rounds of boxing, Golota quit. Apparently he had given up in the face of calls from his trainer Al Certo to think of the people of Poland. Golota has a stammer from his childhood and is known to have anxiety attacks. He was branded a coward, but after complaining of dizziness he was admitted to hospital and discovered to have injured vertebrae which doctors said could have led to paralysis. Whether or not this had anything to do with his decision to quit is not known but Golota's family subsequently received death threats, many refusing to give credence to the diagnosis.

Away from the heavyweight division, there was mixed success for British boxers at world level. Naseem Hamed remained undefeated, although ended the year with no world title. Having beaten Vuyani Bungu and Augie Sanchez, he too lost his crown - this time a WBO one - after failing to fight the No1 challenger Istvan Kovacs.

Joe Calzaghe and Johnny Nelson held on to their WBO belts at super-middleweight and cruiserweight respectively, but the world of boxing rates the WBO titles as only fourth in the pecking order and most US lists do not even bother to include them any more. Unfortunately, British fighters in the other three lists fared badly. Glenn Catley lost the WBC version of the super-middleweight crown that he had won in May in his first defence, against the South African Dingaan Thobela. World title challenges by Michael Brodie, Junior Witter, Micky Cantwell and Robert McCracken all failed.

The sorriest tale, though, concerns Paul Ingle, the IBF featherweight champion who defeated Junior Jones in April but lost the title to Mbulelo Botile in December. After the Botile fight, Ingle went into a coma, apparently induced by the doctors to protect the brain. As we write he's progressing well.

A Late Developer

Short of super-middleweights for their ranking list, the World Boxing Organisation, the governing body most favoured by British boxers, found an imaginative way around the problem. They ranked a dead boxer. In October, Darrin Morris, died of HIV-related meningitis. Athough he had not fought for a year prior to his death, the WBO still rated him the seventh best super-middleweight in the world. Three months after his death, he was elevated to number five in their rankings, though with a caveat alongside his name that read "period of inactivity". Only when it was pointed out to Francisco Valcarel, the WBO president, that the period of inactivity stemmed from the fact that Morris was dead, was his name removed from the list. "It is regrettable," said a thoughtful Valcarel.

Of course, had it not been brought to the president's attention, at a similar rate of progress over the next 12 months, Morris would have reached the number one slot, thereby achieving in death an eminence that was some way beyond him in life.

Professional World Title Fights

Results are given for world title fights sanctioned by the WBA, IBF, and WBC , in that order. Where the WBA, IBF and WBC titles are held by a single boxer, that is considered an undisputed crown.
Interim title fights are not listed.

HEAVYWEIGHT

WBA/IBF/WBC
New York   Apr 29
Lennox Lewis GBR bt
Michael Grant USA
ko, round 2

London   July 15
Lennox Lewis GBR bt
Frans Botha RSA
tko, round 2

IBF/WBC
Las Vegas   Nov 11
Lennox Lewis GBR bt
David Tua SAM
unanimous pts

WBA
Las Vegas   Aug 12
Evander Holyfield USA bt
John Ruiz USA
unanimous pts

CRUISERWEIGHT

WBA
Paris   Apr 8
Fabrice Tiozzo FRA bt
Valery Vikhor LAT
ko, round 6

Lyon   Dec 9
Virgil Hill USA bt
Fabrice Tiozzo FRA
tko, round 1

IBF
Boise, Idaho   Feb 12
Vassily Jirov USA bt
Saul Montana USA
tko, round 9

WBC
Neuss, Germany   May 6
Juan Carlos Gomez CUB bt
Imamu Mayfield USA
ko, round 3

Essen, Germany   May 6
Juan Carlos Gomez CUB bt
Jorge Castro ARG
ko, round 10

LIGHT-HEAVYWEIGHT

WBA/WBC/IBF
New York   Jan 15
Roy Jones USA bt
David Telesco USA
unanimous pts

Indianapolis   May 13
Roy Jones USA bt
Richard Hall USA
tko, round 11

New Orleans   Sep 9
Roy Jones USA bt
Eric Harding USA
tko, round 11

SUPER-MIDDLEWEIGHT

WBA
Paris   Apr 8
Bruno Girard FRA bt
Byron Mitchell USA
unanimous pts

Chateauroux, France   Sep 16
Bruno Girard FRA bt
Manuel Siaca PUR
majority pts

IBF
Magdeburg   Mar 11
Sven Ottke GER bt
Lloyd Bryan USA
unanimous pts

Karlsruhe   June 3
Sven Ottke GER bt
Tocker Pudwill USA
unanimous pts

Magdeburg   Sep 2
Sven Ottke GER bt
Charles Brewer USA
majority pts

Karlsruhe   June 3
Sven Ottke GER bt
Silvio Branco ITA
unanimous pts

WBC
Riesa, Germany   Jan 29
Marcus Beyer GER bt
Leif Keiski USA
ko, round 7

Frankfurt   May 6
Glenn Catley GBR bt
Markus Beyer GER
ko, round 12

South Africa   Sep 1
Dingaan Thobela RSA bt
Glenn Catley GBR
tko, round 12

MIDDLEWEIGHT

WBA
Tunica, Miss   May 20
William Joppy USA bt
Rito Ruvalcaba MEX
tko, round 1

Las Vegas   Sep 16
William Joppy USA bt
Hacine Cherifi FRA
unanimous pts

Las Vegas   Dec 2
William Joppy USA bt
Jonathan Reid USA
tko, round 4

IBF
Washington DC   Feb 6
Bernard Hopkins USA bt
Syd Vanderpoole CAN
unanimous pts

Las Vegas   Dec 1
Bernard Hopkins USA
Antwun Echols USA
tko, round 10

WBC
London   Apr 29
Keith Holmes USA bt
Robert McCracken GBR
tko, round 11

SUPER-WELTERWEIGHT

WBA
Atlantic City   Mar 3
Felix Trinidad PUR bt
David Reid USA
unanimous pts

Las Vegas   July 22
Felix Trinidad PUR bt
Mamadou Thiam FRA
tko, round 3

WBA/IBF
Las Vegas   Dec 2
Felix Trinidad PUR bt
Fernando Vargas USA
tko, round 12

WBC
Madrid   July 21
Javier Castillejo ESP bt
Tony Marshall USA
unanimous pts

Mexico City   Oct 21
Javier Castillejo ESP bt
Javier Martinez ESP
tko, round 4

WELTERWEIGHT

IBF
Las Vegas   Aug 26
Vernon Forrest USA and
Raul Frank USA no contest
clash of heads, round 3

WBC
Las Vegas   June 17
Shane Mosley USA bt
Oscar De La Hoya USA
majority pts

New York   Nov 4
Shane Mosley USA bt
Antonio Diaz USA
tko, round 6

SUPER-LIGHTWEIGHT

WBA
Las Vegas   Sep 16
Sharmba Mitchell USA bt
Felix Flores PUR
unanimous pts

IBF
Uncasville, Conn   Feb 12
Zab Judah USA bt
Jan Bergman RSA
ko, round 4

Glasgow   June 24
Zab Judah USA bt
Junior Witter GBR
unanimous pts

Uncasville, Conn   Aug 5
Zab Judah USA bt
Terron Millett USA
tko, round 4

Detroit   Oct 20
Zab Judah USA bt
Hector Quiroz MEX
tko, round 8

WBC
Uncasville, Conn   Feb 12
Kostya Tszyu AUS bt
Ahmed Santos MEX
ko, round 8

Phoenix, Arizona   July 22
Kostya Tszyu AUS bt
Julio Cesar Chavez MEX
tko, round 6

LIGHTWEIGHT

WBA
Tokyo   Mar 12
Gilbert Serrano VEN
Hiroyuki Sakamoto JPN
tko, round 5

Tokyo   June 11
Takanori Hatekeyama JPN bt
Gilbert Serrano VEN
tko, round 8

Yokohama   Oct 11
Takanori Hatekeyama JPN bt
Hiroyuki Sakamoto JPN
ko, round 10

IBF
Pittsburgh   May 6
Paul Spadafora USA bt
Mike Griffith USA
tko, round 10

Pittsburgh   May 6
Paul Spadafora USA bt
Billy Irwin CAN
unanimous pts

WBC
Bell Gardens, California June 17
Jose Luis Castillo MEX bt
Steve Johnston USA
majority pts

Denver   Sep 19
Jose Luis Castillo MEX bt
Steve Johnston USA
majority pts

SUPER-FEATHERWEIGHT

WBA
South Korea   Jan 30
Jong Kwon-baek KOR drew with
Choi Kyu-chul KOR
majority draw
Kwon-baek retained title

Kansas City   May 21
Joel Casamayor USA bt
Jong Kwon-baek KOR
tko, round 5

Las Vegas   Sep 16
Joel Casamayor USA bt
Radford Beasley USA
tko, round 5

IBF
Las Vegas   Mar 18
Diego Corrales USA bt
Derrick Gainer USA
tko, round 3

El Paso   Sep 2
Diego Corrales USA bt
Angel Manfredy USA
ko, round 3

Miami   Dec 3
Steve Forbes USA bt
John Brown USA
tko, round 8

WBC
Las Vegas   Mar 18
Floyd Mayweather USA bt
Gregorio Goyo Vargas MEX
unanimous pts

FEATHERWEIGHT

WBA
Nagoya   Jan 30
Freddie Norwood USA bt
Takashi Koshimoto JPN
ko, round 9

Argentina   May 25
Freddie Norwood USA bt
Pablo Chacon ARG
unanimous pts

New Orleans   Sep 9
Derrick Gainer USA bt
Freddie Norwood USA
ko, round 11

IBF
New York   Apr 29
Paul Ingle GBR bt
Junior Jones USA
tko, round 11

Manchester   Dec 16
Mbutelo Botile RSA bt
Paul Ingle GBR
ko, round 12

WBC
Merida, Mexico   Apr 14
Guty Espadas MEX bt
Luisito Espinosa PHI
tko, round 11

Merida, Mexico   June 23
Guty Espadas MEX bt
Wethya Sakmuangklang THA
unanimous pts

SUPER-BANTAMWEIGHT

WBA
Las Vegas   Mar 4
Clarence Adams USA bt
Nestor Garza MEX
unanimous pts

Madison, Wisconsin   Aug 5
Clarence Adams USA bt
Adres Fernandez
tko, round 6

IBF
Bristol   Apr 7
Lehlohonolo Ledwaba RSA bt
Ernesto Grey COL
ko, round 8

Kent   Oct 7
Lehlohonolo Ledwaba RSA bt
Eduardo Alvarez ARG
ko, round 8

WBC
Las Vegas   Feb 19
Erik Morales MEX bt
Marco Antonio Barrera MEX
unanimous pts

Las Vegas   Sept 9
Willie Jorin USA bt
Michael Brodie GBR
majority pts

BANTAMWEIGHT
WBA
Las Vegas   Mar 4
Paulie Ayala USA bt
Johnny Bredahl DEN
majority pts
IBF
Las Vegas   Aug 11
Tim Austin USA bt
Arthur Johnson USA
unanimous pts
WBC
Thailand   Mar 11
Veeraphol Sahaprom THA bt
Adan Vargas MEX
unanimous pts
Takasago, Japan   June 25
Veeraphol Sahaprom THA bt
Toshiaki Nishioka JPN
unanimous pts
Bangkok   Dec 5
Veeraphol Sahaprom THA bt
Oscar Arciniega MEX
tko, round 5

SUPER-FLYWEIGHT
WBA
Nagoya   Apr 23
Hideki Todaka JPN bt
Yokthai Sith Oar THA
tko, round 11
Nagoya   Oct 11
Leo Gamez VEN
Hideki Todaka JPN
ko, round 7
IBF
Tunica, Miss   May 20
Julio Gamboa NCA drew with
Felix Machado VEN
Title remains vacant
Miami   July 22
Felix Machado VEN bt
Julio Gamboa NCA
unanimous pts
Maracay, Venezuela   Dec 16
Felix Machado VEN bt
William de Souza COL
tko, round 3
WBC
Seoul   Jan 2
Cho In-Joo KOR bt
Gerry Penalosa JPN
majority pts
South Korea   May 14
Cho In-Joo KOR bt
Julio Cesar Avila MEX
unanimous pts
Osaka   Aug 27
Masanori Tokuyama JPN bt
Cho In-Joo KOR
unanimous pts

Osaka   Dec 12
Masanori Tokuyama bt
Akihiko Nago JPN
unanimous pts

FLYWEIGHT
WBA
Bangkok   Apr 8
Sornpichai Kratchingdaeng THA
bt Gilberto Gonzalez VEN
tko, round 5
Madison, Wisconsin   Aug 5
Eric Morel PUR bt
Sornpichai Kratchingdaeng THA
unaminous pts
Las Vegas   Oct 9
Eric Morel PUR bt
Alberto Ontiveros
unanimous pts
IBF
El Paso, Texas   Jan 14
Irene Pacheco COL bt
Pedro Pena USA
tko, round 11
Las Vegas   Jan 14
Irene Pacheco COL bt
Masibulele Makepula RSA
majority pts
WBC
Thailand   Feb 25
Medgoen Singsurat THA bt
Masaki Kawabat JPN
unanimous pts
Udonthani, Thailand   May 19
Malcolm Tunacao PHI bt
Medgoen Singsurat THA
tko, round 7
Tokyo   Aug 20
Malcolm Tunacao PHI drew with
Celes Kobayoashi JPN
majority draw

JUNIOR-FLYWEIGHT
WBA
Las Vegas   Aug 12
Beibis Mendoza COL bt
Rosenda Alvarez NCA
dsq, round 6
IBF
Las Vegas   Dec 2
Ricardo Lopez MEX bt
Ratanapol Vorapin THA
tko, round 3
WBC
Seoul   June 17
Choi Yo-sam KOR bt
Chart Kiatpetch THA
ko, round 5

STRAW-WEIGHT
WBA
Tokyo   Aug 20
Joma Gamboa PHI bt
Noel Arambulet VEN
majority pts
Yokohama   Dec 6
Keitaro Hoshino JPN bt
Joma Gamboa PHI
unanimous pts
IBF
Kent   Jun 2
Zolani Lepetelo RSA bt
Micky Cantwell GBR
tko, round 8
Peterborough   Dec 3
Zolani Lepetelo RSA bt
Ernesto Rubillar PUR
pts, 12 rounds
WBC
Thailand   Feb 11
Jose Antonio Aguirre MEX bt
Wandee Charoen THA
majority pts
Tabasco, Mexico   July 7
Jose Antonio Aguirre MEX bt
Jose Luis Zepeda
tko, round 5
Mexico City   Oct 21
Jose Antonio Aguirre MEX bt
Erdene Chuluun
tko, round 4

> **"You need more than a left hook and a haircut to beat me"**
> Lennox Lewis, about the Samoan David Tua.
>
> **"I want your heart. I want to eat your children"**
> Mike Tyson, the comment directed at Lennox Lewis. It was either a witty reference to 'Silence of the Lambs' or Tyson is barking mad. Tricky choice, ay?

Amateur Boxing

European Championships

Tampere, Finland   May 13-20

Light Flyweight (-48kg)

1	Valeri Sidorenko	UKR
2	Sergei Kazakov	RUS
3	Pal Lakatos	HUN

Flyweight (-51kg)

1	Vladimir Sidorenko	UKR
2	Bogdan Dobrescu	ROM
3	Sevdelin Hristov	BUL

Bantamweight (-54kg)

1	Agasi Agagüloglu	TUR
2	Raimkul Malakhbekov	RUS
3	György Fargas	HUN

Featherweight (-57kg)

1	Ramazan Paliani	TUR
2	Boris Georgiev	BUL
3	Falk Huste	GER

David Mulholland ENG elim 1st round

Lightweight (-60kg)

1	Alex Maletin	RUS
2	Filip Palic	CRO
3	Selim Paliani	TUR

Light Welterweight (-63.5kg)

1	Alex Leonev	RUS
2	Dimitar Chtilianov	BUL
3	Nurhan Suleymanoglu	TUR

Welterweight (-67 kg)

1	Bülent Ülüsoy	TUR
2	Valeri Brazhink	UKR
3	Darius Jaseiavicius	LTU

Light Middleweight (-71kg)

1	Adnan Katic	GER
2	Andrei Mishin	RUS
3	Nikola Sjekloca	YUG

Stephen McGuire SCO elim 1st round

Middleweight (-75kg)

1	Zsolt Erdei	HUN
2	Stjepan Bozik	CRO
3	Juha Ruokola	FIN
6	Carl Froch	ENG

Light Heavyweight (-81kg)

1	Alex Lebziak	RUS
2	Claudio Rasco	ROM
3	Milorad Gajovic	YUG

Heavyweight (-91kg)

1	Jackson Chanet	FRA
2	Zultan Ipraghimov	RUS
3	Emil Garai	HUN

Kevin Evans WAL elim 1st round

Super Heavyweight (+91kg)

1	Alexei Lezin	RUS
2	Paolo Vidoz	ITA
3	Cengik Koc	GER

Ian Millarvie SCO elim 1st roun

ABA Champions

Super-heavyweight (+ 91kg) - John McDermott
Heavyweight (-91kg) - David Dolan
Cruiserweight (-86kg) - James Dolan
Light-heavyweight (-81kg) - Peter Haymer
Middleweight (-75kg) - Stephen Swales
Light-middleweight (-71kg) - Chris Bessey
Welterweight (-67kg) - Francis Doherty

Light-welterweight (-63.5kg) - Nigel Wright
Lightweight (-60kg) - Andrew McLean
Featherweight (-57kg) - Henry Castle
Bantamweight (-54kg) - Steve Foster
Flyweight (-51kg) - Dale Robinson
Light-flyweight (-48kg) - James Mulhearn

Canoeing

Strange dealings in canoeing in the Olympic year. In April Paul Ratcliffe was polishing up his technique on the Olympic course at Penrith when he was summoned home to take part in the Olympic trials at Nottingham. This despite the fact that Ratcliffe had been preselected for the K1 slalom class on an 80% vote of support from the officers of the British Canoe Union. The late objections came from the British canoeists who had not been pre-selected. None of them had come close to Ratcliffe's record; none of them had won one World Cup title, let alone three; none of them had won two European titles or finished third in successive world championships; none of them..., well, need we go on? Prompted by the Athletes' Union, who put themselves in the strange position of acting for athletes against an athlete, legal action was threatened and Ratcliffe was recalled from Australia. "It doesn't make a mockery of the pre-selection decision," said John Anderson, the BCU performance director, in a statement which defied logic.

The trials duly saw Ratcliffe reselected, but the selection controversies continued elsewhere. Rachel Crosbee has regularly been the top-placed Briton in international events over the past few seasons. If she has ever been beaten by a Brit, it has been by Heather Corrie. Neither, though, found a way into the Olympic team, the place going to Laura Blakeman who, predictably, struggled in Sydney. Anna Hemmings ahead of Tricia Davey was also an unlikely selection for the women's sprint team, the Shepperton paddler having made her mark in marathons. Hemmings, like Blakeman, was found wanting in Sydney.

We should, though, dwell a little on the athletes in Sydney who were not found wanting. Paul Ratcliffe didn't win gold (no British canoeist ever has) and his challenge wasn't helped by going fishing at the end of the first run. Had Ratcliffe crossed the line with his head underwater that would have been it - instant disqualification - but he got his head up and his confidence back for the second run and while he never got within range of the German Thomas Schmidt, no one else did either. Silver equals Britain's best, Gareth Marriott having won that medal in the C1 class at Barcelona.

Stuart Bowman and Nick Smith could not quite manage to step on the podium after Ratcliffe, but came frustratingly close in the C2 class, missing the bronze medal by less than half a second. Another medal did come, but British fans had to wait over a week for it. No Briton has ever finished higher than fifth in the sprint events, and two of the three times that happened came in Los Angeles in 1984 when most of the best paddlers in the world stayed at home. Tim Brabants, who studies medicine at Nottingham University in a normal year, had scraps of form that suggested he could get into the argument in Sydney. The 23-year-old from Walton-on-Thames was fourth at a World Cup event in Hazewinkel, Belgium in May and sixth at the European Championships at Poznan, Poland in July. For Brabants to win a medal, he clearly had to raise his game at Penrith and he did just that. On the same lake that the British rowers relished, Brabants came like a storm at the end of the 1000m race to snatch third place. There was even a suggestion that the Bulgarian Petar Merkov might lose the silver medal, but that came to nothing. Still, third's not bad, is it?

Sprint

European Championships

Poznan, Poland   *July 6-9*

Men

K1 200
1 Alvydas Duonela LTU   36.967
2 Alexei Slivinskiy UKR   36.991
3 Jaime Acuna Iglesias ESP 36.999
Ian Wynne GBR elim semi-final

K1 500
1 Akos Vereckei HUN   1:37.944
2 Mickael Kolganov ISR   1:38.400
3 Petar Merkov BUL   1:39.144

K1 1000
1 Mickael Kolganov ISR   3:36.502
2 Petar Merkov BUL   3:36.682
3 Lutz Liwowski GER   3:37.876
6 Tim Brabants GBR   3:42.034

K2 200
1 Zaichenkov/Luchnik UKR   33.722
2 Rauhe/Wieskoetter GER   33.975
3 Kuzel/Chorvath SVK   33.942
Tingay/Bourne GBR elim semi/final

K2 500
1 Rauhe/Wieskoetter GER1:29.859
2 Zaruba/Holubar CZE   1:30.117
3 Fejervari/Bee HUN   1:31.269
Sabberton/Darby-Dowman GBR elim semi-final

K2 1000
1 Fjeldheim/Larsen NOR   3:18.299
2 Bartafi/Vereb HUN   3:19.199
3 Salakhov/Gorobi RUS   3:19.349
6 Sabberton/D-Dowman   3:20.843

K4 200
1 Slovakia   31.818
2 Ukraine   31.974
3 Hungary   32.106

K4 500
1 Germany   1:21.513
2 Slovakia   1:21.945
3 Russia   1:22.203

K4 1000
1 Germany   2:58.890
2 Hungary   3:00.498
3 Bulgaria   3:00.846

C1 200
1 Dmitro Sablin UKR   41.596
2 Andreas Dittmer GER   41.724
3 Martin Doktor CZE   41.744

C1 500
1 Maxim Opalev RUS   1:49.107
2 Andreas Dittmer GER   1:49.147
3 Nikolay Bouhalov BUL   1:50.517

C1 1000
1 Martin Doktor CZE   4:02.227
2 Andreas Dittmer GER   4:03.067
3 Maxim Opalev RUS   4:06.637

C2 200
1 Jedraszko/Baraszkiewicz POL
   38.533
2 Prochazka /Brecka CZE   38.737
3 Fomitchev/Artemida RUS   38.985
Crowther/Crowther GBR elim semi-final

C2 500
1 Jedraszko/Baraszkiewicz1:42.309
2 Anisim/Averian ROM   1:42.687
3 Kovalev/Kostoglod RUS 1:43.941
Andrew Train/Stephen Train GBR elim heats

C2 1000
1 Baraszkiewicz/Gajownik POL
3:43.665
2 Anisim/Averian ROM   3:43.815
3 Kovalev/Kostoglod RUS 3:43.869
6 Train/Train GBR   3:47.319

C4 200
1 Czech Republic   35.515
2 Hungary   35.727
3 Ukraine   35.951

C4 500
1 Russia   1:33.090
2 Romania   1:33.648
3 Hungary   1:33.696
GBR Train/Train/Crowther/Crowther elim semi-final

C4 1000
1 Hungary   3:22.784
2 Romania   3:23.954
3 Czech Republic   3:34.338

Women

K1 200
1 Rita Koban HUN   42.624
2 Josefa Idem ITA   42.676
3 Elzbieta Urbanczyk POL   42.824
Rebecca Train GBR elim semi-final

K1 500
1 Rita Koban HUN   1:51.584
2 Katrin Wagner GER   1:52.824
3 Elzbieta Urbanczuk POL 1:54.094
7 Anna Hemmings GBR   1:55.904

K1 1000
1 Josefa Idem ITA   4:04.210
2 Kinga Bota HUN   4:04.744
3 Manuela Mucke GER   4:06.778

K2 200
1 Pastuszka/Sokolowska POL
39.306
2 Fischer/Kieseler GER   40.854
3 Manchon/Sanchez ESP   41.210
4 Rebecca Train/Rachel Train GBR
   41.534

K2 500
1 Pastuszka/Sokolowska POL
1:40.150
2 Kovacs/Bota HUN   1:40.348
3 Fischer/Kieseller GER   1:42.616
Train/Train GBR elim semi-final

K2 1000
1 Fischer/Kieseller GER   3:44.434
2 Szadovski/Viski HUN   3:48.058
3 Pastuszka/Sokolowska POL
3:48.358

K4 200
1 Hungary   35.768
2 Germany   36.588
3 Spain   36.816

K4 500
1 Germany   1:31.755
2 Hungary   1:31.895
3 Spain   1:34.899

World Cup

Final Standings

K1/K2 Men
1 Alvydas Duonela LTU   168
2 Knut Holmann NOR   98
3 Bartosz Wolski USA   67

C1/C2 Men
1 Martin Doktor CZE   224
2 Andreas Dittmar GER   80
3 Zhomart Satubaldin KAZ   80

K1/K2 Women
1 Katrin Borchert AUS   120
2 Ruth Nortje NOR   110
3 Josefa Idem ITA   108

Slalom

European Championships

Mezzana, Italy   Jun 23-25

Men
K1
1	Pierpaolo Ferrazzi ITA	216.13
2	Thomas Becker GER	216.44
3	Laurent Burtz FRA	217.09
10	Anthony Brown GBR	219.88
11	Campbell Walsh GBR	220.63
14	Tim Morrison GBR	222.78
15	Ian Raspin GBR	223.29

C1
1	Tony Estanguet FRA	226.90
2	Juraj Mincik SVK	227.47
3	Lukas Pollert CZE	228.07
15	Stuart McIntosh GBR	238.32

C2
1	Hochschorner/Hochschorner SVK	233.96
2	Disson/Forgues FRA	235.39
3	Kolomanski/Staniszewski CZE	235.85
9	Bowman/Smith GBR	241.57

Women
K1
1	Stepanka Hilgertova CZE	236.83
2	Brigitte Guibal FRA	237.65
3	Irene Pavelkova CZE	238.93
9	Heather Corrie GBR	244.32
12	Rachel Crosbee GBR	247.66
13	Laura Blakeman GBR	249.66

World Cup
Final Standings

K1 Men
1	Paul Ratcliffe GBR	76
2	Scott Shipley USA	67
3	Pierpaolo Ferrazzi ITA	67
12	Ian Raspin GBR	34
14	Tim Morrison GBR	17

C1 Men
1	Michal Martikan SVK	85
2	Juraj Mincik SVK	80
3	Patrice Estanguet FRA	70
4	Stuart McIntosh GBR	54

C2 Men
1	Pavol/Peter HochschornerSVK	85
2	Kolomanski/Staneszewski POL	85
3	Jiras/Mader CZE	58
9	Smith/Bowman GBR	46

K1 Women
1	Elena Kaliska SVK	80
2	Mandy Planert GER	80
3	Susanne Hirt GER	60
9	Heather Corrie GBR	33

Placing in last round determines final placing in event of a tie

Marathon

World Championships
Dartmouth, Canada   Sept 2-3

Men
K-1
1	Manuel Busto ESP	2:22:30
2	Istvan Salga HUN	2:22:32
3	Michael Leverett AUS	2:22:32
5	Conor Holmes GBR	2:23:16
6	Ivan Lawler GBR	2:23:17

K-2
1	Guerrero/Alonso ESP	2:12:44
2	Martinez/Quevedo ESP	2:12:45
3	Pinto/Gomes POR	2:12:46

C-1
1	Carsten Scales DEN	2:40:19
2	Pavel Bednar CZE	2:40:19
3	Pal Petervari HUN	2:40:37
11	James Lee GBR	2:53:38

C-2
1	Csabai/Gyore HUN	2:31:07
2	Dalton/Scarola CAN	2:31:11
3	Clauss/Kubicek GER	2:32:08

Women
K1
1	Maria Santos ESP	2:34:20
2	Kornelia Szonda HUN	2:34:22
3	Chantal Meek AUS	2:34:22
7	Abigail Cattle GBR	2:43:47
10	Yael Ford GBR	2:47:44

K2
1	Csay/Pitz HUN	2:25:27
2	Szonda/Javorszky DEN	2:26:07
3	Barford/Knudsen DEN	2:26:08
6	Dallaway/Gilby GBR	2:36:13
9	Hardy/Campbell GBR	2:44:47

Wildwater

World Championships
Treignac, France   June 1-4

Men
K1
1	Thomas Koelmann GER	16:25.49
2	Florian Wohlers GER	16:26.80
3	Robert Pontarollo ITA	16:28.73
22	Ian Tordoff GBR	17:10.53
32	Peter Keron GBR	17:29.00
34	Michael Mason GBR	17:31.68

K1 Team
1	Czech Republic	16:44.40
2	Germany	16:48.30
3	France	16:48.79
9	Great Britain	17:31.25
	(Tordoff/Keron/Mason)	

C1
1	Vladi Panato ITA	17:58.93
2	Stephane Santamaria FRA	18:11.41
3	Mirko Spelli ITA	18:14.50
17	Robert Pumphrey GBR	18:55.28
25	Andrew Reeves GBR	20:46.89
26	David Bradburn GBR	20:59.18
27	Paul Anderson GBR	21:10.63

C1 Team
1	Croatia	18:32.12
2	France	18:37.60
3	Slovenia	18:51.36
6	Great Britain	21:16.95
	(Pumphrey/Reeves/Bradburn)	

C2
1	Vala/Slucik SVK	17:21.58
2	Sutek/Grega SVK	17:34.22
3	Aymard/Pigeron FRA	17:34.71
16	Belbin/Caunt GBR	18:47.90
17	Lee/Pearton GBR	18:55.88
19	Terry/Gordon Walling	19:90.58

C2 Team
1	Slovakia	18:15.07
2	Germany	18:15.87
3	France	18:31.18
4	Great Britain	
	(Belbin/Caunt - Lee/Pearton - Walling/Walling)	

Women
K1
1	Michaela Strnadova CZE	17:42.63
2	Magali Thiebault FRA	17:43.10
3	Anne Crochet FRA	17:51.78
17	Cynthia Berry GBR	18:45.10
18	Tina Parsons GBR	18:52.32
22	Elizabeth Holmes GBR	19:18.93
DNF	Yael Ford GBR	

K1 Team
1	France	18:14.50
2	Germany	18:33.74
3	Slovenia	18:40.44
5	Great Britain	19:30.38
	(Berry/Parsons/Ford)	

Cricket

Eighteen months ago, the England fans were chanting "We've got the worst team in the world" as England slumped to defeat in a home series against New Zealand. Four series victories later and the fans can confidently sing from a different song-sheet. "We've got the third, maybe the fourth best team in the world," or something like that. We wouldn't get more excited than that - yet.

Duncan Fletcher and Nasser Hussain is the axis around which the new England team revolves. The bulk of the team, Atherton, Stewart, Thorpe, Caddick, Gough and Hussain himself have been around for years, which suggests that it was not lack of ability which took England down to the depths of the international game.

While New Zealand series was surely the darkest hour, England still had to negotiate a series in South Africa before things turned around. It was Fletcher's first assignment, but that's not what the series became famous for. England struggled in the first Test, losing by an innings after having had four wickets fall for two runs - and lost the fourth Test by an inning too, which settled the series. However, the final Test at Centurion Park is the one that posterity will be interested in. In a rain-affected game, Hansie Cronje came to an agreement with Hussain that each team should forfeit an innings in a bid to arrive at a result.

It ws three months later in April that news broke from India of match-fixing allegations relating to a one-day series there. Hansie Cronje, as well as other South African players, Nicky Boje, Pieter Strydom and Herschelle Gibbs, were implicated. For a while there was nothing but denial. Eventually, though, the truth emerged. Cronje was first sacked as captain, after he admitted to accepting $10-15,000 from bookmakers for providing information on the triangular series between England, Zimbabwe and South Africa in January 2000. Cronje continued to deny match-fixing, but the damage was done.

In the evidence he gave to the King Commission in June, Cronje denied that any South African matches were fixed, but admitted to receiving $100,000 from bookmakers in his time as captain. For the final Test against England at Centurion, he admitted accepting $5,000 for producing a result, though Hussein was not implicated. Cronje's evidence led to Henry Williams and Gibbs being banned from the South African team after accepting money to perform badly in one-day internationals. The ex-captain also pointed the finger at the former captains of Pakistan and India, Salim Malik and Mohammad Azharuddin. Both players would later be banned for life by their respective cricket boards. Cronje further admitted that he had put a $200,000 offer to his players to throw a 1996 one-day international against India. The offer was rejected, and Cronje continued to argue that he had never actually thrown a match, though by this stage his credibility was about nil.

Cronje's cricket career was over, though he still had the gall to appeal over his lifetime ban. Cricket was horribly tarnished. Once you know that corruption exists, it becomes almost impossible to contain the suspicions. The India enquiry even mentioned Alec Stewart in its despatches. The ECB dealt with that in a perfunctory fashion. Our Alec, never, they said.

PricewaterhouseCoopers Ratings

As at December 30th 2000

Batsmen

	Player	Team	Pts	Ave
1	Sachin Tendulkar	Ind	875	57.28
2	Steve Waugh	Aus	856	50.77
3	Andy Flower	Zim	831	51.05
4	Inzamam-ul-Haq	Pak	801	46.22
5	Ricky Ponting	Aus	769	46.34
6	Saeed Anwar	Pak	767	46.30
7	Brian Lara	WI	756	48.56
8	Michael Atherton	Eng	749	39.13
8	Rahul Dravid	Ind	749	53.58
10	Mahela Jayawardene	Sri	748	44.02
11	Justin Langer	Aus	726	40.44
12	Jacques Kallis	SA	719	43.09
13	Mark Waugh	Aus	707	42.37
14	Gary Kirsten	SA	701	41.70
15	Yousuf Youhana	Pak	699	40.30
16	Adam Gilchrist	Aus	691	52.20
17	Daryll Cullinan	SA	678	42.77
18	Chris Cairns	NZ	677	32.55
19	Aravinda de Silva	Sri	673	42.42
20	Craig McMillan	NZ	672	41.88
21	Alec Stewart	Eng	670	39.81
22	Shivnarine Chanderpaul	WI	665	40.63
23	Michael Slater	Aus	658	43.18
24	Sourav Ganguly	Ind	629	46.74
25	Sanath Jayasuriya	Sri	622	41.84
26	Lance Klusener	SA	621	37.60
27	Nathan Astle	NZ	616	36.70
28	Marvan Atapattu	Sri	612	34.58
29	Nasser Hussain	Eng	601	35.48
30	Graham Thorpe	Eng	598	39.39
31	Stephen Fleming	NZ	595	36.40
32	Jimmy Adams	WI	578	42.21
33	Ijaz Ahmed, snr	Pak	559	38.61
34	Jonty Rhodes	SA	553	35.66
35	Mark Richardson	NZ	546	47.22
36	Sadagopan Ramesh	Ind	540	43.77
37	Mathew Sinclair	NZ	527	40.50
38	Michael Vaughan	Eng	513	28.69
39	Ridley Jacobs	WI	508	24.07
40	Wavell Hinds	WI	506	31.22
41	Greg Blewett	Aus	505	34.02
42	Mark Boucher	SA	502	29.57
43	Guy Whittall	Zim	481	29.70
44	Russel Arnold	Sri	480	30.84
45	Sherwin Campbell	WI	479	32.03
46	Aamir Sohail	Pak	474	35.28
47	Moin Khan	Pak	473	28.11
47	Damien Martyn	Aus	473	42.53
47	Herschelle Gibbs	SA	473	32.29
50	Graeme Hick	Eng	465	32.26

Bowlers

	Player	Team	Pts	Ave
1	Glenn McGrath	Aus	903	21.94
2	Shaun Pollock	SA	902	20.26
3	Allan Donald	SA	850	21.46
4	Muttiah Muralitharan	Sri	849	25.17
5	Courtney Walsh	WI	774	24.56
6	Brett Lee	Aus	739	16.07
7	Jason Gillespie	Aus	714	20.22
8	Darren Gough	Eng	708	27.74
9	Anil Kumble	Ind	701	28.01
10	Wasim Akram	Pak	698	23.17
11	Waqar Younis	Pak	690	22.50
12	Javagal Srinath	Ind	689	29.84
13	Chris Cairns	NZ	683	29.21
14	Saqlain Mushtaq	Pak	675	29.55
15	Colin Miller	Aus	673	25.07
16	Damien Fleming	Aus	671	24.90
17	Andrew Caddick	Eng	641	28.74
18	Shane Warne	Aus	626	25.96
18	Heath Streak	Zim	626	25.00
20	Dion Nash	NZ	622	27.48
21	Dominic Cork	Eng	583	28.50
22	Arshad Khan	Pak	569	28.40
23	Daniel Vettori	NZ	554	32.62
24	Stuart MacGill	Aus	545	24.77
25	Simon Doull	NZ	543	29.30
26	Makhaya Ntini	SA	506	27.34
27	Shayne O'Connor	NZ	505	31.26
28	Jacques Kallis	SA	493	29.75
29	Chaminda Vaas	Sri	488	31.54
30	Reon King	WI	460	27.91
31	Paul Strang	Zim	452	35.28
32	Mushtaq Ahmed	Pak	451	31.96
33	Ashley Giles	Eng	448	28.66
34	Craig White	Eng	445	29.15
35	Paul Adams	SA	434	31.55
36	Alan Mullally	Eng	432	30.58
36	Nicky Boje	SA	432	26.83
38	Venkatesh Prasad	Ind	429	34.70
39	Chris Martin	NZ	421	22.68
40	Pommie Mbangwa	Zim	408	31.43
41	Sunil Joshi	Ind	392	35.85
42	Nantie Hayward	SA	389	26.68
43	Mervyn Dillon	WI	384	33.00
44	Shoaib Akhtar	Pak	381	35.84
45	Henry Olonga	Zim	356	36.42
46	Pramodya Wickremasinghe	Sri	345	42.26
47	Phil Tufnell	Eng	340	36.55
48	Michael Kasprowicz	Aus	338	34.68
49	Lance Klusener	SA	329	36.90
49	Franklyn Rose	WI	329	30.88

The England v West Indies series came along at just the right time and although the quality of the cricket was in sometimes in doubt, nobody suggested that England bought their first five-Test series victory against the Windies in England since 1957. England had already beaten Zimbabwe, with a comfortable innings victory at Lord's before a drawn match at Trent Bridge. The Zimbabweans looked out of their depth, although the political unrest at home provided an unwelcome distraction and it is a wonder that they could play at all.

The triangular one-day tournament between England, Zimbabwe and the West Indies saw Alec Stewart in prime form, his scores in the last four games were 74*, 101, 100*, 97. Stewart also captained the side for much of the tournament as Nasser Hussain recovered from a second broken digit in two summers. Stewart's partner at the top of the order was Marcus Trescothick, who became one of the only England players of recent times to establish himself in the national side in his first few matches. The Somerset player scored half-centuries in his first innings in one-day international and Test matches.

England took their good summer record to the sub-continent and against all expectation came back with a further two Test series victories. Before Christmas, the team fought an attritional battle with Pakistan, pinching the series in a last day run chase, in the Karachi gloom. In the New Year they went to Sri Lanka and after a heavy defeat in the First Test, took the Second and Third.

As bright as England's revival was, they could not match the all-conquering Australia team which, under Steve Waugh, accumulated a record streak of 16 Tests wins in-a-row before crumbling in India.

Donald Bradman, Australia's and cricket's finest batsman (we brook no arguments) could have noted 15 of those victories, but in February he died at the age of 92. Bradman retired from the game in 1948 with an unassailable Test average of 99.94. Even if anyone does ever surpass it, no one will ever credit them with being better than Bradman.

Australia's Victory Roll

1
Oct 14-17, 1999, Harare
bt Zimbabwe - 10 wickets

2
Nov 5-9, 1999, Brisbane
bt Pakistan - 10 wickets

3
Nov 18-22, 1999, Hobart
bt Pakistan - 4 wickets

4
Nov 26-30, 1999, Perth
bt Pakistan - innings & 20 runs

5
Dec 10-14, 1999, Adelaide
bt India - 285 runs

6
Dec 26-30, 1999, Melbourne
bt India - 180 runs

7
Jan 2-6, 2000, Sydney
bt India - innings & 141 runs

8
Mar 11-15, 2000, Auckland
bt New Zealand - 62 runs

9
Mar 24-27, 2000, Wellington
beat New Zealand - 6 wickets

10
Mar 31-Apr 4, 2000, Hamilton
bt New Zealand - 6 wickets

11
Nov 23-25, Brisbane
bt West Indies - innings & 126 runs

12
Dec 1-3, Perth
bt West Indies - innings & 27 runs

13
Dec 15-19, Adelaide
bt West Indies - five wickets

14
Dec 26-30, 2000, Melbourne
bt West Indies - 352 runs

15
Jan 2-6, 2001, Sydney
bt West Indies - 6 wickets

16
March 18-22, 2001, Chennai
bt India - 2 wickets

"Mr Hussain, you are a nice bloke. I do not want to see you get hurt by the great Waqar Younis. Would you mind going off?"

Shahid Afridi, the Pakistan player, trying to get Nasser Hussain to go off for bad light during the Third Test in Karachi. .

"I have spoken to Hansie Cronje and he says it is absolute rubbish. There is nothing at all in it"

Dr Ali Bacher, the United Cricket Board president, on the day that match-fixing allegations surfaced.

"I am more inclined to believe that the Pope is guilty of multiple bigamy than to believe Hansie is guilty of being involved in bribery and corruption"

A caller to an SABC radio show on the same day.

"There were dark moments when I wondered if it was still worth living. I'd think: 'Hansie, you've fallen so far anyway. A few more feet won't matter' "

Hansie Cronje, disgraced former South Africa captain, after he had admitted everything.

"In future, whenever there is a close finish, people will always suspect that the match has been fixed. But at least he has the guts to admit his fault. I wonder if other players will do the same"

Ajit Wadekar, the former Indian batsmen, lends some unwanted perspective to the match-fixing scandal.

"If you can't beat 'em, bribe 'em"

A banner at a one-day international after the scandal.

"It's a shemozzle. Not just an ordinary shemozzle but a straight-out, full blown shemozzle"

Ritchie Benaud, supposedly talking about Shoaib Akhtar's return to international cricket after being suspended for 'throwing'. Answers on a postcard please.

"It's one out of the coaching books, but unfortunately it's from the farmers weekly"

Barry Richards, describing England player Chris Schofield's so-called reverse-slog.

"I think we can keep creating a new world record every game"

Steve Waugh, the super-confident Australian captain, on his side beating the world record of 11 straight Test wins. They extended the record to 16 before losing to India.

Pakistan v England

The English press was unanimous. After fourteen days of the fifteen-day series, the only winner was the pitch, or pitches. The play had been steady or just plain slow and in each of the Tests, there had never appeared the remotest chance of a result. Until the final day, when Pakistan threw it all away (or did England grab it gloriously?).

The Pakistanis prepared dead slow pitches, in the belief that Saqlain would spin them to victory. That tactic was not without foundation given that Saqlain had been the scourge of English county batsmen for the past two years. Take into account England's notoriously bad record of playing spin in Test matches, plus the fact that no England team had toured Pakistan since 1987 (even India and Sri Lanka had not been visited since 1993), and it appeared a reasonable strategy. But Pakistan were proved wrong, Graham Thorpe leading a dogged batting performance and Ashley Giles inspiring the bowlers as the series was snatched on that final day.

There was expected to be an edge between the two teams, given the history. Much mileage was made of Mike Gatting's spat with Shakhoor Rana (who died shortly after the series ended) on the 1987 tour. However the series passed off without real incident and only when Moin's stalling tactics rebounded on him in the final Test was there any acrimony. Steve Bucknor dealt admirably with that, waving away Moin's claims that the fielders could not see – and they really couldn't see – reasoning that his side by deliberately bowling slowly had created the situation in the first place.

England made 480 in the First Test, Saqlain taking all eight wickets to fall. A Graham Thorpe hundred was the highlight, even though he hit just one boundary before reaching three figures, which was thought to be a record. Pakistan also reached 400 and despite a slight wobble, England forced the draw comfortably enough in the second innings. The Second Test followed the same pattern, with both sides making 300 in the first innings. Despite a top order collapse second time round, England were never in danger.

And so to the National Stadium in Karachi. England had already won a remarkable one-day international there (although they lost the series 2-1) scoring 306 batting second with Andrew Flintoff's 84 winning him Man of the Match. But although Pakistan had lost their three previous home series, against Sri Lanka, Australia and Zimbabwe, there was little indication that they would crumble. However, after an inspired caught and bowled from Ashley Giles, Pakistan lost their last eight wickets in the first innings for 88. England's deliberate batting saw them reach 388 in 179.1 overs before the pressure told on the hosts. The could muster only 158 in their second innings, leaving England 176 to win.

Again England were in no hurry to make the winning runs. Graham Thorpe came in and played a beautifully measured innings, but when Graeme Hick was out for 40, England still needed 20 runs to win with gloom rapidly descending. Thorpe and Hussein somehow managed to see just enough of the ball and steered England home to a famous Test and series victory. The result was well worth waiting for, even if many, including those on the field, could barely see the winning runs being struck and no one could see the scoreboard.

First Test
Gaddafi Stadium   *Nov 15-19*

ENGLAND - First Innings

				balls	4/6
M Atherton	c Yousuf	b Saqlain	**73**	190	3/-
M Trescothick	c Saleem	b Saqlain	**71**	193	6/-
G Thorpe		c & b Saqlain	**118**	301	2/-
A Stewart†	lbw	b Saqlain	**3**	7	-/-
N Hussain*	c Wasim	b Saqlain	**7**	13	1/-
G Hick	lbw	b Saqlain	**16**	75	-/-
C White	c Yousuf	b Saqlain	**93**	199	9/2
I Salisbury	lbw	b Saqlain	**31**	97	1/-
A Giles	not out		**37**	104	1/-
A Caddick	not out		**5**	6	-/-
Extras (B3, LB13, NB10)			**26**		
TOTAL (8 wickets dec, 196 overs)			**480**		

Did not Bat: D Gough

Fall of wickets: 1-134 (Trescothick, 54.6 ov), 2-169 (Atherton, 70.5), 3-173 (Stewart, 72.4), 4-183 (Hussain, 76.4), 5-225 (Hick, 98.6), 6-391 (Thorpe, 158.5), 7-398 (White, 164.6), 8-468 (Salisbury, 194.1)

Bowling: Wasim Akram 22-8-40-0 (4nb), **Abdur Razzaq** 22-6-55-0 (2nb), **Saqlain Mushtaq** 74-20-164-8 (3nb), **Mushtaq Ahmed** 44-6-132-0 (1nb), **Shahid Afridi** 18-6-38-0, **Qaisar Abbas** 16-3-35-0

PAKISTAN - First Innings

				balls	4/6
Saeed Anwar	lbw	b Hick	**40**	85	4/-
Shahid Afridi	c Gough	b Giles	**52**	68	6/1
Saleem Elahi		b White	**44**	147	1/-
Inzamam-ul-H		b Giles	**63**	104	9/-
Yousuf Y	c Stewart	b Giles	**124**	308	8/1
Qaiser Abbas	c Hick	b White	**2**	15	-/-
Moin Khan†*	lbw	b Caddick	**17**	40	1/-
Abdur Razzaq	lbw	b White	**10**	37	1/-
Wasim Akram	c White	b Giles	**1**	6	-/-
Saqlain M	not out		**32**	167	2/-
Mushtaq A		c & b White	**0**	8	-/-
Extras (B3, LB5, NB8)			**16**		
TOTAL (163.3 overs)			**401**		

Fall of wickets: 1-63 (Saeed, 21.2 ov), 2-101 (Shahid, 32.1), 3-199 (Saleem, 66.2), 4-203 (Inzamam, 69.3), 5-210 (Qaisar, 74.1), 6-236 (Moin Khan, 84.6), 7-272 (Abdur, 99.2), 8-273 (Wasim, 100.4), 9-400 (Yousuf, 160.1), 10-401 (Mushtaq, 163.3)

Bowling: Gough 17-6-45-0 (2nb), **Caddick** 24-4-68-1, **Giles** 59-20-113-4, **Salisbury** 31-5-71-0, **Hick** 8-0-42-1 **White** 24.3-5-54-4 (2nb)

ENGLAND - Second Innings

				balls	4/6
M Atherton	lbw	b Mushtaq	**20**	58	2/0
M Trescothick	lbw	b Wasim	**1**	21	0/0
N Hussain*	retired hurt		**0**	3	0/0
G Thorpe	c Razzaq	b Saqlain	**5**	26	0/0
A Stewart†	not out		**27**	53	4/0
G Hick		b Shahid	**14**	34	0/0
Extras (LB7, NB3)			**10**		
Total (4 wickets dec, 32.1 overs)			**77**		

Did Not Bat: C White, I Salisbury, A Giles, A Caddick, D Gough

Fall of wickets: 1-4 (Trescothick, 4.6 ov), 2-29 (Thorpe, 16.1), 3-39 (Atherton, 19.1), 4-77 (Hick, 32.1)

Bowling: Wasim Akram 6-5-1-1, **Razzaq** 7-0-21-0 (2nb), **Saqlain Mushtaq** 10-2-14-1, **Mushtaq** 8-0-32-1, (1nb), **Shahid Afridi** 1.1-0-2-1

Toss: **England**
Umpires: **D B Hair (Australia) and Riazuddin**
TV Umpire: **Saleem Badar**

Man of the Match: **Saqlain Mushtaq**
MATCH DRAWN

Second Test

Iqbal Stadium, Faisalabad   Nov 29-Dec 3

PAKISTAN - First Innings

Saeed Anwar	c Thorpe	b Giles	53	52	7/-
Shahid Afridi	c Thorpe	b Gough	10	22	1/-
Saleem Elahi	c Atherton	b Giles	41	93	5/-
Inzamam-ul-H		b Giles	0	2	-/-
Yousuf Y	c Thorpe	b Gough	77	227	8/-
Abdur Razzaq		b White	9	27	1/-
Moin Khan†*	c Hussain	b Giles	65	116	6/2
Wasim Akram	st Stewart	b Giles	1	12	-/-
Saqlain M	c Trescothick	b Gough	34	84	3/-
Arshad Khan	c Thorpe	b White	2	9	-/-
Danish K	not out		8	8	1/-
Extras (B1, LB12, NB3)			16		
TOTAL (108.1 overs)			316		

Fall of wickets: 1-33 (Shahid Afridi, 6.5), 2-96 (Saeed, 21.1), 3-96 (Inzamam-ul-Haq, 21.3), 4-130 (Saleem, 35.6), 5-151 (Razzaq, 44.6), 6-271 (Yousuf Youhana, 88.5), 7-271 (Moin Khan, 89.3), 8-276 (Wasim, 93.5), 9-283 (Arshad, 98.4), 10-316 (Saqlain, 108.1).

Bowling: Gough 23.1-2-79-3 (1nb), **Caddick** 15-3-49-0 (2nb), **White** 25-6-71-2, **Giles** 35-13-75-5, **Salisbury** 10-0-29-0

PAKISTAN - Second Innings

Saleem Elahi	c Stewart	b Giles	72	116	10/-
Shahid Afridi	c Giles	b Gough	10	10	2/-
Abdur Razzaq	not out		100	225	12/-
Inzamam-ul-H	c Hick	b Salisbury	71	122	3/1
Wasim Akram	not out		4	10	-/-
Extras (B6, LB5, NB1)			12		
TOTAL (3 wickets dec, 80.2 overs)			269		

Did Not Bat: Saeed Anwar, Moin Khan†*, Yousuf Youhana, Saqlain Mushtaq, Danish Kaneria, Arshad Khan.

Fall of wickets: 1-13 (Shahid Afridi, 4.3 ov), 2-111 (Saleem Elahi, 35.2 ov)

Bowling: Gough 10.2-1-32-1, **Caddick** 18-1-49-0 (1nb), **Giles** 26-3-90-1, **White** 19-3-55-0, **Salisbury** 7-0-32-1

ENGLAND - First Innings

M Atherton	c Yousuf	b Saqlain	32	100	2/-
M Trescothick	st Moin Khan	b Danish	30	55	3/1
N Hussain*	lbw	b Saqlain	23	102	3/-
I Salisbury	c Yousuf	b Arshad	33	136	4/-
G Thorpe	lbw	b Wasim	79	246	8/-
A Stewart†	c Razzaq	b Danish	13	69	2/-
G Hick	c Yousuf	b Razzaq	17	43	2/-
C White		b Saqlain	41	46	3/2
A Giles	c Shahid	b Razzaq	0	2	-/-
A Caddick	c Moin Khan	b Razzaq	5	21	-/-
D Gough	not out		19	30	2/-
Extras (B4, LB14, NB32)			50		
TOTAL (136.4 overs)			342		

Fall of wickets: 1-49 (Trescothick, 13.2), 2-105 (Atherton, 37.6), 3-106 (Hussain, 41.3), 4-203 (Salisbury, 86.3), 5-235 (Stewart, 107.4), 6-274 (Thorpe, 119.6), 7-274 (Hick, 120.1), 8-275 (Giles, 120.4), 9-295 (Caddick), 10-342 (White, 136.4)

Bowling: Wasim Akram 26-6-69-1 (7nb), **Abdur Razzaq** 20-0-74-3 (10nb), **Danish Kaneria** 34-9-89-2 (3nb), **Saqlain Mushtaq** 30.4-8-62-3 (9nb), **Arshad Khan** 25-12-29-1, **Shahid Afridi** 1-0-1-0 (1nb)

ENGLAND - Second Innings

M Atherton	not out		65	178	5/-
M Trescothick		b Saqlain	10	51	1/-
N Hussain*	c Moin Khan	b Arshad	5	9	1/-
G Thorpe		b Arshad	0	2	-/-
A Stewart†	c Yousuf	b Shahid	22	76	4/-
G Hick		b Shahid	0	10	-/-
C White	not out		9	26	1/-
Extras (LB4, NB10)			14		
TOTAL (5 wickets, 57 overs)			125		

Did Not Bat: A Giles, I Salisbury, A Caddick, D Gough.

Fall of Wickets: 1-44 (Trescothick, 17.5), 2-57 (Hussain, 20.6), 3-57 (Thorpe, 22.2), 4-108 (Stewart, 44.6), 5-110 (Hick, 48.5)

Bowling: Wasim Akram 5-1-13-0 (2nb), **Abdur Razzaq** 1-1-0-0, **Saqlain Mushtaq** 19-4-26-1 (4nb), **Danish Kaneria** 7-0-30-0, **Arshad Khan** 13-4-31-2, **Shahid Afridi** 12-3-21-2 (4nb)

Toss: **Pakistan**
Umpires: **S A Bucknor (West Indies) and Mian Mohammad Aslam**
TV Umpire: **Shakeel Khan**

Man of the Match: **Abdur Razzaq**
MATCH DRAWN

Third Test
National Stadium, Karachi   Dec 7-11

PAKISTAN - First Innings

Saeed Anwar	lbw	b Gough	8	17	-/-
Imran Nazir	c Giles	b Trescothick	20	42	2/-
Saleem Elahi		b Caddick	28	54	4/-
Inzamam-ul-H	c Trescothick	b White	142	257	22/-
Yousuf Y	c &	b Giles	117	242	14/1
Abdur Razzaq	c Hussain	b Giles	21	65	3/-
Moin Khan†*	c Hick	b Giles	13	17	1/-
Shahid Afridi		b Giles	10	14	1/-
Saqlain Mushtaq		b Gough	16	80	-/-
Waqar Younis		b Gough	17	55	2/-
Danish K	not out		0	2	-/-
Extras (B3, LB3, NB7)			13		
TOTAL (139.4 overs)			**405**		

Fall of wickets: 1-8 (Saeed, 4.4), 2-42 (Imran, 14.4), 3-64 (Saleem, 22.1), 4-323 (Yousu, 100.1), 5-325 (Inzamam-ul-Haq, 103.1), 6-340 (Moin Khan, 106.6), 7-359 (Shahid, 112.1), 8-374 (Razzaq, 120.5), 9-402 (Saqlain, 137.5), 10-405 (Waqar, 139.4)

Bowling: Gough 27.4-5-82-3 (3nb), **Caddick** 23-1-76-1 (2nb), **Trescothick** 14-1-34-1 (2nb), **White** 22-3-64-1 **Salisbury** 18-3-49-0, **Giles** 35-7-94-4

PAKISTAN - Second Innings

Saeed Anwar	c Thorpe	b Caddick	21	33	3/-
Imran Nazir	c Stewart	b Gough	4	16	1/-
Saleem Elahi	c Thorpe	b Giles	37	136	3/-
Inzamam-ul-Haq		b Giles	27	45	4/-
Saqlain M	lbw	b Gough	4	19	1/-
Yousuf Y	c Stewart	b White	24	64	4/-
Abdur Razzaq	c Atherton	b Giles	1	41	-/-
Moin Khan†*	c Hussain	b White	14	33	1/-
Shahid Afridi	not out		15	25	2/-
Waqar Younis	run out (Stewart)		0	2	-/-
Danish K	lbw	b Gough	0	9	-/-
Extras (B3, LB5, NB3)			11		
TOTAL (70 overs)			**158**		

Fall of Wickets: 1-24 (Imran, 6.1), 2-26 (Saeed, 9.1), 3-71 (Inzamam-ul-Haq, 24.2), 4-78 (Saqlain, 29.4), 5-128 (Yousuf, 51.1), 6-128 (Saleem, 52.3), 7-139 (Razzaq, 62.6), 8-143 (Moin Khan, 63.6), 9-149 (Waqar, 66.4), 10-158 (Danish, 69.6)

Bowling: Gough 13-4-30-3 (2nb), **Caddick** 15-2-40-1 (1nb), **Giles** 27-12-38-3, **Salisbury** 3-0-12-0, **White** 12-4-30-2

ENGLAND

M Atherton	c Moin Khan	b Razzaq	125	430	9/-
M Trescothick	c Imran	b Waqar	13	27	2/-
N Hussain*	c Inzamam	b Shahid	51	209	4/1
G Thorpe	lbw	b Waqar	18	39	1/-
A Stewart†	c Yousuf	b Saqlain	29	74	5/-
G Hick	c Shahid	b Waqar	12	29	2/-
C White	st Moin Khan	b Danish	35	96	3/1
A Giles		b Waqar	19	44	2/-
I Salisbury	not out		20	82	1/-
A Caddick	c Moin Khan	b Danish	3	11	-/-
D Gough	c Yousuf	b Saqlain	18	58	1/-
Extras (B12, LB9, NB24)			45		
TOTAL (179.1 overs)			**388**		

Fall of Wickets: 1-29 (Trescothick, 10.4), 2-163 (Hussain, 80.3), 3-195 (Thorpe, 91.4), 4-256 (Stewart, 114.2), 5-278 (Hick, 123.5), 6-309 (Atherton, 137.3), 7-339 (Giles, 151.1), 8-345 (White, 154.6), 9-349 (Caddick, 158.4), 10-388 (Gough, 179.1)

Bowling: Waqar Younis 36-5-88-4, **Abdur Razzaq** 28-8-64-1 (8nb), **Shahid Afridi** 16-3-34-1 (1nb), **Saqlain Mushtaq** 52.1-17-101-2 (15nb), **Danish Kaneria** 47-17-80-2

ENGLAND - Second Innings

M Atherton	c Saeed	b Saqlain	26	33	5/-
M Trescothick	c Inzamam	b Saqlain	24	29	3/1
A Stewart†	c Moin Khan	b Saqlain	5	16	-/-
G Thorpe	not out		64	98	4/-
G Hick		b Waqar	40	64	2/-
N Hussain*	not out		6	8	-/-
Extras (B8, LB2, W1)			11		
TOTAL (4 wickets, 41.3 overs)			**176**		

Did Not Bat: C White, A Giles, I Salisbury, A Caddick, D Gough.

Fall of Wickets: 1-38 (Atherton, 8.6), 2-51 (Trescothick, 10.3), 3-65 (Stewart, 16.6), 4-156 (Hick, 38.4)

Bowling: Waqar Younis 6-0-27-1, **Abdur Razzaq** 4-0-17-0, **Saqlain Mushtaq** 17.3-1-64-3 (1w), **Danish Kaneria** 3-0-18-0, **Shahid Afridi** 11-1-40-0

Toss: **Pakistan**
Umpires: **S A Bucknor (West Indies) & Mohammad Nazir**
TV Umpire: **R S Madugalle (Sri Lanka)**

Man of the Match: **Michael Atherton**
ENGLAND WON BY 6 WICKETS
Man of the Series: **Yousuf Youhana**
ENGLAND WON SERIES 1-0

1st One-day International
National Stadium, Karachi   Oct 24

PAKISTAN

Saeed Anwar	c Stewart	b White	24	27	4/0
Imran Nazir		b Caddick	30	47	2/1
Saleem Elahi	c Stewart	b Ealham	28	24	4/0
Inzamam-ul-H	c Flintoff	b Ealham	71	87	6/0
Yousuf Y	c Stewart	b Gough	35	64	1/0
Abdur Razzaq	not out		75	40	5/3
Moin Khan†*	c sub (Solanki) b White		18	12	2/0
Wasim Akram	run out (Giles/Gough)		0	0	0/0
Waqar Younis	run out (Giles)		1	1	0/0
Saqlain M		b Gough	3	3	0/0
Mushtaq A	not out		2	1	0/0
Extras (LB7, W4, NB6)			17		
TOTAL (9 wickets, 50 overs)			304		

Fall of Wickets: 1-39 (Saeed, 6.1), 2-87 (Saleem, 13.3), 3-97 (Imran, 18.1), 4-197 (Yousuf, 39.4 ov), 5-219 (Inzamam, 42.2), 6-267 (Moin, 46.5), 7-271, (Wasim, 47.2), 8-277 (Waqar, 47.5), 9-302 (Saqlain, 49.5)

Bowling: Caddick 10-1-53-1 (3nb, 4w), **Gough** 10-0-71-2 (2nb), **White** 9-0-69-2 (1nb), **Ealham** 10-0-49-2, **Giles** 8-0-37-0, **Trescothick**-3-0-18-0

Toss: **Pakistan**
Umpires: **Riazuddin and Saleem Badar**
TV Umpire: **Feroz Butt**

ENGLAND

M Trescothick	c Mushtaq	b Waqar	11	15	1/0
A Stewart†	c Moin Khan	b Wasim	0	1	0/0
N Hussain*	st Moin Khan	b Mushtaq	73	99	8/0
G Hick	c Moin Khan	b Razzaq	56	51	3/1
G Thorpe	not out		64	66	4/0
A Flintoff	c Moin Khan	b Razzaq	84	60	6/3
C White	not out		0	0	0/0
Extras (LB4, W5, NB9)			18		
TOTAL (5 wickets, 47.2 overs)			306		

Did Not Bat: M Ealham, A Giles, A Caddick, D Gough

Fall of Wickets: 1-2 (Stewart, 0.3), 2-13 (Trescothick, 3.4), 3-127 (Hick, 21.1), 4-164 (Hussain, 30.1), 5-302 (Flintoff, 46.6)

Bowling: Wasim Akram 8-0-59-1 (5nb, 1w), **Waqar Younis** 10-0-66-1 (3nb), **Abdur Razzaq** 10-0-71-2 (1nb, 2w), **Saqlain Mushtaq** 9.2-0-54-0 (2w), **Mushtaq Ahmed** 10-0-52-1

Man of the Match: **Andrew Flintoff**
ENGLAND WON BY 5 WICKETS

2nd One-day International
Gaddafi Stadium, Lahore   Oct 27

ENGLAND

M Trescothick	c sub (Imran)	b Shahid	65	74	5/1
A Stewart†	st Moin Khan	b Mushtaq	22	34	2/0
N Hussain*	st Moin Khan	b Shahid	54	89	5/0
G Hick	run out (Shoaib/Imran-subs)		1	9	0/0
G Thorpe		b Shahid	20	29	1/0
A Flintoff		b Saqlain	17	22	0/0
C White	st Moin Khan	b Mushtaq	0	4	0/0
M Ealham		b Saqlain	3	9	0/0
A Giles		b Shahid	3	13	0/0
D Gough	not out		6	8	0/0
A Caddick	not out		6	8	1/0
Extras (B2, LB6, W6)			14		
TOTAL (9 wickets, 50 overs)			211		

Fall of Wickets: 1-66 (Stewart, 12.1), 2-116 (Trescothick, 25.5), 3-122 (Hick, 28.4), 4-171 (Thorpe, 38.4), 5-178 (Hussain, 40.2), 6-178 (White, 40.6), 7-185 (Ealham, 43.5), 8-194 (Giles, 46.5), 9-198 (Flintoff, 47.5)

Bowling: Wasim Akram 6-0-30-0 (4w), **Abdur Razzaq** 10-1-38-0 (1w), **Azhar Mahmood** 4-0-27-0 (1w), **Mushtaq Ahmed** 10-1-34-1, **Saqlain Mushtaq** 10-0-34-2, **Shahid Afridi** 10-1-40-5

Toss: **Pakistan**
Umpires: **Aleem Dar & Mohammad Nazir**
TV Umpire: **Afzal Ahmed**

PAKISTAN

Saeed Anwar	c Thorpe	b Giles	41	59	4/0
Shahid Afridi	c Thorpe	b Giles	61	69	8/1
Saleem Elahi	not out		58	72	7/0
Yousuf Y	not out		39	73	2/0
Extras (LB1, W6, NB8)			15		
TOTAL (2 wickets, 44.2 overs)			214		

Did Not Bat: Inzamam-ul-Haq, Abdur Razzaq, Moin Khan†*, Wasim Akram, Azhar Mahmood, Saqlain Mushtaq, Mushtaq Ahmed

Fall of Wickets: 1-76 (Saeed Anwar, 17.1), 2-123 (Shahid Afridi, 25.3)

Bowling: Caddick 10-1-37-0 (2nb, 2w), **Gough** 10-0-51-0 (6nb, 1w), **White** 8.2-0-43-0, **Giles** 10-1-45-2, **Ealham** 4-0-23-0, **Hick** 2-0-14-0 (1w)

Man of the Match: **Shahid Afridi**
PAKISTAN WON BY 8 WICKETS

3rd One-day International
Rawalpindi Cricket Stadium Oct 30

ENGLAND

M Trescothick		b Saqlain	36	48	5/0
A J Stewart†	c Moin Khan	b Razzaq	18	33	2/0
N Hussain*	lbw	b Wasim	1	6	0/0
G A Hick		b Saqlain	3	10	0/0
G P Thorpe	run out (Azhar/Moin/Shahid)		39	71	1/0
A Flintoff	c Azhar	b Shahid	10	21	1/0
C White	c Mushtaq	b Saqlain	0	4	0/0
M A Ealham		b Razzaq	23	48	2/0
A F Giles	lbw	b Saqlain	11	19	0/0
D Gough		b Saqlain	0	2	0/0
A R Caddick	not out		1	2	0/0
Extras (LB5, W4, NB7)			16		
TOTAL (42.5 overs)			158		

Fall of Wickets: 1-36 (Stewart, 9.3), 2-38 (Hussain, 10.2), 3-63 (Hick, 15.1), 4-64 (Trescothick, 15.5), 5-85 (Flintoff, 22.3), 6-86 (White, 23.2), 7-133 (Ealham, 36.3), 8-156 (Giles, 41.4), 9-156 (Gough, 41.6), 10-158 (Thorpe, 42.5)

Bowling: Wasim Akram 7-0-27-1 (1nb), **Abdur Razzaq** 10-0-40-2 (4nb, 4w), **Azhar Mahmood** 1-0-3-0, **Mushtaq Ahmed** 10-0-42-0, **Saqlain Mushtaq** 8-0-20-5, **Shahid Afridi** 6.5-1-21-1 (2nb)

Toss: **Pakistan**
Umpires: **Mian Mohammad Aslam & Z I Pasha**
TV Umpire: **Aleem Dar**

PAKISTAN

Imran Nazir	c Hick	b Caddick	0	6	0/0
Shahid Afridi	c Hussain	b Caddick	9	7	2/0
Saleem Elahi	c Hussain	b Giles	23	43	2/0
Inzamam-ul-H	not out		60	108	7/0
Yousuf Y		b White	31	90	2/0
Abdur Razzaq	not out		17	9	4/0
Extras (LB6, W12, NB3)			21		
TOTAL (4 wickets, 43.3 overs)			161		

Did Not Bat: Moin Khan, Wasim Akram, Azhar Mahmood, Saqlain Mushtaq, Mushtaq Ahmed

Fall of Wickets: 1-0 (Imran Nazir, 0.6), 2-9 (Shahid Afridi, 2.1), 3-51 (Saleem Elahi, 14.6), 4-128 (Yousuf Youhana, 39.5)

Bowling: Caddick 9-1-46-2 (2w), **Gough** 8-2-25-0 (1nb), **White** 9.3-2-30-1 (1nb, 1w), **Giles** 10-0-36-1 (2w), **Ealham** 5-0-9-0, **Hick** 2-0-9-0 (3w)

Man of the Match: **Saqlain Mushtaq**
PAKISTAN WON BY 6 WICKETS
PAKISTAN WON SERIES 2-1

England Test Averages

BATTING

	M	I	NO	Rns	HS	Av	100	50
M A Atherton	3	6	1	341	125	68.20	1	2
C White	3	4	1	178	93	59.33	-	1
G P Thorpe	3	6	1	284	118	56.80	1	2
I D K Salisbury	3	3	1	84	33	42.00	-	-
D Gough	3	2	1	37	19*	37.00	-	-
A F Giles	3	3	1	56	37*	28.00	-	-
M E Trescothick	3	6	0	149	71	24.83	-	1
N Hussain	3	6	2	92	51	23.00	-	1
A J Stewart	3	6	1	99	29	19.80	-	-
G A Hick	3	6	0	99	40	16.50	-	-
A R Caddick	3	3	1	13	5*	6.50	-	-

BOWLING

	M	Ovrs	Md	R	W	Av	Best
A F Giles	3	182.0	55	410	17	24.11	5-75
D Gough	3	91.1	18	268	10	26.80	3-30
C White	3	102.3	21	274	9	30.44	4-54
M E Trescothick	3	14.0	1	34	1	34.00	1-34
G A Hick	3	8.0	0	42	1	42.00	1-42
A R Caddick	3	95.0	11	282	3	94.00	1-40
I D K Salisbury	3	69.0	8	193	1	193.00	1-32

Pakistan Test Averages

BATTING

	M	I	NO	Rns	HS	Av	100	50
Yousuf Youhana	3	4	0	342	124	85.50	2	1
Inzamam-ul-Haq	3	5	0	303	142	60.60	1	2
Saleem Elahi	3	5	0	222	72	44.40	-	1
Abdur Razzaq	3	5	1	141	100*	35.25	1	-
Saeed Anwar	3	4	0	122	53	30.50	-	1
Saqlain Mushtaq	3	4	1	86	34	28.66	-	-
Moin Khan	3	4	0	109	65	27.25	-	1
Shahid Afridi	3	5	1	97	52	24.25	-	1
Imran Nazir	1	2	0	24	20	12.00	-	-
Waqar Younis	1	2	0	17	17	8.50	-	-
Danish Kaneria	2	3	2	8	8*	8.00	-	-
Wasim Akram	2	3	1	6	4*	3.00	-	-
Arshad Khan	1	1	0	2	2	2.00	-	-
Qaisar Abbas	1	1	0	2	2	2.00	-	-
Mushtaq Ahmed	1	1	0	0	0	0.00	-	-

BOWLING

	M	Ovrs	Md	Runs	W	Av	Best
Arshad Khan	1	38	16	60	3	20.00	2-31
Waqar Younis	1	42	5	115	5	23.00	4-88
Saqlain Mushtaq	3	203.2	52	431	18	23.94	8-164
Shahid Afridi	3	59.1	13	136	4	34.00	2-21
Danish Kaneria	2	91	26	217	4	54.25	2-80
Abdur Razzaq	3	82	15	231	4	57.75	3-74
Wasim Akram	2	59	20	123	2	61.50	1-1
Mushtaq Ahmed	1	52	6	164	1	164.00	1-32
Qaisar Abbas	1	16	3	35	0	-	-

England v West Indies

F inally England beat the West Indies. It was something they had not done in a series of any kind since 1969, in a five-Test series since 1967-68 and in a five-Test series in England since 1957. To say that the West Indies are not the force they once were is an understatement, but the series had to be won and it was done with some of the most breathless cricket seen in England for many years.

It seemed like business as usual in the First Test at Edgbaston. England crumbled to 179 all out in their first knock – Nick Knight top-scoring with 26 and Darren Gough and Andy Caddick the next best. In reply Sherwin Campbell, Brian Lara, Shivnarine Chanderpaul and Jimmy Adams all made half-centuries to give the West Indies a lead of over 200. It proved more than enough with Courtney Walsh earning Man of the Match honours after reducing England to 14-3 in the second innings. The final margin was an innings and 93 runs.

For much of the Second Test, it looked as though the series lead would stretch to 2-0. Although the West Indies could only muster 267 in their first innings at Lord's, England's frail batting meant that that total was good enough for a first innings lead of 133. What happened in the next 26.4 overs set the pulse racing. Caddick, Gough and Dominic Cork flattened the opposition batsmen and only wicketkeeper Ridley Jacobs was able to get into double figures. The innings closed on 54. Not quite as low as the famous 46 in Trinidad in 1993-94, but low enough to seriously damage the morale of the visitors. Even so, the match was far from settled, the total of 188 to win no easy picking.

Furthermore, when Courtney Walsh took the first six wickets to fall – breaking up a partnership of 92 between Vaughan and Atherton, in the process – the goal looked even more distant. It took a feisty knock of 33 (including a six) from long-term absentee Dominic Cork to steer the England ship to victory. The win was greeted as if it were the salvation of English cricket. Maybe it was.

The Third Test saw the West Indies fight back, Brian Lara finally making a century. The match honours, though, went to Alec Stewart, who scored a hundred in his (and Atherton's) 100th Test match. On the Queen Mother's 100th birthday to boot. With that match drawn, the series moved to Headingley. If Lord's was dramatic, Headingley was chaotic. The tourists could manage only 172, but when Curtly Ambrose took his 400th Test wicket, England were 10-2 in reply. Vaughan and Graeme Hick, coming in at number eight, put on 98 to help England towards a lead of 100, before the West Indies fell apart for a second time. They lasted two balls fewer than they had done at Lord's and scored just 61, Andy Caddick taking four wickets in an single over. England led 2-1 and the West Indies morale, already chipped was now in pieces.

In the Fifth Test at The Oval, the West Indies were set 374 to win in their second innings and it was never in sight. England won the match by 158 runs and formed a guard of honour to salute, Ambrose and Walsh, in their last Tests in England. Ambrose retired immediately after this win although Walsh carried on and on, still trying (almost single-handedly sometimes) to arrest the decline of the West Indies team.

First Test
Edgbaston   *June 15-17*

ENGLAND - First Innings

M Atherton	c Jacobs	b Walsh	20	52	4/0
M Ramprakash	c Hinds	b Walsh	18	48	4/0
N Hussain*	c Jacobs	b Rose	15	82	2/0
G Hick	c Campbell	b Walsh	0	7	0/0
A Stewart†		b Ambrose	6	25	0/0
N Knight	c Lara	b King	26	56	4/0
A Flintoff	c Lara	b Walsh	16	20	3/0
R Croft	c Jacobs	b Walsh	18	19	4/0
A Caddick	not out		21	67	0/0
D Gough	run out (Jacobs)		23	36	4/0
E Giddins	c Jacobs	b King	0	11	0/0
Extras (LB6, W1, NB9)			16		
TOTAL (69 overs)			179		

Fall of Wickets: 1-26 (Ramprakash, 13.5), 2-44 (Atherton, 17.4), 3-45 (Hick, 19.4), 4-57 (Stewart, 28.5), 5-82 (Hussain, 39.5), 6-112 (Knight, 46.4), 7-112 (Flintoff, 47.2), 8-134 (Croft, 53.5), 9-173 (Gough, 65.4), 10-179 (Giddins, 68.6).

Bowling: Ambrose 20.5-10-32-1 (2nb), **Walsh** 21-9-36-5 (4nb), **King** 14.1-2-60-2 (2nb, 1w), **Rose** 13-3-45-1 (1nb)

ENGLAND - Second Innings

M Atherton		b King	19	75	2/0
M Ramprakash	lbw	b Walsh	0	3	0/0
N Hussain*	c Jacobs	b Walsh	8	26	2/0
G Hick	c Jacobs	b Walsh	0	5	0/0
A Stewart†		b Rose	8	12	1/0
N Knight	c Hinds	b Adams	34	103	1/0
A Flintoff		b King	12	22	3/0
R Croft	c Hinds	b King	1	14	0/0
A Caddick	c Hinds	b Rose	4	27	1/0
D Gough	not out		23	52	2/0
E Giddins		b Adams	0	17	0/0
Extras (LB7, W1, NB8)			16		
TOTAL (58 overs)			125		

Fall of Wickets: 1-0 (Ramprakash, 1.3), 2-14 (Hussain, 9.4), 3-14 (Hick, 11.4), 4-24 (Stewart, 14.5), 5-60 (Atherton, 25.2), 6-78 (Flintoff, 29.4), 7-83 (Croft, 33.2), 8-94 (Caddick, 42.2), 9-117 (Knight, 53.3), 10-125 (Giddins, 57.6).

Bowling: Ambrose 14-8-16-0 (2nb), **Walsh** 19-10-22-3, **Rose** 10-1-43-2 (5nb), **King** 9-4-28-3 (1nb), **Gayle** 3-0-4-0, **Adams** 3-1-5-2

WEST INDIES - First Innings

S Campbell		b Gough	59	120	7/0
C Gayle	lbw	b Gough	0	8	0/0
W Hinds	c Hussain	b Caddick	12	11	2/0
B Lara	c Stewart	b Gough	50	93	9/0
S Chanderpaul	c Stewart	b Flintoff	73	119	11/0
J Adams*	c Flintoff	b Gough	98	299	9/0
R Jacobs†	c Stewart	b Caddick	5	21	1/0
C Ambrose	lbw	b Croft	22	50	3/0
F Rose	lbw	b Gough	48	54	7/1
R King	st Stewart	b Croft	1	40	0/0
C Walsh	not out		3	12	0/0
Extras (B6, LB14, NB6)			26		
Total (136.5 overs)			397		

Fall of Wickets: 1-5 (Gayle, 2.5), 2-24 (Hinds, 7.4), 3-123 (Campbell, 36.1), 4-136 (Lara, 40.5), 5-230 (Chanderpaul, 76.5), 6-237 (Jacobs, 81.6), 7-292 (Ambrose, 99.5), 8-354 (Rose, 116.1), 9-385 (King, 131.2), 10-397 (Adams, 136.5)

Bowling: Gough 36.5-6-109-5 (3nb), **Caddick** 30-6-94-2 **Giddins** 18-4-73-0 (3nb), **Croft** 29-9-53-2, **Flintoff** 23-8-48-1

Toss: **West Indies**
Umpires: **D R Shepherd & S Venkataraghavan (India)**
TV Umpire: **B Dudleston**

Man of the Match: **Courtney Walsh**
WEST INDIES WON BY AN INNINGS AND 93 RUNS

Second Test

Lord's   June 29-July 1

WEST INDIES - First Innings

S Campbell	c Hoggard	b Cork	82	155	11/0
A Griffith	run out (Caddick/Stewart)		27	91	1/0
W Hinds	c Stewart	b Cork	59	120	10/0
B Lara	c Stewart	b Gough	6	17	1/0
S Chanderpaul		b Gough	22	61	2/0
J Adams*	lbw	b Gough	1	9	0/0
R Jacobs†	c Stewart	b Cork	10	28	1/0
C Ambrose	c Ramp'kash	b Cork	5	12	1/0
F Rose	lbw	b Gough	29	29	4/1
R King	not out		12	13	3/0
C Walsh		b Caddick	1	4	0/0
Extras	(B1, LB8, W2, NB2)		13		
TOTAL	(89.3 overs)		267		

Fall of Wickets: 1-80 (Griffith, 30.2), 2-162 (Campbell, 55.2), 3-175 (Lara, 62.3), 4-185 (Hinds, 67.1), 5-186 (Adams, 68.4), 6-207 (Jacobs, 77.4), 7-216 (Ambrose, 79.5), 8-253 (Rose, 86.2), 9-258 (Chanderpaul, 88.1), 10-267 (Walsh, 89.3)

Bowling: Gough 21-5-72-4 (2nb), **Caddick** 20.3-3-58-1, **Hoggard** 13-3-49-0 (1w), **Cork** 24-8-39-4, **White** 8-1-30-0, **Vaughan** 3-1-10-0

ENGLAND - First Innings

M Atherton	c Lara	b Walsh	1	7	0/0
M Ramprakash	c Lara	b Ambrose	0	5	0/0
M Vaughan		b Ambrose	4	24	1/0
G Hick		b Ambrose	25	33	5/0
A Stewart†*	c Jacobs	b Walsh	28	68	4/0
N Knight	c Campbell	b King	6	17	0/0
C White	run out (Adams)		27	59	4/0
D Cork	c Jacobs	b Walsh	4	24	1/0
A Caddick	c Campbell	b Walsh	6	14	1/0
D Gough	c Lara	b Ambrose	13	24	0/1
M Hoggard	not out		12	18	1/0
Extras	(LB5, NB3)		8		
Total	(8.2 overs)		134		

Fall of Wickets: 1-1 (Ramprakash, 0.6), 2-1 (Atherton, 1.6), 3-9 (Vaughan, 8.5), 4-37 (Hick, 14.2), 5-50 (Knight, 20.1), 6-85 (Stewart, 31.5), 7-100 (White, 38.4), 8-100 (Cork, 39.3), 9-118 (Caddick, 43.4), 10-134 (Gough, 48.2)

Bowling: Ambrose 14.2-6-30-4, **Walsh** 17-6-43-4 (1nb), **Rose** 7-2-32-0 (2nb), **King** 10-3-24-1

WEST INDIES - Second Innings

S Campbell	c Gough	b Caddick	4	8	0/0
A Griffith	c Stewart	b Gough	1	27	0/0
W Hinds	c Ramp'kash	b Caddick	0	2	0/0
B Lara	c Cork	b Caddick	5	19	1/0
S Chanderpaul	c Ramp'kash	b Gough	9	16	1/0
J Adams*	lbw	b Cork	3	40	0/0
R Jacobs†	c Atherton	b Caddick	12	23	2/0
C Ambrose	c Ramp'kash	b Caddick	0	5	0/0
F Rose	c &	b Cork	1	4	0/0
R King	lbw	b Cork	7	12	0/0
C Walsh	not out		3	5	0/0
Extras	(LB8, NB1)		9		
TOTAL	(26.4 overs)		54		

Fall of Wickets: 1-6 (Campbell, 3.3), 2-6 (Hinds, 3.5), 3-10 (Griffith, 8.1), 4-24 (Lara, 11.2), 5-24 (Chanderpaul, 12.3), 6-39 (Jacobs, 21.2), 7-39 (Adams, 22.6), 8-39 (Ambrose, 23.1), 9-41 (Rose, 24.3), 10-54 (King, 26.4)

Bowling: Gough 8-3-17-2 (1nb); **Caddick** 13-8-16-5, **Cork** 5.4-2-13-3

ENGLAND - Second Innings

M Atherton	lbw	b Walsh	45	143	6/0
M Ramprakash		b Walsh	2	16	0/0
M Vaughan	c Jacobs	b Walsh	41	93	6/0
G Hick	c Lara	b Walsh	15	24	3/0
A Stewart†*	lbw	b Walsh	18	25	2/0
N Knight	c Jacobs	b Rose	2	46	0/0
C White	c Jacobs	b Walsh	0	3	0/0
D Cork	not out		33	49	4/1
A Caddick	lbw	b Ambrose	7	13	1/0
D Gough	not out		4	19	0/0
Extras	(B 3, LB 8, W1, NB12)		24		
TOTAL	(8 wickets, 69.5 overs)		191		

Did Not Bat: M Hoggard.

Fall of Wickets: 1-3 (Ramprakash, 5.3), 2-95 (Vaughan, 36.3), 3-119 (Hick, 44.3), 4-120 (Atherton, 44.5), 5-140 (Stewart, 54.2), 6-140 (White, 54.5), 7-149 (Knight, 57.5), 8-160 (Caddick, 60.6)

Bowling: Ambrose 22-11-22-1, **Walsh** 23.5-5-74-6 (7nb), **Rose** 16-3-67-1 (5nb, 1w), **King** 8-2-17-0

Toss: **England**
Umpires: **J H Hampshire and S Venkataraghavan (India)**
TV Umpire: **R Julian**

Man of the Match: **Dominic Cork**
ENGLAND WON BY 2 WICKETS

Third Test
Old Trafford   Aug 3-7

WEST INDIES - First Innings

S Campbell	c Thorpe	b Gough	2	11	0/0
A Griffith	lbw	b Caddick	2	19	0/0
W Hinds	c Stewart	b Cork	26	70	2/0
B Lara	c Thorpe	b Gough	13	74	2/0
J Adams*	c Thorpe	b White	22	92	2/0
R Sarwan	lbw	b Cork	36	100	2/0
R Jacobs†	b Caddick		7	20	1/0
F Rose	lbw	b Cork	16	20	1/0
C Ambrose	c Hussain	b Caddick	3	5	0/0
R King	not out		3	17	0/0
C Walsh	lbw	b Cork	7	6	0/0
Extras (B1, LB12, NB7)			20		
TOTAL (71.1 overs)			**157**		

Fall of Wickets: 1-3 (Campbell, 2.5), 2-12 (Griffith, 5.5), 3-49 (Hinds, 27.3), 4-49 (Lara, 28.5), 5-118 (Sarwan, 57.1), 6-126 (Jacobs, 63.1), 7-130 (Adams, 64.1), 8-135 (Ambrose, 65.3), 9-148 (Rose, 69.1), 10-157 (Walsh, 71.1)

Bowling: Gough 21-3-58-2 (4nb), **Caddick** 24-10-45-3 (3nb), **Cork** 17.1-8-23-4, **White** 9-1-18-1

ENGLAND - First Innings

M Atherton	c Campbell	b Walsh	1	16	0/0
M Trescothick		b Walsh	66	163	6/1
N Hussain*	c Adams	b Walsh	10	36	0/1
G Thorpe	lbw	b Walsh	0	1	0/0
A Stewart†	c Jacobs	b Ambrose	105	153	13/0
M Vaughan	c Lara	b Ambrose	29	100	0/0
C White		b King	6	30	0/0
D Cork	c Jacobs	b Ambrose	16	35	2/0
R Croft	not out		27	44	2/0
A Caddick	lbw	b Ambrose	3	7	0/0
D Gough	c Ambrose	b King	12	11	1/0
Extras (B10, LB6, NB12)			28		
Total (97.2 overs)			**303**		

Fall of Wickets: 1-1 (Atherton, 3.6), 2-17 (Hussain, 13.4), 3-17 (Thorpe, 13.5), 4-196 (Stewart, 58.2), 5-198 (Trescothick, 63.2), 6-210 (White, 71.4), 7-251 (Cork, 82.4), 8-275 (Vaughan, 90.4), 9-283 (Caddick, 92.3), 10-303 (Gough, 97.2)

Bowling: Ambrose 27-7-70-4 (1nb), **Walsh** 27-14-50-4 **Rose** 20-3-83-0 (7nb), **King** 12.2-3-52-2 (3nb), **Adams** 11-4-32-0 (1nb)

WEST INDIES - Second Innings

S Campbell	c Cork	b White	55	101	9/0
A Griffith	lbw	b Croft	54	196	6/0
W Hinds	c Stewart	b Gough	25	58	6/0
B Lara	run out (Hussain)		112	158	13/1
J Adams*	lbw	b Cork	53	215	5/0
R Sarwan	lbw	b Caddick	19	38	0/0
R Jacobs†	not out		42	111	4/0
F Rose	lbw	b White	10	21	1/0
C Ambrose	not out		36	45	1/1
Extras (B14, LB4, W2, NB12)			32		
TOTAL (7 wickets dec, 155 overs)			**438**		

Did Not Bat: R King, C Walsh.

Fall of Wickets: 1-96 (Campbell, 36.5), 2-145 (Hinds, 54.5), 3-164 (Griffith, 61.6), 4-302 (Lara, 104.1), 5-335 (Sarwan, 118.2), 6-373 (Adams, 135.1), 7-384 (Rose, 140.4)

Bowling: Gough 27-5-96-1 (11nb), **Caddick** 23-4-64-1 (1nb), **Cork** 28-9-64-1, **Croft** 47-8-124-1, **White** 27-5-67-2, **Trescothick** 1-0-2-0 (2w), **Vaughan** 2-1-3-0

ENGLAND - Second Innings

M Atherton	c Jacobs	b Walsh	28	63	3/0
M Trescothick	not out		38	101	6/0
N Hussain*	not out		6	41	0/0
Extras (B 4, LB 1, NB 3)			8		
TOTAL (1 wicket, 33.4 overs)			**80**		

Did Not Bat: G Thorpe, A Stewart, M Vaughan, C White, D Cork, R Croft, A Caddick, D Gough.

Fall of Wicket: 1-61 (Atherton, 21.1)

Bowling: Ambrose 12-2-31-0 (2nb), **Walsh** 14-6-19-1, **King** 2.4-0-15-0, **Adams** 5-1-10-0 (1nb)

Toss: **West Indies**
Umpires: **D B Cowie (New Zealand) and P Willey**
TV Umpire: **K E Palmer**

Man of the Match: **Alec Stewart**
MATCH DRAWN

Fourth Test
Headingley   *Aug 17-18*

WEST INDIES - First Innings

S Campbell	c Trescothick	b Gough	8	11	1/0
A Griffith	c Stewart	b Gough	22	51	2/0
W Hinds	c Stewart	b White	16	47	2/0
B Lara	lbw	b White	4	7	1/0
J Adams*		b White	2	9	0/0
R Sarwan	not out		59	82	9/0
R Jacobs†	c Caddick	b Cork	35	57	7/0
N McLean	c Stewart	b White	7	17	1/0
C Ambrose		b Cork	1	2	0/0
R King	lbw	b Gough	6	11	1/0
C Walsh	c Caddick	b White	1	6	0/0
Extras (LB2, NB9)			11		
TOTAL (48.4 overs)			172		

Fall of Wickets: 1-11 (Campbell, 2.5), 2-50 (Hinds, 16.1), 3-54 (Lara, 18.2), 4-56 (Griffith, 19.2), 5-60 (Adams, 20.5), 6-128 (Jacobs, 37.2), 7-143 (McLean, 42.3), 8-148 (Ambrose, 43.1), 9-168 (King, 47.2), 10-172 (Walsh, 48.4)

Bowling: Gough 17-2-59-3 (6nb), **Caddick** 10-3-35-0 (2nb), **White** 14.4-4-57-5, **Cork** 7-0-19-2

ENGLAND - First Innings

M Atherton	c Lara	b Ambrose	6	18	1/0
M Trescothick	c Lara	b Ambrose	1	7	0/0
N Hussain*	lbw	b Walsh	22	74	3/0
G Thorpe	lbw	b Walsh	46	103	7/0
A Stewart†	c Campbell	b Walsh	5	18	0/0
M Vaughan	c Jacobs	b Ambrose	76	132	7/0
A Caddick	c Jacobs	b Ambrose	6	29	0/0
G Hick	st Jacobs	b Adams	59	95	8/0
C White	c Jacobs	b McLean	0	7	0/0
D Cork	not out		11	19	1/0
D Gough	c Griffith	b Walsh	2	7	0/0
Extras (B4, LB13, W3, NB18)			38		
TOTAL (81.5 overs)			272		

Fall of Wickets: 1-7 (Trescothick, 2.5), 2-10 (Atherton, 4.6), 3-80 (Hussain, 28.3), 4-93 (Thorpe, 34.4), 5-96 (Stewart, 36.4), 6-124 (Caddick, 47.3), 7-222 (Hick, 72.2), 8-223 (White, 73.4), 9-269 (Vaughan, 80.1), 10-272 (Gough, 81.5)

Bowling: Ambrose 18-3-42-4 (5nb), **Walsh** 24.5-9-51-4 (6nb), **King** 11-2-48-0 (4nb, 3w), **McLean** 22-5-93-1 (3nb), **Adams** 6-1-21-1

WEST INDIES - Second Innings

S Campbell	c Hick	b Gough	12	35	2/0
A Griffith		b Gough	0	1	0/0
W Hinds	lbw	b Gough	0	1	0/0
B Lara	lbw	b Gough	2	10	0/0
J Adams*		b Cork	19	43	2/0
R Sarwan	not out		17	56	3/0
R Jacobs†	lbw	b Caddick	1	5	0/0
N McLean		b Caddick	0	2	0/0
C Ambrose		b Caddick	0	1	0/0
R King		b Caddick	0	3	0/0
C Walsh		b Caddick	3	5	0/0
Extras (LB3, NB4)			7		
TOTAL (26.2 overs)			61		

Fall of Wickets: 1-3 (Griffith, 2.1), 2-3 (Hinds, 2.2), 3-11 (Lara, 4.3), 4-21 (Campbell, 10.4), 5-49 (Adams, 19.5), 6-52 (Jacobs, 22.1), 7-52 (McLean, 22.3), 8-52 (Ambrose, 22.4), 9-53 (King, 22.6), 10-61 (Walsh, 26.2)

Bowling: Gough 10-3-30-4 (3nb), **Caddick** 11.2-5-14-5 (1nb), **Cork** 5-0-14-1

Toss: West Indies
Umpires: **D B Cowie (New Zealand) and G Sharp**
TV Umpire: **D J Constant**

Man of the Match: **Michael Vaughan**
ENGLAND WON BY AN INNINGS AND 39 RUNS

Fifth Test
The Oval   Aug 31-Sep 4

ENGLAND - First Innings

M Atherton		b McLean	83	214	12/0
M Trescothick	c Campbell	b Nagamootoo	78	192	12/0
N Hussain*	c Jacobs	b Nagamootoo	0	2	0/0
G Thorpe	lbw	b Walsh	40	158	1/0
A Stewart†	lbw	b McLean	0	3	0/0
M Vaughan	lbw	b Ambrose	10	26	2/0
G Hick	lbw	b Ambrose	17	73	0/0
C White	not out		11	40	1/0
D Cork	lbw	b McLean	0	6	0/0
A Caddick	c Hinds	b Walsh	4	17	1/0
D Gough		b Walsh	8	21	1/0
Extras (B4, LB15, W1, NB10)			30		
TOTAL (123.4 overs)			281		

Fall of Wickets: 1-159 (Trescothick, 61.3), 2-159 (Hussain, 61.5), 3-184 (Atherton, 72.1), 4-184 (Stewart, 72.4), 5-214 (Vaughan, 82.3), 6-254 (Hick, 108.6), 7-254 (Thorpe, 109.5), 8-255 (Cork, 112.5), 9-264 (Caddick, 119.3), 10-281 (Gough, 123.4).

Bowling: Ambrose 31-8-38-2 (5nb), **Walsh** 35.4-16-68-3 (5nb), **McLean** 29-6-80-3 (1w), **Nagamootoo** 24-7-63-2, **Adams** 4-0-13-0

WEST INDIES - First Innings

S Campbell		b Cork	20	74	3/0
A Griffith	c Hick	b White	6	64	0/0
W Hinds	lbw	b Cork	2	7	0/0
B Lara		b White	0	1	0/0
J Adams*	c Hick	b Cork	5	17	0/0
R Sarwan	c Trescothick	b White	5	8	0/0
R Jacobs†	not out		26	61	1/0
M Nagamootoo	c Trescothick	b Gough	18	22	3/0
C Ambrose	lbw	b Caddick	0	1	0/0
N McLean		b White	29	46	5/0
C Walsh		b White	5	10	1/0
Extras (LB3, NB6)			9		
TOTAL (50.5 overs)			125		

Fall of Wickets: 1-32 (Campbell, 21.3), 2-32 (Griffith, 22.4), 3-32 (Lara, 22.5), 4-34 (Hinds, 23.4), 5-39 (Sarwan, 24.6), 6-51 (Adams, 29.5), 7-74 (Nagamootoo, 34.6), 8-75 (Ambrose, 35.6), 9-119 (McLean, 48.5), 10-125 (Walsh, 50.5).

Bowling: Gough 13-3-25-1 (4nb), **Caddick** 18-7-42-1 (2nb), **White** 11.5-1-32-5, **Cork** 8-3-23-3

ENGLAND - Second Innings

M Atherton	c Jacobs	b Walsh	108	331	13/0
M Trescothick	c Lara	b Ambrose	7	36	1/0
N Hussain*	lbw	b McLean	0	15	0/0
G Thorpe	c Griffith	b Walsh	10	56	0/0
A Stewart†	c Campbell	b Nagamootoo	25	104	3/0
M Vaughan	lbw	b Walsh	9	46	0/0
G Hick	c Campbell	b Walsh	0	2	0/0
C White	run out (Griffith)		18	25	3/0
D Cork	lbw	b McLean	26	27	4/1
A Caddick	c Jacobs	b McLean	0	3	0/0
D Gough	not out		1	8	0/0
Extras (B1, LB7, NB5)			13		
TOTAL (108 overs)			217		

Fall of Wickets: 1-21 (Trescothick, 12.5), 2-29 (Hussain, 18.3), 3-56 (Thorpe, 37.3), 4-121 (Stewart, 71.1), 5-139 (Vaughan, 85.2), 6-139 (Hick, 85.4), 7-163 (White, 93.1), 8-207 (Cork, 104.3), 9-207 (Caddick, 104.6), 10-217 (Atherton, 107.6).

Bowling: Ambrose 22-8-36-1 (4nb), **Walsh** 38-17-73-4 (1nb), **McLean** 22-5-60-3, **Nagamootoo** 19-7-29-1, **Adams** 7-3-11-0

WEST INDIES - Second Innings

S Campbell	c Hick	b Gough	28	49	5/0
A Griffith	c Stewart	b Caddick	20	67	2/0
B Lara	lbw	b Gough	47	104	7/0
W Hinds	lbw	b Caddick	7	15	1/0
J Adams*	c White	b Caddick	15	58	1/0
R Sarwan	run out (Thorpe)		27	31	4/0
R Jacobs†	c Hick	b Caddick	1	4	0/0
M Nagamootoo	lbw	b Gough	13	15	2/0
N McLean	not out		23	41	3/0
C Ambrose	c Atherton	b Cork	28	36	3/0
C Walsh	lbw	b Cork	0	2	0/0
Extras (LB3, W1, NB2)			6		
TOTAL (70 overs)			215		

Fall of Wickets: 1-50 (Campbell, 18.3), 2-50 (Griffith, 19.3), 3-58 (Hinds, 25.1), 4-94 (Adams, 43.4), 5-140 (Sarwan, 52.2), 6-142 (Jacobs, 53.2), 7-150 (Lara, 54.3), 8-167 (Nagamootoo, 58.5), 9-215 (Ambrose, 69.4), 10-215 (Walsh, 69.6).

Bowling: Gough 20-3-64-3 (2nb, 1w), **Caddick** 21-7-54-4, **White** 11-2-32-0, **Cork** 15-1-50-2, **Vaughan** 3-1-12-0

Man of the Match: **Michael Atherton**
ENGLAND WON BY 158 RUNS

Toss: **West Indies**
Umpires: **D J Harper (Australia) and D R Shepherd**
TV Umpire: **B Leadbeater**

Men of the Series: **Darren Gough and Courtney Walsh**
ENGLAND WON THE SERIES 3-1

England Test Averages

BATTING

	M	I	NO	Rns	HS	Av	100	50
M J Hoggard	1	1	1	12	12*	-	-	-
M E Trescothick	3	5	1	190	78	47.50	-	2
M A Atherton	5	9	0	311	108	34.55	1	1
M P Vaughan	4	6	0	169	76	28.16	-	1
A J Stewart	5	8	0	195	105	24.37	1	-
G P Thorpe	3	4	0	96	46	24.00	-	-
R D B Croft	2	3	1	46	27*	23.00	-	-
D G Cork	4	5	2	90	33*	22.50	-	-
D Gough	5	8	3	86	23*	17.20	-	-
N V Knight	2	4	0	68	34	17.00	-	-
G A Hick	4	7	0	116	58	16.57	-	1
A Flintoff	1	2	0	28	16	14.00	-	-
C White	4	6	1	62	27	12.40	-	-
N Hussain	4	7	1	61	22	10.16	-	-
A R Caddick	5	8	1	51	21*	7.28	-	-
M R Ramprakash	2	4	0	20	18	5.00	-	-
E S H Giddins	1	2	0	0	0	0.00	-	-

BOWLING

	O	M	R	W	Av	BB
D G Cork	4	109.5	31	245	20	12.25	4-23
C White	4	81.3	14	236	13	18.15	5-32
A R Caddick	5	170.5	53	422	22	19.18	5-14
D Gough	5	173.5	33	530	25	21.20	5-109
A Flintoff	1	23	8	48	1	48.00	1-48
R D B Croft	2	76	17	177	3	59.00	2-53
M E Trescothick	3	1	0	3	0	-	-
M P Vaughan	4	8	3	25	0	-	-
M J Hoggard	1	13	3	49	0	-	-
E S H Giddins	1	18	4	73	0	-	-

West Indies Test Averages

BATTING

	M	I	NO	Rns	HS	Av	100	50
R R Sarwan	3	6	2	163	59*	40.75	-	1
S Chanderpaul	2	3	0	104	73	34.66	-	1
S L Campbell	5	9	0	270	82	30.00	-	1
B C Lara	5	9	0	239	112	26.55	1	1
J C Adams	5	9	0	218	98	24.22	-	2
F A Rose	3	5	0	104	48	20.80	-	-
R D Jacobs	5	9	2	139	42*	19.85	-	-
N A M McLean	2	4	1	59	29	19.66	-	-
A F G Griffith	4	8	0	132	54	16.50	-	1
W W Hinds	5	9	0	147	59	16.33	-	1
M V Nagamootoo	1	2	0	31	18	15.50	-	-
C E L Ambrose	5	9	1	95	36*	11.87	-	-
R D King	4	6	2	29	12*	7.25	-	-
C A Walsh	5	8	2	23	7	3.83	-	-
C H Gayle	1	1	0	0	0	0.00	-	-

BOWLING

	O	M	R	W	Av	BB
C A Walsh	5	220.2	92	436	34	12.82	6-74
C E L Ambrose	5	181.1	63	317	17	18.64	4-30
R D King	4	67.1	16	244	8	30.50	3-28
J C Adams	5	36	10	92	3	30.66	2-5
M V Nagamootoo	1	43	14	92	3	30.66	2-63
N A M McLean	2	73	16	233	7	33.28	3-60
F A Rose	3	66	12	270	4	67.50	2-43
C H Gayle	1	3	0	4	0	-	-

England Test Averages

BATTING

	M	I	NO	Rns	HS	Av	100	50
M A Atherton	2	3	0	225	136	75.00	1	1
A J Stewart	2	3	1	148	124*	74.00	1	-
G A Hick	2	3	0	135	101	45.33	1	-
M R Ramprakash	2	3	0	75	56	25.00	-	1
C P Schofield	2	3	0	67	57	22.33	-	1
N V Knight	2	3	0	51	44	17.00	-	-
A R Caddick	2	3	0	38	13	12.66	-	-
A Flintoff	2	3	0	33	16	11.00	-	-
N Hussain	2	3	0	31	21	10.33	-	-
E S H Giddins	2	3	2	10	7	10.00	-	-
D Gough	2	3	0	17	9	5.66	-	-

BOWLING

	O	M	R	W	Av	BB
E S H Giddins	2	30	10	88	8	11.00	5-15
A R Caddick	2	44.5	13	132	8	16.50	4-38
D Gough	2	49.3	6	174	9	19.33	4-57
M R Ramprakash	2	1	0	1	0	-	-
A Flintoff	2	13	5	35	0	-	-
C P Schofield	2	18	2	73	0	-	-

Zimbabwe Test Averages

BATTING

	M	I	NO	Rns	HS	Av	100	50
M W Goodwin	2	4	2	178	148*	89.00	1	-
B C Strang	1	2	1	37	37*	37.00	-	-
G J Whittall	2	4	1	78	28	26.00	-	-
N C Johnson	2	3	0	74	51	24.66	-	1
A Flower	2	3	0	68	42	22.66	-	-
M Mbangwa	2	2	1	9	8	9.00	-	-
B A Murphy	2	3	1	14	14	7.00	-	-
G W Flower	2	4	0	18	12	4.50	-	-
T R Gripper	1	2	0	6	5	3.00	-	-
A D R Campbell	2	2	0	4	4	2.00	-	-
H H Streak	2	2	0	4	4	2.00	-	-
S V Carlisle	1	0	-	-	-	-	-	-
M L Nkala	1	0	-	-	-	-	-	-

BOWLING

	O	M	R	W	Av	BB
G J Whittall	2	34	10	88	8	11.00	3-14
H H Streak	2	84.5	27	182	9	20.22	6-87
M L Nkala	1	42	11	104	5	20.80	3-82
B A Murphy	2	49.2	13	112	3	37.33	1-19
M Mbangwa	2	54	19	134	2	67.00	2-40
G W Flower	2	1	0	2	0	-	-
B C Strang	1	27	4	86	0	-	-

England v Zimbabwe

First Test
Lord's   May 18-21

ZIMBABWE - First Innings

G Flower		b Caddick	4	17	0/0
T Gripper	c Stewart	b Caddick	1	7	0/0
M Goodwin	c Knight	b Gough	18	43	1/0
A Campbell	c Stewart	b Caddick	0	5	0/0
A Flower†*	c Atherton	b Giddins	24	38	5/0
N Johnson	c Gough	b Giddins	14	33	1/0
G Whittall		b Giddins	15	18	2/0
H Streak	c Atherton	b Giddins	4	7	1/0
B Strang	c Ramp'kash	b Giddins	0	4	0/0
B Murphy	c Stewart	b Gough	0	9	0/0
M Mbangwa	not out		1	2	0/0
Extras (LB2)			2		
TOTAL (30.3 overs)			83		

Fall of Wickets: 1-5 (G Flower, 3.4), 2-8 (Gripper, 5.1), 3-8 (Campbell, 5.6), 4-46 (A Flower, 17.4), 5-48 (Goodwin, 18.4), 6-67 (Whittall, 23.5), 7-77 (Streak, 25.6), 8-79 (Strang, 27.3), 9-82 (Johnson, 29.6), 10-83 (Murphy, 30.3)

Bowling: Gough 12.3-1-36-2, **Caddick** 8-3-28-3, **Flintoff** 3-2-2-0, **Giddins** 7-2-15-5

ZIMBABWE - Second Innings

G Flower	lbw	b Gough	2	6	0/0
T Gripper	c Knight	b Gough	5	12	1/0
M Goodwin	lbw	b Caddick	11	29	2/0
A Campbell	lbw	b Gough	4	6	1/0
B Murphy	lbw	b Giddins	14	63	1/0
A Flower†*	lbw	b Gough	2	3	0/0
N Johnson	c Hick	b Caddick	9	17	1/0
G Whittall	c Hick	b Caddick	23	49	2/0
H Streak	c Knight	b Giddins	0	2	0/0
B Strang	not out		37	37	7/0
M Mbangwa		b Caddick	8	13	2/0
Extras (LB1, NB7)			8		
TOTAL (38.2 overs)			123		

Fall of Wickets: 1-2 (G Flower, 0.6), 2-7 (Gripper, 4.5), 3-18 (Campbell, 6.6), 4-33 (Goodwin, 9.5), 5-36 (A Flower, 10.5), 6-49 (Johnson, 17.2), 7-74 (Murphy, 27.4), 8-74 (Streak, 27.6), 9-92 (Whittall, 34.1), 10-123 (Mbangwa, 38.2).

Bowling: Gough 15-3-57-4 (3nb), **Caddick** 16.2-5-38-4 (4nb), **Giddins** 7-3-27-2

ENGLAND - First Innings

M Atherton	lbw	b Streak	55	120	5/0
M Ramprakash	lbw	b Streak	15	38	1/0
N Hussain*	c Murphy	b Streak	10	22	2/0
G Hick	lbw	b Streak	101	197	3/0
A Stewart†	not out		124	283	21/0
N Knight	c Johnson	b Whittall	44	107	4/0
A Flintoff	c Streak	b Whittall	1	12	0/0
C Schofield	c Johnson	b Whittall	0	3	0/0
A Caddick	c A Flower	b Whittall	13	23	2/0
D Gough	c Campbell	b Murphy	5	11	1/0
E Giddins	c Strang	b Streak	7	4	1/0
Extras (B5, LB29, W1, NB5)			40		
TOTAL (135.5 overs)			415		

Fall of Wickets: 1-29 (Ramprakash, 11.2), 2-49 (Hussain, 19.2), 3-113 (Atherton, 39.4), 4-262 (Hick, 85.3), 5-376 (Knight, 121.1), 6-378 (Flintoff, 123.3), 7-378 (Schofield, 123.6), 8-398 (Caddick, 131.6), 9-407 (Gough, 134.5), 10-415 (Giddins, 135.5)

Bowling: Streak 35.5-12-87-6 (1nb, 1w), **Strang** 27-4-86-0, **Mbangwa** 21-5-69-0 (1nb), **Johnson** 20-5-55-0 (1nb), **Whittall** 7-0-27-3 (2nb), **Murphy** 25-6-57-1

Toss: **England**
Umpires: **D L Orchard (South Africa) and P Willey**
TV Umpire: **J W Holder**

Man of the Match: **Ed Giddins**
ENGLAND WON BY AN INNINGS AND 209 RUNS

CRICKET

Second Test
Trent Bridge   *June 1-5*

ENGLAND - First Innings

M Atherton	c G Flower	b Mbangwa	136	330	19/1
M Ramprakash	c G Flower	b Johnson	56	142	9/0
N Hussain*	c Streak	b Nkala	21	57	5/0
G Hick	c Murphy	b Nkala	5	8	1/0
A Stewart†	lbw	b Whittall	9	29	1/0
N Knight	lbw	b Whittall	1	14	0/0
A Flintoff	lbw	b Mbangwa	16	46	3/0
C Schofield		b Murphy	57	119	7/0
A Caddick	c G Flower	b Nkala	13	38	2/0
D Gough	c Campbell	b Streak	9	28	1/0
E Giddins	not out		3	11	0/0
Extras	(B9, LB13, W16, NB10)		48		
TOTAL	(135.2 overs)		374		

Fall of Wickets: 1-121 (Ramprakash, 48.4), 2-182 (Hussain, 66.5), 3-188 (Hick, 68.4), 4-209 (Stewart, 77.5), 5-221 (Knight, 81.5), 6-264 (Flintoff, 97.3), 7-303 (Atherton, 110.6), 8-335 (Caddick, 123.1), 9-358 (Gough, 130.5), 10-374 (Schofield, 135.2)

Bowling: Streak 32-7-82-1 (1w), **Nkala** 31-6-82-3 (3nb, 4w), **Johnson** 22-7-63-1 (2nb, 2w), **Mbangwa** 18-6-40-2 (1nb), **Murphy** 12.2-1-36-1, **Whittall** 19-7-47-2 (4nb, 1w), **G Flower** 1-0-2-0

ENGLAND - Second Innings

N Knight		b Streak	6	42	0/0
M Ramprakash	c A Flower	b Nkala	4	6	1/0
N Hussain*	lbw	b Nkala	0	8	0/0
G Hick	c A Flower	b Johnson	30	110	3/0
A Stewart†	c A Flower	b Johnson	15	18	3/0
A Flintoff	c A Flower	b Streak	16	62	1/1
M Atherton	c G Flower	b Whittall	34	94	6/0
C Schofield	c Campbell	b Murphy	10	24	1/0
A Caddick	c A Flower	b Whittall	12	57	2/0
D Gough	c Murphy	b Whittall	3	23	0/0
E Giddins	not out		0	9	0/0
Extras	(B5, LB8, W1, NB3)		17		
TOTAL	(75 overs)		147		

Fall of Wickets: 1-6 (Ramprakash, 1.6), 2-6 (Hussain, 5.1), 3-12 (Knight, 12.5), 4-44 (Stewart, 18.2), 5-73 (Flintoff, 34.5), 6-95 (Hick, 44.1), 7-110 (Schofield, 51.3), 8-139 (Caddick, 68.2), 9-140 (Atherton, 70.6), 10-147 (Gough, 74.6)

Bowling: Streak 17-8-13-2 (1w), **Nkala** 11-5-22-2 (1nb), **Johnson** 12-2-41-2 (2nb), **Mbangwa** 15-8-25-0, **Whittall** 8-3-14-3, **Murphy** 12-6-19-1

ZIMBABWE - First Innings

G Flower	c Ramprakash	b Gough	0	6	0/0
G Whittall	lbw	b Giddins	28	28	4/0
M Goodwin	not out		148	250	20/0
N Johnson	c Stewart	b Gough	51	100	8/0
A Flower†*		b Gough	42	113	4/0
B Murphy	not out		0	4	0/0
Extras	(B5, LB5, NB6)		16		
TOTAL	(4 wickets dec, 82.3 overs)		285		

Did Not Bat: S Carlisle, H Streak, A Campbell, M Nkala, M Mbangwa.

Fall of Wickets: 1-1 (G Flower, 0.5), 2-33 (Whittall, 7.4), 3-162 (Johnson, 42.6), 4-284 (A Flower, 81.3)

Bowling: Gough 20-2-66-3 (4nb), **Caddick** 18.3-4-57-0 (2nb), **Giddins** 16-5-46-1, **Schofield** 18-2-73-0, **Flintoff** 10-3-33-0

ZIMBABWE - Second Innings

G Flower	c Hick	b Caddick	12	9	3/0
G Whittall	not out		12	18	2/0
M Goodwin	not out		1	3	0/0
Extras			0		
TOTAL	(1 wicket, 5 overs)		25		

Did Not Bat: A Campbell, A Flower†*, N Johnson, S Carlisle, H Streak, B Murphy, M Nkala, M Mbangwa.

Fall of Wickets: 1-17 (G Flower, 1.5)

Bowling: Gough 2-0-15-0, **Caddick** 2-1-9-1, **Ramprakash** 1-0-1-0

Man of the Match: **M Goodwin**
MATCH DRAWN

Men of the Series: **Michael Atherton and Heath Streak**
ENGLAND WON SERIES 1-0

Toss: **England**
Umpires: **M J Kitchen and D L Orchard (South Africa)**
TV Umpire: **J W Lloyds**

NatWest International Series

First Match
Bristol   July 6

WEST INDIES

A Griffith	c Brent	b Nkala	10	32	0/0
C Gayle	run out (G Flower/Whittall)		41	86	6/0
W Hinds	c Wishart	b G Flower	51	74	5/1
B Lara	c Johnson	b G Flower	60	63	6/1
R Powell	c G Flower	b Brent	36	23	5/1
R Jacobs†	not out		16	17	0/0
F Rose	lbw	b Brent	0	4	0/0
N McLean	run out (G Flower/A Flower)		2	2	0/0
J Adams*	not out		2	2	0/0
Extras (LB4, W7, NB3)			14		
TOTAL (7 wickets, 50 overs)			232		

Did Not Bat: R King, M Dillon

Fall of Wickets: 1-33 (Griffith, 11.1), 2-101 (Gayle, 28.1), 3-135 (Hinds, 35.5), 4-191 (Powell, 42.6), 5-222 (Lara, 47.5), 6-223 (Rose, 48.4), 7-225 (McLean, 49.1).

Bowling: Strang 10-2-32-0, **Nkala** 8-2-40-1 (3nb, 2w), **Johnson** 3-0-14-0 (3w), **Brent** 10-1-59-2 (1w), **Viljoen** 10-0-41-0, **Whittall** 3-0-15-0 (1w), **G Flower** 6-0-27-2

ZIMBABWE

N Johnson	not out		95	128	9/0
C Wishart	c Powell	b Rose	7	19	1/0
M Goodwin	c Hinds	b Rose	23	23	4/0
A Campbell	c Jacobs	b Dillon	17	26	1/0
A Flower†*	c Gayle	b King	42	59	4/0
G Flower	not out		26	25	2/1
Extras (LB6, W8, NB9)			23		
TOTAL (4 wickets, 45 overs)			233		

Did Not Bat: G Whittall, D Viljoen, M Nkala, B Strang, G Brent

Fall of Wickets: 1-24 (Wishart, 5.2), 2-57 (Goodwin, 9.6), 3-90 (Campbell, 17.5), 4-160 (A Flower, 35.1)

Bowling: King 9-0-43-1 (5nb, 2w), **Rose** 10-0-50-2 (4nb) **McLean** 9-0-63-0 (2w), **Dillon** 9-0-35-1 (2w), **Gayle** 8-1-35-0, **Adams** 0-0-1-0 (1w)

Toss: **West Indies**
Umpires: **J Lloyds and P Willey**
TV Umpire: **A Jones**

Man of the Match: **Neil Johnson**
ZIMBABWE WON BY 6 WICKETS

Second Match
The Oval   July 8

ENGLAND

M Trescothick	c Campbell	b P Strang	79	102	7/0
A Stewart†*	lbw	b Johnson	12	23	1/0
G Hick	c G Flower	b P Strang	50	58	4/1
M Maynard		b P Strang	3	9	0/0
G Thorpe	c &	b Viljoen	12	24	0/0
A Flintoff	c Whittall	b B Strang	2	3	0/0
M Ealham	c Whittall	b G Flower	32	56	1/0
R Croft	c Whittall	b Viljoen	5	13	0/0
A Caddick		b G Flower	2	4	0/0
D Gough	not out		3	7	0/0
A Mullally	c Whittall	b G Flower	0	1	0/0
Extras (LB2, W5)			7		
TOTAL (50 overs)			207		

Fall of Wickets: 1-30 (Stewart, 8.3), 2-136 (Hick, 27.6), 3-150 (Trescothick, 31.4), 4-150 (Maynard, 31.6), 5-153 (Flintoff, 32.4), 6-183 (Thorpe, 42.5), 7-191 (Croft, 46.1), 8-197 (Caddick, 47.5), 9-206 (Ealham, 49.2), 10-207 (Mullally, 49.6)

Bowling: Johnson 8-1-25-1 (1w), **B Strang** 10-1-39-1, **Brent** 7-0-42-0, **Viljoen** 10-0-45-2 (1w), **P Strang** 10-0-36-3, **Whittall** 2-0-9-0 (1w), **G Flower** 3-0-9-3

ZIMBABWE

N Johnson	c Maynard	b Caddick	0	3	0/0
C Wishart	lbw	b Caddick	2	13	0/0
M Goodwin	lbw	b Ealham	11	26	0/0
A Campbell	lbw	b Croft	80	136	8/0
A Flower†*		b Mullally	61	88	3/0
G Flower	not out		33	29	3/1
G Whittall	not out		4	1	1/0
Extras (B4, LB5, W4, NB6)			19		
TOTAL (5 wickets, 48.2 overs)			210		

Did Not Bat: D Viljoen, B Strang, G Brent, P Strang.

Fall of Wickets: 1-0 (Johnson, 0.3), 2-9 (Wishart, 4.4), 3-35 (Goodwin, 11.2), 4-158 (Campbell, 40.2), 5-206 (A Flower, 48.1)

Bowling: Caddick 10-2-27-2 (1nb), **Gough** 10-0-47-0 (5nb, 1w), **Ealham** 10-0-44-1 (2w), **Mullally** 9.2-2-33-1 (1w), **Croft** 5-0-30-1, **Flintoff** 4-0-20-0

Toss: **England**
Umpires: **K Palmer and D Shepherd**
TV Umpire: **J Lloyds**
Man of the Match: **Alistair Campbell**
ZIMBABWE WON BY 6 WICKETS

Third Match
Lord's   July 9

ENGLAND

M Trescothick		c & b Gayle	49	79	5/0
A Stewart†*	c Gayle	b McLean	12	20	2/0
G Hick	c Jacobs	b McLean	12	16	2/0
M Maynard		b Collymore	0	5	0/0
G Thorpe	c Dillon	b Rose	42	76	2/0
C White	c Jacobs	b Rose	10	29	0/0
M Ealham		b Gayle	17	24	1/0
R Croft	not out		5	7	0/0
A Caddick	c Gayle	b Rose	0	6	0/0
D Gough	not out		2	4	0/0
Extras (LB4, W3, NB2)			9		
TOTAL (8 wickets, 43.5 overs)			158		

Did Not Bat: A Mullally.

Fall of Wickets: 1-23 (Stewart, 6.3), 2-41 (Hick, 10.4), 3-47 (Maynard, 13.2), 4-99 (Trescothick, 25.5), 5-120 (White, 34.2), 6-148 (Thorpe, 40.2), 7-152 (Ealham, 41.1), 8-153 (Caddick, 42.2).

Bowling: McLean 8-2-25-2 (1w), **Collymore** 10-0-46-1 (2w), **Rose** 9-1-42-3 (2nb), **Gayle** 10-1-28-2, **Dillon** 6.5-3-13-0

WEST INDIES - Did Not Bat

S Campbell, C Gayle, W Hinds, B Lara, R Powell, J Adams, R Jacobs, F Rose, M Dillon, C Collymore, N McLean

Toss: **West Indies**
Umpires: **R Julian and K Palmer**
TV Umpire: **B Dudleston**

MATCH ABANDONED - 1 POINT APIECE

Fourth Match
St Lawrence Ground, Canterbury   July 11

ZIMBABWE

N Johnson	run out (Hinds/Jacobs)		51	68	5/0
G Whittall	c Hinds	b Rose	83	111	5/0
M Goodwin		b Gayle	16	28	0/0
A Campbell	not out		77	78	1/1
G Flower	c Campbell	b Rose	6	7	0/0
A Flower†*	not out		7	8	0/0
Extras (B2, LB7, W7)			16		
TOTAL (4 wickets, 50 overs)			256		

Did Not Bat: S Carlisle, D Viljoen, H Streak, P Strang, B Strang.

Fall Of Wickets: 1-89 (Johnson, 18.6), 2-118 (Goodwin, 27.1), 3-214 (Whittall, 44.2), 4-229 (G Flower, 46.4)

Bowling: McLean 8-0-46-0 (2w), **Collymore** 7-0-40-0 (1w), **Dillon** 10-1-44-0, **Rose** 10-0-47-2, **Gayle** 10-0-42-1 (1w), **Adams** 5-0-28-0 (3w)

Toss: **West Indies**
Umpires: **B Dudleston and R Julian**
TV Umpire: **A Whitehead**

WEST INDIES

C Gayle	c Streak	b Johnson	6	13	1/0
S Campbell	c G Flower	b Johnson	2	4	0/0
W Hinds	c &	b B Strang	9	13	1/0
B Lara		b Streak	3	21	0/0
J Adams*	run out (Carlisle/Streak)		10	23	0/0
R Powell		b Viljoen	14	23	2/0
R Jacobs†	lbw	b G Flower	37	78	1/1
F Rose	lbw	b P Strang	30	31	2/2
N McLean	not out		50	70	3/0
M Dillon	not out		6	24	0/0
Extras (LB4, W15)			19		
TOTAL (8 wickets, 50 overs)			186		

Did Not Bat: C Collymore.

Fall of Wickets: 1-7 (Campbell, 2.1), 2-18 (Gayle, 4.1), 3-23 (Hinds, 5.5), 4-40 (Adams, 12.1), 5-40 (Lara, 12.2), 6-57 (Powell, 19.2), 7-103 (Rose, 28.3), 8-157 (Jacobs, 42.3).

Bowling: Johnson 6-0-16-2 (7w), **B Strang** 10-2-35-1 (2w), **Streak** 8-0-23-1 (2w), **Viljoen** 9-1-26-1 (1w), **P Strang** 10-0-58-1 (2w), **G Flower** 5-0-18-1, **Whittall** 2-0-6-0

Man of the Match: **Guy Whittall**
ZIMBABWE WON BY 70 RUNS

Fifth Match

Old Trafford　　　*July 13*

ZIMBABWE

N Johnson	c Stewart	b Caddick	7	13	1/0
G Whittall	c Stewart	b Gough	15	25	2/0
M Goodwin		b Ealham	21	67	2/0
A Campbell	run out (Tresco'k/Stewart)		10	22	2/0
A Flower†*	c Stewart	b White	28	57	3/0
B Strang		b Mullally	1	6	0/0
G Flower		b Mullally	0	4	0/0
S Carlisle	c Stewart	b Trescothick	19	41	1/0
D Viljoen	c Stewart	b White	0	4	0/0
H Streak	not out		0	0	0/0
P Strang	lbw	b Trescothick	0	1	0/0
Extras (B1, LB4, NB8)			13		
TOTAL (38.4 overs)			114		

Fall of Wickets: 1-14 (Johnson, 2.3), 2-38 (Whittall, 9.4), 3-55 (Campbell, 16.5), 4-64 (Goodwin, 22.5), 5-65 (B Strang, 23.5), 6-65 (G Flower, 25.3), 7-114 (A Flower, 37.2), 8-114 (Viljoen, 37.6), 9-114 (Carlisle, 38.3), 10-114 (P Strang, 38.4).

Bowling: Caddick 8-2-26-1 (2nb), **Gough** 8-1-31-1 (5nb), **Mullally** 8-2-13-2 (1nb), **Ealham** 10-4-19-1, **White** 3-0-13-2, **Trescothick** 1.4-0-7-2

ENGLAND

M Trescothick	lbw	b Streak	29	37	3/1
A Stewart†*	lbw	b Streak	12	23	1/0
A Flintoff	not out		42	45	3/2
G Hick	not out		23	23	2/1
Extras (LB1, W3, NB5)			9		
TOTAL (2 wickets, 20.3 overs)			115		

Did Not Bat: M Maynard, G Thorpe, C White, M Ealham, A Caddick, D Gough, A Mullally.

Fall of Wickets: 1-28 (Stewart, 8.1), 2-57 (Trescothick, 13.1).

Bowling: Johnson 3-0-12-0 (1nb, 2w), **B Strang** 6-1-22-0, **Streak** 6-0-32-2 (4nb, 1w), **Whittall** 2-1-15-0, **P Strang** 2.3-0-28-0, **Viljoen** 1-0-5-0

Toss: **Zimbabwe**
Umpires: **J Holder and G Sharp**
TV Umpire: **R Palmer**

Man of the Match: **Andrew Flintoff**
ENGLAND WON BY 8 WICKETS

Sixth Match

Riverside Ground, Chester-le-Street July 15

WEST INDIES

S Campbell	c White	b Mullally	14	36	0/0
W Hinds	lbw	b Gough	1	7	0/0
B Lara	c Flintoff	b Ealham	54	101	3/0
J Adams*		b Mullally	0	3	0/0
C Gayle	c Thorpe	b Caddick	26	59	3/0
R Powell	c Trescothick	b Mullally	15	30	2/0
R Jacobs†	c Stewart	b White	25	43	1/0
F Rose	c Flintoff	b Gough	18	22	2/0
N McLean	not out		3	5	0/0
M Dillon	not out		0	0	0/0
Extras (B1, LB6, NB6)			13		
TOTAL (8 wickets, 50 overs)			169		

Did Not Bat: R King.

Fall of Wickets: 1-6 (Hinds, 1.2), 2-41 (Campbell, 13.6), 3-43 (Adams, 15.2), 4-104 (Lara, 32.3), 5-104 (Gayle, 34.3), 6-134 (Powell, 42.5), 7-162 (Jacobs, 48.3), 8-168 (Rose, 49.4).

Bowling: Caddick 10-1-30-1 (2nb), **Gough** 10-1-38-2 (3nb), **Mullally** 10-1-27-3 (1nb), **Ealham** 10-2-31-1, **Trescothick** 2-0-13-0, **White** 8-1-23-1

ENGLAND

M Trescothick	not out		87	107	8/1
A Stewart†*	not out		74	110	4/1
Extras (lb 4, w 1, nb 5)			10		
TOTAL (0 wickets, 35.2 overs)			171		

Did Not Bat: A Flintoff, G Hick, M Maynard, G Thorpe, C White, M Ealham, A Caddick, D Gough, A Mullally.

Bowling: King 6-0-30-0 (1nb, 1w), **McLean** 6-1-22-0 (2nb), **Dillon** 6-0-24-0 (1nb), **Rose** 5-0-31-0 (1nb), **Gayle** 8-0-34-0, **Adams** 4-0-20-0, **Powell** 0.2-0-6-0

Toss: **England**
Umpires: **J Hampshire and G Sharp**
TV Umpire: **V Holder**

Man of the Match: **Marcus Trescothick**
ENGLAND WON BY 10 WICKETS

Seventh Match
Riverside Ground, Chester-le-Street July 16

WEST INDIES

S Campbell	c Campbell	b Viljoen	105	137	8/0
W Hinds	c Carlisle	b Viljoen	42	64	7/0
B Lara		b Viljoen	87	76	6/3
R Powell	run out (Streak/A Flower)		12	12	1/0
C Gayle	c Campbell	b Streak	3	4	0/0
R Jacobs†	not out		7	10	0/0
M Nagamootoo	not out		2	2	0/0
Extras	(B2, LB8, W14, NB5)		29		
TOTAL	(5 wickets, 50 overs)		287		

Did Not Bat: J Adams, N McLean, M Dillon, R King.

Fall of Wickets: 1-86 (Hinds, 20.3), 2-259 (Lara, 45.1), 3-260 (Campbell, 45.3), 4-265 (Gayle, 46.3), 5-284 (Powell, 49.3).

Bowling: Strang 10-1-50-0 (3w), **Rennie** 10-1-48-0 (2nb, 4w), **Streak** 10-0-47-1 (3nb, 4w), **Viljoen** 10-0-75-3, **Whittall** 6-0-33-0 (2w), **G Flower** 3-0-16-0, **Campbell** 1-0-8-0

Toss: **West Indies**
Umpires: **J Hampshire and J Holder**
TV Umpire: **T Jesty**

ZIMBABWE

N Johnson	c Jacobs	b Dillon	4	15	0/0
G Whittall	c Powell	b Dillon	23	31	1/0
M Goodwin	not out		112	137	7/0
A Campbell	run out (Nagamootoo)		12	14	0/0
A Flower†*	run out (Gayle)		11	17	1/0
G Flower	not out		96	87	8/1
Extras	(LB12, W14, NB6)		32		
TOTAL	(4 wickets, 49.1 overs)		290		

Did Not Bat: S Carlisle, D Viljoen, H Streak, JA Rennie, B Strang.

Fall of Wickets: 1-18 (Johnson, 3.6), 2-55 (Whittall, 12.5), 3-79 (Campbell, 17.2), 4-104 (A Flower, 22.2)

Bowling: King 9.1-1-42-0 (3nb, 4w), **Dillon** 10-1-52-2 (1nb, 5w), **McLean** 10-0-63-0 (2nb, 1w), **Nagamootoo** 9-0-49-0 (1w), **Gayle** 4-0-27-0, **Adams** 7-0-45-0 (1w)

Man of the Match: **Murray Goodwin**
ZIMBABWE WON BY 6 WICKETS

Eighth Match
Edgbaston July 18

ENGLAND

M Trescothick		b Streak	20	20	2/1
A Stewart†		b Viljoen	101	144	8/0
A Flintoff	c A Flower	b Johnson	24	28	4/0
G Hick	lbw	b Johnson	0	2	0/0
G Thorpe		b G Flower	33	49	1/0
N Hussain*	c Viljoen	b Whittall	34	37	4/0
C White	c Johnson	b Streak	21	11	0/2
M Ealham	not out		9	6	1/0
A Caddick		b Streak	1	2	0/0
D Gough	not out		2	2	0/0
Extras	(LB5, W11, NB1)		17		
TOTAL	(8 wickets, 50 overs)		262		

Did Not Bat: A Mullally.

Fall of Wickets: 1-41 (Trescothick, 6.1), 2-85 (Flintoff, 16.1), 3-85 (Hick, 16.3), 4-166 (Thorpe, 35.2), 5-218 (Stewart, 45.1), 6-246 (White, 47.4), 7-251 (Hussain, 48.3), 8-259 (Caddick, 49.3)

Bowling: Streak 10-0-59-3 (3w), **Johnson** 7-0-37-2 (3w), **Mbangwa** 10-0-43-0 (2w), **Viljoen** 7-0-27-1 (2w), **Strang** 4-0-20-0, **Whittall** 7-0-31-1 (1nb, 1w), **G Flower** 5-0-40-1

Toss: **England**
Umpires: **D Constant and M Kitchen**
TV Umpire: **B Leadbeater**

ZIMBABWE

N Johnson	c Stewart	b Hick	52	74	5/1
G Whittall	c White	b Caddick	3	21	0/0
A Campbell	c Hussain	b White	60	95	5/0
S Carlisle	c Stewart	b Hick	0	1	0/0
M Goodwin	run out (Flintoff/Hick)		3	2	0/0
G Flower	run out (Ealham/Hick)		9	21	0/0
A Flower†*	c Stewart	b White	4	9	0/0
D Viljoen	c Stewart	b White	6	12	0/0
H Streak	c Flintoff	b Gough	45	52	5/0
P Strang	not out		7	16	0 0
M Mbangwa	not out		5	3	1/0
Extras	(B1, LB5, W4, NB6)		16		
TOTAL	(9 wickets, 50 overs)		210		

Fall of Wickets: 1-25 (Whittall, 8.3), 2-87 (Johnson, 22.2), 3-87 (Carlisle, 22.3), 4-90 (Goodwin, 22.6), 5-110 (G Flower, 28.3), 6-123 (A Flower, 30.5), 7-133 (Viljoen, 34.1), 8-172 (Campbell, 44.2), 9-203 (Streak, 49.3).

Bowling: Caddick 8-3-22-1 (2w), **Gough** 8-1-43-1 (6nb), **Mullally** 9-1-37-0 (1w), **Hick** 7-0-37-2 (1w), **Ealham** 10-1-31-0 (1w), **White** 8-0-34-3

Man of the Match: **Alec Stewart**
ENGLAND WON BY 52 RUNS

Ninth Match
Trent Bridge   *July 20*

WEST INDIES

S Campbell		b Gough	1	20	2/0
C Gayle	c White	b Ealham	37	71	4/0
W Hinds	c Hussain	b Ealham	10	32	2/0
J Adams˙		b Mullally	36	59	4/0
R Sarwan		b White	20	36	1/0
R Powell		b White	1	4	0/0
R Jacobs	run out (Thorpe/Stewart)		5	18	0/0
M Nagamootoo	c Ealham	b Gough	11	25	0/0
F Rose	c Franks	b White	29	26	3/0
M Dillon	not out		14	15	2/0
R King	not out		1	2	0/0
Extras (B2, LB4, W5, NB8)			19		
TOTAL (9 wickets, 50 overs)			195		

Fall of Wickets: 1-34 (Campbell, 7.3), 2-63 (Hinds, 17.6), 3-70 (Gayle, 19.6), 4-101 (Sarwan, 30.2), 5-107 (Powell, 32.1), 6-132 (Jacobs, 37.3), 7-139 (Adams, 38.6), 8-170 (Nagamootoo, 46.1), 9-189 (Rose, 49.1).

Bowling: Franks 9-0-48-0 (5nb, 1w), Gough 10-0-34-2 (2nb, 2w), **Mullally** 10-0-29-1 (1nb, 1w), **Ealham** 10-0-37-2, **White** 10-0-35-3 (1w), **Hick** 1-0-6-0

Toss: England
Umpires: **M Kitchen and B Leadbeater**
TV Umpire: **G Burgess**

ENGLAND

M Trescothick	c Jacobs	b King	23	36	5/0
A Stewart†	not out		100	147	11/0
A Flintoff	c Jacobs	b King	2	7	0/0
G Hick		b King	0	1	0/0
G Thorpe	run out (Rose/Nagamootoo)		5	6	0/0
N Hussain˙	c Jacobs	b Nagamootoo	3	13	0/0
C White	run out (Powell/Jacobs)		19	44	2/0
M Ealham	c Gayle	b Rose	16	32	2/0
P Franks	run out (Nagamootoo)		4	17	0/0
D Gough		b Gayle	0	1	0/0
A Mullally	lbw	b Gayle	0	2	0/0
Extras (LB6, W7, NB7)			20		
Total (49.5 overs)			192		

Fall of Wickets: 1-46 (Trescothick, 10.4), 2-49 (Flintoff, 12.5), 3-49 (Hick, 12.6), 4-56 (Thorpe, 15.4), 5-75 (Hussain, 21.5), 6-138 (White, 37.4), 7-170 (Ealham, 44.5), 8-191 (Franks, 49.1), 9-192 (Gough, 49.3), 10-192 (Mullally, 49.5)

Bowling: King 10-1-30-3 (2w), Dillon 10-1-52-0 (4nb, 3w), **Rose** 10-0-31-1 (2nb), **Nagamootoo** 10-1-41-1, **Gayle** 6.5-0-21-2, **Adams** 3-0-11-0 (1nb, 2w)

Man of the Match: **Chris Gayle**
WEST INDIES WON BY 3 RUNS

FINAL
Lord's   *July 22*

ZIMBABWE

N Johnson		b Caddick	21	55	5/0
G Whittall	c Hick	b Gough	0	1	0/0
M Goodwin		b Gough	3	11	0/0
A Campbell	c White	b Mullally	1	19	0/0
A Flower†˙	c Stewart	b White	48	81	4/0
G Flower	not out		53	102	4/0
S Carlisle	c Caddick	b White	14	20	2/0
H Streak	lbw	b Gough	18	12	0/2
B Strang	not out		0	1	0/0
Extras (B1, LB6, W2, NB2)			11		
TOTAL (7 wickets, 50 overs)			169		

Did Not Bat: D Viljoen, M Nkala.

Fall of Wickets: 1-4 (Whittall, 1.1), 2-12 (Goodwin, 5.2), 3-21 (Campbell, 11.5), 4-31 (Johnson, 14.4), 5-120 (A Flower, 41.2), 6-143 (Carlisle, 46.2), 7-169 (Streak, 49.5)

Bowling: Caddick 10-2-23-1, Gough 10-2-20-3 (2nb, 1w), **Mullally** 10-1-32-1 (1w), **White** 10-2-46-2, **Ealham** 10-0-41-0

Toss: England
Umpires: **D Shepherd and P Willey**
TV Umpire: **D Constant**

ENGLAND

M Trescothick	c Campbell	b Streak	1	5	0/0
A Stewart†	c A Flower	b Streak	97	123	14/0
A Flintoff		b Streak	0	4	0/0
G Hick		c & b Viljoen	41	95	1/0
G Thorpe	not out		10	26	0/0
N Hussain˙	not out		9	21	1/0
Extras (LB5, W5, NB2)			12		
TOTAL (4 wickets, 45.2 overs)			170		

Did Not Bat: C White, M Ealham, A Caddick, D Gough, A Mullally.

Fall of Wickets: 1-9 (Trescothick, 2.1), 2-9 (Flintoff, 2.5), 3-143 (Stewart, 36.3), 4-149 (Hick, 39.3)

Bowling: Streak 10-3-30-3 (2w), Nkala 5-0-30-0 (1w), Strang 10-3-26-0 (1nb), Johnson 6-0-22-0 (1nb), Viljoen 10-0-35-1, Whittall 4-0-20-0 (1w), Campbell 0.2-0-2-0

Man of the Match: **Alec Stewart**
ENGLAND WON BY 6 WICKETS

Player of the Tournament: **Alec Stewart**

South Africa v England

First Test
Johannesburg   *Nov 25-29, 1999*

ENGLAND - First Innings

M Butcher	c Boucher	b Donald	1	11	0/0
M Atherton		b Donald	0	2	0/0
N Hussain*	c Klusener	b Pollock	0	3	1/0
M Vaughan	c Boucher	b Pollock	33	84	5/0
A Stewart†	lbw	b Donald	0	1	0/0
C Adams	c Boucher	b Donald	16	31	3/0
A Flintoff	c Boucher	b Pollock	38	48	7/0
G Hamilton	c Pollock	b Donald	0	6	0/0
A Caddick	c Boucher	b Donald	4	10	1/0
D Gough	not out		15	39	2/0
A Mullally	lbw	b Pollock	10	15	0/1
Extras (LB3, W2)			5		
TOTAL (41.4 overs)			122		

Fall of Wickets: 1-1 (Atherton, 0.6 overs), 2-2 (Hussain, 1.6), 3-2 (Butcher, 2.4), 4-2 (Stewart, 2.5), 5-34 (Adams, 12.6), 6-90 (Vaughan, 29.3), 7-91 (Hamilton, 30.5), 8-91 (Flintoff, 31.1), 9-103 (Caddick, 34.6), 10-122 (Mullally, 41.4)

Bowling: Donald 15-3-53-6 (2w), **Pollock** 14.4-6-16-4, **Cronje** 5-2-15-0, **Klusener** 6-1-30-0, **Adams** 1-0-5-0

ENGLAND- Second Innings

M Butcher	lbw	b Donald	32	138	4/0
M Atherton	c Boucher	b Pollock	0	1	0/0
N Hussain*		b Pollock	16	27	2/1
M Vaughan	lbw	b Donald	5	38	1/0
A Stewart†	c Rhodes	b Donald	86	130	14/1
C Adams	c Boucher	b Donald	1	4	0/0
A Flintoff		c & b Adams	36	62	7/0
G Hamilton	c Pollock	b Donald	0	3	0/0
A Caddick		b Pollock	48	72	7/1
D Gough	not out		16	26	2/0
A Mullally	c Kallis	b Pollock	0	2	0/0
Extras (B4, LB10, W6)			20		
TOTAL (83.4 overs)			260		

Fall of Wickets: 1-0 (Atherton, 1.1), 2-31 (Hussain, 9.4), 3-41 (Vaughan, 19.5), 4-145 (Butcher, 54.1), 5-147 (Adams, 54.6), 6-166 (Stewart, 58.4), 7-166 (Hamilton, 60.1), 8-218 (Flintoff, 74.3), 9-260 (Caddick, 83.2), 10-260 (Mullally, 83.4).

Bowling: Donald 23-7-74-5 (1w), **Pollock** 24.4-11-64-4 (1w), **Klusener** 19-4-55-0, **Adams** 11-0-31-1, **Cronje** 6-3-22-0

SOUTH AFRICA - First Innings

G Kirsten	lbw	b Mullally	13	47	1/0
H Gibbs		b Mullally	85	222	11/0
J Kallis	c Stewart	b Gough	12	83	1/0
D Cullinan		b Caddick	108	170	17/0
W Cronje*		b Gough	44	121	8/0
J Rhodes	lbw	b Mullally	26	81	1/0
L Klusener		b Gough	72	85	11/0
S Pollock	c Stewart	b Gough	2	21	0/0
M Boucher†	not out		4	9	0/0
A Donald		b Gough	0	1	0/0
P Adams	not out		0	0	0/0
Extras (B7, LB18, W2, NB10)			37		
TOTAL (9 wickets dec, 138 overs)			403		

Fall of Wickets: 1-37 (Kirsten, 16.1), 2-79 (Kallis, 41.2), 3-175 (Gibbs, 72.2), 4-284 (Cullinan, 102.2), 5-299 (Cronje, 107.1), 6-378 (Rhodes, 127.6), 7-398 (Klusener, 133.2), 8-403 (Pollock, 1317.5), 9-403 (Donald, 137.6)

Bowling: Gough 30-8-70-5 (7nb), **Caddick** 34-12-81-1 (2nb), **Mullally** 34-7-80-3 (1nb, 1w), **Flintoff** 14-5-45-0, **Hamilton** 15-1-63-0 (1w), **Vaughan** 11-2-39-0

Toss: **South Africa**
Umpires: **D L Orchard and S Venkataraghavan (India)**
TV Umpire: **R E Koertzen**

Man of the Match: **Allan Donald**
SOUTH AFRICA WON BY AN INNINGS AND 21 RUNS

Second Test
Port Elizabeth   *Dec 9-13, 1999*

SOUTH AFRICA - First Innings

G Kirsten	c Hussain	b Caddick	15	29	2/0
H Gibbs	run out (Flintoff)		48	98	8/0
J Kallis	c Caddick	b Silverwood	1	30	0/0
D Cullinan	st Stewart	b Tufnell	58	99	8/0
W Cronje*	c Flintoff	b Tufnell	2	4	0/0
J Rhodes	c Atherton	b Flintoff	50	132	5/0
L Klusener	c Adams	b Gough	174	221	25/2
S Pollock	c Vaughan	b Flintoff	7	13	0/0
M Boucher†	c Stewart	b Tufnell	42	119	5/0
A Donald	c Hussain	b Tufnell	9	18	2/0
M Hayward	not out		10	24	2/0
Extras (B7, LB5, W1, NB18)			34		
TOTAL (128.1 overs)			450		

Fall of Wickets: 1-28 (Kirsten, 7.5), 2-57 (Kallis, 17.3), 3-87 (Gibbs, 31.6), 4-91 (Cronje, 33.4), 5-146 (Cullinan, 51.1), 6-252 (Rhodes, 75.5), 7-268 (Pollock, 79.2), 8-387 (Boucher, 115.3), 9-401 (Donald, 119.6), 10-450 (Klusener, 128.1)

Bowling: Gough 21.1-1-107-1 (11nb, 1w), Caddick 31-5-100-1 (2nb), Silverwood 24-4-57-1 (3nb), Tufnell 42-9-124-4 (2nb), Vaughan 3-0-16-0, Flintoff 7-0-31-2

SOUTH AFRICA - Second Innings

G Kirsten	c Vaughan	b Gough	2	23	0/0
H Gibbs	c Flintoff	b Caddick	10	38	1/0
J Kallis	not out		85	260	4/0
D Cullinan		b Caddick	18	45	2/0
W Cronje*	c Vaughan	b Flintoff	27	55	3/0
J Rhodes	not out		57	145	6/0
Extras (B4, LB11, W1, NB9)			25		
TOTAL (4 wickets, dec, 92.5 overs)			224		

Did Not Bat: S Pollock, L Klusener, M Boucher†, A Donald, M Hayward

Fall of Wickets: 1-5 (Kirsten, 4.4), 2-17 (Gibbs, 13.2), 3-50 (Cullinan, 29.6), 4-98 (Cronje, 47.2)

Bowling: Gough 19-6-52-1 (4nb), Caddick 18-4-29-2 (3nb), Silverwood 10-1-24-0 (1w), Tufnell 35-9-71-0 (1nb), Vaughan 2-0-9-0, Flintoff 8.5-2-24-1

ENGLAND - First Innings

M Butcher		b Pollock	4	11	1/0
M Atherton		b Hayward	108	274	15/0
N Hussain*	c Boucher	b Donald	82	154	10/2
M Vaughan		b Hayward	21	99	3/0
A Stewart†		b Donald	15	36	2/0
C Adams	c Kallis	b Pollock	25	65	2/0
A Flintoff		b Pollock	42	37	9/0
A Caddick		b Hayward	35	96	4/0
D Gough		b Donald	6	28	1/0
C Silverwood	c Klusener	b Hayward	6	23	1/0
P Tufnell	not out		7	13	1/0
Extras (B1, LB8, NB13)			22		
TOTAL (137.1 overs)			373		

Fall of Wickets: 1-5 (Butcher, 1.6), 2-160 (Hussain, 51.2), 3-228 (Vaughan, 87.1), 4-229 (Atherton, 89.1), 5-264 (Stewart, 102.1), 6-281 (Adams, 106.2), 7-336 (Flintoff, 116.5), 8-349 (Gough, 125.4), 9-364 (Silverwood, 133.5), 10-373 (Caddick, 137.1)

Bowling: Donald 34-9-109-3, Pollock 34-7-112-3 (9nb), Hayward 28.1-7-75-4 (2nb), Klusener 25-9-48-0 (2nb), Cronje 16-5-20-0

ENGLAND - Second Innings

M Butcher	lbw	b Hayward	1	20	0/0
M Atherton		b Pollock	3	14	0/0
N Hussain*	not out		70	211	9/1
M Vaughan	c Boucher	b Kallis	29	108	2/0
A Stewart†	lbw	b Pollock	28	55	4/1
C Adams	c Rhodes	b Cronje	1	32	0/0
A Flintoff	c Boucher	b Kallis	12	19	2/0
A Caddick	not out		4	6	1/0
Extras (LB2, NB3)			5		
TOTAL (6 wickets, 77 overs)			153		

Did Not Bat: D Gough, C Silverwood, P Tufnell

Fall of Wickets: 1-5 (Atherton, 5.2), 2-5 (Butcher, 6.1), 3-80 (Vaughan, 42.1), 4-125 (Stewart, 59.2), 5-137 (Adams, 70.5), 6-149 (Flintoff, 74.6)

Bowling: Donald 13-4-37-0, Pollock 17-8-18-2 (3nb), Hayward 20-8-55-1, Kallis 7-1-22-2, Klusener 14-9-17-0, Cronje 6-4-2-1

Toss: England
Umpires: R E Koertzen and S A Bucknor (W Indies)
TV Umpire: D L Orchard

Man of the Match: Lance Klusener
MATCH DRAWN

Third Test
Durban   Dec 26-30, 1999

ENGLAND - First Innings

M Butcher	c Klusener	b Adams	48	160	4/0
M Atherton		b Hayward	1	20	0/0
N Hussain*	notout		146	463	17/0
D Maddy	c Adams	b Donald	24	120	3/0
A Stewart†	lbw	b Hayward	95	149	15/0
C Adams		b Adams	19	36	3/0
A Flintoff	lbw	b Cronje	5	19	1/0
A Caddick	lbw	b Cronje	0	1	0/0
D Gough	c Klusener	b Donald	9	25	1/0
C Silverwood	c Boucher	b Pollock	0	4	0/0
P Tufnell	not out		0	5	0/0
Extras (B1, LB14, W3, NB1)			19		
TOTAL (9 wickets dec, 166.4 overs)			366		

Fall of Wickets: 1-7 (Atherton, 8.5), 2-82 (Butcher, 48.6), 3-138 (Maddy, 86.5), 4-294 (Stewart, 136.3), 5-336 (Adams, 148.6), 6-345 (Flintoff, 155.2), 7-345 (Caddick, 155.3), 8-362 (Gough, 162.6), 9-362 (Silverwood, 163.4)

Bowling: Donald 23.4-3-67-2, **Pollock** 33-14-55-1, **Hayward** 20-3-74-2 (2w), **Kallis** 23-9-38-0 (1w), **Klusener** 17-5-38-0 (1nb), **Adams** 43-17-74-2, **Cronje** 7-5-5-2

SOUTH AFRICA - First Innings

G Kirsten	c Stewart	b Caddick	11	31	2/0
H Gibbs	c Stewart	b Caddick	2	12	0/0
J Kallis	c Stewart	b Caddick	0	4	0/0
D Cullinan		b Gough	20	45	2/0
W Cronje*	c Stewart	b Caddick	28	65	2/0
L Klusener	c Maddy	b Tufnell	15	10	3/0
S Pollock		b Caddick	64	89	8/1
M Boucher†		b Caddick	0	2	0/0
A Donald	c Atherton	b Caddick	0	2	0/0
P Adams	c Silverwood	b Gough	9	41	0/0
M Hayward	not out		0	3	0/0
Extras (B4, LB1, W1, NB1)			7		
TOTAL (50.5 overs)			156		

Fall of Wickets: 1-11 (Gibbs, 5.3), 2-11 (Kallis, 7.1), 3-24 (Kirsten, 9.1), 4-57 (Cullinan, 21.4), 5-74 (Klusener, 24.3), 6-84 (Cronje, 31.1), 7-84 (Boucher, 31.3), 8-84 (Donald, 31.5), 9-154 (Pollock, 49.3), 10-156 (Adams, 50.5)

Bowling: Gough 15.5-6-36-2 (1w), **Caddick** 16-5-46-7, **Silverwood** 6-1-38-0, **Tufnell** 10-1-24-1, **Flintoff** 3-0-7-0 (1nb)

SOUTH AFRICA - Second Innings (Following on)

G Kirsten		b Butcher	275	642	26/0
H Gibbs	c Maddy	b Caddick	26	45	5/0
J Kallis	c Stewart	b Gough	69	204	7/0
D Cullinan	c Stewart	b Flintoff	16	50	2/0
W Cronje*	c Stewart	b Flintoff	1	7	0/0
M Boucher†	c Stewart	b Adams	108	220	14/1
L Klusener		b Butcher	45	58	6/0
S Pollock	not out		7	35	0/0
Extras (B5, LB13, W2, NB35)			25		
TOTAL (7 wkts, 209.2 overs)			572		

Did Not Bat: A Donald, P Adams, M Hayward

Fall of Wickets: 1-41 (Gibbs, 14.2), 2-193 (Kallis, 83.2), 3-242 (Cullinan, 104.6), 4-244 (Cronje, 106.2), 5-436 (Boucher, 174.4), 6-537 (Klusener, 197.4), 7-572 (Kirsten, 209.2)

Bowling: Caddick 36-12-70-1 (3nb), **Silverwood** 30-6-89-0 (1w), **Gough** 28-5-82-1 (1w), **Flintoff** 30-9-67-2, **Tufnell** 45-6-117-0 (2nb), **Adams** 13-3-42-1, **Maddy** 14-1-40-0, **Butcher** 8.2-0-32-2, **Hussain** 5-0-15-0

Toss: **England**
Umpires: **D L Orchard and D B Cowie (New Zealand)**
TV Umpire: **W A Diedricks**

Men of the Match: **Andy Caddick and Gary Kirsten**
MATCH DRAWN

Fourth Test
Cape Town Jan 2-6

ENGLAND - First Innings

M Butcher	c Kirsten	b Donald	40	168	6/0
M Atherton	c Kirsten	b Donald	71	124	8/0
N Hussain*	c Boucher	b Adams	15	70	1/0
M Vaughan	c Kirsten	b Donald	42	131	3/0
A Stewart†	c Kirsten	b Donald	40	65	6/0
A Caddick	c Cullinan	b Donald	0	7	0/0
C Adams	c Pollock	b Kallis	10	48	1/0
A Flintoff	c Rhodes	b Klusener	22	47	3/0
D Gough	c Boucher	b Klusener	4	12	0/0
C Silverwood	not out		1	2	0/0
P Tufnell		b Kallis	2	6	0/0
Extras (LB6, W2, NB3)			11		
TOTAL (113 overs)			258		

Fall of Wickets: 1-115 (Atherton, 42.3), 2-125 (Butcher, 52.5), 3-141 (Hussain, 65.4), 4-213 (Stewart, 85.6), 5-213 (Caddick, 88.6), 6-218 (Vaughan, 98.1), 7-231 (Adams, 106.4), 8-253 (Flintoff, 111.1), 9-255 (Gough, 111.4), 10-258 (Tufnell, 112.6)

Bowling: Donald 26-13-47-5, **Pollock** 27-8-59-0 (1nb,1w), **Kallis** 20-4-61-2 (1w), **Klusener** 16-5-42-2 (2nb), **Cronje** 3-2-5-0, **Adams** 21-9-38-1

SOUTH AFRICA - First Innings

G Kirsten	c Stewart	b Silverwood	80	196	8/0
H Gibbs	c Vaughan	b Silverwood	29	49	4/0
J Kallis	c Atherton	b Gough	105	229	10/2
D Cullinan	c Vaughan	b Tufnell	120	255	10/1
W Cronje*	c Vaughan	b Caddick	0	4	0/0
J Rhodes	c Adams	b Silverwood	16	29	2/0
L Klusener		b Gough	3	10	0/0
S Pollock	c Adams	b Caddick	4	22	0/0
M Boucher†	lbw	b Silverwood	36	100	3/0
A Donald	c Adams	b Silverwood	7	8	1/0
P Adams	not out		3	30	0/0
Extras (B1, LB7, NB10)			18		
TOTAL (153.4 overs)			421		

Fall of Wickets: 1-43 (Gibbs, 13.4), 2-201 (Kirsten, 67.3), 3-246 (Kallis, 88.5), 4-247 (Cronje, 91.1), 5-279 (Rhodes, 101.1), 6-290 (Klusener, 104.6), 7-307 (Pollock, 111.6), 8-397 (Boucher, 143.6), 9-405 (Donald, 145.3), 10-421 (Cullinan, 153.4)

Bowling: Gough 37-6-88-2 (6nb), **Caddick** 31-6-95-2 (1nb), **Silverwood** 32-6-91-5, **Flintoff** 4-0-16-0, **Tufnell** 39.4-10-97-1 (3nb), **Butcher** 3-0-9-0, **Adams** 7-2-17-0

ENGLAND - Second Innings

M Butcher	c Boucher	b Pollock	4	9	1/0
M Atherton	c Cullinan	b Pollock	35	109	3/0
N Hussain*	lbw	b Klusener	16	38	2/1
M Vaughan	c Boucher	b Klusener	5	32	0/0
A Stewart†		b Adams	5	28	0/0
C Adams		b Adams	31	59	4/0
A Caddick	c Cullinan	b Donald	14	47	2/0
D Gough	c Donald	b Kallis	8	23	0/0
C Silverwood	not out		5	12	0/0
P Tufnell	c Cullinan	b Adams	0	6	0/0
A Flintoff	absent injured		0	0	0/0
Extras (LB3)			3		
TOTAL (60.3 overs)			126		

Fall of Wickets: 1-4 (Butcher, 2.3), 2-40 (Hussain, 16.3), 3-59 (Vaughan, 27.5), 4-62 (Atherton, 33.5), 5-66 (Stewart, 38.1), 6-105 (Caddick, 51.6), 7-113 (Adams, 54.5), 8-125 (Gough, 59.3), 9-126 (Tufnell, 60.3)

Bowling: Adams 19.3-5-42-2, **Donald** 10.4-2-35-1, **Pollock** 14-8-19-2, **Kallis** 9.2-2-19-1, **Klusener** 7-4-8-2

Toss: **England**
Umpires: **C J Mitchley and B C Cooray (Sri Lanka)**
TV Umpire: **I J Howell**

Man of the Match: **Daryll Cullinan**
SOUTH AFRICA WON BY AN INNINGS AND 37 RUNS

CRICKET

Fifth Test
Centurion   Jan 14-18

SOUTH AFRICA - First Innings

G Kirsten	c Adams	b Gough	0	7	0/0
H Gibbs	c Adams	b Caddick	3	21	0/0
J Kallis		b Caddick	25	61	2/1
D Cullinan		c & b Mullally	46	91	5/0
W Cronje*	c Maddy	b Gough	0	6	0/0
P Strydom	c Stewart	b Silverwood	30	41	5/0
L Klusener	not out		61	96	7/1
S Pollock	run out (Hussain)		30	64	3/0
M Boucher†		b Mullally	22	48	4/0
P Adams	not out		4	8	1/0
Extras (B2, LB11, W3, NB11)			27		
TOTAL (8 wickets dec, 72 overs)			421		

Did not bat: M Hayward

Fall of Wickets: 1-1 (Kirsten, 0.6), 2-15 (Gibbs, 7.6), 3-50 (Kallis, 18.1), 4-55 (Cronje, 19.6), 5-102 (Strydom, 33.1), 6-136 (Cullinan, 40.3), 7-196 (Pollock, 56.6), 8-243 Boucher, 70.3)

Bowling: Gough 20-2-92-2 (10nb, 1w), **Caddick** 19-7-47-2, **Mullally** 24-10-42-2 (1nb, 1w), **Silverwood** 7-1-45-1 (1w), **Vaughan** 2-0-9-0

SOUTH AFRICA - Second Innings

FORFEITED

ENGLAND - First Innings

FORFEITED

ENGLAND - Second Innings

M Butcher	lbw	b Klusener	36	84	6/0
M Atherton	c Boucher	b Pollock	7	29	0/0
N Hussain*	c Gibbs	b Pollock	25	69	2/0
A Stewart†	c Boucher	b Hayward	73	140	10/1
C Adams	c Boucher	b Hayward	1	10	/0
M Vaughan		b Hayward	69	108	9/0
D Maddy	run out (Kirsten/Boucher)		3	6	0/0
A Caddick	c Boucher	b Pollock	0	2	0/0
D Gough	not out		6	3	1/0
C Silverwood	not out		7	7	1/0
Extras (B4, LB9, W4, NB7)			24		
TOTAL (8 wkts, 75.1 overs)			251		

Did not bat: A Mullally

Fall of Wickets: 1-28 (Atherton, 10.1), 2-67 (Butcher, 25.5), 3-90 (Hussain, 32.1), 4-102 (Adams, 37.1), 5-228 (Stewart, 69.3), 6-236 (Maddy, 72.2), 7-236 (Caddick, 72.4), 8-240 (Vaughan, 73.5)

Bowling: Pollock 20-7-53-3 (3nb), **Hayward** 17.1-3-61-3 (3nb, 3w), **Klusener** 14-4-38-1 (1nb), **Kallis** 13-2-44-0 (1w), **Cronje** 5-3-15-0, **Strydom** 6-0-27-0

Man of the Match: **Michael Vaughan**
ENGLAND WON BY 2 WICKETS

Man of the Series: **Daryll Cullinan**
SOUTH AFRICA WON SERIES 2

Toss: **England**
Umpires: **R E Koertzen and D B Hair (Australia)**
TV Umpire: **C J Mitchley**

England Test Averages

BATTING

	M	I	NO	Rns	HS	Av	100	50
N Hussain	5	8	2	370	146*	61.66	1	2
A J Stewart	5	8	0	342	95	42.75	-	3
M P Vaughan	4	7	0	204	69	29.14	-	1
M A Atherton	5	8	0	225	108	28.12	1	1
A Flintoff	4	6	0	155	42	25.83	-	-
M A Butcher	5	8	0	166	48	20.75	-	-
D Gough	5	7	3	64	16*	16.00	-	-
A R Caddick	5	8	1	105	48	15.00	-	-
D L Maddy	2	2	0	27	24	13.50	-	-
C J Adams	5	8	0	104	31	13.00	-	-
C E W Silverwood	4	5	3	19	7*	9.50	-	-
A D Mullally	2	2	0	10	10	5.00	-	-
P C R Tufnell	3	4	2	9	7*	5.00	-	-
G M Hamilton	1	2	0	0		0.00	-	-

BOWLING

M A Butcher	5	11.2	0	41	2	20.50	2-32
A D Mullally	2	58	17	122	5	24.40	3-80
A R Caddick	5	185	51	468	16	29.25	7-46
D Gough	5	170.4	34	527	14	37.64	5-70
A Flintoff	4	66.5	16	190	5	38.00	2-31
C E W Silverwood	4	109	19	344	7	49.14	5-91
C J Adams	5	20	5	59	1	59.00	1-42
P C R Tufnell	3	171.4	35	433	6	72.16	4-124
N Hussain	5	5	0	15	0	-	-
D L Maddy	2	14	1	40	0	-	-
G M Hamilton	1	15	1	63	0	-	-
M P Vaughan	4	18	2	73	0	-	-

One-day Tournament

Round Robin Matches

SOUTH AFRICA V ZIMBABWE Day/Night
Johannesburg   Jan 21
Zimbabwe 226 (49.5) (M W Goodwin 73)
South Africa 229-4 (48.1) (HH Gibbs 65, WJ Cronje 83*)
South Africa won by 6 wickets

SOUTH AFRICA V ENGLAND
Bloemfontein   Jan 23
South Africa 184 (49.5) (J H Kallis 57, Gough 4-29)
England 185-1 (39.3) (N Hussain 85, N V Knight 71*)
England won by 9 wickets

SOUTH AFRICA V ENGLAND D/N
Cape Town   Jan 26
South Africa 204-7 (50)
England 203-9 (50) (N Hussain 85, N V Knight 71*)
South Africa won by 1 run

ZIMBABWE V ENGLAND D/N
Cape Town   Jan 28
Zimbabwe 211-7 (50) (N C Johnson 97)
England 107 (34.2) (Olonga 6-19)
Zimbabwe won by 104 runs

ZIMBABWE V ENGLAND
Kimberley   Jan 30
Zimbabwe 161-9 (50) (Ealham 5-15)
England 162-2 (32.1) (N Hussain 64, N V Knight 72*)
England won by 8 wickets

South Africa Test Averages

BATTING

	M	I	NO	Rns	HS	Av	100	50
M Hayward	3	2	2	10	10*	-	-	-
L Klusener	5	6	1	370	174	74.00	1	2
G Kirsten	5	7	0	396	275	56.57	1	1
D J Cullinan	5	7	0	386	120	55.14	2	1
J N Rhodes	3	4	1	149	57*	49.66	-	2
J H Kallis	5	7	1	297	105	49.50	1	2
M V Boucher	5	6	1	212	108	42.40	1	-
P C Strydom	1	1	0	30	30	30.00	-	-
H H Gibbs	5	7	0	203	85	29.00	-	1
S M Pollock	5	6	1	114	64	22.80	-	1
P R Adams	4	4	3	16	9	16.00	-	-
W J Cronje	5	7	0	102	44	14.57	-	-
A A Donald	4	4	0	16	9	4.00	-	-

BOWLING

A A Donald	4	145.2	41	422	22	19.18	6-53
S M Pollock	5	184.2	69	396	19	20.84	4-16
M Hayward	3	85.2	21	265	10	26.50	4-75
P R Adams	4	95.3	31	190	7	27.14	3-42
W J Cronje	5	48	24	84	3	28.00	2-5
J H Kallis	5	72.2	18	184	5	36.80	2-22
L Klusener	5	118	41	276	5	55.20	2-8
P C Strydom	1	6	0	27	0	-	-

SOUTH AFRICA V ZIMBABWE D/N
Durban   Feb 2
South Africa 222-7 (50) (J H Kallis 52, L Klusener 65*)
Zimbabwe 223-8 (50) (A Flower 59)
Zimbabwe won by 2 wickets

SOUTH AFRICA V ENGLAND D/N
East London   Feb 4
England 231-6 (50) (N V Knight 64, M V Alleyne 53)
South Africa 233-8 (49.4)
South Africa won by 2 wickets

SOUTH AFRICA V ZIMBABWE
Port Elizabeth   Feb 6
South Africa 204-7 (50) (J H Kallis 98*)
Zimbabwe 151 (46) (N C Johnson 56)
South Africa won by 53 runs

ZIMBABWE V ENGLAND D/N
Centurion   Feb 9
Match abandoned without a ball bowled; one point each

Round Robin Final Standings

	P	W	L	NR	T	Pts	RRate
South Africa	6	4	2	-	-	8	+0.074
England	6	2	3	1	-	5	+0.029
Zimbabwe	6	2	3	1	-	5	-0.124

FINAL
SOUTH AFRICA V ENGLAND D/N
Johannesburg   Jan 26
South Africa 149 (45) (W J Cronje 56, Caddick 4-19)
England 111 (43) (Pollock 5-20)
South Africa won by 38 runs

Other one-day matches

ZIMBABWE V ENGLAND
Bulawayo Feb 16
Zimbabwe 194-7 (G W Flower 55*)
England 199-5 (G A Hick 87*)
England won by 5 wickets (D/L method)

ZIMBABWE V ENGLAND
Bulawayo Feb 18
Zimbabwe 131 (White 5-21)
England 134-9
England won by 1 wicket

ZIMBABWE V ENGLAND
Harare Feb 20
England 248-7 (G A Hick 80, D L Maddy 53)
Zimbabwe 163 (Hick 5-33)
England won by 1 wicket

ZIMBABWE V ENGLAND
Harare Feb 23
Match abandoned without a ball bowled

ENGLAND WON SERIES 3-0

ICC Knockout Trophy
PRELIMINARY QUARTER-FINALS

KENYA V INDIA
Nairobi Oct 3
Kenya 208-9 (50) (R D Shah 60, M O Oumbe 51)
India 209-2 (42.3) (S C Ganguly 66, R Dravid 68*)
India won by 8 wickets

SRI LANKA V WEST INIDIES
Nairobi Oct 4
Sri Lanka 287-6 (50) (Gunawardene 132,
Jayawardene 72)
West Indies 179 (46.4)
Sri Lanka won by 108 runs

ENGLAND V BANGLADESH
Nairobi Oct 5
Bangladesh 232-8 (50) (Javed Omar 63*)
England 236-2 (43.5) (A J Stewart 87*, N Hussain 95)
England won by 8 wickets

QUARTER-FINALS

AUSTRALIA V INDIA
Nairobi Oct 7
India 265-9 (50) (Yuvraj Singh 84)
Australia 245 (46.4)
India won by 20 runs

PAKISTAN V SRI LANKA
Nairobi Oct 8
Sri Lanka 194 (45.4)
Pakistan 195-1 (43.2) (Saeed Anwar 105*)
Pakistan won by 9 wickets

NEW ZEALAND V ZIMBABWE
Nairobi Oct 9
New Zealand 265-7 (50) (R G Twose 85,
C D McMillan 52)
Zimbabwe 201 (42.2) (S V Carlisle 67)
New Zealand won by 64 runs

ENGLAND V SOUTH AFRICA
Nairobi Oct 10
England 182 (44.1) (G A Hick 65)
South Africa 184-2 (39.1) (J H Kallis 78*,
H H Dippenaar 65*)
South Africa won by 8 wickets

SEMI-FINALS

NEW ZEALAND V PAKISTAN
Nairobi Oct 11
Pakistan 252 (49.2) (Saeed Anwar 104, O'Connor 5-46)
New Zealand 255-6 (49)
(R G Twose 87, C D McMillan 51*, Azhar Mahmood 4-65)
New Zealand won by 4 wickets

INDIA V SOUTH AFRICA
Nairobi Oct 13
India 295-6 (50) (S C Ganguly 141*, R Dravid 58)
South Africa 200 (41) (M V Boucher 60)
India won by 95 runs

FINAL

NEW ZEALAND V INDIA
Nairobi Oct 15
India 264-6 (50) (S C Ganguly 117, S R Tendulkar 69)
New Zealand 265-6 (49.4) (C L Cairns 102*)
New Zealand won by 4 wickets

Domestic Cricket

There was much pouring of scorn over Gloucestershire's achievements in 1999. They won the Super Cup, it was said, because there were only eight teams in it and when they added the NatWest in the same month, it was because they were one-day specialists and not a proper cricket team. Well, Gloucestershire went one better in 2000, winning all three one-day trophies on offer to make the critics eat their words and then some. There was a measure of good fortune along the way. An eagle-eyed official spotted that Worcestershire, who beat Gloucestershire in the third round of the NatWest Trophy, had fielded Kabir Ali, who had already played in an earlier round for Worcestershire's Cricket Board XI (teams made up of club and second XI players). The match was replayed and Gloucestershire won. However winning three one-day titles was a still fair effort.

They bagged a full-size Super Cup in June, beating Glamorgan in the final (we'll call it by it's old names cos we don't tolerate tobacco sponsors in this book). They then beat Warwickshire in the last NatWest Trophy final – having played the replayed Worcestershire game and the fourth round with Leicestershire on consecutive days. The NatWest final was rain-ruined and Gloucestershire won on the Duckworth-Lewis method. Allan Donald was given the Man of the Match award, according to adjudicator David Gower, for what he might have done with his remaining overs. Good imagination, that Gower, but it was a little harsh on Mike Smith whose 3-18 in 10 overs put the block on Warwickshire's progress. That win gave Gloucestershire win in four consecutive Lord's finals. We'll give them some credit for that.

Not for their accounting though, for in spite of all the winning (the two knockout finals and the First Division of the Norwich Union one-day league) the club made a loss on the season of £38,700. The books were not helped by the fact that the counties received only six percent of the gate receipts for the Lord's finals in 2000. In addition the ECB handout to the counties fell by £50,000.

As it was the first season of two-division championship cricket, it would be technically inaccurate to say Surrey retained their county title, though to all intents and purposed they did so. Surrey have such depth in their four-day squad that they could almost become the first county side to play a squad rota system. Though we don't like to make predictions, we can't see many counties ruffling their feathers this year either. Hampshire, Derbyshire and Durham went down, all a long way from safety. Northamptonshire won the second division, Essex and Glamorgan also gaining promotion. In the Norwich Union National League, Lancashire Lightning, who won in 1999, Worcester and Sussex were relegated. They passed Surrey, winners of the division two, Nottinghamshire and Warwickshire on the way

The averages – as always – were dominated by overseas players, notably Australians. Yet Shane Warne's much trumpeted season with Hampshire did not amount to much. He barely scored a run in the early season and although he eventually took 70 wickets he hit the headlines more for off-field antics, eventually losing the vice-captaincy of Australia. The surf wasn't up to much on the south coast either.

PPP Healthcare County Championship

FIRST DIVISION

		P	W	L	D	Bt	Bl	Pts
1	Surrey	16	9	2	5	44	41	213
2	Lancashire	16	7	1	8	35	42	193
3	Yorkshire	16	7	2	7	36	48	188
4	Leicestershire	16	4	3	9	42	39	165
5	Somerset	16	2	4	10	41	40	145
6	Kent	16	4	4	8	18	42	140
7	Hampshire	16	3	9	4	20	48	112
8	Durham	16	2	9	5	27	41	112
9	Derbyshire	16	2	6	8	19	44	111

Derby docked 8 points for a poor pitch (Surrey, June 9)
Yorks docked 8 points for a poor pitch (Surrey, Aug 8)
Hants docked 8 points for a poor pitch (Yorks, Sep 16)

SECOND DIVISION

		P	W	L	D	Bt	Bl	Pts
1	Northamptonshire	16	7	4	5	39	45	188
2	Essex	16	5	2	9	28	41	165
3	Glamorgan	16	5	3	8	27	41	160
4	Gloucestershire	16	6	4	6	20	42	158
5	Worcestershire	16	5	5	6	25	42	151
6	Warwickshire	16	2	3	11	47	35	150
7	Nottinghamshire	16	2	4	10	41	43	148
8	Middlesex	16	2	6	8	36	46	138
9	Sussex	16	3	6	7	31	39	134

COUNTY CHAMPIONSHIP STATISTICS

Top Individual Scores

Division One
295* A D Brown (Surrey)

Division Two
309* S P James (Glamorgan)

Leading Run Scorers

1	1477	D S Lehmann (Yorkshire)
	1090	P D Bowler (Somerset)
	1089	S M Katich (Durham)
	1039	R Dravid (Kent)
	1038	A Habib (Leicestershire)
2	1472	J L Langer (Middlesex)
	1352	S G Law (Essex)
	1270	M L Hayden (Northamptonshire)
	1175	R C Irani (Sussex)
	1124	M G Bevan (Sussex)

Leading Wicket Takers

1	70	S K Warne (Hampshire)
	66	Saqlain Mushtaq (Surrey)
	60	M P Bicknell (Surrey)
	57	M J Saggers (Kent)
	56	S E J Brown (Durham)
2	76	G D McGrath (Worcestershire)
	67	D M Cousins (Northamptonshire)
	65	P C R Tufnell (Middlesex)
	63	R J Kirtley (Sussex)
	57	J F Brown (Northamptonshire)

Best Bowling (Innings)

1 9-47 M P Bicknell (Surrey)

2 8-41 G D McGrath (Worcestershire)

Leading Catchers

1 30 D P Fulton (Kent)

2 25 J L Langer (Middlesex)

Leading Wicketkeeper

1 43 (41c/2s) P A Nixon (Kent)

2 51 (45c/6s) B J Hyam (Essex)

2000 Final Averages - All First-class Matches

BATTING

	M	In	NO	Rns	HS	Avge	100	50
M G Bevan (Sus)	12	18	3	1124	174	74.93	5	1
M Richardson (NZA)	6	11	2	642	212*	71.33	1	4
D S Lehmann (Yo)	16	23	1	1477	136	67.13	4	9
M W Goodwin (Zi)	8	12	2	651	194	65.10	3	1
PD Bowler (So)	18	26	5	1305	157*	62.14	5	4
J L Langer (Mx)	16	27	3	1472	213*	61.33	5	7
M L Hayden (Nor)	15	22	0	1270	164	57.72	4	6
R Dravid (Kt)	16	25	1	1221	182	55.50	2	8
SG Law (Es)	16	27	2	1385	189	55.40	5	6
RC Irani (Es)	17	29	7	1196	168*	54.36	1	9
A D Brown (Su)	16	23	5	935	295*	51.94	2	4
M T G Elliott (Gla)	13	21	0	1076	177	51.23	4	4
D P Ostler (Wa)	16	24	2	1096	145	49.81	2	7
M Ramprakash (M)	17	28	4	1183	120*	49.29	4	7
R J Bailey (De)	13	19	4	728	118	48.53	2	5
A Habib (Le)	17	23	1	1038	172*	47.18	2	8
N Fairbrother (La)	15	23	5	823	138	45.72	2	3
K J Barnett (Glo)	11	16	2	640	118*	45.71	2	3
M Wagh (Wa)	9	16	3	592	137	45.53	2	3
J P Crawley (La)	15	22	1	951	156	45.28	5	-
P DeFreitas (Le)	14	18	3	677	123*	45.13	1	4
U Afzaal (Not)	16	26	3	1018	151*	44.26	3	4
V Solanki (Wo)	16	28	2	1138	161*	43.76	2	8
M Powell (Wa)	17	26	2	1046	145	43.58	2	8
S Katich (Du)	16	28	3	1089	137*	43.56	3	5
M Trescothick (So)	12	19	2	738	105	43.41	1	5
M Vaughan (Yo)	13	21	1	866	155*	43.30	2	4
M Butcher (Su)	16	25	4	891	191	42.42	2	3
D Cork (De)	14	17	4	542	200*	41.69	1	2
J Dakin (Le)	9	12	1	458	135	41.63	1	3
A Penberthy (Nor)	15	21	2	785	116	41.31	1	5
W Kendall (Ha)	18	31	3	1156	161	41.28	3	5
S James (Gla)	17	28	2	1070	309*	41.15	3	2
M Burns (So)	15	20	1	775	160	40.78	2	5
T Penney (Wa)	13	18	4	569	100*	40.64	1	2
I Ward (Sur)	16	25	3	894	158*	40.63	3	3
A Giles (Wa)	13	14	3	444	128*	40.36	1	1
C J Adams (Sus)	16	26	3	913	156	39.69	1	7
N Knight (Wa)	10	15	0	593	233	39.53	1	1
J Cox (So)	17	26	1	983	171	39.32	3	3
G D Rose (So)	15	18	5	510	124	39.23	2	1
D Leatherdale (Wo)	17	30	5	975	132*	39.00	2	7
D Brown (Wa)	16	22	6	622	203	38.87	1	2
M Atherton (La)	18	29	1	1068	136	38.14	3	6
D L Hemp (Wa)	17	24	2	834	129	37.90	1	5
K Parsons (So)	15	22	2	745	193*	37.25	2	1
M Windows (Glo)	19	31	3	1042	166	37.21	2	6
W Hinds (WI)	11	19	1	669	150	37.16	3	3
A Campbell (ZIM)	8	10	2	292	150*	36.50	1	1
N Shahid (Sur)	9	12	0	434	80	36.16	-	3
D Sales (Nor)	13	20	0	713	276	35.65	1	5
A D Shaw (Glam)	12	18	5	462	88*	35.53	-	3
W Hegg (La)	17	23	5	639	128	35.50	1	4
J Snape (Glo)	15	20	3	598	69	35.17	-	4
G A Hick (Wo)	14	24	2	773	122	35.13	3	3
D Robinson (Es)	12	19	3	561	93*	35.06	-	4
A Flintoff (La)	13	19	1	631	119	35.05	1	4
A Dale (Glam)	17	27	3	837	81	34.87	-	5
R Warren (No)	9	13	1	417	151	34.75	1	2
J Gallian (Not)	16	26	3	796	150	34.60	3	-

BOWLING

	O	M	R	W	Avge	Best
C A Walsh (WI)	242.2	106	457	40	11.42	6-74
R Sidebottom (Yo)	134.2	46	300	24	12.50	6-16
G D McGrath (Wo)	415.4	132	1057	80	13.21	8-41
M Mbangwa (ZIM)	211.5	86	428	30	14.26	6-14
Saqlain M (Su)	451.2	127	1016	66	15.39	7-11
A R Caddick (So)	329.4	98	848	55	15.41	7-64
P J Martin (La)	236.2	83	464	30	15.46	7-67
G Sulzberger (NZA)	189.3	61	458	28	16.35	5-55
I J Harvey (Glo)	254.2	79	658	40	16.45	6-19
A D Mullally (Ha)	343.5	105	832	49	16.97	9-93
O T Parkin (Gla)	108.0	32	291	17	17.11	4-14
C White (Yo)	157.3	32	430	25	17.20	5-32
M P Bicknell (Su)	413.2	115	1052	60	17.53	9-47
K J Dean (De)	246	57	785	44	17.84	8-52
G J Whittall (ZIM)	106	31	290	16	18.12	3-14
M M Betts (Du)	354	91	832	44	18.90	7-30
I Salisbury (Su)	380.3	101	984	52	18.92	8-60
D Gough (Yo)	324.1	61	949	50	18.98	6-63
H Streak (ZIM)	156.1	50	346	18	19.22	6-87
A Flintoff (La)	135.2	47	290	15	19.33	4-18
D M Cousins (Nor)	510.4	143	1318	67	19.67	5-123
K Newell (Gla)	51.0	23	100	5	20.00	2-18
M J Saggers (Kt)	425.2	99	1148	57	20.14	7-79
L Hamilton (NZA)	94	22	287	14	20.50	5-55
J F Brown (Nor)	517.5	142	1258	61	20.62	7-78
A M Smith (Glo)	250.4	70	623	30	20.76	5-52
J Lewis (Glo)	562.3	169	1506	72	20.91	8-95
S R Lampitt (Wo)	412.5	108	1173	56	20.94	7-45
M Smethurst (La)	380.1	90	1176	56	21.00	7-37
D G Cork (De)	356.4	94	886	42	21.09	6-41
M Cawdron (Glo)	199.5	64	534	25	21.36	6-25
K P Dutch (Mx)	142.4	45	365	17	21.47	6-62
S Brown (Du)	442.2	110	1208	56	21.57	7-51
G Hamilton (Yo)	313.4	80	866	40	21.65	5-22
C J Elstub (Yo)	70.1	13	175	8	21.87	3-37
S L Watkin (Gla)	389.4	108	1067	48	22.22	6-26
A L Penberthy (Nor)	131.0	30	358	16	22.37	5-54
C Ambrose (WI)	207.1	65	403	18	22.38	4-30
M R Strong (Nor)	84.2	15	269	12	22.41	4-46
J P Taylor (Nor)	212.3	50	540	24	22.50	6-27
A J Tudor (Su)	304.3	71	1071	47	22.78	7-48
N McLean (WI)	271.3	68	803	35	22.94	5-30
P Tufnell (Mx)	738.3	255	1500	65	23.07	6-48
A F Giles (Wa)	526.4	163	1200	52	23.07	8-90
S K Warne (Ha)	639.4	183	1620	70	23.14	6-34
A Fraser (Mx)	475.3	150	1112	48	23.16	6-64
D R Tuffey (NZA)	116	23	373	16	23.31	5-74
M E Cassar (De)	212.2	54	702	30	23.40	6-76
J C Scuderi (La)	120	28	333	14	23.78	4-58
J N Snape (Glo)	113.3	44	239	10	23.90	3-70
G Chapple (La)	431.5	101	1175	49	23.97	6-42
R C Irani (Es)	407.3	120	1008	42	24.00	5-79
D D Masters (Kt)	435.2	104	1161	48	24.18	6-27
C Collymore (WI)	126.4	44	369	15	24.60	3-18
R D King (WI)	195.1	45	618	25	24.72	3-28
R J Kirtley (Sus)	521.4	138	1559	63	24.74	6-41
J Middlebrook (Yo)	281.1	68	771	31	24.87	6-82
A P Cowan (Es)	398.5	98	1175	47	25.00	5-54
C vd Gucht (Ha)	22	7	75	3	25.00	3-75
B C Strang (ZIM)	187.3	59	452	18	25.11	5-68

The Super Cup
Group Stage *50-over competition*

NORTH DIVISION
County Ground, Derby   Apr 15
Leicestershire 86 (37 overs)
Derbyshire 22-3 (45.3)
No result - 1 point apiece

Riverside, Chester-le-Streer Apr 15
Durham 178 (40)
Yorkshire 168-9 (40)
Durham won by 10 runs

Old Trafford, Manchester Apr 15
Nottinghamshire 164-7 (37)
Lancashire 165-2 (46.5)
Lancashire won by 8 wickets

Grace Road, Leicester   Apr 16
Leicestershire 187 (49.3)
Durham 167 (50)*
Leicestershire won by 20 runs

Trent Bridge, Nottingham Apr 16
Nottinghamshire 94 (33.3)
Derbyshire 98-1 (11.4)
Derbyshire won by 9 wickets

Headingley, Leeds Apr 16
Lancashire 166 (50)
Yorkshire 167-6 (45.3)*
Yorkshire won by 4 wickets

Riverside, Chester-le-Streer Apr 18
Durham 53-8 (10)
Lancashire 55-1 (6.5)
Lancashire won by 9 wickets

Headingley, Leeds Apr 19
Leicestershire 191 (50)
Yorkshire 192-5 (45.5)
Yorkshire won by 5 wickets

County Ground, Derby   Apr 20
Lancashire 218-6 (50)
Derbyshire 219-4 (49)
Derbyshire won by 6 wickets

Trent Bridge, Nottingham Apr 20
Durham 174-8 (28)
Nottighamshire 172-7 (28)
Durham won by 2 runs

County Ground, Derby   Apr 22
Yorkshire 82-2 (21.2) **v Derbyshire**
No result - 1 point apiece

Grace Road, Leicester   Apr 22
Leicestershire v Nottinghamshire
No result - 1 point apiece

Riverside, Chester-le-Streer Apr 24
Durham 245-9 (50)
Derbyshire 107 (40.4)*
Durham won by 138 runs

Old Trafford, Manchester Apr 24
Leicstershire 172 (47.3)
Lancashire 176-9 (46.3)
Lancashire won by 1 wicket

Trent Bridge, Nottingham Apr 24
Nottinghamshire 129-8 (35)
Yorkshire 119-4 (28.2)
Yorkshire won by 6 wickets (D/L)

	W	L	NR	Pts	RR
Yorks	3	1	1	6	+0.315
Durham	3	2	0	6	+0.649
Lancs	3	2	0	6	+0.070
Derbys	2	1	2	6	+0.118
Leics	1	2	2	4	-0.043
Notts	0	4	1	1	-1.480

MIDLANDS/WALES/WEST DIV
*The following games were
abandoned without a ball bowled.*
Northampton v Worcestershire
Warwckshire v Northamptonshire
Worcestershire v Gloucestershire
Somerset v Glamorgan
Northampton v Gloucestershire
Somerset v Worcestershire
Glamorgan v Warwickshire

Sophia Gardens, Cardiff Apr 15
Gloucestershire 148-6 (25)
Glamorgan 150-7 (24.4)
Glamorgan won by 3 wickets

Edgbaston, Birmingham Apr 15
Somerset 48-2(14) **v Warwicks**
No result - 1 point apiece

County Ground, Bristol   Apr 16
Warwickshire 94 (35.4)
Gloucestershire 96-5 (28.1)
Gloucestershire won by 5 wickets

County Ground, Taunton Apr 16
Somerset 257-7 (50)
Northamptonshire 190-3 (40.1)
Glamorgan won by 3 wickets

New Road, Worcester Apr 16
Glamorgan 147 (46.4)
Worcestershire 148-1 (29.4)
Worcestershire won by 9 wickets

County Ground, Bristol   Apr 24
Somerset 225 (49.5)
Gloucestershire 154-5 (35)
Somerset won by 10 runs D/L

County Ground Northampton Apr 24
Glamorgan 238-8 (50)
Northamptonshire 199 (46)
Glamorgan won by 39 runs

Edgbaston, Birmingham Apr 24
Worcestershire 91-4 (10)
Warwickshire 92-3 (9.5)
No result - 1 point apiece

	W	L	NR	Pts	RR
Gloucs	2	1	2	6	+1.036
Glamorgan	2	1	2	6	-0.438
Worcs	1	1	3	5	+2.031
Northants	1	1	3	5	-0.356
Warwicks	1	1	3	5	-1.791
Somerset	0	2	3	3	-0.232

SOUTH DIVISION
*The following games were
abandoned without a ball bowled.*
Essex v Surrey
Hampshire v Middlesex
Kent v Sussex
Middlesex v Essex
Surrey v Kent
Hampshire v Kent
Middlesex v Sussex
Middlesex v Surrey

St Lawrence, Canterbury, Apr 18
Essex 175-8 (39)
Kent 173-5 (39)
Essex won by 2 runs

Hove, Apr 18
Sussex 97 (44)
Surrey 61-2 (20)
Surrey won by 35 runs D/L

County Ground, Chelmsford Apr 19
Essex 201-9 (50)
Hampshire 202-5 (47.3)
Hampshire won by 5 wickets

Hove, Apr 23
Hampshire 166-9 (50)
Sussex 170-8 (49.2)
Sussex won by 2 wickets

County Ground, Chelmsford, Apr 24
Sussex 316-3 (50)
Essex 254-8 (50)
Sussex won by 62 runs

St Lawrence, Canterbury, Apr 24
Kent 204-9 (50)
Middlesex 127 (36.2)
Kent won by 77 runs

Oval, Apr 24
Hampshire 87-7 (10)
Surrey 85-5 (10)
Hampshire won by 2 runs

	W	L	NR	Pts	RR
Sussex	2	1	2	6	+0.282
Hampshire	2	1	2	6	+0.062
Surrey	1	1	3	5	+2.031
Kent	1	1	3	5	-0.356
Essex	1	2	2	4	-1.791
Middlesex	0	1	4	4	-0.232

Continued on page151

The Super Cup Final

Lord's June 10

GLAMORGAN

R D B Croft	c Lewis	b Harvey	11
M T G Elliott		b Harvey	9
M J Powell		c & b Snape	48
M P Maynard*	run out (Barnett)		104
A Dale	run out (Windows/Russell)		5
S P James		b Averis	7
K Newell	c Cunliffe	b Harvey	1
A D Shaw†	c Barnett	b Averis	1
A G Wharf	lbw	b Harvey	8
S L Watkin		b Harvey	10
O T Parkin	not out		0
Extras (LB5, W8, NB8)			21
Total (50 overs)			225

Fall of wickets: 1-18, 2-24, 3-161, 4-178, 5-192, 6-195, 7-202, 8-213, 9-225

Bowling: Harvey 9.3-1-34-5, **Smith** 10-1-44-0, **Lewis** 5-0-23-0, **Averis** 10-0-49-2, **Alleyne** 7-0-33-0, **Snape** 8-0-37-1

Toss: Glamorgan
Umpires: **K E Palmer & G Sharp**

GLOUCESTERSHIRE

T H C Hancock		c & b Parkin	60
K J Barnett		b Croft	39
R J Cunliffe	c Shaw	b Watkin	24
M G N Windows	not out		53
M W Alleyne*	run out		40
Extras (B1, LB4, W3, NB2)			10
Total (3 wkts, 46.5 overs)			226

Did not bat: I J Harvey, J N Snape, R C Russell, J Lewis, J M M Averis, A M Smith

Fall of wickets: 1-80, 2-118, 3-131

Bowling: Parkin 8-1-46-1, **Watkin** 10-1-42-1, **Wharf** 5-0-32-3, **Croft** 10-0-39-1, **Dale** 8.5-0-46-0

Gold Award: **M P Maynard**
GLOUCESTERSHIRE WON BY SEVEN WICKETS

NatWest Trophy Final

Lord's Aug 26 & 27

WARWICKSHIRE

N V Knight	c Russell	b Smith	1
A Singh		b Smith	10
A F Giles	c Barnett	b Hancock	60
D P Ostler	c Harvey	b Averis	19
T L Penney	c Alleyne	b Smith	20
M J Powell		b Harvey	20
D R Brown	c Barnett	b Hancock	4
N M K Smith*	not out		28
K J Piper†	not out		8
Extras (LB12, W22)			34
Total (7 wkts, 50 overs)			205

Did not bat: A A Donald, E S H Giddins

Fall of wickets: 1-9, 2-32, 3-81, 4-129, 5-134, 6-147, 7-170

Bowling: Harvey 10-0-47-1, **Smith** 10-3-18-3, **Averis** 10-1-50-1, **Alleyne** 6-0-28-0, **Hancock** 10-0-34-2, **Ball** 4-0-16-0

Toss: Gloucestershire
Umpires: **J H Hampshire & R Julian**

GLOUCESTERSHIRE

T H C Hancock		b Donald	18
K L Barnett		b Donald	45
I J Harvey	c Powell	b Brown	47
R C Russell†	not out		6
Extras (LB5, W1)			6
Total (29.4 overs)			122

Did not bat: M G N Windows, C G Taylor, M W Alleyne, J N Snape, MC J Ball, J M M Averis, A M Smith

Fall of wickets: 1-40, 2-93, 3-122

Bowling: Brown 5.4-0-38-1, **Giddins** 7-0-20-0, **Donald** 6-2-7-2, **Smith** 4-0-23-0, **Giles** 7-0-29-0

Match Award: **A A Donald**
GLOUCESTERSHIRE WON BY 22 RUNS (D/L)

NatWest Trophy
*50 overs; * Denotes team batting first*

First Round *May 2*

Lincolnshire 204-9 (50) bt **Cheshire 204*** (50) on fewer wickets lost
Norfolk 171-6 (47.5) bt **Cornwall 170-6*** (50)
Durham Cricket Board 195-7 (49.5) bt **Leicestershire CB 192-9*** (50)
Gloucestershire CB 126-2 (28.5) bt **Nottinghamshire CB 125-9*** (50)
Huntingdonshire 148-8* (50) bt **Hamphire CB 120** (46)
Sussex CB 215-7* (50) bt **Herefordshire 209-9** (50)
Cambridgeshire 115-6 (46) bt **Hertfordshire 114*** (47.1)
Shropshire 141-5 (49) bt **Ireland 140*** (50)
Northumberland 175-4 (48.2) bt **Northamptonshire CB 173-8*** (50)
Staffordshire 127-3 (29) bt **Somerset CB 124*** (45.4)
Lancashire CB 146-6 (38.2) bt **Suffolk 145*** (49.4)
Wales Minor Counties 212-6* (50) bt **Buckinghamshire 201-9** (50)
Wiltshire 94-3 (31.1) bt **Scotland 93*** (29.5)
Kent CB 239-9* (50) bt **Worcestershire CB 189** (44.2)

Second Round *May 16*

Cumberland 126-1 (32.2) bt **Cambridgeshire 123*** (45.1)
Derbyshire CB 222-8* (50) bt **Gloucestershire CB 172** (43.3)
Devon 238* (49.5) bt **Staffordshire 46** (20.5)
Dorset 181-8* (50) bt **Norfolk 71** (33.2)
Durham CB 223-5 (38.3) bt **Denmark 218*** (50)
Essex CB 266* (50) bt **Lancashire CB 251-9** (50)
Yorkshire CB 207-5 (45) bt **Huntingdonshire 204-8*** (50)
Lincolnshire 210-8* (50) bt **Holland 115** (37.2)
Middlesex CB 203-8* (50) bt **Wiltshire 200-9** (50)
Northumberland 167-3 (33.2) bt **Bedfordshire 164*** (48)
Shropshire 239-4 (49.2) bt **Surrey CB 233-9*** (50)
Berkshire 207-5 (47.2) bt **Sussex CB 206*** (49.4)
Wales Minor Counties 122-2 (35.3) bt **Oxfordshire 120*** (49.1)
Kent CB 208-8* (50) bt **Warwickshire CB 163** (47.3)

Third Round *June 21 & July 4*

Durham 140* (49.4) bt **Berkshire 97** (28.5)
Kent 141-4 (39) bt **Cumberland 140*** (48.1)
Lancashire 193-0 (30) bt **Lincolnshire 190-9*** (50)
Somerset 262-6* (50) bt **Shropshire 235-9** (50)
Hampshire 150-2 (36.5) bt **Kent CB 149*** (50)
Surrey 198-2 (44) bt **Devon 194-6*** (50)
Sussex 154-1 (27.1) bt **Middlesex CB 153*** (50)
Essex 154* (48.1) bt **Wales Minor Counties 51** (21)
Derbyshire 356-2* (50) bt **Derbyshire CB 133-9** (50)
Northants 169-2 (32.2) bt **Durham CB 167*** (49.5)
Warwickshire 214-8* (50) bt **Essex CB 203-8** (50)
Glamorgan 333-4* (50) bt **Dorset 194** (48.5)
Yorkshire 240-5* (50) bt **Yorkshire CB 110** (38.5)
Middlesex 274-5* (50) bt **Nottinghamshire 146** (37)
Leicesters 328-9* (50) bt **Northumberland 102** (33.3)
Worcs 212-7 (48.5) bt **Gloucestershire 211-8*** (50)
This match had to be replayed as Worcestershire fielded Kabir Ali, who had played for the Worcestershire CB in the first round
Gloucs 163* (49.3) bt **Worcestershire 158** (49.3)

Fourth Round *July 5*

Durham 91 (42.4)
Hampshire 92-5 (24.3)
Hampshire won by 5 wickets

Kent 121 (48.4)
Glamorgan 122-5 (37.1) K Newell 62*, Ealham 4-36
Glamorgan won by 5 wickets

Lancashire 251-5 (50) M Atherton 70, S Ganguly 97
Essex 183 (42.3) Schofield 4-34
Lancashire won by 68 runs

Gloucestershire 210-8 (50) K Barnett 86
Leicestershire 200 (48.1) D Stevens 55, D Maddy 72, Harvey 4-40
Gloucestershire won by 10 runs

Middlesex 223-4 (50) P Weekes 71*
Somerset 58 (28.3) Bloomfield 4-17
Middlesex won by 165 runs

Northamptonshire 252 (50) M Hayden 63, D Sales 65, Gough 4-36
Yorkshire 183 (43.5) A McGrath 64
Northamptonshire won by 69 runs

Sussex 192-9 (50) R Montgomerie 53, M Bevan 60
Surrey 196-3 (47.4) M Butcher 87*
Surrey won by 7 wickets

Warwickshire 257-8 (50) A Giles 107
Derbyshire 217 (46.5) M Di Venuto 84, Donald 4-42
Derbyshire won by 40 runs

Quarter-finals *July 25 & 26*

Middlesex 127 (44) Mascarenhas 4-25
Hampshire 128-3 (34.5)
Hampshire won by 7 wickets

Warwickshire 273-7 (50) N Knight 118, D Ostler 63
Glamorgan 192 (44.4)
Warwickshire won by 81 runs

Gloucestershire 280-8 (50) T Hancock 110, K Barnett 51
Northamptonshire 218-9 (50) A Penberthy 54, Harvey 4-37
Gloucestershire won by 62 runs

Surrey 210-7 (50) G Thorpe 55, Schofield 4-41
Lancashire 214-3 (36) S Ganguly 51, A Flintoff 135*
Lancashire won by 8 wickets

Semi-finals

Aug 12
Warwickshire 262-4 (50) N Knight 100, A Singh 85
Hampshire 243-7 (50) R Smith 61
Warwickshire won by 19 runs

Aug 13
Gloucestershire 248-7 (50) K J Barnett 80, R Russell 55
Lancashire 150 (45.2)
Gloucestershire won by 98 runs

Norwich Union National League

2000 FINAL TABLES
One-day matches - 45 overs each
(Last year's position in brackets)

Division 1

		P	W	L	NR	T	Pts	RR
1	Gloucs Gladiators (4)	16	9	6	0	1	38	+1.258
2	Yorkshire Phoenix (5)	16	9	7	0	0	36	+5.975
3	Northants Steelbacks (-)	16	9	7	0	0	36	-3.983
4	Leicester Foxes (6)	16	7	6	1	2	34	-0.458
5	Kent Spitfires (3)	16	7	7	2	0	32	+6.177
6	Somerset Sabres (-)	16	7	8	1	0	30	-0.594
7	Worcester Royals (2)	16	6	8	2	0	28	-4.236
8	Lancs Lightning (1)	16	6	8	1	0	28	-5.829
9	Sussex Sharks (-)	16	5	8	2	1	26	+0.345

Division 2

		P	W	L	NR	T	Pts	RR
1	Surrey Lions (6)	16	11	3	2	0	48	+11.93
2	Notts Outlaws (5)	16	11	4	1	0	46	-2.177
3	Warwickshire Bears (-)	16	10	5	0	0	42	+7.098
4	Middx Crusaders (7)	16	8	5	2	1	38	-0.260
5	Essex Eagles (-)	16	7	7	2	0	32	+0.359
6	Glamorgan Dragons (4)	16	7	7	0	2	32	-2.184
7	Durham Dynamoes (9)	16	5	11	0	0	20	+0.327
8	Hampshire Hawks (-)	16	5	11	0	0	20	-5.780
9	Derby Scorpions (8)	16	2	13	1	0	10	-8.999

Season's Statistics

Top Scoring Batsmen
Average in brackets

1	P D Collingwood (Durham)	607 (46.69)
2	S M Katich (Durham)	598 (46.00)
3	D J Bicknell (Notts)	537 (41.30)
4	M P Maynard (Glamorgan)	501 (41.75)
5	R A Smith (Hampshire)	464 (35.69)
6	S P James (Glamorgan)	439 (39.90)
7	J E R Gallian (Notts)	439 (31.35)
8	M T G Elliott (Glamorgan)	429 (47.66)
9	I J Ward (Surrey)	429 (35.75)
10	S G Law (Essex)	413 (34.41)

Highest Scores

126* G P Thorpe (Surrey)
126 M E Cassar (Derbyshire)

Top Wicket-taking Bowlers

1	N Kileen (Durham)	29 (14.31)
2	S K Warne (Hampshire)	25 (17.52)
3	D R Brown (Warwickshire)	25 (17.88)
4	P J Franks (Notts)	25 (22.48)
5	N C Phillips (Durham)	24 (21.54)
6	A J Hollioake (Surrey)	23 (11.43)
7	A P Cowan (Essex)	22 (19.68)
8	A F Giles (Warwicks)	22 (19.77)
9	R L Johnson (Middlesex)	21 (16.09)
10	A D Mascarenhas (Hampshire)	21 (25.71)

Best Analyses

6-27 P J Franks (Notts)
6-31 N Kileen (Durham)

Top Wicketkeepers

1	C M W Read (Notts)	27 (25/2)
2	K J Piper (Warwicks)	22 (15/7)
3	A N Aymes (Hampshire)	16 (11/5)
4	D Alleyne (Middlesex)	15 (10/5)
5	M P Speight (Durham)	15 (12/3)
6	K M Krikken (Derbyshire)	12 (7/5)
7	D A Kenway (Hampshire)	11 (7/4)
8	M P Maynard (Glamorgan)	11 (10/1)
9	L D Sutton (Derbyshire)	10 (8/2)
10	B J Hyam (Essex)	9 (6/3)

Top Catchers

1	P D Collingwood (Durham)	11
1	J L Langer (Middlesex)	11
3	T J Mason (Essex)	9
3	N M K Smith (Warwicks)	9
5	D G Cork (Derbyshire)	8
5	T L Penney (Warwicks)	8
5	S M Katich (Durham)	8

THE SUPER CUP, cont

QUARTER-FINALS

Sophia Gardens, Cardiff, May 9
Glamorgan 182-6 (50)
Hampshire 69 (34.2)
Glamorgan won by 113 runs

Old Trafford, Manchester, May 9
Durham 154 (46.5)
Lancashire 158-7 (45)
Lancashire won by 3 wickets

Hove, May 9
Gloucestershire 237-7 (50)
Sussex 208-9 (50)
Gloucestershire won by 29 runs

Headingley, Leeds, May 9
Surrey 198-6 (50)
Yorkshire 191 (49.5)
Yorkshire won by 7 runs

SEMI-FINALS

Sophia Gardens, Cardiff, May 27-28
Glamorgan 251 (49.1)
Surrey 212 (43)
Glamorgan won by 32 runs

County Ground, Bristol, May 28-29
Gloucestershire 220-6 (50)
Lancashire 205-9 (50)
Gloucestershire won by 15 runs

World Cup
Round Robin Matches

AUSTRALIA V NEW ZEALAND
BIL Oval, Lincoln   Nov 29
New Zealand 166 (E C Drumm 74, T A McGregor 4-18)
Australia 167-4 (K L Rolton 51*, L M Keightley 44)
Australia won by 6 wickets

ENGLAND V NETHERLANDS
BIL Oval, Lincoln   Nov 30
England 256-3 (C M Edwards 139*, B Daniels 79)
Netherlands 116 (S V Collyer 5-32)
England won by 140 runs

INDIA V SOUTH AFRICA
Hagley Oval, Christchurch   Nov 30
South Africa 128-8 (Y vd Merwe 42*, R Purnima 3-12)
India 129-2 (R Mithali 69*)
India won by 8 wickets

AUSTRALIA V SRI LANKA
Hagley Oval, Christchurch   Dec 1
Australia 282-3 (K L Rolton 154*, L M Keightley 56)
Sri Lanka 82 (A J Fahey 3-11)
Australia won by 200 runs

IRELAND V NEW ZEALAND
BIL Oval, Lincoln   Dec 1
Ireland 99 (C M Beggs 31, H M Tiffin 2-14)
New Zealand 102-2 (P B Flannery 49*)
New Zealand won by 8 wickets

ENGLAND V SOUTH AFRICA
BIL Oval, Lincoln   Dec 2
England 143 (B Daniels 46, Y van der Merwe 3-25)
South Africa 144-5 (S Viljoen 54*)
South Africa won by 5 wickets

INDIA V NETHERLANDS
Lincoln Green   Dec 2
India 275-4 (A Chopra 69, H Kala 56, R Mithali 51)
Netherlands 121-6 (C Verheul 46*)
India won by 154 runs

AUSTRALIA V IRELAND
Hagley Park, Christchurch   Dec 3
Ireland 90 (C O'Neill 28, Z J Goss 4-10)
Australia 91-0 (L M Keightley 49*, B J Clark 40*)
Australia won by 10 wickets

NEW ZEALAND V SRI LANKA
Lincoln Green   Dec 3
New Zealand 210-4 (A M O'Leary 91*, H M Tiffin 58)
Sri Lnka 88 (A D H Abeysinghe 30)
New Zealand won by 122 runs

INDIA V ENGLAND
Lincoln Green   Dec 4
India 155-7 (C Kaul 45)
England 147 (S C Taylor 60, S Rupanjali 3-25)
India won by 8 runs

NETHERLANDS V SOUTH AFRICA
Hagley Park, Christchurch   Dec 4
Netherlands 92 (M A Koster 36, L P Lewis 4-20)
South Africa 93-6 (M Terblanche 37*)
South Africa won by 4 wickets

SRI LANKA V IRELAND
Lincoln Green   Dec 5
Sri Lanka 129 (A D H Abersinghe 52)
Ireland 119 (C R Senevirathne 3-18)
Sri Lanka won by 10 runs

AUSTRALIA V INDIA
BIL Oval, Lincoln   Dec 6
Australia 223 (L M Keightley 74, K R Rolton 61)
India 172 (A Chopra 47, T A McGregor 3-38)
Australia won by 51 runs

NETHERLANDS V NEW ZEALAND
Hagley Park, Christchurch   Dec 6
Netherlands 80 (H M Watson 3-28)
New Zealand 81-2 (P B Flannery 36*)
New Zealand won by 8 wickets

ENGLAND V IRELAND
BIL Oval, Lincoln   Dec 7
Ireland 103 (C E Taylor 4-25)
England 105-2 (A Thompson 44*)
England won by 8 wickets

SOUTH AFRICA V SRI LANKA
Lincoln Green   Dec 8
Sri Lanka 134
South Africa 135 (M Terblanche 53*)
South Africa won by 6 wickets

INDIA V NEW ZEALAND
BIL Oval, Lincoln   Dec 9
New Zealand 224-5 (A M O'Leary 89, D A Hockley 53)
India 150-7 (C Kaul 59*)
New Zealand won by 74 runs

NETHERLANDS V SRI LANKA
Hagley Park, Christchurch   Dec 10
Sri Lanka 139 (S A R C Silva 53, T van der Gun 3-18)
South Africa 113 (H Rambaldo 38, C Sevevirathne 4-23)
Sri Lanka won by 26 runs

AUSTRALIA V ENGLAND
Lincoln Green   Dec 10
Australia 190-7 (Z J Goss 49, C E Taylor 3-30)
England 136 (S C Taylor 45, C L Mason 3-20)
Australia won by 54 runs

NEW ZEALAND V SOUTH AFRICA
Lincoln Green   Dec 11
New Zealand 265-5 (E C Drumm 108*)
South Africa 107 (C E Eksteen 47*, H M Watson 3-14)
New Zealand won by 158 runs

INDIA V IRELAND
Hagley Park, Christchurch   Dec 11
India 199-9 (A Chopra 70, H Kala 40, C O'Neil 3-33)
Ireland 169
India won by 30 runs

ENGLAND V SRI LANKA
Lincoln Green   Dec 8
England 242-4 (S C Taylor 137*, J Cassar 63*)
Sri Lanka 137-9 (A D H Abeysinghe 57, K M Leng 3-16)
England won by 105 runs

AUSTRALIA V SOUTH AFRICA
BIL Oval, Lincoln   Dec 13
South Africa 169-8 (C E Eksteen 46, C L Mason 3-29)
Australia 171-1 (K L Rolton 107*, B J Clark 49*)
Australia won by 9 wickets

ENGLAND V NEW ZEALAND
BIL Oval, Lincoln   Dec 14
New Zealand 238-8 (R J Rolls 65)
England 145 (K M Keenan 3-16)
New Zealand won by 93 runs

IRELAND V NETHERLANDS
Hagley Park, Christchurch   Dec 14
Ireland 232-6 (C M Beggs 66*, A Linehan 54)
Netherlands 191-8 (R C Milburn 71)
Ireland won by 41 runs

INDIA V SRI LANKA
Lincoln Green   Dec 15
India 230-4 (C Kaul 80, A Chopra 68*)
Sri Lanka 89
India won by 141 runs

AUSTRALIA V NETHERLANDS
Lincoln Green   Dec 16
Netherlands 107-7 (P te Beest 42, A J Fahey 3-19)
Australia 109-0 (L M Keightley 51*, B J Clark 48*)
Australia won by 10 wickets

IRELAND V SOUTH AFRICA
Halgey Park, Christchurch   Dec 16
Ireland 176 (A Linehan 40, S Viljoen 3-27)
South Africa 177-1 (L Olivier 101*)
South Africa won by 9 wickets

Round Robin Final Standings

	P	W	L	NR	T	Pts	RRate
Australia	7	7	-	-	-	14	+1.984
New Zealand	7	6	1	-	-	12	+2.002
India	7	5	2	-	-	10	+0.711
South Africa	7	4	3	-	-	8	-0.403
England	7	3	4	-	-	6	+0.440
Sri Lanka	7	2	5	-	-	4	-1.572
Ireland	7	1	6	-	-	2	-0.975
Netherlands	7	-	7	-	-	0	-2.098

Semi-finals

AUSTRALIA V SOUTH AFRICA
BIL Oval, Lincoln   Dec 18
South Africa 180-8 (L Olivier 41, C L Mason 3-39)
Australia 181-1 (L M Keightley 91*, B J Clark 75)
Australia won by 9 wickets

INDIA V NEW ZEALAND
BIL Oval, Lincoln   Dec 20
India 117 (R Purnima 67)
New Zealand 121-1 (A M O'Leary 50*, E C Drumm 47*)
New Zealand won by 9 wickets

THE FINAL
BIL Oval, Lincoln, New Zealand   Dec 23

NEW ZEALAND

				balls
A M O'Leary		b McGregor	1	8
R J Rolls†	c McGregor	b Mason	34	47
E C Drumm*	c Price	b McGregor	21	29
D A Hockley	lbw	b Fahey	24	69
H M Tiffin	c Bambury	b Goss	14	33
K A Ramel	c Clark	b Fitzpatrick	41	63
H M Watson	c Price	b Mason	11	15
C M Nicholson		b Mason	11	21
R J Pullar	not out		9	5
K M Keenan		b Fitzpatrick	0	2
C A Campbell	run out		0	1
Extras (LB9, W8, NB1)			18	
TOTAL (48.4 overs)			**184**	

Fall of Wickets: 1-17, 2-60, 3-60, 4-92, 5-121), 6-136, 7-172, 8-175, 9-184, 10-184

Bowling: Fitzpatrick 9.4-2-52-3, **McGregor** 10-5-26-2 **Mason** 9-2-30-2, **Magno** 6-0-22-0, **Goss** 4-0-14-1 **Rolton** 6-0-12-0, **Fahey** 4-0-19-1

Toss: **New Zealand**
Umpires: **P D Parker & D M Quested (B G Gerling - TV)**

AUSTRALIA

				balls
L M Keightley	c Rolls	b Keenan	0	4
B J Clark*		b Nicholson	91	102
K L Rolton	run out (Watson)		1	7
C Bambury	c Hockley	b Pullar	14	57
Z J Goss		b Campbell	1	11
O J Magno		b Keenan	4	13
J C Price†		b Pullar	10	28
T A McGregor	run out (Watson)		19	37
C L Fitzpatrick		b Ramel	6	19
C L Mason	c Rolls	b Nicholson	11	13
A J Fahey	not out		3	4
Extras (B1, LB6, W12, NB1)			20	
TOTAL (49.1 overs)			**180**	

Fall of Wickets: 1-0, 2-2, 3-85, 4-88, 5-95, 6-115, 7-150, 8-159, 9-175, 10-180

Bowling: Keenan 10-3-19-2, **Pullar** 10-0-35-2, **Tiffen** 5-1-27-0, **Ramel** 5-0-26-1, **Campbell** 10-2-28-1, **Nicholson** 9.1-1-38-2

Player of the Match: **B J Clark (AUS)**
Player of the Tournament: **L M Keightley (NZL)**
NEW ZEALAND WON BY 4 RUNS

Curling

World Championships
Braehead, Glasgow   April 1-9

Men
ROUND ROBIN
1st Draw: Norway 5 Denmark 6;
Switzerland 6 Scotland 7; Finland 7 Sweden 8;
USA 10 Japan 4; France 2 Canada 8;
2nd Draw: Japan 1 Scotland 8; Canada 9 Finland 2;
Norway 4 Switzerland 10; Sweden 10 France 2;
Denmark 9 USA 10
3rd Draw: Finland 7 Norway 3; Sweden 9 USA 6;
Scotland 3 France 7; Canada 11 Denmark 7;
Switzerland 9 Japan 5
4th Draw: Denmark 8 Switzerland 6; France 6 Norway 5;
Japan 2 Canada 11; Scotland 2 Sweden 10;
USA 4 Finland 9
5th Draw: Sweden 3 Canada 9; USA 8 Switzerland 4;
France 5 Finland 9; Japan 1 Norway 14;
Scotland 8 Denmark 5
6th Draw: France 3 Japan 11; Scotland 4 Canada 7;
USA 5 Norway 7; Denmark 6 Finland 11;
Sweden 8 Switzerland 5
7th Draw: Scotland 2 USA 8; Finland 7 Japan 6;
Sweden 8 Denmark 4; France 4 Switzerland 8;
Canada 6 Norway 4
8th Draw: Switzerland 7 Finland 10;
Denmark 7 France 4; Canada 8 USA 4;
Norway 7 Scotland 3; Japan 6 Sweden 10
9th Draw: USA 4 France 2; Norway 6 Sweden 2;
Denmark 10 Japan 3; Switzerland 8 Canada 7;
Finland 7 Scotland 3

Round Robin Ranking

	W	L
1 Canada	8	1
2= Sweden	7	2
2= Finland	7	2
4 USA	5	4
5= Denmark	4	5
5= Switzerland	4	5
5= Norway	4	5
8 Scotland	3	6
9 France	2	7
10 Japan	1	8

Semi-finals

Sweden 9	Finland 2
Canada 11	USA 3

3rd/4th Place Play-off

Finland 9	USA 4

FINAL

	1	2	3	4	5	6	7	8	9	10	11	Total
Canada	1	1	0	2	1	0	2	0	0	0	0	**7**
Sweden	0	0	2	0	0	1	0	1	0	0	0	**4**

Final Ranking: 1. Canada; 2. Sweden; 3. Finland;
4. USA; 5. Denmark; 6. Switzerland; 7. Norway;
8. Scotland; 9. France; 10. Japan

Women
ROUND ROBIN
1st Draw: France 4 Canada 9; USA 8 Denmark 5;
Sweden 9 Japan 7; Norway 9 Germany 2;
Scotland 2 Switzerland 10
2nd Draw: Germany 5 Denmark 11;
Switzerland 6 Sweden 5; France 2 USA 8;
Japan 1 Scotland 9; Canada 9 Norway 5
3rd Draw: Sweden 13 France 5; Japan 6 Norway 10;
Denmark 8 Scotland 10; Switzerland 6 Canada 5;
USA 4 Germany 8
4th Draw: Canada 7 USA 6; Scotland 9 France 2;
Germany 8 Switzerland 3; Denmark 10 Japan 2;
Norway 7 Sweden 6
5th Draw: Japan 1 Switzerland 8;
Norway 8 USA 7; Scotland 9 Sweden 4;
Germany 7 France 5; Denmark 1 Canada 8
6th Draw: Scotland 6 Germany 8;
Denmark 11 Switzerland 6; Norway 6 France 3;
Canada 7 Sweden 3; Japan 2 USA 11
7th Draw: Denmark 7 Norway 8; Sweden 13 Germany 3;
Japan 4 Canada 6; SCotland 8 USA 7;
Switzerland 9 France 4
8th Draw: USA 6 Sweden 12; Canada 6 Scotland 9;
Switzerland 6 Norway 5; France 4 Denmark 9;
Germany 6 Japan 8
9th Draw: Norway 8 Scotland 7; Japan 7 France 6;
Canada 8 Germany 7; USA 8 Switzerland 6;
Sweden 9 Denmark 3

Round Robin Ranking

	W	L
1= Canada	7	2
1= Norway	7	2
3= Switzerland	6	3
3= Scotland	6	3
5 Sweden	5	4
6= Denmark	4	5
6= Germany	4	5
6= USA	4	5
9 Japan	2	7
10 France	0	10

Semi-finals

Canada 10	Scotland 6
Switzerland 5	Norway 4

3rd/4th Place Play-off

Norway 10	Scotland 5

FINAL

	1	2	3	4	5	6	7	8	9	10	11	Total
Canada	1	0	2	0	1	0	1	1	0	1	0	**7**
Switzerland	0	2	0	1	0	1	0	0	2	0	0	**6**

Final Ranking: 1. Canada; 2. Switzerland; 3. Norway;
4. Scotland; 5. Sweden; 6. Denmark; 7. Germany;
8. USA; 9. Japan; 10. France

Cycling

I n 1990, the sprinter Angella Issayenko giving evidence to the Dubin report, the Canadian government investigation which followed the Ben Johnson positive at the Seoul Games, described the code of silence of the athletes. "Deny, deny, deny," she said. Richard Virenque followed the code to the letter, for the Frenchman denied and denied and denied. Two years after the event, in a courtroom in Lille, he finally told the truth. "I took doping substances, but I didn't have the choice. I was the sheep," he said.

Even then, his statement did not tally with that of his soigneur (or should it be fixeur) Willy Voet, whose words when Virenque was still in denial did not suggest he was ever force-fed any drugs - quite the opposite. "You bastard, you'd be dead if I'd agreed to inject all the products that you'd asked me to," said Voet at the time. Virenque comes out of the affair with no credit at all. There was no dignity even in the confessional, the fallen idol so sad that he would not even accept responsibility for his own actions. At least Issayenko came clean.

The Virenque affair left a more abiding message; that only government agencies are equipped to tackle the drugs issue in sport. It was Marie-George Buffet, the French minister of youth and sport, who has led the fight against drugs in cycling; who initiated the action against the Tour in 1998; and who has subsequently used the success of the anti-drug policy as the platform for the Paris 2008 Olympic bid. It was the Canadian government, way ahead of the game, which established the precedent.

The Tour de France was not a close affair. Lance Armstrong, the winner in 1999, took the race lead on the tenth stage and never lost it. His time trial victory from Frieburg to the Alsatian capital of Mulhouse, was embarrassingly emphatic. The French frowned into their glasses of pastis. 'If Virenque can't do it at half the speed without drugs, how can he?' was the question they were ungraciously asking. Armstrong refused to speak French in case he was misinterpreted, but dopage is a word that is comprehensible in any tongue.

It won't go away. Not yet. As athletics discovered, you cannot simply bury the past, for it has the unconcernable habit of revisiting the future. Just when you least expect it.

For British cycling, nothing but unalloyed joy. David Millar had a couple of days in the Maillot Jaune and Chris Boardman (who's done that too) retired at Manchester, exiting the sport with a record for the one-hour that was slower than his last record for the same distance. This conundrum came about courtesy of the ICU who re-invented the wheel as far as road bikes were concerned, making them more primitive. From next year they will all have solid tyres and be preceded by an official with a flag.

And we've relegated poor Yvonne McGregor to the bottom of the page, which is unfair but sometimes how it pans out. McGregor couldn't contain her own wonderment when she took the world pursuit title at Manchester and neither could those of us there. If ever there was a cyclist who embodied the spirit of the sport, who showed modesty and warmth and commitment, it has been McGregor. In her year of miracles, the 39-year-old won Olympic bronze and a world title. Virenque, go train with her. It could be your salvation.

Road Racing

Tour de France

Date	Stage	Start-Finish (Distance)	Stage Winner	Overall Leader
July 1	1	Futuroscope (16.5km)*	David Millar (Cofidis) GBR	David Millar
July 2	2	Futuroscope - Loudun (194km)	Tom Steels (Mapei) BEL	Millar
July 3	3	Loudon - Nantes (161.5km)	Tom Steels (Mapei) BEL	Millar
July 4	4	Nantes - St Nazaire (70km)**	ONCE ESP	Laurent Jalabert
July 5	5	Vannes - Vitré (202km)	Marcel Wüst (Festina) GER	Jalabert
July 6	6	Vitré - Tours (198.5km)	Leon van Bon (Rabobank) NED	Alberto Elli
July 7	7	Tours - Limoges (205.5km)	Christophe Agnolutto (AG2) FRA	Elli
July 8	8	Limoges - Villneuve-sur-Lot (203.5km)	Erik Dekker (Rabobank) NED	Elli
July 9	9	Agen - Dax (181km)	Paolo Bettini (Mapei) ITA	Elli
July 10	10	Dax - Lourdes-Hautacam (205km)	Javier Otxoa (Kelme) ESP	Lance Armstrong
July 11	11	Bagnères-de-Bigorre - Revel (218.5km)	Erik Dekker (Rabobak) NED	Armstrong
July 13	12	Carpentras - Le Mont Ventoux (149km)	Marco Pantani (Mercatone) ITA	Armstrong
July 14	13	Avignon - Dragiugnan (185.5km)	Vicente Garcia-Acosta (Ban) ESP	Armstrong
July 15	14	Draguignan - Briançon (249.5km)	Santiago Botero (Kelme) COL	Armstrong
July 16	15	Briançon - Courcheval (173.5km)	Marco Pantani (Mercatone) ITA	Armstrong
July 18	16	Courcheval - Morzine (196.5km)	Richard Virenque (Polti) FRA	Armstrong
July 19	17	Evian-les-Bains - Lausanne (155km)	Erik Dekker (Rabobank) NED	Armstrong
July 20	18	Lausanne - Friborg-en-Brisgau (246.5km)	Salvatore Commesso (Saeco) ITA	Armstrong
July 21	19	Friborg-en-Brisgau - Mulhouse (58.5km)*	Lance Armstrong (US Postal) USA	Armstrong
July 22	20	Belfort - Troyes (254.5 km)	Erik Zabel (Telekom) GER	Armstrong
July 23	21	Paris - Champs-Elysées (138km)	Stefano Zanini (Mapei) ITA	Armstrong

* Time Trial
** Team Time Trial   Total Finishers

Final Classification

	Rider	Ctry	Time
1	Lance Armstrong (US Postal)	USA	92:33:08
2	Jan Ullrich (Telekom)	GER	at 6:02
3	Joseba Beloki (Festina)	ESP	at 10:04
4	Christophe Moreau (Festina)	FRA	at 10:34
5	Roberto Heras (Kelme)	ESP	at 11:50
6	Richard Virenque (Polti)	FRA	at 12:13
7	Santiago Botero (Kelme)	COL	at 14:18
8	Fernando Escartin (Kelme)	ESP	at 17:21
9	Francisco Mancebo (Banesto)	ESP	at 18:09
10	Daniele Nardello (Mapei)	ITA	at 18:25
11	Manuel Beltran (Mapei)	ESP	at 21:11
12	Pascal Herve (Polti)	FRA	at 23:13
13	Javier Otxoa (Kelme)	ESP	at 25:00
14	Felix Garcia Casas (Festina)	ESP	at 32:04
15	Alexandre Vinokourov (Telekom)	KZK	at 32:26
16	Roberto Conti (Vini)	ITA	at 34:18
17	Kurt Van De Louwer (Lotto)	BEL	at 34:29
18	Guido Trentin (Vini)	ITA	at 35:57
19	Jean-Cyril Robin (Bonjour)	FRA	at 43:12
20	Geert Verheyen (Lotto)	BEL	at 46:24
62	David Millar (Cofidis)	GBR	at 2:13:03

Points Standings (Green Jersey)

1	Erik Zabel (Telekom)	GER	321
2	Robbie McEwen (Farm Frites)	AUS	203
3	Romans Vainsteins (Vini)	LAT	184
25	David Millar (Cofidis)	GBR	54

King of the Mountains (Polka DOt Jeroey)

1	Santiago Botero (Kelme)	COL	347
2	Javier Otxoa (Kelme)	ESP	283
3	Richard Virenque (Polti)	FRA	267
39	David Millar (Cofidis)	GBR	13

Young Rider (Under-25)

1	Francisco Mancebo (Banesto)	ESP	92:51:17
2	Guido Trentin (Vini)	ITA	at 17:48
3	Guicha Niermann (Rabobank)	GER	at 33:57
5	David Millar (Cofidis)	GBR	at 1:54:54

Teams

1	Kelme-Costa Blanca	278:10:47
2	Festina Watches	at 13:42
3	Banesto	at 18:21

Giro d'Italia
Rome-Milan   May 13-June 4

STAGE WINNERS		*Overall*
P **Jan Hruska** (Vitalicio Seguros)	CZE	Hruska
(Rome 6km*)		
1 **Ivan Quaranta** (Mobilvetta)	ITA	Cipollini
(Rome-Teracini 125km)		
2 **Cristian Moreni** (Liquigas-Pata)	ITA	Moreni
(Terracina-Maddeloni 229km)		
3 **Jan Svorada** (Lampre-Daikin)	CZE	Moreni
(Paestum-Scalea 174km)		
4 **Mario Cipollini** (Saeco)	ITA	Moreni
(Scale-Matera 227km)		
5 **Danilo Di Luca** (Cantina Tollo)	ITA	Tosatto
(Lauria-Foggia 242km)		
6 **Dmitri Konyshev** (Fassa B)	RUS	Tosatto
(Peschici-Vasto 160km)		
7 **David McKenzie** (McCartney)	AUS	Tosatto
(Vasto-Teramo 182km)		
8 **Axel Merckx** (Mapei)	BEL	Cataluna
(Corinaldo-Prato 257km)		
9 **Francesco Casagrande** (Vini C)	ITA	Casagrande
(Ancona-San Sepolcro 179km)		
10 **Ivan Quaranta** (Mobilvetta)	ITA	Casagrande
(San Marcello Pistoiese-Padova 257km)		
11 **Victor Pena Grisales** (Vitalicio)	COL	Casagrande
(Lignano Sabbiadoro 45km*)		
12 **Enrico Cassani** (Polti)	ITA	Casagrande
(Bibione-Feltra 191km)		
13 **Jose Luis Rubiera** (Kelme)	ESP	Casagrande
(Feltre-Selva Gardena 195km)		
14 **Gilberto Simoni** (Lampre)	ITA	Casagrande
(Selva Gardena-Bormio 203km)		
15 **Biagio Conte** (Saeco)	ITA	Casagrande
(Biella-Lumezzane 241km)		
16 **Fabrizio Guidi** (FDJ)	ITA	Casagrande
(Brescia-Meda 102km)		
17 **Alvaro Gonzalez** (Vitalicio)	ESP	Casagrande
(Meda-Genova 236km)		
18 **Stefano Garzelli** (Mercatone)	ITA	Casagrande
(Genova-Prato Nevoso 173km)		
19 **Paolo Lanfranchi** (Mapei)	ITA	Casagrande
(Saluzzo-Briancon 177km)		
20 **Jan Hruska** (Vitalicio)	CZE	Garzelli
(Briancon-Sestriere 34km*)		
21 **Mariano Piccoli** (Lampre)	ITA	Garzelli
(Torino-Milano 189km)		

FINAL CLASSIFICATION

1 Stefano Garzelli (Mercatone)	ITA	98:30:14
2 Francesco Casagrande (Vini C)	ITA	at 1:27
3 Gilberto Simoni (Lampre)	ITA	1:33
4 Andrea Noe (Mapei)	ITA	4:58
5 Pavel Tonkov (Mapei)	RUS	5:28
6 Hernan Buenahora (Nec)	COL	5:48
7 Wladimir Belli (Fassa Bortolo)	ITA	7:38
8 José Luis Rubiera (Kelme)	ESP	8:08
9 Sergey Gonchar (Liquigas)	UKR	8:14
10 Leonardo Piepoli (Banesto)	ITA	8:32

Mountains: Francesco Casagrande (Vini Caldirolo) ITA
Points: Dmitry Konyshev (Fassa Bortolo) RUS
Team: Mapei-Quickstep

Vuelta a España
Malaga-Madrid   Aug 26-Sept 17

STAGE WINNERS

1 **Alex Zülle** (Banesto)	SUI	Zülle
(Malaga-Malaga 13.3km*)		
2 **Oscar Freire Gomez** (Mapei)	ESP	Zülle
(Malaga-Cordoba 167.5km)		
3 **Jans Koerts** (Farm Frites)	NED	Zülle
(Montoro-Valdepenas 198.4km)		
4 **Oscar Freire Gomez** (Mapei)	ESP	Zülle
(Valdepenas-Albacete 159km)		
5 **Eladio Sanchez** (Banesto)	ESP	Zülle
(Albacete-Xorret del Cati 152.3km)		
6 **Paolo Bossoni** (Cantina Tollo)	ITA	Zülle
(Benidorm-Valencia 155.5 km)		
7 **Roberto Heras** (Kelme)	ESP	Zülle
(Valencia-Morella 175km)		
8 **Alessandro Petacchi** (Fassa)	ITA	Zülle
(Vinaroz-Port Aventura 168.5km)		
9 **Abraham Olano** (ONCE)	ESP	Olano
(Tarragona-Tarragona 37.6km*)		
10 **Felix Cardenas Ravalo** (Kelme)	COL	Capilla
(Sabadell-Supermolina 165.8km)		
11 **Roberto Laiseka Jaio** (Euskalte)	ESP	Moreno
(Alp-Arcalis 136.5km)		
12 **Alessandro Petacchi** (Fassa)	ITA	Moreno
(Zaragoza-Zaragoza 131.5km)		
13 **Mariano Piccoli** (Lampre)	ITA	Moreno
(Santander-Santander 143.3km)		
14 **Andrei Zintchenko** (LA-Pecol)	RUS	Heras
(Santander-Lagos de Covadonga 146.5km)		
15 **Alvaro Gonzalez** (Vitalicio)	ESP	Heras
(CAngas de Onis-Gijon 164.2km)		
16 **Gilberto Simoni** (Lampre)	ITA	Heras
(Oviedo-El Angliru 168km)		
17 **Davide Bramati** (Mapei)	ITA	Heras
(Benavente-Salamanca 155.5km)		
18 **Alexandre Vinokourov** (Telekom)	KZK	Heras
(Bejar-Ciudad Rodrigo 159km)		
19 **Mariano Piccoli** (Lampre)	ITA	Heras
(Salamanca-Avila 130km)		
20 **Roberto Heras** (Kelme)	ESP	Heras
(Avila-Alto de Abantos 128.2km)		
21 **Santos Capilla** (ONCE)	ESP	Heras
(Madrid-Madrid 38km*)		

FINAL CLASSIFICATION

1 Roberto Heras (Kelme)	ESP	70:26:14
2 Angel Moreno (Festina)	ESP	at 2:33
3 Pavel Tonkov (Mapei)	RUS	4:55
4 Santos Capilla (ONCE)	ESP	5:52
5 Raimondas Rumsas (Fassa)	LTU	7:38
6 Roberto Laiseka Jaio (Euskatel)	ESP	10:16
7 Fernando Escartin (Kelme)	ESP	11:17
8 Carlos Sastre Candil (ONCE)	ESP	12:16
9 Massimiliano Gentili (Cantina)	ITA	13:10
10 Haimar Zubielda (Euskatel)	ESP	13:14

Mountains: Carlos Sastre Candil (ONCE) ESP
Points: Roberto Heras (Kelme) ESP
Sprints: Gianni Faresin (Mapei) ITA
Team: Kelme

World Championships
Plouay, France   Oct 11-15

Time Trial
Men

1	Sergey Gonchar	UKR	56:21.75
2	Michael Rich	GER	+10.20
3	Laszlo Bodrogi	HUN	+24.02
4	Chris Boardman	GBR	+1:16.32
25	Stuart Dangerfield	GBR	+4:30.14

Women

1	Mari Holden	USA	33:14.62
2	Jeannie Longo-Ciprelli	FRA	+3.71
3	Rasa Polikeviciute	LTU	+46.91
5	Ceris Gilfillan	GBR	+57.72
19	Sarah Symington	GBR	+2:25.73

Road Race
Men

1	Romans Vainsteins	LAT	6:15.28
2	Zbigniew Spruch	POL	st
3	Oscar Freire	ESP	st
17	Max Sciandri	GBR	st
80	Charlie Wegelius	GBR	+12:20

Women

1	Zinaida Stahurskaia	BLR	3:17:39
2	Chantal Beltman	NED	+1:27
3	Madeleine Lindberg	SWE	+1:50
6	Sarah Symington	GBR	st
18	Caroline Alexander	GBR	st
48	Susan Carter	GBR	+18:17
56	Melanie Sears	GBR	+22:26

World Cup
Final Classification, men

1	**Erik Zabel (Telekom)**	**GER**	**347**
2	Andrei Tchmil (Lotto)	BEL	285
3	Francesco Casagrande (Vini)	ITA	230
4	Paolo Bettini (Mapei)	ITA	217
5	Romans Vainsteins (Vini)	LAT	204
6	Oscar Freire (Mapei)	ESP	164
6	Davide Rebellin (Liquigas Pata)	ITA	164
8	Fabio Baldato (Fassa Bortolo)	ITA	145
9	Zbigniew Spruch (Lampre)	POL	144
10	Peter Van Petegem (Farm Frites)	BEL	135

Final Classification, women

1	**Diana Ziliute**	**LTI**	**230**
2	Pia Sundstedt	FIN	215
3	Mirjam Melchers	NED	140
4	Chantal Beltman	NED	122
5	Fabiana Luperini	ITA	100
30	Megan Hughes	GBR	27
34	Sara Symington	GBR	24
45	Ceris Gilfillan	GBR	12

World Cup, men

Milan-San Remo (294km)
Mar 18

1	Erik Zabel (Telekom)	GER	7:11:29
2	Fabio Baldato (Fassa Bortolo)	ITA	same time
3	Oscar Freire Gomez (Mapei)	ESP	s.t.

Tour of Flanders (269km)
Apr 2

1	Andrei Tchmil (Lotto)	BEL	6:48:17
2	Dario Pieri (Saeco)	ITA	at 0:04
3	Romans Vainsteins (Vini Caldirola)	LAT	s.t.

Paris-Roubaix (273km)
Apr 9

1	Johan Museeuw (Mapei)	BEL	6:47:00
2	Peter Van Petegem (Farm Frites)	BEL	at 0:15
3	Erik Zabel (Telekom)	GER	s.t.

Liège-Bastogne-Liège (264km)
Apr 16

1	Paolo Bettini (Mapei)	ITA	6:28:32
2	David Etxebarria (ONCE)	ESP	s.t.
3	Davide Rebellin (Liquigas Pata)	ITA	s.t.

Amstel Gold (256m)
Maastricht   Apr 22

1	Erik Zabel (Telekom)	GER	6:13:37
2	Michael Boogerd (Rabobank)	NED	s.t.
3	Marcus Zberg (Rabobank)	SUI	s.t.

HEW-Cyclasssics Cup (250.8km)
Hamburg   Aug 6

1	Gabriele Missaglia (Lampre)	ITA	6:17:22
2	Francesco Casagrande (Vini Caldirola)	ITA	s.t.
3	Fabio Baldato (Fassa Bortolo)	ITA	at 0:02

San Sebastian Classic (232km)
Aug 12

1	Erik Dekker (Rabobank)	NED	5:16:01
2	Andrei Tchmil (Lotto)	BEL	at 0:04
3	Romans Vainsteins (Vini Caldirola)	LAT	s.t.

Meisterschaft van Zurich (248m)
Aug 20

1	Laurent Dufaux (Saeco)	SUI	6:07:21
2	Jan Ullrich (Telekom)	GER	s.t.
3	Francesco Casagrande (Vini Caldirola)	ITA	s.t.

Paris-Tours (254m)
Oct 8

1	Andrea Tafi (Mapei)	ITA	6:38:14
2	Andrei Tchmil (Lotto)	BEL	at 0:39
3	Daniele Nardello (Mapei)	ITA	s.t.

Tour of Lombardy (258km)
Oct 21

1	Raimondas Rumsas (Fassa Bortolo)	LTU	6:18:36
2	Francesco Casagrande (Vini Caldirola)	ITA	s.t.
3	Niklas Axelsson (Ceramica)	SWE	at 0:04

World Cup, women

Canberra (102km)
Mar 12

1	Anna Wilson	AUS	2:45:43
2	Mirella Van Melis	NED	s.t.
3	Mirjam Melchers	NED	s.t.

La Primavera Rosa (118km)
Sivona-San Remo   Mar 18

1	Diana Ziliute	LTU	3:06:27
2	Ina-Yoko Teutenberg	GER	s.t.
3	Giovanna Troldi	ITA	s.t.
45	Louise Jones	GBR	at 1:03
51	Susan Carter	GBR	at 1:48

La Flèche Wallone (198km)
Huy, Belgium   Apr 12

1	Genevieve Jeanson	CAN	2:38:09
2	Pia Sundstedt	FIN	at 0:10
3	Fany Lecourtois	FRA	at 0:23
17	Ceris Gilfillan	GBR	at 2:32
24	Yvonne McGregor	GBR	at 2:45

Montreal (96.8km)
May 28

1	Pia Sundstedt	FIN	2:46:41
2	Fabiana Luperini	ITA	s.t.
3	Diana Ziliute	LTU	at 1:03
13	Ceris Gilfillan	GBR	at 2:31
29	Yvonne McGregor	GBR	at 6:07

First Union Liberty Classic (115.9km)
Philadelphia   June 4

1	Petra Rossner	GER	3:00:02
2	Diana Ziliute	LTU	s.t.
3	Vera Hohlfield	GER	s.t
5	Megan Hughes	GBR	s.t.
6	Sara Symington	GBR	s.t.
22	Melanie Sears	GBR	s.t.

Rotterdam Tour (140km)
Aug 27

1	Chantal Beltman	NED	3:31:33
2	Leontien Zijlaard Van Moorsel	NED	at 2:40
3	Goulnara Ivanova	RUS	s.t.

GP Suisse Féminin (133.1km)
Embrach   Sept 3

1	Pia Sundstedt	FIN	3:42:12
2	Fabiana Luperini	ITA	s.t.
3	Mirjam Melchers	ITA	at 3:46

National Champions

Road Race

Men
1. John Tanner
2. Jon Clay
3. David Millar

Women
1. Ceris Gilfian
2. Caroline Alexander
3. Yvonne McGregor

Time Trial

Men
1. Chris Newton
2. Tim Buckle
3. Matt Bottrill

Women
1. Ceris Gilfillan
2. Sara Symington
3. Yvonne McGregor

"That was horrendous. Eight and a half hours in the saddle is not sport, it's sado-masochism on a major level"

David Millar, the first leader in the 2000 Tour de France, coming to terms with life in the mountains.

"I love this race, the people and the Champs Elysées. This is what it is all about and what you train so hard for"

David Millar at the end of the Tour, and thinking about the job.

"Armstrong rides at an average speed of 54kph. I find this scandalous. It's a nonsense. Indirectly, it proves he is on dope"

Antoine Vayer, a former Festina trainer, during the trial at Lille in October.

Track Racing

World Championships
Manchester   Oct 25-29

Men
Kilometre Time Trial

1	Arnaud Tournant	FRA	1:01.619
2	Soren Lausberg	GBR	1:01.744
3	Jason Queally	GBR	1:02.449

4000m Individual Pursuit

1	Jens Lehmann	GER	4:21.836 bt
2	Stefan Steinweg	GER	4:26.704
3	Rob Hayles	GBR	

Sprint

1	Jan Van Eijden	GER	2-0
2	Laurent Gane	FRA	

No bronze awarded
Chris Hoy GBR elim 1st round repechages

Olympic Sprint, Team

1	France	44.627
2	Great Britain	45.969
	Hoy/MacLean/Queally	
3	Spain	

4000m Team Pursuit

1	Germany	4:01.322
2	Great Britain	4:03.110
	(Manning/Newton/Clay/Wiggins)	
3	France	

Points Race (40km)

1	Juan Llaneras Rosello	ESP	19pts
2	Matthew Gilmore	BEL	18pts
3	Franz Stocher	AUT	17pts
9	Rob Hayles	GBR	10pts - 1 lap

Keirin

1	Frédéric Magne	FRA	10.695
2	Jens Fiedler	GER	
3	Pavel Buran	CZE	
7	Craig MacLean	GBR	*(1st in 7th-12th race)*

Madison

1	Steinweg/Weispfennig	GER	28
2	Lopez/Llaneras Rosello	ESP	15
3	Curuchet/Simon	ARG	8

Women
500m Time Trial

1	Natalia Markovnichenko	BLR	34.838
2	Jiang Cuihua	CHN	35.461
3	Wang Yan	CHN	35.478
12	Julie Forrester	GBR	36.279

3000m Individual Pursuit

1	Yvonne McGregor	GBR	3:35.274
2	Judith Arndt	GER	3:36.547
3	Elena Tchalykh	RUS	

Sprint

1	Natalia Markovnichenko	BLR	2-1
2	Lori-Ann Muenzer	CAN	
3	Katrin Meinke	GER	

Points Race (30km)

1	Marion Clignet	FRA	15pts
2	Judith Arndt	GER	27pts - 1 lap
3	Olga Slioussareva	RUS	23pts - 1 lap

National Champions

Men
Kilometre Time Trial
1 Jason Queally

4000m Individual Pursuit
1 Rob Hayles

Sprint
1 Craig MacLean

Olympic Sprint
1 City of Edinburgh

Points Race
1 Rob Hayles

Keirin
1 Craig MacLean

Madison
1 James Taylor/Tony Gibb

Women
500m Time Trial
1 Julie Forrester

3000m Individual Pursuit
1 Yvonne McGregor

Sprint
1 Wendy Everson

Points Race
1 Francis Newstead

Mountain Biking

World Championships
Sierra Nevada, Spain   June 3-11

Men

Cross-Country

1	Miguel Martinez	FRA	2:17:38
2	Roland Green	CAN	2:20:30
3	Bart Brentjens	NED	2:22:29

Also

37	Oliver Beckingsale	GBR	2:35:17
60	Paul Lasenby	GBR	2:46:44

Downhill

1	Myles Rockwell	USA	3:55.01
2	Steve Peat	GBR	3:55.59
3	Mickael Pascal	FRA	3:55.69

Also

21	Rob Warner	GBR	4:04.38
24	Nigel Page	GBR	4:06.22
27	Tim Ponting	GBR	4:06.52
32	Will Longden	GBR	4:07.62
49	Crawford Carrick-Anderson	GBR	4:12.35

Dual

1	Wade Bootes		AUS
2	Brian Lopes		USA
3	Mickael Deldycke		FRA

Also

Last 8: Steve Peat GBR
Last 16: Scott Beaumont GBR
Last 32: Nigel Page GBR; Tim Ponting GBR

Women

Cross-Country

1	Margarita Fullana	ESP	2:07:42
2	Alison Sydor	CAN	2:11:09
3	Paola Pezzo	ITA	2:11:56

Also

	Caroline Alexander	GBR	DNF
	Louise Robinson	GBR	DNF

Downhill

1	Anne-C Chausson	FRA	4:18.13
2	Katja Repo	FIN	4:19.26
3	Marla Streb	USA	4:20.03

Also

6	Helen Mortimer	GBR	4:27.84
18	Adele Croxon	GBR	4:42.81

Dual

1	Anne-Caroline Chausson		FRA
2	Tara Llanes		USA
3	Sabrina Jonnier		FRA

Also

Last 16: Helen Mortimer GBR; Jo Leigh GBR

Team Relay (3men, 1 woman)

1	Spain	2:08:14
2	Switzerland	2:13:04
3	Italy	2:14:17
6	Great Britain	2:18:31

Cyclo-cross

World Championships
Poprad, Slovakia

1	Richard Groenendaal	NED
2	Mario De Clercq	BEL
3	Sven Nijs	BEL

BMX

World Championships
Cordoba, Argentina   July 24-29

Men

1	Thomas Allier	FRA
2	Christophe Leveque	FRA
3	Dale Holmes	GBR
8	Jamie Staff	GBR

Women

1	Natarsha Williams	AUS
2	Ellen Bollansee	BEL
3	Maria Gabriela Diaz	ARG

World Cup
South Park, PA, USA   July 1

Men

1	Mario Anderes Soto	COL	324.0
2	Matt Haden	USA	283.5
3	Matt Pohlkamp	USA	259.2
6	Jamie Staff	GBR	202.5

Women

1	Natarsha Williams	AUS	320.0
2	Michelle Cairns	USA	280.0
3	Jamie Lilly	USA	256.0

European BMX Series
Final Standings

Men

1	Robert De Wilde	NED	263
2	Florent Boutte	FRA	245
3	Leiv Ove Nordmark	NOR	185
18	Dylan Clayton	GBR	88
19	Scott Edworth	GBR	85
20	Kelvin Batey	GBR	83
23	Martin Murray	GBR	46
46	Marcus Bloomfield	GBR	8
54=	Darren O'Neill	GBR	5

Women

1	Ellen Bollansee	BEL	236
2	Karine Chambonneau	FRA	197
3	Dagmara Polakova	SVK	185

Darts

Skol World Championship

Circus Tavern, Purfleet   Dec 29-Jan 4
Semi-finals
Dennis Priestley ENG bt Peter Manley ENG 5-2
Phil Taylor ENG bt Dennis Smith ENG 5-0

FINAL
Phil Taylor ENG bt Dennis Priestley ENG 7-3

World Matchplay

Winter Gardens, Blackpool   July 24-29
Round 1
Seedings in brackets
Phil Taylor ENG (1) bt Jamie Harvey SCO 10-2
Nigel Justice ENG bt Colin Lloyd ENG 10-7
John Lowe ENG bt Keith Deller ENG (8) 10-7
Chris Mason ENG bt Gary Mawson CAN 10-4
Dennis Priestley ENG (5) bt Steve Raw ENG 10-1
Ritchie Burnett WAL bt Les Fitton ENG 10-7
Rod Harrington ENG (4) bt Roland Scholten NED 11-9
Bob Anderson ENG bt Graham Stoddart ENG 10-1
Ronnie Baxter ENG bt Peter Manley ENG (2) 10-6
Dennis Ovens ENG bt Dave Askew ENG 10-3
Dennis Smith ENG bt John Part CAN (7) 10-8
Steve Brown USA bt John Ferrell ENG 10-2
Alan Warriner ENG (6) bt Reg Harding ENG 10-8
Mick Manning ENG bt Andy Jenkins ENG 15-13
Shane Burgess ENG (3) bt Martin Adams ENG 15-13
Alex Roy ENG bt Peter Evison ENG 10-5

Round 2
Taylor bt Justice 13-3
Lowe bt Mason 13-11
Burnett bt Priestley 14-12
Harrington bt Anderson 13-7
Baxter bt Ovens 13-3
Brown bt Smith 13-11
Warriner bt Manning 13-8
Roy bt Burgess 18-16

Quarter-finals
Taylor bt Lowe 16-4
Burnett bt Harrington 16-13
Baxter bt Brown 16-5
Warriner bt Roy 16-10

Semi-finals
Taylor bt Burnett 17-9
Warriner bt Baxter 17-9

FINAL
Phil Taylor ENG bt Alan Warriner ENG 18-12

BDO World Championship

Lakeside CC, Frimley Green   Jan 1-9
Round 1
Chris Mason ENG bt Raymond Barneveld NED (1) 3-1
Matt Clark ENG bt Wayne Mardle ENG 3-1
Steve Beaton ENG bt Graham Hunt AUS 3-1
Andy Fordham ENG bt Peter Johnstone SCO (8) 3-0
Ted Hankey ENG (5) bt Bob Taylor SCO 3-0
Steve Douglas ENG bt Garry Spedding USA 3-0
Kevin Painter ENG bt Paul Williams ENG 3-1
Robbie Widdows ENG (4) bt Andy Hayfield ENG 3-1
Ronnie Baxter ENG (2) bt Scott Wollaston USA 3-0
Bobby George ENG bt Dennis Ovens ENG 3-1
Colin Monk ENG bt Andy Jenkins ENG 3-2
Ritchie Davies WAL bt Les Wallace SCO (7) 3-0
Martin Adams ENG (7) bt Steve Coote ENG 3-2
Co Stompe NED bt Andy Smith ENG 3-0
Steve Duke AUS bt Sean Palfrey WAL 3-2
Mervyn King ENG (3) bt Les Fitton ENG 3-2

Round 2
Mason bt Clark 3-2
Fordham bt Beaton 3-2
Hankey bt Douglas 3-0
Painter bt Widdows 3-1
Baxter bt George 3-0
Monk bt Davies 3-2
Stompe bt Coote 3-1
King bt Duke 3-0

Quarter-finals
Mason bt Fordham 5-3
Hankey bt Painter 5-2
Baxter bt Monk 5-4
Stompe bt King 5-2

Semi-finals
Hankey bt Mason 5-4
Baxter bt Stompe 5-2

FINAL
Ted Hankey ENG bt Ronnie Baxter ENG 6-0

> **"The worst thing you can do as a dart player is think. You look at all the great darts players and they're not mensa"**
>
> John Part, doing down his own.

Equestrianism

No joy again for Britain's showjumpers, who once upon a time found Olympic medal-winning an almost mundane affair. In seven post-war Games, eight medals were won, including a precious gold in 1952. Since Munich only a team silver in 1984 has graced the trophy cabinet and the mantle has fallen upon the eventing team to bring home the bacon (if the horses will excuse the metaphor).

Horse trials may make more intensive demands on horse and rider, but none would pretend that the competition is as fierce as in the jumping events. Britain arrived in Sydney as European three-day champions and any final ranking lower than fourth was hard to envisage, with Australia, USA and New Zealand the only viable challengers. That's how it panned out, with all the medals going to those four nations, Britain's turn coming in the team event, with Jeanette Bracewell, Leslie Law and Pippa Funnell, all at their first Olympics, hanging on for the silver medal behind the all-powerful Australians. The brief dream of gold evaporated in the cross-country phase.

Andrew Hoy came passably close to an Australian double, finishing second in the individual on his other horse. That individual title went to David O'Connor, with the New Zealander Mark Todd finishing only third. Todd could be content with that; he's won enough anyway. He has two Olympic titles (1984 & 1988), three Badmintons, five Burghleys, a European Open, three British Opens and a host of other victories. Based in Moreton in the Marsh for the past 17 summers - since he sold his dairy herd to fund his Olympic ambitions in 1984 - the New Zealander has been an auspicious addition to the British scene. His most remarkable victory came at Badminton in 1994, when he won on Horton Point, a horse he had never ridden before that week.

Todd bowed out after Sydney, packed up and went home to New Zealand, with the intention of breeding and selling racehorses, and maybe training a few. If that business takes off, we might yet see him based at Newmarket the next time around.

FEI-BCM WORLD JUMPING RANKINGS
as at 1/4/01

1	Ludger Beerbaum	GER	2712.83
2	Rodrigo Pessoa	BRA	2060.00
3	Lars Nieberg	GER	1986.96
4	Markus Fuchs	SUI	1954.77
5	Willi Melliger	SUI	1905.00
6	Jeroen Dubbeldam	NED	1871.56
7	Ludo Philippaerts	BEL	1821.81
8	Jos Lansink	BEL	1791.44
9	Beat Mändli	SUI	1783.13
10	Hugo Simon	AUT	1707.50
11	Michael Whitaker	GBR	1650.00
12	Marcus Ehning	GER	1509.09
13	Otto Becker	GER	1505.94
14	Franke Sloothaak	GER	1348.34
15	Rolf-Göran Bengtsson	SWE	1120.00
16	Markus Beerbaum	GER	1087.50
17	Alexandra Ledermann	FRA	1016.25
18	René Tebbel	GER	970.00
19	Jessica Kürten	IRL	947.33
20	John Whitaker	GBR	927.67
22	Peter Charles	IRL	891.73
39	Geoff Billington	GBR	642.75

Show Jumping

World Cup Final
Las Vegas   April 19-23
1 Rodrigo Pessao   BRA   0.0
   (Gandini Baloubet du Rouet)
2 Markus Fuchs   SUI   7.50
   (Tinka's Boy)
3 Beat Mändli   SUI   10.00
   (Pozitano)
Did not qualify for second round
19 Geoff Billington   GBR
   (Virtual Village It's Otto)
32 Michael Whitaker   GBR
   (Virtual Village Steps Helsinki)

Nations Cup Final
Rome   July 11-16
1 Germany   14
2 United States   16
3 Italy   20
7 Great Britain   27

International Horse Show
Hickstead   July 7-11

Traxdata King George V Gold Cup
1 Cameron Hanley   IRL   47.12
   (Ballaseyr Twilight)
2 Rob Hoekstra   GBR   48.74
   (Lionell II)
3 Lutz Gripshover   GER
   (Warren NRW)

The British Jumping Derby
Hickstead   Aug 28
Peugeot British Jumping Derby
1 John Whitaker   GBR   86.56
   (Virtual Village Welham)
2 Tim Stockdale   GBR   95.62
   (Traxdata Wiston Bridget)
3 Rob Hoekstra   GBR   92.93
   (Lionel II)

Horse of the Year Show
Wembley   Sept 27-Oct 1
Traxdata Grand Prix
1 Robert Smith   GBR   34.80
   (Senator Mr Springfield)
2 Dirk Demeersman   BEL   34.88
   (First Samuel)
3 Billy Twomey   IRL   35.01
   (Hilton III)

The Olympia International
Olympia   Dec 14-18
The Traxdata Grand Prix
1 Lars Nieberg   GER   34.96
   (Loro Piana Esprit FRH)
2 Herve Godignon   FRA   35.84
   (Diams III)
3 Ludger Beerbaum   GER   36.34
   (Goldfever)

Horse Trials

Badminton
May 5-7
1 Mary King (Star Appeal)   GBR   37.80
2 Leslie Law (Shear H20)   GBR   46.80
3 Rodney Powell (Flintstone)   GBR   50.40

Bramham
June 9-11
1 Paul Tapner (Highpoint)   AUS   59.40
2 Blyth Tait (Chesterfield)   NZL   60.00
3 Gary Parsonage (Toucan)   GBR   60.80

British Championships
Gatcombe Park   Aug 15-16
1 William Fox-Pitt (Moon Man)   57.20
2 Chris Bartle (Word Perfect II)   57.40
3 Karen Dixon (Too Smart)   60.80

Burghley
Aug 31-Sep 3
1 Andrew Nicholson (Mr Smiffy)   NZL   53.80
2 Merran Wallis (Gershwin III)   AUS   60.40
3 Clea Hoeg-Mudd (Feast of Florios)   GBR   62.60

Blenheim
Sep 7-10
1 William Fox-Pitt (Stunning)   GBR   47.00
2 William Fox-Pitt (Tamarillo)   GBR   47.40
3 Lucinda Fredericks(Rumpy Pumpy)   AUS   53.60

Dressage

World Cup Final
's-Hertogenbosch, Netherlands   July 1-4
Individual
1 Anky Van Grunsven   NED   100
   (Gestion Bonfire)
2 Coby van Baalen   NED   95
   (Olympic Ferro)
3 Arjen Teeuwissen   NED   90
   (Gestion Goliath T)

Fencing

European Championships
Madeira, Portugal,   *April*

Men
Foil Kristian Hellstrom SWE
Epee Robert Andrzejuk POL
Sabre Fernando Casares ESP

Women
Foil Bianca Becker GER
Epée Laura Flessel-Colovic FRA
Sabre Cecile Argiolas FRA

World Cup
FINAL STANDINGS

Men

Individual Epée

1	Peter Vanky SWE	181
2	Pavel Kolobkov RUS	180
3	Alfredo Rota ITA	142
4	Fabrice Jeannet FRA	141
5	Hugues Obry FRA	140
76	Thomas Cadman GBR	25
140	Greg Allen GBR	10

Individual Foil

1	Ralf Bissdorf GER	274
2	Serge Goloubitsky UKR	139
3	Jean-Noel Ferrari FRA	139
4	Kim Young-Ho KOR	117
5	Ruchard Breutner GER	113
110	Donnie McKenzie GBR	10
137	James Beevers GBR	8

Individual Sabre

1	Sergej Charikov RUS	229
2	Stanislaw Pozdniakov RUS	215
3	Domonkos Ferjancsik HUN	193
4	Mihai Covaliu ROM	1822
5	Zsolt Nemcsik HUN	171
29	James Williams GBR	48
120	Dominic Flood GBR	6

Women

Individual Epée

1	Imke Duplitzer GER	167
2	Margherita Zalaffi ITA	166
3	Cristiana Cascioli ITA	156
4	Gian Hablutzel-Burki SUI	153
5	Tatiana Logounoa RUS	151
38	Georgina Usher GBR	46
105	Debbie Catchpole GBR	12

Individual Foil

1	Valentina Vezzali ITA	311
2	Laura Carlescu Badea ROM	231
3	Giovanna Trillini ITA	219
4	Sabine Bau GER	157
5	Roxana Scarlat ROM	153
64	Eloise Smith GBR	20
85	Linda Strachan GBR	13

Individual Sabre

1	Anne-Lise Touya FRA	224
2	Elena Jemaeva AZE	205
3	Gioia Marzocca ITA	185
4	Sandra Benad GER	174
5	Ilaria Bianco ITA	155
28	Caroline Stevenson GBR	36
49	Charlotte Brown GBR	21
51	Louise Bond-Williams GBR	20

Golf

I t barely seems believable now that Tiger Woods went through two and a half years without winning a Major - the drought lasting from his success at Augusta in 1997, until he demoralised the field at Medinah in the US PGA In August 1999. They were hard times for Tiger; only six PGA Tour wins and about $50 million in the bank to console him during that bleak spell. The bad old days, he probably calls them now.

After winning at Medinah, he could relax a little. He took the World Golf Championships (which in spite of the name it palpably isn't), eased back to prepare for the Ryder Cup, which he helped win, then closed the season with three successive tour victories. The 2000 season began in a similar vein, with two more wins to take the victorious sequence to six, thus equalling the run of Ben Hogan's in 1948, though falling some way short of Byron Nelson's 11-in-a-row which was achieved shortly after the war. Of course, it was all so different then, as the 88-year-old Nelson was first to admit. He won just over $63,000 in war bonds for his streak, Woods accumulated slightly in excess of $4.5 million. Nelson quit the game as soon as he had enough to buy a ranch in Texas, Woods already has enough to buy Texas.

Anyway, the sequence dried up in March when the great one had the indignity of back-to-back second places. He stumbled along thereafter, winning just the once in March, at Bay Hills, not at all in April (how humiliating), and only once in May, at Orlando.

In June, at the US Open he slipped comfortably back into the old routine, embarrassing the best golfers in the world with a record 15-stroke win, two strokes better than Old Tom Morris (as opposed to his son Young Tom Morris) had managed when he won the third Open Championship in 1862. They all knew the blitz from Woods was coming, but in those quiet moments of reflection, and prayer when reflection wasn't enough, they still could not have envisioned this. Then it got worse.

Two more Majors later, Woods had equalled another Hogan record, that of three Majors in a season. Hogan hit his three-timer in 1953, and could not have made a fourth as he had to choose between the US PGA and the Open Championship when they clashed. He went to Carnoustie to challenge for the oldest title in the book and came away with his sole success in the Open. Throughout his career, Ben Hogan won nine Majors, but you can't compare it to Woods, who took his fifth Major at Valhalla, when he was barely out of short trousers.

When you wrapped up Tiger Woods' season in a little ball, it amounted to nine Tour victories and over nine million dollars in prize money in the US, plus the Johnny Walker at Bangkok in November, his other victory on the European Tour. As for the world ranking, he almost made it redundant for he started the year on top and ended the year in the same position. In December, he was a modest six points clear of David Duval (as close as anyone got all year), but back in September shortly after winning the Canadian Open he established a lead of 17.59 points over the South African Ernie Els. This amounted to the highest-ever lead in the world ranking list since its inception. At the time, it was probably hard to imagine that it would ever be bettered, but of course it was. But that's another yearbook.

Tiger Woods dwarfed everything and everyone in golf, so when the redoubtable Colin Montgomerie failed to win his eighth Volvo Order of Merit title, no one much noticed. That's how he would have wanted it anyway. As for a first Major for Montgomerie, well those hopes took flight and who's to say they will ever land again.

Lee Westwood stepped in Monty's shoes, winning his first Volvo title. Prior to the German Open in May, the Worksop golfer seemed more likely to hang up his boots, than step into anyone's, for he was so far out of sorts that he stood only 39th on the money list. But what a difference a win makes, especially when Woods is hanging on your coat-tails. Westwoood earned a healthy £269,000 for his win at Gut Kaden and leapt to third on the Volvo Order of Merit. Thereafter, it was fine. The demons has left him for some other poor golfer and Westwood romped through the rest of the summer and autumn posting another five Tour wins and over £1.8m in prize money.

Darren Clarke was second, the only one close to Westwood's earnings, the Ulsterman's finest hour also coming when he beat Woods, by a substantial 4 & 3 in the World Golf Championship (here we go again) match-play event at Carlsbad.

Talk of money leads us to Padraig Harrington's tale of woe. Ahead by five strokes after three days of the International Open at Sutton Coldfield in May, the Irishman looked an assured winner. Prior to the start of the final day's play, however, Harrington was disqualified for not signing his scorecard. New Zealander Michael Campbell, one of his playing partners, had signed it instead. Harrington, though, was blaming no one but himself - which took some doing - for the cost to the Irishman, was almost certainly a cool £166,599.

"So far he has dominated more than any man has dominated golf. He is the first man who doesn't really have any weakness"
Gary Player.

"It was almost sad hearing the other players talk about him. They all seem baffled as to what they can do"
Michael Bonnallack, secretary of the Royal & Ancient at St Andrew's.

"Logic dictates that he must suffer a loss in form some time...but who knows, it may go on forever"
John Jacobs, coach.

"It's almost as though now guys will play the Tigerless tour to have a chance to win"
Nick Faldo.

"He has raised the bar to a level that only he can jump"
Tom Watson.

"We are all mortal and he's not"
Rocco Mediate, after Woods won the US Open by 15 shots.

"I am in awe"
Ernie Els, after finishing second behind Woods in the US Open.

"Set to overtake Elvis as the greatest-ever American"
BBC reporter, after Woods' sixth successive PGA Tour victory.

"Tiger Woods"
Stuart Appleby, when asked what he would need to shoot to win the US PGA title.

The 129th Open Championship

St Andrews   *July 20-23*
Par: 72

269	**Tiger Woods USA**	**67 66 67 69**		Lucas Parsons AUS	70 72 71 74
(-19)	(£500,000)			Tsuyoshi Yoneyama JPN	74 69 70 74
277	Ernie Els RSA	66 72 70 69		(£10,345 each)	
(-11)	Thomas Björn DEN	69 69 68 71	288	Mike Weir CAN	75 68 70 75
	(£245,000 each)		(level)	Ian Garbutt ENG	68 75 70 75
278	Tom Lehman USA	68 70 70 70		Rocco Mediate USA	74 69 76 69
(-10)	David Toms USA	69 67 71 71		(£8,400 each)	
	(£130,000 each)		289	David Frost RSA	73 71 71 74
279	Fred Couples USA	70 68 72 69	(+1)	Tom Watson USA	73 71 72 73
(-9)	(£100,000)			Shigeki Maruyama JPN	68 76 69 76
280	Loren Roberts USA	69 68 70 73		Greg Owen ENG	70 74 72 73
(-8)	Paul Azinger USA	69 72 72 67		Andrew Coltart SCO	70 72 73 74
	Pierre Fulke SWE	69 72 70 69		(£7,800 each)	
	Darren Clarke NIR	70 69 68 73	290	Christy O'Connor jr IRL	69 75 72 74
	(£66,250 each)		(+2)	Jeff Sluman USA	72 68 75 75
281	Bernhard Langer GER	74 70 66 71		Steve Elkington AUS	73 69 74 74
(-7)	Mark McNulty ZIM	69 72 70 70		Kirk Triplett USA	73 71 74 72
	David Duval USA	70 70 66 75		(£7,425 each)	
	Stuart Appleby AUS	73 70 68 70	291	Desvonde Botes RSA	71 70 76 74
	Davis Love III USA	74 66 74 67	(+3)	Ian Poulter ENG	74 69 73 75
	Vijay Singh FIJ	70 70 73 68		Per-Ulrik Johnsson SWE	72 69 76 74
	Phil Mickelson USA	72 66 71 72		Lee Westwood ENG	70 70 76 75
	Bob May USA	72 72 66 71		(£7,225 each)	
	Dennis Paulson USA	68 71 69 73	292	Gordon Brand jr SCO	69 72 80 71
	(£37,111 each)		(+4)	Ian Woosnam WAL	72 72 73 75
282	Steve Flesch USA	67 70 71 74		(£7,075 each)	
(-6)	Padraig Harrington IRL	68 72 70 72	294	Tom Kite USA	72 72 76 74
	Steve Pate USA	73 70 71 68	(+6)	Kazuhiko Hosokawa JPN	75 69 77 73
	Bob Estes USA	72 69 70 71		(£7,000 each)	
	Paul McGinley IRL	69 72 71 70	295	Peter Senior AUS	71 71 74 79
	Notah Begay III USA	69 73 69 71	(+7)	Lionel Alexandre FRA	75 68 76 76
	(£25,500 each)			(£7,000 each)	
283	Mark O'Meara USA	70 73 69 71			
(-5)	Colin Montgomerie SCO	71 70 72 70			
	Miguel Angel Jiménez ESP	73 71 71 68			
	Mark Calcavecchia USA	73 70 71 69			
	Dean Robertson SCO	73 70 68 72			
	(£20,000 each)				
284	José Maria Olazábal ESP	72 70 71 71			
(-4)	Jean van der Velde FRA	71 68 72 73			
	Steve Jones USA	70 70 72 72			
	Jarmo Sandelin SWE	70 70 75 69			
	(£16,750 each)				
285	Eduardo Romero ARG	71 68 72 74			
(-3)	(£15,500)				
286	Sergio Garcia ESP	68 69 73 76			
(-2)	Jesper Parnevik SWE	73 69 72 72			
	Craig Parry AUS	72 72 71 71			
	José Coceres ARG	74 66 69 77			
	Robert Allenby AUS	72 71 72 71			
	(£14,000 each)				
287	Nick Faldo ENG	70 71 75 71			
(-1)	Justin Leonard USA	70 74 72 71			
	Stewart Cink USA	69 73 76 69			
	Jim Furyk USA	69 71 75 72			
	Nick O'Hern AUS	69 74 70 74			
	Jarrod Moseley AUS	70 71 70 76			
	Gary Orr SCO	72 71 72 72			
	Jeff Maggert USA	72 71 69 75			
	Retief Goosen RSA	72 72 71 72			

The following did not make the cut:
145: Katuyoshi Tomuri JPN 73 72, Marc Farry FRA 72 73, Maarten Lafeber NED 73 72, Stephen Leaney AUS 75 70, Fred Funk USA 71 74, Jamie Spence ENG 74 71, Nobuhito Sato JPN 75 70, Scott Verplank USA 72 73, Hal Sutton USA 75 70, Jim Carter USA 72 73, Hirofumi Miyase JPN 72 73, Michael Campbell NZL 72 73, Mikko Ilonen FIN 74 71, Yasuharu Imano JPN 77 68 (£1,300 each); **146:** Jean-Francois Remesy FRA 69 77, Nick Price ZIM 76 70, Paul Eales ENG 74 72, Phillip Price WAL 75 71, John Houston USA 76 70, Angel Cabrera ARG 74 72, Scott Dunlap USA 68 78, Manuel Zerman ITA 78 68, Simon Dyson ENG 72 74 (£1,080 each); **147:** Seve Ballesteros ESP 78 69, Bob Charles NZL 72 75, Andrew Oldcorn SCO 71 76, Sam Torrance SCO 72 75, Steve Stricker USA 73 74, Steve Wenster ENG 74 73, Steen Tinning DEN 76 71, David Sutherland ENG 75 72, Jyoti Randhawa INA 73 74, Mark Brooks USA 74 73, Lee Jansen USA 75 72, John Bickerton ENG 75 72, Nic Henning RSA 78 69, Ted Tryba USA 73 74, Yeh Wei-Tze TPE 77 70, Adam Scott AUS 72 75 (£1,080 each); **148:** Roger Chapman ENG 75 73, Brian Marchbank SCO 74 74, Corey Pavin USA 73 75, Alex Cejka GER 78 70, Carlos Daniel Franco PAR 75 73, Simon Kahn ENG 76 72, Patrik Sjoland

SWE 76 72, John Daley USA 76 72, Yoshinori Mizumaki JPN 74 74, Luke Donald* ENG 73 75, Chris DiMarco USA 72 76, Philip Rowe* ENG 72 76, Shingo Katayama 71 77 (£964 each); **149:** Sandy Lyle SCO 71 78, Naomichi Ozaki JPN 79 70, Brian Davis ENG 72 77, José Manuel Carriles ESP 77 72, Chris Perry USA 74 75, Tim Herron USA 77 72, David Gossett USA 71 78 (£964 each); **150:** Jack Nicklaus USA 77 73, Scott Watson ENG 76 74, Raymond Russell SCO 74 76 (£700 each); **151:** Mark James ENG 76 75, Tom Scherrer USA 77 74, Bob Tway USA 73 78, Stuart Little ENG 79 72, Paul Dwyer ENG 76 75 (£700 each); **152:** Kyi Hla Han MYA 71 81 (£700);

153: Philip Golding ENG 78 75, Robert Karlsson SWE 80, 73, Paul Lawrie SCO 78 75, Adilson da Silva BRA 79 74 (£700 each); **154:** Tony Johnstone ZIM 79 75, Jamie Harris ENG 76 78 (£700 each); **155:** Gary Emerson ENG 79 76, Fredrik Jacobson SWE 82 73 (£700 each); **156:** Gary Player RSA 77 79 (£700); **157:** Lee Trevino USA 80 77, Darren Fichardt RSA 81 76, Paul Affleck WAL 76 81 (£700 each); **159:** Michael Jonzon SWE 76 83 (£700); **160:** Colin Gillies SCO 80 80

Withdrawn: Dudley Hart USA 69 74

* *Denotes amateur*

Oh dear, this was the moment when every other golfer on the tour swallowed hard. Of course, they knew it was coming, Woods had already lit the blue touch paper with wins in the other three Majors, and a walloping great 15-stroker in the US Open just five weeks before. But for five years, including the first two as an amateur (in 1995 and 1996), the Open had resisted him. Well, this time, Woods against the Old Course was a one-horse race. He was one stroke down on Ernie Els after day one, three strokes ahead of David Toms after day two, and six strokes ahead of Thomas Bjorn and David Duval after day three. The final round would have been no more than a lap of honour, had it not been for the early sparkle of his compatriot Duval.

The underdog started out as if anything were possible. He birdied the second, third, sixth and seventh holes and if his playing partner had any knowledge of anxiety (and that's in question) he would have felt it then. At the turn, the six-stroke lead had contracted to just three, and Woods was no longer the stone cold certainty. Not for a hole, anyway, for by the time the tenth was all over, Duval's challenge had evaporated. It hinged on a putt, or more accurately two putts. Duval missed his 11-footer, while Woods, taking an eternity to prepare, holed his nine-footer. The lead was back to four shots, and if the pendulum had started to swing away from Woods, it was flying his way now.

Duval hung around in second place until he reached the 17th, when despondency turned to disaster. The Road Hole rose up to greet him, took by him the throat and shook whatever life was left out of his game. When it released him, Duval had an eight on the card and, some minutes later, had a 43 inward half to contemplate. He had not only forfeited second place, he had claimed a share of 11th. Did that feel bad? You bet.

Thomas Bjorn was the first European home, the Dane finishing joint second with Els for his best-ever finish in a Major. Darren Clarke was the first Briton home, sacrifiing a real chance of at least a share of the second-place slot with a final round of 73. Colin Montgomerie was wonderfully consistent, but that mattered not a jot for his putting continually let him down as he finished 14 strokes behind the leader. Montgomerie bridled at reporters' questions afterwards. "I've just finished my round, you know, it's very difficult to ask someone their reflections on a week like this when he's just finished his round. Give me a week...or a month," he said.

US Masters

Augusta National Course, Georgia   Apr 6-9
Par: 72, US unless stated

278	**Vijay Singh FIJ**	**72 67 70 69**
(-10)	($828,000)	
281	Ernie Els RSA	72 67 74 68
(-7)	($496,800)	
282	Loren Roberts	73 69 71 69
(-6)	David Duval	73 65 74 70
	(£266,800 each)	
284	Tiger Woods	75 72 68 69
(4)	($184,000)	
285	Tom Lehman	69 72 75 69
(-3)	($165,600)	
286	Davis Love III	75 72 68 71
(-2)	Phil Mickelson	71 68 76 71
	Carlos Franco PAR	79 68 70 69
	($143,367 each)	
287	Hal Sutton	72 75 71 69
(-1)	($124,200)	
288	Nick Price ZIM	74 69 73 72
(level)	Greg Norman AUS	80 68 70 70
	Fred Couples	76 72 70 70
	($105,800)	
289	Dennis Paulson	68 76 73 72
(+1)	Jim Furyk	73 74 71 71
	Chris Perry	73 75 72 69
	John Huston	77 69 72 71
	($80,500 each)	
290	Jeff Sluman	73 69 77 71
(+2)	($69,000)	
291	Glen Day	79 67 74 71
(+3)	Padraig Harrington IRL	76 69 75 71
	Colin Montgomerie SCO	76 69 77 69
	Jean van der Velde FRA	76 70 75 70
	Bob Estes	72 71 77 71
	Steve Stricker	70 73 75 73
	($58,820 each)	
292	Larry Mize	78 67 73 74
(+4)	Craig Parry AUS	75 71 72 74
	Steve Jones	71 70 76 75
	($37,567 each)	
293	Mike Weir CAN	75 70 70 78
(+5)	Bernhard Langer GER	71 71 75 76
	Dudley Hart	75 71 72 75
	Stewart Cink	75 72 72 74
	Jumbo Ozaki JPN	72 72 74 75
	Nick Faldo ENG	72 72 74 75
	Thomas Björn DEN	71 77 73 72
	Justin Leonard	72 71 77 73
	Paul Azinger	72 72 77 72
	($28,673 each)	
294	Fred Funk	75 68 78 73
(+6)	Jay Haas	75 71 75 73
	Notah Begay III	74 74 73 73
	($21,620 each)	
295	Sergio Garcia ESP	70 72 75 78
(+7)	Mark Brooks	72 76 73 74
	Jesper Parnevik SWE	77 71 70 77
	Ian Woosnam WAL	74 70 76 75
	Darren Clarke NIR	72 71 78 74
	Retief Goosen RSA	73 69 79 74
	($17,480 each)	
296	Scott Gump	75 70 78 73
(+8)	Shigeki Maruyama JPN	76 71 74 75
	($13,800 each)	
297	Brandt Jobe	73 74 76 74
(+9)	($12,604)	
298	Steve Pate	78 69 77 74
(+10)	Miguel Angel Jiménez ESP	76 71 79 72
	David Toms	74 72 73 79
	($11,623 each)	
299	Rocco Mediate	71 74 75 79
(+11)	Steve Elkington AUS	74 74 78 73
	($10,948 each)	
303	David Gossett*	75 71 79 78
(+15)	Jack Nicklaus	74 70 81 78
	($10,672)	
308	Skip Kendall	76 72 77 83
(+20)	($10,580)	
313	Tommy Aaron	72 74 86 81
(+25)	($10,488)	

The following did not make the cut:
149: José Maria Olazábal ESP 72 77, Bob Tway 77 72, Scott Hoch 78 71, Jeff Maggert 77 72, Duffy Waldorf 78 71, Aaron Baddeley* AUS 77 72, Danny Green* 73 76; **150:** Corey Pavin 80 70, Gary Player RSA 76 74, Mark O'Meara 75 75, Craig Stadler 73 77, Stuart Appleby AUS 73 77, Angel Cabrera ARG 74 76, Brent Geiberger 76 74, Kim Sung-Yoon* KOR 75 75; **151:** Sandy Lyle SCO 79 72, Tom Watson 75 76, Gabriel Hjertstedt SWE 78 73; **152:** Naomichi Ozaki JPN 75 77, Lee Janzen 76 76, Lee Westwood ENG 77 75; **153:** Paul Lawrie SCO 79 74, John Daly 80 73, Hunter Haas*; **155:** Ben Crenshaw 79 76, Charles Coody 81 74, Kirk Triplett 76 79; **156:** Fuzzy Zoeller 82 74, Ted Tryba 75 81; **157:** Brian Watts 78 79; **158:** Raymond Floyd 80 78, Tim Herron 84 74; **159:** Graeme Storm* ENG 83 76; **160:** Arnold Palmer 78 82; **162:** Seve Ballesteros ESP 81 81, Gay Brewer 84 78

* Denotes Amateur

David Duval arrived at the Masters in 1999 in the form of his life. Four tournament victories, including the two tournaments prior to Augusta, had cast him as the favourite. Yet, he barely got in a blow, only finding his line on the final day, when it was all too late anyway. So Duval tried a different strategy, turning up at Augusta with no wins under his belt, but fresh as Georgia daisy. In horse racing parlance, he had been laid out for this one.

Well, as he returned to the clubhouse at the end of the second round, Duval was possibly thinking that it was all going according to plan. He had mastered Augusta with a second round of 65, which was as good as anyone would manage, and which took him to the top of the leaderboard. He did not, however, use the third day to consolidate, and his 74 ceded four shots to Vijay Singh, three to Loren Roberts and six to Tiger Woods, who was belatedly throwing his hat in the ring. The final round began with Singh on 209 three shots clear of Duval, with Roberts and Ernie Els a shot further back. A handful of players sat on 215, but only Woods hinted that he could get closer.

It needed a charge to bring Singh back to the pack and it came from both Duval and Woods, the former galloping through the opening nine holes in 32, which was better even than his halfway score in the second round. Woods made it in 33. While they were on horseback, Singh was not. At the 11th hole, the Fijian hit a poor second shot into the lake which, in most years would have been his goodbye note to the championship. However, such was the pin position, that Singh was able to make his drop on the green side of the lake (not in the drop zone) leaving him a chip and the loss of just one stroke to par. Clearly believing that Destiny was his companion, Singh then tried another shot of wild abandon on the 12th which flew into the rough behind the green and, lo and behold, bounced back out and into the bunker, thereby proving him absolutely correct. Singh needed no further encouragement, dropping his sand shot to within 18 inches of the hole. From that moment, Singh was back on course.

Nevertheless, it still needed Duval to get down from his horse, which he duly did on the 13th. Not one golfer had been aggressive in their approach to that hole all day, so difficult was the pin position. Duval clearly couldn't see properly through the dark glasses, or perhaps he thought that Destiny was riding with him, not Singh. Unerringly, his shot found the creek and the hole took him six shots. Singh made par and the single stroke between them became three again, just as it was when the day started.

There were no more flutters, Singh going on to take his second Major title (he won the US PGA in 1998). Again, the story of his two-year suspension by the Indonesian PGA when he played on the Asian Tour in 1983 hit the headlines. Singh denies that he had tried to cheat that day, maintaining that his marker had simply got the score wrong. He'll never quite shake off the tale, though, for in golf you can be sexist or racist (as they were in Augusta for many, many years) but you mustn't cheat.

Colin Montgomerie was the best of British, and the best of the Europeans too, though that rather cast an aspersion on the rest, for the Scot's switchback ride - bad round, good round, bad round, good round - left him 13 shots adrift in 19th place and, in his 37th year - yet another Major had passed him by.

US Open

Pebble Beach, California   *June 15-18*
Par: 71, US unless stated

272	**Tiger Woods**	**65**	**69**	**71**	**67**
(-12)	**($800,000)**				
287	Ernie Els RSA	74	73	68	72
(+3)	Miguel A Jiménez ESP	66	74	76	71
	($390,150 each)				
288	John Huston	67	75	76	70
(+4)	($212,779)				
289	Padraig Harrington IRL	73	71	72	73
(+5)	Lee Westwood ENG	71	71	76	71
	($162,526 each)				
290	Nick Faldo	69	74	76	71
(+6)	($137,203)				
291	Stewart Cink	77	72	72	70
(+7)	David Duval	75	71	74	71
	Loren Roberts	68	78	73	72
	Vijay Singh FIJ	70	73	80	68
	($112,766 each)				
292	Paul Azinger	71	73	79	69
(+8)	Michael Campbell	71	77	71	73
	Retief Goosen RSA	77	72	72	71
	José Maria Olazábal ESP	70	71	76	75
	($86,223 each)				
293	Fred Couples	70	75	75	73
(+9)	Scott Hoch	73	76	75	69
	Justin Leonard	73	73	75	72
	Phil Mickelson	71	73	76	76
	David Toms	73	76	72	72
	Mike Weir CAN	76	72	76	69
	($65,214 each)				
294	Notah Begay III	74	75	72	73
(+10)	($53,105)				
295	Mike Brisky	71	73	79	72
(+11)	Tom Lehman	71	73	78	73
	Bob May	72	76	75	72
	Hal Sutton	69	73	83	70
	($45,537 each)				
296	Hale Irwin	68	78	81	69
(+12)	Steve Jones	75	73	75	73
	Nick Price ZIM	77	70	78	71
	Steve Stricker	75	74	75	72
	Tom Watson	71	74	78	73
	($34,066 each)				
297	Tom Kite	72	77	77	71
(+13)	Rocco Mediate	69	76	75	77
	Chris Perry	75	72	78	72
	Lee Porter	74	70	83	70
	Richard Zokol	74	74	80	69
	($28,247 each)				
298	Woody Austin	77	70	78	73
(+14)	Angel Cabrera ARG	69	76	79	74
	Bobby Clampett	68	77	79	74
	Lee Janzen	71	73	79	75
	Jerry Kelly	73	73	81	71
	Larry Mize	73	72	76	77
	Craig Parry AUS	73	74	76	75
	Ted Tryba	71	73	79	75
	Charles Warren III	75	74	75	74
	($22,056 each)				
299	Thomas Björn DEN	70	70	82	77
(+15)	Sergio Garcia ESP	75	71	81	72
	Rick Hartmann	73	75	75	76
	Colin Montgomerie SCO	73	74	79	73
	Scott Verplank	72	74	78	75
	($15,891 each)				
300	Mark O'Meara	74	74	78	74
(+16)	Warren Schutte	74	75	74	77
	($13,578 each)				
301	Darren Clarke NIR	71	75	83	72
(+17)	Keith Clearwater	74	74	80	73
	($12,747 each)				
302	Kirk Triplett	70	71	84	77
(+18)	($12,153)				
303	Dave Eichelberger	78	69	77	79
(+19)	Jimmy Green	74	75	77	77
	($11,760 each)				
304	Jeffrey Wilson*	74	72	82	76
(+20)					
305	Jim Furyk	72	74	84	75
(+21)	($11,425)				
306	Brandel Chamblee	70	77	82	77
(+19)	Carlos Franco PAR	74	75	75	82
	($11,144 each)				
313	Robert Damron	72	73	84	84
(+29)	($10,862	73	74	79	75

The following did not make the cut:

150: Corey Pavin 72 76, Kevin Johnson 74 76, Fred Funk 76 74, Tim Herron 75 75, Dudley Hart 77 73, Don Pooley 76 74, Bob Estes 73 77, Brian Henninger 77 73, Todd Fischer 78 72, Mike Burke jr 77 73, Ryuji Imada 75 75, J Brian Gay 72 78; **151:** Tommy Armour III 76 75, Craig Stadler 79 72, Frank Nobilo NZL 75 76, Stuart Appleby AUS 75 76, Mark Brooks 74 77, Jeff Maggert 72 79, Duffy Waldorf 73 78, Dennis Paulson 75 76, Brandt Jobe 72 79, Mark Slawter 77 74, Chad Campbell 74 77, Brent Geiberger 73 78, Bill van Orman 76 75, Chris Kaufman 76 75, Matt Gogel 72 79; **152:** David Frost RSA 76 76, Jeff Sluman 78 74, Jim McGovern 76 76, Darrell Kestner 74 78, Jean van der Velde FRA 76 76, Ed Fryatt ENG 78 74, Jonathan Kaye 74 78, Joe Daley 83, 69; **153:** Andrew Magee 74 79, Jesper Parnevik SWE 73 80, Chris Tidland 77 76, Paul Goydos 75 78, Brett Quigley 75 78, Aaron Baddeley* AUS 79 74, Ricky Barnes* 80 73; **154:** Andy Bean 77 77, Davis Love III 75 79, Steve Pate 74 80, Robert Gamez 75 79, David Berganio jr 77 77, Mike Borich URU 77 77, Rory Sabbatini 79 75; **155:** Jack Nicklaus 73 82, J P Hayes 76 79, John Cook 79 76, David Gossett* 78 77, Andrew Sanders 77 78, Jason Buha 80 75, Jake Reeves 74 81, Michael Harris 77 78; **156:** Cameron Beckman 78 78, Brad Faxon 80 76, Paul Gow AUS 77 79, Scott Gump 74 82, Taggart Ridings 80 76, Craig Lile* 78 78, Zoran Zorkic 80 76, Javier Sanchez 77 79, Brad Elder 77 79;

157: Bernhard Langer GER 77 80, Shigeki Maruyama JPN 77 80, Glen Day 77 80, Jarmo Sandelin SWE 77 80, John Levitt 79 78, Edward Whitman 82 75, Mike Malizia 76 81, Jeff Lee 79 78; **158:** Billy Mayfair 83 75, Jim Carter 76 82, Frank Lickliter 81 77, Jed McLuen* 79 79; **159:** Greg Norman AUS 77 82, Rodney Butcher 84 75, Craig Spence AUS 76 83, J L Lewis 77 82, Rick Stimmel 76 83, Mario Tiziani 80 79;

160: Graham Davidson SCO 81 79, Ken Krieger 81 79, Rich Heath 79 81, Mike Troy 79 81; **161:** Clark Renner 85 76; **162:** Curtis Strange 81 81, Colin Amaral 79 83;

Withdrawn: John Daly 83
Disqualified: Kyle Blackman 78

One month prior to the US Open, Tiger Woods lost the Deutsche Bank Open at Hamburg. Nothing spectacular in that, you may think, even Tiger Woods loses occasionally. And so he does, but not when he starts the final round in the lead. At Hamburg, he was two strokes ahead of Lee Westwood at the start of the final round and his subsequent defeat was the first time he had given away a last-day advantage in 18 tournaments, the first time he had lost from that position as a professional.

Well, he was certainly taking no chances on that happening again at Pebble Beach. By the time the final day's play got underway on Sunday, Woods was so far ahead he could have played the final round with one of those elastic kids' clubs you get in Toys 'R' Us and he still would have won easily. As it was, with the proper clubs, he took a starting lead of nine shots and extended it to 15.

"He's just better in all aspects of the game, especially mentally. In some people, it brings out the best. Others fold like deck chairs. He has something. I don't know what it is and he's not going to tell us," said Rocco Mediate, who finished back in the pack. though, this was a tournament where you could realistically say that everyone finished in the pack.

Woods did have a moment in the last round when his feet, if not made of clay, were at least brushed with dirt. It was on the sixth, when his ball actually landed in the rough and grown men hid their eyes and women swooned. But it only happened the once. "I had this sense of calm. I felt very tranquil inside, even in the stormy conditions," said Woods, who magically seemed to avoid all those stormy conditions. Even Nicklaus suggested that he was getting assistance from more than just his caddie when - for the second time - the winds dropped just as Woods started his round.

Miguel Angel Jiménez was the best of the Europeans, in a distant second place with Ernie Els, while Lee Westwood shared fifth with the Irishman Padraig Harrington. Nick Faldo, in seventh, made his first impact in a Major since we don't know when. Even so, Faldo was still 18 shots behind the leader, so looking at it like that maybe it wasn't such a special show.

Darren Clarke was deeply despondent, having hit a third-round 83 that left him a mountainous 24 shots behind Woods going into the final round. The Ulsterman conceded another five strokes in the last round and must have been left wondering if he had ever finished 29 shots behind anyone ever. Colin Montgomerie, who finished two shots ahead of Clarke, actually topped one of the statistical tables for accuracy on the fairways. "Maybe they should put the pins on the fairways," squeaked the Scot sardonically.

US PGA Championship

Valhalla Golf Club, Louisville, Kentucky Aug 17-20
Par: 72, US unless stated

270	**Tiger Woods**	**66 67 70 67**
(-18)	($900,000)
	Won in a three-hole play-off
	Bob May	72 66 66 66
	($540,000)
275	Thomas Björn DEN	72 68 67 68
(-13)	($340,000)
276	Greg Chalmers AUS	71 69 66 70
(-12)	José Maria Olazábal ESP	76 68 63 69
	Stuart Appleby AUS	70 69 68 69
	($198,666 each)
277	Franklin Langham	72 71 65 69
(-11)	($157,000)
278	Notah Begay III	72 66 70 70
(-10)	($145,000)
279	Tom Watson	76 70 65 68
(-9)	Fred Funk	69 68 74 68
	Davis Love III	68 69 72 70
	Darren Clarke NIR	68 72 72 67
	Scott Dunlap	66 68 70 75
	Phil Mickelson	70 70 69 70
	($112,500 each)
280	Stewart Cink	72 71 70 67
(-8)	Lee Westwood ENG	72 72 69 67
	Chris DiMarco	73 70 69 68
	Michael Clark II	73 70 67 70
	($77,500 each)
281	Tom Kite	70 72 69 70
(-7)	J P Hayes	69 68 68 76
	Angel Cabrera ARG	72 71 71 67
	Robert Allenby AUS	73 71 68 69
	Lee Janzen	76 70 70 65
	($56,200 each)
282	Paul Azinger	72 71 66 73
(-6)	Steve Jones	72 71 70 69
	Jarmo Sandelin SWE	74 72 68 68
	($41,000 each)
283	Brad Faxon	71 74 70 68
(-5)	Skip Kendall	72 72 69 70
	Tom Pernice	74 69 70 70
	($34,166 each)
284	Mike Weir CAN	76 69 68 71
(-4)	Jean van der Velde FRA	70 74 69 71
	Stephen Ames TRI	69 71 71 73
	Kenny Perry	78 68 70 68
	($28,875 each)
285	Sergio Garcia ESP	74 69 73 69
(-3)	Chris Perry	72 74 70 69
	Mark Calcavecchia	73 74 71 67
	Ernie Els RSA	74 68 72 71
	Blaine McCallister	73 71 70 71
	($24,000 each)
286	Toshimitsu Izawa JPN	73 73 71 69
(-2)	Colin Montgomerie SCO	74 72 70 70
	($20,500 each)

287	Jeff Sluman	73 69 72 73
(-1)	Justin Leonard	73 73 71 70
	Paul Stankowski	75 72 68 72
	Steve Pate	75 70 74 68
	David Toms	72 68 72 75
	($17,000 each)
288	Bernhard Langer GER	75 69 73 71
(level)	Mark O'Meara	71 72 70 75
	Shigeki Maruyama JPN	77 69 71 71
	Duffy Waldorf	75 70 71 72
	Brian Henninger	70 74 71 73
	($12,650 each)
289	Nick Faldo ENG	79 68 69 73
(+1)	Jesper Parnevik SWE	72 74 70 73
	Steve Lowery	73 74 73 69
	Brian Watts	72 74 73 70
	Glen Day	76 71 71 71
	Andrew Coltart SCO	74 71 73 71
	Jonathan Kaye	69 74 71 75
	($10,964 each)
290	Padraig Harrington IRL	75 72 69 74
(+2)	Loren Roberts	74 72 71 73
	Curtis Strange	72 70 76 72
	Carlos Franco PAR	72 74 74 70
	Dennis Paulson	72 75 70 73
	Joe Ogilvie	73 74 71 72
	($10,250 each)
291	Wayne Grady AUS	71 74 68 78
(+3)	Craig Stadler	74 69 71 77
	Bill Glasson	73 74 71 73
	Miguel Angel Jiménez ESP	70 77 74 70
	Jay Haas	73 74 68 76
	($9,700 each)
292	Greg Kraft	71 73 75 73
(+4)	Kirk Triplett	76 71 73 72
	($9,425 each)
293	John Huston	75 72 74 72
(+5)	($9,350)
294	Jim Furyk	74 71 74 75
(+6)	Paul Lawrie SCO	75 71 73 75
	($9,275 each)
297	Robert Damron	72 74 81 70
(+9)	Billy Mayfair	74 73 76 74
	Scott Hoch	73 70 75 79
	($9,150 each)
299
(+11)	Rory Sabbatini	74 71 76 78
	($9,050)
300	Masashi Ozaki JPN	74 71 76 79
(+12)	($9,000)
301	Hidemichi Tanaka JPN	72 73 77 79
(+13)	($8,950)
313	Frank Dobbs	75 72 88 78
	($8,900)

The following did not make the cut
148: Andrew Magee 75 73, Jack Nicklaus 77 71, Ian Woosnam WAL 73 75, Steve Flesch 76 72, Jerry Kelly 74 74, Ed Fryatt ENG 69 79, Vijay Singh FIJ 77 71, Bob Estes 74 74, Peter O'Malley AUS 74 74, Gary Orr SCO 77 71, Jay Don Blake 73 75, Jeff Maggert 73 75, Retief Goosen RSA 75 73, Kevin Sutherland 74 74, James Blair III 75 73, Mark Brown 71 77, Tim Dunlavey 76 72; **149:** Nick Price ZIM 77 72, Tim Herron 72 77, Fred Couples 79 70, Scott Verplank 75 74, Hal Sutton 74 75, Paul McGinley IRL 74 75, Mark Brooks 78 71, Ted Tryba 75 74, Bob Boyd 74 75, Harrison Frazar 75 74; **150:** Bob Tway 77 73, Russ Cochrane 74 76, Ed Sabo 78 72; **151:** Shaun Kelly ENG 74 77, Todd Smith 78 73; **152:** Greg Norman AUS 75 77, Karl Kimball 75 77, Philip Price WAL 77 75, Mathias Grönberg SWE 78 74, Eddie Terasa 76 76; **153:** Eduardo Romero ARG 75 78, Steve Stricker 80 73, Jeff Freeman 76 77, Brent Geiberger 75 78; **154** Corey Pavin 79 75, Robert Gaus 76 78, Greg Turner NZL 77 77, Bradley Shafley 80 74, José Coceres ARG 75 79, Steve Brady 78 76, Robert Wilkin 76 78; **155:** Craig Parry AUS 80 75, Shingo Katayama JPN 76 79, Jim Woodward 78 77; **156:** Naomichi Ozaki JPN 81 75, John Daly 74 82, Brian Gaffney 79 77; **157:** Michael Campbell NZL 84 73; **158:** Mike Gill 81 77; **159:** Lanny Wadkins 76 83, Kevin Burton 80 79; **160:** Sam Torrance SCO 82 78; **163:** Rick Morton 84 79; **164:** Tim Thelen 85 79; **165:** Ronald Stelten 86 79; **166:** Jamie Elliott 87 79; **167:** Tony Kelley 84 83

Withdrawn: Ben Crenshaw 83, Tom Scherrer 77, Jim Carter 85, Rocco Mediate 77, Tom Lehman 82

If you'd have stuck a pin in the telephone directory, there was a tiny chance you would have stuck it in the name Bob May. If you'd have been offered a choice as to which player would take Tiger Woods to a play-off in the US PGA, the chances are even smaller that you would have come up with May, who was best known in England for his victory in the British Masters a year earlier, but completely unknown in his native USA. May finished the 1999 Volvo Tour in 11th position, which was a fair performance but hardly indicated that he was the man to challenge Woods' absolute and utter pre-eminence. But he did.

Woods led going into the final round, but only by a single shot from May and his fellow American Scott Dunlap. Dunlap faded fast on the final round, but rather than Woods asserting his authority, it was May, homeward bound, who put on the pressure. Birdies at the 11th, 12th and 14th gave May a lead that he clung on to till the 17th hove into view. At that hole, Woods hit his sand-iron shot to four-feet and reclaimed a share of the lead. At the final hole, Woods was set for the title when May weaved his 15-foot putt into the cup.

The play-off was over the last three holes, with Woods immediately going one-up. Another day, any other day and Woods would have closed it there and then, but on the second extra hole he shot into the rough to prolong the agony. The 18th was scrappy, but Woods' five was enough for the title. May took home $540,000 and established his reputation in his native America.

Thomas Bjorn scored a final-round 68, to make the third spot his own, five shots adrift of May and Woods. While Darren Clarke, four shots further back, was the leading UK player. Clarke actually finished 20 shots closer to Woods than he had in the US Open three months earlier. Did it all mean that Woods was losing the magic? Well, if you listened to May you might believe that.

"I see Tiger walk around the locker room joking and laughing with everybody and, if there was an intimidation thing in there, you wouldn't see other people joking back with him," said the runner-up.

Believe that Bob, and you'll believe anything.

World Ranking

as at December 12

	Player	Ctry	Average			Player	Ctry	Average
1	Tiger Woods	USA	19.98		51	Bernhard Langer	GER	3.06
2	David Duval	USA	13.15		52	Billy Mayfair	USA	3.05
3	Colin Montgomerie	SCO	10.36		53	Bob May	USA	2.96
4	Davis Love III	USA	9.48		54	Ted Tryba	USA	2.95
5	Ernie Els	RSA	8.64		55	Rocco Mediate	USA	2.92
6	Lee Westwood	ENG	7.85		56	Andrew Magee	USA	2.82
7	Vijay Singh	FIJ	7.82		57	Mike Weir	CAN	2.80
8	Nick Price	ZIM	7.20		58	Mike Calcavecchia	USA	2.79
9	Phil Mickelson	USA	6.58		59	Shigeki Maruyama	JPN	2.78
10	Mark O'Meara	USA	6.52		60	Bill Glasson	USA	2.77
11	Jim Furyk	USA	6.36		61	Angel Cabrera	ARG	2.77
12	Sergio Garcia	ESP	6.20		62	Brandt Jobe	USA	2.75
13	Justin Leonard	USA	6.14		63	Olin Browne	USA	2.71
14	Hal Sutton	USA	6.11		64	Duffy Waldorf	USA	2.69
15	Jesper Parnevik	SWE	5.43		65	Dennis Paulson	USA	2.67
16	John Huston	USA	5.36		66	John Cook	USA	2.50
17	Jeff Maggert	USA	5.34		67	Robert Karlsson	SWE	2.43
18	Carlos Franco	PAR	5.30		68	Jarmo Sandelin	SWE	2.38
19	Darren Clarke	NIR	5.29		69	Jay Haas	USA	2.37
20	Fred Couples	USA	5.18		70	Skip Kendall	USA	2.36
21	Miguel Angel Jiménez	ESP	4.91		71	Paul Azinger	USA	2.36
22	Tom Lehman	USA	4.83		72	Ian Woosnam	WAL	2.29
23	Chris Perry	USA	4.42		73	Scott Verplank	USA	2.27
24	David Toms	USA	4.40		74	Greg Turner	NZL	2.24
25	Steve Elkington	AUS	4.29		75	Toshi Izawa	JPN	2.21
26	José Maria Olazábal	ESP	4.24		76	Scott Dunlap	USA	2.18
27	Steve Pate	USA	4.15		77	Frank Lickliter	USA	2.17
28	Jeff Sluman	USA	4.03		78	Eduardo Romero	ARG	2.17
29	Steve Stricker	USA	3.95		79	Peter O'Malley	AUS	2.14
30	Bob Estes	USA	3.86		80	Kirk Triplett	USA	2.12
31	Stuart Appleby	AUS	3.85		81	Mark James	ENG	2.09
32	Tim Herron	USA	3.83		82	Andrew Coltart	SCO	2.08
33	Stewart Cink	USA	3.81		83	Kazuhiko Hosokawa	JPN	2.06
34	Retief Goosen	RSA	3.76		84	David Frost	RSA	2.04
35	Dudley Hart	USA	3.75		85	Hidemichi Tanaka	JPN	1.97
36	Glen Day	USA	3.73		86	Patrik Sjöland	SWE	1.97
37	Jumbo Ozaki	JPN	3.68		87	Notah Begay III	USA	1.96
38	Thomas Björn	DEN	3.63		88	Stephen Ames	TRI	1.95
39	Lee Janzen	USA	3.63		89	Stephen Leaney	AUS	1.95
40	Brian Watts	USA	3.61		90	Tsuyoshi Yoneyama	JPN	1.94
41	Craig Parry	AUS	3.61		91	Jean van der Velde	FRA	1.92
42	Scott Hoch	USA	3.54		91	Greg Kraft	USA	1.91
43	Greg Norman	AUS	3.45		93	Craig Stadler	USA	1.90
44	Paul Lawrie	SCO	3.38		94	Alexander Cejka	GER	1.85
45	Bob Tway	USA	3.36		95	Brandel Chamblee	USA	1.84
46	Naomichi Joe Ozaki	JPN	3.36		96	Brad Faxon	USA	1.82
47	Brent Geiberger	USA	3.32		97	Steve Flesch	USA	1.80
48	Fred Funk	USA	3.28		98	Tom Watson	USA	1.77
49	Loren Roberts	USA	3.27		99	Steve Jones	USA	1.77
50	Padraig Harrington	IRL	3.07		100	Frankie Minoza	PHI	1.77

Averages are shown to two decimal places, where necessary they have been taken to further decimal places to determine final positions.

European Tour

Date		Tournament	Venue	Winner	Score	1st Prize	Runner(s)-up	Margin
Jan	13	South African	Houghton GC	**Anthony Wall**	204	£79,100	Phillip Price WAL	2
	16	PGA	Johannesburg	ENG	(-12)		Gary Orr SCO	
Jan	20	Mercedes-Benz	Randpark GC	**Mathias Grönberg**	274	£97,050	Fichardt RSA	1
	23	S AfricanOpen	Johannesburg	SWE	(-14)		Price ZIM, Gonzalez ARG	
Jan	27	Heineken Classic	The Vines Resort	**Michael Campbell**	268	£121,767	Thomas Björn	6
Jan	30		Perth, Australia	NZL	(-20)		DEN	
Feb	3	Greg Norman	The Lakes GC	**Lucas Parsons**	273	£145,456	Peter Senior	4
	6	Holden International	Sydney	AUS	(-19)		AUS	
Feb	10	Malaysian	Templer Park GC	**Yeh Wei-tze**	278	£83,720	Harrington	1
	13	Open	Kuala Lumpur	TPE	(-10)		Hainline, Terblanche	
Feb	17	Algarve	Le Meridian Penina	**Gary Orr**	275	£103,030	Phillip Price	1
Feb	20	Portuguese Open	Algarve	SCO	(-13)		WAL	
Feb	23	WGC Andersen	La Costa	**Darren Clarke**		£625,626	Tiger Woods	4 & 3
Feb	27	Matchplay	Carlsbad, CAL	NIR			USA	
Mar	2	Dubai Desert	Dubai Creek	**José Coceres**	274	£141,610	Paul McGinley IRL	2
	5	Classic	Golf & Yacht Club	ARG	(-14)		Patrik Sjöland SWE	
Mar	9	Qatar Masters	Doha GC	**Rolf Muntz**	280	£79,064	Ian Woosnam	5
	12		Qatar	NED	(-8)		WAL	
Mar	16	Madeira Island	Santo da Serra	**Niclas Fasth**	279	£56,041	Drummond SCO	2
	19	Open		SWE	(-9)		Davis ENG, Johnson SWE	
Mar	23	Rio de Janeiro	Itanhangá	**Roger Chapman**	270	£68,952	Padraig Harrington play	
	26	500 Years Open	Rio	ENG	(-18)		IRL	-off
Mar	30	Sao Paolo	Sao Paolo GC	**Padraig Harrington**	270	£78,566	Gerry Norquist	2
Apr	2	500 Years Open		IRL	(-14)		USA	
Apr	6	**US Masters**	Augusta National	**Vijay Singh**	278	£520,035	Ernie Els	3
	9		Georgia, USA	FIJ	(-10)		RSA	
Apr	14	Eurobet Seve	Sunningdale GC	**Continental Europe**			GB & Ireland	
	16	Ballesteros Open	Berkshire	13½-12½				
Apr	20	Moroccan Open	Golf D'Amelkis	**Jamie Spence**	266	£66,640	Delagrange FRA	4
	23	Meditel	Marrakech	ENG	(-22)		Poulter ENG, Levet FRA	
Apr	28	Peugeot Open	PGA Golfe de	**Brian Davis**	274	£98,988	Markus Brier	3
May	1	de España	Catalunya, Girona	ENG	(-14)		AUT	
May	4	Novotel Perrier	Le Golf National	**Colin Montgomerie**	272	£116,778	Jonathan Lomas	2
	7	Open de France	Paris	SCO	(-16)		ENG	
May	11	International Open	The De Vere Belfry	**José Maria Olazábal**	275	£166,599	Phillip Price	3
	14		Sutton Coldfield	SCO	(-13)		WAL	
May	18	Deutsche Bk Open	Gut Kaden	**Lee Westwood**	273	£269,311	Emanuele	3
	21	TPC of Europe	Hamburg	ENG	(-15)		Canonica ITA	
May	26	Volvo PGA	The Wentworth	**Colin Montgomerie**	271	£250,000	Westwood ENG	5
	29	Championship	Club, Surrey	SCO	(-17)		Clarke ENG, Coltart SCO	
June	1	The Compass	Marriott Forest	**Darren Clarke**	275	£130,390	Mark James ENG	1
	4	English Open	of Arden, Warwicks	NIR	(-13)		Michael Campbell NZL	
June	8	The Celtic Manor	Celtic Manor Resort	**Steen Tinning**	273	£125,000	David Howell	1
	11	Wales Open	Newport	DEN	(-15)		ENG	
June	15	**US Open**	Pebble Beach	**Tiger Woods**	272	£530,539	Miguel Angel	15
	18		California	USA	(-12)		Jiménez ESP	
June	22	Compaq European	De Vere Slaley Hall	**Lee Westwood**	276	£108,330	Fredrick Jacobson	3
	25	Grand Prix	Northumberland	ENG	(-12)		SWE	

Date	Tournament	Venue	Winner	Score	Prize	Runner-up	
June 29 / July 2	Murphy's Irish Open	Ballybunion GC County Kerry	**Patrik Sjöland** SWE	270 (-14)	£166,660	Fredrik Jacobsen SWE	2
July 6 / 9	Smurfit European Open	The K Club Dublin	**Lee Westwood** ENG	276 (-12)	£250,000	Angel Cabrera ARG	1
July 12 / 15	Standard Life Loch Lomond	Loch Lomond Glasgow	**Ernie Els** RSA	273 (-11)	£183,330	Tom Lehman USA	1
July 20 / 23	**The 129th Open Golf Championship**	St Andrews Fife	**Tiger Woods** USA	269 (-19)	£500,000	Ernie Els RSA Thomas Bjorn DEN	8
July 27 / 30	TNT Dutch Open	Nordwijkse GC	**Stephen Leaney** AUS	269 (-19)	£138,602	Bernhard Langer GER	4
Aug 3 / 6	Volvo Scandinavian Masters	Kungsängen Stockholm	**Lee Westwood** ENG	270 (-14)	£164,095	Michael Campbell NZL	3
Aug 10 / 13	Victor Chandler British Masters	Woburn Milton Keynes	**Gary Orr** SCO	267 (-21)	£133,330	Per-Ulrik Johansson SWE	2
Aug 17 / 20	**US PGA Championship**	Valhalla GC Louisville	**Tiger Woods** USA	270 (-18)	£598,404	Bob May USA	play -off
Aug 17 / 20	North West of Ireland Open	Slieve Russell Hotel County Cavan	**Massimo Scarpa** ITA	275 (-13)	£35,083	Mikael Lundberg SWE	1
Aug 24 / 27	WGC-NEC Invitational	Firestone CC Akron, Ohio	**Tiger Woods** USA	259 (-21)	£598,404	Phillip Price WAL Justin Leonard USA	11
Aug 24 / 27	Scottish PGA Championships	Gleneagles Hotel	**Pierre Fulke** SWE	271 (-17)	£66,660	Henrik Nystrom SWE	2
Aug 31 / Sep 3	BMW International Open	Crans-sur Sierre Switzerland	**Thomas Björn** DEN	268 (-20)	£153,000	Bernhard Langer GER	3
Sep 7 / 10	Canon European Masters	Crans-sur-Sierre Switzerland	**Eduardo Romero** ARG	261 (-23)	£153,937	Thomas Björn DEN	10
Sep 14 / 17	Trophé Lancôme Paris	St Nom la Bretéche Paris	**Retief Goosen** RSA	271 (-13)	£133,330	Darren Clarke NIR Michael Campbell NZL	1
Sep 21 / 24	Belgacom Open	Royal Zoute Belgium	**Lee Westwood** ENG	266 (-4)	£102,006	Eduardo Romero ARG	4
Sep 28 / Oct 4	Linde German Masters	Gut Lärchenhof Cologne	**Michael Campbell** NZL	197 (-19)	£271,612	Jose Coceres ARG	1
Oct 5 / 8	Cisco World Match Play Championship*	Wentworth Club Surrey	**Lee Westwood** ENG		£250,000	Colin Montgomerie SCO	at 38th
Oct 12 / 15	World Cup of Golf*	St Andrews Fife	**Spain** (Martin/Jiménez/Olazábal)	2-1	£300,000	South Africa (Frost/Goosen/Els)	
Oct 19 / 22	BBVA Open Turespaña Masters	Club de Campo Madrid	**Padraig Harrington** IRL	267 (-17)	£97,824	Gary Orr SCO	2
Oct 26 / 29	Italian Open	Is Molas Sardinia	**Ian Poulter** ENG	267 (-21)	£96,895	Gordon Brand jr SCO	1
Nov 2 / 5	Volvo Masters	Montecastillo Jerez, Spain	**Pierre Fulke** SWE	272 (-16)	£333,330	Darren Clarke NIR	1
Nov 9 / 12	WGC - American Express Chps	Club de Golf Valderrama	**Mike Weir** CAN	277 (-11)	£690,417	Lee Westwood ENG	2
Nov 16 / 19	Johnny Walker Classic**	Alpine G & SC Bangkok	**Tiger Woods** USA	263 (-25)	£128,735	Geoff Ogilvy AUS	3

* Denotes Approved Special Events

** This event is part of the 2001 Tour

European Money List
Final Standing

	Player	Ctry	Evts	£Sterling
1	Lee Westwood	ENG	23	1,858,602
2	Darren Clarke	NIR	22	1,616,441
3	Ernie Els	RSA	11	1,199,707
4	Michael Campbell	NZL	21	1,185,613
5	Thomas Björn	DEN	27	1,147,614
6	Colin Montgomerie	SCO	23	1,035,366
7	Padraig Harrington	IRL	24	803,426
8	Phillip Price	WAL	26	791,930
9	José Maria Olazábal	ESP	21	698,542
10	Gary Orr	SCO	26	600,358
11	Miguel Angel Jiménez	ESP	19	597,381
12	Pierre Fulke	SWE	16	584,661
13	José Coceres	ARG	21	558,926
14	Angel Cabrera	ARG	26	555,680
15	Retief Goosen	RSA	24	530,946
16	Eduardo Romero	ARG	23	485,557
17	Andrew Coltart	SCO	28	476,368
18	Paul McGinley	SCO	26	457,395
19	Bernhard Langer	GER	22	451,932
20	Mathias Grönberg	SWE	29	369,143
21	Sergio Garcia	ESP	13	356,383
22	Per-Ulrik Johansson	SWE	20	342,575
23	Patrik Sjöland	SWE	24	341,219
24	Ian Woosnam	WAL	26	330,669
25	Fredrik Jacobsen	SWE	23	322,046
26	Paul Lawrie	SCO	19	304,531
27	Emanuele Canonica	ITA	21	301,639
28	Stephen Leany	AUS	21	287,327
29	Brian Davis	ENG	26	276,746
30	Steen Tinning	DEN	26	270,949
31	Ian Poulter	ENG	28	266,143
32	Jean van der Velde	FRA	13	249,378
33	Roger Chapman	ENG	28	231,836
34	Ricardo Gonzalez	ARG	26	229,627
35	Roger Wessels	RSA	31	229,400
36	Jamie Spence	ENG	20	223,470
37	Lucas Parsons	AUS	22	219,077
38	Jarmo Sandelin	SWE	26	217,775
39	Greg Owen	ENG	28	217,001
40	David Howell	ENG	30	204,771
41	Peter Senior	AUS	13	203,312
42	Nick O'Hern	AUS	22	200,683
43	Ignacio Garrido	ESP	24	199,975
44	Anthony Wall	ENG	24	196,531
45	Niclas Fasth	SWE	22	191,951
46	Alastair Forsyth	SCO	30	188,862
47	Peter O'Malley	AUS	22	188,642
48	Geoff Ogilvy	AUS	20	186,257
49	Mark McNulty	ZIM	19	184,227
50	Dean Robertson	SCO	23	179,917

US PGA Money List
Final Standing

	Player	Ctry	Evts	USDollars
1	Tiger Woods	USA	20	9,188,321
2	Phil Mickelson	USA	23	4,746,457
3	Ernie Els	RSA	20	3,469,405
4	Hal Sutton	USA	25	3,061,444
5	Vijay Singh	FIJ	26	2,573,835
6	Mike Weir	CAN	28	2,547,829
7	David Duval	USA	19	2,462,846
8	Jesper Parnevik	SWE	20	2,413,345
9	Davis Love III	USA	25	2,337,765
10	Stewart Cink	USA	27	2,169,727
11	Kirk Triplett	USA	28	2,099,943
12	Tom Lehman	USA	21	2,068,499
13	Steve Flesch	USA	32	2,025,781
14	Justin Leonard	USA	28	2,023,465
15	David Toms	USA	31	2,002,068
16	Robert Allenby	AUS	26	1,968,685
17	Jim Furyk	USA	25	1,940,519
18	Loren Roberts	USA	24	1,932,280
19	Chris DiMarco	USA	33	1,842,221
20	Notah Begay III	USA	24	1,819,323
21	Nick Price	ZIM	18	1,804,433
22	Scott Verplank	USA	28	1,747,643
23	Mark Calcavecchia	USA	28	1,702,317
24	Stuart Appleby	AUS	24	1,642,221
25	John Huston	USA	23	1,631,695
26	Franklin Langham	USA	28	1,604,952
27	Paul Azinger	USA	20	1,597,139
28	Chris Perry	USA	31	1,563,115
29	Bob May	USA	26	1,557,720
30	Carlos Franco	PAR	24	1,550,592
31	Steve Lowery	USA	30	1,543,818
32	Duffy Waldorf	USA	23	1,384,508
33	Scott Hoch	USA	29	1,368,888
34	Rocco Mediate	USA	24	1,320,278
35	Tom Scherrer	USA	33	1,263,585
36	Rory Sabbatini	USA	26	1,262,535
37	Shigeki Maruyama	JPN	26	1,207,104
38	Grant Waite	USA	26	1,142,789
39	Jeff Maggert	USA	27	1,138,749
40	Jonathan Kaye	USA	34	1,096,131
41	Greg Chalmers	USA	28	1,063,456
42	Sergio Garcia	ESP	16	1,054,338
43	Dudley Hart	USA	24	1,048,166
44	Scott Dunlap	USA	30	1,040,244
45	Billy Andrade	USA	31	1,004,827
46	Brad Faxon	USA	29	999,460
47	Fred Couples	USA	19	990,215
48	Jim Carter	USA	30	964,346
49	Blaine McCallister	USA	30	963,974
50	Skip Kendall	USA	32	947,118

US PGA Tour

Date	Tournament	Venue	Winner	Score	1st Prize	Runner(s)-up	Margin
Jan 3 9	Mercedes Championship	The Plantation Kapalua, Hawaii	**Tiger Woods** USA	276 (-16)	$522,000	Ernie Els RSA	play -off
Jan 10 16	Sony Open in Hawaii	Waialae CC Honolulu	**Paul Azinger** USA	261 (-19)	$522,000	Stuart Appleby AUS	7
Jan 17 23	Bob Hope Chrysler Classic	Indians Wells California	**Jesper Parnevik** SWE	331 (-27)	$540,000	Rory Sabbatini USA	1
Jan 24 26	Phoenix Open	TPC of Scottsdale Arizona	**Tom Lehman** USA	270 (-14)	$576,000	Rocco Mediate USA 1 Robert Allenby AUS	
Jan 31 Feb 6	AT&T National Pro-Am	Pebble Beach California	**Tiger Woods** USA	273 (-15)	$720,000	Mat Gogel USA Vijay Singh FIJ	2
Feb 7 13	Buick Invitational	Torrey Pines GC La Jolla, CA	**Phil Mickelson** USA	270 (-18)	$540,000	Shigeki Maruyama Tiger Woods	4
Feb 14 20	Nissan Open	Riviera CC, Pacific Palisades CA	**Kirk Triplett** USA	270 (-14)	$558,000	Jesper Parnevik SWE	1
Feb 21 27	World Golf Chps Match Play	La Costa Resort Carlsbad, CA	**Darren Clarke** NIR		$1,000,000	Tiger Woods USA	4 & 3
Feb 21 27	Touchstone Tucson Open	Tucson National Arizona	**Jim Carter** USA	269 (-19)	$540,000	Di Marco, Scherrer Fehr, Van de Velde	1
Feb 28 Mar 5	Doral-Ryder Open	Doral Resort & CC Miami, Florida	**Jim Furyk** USA	265 (-23)	$540,000	Franklin Langham USA	2
Mar 6 12	Honda Classic	TPC at Heron Bay Coral Springs, FL	**Dudley Hart** USA	269 (-19)	$522,000	Kevin Wentworth J P Hayes	1
Mar 13 19	Bay Hills Invitational	Bay Hill Club Orlando, Florida	**Tiger Woods** USA	270 (-18)	$450,000	Davis Love III USA	4
Mar 20 26	The Players Championship	TPC at Sawgrass Ponte Vedre, FL	**Hal Sutton** USA	278 (-10)	$1,080,000	Tiger Woods USA	1
Mar 27 Apr 2	BellSouth Classic	Sugarloaf Duluth, Georgia	**Phil Mickelson** USA	205 (-11)	$504,000	Gary Nicklaus USA	play -off
Apr 6 9	**The Masters Tournament**	Augusta National Augusta, GA	**Vijay Singh** FIJ	278 (-10)	$828,000	Ernie Els RSA	3
Apr 10 16	MCI Classic	Harbour Town GL Hilton Head, SC	**Stewart Cink** USA	270 (-14)	$540,000	Tom Lehman USA	2
Apr 17 23	Greater Greensboro Chrysler Classic	Forest Oaks CC Greensboro, NC	**Hal Sutton** USA	274 (-14)	$540,000	Andrew Magee USA	3
Apr 24 30	Shell Houston Open	TPC at Woodlands The Woodlands, TX	**Robert Allenby** AUS	275 (-13)	$504,000	Craig Stadler USA	play -off
May 1 7	Compaq Classic of New Orleans	English Turn GC New Orleans	**Carlos Franco** PAR	270 (-18)	$612,000	Blaine McCallister USA	play -off
May 8 14	GTE Byron Nelson Classic	TPC at Las Colinas Irving, TX	**Jesper Parnevik** SWE	269 (-11)	$720,000	Phil Mickelson Davis Love III	play -off
May 15 21	Mastercard Colonial	Colonial CC Fort Worth, TX	**Phil Mickelson** USA	268 (-12)	$594,000	Stewart Cink Davis Love III	2
May 22 28	Memorial Tournament	Muirfield Village Dublin, OH	**Tiger Woods** USA	269 (-19)	$558,000	Ernie Els RSA Justin Leonard USA	5
May 29 June 4	Kemper Insurance Open	TPC at Avenel Potomac. MD	**Tom Scherrer** USA	271 (-13)	$540,000	Hosokawa, Chalmers 2 Leonard, Lowery, Langham	
June 5 11	Buick Classic	Westchester CC Harrison, NY	**Dennis Paulsen** USA	276 (-8)	$540,000	David Duval USA	play -off

Date	Tournament	Venue	Winner	Score	Prize	Runner-up	
June 12 18	**US Open Championship**	Pebble Beach California	**Tiger Woods** USA	272 (-12)	$800,000	Ernie Els RSA	15
June 19 25	FedEx St Jude Classic	TPC at Southwind Memphis	**Notah Begay III** USA	271 (-13)	$540,000	Chris DiMarco Bob May	1
June 26 July 2	Canon Greater Hartford Open	River Highlands Cromwell, CT	**Notah Begay III** USA	260 (-20)	$504,000	Mark Calcavecchia USA	1
July 3 9	Advil Western Open	Cog Hill G & CC Lemont, Illinois	**Robert Allenby** AUS	274 (-14)	$540,000	Nick Price ZIM	play -off
July 10 16	Greater Milwaukee Open	Brown Deer Park Milwaukee, WI	**Loren Roberts** USA	260 (-24)	$450,000	Franklin Langham USA	8
July 17 23	**The Open***	St Andrews Fife	**Tiger Woods** USA	269 (-19)	£500,000	Thomas Björn DEN	8
July 17 23	BC Open	En-Joie GC Endicott, NY	**Brad Faxon** USA	270 (-18)	$360,000	Esteban Toledo MEX	1
July 24 30	John Deere Classic	TPC at Deere Run Silvis, IL	**Michael Clark II** USA	265 (-19)	$468,000	Kirk Triplett USA	play -off
July 31 Aug 6	The International	Castle Pines GC Castle Rock, CO	**Ernie Els** RSA	48pts	$630,000	Phil Mickelson USA	4pts
Aug 7 13	Buick Open	Warwick Hills CC Grand Blanc, MI	**Rocco Mediate** USA	268 (-20)	$486,000	Chris Perry USA	1
Aug 14 20	**PGA Championship**	Valhalla GC Louoisville, KY	**Tiger Woods** USA	270 (-18)	$900,000	Bob May USA	play -off
Aug 21 27	World Golf Championships	Firestone CC Akron, OH	**Tiger Woods** USA	259 (-21)	$1,000,000	Phillip Price WAL Justin Leonard USA	11
Aug 21 27	Reno-Tahoe Open	Montreux G & CC Reno, Nevada	**Scott Verplank** USA	275 (-13)	$540,000	Jean vd Velde FRA	play -off
Aug 28 Sep 3	Air Canada Championship	Northview G & CC Surrey BC	**Rory Sabbatini** USA	268 (-16)	$540,000	Grant Waite USA	1
Sep 4 10	Bell Canadian Open	Glen Abbey GC Oakville, Ontario	**Tiger Woods** USA	266 (-22)	$594,000	Grant Waite USA	1
Sep 11 17	SEI Pennsylvania Classic	Waynesboro CC Paoli, PA	**Chris DiMarco** USA	270 (-14)	$576,000	Mark Calcavecchia USA	6
Sep 18 24	Westin Texas Open	La Cantera GC San Antonio TX	**Justin Leonard** USA	261 (-19)	$468,000	Mark Wiebe USA	5
Sep 25 Oct 1	Buick Challenge	Calloway Gdns Pine Mountain, GA	**David Duval** USA	269 (-19)	$414,000	Jeff Maggert USA Nick Price ZIM	2
Oct 2 8	Michelob Championship	KingsMill GC Williamsburg, VA	**David Toms** USA	271 (-13)	$540,000	Mike Weir CAN	play -off
Oct 9 15	Invensys Classic	TPC at Summerlin Las Vegas, NV	**Billy Andrade** USA	332 (-28)	$765,000	Phil Mickelson USA	1
Oct 17 22	The Presidents Cup	Robert Trent Jones Gainesville, VA	**USA**	21½-10½		International Team	
Oct 16 22	Tampa Bay Classic	Westin Innisbrook Tampa Bay, FL	**John Huston** USA	271 (-13)	£432,000	Carl Paulson USA	3
Oct 23 29	Walt Disney World/ National Car Rental	Lake Buena Vista, Florida	**Duffy Waldorf** USA	262 (-26)	$540,000	Steve Flesch USA	1
Oct 30 Nov 5	THE TOUR Championship	East Lake GC Atlanta	**Phil Mickelson** USA	267 (-13)	$900,000	Tiger Woods USA	1
Oct 30 Nov 5	Southern Fare Bureau Classic	Annandale GC Madison	**Steve Lowery** USA	266 (-22)	$396,000	Skip Kendall USA	play -off
Nov 9 12	WGC - American Express Chps	Club de Golf Valderrama	**Mike Weir** CAN	277 (-11)	£690,417	Lee Westwood ENG	2

Women's Golf

When the weather closed in on Loch Lomond on Saturday afternoon, it looked ominous enough to wonder if Europe were about to win the Solheim Cup for the first time in eight years without playing the final day singles. The skies were black, the rain was falling in buckets and Europe led by five points. A wash-out would have been a particularly fine idea, especially appealing to those who could remember the last time the Solheim was played on British soil and what happened in the singles then.

At Chepstow in 1996, Europe entered the final day leading by nine points to seven. They won the first singles in the clubhouse, too, Annika Sorenstam beating Pat Bradley 2 & 1. But that was it for winning. Liselotte Neumann and Alison Nicholas halved their matches and everyone else lost. The USA came home winners 17-11, taking nine of the 12 singles. You'd sleep in your mum and dad's room for a few weeks after that.

Well, the nightmare did not return. Perhaps, the sting was taken out of the American tail by the fact that four pairs had still to be completed on that final day and those matches were decided three-one in favour of the Europeans. The USA had no time to lick their wounds, no time to re-assert their team morale, they just had to get back out and squelch their way through the singles.

Juli Inkster had endured a pretty moderate weekend, but she found some compensation in the first singles by eclipsing Annika Sorenstam 5 & 4. Unfortunately, Sorenstam was probably still dwelling upon an incident in the early morning fourball when she had been paired with Janice Moodie against the Americans Pat Hurst and Kelly Robbins. On the 13th hole, Sorenstam chipped in, a shot which looked likely to keep the Europeans just one hole down. However, as soon as the ball went in the US pair called in their captain Pat Bradley and an official complaint was recorded that Sorenstam had played out of turn. The match referee Pat Trammel paced out the distance (which is a pretty crude measure at the best of times) and agreed with the Americans. The Swede was desolate, knowing that the Americans had watched her line up the shot and had only complained after the ball had gone in the hole. "The more I think about it, the more mad I get...if someone in my team had done it, I would have been outraged," said Sorenstam. The shot had to be played again, but Sorenstam could not repeat the magic, the tearful blur probably not helping. They went on to lose the fourball 2 & 1. Still, at least on this occasion the Europeans weren't just the moral victors, they were the real ones too.

Even after Sorenstam, it wasn't plain sailing, as Sophie Gustafson also took a hammering, from Brandie Burton. Helen Alfredsson, a wild-card selection for the team, stopped the rot when she beat Beth Daniel, but successive losses by Trish Johnson (to a relatively well-behaved Dottie Pepper) and Laura Davies (who didn't muster a win all weekend) brought the US to within two points of Europe and, when Patricia Lebouc last to Meg Mallon, it was down to just one. It had come to the crunch and, for once, it was not the US who came up with the goods. Katrin Nilsmark, Carin Koch and Janice Moodie won three of the last four matches out on the course and Europe had triumphed.

Solheim Cup

Loch Lomond   Oct 6-8
European names first, winners in bold

FRIDAY MATCHES
FOURSOMES
Laura Davies/Alison Nicholas beat
Dottie Pepper/Juli Inkster 4 & 3

Trish Johnson/Sophie Gustafson beat
Kelly Robbins/Pat Hurst 3 & 2

Catrin Nilsmark/Carin Koch beat
Meg Mallon/Beth Daniel 1 up

Annika Sorenstam/Janice Moodie beat
Meg Mallon/Beth Daniel 1 up

Laura Davies/Alison Nicholas lost to
Becky Iverson/Rosie Jones 6 & 5

Trish Johnson/Sophie Gustafson halved with
Juli Inkster/Sherri Steinhauer

Liselotte Neumann/Helen Alfredsson lost to
Kelly Robbins/Pat Hurst 1 up

Janice Moodie/Annika Sorenstam beat
Meg Mallon/Beth Daniel 1 up

SATURDAY MATCHES
FOURBALLS
Trish Johnson/Sophie Gustafson beat
Rosie Jones/Becky Iverson 3 & 2

Alison Nicholas/Helen Alfredsson beat
Juli Inkster/Sherri Steinhauer 3 & 2

Catrin Nilsmark/Carin Koch beat
Nancy Scranton/Michele Redman 2 & 1

Liselotte Neumann/Patricia M Lebouc halved with
Dottie Pepper/Brandie Burton

Laura Davies/Raquel Carriedo halved with
Meg Mallon/Beth Daniel

Annika Sorenstam/Janice Moodie lost to
Pat Hurst/Kelly Robbins 2 & 1
Great Britain & Ireland 2   USA 7

SUNDAY MATCHES
SINGLES
Annika Sorenstam lost to **Juli Inkster** 5 & 4
Sophie Gustafson lost to **Brandie Burton** 4 & 3
Helen Alfredsson beat Beth Daniel 4 & 3
Trish Johnson lost to **Dottie Pepper** 2 & 1
Laura Davies lost to **Kelly Robbins** 3 & 2
Liselotte Neumann halved with **Pat Hurst**
Alison Nicholas halved with **Sherri Steinhauer**
Patricia Meunier Lebouc lost to **Meg Mallon** 1 up
Catrin Nilsmark beat Rosie Jones 1 up
Raquel Carriedo lost to **Becky Iversen** 3 & 2
Carin Koch beat Michele Redman 2 & 1
Janice Moodie beat Nancy Scranton 1 up

FINAL SCORE
Europe 14½   USA 11½

No woman has ever won the Women's Open three times in succession and Sherri Steinhauer did not have to wait long to know that she wasn't about to be the first. The American's first round of 77 was only marginally bettered by a second round of 75 which left her two shots adrift of the cut. She was in good company, Alison Nicholas made the same halfway score, but when you're hitting your head against a brick wall, it doesn't matter much who you do it with.

Sophie Gustafson won the title, but the Swede seemed quite prepared to give the prize to someone else, as it came within her grasp. On the 17th, Gustafson took a bogey six that took her back to nine under par. Her playing partner Meg Mallon took encouragement, for she was just two shots behind Gustafsson, while in the clubhouse watching them both play the 18th hole, were Becky Iverson, Liselotte Neumann and Kirsty Taylor, who were eight under par.

Kirtsty Taylor, from the nearby Clitheroe club, had hit a superb 67 to put herself in contention, but they all needed the Swede to stumble again at the last. Instead, Gustafson made a five-foot putt for a birdie and the Gothenburg collected the biggest pay pack of her career, £120,000.

It was not quite enough to take Gustafson to the top the European money list, Annika Sorenstam earning almost a thousand pounds more in total (£208,283-£207,288), but such sums paled in comparison with the earnings on the US LPGA Tour. Karrie Webb was out on her own in the US, winning six tournaments including the US Open and the Nabisco. She also won her native Australian Masters and aggregated $1,876,853 - a US LPGA record - to finish nearly half a million dollars clear of Annika Sorenstam.

European Tour

Date	Tournament	Venue	Winner	Score	1st Prize	Runner(s)-up	Margin
May 6 8	AAMI Australian Open*	Tarra Yarra GC	**Karrie Webb** AUS	270 (-22)	$AU36,694	Rachel Hetherington AUS	3
May 18 May 21	Italian Open	Poggio dei Medici Florence	**Sophie Gustafson** SWE	284 (-8)	£15,000	S Cavalleri ITA V Van Ryckeghem BEL	3
May 26 May 28	Hannover Expo 2000 Open	Rethmar GC Hanover	**Alison Munt** AUS	212 (-4)	£15,000	Valerie Van Ryckeghem BEL	1
June 1 8	Chrysler Open	Halmstad GC Sweden	**Carin Koch** SWE	277 (-11)	£22,500	Samantha Head ENG	4
June 8 11	Waterford Crystal Irish Open	Faithlegg GC	**Sophie Gustafson** SWE	282 (-6)	£15,000	Marine Monnet FRA	1
June 14 June 17	Evian Open	Royal Golf Club Evian-les-Bains	**Annika Sorenstam** SWE	276 (-12)	£177,433	Karrie Webb AUS	play -off
June 29 July 2	French Open	Le Golf d'Arras	**Patricia M Lebouc** FRA	271 (-17)	£15,000	R Carriedo ESP Asa Gottmo SWE	1
July 6 9	German Open	Marriott Hotel Treudelberg	**Joanne Morley** ENG	274 (-14)	£15,000	Raquel Carriedo ESP	2
July 13 15	Austrian Open	Steiermärkischer GC, Frohnleiten	**Patricia M Lebouc** FRA	206 (-10)	£15,000	Trish Johnson L Hed, A B Sanchez	1
Aug 4 6	Ladies British Masters	Mottram Hall GC Cheshire	**Trish Johnson** ENG	207 (-9)	£15,000	Vibeke Stensrud NOR	2
Aug 12 15	Weetabix Women's British Open	Woburn G & CC Milton Keynes	**Sophie Gustafson** SWE	282 (-10)	£120,000	K Taylor, Iverson, Neumann & Mallon	2
Aug 19 22	Compaq Open	Österåkers GC Stockholm	**Julie Inkster** USA	282 (-6)	£45,000	Sophie Gustafson SWE	1
Aug 31 Sep 2	Kronenbourg 1664 Chart Hills Classic	Biddenden Kent	**Gina Marie Scott** NZL	207 (-9)	£15,000	Isabella Maconi ITA	play- off
Sep 15 17	Ladies World Cup	Adare Manor GR Ireland	**Sweden**	425 (-7)		England	5
Sep 21 23	Mexx Sport Open	Zandvoort Netherlands	**Tina Fischer** GER	211 (-5)	£15,000	Kirsty Taylor ENG Raquel Carriedo ESP	3
Oct 13 15	Marrakech Palmeraie Open	Marrakech Morocco	**Alison Munt** AUS	207 (-9)	£15,000	Trish Johnson ENG	3

European Tour Final Money List

	Player	Ctry	Events	£		Player	Ctry	Events	£
1	Annika Sorenstam	SWE	3	208,283	11	Carin Koch	SWE	4	44,541
2	Sophie Gustafson	SWE	8	207,288	12	Valerie Van Ryckegham	BEL	14	42,151
3	Kirsty Taylor	ENG	15	82,908	13	Joanne Morley	ENG	5	41,078
4	Alison Nicholas	ENG	9	72,710	14	Laura Davies	ENG	8	40,743
5	Trish Johnson	ENG	12	69,638	15	Silvia Cavalleri	ITA	6	39,814
6	Raquel Carriedo	ESP	12	62,619	16	Kathryn Marshall	SCO	5	38,185
7	Liseloote Neumann	SWE	3	59,665	17	Samantha Head	ENG	14	35,449
8	Marine Monnet	FRA	14	59,162	18	Sandrine Mendiburu	FRA	15	31,858
9	Alison Munt	AUS	15	55,172	19	Janice Moodie	SCO	3	30,879
10	Patricia Meunier Lebouc	FRA	13	47,795	20	Johanna Head	ENG	14	29,870

Weetabix British Open

Royal Birkdale   Aug 17-20
Par: 73

282	**Sophie Gustafson SWE**	70 66 71 75	
(-10)	**(£120,000)**		
284	Kirsty Taylor ENG	71 74 72 67	
(-8)	Becky Iverson USA	70 70 75 69	
	Liselotte Neumann SWE	71 73 71 69	
	Meg Mallon USA	74 69 71 70	
	(£50,712 each)		
285	Laura Philo USA	72 73 72 68	
(-7)	(£27,500)		
286	Karrie Webb AUS	68 75 72 71	
(-6)	(£23,250)		
287	Janice Moodie SCO	73 74 73 67	
(-5)	Vicki Goetze-Ackerman USA	77 69 73 68	
	(£19,500 each)		
288	Maggie Will USA	74 72 76 66	
(-4)	Michelle McGann USA	72 76 69 71	
	Juli Inkster USA	70 69 77 72	
	Jenny Lidback PER	71 71 73 73	
	Trish Johnson ENG	71 72 72 73	
	Kellee Booth USA	73 71 71 73	
	Kathryn Marshall SCO	72 69 73 74	
	(£13,250 each)		
289	Pat Bradley USA	74 71 74 70	
(-3)	Rosie Jones USA	72 72 73 72	
	Annika Sorenstam SWE	70 76 71 72	
	(£9,850 each)		
290	Kelly Robbins USA	73 74 73 70	
(-2)	Karen Weiss USA	73 70 75 72	
	Rachel Hetherington AUS	71 74 73 72	
	Brandie Burton USA	72 74 71 73	
	(£8,475 each)		
291	Michele Redman USA	74 73 73 71	
(-1)	Alicia Dibos PER	72 73 74 72	
	Marine Monnet FRA	72 73 74 72	
	Raquel Carriedo ESP	76 71 72 72	
	(£7,275 each)		
292	Riko Higashio JPN	74 72 76 70	
(level)	Susan Redman USA	70 78 71 73	
	Jill McGill USA	71 71 76 74	
	Mhairi McKay SCO	74 71 71 76	
	(£6,312 each)		
293	Shani Waugh AUS	73 74 76 70	
(+1)	Michelle Estill USA	72 75 75 71	
	Sofia G Whitmore SWE	80 69 73 71	
	Gail Graham CAN	79 71 71 72	
	Betsy King USA	74 73 73 73	
	(£5,400 each)		
294	Giulia Sergas ITA	77 70 78 69	
(+2)	Maria Hjorth SWE	76 72 75 71	
	Tina Barrett USA	77 72 72 73	
	Leigh Ann Mills USA	74 72 74 74	
	Julie Forbes SCO	72 73 74 75	
	Wendy Daden ENG	77 71 71 75	
	Pernilla Sterner SWE	77 72 70 75	
	Laura Davies ENG	76 70 72 76	
	(£4,118 each)		

295	Anna Berg SWE	73 77 75 70	
(+3)	Yu Ping Lin TPE	73 74 77 71	
	Aki Takamura JPN	73 76 75 71	
	Karen Pearce USA	74 76 74 71	
	(£3,125 each)		
296	Silvia Cavalleri ITA	79 70 74 73	
(+4)	Stephanie Arricau FRA	78 71 74 73	
	Sara Eklund SWE	75 75 73 73	
	Karen Stupples ENG	73 77 73 73	
	Sandrine Mendiburi FRA	77 72 73 74	
	Jenifer Feldott USA	75 71 74 76	
	Helen Alfredsson SWE	78 71 71 76	
	Anne-Marie Knight AUS	73 71 75 77	
	(£2,287 each)		
297	Federica Dassu ITA	77 73 73 74	
(+5)	(£1,800)		
298	Kristal Parker-Gregory USA	75 74 75 74	
(+6)	Elisabeth Esterl GER	75 75 72 76	
	(£1,650 each)		
299	Catrin Nilsmark SWE	77 72 78 72	
(+7)	Smriti Mehra IND	75 75 73 76	
	Johanna Head ENG	77 73 71 78	
	(£1,400 each)		
300	Mardi Lunn AUS	80 69 78 73	
(+8)	Mandy Adamson RSA	78 71 78 73	
	Dale Reid SCO	76 71 78 75	
	(£1,200 each)		
301	Hiromi Kobayashi JPN	75 74 76 76	
(+9)	Lisa DePaulo USA	76 74 71 80	
	(£800 each)		
303	Hsui Feng Tseng CHN	76 73 81 73	
(+11)	Nina Karlsson SWE	77 73 76 77	
	Judith Van Hagen NED	76 74 75 78	
	(£800 each)		
304	Emilee Klein USA	72 77 77 78	
(+12)	Gina Marie Scott NZL	78 72 76 78	
	Laurette Maritz RSA	71 76 77 80	
	(£800 each)		
306	Lora Fairclough ENG	76 71 80 79	
(+14)	(£800)		

Those who missed the cut includes:
151: Corinne Dibnah AUS 76 75, Catriona Matthew SCO 78 73, Joanne Morley ENG 76 75, Stefania Croce ITA 77 74
152: Charlotta Sorenstam SWE 77 75, Sherri Steinhauer USA 77 75
153: Alison Nicholas ENG 78 75, Kirsty Taylor* ENG 78 76
155: Helen Dobson ENG 76 79
156: Patricia Meunieer Lebouc FRA 77 79
157: Carin Koch SWE 78 79, Karen Lunn AUS 78 79

GOLF

US LPGA Tour

Date	Tournament	Venue	Winner	Score	1st Prize	Runner(s)-up	Margin
Jan 13 16	The Office Depot	Ibis G & CC West Palm Beach	**Karrie Webb** AUS	281 (-7)	$112,500	Juli Inkster USA	4
Jan 20 23	Subaru Memorial of Naples	Club at the Strand Naples, Florida	**Nancy Scranton** USA	275 (-13)	$112,500	Maria Hjorth SWE	play -off
Feb 11 13	Los Angeles Championship	Wood Ranch GC Simi Valley, CA	**Laura Davies** ENG	211 (-5)	$97,500	Koch, Redman Moodie	3
Feb 18 20	Cup Noodles Hawaiian Open	Kapolei GC Oahu	**Betsy King** USA	204 (-12)	$97,500	Brandie Burton USA	2
Feb 24 27	Australian Masters*	Royal Pines Resort Queensland	**Karrie Webb** AUS	274 (-14)	$112,500	Lorie Kane USA	1
Mar 2 4	Takefuji Classic	Kona CC Hawaii	**Karrie Webb** AUS	207 (-9)	$120,000	A Sorenstam SWE	play -off
Mar 9 12	Welch's/Circle K Championship	Randolph Pk GC Tucson, AZ	**Annika Sorenstam** SWE	269 (-19)	$105,000	Pat Hurst USA	play -off
Mar 16 19	Standard Register PING	Legacy GC Phoenix, AZ	**Charlotta Sorenstam** SWE	276 (-12)	$127,500	Karrie Webb AUS	2
Mar 23 26	**Nabisco Championship**	Mission Hills CC Rancho Mirage, CA	**Karrie Webb** AUS	274 (-14)	$187,500	Dottie Pepper USA	10
Apr 13 16	Longs Drugs Challenge	Twelve Bridges GC Lincoln, CA	**Juli Inkster** USA	275 (-10)	$105,000	Brandi Burton USA	5
Apr 28 30	Chick-fil-A Charity Championship	Eagles Landing CC Stockbridge, GA	**Sophie Gustafson** SWE	206 (-10)	$135,000	Kelly Robbins USA	1
May 4 7	The Phillips Invitational	Onion Creek Club Austin, Texas	**Laura Davies** ENG	275 (-5)	$127,500	Dottie Pepper USA	2
May 11 14	Electrolux USA Championship	Legends Club of Tennessee	**Pat Hurst** USA	275 (-13)	$120,000	Juli Inkster USA	4
May 19 21	Firstar LPGA Classic	CC of the North Beavercreek, Ohio	**Annika Sorenstam** SWE	197 (-19)	$97,500	Cristie Kerr USA Karrie Webb AUS	1
May 25 28	Corning Classic	Corning CC Corning, New York	**Betsy King** USA	276 (-12)	$120,000	K Keuhne V G-Ackerman	play -off
June 1 4	Kathy Ireland Classic	Wacheslaw GC Murrels Inlet, SC	**Grace Park** USA	274 (-14)	$112,500	Pat Hurst USA Juli Inkster USA	1
June 8 11	Wegmans Rochester	Locust Hill CC Pittsford, NY	**Meg Mallon** USA	280 (-8)	$150,000	Wendy Doolan AUS	2
June 22 25	**McDonald's Championship**	Dupont CC Wilmington, DE	**Juli Inkster** USA	281 (-3)	$210,000	Stefania Croce ITA	play -off
June 30 July 2	ShopRite Classic	Marriott Seaview Atlantic City	**Janice Moodie** SCO	203 (-10)	$165,000	Pat Hurst USA Grace Park USA	2
July 6 9	Jamie Farr Kroger Classic	Highland Meadows Sylvania, Ohio	**Annika Sorenstam** SWE	274 (-10)	$150,000	Rachel Hetherington AUS	play -off
July 15 18	JAL Big Apple Classic	Wykagyl CC New Rochelle, NY	**Annika Sorenstam** SWE	206 (-7)	$135,000	Rosie Jones USA	1
July 20 23	**US Open Championship**	Merit Club, Libertyville, ILL	**Karrie Webb** AUS	282 (-6)	$500,000	Cristie Kerr USA Meg Mallon USA	5
July 28 30	Giant Eagle Classic	Avalon Lakes GC Warren, OH	**Dorothy Delasin** USA	205 (-11)	$150,000	Pat Hurst USA	play -off
Aug 4 6	Michelob Light Classic	Fox Run GC St Louis, MI	**Lorie Kane** CAN	205 (-11)	$120,000	Kristie Albers USA	3

Aug 10 13	**du Maurier Classic**	Royal Ottawa GC Aylmer, Canada	**Meg Mallon** USA	282 (-6)	$180,000	Rosie Jones USA	1
Aug 24 27	Oldsmobile Classic	Walnut Hills CC E Lansing, Michigan	**Karrie Webb** AUS	265 (-23)	$112,500	Meg Mallon USA	2
Sep 1 3	State Farm Rail Classic	The Rail GC Springfield, Illinois	**Laurel Kean** USA	198 (-18)	$135,000	D Ammaccapane Kim Mi-Hyun	6
Sep 8 10	First Union Betsy King Classic	Berkleigh CC Kutztown, Penn	**Michele Redman** USA	202 (-14)	$120,000	Meg Mallon Jean Bartholomew	3
Sep 22 24	The Safeway Championship	Columbia Edgewater Portland, Oregon	**Kim Mi-Hyun** KOR	215 (-1)	$120,000	Jeong Jang KOR	play -off
Sep 28 Oct 1	New Albany Classic	New Albany CC New Albany, Ohio	**Lorie Kane** CAN	277 (-11)	$150,000	Kim Mi-Hyun KOR	play -off
Oct 6 8	**The Solheim Cup**	Loch Lomond GC Luss, Scotland					
Oct 12 15	Samsung World Championship		**Juli Inkster** USA	274 (-14)	$152,000	Annika Sorenstam SWE	4
Oct 19 22	AFLAC Champions	Robert Trent Trail Mobile, Alabama	**Karrie Webb** AUS	273 (-15)	$122,000	Dottie Pepper USA	play -off
Nov 16 19	Arch Wireless Championship	Daytona Beach Legends Course	**Dottie Pepper** USA	279 (-9)	$215,000	Rachel Teske AUS	3

US LPGA 2000 ORDER OF MERIT
Final Standing

	Player	Ctry	Events	$
1	Karrie Webb	AUS	22	1,876,853
2	Annika Sorenstam	SWE	22	1,404,948
3	Meg Mallon	USA	26	1,146,360
4	Juli Inkster	USA	19	980,330
5	Lorie Kane	CAN	30	929,189
6	Pat Hurst	USA	26	840,161
7	Kim Mi-Hyun	KOR	27	825,720
8	Dottie Pepper	USA	19	786,695
9	Rosie Jones	USA	25	643,054
10	Michele Redman	USA	28	585,694
11	Laura Davies	ENG	22	557,158
12	Se Ri Pak	KOR	23	550,376
13	Sophie Gustafson	SWE	21	544,390
14	Janice Moodie	SCO	28	534,833
15	Cristie Kerr	USA	24	530,751
16	Sherri Steinhauer	USA	30	460,370
17	Rachel Teske (née Hetherington)	AUS	28	447,180
18	Nancy Scranton	USA	29	431,452
19	Grace Park	USA	25	427,055
20	Charlotta Sorenstam	SWE	28	421,687
21	Betsy King	USA	27	402,689
22	Kelly Robbins	USA	23	384,266
23	Brandy Burton	USA	25	379,189
24	Leta Lindley	USA	27	351,195
25	Dorothy Delasin	USA	29	339,112
26	Kelli Kuehne	USA	23	337,406
27	Beth Daniel	USA	24	334,411
28	Carin Koch	USA	25	329,377
29	Becky Iverson	USA	28	319,959
30	Wendy Doolan	AUS	19	295,277
Also				
32	Catriona Matthew	SCO	28	278,382
43	Alison Nicholas	ENG	15	199,334
48	Liselotte Neumann	SWE	25	185,309

Amateur Golf

The Curtis Cup

Ganton, Yorkshire   June 25-26
Great Britain and Ireland names first

SATURDAY MATCHES
Foursomes
Kim Andrew/Becky Morgan lost to
Beth Bauer/Carol Semple Thompson   1 hole

Becky Brewerton/Rebecca Hudson lost to
Stephanie Keever/Angela Stanford   1 hole

Emma Duggleby/Suzanne O'Brien halved with
Hilary Homeyer/Virginia Derby Grimes

Singles
Andrew lost to **Bauer** 3 & 2
Hudson lost to **Keever** 4 & 2
Fiona Brown lost to **Robin Weiss** 1 hole
Lesley Nicholson halved with Stanford
O'Brien bt Leland Beckel 3 & 1
Duggleby lost to **Homeyer** 1 hole

Great Britain & Ireland 2   USA 7

SUNDAY MATCHES
Foursomes
Brewerton/Hudson bt
Bauer/Semple Thompson 2 & 1

Duggleby/O'Brien bt
Keever/Stanford 7& 6

Andrew/Morgan lost to
Homeyer/Derby Grimes 3 & 1

Singles
Hudson lost to **Bauer** 1 hole
O'Brien bt Weiss 3 & 2
Duggleby bt Keever 4 & 2
Brewerton lost to **Homeyer** 3 & 2
Morgan bt Stanford 5 & 4
Andrew bt Grimes 6 & 5

Final Score
Great Britain & Ireland 8   USA 10

The Amateur Championship

Royal Liverpool   June 10

FINAL
Mikko Ilonen (Finland) bt
Christian Reimbold (Germany) 2 & 1

Gymnastics

W hen Andreea Raducan returned home from the Olympic Games, the association of Romanian jewellers had a gold medal waiting for her. Made of real gold it was worth a small fortune, but Raducan would have exchanged it any day of the week for a worthless old alloy - the Olympic gold medal. Raducan and her teammates had already upset the Russians to take team gold and, when they posted first, second and third in the all-around event as well, it was the first time since 1960, that a single country had been so dominant.

When the news came through that Raducan, the first Romanian since Nadia Comaneci in 1976 to win the all-around title, had tested positive for pseudoephedrine the Romanians were stunned. Raducan had been given Nurofen, by the team doctor, Ioachin Oana, for a cold. This held no sway with the IOC, the drug was on the banned list and Raducan was stripped of her all-around gold medal. Simona Amanar was elevated to gold, Maria Olaru moved up to silver and Liu Xuan of China took the bronze. Raducan, who was not tested after the team competition, was allowed to keep that gold medal.

For Svetlana Khorkina, who many expected to challenge strongly for the all-around title, it was a games salvaged only on the final day. The Russian team silver was one place lower than expected and, while she qualified for the all-around first in place, she succumbed to nerves in the final. She fell in the vault and, spectacularly, parted company with the uneven bars. Her Olympic title came, ironically, when she returned to the uneven bars for the apparatus finals. It stemmed the flow of tears, but was no more than a consolation prize in what was her last Olympics.

Men's gymnastics is always slightly in the shadow and Sydney was no different. China won the team gold, Alexei Nemov of Russia was all-around champion. The six apparatus finals went to six different countries, the most surprising of which was Igors Vihrovs win on the floor to give Latvia its solitary success in Sydney.

For the British, the Games was a qualified success. The results were the best ever and set standards for the future, but a wholesale post-games retirement may have put Britain on the back foot as the Olympic cycle begins again. Craig Heap, the only man in Sydney, reached the all-around final and came 32nd. The women's team competing for the first time came a respectable 10th out of the 12 teams and individually Lisa Mason, Annika Reeder and Emma Williams made the all-around final, Mason with the best finish of 23rd. However, of the seven-strong British team, four have now retired, and the futures of Mason and Heap are still undecided, which leaves just Williams and a big gap to fill after such a promising Games.

> "The medical committee said that they knew the pills didn't help the athlete. In fact they are bad for the gymnast. The only time they will have a pill for gymnastics it will have to be a very smart one, so that the competitor can say to the pill, 'I'm on the beam now, can you help?, I'm on the vault now...'"
>
> Octavian Belu, Andreea Raducan's coach, outraged by the disqualification.

Artistic

European Championships, Men

Bremen   May 25-28

Team

1 Russia		171.071
2 Romania		170.844
3 Ukraine		170.608

All-Around

1 Olexandr Beresch	UKR	57.787
2 Ivan Ivankov	BLR	57.598
3 Marian Dragulescu	ROM	57.448
16 Craig Heap	GBR	54.849

Floor

1 Marian Dragulescu	ROM	9.687
2 Gervasio Deferr	ESP	9.675
3 Alexei Bondarenko	RUS	9.587

Pommel

1 Marius Urzica	ROM	9.762
2 Eric Poujade	FRA	9.750
3 Olexandr Beresch	UKR	9.662

Rings

1 Dimothenis Tambakos	GRE	9.737
2 Szilveszter Csollany	HUN	9.675
3 Ivan Ivankov	BLR	9.650

Vault

1 Ioan Suciu	ROM	9.631
2 Dimitri Karbanenko	FRA	9.625
3 Olexandr Svetlichnyi	UKR	9.606
8 Kanukai Jackson	GBR	9.174

Parallel Bars

1 Mitja Petykovsek	SLO	9.800
2 Ivan Ivankov	BLR	9.775
3 Alexei Bondarenko	RUS	9.725

High Bar

1 Olexandr Beresch	UKR	9.737
2 Ivan Ivankov	BLR	9.725
3 Aljaz Pegan	SLO	9.687

European Championships, Women

Paris   May 12-14

Team

1 Russia		115.760
2 Ukraine		115.302
3 Romania		114.703
7 Great Britain		110.482

All-Around

1 Svetlana Khorkina	RUS	38.749
2 Elena Zamolodchikova	RUS	38.624
3 Vyktoria Karpenko	UKR	38.456
10 Lisa Mason	GBR	37.368

Vault

1 Simona Amanar	ROM	9.674
2 Elena Zamolodchikova	ROM	9.668
3 Esther Moya	ESP	9.574

Uneven Bars

1 Svetlana Khorkina	RUS	9.837
2 Vyktoria Karpenko	UKR	9.800
3 Elena Produnova	RUS	9.775

Beam

1 Svetlana Khorkina	RUS	9.837
2 Simona Amanar	ROM	9.800
3 Elena Zamolodchikova	RUS	9.762
7 Lisa Mason	GBR	9.275

Floor

1 Ludivine Furnon	FRA	9.875
2 Vyktoria Karpenko	UKR	9.812
2 Andreea Raducan	ROM	9.812
2 Elena Produnova	RUS	9.812

Grand Prix Final

Glasgow   Dec 9-10

Men

Floor Final

1 Gervasio Deferr	ESP	9.725
2= Keyle Shewfelt	CAN	9.650
2= Jordan Jovtchev	BUL	9.650

Pommel Horse Final

1 Marius Urzica	ROM	9.837
2 Ivan Ivankov	BLR	9.750
3 Aowei Xing	CHN	9.700

Rings Final

1 Szilveszter Csollany	HUN	9.812
2 Jordan Jovtchev	BUL	9.800
3 Ivan Ivankov	BLR	9.787

Vault Final

1 Marian Dragulescu	ROM	9.700
2 Gervasio Deferr	ESP	9.625
3 Evgeni Sapronenko	LAT	9.606
6 Kanukai Jackson	GBR	9.356

Parallel Bars Final

1 Mitja Petkovsek	SLO	9.800
2 Alexei Bondarenko	RUS	9.725
3 Aljaz Pegan	SLO	9.675

High Bar Final

1 Alexander Beresch	UKR	9.762
2 Aljaz Pegan	SLO	9.750
3 Ivan Ivankov	BLR	9.700

Women

Vault Final

1 Elena Zamolodchikova	RUS	9.581
2 Simona Amanar	ROM	9.387
3 Yoanna Skowronska	POL	9.374
6 Emma Williams	GBR	9.281

Asymmetric Bars Final

1 Ling Jie	CHN	9.800
2 Alana Slater	AUS	9.662
3 Andreea Raducan	ROM	9.425

Beam Final

1 Ling Jie	CHN	9.800
2 Alana Slater	AUS	9.662
3 Andreea Raducan	ROM	9.425

Floor Final

1 Andreea Raducan	ROM	9.687
2 Elena Zamolodchikova	RUS	9.675
3 Dong Fangxiao	CHN	9.662

British Championships

All Around

Men: Kanukai Jackson	Harrow		53.400
Women: Emma Williams	Liverpool		

Rhythmic

European Championships
Zaragoza, Spain   June 1-4

Team
1	Russia	79.949
2	Belarus	79.666
3	Ukraine	79.515
22	Great Britain	76.156

All-Around
1	Alina Kabaeva	RUS	39.983
2	Yulia Raskina	BLR	39.983
3	Youlia Barsoukova	RUS	39.916

Rope
1	Youlia Barsoukova	RUS	9.983
2	Tamara Yerofeeva	UKR	9.983
3	Alina Kabaeva	RUS	9.966

Hoop
1	Alina Kabaeva	RUS	10.000
1	Eva Serrano	FRA	10.000
3	Youlia Barsoukova	RUS	10.000

Ball
1	Alina Kabaeva	RUS	9.966
2	Yulia Raskina	BLR	10.000
3	Youlia Barsoukova	RUS	10.000

Ribbon
1	Alina Kabaeva	RUS	10.000
2	Eva Serrano	FRA	10.000
3	Yulia Raskina	BLR	9.966

Grand Prix Final
Glasgow   Dec 9-10

Rope
1 Alina Kabaeva RUS 9.875
2 Youlia Barsoukova RUS 9.825
3 Irina Tschaschina RUS 9.725

Hope
1Youlia Barsoukova RUS 9.850
2 Alina Kabaeva RUS 9.837
3 Yukia Raskina BLR 9.812

Ball
1 Alina Kabaeva RUS 9.875
2 Youlia Barsoukova RUS 9.837
3 Yukia Raskina BLR 9.775

Ribbon
1 Alina Kabaeva RUS 9.900
2 Youlia Barsoukova RUS 9.750
3 Yukia Raskina BLR 9.725

Sports Aerobics

World Championships
Riesa, Germany   June 2-4

Individual Men
1	Jonathan Canada	ESP	19.000
2	Kwang-Soo Park	KOR	18.600
3	Claudiu Moldovan	ROM	18.300

Individual Women
1	Izabela Lacatus	ROM	19.050
2	Isamara Secati	BRA	18.900
3	Ludmila Kovatcheva	BUL	18.650
24	Joanne Stevens	GBR	15.750
40	Sarah Hamm	GBR	13.200

Mixed Pair
1	Russia		19.850
2	Romania		19.150
3	Korea		18.850
19	McGuinnes/Russel	GBR	15.300

Trios
1	Romania 2	19.050
2	Korea	18.366
3	Russia	18.200

Sports Acrobatics

World Championships
Wroclaw, Poland   Nov 2-5

Men's Pairs
Overall
1	Anikin/Batrakov	RUS	29.875
2	Baravikov/Liubezny	BLR	29.475
3	Ivanov/Nikalov	BUL	29.400
8	Flores/Smith	GBR	25.550

Balance
1	Li/Song	CHN	19.950
2	Anikin/Batrakov	RUS	19.875
3	Flores/Smith	GBR	19.825

Tempo
1	Anikin/Batrakov	RUS	19.825
2	Ivanov/Nikalov	BUL	19.550
3	Koleschnikov/Menshykh	UKR	19.525

Men's Group
Overall
1	China	29.825
2	Russia	29.525
3	Bulgaria	28.050

Balance
1	China	19.850
2	Russia	19.825
3	Bulgaria	19.525

Tempo
1	China	19.875
2	Russia	19.725
3	Belarus	19.575

Women's Pairs
Overall
1	Lopatkina/Mochova	RUS	29.850
2	Shi/Sun	CHN	29.600
3	Clarke/Middleton	GBR	29.225

Balance
1	Lopatkina/Mochova	RUS	19.875
2	Shi/Sun	CHN	19.775
3	Klokova/Kovzalyuk	UKR	19.750
4	Clarke/Middleton	GBR	19.450

Tempo
1	Lopatkina/Mochova	RUS	19.825
2	Shi/Sun	CHN	19.675
3	Vd Weghe/V Maldegam	BEL	19.400
4	Clarke/Middleton	GBR	19.400

Women's Group
Overall
1	Russia	29.800
2	China	29.725
3	Great Britain	29.700
	(Collins/Crocker/Cox)	

Balance
1	Russia	19.900
2	China	19.850
3	Belarus	19.825
4	Great Britain	19.775

Tempo
1	Russia	19.875
2	China	19.800
3	Great Britain	19.700

Mixed Pairs
Overall
1	Jakovlev/Lymareva	RUS	30.000
2	Todorova/Katzov	BUL	29.525
3	Chen/Wu	CHN	29.500
6	Wharton/Wood	GBR	29.250

Balance
1	Jakovlev/Lymareva	RUS	20.000
2	Todorova/Katzov	BUL	19.750
3	Hauryliuk/Dvorak	BLR	19.650
7	Wharton/Wood	GBR	19.550

Tempo
1	Jakovlev/Lymareva	RUS	19.950
2	Dzyuba/Klymenko	UKR	19.825
3	Broncatello/Davis	UKR	19.650

Trampolining

European Championships
Eindhoven, Netherlands   Oct 16-22

Men
Individual
1	German Khnytchev	RUS	108.60
2	David Martin	FRA	107.70
3	Vladimir Kakorko	BLR	105.30
15	Paul Smyth	GBR	64.90
16	Simon Milnes	GBR	64.70
18	Lee Brearley	GBR	64.50
24	Mark Alexander	GBR	62.90
39	Jamie Crisp	GBR	58.20

Team
1	France	116.70
2	Belarus	116.20
3	Great Britain	114.10
	(Alexander/Smyth/Milnes/Brearley)	

Synchronised
1	Khnytchev/Moskaleko	RUS	136.00
2	Serth/Reithofer	GER	134.10
3	Milnes/Alexander	GBR	133.30

Individual Double Mini
1	Nuno Merino	POR	24.59
2	Uwe Maraquadt	GER	23.40
3	Vladimir Cojoc	MDA	22.88

Individual Tumbling
1	Levon Petrosian	RUS	85.89
2	Ruslan Gruzda	UKR	81.08
3	Andriy Kozlenko	UKR	79.80
4	Ross Gibson	GBR	79.16
9	Robert Small	GBR	67.99
12	Robert Proctor	GBR	52.62
15	Richard Barker	GBR	48.89

Team Tumbling
1	Russia	90.46
2	Great Britain	81.73
	(Barker/Gibson/Proctor/Small)	
3	France	81.32

Women
Individual
1	Irina Karavaeva	RUS	105.90
2	A Dogonadze-Lilkendey	GER	104.50
3	Oksana Tsyguleva	UKR	103.30
9	Kirsten Lawton	GBR	99.00
13	Claire Wright	GBR	62.60
15	Elenor Dixon Jackson	GBR	62.30
19	Victoria Pollard	GBR	61.60

Team
1	Russia	112.00
2	Belarus	110.50
3	Germany	109.20
5	Great Britain	108.90
	(Pollard/Wright/Lawton/Jackson)	

Synchronised
1	Lebedeva/Karpenkova	BLR	130.00
2	Ludwig/D-Lilkendey	GER	129.70
3	Wright/Lawton	GBR	127.00

Individual Double Mini
1	Katarina Prokesova	SLO	22.20
2	Teodora Sinilkova	BUL	21.53
3	Antonia Ivanova	BUL	21.06

Individual Tumbling
1	Elena Bloujina	RUS	78.92
2	Natalia Rakhmanova	RUS	77.05
3	Chrystel Robert	FRA	75.25
9	Andrea Linford	GBR	62.63
10	Zoe Styles	GBR	61.82
16	Kathryn Perbedy	GBR	39.83
18	Elizabeth Gough	GBR	37.16

Team Tumbling
1	France	76.22
2	Ukraine	70.66
3	Belarus	69.92
5	Great Britain	64.69
	(Gough/Linford/Styles/Perbedy)	

Hockey

The 8-1 defeat by Pakistan in Sydney was the worst ever for British men in Olympic history. It was worse than in 1948, when India inflicted on Britain its first-ever Olympic defeat, winning the final 4-0. Worse than losing to 7-0 to Australia in the 1964 Olympics. Worse than defeats by Spain and Germany and everyone else over the years. Even in Atlanta, where we finished a regulation seventh place, Britain only lost to Pakistan 2-1. No, this was the worst of the worst. Having thus written off their chances, the British men had the regulation response, playing far better once their cause was hopeless, than they ever did when it was hopeful - this is a trait particularly shared with the England cricket team. The British men remained undefeated in their last three pool games, including a 2-1 defeat of Germany, but their defeat by the same team at the classification stage consigned them to sixth overall. This was exactly where you would have expected to find them.

Going into the Games, the Russell Garcia affair did little for team moral. Garcia, the last competitive member of the 1988 gold medal winning squad, had tested positive for cocaine in 1999 and was banned for three months. A lifelong ban, imposed by the British Olympic Association, was the automatic consequence. However, in its wisdom, the BOA rescinded its ban (though not for swimmer Mike Fibbens for the same offence?) and Garcia was eligible again for the squad. Two months before the Games, though, Garcia himself withdrew from the squad claiming "lack of motivation".

The women could manage only a single victory, over Spain, on their way to eighth place out of ten. They lost only by the single goal to Australia, the game ending prematurely as officials deemed that British goalkeeper, Hilary Rose, should not have come up for an extra-time penalty corner without wearing her helmet. Coach Jon Royce was quieter spoken than usual in such circumstances, conceding that the best team had won anyway. He wasn't quite as constrained against Argentina, though, using language defined as "crude and offensive" against a drug-testing official. A touchline ban for Royce was the immediate result; six months later, after comments by the captain, Pauline Stott, to *Scotland on Sunday* newspaper, Royce found himself the subject of an official enquiry.

The Australians were clear favourites to win the women's title, as they had done in Atlanta. For the four-year cycle leading up to Sydney, they had been the dominant team in women's hockey, almost the only hiccup coming when they finished just third in the Champions Trophy in Amstelveen. In Sydney, the only blot on Australia's perfect record came when they drew with Spain, and the poor Netherlands, having beaten Australia 2-1 on the way to the Champions Trophy, were blown away 5-0 at the Olympics.

The Netherlands men took a very different route to the Australian women, scoring only a point from their first two matches, and ending the tournament with the extraordinary record for champions in that, at full-time in five of their seven matches, they had been level or losing. The final, against Argentina was one of them, Holland's second successive match that went to penalty strokes, but they held their nerve and held their Olympic title.

Men's Hockey

Champions Trophy

Netherlands   *May 26-June 4*

Pool Matches

Spain 2 Germany 1; Australia 2 Korea 0; Great Britain 1
Netherlands 2; Australia 1 Spain 1; Korea 0
Netherlands 1; Great Britain 0 Germany 4; Australia 3
Great Britain 3; Spain 0 Korea 1; Netherlands 3
Germany 2; Germany 3 Korea 1; Great Britain 1 Spain 5;
Netherlands 3 Australia 1; Netherlands 1 Spain 0;
Germany 4 Australia 2; Korea 3 Great Britain 1

Pool Standings

		P	W	D	L	GF	GA	Pts
1	Netherlands	5	5	0	0	10	4	10
2	Germany	5	3	0	2	14	8	6
3	Spain	5	2	1	2	8	5	5
4	Korea	5	2	0	3	5	7	4
5	Australia	5	1	2	2	9	11	4
6	Great Britain	5	0	1	4	6	17	1

5/6th Place Play-off

Australia 3   Great Britain 2

3rd/4th Place Play-off

Spain 0   Korea 3

FINAL

Netherlands 2   Germany 1

Final Standings:

1. Netherlands; 2. Germany; 3. Korea; 4. Spain;
5. Australia; 6. Great Britain

Olympic Qualifying

Osaka, Japan   *Mar 9-20*

Pool A Matches

Great Britain 4 Japan 2; Belgium 1 Korea 2;
New Zealand 2 Great Britain 2; Korea 4 Poland 1;
New Zealand 5 Belgium 4; Poland 0 Japan 2;
Great Britain 1 Korea 4; Japan 2 New Zealand 0;
Belgium 1 Poland 3; Japan 1 Korea 5; Poland 5
Great Britain 2; Korea 5 New Zealand 1; Great Britain 4
Belgium 3; New Zealand 1 Poland 2; Belgium 3 Japan 3

Pool A Table

		P	W	D	L	GF	GA	Pts
1	Korea	5	5	0	0	20	6	15
2	Poland	5	3	0	2	11	10	9
3	Japan	5	2	1	2	10	12	7
4	Great Britain	5	2	1	2	13	16	7
5	New Zealand	5	1	1	3	10	15	4
6	Belgium	5	0	1	4	12	17	1

Pool B Matches

Malaysia 1 Spain 7; Argentina 1 Switzerland 3; Belarus 1
Malaysia 7; Pakistan 7 Switzerland 3; Belarus 0
Argentina 6; Spain 4 Argentina 4; Malaysia 4 Argentina 4;
Switzerland 0 Spain 3; Pakistan 6 Belarus 0;
Switzerland 2 Malaysia 4; Argentina 3 Spain 6;
Malaysia 2 Pakistan 5; Spain 5 Belarus 0; Pakistan 3
Argentina 4; Belarus 1 Switzerland 2

Pool B Table

1	Spain	5	4	1	0	25	8	13
2	Pakistan	5	3	1	1	25	13	10
3	Argentina	5	2	1	2	18	16	7
4	Malaysia	5	2	1	2	18	19	7
5	Switzerland	5	2	0	3	10	16	6
6	Belarus	5	0	0	5	2	16	0

Classification matches 9th-12th

New Zealand 6 Belarus 3; Switzerland 1 Belgium 6

11/12th Place Play-off

Belarus 1 Switzerland 6

9/10th Place Play-off

Belgium 1 New Zealand 0

Classification matches 5th-8th

Great Britain 3 Argentina 0; Malaysia 2 Japan 1

7/8th Place Play-off

Argentina 1 Japan 0

5/6th Place Play-off

Malaysia 1 Great Britain 2

Semi-finals

Korea 1 Pakistan 3
Spain 4 Poland 0

Bronze Medal match

Korea 2 Poland 1

Final

Spain 3 Pakistan 1

Final standings: 1. Spain; 2. Pakistan; 3.
Korea; 4. Poland; 5. Great Britain; 6. Malaysia;
7. Argentina; 8. Japan; 9. Belgium; 10. New Zealand;
11. Belarus; 12. Switzerland
The top six countries qualified for Sydney

European Club Championship
A Division
Cannock   *June 9-12*

Pool A
Bloemendaal 8 Eagles 0; Pocztowiec 0 Cannock 1;
Bloemendaal 4 Cannock 0; Pocztowiec 4 Eagles 1;
Bloemendaal 2 Pocztowiec 0; Cannock 3 Eagles 1
Standings
1. Bloemendaal ; 2. Cannock; 3. Pocztowiec ; 4. Eagles

Pool B
Egara 6 Cernusco 1; Club an der Alster 4 Lille 1;
Egara 8 Lille 0; Club an der Alster 9 Cernusco 1;
Lille 6 Cernusco 2; Egara 2 Club an der Alster 4
Standings
1. Club an der Alster; 2. Egara; 3. Lille; 4. Cernusco

3rd/4th place play-off
Cannock 0 Egara 3

Final
Bloemendaal 1 Club an der Alster 1
Club an der Alster won 5-3 on penalty strokes

Final Standings
1. Club an der Alster GER; 2. Bloemendaal NED; 3. Club Egara ESP; 4. Cannock ENG; 5. Lille FRA & Pocztowiec POL; 7. Eagles GIB & Cernusco ITA
Gibraltar and Italy relegated to B Division

B Division Final Standings
Ireland   June 9-12
1. Western SCO; 2. Instonians IRL; 3. Olten SUI; 4. Dragons Brasschaat BEL; 5. Brest BLR & Slavia Prague CZE; 7. Olimpic Vinnitsa UKR & WAC AUT
Ireland & Scotland promoted to A;
Austria and Ukraine relegated to C

C Division Final Standings
Whitchurch, Wales   June 9-12
1. SKA Samara RUS; 2. Valhalla SWE; 3. Slagelse DEN; 4. Zorka Subotica YUG; 5. Grupo Desportivo do Viso POR & Whitchurch WAL; 7. Kedainiai TUR & Ramaldense POR *Russia and Sweden promoted to B*

European Cup Winners' Cup
A Division
Spain   Apr 21-24

Pool A
Oranje Zwart 4 Rotweiss Wettingen 4; Reading 4 Racing Club 0; Oranje Zwart 2 Racing Club 0; Reading 2 Rotweiss Wettingen 2; Oranje Zwart 2 Racing Club 0; Reading 2 Rotweiss Wettingen 2
Standings
1. Reading; 2. Oranje Zwart; 3. Rotweiss Wettingen; 4. Racing Club

Pool B
Grunwald 2 Cork 0; Atlétic Terrassa 3 Harvesthüder 2; Grunwald 1 Harvesthüder 1; Atlétic Terrassa 0 Cork 1; Cork 1 Harvesthüder 5; Atlétic Terrassa 3 Grunwald 0
Standings
1. Atlétic Terrassa; 2. Harvesthüder; 3. Grunwald; 4. Cork

3rd/4th place play-off
Harvesthüder 4 Oranje Zwart 2

Final
Reading 3 Atlétic Terrassa 4

A Division Final Standings
1. Atletic Terassa ESP; 2. Reading ENG; 3.Harvethüder GER; 4. Oranje Zwart NED; 5. Grunwald POL & Rotweiss Wettingen SUI; 7. Racing Club FRA & Cork IRL
France and Ireland relegated to B Division

B Division Final Standings
Stroitel Brest, Belarus   Apr 21-24
1. Leuven BEL; 2. Amsicora ITA; 3. Ekaterinaburg RUS; 4. Stroitel Brest BEL; 5. Vinnitsa UKR & Airways Wanderers SCO; 7. Praga CZE & Grammarians GIB
Belgium and Italy promoted to A Division
Czech Republic and Gibraltar relegated to C Division

C Division Final Standings
Vienna   Apr 21-24
1. AHTC Vienna AUT; 2. GD Viso POR; 3. Moravske Toplce SLO; 4. Vetan Baku AZE; 5. Dinamo Pancevo YUG & ABC Team FIN; 7. UCW Swansea WAL & SKA Imerti GEO
Austria and Portugal promoted to B Division

Indoor Club Championship
A Division
Bad Dürkheim GER   Feb 18-20

Pool A Standings
1. Slagelse; 2. Ekaterinaburg; 3. Pocztowiec; 4. Atlétic Terrassa

Pool B Standings
1. Durkheimer; 2.Montrouge; 3. Vienna; 4. Dundee

Semi-finals
Slagelse 8 Montrouge 7
Durkheimer 11 Ekaterinaburg 4

3rd/4th place play-off
Montrouge 3 Ekaterinaburg 2

Final
Durkheimer 6 Slagelse 3

A Division Final Standings
1. Durkheimer GER; 2. Slagelse DEN; 3. Montrouge FRA; 4.Ekaterinaburg RUS; 5. Atlétic Terrassa; 6. Pocztowiec POL; 7. Dundee SCO; 8. Vienna AUT
Dundee and Vienna relegated to B Division

B Division Final Standings
Prague, Czech Republic Feb 18-20
1. Rotweiss Wettingen SUI; 2. Slavia Prague CZE; 3.Valhalla SWE; 4. Marathon CRO; 5. Southgate ENG; 6.CUS Bologna ITA; 7. Rosco HUN; 8. Northop Hall WAL
Switzerland and Czech Rep promoted to A Division
Hungary and Wales relegated to C Division

C Division Final Standings
Rosco, Hungary   Feb 19-21
1. Venlo NED; 2. A A Espinho POR; 3. Vinnitsa UKR; 4. Svoboda SLO; 5. Palma Senkvice SVK; 6. Hockey Team 85 FIN; 7. Avoca IRL; 8. Loco Sofia BUL
Netherlands and Portugal promoted to B Division

Domestic Hockey
National Hockey League
Premier Division

	P	W	D	L	GF	GA	Pts
1 Canterbury	18	13	2	3	68	43	41
2 Cannock	18	13	1	4	62	35	40
3 Reading	18	12	3	3	71	37	39
4 Guildford	18	10	3	5	53	43	33
5 Surbiton	18	7	4	7	46	44	25
6 Old Loughtonians	18	5	8	5	46	46	23
7 Southgate	18	4	2	12	38	52	14
8 Bourneville	18	4	2	12	34	55	14
9 Teddington	18	3	5	10	35	64	14
10 Beeston	18	3	2	13	36	70	11

Premiership Final

Cannock 3   Canterbury 2

Cannock won 4-3 on penalty strokes

Division One

	P	W	D	L	GF	GA	Pts
1 Loughboro' Students	18	13	2	3	68	43	41
2 Lewes	18	12	4	2	71	34	40
3 Doncaster	18	10	4	4	67	30	34
4 Chelmsford	18	8	5	5	55	48	29
5 Stourport	18	7	2	9	40	38	23
6 Barford Tigers	18	6	5	7	37	39	23
7 Brooklands	18	5	6	7	34	45	21
8 East Grinstead	18	6	3	9	34	56	21
9 Indian Gymkhana	18	4	1	13	34	63	13
10 Hounslow	18	2	1	15	24	86	7

Division Two

	P	W	D	L	GF	GA	Pts
1 Hampstead	22	19	2	1	79	28	59
2 St Albans	22	17	2	3	63	24	53
3 Firebrands	22	9	5	8	49	46	32
4 Peterborough Town	22	6	10	6	33	39	28
5 Harleston Magpies	22	7	7	8	45	54	28
6 Bromley	22	8	3	11	44	53	27
7 Formby	22	7	5	10	36	41	26
8 Oxford Hawks	22	7	4	11	39	40	25
9 Oxford Univerity	22	6	7	9	35	38	25
10 Havant	22	7	4	11	37	52	25
11 Isca	22	6	4	12	36	48	22
12 Eastcote	22	4	5	13	33	66	17

EHA Cup
Final

Milton Keynes   *May 7*

Reading 3   Old Loughtonians 2

EHA Trophy
Final

Bournemouth 5   Wisbech 0

EHA Vintage
Final

Eastcote 2   Trojans 4

Women's Hockey
Champions Trophy
Netherlands   May 26-June 4

Pool Matches
Germany 2 Argentina 1; New Zealand 1 Australia 4;
South Africa 2 Netherlands 3; Australia 3 Argentina 0;
South Africa 1 Germany 3; Netherlands 3
New Zealand 0; Germany 2 Australia 1; South Africa 1
New Zealand 1; Argentina 1 Netherlands 0;
New Zealand 2 Germany 2; Argentina 2 South Africa 2;
Netherlands 2 Australia 1; New Zealand 1 Argentina 3;
Netherlands 2 Germany 0; Australia 6 South Africa 0

Pool Standings

	P	W	D	L	GF	GA	Pts
1 Netherlands	5	4	0	1	10	4	8
2 Germany	5	3	1	1	9	7	7
3 Australia	5	3	0	2	15	6	6
4 Argentina	5	2	1	2	7	8	5
5 New Zealand	5	0	2	3	5	13	2
6 South Africa	5	0	2	3	6	15	2

5/6th Place Play-off

New Zealand 0   South Africa 2

3rd/4th Place Play-off

Australia 1   Argentina 0

FINAL

Netherlands 3   Germany 2

Final Standings:
1. Netherlands; 2. Germany; 3. Australia; 4. Argentina;
5. South Africa; 6. New Zealand

European Nations Cup
Vienna   Jan 28-30

Pool A
Germany 7 Belarus 2; Scotland 3 Slovakia 3; Germany
13 Slovakia 1; Scotland 4 Belarus 3; Germany 6 Scotland
1; Slovakia 5 Belarus 7
Final Standings
1. Germany; 2. Scotland; 3. Belarus; 4. Slovakia
Pool B
England 3 Czech Republic 4; Austria 7 Russia 11;
England 5 Russia 4; Austria 2 Czech Republic 2; England
1 Austria 1; Russia 4 Czech Republic 1
Final Standings
1. Russia; 2. Czech Republic; 3. England; 4. Austria
Classification matches 5th-8th
Slovakia 1 England 0; Belarus 7 Austria 6
7th-8th place play-off
England 3 Austria 7
5th-6th place play-off
Slovakia 4 Belarus 4 *Slovakia won 4-3 on penalties*
Semi-finals
Scotland 2 Russia 8; Germany 5 Czech Republic 0
Bronze medal match
Scotland 1 Czech Republic 4
Final
Russia 1 Germany 9
England and Austria relegated to B division

B Division Final Standings
Lievin, France   Jan 28-29
1. Lithuania; 2. France; 3. Poland; 4. Denmark; 5. Finland; 6. Greece
Lithuania and France promoted to A Division;

Olympic Qualifying

Milton Keynes   Mar 23-Apr 2

Pool A Matches
India 1 Spain 3; Germany 4 USA 1; Ireland 1 India 0; Spain 1 Germany 1; USA 1 Ireland 1; India 0 Germany 4; Spain 2 USA 2; Germany 2 Ireland 1; USA 2 India 1; Ireland 0 Spain 2

Pool A Table

		P	W	D	L	GF	GA	Pts
1	Germany	4	3	1	0	11	3	10
2	Spain	4	2	2	0	8	4	8
3	USA	4	1	2	1	6	8	5
4	Ireland	4	1	1	2	3	5	4
5	India	4	0	0	4	2	10	0

Pool B Matches
Russia 1 China 3; New Zealand 0 Japan 4; Great Britain 5 Russia 9; China 0 New Zealand 0; Great Britain 2 Japan 0; Russia 0 New Zealand 8; China 1 Japan 0; New Zealand 1 Great Britain 0; Japan 2 Russia 1; Great Britain 1 China 0

Pool B Table

1	Great Britain	4	3	0	1	8	4	9
2	New Zealand	4	2	1	1	9	4	7
3	China	4	2	1	1	4	2	7
4	Japan	4	2	0	2	7	4	6
5	Russia	4	0	0	4	2	18	0

9/10th Place Play-off
Russia 2   India 1

Classification matches 5th-8th
USA 2   Japan 0
Ireland 0   China 1

7/8th Place Play-off
Japan 3   Ireland 0

5/6th Place Play-off
USA 0   China 2

Semi-finals
Spain 1   Great Britain 2
Germany 1   New Zealand 2

Bronze Medal Match
Spain 0   Germany1

Final
Great Britain 0   New Zealand 1

Final Standings:
1. New Zealand; 2. Great Britain; 3 Germany; 4. Spain 5. China; 6. USA; 7. Japan; 8. Ireland

The top five qualified for Sydney

European Club Championship
A Division
Glasgow   June 9-12

Pool A
Berliner 2 Cambrai 0; Western 1 Ritm Grodno 0; Berliner 2 Ritm Grodno 0; Western 4 Cambrai 0; Berliner 4 Western 2; Ritm Grodno 1 Cambrai 1
Standings
1. Berliner; 2. Western; 3. Ritm Grodno; 4. Cambrai

Pool B
's-Hertogenbosch 6 Pegasus 0; Slough 1 Borispol 1; 's-Hertogenbosch 5 Borispol 3; Slough 3 Pegasus 2; 's-Hertogenbosch 7 Slough 0; Borispol 3 Pegasus 2
Standings
1. 's-Hertogenbosch; 2. Borispol; 3. Slough; 4. Pegasus

3rd/4th place play-off
Western 1 Borispol 2

Final
's-Hertogenbosch 7 Berliner 0

Final Standings
1. 's-Hertogenbosch NED; 2. Berliner GER; 3. Kolos Borispol UKR; 4. Western SCO; 5. Ritm Grodno BLR & Slough ENG; 7. Cambrai FRA & Pegasus IRL
France and Ireland relegated to B Division

B Division Final Standings
Prague   June 9-12
1. Moscow Pravda RUS; 2. Real Sociedad ESP; 3. HC Siauliai LTU; 4. Swansea WAL; 5.Slavia Prague CZE & Leuven BEL; 7. Rabitachi Baku AZE & Arminen Koller Transport AUT
Russia and Spain promoted to A Division; Austria and Azerbaijan relegated to C Division

C Division Final Standings
Wettingen, Sitzerland   June 9-12
1.Libertas San Saba ITA; 2. Polar Wroclaw POL; 3. HC Rotweiss Wettingen SUI; 4. ABC Team FIN; 5. Raca SVK
Italy and Poland promoted to B Division

European Cup Winners' Cup
A Division
Cologne   April 21-24
Pool A
Club Campo 0 Leicester 4; Amsterdam 8 Uccle Sport 0; Club Campo 0 Uccle Sport 3; Amsterdam 2 Leicester 1; Leicester 7 Uccles Sport 1; Amsterdam 9 Club Campo 0
Standings
1. Amsterdam; 2. Leicester; 3. Uccle Sport; 4. Club de Campo

Pool B
Sumy 2 Edinburgh 0; Stadion Rot-Weiss 2 Hermes 0; Sumy 1 Hermes 4; Stadion Rot-Weiss 2 Edinburgh 0; Edinburgh 1 Hermes 2; Stadion Rot-Weiss 5 Sumy 0
Standings
1.Stadion Rot-Weiss; 2. Hermes; 3. Edinburgh; 4. Sumy

3rd/4th place play-off
Leicester 2 Hermes 2
Hermes won 3-0 on penalties

Final
Amsterdam 2 Stadion Rot-Weiss 3

HOCKEY

A Division Final Standings
1. Stadion Rot-Weiss Cologne GER; 2. Amsterdam NED;
3. Hermes IRL; 4. Leicester ENG; 5. Dinamo Sumy UKR
& Grange Edinburgh SCO; 7. Club de Campo ESP &
Uccle Sport BEL
Spain and Belgium relegated to B Division

B Division Final Standings
Terassa   April 21-24
1. Atlétic Terrassa ESP; 2. Reading ENG; 3.
Harvesthüder; 4. Oranje Zwart NED; 5. Grunwald POL &
Rotweiss Wettingen SUI; 7. Racing Club FRA & Cork IRL
Spain and England promoted to A Division

Indoor Club Championship
A Division
Cambrai, France   Feb 25-27

One Pool
Russelsheimer 8 Slough 3; Ritm Grodno 5 Siauliai 2;
Klipper 5 Cambrai 4; Slough 3 Club de Campo 4; Siauliai
3 Russelsheimer 12; Cambrai 4 Ritm Grodno 2; Club de
Campo 1 Klipper 9; Ritm Grodno 3 Klipper 4; Siauliai 7
Club de Campo 3; Russelsheimer 9 Cambrai 0; Slough 1
Ritm Grodno 4; Club de Campo 1 Russelsheimer 10;
Klipper 10 Slough 0; Cambrai 4 Siauliai 4; Siauliai 7
Slough 2; Russelsheimer 8 Ritm Grodno 3; Club de
Campo 3 Cambrai 4; Siauliai 1 Klipper 5; Ritm Grodno 4
Club de Campo 4; Cambrai 2 Slough 3; Russelsheimer 8
Klipper 2

A Division Final Standings
1. Russelsheimer GER; 2. Klipper THC GER; 3. Ritm
Grodno; 4. Siauliai LTU; 5. Cambrai FRA; 6. Club de
Campo ESP; 7. Slough ENG
England are relegated to B Division

B Division Final Standings
Vienna   Feb 25-27
1. WR Neudorf AUT; 2. Glasgow Western SCO; 3. CKS
Vysehard CZE;4. Rotweiss Wettingen SUI; 5. Slagelse
DEN; 6. HC Raca SVK; 7. AZS AWF POL
Austria and Scotland promoted A Division
Poland relegated to C Division

C Division Final Standings
Rome   Feb 25-27
1. Rotterdam NED; 2. Libertas San Saba ITA; 3.
Pontypridd WAL; 4. Partille SWE; 5 ABC Team FIN; 6
Triglav SLO
Netherlands and Italy promoted B Division

Domestic Hockey
National League
Premier Division
		P	W	D	L	GF	GA	Pts
1	Hightown	18	13	1	4	49	21	40
2	Ipswich	18	19	4	4	53	36	34
3	Fyffes Leicester	18	9	6	3	38	22	33
4	Canterbury	18	9	3	6	36	29	30
5	Clifton	18	9	2	7	28	25	29
6	Slough	18	7	5	6	40	35	26
7	Sutton Coldfield	18	6	3	9	30	43	21
8	Olton & West Warwick	18	5	5	8	31	41	20
9	Chelmsford Highway	18	4	5	9	26	36	17
10	Doncaster	18	1	0	17	12	55	3

Premiership Final
Hightown 3   Ipswich 1

Division One
		P	W	D	L	GF	GA	Pts
1	Loughboro' Students	18	17	1	0	65	15	52
2	Bradford	18	11	4	3	35	18	37
3	Old Loughtonians	18	11	2	5	39	22	35
4	Wimbledon	18	9	2	7	27	22	29
5	Woking	18	7	2	9	38	41	23
6	Trojans	18	7	2	9	29	36	23
7	Ealing	18	4	5	9	17	32	17
8	Sunderland Ashbrooke	18	4	5	9	21	45	17
9	Aldridge	18	3	5	10	21	28	14
10	Bracknell	18	2	2	14	14	47	8

Division Two
		P	W	D	L	GF	GA	Pts
1	Harleston Magpies	18	17	0	1	53	13	40
2	Deeside Ramblers	18	12	3	3	39	21	39
3	Poynton	18	11	3	4	53	29	36
4	Bedford	18	7	5	6	31	29	26
5	Sherwood	18	6	4	8	19	27	22
6	St Albans	18	5	5	8	34	38	20
7	Exmouth	18	5	5	8	32	41	20
8	Kettering	18	6	0	12	21	39	18
9	Hampton in Arden	18	3	4	11	38	43	13
10	Dulwich	18	3	1	14	18	58	10

AEWHA Cup
Final
Milton Keynes   May 7
Clifton 4   Sutton Coldfield 2

Horse Racing

Poor Sinndar, the Aga Khan's colt wins the Epsom Derby, the Irish Derby and the Arc - an unprecedented feat - and is still rated below Helissio, the 1996 Arc winner. As Helissio's victory figures in no one's collection of great moments of the twentieth century, then it doesn't say much for Sinndar's chances with posterity. After the Arc, the Aga Khan, as is his wont, immediately retired the horse to Gilltown Stud in County Kildare where, if you've got a spare 30,000 Irish punts, you could get your own little Sinndar.

Poor Sinndar again, for as well as being given scant credit by the official handicappers in his own age group, he was also measured against two four-year-olds who didn't just look good, but in their best moments, looked utterly sensational. Dubai Millennium only once lost a race and that was the Epsom Derby in 1999, when he started favourite and finished sixth behind Oath. Not until the Dubai World Cup in March, though, did the adjectives move up several gears - from very good to incomparable. Bizarrely, after walloping the best in the world, he started at odds against when he met Sendawar in the Prince of Wales's Stakes at Ascot. Was it a giveaway? Just a bit. For the second time, there was no real strategy, just lead from the start and run the legs off the rest. It worked in Dubai on dirt, and at Ascot on turf. Dubai Millennium won in Dubai by six lengths, at Ascot by eight lengths.

Godolphin maintained that Dubai Millennium was the best horse in the world, but it was by no means clear cut. Montjeu had won the French Derby, the Irish Derby and the Arc as a three-year-old, but never looked better than in the King George VI and Queen Elizabeth Diamond Stakes at Ascot when he won a Group 1 contest without coming off the bit. Even Sheikh Mohammed was impressed that day.

Initially, the Sheikh was not enthusiastic about a match. When he'd come around to the idea of a $4m head-to-head, it was too late. On August 5th on the Newmarket gallops, Dubai Millennium cracked a bone in his right hind leg. He was retired to stud. Within nine months, the horse would be dead. He covered 82 mares in his short time at the Gilltown Stud. There will, at least, be a racing heritage.

Montjeu carried on racing, won his Arc warm-up in the Prix Foy, at 10/1 on, without effort and then the bubble burst. In the Arc, he was a more modest odds-on, at 4/5, but had no answer when Sinndar put his foot down. The odds were still on for the Champion Stakes, but Kalanisi was his match and, as Churchill Downs hove into view, the bookmakers were at last willing to extend the odds, though, remarkably, he still started favourite.

In a career that spanned 16 races, Montjeu had only once not started favourite - in his first race at Chantilly in September 1998 - and eight times (six in Group 1 races) had started as an odds-on shot. If Montjeu had fractured a pastern in September, he would be up there alongside Hyperion.

As if all this wasn't enough, there was still Giant's Causeway. Aidan O'Brien's charge raced in nine Group 1 races throughout the year, won five and placed second in the rest, Only in one race - the 2000 Guineas - was it beaten by more than half a length.

The jockeys' title went for the first time to Kevin Darley. It was well-earned, though Fate had a hand in affairs. In a plane crash at Newmarket on June 1st, in which the pilot Patrick Mackey died, Frankie Dettori and Ray Cochrane were fortunate enough to walk away, though the injuries to Dettori, kept him out of race riding for two months.

Aidan O'Brien was responsible for the National Hunt horse of the year, and last year, and the year before. Istabraq made it three Champion Hurdles, to match Hatton's Grace, Sir Ken, Persian War and See You Then, and the third was as easy as the rest.

Martin Pipe won the last Champion Hurdle before Istabraq with Make a Stand in 1997. It has so far been his only victory in the race. Pipe has never though won the Gold Cup - Gloria Victis, his brilliant novice, was put down after being injured in the 2000 race - but while there are still a few gaps in the quality races, the Somerset trainer has no peer as far as quantity goes. In February, at Folkestone, Through The Rye became the winner number 2,989 to overtake the record of Arthur Stephenson. Later that afternoon at the same course, Mr Cool made the tally 2,990. By the time you read this, Pipe will probably have reached about four million. Will it make him happy? Probably not, but that's not why he's done it.

Looks Like Trouble won the Gold Cup for Noel Chance and Papillon won the Grand National, like last year's, an Irish father and son combination successful.

As a passing note, we should mention the television deal for racing which first hit the news in March, 2000. It has subsequently become the most protracted negotiation of any deal in the world of sport, on and off at a rate they'd be envious of at the National Stud.

Johnny Murtagh
Group 1 wins in 2000

June 10	The Derby (Epsom) **Sinndar**	£609,000
June 27	Irish Derby (Curragh) **Sinndar**	£482,400
July 16	Irish Oaks (Curragh) **Petrushka**	£112,425
July 30	Grosser Dallmayr Preis (Munich) **Greek Dance**	£79,442
Aug 23	Yorkshire Oaks (York) **Petrushka**	£127,600
Oct 1	Prix de l'Abbaye (Longchamp) **Namid**	£48,031
Oct 1	Prix de l'Arc de Triomphe (Longchamp) **Sinndar**	£576,369
Oct 1	Prix de l'Opera (Longchamp) **Petrushka**	£67,243
Oct 14	Champion Stakes (Newmarket) **Kalanisi**	£232,000
Oct 21	Racing Post Trophy (Doncaster) **Dilshaan**	£105,000
Nov 4	Breeders' Cup Turf (Kentucky) **Kalanisi**	£786,341

Giant's Causeway
Group 1 races in 2000

May 6	2000 Guineas (Newmarket) **2nd**	£66,000
May 27	Irish 2000 Guineas (Curragh) **2nd**	£38,600
June 20	St James' Palace Stakes (Ascot) **1st**	£156,600
July 8	Eclipse Stakes (Sandown) **1st**	£216,000
Aug 2	Sussex Stakes (Goodwood) **1st**	£159,500
Aug 22	Juddmonte Stakes (York) **1st**	£261,000
Sep 9	Irish Champion Stakes (Leopardstown) **1st**	£486,200
Sep 23	Queen Elizabeth Stakes (Ascot) **2nd**	£75,900
Nov 4	Breeders' Cup Classic (Kentucky) **2nd**	£581,707

Giant's Causeway won a total of £2,041,507 win and place money during 2000

Flat Racing

Vodafone Derby Stakes

Epsom, June 10   3yo c&f 1m 4f 10y   15 ran

1 Sinndar (9-0)	Johnny Murtagh	7/1
John Oxx	*£609,000*	
2 Sakhee (9-0)	Richard Hills	4/1
John Dunlop	*£231,000*	
3 Beat Hollow (9-0)	Richard Quinn	7/2F
Henry Cecil	*£115,500*	
4 Best Of The Bests (9-0)	Chris McCarron	12/1
Saeed bin Suroor	*£52,500*	
5 Wellbeing (9-0)	Willie Ryan	7/1
6 Hatha Anna (9-0)	Kevin Darley	66/1
7 St Expedit (9-0)	Richard Hughes	28/1
8 Barathea Guest (9-0)	Philip Robinson	12/1
9 Zyz (9-0)	Jimmy Fortune	100/1
10 Aristotle (9-0)	Mick Kinane	5/1
11 Inchlonaig (9-0)	Pat Eddery	16/1
12 Broche (9-0)	Christophe Soumillon	40/1
13 Going Global (9-0)	John Reid	25/1
14 Cracow (9-0)	Michael Hills	66/1
15 Kingsclere (9-0)	Olivier Peslier	16/1

Distances: 1, 5, 4, 3, ½, ½, 1¼, 2½, nk,1¼, 7, ¾, hd, dist
Winning Owner: HH The Aga Khan
Time: 2:36.75 (+1.95)

The Other Classics

Sagitta 2000 Guineas Stakes

Newmarket, May 6   3yo c&f 1m   16 ran

King's Best (9-0)	Kieren Fallon	13/2
Giant's Causeway (9-0)	Mick Kinane	7/2F
Barathea Guest (9-0)	Philip Robinson	12/1
Sir Michael Stoute £173,300		

Sagitta 1000 Guineas Stakes

Newmarket, May 7   3yo f 1m   27 ran

Lahan (9-0)	Richard Hills	14/1
Princess Ellen (9-0)	Kevin Darley	66/1
Petrushka (9-0)	Kieren Fallon	6/4F
John Gosden £145,000		

Vodafone Oaks Stakes

Epsom, June 9   3yo f 1m 4f 10y   16 ran

Love Divine (9-0)	Richard Quinn	9-4F
Kalypso Katie (9-0)	Mick Kinane	7-2
Melikah (9-0)	Chris McCarron	10-1
Henry Cecil £191,400		

Pertemps St Leger Stakes

Doncaster, Sep 9   3yo c&f   1m 6f 132y   11 ran

Millenary (9-0)	Richard Quinn	11/4F
Air Marshall (9-0)	John Reid	3/1
Chimes At Midnight (9-0)	John Carroll	40/1
John Dunlop £222,000		

2000 UK Group One Wins By Trainer

Last years win count in brackets

Sir Michael Stoute 6 (-)
2000 Guineas, Coronation Cup, Yorkshire Oaks,
Cheveley Park Stakes, Champion Stakes, Racing Post Trophy

Aidan O'Brien 5 (3)
Eclipse, Sussex Stakes, Juddmonte International,
Middle Park Stakes, St James's Palace Stakes

Saeed Bin Suroor 3 (9)
Lockinge, Prince of Wales's Stakes, Ascot Gold Cup

John Gosden 3 (-)
1000 Guineas , Queen Elizabeth II Stakes, Fillies' Mile

John Hammond 2 (-)
King George VI & Queen Elizabeth Stakes, Nunthorpe

Clive Brittain 1 (1) Nassau Stakes   **Henry Cecil 1** (5) Oaks
Mick Channon 1 (1) Dewhurst Stakes **John Dunlop 1** (-) St Leger
Tim Easterby 1 (-) Sprint Cup **Hideyuki Mori 1** (-) July Cup   **John Oxx 1** (1) Derby

Group One

(see also Ascot)

Juddmonte Lockinge Stakes
Newbury, May 20   4yo+ 1m   7 ran

Aljabr (4-9-0)	Frankie Dettori	8/13F
Trans Island (5-9-0)	Kieren Fallon	13/2
Indian Lodge (4-9-0)	Mick Kinane	5/1

Saeed Bin Suroor   £81,000

Vodafone Coronation Cup Stakes
Epsom, June 9   4yo+ 1m 4f 10y   4 ran

Daliapour (4-9-0)	Kieren Fallon	11/8F
Fantastic Light (4-9-0)	Chris McCarron	7/4
Border Arrow (5-9-0)	Jimmy Fortune	6/1

Sir Michael Stoute   £150,000

Coral-Eclipse Stakes
Sandown, July 8   3yo+ 1m 2f 7y   8 ran

Giant's Causeway (3-8-10)	George Duffield	8/1
Kalanisi (4-9-7)	Pat Eddery	7/2
Shiva (5-9-4)	Richard Quinn	4/1

Aidan O'Brien (IRL)   £216,000

Darley July Cup Stakes
Newmarket, July 13   3yo+ 6f   10 ran

Agnes World (5-9-5)	Yutaka Take	4/1F
Lincoln Dancer (3-8-13)	Michael Roberts	9/2
Pipalong (4-9-2)	Kevin Darley	10/1

Hideyuki Mori (JPN)   £95,700

King George VI & Queen Eliz'th Diamond Stks
Ascot, July 29   3yo+ 1m 4f   7 ran

Montjeu (4-9-7)	Mick Kinane	1/3F
Fantastic Light (4-9-7)	John Reid	12/1
Daliapour (4-9-7)	Johnny Murtagh	13/2

John Hammond (FRA)   £435,000

Champagne Lanson Sussex Stakes
Goodwood, Aug 2   3yo+ 1m   10 ran

Giant's Causeway (3-9-0)	Mick Kinane	3/1JF
Dansili (4-9-7)	Olivier Peslier	3/1JF
Medicean (4-9-0)	Johnny Murtagh	12/1

Aidan O'Brien (IRL)   £159,500

Vodafone Nassau Stakes
Goodwood, Aug 5   3yo+ f&m 1m 1f 192y   7 ran

Crimplene (3-8-6)	Philip Robinson	7/4F
Ela Athena (4-9-1)	Michael Roberts	7/1
Princess Ellen (3-8-6)	Kevin Darley	7/2

Clive Brittain   £78,300

Juddmonte International Stakes
York, Aug 22   3yo+ 1m 2f 85y   6 ran

Giant's Causeway (3-8-11)	Mick Kinane	10/11F
Kalanisi (4-9-5)	Pat Eddery	5/4
Lear Spear (5-9-5)	Richard Quinn	14/1

Aidan O'Brien (IRL)   £261,000

Aston Upthorpe Yorkshire Oaks
York, Aug 23   3yo+ f&m 1m 3f 195y   6 ran

Petrushka (3-8-8)	Johnny Murtagh	5/4F
Love Divine (3-8-8)	Richard Quinn	2/1
Ramruma (4-9-4)	Mick Kinane	15/2

Sir Michael Stoute   £127,600

Victor Chandler Nunthorpe Stakes
York, Aug 24   2yo+ 5f   13 ran

Nuclear Debate (5-9-9)	Gerard Mosse	5/2F
Bertolini (4-9-9)	Frankie Dettori	13/2
Pipalong (4-9-6)	Kevin Darley	7/1

John Hammond (FRA)   £101,500

Stanley Leisure Sprint Cup Stakes
Haydock, Sep 2   3yo+ 6f   13 ran

Pipalong (4-9-0)	Kevin Darley	3/1
Sampower Star (4-9-0)	Ted Durcan	6/1
Tomba (6-9-0)	Philip Robinson	11/1

Tim Easterby   £87,000

Queen Elizabeth II Stakes
Ascot, Sep 23   3yo+ 1m   12 ran

Observatory (3-8-11)	Kevin Darley	14/1
Giant's Causeway (3-8-11)	Mick Kinane	11/10F
Best Of The Bests (3-8-11)	Frankie Dettori	7/1

John Gosden   £200,100

Mean Valley Stud Fillies' Mile Stakes
Ascot, Sep 23   2yo f 1m   9 ran

Crystal Music (8-10)	Frankie Dettori	4/1
Summer Symphony (8-10)	Jamie Spencer	2/1F
Hotelgenie Dot Com (8-10)	Craig Williams	7/2

John Gosden   £116,000

Shadwell Stud Cheveley Park Stakes
Newmarket, Sep 26   2yo f 6f   13 ran

Regal Rose (8-11)	Frankie Dettori	11/2
Toroca (8-11)	Paul Scallan	66/1
Mala Mala (8-11)	Warren O'Connor	25/1

Sir Michael Stoute   £75,400

Middle Park Stakes
Newmarket, Sep 28   2yo c 6f   10 ran

Minardi (8-11)	Mick Kinane	5/6F
Endless Summer (8-11)	Jimmy Fortune	9/1
Red Carpet (8-11)	Johnny Murtagh	25/1

Aidan O'Brien (IRL)   89,320

Darley Dewhurst Stakes
Newmarket, Oct 14   2yo c&f 7f   10 ran

Tobougg (9-0)	Craig Williams	7/4F
Noverre (9-0)	Frankie Dettori	7/1
Tempest (9-0)	Johnny Murtagh	40/1

Mick Channon   £124,700

Dubai Champion Stakes
Newmarket, Oct 14   3yo+ 1m 2f   15 ran

Kalanisi (4-9-2)	Johnny Murtagh	5/1
Montjeu (4-9-2)	Mick Kinane	10/11F
Distant Music (3-8-11)	Michael Hills	20/1

Sir Michael Stoute   £232,000

Racing Post Trophy Stakes
Doncaster, Oct 21   2yo c&f 1m   10 ran

Dilshaan (9-0)	Johnny Murtagh	14/1
Tamburlaine (9-0)	Richard Hughes	11/4
Bonnard (9-0)	George Duffield	25/1

Sir Michael Stoute   £105,000

Royal Ascot

Queen Anne Stakes (Group 2)

June 20   *3yo+ 1m*   *11 ran*

Kalanisi (4-9-2)	Kieren Fallon	11/2
Dansili (4-9-5)	Olivier Peslier	10/3
Swallow Flight (4-9-2)	Michael Roberts	11/1

Sir Michael Stoute £72,000

King's Stand Stakes (Group 2)

June 20   *3yo+ 5f*   *23 ran*

Nuclear Debate (5-9-2)	Gerard Mosse	16/1
Agnes World (5-9-5)	Yutaka Take	16/1
Bertolini (4-9-2)	Jerry Bailey	7/1

John Hammond (FRA) £81,000

St James's Palace Stakes (Group 1)

June 20   *3yo c 1m*   *11 ran*

Giant's Causeway (9-0)	Mick Kinane	7/2F
Valentino (9-0)	Gerard Mosse	16/1
Medicean (9-0)	Kieren Fallon	16/1

Aidan O'Brien (IRL) £156,600

Coventry Stakes (Group 3)

June 20   *2yo 6f*   *12 ran*

CD Europe (8-12)	Steve Drowne	8/1
Bram Stoker (8-12)	Richard Hughes	4/1
Modgliani (8-12)	Mick Kinane	7/2F

Mick Channon £36,000

Queen's Vase Stakes (Group 3)

June 20   *3yo 2m 45y*   *13 ran*

Dalampour (8-11)	Kieren Fallon	3/1F
Dutch Harrier (8-11)	Stephen Craine	33/1
Samsaam (8-11)	Richard Hills	11/2

Sir Michael Stoute £36,000

Duke of Edinburgh Handicap (Class B)

June 20   *3yo+ 1m 4f*   *20 ran*

Katiykha (4-9-9)	Johnny Murtagh	10/1
Gallery God (4-8-9)	Yutaka Take	14/1
Veridian (7-8-4)	Pat Eddery	12/1
National Anthem (4-9-12)	Kieren Fallon	5/2F

John Oxx (IRL) £35,750

Jersey Stakes (Group 3)

June 21   *3yo 7f*   *19 ran*

Observatory (8-11)	Kevin Darley	11/2
Umistim (9-3)	Dane O'Neill	16/1
Hunting Lion (8-11)	Craig Williams	25/1

John Gosden £42,000

Queen Mary Stakes (Group 3)

June 21   *2yo f 5f*   *20 ran*

Romantic Myth (8-8)	Kevin Darley	4/1F
Al Ihsas (8-8)	Richard Hills	11/2
Little Firefly (8-8)	Mick Kinane	7/1

Tim Easterby £33,000

Prince of Wales's Stakes (Group 1)

June 21   *3yo+ 1m 2f*   *6 ran*

Dubai Millenium (4-9-0)	Jerry Bailey	5/4
Sumitas (4-9-0)	Terry Hellier	66/1
Beat All (4-9-0)	Kieren Fallon	14/1

Saeed Bin Suroor £144,000

Royal Hunt Cup Handicap (Class B)

June 21   *3yo+ 1m*   *32 ran*

Caribbean Monarch (5-8-10)	Kieren Fallon	11/2
John Ferneley (5-8-9)	Kevin Darley	12/1
Persiano (5-8-6)	David Harrison	14/1
Pythios (4-9-0)	Richard Quinn	16/1

Sir Michael Stoute £69,600

Chesham Stakes (Listed)

June 21   *2yo 7f*   *15 ran*

Celtic Silence (8-12)	Kieren Fallon	15/8F
Baaridd (9-0)	Philip Robinson	7/1
Leopard Spot (8-12)	Mick Kinane	13/2

Mark Johnston £24,375

Ascot Stakes Handicap (Class C)

June 21   *4yo+ 2m 4f*   *24 ran*

Barba Papa (6-9-7)	Johnny Murtagh	10/1
Seliana (4-8-5)	Francis Norton	25/1
Heros Fatal (6-9-7)	Richard Hughes	9/4F
Thames Dancer (4-9-2)	Ted Durcan	16/1

Tony Martin (IRL) £29,900

Ribblesdale Stakes (Group 2)

June 22   *3yo f 1m 4f*   *10 ran*

Miletrian (8-8)	Michael Roberts	10/1
Teggiano (8-8)	Jose Velazquez	7/2F
Interlude (8-8)	Richard Hughes	7/2F

Mick Channon £81,000

Norfolk Stakes (Group 3)

June 22   *2yo 5f*   *11 ran*

Superstar Leo (8-7)	Richard Quinn	5/1
Bouncing Bowdler (8-12)	Daryll Holland	14/1
Pan Jammer (8-12)	Steve Drowne	9/1

William Haggas £33,000

Gold Cup Stakes (Group 1)

June 22   *4yo+ 2m 4f*   *11 ran*

Kayf Tara (6-9-2)	Mick Kinane	11/8F
Far Cry (5-9-2)	Kevin Darley	20/1
Compton Ace (4-9-0)	Richard Hughes	11/1

Saeed bin Suroor £121,275

Cork And Orrery Stakes (Group 2)

June 22   *3yo+ 6f*   *16 ran*

Superior Premium (6-9-0)	Johnny Murtagh	20/1
Sampower Star (4-9-0)	Jose Velazquez	14/1
Lend A Hand (5-9-0)	Jerry Bailey	7/4F

Richard Fahey £72,000

King George V Handicap (Class B)

June 22   *3yo 1m 4f*   *16 ran*

Give The Slip (9-4)	Pat Eddery	8/1
Water Jump (8-13)	Richard Quinn	11/2F
Film Script (9-5)	Richard Hughes	10/1
Bonaguil (8-10)	Richard Mullen	14/1

Amanda Perrett £35,750

Royal Ascot

(continued)

Britannia Handicap (Class B)

June 22	*3yo c&g 1m*	*32 ran*
El Gran Papa (8-4)	Francis Norton	4/1F
Sign Of Hope (8-5)	John Egan	14/1
Kookaburra (8-12)	Gerard Mosse	25/1
Man O'Mystery (8-13)	Pat Eddery	12/1
John Gosden £35,750		

King Edward VII Stakes (Group 2)

June 23	*3yo c&g 1m 4f*	*7 ran*
Subtle Power (8-8)	Richard Quinn	7/4F
Zafonium (8-8)	Pat Eddery	6/1
Roscius (8-8)	Jose Velazquez	7/1
Henry Cecil £81,000		

Hardwicke Stakes (Group 2)

June 23	*4yo+ 1m 4f*	*9 ran*
Fruits Of Love (5-8-12)	Olivier Peslier	9/2
Yavana's Pace (8-8-9)	Darryll Holland	25/1
Blueprint (5-8-12)	Pat Eddery	11/4F
Mark Johnston £81,000		

Coronation Stakes (Group 1)

June 23	*3yo f 1m*	*9 ran*
Crimplene (9-0)	Philip Robinson	4/1J
Princess Ellen (9-0)	Kevin Darley	6/1
Bluemamba (9-0)	Olivier Peslier	7/1
Clive Brittain £156,000		

Wokingham Handicap (Class B)

June 23	*3yo+ 6f*	*29 ran*
Harmonic Way (5-9-6)	Richard Hughes	12/1
Tussle (5-8-7)	Richard Quinn	14/1
Strahan (3-8-10)	Kevin Darley	11/2F
Deep Space (5-9-9)	John Reid	16/1
Roger Charlton £58,000		

Windsor Castle Stakes (Class B)

June 23	*2yo 5f*	*11 ran*
Autumnal (8-8)	Pat Eddery	4/1
Give Back Calais (8-11)	Seb Sanders	13/2
Zietunzeen (8-6)	John Carroll	20/1
Brian Meehan £20,300		

Queen Alexandra Stakes (Class B)

June 23	*4yo+ 2m 6f 34y*	*8 ran*
Dominant Duchess (6-8-9)	Richard Quinn	7/1
Three Cheers (6-9-5)	S Guillot	9/4F
Spirit of Love (5-9-5)	Daryll Holland	8/1
John Hills £20,300		

Leading Jockeys

	1st	2nd	3rd
Kieren Fallon	4	-	2
Richard Quinn	3	2	-
Johnny Murtagh	3	-	-

Leading Trainer

Sir Michael Stoute	3

"My head said we shouldn't run him, but my heart said we should"

Aidan O'Brien, after Istabraq had a nose-bleed in his box at Cheltenham.

"We're dead mate, this is it, we're gone"

Frankie Dettori, to Ray Cochrane moments before their plane crash.

"It's been an awful season but I have no thoughts of giving up. The other jocks keep encouraging me and I go out there every day thinking my luck will change soon"

Richie Forristal, after riding 133 consecutive losers.

"This'll mean the world to Dad. He eats drinks and sleeps horses. Nothing else matters. If you asked him who Liverpool were playing tomorrow, he would ask who Liverpool were"

Ruby Walsh, who won the Grand National aboard Papillon, trained by his dad, Ted.

"When the sacking fell apart one of the lads said we've found Shergar at last. We examined it and put two and two together"

Tom Foley, a Tralee councillor, on the moment he thought that he had found Shergar's skull. After forensic tests, the skull turned out **not** to belong to Shergar.

Group 2

(see also Ascot)

KLM UK Mile Stakes
Sandown, Apr 28   4yo+ 1m 14y
Indian Lodge (4-9-0)
Mick Kinane   9-4F
Amanda Perrett   £36,000

Sagitta Jockey Club Stakes
Newmarket, May 5   4yo+ 1m 4f
Blueprint (5-8-9)
Kieren Fallon   9-2
Sir Michael Stoute   £34,800

JWE Telecom
Dante Stakes
York, May 17   3yo 1m2f 85yds
Sakhee (8-11)
Richard Hills   5-2JF
John Dunlop   £86,275

Merewood Yorkshire Cup
York, May 18   4yo+ 1m 5f 194y
Kayf Tara (6-9-0)
Frankie Dettori   15-8F
Saeed Bin Suroor   £78,300

Tripleprint Temple Stakes
Sandown, May 29   3yo+ 5f 6y
Perryston View (8-9-3)
John Reid   8/1
Jeremy Glover   £36,000

Thehorsesmouth.co.uk
Cherry Hinton
Newmarket, July 11   2yo f 6f
Dora Carrington (8-9)
Richard Quinn   12-1
Peter Harris   £29,000

Princess Of Wales' Stakes
Newmarket, July 11   3yo+ 1m 4f
Little Rock (4-9-2)
Pat Eddery   10-3
Sir Michael Stoute   £34,800

Falmouth Stakes
Newmarket, July 12   3yo+ f&m 1m
Alshakr (3-8-6)
Richard Hills   9-2
Ben Hanbury   £34,800

Richmond Stakes
Goodwood, Aug 3   2yo c&g 6f
Endless Summer (8-11)
Jimmy Fortune   2-1F
John Gosden   £29,000

J P Morgan Goodwood Cup
Goodwood, Aug 3   3yo+ 2m
Royal Rebel (4-9-2)
Mick Kinane   10-1
Mark Johnston   £46,400

Geoffrey Freer Stakes
Newbury, Aug 19   3yo+ 1m 5f 61y
Murghem (5-9-3)
Darryll Holland   7/4F
Mark Johnston   £36,000

Great Voltigeur Stakes
York, Aug 22   3yo c&g 1m 3f 195y
Air Marshall (8-9)
Johnny Murtagh   7/2
Sir Michael Stoute   £89,250

Gimcrack Stakes
York, Aug 23   2yo c&g 6f
Bannister (8-11)
Johnny Murtagh   11-1
Richard Hannon   £72,500

Peugeot Lowther Stakes
York, Aug 24   2yo f 6f
Enthused (9-0)
Johnny Murtagh   9/4
Sir Michael Stoute   £46,400

Celebration Mile Stakes
Goodwood, Aug 26   3yo+ 1m
Medicean (3-8-9)
Pat Eddery   5/2
Sir Michael Stoute   £46,400

Champagne Stakes
Doncaster, Sep 8   2yo c&g 7f
Noverre (9-0)
Frankie Dettori   7/2
David Loder   £60,000

Flying Childers Stakes
Doncaster, Sep 9   2yo 5f
Superstar Leo (8-12)
Michael Hills   2/1F
William Haggas   £27,000

Mill Reef Stakes
Newbury, Sep 16   2yo 6f 8y
Bouncing Bowdler (8-12)
Richard Hills   10/1
Mark Johnston   £30,000

Sodexho Diadem Stakes
Ascot Sep 24   3yo+ 6f
Sampower Star (4-9-0)
Frankie Dettori   7-4F
Saeed Bin Suroor   £60,000

Royal Lodge Stakes
Ascot, Sep 24   2yo c&g 1m
Atlantis Prince (8-11)
Frankie Dettori   11/2
Sean Woods   £72,000

Peugeot Sun Chariot Stakes
Newmarket, Sep 30 3yo+ f&m 1m 2f
Danceabout (3-8-9)
Darryll Holland   9/2
Geoff Wragg   £34,800

Victor Chandler Challenge St
Newmarket, Oct 14   3yo+ 7f
Last Resort (3-8-9)
Michael Hills   20/1
Barry Hills   £58,000

Owen Brown Rockfel Stakes
Newmarket, Oct 14   2yo f 7f
Sayedah (8-9)
Richard Hills   25/1
Marcus Tregoning   £29,000

Group 3

(see also Ascot)

Lanes End Greenham Stakes
Newmarket, Apr 18   3yo c&g 7f
Barathea Guest (9-0)
Philip Robinson   13/2
George Margarson   £18,000

Shadwell Nell Gwyn Stakes
Newmarket, Apr 18   3yo c&g 7f
Petrushka (8-9)
Kieren Fallon   7/2F
Sir Michael Stoute   £20,300

Earl of Sefton Stakes
Newmarket, Apr 19 4yo+ 1m 110y
Indian Lodge (4-8-10)
Mick Kinane   10/1
Amanda Perrett   £20,300

Craven Stakes
Newmarket, Apr 20   3yo c&g 1m
Umistim (8-9)
Richard Hughes   8/1
Richard Hannon   £20,300

John Porter Stks
Newbury, Apr 22   4yo+ 1m 3f 200y
Yavana's Pace (8-9-1)
Darryll Holland   7/1
Mark Johnston   £21,000

Levy Bd Leicestershire Stakes
Doncaster, Apr 29   4yo+ 7f
Sugarfoot (6-9-1)
Ray Cochrane   4/1
Nigel Tinkler   £20,300

Thresher Classic Trial Stks
Sandown, Apr 29   3yo 1m 2f 7y
Sakhee (8-11)
Richard Hills   11/4
John Dunlop   £36,000

Marriott Hotels
Gordon Richard Stakes
Sandown, Apr 29   4yo+ 1m 2f 7y
Little Rock (4-8-10)
Kieren Fallon   5/2F
Sir Michael Stoute   £24,000

Bovis Homes Sagaro Stakes
Ascot, May 3   4yo+ 2m 45y
Orchestra Stall (8-8-12)
Kevin Darley   6/1
John Dunlop   £25,200

Victor Chandler
Palace House Stakes
Newmarket, May 6   3yo+ 5f
Pipalong (4-8-9)
Kevin Darley   9/1
Tim Easterby   £23,200

Victor Chandler Chester Vase
Chester, May 9   3yo 1m 4f 66y
Millenary (8-10)
Pat Eddery   8/1
John Dunlop   £36,000

Ormonde Stakes
Chester, May 11   4yo+ 1m 5f 89y
Daliapour (4-8-11)
Kieren Fallon   11/8F
Sir Michael Stoute   £36,000

Pertemps Derby Trial Stakes
Lingfield, May 13   3yo 1m 3f 106y
Saddler's Quest (8-7)
Kevin Darley   100/30F
Gerard Butler   £34,800

Tattersalls Musidora Stks
York, May 16   3yo f 1m 2f 85y
Kalypso Katie (8-8)
Mick Kinane   100/30
Jeremy Noseda   £26,100

Duke Of York Victor Chandler Stakes
York, May 18   3yo+ 6f
Lend A Hand (5-9-5)
Frankie Dettori   100/30
Saeed Bin Suroor   £36,000

Bonusprint Henry II Stakes
Sandown, May 29   4yo+ 2m 78y
Persian Punch (7-8-12)
Philip Robinson   11/2
David Elsworth   £24,000

Brigadier Gerard Stakes
Sandown, May 30   4yo+ 1m 2f 7y
Shiva (5-9-0)
Richard Quinn   7/2F
Henry Cecil   £24,000

Vodafone Diomed Stakes
Epsom, June 10   3yo+ 1m 114y
Trans Island (5-9-9)
Kieren Fallon   5/4F
Ian Balding   £30,000

Van Geest Criterion Stakes
Newmarket, July 1   3yo+ 7f
Arkadian Hero (5-9-1)
Jamie Spencer   100/30F
Luca Cumani   £20,300

Unigate Food Service Lancashire Oaks Stakes
Haydock, July 8   3yo+ f&m 1m 4f
Ela Athena (4-9-3)
Philip Robinson   5/1
Michael Jarvis   £24,000

TNT Aviation July Stakes
Newmarket, July 12   2yo c&g 6f
Noverre (8-13)
Jimmy Fortune   5/2F
David Loder   £20,300

Sodexho Prestige Classic Stakes
Ayr, July 17   3yo+ 1m 2f
Endless Hall (4-9-9)
Jamie Spencer   7/1
Luca Cumani   £20,300

Princess Margaret Stakes
Ascot, July 29   2yo f 6f
Enthused (8-9)
Johnny Murtagh   2/1F
Sir Michael Stoute   £24,000

King George Stakes
Goodwood, Aug 1   3yo+ 5f
Cassandra Go (4-8-10)
Michael Roberts   11/2
Geoff Wragg   £30,000

Peugeot Gordon Stakes
Goodwood, Aug 1   3yo 1m 4f
Millenary (8-13)
Richard Quinn   9/1
John Dunlop   £29,000

Lanson Champagne Vintage Stakes
Goodwood, Aug 2   2yo 7f
No Excuse Needed (8-11)
Johnny Murtagh   12/1
Sir Michael Stoute   £30,000

Theo Fennell Lennox Stakes
Goodwood, Aug 4   3yo+ 7f
Observatory (3-8-12)
Kevin Darley   11/4
John Gosden   £30,000

The Queen Mother's 100th B'day Molecomb Stakes
Goodwood, Aug 4   2yo 5f
Misty Eyed (8-10)
Lee Newman   3/1F
Nerys Dutfield   £24,000

Petros Rose Of Lancaster St
Haydock, Aug 12 3yo+ 1m 2f 120y
Ekraar (3-8-7)
Richard Hills   7/4F
Marcus Tregoning   £23,200

The Horsesmouth.co.uk Hungerford Stakes
Newbury, Aug 18   3yo+ 7f 64y
Arkadian Hero (5-9-2)
Jamie Spencer   5/2
Luca Cumani   £21,000

Ford Solario Stakes
Sandown, Aug 19   2yo 7f 16y
King's Ironbridge (8-11)
Richard Hughes   10/1
Richard Hannon   £18,000

Wetherbys Lonsdale Stakes
York, Aug 22 3yo+ 1m 7f 195y
Royal Rebel (4-9-6)
Mick Kinane   2/1JF
Mark Johnston   £44,625

Winter Hill Stakes
Windsor, Aug 26   3yo+ 1m 2f 7y
Adilabad (3-8-6)
Pat Eddery   6/4F
Sir Michael Stoute   £23,400

ATS Euromaster Prestige St
Goodwood, Aug 27   2yo f 7f
Freefourracing (8-9)
Richard Quinn   8/1
Brian Meehan   £24,000

Milcars September Stakes
Kempton, Sep 2   3yo+ 1m 4f
Mutamam (5-9-0)
Richard Hills   5/2F
Alec Stewart   £21,000

Park Hill Stakes
Doncaster, Sep 6
3yo+ f&m 1m 6f 132y
Miletrian (3-8-10)
Craig Williams   10/1
Mick Channon   £24,000

G.N.E.R Park Stakes
Doncaster, Sep 7   3yo+ 1m
Distant Music (3-8-9)
Michael Hills   4/1
Barry Hills   £21,000

May Hill Stakes
Doncaster, Sep 7   2yo f 1m
Karasta (8-9)
Johnny Murtagh   5/4F
Sir Michael Stoute   £24,000

GNER Doncaster Cup Stakes
Doncaster, Sep 7   3yo+ 2m 2f
Enzeli (5-9-7)
Johnny Murtagh   15/2
John Oxx (IRL)   £24,000

Flutter.com Select Stakes
Goodwood, Sep 9   3yo+
1m1f192yds
Ekraar (3-8-10)
Richard Hills   10/11F
Marcus Tregoning   £24,000

Old Vic Cumberland Lodge
Ascot, Sep 23   3yo+ 1m 4f
Mutamam (5-9-3)
Richard Hills   4/6F
Alec Stewart   £32,400

Somerville Tattersall Stakes
Newmarket, Sep 29   2yo c&g 7f
King Charlemagne (8-9)
Mick Kinane   11/2
Aidan O'Brien   £20,300

Princess Royal Stakes
Ascot, Oct 13   3yo+ f&m 1m 4f
Sacred Song (3-8-7)
Richard Quinn   12/1
Henry Cecil   £16,200

Jockey Club Cup
Newmarket, Oct 14   3yo+ 2m
Persian Punch (7-9-5)
Richard Hughes   7/1
David Elsworth   £29,000

Vodafone Cornwallis Stakes
Newbury, Oct 20   2yo 5f
Danehurst (8-7)
George Duffield   7/2F
Sir Mark Prescott   £16,950

Vodafone Horris Hill Stakes
Newbury, Oct 20   2yo c&g 7f 64y
Clearing (8-9)
Jimmy Fortune   9/2
John Gosden   £21,000

Perpetual St Simon Stakes
Newbury, Oct 21   3yo+ 1m4f 5yds
Wellbeing (3-8-7)
Richard Quinn   4/7F
Henry Cecil   £21,000

Other Major Races

Worthington Lincoln H'cap
Doncaster, Mar 25   1m
John Ferneley (5-8-10)
Jimmy Fortune   7/1JF
Paul Cole   £43,761

Tote Chester Cup
Chester, May 10   4yo+ 2m 2f 147y
Bangalore (4-7-10)
Gary Bardwell   16/1
Amanda Perrett   £65,000

Tote Silver Bowl Handicap
Haydock, May 27   3yo 1m 30yds
Atlantic Rhapsody (8-3)
Joe Fanning   11/1
Mark Johnston   £43,875

William Hill Trophy Handicap
York, June 17   3yo 6f
Cotton House (8-13)
Craig Williams   25/1
Mick Channon   £38,532

Foster's Lager
Northumberland Plate
Newcastle, July 1   3yo+ 2m 19y
Bay Of Islands (8-8-4)
Kevin Darley   7/1
David Morris   £75,400

Tote Exacta Handicap
Sandown, Jul 7   3yo+ 1m2f 7yds
Lady Angharad (4-8-1)
Richard Mullen   14/1
James Fanshawe   £58,000

Letheby & Christopher
Old Newton Cup Handicap
Haydock, July 8   3yo+ 1m 3f 200y
Radas Daughter (4-8-11)
Kevin Darley   11/1
Ian Balding   £36,888

John Smith's Cup Handicap
York, July 15   3yo+ 1m 2f 85y
Sobriety (3-8-8)
John Reid   20/1
Fulke Johnson Houghton   £87,750

Wetherbys Super Sprint
Newbury, July 22   2yo 5f 34y
Superstar Leo (8-6)
Michael Hills   9/2
William Haggas   £72,500

Tote International Handicap
Ascot, Jul 29   3yo+ 7f
Tillerman (4-8-10)
Mick Kinane   10/1
Amanda Perrett   £87,000

Jockey Club Sprint Handicap
Ascot, Jul 30   3yo+ 5f
Magic Rainbow (5-7-5)
Jamie Mackay   8/1
Michael Bell   £46,000

Tote Gold Trophy
Goodwood, Aug 2   3yo 1m 4f
Blue Gold (9-1)
John Reid   14/1
Richard Hannon   £45,500

William Hill Mile Handicap
Goodwood, Aug 3   3yo+ 1m
Persiano (5-8-12)
David Harrison   10/1
James Fanshawe   £65,000

Volvo Globetrotter Handicap
Goodwood, Aug 4   3yo 1m 2f
Happy Diamond (9-6)
John Reid   15/2
Mark Johnston   £32,500

Vodafone Stewards' Cup
Goodwood, Aug 5   3yo+ 6f
Tayseer (6-8-11)
Richard Hughes   13/2
David Nicholls   £55,250

Ritz Club Shergar Sprint Cup
Ascot, Aug 12   3yo 6f
Bernstein (8-12)
Mick Kinane   5/1
Aidan O'Brien   £50,000

Dubai Internet Shergar Cup
Ascot, Aug 12   3yo 6f
Arctic Owl (6-9-3)
Johnny Murtagh   9/2
James Fanshawe   £56,000

Tote Ebor Handicap
York, Aug 23   3yo+ 1m 5f 194y
Give The Slip (3-8-8)
Pat Eddery   8/1
Amanda Perrett   £113,750

St Leger Yearling Stakes
Doncaster, Sep 6   2yo 6f
Goggles (8-11)
Chris Rutter   14/1
Henry Candy   £155,950

Courage Best Handicap
Newbury, Sep 16   3yo+ 1m 2f 6y
Komistar (5-8-6)
Philip Robinson   16/1
Peter Harris   £43,500

Ladbroke Ayr Gold Cup
Ayr, Sep 16   3yo+ 6f
Bahamian Pirate (5-8-0)
Adrian Nicholls   33/1
David Nicholls   £65,000

Tote Trifecta Handicap
Ascot, Sep 23   3yo+ 7f
Duke Of Modena (3-8-6)
Steve Carson   9/1
Toby Balding   £43,500

Coral Eurobet Handicap
Ascot, Sep 24   3yo+ 1m 4f
Kind Regards (3-8-4)
Craig Williams   15/2
Mark Johnston   £45,500

Tattersalls Houghton Sales Stakes
Newmarket, Sep 26   2yo 7f
Mozart (9-0)
Mick Kinane   11/10F
Aidan O'Brien (IRL)   £229,200

Tote Cambridgeshire
Newmarket, Sep 30   3yo+ 1m 1f
Katy Nowaitee (4-8-8)
John Reid   6/1
Peter Harris   £69,600

Betabet.com Two-Year-Old Trophy Stakes
Redcar, Sep 30   2yo 6f
Dim Sums (8-4)
Kevin Darley   6/4F
David Barron   £58,000

Tattersalls Autumn Auction Stakes
Newmarket, Oct 13   2yo 6f
Goodie Twosues (8-1)
Lee Newman   5/1
Richard Hannon   £50,825

Tote Cesarewitch Handicap
Newmarket, Oct 14   3yo+ 2m2f
Heros Fatal (6-8-0)
Gary Carter   11/1
Martin Pipe   £78,000

Top Flat Trainers

Turf Only, Listed by Total Money

		1st	2nd	3rd	4th	Total	%	Win Money	Total Money	£1 Stake
1	Sir Michael Stoute	90	72	61	56	464	19	1,923,458	2,962,790	-112.27
2	John Dunlop	97	76	59	55	561	17	1,016,785	1,702,229	-117.36
3	Richard Hannon	117	128	113	106	1023	11	881,936	1,659,695	-214.55
4	Mark Johnston	114	114	91	86	732	15	1,063,657	1,606,526	-136.55
5	Aidan O'Brien	10	10	6	8	61	16	1,226,912	1,597,199	-20.29
6	John Gosden	79	76	50	52	428	18	1,069,067	1,543,363	-48.47
7	Saeed Bin Suroor	17	15	17	10	105	16	643,674	1,361,035	-55.55
8	Mick Channon	88	94	87	88	775	11	743,741	1,171,909	-104.07
9	Henry Cecil	60	40	32	29	252	23	683,480	1,147,814	-45.47
10	Barry Hills	58	74	57	67	622	9	407,972	888,844	-241.97
11	John Hammond	4	2	0	1	9	44	646,500	742,094	+16.58
12	Paul Cole	48	37	27	37	304	15	450,193	705,839	-54.54
13	David Nicholls	55	42	61	41	608	9	444,183	698,431	-206.83
14	John Oxx	3	1	0	0	7	42	668,750	689,640	+20.50
15	Tim Easterby	57	49	64	53	640	8	417,234	661,332	-280.45
16	James Fanshawe	34	38	32	36	279	12	398,351	572,726	-59.79
17	Mrs Amanda Perrett	25	14	24	20	181	13	495,026	570,110	-13.44
18	Ian Balding	46	37	42	38	416	11	325,444	564,148	-144.29
19	William Haggas	41	33	25	8	199	20	383,373	562,812	-9.06
20	Jack Berry	62	68	82	64	716	8	269,214	529,988	-335.83
21	Ed Dunlop	51	32	46	32	341	14	333,365	513,353	-75.36
22	Michael Jarvis	34	35	24	22	242	14	234,183	512,119	+0.19
23	David Elsworth	30	35	22	31	327	9	253,575	491,518	-119.51
24	Peter Harris	33	32	30	40	377	8	363,178	484,826	-130.13
25	Micahel Bell	45	47	41	41	372	12	280,729	483,815	-78.55

Top Flat Jockeys

Turf Only, Listed by Races Won

		1st	2nd	3rd	4th	Total	%	Win Money	Total Money	£1 Stake
1	Kevin Darley	147	134	107	102	951	15.5	1,426,683	2,271,488	-209.86
2	Richard Quinn	138	118	86	81	764	18.0	1,538,017	2,398,260	-46.33
3	Pat Eddery	127	90	79	74	808	15.7	1,106,421	1,913,265	-150.01
4	Richard Hughes	97	97	79	92	764	12.7	812,559	1,426,436	-200.62
5	Jimmy Fortune	90	78	63	71	665	13.5	675,965	1,146,362	-119.77
6	Richard Hills	81	49	56	42	459	17.6	1,003,945	1,616,370	+43.73
7	Tony Culhane	73	82	66	63	690	10.6	345,814	548,057	-112.69
8	John Reid	69	62	98	60	720	9.6	701,898	1,357,364	-157.91
9	Darryll Holland	67	70	47	57	497	13.5	462,745	751,590	-149.55
10	Seb Sanders	60	61	70	47	632	9.5	386,277	612,820	-172.12
11	Gary Carter	58	43	41	41	446	13.0	316,046	491,339	-146.49
12	George Duffield	57	48	64	50	639	8.9	490,457	664,127	-246.90
13	Michael Hills	57	73	46	61	515	11.1	519,596	979,270	-148.53
14	Lee Newman	56	36	39	58	487	11.5	362,596	504,908	+45.71
15	Philip Robinson	55	28	43	43	426	12.9	631,649	872,727	+0.20
16	Kieren Fallon	55	47	37	32	309	17.8	1,016,743	1,372,952	-69.33
171	Jamie Spencer	54	41	42	44	452	11.9	334,693	622,117	-141.54
18	John Carroll	53	57	63	60	581	9.1	226,173	480,586	-254.97
19	Fergal Lynch	49	51	42	46	452	10.8	218,444	341,908	-98.84
20	Willie Supple	48	49	55	64	554	8.7	261,064	423,256	-203.09
21	Michael Roberts	48	40	37	38	396	12.1	426,182	692,898	-125.91
22	Francis Norton	45	57	56	51	556	8.0	304,594	568,307	-134.90
23	Joe Fanning	45	49	43	61	469	9.6	238,546	366,439	-124.80
24	Frankie Dettori	45	34	25	23	245	18.4	872,797	1,296,523	-35.62
25	Jason Weaver	43	38	44	37	430	10.0	207,316	337,968	-95.59

All-Weather Tables

Jockeys

	Wins
Neil Callan	52
Francis Norton	32
George Baker	31
Lee Newman	31
Martin Dwyer	30
Paul Doe	27
Ian Mongan	27
Tom McLaughlin	25
Tony Clark	25
Michael Tebbutt	24
Jamie Spencer	24
Paul Quinn	22
Seb Sanders	20
Robbie Fitzpatrick	19
Tony Culhane	19
Joe Fanning	18
Mark Henry	16
Stanley Finnamore	16
Jason Weaver	16
Michael Hills	16
Jason Tate	15
Chris Catlin	14
Michael Fenton	14
Carl Lowther	14
Fergus Sweeney	14

Trainers

	Wins
Nick Littmoden	32
David Barron	27
Karl Burke	27
Sir Mark Prescott	25
Reg Hollinshead	22
Gary Moore	22
Pat Haslam	21
Richard Hannon	18
Andrew Reid	18
David Nicholls	18
Norma McCauley	17
Brian McMahon	17
Derek Shaw	17
Mark Polglase	16
Mark Johnston	16
David Chapman	15
Terry Mills	15
Barry Hills	14
Peter Makin	14

Overseas Races

Australia

Fosters Melbourne Cup
Flemington, Nov 7   3yo+ 2m
Brew (6-7-10)
Kerrin McEvoy   14/1
Michael Moroney NZL   AUS$2m

Canada

Atto Mile
Woodbine, Sep 10   3yo+ 1m turf
Riviera (6-8-5)
Jose Velazquez   106/10
Bobby Frankel (USA) £253,165

Canadian International
Woodbine, Oct 17   3yo+
1m 4f turf
Mutafaweq (5-9-0)
Frankie Dettori   4/1
Saeed bin Suroor   £379,747

Dubai

Dubai Turf Classic
Nad Al Sheba, Mar 25
4yo+   1m 4f turf
Fantastic Light (4-8-9)
Kieren Fallon
Sit Michael Stoute   £731,707

Dubai Duty Free
Nad Al Sheba, Mar 25
4yo+   1m 2f dirt
Rhythm Band (4-9-0)
Ted Durcan
Saeed bin Suroor   £731,707

Dubai World Cup
Nad Al Sheba, Mar 25
4yo+   1m 2f dirt
Dubai Millennium (4-9-0)
Frankie Dettori
Saeed bin Suroor   £2,195,122

France

Prix Ganay
Longchamp, Apr 30
4yo+   1m 2f 110y
Indian Danehill (4-9-2)
Olivier Peslier   3/5F
Andre Fabre (FRA) £48,031

Prix Lupin
Longchamp, May 14 3yo c&f
1m 2f 110y
Ciro (9-2)
Olivier Peslier   211/31
Aidan O'Brien (IRL)   £48,031

Poule d'Essai des Poulains
Longchamp, May 14 3yo c 1m
Bachir (9-2)
Frankie Dettori   31/10
Saeed bin Suroor   £96,061

Dubai Poule d'Essai des Pouliches
Longchamp, May 14   3yo f 1m
Bluemamba (9-0)
Thierry Jarnet   184/10
P Bary (FRA)   £96,061

Prix Saint-Alary
Longchamp, May 21 3yo f 1m 2f
Reve Doscar (9-0)
Alain Badel   96/10
Mme B Badel (FRA) £48,031

Prix d'Ispahan
Longchamp, May 23
4yo+ c&f 1m 1f 55y
Sendawar (4-9-2)
Gerard Mosse   4/5F
A de Royer Dupre (FRA) £48,031

Les Emirates Arabes Unis Prix du Jockey-Club
Chantilly, June 4 3yo c&f 1m 4f
Holding Court (9-2)
Philip Robinson   61/10
Michael Jarvis   £240,154

Prix Jean Prat
Chantilly, June 4   3yo 1m 1f
Suances (9-2)
Gerard Mosse   26/10
M Delcher-Sanchez (ESP) £43,057

Prix de Diane Hermès
Chantilly, June 11 3yo f
1m 2f 110y
Egyptband (9-0)
Olivier Doleuze   58/10
Mme Christine Head (FRA) £134.486

Grand Prix de Paris
Longchamp, June 25 3yo c&f 1m 2f
Beat Hollow (9-2)
Richard Quinn   7/5F
Henry Cecil   £115,274

Grand Prix de Saint-Cloud
Saint-Cloud, July 2 3yo+ 1m 4f
Montjeu (4-9-8)
Cash Asmussen   1/5F
John Hammond (FRA)   £129,171

Prix Maurice de Gheest
Deauville, Aug 6 3yo+ 6f 110y
Bold Edge (5-9-2)
Dane O'Neill   91/10
Richard Hannon   £48,031

Prix du Haras
Deauville, Aug 13   3yo+ c&f 1m
Muhtathir (5-9-4)
Frankie Dettori   215/10
Saeed bin Suroor   £115,274

Prix Morny
Deauville, Aug 20   2yo c&f 6f
Bad As I Wanna Be (9-0)
Gerard Mosse   144/10
Brian Meehan   £76,849

Prix du Moulin
Longchamp, Sep 3 3yo+ c&f 1m
Indian Lodge (4-9-2)
Cash Asmussen   1.80FF
Amanda Perrett   £86,465

Prix Vermeille
Longchamp Sep 10 3yo f 1m 4f
Volvoreta (9-0)
Mick Kinane   1.80FF
C Lerner (FRA)   £76,849

Prix de la Salamandre
Longchamp Sep 16 2yo 7f
Tobougg (9-0)
Craig Williams   38/10
Mick Channon   £38,425

Prix Marcel Boussac
Longchamp, Oct 1 2yo 1m
Amonita (8-11)
Thierry Jarnet   115/10
P Bary FRA   £76,849

Prix de L'Abbaye
Longchamp, Oct 1 2yo+ 5f
Namid (8-11)
Johnny Murtagh   68/10
John Oxx IRL

Prix de L'Arc de Triomphe
Longchamp, Oct 1 3yo+ 1m 4f
Sinndar (3-8-10)
Johnny Murtagh   8/5
John Oxx IRL   £576,369

Prix de l'Opera
Longchamp, Oct 1 3yo f 1m 2f
Petrushka (9-0)
Johnny Murtagh   9/10F
Sir Michael Stoute   £67,243

Prix du Cadran
Longchamp, Oct 1 2yo 1m
San Sebastian (9-0)
Davy Bonilla   122/10
John Dunlop   £48,031

Grand Criterium
Longchamp, Oct 10 2yo 1m
Okawango (9-0)
Olivier Doleuze   6/5JF
Mme C Head (FRA)   £107,643

Prix de la Foret
Longchamp, Oct 15 3yo+ 7f
Indian Lodge (4-9-2)
Pat Eddery   36/10
Amanda Perrett   £48,031

Prix Royal-Oak
Longchamp, Oct 22
3yo+ 1m 7f 110y
Amilynx (4-9-4)
Olivier Peslier   13/10F
Andre Fabre FRA   £38,425

Criterium de St-Cloud
St-Cloud, Oct 29   2yo 1m 2f
Sagacity (9-0)
Olivier Peslier   24/10
Andre Fabre FRA   £38,425

Germany

BMW Deutsches Derby
Hamburg, July 2 3yo c&f 1m 4f
Samum (9-2)
Andrasch Starke
Andreas Schutz GER

WGZ Bank-Deutschlandpreis
Dusseldorf, July 23 3yo+ 1m 4f
Mutafaweq (4-9-6)
Richard Hills
Saeed bin Suroor   £64,516

Grosser Dallmayr Preis
Munich, July 30 3yo+ 1m 2f
Greek Dance (5-9-6)
Johnny Murtagh
Sir Michael Stoute   £79,442

Grosser Preis Von Baden
Baden-Baden, Sep 3 3yo+ 1m 4f
Samum (3-8-9)
Andrasch Starke   16/10F
Andreas Schultz (GER) £322,581

Pries von Europa
Cologne, Sep 24   3yo+ 1m 4f
Golden Snake (4-9-6)
Davy Bonilla
John Dunlop   £96,774

Ireland

Irish 2000 Guineas
Curragh, May 27   3yo c&f 1m
Bachir (9-0)
Frankie Dettori   4/1
Saeed bin Suroor   £116,600

Irish 1000 Guineas
Curragh, May 28   3yo f 1m
Crimplene (9-0)
Philip Robinson   16/1
Clive Brittain   £112,600

Tattersall's Gold Cup
Curragh, May 28 4yo+ 1m 2f 110y
Montjeu (4-9-0)
Mick Kinane   1/3F
H R A Cecil   IR£62,000

Irish Derby
Curragh, June 27 3yo c&f 1m 4f
Sinndar (9-0)
Johnny Murtagh   11/10F
John Oxx (IRL)   £482,400

Irish Oaks
Curragh, July 16   3yo f 1m 4f
Petrushka (9-0)
Johnny Murtagh   11/2
Sir Michael Stoute   £112,425

Heinz 57 Phoenix Stakes
Leopardstown, Aug 13 2yo c&f 6f
Minardi (9-0)
Mick Kinane   7/2
Aidan O'Brien (IRL)   £98,350

Tattersalls Breeders
Curragh, Aug 26 2yo c&f 6f
Blue Goddess (8-7)
David Harrison   5/1F
Richard Hannon   £98,000

Moyglare Stud Stakes
Curragh, Sep 5 2yo f 7f
Sequoyah (8-11)
J P Spencer   9/4F
Aidan O'Brien (IRL)   IR£98,250

Champion Stakes
Leopardstown, Sep 11 3yo+ c&f
1m 2f
Giants Causeway (3-8-11)
Mick Kinane   8/11F
Aidan O'Brien (IRL)   £486,200

Irish St Leger
Curragh, Sep 16   3yo+ 1m 6f
Arctic Owl (6-9-8)
David Harrison   7/2
James Fanshawe   £101,800

National Stakes
Curragh, Sep 17   2yo c&f 1m
Beckett (9-0)
James Heffernan   7/1
Aidan O'Brien (IRL)   £114,600

Italy

Premio Presidente della Repubblica
Capannelle , May 14 4yo+ 1m 2f
Timboroa (4-9-2)
Mirco Demuro
Roberto Brogi (ITA)   £192,261

Oaks D'Italia
San Siro, May 21 3yo f 1m 3f
Timi (8-11)
Mirco Demuro   57/10
Lorenzo Brogi (ITA)   £92,390

Derby Italiano
Capannelle, May 28 3yo c&f 1m 4f
Kallisto (9-2)
Andreas Boschert   34/10
Hans Blume (GER)   £210,544

Gran Premio Di Milano
San Siro, June 18 3yo+ 1m 4f
Endless Hall (4-9-6)
Fernando Jovine   14L
Luca Cumani   £100,685

GP Del Jockey-Club
San Siro, Oct 22   3yo+ 1m 4f
Golden Snake (4-9-4)
Pat Eddery   13/10
John Dunlop   £106,053

Japan

Yasuda Kinen
Fuchu, Tokyo, June 13 3yo+ 1m
Fairy King Prawn (4-9-2)
Robert Fradd
Ricky Yiu Poon-fai (Japan)
£581,037

Tokyo Cup
Fuchu, Tokyo, Nov 26 3yo+ 1m 4f
TM Opera O (4-9-0)
Ryuiji Wada   1.5/1
Ichizo Iwamoto JPN   £581,037

Singapore

International Cup
Kranji, Mar 4 3yo+ 1m 2f
Timahs (4-9-0)
Frankie Dettori
Saeed bin Suroor   £666,667

United States

Kentucky Derby
Louisville, May 6 3yo   1m 2f
Fusaichi Pegasus (9-0)
Kent Desormeaux
Neil Drysdale (USA)   £541,585

Preakness Stakes-
Pimlico, May 20 3yo 1m 1f 110y dirt
Red Bullet (9-0)
Jerry Bailey
Joe Orseno USA $650,000

Belmont Stakes
Belmont Park, June 10
3yo 1m 4f dirt
Commendable (9-0)
Pat Day
D Wayne Lukas USA $600,000

Turf Classic
Belmont Park, Oct 7
3yo+ 1m 2f dirt
Johns Call (9-9-0)
Jean-Luc Samyn   104/10
Tony Voss (USA)   £274,390

Breeders' Cup
Churchill Downs, Kentucky   Nov 4

Distaff
3yo f & m 1m 110y (dirt)
Spain (8-11)
Victor Espinoza
D Wayne Lukas USA $1,227,200

Juvenile Fillies
2yo f 1m 110y (dirt)
Caressing (8-7)
JoseVelazquez
David Vance USA $582,400

Mile
3yo+ 1m (turf)
War Chant (3-8-11)
Gary Stevens
Neil Drysdale USA $608,400

Sprint
3yo+ 6f (dirt)
Kona Gold (6-9-0)
Alex Solis
Bruce Headley USA $520,000

Filly & Mare
3yo+ f & m 1m 3f (turf)
Perfect Sting (4-8-11)
Jerry Bailey
Joe Orseno USA $629,200

Juvenile
2yo c & g 1m 110y (dirt)
Macho Uno (2-8-10)
Jerry Bailey
Joe Orseno USA $556,400

Turf
3yo+ 1m 4f (turf)
Kalanisi (4-9-0)
Johnny Murtagh
Sir Michael Stoute $1,289,600

Classic
3yo+ 1m 2f (dirt)
Tiznow (3-8-10)
Chris McCarron
Jay Robbins USA $2,438,80

National Hunt Racing

1999/2000 Season

Axminster 100 Desert Orchid Pattern Handicap Chase
Wincanton, Oct 21   2m 5f
No Retreat (6-10-3)
Tony Dobbin   4-1
Steve Brookshaw   £19,350

Peterhouse Group Charlie Hall Chase
Wetherby, Oct 30   3m 1f
See More Business (9-11-12)
Mick Fitzgerald   11/4JF
Paul Nicholls   £23,800

William Hill Haldon Gold Handicap Chase
Exeter, Nov 2   2m 1f 110y
Flagship Uberalles (5-10-13)
Joe Tizzard   7-4F
Paul Nicholls   £19,050

Tote Silver Trophy Handicap Hurdle
Chepstow, Nov 6   2m 4f 110y
Carlovent (4-10-7)
David Casey   12/1
Martin Pipe   £22,074

Badger Beer H'cap Chase
Wincanton, Nov 6   3m1f110yds
Flaked Oats (10-10-0)
Robert Widger   25/1
Paul Nicholls   £20,875

Sporting Index Cross-country Chase
Cheltenham, Nov 12   3m 7f
Linden's Lotto (10-11-8)
Paul Carberry   7-4F
Tony Martin (IRL)   £17,181

Murphy's Gold Cup Handicap Chase
Cheltenham, Nov 13   2m 4f 110y
The Outback Way (9-10-0)
Norman Williamson   9/1
Venetia Williams   £46,100

Edward Hanmer Memorial Limited H'cap Chase
Haydock, Nov 13   3m
The Last Fling (9-10-5)
Seamus Durack   25/1
Sue Smith   £25,000

Murphy's Handicap Hurdle
Cheltenham, Nov 14   2m 110y
Rodock (5-10-0)
Tony McCoy   11-4JF
Martin Pipe   £31,728

Pricewaterhouse Ascot Hdle
Ascot, Nov 19   2m4f
Wahiba Sands (6-11-4)
Tony McCoy   5-4F
Martin Pipe   £15,475

First National Bank Chase
Ascot, Nov 20   2m 3f 110y
Nordance Prince (8-10-9)
Richard Johnson   8/1
Venetia Williams   £29,775

Victor C Peterborough Chase
Huntingdon, Nov 20   3m 3f
Edredon Bleu (7-11-10)
Jim Culloty   11/8F
Henrietta Knight   £23,750

Tote Becher Handicap Chase
Aintree, Nov 21   3m 3f
Feels Like Gold (11-10-0)
Tony Dobbin   9-1
Nicky Richards   £28,750

Ladbrokes Handicap Hurdle
Newbury, Nov 27   3m 2f 110y
Picket Piece (8-10-8)
Richard Johnson   13/8F
David Nicholson   £20,832

Hennessy Cognac Gold Cup
Newbury, Nov 27   3m 2f 110y
Ever Blessed (7-10-0)
Timmy Murphy   9/2F
Mark Pitman   £48,880

Pertemps Fighting Fifth Hdle
Newcastle, Nov 27   2m
Dato Star (8-11-8)
Lorcan Wyer   4/9F
Malcolm Jefferson   £22,025

Mitsubishi Shogun Tingle Creek Trophy
Sandown, Dec 4   2m
Flagship Uberalles (5-11-7)
Joe Tizzard   100/30
Paul Nicholls   £38,700

William Hill Handicap Hurdle
Sandown, Dec 4   2m 110y
Copeland (4-10-5)
David Casey   7/1
Martin Pipe   £34,900

Coral Rehearsal H'cap Chase
Chepstow, Dec 4   3m
Dr Leunt (8-10-10)
Andrew Thornton   9/4F
Philip Hobbs   £20,850

Tripleprint Gold Cup Chase
Cheltenham, Dec 11   2m 5f
Legal Right (6-10-13)
Richard Johnson   6/1
Jonjo O'Neill   £46,100

Bonusprint Bula Hurdle
Cheltenham, Dec 11   2m 1f
Relkeel (10-11-8)
Richard Johnson   13/2
Alan King   £21,425

Tommy Whittle Chase
Haydock, Dec 11   3m
Bobby Grant (8-11-3)
Robbie Supple   5/1
Peter Beaumont   £25,000

Long Walk Hurdle
Ascot, Dec 18   3m 1f 110y
Anzum (8-11-7)
Richard Johnson   4/1
Alan King   £32,750

Tote Silver Cup H'cap Chase
Ascot, Dec 18   3m 110y
Tresor De Mai (5-11-1)
Tony McCoy   10/1
Martin Pipe   £29,050

Feltham Novices Chase
Kempton, Dec 27   3m
Gloria Victis (5-11-7)
Tony McCoy   2-1F
Martin Pipe   £23,815

King George VI Chase
Kempton, Dec 27   3m
See More Business (9-11-10)
Mick Fitzgerald   5-2F
Paul Nicholls   £65,500

Scott Taylor Castleford Chase
Wetherby, Dec 27   2m
Nordance Prince (8-10-6)
Tony Dobbin   3-1JF
Venetia Williams   £19,300

Finale Junior Hurdle
Chepstow, Dec 28   2m 110y
Mister Banjo (3-11-0)
Mick Fitzgerald   8-11F
Nicky Henderson   £17,250

Coral Welsh National Handicap Chase
Chepstow, Dec 28   3m 5f 110y
Edmond (7-10-0)
Richard Johnson   4-1
Henry Daly   £40,300

Pertemps Christmas Hdle
Kempton, Dec 28   2m
Dato Star (8-11-7)
Lorcan Wyer   11-8
Malcolm Jefferson   £29,730

Challow Hdle
Cheltenham, Dec 31   2m4f 110 yds
Bindaree (5-11-7)
Carl Llewellyn   5-2
Nigel Twiston-Davies   £16,375

Coral Mildmay, Peter Cazalet H'cap Chase
Sandown, Jan 8   3m 5f 110y
Lancastrian Jet (9-10-10)
Andrew Thornton   4/1
Henry Daly   £20,800

Victor Chandler H'cap Chase
Ascot, Jan 15   2m
Nordance Prince (9-10-0)
Tony McCoy   13/8F
Venetia Williams   £30,000

Direct Bet Peter Marsh Limited Handicap Chase
Haydock, Jan 22   3m
The Last Fling (10-10-12)
Seamus Durack   11/2
Sue Smith   £25,500

Tote Lanzarote H'cap Hurdle
Kempton, Jan 22   2m
Heart (7-10-6)
Carl Rafter   10/1
Henrietta Knight   £21,450

Pillar Property Chase
Cheltenham, Jan 29   3m 1f 110y
Looks Like Trouble (8-11-6)
Norman Williamson   100/30
Noel Chance   £30,000

Marchpole Cleeve Hurdle
Cheltenham, Jan 29   2m 5f 110y
Lady Rebecca (8-11-3)
Norman Williamson   EvsF
Venetia Williams   £30,000

Pertemps Great Yorkshire Handicap Chase
Doncaster, Jan 29   3m
Beau (7-11-0)
Tom Jenks   16/1
Nigel Twiston-Davies   £30,914

Wetherbys Scilly Isles Novices Chase
Sandown, Feb 5   2m 4f 110y
Upgrade (6-11-6)
Tony McCoy   11/2
Martin Pipe   £24,000

Agfa Diamond Limited Handicap Chase
Sandown, Feb 5   3m 110y
Trouble Ahead (9-11-4)
Norman Williamson   8/1
Kim Bailey   £19,140

Tote Handicap Hurdle
Sandown, Feb 5   2m 6f
Rubhahunish (9-10-6)
Jamie Goldstein   11/2
Nigel Twiston Davies   £27,000

National Trial H'cap Chase
Uttoxeter, Feb 5   3m 4f
Young Kenny (9-11-13)
Russ Garritty   8/1
Peter Beaumont   £34,800

Mitsubishi Shogun Game Spirit Chase
Newbury, Feb 12   2m 1f
Flagship Uberalles (6-11-13)
Joe Tizzard   1/4F
Paul Nicholls   £20,150

Tote Gold Trophy H'p Hurdle
Newbury, Feb 12   2m 110y
Geos (5-11-3)
Mick Fitzgerald   15/2
Nicky Henderson   £58,000

Mitsubishi Shogun Chase
Ascot, Feb 19   2m 3f 110y
Rockforce (8-11-7)
Joe Tizzard   2/1F
Paul Nicholls   £39,000

Tote Northern National Handicap Chase
Newcastle, Feb 19   4m 1f
Scotton Green (9-10-2)
Lorcan Wyer   8/1
Tim Easterby   £29,000

De Vere Gold Cup Chase
Haydock, Feb 26   3m 4f 110y
The Last Fling (10-11-1)
Seamus Durack   5/1
Sue Smith   £59,500

Racing Post Handicap Chase
Kempton, Feb 26   3m
Gloria Victis (6-11-10)
Richard Johnson   100/30F
Martin Pipe   £43,500

Sunderlands Imperial Cup Handicap Hurdle
Sandown, Mar 11   2m 110y
Magic Combination (7-10-0)
David Casey   11/1
Barney Curley   £21,450

Marstons Midlands Grand National Handicap Chase
Uttoxeter, Mar 18   4m 2f
Ackzo (7-10-0)
Adrian Maguire   15/8F
Ferdy Murphy   £43,500

Grosvenor Casinos Long Distance Hurdle
Ascot, Apr 1   3m
Teeatral (6-11-7)
Dean Gallagher   4/1
Charlie Egerton   £18,600

Barton and Guestier Top Novices' Hurdle
Aintree, Apr 6   2m 110y
Phardante Flyer (6-11-0)
Richard Johnson   5-1
Philip Hobbs   £21,000

Martell Cup Chase
Aintree, Apr 6   3m 1f
See More Business (10-12-0)
Mick Fitzgerald   5/4F
Paul Nicholls   £46,900

Sandeman Novices' Chase
Aintree, Apr 6   2m
Cenkos (6-11-4)
David Casey   7-2
Oliver Sherwood   £36,000

Glenlivet Novices Hurdle
Aintree, Apr 6   2m 110y
Lord Brex (4-11-0)
Richard Johnson   15-2
Philip Hobbs   £24,000

Martell Mersey Novices Hdle
Aintree, Apr 7   2m 4f
Best Mate (5-11-1)
Jim Culloty   4-11F
Henrietta Knight   £21,000

Mumm Melling Chase
Aintree, Apr 7   2m 4f
Direct Route (9-11-10)
Norman Williamson   11-8JF
H Johnson   £60,000

Mumm Mildmay Novices' Chase
Aintree, Apr 7   3m 1f
High Game (6-11-4)
Norman Williamson   9-1
Oliver Sherwood   £27,000

John Hughes Trophy Handicap Chase
Aintree, Apr 7   2m 6f
Northern Starlight (9-11-5)
Tony McCoy   7-1
Martin Pipe   £26,000

Sefton Novices' Hurdle
Aintree, Apr 7   3m 110y
Sackville (7-11-4)
Barry Geraghty   12-1
Frances Crowley   £27,000

Martell Red Rum Limited Handicap Chase
Aintree, Apr 8   2m
Jungli (7-10-7)
Jimmy McCarthy   12/1
Paul Webber   £30,000

Martell Aintree Hurdle
Aintree, Apr 8   2m 4f
Mister Morose (10-11-7)
Carl Llewellyn   16/1
Nigel Twiston-Davies   £60,000

Ladbroke Casinos Scottish Grand National
Ayr, Apr 15   4m 1f
Paris Pike (8-11-0)
Adrian Maguire   5/1JF
Ferdy Murphy   £42,000

Whitbread Gold Cup Handicap Chase
Sandown, Apr 29   3m 5f 110y
Beau (7-10-9)
Carl Llewellyn   6/1JF
Nigel Twiston-Davies   £66,700

Martell Grand National

Aintree, Apr 8　　　*4m 4f*　　　　*40 ran*

1	**Papillon** (9-10-12) Ruby Walsh	-	10/1
	Ted Walsh (IRL)　£290,000		
2	**Mely Moss** (9-10-1) N. Williamson	1	25/1
	Charlie Egerton　£110,000		
3	**Niki Dee** (10-10-13) Robbie Supple	12	25/1
	Peter Beaumont　£55,000		
4	**Brave Highlander** (12-10-0) Phillip Hide	7	50/1
	Josh Gifford　£25,000		
5	**Addington Boy** (12-11-2) A Maguire	Nk	33/1
	Ferdy Murphy　£12,500		
6	**Call It A Day** (10-10-11) Barry Geraghty	3	50/1
	Alan King　£7,500		
7	**The Last Fling** (10-11-5) Seamus Durack	4	14/1
	Sue Smith		
8	**Lucky Town** (9-10-5) David Casey	9	20/1
	Enda Bolger (IRL)		
9	**Djeddah** (9-11-8) Thierry Doumen	2	16/1
	Francois Doumen (FRA)		
10	**Hollybank Buck** (10-10-4) Peter Niven	27	33/1
	Tony Martin (IRL)		
11	**Bobbyjo** (10-11-6) Paul Carberry	7	12/1
	Tommy Carberry (IRL)		
12	**Kendal Cavalier** (10-10-6) Barry Fenton	4	33/1
	Toby Balding		
13	**Suny Bay** (11-11-12) Chris Maude	1½	66/1
	Simon Sherwood		
14	**Feels Like Gold** (12-10-7) Brian Harding	11	28/1
	Nicky Richards		
15	**Camelot Knight** (14-10-0) Ollie McPhail	¾	28/1
	Nigel Twiston-Davies		
16	**Kingdom of Shades** (10-10-4) T Jenks	17	50/1
	Venetia Williams		
17	**Celtic Giant** (10-10-0) Bruce Gibson	22	100/1
	Len Lungo		

Non-finishers

The right-hand number shows the fence at which the horse fell or unseated rider. Where the horse has pulled up, the last fence jumped is given.

F	Micko's Dream (8-10-10) Jason Titley	14/1	1
F	Senor El Betrutti (11-10-12) Carl Llewellyn	100/1	1
F	Art Prince (10-10-0) Dean Gallagher	100/1	1
F	Royal Predica (6-10-4) Glenn Tormey	50/1	1
F	Trinitro (9-10-3) Robert Bellamy	100/1	1
U	Sparky Gayle (10-10-8) Brian Storey	33/1	2
U	Dark Stranger (9-10-1) Tony McCoy	9/1F	3
F	Earthmover (9-10-5) Joe Tizzard	14/1	4
F	Choisty (10-10-0) Robert Widger	50/1	4
F	Red Marauder (10-11-2) Richard Guest	18/1	6
F	Young Kenny (9-12-0) Brendan Powell	14/1	10
U	Druid's Brook (11-10-0) Rupert Wakley	66/1	11
F	The Gopher (11-10-3) Warren Marston	66/1	13
F	Torduff Express (9-10-3) Robert Thornton	50/1	13
U	Merry People (12-10-0) Garret Cotter	40/1	14
P	Listen Timmy (11-11-5) Tony Dobbin	50/1	17
F	Village King (7-10-11) Jim Culloty	50/1	20
F	Flaked Oats (11-10-0) Timmy Murphy	50/1	20
U	Stormy Passage (10-11-3) Andy Thornton	50/1	22
F	Esprit de Cotte (8-10-8) Mick Fitzgerald	50/1	22
F	Buck Rogers (11-11-0) Ken Whelan	50/1	24
P	Star Traveller (9-10-11) Richard Johnson	10/1	27
U	Escartefigue (8-11-9) Jimmy McCarthy	50/1	30

F=Fell, P=Pulled Up, U=Unseated

40 ran
Time: 9:09.70 (Fast by 12.2s)
Winning Owner: Mrs J Maxwell Moran
Winning Breeder: E McCormack
Second Owner: Darren C Mercer
Third Owner: George Dilger

TOTE returns:
Win £13.00 ; Places £2.70, £6.30, £6.40, £9.60;
Exacta £293.30; CSF £224.07; Tricast £5519.81;
Trifecta £20164.80

Total SP 138%

Cheltenham Festival

Capel Cure Sharp Novices' Hurdle

Mar 14	2m 110y	15 ran
Sausalito Bay (6-11-8)	Paul Carberry	14/1
Best Mate (5-11-8)	Jim Culloty	6/1
Youlneverwalkalone (6-11-8)	Conor o'Dwyer	5/4F

Noel Meade (IRL) £46,400

Irish Independent Arkle Challenge Chase

Mar 14	2m	12 ran
Tiutchev (7-11-8)	Mick Fitzgerald	8/1
Cenkos (6-11-8)	David Casey	10/1
Decoupage (8-11-8)	Norman Williamson	7/4F

Nicky Henderson £66,700

Smurfit Champion Hurdle Trophy

Mar 14	2m 110y	12 ran
Istabraq (8-12-0)	Charlie Swan	8/15F
Hors La Loi III (5-12-0)	Dean Gallagher	11/1
Blue Royal (5-12-0)	Mick Fitzgerald	16/1

Aidan O'Brien (IRL) £145,000

William Hill National Hunt Handicap Chase

Mar 16	3m 1f	12 ran
Marlborough (8-10-3)	Mick Fitzgerald	11/2
Beau (7-10-2)	Carl Llewellyn	5/1JF
Star Traveller (9-10-0)	Andrew Thornton	6/1

Nicky Henderson £39,000

Fulke Walwyn Kim Muir Challenge Cup Amateur Handicap Chase

Mar 14	3m 1f	23 ran
Honey Mount (9-9-12)	Robert Walford	8/1
Marching Marquis (9-10-0)	Tom Gibney	33/1
Supreme Charm (8-10-9)	Des Flavin	16/1
Clifton Set (9-9-11)	Ben Hitchcott	20/1

Robert Alner £22,750

Ladbrokes Casinos Handicap Hurdle Final

Mar 14	3m 2f	24 ran
Rubhahunish (9-11-2)	Carl Llewellyn	8/1
Take Five (7-10-0)	Norman Williamson	7/1
Font Romeu (7-10-6)	Barry Fenton	14/1
Darapour (6-10-5)	Charlie Swan	4/1F

Nigel Twiston Davies £29,250

Royal & Sun Alliance Novice Hurdle

Mar 15	2m 5f	14 ran
Monsignor (6-11-7)	Norman Williamson	5/4F
No Discount (6-11-7)	Charlie Swan	20/1
Gentle Rivage (6-11-7)	Tom Jenks	50/1

Mark Pitman £46,400

Queen Mother Champion Chase

Mar 15	2m	9 ran
Edredon Bleu (8-12-0)	Tony McCoy	7/2
Direct Route (9-12-0)	Norman Williamson	5/1
Flagship Uberalles (6-12-0)	Joe Tizzard	11/10F

Henrietta Knight £107,300

Coral Cup Handicap Hurdle

Mar 15	2m 5f	26 ran
What's Up Boys (6-10-3)	Paul Flynn	33/1
Native Dara (7-10-4)	Paul Carberry	25/1
Ross Moff (7-10-3)	Charlie Swan	15/2
Vanilla Man (7-10-0)	Tom Treacy	25/1

Philip Hobbs £39,000

Royal SunAlliance Novices' Chase

Mar 15	3m 1f	9 ran
Lord Noelie (7-11-4)	Jim Culloty	9/2
Alexander Banquet (7-11-4)	Ruby Walsh	9/2
Toto Toscato (6-11-4)	Richard Johnson	11/1

Henrietta Knight £66,700

National Hunt Chase Challenge Cup

Mar 15	4m	21 ran
Relaxation (8-12-0)	Mark Bradburne	8/1
Inch Rose (6-11-13)	Philip Scouller	9/1
Mister One (9-12-7)	J D Moore	11/2

Henry Daly £21,125

Mildmay Of Flete Challenge Cup H'p Chase

Mar 15	2m 4f 110y	18 ran
Dark Stranger (9-10-3)	Richard Johnson	14/1
Native Charm (8-11-0)	Jimmy McCarthy	13/2F
Inn At The Top (8-10-8)	Robbie Supple	7/1
Sir Dante (9-10-7)	Barry Fenton	10/1

Martin Pipe £35,750

Wetherbys Bumper Open NH Flat Race

Mar 15	2m 110y	17 ran
Joe Cullen (5-11-6)	Charlie Swan	14/1
Inca (5-11-6)	Mick Fitzgerald	2/1F
Be My Royal (6-11-6)	J A Nash	16/1

Willie Mullins (IRL) £18,000

Elite Racing Daily Express Triumph Hurdle

Mar 16	2m 1f	28 ran
Snow Drop (4-10-9)	Thierry Doumen	7/1F
Regal Exit (4-11-0)	Barry Geraghty	20/1
General Cloney (4-11-0)	Ruby Walsh	20/1

Francois Doumen (FRA) £46,400

Bonusprint Stayers' Hurdle

Mar 16	3m 110y	10 ran
Bacchanal (6-11-10)	Mick Fitzgerald	11/2
Limestone Lad (8-11-10)	Shane McGovern	3/1
Behrajan (5-11-10)	Richard Johnson	8/1

Nicky Henderson £66,700

Tote Cheltenham Gold Cup Chase

Mar 16	3m 2f 110y	12 ran
Looks Like Trouble (8-12-0)	Richard Johnson	9/2
Florida Pearl (8-12-0)	Ruby Walsh	9/2
Strong Promise (9-12-0)	Robert Thornton	20/1

Noel Chance £162,400

Cheltenham

Continued

Christies Foxhunter Challenge Cup Chase

Mar 16	*3m 2f 110y*	*24 ran*
Cavalero (11-12-0)	Alex Charles-Jones	16/1
Real Value (9-12-0)	Ben Hitchcott	8/1
Trade Dispute (8-12-0)	Grant Tuer	9/1
John Manners £19,500		

Grand Annual Challenge Cup H'cap Chase

Mar 16	*2m 110y*	*16 ran*
Samakaan (7-10-11)	Norman Williamson	9/2F
Green Green Desert (9-10-13)	Joe Tizzard	12/1
Aghawadda Gold (8-11-10)	Russ Garritty	10/1
Clifton Beat (9-10-9)	Richard Johnson	14/1
Venetia Williams £32,500		

Cathcart Challenge Cup Chase

Mar 16	*2m 5f*	*8 ran*
Stormyfairweather (8-11-12)	Mick Fitzgerald	11/2
Fadalko (7-11-3)	Joe Tizzard	10/1
Majadou (6-11-3)	Tony McCoy	4/1
Nicky Henderson £36,000		

Vincent O'Brien County Handicap Hurdle

Mar 16	*2m 1f*	*21 ran*
Master Tern (5-10-3)	Tony Dobbin	9/2F
Danegold (8-10-2)	Timmy Murphy	25/1
Spokesman (6-10-2)	Paul Moloney	10/1
Auetaler (6-11-9)	Rodi Greene	12/1
Jonjo O'Neill £30,000		

Leading Cheltenham Jockeys

Jockey	*1st*	*2nd*	*3rd*
Mick Fitzgerald	4	1	1
Norman Williamson	2	2	1
Richard Johnson	2	-	2
Charlie Swan	2	-	1

Leading Cheltenham Trainers

Trainer	*Winners*
Nicky Henderson	4
Henrietta Knight	2

Overseas

1999/2000 Races

Czech Republic

Velka Pardubicka Ceske Pojistovny Chase
Pardubice, Cze, Oct 10
6yo+ 4m 2f 110y
Peruan (11-10-7)
Zdenek Matysik
Lenka Horakova (Cze)   £34,027

France

Gras Savoye Grand Steeple-Chase de Paris
Auteuil, May 28   3m 5f
Vieux Beaufai (7-10-3)
P Bigot   3.20FF
F Danloux (France)   £134,486

Ireland

Punchestown Chase
Punchestown, Dec 4   2m 4f
Buck Rogers (10-11-8)
Ken Whelan   16/1
Victor Bowens (Ireland)   IR£32,500

Paddy Power Chase
Leopardstown, Dec 27 3m
Inis Cara (7-10-8)
Robbie McNally   11/1
Michael Hourigan (Ireland)
£IR71,250

Ericsson Chase
Leopardstown, Dec 28 3m
Rince Ri (6-12-0)
Conor O'Dwyer   9/2
Ted Walsh (Ireland) £IR49,000

Pierse Leopardstown Handicap Chase
Leopardstown, Jan 8   3m
Buck Rogers (11-11-11)
Ken Whelan   6/1
V ictor Bowens (Ireland) £IR32,500

Ladbroke Handicap Hurdle
Leopardstown, Jan 8   2m
Mantles Prince (6-9-12)
Francis Berry   12/1
Pat Hughes (Ireland) £IR65,300

AIG Champion Hurdle
Leopardstown, Jan 23   2m
Istabraq (8-11-10)
Charlie Swan   2/9F
Aidan O'Brien (Ireland) £IR50,250

Dr P J Moriarty Novices' Chase
Leopardstown, Feb 6 2m 5f
Native Upmanship (7-12-0)
Conor O'Dwyer   9/4JF
Arthur Moore (Ireland) £IR32,500

Hennessy Cognac Gold Cup
Leopardstown, Feb 6 3m
Florida Pearl (8-12-0)
Paul Carberry   8/11F
Willie Mullins (Ireland) £IR67,100

Powers Irish National Handicap Chase
Fairyhouse, Apr 24   3m 5f
Commanche Court (7-11-4)
Ruby Walsh   8/1F
Ted Walsh (Ireland) £IR78,350

Power Gold Cup Chase
Fairyhouse, Apr 25   2m 4f
Native Upmanship (7-11-7)
Conor O'Dwyer   5/4F
Arthur Moore (Ireland) £IR38,850

Power Handicap Hurdle
Fairyhouse, Apr 25   2m 4f
Killultagh Storm (6-9-8)
David Casey   12/1
Willie Mullins (Ireland) £IR48,750

**Country Pride
Champion Novices' Hurdle**
Punchestown, Apr 27 2m
Cardinal Hill (5-11-13)
Charlie Swan   1/2F
N Meade (Ireland)   IR£32,860

BMW Chase
Punchestown, May 2   2m
Get Real (9-11-6)
Mick Fitzgerald   3/1
Nicky Henderson   IR£37,400

**Evening Herald
Champion Novice Hurdle**
Punchestown, May 2 2m
Moscow Flyer (6-12-0)
Barry Geraghty   10/1
*Mrs Jessica Harrington (Ireland)
IR£31,000*

**Stanley Cooker
Champion Novice Hurdle**
Punchestown, May 3 2m 4f
What's Up Boys (6-12-0)
Richard Johnson   6/1
Philip Hobbs   IR£31,000

Heineken Gold Cup Chase
Punchestown, May 3 3m 1f
Commanche Court (7-11-9)
Ruby Walsh   100/30
Ted Walsh (Ireland)   IR£74,400

I.A.W.S Four Year Old Hurdle
Punchestown, May 3 2m
Topacio (4-11-0)
Charlie Swan   10/1
Pat Hughes (Ireland) IR£43,400

**Swordlestown Cup Novices'
Chase**
Punchestown, May 3 2m
Tuitchev (7-11-9)
Mick Fitzgerald   9/10F
Nicky Henderson   IR£31,000

Shell Champion Hurdle
Punchestown, May 5 2m
Grimes (7-11-9)
Charlie Swan   6/1
Christy Roche (Ireland) IR£66,000

**Dave Austin Memorial
Chase (Novices Handicap)**
Punchestown, May 5 3m 1f
Feathered Leather (8-10-12)
Norman Williamson   6/1
Arthur Moore (Ireland) IR£37,200

"He was fantastic, but I'd loved to have been in his slipstream on the Brigadier"

Joe Mercer, the only dissenting voice after Dubai Millennium won the Prince of Wales's Stakes at Ascot by eight lengths. The rest of the world queued up to proclaim the horse the best in the world.

"You don't light a candle towards the sun"

Sheikh Mohammed, in July on the chance of Dubai Millennium taking on Montjeu. The Sheikh had just watched Montjeu's effortless victory in the King George VI and Queen Elizabeth Diamond Stakes at Ascot. Sheikh Mohammed would later agree to the two horses meeting, but Dubai Millennium was injured on the Newmarket gallops on August 5th and the horse was retired.

NATIONAL HUNT 1999-2000

Top Trainers
Listed by Total Money

	1st	2nd	3rd	4th	Total	%	Win Money	Total Money	£1Stake
Martin Pipe	243	119	90	85	903	26.9	1,264,386	1,677,603	+8.86
Paul Nicholls	71	58	47	31	325	21.8	644,248	940,101	-57.22
Philip Hobbs	120	84	65	56	514	23.3	605,295	894,401	+67.13
Nicky Henderson	67	45	41	32	315	21.3	641,371	864,093	-5.33
Nigel Twiston-Davies	87	67	63	47	513	17.0	600,971	835,085	-33.74
Venetia Williams	73	46	37	20	290	25.2	520,758	699,642	-30.14
Mary Reveley	106	71	55	34	439	24.1	416,804	555,644	-20.85
Henrietta Knight	40	34	24	19	222	18.0	388,158	510,533	+12.60
Alan King	27	39	29	22	208	13.0	189,242	412,954	-88.48
Mark Pitman	36	32	30	25	208	17.3	297,183	404,115	-21.32
Henry Daly	38	40	26	29	255	14.9	256,663	390,473	-21.14
Sue Smith	39	32	48	43	318	12.3	272,915	359,375	-65.96
Jonjo O'Neill	44	36	45	24	291	15.1	261,388	344,123	-29.13
Ferdy Murphy	34	26	28	15	200	17.0	226,352	320,037	-31.54
Tom Walsh	1	0	0	0	3	33.3	290,000	290,000	+8.00
Noel Chance	15	8	16	8	78	19.2	238,764	266,498	+38.27
Peter Beaumont	14	29	20	14	159	8.8	109,509	260,847	-70.08
Mick Hammond	37	45	26	36	275	13.5	178,041	250,604	-84.67
Josh Gifford	28	32	36	36	230	12.2	128,915	249,634	-79.34
Charlie Egerton	18	9	10	2	64	28.1	103,574	246,268	+3.97
Oliver Sherwood	23	30	22	12	148	15.5	133,139	237,016	-68.68
Ian Williams	42	28	21	20	234	17.9	185,196	234,484	-20.64
Howard Johnson	19	19	21	15	166	11.4	122,102	233,230	-59.83
Malcolm Jefferson	26	27	13	17	179	14.5	152,388	230,838	+16.68
Paul Webber	29	18	21	19	209	13.9	156,113	222,903	-29.78

Top Jockeys
Listed by races won

		1st	2nd	3rd	4th	Total	%	Win Money	Total Money	£1 Stake
1	Tony McCoy	245	136	91	58	803	30.5	1,329,379	1,737,964	+10.46
2	Richard Johnson	142	154	128	116	858	16.6	1,007,596	1,539,022	-137.81
3	Norman Williamson	123	70	69	49	540	22.8	851,635	1,304,271	-4.68
4	Mick Fitzgerald	107	99	76	58	549	19.5	959,062	1,280,024	-79.04
5	Tony Dobbin	71	39	42	34	406	17.5	359,903	452,451	+4.98
6	Carl Llewellyn	68	55	62	42	469	14.5	481,289	691,151	-93.85
7	Andy Thornton	66	66	58	64	511	12.9	371,358	575,769	-118.22
8	Tim Murphy	64	49	43	66	450	14.2	344,951	532,056	-54.66
9	Adrian Maguire	63	57	68	48	461	13.7	373,546	570,477	-133.77
10	Joe Tizzard	63	59	57	41	400	15.8	394,808	645,377	-110.08
11	Seamus Durack	57	46	37	39	435	13.1	363,877	492,250.	-132.46
12	Dean Gallagher	51	34	34	39	312	16.3	260,623	415,273	+45.61
13	Alan Dempsey	51	36	25	30	276	18.5	208,041	275,764	-66.98
14	Warren Marston	44	44	48	46	440	10.0	171,411	286,973	-115.88
15	Jim Culloty	42	40	27	36	329	12.8	275,017	397,197	-19.55
16	Paul Flynn	41	39	36	35	262	15.6	168,211	258,916	+64.61
17	Barry Fenton	39	46	50	42	386	10.1	187,201	306,802	-148.00
18	Jamie Mogford	39	38	34	36	374	10.4	126,990	196,164	-45.14
19	Brian Harding	39	45	25	35	360	10.8	186,625	270,421	-116.02
20	John Crowley	36	23	38	46	291	12.4	124,033	178,523	+19.82
21	Lorcan Wyer	35	28	22	14	189	18.5	224,054	304,223	-44.54
22	Adie Smith	33	38	41	33	346	9.5	119,231	190,371	-52.02
23	James McCarthy	33	49	32	23	286	11.5	185,534	347,992	-140.96
24	Robbie Supple	32	36	50	29	322	9.9	162,217	331,993	-139.31
25	Philip Hide	32	34	35	35	263	12.2	129,678	251,916	-68.34

Ice Hockey

G reat Britain's ice hockey team have become the nearly men. In April 1999 the team were second in Pool B of the world championships, with only the top team reaching Pool A. In November they had a second chance in the Pool A qualifiers. They came third of four teams after conceding a goal in the last two seconds against Kazakhstan. Even then they could have reached Pool A for the 2000 world championships by beating Norway in a qualifying play-off in Eindhoven. They lost that as well, though, 2-1. Good riddance, 1999.

In 2000, the British team had two objectives. The first, in February, was to try and progress in the qualifying for the 2002 Winter Olympics. The second, in April, was yet another attempt to reach Pool A of the world championships. The squad for the Olympic qualifiers was severely depleted by injuries and because Superleague clubs would not agree to release players or postpone fixtures, the national side used British National League players to make up the squad numbers. It was no surprise, then, that Britain fell short. After beating Romania, narrow defeats by the French hosts and Poland ended the Olympic dream for another four years.

As for the world championships, Britain were undone in their first game. A 6-5 defeat by Estonia was the worst possible start. In following that up with a 3-3 draw with Slovenia, who finished seventh of the eight teams, they looked to have killed off their chances. But lost causes are always great motivators (see also hockey and cricket sections) and Britain bounced back with a 9-0 defeat of the hapless Dutch team, backing that victory up with wins over Poland, Denmark and Kazakhstan, to put them in sight of the top table. The Germans, as the hosts of 2001 would have qualified anyway, but Britain needed to finish top in order to get promoted, which meant beating the Germans. However, it was not to be. Britain stumbled badly at the final hurdle, a hefty 5-0 defeat by the Germans condemning them to another year in Pool B.

The British coach Peter Woods left his position in June, to be replaced by Chris McSorley, the man who coached London Knights to the Superleague play-off title. McSorley had made news earlier in the year, pledging to sign his brother Marty for the Knights. Marty, while playing for the Boston Bruins, had received the longest suspension in NHL history - 23 games - for on-ice violence and was later convicted by a Vancouver court for assault with a weapon. Maybe it wasn't such a good pledge, after all.

The Stanley Cup in 2000 went to the New Jersey Devils, who beat the defending champions the Dallas Stars 4-2 in the best-of-seven series. It was the second Stanley Cup for the team, the first coming in 1995. In the sixth game Jason Arnott's goal in the second period of sudden-death overtime clinched victory.

In Pool A of the world championships, the Czech Republic won a second consecutive title. The Czechs only blip came in the second phase, when they lost to Finland 6-4. It did not matter as they still comfortably qualified for the semi-finals, where they beat Canada. In the final, they defeated the Slovakians, who would once have been their teammates, 5-3.

World Championship
St Petersburg, Russia   April 29-May 16

Pool A

The top three teams in Groups A & D, qualify for Group E.The top three in B & C qualify for Group F. In Groups E & F, teams play the three teams they have not yet played, whilst carrying forward the points from the games against the teams they already have played. Apparently. The top four of the six team Groups E & F, go forward to the quarter-finals where normality is restored. As for the bottom teams from Groups A-D, well, they play in Group G. The bottom two in that final Group get relegated from Pool A of the world championships. Enjoy.

Group A
Belarus 7 Ukraine 3; Latvia 1 Sweden 3; Belarus 3 Latvia 6; Sweden 7 Ukraine 2; Ukraine 1 Latvia 2; Sweden 7 Belarus 0

Standings	P	W	D	L	GF	GA	Pts
1 Sweden	3	3	0	0	17	3	6
2 Latvia	3	2	0	1	9	7	4
3 Belarus	3	1	0	2	10	16	2
4 Ukraine	3	0	0	3	6	16	0

Group B
Slovakia 2 Austria 0; Italy 0 Finland 6; Slovakia 6 Italy 2; Finland 3 Austria 3; Austria 0 Italy 3; Finland 2 Slovakia 2

Standings	P	W	D	L	GF	GA	Pts
1 Slovakia	3	2	1	0	10	4	5
2 Finland	3	1	2	0	11	5	4
3 Italy	3	1	0	2	5	12	2
4 Austria	3	0	1	2	3	8	1

Group C
Canada 6 Japan 0; Norway 0 Czech Republic 4; Czech Republic 6 Japan 3; Canada 3 Norway 4; Japan 0 Norway 9; Czech Republic 2 Canada 1

Standings	P	W	D	L	GF	GA	Pts
1 Czech Republic	3	3	0	0	12	4	6
2 Norway	3	2	0	1	13	7	4
3 Canada	3	1	0	2	10	6	2
4 Japan	3	0	0	3	3	21	0

Group D
USA 3 Switzerland 3; Russia 8 France 1; Switzerland 2 France 4; Russia 0 USA 3; France 2 USA 3; Switzerland 3 Russia 2

Standings	P	W	D	L	GF	GA	Pts
1 USA	3	2	1	0	9	5	5
2 Switzerland	3	1	1	1	8	9	3
3 Russia	3	1	1	1	10	7	2
4 France	3	1	0	2	7	13	2

Group E
Sweden 2 Russia 4; Sweden 1 Switzerland 1; USA 1 Belarus 0; Latvia 3 Russia 2; Switzerland 3 Belarus 5; Sweden 3 USA 5; Latvia 1 Switzerland 4; USA 1 Latvia 1; Russia 0 Belarus 1

Standings	P	W	D	L	GF	GA	Pts
1 USA	5	3	2	0	13	7	8
2 Switzerland	5	2	2	1	14	12	6
3 Sweden	5	2	1	2	16	11	5
4 Latvia	5	2	1	2	12	13	5
5 Belarus	5	2	0	3	9	17	4
6 Russia	5	1	0	4	8	12	2

Group F
Slovakia 3 Canada 4; Finland 1 Canada 5; Czech Republic 4 Finland 6; Slovakia 9 Norway 1; Norway 4 Finland 7; Czech Republic 9 Italy 2; Norway 1 Italy 1; Czech Republic 6 Slovakia 2; Canada 6 Italy 0

Standings	P	W	D	L	GF	GA	Pts
1 Czech Republic	5	4	0	1	25	11	8
2 Finland	5	3	1	1	22	15	7
3 Canada	5	3	0	2	19	10	6
4 Slovakia	5	2	1	2	22	15	5
5 Norway	5	1	1	3	10	24	3
6 Italy	5	0	1	4	5	28	1

Group G - Losers' Round
Playoff for places 13 to 16
Ukraine 4 Japan 0; France 7 Japan 2; Austria 3 Ukraine 2; Austria 5 Japan 3; France 2 Ukraine 3; France 3 Austria 3

Standings	P	W	D	L	GF	GA	Pts
13 Austria	3	2	1	0	11	8	5
14 Ukraine	3	2	0	1	9	5	4
15 France	3	1	1	1	12	8	3
16 Japan	3	0	0	3	5	16	0

France relegated and Japan goes to Far East qualifying pool.

Quarter-finals
USA 1 Slovakia 4; Finland 2 Sweden 1; Switzerland 3 Canada 5; Czech Republic 3 Latvia 1

Semi-finals
Canada 1 Czech Republic 2; Slovakia 3 Finland 1

Play-off for 3rd/4th place
Canada 1 Finland 2

FINAL
Slovakia 3 Czech Republic 5

Pool B
Katowice, Poland   Apr 12-21

Great Britain 5 Estonia 6; Germany 7 Slovenia 2; Netherlands 3 Kazakhstan 5; Denmark 3 Poland 3; Slovenia 3 Great Britain 3; Germany 5 Netherlands 1; Estonia 0 Denmark 4; Kazakhstan 5 Poland 2; Great Britain 9 Netherlands 0; Denmark 4 Slovenia 2; Kazakhstan 4 Estonia 2; Germany 2 Poland 6; Slovenia 4 Kazakhstan 9; Estonia 2 Germany 3; Denmark 2 Netherlands 2; Poland 4 Great Britain 6; Netherlands 2 Slovenia 2; Kazakhstan 2 Germany 5; Denmark 4 Great Britain 5; Estonia 1 Poland 5; Great Britain 3 Kazakhstan 1; Germany 3 Denmark 2; Netherlands 4 Estonia 3; Poland 3 Slovenia 1; Slovenia 2 Estonia 3; Great Britain 0 Germany 5; Kazakhstan 4 Denmark 3; Poland 5 Netherlands 1

Standings	P	W	D	L	GF	GA	Pts
1 Germany	7	6	0	1	30	15	12
2 Kazakhstan	7	5	0	2	30	22	10
3 Great Britain	7	4	1	2	28	19	9
4 Poland	7	4	1	2	28	19	9
5 Denmark	7	2	2	3	22	19	6
6 Estonia	7	3	0	4	19	27	6
7 Slovenia	7	0	2	5	16	31	2
8 Netherlands	7	0	2	5	13	33	2

Germany promoted to pool A

2002 Olympic Pre-qualifying tournament

Gdansk, Poland   *Feb 10-13*

Group Three

Great Britain 4 Romania 0; Poland 2 France 5; France 9 Romania 1; Great Britain 2 Poland 4; France 5 Great Britain 4; Romania 2 Poland 11

Standings	P	W	D	L	GF	GA	Pts
1 France	3	3	0	0	19	7	6
2 Poland	3	2	0	1	17	9	4
3 Great Britain	3	1	0	2	10	9	2
4 Romania	3	0	0	3	3	24	0

France progress to the final qualifying round

Women's World Championship 2000

Canada   *April 3-9*

Group A

Sweden 1 China 1; Japan 0 Canada 9; Sweden 10 Japan 0; Canada 8 China 1; China 3 Japan 0; Canada 4 Sweden 0

Standings	P	W	D	L	GF	GA	Pts
1 Canada	3	3	0	0	21	1	6
2 Sweden	3	1	1	1	11	5	3
3 China	3	1	1	1	5	9	3
4 Japan	3	0	0	3	0	22	0

Group B

Finland 7 Russia 1; Germany 1 USA 16; Finland 4 Germany 1; USA 15 Russia 0; Russia 7 Germany 2; USA 4 Finland 3

Standings	P	W	D	L	GF	GA	Pts
1 USA	3	3	0	0	35	4	6
2 Finland	3	2	0	1	14	6	4
3 Russia	3	1	0	2	8	24	2
4 Germany	3	0	0	3	4	27	0

5th-8th Play-off matches

China 3 Germany 0; Russia 8 Japan 4

7th/8th place Play-off

Japan 2 Germany 3

5th/6th place Play-off

China 0 Russia 4

Semi-finals

Canada 3 Finland 2; USA 7 Sweden 1

Play-off for 3rd/4th place

Finland 7 Sweden 1

Final

United States 2 Canada 3

Pool B

Final Standings

1. Kazakhstan; 2. Switzerland; 3. Norway; 4. Denmark; 5. France; 6. Latvia; 7. Czech Republic; 8. Italy

Kazakhstan promoted to pool A

Italy relegated to pool B qualification

Pool B qualification

Final Standings

1. North Korea; 2. Slovakia; 3. Great Britain; 4. Belgium; 5. Netherlands; 6. Hungary; 7. Australia; 8. South Africa

Korea qualify for pool B

Domestic Leagues

Sekonda Superleague

	P	W	L	D	GF	GA	Pts
1 Bracknell Bees	42	24	15	3	181	138	56
2 Sheffield Steelers	42	24	16	2	188	155	52
3 Manchester Storm	42	23	17	2	155	138	51
4 London Knights	42	23	16	3	135	125	50
5 Ayr Scottish Eagles	42	17	20	5	144	147	43
6 Nottingham Panthers	42	18	21	3	140	165	40
7 Cardiff Devils	42	17	21	4	138	149	40
8 Newcastle Riverkings	42	11	31	0	113	177	24

Teams get an extra point for overtime losses.

Superleague Play-offs

Manchester   *Mar 1-28*

Group A Final Standings

1 London Knights	6	5	1	0	28	14	10
2 Newcastle Riverkings	6	3	2	1	14	12	9
3 Bracknell Bees	6	3	2	1	22	19	7
4 Nottingham Panthers	6	0	6	0	7	26	1

Group B Final Standings

1 Sheffield Steelers	6	4	0	2	26	14	10
2 Ayr Scottish Eagles	6	2	3	1	12	19	6
3 Cardiff Devils	6	2	3	1	15	16	5
4 Manchester Storm	6	1	3	2	12	16	5

Semi-Finals

Newcastle Riverkings 3 Sheffield Steelers 1

London Knights 2 Ayr Scottish Eagles 1 overtime

SEKONDA SUPERLEAGUE PLAY-OFF FINAL

London Knights 7 Newcastle Riverkings 3

Challenge Cup

Nottingham Panthers 1 Sheffield Steelers 2

Benson & Hedges Cup

Manchester Storm 3 London Knights 3 overtime

Manchester won 1-0 on penalty shots

British National League

	P	W	L	GF	GA	Pts
1 Fife Flyers	36	29	7	176	89	58
2 Guildford Flames	36	27	9	185	99	56
3 Basingstoke Bison	36	25	11	139	85	50
4 Hull Thunder	36	23	12	149	132	47
5 Peterborough Pirates	36	23	13	171	128	46
6 Slough Jets	36	19	17	109	100	41
7 Solihull Blaze	36	14	22	161	172	30
8 Edinburgh Capitals	36	10	26	118	192	21
9 Milton Keynes Kings	36	5	31	114	202	13
10 Paisley Pirates	36	5	31	103	226	11

British National League Play-off Final

Fife Flyers bt Basingstoke Bison three games to zero

English Premier League

	P	W	D	L	GF	GA	Pts
1 Chelmsford Chieftains	24	19	1	4	144	90	39
2 Isle of Wight Raiders	24	13	3	8	141	103	29
3 Swindon Chill	24	10	1	13	90	111	21
4 Invicta Dynamoes	24	8	3	13	117	138	19
5 Romford Raiders	24	5	2	17	83	133	12

English Premier League Play-off Final (aggregate)

Chelmsford Chieftians 7 Swindon Chill 4

National Hockey League

Eastern Conference

NORTHEAST DIVISION	P	W	L	T	Pts
Toronto Maple Leafs	82	45	7	27	100
Ottawa Senators	82	41	11	28	95
Buffalo Sabres	82	35	11	32	85
Montreal Canadiens	82	35	9	34	83
Boston Bruins	82	24	19	33	73

ATLANTIC DIVISION	P	W	L	T	Pts
Philadelphia Flyers	82	45	12	22	105
New Jersey Devils	82	45	8	24	103
Pittsburgh Penguins	82	37	8	6	88
New York Rangers	82	29	12	3	73
New York Islanders	82	24	9	1	58

SOUTHEAST DIVISION	P	W	L	T	Pts
Washington Capitals	82	44	12	24	102
Florida Panthers	82	43	6	27	98
Carolina Hurricanes	82	37	10	35	84
Tampa Bay Lightening	82	19	9	47	54
Atlanta Thrashers	82	14	7	57	39

Western Conference

CENTRAL DIVISION	P	W	L	T	Pts
St. Louis Blues	82	51	11	19	114
Detroit Red Wings	82	48	10	22	108
Chicago Blackhawks	82	33	10	37	78
Nashville Predators	82	28	7	40	70

PACIFIC DIVISION	P	W	L	T	Pts
Dallas Stars	82	43	10	23	102
Los Angeles Kings	82	39	12	27	94
Phoenix Coyotes	82	39	8	31	90
San Jose Sharks	82	35	10	30	87
Mighty Ducks of Anaheim	82	34	12	33	83

NORTHWEST DIVISION	P	W	L	T	Pts
Colorado Avalanche	82	42	11	28	96
Edmonton Oilers	82	32	16	26	88
Vancouver Canucks	82	30	15	29	83
Calgary Flames	82	31	10	36	77

Conference Quarter-finals

EASTERN CONFERENCE *(Best of 7 Series)*
Philadelphia Flyers bt Buffalo Sabres 4-1
Pittsburgh Penguins bt Washington Capitals 4-1
New Jersey Devils bt Florida Panthers 4-0
Toronto Maple Leafs bt Ottowa Senators 4-2

WESTERN CONFERENCE *(Best of 7 Series)*
Colorado Avalanche bt Phoenix Coyotes 4-1
Detroit Red Wings bt Los Angeles Kings 4-0
Dallas Stars bt Edmonton Oilers 4-1
San Jose Sharks bt St Louis Blues 4-3

Conference Semi-finals

EASTERN CONFERENCE
Philadelphia Flyers bt Pittsburgh Penguins 4-2
New Jersey Devils bt Toronto Maple Leafs 4-2

WESTERN CONFERENCE
Dallas Stars bt San Jose Sharks 4-1
Colorado Avalanche bt Detroit Red Wings 4-1

Conference Finals
EASTERN DIVISION
Philadelphia Flyers bt New Jersey 4-3
WESTERN DIVISION
Dallas Stars bt Colorado Avalanche 4-3

NHL Stanley Cup Championship
Best of 7 series
Game 1: Dallas Stars 3 New Jersey Devils 7
Game 2: Dallas Stars 2 New Jersey Devils 1
Game 3: New Jersey Devils 2 Dallas Stars 1
Game 4: New Jersey Devils 3 Dallas Stars 1
Game 5: Dallas Stars 1 New Jersey Devils 0
Game 6: New Jersey Devils 2 Dallas Stars 1

New Jersey Devils won the Stanley Cup 4-2

NHL Leading Scorers

Goals score two points, assists a single point

	Player	Team	GP	G	A	Pts
1	Jaromir Jagr	Pittsburgh	63	42	54	96
2	Pavel Bure	Florida	74	58	36	94
3	Mark Recch	Philadelphia	82	28	63	91
4	Paul Kariya	Anaheim	74	42	44	86
5	Tony Amonte	Chicago	82	43	42	85
6	Teemu Selanne	Anaheim	79	33	52	85
7	Owen Nolan	San Jose	78	44	40	84
8	Joe Sakic	Colorado	60	28	54	82
9	Mike Modano	Dallas	77	38	43	81
10	Steve Yzerman	Detroit	78	35	44	79
11	B Shanahan	Detroit	78	41	37	78
12	Jeremy Roenick	Phoenix	75	34	44	78
13	John Leclair	Philadelphia	82	40	37	77
14	Valeri Bure	Calgary	82	35	40	75
15	Pavol Demitra	St Louis	71	28	47	75
16	Luc Robitaille	Los Angeles	71	36	37	73
17	Mats Sundin	Toronto	73	32	41	73
18	Doug Gilmour	Buffalo	74	25	48	73
19	Nicklas Lidstrom	Detroit	81	20	53	73
20	Milan Hejduk	Colorado	82	36	36	72

NHL Leading Goaltenders

In order of percentage of shots saved,
then average goals conceded. 10 games+

	Player	Team	GP	Av	%S
1	Manny Fernandez	Dallas	24	2.13	.920
2	Ed Belfour	Dallas	62	2.10	.919
3	Jose Theodore	Montreal	30	2.10	.919
4	Dominik Hasek	Buffalo	35	2.21	.919
5	Mike Vernon	Florida	49	2.47	.919
6	Brian Boucher	Philadelphia	35	1.91	.918
7	Olaf Kolzig	Washington	73	2.24	.917
8	Marc Denis	Colorado	23	2.54	.917
9	Curtis Joesph	Toronto	63	2.49	.915
10	Trevor Kidd	Florida	28	2.63	.915

Ice Skating

Life was generally predictable on the ice; Michelle Kwan won her third world title in five years; Russia's Alexei Yagudin won his third in three years; and British skaters were nowhere to be seen, not even in the distance. In Nice, Matthew Davies was 29th and Tamsin Sear finished 37th. We did wonder if this was the worst-ever British performance in the individual events at a world championships, but a quick check on the previous year's results showed that Clive Shorten was the top man in 31st place and there was no British woman. So, the Nice results were just business as usual.

"The reason we are in this predicament is not because of this year or even the last five years. While Britain reflected on its history, and it was a glorious history, the rest of the world evolved. It's only now that it's starting to change," said Andre Bourgeois, the performance director of British skating, whose benchmark for success is to produce homegrown talent. "John Curry and Robin Cousins had to leave the country to win Olympic titles, and even Torvill and Dean had to go to Germany when they made their comeback in 1994," he pointed out. It remains ironic that the Lottery has funded the Nottingham ice rink to the tune of £22m, but for the season 2000-2001 not a single British skater will be funded to use it. Young skaters like Alan Street are making progress, but the Salt Lake City Games will come far too soon for the younger brigade of skaters.

In ice dancing, there were new world champions, the French couple Marina Anissina and Gwendal Peizerat, who were thought unfortunate to have finished second to the Russians Anjelika Krylova and Oleg Ovsyannikov, a year earlier. Krylova's neck and back injuries had forced her into retirement leaving the way clear for the French. Julie Keeble and Lukasz Zalewski finished 21st, the highest British placing at the championships.

In the pairs, there was controversy, when the Russians Elena Berezhnaya and Anton Sikharulidze withdrew after Berezhnaya tested positive for a banned stimulant. Their compatriots, Maria Petrova and Alexei Tikhonov took the title in their absence after finishing second to them in Vienna.

> **"They gave Mike Tyson a second chance and he was convicted of rape. Why can't I get a second chance?"**
>
> Tonya Harding attempting a comeback after five-and-a-half years.

> **"I've tried some of the moves Torvill and Dean made look so easy and believe me, if things go wrong, you could kill yourself"**
>
> Gary Hoppe, coach to the British ice dance champions, Julie Keeble and Lukasz Zalewski.

> **"Pitiful I would say. It's at the lowest of the low. Not through lack of effort, but through lack of cohesion"**
>
> Robin Cousins.

World Championships
Nice   *Mar 23-Apr 3*

ICE DANCING
Four elements; two compulsory, original and free dances

			Pts
1	Marina Anissina	FRA	2.6
	Gwendal Peizerat		
2	Babara Fusar-Poli	ITA	3.4
	Maurizio Margaglio		
3	Margarita Drobiazko	CAN	7.0
	Povilas Vanagas		
21	Julie Keeble	GBR	44.2
	Lukacz Zalewski		

PAIRS
Two elements; technical & free-skating

1	Maria Petrova	RUS	2.0
	Alexei Tikhonov		
2	Shen Xue	CHN	2.5
	Zhao Hongbo		
3	Sarah Abitbol	FRA	5.0
	Stephane Bernadis		

FIGURE SKATING
Men
Two elements; technical & free-skating

1	Alexei Yagudin	RUS	2.0
2	Elvis Stojko	CAN	5.4
3	Michael Weiss	USA	5.6
29	Matthew Davies	GBR	

Women

1	Michelle Kwan	USA	2.0
2	Irina Slutskaya	RUS	3.6
3	Maria Butyrskaya	RUS	4.0
37	Tamsin Sear	GBR	

European Championships
Vienna   *Feb 6-13*

Ice Dancing

1	Marina Anissina	FRA	2.0
	Gwendal Peizerat		
2	Barbara Fusar-Poli	ITA	4.0
	Maurizio Maragalio		
3	Margarita Drobiazko	LTU	6.8
	Povilas Vanagas		
16	Julie Keeble	GBR	32.0
	Lukacz Zalewski		

Pairs

1	Elena Berezhnaya	RUS	2.0
	Anton Sikharulidze		
2	Maria Petrova	POL	2.5
	Alexei Tikhonov		
3	Dorota Zagorska	POL	4.5
	Mariusz Siudek		

FIGURE SKATING
Men

1	Evgeny Plushenko	RUS	2.6
2	Alexei Yagudin	RUS	3.0
3	Dmitri Dmitrenko	RUS	5.6
18	Matthew Davies	GBR	32.8

Women

1	Irina Slutskaya	RUS	2.0
2	Maria Butyrskaya	RUS	4.8
3	Viktoria Volchkova	RUS	6.0
23	Tamsin Sear	GBR	41.0

Grand Prix Final
Lyon   *Jan 14-16*

ICE DANCING

1	Marina Anissina/Gwendal Peizerat	FRA
2	Barbara Fusi-Poli/Maurisio Margaglio	ITA
3	Margarita Drobiazko / Povilas Vanagas	LTU

PAIRS

1	Shen Xue/Zhao Hongbo	CHN
2	Sarah Abitol/Stéphane Bernadis	FRA
3	Elena Berezhnaya/Anton Sikharulidze	RUS

FIGURE SKATING
Men

1	Evgeny Plushenko	RUS
2	Elvis Stojko	CAN
3	Timothy Gabel	USA

Women

1	Irina Slutskaya	RUS
2	Michelle Kwan	USA
3	Maria Butyrskaya	RUS

Synchronised World Championships
Minneapolis   *Apr 5-8*

1	Sweden	1.5
2	Canada	3.0
3	Finland	4.5
15	Great Britain	23.5

British Championships
Belfast   *Nov 11-14, 1999*

Ice Dance: Julie Keeble/Lukacz Zalewski
Pairs: Sarah Kemp/Daniel Thomas
Men: Neil Wilson
Women: Tamsin Sear

Judo

Kate Howey has never won an Olympic title, but she hasn't missed out on much else. In a senior career that has now spanned 10 years, Howey has won medals at 12 different major championships. In Sydney, she saved the reputation of British judo by winning silver, as she had three years earlier at the world championships in Paris. On that occasion, the British judo team was still reeling from the effects of a disastrous Atlanta Games. The first tranches of Lottery money were just being allocated and there was nothing more important to the federation than a world title. Howey obliged.

In Sydney the Atlanta nightmares were lurking. Vicki Dunn, the first Briton to fight, at least won a bout, though successive defeats in the main draw and repechage halted her challenge. John Buchanan had one fight and one defeat, against the Spaniard Oscar Penas, and by the end of day one, the British score read fought four, lost three. It was the kind of dodgy start you could easily have recovered from, except backstage another drama was unfolding that would match any from Atlanta.

Debbie Allan had no time to sleep on Monday night, but it didn't halt the nightmare. She was on the scales before five o'clock on Tuesday morning desperately praying that a couple of pounds of excess weight that she was carrying had been worried away. No such luck. She worried some more, sweated some more, cut off her hair, took off her clothes and all to no avail. When the deadline came at 8 am, the 25-year-old was 50gms above the limit. She was out without having stepped on the mat.

A sub-plot emerged; that the official testing scales had been tampered with. Allan, argued British Judo, was the injured innocent. There was outrage and indignation, and blame was peppered in all directions. But times had changed. In the age of professional sport, there are no innocents, responsibility stops at your own door. Mark Earle, Allan's coach, would later accept this, tendering his resignation to the BJA. And poor Allan, having qualified for the Games by courageously contesting her last bout at the Birmingham world championships with only one good arm, never got the chance to fight in Sydney with two.

While Allan lamented David Somerville won a single bout on Monday. On Tuesday, Cheryl Peel was tumbled out in her first fight by the Japanese Kie Kusakabe. On Wednesday, it got worse. Graeme Randall was one of only three reigning world champions in the British Olympic team (Colin Jackson and coxless four were the others) and his rapid dismissal of the Tunisian Abdessalem Arous in his first fight augured well. In his second bout, Randall was coasting, when his sharply-honed instincts suddenly failed him. As T S Eliot once said, between the essence and the existence falls the shadow, and Randall was caught in it. He dwelt in inactivity not once, but three times, earning penalties for each, losing a bout he was easily winning.

Karen Roberts won one bout the same day, albeit a fine result against the Cuban Kenia Gonzalez. Chloe Cowen would win only once on Friday; Karina Bryant just the once on Saturday. Thank goodness for Howey on Thursday.

European Championships

Wroclaw, Poland   May 18-22
British fighters shown if they finished in the top eight

Men

-60Kg

1	Elchin Ismaylov	AZE
2	Eric Despezelle	FRA
3	Cedric Taymans	BEL
3	Nestor Khergiani	GEO
5	John Buchanan	GBR

-66Kg

1	Patrick Van Kalken	NED
2	Jozsef Csak	HUN
3	Gueorgui Gueourguiev	BUL
3	Girolamo Giovinazzo	ITA

-73Kg

1	Michel Almeida	POR
2	Vitali Makarov	RUS
3	Georgi Revazishvili	GEO
3	Ferrid Kheder	FRA

-81kg

1	Sergei Ashwanden	SUI
2	Ricardo Martin	ESP
3	Aleksei Budolin	EST
3	Robert Krawczyk	POL

-90kg

1	Adrian Croitoru	ROM
2	Mark Huizinga	NED
3	Rassoul Salimov	AZE
3	Ruslan Mashurenko	UKR

-100kg

1	Yuri Stepkine	RUS
2	Daniel Gurschner	GER
3	Iveri Jikarauli	GEO
3	Franz Birkfellner	AUT

+100kg

1	Dennis Van Der Geest	NED
2	Tamerlan Tmenov	RUS
3	Ernesto Perez-Lobo	ESP
3	Frank Moller	GER

Women

-48Kg

1	Laura Moise	ROM
2	Lioubov Brouletova	RUS
3	Sarah Nichilo-Rosso	FRA
3	Julia Matijass	GER

-52Kg

1	Laetitia Tignola	FRA
2	Georgina Singleton	GBR
3	Ioana Dinea	ROM
3	Deborah Gravenstijn	NED

-57Kg

1	Barbara Harel	FRA
2	Pernilla Andersson	SWE
3	Micaela Vernerova	CZE
3	Jessica Gal	NED
5	Jennifer Brien	GBR

-63kg

1	Gella Vandencaveye	BEL
2	Severine Vandenhende	FRA
3	Sara Alvarez-Menendez	ESP
3	Anna Saraeva	RUS

-70kg

1	Ursula Martin	ESP
2	Kate Howey	GBR
3	Ulla Werbrouck	BEL
3	Ylenia Scapin	ITA

-78kg

1	Celine Lebrun	FRA
2	Chloe Cowen	GBR
3	Uta Kuhnen	GER
3	Anastasia Matrosova	UKR

+78kg

1	Karina Bryant	GBR
2	Irina Rodina	RUS
3	Johanna Hagn	GER
3	Christine Cicot	FRA

European Team Championships

Aalst, Belgium   Nov 18-19

Men

Final Standings

1. France; 2. Great Britain; 3= Belgium; 3= Germany 5= Netherlands; 5= Romania

Final

France bt Great Britain 5-2
-60kg: James Johnson beat Eric Despezelle
-66kg: James Warren beat Laurent Cormao
-73kg: Eric Bonti lost to Daniel Fernandes
-81kg: Luke Preston lost to Andre Allard
-90kg: Winston Gordon lost to Frederi Demontfaucon
-100kg: Keith Davis lost to Ghislain Lemaire
+100kg: Robert Stilwell lost to Jerome Dreyfus

Women

Final Standings

1. France; 2. Romania; 3= Belgium; 3= Netherlands; 5= Great Britain; 5= Russia

Paris 'A' Tournament
Paris   Feb 12-13

Men

-60kg

1	Tadahiro Nomura	JPN
2	Manoulo Poulot	CUB
3	Yacine Douma	FRA
3	Denilson Lourenco	BRA

-66kg

1	Yordanis Arenciba	CUB
2	Franck Bellard	FRA
3	Javier Delgado	ESP
3	Amar Meridja	ALG

-73kg

1	Ferrid Kheder	FRA
2	Thiago Camilo	BRA
3	Christophe Gagliano	FRA
3	Christophe Massina	FRA

-81kg

1	Maarten Arens	NED
2	Djamel Bouras	FRA
3	Ryuichi Murata	JPN
3	Alexeksei Budolin	EST

-90kg

1	Frederic Demontfaucon	FRA
2	Yosvane Despaigne	CUB
3	Kamol Muradov	UZB
3	Keith Morgan	CAN

-100kg

1	Kosei Inoue	JPN
2	Stephane Traineau	FRA
3	Armen Bagdasarov	UZB
3	Pawel Nastula	POL

+100kg

1	Yasuyuki Muneta	JPN
2	Angel Sanchez	CUB
3	Eric Krieger	AUT
3	Indrek Pertelson	EST

Women

-48kg

1	Atsuku Nagai	JPN
2	Frederique Jossinet	FRA
3	Huang Lihong	CHI
3	Amarilis Savon	CUB

-52kg

1	Liu Yuxiang	CHI
2	Legna Verdecia	CUB
3	Oxana Karzakova	RUS
3	Kim Hye-Suk	KOR

-57kg

1	Magali Baton	FRA
2	Isabelle Fernandez	ESP
3	Driulis Gonzalez	CUB
3	Kim Hwa-Soo	KOR

-63kg

1	Jung Sung-Sook	KOR
2	Severine Vandenhende	FRA
3	Gella Vandecaveye	BEL
3	Nami Kimoto	JPN

-70kg

1	Ulla Werbrouck	BEL
2	Cho Min-Sun	KOR
3	Claudia Zwiers	NED
3	Elena Kotelnikova	RUS

-78kg

1	Edinanci F Silva	BRA
2	Mizuko Matsuzaki	JPN
3	Michelle Rogers	GBR
3	Celine Lebrun	FRA

+78kg

1	Yuan Hua	CHI
2	Sandra Koppen	GER
3	Mayumi Yamashita	JPN
3	Daima Beltran	CUB

British Open
Birmingham   Apr 15-16

Men

-60kg

1	Takeshi Ogawa	JPN
2	John Buchanan	GBR
3	Amine Benabeloumed	FRA
3	David Johnson	GBR

-66kg

1	Gregory Leroux	FRA
2	Stephane Biez	FRA
3	Ludovic Bimont	FRA
3	Hirano Yukihide	JPN

-73kg

1	Lee Burbridge	GBR
2	Ian Francis	GBR
3	José-Leon Ruiz	ESR
3	Daniel Hawkins	GBR

-81kg

1	Alvaro-S Paseiro	URU
2	Luke Preston	GBR
3	Darren Warner	GBR
3	Aeron Cohen	USA

-90kg

1	Peter Cousins	GBR
2	Steven Vidler	GBR
3	Nedy Girard	FRA
3	Chrystian Lorsei	FRA

-100kg

1	Alexander Borderieux	FRA
2	Sebastien Guagenti	FRA
3	Keith Davies	GBR
3	Ato-V Hand	USA

+100kg

1	Takaiwa Isao	JPN
2	Nacanieli Takayawa	VEN
3	Jeroen Tammeling	NED
3	Robert Stilwell	GBR

Women

-48kg

1	Fiona Robertson	GBR
2	Nathalie Lepage	FRA
3	Elise Summers	GBR
3	Birte Siemens	GER

-52kg

1	Georgina Singleton	GBR
2	Virgine Marte	FRA
3	Matilde Sevestre	FRA
3	Myriam Boccieri	FRA

-57kg

1	Debbie Allan	GBR
2	Karine Paillard	FRA
3	Jennifer Brien	GBR
3	Alexa von Schichow	GER

-63kg

1	Gemma Hutchins	GBR
2	Karen Roberts	GBR
3	Orit Baron	ISR
3	Celita Schutz	USA

-70kg

1	Kate Howey	GBR
2	Rachel Wilding	GBR
3	Amanda Costello	GBR
3	Yvonne Wansart	GBR

-78kg

1	Barbara Telle	FRA
2	Joanna Melen	GBR
3	Cindy Sneevliet	NED
3	Aurelia Javault	FRA

+78kg

1	Karina Bryant	GBR
2	Simone Callender	GBR
3	Daniela Lodahl	GER
3	Marit Papenhousen	GER

Modern Pentathlon

For the first time ever, there was no British entry in the men's pentathlon events at the Olympic Games. Richard Phelps had flown the flag for the past four, but even he could not perpetually withstand the ravages of time. So it was down to the women, who were at the Olympics for the first time, their event having been exchanged for the men's team event, though the UIPM (the governing body) hadn't meant it to be that way.

The inclusion of the women's event was always good news for Britain, but even at the end of a fortnight when just about every other British plan had worked to perfection, it was still hard to envisage it would be quite that good. Stephanie Cook was some way short of a sure thing. Nobody disputed that the doctor could run, but while she might be a dapper hand with a suture needle, she is decidedly less assured with an épée. In short, Cook is a dodgy fencer and with that event being the second of the five, the 28-year-old needed not just to be close to her best in the other events, but could also be dependent on others' failings.

Cook kept up her standards, swimming her fastest-ever time, but was still only ranked 14th overall behind the Russian Elizaveta Suvorova after three events. If there was a moment when Cook needed a little help, it came in the riding. Good and bad horsewomen come unstuck and Suvorova can thank the mulish Riverina for the end of her Olympic hopes. The horse didn't like the look of either the second or the third obstacle, and Suvorova could do nothing. The lead went to the American Emily deRiel, who knew only too well (having been to Oxford with Cook) that 49 points was nowhere near enough of a lead.

Both the run and ride took place in the Baseball Stadium in Olympic Park. It was ideal for the ride - sharp turns make showjumping a truer test of control. For the run, however, it was like a primary school sports day, with the running path interlacing itself so many times that it was impossible to sustain pace and almost impossible for the spectators to follow. There was a slight worry that the tortuous route might militate against Cook, who was by some distance the best runner in the field, but the anxiety was short-lived.

Cook had seven women start before her (the athletes starting according to their points scores so first past the post would be the winner) and made up the ground so quickly that the flags were out almost before the end of the first kilometre. Kate Allenby, who had started the run in third place, looked to be treading water as Cook passed, but it was only relative and she would still stay on for the bronze medal. DeRiel made no attempt to take on Cook as the Bath athlete strode into the lead and the merest uncertainty came when the good doctor, having established a 10-metre lead, could not extend it. Still 10 metres is enough for gold and when Allenby crossed the line too, the mutual ecstasy was something to behold.

Cook will stay in training until the Millfield world championships in July, before going off to become a doctor again. The sport will be in good hands though. As we write, Georgina Harland has already registered her second World Cup win of the 2001 season. There'll be much to write about next year too.

Event sequence for all competitions: Shoot, Fence, Swim, Ride & Run

World Championships
Pessaro, Italy   June 12-18

Men
Individual

			Total
1	Andrejus Zadneprovskis	LTU	5577
	(1144, 880 ,1263, 1100 ,1190)		
2	Gabor Balogh	HUN	5551
	(1192, 940, 1195, 1070, 1154)		
3	Nicolae Papuc	ROM	5444
	(1084, 970, 1168, 1088, 1134)		
29	Richard Phelps	GBR	4875
	(880, 790, 1202, 947, 1056)		

Team
1	USA	15867
	Gregory/Iliev/Senior	
2	Poland	15123
	Horbacz/Stefanek/Warabida	
3	Sweden	14295
	Brandt/Danielsson/Johansson	
14	Great Britain	12436
	Alexander Buirski/Richard Phelps/Greg Whyte	

Relay
1	USA	5459
	Iliev/Jagorachvili/Senior	
2	Russia	5313
	Kuharev/Sabirhusin/Stoikov	
3	Hungary	5203
	Kallai/Kovacs/Madaras	

Women
Individual

			Total
1	Pernille Svarre	DEN	5341
	(964, 970, 1052, 1067, 1288)		
2	Paulina Boenisz	POL	5270
	(1156, 820, 1123, 991, 1180)		
3	Elen Rublevska	LAT	5256
	(1132, 910, 1112, 1030 ,1072)		
6	Kate Allenby	GBR	5219
	(1012, 850, 1157, 1100, 1100)		
9	Stephanie Cook	GBR	5199
	(1024, 640, 1119, 1034, 1382)		
17	Georgina Harland	GBR	5036
	(892, 640, 1228, 1040, 1236)		

Team
1	Poland	15479
	Boenisz/Idzi/Sulima	
2	Great Britain	15454
	Kate Allenby/Stephanie Cook/Georgina Harland	
3	Italy	15345
	Cerutti/Fares/Gabella	

Relay
1	Hungary	4950
	Mahte/Simoka/Voros	
2	Great Britain	4937
	Stephanie Cook/Gwen Kinsey/Sian Lewis	
3	Belarus	4749
	Baschlakova/Shubenok/Vnukova	

European Championships
Szekesfehervar, Hungary   July 2-3

Men
Individual

			Total
1	Imre Tiideman	EST	5427
	(1252, 850, 1120, 1027, 1178)		
2	Nicolae Papuc	ROM	5406
	(1132, 910, 1175, 1079, 1110)		
3	Adrian Toader	ROM	5378
	(1180, 760, 1228, 1100, 1110)		

Team
1	Russia	15,624
	Alexey Turkin/Rustem Sabirkhouzin/Denis Stoikov	
2	Germany	15,603
3	France	15,552

Relay
1	Hungary	5087
	Akos Hanzely/Peter Sarfalvi/Gabor Balogh	
2	France	4953
3	Sweden	4907

Women
Individual

			Total
1	Zsuszanna Voros	HUN	5485
	(1168/969/1228/1100/1020)		
2	Stephanie Cook	GBR	5321
	(1108/690/1125/1100/1298)		
3	Tatiana Mouratova	RUS	5265
	(1108/938/1139/1100/980)		
7	Georgina Harland	GBR	5187
	(1036/659/1238/1070/1184)		
14	Sian Lewis	GBR	5056
	(1036/721/1129/1040/1130)		
21	Emily Bright	GBR	4921
	(964/721/1192/1100/944)		

Team
1	Hungary	15,593
	Scsilla Furi/Zsuszanna Voros/Bea Simoka	
2	Great Britain	15,564
	Georgina Harland/Sian Lewis/Stephanie Cook	
3	France	15,203

Relay
1	Great Britain	4727
	Georgina Harland/Stephanie Cook/Kate Allenby	
2	Germany	4594
3	Hungary	4530

World Cup Final
Aix-en-Provence   *Oct 14-15*

Men
1   Vadim Tkachuk   UKR   5351
    (1168, 963, 1122, 1100, 988)
2   Eric Walther   GER   5316
    (1132, 815, 1289, 1040, 1040)
3   Igor Warabida   POL   5255
    (1108, 889, 1160, 1040, 1058)

Women
1   Caroline Delemer   FRA   5104
    (1024, 852, 1120, 1070, 1038)
2   Elena Rublevska   LAT   5080
    (1060, 963, 1059, 1100, 898)
3   Axelle Guiguet   FRA   5072
    (1132, 963, 1093, 1070, 814)
5   Georgina Harland   GBR   5052
    (964, 630, 1237, 1085, 1136)
9   Sian Lewis   GBR   4886
    (1096, 704, 1114, 942, 1030)
13   Gwen Kinsey   GBR   4796
    (928, 778, 1020, 1094, 976)

British Championships
Sandhurst   *Aug 12-13*

Men
Individual   *Total*
1   Richard Phelps   Spartan   5249
    (880, 1031, 1200, 1100, 1038)
2   Matt Barnes   5207
    (856, 1062, 1108, 1037, 1144)
3   James Greenwell   4958
    (892, 1000, 1090, 944, 1032)

Women
Individual   *Total*
1   Sian Lewis   Spartan   5470
    (1168, 1037, 1133, 1070, 1062)
2   Stephanie Cook   5375
    (1132, 778, 1103, 1070, 1292)
3   Kate Allenby   5280
    (1060, 963, 1161, 1070, 1026)

Motor Cycling

T here were moments of celebration for British biking, courtesy of Neil Hodgson at Donington in May and Brands Hatch in August, but this was a summer of sadness, marked by the passing of Joey Dunlop on a street in Estonia, a thousand miles or more from his home in Ballymoney, Northern Ireland, and Joey's Bar, the public house on the local station that was a magnet for motorbike fans.

Dunlop had earned his legendary status by his mastery of the Isle of Man races. His first victory came in 1977 in the Jubilee Classic - his second year racing on the Island - and for the next 23 years Dunlop continued on the greatest victory roll in the sport. In all, he took the chequered flag in 26 TT races; the last three added in June when he was 48. It was a measure of how far he was above the rest, that the next best tally was just 14 wins, and belonged to Mike Hailwood, an imperious rider who once won seven world titles in a row.

Dunlop began racing on a 199cc Tiger Cub for which, in 1969, he had paid £50. His first two TT victories came on Yamahas, but in 1983 he switched to Honda and his plain yellow helmet became a beacon to the supporters who idolised the Irishman. His passion mirrored theirs: in 1989 he arrived at the Island on crutches ready to race, but the organisers refused to let him. Two years ago, he had arrived for the week of racing, severely bruised and beaten by a tumble at the 100-mile Tandragree road race, the fall breaking his pelvis, collarbone and costing him the third finger of his left hand, yet he still won the lightweight TT.

Another man might have chosen another venue to make his name, for there can be no more fearsome challenge in mainstream sport than the 37-mile circuit that swoops down dales and up hills, and is bordered by stone walls, lampposts, sheep fencing, houses and sheer drops. On a conventional racetrack, you can slide off into the gravel, and walk away. On the Isle of Man, you can't. "It's a dangerous track. You have to be cautious. If you do that, it's the most exciting fortnight of your racing career," he said.

In 1999 Dunlop had a disappointing summer, retirement seemed to draw closer. Dunlop didn't see it that way, though, and last summer, in inspired form, he rattled off three more superb victories; in the Formula 1, the lightweight and the ultra-lightweight classes.

There were honours off the bike; an MBE, in 1986, which was elevated to an OBE 10 years later - for services to charity, which had included solo drives to Romania, Bosnia and Albania, in a van packed with food, clothes and medication.

Dunlop died on July 2nd, while racing in Tallinn, the Estonian capital. Like the Isle of Man, the Pirita-Kose-Kloostrimetsa race takes place on a circuit adapted from public roads. In the Estonian race, though, there had been no fatal accidents since 1961, the year of its inception. Dunlop had already won two races at the festival when, in the 125cc race, he came off the bike, crashed into trees by the roadside and died instantly.

"I never really wanted to be a superstar," said Dunlop before last year's TT races. "I just wanted to be myself. I hope people remember me that way."

Carl Fogarty could claim one of the few Isle of Man records that Dunlop didn't own, snaking through the Island course at a breath-taking 123.61mph when his star was still on the rise. Fogarty would abandon the Isle of Man and forge his career in the Superbike championship, becoming as dominant in that sphere as Dunlop became on the island. Fogarty's first Superbike victory came in 1992, the fifth season of that series and, by the time of his enforced retirement in September, he had won four championships and completed 59 wins, 32 ahead of the next best record, that of American Doug Polen.

With British riders struggling in the Grand Prix series, it was left to Fogarty to single-handedly revive British track racing and the 120,000-plus who turned out at Brands Hatch in 1999, his final championship-winning year, was testimony to his success. There was another huge crowd at Brands again the following year for his final spin on the Ducati, at a caterpillar's pace around the famous circuit.

The 34-year-old completed two unsteady circuits, still troubled by the weakness in his upper right arm, broken in a crash at Philip Island in April. After he dismounted, the familiar rituals were completed; his helmet, his leathers and even his boots flung into the crowd. This was Foggy's fond farewell, though he did not admit it until mid-September, when British sports watchers were absorbed with the Sydney Olympics. Maybe he wanted to go quietly.

Having waited so long for a winner, it came as something of a shock when Neil Hodgson, who had already spent three years hanging around in World Superbike from 1996-1998 without any notable success, returned to the series at Donington and finished third in the first race and won the second. It was just three weeks after Fogarty's crash. Hodgson and his GSE Ducati team had been given a wild card for Donington and they were given another one for Brands in August.

Fogarty was there to lead the applause when Hodgson did it again at Brands, winning the second race after a podium place in the first. The mantle had been passed; from Blackburn's hero, to the Burnley boy. Well, not quite. These days, Hodgson lives on the Isle of Man. That's where people go when they are rich and famous. Hodgson, we hope, has not been premature.

Joey Dunlop

1952-2000

Isle of Man TT Races
98

Isle of Man TT Wins
26

1977
Jubilee Classic
1980
1000cc Classic
1983
Formula 1
1984
Formula 1
1985
Formula 1
Junior 250cc
Senior TT
1986
Formula 1
1987
Formula 1
Senior TT
1988
Formula 1
Senior TT
Junior 350cc TT
1992
Ultra Lightweight 125cc
1993
Ultra Lightweight 125cc
1994
Ultra Lightweight 125c
Lightweight 350cc
1995
Lightweight 250cc
Senior TT
1996
Ultra Lightweight 125cc
Lightweight 250cc
1997
Lightweight 250cc
1998
Lightweight 250cc
2000
Formula 1
Lightweight 250cc
Ultra Lightweight 125cc

Grands Prix (MotoGP)

South African GP
Welkom   Mar 19

500CC (28 laps, total distance 118.125km)
1	Garry McCoy (Yamaha)	AUS	45:38.775	25
2	Carlos Checa (Yamaha)	ESP	+0.366	20
3	Loris Capirossi (Honda)	ITA	1.590	16

Not Classified: Jeremy McWillliams (Aprilia) GBR

250CC (26 laps, total distance 110.457km)
1	Shinya Nakano (Yamaha)	JPN	42:34.085	25
2	Daijiro Katoh (Honda)	JPN	+0.875	20
3	Tohru Ukawa (Honda)	JPN	+13.813	16
9	Jason Vincent (Honda)	GBR	+1:07.732	7
11	Jamie Robinson (Aprilia)	GBR	+1:23.219	5

NC: Adrian Coates GBR

125CC (24 laps, total distance 101.820km)
1	Arnaud Vincent (Aprilia)	FRA	41:35.310	25
2	Mirko Giansanti (Honda)	ITA	+1.937	20
3	Emilio Alzamora (Honda)	ESP	+2.057	16
22	Leon Haslam (Italjet)	GBR	+1:28.648	-

Malaysian GP
Sepang   Apr 2

500CC (15 laps, total distance 83.191km)
1	Kenny Roberts Jr (Suzuki)	USA	31:58.102	25
2	Carlos Checa (Yamaha)	ESP	+1.870	20
3	Garry McCoy (Yamaha)	AUS	+7.190	16
10	Jeremy McWilliams (Aprilia)	GBR	+35.874	6

Points after round 2: McCoy 41, Checa 40, Roberts 35

250CC (20 laps, total distance 110.582)
1	Shinya Nakano (Yamaha)	JPN	43:20.928	25
2	Olivier Jacque (Honda)	FRA	+4.402	20
3	Daijiro Katoh (Honda)	JPN	+6.270	16
12	Jason Vincent (Honda)	GBR	+59.380	4

Points after round 2: Nakano 50, Katoh 36, Jacque 33

125CC (19 laps, total distance 105.343km)
1	Roberto Locatelli (Aprilia)	ITA	43:30.905	25
2	Youichi Ui (Derbi)	JPN	+0.161	20
3	Mirko Giansanti (Honda)	ITA	+0.163	16
19	Leon Haslam (Italjet)	GBR	+1:25.423	-

Points after round 2: Locatelli 38, Giansanti 36

Japanese GP
Motegi   Apr 9

500CC (21 laps, total distance 123.185km)
1	Norick Abe (Yamaha)	JPN	45:16.657	25
2	Kenny Roberts Jr (Suzuki)	USA	+0.279	20
3	Tadayuki Okada (Honda)	JPN	+1.912	16
8	Jeremy McWilliams (Aprilia)	GBR	+4.902	8

Points after round 3: Roberts 55, Checa 51, McCoy 48, Abe 34, Aoki 32, Barros 30, Okada 26, Crivillé 21

250CC (19 laps, total distance 111.230km)
1	Daijiro Katoh (Honda)	JPN	41:00.361	25
2	Tohru Ukawa (Honda)	JPN	+0.129	20
3	Shinya Nakano (Yamaha)	JPN	+0.231	16
16	Jason Vincent (Honda)	GBR	+1:14.678	-

Points after round 3: Nakano 66, Katoh 61, Jacque 46, Ukawa 36, West 31, Melandri 25

125CC (18 laps, total distance 105.199km)
1	Youichi Ui (Derbi)	JPN	41:04.264	25
2	Noboru Ueda (Honda)	JPN	+7.848	20
3	Masao Azuma (Honda)	JPN	+8.667	16

Points after round 3: Locatelli 54, Ui 45, Ueda 42, Alzamora 40, Giansanti 36

Spanish GP
Jerez de la Frontera   Apr 30

500CC (26 laps, total distance 114.416km)
1	Kenny Roberts Jr (Suzuki)	USA	45:52.311	25
2	Carlos Checa (Yamaha)	ESP	+0.859	20
3	Valentino Rossi (Honda)	ITA	+3.525	16

NC: Jeremy McWilliams (Aprilia) GBR

Points after round 4: Roberts 80, Checa 71, McCoy 48, Barros & Aoki 41, Crivillé 34, Okada 32

250CC (26 laps, total distance 114.190km)
1	Ralf Waldmann (Aprilia)	GER	45:56.451	25
2	Daijiro Katoh (Honda)	JPN	+5.188	20
3	Tohru Ukawa (Honda)	JPN	+6.052	16
12	Jason Vincent (Aprilia)	GBR	+56.202	4
21	Adrian Coates (Aprilia)	GBR	+1:25.101	-

Points after round 4: Katoh 81, Nakano 67, Jacque 59, Ukawa 52, Waldmann 47, West 42

125CC (23 laps, total distance 101.197km)
1	Emilio Alzamora (Honda)	ESP	42:19.740	25
2	Mirko Giansanti (Honda)	ITA	+1.047	20
3	Roberto Locatelli (Aprilia)	ITA	+5.076	16
17	Leon Haslam (Italjet)	GBR	+1:16.185	-

Points after round 4: Alzamora 65, Giansanti 56, Locatelli 54, Ueda 53, Ui 45, Azuma 44, Vincent 41

French GP
Le Mans   May 14

500CC (28 laps, total distance 120.470km)
1	Alex Crivillé (Honda)	ESP	47:15.363	25
2	Norick Abe (Yamaha)	JPN	+0.321	20
3	Valentino Rossi (Honda)	ITA	+1.155	16
12	Jeremy McWilliams (Aprilia)	GBR	+42.085	4

Points after round 5: Roberts 90, Checa 80, McCoy 61, Crivillé 59, Abe 54, Aoki 46

250CC (26 laps, total distance 111.188km)
1	Tohru Ukawa (Honda)	JPN	44:42.954	25
2	Shinya Nakano (Yamaha)	JPN	+0.279	20
3	Olivier Jacque (Yamaha)	FRA	+2.521	16

Points after round 5: Katoh 91, Nakano 87, Ukawa 77, Jacque 76, West 53, Melandri 48

125CC (24 laps, total distance 103.766km)
1	Youichi Ui (Derbi)	JPN	43:43.690	25
2	Mirko Giansanti (Honda)	ITA	+1.655	20
3	Emilio Alzamora (Honda)	ESP	+1.857	16

Points after round 5: Alzamora 81, Giansanti 76, Ui 70, Locatelli 67, Ueda 53, Vincent 52, Azuma 44

Italian GP
Mugello   May 28

500CC (23 laps, total distance 120.239km)
1 Loris Capirossi (Honda)   ITA   44:04.220   25
2 Carlos Checa (Yamaha)   ESP   +2.876   20
3 Jeremy McWilliams (Aprilia) GBR   +8.041   16
NC: Callum Ramsay (Honda) GBR
Points after round 6: Checa 100, Roberts 100, Abe 65, Capirossi 63, McCoy 61, Aoki 59

250CC (21 laps, total distance 110.168km)
1 Shinya Nakano (Yamaha)   JPN   40:30.142   25
2 Olivier Jacque (Yamaha)   FRA   +0.786   20
3 Daijiro Katoh (Honda)   JPN   +15.233   16
14 Adrian Coates (Aprilia)   GBR   1 lap   2
NC: Jason Vincent & Jamie Robinson GBR
Points after round 6: Nakano 112, Katoh 107, Jacque 95, Ukawa 87, West 62, Melandri 61

125CC (20 laps, total distance 104.976km)
1 Roberto Locatelli (Aprilia) ITA   40:36.753   25
2 Mirko Giansanti (Honda)   ITA   +6.212   20
3 Masao Azuma (Honda)   JPN   +6.258   16
22 Leon Haslam (Italjet)   GBR   +1:16.759   -
Points after round 6: Giansanti 96, Locatelli 92, Alzamora 90, Ui 70, Ueda 63, Azuma & Vincent 60

Catalunyan GP
Barcelona   June 11

500CC (25 laps, total distance 118.612km)
1 Kenny Roberts Jr (Suzuki)   USA   51:31.504   25
2 Norick Abe (Yamaha)   JPN   +4.454   20
3 Valentino Rossi (Honda)   ITA   +5.087   16
12 Jeremy McWilliams (Aprilia) GBR   1 lap   4
Points after round 7: Roberts 125, Checa 100, Abe 75, Capirossi 73, Aoki 72, McCoy 61

250CC (23 laps, total distance 108.819km)
1 Olivier Jacque (Yamaha)   FRA   48:23.116   25
2 Tohru Okawa (Honda)   JPN   +4.025   20
3 Shinya Nakano (Yamaha)   JPN   +8.177   16
10 Jamie Robinson (Aprilia)   GBR   +56.066   6
19 Jason Vincent (Aprilia)   GBR   +1:38.584   -
21 Adrian Coates (Aprilia)   GBR   +1:54.290   -
Points after round 7: Nakano 128, Katoh & Jacque 120, Ukawa 107, Melandri 71, West 70

125CC (22 laps, total distance 103.246km)
1 Simone Sanna (Aprilia)   ITA   47:54.390   25
2 Masao Azuma (Honda)   JPN   +10.770   20
3 Gino Borsoi (Aprilia)   ITA   +11.012   16
10 Leon Haslam (Italjet)   GBR   +1:46.951   6
Points after round 7: Giansanti 96, Locatelli 92, Alzamora 90, Azuma 80, Vincent 73, Ui 70, Borsoi 67

Dutch GP
Assen   June 24

500CC (20 laps, total distance 120.72km)
1 Alex Barros (Honda)   BRA   42:46.142   25
2 Alex Crivillé (Honda)   ESP   +2.077   20
3 Loris Capirossi (Honda)   ITA   +2.907   16
NC: Phil Giles & Jeremy McWilliams GBR
Points after round 8: Roberts 125, Checa 111, Abe 81, Capirossi 89, Crivillé 79, Barros 77, Aoki 75, Rossi 67

250CC (18 laps, total distance 108.989km)
1 Tohru Ukawa (Honda)   JPN   42:58.958   25
2 Oliver Jacque (Yamaha)   FRA   +5.954   20
3 Shinya Nakano (Yamaha)   JPN   +7.986   16
6 Jamie Robinson (Aprilia)   GBR   +46.491   10
19 Jason Vincent (Aprilia)   GBR   1 lap   -
NC: Adrian Coates GBR
Points after round 8: Nakano 144, Jacque 140, Ukawa 132, Katoh 128, West 83, Melandri 71

125CC (17 laps, total distance 102.641km)
1 Youichi Ui (Derbi)   JPN   42:04.508   25
2 Noboru Ueda (Honda)   JPN   +2.380   20
3 Manuel Poggiali (Derbi)   SMR   +2.781   16
Points after round 8: Locatelli 102, Giansanti 96, Ui 95, Alzamora 90, Azuma 87, Ueda 83, Vincent 76

British GP
Donington   July 9

500CC (30 laps, total distance 120.614km)
1 Valentino Rossi (Honda)   ITA   52:37.246   25
2 Kenny Roberts Jr (Suzuki)   USA   +0.395   20
3 Jeremy McWilliams (Aprilia) JPN   +0.944   16
13 John McGuinness (Honda)   GBR   +1:03.534   3
NC: Phil Giles GBR
Points after round 9: Roberts 145, Checa 116, Capirossi 102, Rossi 92, Abe 91, Crivillé 88, Barros 79

250CC (27 laps, total distance 108.172km)
1 Ralf Waldmann (Aprilia)   GER   49:41.073   25
2 Olivier Jacque (Yamaha)   FRA   +0.344   20
3 Naoki Matsudo (Yamaha)   JPN   +1.609   16
5 Jason Vincent (Aprilia)   GBR   +22.714   11
13 Gary Haslam (Honda)   GBR   +1:54.697   3
19 Jason Davis (Honda)   GBR   1 lap   -
Points after round 9: Jacque 160, Nakano 153, Ukawa 145, Katoh 134, Waldmann 89, West 83

125CC (26 laps, total distance 104.363km)
1 Youichi Ui (Derbi)   JPN   43:28.374   25
2 Emilio Alzamora (Honda)   ESP   +0.752   20
3 Noboru Ueda (Honda)   JPN   +3.104   16
19 Leon Haslam (Italjet)   GBR   +1:23.679   -
20 Stuart Eaton (Honda)   GBR   +1:46.031   -
23 Paul Robinson (Honda)   GBR   +2:15.991   -
NC: Kenny Tibble GBR
Points after round 9: Ui 120, Locatelli 115, Alzamora 110, Giansanti 106, Ueda 99, Azuma 98, Vincent 79

German GP
Sachsenring   July 23

500CC (31 laps, total distance 108.594km)
1 Alex Barros (Honda)   BRA   43:54.632   25
2 Valentino Rossi (Honda)   ITA   +0.078   20
3 Kenny Roberts Jr (Suzuki)   USA   +0.864   16
NC: Jeremy McWilliams GBR
Points after round 10: Roberts 161, Checa 123, Rossi & Capirossi 112, Barros 104, Abe 96, Crivillé 88, Aoki 78

250CC (30 laps, total distance 105.441km)
1 Olivier Jacque (Yamaha)   FRA   42:15.207   25
2 Tohru Ukawa (Honda)   JPN   +11.689   20
3 Shinya Nakano (Yamaha)   JPN   +21.180   16
21 Jason Vincent (Aprilia)   GBR   +1 lap   -
24 Adrian Coates (Aprilia)   GBR   +1 lap   -
NC: Jamie Robinson GBR
Points after round 10: Jacque 185, Nakano 169, Ukawa 165, Katoh 147, Waldmann 97, West 89

125CC (29 laps, total distance 101.204km)
1 Youichi Ui (Derbi) JPN 42:02.197 25
2 Roberto Locatelli (Aprilia) ITA +7.530 20
3 Simone Sanna (Aprilia) ITA +17.306 16
NC: Leon Haslam GBR
Points after round 10: *Ui 145, Locatelli 135, Giansanti 117, Alzamora 110, Ueda 102, Azuma 98, Vincent 92*

Czech GP
Brno   Aug 20

500CC (22 laps, total distance 118.636km)
1 Max Biaggi (Yamaha) ITA 45:31.918 25
2 Valentino Rossi (Honda) ITA +6.641 20
3 Garry McCoy (Yamaha) AUS +8.627 16
9 Jeremy McWilliams (Aprilia) GBR +23.002 7
19 Phil Giles (Honda) GBR +1 lap -
Points after round 11: *Roberts 174, Rossi 132, Checa 128, Capirossi 123, Barros 104, Crivillé 97, Abe 96*

250CC (20 laps, total distance 108.305km)
1 Shinya Nakano (Yamaha) JPN 41:44.845 25
2 Tohru Ukawa (Honda) JPN +3.994 20
3 Olivier Jacque (Yamaha) FRA +4.987 16
15 Jamie Robinson (Aprilia) GBR +1:15.068 1
22 Adrian Coates (Aprilia) GBR +1:35.776 -
NC: Jason Vincent
Points after round 11: *Jacque 201, Nakano 194, Ukawa 185, Katoh 157, Waldmann 108*

125CC (19 laps, total distance 102.660km)
1 Roberto Locatelli (Aprilia) ITA 41:19.190 25
2 Youichi Ui (Derbi) JPN +1.533 20
3 Emilio Alzamora (Honda) ESP +1.716 16
17 Leon Haslam (Italjet) GBR +1:35.984 -
Points after round 11: *Ui 165, Locatelli 160, Giansanti & Alzamora 126, Ueda 113, Vincent 102, Azuma 98*

Portuguese GP
Estoril   Sep 3

500CC (28 laps, total distance 117.981km)
1 Garry McCoy (Yamaha) AUS 48:07.663 25
2 Kenny Roberts Jr (Suzuki) USA +4.941 20
3 Valentino Rossi (Honda) ITA +5.182 16
11 Jeremy McWilliams (Aprilia) GBR +32.421 5
19 Phil Giles (Honda) GBR +1 lap -
Points after round 12: *Roberts 194, Rossi 148, Checa 132, Capirossi 126, Barros 110, McCoy 109, Crivillé 107*

250CC (26 laps, total distance 108.560km)
1 Daijiro Katoh (Honda) JPN 45:07.769 25
2 Olivier Jacque (Yamaha) FRA +10.954 20
3 Marco Melandri (Aprilia) ITA +28.317 16
7 Jason Vincent (Aprilia) GBR +40.375 9
15 Jamie Robinson (Aprilia) GBR 1:24.133 1
NC: Adrian Coates GBR
Points after round 12: *Jacque 221, Nakano 194, Ukawa 185, Katoh 182, Waldmann 108, West 107*

125CC (24 laps, total distance 100.816km)
1 Emilio Alzamora (Honda) ESP 43:22.891 25
2 Roberto Locatelli (Aprilia) ITA +3.691 20
3 Arnaud Vincent (Aprilia) FRA +12.233 16
Points after round 12: *Locatelli 180, Ui 165, Alzamora 151, Giansanti 126, Vincent 118, Ueda 113, Azuma 98*

Valencia GP
Valencia   Sep 17

500CC (30 laps, total distance 120.751km)
1 Garry McCoy (Yamaha) AUS 48:27.799 25
2 Kenny Roberts Jr (Suzuki) USA +5.005 20
3 Max Biaggi (Yamaha) ITA +5.978 16
15 Phil Giles (Honda) GBR +1 lap 1
NC: Jeremy McWilliams
Points after round 13: *Roberts 214, Rossi 148, Checa 141, McCoy 136, Capirossi 126, Barros 121, Biaggi 118*

250CC (27 laps, total distance 108.650km)
1 Shinya Nakano (Yamaha) JPN 43:49.140 25
2 Olivier Jacque (Yamaha) FRA +4.285 20
3 Marco Melandri (Aprilia) ITA +14.848 16
9 Jason Vincent (Aprilia) GBR +40.271 7
19 Jamie Robinson (Aprilia) GBR +1:22.270 -
23 Adrian Coates (Aprilia) GBR +1 lap -
Points after round 13: *Jacque 241, Nakano 219, Ukawa 198, Katoh 193, Melandri & West 116*

125CC (25 laps, total distance 100.491km)
1 Roberto Locatelli (Aprilia) ITA 42:27.505 25
2 Masao Azuma (Honda) JPN +0.433 20
3 Youichi Ui (Derbi) JPN +7.925 16
22 Leon Haslam (Italjet) GBR +1:17.512 -
Points after round 13: *Locatelli 205, Ui 181, Alzamora 162, Giansanti 129, Vincent 124, Ueda & Azuma 118*

Brazilian GP
Rio de Janeiro   Oct 7

500CC (24 laps, total distance 118.544km)
1 Valentino Rossi (Honda) ITA 45:22.624 25
2 Alex Barros (Honda) BRA +0.970 20
3 Garry McCoy (Yamaha) AUS +3.446 16
NC: Jeremy McWilliams GBR
Points after round 14: *Roberts 224, Rossi 173, McCoy 150, Checa 142, Barros 141, Biaggi 140*

250CC (22 laps, total distance 108.130km)
1 Daijiro Katoh (Honda) JPN 42:14.822 25
2 Tohru Ukawa (Honda) JPN +0.064 20
3 Marco Melandri (Aprilia) ITA +0.190 16
9 Jason Vincent (Aprilia) GBR +41.546 7
18 Adrian Coates (Aprilia) GBR +1:12.784 -
NC: Jamie Robinson GBR
Points after round 14: *Jacque 241, Nakano 232, Ukawa & Katoh 218, Melandri 132, West 127*

125CC (21 laps, total distance 103.156km)
1 Simone Sanna (Aprilia) ITA 42:14.265 25
2 Masao Azuma (Honda) JPN +0.131 20
3 Youichi Ui (Derbi) JPN +5.680 16
NC: Leon Haslam GBR
Points after round 14: *Locatelli 205, Ui 197, Alzamora 170, Azuma 138, Giansanti 129, Ueda 128, Vincent 124*

Pacific GP
Motegi Twin-Ring   *Oct 15*

500CC (25 laps, total distance 120.242km)
1	Kenny Roberts Jr (Suzuki)	USA	46:23.327	25
2	Valentino Rossi (Honda)	ITA	+6.175	20
3	Max Biaggi (Yamaha)	ITA	+6.360	16
14	Jeremy McWilliams (Aprilia)	GBR	+55.657	2

Points after round 15: Roberts 249, Rossi 193, Biaggi 156, Checa 155, McCoy & Barros 150

250CC (23 laps, total distance 110.518km)
1	Daijiro Katoh (Honda)	JPN	43:26.394	25
2	Shinya Nakano (Yamaha)	JPN	+0.707	20
3	Marco Melandri (Aprilia)	ITA	+19.677	16
9	Jason Vincent (Aprilia)	GBR	+1:08.330	7

NC: Jamie Robinson GBR

Points after round 15: Jacque 254, Nakano 252, Katoh 243, Ukawa 229, Melandri 148, West 137

125CC (21 laps, total distance 100.307km)
1	Roberto Locatelli (Aprilia)	ITA	41:55.152	25
2	Emilio Alzamora (Honda)	ESP	+13.790	20
3	Simone Sanna (Aprilia)	ITA	+16.429	16

NC: Leon Haslam GBR

Points after round 15: Locatelli 230, Ui 197, Alzamora 190, Azuma 149, Ueda 136, Giansanti 129, Sanna 126

Australian GP
Philip Island   *Oct 29*

500CC (27 laps, total distance 120.561km)
1	Max Biaggi (Yamaha)	ITA	42:29.792	25
2	Loris Capirossi (Honda)	ITA	+0.182	20
3	Valentino Rossi (Honda)	ITA	+0.288	16
8	Jeremy McWilliams (Aprilia)	GBR	+0.426	8

Points after round 16: Roberts 258, Rossi 209, Biaggi 170, Barros 163, McCoy 161, Checa 155

250CC (25 laps, total distance 111.641km)
1	Olivier Jacque (Yamaha)	FRA	39:19.795	25
2	Shinya Nakano (Yamaha)	JPN	+0.014	20
3	Daijiro Katoh (Honda)	JPN	+14.525	16
8	Jason Vincent (Aprilia)	GBR	+59.170	8

NC: Adrian Coates GBR

Points after round 116: Jacque 279, Nakano 272, Katoh 259, Ukawa 239, Melandri 159, West 146

125CC (23 laps, total distance 102.451km)
1	Masao Azuma (Honda)	JPN	39:09.128	25
2	Youichi Ui (Derbi)	JPN	+0.622	20
3	Noboru Ueda (Honda)	JPN	+4.088	16
17	Leon Haslam (Italjet)	GBR	+1:24.320	-

Points after round 16: Locatelli 230, Ui 217, Alzamora 203, Azuma 174, Ueda 152, Sanna 132

World GP Championships
Final Standings
Top 12 and British

500CC
1	Kenny Roberts Jr	USA	258
2	Valentino Rossi	ITA	209
3	Max Biaggi	ITA	170
4	Alex Barros	BRA	163
5	Garry McCoy	AUS	161
6	Carlos Checa	ESP	155
7	Loris Capirossi	ITA	154
8	Norick Abe	JPN	147
9	Alex Crivillé	ESP	122
10	Nobuatsu Aoki	JPN	116
11	Tadayuki Okada	JPN	107
12	Regis Laconi	ITA	106
14	Jeremy McWilliams	GBR	76
24	John McGuinness	GBR	3
29	Phil Giles	GBR	1

Constructors' Championship
1. Yamaha 318; 2. Honda 311; 3. Suzuki 264;
4. Aprilia 94; 5. TSR-Honda 85; 6. Modenas 30

250CC
1	Olivier Jacque	FRA	279
2	Shinya Nakano	JPN	272
3	Daijiro Katoh	JPN	259
4	Tohru Ukawa	JPN	239
5	Marco Melandri	ITA	159
6	Anthony West	AUS	146
7	Ralf Waldmann	GER	143
8	Franco Battaini	ITA	96
9	Sebastian Porto	ARG	83
10	Naoki Matsudo	JPN	79
11	Jason Vincent	GBR	64
12	Klaus Nöhles	GER	45
19	Jamie Robinson	GBR	23

Constructors' Championship
1. Yamaha 342; 2. Honda 324;
3. Aprilia 232; 4. TSR-Honda 58

125CC
1	Roberto Locatelli	ITA	230
2	Youichi Ui	JPN	217
3	Emilio Alzamora	ESP	203
4	Masao Azuma	JPN	174
5	Noboru Ueda	JPN	152
6	Simone Sanna	ITA	132
7	Arnaud Vincent	FRA	131
8	Mirko Giansanti	ITA	129
9	Gino Borsoi	ITA	112
10	Ivan Goi	ITA	107
11	Lucio Cecchinello	ITA	104
12	Steve Jenkner	GER	73
27	Leon Haslam	GBR	6

Constructors' Championship
1. Honda 318; 2. Aprilia 313;
3. Derbi 250; 4. Italjet 31; 5. Yamaha 1

Superbikes

South African WSB
Kayalami (25 x 4.2606km)   *Apr 2*

RACE 1

1	Colin Edwards (Honda)	USA	43:21.141	25
2	Noriyuki Haga (Yamaha)	JPN	+0.133	20
3	Carl Fogarty (Ducati)	GBR	+0.225	16

RACE 2

1	Noriyuki Haga (Yamaha)	JPN	43:22.756	25
2	Colin Edwards (Honda)	USA	+6.482	20
3	Pierfrancesco Chili (Suzuki)	ITA	+11.967	16

Haga, who finished 2nd in race 1 and 1st in race 2, was later disqualified for failing a drugs test

Australian WSB
Philip Island (22 x 4.450km)   *Apr 23*

RACE 1

1	Anthony Gobert (Bimota)	AUS	40:48.406	25
2	Carl Fogarty (Ducati)	GBR	+29.542	20
3	Vittoriano Guareschi (Yamaha)	ITA	+41.205	16

RACE 2 (15 laps only)

1	Troy Corser (Aprilia)	AUS	25:45.786	25
2	Noriyuki Haga (Yamaha)	JPN	+1.994	20
3	Pierfrancesco Chili (Suzuki)	ITA	+4.330	16

Japanese WSB
Sugo (25 laps x 3.737km)   *Apr 30*

RACE 1

1	Hitoyasu Izutsu (Kawasaki)	JPN	37:57.425	25
2	Noriyuki Haga (Yamaha)	JPN	+3.812	20
3	Pierfrancesco Chili (Suzuki)	ITA	+4.093	16

RACE 2

1	Hitoyasu Izutsu (Kawasaki)	JPN	34:47.120	25
2	Wataru Yoshikawa (Yamaha)	JPN	+0.223	20
3	Colin Edwards (Honda)	USA	+4.302	16

British WSB
Donington (25 x 4.023km)   *May 14*

RACE 1

1	Colin Edwards (Honda)	USA	39:26.879	25
2	Pierfrancesco Chili (Suzuki)	ITA	+1.079	20
3	Neil Hodgson (Ducati)	GBR	+6.177	16

RACE 2

1	Neil Hodgson (Ducati)	GBR	39:32.446	25
2	Chris Walker (Suzuki)	GBR	+0.830	20
3	Pierfrancesco Chili (Suzuki)	ITA	+2.746	16

Italian WSB
Monza (18 x 5.770km)   *May 21*

RACE 1

1	Pierfrancesco Chili (Suzuki)	ITA	31:59.010	25
2	Colin Edwards (Honda)	USA	+0.028	20
3	Akira Yanagawa (Kawasaki)	JPN	+11.901	16

RACE 2

1	Colin Edwards (Honda)	USA	32:07.510	25
2	Pierfrancesco Chili (Suzuki)	ITA	+0.031	20
3	Akira Yanagawa (Kawasaki)	JPN	+2.552	16

German WSB
Hockenheim   *June 4*

RACE 1

1	Troy Bayliss (Ducati)	USA	28:20.273	25
2	Akira Yanagawa (Kawasaki)	JPN	+0.202	20
3	Noriyuki Haga (Yamaha)	JPN	+0.748	16

RACE 2

1	Noriyuki Haga (Yamaha)	JPN	28:20.519	25
2	Colin Edwards (Honda)	USA	+0.170	20
3	Pierfrancesco Chili (Suzuki)	ITA	+0.406	16

San Marino WSB
Misano (25 x 4.060km)   *June 18*

RACE 1

1	Troy Corser (Aprilia)	AUS	40:28.677	25
2	Troy Bayliss (Ducati)	AUS	+8.573	20
3	Katsuaki Fujiwara (Suzuki)	JPN	+9.146	20

RACE 2

1	Troy Corser (Aprilia)	AUS	37:10.504	25
2	Troy Bayliss (Ducati)	AUS	+4.776	20
3	Ben Bostrom (Ducati)	USA	+5.538	16

Spanish WSB
Valencia (4.005km)   *June 25*

RACE 1

1	Troy Corser (Aprilia)	AUS	37:17.084	25
2	Ben Bostrom (Ducati)	USA	+8.703	20
3	Noriyuki Haga (Yamaha)	JPN	+13.934	16

RACE 2

1	Noriyuki Haga (Yamaha)	JPN	37:27.788	25
2	Ben Bostrom (Ducati)	USA	+1.227	20
3	Troy Bayliss (Ducati)	AUS	+3.056	16

United States WSB
Laguna Seca (28 x 3.610km)   *July 9*

RACE 1

1	Noriyuki Haga (Yamaha)	JPN	40:40.379	25
2	Colin Edwards (Honda)	USA	+2.664	20
3	Troy Corser (Ducati)	AUS	+3.571	16

RACE 2

1	Troy Corser (Ducati)	AUS	40:38.714	25
2	Noriyuki Haga (Yamaha)	JPN	+7.715	20
3	Ben Bostrom (Ducati)	USA	+9.011	16

European WSB
Brands Hatch (25 x 4.184km)   *Aug 6*

RACE 1

1	Troy Bayliss (Ducati)	AUS	36:35.753	25
2	Neil Hodgson (Ducati)	GBR	+0.235	20
3	Chris Walker (Suzuki)	GBR	+8.782	16

RACE 2

1	Neil Hodgson (Ducati)	GBR	36:33.880	25
2	Troy Bayliss (Ducati)	AUS	+0.732	20
3	Pierfrancesco Chili (Suzuki)	ITA	+4.759	16

Dutch WSB
Assen (16 x 6.049km)   *Sep 3*

RACE 1

1	Colin Edwards (Honda)	USA	37:19.466	25
2	Juan Batista Borja (Ducati)	ESP	+9.890	20
3	Noriyuki Haga (Yamaha)	JPN	+19.715	16

RACE 2

1	Noriyuki Haga (Yamaha)	JPN	33:44.824	25
2	Akira Yanagawa (Kawasaki)	JPN	+5.884	20
3	Aaron Slight (Honda)	NZL	+8.606	16

German WSB

Oschersleben (3.667km) *Sep 10*

RACE 1

1	Colin Edwards (Honda)	USA	41:50.041	25
2	Gregorio Lavilla (Kawasaki)	ITA	+5.642	20
3	Troy Bayliss (Ducati)	AUS	+7.064	16

RACE 2

1	Colin Edwards (Honda)	USA	+41:48.277	25
2	Troy Bayliss (Ducati)	AUS	+4.199	20
3	Akira Yanagawa (Kawasaki)	JPN	+5.808	16

British WSB

Donington (25 x 4.318km) *Oct 15*

RACE 1

1	John Reynolds (Ducati)	GBR	40:09.855	25
2	Troy Bayliss (Ducati)	AUS	+0.458	20
3	Chris Walker (Suzuki)	GBR	+3.556	16

RACE 2

1	Colin Edwards (Honda)	USA	36:37.860	25
2	Pierfrancesco Chili (Suzuki)	AUS	+1.016	20
3	Troy Corser (Aprilia)	AUS	+4.766	16

World Superbike

Final Standings

1	Colin Edwards USA	400
2	Noriyuki Haga JPN	335
3	Troy Corser AUS	310
4	Pierfrancesco Chili ITA	258
5	Akira Yanagawa JPN	247
6	Troy Bayliss AUS	243
7	Ben Bostrom USA	174
8	Aaron Slight NZL	153
9	Katsuaki Fujiwara	151
10	Georgio Lavilla ITA	133
11	Juan Batista Borja ESP	123
12	Neil Hodgson GBR	99
13	Andreas Meklau AUT	91
14	Chris Walker GBR	82
15	Alessandro Antonello ITA	72
16	Robert Ulm AUT	67
17	John Reynolds GBR	57
18	Haruchika Aoki JPN	56
19	Hitoyasu Izutsu JPN	50
20	Vittoriano Guareschi ITA	46
26	Carl Fogarty GBR	36
28	James Hayden GBR	24

Constructors' Championship

1. Ducati 403; 2. Kawasaki 348; 3. Honda 313;
4. Yamaha 145; 5. Suzuki 12

2001 Superbike Entry List

1	Colin Edwards (Honda)	USA
3	Troy Corser (Ducati)	AUS
4	Pierfrancesco Chili (Suzuki)	ITA
5	Akira Yanagawa (Kawasaki)	JPN
6	Gregorio Lavilla (Kawasaki)	ESP
7	Juan Batista Borja (Yamaha)	ESP
8	Tadayuki Okada (Honda)	JPN
11	Ruben Xaus (Ducati)	ESP
13	Andreas Meklau (Ducati)	AUT
14	Peter Goddard (Benelli)	AUS
19	Hitoyasu Izutsu (Kawasaki)	JPN
20	Marco Borciani (Ducati)	ITA
21	Troy Bayliss (Ducati)	AUS
22	Lucio Pedercini (Ducati)	ITA
23	Jiri Mrkyvka (Ducati)	CZE
24	Stéphane Chambon (Suziki)	FRA
25	Javier Rodriguez Hernandez (Honda)	ESP
26	Warwick Nowland (Ducati)	AUS
27	Bertrand Stey (Honda)	FRA
31	Michele Malatesta (Kawasaki)	ITA
33	Robert Ulm (Ducati)	AUT
34	Jean-Marc Deletang (Yamaha)	FRA
35	Giovanni Bussei (Ducati)	ITA
36	Broc Parkes (Ducati)	AUS
39	Alex Gramigni (Yamaha)	ITA
41	Ludovic Holon (Kawasaki)	FRA
51	Martin Andrew Craggill (Ducati)	AUS
52	James Toseland (Ducati)	GBR
55	Régis Laconi (Aprilia)	FRA
99	Steve Martin (Ducati)	AUS
100	Neil Hodgson (Ducati)	GBR
155	Ben Bostrom (Ducati)	USA

Supersport

World Championship

Final Standings

1	Jorge Teuchert (Yamaha) GER	136
2	Paolo Casoli (Ducati) ITA	133
3	Stephane Chambon (Suzuki) FRA	133
4	Christian Kellner (Yamaha) GER	122
5	Karl Muggeridge (Honda) AUS	113
6	Jamie Whitham (Yamaha) GBR	104
7	Ruben Xaus (Ducati) ESP	77
8	Iain McPherson (Kawasaki) GBR	74
9	Fabrizio Pirovano (Suzuki) ITA	61
10	Andrew Pitt (Kawasaki) AUS	60

Sidecar World Cup

South Africa
Kyalami   *Apr 2*

1	Klaffenbock/Hanni (Suzuki)	AUT	47:08.339	25
2	Webster/Woodhead (Suzuki)	GBR	+4.890	20
3	Steinhausen/Parzer (Suzuki)	GER	+54.081	16

Australia
Philip Island   *Apr 23*

1	Webster/Woodhead (Suzuki)	GBR	35:23.088	25
2	Steinhausen/Parzer (Suzuki)	GER	+43.562	20
3	Soutar/Hetherington (ADM)	AUS	+53.042	16

Great Britain
Donington   *May 14*

1	Webster/Woodhead (Suzuki)	GBR	30:11.487	25
2	Steinhausen/Parzer (Suzuki)	GER	+6.849	20
3	Janssen/Hopkinson (BRN)	NED	+31.797	16

Italy
Monza   *May 21*

1	Webster/Woodhead (Suzuki)	GBR	27:10.964	25
2	Klaffenbock/Hanni (Suzuki)	AUT	+9.401	20
3	Abbott/Biggs (Yamaha)	GBR	+36.337	16

Germany
Hockenheim   *June 4*

1	Steinhausen/Parzer (Suzuki)	GER	22:03.659	25
2	Webster/Woodhead (Suzuki)	GBR	+0.410	20
3	Klaffenbock/Hanni (Suzuki)	AUT	+1.070	16

San Marino
Misano   *June 18*

1	Webster/Woodhead (Suzuki)	GBR	39:17.635	25
2	Klaffenbock/Hanni (Suzuki)	AUT	+7.776	20
2	Muldoon/Gusman (ADM)	GBR	+8.336	16

Spain
Valencia   *June 25*

1	Klaffenbock/Hanni (Suzuki)	AUT	39:45.798	25
2	Webster/Woodhead (Suzuki)	GBR	+0.204	20
3	Steinhausen/Parzer (Suzuki)	GER	+24.934	16

Great Britain
Brands Hatch   *Aug 6*

1	Klaffenbock/Hanni (Suzuki)	AUT	35:51.561	25
2	Webster/Woodhead (Suzuki)	GBR	+0.211	20
3	Steinhausen/Parzer (Suzuki)	GER	+1.813	16

Netherlands
Assen   *Sep 3*

1	Steinhausen/Parzer (Suzuki)	GER	35:47.306	16
2	Klaffenbock/Hanni (Suzuki)	AUT	+3.026	25
3	Abbott/Biggs (Yamaha)	GBR	+17.931	16

Germany
Oschersleben   *Sep 10*

1	Klaffenbock/Hanni (Suzuki)	AUT	44:13.093	25
2	Webster/Woodhead (Suzuki)	GBR	+0.276	20
3	Steinhausen/Parzer (Suzuki)	GER	+6.156	16

Great Britain
Brands Hatch   *Oct 15*

1	Klaffenbock/Hanni (Suzuki)	AUT	31:05.582	25
2	Webster/Woodhead (Suzuki)	GBR	+4.709	20
3	Abbott/Biggs (Yamaha)	GBR	+5.652	16

Final Standings: Webster/Woodhead 220,
Klaffenbock/Hanni 212, Steinhausen/Parzer 178,
Janssen/Hopkinson 96, Hauzenberger/Crone 94,
Muldoon/Gusman 93, Abbott/Biggs 71

Motocross

World Championships
Final Standings (16 rounds)

500CC

1	Joel Smets (KTM)	BEL	583
2	Marnicq Berboets (Yamaha)	BEL	432
3	Peter Johansson (KTM)	SWE	397
14	Christian Burnham (Vor)	GBR	106
18	James Marsh (KTM)	GBR	68

250CC

1	Frederic Bolley (Honda)	FRA	421
2	Mickael Pichon (Suzuki)	FRA	367
3	Pit Beirer (Kawasaki)	GER	340
8	Paul Cooper (Husqvarna)	GBR	249
22	Justin Morris (Yamaha)	GBR	38

125CC

1	Grant Langston (KTM)	RSA	493
2	James Dobb (KTM)	GBR	419
3	Mike Brown (Honda)	USA	379
10	Carl Nunn (Yamaha)	GBR	155
15	Stephen Sword (Honda)	GBR	77

Endurance

World Championship
Final Standings (6 rounds)

1	Peter Linden (Suzuki) SWE	137
1	Warwick Nowland (Suzuki) AUS	137
3	Stephane Mertens (Suzuki) BEL	130
4	Sebastien Scarnato (Kawasaki) FRA	112
4	Nicola Dussauge (Kawasaki) FRA	112
4	Christophe Guyot (Kawasaki) FRA	112
7	Mark Willis (Yamaha) AUS	100
7	Jean-Marc Deletang (Yamaha) FRA	100
7	Fabien Foret (Yamaha) FRA	100

Trials

World Championship
Final Standings (10 rounds/20 races)

1	Dougie Lampkin (Montesa) GBR	379
2	Takahasi Fujinami (Honda) JPN	294
3	Marc Colomer (Montesa) ESP	282
4	Marc Freixa (Gas Gas) ESP	229
5	Kenichi Kuroyama (Beta) JPN	189
6	Steve Colley (Gas Gas) GBR	178
7	Albert Cabestany (Beta) ESP	164
8	Marcel Justribo (Montesa) ESP	160
9	Adam Raga (Gas Gas) ESP	154
10	David Cobos (Sherco) ESP	141

Speedway

World Championship - Grand Prix

Czech Rep GP
Prague   May 6
Standings: 1. Billy Hamill USA 25;
2. Mark Loram GBR 20; 3. Chris Louis GBR 18;
4. Todd Wiltshire AUS 16; 5. Tomasz Gollob POL 15

Swedish GP
Linkoping   June 3
Standings: 1. Jason Crump GBR 25; 2. Mark Loram 20;
3. Todd Wiltshire AUS 18; 4. Tony Rickardsson SWE 16;
5. Jimmy Nilsen SWE 15

Polish GP
Wroclaw   July 1
Standings: 1. Tony Rickardsson 25; 2. Billy Hamill 20;
3. Chris Louis 18; 4. Leigh Adams USA 16;
5. Mark Loram 15

British GP
Coventry   July 29
Standings: 1. Martin Dugard SWE 25;
2. Ryan Sullivan AUS 20; 3. Mark Loram 18;
4. Jason Lyons AUS 16; 5. Leigh Adams 15

Denmark GP
Vojens   Sep 2
Standings: 1. Greg Hancock USA 25;
2. Jason Crump 20; 3. Stefan Danno SWE 18;
4. Nicki Pedersen DEN 16; 5. Mark Loram 15

Polish II GP
Bydgoszcz   Sep 23
Standings: 1. Billy Hamill 25;
2. Greg Hancock 20; 3. Tony Rickardsson 18;
4. Jason Crump 16; 5. Tomasz Gollob 15

World Championship Final Standings:

1	Mark Loram GBR	102
2	Billy Hamill USA	95
3	Tony Rickardsson SWE	94
4	Jason Crump GBR	88
5	Greg Hancock USA	76
6	Leigh Adams USA	65
7	Tomasz Gollob POL	64
8	Todd Wiltshire AUS	63
9	Ryan Sullivan AUS	62
10	Chris Louis GBR	60

Elite League

Final Standings

	P	W	L	D	B*	Pts
Eastbourne	32	16	0	0	13	62
Kings Lynn	32	16	0	0	14	60
Ipswich	32	16	3	13	11	46
Coventry	32	11	1	4	8	43
Poole	32	14	4	14	8	40
Wolverhampton	32	15	3	14	6	39
Peterborough	32	11	2	19	7	31
Oxford	32	9	1	21	4	23
Belle Vue	32	5	3	23	1	14

* Bonus points

Elite League Knock-out Cup

Kings Lynn 58 Coventry 32
Coventry 48 Kings Lynn 42
Kings Lynn won 100-80 on aggregate

Premier League

Final Standings

Exeter	26	15	1	10	13	44
Swindon	26	18	0	8	8	44
Hull	23	16	2	8	9	43
Sheffield	26	16	1	9	9	42
Workington	26	15	2	9	10	42
Edinburgh	26	15	1	10	8	39
Stoke	26	12	2	12	5	31
Newcastle	26	11	1	14	7	30
Glasgow	26	10	2	14	5	27
Newport	26	10	1	15	5	26
Isle of Wight	26	8	2	16	6	24
Berwick	26	10	0	16	3	23
Arena Essex	26	11	0	15	1	23
Reading	26	7	1	18	2	17

Motor Racing

All those years, all those famous drivers - Alain Prost, Gilles Villeneuve and Nigel Mansell included - and not one of them could do what Jody Scheckter had done in 1979 and bring the drivers' title back to Ferrari. The Tifosi had become the Morosi, as championship after championship had passed them by. Then along came Michael Schumacher, for £25m smackers and a winning record second to none in the sport, and Ferrari still didn't win the title.

In 1997, Schumacher finished runner-up, but was disqualified after taking a sudden dislike to Jacques Villeneuve's car at Jerez, in the final Grand Prix of the season, and driving his car into it. In 1998, he managed to get the runners-up spot and keep it. Some improvement there, then. In 1999, his season was effectively ended when he broke his leg at the British Grand Prix in July. When Schumacher returned to the title chase in October, he had no chance of making up the ground, but his teammate Eddie Irvine was in there fighting for the title. When Irvine needed Schumacher, though, in the final race of the year, the German was noticeable by his reticence to get involved. Irvine lost the title to Mika Hakkinen, went off to Jaguar for a fee adjacent to £5m a year and was probably happy, even though he didn't come near winning a race in 2000 and ended up the season with just four points.

Schumacher meanwhile finally gave Ferrari what it wanted. Starting the 2000 season at a gallop, Schumacher faltered during the late summer, before going back on the bridle in the autumn. The German won the first three races and the last three races to give his season a certain symmetry. Hakkinen, who had led during August, eventually finished 19 points adrift. Ferrari also retained the constructors' championship, with the Brazilian Rubens Barrichello replacing Irvine as the second man. In some ways, Barrichello was the perfect foil for Schumacher for the Brazilian had never won a GP race before joining Ferrari - no threat to you there then, Michael? Barrichello contributed a valuable 62 points towards the team effort, but the 10 points that came at Hockenheim made it the most important of the 28-year-old Brazilian's life. After eight years and 123 races, Barrichello had finally won a Grand Prix and he was seriously, seriously happy.

Of the home drivers, David Coulthard had the best season, winning three times, including the Silverstone and the Monaco races (the latter event not having been won by a Briton since Jackie Stewart was successful in 1973). Coulthard finished in third place in the championship, coming back from a plane accident in May which came perilously close to costing him his life. The two co-pilots were killed in the crash, but Coulthard and his partner Heidi both escaped with minor injuries. A week after the crash, at Barcelona, Coulthard finished second.

In its first season, Jaguar had a modest start, with just two finishes in the points, Irvine's fourth in Monaco and the same driver's sixth in Malaysia. Johnny Herbert was the team's second man, but he'd had enough of Formula 1 and announced his decision to move on. Herbert's career highlight was his unexpected victory at the 1995 British Grand Prix.

Jenson Button was barely out of his teens when the season began in Australia, but he justified Frank Williams' faith in him, finishing in the points on six occasions and ending up in eighth place in the table. Nevertheless, by the end of the season it was clear that Williams wanted to bring in the Cart champion Juan-Pablo Montoya and Button was sent out "on loan" to the Benetton team for 2001.

The British Grand Prix moved to April and the event was an unmitigated disaster. The car parks turned into quagmires because of the unremitting rain and on race-day - with nowhere to park the cars - there were 15-mile traffic jams. Many people could not get anywhere near the course and missed the event, including the family of David Coulthard, who would quite like to have seen him win the race. The debacle was reckoned to have cost the circuit £3 million in revenue. At least the Easter experiment was later abandoned and the race scheduled for its traditional, and sensible, July slot.

While Silverstone bemoaned the loss of three million, SLEC, the parent company of F1 had 50% of its shares sold off for the sum of £1.1 billion to the German media group EM TV.

Elsewhere in the motor sport world, the Williams target Montoya could not hold on to his Cart title, Gil de Ferran of Brazil the new champion, with Montoya down in ninth, the Scot, Dario Franchitti in 13th and England's Mark Blundell in 21st.

In the world rally championships, Colin McRae again failed in his quest to add to his single world title. At the Tour of Corsica in October, he plunged off the road at 80mph, was concussed and shattered his cheekbone, but amazingly still came back to compete at San Remo later in the month. Even so, he was only the second ranked British driver at the season's end. Richard Burns pushed the champion Marcus Gronhölm all the way, winning four races during the year. His last victory came in the Rally of Great Britain, but as Gronhölm followed him home in second place, Burns had to concede the title to the Flnn.

2001 F1 Teams

Ferrari
Michael Schumacher
Rubens Barrichello
McLaren-Mercedes
Mika Hakkinen
David Coulthard
Williams-BMW
Ralf Schumacher
Juan-Pablo Montoya
Benetton-Renault
Giancarlo Fisichella
Jenson Button
BAR-Honda
Olivier Panis
Jacques Villeneuve
Jordan-Honda
Heinz-Harald Frentzen
Jarno Trulli
Arrows-Asiatech
Jos Verstappen
Enrique Bernoldi
Sauber-Petronas
Nick Heidfeld
Kimi Raikkonen
Jaguar
Eddie Irvine
Luciano Burti/Pedro dl Rosa
Minardi-European
Fernando Alonso
Tarso Marques
Prost-Acer
Jean Alesi
Gaston Mazzacane/L Burti

Formula One

Australian Grand Prix
Melbourne   *Mar 12*
Laps: 57 x 5.303km   *Total distance: 302.271km*

1	Michael Schumacher (Ferrari) GER	1:34:01.987
		(196.255 kph)
2	Rubens Barrichello (Ferrari) BRA	+11.415
3	Ralf Schumacher (Williams) GER	+20.009
4	Jacque Villeneuve (BAR) CAN	+44.447
5	Giancarlo Fisichella (Benetton) ITA	+45.165
6	Ricardo Zonta (BAR) BRA	+46.468

Pole Position: Hakkinen
Fastest Lap: Barrichello 1:31.481

WORLD CHAMPIONSHIP STANDINGS
Drivers: *M Schumacher 10, Barrichello 6,*
R Schumacher 4, Villeneuve 3, Fisichella 2, Zonta 1
Constructors: *Ferrari 16, Williams & BAR 4, Benetton 2*

Brazilian Grand Prix
Interlagos   *Mar 26*
Laps: 72 x 4.292km   *Total distance: 308.994km*

1	Michael Schumacher (Ferrari) GER	1:31:35.271
		(200.423 kph)
2	Giancarlo Fisichella (Benetton) ITA	+39.898
3	Heinz-Harald Frentzen (Jordan) GER	+42.268
4	Jarno Trulli (Jordan) ITA	+ 1:12.780
5	Ralf Schumacher (Williams) GER	1 lap
6	Jenson Button (Williams) GBR	1 lap

Pole Position: Hakkinen
Fastest Lap: M Schumacher 1:14.755

Drivers: *M Schumacher 20, Fisichella 8, Barrichello 6, R*
Schumacher 6, Frentzen 4, Villeneuve & Trulli 3,
Button & Zonta 1
Constructors: *Ferrari 26, Benetton 8,*
Jordan & Williams 7, BAR 4

San Marino Grand Prix
Imola   *Apr 9*
Laps: 62 x 4.930km   *Total distance: 305.428km*

1	Michael Schumacher (Ferrari) GER	1:31:39.776
		(200.043 kph)
2	Mika Hakkinen (McLaren) FIN	+01.168
3	David Coulthard (McLaren) GBR	+51.008
4	Rubens Barrichello (Ferrari) BRA	+1:29.276
5	Jacques Villeneuve (BAR) CAN	1 lap
6	Mika Salo (Sauber Petronas) FIN	1 lap

Pole Position: Hakkinen
Fastest Lap: Hakkinen 1:26.523

Drivers: *M Schumacher 30, Barrichello 9, Fisichella 8,*
Hakkinen & R Schumacher 6, Villeneuve 5, Coulthard &
Frentzen 4, Trulli 3, Button, Zonta & Salo 1
Constructors: *Ferrari 39, McLaren 10, Benetton 8,*
Williams & Jordan 7, BAR 6, Sauber 1

British Grand Prix
Silverstone   *Apr 23*
Laps: 61 x 5.140km   *Total distance: 307.196km*

1	David Coulthard (McLaren) GBR	1:28.50.108
		(308.400 kph)
2	Mika Hakkinen (McLaren) FIN	+1.477
3	Michael Schumacher (Ferrari) GER	+19.917
4	Ralf Schumacher (Williams) GER	+41.312
5	Jenson Button(Williams) GBR	+57.759
6	Jarno Trulli (Jordan) ITA	+1:19.273

Pole Position: Barrichello
Fastest Lap: Barrichello 1:26.217

Drivers: *M Schumacher 34, Coulthard 14, Hakkinen 12,*
Barrichello & R Schumacher 9, Fisichella 8, Villeneuve 5,
Frentzen & Trulli 4, Button 3, Salo & Zonta 1
Constructors: *Ferrari 43, McLaren 26, Williams 12,*
Benetton & Jordan 8, BAR 6, Sauber 1

Spanish Grand Prix
Barcelona   *May 7*
Laps: 65 x 4.728km   *Total distance: 307.196km*

1	Mika Hakkinen (McLaren) FIN	1:33:50.39
		(196.498 kph)
2	David Coulthard (McLaren) SCO	+16.066
3	Rubens Barrichello (Ferrari) BRA	+29.112
4	Ralf Schumacher (Williams) GER	+37.311
5	Michael Schumacher (Ferrari) GER	+47.983
6	Heinz-Harald Frentzen (Jordan) GER	+1:21.925

Pole Position: Hakkinen
Fastest Lap: Hakkinen 1:24.982

Drivers: *M Schumacher 36, Hakkinen 22, Coulthard 20,*
Barrichello 13, R Schumacher 12, Fisichella 8, Frentzen
& Villeneuve 5, Trulli 4, Button 3, Salo & Zonta 1
Constructors: *Ferrari 49, McLaren 42, Jordan 16,*
Williams 15, Jordan 9, Benetton 8, BAR 6,
Sauber 1

European Grand Prix
Nurburgring   *May 21*
Laps: 67 x 4.556km   *Total distance: 305.235km*

1	Michael Schumacher (Ferrari) GER	1:42:00.307
		(179.541kph)
2	Mika Hakkinen (McLaren) FIN	+13.822
3	David Coulthard (McLaren) GBR	+1 lap
4	Rubens Barrichello (Ferrari) BRA	+1 lap
5	Giancarlo Fisichella (Benetton) ITA	+1 lap
6	Pedro de la Rosa (Arrows) ESP	+1 lap

Pole Position: David Coulthard
Fastest Lap: M Schumacher 1:22.269

Drivers: *M Schumacher 46, Hakinnen 28, Coulthard 24,*
Barrichello 16, R Schumacher 12, Fisichella 10, Frentzen
& Villeneuve 5, Trulli 4, Button 3, De la Rosa, Salo &
Zonta 1
Constructors: *Ferrari 62, McLaren 52, Williams 15,*
Benetton 10, Jordan 9, BAR 6, Arrows & Sauber 1

Monaco Grand Prix
Monte Carlo   *June 4*
Laps: 78 x 3.370km   *Total distance: 262.860km*
1   David Coulthard (McLaren) GBR   1:49:28.213
                                  (144.072kph)

2   Rubens Barrichello (Ferrari) BRA   +15.889
3   Giancarlo Fisichella (Benetton) ITA   +18.522
4   Eddie Irvine (Jaguar) GBR   +1:05.924
5   Mika Salo (Sauber) FIN   +1:20.775
6   Mika Hakkinen (McLaren) FIN   +1 lap
Pole Position: M Schumacher
Fastest Lap: Hakkinen 1:21.571
Drivers: *M Schumacher 46, Coulthard 34, Hakinnen 29, Barrichello 22, Fisichella 14, R Schumacher 12, Frentzen & Villeneuve 5, Trulli 4, Button, Irvine & Salo 3, De la Rosa & Zonta 1*
Constructors: *Ferrari 68, McLaren 63, Williams 15, Benetton 14, Jordan 9, BAR 6, Jaguar 3, Sauber 2, Arrows 1*

Canadian Grand Prix
Montreal   *June 18*
Laps: 69 x 4.421km   *Total distance: 305.049km*
1   Michael Schumacher (Ferrari) GER   1:41:12.313
                                  (180.850kph)

2   Rubens Barrichello (Ferrari) BRA   +0.174
3   Giancarlo Fisichella (Benetton) ITA   +15.365
4   Mika Hakkinen (McLaren) FIN   +18.561
5   Jos Verstappen (Arrows) NED   +52.208
6   Jarno Trulli (Jordan) ITA   +1:01.687
Pole Position: M Schumacher
Fastest Lap: Hakkinen 1:19.049
Drivers: *M Schumacher 56, Coulthard 34, Hakkinen 32, Barrichello 28, Fisichella 18, R Schumacher 12, Frentzen & Villeneuve & Trulli 5, Button, Irvine & Salo 3, Verstappen 2, De la Rosa & Zonta 1*
Constructors: *Ferrari 84, McLaren 66, Benetton 18, Williams 15, Jordan 10, BAR 6, Jaguar 3, Sauber 2, Arrows 2*

French Grand Prix
Magny-Cours   *July 2*
Laps: 72 x 4.251km   *Total distance: 305.886km*
1   David Coulthard (McLaren) GBR   1:38:05.538
                                  (187.101kph)

2   Mika Hakkinen (McLaren) FIN   +14.748
3   Rubens Barrichello (Ferrari) BRA   +32.409
4   Jacques Villeneuve (BAR) CAN   +1:01.322
5   Ralf Schumacher (Willliams) GER   +1:03.981
6   Jarno Trulli (Jordan) ITA   +1:15.605
Pole Position: M Schumacher
Fastest Lap: Coulthard 1:19.479
Drivers: *M Schumacher 56, Coulthard 44, Hakinnen 38, Barrichello 32, Fisichella 18, R Schumacher 14, Villeneuve 8, Trulli 6, Frentzen 5, Button, Irvine & Salo 3, Verstappen 2, De la Rosa & Zonta 1*
Constructors: *Ferrari 88, McLaren 82, Benetton 18, Williams 17, Jordan 11, BAR 9, Jaguar 3, Sauber 2, Arrows 2*

Austrian Grand Prix
A1-Ring   *July 2*
Laps: 71 x 4.326km   *Total distance: 307.146km*
1   Mika Hakkinen (McLaren) FIN   1:28:15.818
                                  (208.792kph)

2   David Coulthard (McLaren) GBR   +12.535
3   Rubens Barrichello (Ferrari) BRA   +30.795
4   Jacques Villeneuve (BAR) CAN   +1 lap
5   Jenson Button (Willliams) GBR   +1 lap
6   Mika Salo (Sauber) FIN   +1 lap
Pole Position: Hakkinen
Fastest Lap: Coulthard 1:11.783
Drivers: *M Schumacher 56, Coulthard 50, Hakkinen 48, Barrichello 36, Fisichella 18, R Schumacher 14, Villeneuve 11, Trulli 6, Frentzen & Button 5, Salo 4, Irvine 3, Verstappen 2, De la Rosa & Zonta 1*
Constructors: *Ferrari 88, McLaren 82, Benetton 18, Williams 17, Jordan 11, BAR 9, Jaguar 3, Sauber & Arrows 2*

German Grand Prix
Hockenheim   *July 30*
Laps: 45 x 6.823km   *Total distance: 307.125km*
1   Rubens Barrichello (Ferrari) BRA   1:25:34.418
                                  (kph)

2   Mika Hakkinen (McLaren) FIN   +7.452
3   David Coulthard (McLaren) GBR   +21.168
4   Jenson Button (Williams) GBR   +22.685
5   Mika Salo (Sauber) FIN   +27.112
6   Pedro de la Rosa (Arrows) ESP   +29.079
Pole Position: Coulthard
Fastest Lap: Barrichello 1:44.300
Drivers: *M Schumacher 56, Coulthard & Hakkinen 54, Barrichello 46, Fisichella 18, R Schumacher 14, Villeneuve 11, Button 8, Trulli & Salo 6, Frentzen 5 , Irvine 3, Verstappen & De la Rosa 2, Zonta 1*
Constructors: *Ferrari 98, McLaren 92, Williams 20, Benetton 18, Jordan 11, BAR 9, Sauber 4 Jaguar & Arrows 3*

Hungarian Grand Prix
Hungaroring, Budapest   *Aug 13*
Laps: 77 x 3.975km   *Total distance: 306.075km*
1   Mika Hakkinen (McLaren) FIN   1:45.33.869
                                  (kph)

2   Michael Schumacher (Ferrari) GER   +7.916
3   David Coulthard (McLaren) GBR   +8.454
4   Rubens Barrichello (Ferrari) BRA   +44.157
5   Ralf Schumacher (Willliams) GER   +50.437
6   Heinz-Harald Frentzen (Jordan) GER   +1:08.099
Pole Position: M Schumacher
Fastest Lap: Hakkinen 1:20.028
Drivers: *Hakkinen 64, M Schumacher 62, Coulthard 58, Barrichello 49, Fisichella 18, R Schumacher 16, Villeneuve 11, Button 8, Frentzen, Trulli & Salo 6, Irvine 3, Verstappen & De la Rosa 2, Zonta 1*
Constructors: *McLaren 104, Ferrari 103, Williams 22, Benetton 18, Jordan 12, BAR 9, Sauber 4 Jaguar & Arrows 3*

Belgian Grand Prix

Spa-Francorchamps   *Aug 27*
Laps: 44 x 6.968km   *Total distance: 306.592km*
1 Mika Hakkinen (McLaren) FIN   1:28:14.494
                                              (kph)
2 Michael Schumacher (Ferrari) GER   +1.103
3 Ralf Schumacher (Williams) GER   +38.096
4 David Coulthard (McLaren) GBR   +43.280
5 Jenson Button (Williams) GBR   +49.914
6 Heinz-Harald Frentzen (Jordan) GER   +55.985
Pole Position: Hakkinen

Fastest Lap: Barrichello 1:53.803

Drivers: *Hakkinen 74, M Schumacher 68, Coulthard 61,*
Barrichello 49, R Schumacher 20, Fisichella 18,
Villeneuve 11, Button 10, Frentzen 7, Trulli & Salo 6,
Irvine 3, Verstappen & De la Rosa 2, Zonta 1
Constructors: *McLaren 117, Ferrari 109, Williams 28,*
Benetton 18, Jordan 13, BAR 9, Sauber 4 Jaguar &
Arrows 3

Italian Grand Prix

Monza   *Sep 10*
Laps: 53 x 5.783km   *Total distance: 306.234km*
1 Michael Schumacher (Ferrari) GER   1:27:31.638
                                              (kph)
2 Mika Hakkinen (McLaren) FIN   +3.810
3 Ralf Schumacher (Williams) GER   +52.432
4 Jos Verstappen (Arrows) NED   +59.938
5 Alexander Wurz (Benetton) AUT   +1:07.426
6 Ricardo Zonta (BAR) BRA   +1:09.292
Pole Position: M Schumacher

Fastest Lap: Hakkinen 1:25.595

Drivers: *Hakkinen 80, M Schumacher 78, Coulthard 61,*
Barrichello 49, R Schumacher 24, Fisichella 18,
Villeneuve 11, Button 10, Frentzen 7, Trulli & Salo 6,
Verstappen 5, Irvine 3, De la Rosa, Wurz & Zonta 2
Constructors: *McLaren 123, Ferrari 119, Williams 32,*
Benetton 20, Jordan 13, BAR 10, Arrows 6, Sauber 4
Jaguar 3

USA Grand Prix

Indianapolis   *Sep 24*
Laps: 73 x 4.195km   *Total distance: 306.235km*
1 Michael Schumacher (Ferrari) GER   1:36:30.883
                                              (190.376kph)
2 Rubens Barrichello (Ferrari) BRA   +12.118
3 Heinz-Harald Frentzen (Jordan) GER   +17.368
4 Jacques Villeneuve (BAR) CAN   +17.935
5 David Coulthard (McLaren) FRA   +28.813
6 Ricardo Zonta (BAR) BRA   +51.694
Pole Position: M Schumacher

Fastest Lap: Coulthard 1:14.711

Drivers: *M Schumacher 88, Hakkinen 80, Coulthard 63,*
Barrichello 55, R Schumacher 24, Fisichella 18,
Villeneuve 14, Frentzen 11, Button 10, Trulli & Salo 6,
Verstappen 5, Irvine & Zonta 3, De la Rosa & Wurz 2
Constructors: *Ferrari 135, McLaren 125, Williams 32,*
Benetton 20, Jordan 17, BAR 13, Arrows 6, Sauber 4
Jaguar 3

Japanese Grand Prix

Suzuka   *Oct 8*
Laps: 53 x 5.864km   *Total distance: 310.582km*
1 Michael Schumacher (Ferrari) GER   1:29.53.435
                                              (kph)
2 Mika Hakkinen (McLaren) FIN   +1.837
3 David Coulthard (McLaren) GBR   +1:09.914
4 Rubens Barrichello (Ferrari) BRA   +1:19.190
5 Jenson Button (Williams) GBR   +1:25.694
6 Jacques Villeneuve (BAR) CAN   + 1 lap
Pole Position: M Schumacher

Fastest Lap: Hakkinen 1:39.189

Drivers: *M Schumacher 98, Hakkinen 86, Coulthard 67,*
Barrichello 58, R Schumacher 24, Fisichella 18,
Villeneuve 15, Button 12, Frentzen 11, Trulli & Salo 6,
Verstappen 5, Irvine & Zonta 3, De la Rosa & Wurz 2
Constructors: *Ferrari 148, McLaren 135, Williams 34,*
Benetton 20, Jordan 17, BAR 14, Arrows 6, Sauber 4
Jaguar 3

Driver's Championship

Final Standings

1	Michael Schumacher GER *(Ferrari)*	108
2	Mika Hakkinen FIN *(McLaren-Mercedes)*	89
3	David Coulthard GBR *(McLaren/Mercedes)*	73
4	Rubens Barrichello BRA *(Ferrari)*	62
5	Ralf Schumacher GER *(Williams/BMW)*	24
6	Giancarlo Fisichella ITA *(Benetton/Playlife)*	18
7	Jacques Villeneuve CAN *(BAR Honda)*	17
8	Jenson Button GBR *(Williams/BMW)*	12
9	Heinz-Harald Frentzen GER *(Jordan Mugen-Honda)*	11
10	Jarno Trulli ITA *(Jordan Mugen-Honda)*	6
11	Mika Salo FIN *(Sauber/Petronas)*	6
12	Jos Verstappen NED *(Arrows/Supertec)*	5
13	Eddie Irvine GBR *(Jaguar)*	4
14	Ricardo Zonta BRA *(BAR Honda)*	3
15	Alexander Wurz AUT *(Benetton/Playlife)*	2
16	Pedro de la Rosa ESP *(Arrows/Supertec)*	2

Constructors' Final Standings

1.Ferrari 170; 2 McLaren Mercedes 152;
3 Williams BMW 36; 4= Benetton & BAR Honda 20
6 Jordan Mugen-Honda 17; 7 Arrows Supertec 7
8 Sauber Petronas 6; 9 Jaguar 4

Malaysian Grand Prix

Sepang   Oct 22
Laps: 56 x 5.543   *Total distance: 310.408km*

1	Michael Schumacher (Ferrari) GER	1:35:54.230
		(*194.200kph*)
2	David Coulthard (McLaren) GBR	+0.732
3	Rubens Barrichello (Ferrari) BRA	+18.444
4	Mika Hakkinen (McLaren) FIN	+35.259
5	Jacques Villeneuve (BAR) CAN	+1:10.692
6	Eddie Irvine (Jaguar) GBR	+1:12.568

Pole Position: M Schumacher
Fastest Lap: Hakkinen 1:38.543

Formula 3000

Round 1

Imola   Apr 8

1	Nicolas Minassian (SuperNova) FRA	1:11:06.106
2	Bruno Junqueiro (Petrobras) BRA	+2.298
3	Mark Webber (European 3000) AUS	+2.732

Round 2

Silverstone   Apr 22

1	Mark Webber (European 3000) AUS	1:22:24.239
2	Darren Manning (Lukoil Arden) GBR	+0.948
3	Justin Wilson (Nordic) GBR	+4.979

Round 3

Barcelona   May 6

1	Bruno Junqueiro (Petrobras) BRA	1:11:52.069
2	Nicolas Minassian (SuperNova) FRA	+3.563
3	David Saelens (SuperNova) BEL	+4.778

Round 4

Nurburgring   May 20

1	Bruno Junqueiro (Petrobras) BRA	1:24:07.832
2	Fabrizio Gollin (Martello-Coloni) ITA	+10.882
3	Andre Couto POR	+58.488

Round 5

Monte Carlo   June 3

1	Bruno Junqueiro (Petrobras) BRA	1:19:08.755
2	Jamie Davies (Fortec) GBR	+1.599
3	David Saelens (SuperNova) BEL	+7.726

Round 6

Magny Cours   July 1

1	Nicolas Minassian (SuperNova) FRA	1:15:44.627
2	Sebastien Bourdais FRA	+3.559
3	David Saelens (SuperNova) BEL	+7.936

Round 7

A1-Ring   July 15

1	Nicolas Minassian (SuperNova) FRA	1:10:42.354
2	Justin Wilson (Nordic) GBR	+1.414
3	Darren Manning (Lukoil) GBR	+5.909

Round 8

Hockenheim   July 29

1	Tomas Enge (McLaren jr) CZE	1:14:50.567
2	Tomas Scheckter (McLaren jr) RSA	+6.316
3	Mark Webber (European 3000) AUS	+16.323

Round 9

Hungaroring   Aug 12

1	Bruno Junqueiro (Petrobras) BRA	1:21:30.052
2	Fernando Alonso (Astromega) ESP	+0.594
3	Ricardo Mauricio (Red Bull) BRA	+5.813

Round 10

Spa-Francorchamps   Aug 26

1	Fernando Alonso (Astromega) ESP	1:08:04.964
2	Marc Goossens (Astromega) BEL	+14.601
3	Bruno Junqueiro (Petrobras) BRA	+15.336

FINAL STANDINGS

1	Bruno Junqueiro (Petrobras) BRA	48
2	Nicolas Minassian (SuperNova) FRA	45
3	Mark Webber (European 3000) AUS	21
4	Fernando Alonso (Astromega) ESP	17
5	Justin Wilson (Nordic) GBR	16

"Obviously it was Ricardo's fault. He overestimated his ability"

Michael Schumacher after he was shunted out of the Austrian Grand Prix at the first corner by Brazilian driver Ricardo Zonta.

"I don't believe you can go straight from the kindergarten to university; even Einstein probably gained a lot from going through primary and secondary school"

Jackie Stewart's reservations about Williams' rookie driver Jenson Button.

FedEx Championship Series

Round 1

Homestead, Florida   *Mar 26*

	Driver	Cntry	Laps	Status
1	Max Papis	ITA	150	1:22:01.975
	(Reynard/Ford Cosworth)			
2	Roberto Moreno	BRA	150	+0.620
3	Paul Tracy	CAN	150	+3.835
11	Dario Franchitti	SCO	149	+ 1 lap
13	Mark Blundell	ENG	148	+ 2 laps

Round 2

Long Beach, California   *Apr 16*

	Driver	Cntry	Laps	Status
1	Paul Tracy	CAN	82	1:57:11.132
	(Reynard/Honda)			
2	Helio Castroneves	BRA	82	+3.191
3	Jimmy Vasser	USA	82	+3.298
8	Mark Blundell	ENG	82	+7.737
23	Dario Franchitti	SCO	23	Wrecked

Round 3

Rio de Janeiro, Brazil   *Apr 30*

	Driver	Cntry	Laps	Status
1	Adrian Fernandez	MEX	108	1:37:12.490
	(Reynard/Ford Cosworth)			
2	Jimmy Vasser	USA	108	+0.931
3	Paul Tracy	CAN	108	+1.338
7	Mark Blundell	ENG	108	+5.079
11	Dario Franchitti	SCO	107	+1 lap

Round 4

Japan   *May 14*

	Driver	Cntry	Laps	Status
1	Michael Andretti	USA	201	1:58:52.201
	(Lola/Ford Cosworth)			
2	Dario Franchitti	SCO	201	+0.546
3	Roberto Moreno	BRA	201	+2.825
19	Mark Blundell	ENG	161	Wrecked

Round 5

Nazareth   *May 27*

	Driver	Cntry	Laps	Status
1	Gil de Ferran	BRA	225	2:06:10.334
	(Reynard/Honda)			
2	Mauricio Gugelmin	BRA	225	+0.815
3	Kenny Brack	SWE	225	+1.880
17	Mark Blundell	ENG	166	Wrecked
23	Dario Franchitti	SCO	0	Wrecked

Round 6

Milwaukee   *Jun 5*

	Driver	Cntry	Laps	Status
1	Juan Montoya	COL	225	1:37:38.526
	(Lola/Toyota)			
2	Michael Andretti	USA	225	+1.015
3	Patrick Carpentier	CAN	225	+8.457
6	Dario Franchitti	SCO	225	+15.633
17	Mark Blundell	ENG	224	+1 lap

Round 7

Detroit   *June 18*

	Driver	Cntry	Laps	Status
1	Helio Castroneves	BRA	84	2:01:23.607
	(Reynard/Honda)			
2	Max Papis	ITA	84	+4.415
3	Oriol Seriva	ESP	84	+10.465
4	Dario Franchitti	SCO	84	+13.637
11	Mark Blundell	ENG	81	+ 3 laps

Round 8

Portland   *June 25*

	Driver	Cntry	Laps	Status
1	Gil de Ferran	BRA	112	2:00:46.002
	(Reynard-Honda)			
2	Roberto Moreno	BRA	112	+3.248
3	Christian Fittipaldi	BRA	112	+9.605
9	Dario Franchitti	SCO	112	+1:02.484
20	Mark Blundell	ENG	31	Mechanical

Round 9

Cleveland, Ohio   *July 2*

	Driver	Cntry	Laps	Status
1	Roberto Moreno	BRA	100	1:52:12.092
	(Reynard/Ford Cosworth)			
2	Kenny Brack	SWE	100	+0.826
3	Cristiano da Matta	BRA	100	+1.967
12	Mark Blundell	ENG	98	+ 2 laps
13	Dario Franchitti	SCO	94	Mechanical

Round 10

Toronto   *July 16*

	Driver	Cntry	Laps	Status
1	Michael Andretti	USA	112	2:00:02.313
	(Lola/Ford Cosworth)			
2	Adrian Fernandez	MEX	112	+6.527
3	Paul Tracy	CAN	112	+9.118
22	Mark Blundell	ENG	19	Mechanical
25	Dario Franchitti	SCO	1	Wrecked

Round 11

Michigan   *July 23*

	Driver	Cntry	Laps	Status
1	Juan Montoya	COL	250	2:48:49.790
	(Lola/Toyota)			
2	Michael Andretti	USA	250	+0.040
3	Dario Franchitti	SCO	250	+1.621
19	Mark Blundell	ENG	131	Mechanical

Round 12

Chicago   *July 30*

	Driver	Cntry	Laps	Status
1	Cristiano da Matta	BRA	225	2:01:23.727
	(Reynard/Toyota)			
2	Michael Andretti	USA	225	+1.690
3	Gil de Ferran	BRA	225	+2.519
20	Dario Franchitti	SCO	74	Wrecked
23	Mark Blundell	ENG	18	Mechanical

Round 13

Mid Ohio   *Aug 13*

	Driver	Cntry	Laps	Status
1	Helio Castroneves (Reynard/Honda))	BRA	83	1:43:59.029
2	Gil de Ferran	BRA	83	+4.686
3	Christian Fittipaldi	BRA	83	+6.173
14	Mark Blundell	ENG	82	+ 1 lap
22	Dario Franchitti	SCO	52	Wrecked

Round 14

Road America   *Aug 20*

	Driver	Cntry	Laps	Status
1	Paul Tracy (Reynard/Honda)	CAN	55	1:37:53.681
2	Adrian Fernandez	MEX	55	+7.450
3	Kenny Brack	SWE	55	+8.836
11	Mark Blundell	ENG	48	Mechanical
12	Dario Franchitti	SCO	43	Mechanical

Round 15

Vancouver   *Sep 3*

	Driver	Cntry	Laps	Status
1	Paul Tracy (Reynard/Honda)	CAN	90	1:53:06.024
2	Dario Franchitti	SCO	90	+0.000
3	Adrian Fernandez	MEX	90	+19.031
25	Mark Blundell	ENG	3	Wrecked

Round 16

Laguna Seca   *Sep 10*

	Driver	Cntry	Laps	Status
1	Helio Castroneves (Reynard/Honda)	BRA	83	1:46:11.800
2	Gil de Ferran	BRA	83	+0.954
3	Dario Franchitti	SCO	83	+2.642
13	Mark Blundell	ENG	83	+25.312

Round 17

Gateway   *Sep 12*

	Driver	Cntry	Laps	Status
1	Juan Montoya (Lola/Toyota)	COL	236	1:55:38.003
2	Patrick Carpentier	CAN	236	+11.804
3	Roberto Moreno	BRA	235	+ 1 lap
23	Mark Blundell	ENG	64	Mechanical
24	Dario Franchitti	SCO	62	Mechanical

Round 18

Houston   *Oct 1*

	Driver	Cntry	Laps	Status
1	Jimmy Vasser (Lola/Toyota)	USA	100	1:59:02.370
2	Juan Montoya	COL	100	+1.914
3	Gil de Ferran	BRA	100	+2.317
20	Mark Blundell	ENG	50	Mechanical
25	Dario Franchitti	SCO	1	Wrecked

Round 19

Gold Coast, Queensland   *Oct 15*

	Driver	Cntry	Laps	Status
1	Adrian Fernandez (Reynard/Ford Cosworth)	MEX	59	2:01:14.605
2	Kenny Brack	SWE	59	+0.324
3	Jimmy Vasser	USA	59	+4.059
19	Mark Blundell	ENG	59	+18.783
25	Dario Franchitti	SCO	0	Wrecked

Round 20

Fontana, California   *Oct 29*

	Driver	Cntry	Laps	Status
1	Christian Fittipaldi (Lola/Ford Cosworth)	BRA	250	3:38:04.376
2	Roberto Moreno	BRA	250	+0.194
3	Gil de Ferran	BRA	250	+0.526
15	Mark Blundell	ENG	129	Mechanical
23	Dario Franchitti	SCO	45	Mechanical

> **"I went through a period when I was perceived as being a soft touch, someone who moves over"**
>
> David Coulthard.
>
> **"I was starting to think that Michael could walk on water because he never seems to have reliability problems, but it seems that he does get wet like the rest of us"**
>
> Couthard, after winning in Monaco. Michael Schumacher failed to finish.
>
> **"I've not had sex for two weeks now. With my cracked ribs and Heidi's bruised chest, it's a bit difficult. The dog is starting to get worried"**
>
> Coulthard, after escaping relatively unscathed from the plane crash that killed both pilots.

CART
FedEx Drivers' Championship

Final Standings

			total
1	Gil de Ferran	BRA	163
2	Adrian Fernandez	MEX	153
3	Roberto Moreno	BRA	147
4	Paul Tracy	CAN	134
5	Kenny Brack	SWE	134
6	Jimmy Vasser	USA	131
7	Helio Castroneves	BRA	129
8	Michael Andretti	USA	127
9	Juan Montoya	COL	126
10	Cristiano da Matta	BRA	112
11	Patrick Carpentier	CAN	101
12	Christian Fittipaldi	BRA	97
13	Dario Franchitti	SCO	92
14	Max Papis	ITA	88
15	Oriol Servia	ESP	60
16	Alexandre Tagliani	CAN	53
17	Mauricio Gugelmin	BRA	39
18	Bryan Herta	USA	26
19	Tony Kanaan	BRA	24
20	Merno Gidley	USA	20
21	Mark Blundell	ENG	18

Rookie of the Year

Final Standings

			total
1	Kenny Brack	SWE	134
2	Oriol Servia	ESP	60
3	Alexandre Tagliani	CAN	53

Constructors' Championship

Final Standings

		total
1	Reynard	394
2	Lola	275
3	Swift	74

Manufacturers' Championship

Final Standings

		total
1	Ford	335
2	Honda	313
3	Toyota	275
4	Mercedes	74

Le Mans 24 Hours

Circuit de la Sarthe   June 17-18
Circuit length: 13.61km

	Drivers	Entrant	Category	Car	Laps
1	Biela/Kristensen/Pirro	Audi Sport/Joest	LMP900	Audi 3596T	368
2	Aiello/McNish/Ortellii	Audi Sport/Joest	LMP900	Audi 3596T	367
3	Abt/Alboreto/Capello	Audi Sport/Joest	LMP900	Audi 3596T	365
4	Bourdais/Clerico/Grouillard	Pescarolo Sport	LMP900	Peugeot 3200T	344
5	O'Connell/Katoh/Raphanel	Panoz Motorsports	LMP900	Ford 6000A	342
6	Suzuki/Mo Kageyama/Mi Kageyama	TV Asahi Team Dragon	LMP900	Ford 6000A	340
7	Beretta/Wendlinger/Dupuy	Viper Team Oreca	LMGTS	Chrysler 8000A	333
8	Tsuchiya/Iida/Kondo	TV Asahi Team Dragon	LMP900	Ford 6000A	330
9	Donohue/Amorim/Beltoise	Viper Team Oreca	LMGTS	Chrysler 8000A	328
10	Pilgrim/Collins/Freon	Corvette Racing/Gary Pratt	LMGTS	Corvette 6991A	327

Winner's Distance Covered: 5,007.988km

Rallying

World Championship

Rallye Automobile Monte Carlo
Jan 20-22

1 Tommi Makinen (Mitsubishi Ralliart) FIN   4:23:35.2
2 Carlos Sainz (M-Sport Ford) ESP   4:25:00.7
3 Juha Kankkunen (Prodrive Subaru) FIN   4:26:57.2

Swedish Rally
Feb 10-13

1 Marcus Grönholm (Peugeot Sport) FIN   3:20:33.3
2 Tommi Makinen (Mitsubishi Ralliart) FIN   3:20:40.1
3 Colin McRae (M-Sport Ford) GBR   3:20:47.0

Safari Rally Kenya
Feb 24-27

1 Richard Burns (Prodrive Subaru) GBR   8:33:13
2 Juha Kankkunen (Prodrive Subaru) FIN   8:37:50
3 Didier Auriol (SEAT) FRA   8:55:57

Portuguese Rally
Mar 16-19

1 Richard Burns (Prodrive Subaru) GBR   4:34:00.0
2 Marcus Grönholm (Peugeot Sport) FIN   4:34:06.5
3 Carlos Sainz (M-Sport Ford) ESP   4:36:09.2

Catalan Rally
Mar 30-Apr 2

1 Colin McRae (M-Sport Ford) GBR   4:07:13.0
2 Richard Burns (Prodrive Subaru) GBR   4:07:18.9
3 Carlos Sainz (M-Sport Ford) ESP   4:07:24.7

Rally Argentina
May 11-14

1 Richard Burns (Prodrive Subaru) GBR   4:10:20.7
2 Marcus Grönholm (Peugeot Sport) FIN   4:11:28.1
3 Tommi Makinen (Mitsubishi Ralliart) FIN   4:11:52.3

Acropolis Rally
June 8-11

1 Colin McRae (M-Sport Ford) GBR   4:56:54.8
2 Carlos Sainz (M-Sport Ford) ESP   4:57:17.9
3 Juha Kankkunen (Prodrive Subaru) FIN   5:03:33.1

Rally New Zealand
July 13-15

1 Marcus Grönholm (Peugeot Sport) FIN   3:45:13.4
2 Colin McRae (M-Sport Ford) GBR   3:45:27.9
3 Carlos Sainz (M-Sport Ford) ESP   3:46:31.8

Rally Finland
Aug 17-20

1 Marcus Grönholm (Peugeot Sport) FIN   3:22:37.1
2 Colin McRae (M-Sport Ford) GBR   3:23:43.5
3 Harri Rovanpera (Grifone) FIN   3:23:46.7

Rally Cyprus
Sep 7-10

1 Carlos Sainz (M-Sport Ford) ESP   5:26:04.9
2 Colin McRae (M-Sport Ford) GBR   5:26:42.2
3 François Delecour (Peugeot Sport) FRA   5:27:35.7

Corsican Rally
Sep 28-Oct 1

1 Giles Panizzi (Peugeot Sport) FRA   4:02:14.2
2 François Delecour (Paugeot Sport) FRA   4:02:47.7
3 Carlos Sainz (M-Sport Ford) ESP   4:03:26.8

San Remo Rally
Oct 19-22

1 Gilles Panizzi (Peugeot Sport) FRA   3:52:07.3
2 François Delecour (Peugeot Sport) FRA   3:52:24.1
3 Tommi Makinen (Mitsubishi Ralliart) FIN   3:53:00.3

Rally Australia
Nov 9-12

1 Marcus Grönholm (Subaru Impreza) FIN   3:43:57.2
2 Richard Burns (Prodrive Subaru) GBR   3:43:59.9
3 François Delecour (Peugeot Sport) FRA   3:45:30.1

Network Q Rally of Great Britain
Nov 23-26

1 Richard Burns (Subaru Impreza) GBR   3:53:44.2
2 Marcus Grönholm (Subaru Impreza) FIN   3:44:07.5
3 Tommi Makinen (Mitsubishi Ralliart) FIN   3:44:16.9

DRIVERS' CHAMPIONSHIP
Final Standings

1 Marcus Grönholm (Peugeot Sport) FIN   65
2 Richard Burns (Prodrive Subaru) GBR   60
3 Carlos Sainz (M-Sport Ford) ESP   46
4 Colin McRae (M-Sport Ford) GBR   43
5 Tommi Makinen (Mitsubishi Ralliart) FIN   36
6 François Delecour (Peugeot Sport) FRA   24
7 Gilles Panizzi (Peugeot Sport) FRA   21
8 Juha Kankkunen (Prodrive Subaru) FIN   20

MANUFACTURERS' CHAMPIONSHIP
Final Standings

1. Peugeot 111; 2. Ford 91; 3. Subaru 88;
4. Mitsubishi 43; 5. SEAT 11; 6. Skoda 8

Mobil 1 British Rally Championship

DRIVERS' CHAMPIONSHIP
Final Standings

1 Marko Ipatti (Mitsubishi Lancer) FIN   45
2 Mark Higgins (Vauxhall Astra) GBR   44
3 Neil Wearden (Poulton-le-Fylde) GBR   35
4 Tapio Laukkanen (Volkswagen Golf) FIN   30
5 Justin Dale (Peugeot 106 Super) GBR   28
6 Mats Andersson (Proton Compact) SWE   26
7 Jarmo Kytoleho (Hyundai Coupe F2) FIN   24
8 Andrew Pinker (Hyundai Coupe F2) GBR   15
9 Charlie Jukes (Proton Compact) GBR   11
10 David Higgins (Peugeot 106 Super) GBR   10

Netball

International Matches

European Championship
Feb 25-27, 2000

Feb 25
England 58 N Ireland 38
Malta 10 Wales 69

Feb 26
England 87 Malta 11
Northern Ireland 41 Scotland 43
England 42 Wales 32
Malta 21 Scotland 49

Feb 27
Northern Ireland 28 Wales 60
England 58 Scotland 30
Malta 19 Northern Ireland 55
Scotland 29 Wales 59

Final Placings
1. England played 4-won 4; 2. Wales 3-1; 3. Scotland 2-2;
4. Northern Ireland 1-3; 5. Malta 0-4

Other Internationals

Cardiff, Jan 30, 1999
Wales 26 England 55

Manchester Feb 22, 1999
England 57 South Africa 54

England v South Africa Test Series, 2000
Wembley, May 13
England 48 South Africa 41
Manchester, May 17
England 42 South Africa 44
Sheffield, May 22
England 57 South Africa 39

England v Jamaica Test Series, 2000
Guildford, Apr 5
England 50 Jamaica 36
Gateshead, Apr 8
England 52 Jamaica 41
Birmingham, Apr 12
England 38 Jamaica 49

Tri-nations
South Africa, Nov 2000
New Zealand 52 Australia 40
Australia 81 South Africa 23
Australia 73 South Africa 33
New Zealand 81 South Africa 35
New Zealand 88 South Africa 34

National Clubs Competition

Semi Finals/Finals Results 1999/2000 Season
30th April, 2000 - Stockland Green Leisure Centre,
Birmingham

Semi Finals
Sheffield Concord v Sheffield Open: 40 - 41
Star v Wealdon: 50- 41

3rd/4th Place Play Off
Wealdon v Sheffield Concord: 55 - 49
FINAL
Star v Sheffield Open: 49 - 30

Inter Counties Championship

Winners: Derbyshire

English Counties League Championship

Winners: Essex Met

Orienteering

World Cup
FINAL STANDINGS
Men

Individual

1	Jani Lakanen	FIN	261
2	Tore Sandvik	NOR	256
3	Allan Mogensen	DEN	252
4	Emil Wingstedt	SWE	251
5=	Valentin Novikov	RUS	241
5=	Bjørnar Valstad	NOR	241
7	Janne Salmi	FIN	236
8	Tomo Karppinen	FIN	230
9	Mikael Bostrom	FIN	221
10	Carl Henrik Bjøerseth	NOR	214
11	Jamie Stevenson	GBR	210
34	Stephen Palmer	GBR	84
37	Jon Duncan	GBR	76
44	Steven Hale	GBR	63
45	David Peel	GBR	62
61=	Daniel Marston	GBR	44
63	Oliver Johnson	GBR	41
87=	Andy Kitchen	GBR	15

Team

1	Sweden	47
2	Norway	45
3	Switzerland	42
4	Finland	40
5	Denmark	31
6	Great Britain	29

Women

Individual

1	Hanne Staff	NOR	276
2	Simone Luder	SUI	261
3	Heather Monro	GBR	255
4	Katarine Allberg	SWE	246
5	Brigitte Wolf	SUI	241
6	Jenny Johansson	SWE	239
7	Reeta Kolkkala	FIN	236
8	Yvette Baker	GBR	233
9	Kirsti Bostrom	FIN	230
10	Emma Engstrand	SWE	225
30	Jenny James	GBR	108
45=	Helene Hargreaves	GBR	59
49=	Kim Buckley	GBR	56
53	Lorna Eades	GBR	52
56=	Sarah Rollins	GBR	48
78	Liz Campbell	GBR	19
109=	Hannah Wootton	GBR	1

Team

1	Norway	55
2	Sweden	49
3	Switzerland	46
4	Great Britain	36
5	Finland	35

World Rankings
As at Mar 31, 2001

Men

1	Bjørnar Valstad	NOR	5606
2	Valentin Novikov	RUS	5582
3	Allan Mogensen	DEN	5556
4	Jani Lakanen	FIN	5474
5	Jamie Stevenson	GBR	5442
6	Tore Sandvik	NOR	5437
7	Emil Wingstedt	SWE	5434
8	Carl Henrik Björseth	NOR	5430
9	Janne Salmi	FIN	5414
10	Jimmy Birklin	SWE	5394

Women

1	Simone Luder	SUI	5691
2	Hanne Staff	NOR	5686
3	Heather Monro	GBR	5604
4	Emma Engstrand	SWE	5574
5	Brigitte Wolf	SUI	5497
6	Reeta Kolkkala	FIN	5477
7	Katarina Allberg	SWE	5468
8	Marika Mikkola	FIN	5440
9	Jenny Johansson	SWE	5424
10=	Cecilia Nilsson	SWE	5415
10=	Maria Sandström	SWE	5415

Rowing

Sir Steven Redgrave

Olympic Games

1984 Los Angeles	Gold	Coxed Four (with Martin Cross/Richard Budgett/Andrew Holmes/Adrian Ellison)
1988 Seoul	Gold	Coxless Pair (with Andrew Holmes)
	Bronze	Coxed Pair (with Andrew Holmes /Patrick Sweeney)
1992 Barcelona	Gold	Coxless Pair (with Matthew Pinsent)
1996 Atlanta	Gold	Coxless Pair (with Matthew Pinsent)
2000 Sydney	Gold	Coxless Four (with James Cracknell/Tim Foster/Matthew Pinsent)

Commonwealth Games

1986 Edinburgh	Gold	Single Scull
	Gold	Coxless Pair (with Andrew Holmes)
	Gold	Coxed Four (with Martin Cross/Adam Cliff/Andrew Holmes/Adrian Ellison)

World Championships

1986 Nottingham	Gold	Coxed Pair (with Andrew Holmes/Patrick Sweeney)
1987 Copenhagen	Gold	Coxless Pair (with Andrew Holmes)
	Silver	Coxed Pair (with Andrew Holmes/Patrick Sweeney)
1989 Bled	Silver	Coxless Pair (with Simon Berrisford)
1990 Tasmania	Bronze	Coxless Pair (with Matthew Pinsent)
1991 Vienna	Gold	Coxless Pair (with Matthew Pinsent)
1993 Roudnice	Gold	Coxless Pair (with Matthew Pinsent)
1994 Indianapolis	Gold	Coxless Pair (with Matthew Pinsent)
1995 Tampere	Gold	Coxless Pair (with Matthew Pinsent)
1997 Aiguebelette	Gold	Coxless Four (with James Cracknell/Tim Foster/Matthew Pinsent)
1998 Cologne	Gold	Coxless Four (with James Cracknell/Tim Foster/Matthew Pinsent)
1999 St Catharines	Gold	Coxless Four (with James Cracknell/Ed Coode/Matthew Pinsent)

Henley Regatta

1981	1st	Double Sculls Challenge Cup
1982	1st	Double Sculls Challenge Cup
	1st	Queen Mother Challenge Cup
1983	1st	Diamond Challenge Sculls
1984	1st	Prince Philip Challenge Cup
1985	1st	Diamond Challenge Sculls
	1st	Prince Philip Challenge Cup
1986	1st	The Silver Goblets & Nickalls Challenge Cup
1987	1st	The Silver Goblets & Nickalls Challenge Cup
1989	1st	The Silver Goblets & Nickalls Challenge Cup
1991	1st	The Silver Goblets & Nickalls Challenge Cup
1993	1st	The Silver Goblets & Nickalls Challenge Cup
	1st	The Stewards Challenge Cup
1994	1st	The Silver Goblets & Nickalls Challenge Cup
1995	1st	The Silver Goblets & Nickalls Challenge Cup
1997	1st	The Stewards Challenge Cup
1998	1st	The Stewards Challenge Cup
1999	1st	The Stewards Challenge Cup
2000	1st	The Stewards Challenge Cup

Since his first appearance at Henley in 1980, Redgrave has rowed in 67 races (including heats and finals) and won 64 of them. He was last defeated in a boat at Henley in 1986.

See also Olympic Games section for rowing comments

World Championships
for non-Olympic events

Zagreb, Croatia   *Aug 3-6*
Crews are listed in order from bow to stroke, with the cox signified by an asterisk.

Men

Coxed Pair
1	United States	7:07
2	Romania	7:10.0
3	France	7:10.6
10	Great Britain	7:14

(Gardner/Simmons/Cormack*)

Coxed Four
1	Great Britain	6:16

(Smith, Williams, Garbett, Dunn, Potts*)
2	United States	6:18
3	Germany	6:21

Lightweight Single Sculls
1	Czech Republic	7:21
2	Ireland	7:22
3	Slovakia	7:27
15	Great Britain	

(Monnickendam)

Lightweight Quad Sculls
1	Japan	6:06
2	Italy	6:08
3	Spain	6:09

No British boat

Lightweight Coxless Pair
1	Canada	6:49
2	Great Britain	6:50.0

(Peter Haining/Nick Strange)
3	Denmark	6:50.2

Lightweight Eight
1	USA	5:55
2	Great Britain	5:58

(Kittoe/Brown/McNiven/Beechey/Middleton/McGarva/Lee/Baker/Cormack*)

Women

Coxless Four
1	Belarus	6:44
2	Poland	6:47
3	Romania	6:49

No GBR boat

Lightweight Single Sculls
1	Finland	8:13
2	Germany	8:20
3	Ireland	8:24
5	Great Britain	8:28

(Langlands)

Lightweight Quad Sculls
1	Germany	6:54
2	Australia	6:56
3	China	6:58
5	Great Britain	7:03

(Casey/Nitsch/Birch/Hall)

Lightweight Coxless Pair
1	Great Britain	7:32

(Myers/Taylor)
2	USA	7:35
3	Germany	7:49

World Cup Series

Non-World Cup events indicated by NWC
British crews shown where they reached a final

Munich Regatta
June 1-3

Men
Single Sculls
1	Vaclav Chalupa	CZE	7:08.68
2	Marcel Hacker	GER	7:09.00
3	Juri Jaanson	EST	7:17.00

Double Sculls
1	Spik/Cop	SLO	6:33.11
2	Tufte/Bekken	NOR	6:35.37
3	Petö/Haller	HUN	6:38.19

Quad Sculls
1	Ukraine	6:05.59
2	Switzerland	6:07.35
3	Netherlands	6:07.95

Coxless Pair
1	Visacki/Stojic	YUG	6:52.52
2	Andrieux/Rolland	FRA	6:57.89
3	G Searle/E Coode	GBR	6:59.76

Coxless Four
1	Great Britain	6:19.59

(Cracknell/Redgrave/Coode/Pinsent)
2	France	6:15.43
3	Norway	6:18.08
5	Great Britain 2	6:23.75

(Smith/Simmons/Garbett/Dunn)

Eight
1	Croatia	5:54.48
2	Great Britain	5:57.05

(Thatcher/Hunt-Davis/Dennis/Attrill/Grubor/West/Scarlett/Trapmore/Douglas)
3	Netherlands	5:59.25

Lightweight Single Sculls (NWC)
1	Tomas Haltsonen	FIN	7:42.76
2	Lubos Fedstapka	SVK	7:44.37
3	Pawel Randa	POL	7:44.94

Lightweight Double Sculls
1	Touron/Chapelle	FRA	6:41.51
2	Kucharski/Sycz	POL	6:45.44
3	Gier/Gier	SUI	6:49.00

Lightweight Coxless Pair (NWC)
1 Dormans/De Groot NED 7:07.08
2 Baker/Legg GBR 7:10.32
3 Fauck/Heindenreich GER 7:12.58
5 Tucker/Davis GBR 7:15.92

Lightweight Coxless Four
1 France 6:16.57
2 Austria 6:19.38
3 Ireland 6:19.74

Women
Single Sculls
1 Ekaterina Karsten BLR 7:50.98
2 Irina Fedotova RUS 7:55.06
3 Katrin Rutschow-Stomporowski
   GER 8:00.04
5 Alison Mowbray GBR 8:05.83

Double Sculls
1 Thieme/Boron GER 7:15.44
2 Lipa/Cochela ROM 7:18.65
3 Liu/Zhang CHN 7:21.68
4 Houghton/Lindsay GBR 7:23.02

Quad Sculls
1 Germany 6:37.28
2 Ukraine 6:38.77
3 Belarus 6:43.64
5 Great Britain 6:44.66
   (G Batten/Winckless/Grainger/M Batten)

Coxless Pair
1 Damian/Ignat ROM 7:34.84
2 Wech/Barth GER 7:37.11
3 Potchitaeva/Ligatcheva RUS 7:40.07
5 Blackie/Bishop GBR 7:44.55

Eight
1 Netherlands 6:33.93
2 Belarus 6:35.09
3 Romania 6:36.07
4 Great Britain 6:37.34
   (Trickey/Zino/Gough/Carroll/Laverick/
   Beever/McKenzie/Eyre/Miller)

Lightweight Single Sculls (NWC)
1 Laila Finska-Bezerra FIN 8:36.38
2 Sinead Jenkins IRL 8:38.52
3 Angelika Brand GER 8:40.29
5 Jane Hall GBR 8:56.36

Lightweight Double Sculls
1 Biehoff/Blasberg GER 7:24.76
2 Van der Volk/Van Eupen NED 7:30.47
3 Barcica/Macoviciuc ROM 7:32.91

Lightweight Quad Sculls (NWC)
1 Great Britain 7:14.49
   (Myers/Casey/McClelland-Brooks/Birch)
2 Ireland 7:22.96
3 Hungary 7:44.00

Vienna Regatta
June 23-25

Men
Single Sculls
1 Xeno Mueller SUI 7:34.81
2 Rob Waddell NZL 7:36.52
3 Vaclav Chalupa CZE 7:38.61

Double Sculls
1 Tufte/Bekken NOR 7:01.47
2 Galtarossa/Sartori ITA 7:04:01
3 Petö/Haller HUN 7:09.99

Quad Sculls
1 Austria 6:22.45
   (Hartl/Nussbaumer/Jonke/Lambing)
2 Italy 6:22.47
3 USA 6:25.90

Coxless Pair
1 Ginn/Tomkins AUS 7:16.54
2 Sorrentino/PanzarinoITA 7:18.42
3 G Searle/Coode GBR 7:18.88

Coxless Four
1 Great Britain 6:34.62
   (Cracknell/Redgrave/Coode/Pinsent)
2 New Zealand 6:36.38
3 Great Britain II 6:37.10
   (Garbett/Williams/Scarlett/Dunn)

Eight
1 Great Britain 5:58.76
   (Thatcher/Hunt-Davis/Grubor/Atrill/Dennis/West/
   Lindsay/Trapmore/Douglas*)
2 Australia 6:00.63
3 Germany 6:03.09

Lightweight Single Sculls (NWC)
1 P Randa POL 7:57.80
2 L Podstupka SVK 7:59.44
3 F Mannucci ITA 8:03.21

Lightweight Double Sculls
1 Basalini/Pittino ITA 7:11.56
2 Luini/Pettinari ITA 7:14.74
3 Gier/Gier SUI 7:21.15

Lightweight Quad Sculls (NWC)
1 Austria 6:39.74
2 United States 6:42.84
3 Canada 6:43.48

Lightweight Coxless Pair (NWC)
1 Strauch/Spaeter GER 7:33.03
2 Pasqualini/Fraquelli ITA 7:39.48
3 Krog/Skov Hansen DEN 7:43.70

Lightweight Coxless Four
1 Austria 6:39.74
2 United States II 6:42.84
3 Canada 6:43.48

Women
Single Sculls
1 X Zhang CHN 8:21.50
2 Katrin Rutschow-Stomporovski GER8:23.13
3 Sonia Waddell NZL 8:37.42

Double Sculls
1 Evers-Swindel x2 NZL 7:51.65
2 Poplavskaja/Sakickiene LTU 7:57.59
3 Skricki/Davidon USA 7:58.61

Quad Sculls
1 Great Britain 7:09.87
  (G Batten/Winckless/Grainger/M Batten)
2 China 7:17.36
3 Romania 7:21.20

Coxless Pair
1 Taylor/Slatter AUS 8:03.71
2 Robinson/Luke CAN 8:06.30
3 Wech/Barth GER 8:09.06

Eight
1 Belarus 6:31.74
2 Romania 6:33.91
3 Australia 6:40.22
5 Great Britain 6:45.53
  (Trickey/Zino/Sanders/Carroll/Laverick/
  Beever/Mckenzie/Eyre/Miller*)

Lightweight Single Sculls (NWC)
1 Finska-Bezerr FIN 8:49.27
2 S Jennings IRL 8:54.42
3 A Brand GER 9:13.08

Lightweight Double Sculls
1 Burcica/Alupei ROM 8:08.60
2 Yu/Ou CHN 8:11.49
3 Plugge/Vogel SUI 8:16.77

Lucerne Regatta
The Rotsee July 14-16

Men
Single Scull
1 Rob Waddell NZL 6:53.13
2 Derek Porter CAN 6:54.15
3 Vaclav Chalupa CZE 6:56.60

Double Scull
1 Spik/Cop SLO 6:33.82
2 Tufte/Bekken NOR 6:37.77
3 Tibor/Haller HUN 6:39.21

Quadruple Scull
1 Italy 5:49.74
  (Raineri/Galtarossa/Sartori/Abbagnale)
2 Netherlands 5:51.44
3 Austria 5:52.50

Coxless Pair
1 Long/Tomkins AUS 6:34.98
2 Sorrentino/Panzarino ITA 6:36.14
3 Kirchhoff/Sens GER 6:36.46
Coode/Searle GBR won the B Final

Coxless Four
1 Italy 6:02.01
  (Molea/Dei Rossi/Carboncinci/Mornati)
2 New Zealand 6:04.40
3 Australia 6:04.60
4 Great Britain 6:08.01
  (Cracknell/Redgrave/Foster/Pinsent)

Eights
1 Great Britain 5:35.48
  (Lindsay/Hunt-Davies/Dennis/Cracknell/Grubor/
  West/Scarlett/Trapmore/Douglas)
2 Australia 5:35.79
3 USA 5:36.50

Lightweight Double Scull
1 Luini/Pettinari ITA 6:29.03
2 Touron/Chapelle FRA 6:31.70
3 Euler/Ruehling GER 6:33.66
4 Kay/Male GBR 6:35.71

Lightweight Coxless Four
1 France 6:00.13
  (Porchier/Bette/Hocde/Dorfman)
2 Austria 6:00.21
3 Italy 6:05.06

Women
Single Scull
1 Ekaterina Karsten BLR 7:31.39
2 Rumyana Neykova BUL 7:32.92
3 Katrin Rutschow-Stomporowski
                     GER 7:39.82

Double Scull
1 Thieme/Boron GER 6:55.32
2 Sakickiene/Paplavskaja LTU 7:00.17
3 Skricki/Davidon USA 7:01.00
6 Houghton/Lindsay GBR 7:09.86

Quadruple Scull
1 Germany 6:19.68
  (Kowalski/Lutze/Evers/Kowalski)
2 Russia 6:21.42
3 USA 6:29.53

Coxless Pair
1 Damian/Ignat ROM 7:12.83
2 Taylor/Slatter AUS 7:15.20
3 Robinson/Luke CAN 7:15.99
Blackie/Bishop GBR won the B final

Eights
1 Romania 6:11.51
  (Damian/Susanu/Olteanu/Ignat/Dumitrache/
  Lipa/Popescu/Cochela)
2 Canada 6:12.85
3 Australia 6:12.93

Lightweight Double Scull
1 Burcica/Alupei ROM 7:07.75
2 Smith Collins/Garner USA 7:09.48
3 Blasberg/Viehoff GER 7:10.81

World Cup
Nations - Finals Standings
1. Germany 143; 2. Australia 100; 3. Great Britain 93;
4. Romania 86; 5. Italy 77

Events - Final Standings
Men
Single Scull
1	Czech Republic	18
2	New Zealand	14
3	Germany	13

Coxless Pair
1	Australia	16
2	Italy	12
3	Germany	11

Double Scull
1	Norway	20
2	Slovenia	16
3	Hungary	15

Coxless Four
1	Great Britain	20
2	Italy	12
3	New Zealand	12

Lightweight Double Scull
1	Italy	16
2	France	14
3	Switzerland	10

Lightweight Coxless Four
1	Austria	20
2	France	16
3	Italy	11

Quadruple Scull
1	Austria	15
2	Italy	14
3	Netherlands	13

Eights
1	Britain	22
2	Croatia	13
3	Australia	12

Women
Single Scull
1	Belarus	16
2	Germany	16
3	Russia	10

Coxless Pair
1	Romania	19
2	Germany	15
3	Australia	13

Double Scull
1	Germany	16
2	Lithuania	15
3	New Zealand	9

Lightweight Double Scull
1	Romania	21
2	Germany	13
3	Switzerland	11

Quadruple Scull
1	Germany	16
2	Britain	11
3	Russia	10

Eights
1	Romania	19
2	Belarus	16
3	Netherlands	12

146th University Boat Race
Putney to Mortlake   Mar 25

Oxford beat Cambridge by three lengths
Times (Oxford first)
Mile: 3:41; 3:42
Hammersmith Bridge: 6:35; 6:34
Chiswick Steps: 10:44; 10:44
Barnes Bridge 14:54; 14:59
Finish: 18:04; 18:12

	Cambridge	Oxford
	B S J Cummings	T H Ayer
	H N F Martin	A M Reid
	J J O'Loghlen	N J Robinson
	T A Stallard	M J Smith
	R P Cantwell	B J Burch
	R A Ehlers	A G G Dunn
	D J Tweedie	E B Lilledahl
	A J West	D R Snow
Cox	G J Glassman	A K MCLaren

Reserve Race
Isis *(Oxford)* beat Goldie *(Cambridge)* by five lengths

Women's Boat Race
Putney to Mortlake   Mar 25
Oxford bt Cambridge
by 2 & 1/4 lengths
6:18

Head of the River
Mortlake to Putney   Mar 18

1	Queen's Tower	17:16.07
2	Leander	17:17.33
3	Oxford Brookes	17:31.53

Henley Regatta

June 23-July 2
All events for men, except where stated

Temple Cup
Eights
Yale University bt Oxford Brookes University
⅔l   6:37

Wyfold Cup
Coxless Four
Worcester Rowing Club bt Queen's Tower
1¾l   7:15

Princess Elizabeth Cup
Eight
St Joseph's Prep School (USA) bt Groton (USA)
1¾l   6:47

Stewards' Cup
Coxless Four
Leander bt Sydney Haberfield
⅔l   6:50

Double Sculls Cup
Kalizan/Samuelsen (DEN) bt Langridge/Wells GBR
easily 7:28

Britannia Cup
Coxed Four
Cambridge University bt Imperial College, London
½   7:19

Visitors' Cup
Coxless Four
Oxford Brookes University
7:04

Diamond Scull
Single Sculls
A H Abdullah (USA) bt S D Goodbrand GBR
⅔l   8:12

Grand Cup
Eight
Australian Institute of Sport bt Leander/Queen's Tower
1½l   6:19

Silver Goblets & Nickalls' Challenge Cup
Coxless Pair
Searle/Coode bt Di Clemente/Cech
1¾l   7:32

Princess Royal Cup (women)
D Flood (Tideway scullers) bt M Brandin
1l   9:12

Fawley Cup
Coxless Four
Leander/Llandaff
7:16

Prince Philip Cup
Coxed Four
Leander/Llandaff bt Tiffin School
3½l   7:08

The Henley Prize
Women's eights
University of Washington
7:29

Women's Plate
Eight
Brown University (USA) bt Rostock & Heidelberg (GER)
1l   6:30

Thames Cup
Eight
Molesey A bt Crabtree
½l   6:36

Queen Mother Cup
Coxless Four
A S R Nereus & D S R Laga (NED) bt
Australian Institute of Sport
3¼l   6:45

Women's Henley

June 19-20

Single Sculls
D Flood (TSS) bt E Butler-Stoney (Wallingford)
easily 5:57

Double Sculls
Mortlake Anglian & Alpha bt Walbrook/Grosvenor
1¼l   6:00

Quad Sculls
Thames Tradesman bt Molesey
2¼l   5:19

Redgrave Coxless Pair
Marlow/Thames bt Kingston/Newcastle University
1¾l   5:41

Coxed Four
Wallingford bt Sons of the Thames
1¾l   5:53

Coxless Four
Univ London/UL Tyrian bt Univ British Columbia
4l 5:29

Eight
University Victoria (CAN) bt UTRC/Kingston
⅔l   5:02

Lightweight Single Sculls
A Holohan (Commercial) bt E Huntington (Lea)
2l   6:01

Lightweight Double Sculls
Wallingford bt Mortlake Anglian & Alpha
3½l

Lightweight Coxless Pair
Tideway scullers bt Wemmer Pan (RSA)
2½l   5:53

Lightweight Coxless Four
Avon County bt Nottingham
2½l   5:28

Rugby League

World Cup is a generous name for a tournament so dominated by a single country. Not only did the Australians have by far and away the best team the tournament, but they helped form most of the others too. The Aussies made up the entire Lebanon team, as well as huge chunks of other squads: 12 for Scotland, 10 for Ireland, seven Russians and even a New Zealand Maori. Their domination of the event was total. From the outset, only Australia could win and the Kangeroos duly delivered. Their supremacy, atrocious weather and some odd scheduling meant that the tournament was destined to make less of an impact than the organisers might have hoped for.

The weather was so bad that three of the Lebanese team, Michael Coorey, George Catrib and Travis Touma, were treated for hypothermia after their opening game against New Zealand at Gloucester. The unbelievable autumn rains, which brought flooding and misery to so many people, left their mark on all six countries that hosted games.

The scheduling errors began with the England v Australia opener, timed for a Saturday evening at Twickenham. This was unsympathethic to the fans, the majority of whom travelled down from the north. The organisers had also failed to secure terrestrial television coverage for the match. The relative success of the 1995 tournament was built upon the opening game between the same two teams, shown live on Grandstand.

Other comparisons between the 1995 World Cup did not reflect well on this tournament. In Wales, the organisers ignored the fact that 15,000 had turned up at the Vetch Field in 1995 and instead gave the Wales against Lebanon match to Stradey Park, home of Llanelli RFC. The game drew a mere 1,497 people. Only in France, which admittedly escaped the worst of the weather, were crowds anything like encouraging. France v Tonga in Carcassone even hit five figures.

The home challenge disappeared in the semi-final, both England and Wales suffering heavy defeats. The final, Australia and New Zealand, was watched by 44,329 at Old Trafford. The Aussies won 40-12, though New Zealand were competitive for long periods before running out of steam.

Domestically, St Helens won the Grand Final, also at Old Trafford, in a frenzied atmosphere that must have made Roy Keane a little envious. The Warriors domination of league, once absolute, is now no more than a fading memory. As is the career of their magnificent scrum-half Shaun Edwards, who was part of the all-conquering team of the nineties, but who gave way to injuries and retired at 33. His career record reads: seven championships, five premierships, nine challenge cups, seven Regal trophies, three world club challenges, five Lancashire cups and three charity shields. Edwards was also a crossover player before union ever dreamed of going professional – he captained England schoolboys at both codes. In all, he played for Great Britain 36 times. "I can't walk for two days after every game and every time I get hit on the right side I get double vision," he said. As tough as he was, even Edwards couldn't ignore what his body was telling him.

World Cup

Group A

Twickenham   *Oct 28*
ENGLAND 2   **AUSTRALIA 22**
Tries: *Sailor 2, Gidley*
    MacDougall
Goals: Farrell   *Rogers 3*
England: Radlinski, Walker, Naylor, Senior, Pryce, Smith, Long, Howard, Rowley, Fielden, Morley, Forshaw, Farrell* *Subs:* Wellens, Sinfield, Fleary, Anderson
Australia: Lockyer, Rogers, Girdler, Gidley, Sailor, Fittler*, Kimmorley, Webcke, Johns, Kearns, Tallis, Fletcher, Hill *Subs:* MacDougall, Croker, Britt, Stevens
Attendance: 33,758. Referee: David Pakieto NZL

Craven Park, Barrow   *Oct 29*
FIJI 38   **RUSSIA 12**
Tries: Vunivalu 3, Tuquiri 2 Iliassov, Rullis
Kuraduadua, Sivatabua
Goals: Tuquiri 5   *Jitsov, Mitrofanov*
Fiji: Tuquiri*, Kuruduadua, Sovatabua, Navale, Tadulala, Smith, Tuiyabayaba, Cakacaka, Robarts, Vaklatawa, Tamani, Marayawa, Vunivalu *Subs:* Tokarei, Lasagavibau, Takayawa, Vuniyayawa
Russia: Iliassov, Mitrofanov, Donovan, Cygler, Romanov, Olari, Gavriline, Rubin*, Lysenkov, Campbell, Sokolov, Findlay, Rullis *Subs:* Kalachkine, Netchaev, Jiltsov, Postnikov
Attendance: 2,187. Referee: Russell Smith ENG

Knowsley Road, St Helens   *Nov 1*
ENGLAND 76   **RUSSIA 4**
Tries: Sinfield 3, Rowley 2
Peacock 2, Long 2, Hay,
Walker, Pryce, Stephenson
Deacon
Goals: Farrell 5, Long 5   *Mitrofanov 2*
England: Wellens, Pryce, Walker, Senior, Rogers, Farrell*, Deacon, Stephenson, Rowley, Fleary, Peacock, Hay, Sinfield *Subs:* Long, Spruce, Howard, Fielden
Russia: Iliassov, Mitrofanov, Doumalkine, Cygler, Romanov, Olari, Gavriline, Rubin*, Lysenkov, Campbell, Sokolov, Findlay, Rullis *Subs:* Kalachkine, Netchaev, Jiltsov, Postnikov
Attendance: 6,346. Referee: Bill Shrimpton NZL

Gateshead Stadium   *Nov 1*
AUSTRALIA 66   **FIJI 8**
Tries: Rogers 4, Kennedy 2 Cakacaka, Tuquiri
Girdler 2, Barrett, Hindmarsh
MacDougall, Gidley
Goals: Rogers 9
Australia: Lockyer, Rogers, Girdler, Gidley, MacDougall, Barrett, Johns, Stevens, Gower, Vella, Kennedy, Hindmarsh, Fittler* *Subs:* Hill, Croker, Kearns, Webcke
Fiji: Tuquiri (c), Kuraduadua, Sovatabua, Navale, Tadulala, Smith, Naisoro, Cakacaka, Robarts, Vaklatawa, Tamani, Marayawa, Vunivalu *Subs:* Tokarei, Navugona, Takayawa, Wawavamia
Attendance: 4,197. Referee: Robert Connolly ENG

Headingley   *Nov 4*
ENGLAND 64   **FIJI 10**
Tries: Peacock 3, Rogers 2 Navale, Tuquiri
Wellens 2, Hay, Naylor
Radlinski, Smith, Farrell
Goals: Farrell 8   *Vunivalu*
England: Spruce, Wellens, Naylor, Radlinski, Rogers, Long, Deacon, Stephenson, Smith, Anderson, Peacock, Hay, Farrell* *Subs:* Sinfield, Walker, Fielden, Howard
Fiji: Tuqiri (capt), Vakararawa, Rakabula, Navale, Bolakaro, Sovatabua, Tuiyabayaba, Vakatawa, Robart, Cakacaka, Wawavamia, Valelala, Vinivalu *Subs:* Tokarei, Lasagavibau, Matakamikamica, Vuniyayawa
Attendance: 10,052. Referee: Thierry Albert ENG

Headingley   *Nov 4*
AUSTRALIA 110   **RUSSIA 4**
Tries: Sailor 4, Girdler 3   *Donovan*
Barrett 2, Croker 2
Hindmarsh 2, MacDougall
Fletcher, Webcke, Tallis
Johns, Gidley
Goals: Girdler 17
Australia: MacDougall, Croker, Girdler, Gidley, Sailor, Barrett, Kimmorley, Webcke, Johns, Kearns, Tallis, Fletcher, Hill *Subs:* Gower, Hindmarsh, Vella, Kennedy
Russia: Mitrofanov, Donovan, Romanov, Iliassov, Chamsoutdinov, Olari, Gavriline, Rubin*, Lysenkov, Campbell, Doumalkine, Garifoulline, Rullis *Subs:* Kalachkine, Goirgas, Kuchumov, Artachine
Attendance: 10,052. Referee: Thierry Alibert FRA

Group B

Kingsholm, Gloucester   *Oct 29*
NEW ZEALAND 64   **LEBANON 0**
Tries: Bennett 2, Carroll 2
Vainikolo 2, Talau 2, Jones 2
Jellick, Swann
Goals: Jones 6, H Paul 2
New Zealand: Barnett*, Jellick, Carroll, Talau, Vainikolo, H Paul, Jones, Smith, Swain, Pongia, Swann, Kearney, Wiki *Subs:* R Paul, J Vagana, Cayless, Rua
Lebanon: H El-Masri, Narjarin, Katrib, Touma, H Saleh, Stanton, Khoury, Maroon*, Semrani, Elamud, Chamoun, Coorey, Lichau *Subs:* Tamer, Nohra, Salem, S El-Masri
Attendance: 2,496. Referee: Bill Harrigan AUS

Rasecourse Ground, Wrexham Oct 29
WALES 38   **COOK ISLANDS 6**
Tries: Tassell 3, Briers   *Temata*
Cunningham, Jenkins
Goals: Harris 7   *Piakura*
Wales: Atcheson, Sterling, Tassell, Critchley, Sullivan, Harris*, Briers, Farrell, Cunningham, Whittle, Morgan, Jenkins, Busby *Subs:* Watson, Davies, Carvell, Highton
Cook Is: Piakura, Tongia, Berryman, Iro*, Temata, Bowen, Joe, Tuakura, Clarke, Temu, Kuru, Pau, Samuel *Subs:* Anderson, Lewis, Glassie, Cooki
Attendance: 5,017. Referee: Thierry Alibert FRA

Stradey Park, Llanelli Oct 29

WALES 24   **LEBANON 22**

Tries: Harris 2, Sterling   *H Saleh 2, Coorey,*
    S El Masri
Cunningham, Davies
Goals: Harris 2   *H El Masri 3*

Wales: Atcheson, Sterling, Tassell, Critchley, Sullivan, Harris*, Briers, Farrell, Cunningham, Whittle, Jenkins, Morgan, Busby *Subs:* Davies, Morley, Highton, Carvell
Lebanon: H. El Masri, S. El Masri, Coorey, H Saleh, Abbas, Elchab, Khoury, Maroon*, Semrani, Elahmad, Chamoun, Goddard, Daher *Subs:* Salem, Lichaa, Touma, Tamei
Attendance: 1,497. Referee: David Pakieto NZL

Madejski Stadium, Reading   *Nov 2*

NEW ZEALAND 84   **COOK ISLANDS 10**

Tries: Barnett 2, R Paul 2   *Voovao, Iro*
Lavea 2, Vaealiki 2, Wiki,
Lauiti'iti, Puleta, Vagana,
Vainikolo, Cayless, Pongia
Goals: Lavea 12   *Piakura*

New Zealand: Barnett*, N. Vagana, Blackmore, Vaealiki, Vainikolo, Lavea, R. Paul, J. Vagana, Swain, Cayless,Lauiti'iti, Puletua, Wiki *Subs:* Jones, Smith, Pongia, Kearney
Cook Is: Piakura, Tongia, Berryman, Iro*, Temata, Bowen, Tuakura, Clarke, Temu, Kuru, Pau, Samuel *Subs:* Anderson, Lewis, Glassie, Cooki
Attendance: 3,982. Referee: Tim Mander AUS

Millenium Stadium, Cardiff   *Nov 5*

COOK ISLANDS 22   **LEBANON 22**

Tries: Berryman 2, Joe,   *H El Masri 2, Touma*
Toa   *H Saleh*
Goals: Berryman 2, Piakura *H El Masri 3*

Cook Is: Piakura, Toa, Lewis, Iro*, Temata, Bowen, Joe, Tuakura, Clarke, Temu, Samuel, Pau, Berryman *Subs:* Andersson, Shepherd, Ruaporo
Lebanon: Chahal, Abbas, H Saleh, H El Masri, Touma, Stanton, S El Masri, Maroon*, N Saleh, Chamoun, Salem, Tamer, Daher *Subs:* Khoury, Lichaa, Katrib, Nohra
Attendance: 5,500. Referee: Bill Shrimpton NZL

Millenium Stadium, Cardiff   *Nov 5*

WALES 18   **NEW ZEALAND 58**

Tries: Briers, Atcheson   *Vainikolo 3, Barnett 2, Talau*
Farrell   *H Paul, Wiki, Carroll,*
    Lauti'iti, N Vagana
Goals: Harris 3   *H Paul 5, Lavea 2*

Wales: Davies, Sterling, O'Hare, Critchley, Sullivan, Harris*, Briers, Farrell, Watson, Whittle, Jenkins, Morgan, Morley *Subs:* Eaton, Atcheson, Highton, Smith
New Zealand: Barnett*, N Vagana, Carroll, Talau, Vainikolo, H Paul, Jones, Smith, Swain, Cayless, Rua, Kearney, Wiki *Subs:* Lavea, J Vagana, Puletua, Lauiti'iti
Attendance: 17,612. Referee: Russell Smith ENG

Group C

Charlety Stadium, Paris   *Oct 28*

FRANCE 20   **PAPUA NEW GUINEA 23**

Tries: Hechiche 2,   *Bai, Krewanty, Buko, Lam*
Benausse, Dekkiche
Goals: Banquet 2   *Wilshere 2, Gene*
Drop Goals: *Lam*

France: Banquet, Benausse, Cassin, Dulac, Dekkiche, Frayssinous, Devecchi*, Jampy, Guisset, Tallec, Teixido, Wulf, Hechich. *Subs:* Sands, El Khalouki, Carrasco, Despin
PNG: Buko, Wilshere, Aila, Songoro, Bai, Gene, Lam*, Kahl, Marum, Solbat, Naawi, Mamando, O'Reilly *Subs:* Mom, Krewanty, Norman, Mondo
Attendance: 4,500. Referee: Steve Ganson ENG

Charlety Stadium, Paris   *Oct 28*

TONGA 66   **SOUTH AFRICA 18**

Tries: Vaikona 4, D Mann 2 *Breytenbach, Barnard, Best*
Liava'a, M Masella, Moala
E Mann, Lomi, L Kaufusi
Mason
Goals: Moala 5, Mason   *Bloem 2, O'Shea*
D Mann

Tonga: Koloi, Moala, Vaikona, G Wolfgramm, L Kaufusi, Howlett, W Wolfgramm, M Masella*, E Mann, Liava'a, Mason, Talou, D Mann *Subs:* Fisi'iahi, Manu, Lomi, Kite
S Africa: O'Shea, Best, Barnard, Johnson, Dames, Breytenbach, Bloem*, Booysen, Skelton, Powell, Rutgerson, De Villiers, Erasmus *Subs:* Jennings, Nel, Mulder, Cloete
Attendance: 3,000. Referee: Darren Hopewell NZL

Stade d'Albert Domec   *Nov 1*

FRANCE 28   **TONGA 8**

Tries: Banquet, Sirvent,   *D Fishi'iahi, P Fishi'iahi*
Dulac, Garcia, Jampy
Goals: Banquet 4

France: Banquet, Garcia, Cassin, Dulac, Sirvent, Devecchi*, Rinaldi, Hechiche, Wulf, Sands, Guisset, Tallec, Jampy *Subs:* Teixido, Carrasco, Sort, Despin
Tonga: Koloi, Moala, Vaikona, D Fisi'iahi, L Kaufusi, Howlett, Hifo, M Masella*, E Mann, Liava'a, Mason, Kite, D Mann *Subs:* P Fisi'iahi, W Mann, Lomi, A Masella
Attendance: 10,288. Referee: Steven Clark AUS

Stade Sept Derniers, Toulouse   *Nov 2*

PAPUA NEW GUINEA 16   **SOUTH AFRICA 0**

Tries: Aila, Wilshere, Paiyo
Goals: Wilshere 2

PNG: Buko, Wilshere, Aila, Songoro, Bai, Gene, Lam*, Kahl, Mom, Mondo, Naawi, Mamando, O'Reilly *Subs:* Paiyo, Krewanty, Norman, Aizue
S Africa: Best, Dames, Johnson, Barnard, Noble, Van Wyke, Bloem*, Booysen, Hurter, Powell, De Villiers, Rutgerson, Erasmus *Subs:* Jennings, Nel, Mulder, Cloete
Attendance: 4,313. Referee: Darren Hopewell NZL

Stade Municipal, Albi	Nov 5
FRANCE 56	**SOUTH AFRICA 6**

Tries: Cassin 3, Jampy 2
Banquet, Guisset, Sirvent
Tallec

De Villiers

Goals: Banquet 10   Bloem

France: Banquet, Garcia, Cassin, Dulac, Sirvent, Devecchi*, Rinaldi, Hechiche, Wulf, Teixido, Guisset, Tallec, Jampy Subs: Despin, Carrasco, Sort, Sands
S Africa: Best, Noble, Barnard, Johnson, Dames, Van Wyke, Bloem*, Booysen, Jennings, Powell, De Villiers, Rutgerson, Erasmus Subs: Hurter, Webb, Mulder, Louw
Attendance: 7,969.   Referee: Steven Clark AUS

Stade Municipal, St Esteve	Nov 6
PAPUA NEW GUINEA 30	**TONGA 22**

Tries: Gene 2, Mondo,   Moala 2, Mason, Vaikona
Buko, Karl

Goals: Wilshere 5   Moala 3

PNG: Buko, Wilshere, Aila, Songoro, Bai, Gene, Lam, Karl, Mom, Mondo, Naawi, Mamando, O'Reilly Subs: Paiyo, Krewanty, Norman, Aizue
Tonga: L. Kaufusi, Moala, Koloi, G. Wolfgramm, Vaikona,Howlett, D. Mann, M. Masella, E. Mann, A. Masella, Mason, M. Kaufusi, Manu Subs: D. Fisi'iahi, W. Wolfgramm, Lomi, Lomu
Attendance: 3,666.   Referee: Steve Ganson ENG

Group D

Windsor Park, Belfast	Oct 28
IRELAND 30	**SAMOA 16**

Tries: Joynt, Ricketson,   Leauma, Milford, Betham
Eagar, Carney, Prescott

Goals: Prescott 5   Geros 2

Ireland: Prescott, Carney, Withers, Eagar, Forster, Martyn, Sheridan, O'Connor*, Williams, McDermott, Joynt, Campion, Ricketson. Subs: Bretherton, Lawless, Barnhill, Southern
Samoa: Milford, Leauma, A Swann, Gulavao, Meli, Geros, W Swann, Puletua, Betham, Seu Seu, Solomona, Peterson, Poching* Subs: Tatupu, Kololo, Leafa, Faafili
Attendance: 3,207.   Referee: Tim Mander AUS

Firhill, Glasgow	Oct 29
SCOTLAND 16	**NZ MAORI 17**

Tries: Bell, Maiden, Penny   Toopi 2, Kidwell
Goals: PCrowther, Mackay   Ngamu 2
Drop: Ngamu

Scotland: Penny, Daylight, Gilmour, Bell, Mackay, Purcell, Horne, Heckenberg, Russell, Laughton, Cram, Logan, Vowles Subs: Maiden, McDonald, Crowther, Shaw
Maori: Toopi, Manuel, Kohe-Love, Kidwell, Hoppe, Ngamu, Te Rangi, Rauhihi, Perenara, Hermansson, Koopu, Smith, Nikau* Subs: Moana, Nahi, Leuluai, Reihana
Attendance: 2,008.   Referee: Stuart Cummings ENG

Tolka Park, Dublin	Nov 1
IRELAND 18	**SCOTLAND 6**

Tries: Sheridan, Withers   Arnold
Goals: Prescott 5   Crowther

Ireland: Prescott, Carney, Withers, Eager, Herron, Martyn, Sheridan, O'Connor*, Lawless, McDermott, Joynt, Campion, Ricketson Subs: Williams, Mathiou, Barnhill, Bradbury
Scotland: Penny, Daylight, Gilmour, Bell, Crowther, Horne, Rhodes, Heckenberg, Russell*, Laughton, Logan, Cram, Vowles Subs: Maiden, Graham, McDonald, Shaw
Attendance: 1,732.   Referee: Russell Smith ENG

Derwent Park, Workington	Nov 1
SAMOA 21	**NZ MAORI 16**

Tries: Faafili 2, W Swann   Matthews, Nelson, Rauhihi
Milford

Goals: Poching 2   Goodwin 2
Drop Goals: W Swann

Samoa: Milford, Meli, A Swann, Galuvao, Leauma, Fa'afili, W Swann, Puletua, Betham, Seu Seu, Solomona, Leafa, Poching* Subs: Tatupu, Geros, Leulhuai, Fala
Maori: Toopi, Mills, Whatuira, Nelson, Matthews, Goodwin, J Smith, Rauhihi, Cook, Reihana, Leuluai, T Smith, Nikau* Subs: Kohe-Love, Moana, Kidwell, Hermannson
Attendance: 4,107.   Referee: Bill Harrigan AUS

Tolka Park, Dublin	Nov 4
IRELAND 30	**NZ MAORI 16**

Tries: Forster, Carney   Nelson, Te Rangi, Koopu
Barnhill, Withers, Sheridan
Goals: Prescott 5   Perenara, Ngamu

Ireland: Prescott, Carney, Withers, Ricketson, Forster, Clinch, Sheridan, O'Connor*, Williams, McDermott, Joynt, Barnhill, Campion Subs: Bretherton, Lawless, Tallon, Southern
Maori: Toopi, Manuell, Kohe-Love, Kidwell, Hoppe, Ngamu, H. Te Rangi, Rauhihi, Perenara, Hermansson, Koopu, T. Smith, Nikau* Subs: Moana, Nelson, Nahi, Reihana
Attendance: 3,164.   Referee: Bill Harrigan AUS

Tynecastle, Edinburgh	Nov 5
SCOTLAND 12	**SAMOA 20**

Tries: Vowles, Rhodes   Leauma 2, Solomona, Milford
Goals: Crowther 2   Laloata 2

Scotland: Arnold, Daylight, Gilmour, Bell, Crowther, Purcell, Horne, Heckenberg, Russell, Laughton, Logan, Cram, Vowles Subs: S. Rhodes, Maiden, McDonald, Shaw
Samoa: Milford, Lima, A. Swann, Laloata, Leauma, Faafili, Talapeau, Puletua, Betham, Seu Seu, Solomona, Tatupu, Poching Subs: W. Swann, Leulhuai, Leafa, Fala
Attendance: 1,579.   Referee: David Pakieto NZL

Final Standings
Group A

Standings	P	W	D	L	PF	PA	Pts
1 Australia	3	3	0	0	198	14	6
2 England	3	2	0	1	144	36	4
3 Fiji	3	1	0	2	56	144	2
4 Russia	3	0	0	3	20	224	0

Group B

Standings	P	W	D	L	PF	PA	Pts
1 New Zealand	3	3	0	0	206	28	6
2 Wales	3	2	0	1	80	86	4
3 Lebanon	3	0	1	2	44	110	1
4 Cook Islands	3	0	1	2	38	144	1

Group C

Standings	P	W	D	L	PF	PA	Pts
1 Papua New Guinea	3	3	0	0	69	42	6
2 France	3	2	0	1	104	37	4
3 Tonga	3	1	0	2	96	76	2
4 South Africa	3	0	0	3	24	138	0

Group D

Standings	P	W	D	L	PF	PA	Pts
1 Ireland	3	3	0	0	78	38	6
2 Samoa	3	2	0	1	57	58	4
3 New Zealand Maori	3	1	0	2	49	67	2
4 Scotland	3	0	0	3	34	55	0

Quarter-finals

Vicarage Road, Watford *Nov 11*
AUSTRALIA 66 **SAMOA 10**
Tries: Fletcher 3, Johns 2 *Solomona, Leauma*
Hill 2, MacDougall 2, Girdler
Fittler, Sailor
Goals: Rogers 9 *Laloata*
Australia: Lockyer, Rogers, Girdler, Gidley, Sailor, Fittler*, Kimmorley, Webcke, Johns, Kearns, Tallis, Fletcher, Hill *Subs:* MacDougall, Croker, Stevens, Britt
Samoa: Milford, Leauma, A Swann, Laloata, Lima, Faafili, W Swann, Puletua, Betham, Seu Seu, Solomona, Leuluai, Poching* *Subs:* Tatupu, Leafa, Fala, Meli
Attendance: 5,404. Referee: Stuart Cummings ENG

Headingley *Nov 11*
ENGLAND 26 **IRELAND 16**
Tries: Senior, Peacock *Withers 2, Martyn*
Smith, Walker
Goals: Farrell 5 *Prescott 2*
England: Wellens, Walker, Radlinski, Senior, Rogers, Long, Deacon, Fielden, Rowley, Anderson, Morley, Forshaw, Farrell* *Subs:* Smith, Naylor, Peacock, Howard
Ireland: Prescott, Carney, Martyn, Eagar, Forster, Withers, Sheridan, O'Connor*, Williams, McDermott, Joynt, Campion, Ricketson *Subs:* Ricketso, Clinch, Barnhill, Mathiou, Southern
Attendance: 15,405. Referee: Tim Mander AUS

Auto Quest Stadium, Widnes *Nov 12*
WALES 22 **PAPUA NEW GUINEA 8**
Tries: Critchley, Briers *Wilshere*
Davies
Goals: Harris 5 *Wilshere 2*
Wales: Atcheson, Sterling, Tassell, Critchley, Sullivan, Harris*, Briers, Farrell, Cunningham, Morgan, Jenkins, Hoghton, Busby *Subs:* Davies, Morley, Devereaux, Moriarty
PNG: Buko, Wilshere, Aila, Songoro, Bai, Gene, Lam*, Karl, Mom, Mondo, Naawi, Mamando, O'Reilly *Subs:* Paiyo, Krewanty, Norman, Aizue
Attendance: 5,211. Referee: David Pakieto NZL

Wheldon Road, Castleford *Nov 12*
NEW ZEALAND 54 **FRANCE 6**
Tries: R Paul 3, Rua, *Sirvent*
Pongia, Smith, Kearney
Jellick, Talau, Blackmore
Goals: H Paul 7 *Banquet*
New Zealand: Barnett*, Jellick, Blackmore, Talau, N Vagana, H Paul, R Paul, Smith, Swain, Pongia, Rua, Kearney *Subs:* Swann, Cayless, J Vagana, Wiki, Carroll
France: Banquet, Garcia, Cassin, Dulac, Sirvemt, Devecchi*, Rinaldi, Hechiche, Wulf, Sands, Guisset, Tallec, Jampy, *Subs:* Despin, Carrasco, Sort, Teixido
Attendance: 5,158. Referee: Bill Harrigan AUS

Semi-finals

Reebok Stadium, Bolton *Nov 18*
ENGLAND 6 **NEW ZEALAND 49**
Tries: Smith *Vainikolo 2, Talua 2,*
 Kearney, Wiki, N Vagana,
 Swann
Goals: Farrell *H Paul 8*
Drop Goals: *H Paul*
England: Radlinski, Walker, Naylor, Senior, Wellens, Deacon, Long, Fielden, Smith, Howard, Sculthorpe, Forshaw, Farrell* *Subs:* Peacock, Hay, Fleary, Anderson
New Zealand: Barnett*, N Vagana, Carroll, Talau, Vainikolo, H Paul, Jones, Smith, Swain, Pongia, Rua, Kearney, Wiki *Subs:* R Paul, J Vagana, Cayless, Swann
Attendance: 5,404. Referee: Tim Mander AUS

McAlpine Stadium, Huddersfield *Nov 19*
AUSTRALIA 46 **WALES 22**
Tries: Fittler 2, Lockyer 2 *Watson, Tassell, Briers*
Kimmorley, Sailor, Fletcher
Gower, Kennedy
Goals: Lockyer 4, Girdler *Harris 4*
Drop Goals: *Briers 2*
Australia: Lockyer, MacDougall, Girdler, Gidley, Sailor, Fittler*, Kimmorley, Webcke, Gower, Vella, Tallis, Fletcher, Hill *Subs:* Barret, Kearns, Kennedy, Hindmarsh
Wales: Harris*, Smith, Tassell, Critchley, Sullivan, Briers, Watson, Farrell, Cunningham, Moriarty, Morgan, Highton, Morley *Subs:* Davies, Atcheson, Devereaux, Luckwell
Attendance: 8,114. Referee: Russell Smith ENG

Final

NEW ZEALAND 12   **AUSTRALIA 40**
Tries: Vainikolo, Carroll   *Sailor 2, Gidley, Hindmarsh*
                            Lockyer, Fittler, Barrett
Goals: H Paul 2   *Rogers 6*
New Zealand: Barnett*, N Vagana, Carroll, Talau, Vainikolo, H Paul, Jones, Smith, Swain, Pongia, Rua, Kearney, Wiki *Subs:* R Paul, J Vagana, Cayless, Swann
Australia: Lockyer, Rogers, MacDougall, Gidley, Sailor, Fittler*, Kimmorley, Webcke, Johns, Kearns, Tallis, Fletcher, Hill *Subs:* Barrett, Hindmarsh, Britt, Stevens
Attendance: 44,329. Referee: Stuart Cummings ENG

> **"I believe it is the best sport in the world. It's got everything - speed and tough, ugly men"**
>
> Terry O'Connor, Ireland captain, who is fast, tough and, er...
>
> **"We shot ourselves with a double-barrelled shotgun in both feet"**
>
> Ellery Hanley, St Helens coach, after his team lost to Bradford Bulls.
>
> **"I've never scored a hat-trick before, not even playing against my sister in the yard at home"**
>
> Bryan Fletcher, Australian forward, who scored a hattrick against Samoa in the World Cup match.

Australian Results

ARL Premiership

	P	W	D	L	F	A	Pts
Brisbane Broncos	26	18	2	6	698	388	38
Sydney Roosters	26	16	0	10	601	520	32
Newcastle Knights	26	15	1	10	686	532	31
Canberra Raiders	26	15	0	11	506	479	30
Penrith Panthers	26	15	0	11	573	562	30
Melbourne Storm	26	14	1	11	672	529	29
Parramatta Eels	26	14	1	11	476	456	29
The Sharks	26	13	0	13	570	463	26
St George-Illawara	26	12	0	14	576	656	24
Wests Tigers	26	11	2	13	519	642	24
The Bulldogs	26	10	1	15	469	553	21
Northern Eagles	26	9	0	17	476	628	18
Auckland Warriors	26	8	2	16	426	662	18
North Queensland Cowboys	26	7	0	19	436	612	12

Play-offs

The top eight teams qualify for the play-offs. In the first round, 1st plays 8th, 2nd plays 7th, etc. From those four matches, the two losers that were the lowest placed in the League are eliminated and the two winners that were highest placed go directly to the preliminary finals. The other four teams play each other; a loser in the qualifying semi-finals paired against a winner in the same round. The winners of the elimination semi-finals go into the preliminary finals, their opponents determined by league placings (lowest meets highest). The preliminary final is, in fact, what earthlings normally call a semi-final and you all understand what that is. If we've got any of this wrong, please don't phone us, phone the ARL.

Qualifying Semi-Finals
Canberra Raiders 34   Penrith Panthers 16
Newcastle Knights 30   Melbourne Storm 16
Parramatta Eels 32   Sydney Roosters 8
Brisbane Broncos 34   Cronulla Sharks 20

Elimination Semi Finals
Parramatta Eels 28   Penrith Panthers 10
Sydney Roosters 38   Canberra Raiders 10

Preliminary Finals
Sydney Roosters 26   Newcastle Knights 20
Brisbane Broncos 16   Parramatta Eels 10

Grand Final
Stadium Australia, Sydney   *Aug 27*
Brisbane Broncos 14   **Sydney Roosters 6**
Tries: Tuquiri, Sailor   *Fitzgibbon*
Goals: De Vere 3   *Phillips*
Crowd: 94,277

World Club Challenge
JJB Stadium, Wigan   *Jan 22*
St Helens 6   **Melbourne Storm 44**

British Results

Super League

	P	W	D	L	F	A	Pts
Wigan	28	24	1	3	960	405	49
St. Helens	28	23	0	5	988	627	46
Bradford Bulls	28	20	3	5	1004	408	43
Leeds Rhinos	28	17	0	11	692	626	34
Castleford Tigers	28	17	0	11	585	571	34
Warrington Wolves	28	13	0	15	735	817	26
Hull	28	12	1	15	630	681	25
Halifax Blue Sox	28	11	1	16	664	703	23
Salford City Reds	28	10	0	18	542	910	20
Wakefield Trinity	28	8	0	20	557	771	16
London Broncos	28	6	0	22	456	770	12
Huddersf'd/Sheffield	28	4	0	24	502	1026	8

Play-offs

The top five teams in the League table qualify for the play-offs. The 2nd and 3rd teams in the League meet in Match A, the 4th and 5th in Match B. The loser of Match B is eliminated. The winner of Match B goes on to play the loser of Match A in Match D. The winner of Match A meets the League champions in Match C. The winner of Match C goes straight to the Grand Final, while the loser meets the winner of Match D in Match E. The winner of Match E meets the winner of Match C in the Grand Final. This format is incomprehensible to anyone new to the sport and usually means that the two teams in the Grand Final have already met about a week earlier in the play-offs.

Match A
St Helens 16   Bradford 11
Match B
Leeds 22   Castleford 14
Match C
St Helens 54   Wigan 16
Match D
Bradford 46   Leeds 12
Match E
Wigan 40   Bradford 12

Grand Final

Old Trafford   Oct 14
St Helens 29   Wigan Warriors 16
Tries: Joynt 2, Hoppe,   Farrell, Hodgson, Smith
Tuilagi, Jonkers
Goals: Long 4   Farrell 2
Drop Goal: Sculthorpe
St Helens: Wellens, Hall, Iro, Hoppe, Sullivan, Martyn, Long, Perelini, Cunningham, O,Neill, Jonkers, Joynt*, Sculthorpe
Subs: Tuilagi, Barrow, Stankevitch, Nickle
Wigan: Robinson, Dallas, Ralinski, Renouf, Hodgson, Smith, Peters, O'Connor, Newton, Cowie, Cassidy, Betts, Farrell*
Subs: Gilmour, Chester, Mestrov, Malam
Attendance: 58,132
Referee: Russell Smith (Castleford)

Northern Ford Premiership

	P	W	D	L	PF	PA	Pts
Dewsbury Rams	28	22	1	5	848	400	45
Keighley Cougars	28	22	0	6	1002	401	44
Doncaster Dragons	28	21	0	7	880	397	42
Leigh Centurions	28	21	0	7	854	476	42
Featherstone R	28	20	1	7	795	523	41
Oldham	28	19	1	8	734	513	39
Hull KR	28	17	1	10	880	397	35
Widnes Vikings	28	17	0	11	698	483	34
Swinton Lions	28	13	2	13	726	733	28
Barrow Border R	28	14	0	14	647	711	28
Whitehaven W	28	11	1	16	533	674	23
Workington Town	28	11	1	16	502	776	23
Rochdale Hornets	28	10	0	18	563	696	20
Sheffield Eagles	28	9	1	18	479	585	19
Hunslet Hawks	28	8	0	12	487	678	16
Batley Bulldogs	28	6	0	22	482	759	12
York Wasps	28	5	1	22	392	859	11
Lancashire Lynx	28	1	0	27	301	1361	2

Play-offs

The preliminary semi-finals consists of 1st v 4th and 2nd v 3rd. The elimination semi-finals see 5th play 8th and 6th against 7th, with the losers being eliminated. The winners of the elimination semi-finals play the losers of the preliminary semi-finals in the minor semi-finals. The losers of the minor semi-finals are eliminated, whereas the winners go on to play the winners of the preliminary semi-finals in the major semi-finals - which really are semi-finals. The winners of the major semi-finals go on to meet in the final. Except it's not a final it's a Grand Final.

Preliminary semi-finals
Dewsbury Rams 12   Leigh Centurions 29
Keighley Cougars 44   Doncaster Dragons 22
Elimination semi-finals
Featherstone Rovers 43   Widnes Vikings 24
Oldham 22   Hull Kingston Rovers 14
Minor semi-finals
Dewsbury Rams 25   Featherstone Rovers 18
Doncaster Dragons 17   Oldham 24
Major semi-finals
Dewsbury Rams 38   Keighley Cougars 12
Leigh Centurions 18   Oldham 10

Grand Final
Dewsbury Rams 13   Leigh Centurions 12

Challenge Cup Final

Murrayfield   Apr 29
Bradford Bulls 24   Leeds Rhinos 18
Tries: Withers 2, McAvoy, Fielden   Hay, St Hilaire
Goals: H Paul 4   Harris 5
Bradford: Spruce, McAvoy, Naylor, Withers, Vaikona, H Paul, R Paul, MCDermott, Lowes, Anderson, Peacock, Forshaw, Mackay *Subs:* Pryce, Boyle, Dwyer, Fielden
Leeds: Harris, Rivett, Blackmore, Senior, Cummins, Powell, Sheridan, Fleary, Lawford, McDermott, Morley, Farrell, Hay *Subs:* St Hilaire, Jackson, Barnhill, Mathiou
Attendance: 67,247; Referee: Steve Presley (Castleford)
Lance Todd Trophy: Henry Paul (Bradford)

Rugby Union

Only Scotland could have done it; lost to the no-hopers of Italy in the first Six Nations match, beaten the champions England in the last. Had they not succeeded against England, who had already secured the championship by the time they met at a rainy and wind-swept Murrayfield, the Scots would have been the first team to finish bottom of the Six Nations. As it was, their win in the last match helped them crawl off the bottom. Italy, who conceded 228 points in their five matches, having a far inferior points difference.

Notwithstanding another bad day at Murrayfield and another lost Grand Slam, England were still by far the best team on show. Even though Clive Woodward persisted with his baseball cap, and jumped up and down rather too much when England scored (against anyone) he nevertheless created a professional set-up for the team, which now had almost as many coaches as the other five nations put together, and the quality was evident. Woodward's reward, in May, was to receive an extended contract leading up to the 2003 World Cup. Six months later, the RFU felt even more secure in their choice, although there was a brief spell where they nearly didn't have a team to be coached, but we'll come to that.

Wales were woeful at Twickenham, scoring not a single point in the second half as they were rolled over 46-12. When your own fitness coach turns on you, you know you've got troubles, and Wales' Steve Black was quick to berate the fitness levels of the players he was responsible for. He blamed the clubs, though, rather than himself.

Wales' woes continued when Shane Howarth and Brett Sinkinson were revealed to have no connection with the Valleys. Everyone knew the New Zealanders weren't Welsh, but their grannies were supposed to be. Then Scotland's Dave Hilton came out of the closet, admitting his grandad wasn't born in Edinburgh, as he thought, but Bristol, which is quite a long way away from the Scottish capital. After 41 caps, this was a bit of a blow. The whole shebang went before the International Rugby Board, which determined that the three should be deemed ineligible for their respective teams, and for a brief spell of 'grannygate' fever, birth, death and marriage certificates were scrutinised like never before.

The midsummer tours saw England in South Africa and Scotland in New Zealand. Having found the Italians a handful in February, it was hardly a shock when the Scots were overwhelmed by the All Blacks, conceding 19 tries in the two games. It difficult to know the value of a tour in which success is a defeat by fewer than 40 points.

The two England Tests in South Africa were more balanced confrontations. England narrowly lost the first amidst squabbles over a Tim Stimpson touchdown, which the video referee determined had not happened. It gave even more of an edge to the second encounter at Bloemfontein, which England won. Jonny Wilkinson, who missed the first Test, was the executioner, scoring every one of his side's 27 points, with eight penalties and a dropped goal. Up until the 80th minute, the South Africans were trailing by 27-15 and only a disputed try by Joost van der Westhuizen gave the scoreline respectability for the home side. For England, it was only the third victory over the South Africans on their soil.

Victory in Bloemfontein would turn out to be a benchmark. It was the moment that signalled to the south hemisphere teams that England had arrived; there were four teams on the top table now. The autumn games would ratify that status; though briefly the strained negotiations between the RFU and the players almost caused the cancellation of the second match, against Argentina. It was yet another argument in the sport that turned eyes away from the performances on the field, sadly because it happened the week after England had posted a superb victory against the World Cup holders, Australia, at Twickenham.

It was a match dominated by defences and which the visitors look to have sealed, leading by four points with seconds to go. An Iain Balshaw chip, chased down by Dan Luger, was followed by anxiety minutes as the video referee scrutinised the replay. Luger was certain he'd touched down and, this time Brian Stirling, the video referee, agreed.

News of the strike threat broke on Monday, just two days after the Australian game. Negotiations between the players' representatives, CSS Stellar, and the RFU had been going on for 12 months, which apparently was not long enough to reach an agreement. The argument did not concern the overall amount on the table - about £60,000 per man - but how much of it came as win bonuses. The RFU wanted to pay 40% of the total that way, the players were seeking a figure closer to 30%. The revised agreement was brokered by Peter Wheeler, the Leicester chief executive, and on Wednesday morning, when it was announced, the choruses were contradictory. While the players asserted that the proportion of win bonus had changed, the RFU forcefully maintained it hadn't. It was all semantics. The RFU had changed the payments - a one-off lump sum of £50,000 apparently added - and the opposing arguments were merely about saving face. While the majority of the media reports came down on the side of the RFU, we wonder what the role of administrators is if not to administrate. It was a deal that should have been settled long before the Argentina game. Clive Woodward made it an emotional issue (as he does most things), but the relationship with the players was bridged sufficiently for a dull 19-0 victory against the Pumas in boggy conditions.

A week later South Africa lined up against England at Twickenham. This was not a vintage South African team, both Wales and Ireland, in earlier tour matches, had got to within striking distance, each going down by 10 points. Jonny Wilkinson (who scored 20 points) was again pivotal for England; Will Greenwood's first-half try was the most significant breakthrough; and though England lost both Richard Hill and Neil Back in the second half, they scored a clear victory against the South Africans. "It was a big, big win for us," said Woodward, and this time no on was arguing.

"It's a common name around here"

Dilwyn Morgan, Bala second row, whose side started its match against Fairwater with 10 players in their team named Jones.

"We have become the laughing stock of the world"

Clive Rowlands, ex-president on the Welsh Rugby Union, on the grannygate scandal.

"Is there a sinister force behind this?"

Clive Woodward, on the players' threats to go on strike.

Six Nations Championship

Rome   *Feb 5*
ITALY 34   **SCOTLAND 20**
Tries: De Carli   *Bulloch, M Leslie*
Conv: Dominguez   *Logan, Townsend*
PG: Dominguez 6   *Townsend*
DG: Dominguez 3   *Townsend*
Italy: M Pini; D Dallan, M Dallan (Rivaro 45), L Martin, C Stoica; D Dominguez, A Troncon* (Mazzantini 79); M Cuttitta, A Moscardi, T Paoletti (De Carli 65), C Checchinato, A Gritti, M Giovanelli, M Bergamasco (Persico 64), W Visser (Lanzi 19-22)
Scotland: G Metcalfe; S Longstaff, J Mayer, J Leslie*, K Logan; G Townsend, B Redpath; T Smith, G Bulloch, M Stewart (Hilton 68), S Murray, S Grimes, M Leslie (McLaren 13), B Pountney, G Simpson (Reid 19-31)
Referee: *J Kaplan RSA*

Twickenham   *Feb 5*
ENGLAND 50   **IRELAND 18**
Tries: Cohen 2,   *Maggs, Galwey*
Healey 2, Back, Tindall
Conv: Wilkinson 4   *Humphreys*
PG: Wilkinson 4   *Humphreys 2*
England: M Perry (Balshaw 70); A Healey, M Tindall, M Catt, B Cohen; J Wilkinson, M Dawson*; J Leonard (Woodman 70), P Greening, P Vickery, G Archer, S Shaw (Corry 76), R Hill, N Back, L Dallaglio
Ireland: C O'Shea (Dempsey 47); J Bishop, B O'Driscoll, M Mullins, K Maggs; D Humphreys, T Tierney; P Clohessy, K Wood*, P Wallace, R Casey (Galwey 40), M O'Kelly, D O'Cuinneagain (Brenna, 47), K Dawson, A Foley
Referee: *S Walsh NZL*

Millennium Stadium   *Feb 5*
WALES 3   **FRANCE 36**
Tries: *Magne, Castaignede,*
    Ntamack
Conv: *Lamaison 3*
PG: N Jenkins   *Lamaison 4*
DG: *Lamaison*
Wales: S Howarth; G Thomas, M Taylor, J Jones-Hughes; D James (S William 72); N Jenkins; R Howley (Smith 76), P Rogers (John 71), G Jenkins (B Williams 78), D Young*, I Gough, C Wyatt (Voyle 69), C Charvis (Lewis 60), B Sinkinson, S Quinnell
France: T Castaignède; E Ntamack, R Dourthe (Venditti 21); T Lombard, C Dominici; C Lamaison (Penaud 80), F Galthié (Loussucq 78); C Califano, M Dal Maso (Ibanez 74), F Tournaire (De Villiers 74), O Brouzet, L Mateiu (Lièvremont 46), A Benazzi, O Magne (Betson 76), F Pelous*
Referee: *C White ENG*

Stade de France   *Feb 19*
FRANCE 9   **ENGLAND 15**
PG: Dourthe 3   *Wilkinson 5*
France: R Dourthe; E Ntamack, D Venditti, T Lombard, C Dominici; T Castaignède, F Galthié; C Califano, M Dal Maso (Ibanez 72), F Tournaire (De Villiers 72), L Matiu (Lièvremont h-t), O Brouzet, A Benazzi (Betsen, 63), O Magne, F Pelous*
England: M Perry (Balshaw 63); A Healey, M Tindall, M Catt, B Cohen; J Wilkinson, M Dawson*; J Leonard, P Greening, P Vickery, G Archer, S Shaw, R Hill (Corry 75), N Back, L Dallaglio
Referee: *S Dickinson AUS*

Millennium Stadium   *Feb 19*
WALES 47   **ITALY 16**
Tries: S Quinnell,   *Visser*
Williams, Bateman,
Howarth
Conv: N Jenkins 3   *Dominguez*
PG: N Jenkins 7   *Dominguez 2*
DG: *Dominguez*
Wales: S Howarth; G Thomas (James 72), A Bateman, M Taylor, S Williams; N Jenkins, R Howley; P Rogers (John 80), G Jenkins (B Williams, 68), D Young*, C Quinnell, C Wyatt (Gough 68), G Lewis (Charvis h-t), B Sinkinson, S Quinnell
Italy: M Pini; C Stoica, L Martin (Francesio 54), M Rivaro, D Dallam; D Dominguez, A Troncon*; M Cuttitta, A Moscordi (Orlandi 23-25), T Paoletti, G Lanzi (Persico 65), A Gritti, C Checchinato, M Bergamasco, V Visser
Referee: *I Ramage SCO*

Lansdowne Road   *Feb 19*
IRELAND 44   **SCOTLAND 22**
Tries: O'Kelly, Horgan,   *Logan, Metcalfe*
O'Driscoll, Humphreys,   *Graham* _
Wood
Conv: O'Gara 2,   *Logan 2*
Humphreys 3
PG: O'Gara 2   *Logan*
Humphreys
Ireland: G Dempsey (Henderson 38); S Horgan, B O'Driscoll, M Mullins, D Hickie; R O'Gara (Humphreys 51), P Stringer; P Clohessy, K Wood*, J Hayes (Fitzpatrick 68), M Galwey (Davidson 57), M O'Kelly, S Easterby, K Dawson, A Foley
Scotland: G Metcalfe; S Longstaff, M Mayer, A Shiel, K Logan; G Townsend, B Redpath* (Nichol 55); T Smith, G Bulloch (Russell, 68), M Stewart (Graham 65-80), S Murray (Weir 51), S Grimes, M Leslie, A Pountney, G Simpson
Referee: *J Dume FRA*

Lansdowne Road | Mar 4
IRELAND 60 | **ITALY 13**
Tries: Wood, Horgan 2 | De Rossi
Dawson, O'Driscoll,
Dempsey
Conv: O'Gara 6 | Dominguez
PG: O'Gara 6 | Dominguez 2

Ireland: G Dempsey; S Horgan, B O'Driscoll, M Mullins (Henderson, 60), D Hickie; R O'Gara, P Stringer; P Clohessy (Fitzpatrick, 65), K Wood*, J Hayes, M Galwey, M O'Kelly, S Easterby (O'Cuinneagain, 58), K Dawson, A Foley
Italy: M Pini (Preo, 31); J-S Francesio, C Stoica (Rivaro, 65), M Dominguez, A Troncon*; M Cuttitta, A Moscardi, T Paoletti (Perugini, 40), C Checchinato, A Gritti (Lanzi, 65), W Visser, M Bergamasco (Travini, 40), A de Rossi
Referee: D Bevan WAL

Murrayfield | Mar 4
SCOTLAND 16 | **FRANCE 28**
Tries: Nichol | Castaignede, Magne 2
Conv: Paterson | Merceron 2
PG: Logan, Paterson 2 | Merceron 3

Scotland: C Paterson; G Metcalfe, J McLaren (Hodge 72), J Leslie*, K Logan; G Townsend, A Nichol; T Smith, S Brotherston, M Stewart (Hilton 67), M Murray, D Weir (Grimes 67), M Leslie, B Pountney, S Reid (Mather 14-19)
France: T Castaignède; E Ntamack, D Venditti, T Lombard, C Dominici; G Merceron (Elissalde 80), C Laussucq; C Califano, M Dal Maso (Ibanez 53), F Tournaire (De Villiers 53), J Daude (Lièvremont 49), O Brouzet, S Chabal (Costas 52), O Magne, F Pelous*
Referee: S Lander ENG

Twickenham | Mar 4
ENGLAND 46 | **WALES 12**
Tries: Greening, Back
Hill, Dallaglio, Cohen
Conv: Wilkinson 3
PG: Wilkinson 5 | N Jenkins 3
DG: | N Jenkins

Italy: M Perry; A Healey, M Tindall, M Catt, B Cohen; J Wilkinson, M Dawson*; J Leonard, P Greening, P Vickery, G Archer, S Shaw (Corry 71), R Hill, N Back, L Dallaglio, M Corry
Wales: S Howarth; G Thomas, A Bateman, M Taylor, S Williams; N Jenkins, R Howley; P Rogers, G Jenkins (B Williams, 71), D Young* (John 23), C Quinnell (Gough 63), C Wyatt, C Charvis (B Williams 52-56), B Sinkinson, S Quinnell (M Williams 70)
Referee: J Fleming SCO

Rome | Mar 18
ITALY 12 | **ENGLAND 59**
Tries: Martin, | Penalty Try, Dawson 2,
Stoica | Healey 3, Cohen 2
Conv: Dominguez | Wilkinson 3, Healey, King
PG: | Wilkinson 2
DG: | Back

Italy: C Pilat; C Stoica, N Zisti, L Martin, D Dallan (Preo 58); D Dominguez, A Troncon*; A Lo Cicero, A Moscardi, T Paoletti (Cuttitta 57), C Checchinato, A Gritti, V Cristofoletto, M Bergamasco (Persico 76), A de Rossi
England: M Perry; A Healey, M Tindall (Balshaw 62), M Catt, B Cohen; J Wilkinson (King 73), M Dawson* (Gomarsall 77); J Leonard (Woodman 70), P Greening (McCarthy 81), D Garforth, G Archer (Corry 78), S Shaw, R Hill (Worsley 70), N Back, L Dallaglio
Referee: A Lewis IRL

Millennium Stadium | Mar 18
WALES 26 | **SCOTLAND 18**
Tries: Williams 2 | M Leslie, Townsend
Conv: S Jones 2 | Hodge
PG: S Jones 4 | Hodge 2

Wales: M Cardey; G Thomas, A Bateman, M Taylor, S Williams; S Jones, R Moon; P Rogers, G Jenkins, D Young*, I Gough, A Moore, N Budgett, C Charvis, G Lewis
Scotland: C Paterson; C Moir, G Townsend, J Leslie*, G Metcalfe; D Hodge, A Nichol; T Smith, S Brotherstone (Bulloch 50), M Stewart (Hilton 80), S Murray, S Grimes, M Leslie, B Pountney, S Reid
Referee: D McHugh IRL

Rome | Mar 18
FRANCE 42 | **ITALY 31**
Tries: Penaud, | Martin, Troncon 2,
Castaignede, Pelous, | Mazzantini
Benazzi, Penaud
Conv: Dourthe 4 | Dominguez 4
PG: Dourthe 3
DG: | Dominguez

France: T Castaignède; P Bernat-Salles (Venditti 23), R Dourthe, E Ntamack, D Bory (Heymans 70); A Penaud, A Hueber; C Califano, M Dal Maso (Ibanex 40), F Tournaire (De Villiers 70), F Pelous*, O Brouzet (Miorin 62), L Mallier, O Magne, T Lièvremont (Benazzi 40)
Italy: M Pini; N Mazzucato, N Zisti (Dallan 52), L Martin, A Stoica; D Dominguez, A Troncon*; A Lo Cicero, A Moscardi (Orlandi 74), T Paoletti, C Checchinato, A Gritti, W Cristofoletto, M Bergamasco, A De Rossi (Visser 52)
Referee: P Deluca ARG

Lansdowne Road   *Apr 1*
IRELAND 19   **WALES 23**
Tries: Horgan   *Budgett, Jones*
Conv: O'Gara   *S Jones 2*
PG: O'Gara 4   *S Jones, N Jenkins 2*
Ireland: G Dempsey; S Horgan (Landsdowne), B O'Driscoll, R Henderson, D Hickie; R O'Gara (Humphreys 66), P Stringer; P Clohessy, K Wood*, J Hayes, M Galwey (Davidson 58), M O'Kelly, S Easterby (Ward 65), K Dawson, A Foley
Wales: R Williams; G Thomas, A Bateman, S Gibbs, S Williams (James 76); S Jones (Jenkins 67), R Moon; P Rogers, G Jenkins (McBryde 69), D Young, I Gough, A Moore, N Budgett, C Charvis, G Lewis
Referee: A Cole AUS

Murrayfield   *Apr 2*
SCOTLAND 19   **ENGLAND 13**
Try: Hodge   *Dallaglio*
Conv: Hodge   *Wilkinson*
PG: Hodge 4   *Wilkinson 2*
Scotland: C Paterson; C Moir, G Townsend, J McLaren, G Metcalfe; D Hodge, A Nichol*; T Smith, S Brotherstone, M Stewart (G McIlwham, 69), S Murray, R Metcalfe, J White, B Pountney, M Leslie (S Reid, 40-41)
England: M Perry; A Healey, M Tindall, M Catt, B Cohen (Balshaw, 57); J Wilkinson, M Dawson*; J Leonard, P Greening, P Vickery, G Archer (Corry, 64), S Shaw, R Hill (Worsley, 80), N Back, L Dallaglio
Referee: C Thomas

Final Six-Nations Table

		P	W	D	L	PF	PA	Diff	Pts
1	England	5	4	0	1	183	70	113	8
2	France	5	3	0	2	140	92	48	6
3	Ireland	5	3	0	2	168	133	35	6
4	Wales	5	3	0	2	111	135	-24	6
5	Scotland	5	1	0	4	95	145	-50	2
6	Italy	5	1	0	4	106	228	-122	2

Other Internationals

Pretoria   *June 17*
SOUTH AFRICA 18   **ENGLAND 13**
Tries: *Luger*
Conv: *Stimpson*
PG: Van Straaten 6   *Stimpson 2*
South Africa: P Montgomery; B Paulse, R Fleck (Delport 21-40, 72), D W Barry (Williams 26-40), P Rossouw; B van Straaten, J van der Westhuizen; R Kempson, C Marais, W Meyer, S Boome (Van den Berg 72), K Otto, R Erasmus (Krige 21, Le Roux 43-45), A Venter, A Vos*
England: M Perry; T Stimpson, M Tindall, M Catt (Lloyd 72), D Luger; A Healey, K Bracken; J Leonard, P Greening, J White (Flatman 58), M Johnson* (Shaw 71), D Grewcock (Worsley 86), R Hill (Regan 42-49), N Back, L Dallaglio
Referee: C Hawke NZL

Dunedin   *June 24*
NEW ZEALAND 69   **SCOTLAND 20**
Tries: Oliver 2, Cribb,   *Metcalfe, Simpson*
Lomu 3, Umaga 2,
Cullen, Alatini, Flavell
Conv: Mehrtens 7   *Hodge 2*
PG: *Hodge 2*
New Zealand: C Cullen (MacDonald, 50); T Umaga, A Ieremia, P Alatini, J Lomu; A Mehrtens, B Kelleher; C Hoeft, A Oliver (Hammett, 65), G Somerville (Dowd, 60), T Blackadder*, N Maxwell (Flavell, 65), T Randell (Kronfield, 50), S Robertson, R Cribb
Scotland: C Paterson; C Moir, G Townsend (Shiel, 57), J McLaren (Joiner, 61), S Longstaff; D Hodge (Edinburgh), A Nichol*; T Smith, G Bulloch, B Stewart (M Stewart, 71), S Murray (Fullerton, 36), R Metcalfe, J White, M Leslie (Simpson, 61), R Beattie
Referee: S Young AUS

Bloemfontein   June 24
SOUTH AFRICA 22   ENGLAND 27
Tries: Van der Westhuizen
Conv: Montgomery
PG: Van Straaten 4   Wilkinson 8
Montgomery
DG: Wilkinson
South Africa: P Montgomery; B Paulse, R Fleck, D W
Barry, P Rossouw; B van Straaten (Williams, 40); J Van
der Westhuizen; R Kempson, C Marais, C Visagie (Le
Roux, 61, S Boome, K Otto, C Krige, A Venter, A Vos*
England: M Perry; A Healey, M Tindall (Lloyd, 71), M
Catt, B Cohen; J Wilkinson, K Bracken; J Leonard, P
Greening, J White (Flatman, 89), M Johnson*, D
Grewcock (Shaw, 54), R Hill (Flatman, 23-28, Worsley,
60), N Back, L Dallaglio
Referee: S Dickinson AUS

Auckland   July 1
NEW ZEALAND 48   SCOTLAND 14
Tries: Kronfield, Cribb   Paterson, Murray
Umaga 2, Ieremia,
Robinson, Marshall,
Cullen
Conv: Mehrtens 3   Hodge 2
Brown
New Zealand: C Cullen; T Umaga (MacDonald, 69), M
Robinson, A Ieremia, J Lomu; A Mehrtens (Borwn, 62), J
Marshall; C Hoeft (Dowd, 56), A Oliver (Hammett, 53-62,
74), K Meeuws, N Maxwell (Randell, 71), T Blackadder*,
R Thorne, J Kronfeld (Robertson, 56), R Cribb
Scotland: C Paterson; C Murray, G Townsend, G Shiel,
C Joiner; D Hodge, A Nicol* (Beveridge, 78); T Smith, G
Bulloch (Scott, 74), B Stewart (McIlwham, 53), I Fullarton,
R Metcalfe (Hines, 64), J White, M Leslie, J Petrie
(Beattie, 67)
Referee: W Erickson AUS

Murrayfield   Nov 4
SCOTLAND 53   USA 6
Tries: Poutney, Leslie 2
Paterson, Townsend 2,
Conv: Townsend 4
PG: Townsend 5   Wells 2
Scotland: C Paterson; C Murray (Joiner, 68), A Bulloch,
J Leslie, J Steel; G Townsend (Hodge, 79), B Redpath
(Beveridge, 79); T Smith, S Brotherstone (Scott, 37-40,
64), G Graham (McIlwham, 57), S Murray (Metcalfe, 71),
S Grimes, J Petrie (White, 64), S Taylor, B Pountney*
USA: K Shuman; J Naivalu, P Eloff, J Grobler, M Delai; G
Wells, K Dalzell; J Clayton, K Khasigian, P Still, L Gross,
P Farner, D Hodges*, O Fifita, D Lyle
Referee: P Deluca ARG

Stade de France   Nov 4
FRANCE 13   AUSTRALIA 18
Tries: Galthie
Conv: Lamaison
PG: Lamaison 2   Burke 6
France: X Garbajosa; T Lombard, F Comba, R Dourthe,
D Bory; C Lamaison, F Galthie; S Marconnet
(F Tournaire 60), F Landreau, C Califano, F Pelous*,
O Brouzet (D Auradou 57), C Moni (S Betson 67), O
Magne, C Juillet (O Azam 61)
Australia: C Latham; M Burke, D Herbert, S Mortlock,
J Roff; R Kafer, S Cordingley; B Young, M Foley
(J Paul 25), F Dyson (G Panaho 54), J Eales*, D Giffin,
M Cockbain, G Smith, T Kefu (J Williams 64)
Referee: P Honiss NZL

Stade de France   Nov 11
FRANCE 26   NEW ZEALAND 39
Tries: Bernat-Salles   Howlett, Cullen
Pelous
Conv: Lamaison 2   Mehrtens
PG: Lamaison 4   Mehrtens 9
France: X Garbajosa; T Lombard (Bernat-Salles, 52), F
Comba, R Dourthe, D Bory; C Lamaison, F Galthié; S
Marconnet, F Landreau, C Califano (De Villiers, 61), F
Pelous*, D Auradou, C Moni (Betson, 61), C Juillet, O
Magne
New Zealand: C Cullen; D Howlett, T Umaga, D Gibson,
J Lomu; A Mehrtens, J Marshall; G Feek, A Oliver, G
Somerville (Slater, 70), T Blackadder*, N Maxwell, R
Thorne, S Robertson, R Cribb
Referee: W Erickson AUS

Lansdowne Road   Nov 11
IRELAND 78   JAPAN 9
Tries: Murphy, Stringer,
Hickie 3, Howe 2,
O'Driscoll 2, Clohessy,
Henderson
Conv: O'Gara 10
PG: O'Gara   Hirose 3
Ireland: G Murphy (Humphreys, 62); D Hickie, B
O'Driscoll, S Horgan (Henderson, 60), D Howe; R
O'Gara, P Stringer; P Clohessy, K Wood*, J Hayes, P
Johns (Longwell, 56), M O'Kelly, A Ward, K Dawson, A
Foley
Japan: D Ohata, M Oda, R Kawai, H Namba, P Tuidraki,
K Hirose (Fuchigami, 54), K Ohara* (Ito, 54), T Fumihara,
N Yasuda, N Nakamura, K Todd, H Tanuma, H
Sugawara, T Ito, K Kubo
Referee: N Whitehouse WAL

Millennium Stadium Nov 11
WALES 50 **SAMOA 6**
Tries: Taylor,
S Williams 2, Gough,
Penalty Try, Bateman
Conv: A Thomas 4
PG: A Thomas 4 Patu, Sanft
Wales: R Williams, A Bateman, M Taylor*, S Gibbs (James, 72), S Williams, A Thomas, R Howley (Moon, 69), I Thomas (N Jenkins, 69), G Jenkins (A Lewis, 50), B Evans (John, 50), I Gough, D Jones (Griffiths, 55), G Lewis, C Charvis, S Quinnell (Budgett, 66)
Samoa: H V Patu, S Faasua (Misa, 70), F Soolefai, F Tuilagi, F Toala, Q Sanft, S Sooialo, T Veiru (Tafeamalii, 70), O Matauiau* (Schwalger, 29), P Asi, O Paletoi (Tone, 50), S Poching, A Vaeluaga, L Mealamu (Mamea, 62), J Maligi
Referee: S Dickinson AUS

Murrayfield Nov 11
SCOTLAND 9 **AUSTRALIA 30**
Tries: Latham, Roff, Burke
Conv: Burke 3
PG: Townsend 3 Burke 3
Scotland: C Paterson; C Murray, A Bulloch, J Leslie, J Steel; G Townsend, B Redpath; T Smith, S Brotherstone (G Bulloch, 51), G Graham (McIlwham, 53), S Murray, S Grimes (Metcalfe, 64), J Petrie (White, 64, Graham, 81), B Pountney*, S Taylor
Australia: C Latham; M Burke, D Herbert, S Mortlock (Gray, 69), J Roff; R Kafer (Fletley, 55), S Cordingley (Whitaker, 76); B Young, M Foley (Paul, 40), F Dyson (Panoho, 46), J Eales*, D Giffin, M Cockbain (Williams, 40), G Smith, T Kefu (Connors, 68)
Referee: C White ENG

Marseille Nov 18
FRANCE 42 **NEW ZEALAND 33**
Tries: Garbajosa, Marshall, Howlett,
Magne, Galthié Slater
Conv: Lamaison 3 Mehrtens 3
PG: Lamaison 5 Mehrtens 4
DG: Lamaison 2
France: J L Sadourny, P Bernat-Salles, F Comba, R Dourthe (M Dourthe, 30-34), X Garbajosa, C Lamaison, F Galthie, S Marconnet, F Alandreau (Azam, 80), P De Villiers (Califano, 52), D Auradou (Brouzet, 52), F Pelous*, C Moni (Betson, 70), O Magne, C Juillet
New Zealand: C Cullen, D Howlett, T Umaga, D Gibson, B Reihana, A Mehrtens, J Marshall, G Feek, A Oliver (Hammett, 78), G Somerville (Slater, 38), T Blackadder*, N Maxwell (Flavell, 84), R Thorne (Randall, 50), S Robertson, R Cribb
Referee: J Kaplan RSA

Murrayfield Nov 18
SCOTLAND 31 **SAMOA 8**
Tries: Petry, Logan, Patu
Smith, Bulluch
Conv: Townsend
PG: Townsend 3 Sanft
Scotland: C Paterson; C Murray, A Bulloch (Hodge, 75), J Leslie, K Logan; G Townsend, B Redpath (Beveridge, 75); T Smith, S Brotherstone (G Bulloch, 68), G Graham (McIlwham, 51), S Murray, R Metcalfe (Grimes, 56), J White (Beattie, 23-34), B Pountney*, J Petrie
Samoa: H V Patu; M Schuster (T Suemai, 26), F So'olefai, F Tuilagi, F Toala; Q Sanft (A Toleafoa, 57), S So'oialo; D Tafaemalii (Schwalger 65), O Matauiau*, P Asi, S Poching, S Tone, A Vaeluaga (T Veirub, 76), L Mealaum (A Mika, 79), J Maligi (J Mamea, 68)
Referee: I Hyde-Lay CAN

Millennium Stadium Nov 18
WALES 42 **USA 11**
Tries: James 2, Taylor, Delai
A Thomas, R Williams,
N Jenkins
Conv: A Thomas 2,
N Jenkins
PG: A Thomas 2 Wells 2
Wales: R Williams; A Bateman, M Taylor* (G Thomas, 60), S Gibbs, D James; A Thomas (N Jenkins, 65), R Howley (Moon, 80); D Morris, G Jenkins (Lewis, 57), B Evans (I Thomas, 55), I Gough (Moore, 70), C Wyatt, N Budgett, C Charvis, S Quinnell (G Lewis, 60)
USA: K Shuman; J Naivalu, P Eloff, J Grobler (Kayter, 60), M Delai; G Wells, K Dalzell; J Clayton, K Khasigian (Flynn), P Still, L Gross, P Farner, D Hodges*, O Fifita (Magelby), D Lyle
Referee: I Ramage SCO

Twickenham Nov 18
ENGLAND 22 **AUSTRALIA 19**
Tries: Luger Burke
Conv: Wilkinson Burke
PG: Wilkinson 4 Burke 4
DG: Wilkinson
England: M Perry; A Healey (Balshaw, 55), M Tindall, M Catt, D Luger; J Wilkinson, K Bracken (Dawson, 55); J Leonard, P Greening (Regan, 85), P Vickery (Flatman, 22-25), M Johnson*, D Grewcock, R Hill, N Back, L Dallaglio
Australia: C Latham; M Burke, D Herbert, S Mortlock, J Roff; R Kafer (Grey, 45), S Cordingley; B Young, M Foley (Paul, 40), F Dyson (Panoho, 30), J Eales*, D Giffin (Cockbain, 78), J Williams, G Smith (Waugh, 76), T Kefu (Connors, 46-58)
Referee: A Watson RSA

Lansdowne Road **Nov 19**
IRELAND 18 **SOUTH AFRICA 28**
Tries: Hickie, Howe *Van der Westhuizen,*
Krige, Venter
Conv: O'Gara *Montgomery, Van Straaten*
PG: O'Gara 2 *Montgomery 2, Van Straaten*
Ireland: G Dempsey (Horgan, 81); D Hickie, B O'Driscoll, R Henderson, T Howe; R O'Gara (Humphreys, 62), P Stringer; P Clohessy, K Wood*, J Hayes (Fitzpatrick, 78); G Longwell, M O'Kelly, E Miller (Ward, 71), K Dawson, A Foley
South Africa: T Delport; C Williams, G Esterhuizen (Fleck, 64), R Fleck (Van Straaten, 40), P Rossouw, P Montgomery, J van der Westhuizen; W Meyer, J Smit, R Kempson, M Andrews, A van den Berg, C Krige, A Venter, A Vos*
Referee: S Lander ENG

Twickenham **Nov 25**
ENGLAND 19 **ARGENTINA 0**
Tries: Cohen
Conv: Wilkinson
PG: Wilkinson 3
DG: Wilkinson
England: I Balshaw; B Cohen, M Tindall (Greenwood, 57); M Catt, D Luger; J Wilkinson, M Dawson; J Leonard (Flatman, 69), M Regan (West, 77), J White (Vickery, 40, Flatman 50-67), M Johnson*, D Grewcock, R Hill (Corry, 74), N Back, L Dallaglio
Argentina: F Contepomi; O Bartolucci, J Orengo, L Arbizu*, I Corleto; G Quesada, A Pichot; R Grau, F Mendez, O Hasan, I Fernandez-Lobbe, A Allub (Ugartemendia, 64), S Phelan, R Martin, G Longo
Referee: A Lewis IRL

Genoa **Nov 25**
ITALY 19 **NEW ZEALAND 56**
Tries: Lo Cicero, *Reihana 2, Tiatia, Howlett,*
Saviozzi *Cribb 2, Marshall, Spencer*
Conv: *Spencer 5*
PG: Pez 3 *Spencer 2*
Italy: C Stoica; M Perziano, L Martin, G Raineri, D Dallan; R Pez (Preo, 54), A Troncon (Frati, 3); A Lo Cicero, A Moscardi*, A Muraro, A Gritti, W Visser (Mastrodomenicio, 63), M Zaffiri (De Rossi, 39), C Caione (Saviozzi, 72), R Piovan
New Zealand: C Cullen (Mehrtens, 77); D Howlett, T Umaga, P Alatini, B Reihana; C Spencer, J Marshall; G Feek, A Oliver (Hammett, 73), G Sommerville (Slater, 54), T Blackadder, T Flavell, F Tiatia (Maxwell, 46), S Robertson (Randall, 73), R Cribb
Referee: R Davies WAL

Millennium Stadium **Nov 26**
WALES 13 **SOUTH AFRICA 23**
Tries: Gibbs *Van der Westhuizen, Paulse*
Conv: N Jenkins *Van Straaten 2*
PG: N Jenkins, *Van Straaten 3*
A Thomas
Wales: R Williams (S Williams, 19); G Thomas, A Bateman, S Gibbs, D James; N Jenkins (A Thomas, 60), R Howley; P Rogers (I Thomas, 41), G Jenkins (A Lewis, 55), D Morris (John, 62), I Gough, C Wyatt, N Budgett, C Charvis, S Quinnell*
South Africa: T Delport (Esterhuizen, 43); B Paulse, B Van Straaten, R Fleck, P Rossouw; P Montgomery, J van der Westhuizen; W Meyer (Le Roux, 76), J Smit, R Kempson, M Andrews, A van den Berg (Venter, 56), C Krige, A Venter, A Vos*
Referee: S Walsh NZL

Twickenham **Dec 2**
ENGLAND 25 **SOUTH AFRICA 17**
Tries: Greenwood *Van Straaten*
Conv: Wilkinson
PG: Wilkinson 6 *Van Straaten 4*
England: M Perry; B Cohen, M Tindall, W Greenwood, D Luger; J Wilkinson, M Dawson; J Leonard, P Greening, J White, M Johnson*, D Grewcock, R Hill, N Back, L Dallaglio
South Africa: P Montgomery; B Paulse, R Fleck, J Mulder, S Terblanche; B van Straaten, J van der Westhuizen; R Kempson, J Smit, W Meyer, A van den Bergh, M Andrews, C Krige, A Venter, A Vos*

Tri-Nations Series

Sydney	*July 15*
AUSTRALIA 35	**NEW ZEALAND 39**
Tries: Mortlock 2,	*Umaga, Alatini, Cullen,*
Latham, Roff, Paul	*Marshall, Lomu*
Conv: Mortlock 2	*Mehrtens 4*
PG: Mortlock 2	*Mehrtens 2*

Australia: C Latham; S Mortlock (A Walker 76),
D Herbert (R Kafer 69), J Little (R Kafer 53-69), J Roff;
S Larkham, G Gregan; R Harry (G Panoho 57), M Foley
(J Paul 40), F Dyson, D Giffin, J Eales*, M Connors,
D Wilson (T Kefu 46), J Williams (T Jacques 78).
New Zealand: C Cullen; T Umaga, A Ieremia, P Alatini,
J Lomu; A Mehrtens (T Brown 65), J Marshall (B Kelleher
70); C Hoeft, A Oliver (M Hammett 72), K Meeuws,
T Blackadder*, N Maxwell (T Flavell 50), T Randell,
S Robertson (J Kronfeld 44), R Cribb
Referee: A Watson RSA

Christchurch	*July 22*
NEW ZEALAND 25	**SOUTH AFRICA 12**
Tries: Cullen 2	
PG: Mehrtens 3, Brown	*Van Straaten 3*
DG: Mehrtens	*Montgomery*

New Zealand: C Cullen (L MacDonald 2-6); T Umaga,
M Robinson, P Alatini, J Lomu; A Mehrtens (T Brown 68),
J Marshall; C Hoeft (C Dowd 51), A Oliver (M Hammett
63), K Meeuws, T Blackadder*, T Flavell (N Maxwell 40),
T Randell, J Kronfeld (S Robertson 74), R Cribb
South Africa: P Montgomery; T Delport, R Fleck (G
Esterhuizen 75), D Barry, B Paulse; B van Straaten, W
Swanepoel (J van der Westhuizen 75); R Kempson (J
Smit 34-40, 71), C Marais, C Visagie (W Meyer 66), A
van den Berg (J Labuschagne 71), A Venter, J Erasmus,
C Krige (W Brosnihan 2-11), A Vos*
Referee: C White ENG

Sydney	*July 29*
AUSTRALIA 26	**SOUTH AFRICA 6**
Tries: Mortlock, Paul	
Conv: Mortlock 2	
PG: Mortlock 4	*Van Straaten 2*

Australia: C Latham; S Mortlock, D Herbert, J Little
(R Kafer 78), J Roff (B Tune, 63); S Larkham, G Gregan;
R Harry, M Foley (J Paul 40), F Dyson (G Panoho 70),
D Giffin, J Eales* (Cockbain 56-58), M Connors
(M Cockbain 58) D Wilson (J Williams 72), J Williams
(T Kefu 46).
South Africa: T Delport; B Paulse, R Fleck, D W Barry,
P Rossouw; B Van Straaten (P Montgomery 65), W
Swanepoel (J van der Westhuizen 65); R Kempson,
C Marais (J Smit 64), C Visagie (O le Roux 63), A Van
den Berg (W Brosnihan 70), M Andrews (W Brosnihan
56-70), C Krige, A Venter, A Vos*
Referee: E Morrison ENG

Wellington	*Aug 5*
NEW ZEALAND 23	**AUSTRALIA 24**
Tries: Cullen 2	*Mortlock, Roff*
Conv: Mehrtens 2	*Mortlock*
PG: Mehrtens 3	*Mortlock 3, Eales*

New Zealand: C Cullen; T Umaga, A Ieremia, P Alatini,
J Lomu; A Mehrtens (T Brown 62), J Marshall
(B Kelleher 66); R Cribb, J Kronfeld (R Thorne 54),
T Randell, N Maxwell, T Blackadder*, K Meeuws,
A Oliver (M Hammett 76), C Hoeft (C Dowd 70)
Australia: C Latham; S Mortlock (J Roff 76), D Herbert,
J Little, J Roff (B Tune 40); S Larkham, G Gregan;
R Harry, M Foley (J Paul 35), F Dyson, D Giffin, J Eales*,
J Williams (M Connors 46), D Wilson, T Kefu
(J Williams 62)
Referee: J Kaplan RSA

Johannesburg	*Aug 19*
SOUTH AFRICA 46	**NEW ZEALAND 40**
Tries: Williams, Fleck 2,	*Umaga 2, Cullen 2*
Swanepoel 2, Delport	
Conv: Van Straaten 5	*Mehrtens 4*
PG: Van Straaten 2	*Mehrtens 3*
DG:	*Mehrtens*

South Africa: T Delport; C Williams, G Eesterhuizen,
R Fleck (J van der Westhuyzen 80), B Paulse; B Van
Straaten, W Swanepoel; A Vos (capt), C Krige
(W Brosnihan 75), J Erasmus, M Andrews (A van der
Berg 75), A Venter, C Visage (W Meyer 79), C Marais,
O le Roux (J Smit 61)
New Zealand: C Cullen (L MacDonald 55); T Umaga,
A Ieremia, P Alatini, J Lomu; A Mehrtens, J Marshall;
R Cribb, J Kronfield (S Robertson 74), T Randell,
N Maxwell (T Flavell 45), T Blackadder*, K Meeuws,
A Oliver (M Hammett 52), C Hoeft (G Somerville 40)
Referee: A Cole AUS

Durban	*Aug 26*
SOUTH AFRICA 18	**AUSTRALIA 19**
Tries:	*Latham*
Conv:	*Mortlock*
PG: Van Straaten 6	*Mortlock 4*

South Africa: T Delport; C Williams, G Esterhuizen,
R Fleck, B Paulse; B Van Straaten, W Swanepoel;
R Kempson (O le Roux 40), C Marais (J Smit 76),
C Visagie, A Venter, M Andrews (A van den Berg 70),
J Erasmus (A van den Berg 55-70), C Krige, A Vos*
(W Brosnihan 40)
Australia: C Latham; S Mortlock, D Herbert, J Little,
J Roff (B Tune 70, R Kafer 73); S Larkham, G Gregan;
R Harry, M Foley (J Paul 31), F Dyson, D Giffin, J Eales
(capt), M Connors (T Kefu 50), D Wilson (M Cockbain
53-70), J Williams (M Cockbain 70)
Referee: P Honiss NZL

AUSTRALIA WON THE TRI-NATIONS SERIES

Heineken Cup

Quarter-finals

Les Sept Derniers	*Apr 15*
Toulouse 31	Montferrand 18
Stradey Park	*Apr 15*
Llanelli 22	Cardiff 3
Limerick	*Apr 15*
Munster	Stade Français 10
Franklin Park	*Apr 16*
Northampton 25	Wasps 22

Semi-finals

Madejski Stadium	*May 7*
Northampton 31	Llanelli 28
Bordeaux	*May 6*
Toulouse 25	Munster 31

Final

Twickenham   *May 27*
MUNSTER 8   **NORTHAMPTON 9**
Tries: Wallace
PG: Grayson 3
DG: Holland

Munster: D Crotty; J Kelly, M Mullins, J Holland, A Horgan; R O'Gara, P Stringer; P Clohessy, K Wood*, J Hayes, M Galwey, J Langford, E Halvey, D Wallace, A Foley
Colomiers: P Grayson; C Moir, A Bateman, M Allen, B Cohen; A Hepher, D Malone; G Pagel, F Mendez, M Stewart, A Newman, T Rodber, D MacKinnon, B Pountney, P Lam*
Referee: Dume
Attendance: 66,441

Heineken Shield

FINAL
Toulouse   *May 27*
PAU 34   **CASTRES 21**

"Unbelievable. I'm so bloody proud I could cry. F* the film, I'm going on the lash"**

Richard Harris, on learning while filming in the Mexican jungle that his team, Munster, had won their Heineken European Cup semi-final against Toulouse.

"I live round the corner from Twickenham and every day I will have to stare at this monument to despair and defeat. I might have to buy a pair of dark glasses so I can't see it"

Keith Wood, the Munster captain, after the Heineken Cup defeat by Northampton in the final.

"They started warming up like professionals and we just stood about smoking a few cigarettes knowing we were in real trouble"

Rod Thomas, of vets side Dorchester Gladiators, who mistakenly arranged a fixture against the best team in Romania, national champions Steaua Bucharest. Steaua won 61-17.

"Czech Rugby is not big but who cares? We have Prague, Brno and all the nice places in our country. Rugby gives us the opportunity to get out there on Saturdays, have a bit of a fight with our old enemies and enjoy a pint afterwards. We love it"

Czech Republic rugby website, www.rugby.cz/english.

Domestic Results

Allied Dunbar Premiership

Division 1	P	W	D	L	F	A	Pts
1 Leicester	22	18	1	3	687	425	51
2 Bath	22	15	2	5	690	425	43
3 Gloucester	22	15	0	7	628	490	40
4 Saracens	22	14	0	8	729	514	37
5 Northampton	22	13	1	8	551	480	35
6 Bristol*	22	12	1	9	632	602	34
7 Wasps	22	11	1	10	640	461	31
8 London Irish	22	9	1	12	613	616	25
9 Newcastle	22	6	2	14	377	630	19
10 Harlequins	22	7	0	15	441	687	18
11 Sale	22	7	0	15	381	633	18
12 Bedford	22	1	0	21	396	802	3

*Until the end of the World Cup (Nov 6) two points were awarded for wins rather than three. *Two points deducted*

Premiership Play-off

May 24
Rotherham 40   Bedford 20
May 28
Bedford 14   Rotherham 0
Rotherham promoted (40-34 on aggregate) to Premiership

Allied Dunbar Premiership 2

	P	W	D	L	F	A	Pts
1 Rotherham	26	24	0	2	1045	267	48
2 Leeds	26	22	0	4	794	269	44
3 Worcester	26	19	0	7	865	450	38
4 Exeter	26	19	0	7	742	466	38
5 London Welsh	26	16	0	10	712	476	32
6 Coventry	26	15	0	11	714	589	30
7 Moseley	26	14	0	12	595	526	28
8 Manchester	26	11	0	15	513	671	22
9 Henley	26	10	1	15	599	696	21
10 Wakefield	26	10	0	16	547	638	20
11 Orrell	26	7	0	19	388	682	14
12 Waterloo	26	6	2	18	441	830	14
13 Rugby	26	6	1	19	408	905	13
14 West Hartlepool	26	1	0	25	216	1114	2

National League Division 1

	P	W	D	L	F	A	Pts
1 Otley	26	22	1	3	817	399	45
2 B'ham/Solihull	26	21	1	4	659	346	43
3 Wharfedale	26	19	1	6	646	317	39
4 Rosslyn Park	26	17	2	7	694	371	36
5 Newbury	26	15	1	10	550	483	31
6 Harrogate	26	14	1	11	508	449	29
7 Bracknell	26	14	0	12	558	408	28
8 Preston G	26	12	0	14	608	580	24
9 Fylde	26	10	1	15	387	485	21
10 Lydney	26	9	2	15	496	632	20
11 Nottingham	26	8	1	17	460	574	17
12 Camberley	26	7	0	19	398	832	14
13 Reading	26	6	0	20	442	626	12
14 Blackheath	26	2	1	23	316	1037	5

National League Division 2 North

	P	W	D	L	F	A	Pts
1 Kendal	26	24	0	2	817	305	48
2 Stourbridge	26	21	1	4	730	411	43
3 New Brighton	26	21	0	5	784	283	42
4 Walsall	26	16	0	10	588	419	32
5 Sedgley Park	26	14	2	10	689	484	30
6 Doncaster	26	12	2	12	656	542	26
7 Morley	26	12	1	13	614	547	25
8 Nuneaton	26	11	1	14	610	665	23
9 Bedford Ath	26	11	0	15	563	729	22
10 Sandal	26	9	3	14	471	549	21
11 Whitchurch	26	9	1	16	430	794	19
12 Aspatria	26	8	0	18	483	697	16
13 Liverpool St H	26	5	0	21	335	848	10
14 Sheffield	26	3	1	22	291	788	7

National League Division 2 South

	P	W	D	L	F	A	Pts
1 Esher	26	23	0	3	1018	356	46
2 Penzance/N	26	20	1	5	1055	479	41
3 Nth Walsham	26	19	0	7	792	358	38
4 Plymouth	26	17	2	7	664	382	36
5 Redruth	26	16	0	10	597	523	32
6 Barking	26	15	0	11	628	523	30
7 Clifton	26	12	1	13	575	549	25
8 Tabard	26	11	1	14	550	627	23
9 Westcombe P	26	11	0	15	550	706	22
10 Cheltenham	26	10	1	15	503	678	21
11 Weston-s-M	26	11	0	15	512	598	20
12 Bridgwater	26	8	0	18	523	729	16
13 Norwich	26	6	0	20	321	695	12
14 Met Police	26	0	0	26	223	1308	0

Tetley's Bitter Cup

Final

Twickenham   May 13
Wasps 31   **Northampton 23**
Tries: Lewsey, Leota,   *Pountney*
Logan, Denney
Conv: Logan
PG: King 3   *Grayson 6*

Wasps: J Lewsey; S Roiser, M Denney, R Henderson, K Logan, M Wood; D Molloy, T Leota, W Green (A Le Chevalier 57-65), A Reed (M Weedon 65), S Shaw, J Worsley, P Volley, L Dallaglio*

Northampton: N Beal; C Moir, A Bateman, M Allen, B Cohen; P Grayson, M Dawson; G Pagel, F Mendez, M Stewart (M Scelzo 73), A King, M Wood; D Molloy, T Leota, W Green (A Newman (J Phillips 60), R Metcalfe, T Rodber, B Pountney, P Lam* (S Walter 33-39, D Mackinnon 65)

Tetley's Bitter County Championships

Twickenham   May 20
Yorkshire 16   Devon 9

Welsh/Scottish League

		P	W	D	L	PF	PA	Pt
1	Cardiff	21	18	1	2	839	463	59
2	Newport	22	15	1	6	773	453	49
3	Swansea	21	13	1	7	650	469	43
4	Pontypridd	21	13	2	6	637	466	41
5	Llanelli	21	13	0	8	736	498	38
6	Ebbw Vale	22	12	0	10	647	569	38
7	Neath	22	11	2	9	664	553	35
8	Edinburgh R'rs	22	10	1	11	564	654	34
9	Bridgend	22	8	1	13	427	564	27
10	Glasgow Caley	22	8	1	13	488	621	25
11	Caerphilly	22	2	1	19	427	939	6
12	Dunvant	22	1	1	20	357	960	5

BT Scotland Premiership 1

		P	W	D	L	PF	PA	Pt
1	Heriot's FP	18	16	0	2	707	274	74
2	Glasgow Hawks	18	13	0	5	566	277	63
3	Melrose	18	11	0	7	446	396	52
4	Currie	18	10	0	8	436	442	52
5	Gala	18	9	0	9	457	448	46
6	Hawick	18	9	1	8	466	472	46
7	Jed-Forest	18	8	1	9	361	416	43
8	Watsonians	18	6	0	12	395	490	34
9	Kelso	18	5	0	13	323	531	27
10	West of Scotland	18	2	0	16	276	687	13

BT Cellnet Cup
Final

Murrayfield　　　　*April 23*
Boroughmuir 35　　**Glasgow Hawks 10**
Tries: Couper 2,　　*Penalty Try*
McCallum, Davidson
Conv: Howarth 3　　*Aitkin*
PG: Howarth 3　　*Aitkin*
Boroughmuir: T Lightoller (T Dowling 64); D Stark, L
Graham, G Kiddie, R Couper (M Murray 81); C Howarth,
D Roberts (C Cusiter 73); A Green (D Rutterford 81), D
Cunningham (N Dickson 24), S Penman*, A Davidson, G
McCallum, N Bruce (E MacDonald 77), R Muir, O Brown
(J McKinlay 81)
Glasgow Hawks: C Aitken (T Matthewson 58); K Baillie,
C Simmers, R Munday (N Barrett 81), G Hawkes; E
Martin, C Little (K Sinclair 69); C Hanvey, C Docherty (D
MacNeill 81), G Walsh (G Francis 72), I Smith, C
Afuakwah, S Hutton*, R McKay, R Niven

Welsh National League

Division 1		P	W	D	L	PF	PA	B	Pts
1	Llanelli	20	15	1	4	768	341	18	64
2	Pontypridd	20	12	0	8	646	468	10	46
3	Neath	20	12	0	8	568	491	8	44
4	Ebbw Vale	20	12	1	7	541	468	7	44
5	Caerphilly	20	10	2	8	550	562	5	37
6	Bridgend	20	9	2	9	522	597	5	34
7	Newport	20	5	0	15	499	629	8	23
8	Aberavon	20	2	0	18	391	929	4	10

Welsh Challenge Cup
Final

Millennium Stadium　　*May 20*
Llanelli 22　　　　**Swansea 12**
Tries: Gillies
Conv: S Jones
PG: S Jones 5　　　　*Thomas 4*
Llanelli: M Cardey; W Proctor*, D James, N Boobyer
(M Jones 40); S Finau; S Jones, R Moon; P Booth,
R McBryde, J Davies, C Wyatt, C Gillies, S Easterby,
I Boobyer (M Thomas 20-30), S Quinnell
Swansea: K Morgan; R Rees, M Taylor, S Gibbs*, S
Payne; A Thomas, R Jones; D Morris, G Jenkins
(C Wells 69), B Evans (C Anthony 69), J Griffiths,
T Maullin, P Moriarty, C Charvis, L Jones (C Wells 35-45,
D Thomas 60)

AIB Irish League

Division 1		P	W	D	L	PF	PA	Pts
1	St Mary's	11	8	0	3	265	121	36
2	Terenure	11	8	0	3	235	229	36
3	Lansdowne	11	7	1	3	265	149	33
4	Ballymena	11	7	0	4	267	282	32
5	Garryowen	11	6	0	5	245	199	29
6	Cork Constitution	11	6	0	5	259	258	28
7	Young Munster	11	6	0	5	175	243	25
8	Buccaneers	11	5	0	6	205	196	22
9	Shannon	11	4	0	7	222	229	22
10	Dungannon	11	4	0	7	235	252	19

Sailing

A revolution in sleepy old Rushcutters Bay, who'd have thought it? Well, there was a belief amongst the sailors, the coaches and the specialist press that something could happen, though none would have predicted such excessive glee. The last time that Britannia ruled the Olympic waves was in 1908, when the races on the Solent yielded four British titles. As three of those came in events where the only entrants were British boats, this was not much of an achievement. At Rushcutters Bay, it was very different.

As the Games began, Britain had not a single reigning world sailing champion. Indeed, Ben Ainslie was the only domestic sailor to have won a world title since the last Olympic Games, his Laser class victory coming in 1999. However, Ainslie could not retain the title, at Cancun in March, obliged to give best to his rival Robert Scheidt, the Brazilian on waters he might almost call home. In Sydney, the tables would be turned again.

Iain Percy had been the top-ranked Finn sailor in the world in December 1999, but his championship forays at Weymouth and Mallorca (for the world and European titles) had been fruitless. At Mallorca, Percy had withdrawn after just three races with food poisoning. Yet, coming into Sydney his confidence was surprisingly high.

The last member of the triumvirate was the first to be crowned Olympic champion, and she was the one least expected to claim a title. Shirley Robertson admitted that she was the perpetual bridesmaid of her sport. Frequently a leader in the world rankings, she had never quite brought off the major victory. At Atlanta, she had frustratingly finished fourth.

The Dutchwoman Margriet Matthijsse was the favourite for the Europe class in Sydney, but if her coach is to be believed, threw away her chances by her own obduracity. "Everyone goes right, so you have to go left," he said accusingly. Robertson played it cautiously (the only way with the fickle winds of the harbour switching on and off), so that when the chips were down, she and not Matthijsse had the points in the bag. The Dutchwoman won the final three races, but still couldn't catch Robertson who won the Olympic title by two points. As the Scottish sailor pulled her boat ashore, the British team were ecstatic, the first gold medal was in the bag, the second on its way.

Ben Ainslie *(see also Review section)* had to wait until all the appeals had been considered before he could claim his title, but before supper on Friday, there were two titles in the bag. On Saturday, Percy, who had had controlled the Finn class from start to finish, made it three.

If that were not enough, there were also two silver medals to add to the catch. The first came from the 49er crew of Ian Barker and Simon Hiscocks, the former celebrating his victory with such gusto that it was quite a surprise to see him standing upright the very next day. The second silver medal came in the Star class, with Ian Walker and Mark Covell, a crew only formed when their respective partners, John Merricks and Glyn Charles, died. "There's not a day goes by when we don't think of them," said Walker, who had won his first silver medal in Atlanta with Merricks.

Olympic Classes

470 World Championships
Balatonfured, Hungary   *May 10-20*
Men

1	King/Turnbull	AUS	39
2	Philippe/Cariou	FRA	47
3	Braslavets/Matvyenko	UKR	61
6	Rogers/Glanfield	GBR	96
15	Draper/Newman	GBR	144
22	Vials/Leask	GBR	179

Women

1	Bekatorou/Tsoulfa	GRE	35
2	Armstrong/Stowell	AUS	44
3	Via-Dufresne/Azon	ESP	55
27	Nurton/Watson	GBR	186
28	Rees-Jones/Leask	GBR	193
35	Gibson/Clark	GBR	54
54	Lucas/Parkin	GBR	261
55	Raggatt/Webb	GBR	261

470 European Championships
Dervio, Italy   *June 4-14*
Men

1	Cooke/Nicholas	NZL	44
2	Gildas/Cariou	FRA	53
3	Forester/Merrick	USA	60
6	Rogers/Glanfield	GBR	71
16	Draper/Newman	GBR	120

Women

1	Armstrong/Stowell	AUS	16
2	Bekatorou/Tsoulfa	GRE	34
3	S Ward/M Ward	DEN	50

49er World Championship
Bahia de San Carlos, Mexico   *Mar 14-24*

1	Michael Hestbaek/Jonathan Perrson	DEN	25.0
2	Thomas Johanson/Jyki Jarvi	FIN	27.0
3	S Lopez Vazquez/ Javier de la Plata	ESP	34.0
4	Christoffer Sundby/Vegard Arnhoff	NOR	37.0
5	Marc Audineau/Julien Farnarier	FRA	41.0
6	Marcus Bauer/Philip Barth	GER	43.8
7	Ian Barker/Simon Hiscocks	GBR	46.1
14	Paul Brotherton/Mo Gray	GBR	70.0
15	Andy Budgen/Ian Budgen	GBR	71.0
16	Alister Richardson/Peter Greenhalgh	GBR	74.0
24	Tim Robinson/Zeb Elliot	GBR	84.0

49er European Championship
Medemblik, Netherlands   *June 1-5*

1	Michael Hestbaek/Jonathan Persson	DEN	53
2	Rodian Luka/Georgiy Leonchuk	UKR	53
3	Iker Martinez/Xabier Fernandez	ESP	56
10	Paul Brotherton/Mo Gray	GBR	69
17	Alistair Richardson/Peter Greenhalgh	GBR	92
20	Ian Barker/Simon Hiscocks	GBR	104

Chris Nicholson/Daniel Philips (35pts) won the series, but as they were Australians were awarded the 'Open' title.

Europe World Championship
Sydney   *Jan 6-16*

1	Kristine Roug	DEN	25
2	Shirley Robertson	GBR	41
3	Meg Gaillard	USA	54
36	Jayne Singleton	GBR	245
42	Kit Grime	GBR	263
62	Debbie Winstanley	GBR	185
66	Nicky Muller	GBR	212
77	Kirsty Bonar	GBR	256

Finn Gold Cup
Weymouth   *Jun 10-16*

1	Mateusz Kusznierewicz	POL	13
2	Sebastien Godefroid	BEL	26
3	Emilios Papathanasiou	GRE	44
12	Andrew Simpson	GBR	82
14	David Mellor	GBR	89
18	Iain Percy	GBR	106.25
28	Charlie Cumbley	GBR	155
32	Richard Stenhouse	GBR	173

Finn European Championship
Mallorca   *Apr 7-15*

1	Mateusz Kusznierewicz	POL	12
2	Karlo Kuret	CRO	40
3	David Burrows	IRL	48
11	Jamie Lea	GBR	88
24	Charlie Cumbley	GBR	167
28	David Mellor	GBR	183
34	Chris Brittle	GBR	217
50	Iain Percy	GBR	298

(retired after 3 races - food poisoning)

Mistral World Championships
Mar del Plata ARG   *Feb 10-20*
Men

1	Nikolas Kaklamanakis	GRE	38
2	Aaron McIntosh	NZL	39
3	Carlos Espinola	ARG	47
23	Nick Dempsey	GBR	149
32	Dominic Tidey	GBR	184
42	Wemms	GBR	216

Women

1	Alessandra Sensini	ITA	23
2	Lee Lai Shan	HKG	26
3	Faustine Merret	FRA	35
21	Christine Johnston	GBR	197
29	Helen Cartwright	GBR	248
31	Jessica Ash	GBR	275

Mistral European Championships
Cadiz, Spain   *May 18-28*
Men

1	Alexander Guyader	FRA	28
2	Amit Inbar	ISR	42
3	Julien Bontemps	FRA	53
10	Dominic Tidey	GBR	99
15	Nick Dempsey	GBR	118

Women

1	Alessandra Sensini	ITA	27
2	Faustine Merret	FRA	31
3	Anna Galecka	POL	40
14	Christine Johnston	GBR	111
20	Helen Cartwright	GBR	195

Laser World Championships
Cancun, Mexico   *Mar 13-22*

1	Robert Scheidt	BRA	30.5pts
2	Michael Blackburn	AUS	53pts
3	Ben Ainslie	GBR	64pts
6	Paul Goodison	GBR	80pts
27	Andrew Simpson	GBR	213pts
34	Mark Barron	GBR	253pts
38	Jim Taylor	GBR	264pts
46	Ed Wright	GBR	300pts
60	Dan Holman	GBR	395pts
66	Peter Walker	GBR	408pts

Laser European Championships
Warnemunde, Germany   *June 9-17*

1	Ben Ainslie	GBR	17
2	Paul Goodison	GBR	18
3	Peer Moberg	NOR	28
9	Edward Wright	GBR	48

Soling European Championship
La Rochelle, France   *June 11-17*

1	Bank/Blaksjaer/Jacobsen	DEN	50.70
2	Shaidouko/Khoperski/Kiriliuk	RUS	51.10
3	Pichugin/Korotkov/Timokhov	UKR	58.70
13	Ian Williams/Mark Nicholls/Steve Mitchell		
		GBR	153.00

Star World Championship
Annapolis, Maryland   *May 10-20*

1	Reynolds/Liljedal	USA	30
2	MacDonald/Bjorn	CAN	45
3	Mansfield/O'Brien	IRL	53
5	Walker/Covell	GBR	57

Tornado World Championships
Sydney, Australia   *Jan 2-15*

1	Gaebler/Schwall	GER	46
2	Hagara/Steinacher	AUT	47
3	J-C Mourniac/Philippe Mourniac	FRA	55
8	Hugh Styles/Adam May	GBR	77
22	Rob Wilson/Will Howden	GBR	166
32	John Pierce/Barry Roche	GBR	229
35	Leigh McMillan/Joe Hutchinson	GBR	255

Tornado European Championships
Alassio, Italy   *May 6-12*

1	Roland Gaebler/Rene Schwall GER		20
2	Roman Hagara/Hans Peter Steinacher AUT		21
3	Andreas Hagara/Wolfgang Moser AUT		29
5	Hugh Styles/Adam May	GBR	57
11	Rob Wilson/Will Howden	GBR	89
14	Will Howden/Leigh McMilllan GBR		99
15	Leigh McMillan/Joe Hutchinson GBR		103
37	Mark Littlejohn/Simon Hughes GBR		240

GB Olympic Trials
Weymouth   April 15-24

49er class

1	Ian Barker and Simon Hiscocks	33
2	Paul Brotherton and Moray Gray	34
3	Tim Robinson and Zeb Elliot	44

470 class
Men

1	Chris Drapper/Dan Newman	19
2	Nick Rogers/Joe Glanfield	20
3	Graham Vials/Magnus Leask	27

Women

1	Helena Lucas/Sue Parkin	52
2	Bethan Raggatt/Sarah Webb	54
3	Severine Rees-Jones/Inga Leask	73

Mistral
Men

1	Nick Dempsey	12
2	Dominic Tidey	18
3	Adrian Jones	19

Women

1	Christine Johnston	78
2	Helen Cartwright	94
3	Jessica Ash	179

Finn Class

1	Iain Percy	9
2	Jamie Lea	26
3	Andrew Simpson	37

Tornado Class

1	Hugh Styles and Adam May	15
2	Rob Wilson and Will Howden	17
3	Tim Reid and Trevor Hewitt	29

Soling Match Racing
Andy Beadsworth and Richard Sydenham and Barry Parkin (United Airlines)
beat
Ian Williams and Mark Nicholls and Andy Hemmings (South West RDA) 5 - 0

World Rankings

As at Dec 12
British rankings shown if top 20

470
Men
1	King/Turnbull AUS	5367
2	Foerster/Merrick USA	5336
3	Braslavets/Matvyenko UKR	5224
5	Rogers/Glanfield GBR	5117

Women
1	Armstrong/Stowell AUS	5558
2	Taran/Pakholchyk UKR	5456
3	Via Dufresne/Azon ESP	5242

49er
1	Baur/Barth GER	5172
2	Hestbaek/Persson DEN	5168
3	Nicholson/Phillips AUS	5138
9	Barker/Hiscocks GBR	4815
17	Brotherton/Gray GBR	3941
20	Richardson/Greenhalgh GBR	3822

Europe
1	Sari Multala FIN	5530
2	Kristine Roug DEN	5470
3	Shirley Robertson GBR	5412

Finn
1	Mateusz Kusznierewicz POL	5510
2	Fredrik Loof SWE	5467
3	Sebastien Godefroid BEL	5428
8	Iain Percy GBR	5099

Laser
1	Robert Scheidt BRA	5528
2	Michael Blackburn AUS	5466
3	Kalle Suneson SWE	5458
4	Ben Ainslie GBR	5385
19	Paul Goodison GBR	4412

Boardsailing (Mistral)
Men
1	Lars Kleppich AUS	5418
2	Aaron McIntosh NZL	5220
3	Alexandre Guyader FRA	5205
15	Nick Dempsey GBR	4539

Women
1	Alessandra Sensini ITA	5341
2	Lisa Vidal FRA	5282
3	Jessica Crisp AUS	5276
10	Christine Johnston GBR	4148

Soling
1	Schumann/Bahr/Borlowski GER	5388
2	Bank/Jacobsen/Blakskjaer DEN	5280
3	Beadsworth/Sydenham/Parkin GBR	5122

Star
1	Reynolds/Liljedahl USA	5451
2	Walker/Covell GBR	5401
3	Beashel/Giles AUS	5290

Tornado
1	Hagara/Steinacher AUT	5641
2	Gaebler/Schwall GER	5581
3	Bundock/Forbes AUS	5541
6	Styles/May GBR	5101
20	Wilson/Howden GBR	4133

Skiing

E ven the Olympic downhill champion had to admit defeat. In 1998 Jean-Luc Crétier had been on top of the world, but two years later he was ready to retire. Crétier had not fully recovered from ruptured ligaments, but the lack of a wild card from the sport's governing body had forced his hand. The thought of competing against Hermann Maier could not have helped, the Austrian had another dominant season, winning the overall, downhill, giant slalom and super giant slalom World Cup titles. There wasn't much left for everyone else.

Maier's season, the only one in the four-year cycle of the sport that does not have either a world or Olympic championships, made history when he broke fellow Austrian Franz Klammer's record of 26 World Cup victories. Although Maier has more disciplines to choose from (there was no Super G in the World Cup until 1986 when Klammer had retired), the Flachau skier has done in four winters what it took Klammer 11 to achieve. The only skier close to matching his results, was Christian Mayer in the giant slalom, who came within three points of his fellow Austrian. Maier's final overall score of 2,000 points was 560 ahead of Kjetil Andre Aamodt, the Norwegian who was the only other skier to win a title. The Herminator was flying.

It was reported that Maier's earnings from endorsements grew to a majestic £3m for the season. A handy income which will, of course, be taxable. Alberto Tomba, who was once as famous as Maier, and even richer, appears to have overlooked the matter of tax. Three months before he was due to stand trial on tax evasion charges, Tomba agreed to pay £2.5m in back taxes. The Italian, the son of a textile millionaire, was alleged not to have paid tax on £7 million pounds worth of earnings from his career

Many of the top women were on the sidelines at various points of the 1999-2000 season. Alex Meissnitzer of Austria, Pernilla Wiberg of Sweden, Germany's Hilde Gerg and the promising teenager Janica Kostelic of Croatia were the most notable absentees. In their absence, the World Cup titles were shared around. Renate Götschl won the overall title, on the back of her super giant slalom title; she also won the only combined race of the season. The downhill title went to Germany's Regina Haeusl, although Götschl was just five points behind. Austria's Michaela Dorfmeister was the giant slalom champion, but the big surprise came in the slalom category, where Slovenia Spela Pretnar took the title. It was Slovenia's first skiing title since it became an independent nation in 1991.

Emma Carrick-Anderson was the only Briton to score any points during the season. She finished 87th in the overall standings, 1591 points behind Götschl. However there was a glimmer of hope as the new season began. Britain had two skiers, Alain Baxter and Johnny Moulder-Brown, in the points in a floodlit World Cup slalom in Sestriere, although this was thanks in part to the inability of others to complete the course. There were a few decent juniors emerging as well, such as Amanda Pirie and Chemmy Allcott, and, almost twenty years after Konrad Bartelski's recorded the best-ever World Cup finish by a Briton (second place in Val Gardena) the time is right for a new star to emerge.

Alpine

World Cup Final
Bornio, Italy   *Mar 10-19*

MEN
Downhill
1	Hannes Trinkl AUT	1:58.32
2	Hermann Maier AUT	+0.40
3	Christian Greber AUT	+0.79

Super G
1	Hermann Maier AUT	1:40.08
2	Fritz Strobl AUT	+1.91
3	Andreas Schifferer AUT	+1.98

Giant Slalom
1	Benjamin Raich AUT	2:25.64
2	Christian Mayer AUT	+0.17
3	Heinz Schilchegger AUT	+0.24

Slalom
1	O Christian FurusethNOR	1:52.49
2	Benjamin Raich AUT	+0.39
3	Matjaz Vrhovnik SLO	+0.72

Women
Downhill
1	Regine Cavagnoud FRA	1:33.01
2	Corinne Rey Bellet SUI	+0.73
3	Renate Götschl AUT	+0.79

Super G
1	Renate Götschl AUT	1:17.89
2	Martina Ertl GER	+0.06
3	Brigitte Obermoser AUT	+0.08

Giant Slalom
1	Brigitte Obermoser AUT	2:42.79
2	Michaela Dorfmeister AUT	+0.24
3	Birgit Heeb LIE	+0.76

Slalom
1	Kristina Koznick USA	1:26.23
2	Anja Paerson SWE	+0.13
3	Elisabetta Biavaschi ITA	+0.15

World Cup
Final Standings
MEN
Overall
1	Hermann Maier AUT	2000
2	Kjetil Andre Aamodt NOR	1440
3	Josef Strobl AUT	994
4	Kristian Ghedina ITA	958
5	Andreas Schifferer AUT	905
6	Stephan Eberharter AUT	904

Downhill
1	Hermann Maier AUT	800
2	Kristian Ghedina ITA	677
3	Josef Strobl AUT	533

Super G
1	Hermann Maier AUT	540
2	Werner Franz AUT	371
3	Fritz Strobl AUT	354

Giant Slalom
1	Hermann Maier AUT	520
2	Christian Mayer AUT	517
3	Michael Von Gruenigen SUI	466

Slalom
1	Kjetil Andre Aamodt NOR	598
2	Ole Christian Furuseth NOR	544
3	Matjaz Vrhovnik SLO	538

Combined
1	Kjetil Andre Aamodt NOR	200
2	Hermann Maier AUT	140
3	Fredrik Nyberg SWE	102

WOMEN
Overall
1	Renate Götschl AUT	1631
2	Michaela Dorfmeister AUT	1306
3	Regine Cavagnoud FRA	1036
4	Isolde Kostner ITA	878
5	Brigitte Obermoser AUT	806
87	E Carrick-Anderson GBR	40

Downhill
1	Regina Haeusl GER	529
2	Renate Götschl AUT	524
3	Isolde Kostner ITA	484

Super G
1	Renate Götschl AUT	554
2	Melanie Turgeon CAN	343
3	Mojca Suhadolc SLO	341

Giant Slalom
1	Michaela Dorfmeister AUT	684
2	Sonja Nef SUI	602
3	Anita Wachter AUT	470

Slalom
1	Spela Pretnar SLO	645
2	Christel Saioni FRA	626
3	Anja Paerson SWE	499

Combined
1	Renate Götschl AUT	100
2	Caroline Lalive USA	80
3	Andrine Flemmen NOR	60

Cross-country

World Cup Final Standings
Men Overall
1	Johann Muehlegg ESP	948
2	Jari Isometsa FIN	708
3	Odd-Bjorn Hjelmeset NOR	586

Long Distance
1	Johann Muehlegg ESP	315
2	Mikhail Ivanov RUS	198
3	Michail Botvinov AUT	183

Middle Distance
1	Jari Isometsa FIN	596
2	Johann Muehlegg ESP	592
3	Per Elofsson SWE	350

Sprint
1	Morten Broers NOR	349
2	Odd-Bjorn Hjelmeset NOR	268
3	Haavard Solbakken NOR	239

Women Overall
1	Bente Martinsen NOR	1176
1	Kristina Smigun EST	1165
3	Larissa Lazutina RUS	1008

Long Distance
1	Larissa Lazutina RUS	360
2	Kristina Smigun EST	266
3	Olga Danilova RUS	256

Middle Distance
1	Kristina Smigun EST	601
2	Stefania Belmondo ITA	585
3	Larissa Lazutina RUS	553

Sprint
1	Bente Martinsen NOR	505
2	Anita Moen NOR	300
3	Kristina Smigun EST	298

Nations Cup Overall
1	Norway	9059
2	Russia	8134
3	Italy	4855

Nations Cup Men
1	Norway	5019
2	Italy	2644
3	Finland	2435

Nations Cup Women
1	Russia	6302
2	Norway	4040
3	Italy	2211

Nordic Combined

World Cup

Nations Cup Overall
1	Finland	5534
2	Norway	5183
3	Germany	3179

World Cup Overall
1	Samppa Lajunen FIN	2175
2	Bjarte Engen Vik NOR	1990
3	Ladislav Rygl CZE	1274

World Cup Final

Nations Overall
1	Austria	430.50
2	Finland	430.00
3	Norway	417.20

World Cup Final Standings
1 Samppa Lajunen FIN
2 Kenji Ogiwara JPN
3 Lars Andreas Oestvik NOR

Ski-jumping

World Cup

Final Standings
1	Martin Schmitt GER	1833
2	Andreas Widhoelzl AUT	1452
3	Janne Ahonen FIN	1437

Nations Cup
1	Finland	5219
2	Austria	4409
3	Germany	4395

Freestyle

World Cup

MEN

Overall
1	Janne Lahtala FIN	100.00
2	Nicolas Fontaine CAN	95.20
3	Alexei Grichin BLR	93.60
83=	Sam Temple GBR	3.00

Aerials
1	Nicolas Fontaine CAN	476
2	Alexei Grichin BLR	468
3	Joe Pack USA	456

Moguls
1	Janne Lahtala FIN	500
2	Sami Mustinen FIN	440
3	Pierre-Alexandre Rousseau CAN	424
48	Sam Temple GBR	12

Dual Moguls
1	Janne Lahtala FIN	368
2	Stephane Rochon CAN	357
3	Johann Gregoire FRA	304
20	Sam Temple GBR	48

WOMEN

Aerials
1	Jacqui Cooper AUS	488
2	Veronica Brenner CAN	476
3	Hilde Synnove Lid NOR	432

Moguls
1	Ann Battelle USA	468
2	Marja Elfman SWE	468
3	Sandra Schmitt GER	464

Dual Moguls
1	Kari Traa NOR	372
2	Ann Battelle USA	364
3	Sandra Schmitt GER	356

Snowboarding

World Cup

Final Standings

MEN
Men's Overall		pts
1	Matthieu Bozzetto FRA	1309.00
2	Nicolas Huet FRA	1034.00
3	Felix Stadler AUT	890.71

Giant Slalom
1	Stefan Kaltschuetz AUT	4350
2	Matthieu Bozzetto FRA	3836
3	Nicolas Huet FRA	3360

Slalom
1	Matthieu Bozzetto FRA	7610
2	Nicolas Huet FRA	5540
3	Felix Stadler AUT	4650

Halfpipe
1	Thomas Johansson SWE	5770
2	Magnus Sterner SWE	5070
3	Fredrik Sterner SWE	4571

Snowboard Cross
1	Pontus Stahlkloo SWE	5850
2	Guillaume Nantermod SUI	5230
3	Zeke Steggall AUS	5060

WOMEN

Giant Slalom
1	Margerita Parini ITA	4610
2	Karine Ruby FRA	3600
3	Manuela Riegler AUT	3570

Slalom
1	Isabelle Blanc FRA	6650
2	Manuela Riegler AUT	5220
3	Karine Ruby FRA	4970

Halfpipe
1	Sabine Wehr-Hasler	7650
2	Tricia Bymes USA	6540
3	Anna Hellman SWE	6540

Snowboard Cross
1	Sandra Farmand GER	5240
2	Carmen Ranigler ITA	5220
3	Manuela Riegler AUT	4970

Snooker

In snooker, people have become used to one man dominating the rest. In the 70's it was old Dracula himself, Ray Reardon. Steve Davis was the 80's champion and in the 1990's Stephen Hendry at his peak (which was virtually the whole decade) was considered the best player the sport had ever seen. It must be slightly odd for insiders then, that although Mark Williams became the world number one at the end of the 1999-2000 season, there were four others who could reasonably claim to be the best.

Hendry started the season where he had left off. The Scot who won the world title in 1999 - his seventh - won the British Open in August, however that would be the high point of his campaign. John Higgins, who had started the season as number one, won the Grand Prix and the Welsh Open. Williams himself won the UK championship and the Thailand Masters. The ever-unpredictable Ronnie O'Sullivan won the China Open, the Scottish Open and also checked into The Priory clinic (a unique treble). Finally Matthew Stevens staked his claim by winning the Masters at Wembley.

By the time mid-April rolled around, any one of these five could have felt that victory at the Crucible could be theirs. For Hendry and O'Sullivan though, the challenge would come to an end at the first hurdle. Hendry was sensationally dumped out by Stuart Bingham, 10-7 while O'Sullivan lost to David Gray, who in turn lost 13-1 in his next match. Higgins, Williams and Stevens all made the semi-finals, along with the unheralded Joe Swail of Northern Ireland. Stevens picked the long straw and defeated the Ulsterman, 17-12. Meanwhile Higgins and Stevens had a tense struggle and Higgins cracked. After leading 15-11, the Scot could not cross the finishing line and Williams racked-up six consecutive frames.

So it came down to the first final between two Welshman. Stevens stormed into a 13-7 lead but Williams produced another great comeback, winning seven of the next eight games to level at 14-14. That score was still perfectly balanced at 16-all, but Williams, who forever looks like a man with a mountainous hangover but never plays like one, wrapped up the title with successive frames. Williams, not as convincingly as stablemate Hendry in his pomp, had become the world number one. The first left-handed champion is there to be shot at, which should make a change for snooker, so used to the domination of one.

If Williams was delighted to win the world championship then factory worker, Kevin Bohn, was delirious. In 1989, when Williams was just 14, Bohn staked one week's wages - £140 - that Williams would win the world championships by 2000. Bohn got odds of 300-1 and so pocketed a cool £42,000 - or the better part of six years wages for the man from Llanelli.

As the new season started, The Sportsmasters Network threatened to start a rival tour and provisionally signed some of the top names. Perhaps mindful of what has happened to darts, where there are two world championships, both to an extent discredited, nothing concrete was confirmed but the situation remained an unstable one. As so often in snooker, the game was not administered as well as it was played.

World Championship

Crucible Theatre, Sheffield   *Apr 15-May 1*

ROUND 1	ROUND 2	QUARTER-FINALS	SEMI-FINALS	FINAL

Stuart Bingham (Q) 10
Stephen Hendry (2) 7
    Jimmy White 13
    Stuart Bingham 9
Jimmy White (16) 10
Billy Snaddon (Q) 7
        Matthew Stevens 13
        Jimmy White 7
Matthew Stevens (9) 10
Tony Drago (Q) 2
    Matthew Stevens 13
    Alan McManus 4
Alan McManus (8) 10
Nigel Bond (Q) 7
            Matthew Stevens 17
            Joe Swail 12
John Parrott (5) 10
Gary Wilkinson (Q) 9
    Joe Swail 13
    John Parrott 12
Joe Swail (Q) 10
Paul Hunter (12) 6
        Joe Swail 13
        Dominic Dale 9
Dominic Dale (Q) 10
Peter Ebdon (13) 6
    Dominic Dale 13
    David Gray 1
David Gray (Q) 10
Ronnie O'Sullivan (4) 9

Mark Williams 18
Matthew Stevens 16

Mark Williams (3) 10
John Read (Q) 4
    Mark Williams 13
    Drew Henry 9
Drew Henry (Q) 10
Mark King (14) 8
        Mark Williams 13
        Fergal O'Brien 5
Fergal O'Brien (11) 10
Chris Small (Q) 8
    Fergal O'Brien 13
    Stephen Lee 8
Stephen Lee (6) 10
Kristjan Helgason (Q) 3
            Mark Williams 17
            Joh Higgins 15
Ken Doherty (7) 10
Darren Morgan (Q) 3
    Anthony Hamilton 13
    Ken Doherty 12
Anthony Hamilton (10) 10
Marco Fu (Q) 4
        John Higgins 13
        Anthony Hamilton 3
Steve Davis (15) 10
Graeme Dott (Q) 6
    John Higgins 13
    Steve Davis 11
Joh Higgins (1) 10
Dave Harold (Q) 8

Highest break: 143 Mark Willliams
Williams became the first left-handed player to win the world title.

Major Tournaments 1999-2000

Date	Tournament	Venue	Winner	Score	Runner-up
Sep 8-19	British Open	Plymouth Pavilions	**Stephen Hendry**	9-5	Peter Ebdon
Oct 11-24	Grand Prix	Guild Hall, Preston	**John Higgins**	9-8	Mark Williams
Nov 13-28	L Vic. UK Championship	Bournemouth	**Mark Williams**	10-8	Matthew Stevens
Dec 11-19	China International	Shanghai	**Ronnie O'Sullivan**	9-2	Stephen Lee
Jan 14-22	Nations Cup*	Reading	England	6-4	Wales
Jan 24-30	Welsh Open	Cardiff	**John Higgins**	9-8	Stephen Lee
Feb 5-13	The Masters	Wembley	**Matthew Stevens**	10-8	Ken Doherty
Feb 20-27	Malta Grand Prix	Med CC, Malta	**Ken Doherty**	9-3	Mark Williams
Mar 3-11	Thailand Masters	Bangkok	**Mark Williams**	9-5	Stephen Hendry
Mar 28-Apr 19	Scottish Open	Aberdeen	**Ronnie O'Sullivan**	9-1	Mark Williams

* Non-ranking event

Women's Events
World Championship

Sheffield   Apr 14-21
Final
Kelly Fisher bt Lisa Ingall 4-1

SCOTTISH MASTERS
Final
Kelly Fisher bt Julie Gillespie 4-0

BRITISH OPEN
Final
Kelly Fisher bt June Banks 4-2

GRAND PRIX
Final
Lynette Horsburgh bt Emma Bonney 4-2

LADIES UK CHAMPIONSHIP
Final
Kelly Fisher bt Emma Bonney 4-0

WELSH OPEN
Final
Lynette Horsburgh bt Kelly Fisher 3-1

CONNIE GOUGH NATIONAL OPEN
Final
Kelly Fisher bt Kim Shaw 4-1

"It's official, I'm the No1 now - up yours"

Mark Williams, leaving a message on Stephen Hendry's answering machine.

"I feel like I'm world champion myself"

Kevin Bohn, who staked £140 at 300-1 in 1989 on Mark Williams winning the world championship by 2000. Williams was 14 when Bohn first saw him play.

"While Stephen says he has been playing well, I think in many ways he has been kidding himself"

Ian Doyle, Stephen Hendry's manager after the Scot's first round world championship defeat .

World Rankings

Rankings apply throughout the 2000-2001 season

1	(3)	Mark Willliams WAL	57,100	51	(51)	Rod Lawler ENG	11,390
2	(1)	John Higgins SCO	44,445	52	(60)	David Gray ENG	11,3345
3	(2)	Stephen Hendry SCO	42,570	53	(49)	Gary Ponting ENG	11,325
4	(4)	Ronnie O'Sullivan ENG	32,640	54	(50)	Jason Ferguson ENG	11,240
5	(6)	Stephen Lee ENG	31,605	55	(58)	David Roe ENG	11,120
6	(9)	Matthew Stephens WAL	31,105	56	(56)	Paul Wykes ENG	11,089
7	(7)	Ken Doherty IRL	29,255	57	(47)	Matthew Couch ENG	10,970
8	(8)	Alan McManus SCO	25,510	58	(41)	Gerard Greene NIR	10,951
9	(11)	Fergal O'Brien IRL	24,702	59	(84)	Patrick Wallace NIR	10,855
10	(5)	John Parrott ENG	24,065	60	(68)	Stuart Pettman ENG	10,830
11	(10)	Anthony Hamilton ENG	23,515	61	(59)	Joe Johnson ENG	10,824
12	(13)	Peter Ebdon ENG	23,355	62	(74)	Michael Holt ENG	10,805
13	(17)	Dave Harold ENG	22,737	63	(62)	John Read ENG	10,722
14	(12)	Paul Hunter ENG	22,497	64	(44)	Steve James ENG	10,636
15	(35)	Marco Fu HKG	22,329	65	(54)	Nick Walker ENG	10,484
16	(28)	Joe Swail NIR	21,590	66	(37)	Martin Clark ENG	10, 389
17	(15)	Steve Davis ENG	21,500	67	(72)	John Lardner SCO	10,377
18	(16)	Jimmy White ENG	20,587	68	(69)	Shokat Ali PAK	10,115
19	(25)	Graeme Dott SCO	20,112	69	(55)	Dean Reynolds ENG	10,115
20	(19)	Dominic Dale WAL	19,947	70	(94)	Phaithoon Phonbun THA	10,045
21	(18)	Chris Small SCO	19,497	71	(81)	Leo Fernandez IRL	10,027
22	(14)	Mark King ENG	19,450	72	(57)	Mick Price ENG	9,889
23	(21)	Nigel Bond ENG	18,822	73	(40)	Neal Foulds ENG	9,665
24	(24)	Billy Snaddon SCO	18,412	74	(104)	Kristjan Helgason ISL	9,432
25	(23)	Darren Morgan WAL	17,194	75	(100)	Robert Milkins ENG	9,400
26	(20)	Tony Drago MLT	17,072	76	(75)	Willie Thorne ENG	9,320
27	(22)	James Wattana THA	16,975	77	(78)	Mark Davies ENG	9,285
28	(31)	Brian Morgan ENG	16,235	78	(82)	Martin Dziewialtowski SCO	9,115
29	(45)	Drew Henry SCO	16,200	79	(65)	Tony Jones ENG	9,010
30	(30)	Terry Murphy NIR	15,632	80	(73)	Leigh Griffin ENG	8,995
31	(34)	Joe Perry ENG	15,470	81	(110)	Paul Sweeney	8,820
32	(26)	Quinton Hann AUS	15,445	82	(79)	Mark Gray ENG	8,710
33	(27)	Jamie Burnett SCO	15,315	83	(83)	Wayne Brown ENG	8,665
34	(29)	Gary Wilkinson ENG	15,072	84	(71)	Karl Broughton ENG	8,625
35	(38)	Paul Davies WAL	14,410	85	(89)	Craig MacGillivray SCO	8,515
36	(32)	Andy Hicks ENG	13,650	86	(66)	Nicolas Pearce ENG	8,240
37	(33)	Bradley Jones ENG	13,355	87	(90)	Darren Clarke ENG	8,160
38	(39)	Ian McCullough ENG	13,096	88	(106)	Adrian Gunnell ENG	8,095
39	(52)	Dave Finbow ENG	12,845	89	(64)	Jason Prince NIR	8,064
40	(80)	Anthony Davies WAL	12,610	90	(76)	Tony Chappel WAL	8,005
41	(63)	Jimmy Michie ENG	12,554	91	(112)	Mark Fenton	7,955
42	(46)	Lee Walker WAL	12,489	92	(142)	Allister Carter	7,825
43	(92)	Stuart Bingham ENG	12,320	93	(134)	Mike Dunn ENG	7,825
44	(53)	Jonathan Birch ENG	12,264	94	(85)	Stephen O'Connor IRL	7.670
45	(42)	Peter Lines ENG	12,010	95	(86)	Steve Judd ENG	7,655
46	(67)	Michael Judge NIR	11,815	96	(77)	Dene O'Kane NZL	7,525
47	(48)	Marcus Campbell SCO	11,799	97	(113)	Barry Pinches	7,335
48	(43)	Euan Henderson SCO	11,615	98	(138)	David McLellan ENG	7,280
49	(36)	Alain Robidoux CAN	11,415	99	(87)	Sean Storey ENG	7,175
50	(61)	Alfred Burden ENG	11,399	100	(193)	Stephen Maguire SCO	7,153

Speed Skating

Long Track

Gunda Niemann-Stirnemann is referred to as Gunda Niemann. There is no British participation in any of the Long Track events.

World All Around Championships
Millwaukee   *Feb 5-6*
Men
All Around (Overall)
1 Gianni Romme NED   153.277
2 Ids Postma NED   155.433
3 Rintje Ritsma NED   155.822
500m
1 Jae-Bong Choi KOR   36.010
2 Adne Søndral NOR   36.080
3 Ids Postma NED   36.560
1500m
1 Adne Søndral NOR   1:47.85
2 Petter Andersen NOR   1:49.29
3 Ids Postma NED   1:50.28
5000m
1 Gianni Romme NED   6:26.14
2 Frank Dittrich GER   6:36.02
3 Bart Veldkamp BEL   6:36.78
10000m
1 Gianni Romme NED   13:23.94
2 Bart Veldkamp BEL   13:40.77
3 Frank Dittrich GER   13:42.03
Women
All Around (Overall)
1 Claudia Pechstein GER 163.830
2 Gunda Niemann GER   163.985
3 Maki Tabata JPN   165.296
500m
1 Edel T Hoiseth NOR   39.480
2 Maki Tabata JPN   39.680
3 Emese Hunyady AUT   39.780
1500m
1 Maki Tabata JPN   1:59.52
2 Claudia Pechstein GER   1:59.97
3 Gunda Niemann GER   2:00.62

3000m
1 Claudia Pechstein GER   4:06.44
2 Gunda Niemann GER   4:06.83
3 Maki Tabata JPN   4:13.79
5000m
1 Gunda Niemann GER   7:02.11
2 Claudia Pechstein GER   7:05.87
3 Maki Tabata JPN   7:14.78

Single Distance World Championships
Nagano   *Mar 3-5*
Men
500m
1 Hiroyasu Shimizu JPN   70.49
1000m
1 Adne Søndral NOR   1:09.96
1500m
1 Ids Postma NED   1:47.98
5000m
1 Gianni Romme NED   6:23.31
10000m
1 Gianni Romme NED   13:12.27
Women
500m
1 Monique Garbrecht GER   77.48
1000m
1 Monique Garbrecht GER   1:16.59
1500m
1 Claudia Pechstein GER 1:58.43
3000m
1 Claudia Pechstein GER   4:05.68
5000m
1 Gunda Niemann GER   6:58.71

World Sprint Chps
Seoul Feb 26-27
Final Standings
Men
1 Jeremy Wotherspoon CAN 142.215
Women
1 Monique Garbrecht GER 155.265

European Championships
Hamar, Norway   *Jan 14-16*
Men
500m
1 Adne Søndral NOR   35.72
2 Petter Andersen NOR   36.36
3 Rintje Ritsma NED   36.56
1500
1 Adne Søndral NOR   1:47.23
2 Ids Postma NED   1:48.73
3 Petter Andersen NOR   1:48.90
3000m
1 Eskil Ervik NOR   6:30.53
2 Bart Veldkamp NED   6:33.35
3 Vadim Sayutin RUS   6:34.22
5000m
1 Frank Dittrich GER   13:28.68
2 Knut Morgenstern GER   13:34.98
3 Roberto Sighel ITA   13:38.72
Overall
1 Rintje Ritsma NED   153.608
2 Eskil Ervik NOR   153.858
3 Ids Postma NED   154.585

Women
500m
1 Tonny de Jong NED   39.76
2 Emese Hunyady AUT   39.78
3 Anni Friesinger GER   39.79
1500m
1 Emese Hunyady AUT   1:57.58
2 Renate Groenewold NED 1:58.17
3 Annemarie Thomas NED 1:59.06
3000m
1 Renate Groenewold NED 4:05.44
2 Anni Friesinger GER   4:06.03
3 Gunda Niemann GER   4:06.13
5000m
1 Gunda Niemann GER   6:56.84
2 Claudia Pechstein GER   7:05.99
3 Anni Friesinger GER   7:07.37
Overall
1 Anni Friesinger GER   163.322
2 Gunda Niemann GER   163.348
3 Renate Groenewold NED 163.915

World Records, Set in 1999/2000

MEN

500m	**34.63**	**Jeremy Wotherspoon**	CAN	Calgary, Jan 29
1000m	**1.08.49**	**Jeremy Wotherspoon**	CAN	Calgary, Jan 12
	1.08.35	**Jeremy Wotherspoon**	CAN	Calgary, Mar 18
1500m	**1.45.56**	**Jakko Jan Leeuwangh**	NED	Calgary, Jan 29
3000m	**3.43.76**	**Steven Elm**	CAN	Calgary, Mar 17
5000m	**6.18.72**	**Gianni Romme**	GER	Calgary, Jan 30

WOMEN

3000m	**4.00.51**	**Gunda Niemann-Stirnemann**	GER	Calgary, Jan 30
5000m	**6.56.84**	**Gunda Niemann-Stirnemann**	GER	Hamar, Jan 16

Short Track

World Championships

Sheffield, Mar 10 - 12
The top seven ranked skaters (after the 500m, 1000m & 1500m) qualify for the 3000m.

Men
Overall

1 Ryoung Min KOR	68pts	
2 Eric Bedard CAN	63pts	
3 JiaJun Li CHN	60pts	
14 Nicky Gooch GBR		
22 Matthew Jasper GBR		

500m

1 Eric Bedard CAN	42.009
2 Daniel Weinstein USA	42.058
3 Satoru Terao JPN	42.157
15 Matthew Jasper GBR	
23 Nicky Gooch GBR	

1000m

1 JiaJun Li CHN	1:31.098
2 Yulong An CHN	1:31.212
3 Daniel Weinstein USA	1:33.228
8 Nicky Gooch GBR	
26 Matthew Jasper GBR	

1500m

1 Ryoung Min KOR	2:23.098
2 Eric Bedard CAN	2:23.200
3 Satoru Terao JPN	2:23.286
14 Matthew Jasper GBR	
18 Nicky Gooch GBR	

3000m

1 Ryoung Min KOR	5:02.496
2 JiaJun Li CHN	5:02.934
3 Daniel Weinstein USA	5:03.416
7 Yulong An CHN	5:17.001

DNQ: Nicky Gooch& Matthew Jasper

5000m Relay

1 China	7:09.387
2 Japan	7:09.705
3 Italy	7:09.709
5 Great Britain	

Women
Overall

1 Yang Yang (A) CHN	89pts	
2 Sang-Mi An KOR	52pts	
3 Yang Yang (S) CHN	47pts	
15 Joanna Williams GBR		
20 Debbie Palmer GBR		

500m

1 Evgenia Radanova BUL 44.626	
2 Yang Yang (S) CHN 44.704	
3 Sang-Mi An KOR 46.523	
18 Debbie Palmer GBR	
23 Joanna Williams GBR	

1000m

1 Yang Yang (A) CHN	1:40.363
2 Yang Yang (S) CHN 1:40.683	
3 Min-Jin Joo KOR 1:40.742	
15 Joanna Williams GBR	
20 Debbie Palmer GBR	

1500m

1 Yang Yang (A) CHN	2:32.707
2 Hye-Won Park KOR	2:32.829
3 Min-Jin Joo KOR	2:33.175
16 Joanna Williams GBR	
19 Debbie Palmer GBR	

3000m

1 Sang-Mi An KOR	5:24.272
2 Yang Yang (A) CHN	5:27.445
3 Annie Perreault CAN	5:30.222

3000m Relay

1 China	4:28.267
2 Korea	4:28.388
3 Canada	4:35.417
8 Great Britain	

World Team Championships

The Hague Mar 4-5
Final Standings
Men

1. Canada 46pts; 2. Korea 46;
3. Italy 37; 4. China 28; 5. USA 28
6. Japan 27; 7. Netherlands 19

Women

1. China 60pts; 2. Korea 53;
3. Japan 34; 4. Canada 30;
5. Italy 25; 6. USA 18;
7. Netherlands 16

No British participation

European Championships

Bormio, Italy Jan 21-23
Men
Overall

1 Fabio Carta ITA	73pts	
2 Nicky Gooch GBR	63pts	
3 Nicola Franceschina ITA	60pts	

500m

1 Fabio Carta ITA	42.830
2 Dave Versteeg NED	42.893
3 Kornel Szanto HUN	42.953
4 Nicky Gooch GBR	1:07.488

1000m

1 N Francheschina ITA	1:31.637
2 Michele Antonioli ITA	1:32.180
3 Cees Juffermans NED	1:32.794

1500m

1 Nicky Gooch GBR	2:33.339
2 N Francheschina ITA	2:33.336
3 Michele Antonioli ITA	2:33.526

3000m

1 Fabio Carta ITA	5:18.155
2 Michele Antonioli ITA	5:18.499
3 Bruno Loscos FRA	5:18.518

Relay

1 Italy	7:00.928
2 Great Britain	7:03.919
3 France	7:06.810

Women
Overall

1 Evgenia Radanova BUL	123
2 Katia Zini ITA	76
3 Evelina Rodigari ITA	74
5 Debbie Palmer GBR	17

500m

1 Katia Zina ITA	44.551
2 Evgenia Radanova BUL	44.563
3 Debbie Palmer GBR	45.709

1000m

1 Evgenia Radanova BUL 1:39.261	
2 Evelina Rodigari ITA	1:40.007
3 Yvonne Kunze GER	1:40.138

1500m

1 Evgenia Radanova BUL 2:30.183	
2 Katia Zina ITA	2:30.467
3 Evelina Rodigari ITA	2:31.385
7 Debbie Palmer GBR	2:33.593

3000m

1 Evgenia Radanova BUL 5:57.828	
2 Katia Zina ITA	5:58.197
3 Evelina Rodigari ITA	5:59.536
7 Debbie Palmer GBR	6:00.087

Relay

1 Bulgaria	4:22.540
2 Italy	4:23.989
3 Great Britain	4:31.872

World Cup

Final Standings
Women
Overall
1 Yang Yang (A) CHN 97pts
500m
1 Yang Yang (S) CHN 95
1000m
1 Yang Yang (A) CHN 97
1500m
1 Yang Yang (A) CHN 100
Relay
1. China 100
Team
1. China 100

Men
Overall
1 Kim Dong-Sung KOR 97
500m
1 Li JiaJun CHN 99pts
1000m
1 Kim Dong-Sung JOR 98
1500m
1 Li JiaJun CHN93
Relay
1. Korea 99
Team
1. China 99

British Champions

Men
500m: Matthew Jasper
1000m: Nicky Gooch
1500m: Nicky Gooch
3000m: James Ellis

Women
500m: Debbie Palmer
1000m: Joanna Williams
1500m: Debbie Palmer

Squash

While the rest of the world was relishing the spectacle of the Sydney Olympics, the squash community was looking on gloomily. Olympics recognition has always been the Holy Grail for the sport, but they were left off the timetable for Sydney, when prospects for inclusion had looked half-decent. After the Games, it got worse. Athens announced that there would be no additions for 2004 (rumours emanating that the International Olympic committee had barely enough confidence that Athens could handle the existing sports) and squash was again off the agenda. The next opportunity will be for Beijing, so expect all manner of squash promotions in China, coming very shortly.

Squash also suffered in 2000 from the absence of a men's World Open. Over the past few years, the sport has played brinkmanship with its competitions, most notably the British Open, which was bailed out by the Eye Group in 1999, after having been postponed from it regular April date through lack of sponsorship. The Eye Group supported the event again in 2000 (and would become much more heavily involved in the sport a year on) which had a surprise winner in David Evans, who became the first Welshman - and only the fifth Briton in 71 years - to win the title. Nicol had pulled out of the tournament with an injury. Evans almost managed the rare double of winning the National title as well.

Though Evans won the most prestigious title on offer during the year, the Scot Peter Nicol and the Canadian Jonathon Power were still recognised as the two best players in the world. Their tussle for top place in the rankings continued throughout the season.

England's Cassie Campion went into the year as the women's world champion, but suffered injury problems and could not defend her title at Edinburgh. Sarah Fitz-Gerald, three-times champions from 1996-1998, returned from a long injury absence, but when the championships came around, in November, she was not yet sharp enough.

The final came down to the two women who had dominated the year: Leilani Joyce of New Zealand and Carol Owens, a New Zealand-based Aussie. They had met six times already during the year, Joyce holding a convincing five-one advantage. Joyce was the British Open champion as well, having defeated England's Sue Wright for that title. The final looked to be going to that form book as Joyce forged a two-game advantage and led 7-0 in the third. At 8-4, the defining moment came. "When she had matchball in the third game, I could hear her hyperventilating, she seemed really nervous," said Owens. "I told myself I had nothing to lose - and just went for it." A two-game deficit became a three-two win and Owens became the sixth Australian women to become world champion.

The team championship followed the individual competition, and with the Australians depleted by the absence of Carol Owens, England took the final, by two matches to one. In the European events, there was an air of inevitability as England won both the men's and women's senior titles, as well as the men's junior title. All three with absolute comfort. England should take care, when titles are dominated in this fashion, they lose value. Not only does it turn off spectators when the outcome is predictable, but it turns off sponsors, and is not necessarily beneficial to the fledgling nations in European squash.

Women's World Open

Edinburgh   Nov 11-17

2nd round

Carol Owens AUS bt Vicky Botwright ENG 9-3 9-0 9-2
Tania Bailey ENG bt Sabine Schoene GER 9-2 10-9 9-7
Linda Charman ENG bt Pamela Nimmo SCO 9-5 9-2 9-2
Sarah Fitz-Gerald AUS bt Jenny Tranfield ENG
9-0 9-1 9-2
Stephanie Brind ENG bt Fiona Geaves ENG
9-0 3-9 8-10 9-2 9-2
Natalie Grainger ENG bt Rachael Grinham AUS
9-6 3-9 9-7 9-7
Suzanne Horner ENG bt Rebecca Macree ENG
9-2 9-3 10-8
Leilani Joyce NZL bt Vanessa Atkinson NED
9-2 5-9 9-5 9-5

Quarter-finals

Carol Owens AUS bt Tania Bailey ENG 9-5 9-0 9-1
Sarah Fitz-Gerald AUS bt Linda Charman 9-3 9-0 9-1
Natalie Grainger ENG bt Stephanie Brind ENG
9-2 9-5 9-3
Leilani Joyce NZL bt Suzanne Horner ENG 9-2 9-6 9-0

Semi-finals

Carol Owens AUS bt Sarah Fitz-Gerald AUS
9-6 9-5 7-9 5-9 9-6
Leilani Joyce NZL bt Natalie Grainger ENG
9-6 9-3 9-10 4-9 9-5

Final

Carol Owens AUS bt Leilani Joyce NZL
7-9 3-9 10-8 9-6 9-1

Women's World Team Championships

Sheffield   Nov 19-25

Quarter-finals

England bt Canada 3-0
New Zealand bt South Africa 2-1
Egypt bt Germany 2-1
Australia bt France 3-0

Semi-finals

England bt New Zealand 2-1
Australia bt Egypt 2-1

Final

England bt Australia 2-1
Linda Charman lost to Sarah Fitz-Gerald 5-9 0-9 4-9
Tania Bailey bt Nathalie Grinham 9-1 9-0 9-0
Stephanie Brind bt Robyn Cooper 9-6 9-4 0-9 9-3

3/4th Place Play-off

New Zealand bt Egypt 2-1
Leilani Joyce bt Salma Shabana 9-5 9-4 9-1
Shelley Kitchen lost to Maha Zein 9-10 9-6 10-8 3-9 7-9
Sarah Cook bt Omneya Abdel Kawy 9-2 9-6 10-8

Final Standings: 1. England; 2. Australia; 3. New
Zealand; 4. Egypt; 5. South Africa; 6. Germany; 7.
Canada; 8. France; 9. Scotland; 10. Hong Kong; 11.
Denmark; 12. Malaysia; 13. Switzerland; 14. Netherlands;
15.Ireland; 16. Brazil; 17. Spain; 18. USA; 19. Italy; 20.
Japan; 21. Wales

European Team Championships

Vienna, Austria   Apr 26-29

Men

Semi-finals

England bt Wales 3-1; France bt Finland 4-0

Final

England bt France 4-0
English names first
Simon Parke bt Thierry Lincou 9-6 9-1 3-9 9-3
Del Harris bt Jean-Michel Arcucci 9-6 9-1 9-1
Mark Chaloner bt Gregory Gaultier 9-6 9-6 9-5
Paul Johnson bt RenanLavigne 9-2 9-0

Final Standings: 1. England; 2.France; 3. Finland; 4.
Wales; 5. Germany; 6. Netherlands; 7. Switzerland; 8.
Austria; 9. Sweden; 10. Italy; 11. Belgium; 12. Spain; 13.
Ireland; 14. Denmark; 15. Greece; 16. Slovenia; 17.
Hungary; 18. Israel; 19. Czech Republic; 20. Slovakia

Women

Semi-finals

England bt Netherlands 3-0; Germany bt Scotland 2-1

Final

England bt Germany 3-0
Cassie Campion bt Sabine Schoene 9-1 9-4 9-3
Linda Charman bt Sabine Baum 9-3 9-0 9-1
Stephanie Brind bt Daniela Grzenia 9-4 9-6 9-2

Final Standings: 1. England; 2. Germany;
3. Scotland; 4. Netherlands; 5. Denmark; 6. Spain; 7.
Switzerland; 8. France; 9. Ireland; 10. Belgium; 11. Italy;
12. Wales; 13. Finland; 14. Israel; 15. Norway; 16.
Hungary; 17. Austria; 18. Slovenia; 19. Slovakia

Men's World Junior Championships

Milan   July 12 -29

Final

Kareem Darwish EGY bt Gregory Gaultier FRA
9-1 9-3 9-7

Team Final

England bt Egypt 2-1
English names first
Daryl Selby bt Akram Youssif 9-6 3-9 10-8 9-0
James Willstrop lost to Kareem Darwish
10-8 2-9 10-8 8-10 2-9
Phillip Barker bt Mahmoud Abdel Kader
5-9 2-9 9-2 9-5 9-2

European Junior Championships

Bremen   Apr 10-24

Men's Final

Gregory Gaultier FRA bt James Willstrop ENG
9-7 9-6 4-9 9-4

Women's Final

Dominique Lloyd-Walter ENG bt Amina Helal ENG
9-2 9-3 9-7

Team Final

England bt Spain 2-1
D Lloyd -Walter bt Elisabeth Sado 5-9 9-6 9-2 9-1
James Willstrop lost to Alberto Manso 4-9 8-10 9-10
Phillip Barker bt Borja Golan 9-3 9-4 2-9 9-1

World Rankings

Men

As at April 2001

		Average Pts
1	Jonathon Power CAN	662.500
2	Peter Nicol SCO	645.313
3	David Evans WAL	428.125
4	David Palmer AUS	367.969
5	Paul Price AUS	351.719
6	John White SCO	332.813
7	Simon Parke ENG	319.531
8	Martin Heath SCO	289.063
9	Mark Chaloner ENG	265.969
10	Ahmed Barada EGY	259.375
11	Paul Johnson ENG	248.438
12	Alex Gough WAL	237.500
13	Ong Heng Bee MAS	230.972
14	Stewart Boswell AUS	190.000
15	John Williams AUS	182.969
16	Lee Beachill ENG	180.833
17	Omar Elborolossy EGY	180.556
18	Del Harris ENG	173.438
19	Graham Ryding CAN	172.750
20	Thierry Lincou FRA	164.844
21	Joseph Kneipp AUS	161.563
22	Nick Taylor ENG	151.563
23	Peter Genever ENG	149.531
24	Amr Shabana EGY	145.000
25	Anthony Ricketts AUS	137.656

Women

As at April 2001

1	Leilani Joyce NZL	2221.625
2	Carol Owens AUS	1764.125
3	Sarah Fitz-Gerald AUS	1357.500
4	Linda Charman-Smith ENG	934.938
5	Natalie Grainger ENG	862.111
6	Tania Bailey ENG	859.111
7	Suzanne Horner ENG	701.750
8	Rachael Grinham AUS	687.200
9	Fiona Geaves ENG	671.938
10	Stephanie Brind ENG	610.800
11	Vanessa Atkinson NED	542.475
12	Cassie Campion ENG	540.000
13	Rebecca Macree ENG	539.833
14	Sabine Schoene GER	530.750
15	Sue Wright ENG	408.125
16	Pamela Nimmo SCO	382.361
17	Jenny Tranfield ENG	375.528
18	Vicky Botwright ENG	369.025
19	Natalie Grinham AUS	348.875
20	Ellen Petersen DEN	282.361
21	Omneya Abdel Kawy EGY	279.250
22	Maha Zein EGY	276.944
23	Senga Macfie SCO	270.889
24	Latasha Khan USA	270.833
25	Salma Shabana EGY	268.389

British Open

Edgbaston Priory, Birmingham   *Oct 9-14*

Men

Quarter-finals

Mark Chaloner ENG bt Alex Gough WAL
15-8 15-11 12-15 15-12
Paul Price AUS bt Joseph Kneipp AUS
15-12 15-10 13-15 6-15 17-16
David Evans WAL bt Ong Beng Hee MAS
12-15 15-6 15-13 15-9
David Palmer AUS bt Jonathon Power CAN
17-16 15-14 9-15 7-15 15-12

Semi-finals

Paul Price bt Mark Chaloner 17-16 11-15 15-7 15-5
David Evans bt David Palmer 15-5 15-6 15-11

Final

David Evans bt Paul Price 15-11 15-6 15-10

Women

Quarter-finals

Sue Wright ENG bt Vanessa Atkinson NED
0-9 9-3 7-9 9-3 9-5
Carol Owens AUS bt Sarah Fitz-Gerald AUS 9-5 9-5 9-3
Linda Charman ENG bt Fiona Geaves ENG 9-3 9-3 9-3
Leilani Joyce NZL bt Suzanne Horner ENG 9-4 9-2 9-1

Semi-finals

Sue Wright bt Carol Owens 10-9 9-5 3-9 9-5
Leilani Joyce bt Linda Charman 10-8 9-0 9-4

Final

Leilani Joyce bt Sue Wright 9-7 9-4 9-2

Business Pages National Squash Championships

Manchester Velodrome   Feb 8-12

Men's Final

Peter Marshall (Notts) bt David Evans (WAL)
15-9 15-6 15-11

Women's Final

Cassie Campion (Norfolk) bt Sue Wright (Kent)
9-1 2-9 9-2 2-9 9-3

Other Major Events

Greenwich Open
Jan 21-24
Men's Final
Joseph Kneipp AUS bt Del Harris ENG 15-7 15-10 15-3
Women's Final
Sarah Fitz-Gerald AUS bt Suzanne Horner ENG 9-6 9-0 4-9 9-7

DLJ Direct Tournament of Champions
Grand Central Station, New York   Jan 30-Feb 3
Final
Jonathon Power CAN bt Martin Heath SCO 15-12 15-11 14-15 15-12

Al-Ahram PSA Masters
Hughada, Egypt   Mar 27-Apr 1
Final
Peter Nicol SCO bt Jonathon Power CAN 15-13 15-7 15-6

WISPA World Grand Prix Finals
Hughada, Egypt   Apr 5
Final
Carol Owens AUS bt Cassie Campion ENG 9-1 5-9 5-9 9-2 9-2

Equitable Life Super Series Finals
Broadgate Arena, London   June 5-9
Final
Peter Nicol SCO bt Simon Parke ENG 13-15 15-9 15-12 12-15 15-12

Al-Ahram International
Cairo   Aug 20-26
Men's Final
Peter Nicol SCO bt Ahmed Barada EGY 15-14 9-15 15-3 15-12

Women's Final
Leilani Joyce NZL bt Carol Owens AUS 8-10 9-7 9-5 3-9 9-5

Women's Heliopolis Open
Cairo   Aug 28-Sept 1
Final
Leilani Joyce NZL bt Carol Owens AUS 9-6 7-9 9-3 9-2

Cathay Pacific Hong Kong Open
Hong Kong Aug 28-Sept 1
Final
Peter Nicol SCO bt Jonathon Power CAN 15-11 15-10 15-6

Women's Eat Well Live Well Australian Open
Melbourne   Sept 6-10
Final
Leilani Joyce NZL bt Carol Owens AUS 9/7 9/5 9/3

Women's Carol Weymuller Open
New York   Oct 19-23
Final
Leilani Joyce NZL bt Linda Charman ENG 9-5 9-2 9-1

SG Cowen US Open
Boston   Oct 27-Nov 4
Final
Jonathon Power CAN bt Simon Parke ENG 15-3 11-15 15-12 15-12

Florida Squash Open
Boca Raton Nov 8-13
Final
Jonathon Power CAN bt Martin Heath SCO 12-15 15-11 15-10 15-3

VMG Capital Squash Classic
Toronto   Nov 27-Dec 2
Final
Jonathon Power CAN bt Peter Nicol SCO 15-8 15-4 15-5

Universal Sports Club Classic
London   Dec 4-8
Final
Sarah Fitz-Gerald AUS bt Carol Owens AUS 3-9 9-6 9-3 9-1

Swimming

The remarkable international performances are dealt with elsewhere (see Olympic Games), but this section is concerned with the unremarkable domestic performances. The post-mortems for the Olympics could have begun in Helsinki 10 weeks earlier, because it was already evident that British swimming had meandered off down some unprofitable bywater. "Well, don't I get any credit for coming back to win a medal," said Sue Rolph, after finishing third in the 200m Medley at Helsinki, and she was right, there was none.

There was no credit for Rolph because a year earlier she had stormed home in the 100m at the European championships at Istanbul to set herself up as a genuine Olympic medal candidate. A year later, all those ambitions had been swept away. Inge de Bruijn, within two days at Sheffield, had broken three world records and equalled another. For Rolph, this was a disaster. She had been a foot ahead of De Bruijn when she won the European title in 55.03. In Sheffield, De Bruijn, making spectacular progress in her 27th year, swam 53.80. Deep down in her psyche, Rolph probably believed she could swim 54.5, but never under 54 seconds - and she was only 22. Rolph had lost her Olympic strategy.

Paul Palmer had known his nemesis since the Commonwealth Games in 1998. Ian Thorpe was always going to reconstruct the record books. He was 12 metres ahead of Palmer in the 400m freestyle by May. Palmer toyed with the 1500m - "That event hasn't moved on," he said - but though he swam it at the Games, it was a gesture, no more.

Both Palmer and Rolph saw only disappointment ahead of them in Sydney and nothing emanating from the heart of the sport was about to convince them otherwise. The team that arrived in Sydney was not short of funds, only short of morale; and that - it would be fair to say - was not the fault of the swimmers.

In the months since, the changes have been rung. Bill Sweetenham, from Australia, took over as performance director from Deryk Snelling. Sweetenham's first action of consequence was to drop from the Valencia team arguably the best chance of a title - Zoe Baker in the 50m breast, which surely was not good for morale either.

Mark Foster won another world short course title in Valencia, but his victory did not supply the uplift the sport needs. That came from Joanne Fargus, whose stroking is so clean that she travels with a serenity that swans would envy. Not that many swans try the backstroke. Fargus is the future, so maybe it's not all bad news.

From the Deep End

Deryk Snelling, British performance director, in Sydney

"Like Hiroshima we were decimated..."

"Maybe it [swimming] is not quite as sophisticated as track and field, but neither is it as dirty..."

"Susie O'Neill is more important than Alex Ferguson and Manchester United to the Australians. She is a goddess. She is Madame Butterfly..."

World Long Course (50m) Records

set in 2000

Men

50m Free	**Alexander Popov** RUS	21.64	June 16	Moscow
100m free	**Michael Klim** AUS	48.18	Sep 16	Sydney
	Pieter vd Hoogenband NED	47.84	Sep 19	Sydney
200m free	**Ian Thorpe** AUS	1:45.69	May 14	Sydney
	Ian Thorpe AUS	1:45.51	May 15	Sydney
	Pieter vd Hoogenband NED	1:45.35	Sep 17	Sydney
	Pieter vd Hoogenband NED	1:45.35	Sep 18	Sydney
400m free	**Ian Thorpe** AUS	3:41.33	May 13	Sydney
	Ian Thorpe AUS	3:40.59	Sep 16	Sydney
100m breast	**Roman Sloudnov** RUS	1:00.36	June 15	Moscow
50m butterfly	**Geoff Huegill** AUS	23.60	May 14	Sydney
200m fly	**Tom Malchow** USA	1:55.18	June 17	Charlotte
400m IM	**Tom Dolan** USA	4:11.76	Sep 17	Sydney
4x100m free	**Australia**	3:13.67	Sep 16	Sydney
	(Klim/Fydler/Callus/Thorpe)			
4x200m free	**Australia**	7:07.05	Sep 19	Sydney
	(Thorpe/Klim/Pearson/Kirby)			
4x100m medley	**USA**	3:33.73	23 Sep	Sydney
	(Lenny Krayzelburg, Ed Moses, Ian Crocker, Gary Hall Jr)			

Women

50m free	**Inge de Bruijn** NED	24.51	May 27	Sheffield
	Inge de Bruijn NED	24.39	June 10	Rio
	Inge de Bruijn NED	24.13	Sep 22	Sydney
100m free	**Inge de Bruijn** NED	53.80	May 28	Sheffield
	Inge de Bruijn NED	53.77	Sep 20	Sydney
50m back	**Nina Jivanevskaia** ESP	28.69	April 8	Madrid
	Mai Nakamura JPN	28.67	April 23	Tokyo
	Sandra Volker GER	28.25	June 17	Berlin
50m fly	**Inge de Bruijn** NED	25.83	May 20	Monte Carlo
	Inge de Bruijn NED	25.64	May 26	Sheffield
100m fly	**Inge de Bruijn** NED	56.69	May 27	Sheffield
	Inge de Bruijn NED	56.61	Sep 17	Sydney
200m fly	**Susan O'Neill** AUS	2:05.81	May 17	Sydney
400m IM	**Yana Klochkova** UKR	4:33.59	Sep 16	Sydney
4x100m free	**USA**	3:36.61	Sep 16	Sydney
	(Amy Van Dyken, Dara Torres, Courtney Shealy, Jenny Thompson)			
4x100m medley	**USA**	3:58.30	Sep 23	Sydney
	(B.J. Bedford, Megan Quann, Jenny Thompson, Dara Torres)			

European Championships
Helsinki　　　　*June 30-July 9*

Men

50m Free
1 Alexander Popov	RUS	21.95
2 P vd Hoogenband	NED	22.35
3 Lorenzo Vismara	ITA	22.38
7 Mark Foster	GBR	22.85

100m Free
1 Alexander Popov	RUS	48.61
2 P vd Hoogenband	NED	48.77
3 Lars Frolander	SWE	49.24

200m Free
1 Massi Rosolino	ITA	1:47.31
2 P vd Hoogenband	NED	1:47.62
3 Paul Palmer	GBR	1:49.54

400m Free
1 Emiliano Brembilla	ITA	3:48.56
2 Dragos Coman	ROM	3:48.69
3 Paul Palmer	GBR	3:50.97

1500m Free
1 Igor Chervynsky	UKR	15:05.31
2 Emiliano Brembilla	ITA	15:06.42
3 Dragos Coman	ROM	15:10.97

DNQ: Paul Palmer

50m Back
1 Stev Theloke	GER	25.60
2 Darius Grigalionis	LTU	25.61
3 David Ortega	ESP	26.00
8 Neil Willey	GBR	26.33

100m Back
1 David Ortega	ESP	55.50
2 V Nikolaychuk	UKR	55.64
3 Derya Buyukuncu	TUR	55.84

DNQ: Gregor Tait and Neil Willey

200m Back
1 Gordon Kozulj	CRO	1:58.62
2 Emanuele Merisi	ITA	2:00.02
3 Joab Gath	ISR	2:00.32

DNQ: Gregor Tait

50m Breast
1 Mark Warnecke	GER	27.75
2 Oleg Lisogor	UKR	27.81
3 Remo Lutolf	SUI	27.91

DNQ: James Gibson

100m Breast
1 Domenico Fioravanti	ITA	1:02.02
2 Jarno Pihlava	FIN	1:02.07
3 Dmitri Komornikov	RUS	1:02.11

DNQ: Ian Edmond & James Gibson

200m Breast
1 Dmitri Komornikov	RUS	2:13.09
2 Domenico Fioravanti	ITA	2:14.87
3 Maxim Podoprigora	AUT	2:15.07

DNQ: Ian Edmond

50m Fly
1 Jere Hard	FIN	23.88
2 Lars Frolander	SWE	23.96
3 Mark Foster	GBR	24.02

100m Fly
1 Lars Frolander	SWE	52.23
2 Thomas Rupprath	GER	53.38
3 James Hickman	GBR	53.44

200m Fly
1 Anatoli Poliakov	RUS	1:56.73
2 James Hickman	GBR	1:58.44
3 Ioan Gherghel	ROM	1:58.54

200m IM
1 Massi Rosolino	ITA	2:00.62
2 Christian Keller	GER	2:02.02
3 Xavier Marchand	FRA	2:02.06
8 James Hickman	GBR	2:05.46

400 IM
1 Istvan Bathazi	HUN	4:18.51
2 Cezar Badita	ROM	4:19.42
3 Johann Le Bihan	FRA	4:20.50

4 x 100m Free
1 Russia	3:18.75

Pimankov/Chernyshev/Kapralov/Popov
2 Germany	3:19.16
3 France	3:20.37

4 x 200m Free
1 Italy	7:16.52

Rosolino/Pellicciari/Cercato/Brembilla
2 Germany	7:18.96
3 Netherlands	7:19.91

4 x 100m Medley
1 Russia	3:39.29

Aminov/Komornikov/Chernyshev/Popov
2 Sweden	3:40.43
3 Ukraine	3:40.91

Women

50m Free
1 Therese Alshammar	SWE	24.44
2 Wilma van Rijn	NED	25.46
3 Olga Mukomol	UKR	25.54

100m Free
1 Therese Alshammar	SWE	54.41
2 Martina Moravcova	SVK	54.45
3 Mette Jacobsen	DEN	55.31
4 Karen Pickering	GBR	55.67
7 Sue Rolph	GBR	56.23

200m Free
1 N Baranovskaya	BLR	1:59.51
2 Martin Moravcova	SVK	2:00.08
3 Camelia Potec	ROM	2:00.32

400m Free
1 Yana Klochkova	UKR	4:09.41
2 N Baranouskaya	BLR	4:11.37
3 Camelia Potec	ROM	4:11.76

800m Free
1 Flavia Rigamonti	SUI	8:29.16
2 Chantal Strasser	SUI	8:31.36
3 Kirsten Vlieghuis	NED	8:37.94
4 Rebecca Cooke	GBR	8:46.71

50m Back
1 Nina Zhivanevskaya	ESP	28.76
2 Diana Mocanu	ROM	28.85
3 Ilona Hlavackova	CZE	29.18

100m Back
1 N Zhivanevskaya	ESP	1:01.02
2 Diana Mocanu	ROM	1:01.54
3 Lousie Ornstedt	DEN	1:01.88

200m Back
1 N Zhivanevskaya	ESP	2:09.53
2 Diana Mocanu	ROM	2:11.62
3 A Buschschulte	GER	2:12.04
4 Joanne Fargus	GBR	2:13.35

50m Breast
1 Agnes Kovacs	HUN	31.68
2 Zoe Baker	GBR	32.00
3 Sylvia Gerasch	GER	32.02

100m Breast
1 Agnes Kovacs	HUN	1:08.38
2 Sylvia Gerasch	GER	1:09.28
3 S Bondarenko	UKR	1:09.81

DNQ: Zoe Baker

200m Breast
1 Beatrice Caslaru	ROM	2:26.76
2 Agnes Kovacs	HUN	2:26.85
3 Karine Bremond	FRA	2:28.20

DNQ: Jaime King

50m Fly
1 A-K Kammerling	SWE	26.40
2 Karen Egdal	DEN	26.97
3 Martina Moravcova	SVK	26.98

100m Fly
1 Martina Moravcova	SVK	58.72
2 Otylia Jedrzejczak	POL	58.97
3 Johanna Sjoberg	SWE	59.29

200m Fly
1 Otylia Jedrzejczak	POL	2:08.63
2 Mette Jacobsen	DEN	2:08.77
3 Mireia Garcia	ESP	2:10.44

DNQ: Caroline Smart

200m IM
1 Beatrice Caslaru	ROM	2:12.57
1 Jana Klochkova	UKR	2:12.57
3 Sue Rolph	GBR	2:15.82

400m IM
1 Jana Klochkova	UKR	4:39.78
2 Beatrice Caslaru	ROM	4:41.64
3 Yseult Gervy	BEL	4:46.15

4 x 100m Free
1 Sweden	3:42.38

Johnke/Sjoberg/Kammerling/Alshammar
2 Italy	3:45.31
3 Belgium	3:46.42

4 x 200m Free
1 Romania	8:03.17

Potec/Paduraru/Diaconescu/Caslaru
2 Italy	8:08.14
3 France	8:08.30

4 x 100m Medley
1 Sweden   4:06.00
Alshammar/Igelstrom/Sjoberg/
Johncke
2 Belgium   4:09.52
3 Romania   4:10.05

Diving

Men
1m Springboard
1	Alexander Mesch	GER	370.53
2	Dmitry Baibakov	RUS	363.00
3	Joona Puhakka	FIN	347.16
6	Peter Waterfield	GBR	305.04

3m Springboard
1	Dmitry Sautin	RUS	681.48
2	Stefan Ahrens	GER	641.94
3	A Dobroskok	RUS	634.59
11	Mark Shipman	GBR	564.69

DNQ: Tony Ali

10m Platform
1	Dmitry Sautin	RUS	710.07
2	Heiko Meyer	GER	635.97
3	Igor Loukashin	RUS	634.98
5	Leon Taylor	GBR	618.12
6	Peter Waterfield	GBR	554.37

3m Synchro
1	Schellenberg/Wels	GER	331.98
2	Sautin/Dobroskok	RUS	328.56
3	Gil/Alvarez	ESP	293.46
10	Waterfield/Ali	GBR	240.66

Platform Synchro
1	Sautin/Loukashin	RUS	323.46
2	Volodkov/Skrypnik	UKR	292.74
3	Waterfield/Taylor	GBR	280.20

Women
1m Springboard
1	Vera Ilyina	RUS	272.28
2	Heike Fischer	GER	256.83
3	Natalia Oumyskova	RUS	252.00

DNQ: Jane Smith

3m Springboard
1	Youlia Pakhalina	RUS	578.37
2	Doerte Lindner	GER	528.72
3	Anna Lindberg	SWE	523.77
12	Jane Smith	GBR	425.28

DNQ: Karen Smith

10m Platform
1	S Timoshinina	RUS	482.34
2	Ute Wietzig	GER	476.73
3	Olena Zhupina	UKR	475.86
6	Sally Freeman	GBR	447.33
8	Lesley Ward	GBR	429.69

3m Synchro
1	Pakhalina/Ilyina	RUS	303.12
2	Schmalfuss/Lindner	GER	272.52
3	Sorokina/Zhupina	UKR	263.88

Platform Synchro
1	Piper/Wetzig	GER	268.05
2	Timoshinina/Olshevskaya		
		RUS	265.20
3	Lyeonova/Zhupina	UKR	246.54
5	Freeman/Smith	GBR	237.15

Synchro Swimming
Solo
1	Olga Brusnikina	RUS	99.200
2	Virginie Dedieu	FRA	98.080
3	Gemma Mengual	ESP	96.240
10	Kathy Hooper	GBR	88.000

Duet
1 Brusnikina/Kisseleva
		RUS	99.360
2	Dedieu/Lignot	FRA	97.160
3	Mengual/tirados	ESP	96.080
10	Hooper/Adamson	GBR	87.480

Team
1	Russia		99.520
2	Italy		97.480
3	France		97.000
10	Great Britain		85.520

Open Water
Men
5km
1	Luca Baldini	ITA	55:13.1
2	Fabio Venturini	ITA	55:16.4
3	David Meca	ESP	55:35.3
27	David Fytche	GBR	1:00:59.5

25km
1	Stephane Lecat	FRA	5:05:22.5
2	David Meca	ESP	5:05:28.9
3	Fabio Fusi	ITA	5:06:25.5
14	David Fytche	GBR	5:45.08.7

Women
5km
1	Peggy Büchse	GER	1:00:26.6
2	Britta Kamrau	GER	1:00:40.9
3	Jana Pechanova	CZE	1:00:41.6
16	Paula Wood	GBR	1:01:07.2

25km
1	Peggy Büchse	GER	5:22:11.1
2	Edith van Dijk	NED	5:24:47.0
3	Valeria Casprini	ITA	5:24:52.7

European Championships Medal Table
swimming only

1	Sweden	6	2	2	10	11	Finland	1	1	-	2
2	Russia	6	-	1	7	11	Poland	1	1	-	2
3	Italy	5	5	1	11	14	Croatia	1	-	-	1
4	Spain	4	-	2	6	15	Netherlands	-	4	2	6
5	Romania	3	6	5	14	16	Great Britain	-	2	5	7
6	Ukraine	3	3	3	9	17	Denmark	-	2	2	4
7	Hungary	3	1	-	4	18	Belgium	-	1	2	3
8	Germany	2	5	2	9	19	Lithuania	-	1	-	1
9	Slovakia	1	2	1	4	20	Austria	-	-	1	1
10	Switzerland	1	1	1	3	20	Czech Rep	-	-	1	1
11	Belarus	1	1	-	2	20	Israel	-	-	1	1

World Short Course Championships

Athens   *Mar 16-19*

Men

World Records are shown in bold

50m Free
1	Mark Foster	GBR	21.58
2	Brendon Dedekind	RSA	21.62
3	Stefan Nystrand	SWE	21.80

Elim in ht : Paul Belk GBR

100m Free
1	Lars Frolander	SWE	46.80
2	Stefan Nystrand	SWE	47.73
3	Scott Tucker	USA	47.82

Elim in s-f: Paul Belk GBR
Elim in ht: Gavin Meadows GBR

200m Free
1	Bela Szabados	HUN	1:45.17
2	Massi Rosolino	ITA	1:45.63
3	Chad Carvin	USA	1:45.79
5	James Salter	GBR	1:46.29

Elim in ht: Ed Sinclair GBR

400m Free
1	Chad Carvin	USA	3:41.13
2	Paul Palmer	GBR	3:42.70
3	Massi Rosolino	GBR	3:43.68
4	James Salter	GBR	3:45.02

1500m Free
1	Jorg Hoffman	GER	14:47.57
2	Igor Chervinskiy	UKR	14:48.20
3	Chad Carvin	USA	14:51.23

Stuart Trees GBR 5th in slow heat

50m Back
| 1 | Neil Walker | USA | 23.99 |

(24.04 WR in heat, 23.42 WR in s-f)
2	Lenny Krayzelburg	USA	24.24
3	Rodolfo Falcon	CUB	24.32
4=	Neil Willey	GBR	24.67

Elim in ht: Martin Harris GBR

100m Back
1	Neil Walker	USA	**50.75**
2	Rodolfo Falcon	CUB	52.87
3	Derya Buyukuncu	TUR	52.88
8	Neil Willey	GBR	53.67

Elim in ht: Martin Harris GBR

200m Back
1	Gordon Kozulj	CRO	1:53.31
2	Brad Bridgewater	USA	1:53.87
3	V Nikolaychuk	UKR	1:55.33

Elim in ht: Gregor Tait GBR, David O'Brien GBR

50m Breast
1	Mark Warnecke	GER	27.22
2	Brendon Dedekind	RSA	27.27
3	Oleg Lisogor	UKR	27.30

Elim in s-f: James Gibson GBR

100m Breast
| 1 | Roman Sloudnov | RUS | 58.57 |

(58.51 WR in semi-final)
2	Yi Zhu	CHN	59.99
3	Roman Ivanovski	RUS	1:00.05
8	Darren Mew	GBR	1:01.26

Elim in s-f: James Gibson GBR
Elim in hts: Michael Williamson IRL

200m Breast
1	Roman Sloudnov	RUS	**2:07.59**
2	Terence Parkin	RSA	2:07.91
3	Andrei Ivanov	RUS	2:09.90
4	Adam Whitehead	GBR	2:10.82

Elim in ht : Ian Edmond GBR, Michael Williamson IRL

50m Fly
1	Mark Foster	GBR	23.30
2	Neil Walker	USA	23.46
3	Sabir Muhammad	USA	23.56

(Lars Frolander SWE 23.19 WR in heat; Frolander did not contest final)
Elim in ht : David Bennett GBR

100m Fly
| 1 | Lars Frolander | SWE | **50.44** |

(50.59 WR in heats)
| 2 | James Hickman | GBR | 51.53 |
| 3 | Denis Sylantyev | UKR | 51.84 |

Elim in ht : Aaron Wiles GBR

200m Fly
1	James Hickman	GBR	1:53.57
2	Shamek Pietucha	CAN	1:54.27
3	Anatoli Poliakov	RUS	1:54.47

Elim in ht: Robert Greenwood GBR

100m IM
1	Neil Walker	USA	**52.79**
2	Jani Sievinen	FIN	54.08
3	James Hickman	GBR	54.38

Elim in ht: Michael Cole GBR

200 IM
1	Jani Sievinen	FIN	1:56.27
2	James Hickman	GBR	1:56.86
3	Massi Rosolino	ITA	1:58.05

Elim in ht : Michael Cole GBR

400 IM
1	Jani Sievinen	FIN	4:09.54
2	Terence Parkin	RSA	4:10.56
3	MIchael Halika	ISR	4:10.90

Elim in ht : Michael Cole GBR, Mark Racher GBR

4x100 Free
| 1 | Sweden | | **3:09.57** |

Nystrom/Frolander/Ohlin/Nystrand
2	USA		3:10.98
3	Germany		3:13.69
6	Great Britain		3:15.54

Belk/Meadows/Kidd/Brinn

4x200m Free
| 1 | USA | | **7:01.33** |

Davis/Walker/Tucker/Charvin
| 2 | Great Britain | | 7:03.06 |

Sinclair/Spackman/Palmer/Salter
| 3 | Russia | | 7:05.24 |

4x100m Medley Relay
| 1 | USA | | 3:30.03 |

Krayzelburg/Marrs/Walker/Tucker
| 2 | Germany | | 3:31.77 |
| 3 | Great Britain | | 3:32.08 |

Willey/Mew/Hickman/Meadows

Women

50m Free
1	Therese Alshammar	SWE	**23.59**
2	Sandra Volker	GER	24.77
3	Alison Sheppard	GBR	24.80

Elim in ht : Karen Pickering GBR

100m Free
1	Therese Alshammar	SWE	**52.17**
2	Jenny Thompson	USA	53.14
3	Martina Moravcova	SVK	53.88
5	Karen Pickering	GBR	54.60

Elim in ht : Rosalind Brett GBR

200m Free
1	Yu Yang	CHN	1:56.06
2	Martina Moravcova	SVK	1:56.46
3	N Baranovskaya	BLR	1:57.54
4	Karen Pickering	GBR	1:57.71
7	Karen Legg	GBR	1:58.46

400m Free
1	Lindsay Benko	USA	4:02.44
2	Yana Klochkova	UKR	4:04.39
3	Hua Chen	CHN	4:06.63

Elim in ht : Rebecca Cooke GBR, Karen Legg GBR

800m Free
1	Hua Chen	CHN	8:17.03
2	Brooke Bennett	USA	8:19.66
3	Flavia Rigamonti	SUI	8:21.57
5	Rebecca Cooke	GBR	8:29.87

50m Back
1	Antje Buschschulte	GER	27.90
2	Marylyn Chiang	CAN	28.03
3	Kellie McMillan	AUS	28.06
4	Sarah Price	GBR	28.40

Elim in s-f: Zoe Cray GBR

100m Back
1	Sandra Volker	GER	58.66
2	Marylyn Chinag	CAN	59.33
3	Antje Buschschulte	GER	59.37

Elim in s-f Sarah Price GBR, Zoe Cray GBR

200m Back
1	Antje Buschschulte	GER	2:07.29
2	Clementine Stoney	AUS	2:08.64
3	Lindsay Benko	USA	2:08.85
4	Helen Don-Duncan	GBR	2:09.24

50m Breast
1	Sarah Poewe	RSA	30.66
2	Ping Hao	CHN	31.22
3	Tara Kirk	USA	31.47
8	Zoe Baker	GBR	32.06

Elim in s-f: Heidi Earp GBR
Elim in ht: Louise Robinson IRL

100m Breast
1	Sarah Poewe	RSA	1:06.21
2	Alicja Peczak	POL	1:07.69
3	Elena Bogomazova	RUS	1:08.27

Elim in s-f: Heidi Earp GBR
Elim in ht : Louise Robinson IRL, Zoe Baker GBR

200m Breast
1 Rebecca Brown   AUS 2:23.41
2 Alicja Peczak   POL 2:24.24
3 Brooke Hanson   AUS 2:25.30
8 Jaime King   GBR 2:29.61
Elim in ht : Heidi Earp GBR

50m Fly
1 Jenny Thompson   USA   26.13
2 Anna-K Kammerling SWE   26.16
3 Nicola Jackson   GBR   26.85
7 Caroline Foot   GBR   27.34

100m Fly
1 Jenny Thompson   USA   57.67
(56.56 WR in semi-final)
2 Johanna Sjoberg   SWE   57.96
3 Karen Campbell   USA   58.86
6 Nicola Jackson   GBR   59.51
8 Caroline Foot   GBR   59.87

200m Fly
1 Mette Jacobsen   DEN 2:08.10
2 Katrin Jake   GER 2:09.42
3 Otilia Jedrzejczak GER 2:09.61
Elim in ht : Caroline Smart GBR,
Holly Fox GBR

100m IM
1 Martina Moravcova SVK   59.71
2 Marianne Limpert   CAN 1:02.00
3 Alenka Kejzar   SLO 1:02.24
7 Sarah Whewell   GBR 1:09.91

200m IM
1 Yana Klochkova   UKR 2:08.97
2 Martina Moravcova SVK 2:08.98
3 Marianne Limpert   CAN 2:12.68
Elim in ht : Kathryn Evans GBR,
Sarah Whewell GBR

400m IM
1 Yana Klochkova   UKR 4:32.45
2 Nicole Hetzer   GER 4:37.92
3 Katie Yevak   GER 4:38.80
Elim in ht : Holly Fox GBR

4x100 Free
1 Sweden   3:35.54
Johnke/Alsh'r/Kammerling/Sjoberg
2 Germany   3:37.31
3 Great Britain   3:37.93
Sheppard/Huddart/Legg/Pickering

4x200m Free
1 Great Britain   **7:49.11**
Huddart/Jackson/Legg/Pickering
2 USA   7:50.59
3 China   7:52.70

4x100m Medley Relay
1 Sweden   3:59.53
Alsh'r/Igelstrom/Sjoberg/Kammerling
2 Germany   4:01.47
3 USA   4:02.51
5 Great Britain   4:03.35
Price/King/Jackson/Pickering

World Short Course Medal Table

	G	S	B	Ttl		G	S	B	Ttl
USA	9	7	9	25	Denmark	1	-	-	1
Sweden	7	3	1	11	Hungary	1	-	-	1
Germany	5	6	2	13	Canada	-	4	1	5
Britain	4	4	5	13	Poland	-	2	1	3
S Africa	2	4	-	6	Italy	-	1	2	3
Ukraine	2	2	3	7	Cuba	-	1	1	2
China	2	2	2	6	Israel	-	-	1	1
Finland	2	1	-	3	Switzerland	-	-	1	1
Russia	2	-	5	7	Slovenia	-	-	1	1
Slovakia	1	2	1	4	Turkey	-	-	1	1
Australia	1	1	2	4	Belarus	-	-	1	1
Croatia	1	-	-	1					

European Short Course Championships

Valencia   *Dec 14-17*

Men
World Records are shown in bold

50m Free
1 Stefan Nystrand   SWE   21.52
2 Mark Foster   GBR   21.60
3 Oleksandr Volynets UKR   21.70
Elim ht: Matthew Kidd GBR

100m Free
1 Stefan Nystrand   SWE   47.56
2 Denis Pimankov   RUS   47.69
3 Karel Novy   SUI   47.87

200m Free
1 Masso Rosolino   ITA 1:44.63
2 Kvetoslav Svoboda CZE 1:45.27
3 Paul Palmer   GBR 1:46.24
6 James Salter   GBR 1:47.67
Salter 1:47.19 in ht
Elim ht: Matthew Kidd GBR

400m Free
1 Masso Rosolino   ITA 3:39.59
2 Paul Palmer   GBR 3:44.80
3 Kvetoslav Svoboda CZE 3:47.36
8 James Salter   GBR 3:50.34

1500m Free
1 Masso Rosolino   ITA 14:36.93
2 Frederick Hvid   ESP 14:53.93
3 Igor Schervynsky   UKR 14:56.36
4 Adam Faulkner   GBR 14:58.10

50m Back
1 Ante Maskovic   CRO   24.60
2 Orn Arnarson   ISL   24.81
3 Darius Grigalionis LTU   24.82

100m Back
1 Orn Arnarson   ISL   52.28
2 Gordan Kozulj   CRO   52.57
3 Przemyslan Wilant POL   53.21

200m Back
1 Orn Arnarson   ISL 1:52.90
2 Gordan Kozulj   CRO 1:53.50
3 Blaz Medvesek   SLO 1:54.61
8 Stephen Parry   GBR 1:58.22
Elim ht: Simon Militis GBR

50m Breast
1 Mark Warnecke   GER   27.11
1 Daniel Malek   CZE   27.11
1 Domenico Fioravanti ITA 27.11
4 Darren Mew   GBR   27.32
Elim ht: Adam Whitehead GBR

100m Breast
1 Domenico Fioravanti ITA 58.89
2 Daniel Malek   CZE   59.67
3 Darren Mew   GBR 1:00.04
8 Adam Whitehead   GBR 1:00.78

200m Breast
1 Stephan Perrot   FRA 2:07.58
2 Domenico Fioravanti   ITA 2:08.76
3 Daniel Malek   CZE 2:08.86
5 Ian Edmond   GBR 2:11.49

50m Fly
1 Mark Foster   GBR 23.31
2 Jere Hard   FIN 23.48
3 Jorge Ulibarri   ESP 23.61

100m Fly
1 Thomas Rupprath   GER 51.31
2 Lars Frolander   SWE 51.76
3 Anatoli Poliakov   RUS 52.54
Elim ht: Robert Greenwood GBR
Elim s-f: James Hickman GBR

200m Fly
1 Thomas Rupprath   GER 1:53.28
2 Anatoli Poliakov   RUS 1:54.01
3 Stephen Parry   GBR 1:54.37
4 James Hickman   GBR 1:55.10

100m IM
1 Peter Mankoc   SLO 54.14
2 Indrek Sei   EST 54.22
3 Davide Cassol   ITA 55.10
8 Ian Edmond   GBR 56.47
Elim s-f: James Hickman

200m IM
1 Masso Rosolino   ITA 1:56.62
2 Christian Keller   GER 1:57.68
3 Peter Mankoc   SLO 1:58.14
8 James Hickman   GBR 2:02.88
Elim ht: Michael Cole GBR

400m IM
1 Alessio Boggiatto   ITA 4:10.61
2 Frederick Hvid   ESP 4:12.94
3 Michael Halika   ISR 4:13.48
4 Simon Militis   GBR 4:15.67
8 Darren Wigg   GBR 4:19.49

4x50m Free
1 Sweden   1:27.52
Dahl/Nystrand/Frolander/Andersson
2 Germany   1:27.81
3 Great Britain   1:28.18
Howard/Foster/Parry/Kidd

4x50m Medley
1 Germany   1:36.23
Halgasch/Warnecke/Rupprath/
Winkler
2 Ukraine   1:37.48
3 Croatia   1:37.71
4 Great Britain   1:37.87
Parry/Mew/Hickman/Foster

Women

50m Free
1 Therese Alshammar SWE 24.09
2 Alison Sheppard   GBR 24.48
3 Anna-K Kammerling SWE 24.75
Elim s-f: Sue Rolph GBR

100m Free
1 Therese Alshammar SWE 53.13
2 Johanna Sjöberg   SWE 53.82
3 Martina Moravcova SVK 53.97
5 Karen Pickering   GBR 54.95
Elim s-f: Sue Rolph GBR

200m Free
1 Martina Moravcova SVK 1:56.51
2 Karen Pickering   GBR 1:57.22
3 Karen Legg   GBR 1:57.60

400m Free
1 Irina Oufimtseva RUS 4:06.71
2 Jana Pechanova   CZE 4:09.52
3 Rebecca Cooke   GBR 4:10.80
Elim ht: Vicki Horner GBR

800m Free
1 Chantal Strasser SUI 8:27.23
2 Rebecca Cooke   GBR 8:29.24
3 Jana Pechanova   CZE 8:31.17

50m Back
1 Ilona Hlavackova   CZE 27.84
2 Nina Zhivanevskaya   ESP 28.10
3 Daniela Samulski   GER 28.12
5 Sarah Price   GBR 28.76
8 Katy Sexton   GBR 28.99

100m Back
1 Ilona Hlavackova   CZE 58.82
2 Katy Sexton   GBR 1:00.04
3 Nina Zhivaneskaya   ESP 1:00.09
5 Sarah Price   GBR 1:01.25

200m Back
1 Joanna Fargus   GBR 2:08.19
2 Nina Zhivanevskaya   ESP 2:09.15
3 Anja Carman   SLO 2:10.71
8 Helen Don-Duncan   GBR 2:14.13

50m Breast
1 Emma Igelström   SWE 31.26
2 A Braszkiewicz   POL 31.55
3 A Gulbrandben   NOR 31.70
Elim ht: Jaime King GBR
Elim s-f: Heidi Earp GBR

100m Breast
1 Alicja Peczak   POL 1:06.95
2 Emma Igelström   SWE 1:07.14
3 A Gulbrandben   NOR 1:08.17
5 Heidi Earp   GBR 1:08.77
Elim ht: Jaime King GBR

200m Breast
1 Emma Igelström   SWE 2:24.05
2 Alicja Peczak   POL 2:24.17
3 A Gulbrandben   NOR 2:25.55
4 Heidi Earp   GBR 2:26.20

50m Fly
1 A Kammerling   SWE **25.60**
2 Karen Egdal   DEN 26.72
3 Johanna Sjöberg   SWE 26.74

100m Fly
1 Martina Moravcova   SVK 57.54
2 Johanna Sjöberg   SWE 57.86
3 Mette Jacobsen   DEN 58.91
8 Margaretha Pedder   GBR 1:00.53

200m Fly
1 Annika Mehlhorn   GER 2:05.77
2 Mette Jacobsen   DEN 2:07.70
3 Petra Zahrl   AUT 2:09.29
4 Margaretha Pedder   GBR 2:09.75

100m IM
1 Martina Moravcova   SVK 1:00.58
2 Annika Mehlhorn   GER 1:01.21
3 Sue Rolph   GBR 1:01.25
Elin s-f: Kathryn Evans GBR

200m IM
1 Yana Klochkova   UKR 2:10.75
2 Oxana Verevka   RUS 2:12.15
3 Sue Rolph   GBR 2:12.28
Elim ht: Kathryn Evans GBR

400m IM
1 Yana Klochkova   UKR 4:35.11
2 Annika Mehlhorn   GER 4:39.02
3 Rachel Corner   GBR 4:40.11
Elim ht: Nathalie Brown GBR

4x50m Free
1 Sweden   1:38.21
Lofstedt/Alshammar/Sjöberg/
Kammerling
2 Great Britain   1:38.39
Sheppard/Rolph/Pickering/Brett
3 Germany   1:39.63

4x50m Medley
1 Sweden   1:48.31
Alshammar/Igelström/Kammerling/S
jöberg
2 Germany   1:50.96
3 Great Britain   1:51.20
Price/Earp/Brett/Sheppard

World Cup
Final Standings
1999-2000

Men
50m Free: L Vismara ITA
100/200m Free: Bela Szabados HUN
400/1500m: Chad Charvin USA
50m Back: Tomislav Karlo CRO
100/200m Back:
Lenny Krayzelburg USA
50m Breast: Mark Warnecke GER
100/200m Breast: Phil Rogers AUS
50/100m Fly: Mike Mintenko CAN
200 Fly/400 IM: Massimiliano Eroli ITA
100/200m IM: Xie Xufeng CHN

Women
50/100m Free/50m Fly/100m IM:
Jenny Thompson USA
200m Free: Yang Yu CHN
400/800m Free: Rebecca Cooke GBR
50m Back: Nina Zhivanevskaya ESP
100m Back: Dyana Calub AUS
200m Back: Kelly Stefanyshyn CAN
50m Breast: Janne Schafer GER
100/200m Breast: Alicia Peczak POL
100m Fly: Ruan Yi CHN
200m Fly: Jennifer Button CAN
200/400m IM: Beatrice Caslaru ROM

British Olympic Trials

Sheffield   *Jul 25-30*

Men

50m Free
1	Mark Foster	22.42
2	Matthew Kidd	23.17
3	Anthony Howard	23.24

100m Free
1	Mark Stevens	50.44
2	Paul Belk	50.47
3	Jamie Salter	50.52

200m Free
1	Paul Palmer	1:48.42
2	Jamie Salter	1:48.73
3	Ed Sinclair	1:49.21

400m Free
1	Paul Palmer	3:49.61
2	Jamie Salter	3:53.09
3	Graeme Smith	3:53.83

1500m
1	Paul Palmer	15:17.53
2	Adam Faulkner	15:17.84
3	Graeme Smith	15:31.98

50m Breast
1	Darren Mew	28.39
2	Chris Cook	29.13
3	Greg Haynes	29.85

100m Breast
1	Darren Mew	1:01.78
2	Adam Whitehead	1:02.29
3	James Gibson	1:03.54

200m Breast
1	Adam Whitehead	2:14.14
2	Ian Edmond	2:15.62
3	Chris Cook	2:17.62

50m Fly
1	Greg Phillips	25.04
2	David Jones	25.23
3	Alex Boyce	25.37

100m Fly
1	James Hickman	52.87
2	Robert Greenwood	53.97
3	Aaron Wiles	54.16

200m Fly
1	Stephen Parry	1:57.13
2	James Hickman	1:57.46
3	Robert Greenwood	2:00.67

50m Back
1	Brett Lummis	26.61
2	Alexander Scotcher	27.39
3	Aaron Birch	27.53

100m Back
1	Adam Ruckwood	55.81
2	Neil Willey	56.23
3	Martin Harris	56.57

200m Back
1	Adam Ruckwood	2:00.51
2	Simon Militis	2:00.75
3	Gregor Tait	2:02.43

200m IM
1	James Hickman	2:03,85
2	Michael Cole	2:04.00
2	Brett Lummis	2:06.06

400m IM
1	Simon Militis	4:20.77
2	Darren Wigg	4:27.05
3	Adam Faulkner	4:27.73

Women

50m Free
1	Alison Sheppard	25.20
2	Sue Rolph	25.54
3	Rosalind Brett	25.96

100m Free
1	Karen Pickering	55.58
2	Karen Legg	55.99
3	Rosalind Brett	56.14

200m Free
1	Karen Legg	2:00.45
2	Karen Pickering	2:00.67
3	Nicola Jackson	2:01.31

400m Free
1	Vicki Horner	4:15.91
2	Rebecca Cooke	4:16.24
3	Stacey Houldsworth	4:17.39

800m Free
1	Rebecca Cooke	8:39.18
2	Sarah Collings	8:44.31
3	Nathalie Brown	8:49.53

50m Breast
1	Zoe Baker	32.24
2	Kate Haywood	33.54
3	Jane Davis	33.59

100m Breast
1	Heidi Earp	1:10.16
2	Jaime King	1:10.67
3	Rachel Genner	1:10.91

200m Breast
1	Jaime King	2:29.95
2	Heidi Earp	2:30.44
3	Linda Hindmarsh	2:33.70

50m Fly
1	Caroline Foot	27.73
2	Alexa White	28.27
3	Kerry Martin	28.73

100m Fly
1	Margaretha Pedder	1:00.74
2	Georgina Lee	1:00.99
3	Nicola Jackson	1:01.21

200m Fly
1	Georgina Lee	2:11.36
2	Margaretha Pedder	2:11.59
3	Holly Fox	2:15.77

50m Back
1	Zoe Cray	29.82
2	Sarah Price	29.95
3	Julie Fort	30.76

100m Back
1	Katy Sexton	1:01.80
2	Sarah Price	1:02.18
3	Joanna Fargus	1:03.22

200m Back
1	Helen Don-Duncan	2:11.25
2	Joanna Fargus	2:12.10
3	Katy Sexton	2:13.35

200m IM
1	Sue Rolph	2:14.90
2	Kathryn Evans	2:16.26
3	Rachael Corner	2:18.59

400m IM
1	Rachael Corner	4:49.15
2	Nathalie Brown	4:53.33
3	Sarah Heyes	4:53.52

Table Tennis

W ell, the ball got bigger in October, expanding from the old fly-away 38mm to an it's-so-slow-the British players-can almost-see-it 40mm. Apparently, the increased ball also diminishes spin and with another rule change going through in 2002 which renders masking the ball at service illegal, table tennis could become a game where rallies are commonplace. That, anyway, is the intention.

Given how badly British table tennis has done over the past four years, any changes should help. Only one player qualified for the Olympics, Matthew Syed, and he was about as successful at Sydney as he was nine months afterwards in Wokingham, when he tried to unseat John Redwood. Syed has class, but with a political future mapped out, the Commonwealth Games may be his swansong.

Times were even worse for the home nations (if that's possible) in the world team championships with England, the best of British, ranked only 26th in the men's competition and 27th in the women's. In the European championships, both the men and the women were relegated in their team competitions and in the individual championships, not one player or pair reaching the third round. Desperate times, but the horizons are not entirely bleak. In Andrew Baggaley, Gareth Herbert and the Welshman Adam Robertson, Britain has three players capable of making an impact at international level. With Katy Parker a possible improver in the women's ranks, it bodes well.

In the Olympic final against Kong Linghui, Jan-Ove Waldner, the 1992 Olympic champion, came back from a 2-0 deficit to level at the match at 2-2. Predictably, Kong then took the deciding game by the relatively comfortable margin of 21-13. The remaining finals were all Chinese affairs, Wang Nan winning the women's singles, Wang Liqin and Yan Seng winning the men's doubles and Li Ju and Wang taking the women's doubles gold. The Chinese clean sweep matched their achievement in Atlanta, and from the total of 16 Olympic titles which have been contested since table tennis became an Olympic sport, the Chinese have won 13 of them. Moreover, in nine Olympic finals, they have supplied both contestants. The rest of the world long ago realised that if you can't beat the Chinese, you sign them, and the exodus continued in 2000. Unfortunately, the recruiting techniques in Britain are clearly not up to speed because, since Chen Xinhua moved on, our Chinese signings have been notable by their absence. This despite the fact that Deng Yaping, the greatest of the lot, spent much of the year (and last year) studying English at Nottingham University. Yaping, isn't there anyone you know in back in Zhengzhou who's just aching to play for Britain?

Olympic Qualifying Tournament

Seville, Spain   May 25-28

Men
Carl Prean and Alex Perry, both GBR, failed to qualify from the preliminary group stage.

Women
Great Britain did not have a women representative in the qualifying tournament.

World Team Championships
Kuala Lumpur, Malaysia   Feb 19-26

Men

Quarter-finals
China bt Korea 3-0
Japan bt Chinese Tapei 3-2
Italy bt Netherlands 3-1
Sweden bt Germany 3-0
Semi-finals
China bt Japan 3-0
Sweden bt Italy 3-1
Final
Sweden bt China 3-2
Final GBR & IRL Rankings: England 26th, Wales 38th, Scotland 54th, Ireland 47th

Women

Quarter-finals
China bt Hong Kong 3-0
Korea bt Japan 3-1
Chinese Tapiei bt Germany 3-1
Romania bt Singapore 3-1
Semi-finals
China bt Korea 3-1
Chinese Taipei bt Romania 3-1
Final
China bt Chinese Taipei 3-1
Final Rankings: England 27th, Wales 47th, Ireland 55th

European Championships
Bremen, Germany   Apr 21-May 1
GBR early round matches only given

Men's Singles

Round 1
Alex Perry ENG bt Michal Bardon SVK 21-23, 21-18, 21-10, 21-13
Magnus Mölin SWE bt Terry Young ENG 21-14, 21-16, 24-22
Matthew Syed ENG bt Thierry Miller SUI 21-15, 21-11, 21-10
Round 2
Peter Karlsson SWE bt Alex Perry ENG 21-15, 21-7, 21-11
Marcin Kusinski POL bt Matthew Syed ENG 21-18, 25-23, 13-21, 21-16
Semi-finals
Peter Karlsson SWE bt Petr Korbel CZE 21-19, 21-16, 21-15
Zoran Primorac CRO bt Jan-Ove Waldner SWE 19-21, 21-16, 23-25, 21-17, 21-16
Final
Peter Karlsson bt Zoran Primorac 21-15, 21-18, 21-16

Men's Doubles

Round 1
Adrian Crisan/Andrei Filimon ROM bt Alex Perry/Terry Young ENG 17-21, 21-16, 21-17
Semi-finals
Patrick Chila/Jean-Philip Gatien FRA bt Lars Hielscher/Thomas Keinath GER 21-15, 21-19
Kalnikos Kreanga/Ilija Lupulesku GRE/YUG bt Karl Jindrak/Werner Schlager AUT 21-12, 21-13
Final
Chila/Gatien bt Kreanga/Lupulesku 21-15, 21-12

Women's Singles

Round 1
Asa Svensson SWE bt Kubrat Owlabi ENG 21-19, 21-11, 21-9
Bethan Daunton WAL bt Sara Perez ESP 21-16, 21-14, 21-19
Wang Yu ITA bt Helen Lower ENG 14-21, 21-23, 21-15, 21-13, 21-8
Linda Radford ENG bt Tatiana Logatskaya BLR 21-19, 21-18, 221-13
Round 2
Ni Xia Lian LUX bt Bethan Daunton WAL 21-17, 21-13, 21-10
Jing Tian-Zörner GER bt Linda Radford ENG 21-8, 21-3 21-14
Semi-finals
Qianhong Gotsch GER bt Jie Schöpp GER 21-15, 21-16, 27-25
Mihaela Steff ROM bt Tamara Boros CRO 22-20, 21-15, 15-21, 25-23
Final
Qianhong Gotsch bt Mihaela Steff 16-21, 22-20, 21-15, 13-21, 21-13

Women's Doubles

Round 1
Magdalena Gorowska/Joanna Narkiecicz POL bt Helen Lower/Kurat Owolabi ENG 21-15, 21-13
Agathe Costes/Sabrina Fernandez FRA bt Katy Parker/Linda Radford ENG 21-15, 21-14
Semi-finals
Ni Xia Lian/Peggy Regenwetter LUX bt Elke Schall/Nicole Struse GER 21-18, 21-18
Csilla Bartoki/Krisztina Toth HUN bt Asa Svensson/Marie Svensson SWE 21-17, 22-20
Final
Csilla Bartofi/Krisztinea Toth bt Ni Xia Lian/Peggy Regenwetter 21-13, 20-22, 21-14

Mixed Doubles

Round 1
Jaromir Truska/Eva Odorova SVK bt Herbert/Linda Radford ENG   21-17, 22-20
Matthew Syed/Qianlong Gotsch ENG/GER bt Yordanov/Vitcheva-Gatinsk 21-0, 21-0
Round 2
Matthew Syed/Qianlong Gotsch bt Illas/Popova 21-8, 21-16
Round 3
Ilija Lupulesku/Marie Svensson YUG/SWE bt Matthew Syed/Qianlong Gotsch 14-21, 21-16, 21-9
Semi-finals
Aleksandar Karakasevic/Ruta B-Garkauskaite YUG/LIT bt Ntaniel Tsiokas/Jie Schöpp GRE/GER 21-16, 16-21, 21-14
Ilija Lupulesku/Marie Svensson bt Roko Tosic/Sandra Paovic CRO 18-21, 21-16, 22-20
Final
Aleksandar Karakasevic/Ruta B-Garkauskaite bt Ilija Lupulesku/Marie Svensson 21-19, 21-12

Men's Team

Category 1 - Group A
Group Standings: 1. Sweden 10pts, 2. Denmark, 3. France, 4. Austria, 5. Russia, 6. Yugoslavia
Category 1 - Group B
Poland bt England 4-1; Germany bt England 4-0
Belgium bt England 4-2; Netherlands bt England 4-3
Czech Republic bt England 4-0
Group Standings: 1. Germany 10; 2. Poland 9; 3. Czech Rep 7; 4. Netherlands 7; 5. Belgium 7; 6. England 5
Category 2 - Group C
Final Standings; 1. Greece 10; 2. Hungary 9;
3. Slovenia 8; 4. Romania 7; 5. Slovakia 6; 6. Bulgaria 5
Category 2 - Group D
Group Stadings: 1. Belorus 9; 2. Croatia 9; 3. Italy 8; 4. Norway 8; 5. Spain 6; 6. Ukraine 5
Category 3 - Group E
Group Standings: 1. Finland 10, 2. Luxembourg 9;
3. Estonia 8; 4. Cyprus 7; 5 Azerbiajan 6;
6. Liechtenstein 5
Category 3 - Group F
Scotland bt Moldova 4-1; Scotland bt Albania 4-0;
Scotland bt Bosnia 4-1; Portugal bt Scotland 4-2;
Group Standings: 1. Portugal 8pts; 2. Scotland 7; 3. Bosnia 6; 4. Moldova 5; 5. Albania 4
Category 3 - Group G
Ireland bt Malta 4-1; Ireland bt Iceland 4-3;
Israel bt Ireland 3-0; Lithuania bt Ireland 4-2
Group Standings: 1. Israel 8pts; 2. Lithuania 7; 3.Ireland 6; 4. Iceland 5; 5. Malta 4
Category 3 - Group H
Wales bt Latvia 4-1; Armenia bt Wales 4-0;
Wales bt San Marino 4-1; Turkey bt Wales 4-1;
Wales bt Switzerland 4-1
Group Standings: 1. Armenia 10; 2. Turkey 9; 3. Wales 8; 4. Switzerland 7; 5. Latvia 6; 6. San Marino 5
33rd/36th Places
Wales bt Estonia 4-1
Ireland bt Bosnia 4-3
33rd/34th Place
Wales bt Ireland 4-1
29th/32nd Places
Lithuania bt Scotland 4-2
31st/32nd Place
Turkey bt Scotland 4-2
9/12th Places
Russia bt England 4-3
11th Place
England bt Belgium 4-3
England and Belgium relegated to Category 2
Semi-finals
Sweden bt Poland 4-3; Germany bt Denmark 4-1
Final
Sweden bt Germany 4-1
Final Placings: 1. Sweden; 2. Germany; 3. Poland; 11. England; 32. Scotland; 33. Wales; 34. Ireland

Women's Team

Category 1 - Group A
Group Standings: 1. Germany 10pts, 2. Russia 9, 3. Italy 8; 4. Sweden 7; 5. Romania 6; 6. France 5
Category 1 - Group B
Czech Rep bt England 4-2; England bt Netherlands 4-3;
Hungary bt England 4-0; Belarus bt England 4-0;
Croatia bt England 4-0
Group Standings: 1. Hungary 10; 2. Croatia 9;

3. Belarus 8; 4. Czech Rep 7; 5. England 6;
6. Netherlands 5
Category 2 - Group C
Group Placings: 1. Slovenia 9; 2. Luxembourg 9;
3. Ukraine 8; 4. Austria 7; 5. Ukraine 6; 6. Bulgaria 6
Category 2 - Group D
Group Standings: 1. Belgium 10; 2. Slovakia 9;
3. Yugoslavia 8; 4. Lithuania 7; 5. Spain 6; 6. Greece
Category 3 - Group E
Wales bt Malta 4-2; Turkey bt Malta 4-3;
Wales bt Switzerland 4-1; Poland bt Wales 4-2;
Turkey bt Wales 4-2
Group Standings: 1. Poland 8; 2. Turkey 7; 3. Wales 6; 4. Switzerland 5; 5. Malta 4
Category 3 - Group F
Portugal bt Ireland 4-0; Bosnia bt Ireland 4-0;
Latvia bt Ireland 4-1
Group Standings: 1. Bosnia 6; 2. Portugal 5; 3. Latvia; 4. Ireland 3
Category 3 - Group G
Estonia bt Scotland 4-0; Moldova bt Scotland 4-1;
Scotland bt Azerbaijan 4-2; Denmark bt Scotland 4-0
Group Standings: 1. Denmark 8; 2. Estonia 7;
3. Moldova 6; 4. Scotland 5; 5. Azerbaijan 4
34/36th Places
Switzerland bt Ireland 4-1; Ireland bt Scotland 4-0;
Switzerland bt Scotland 4-0
31st/33rd Places
Lithuania bt Wales 4-2; Moldova bt Wales 4-1
9/12th Places
France bt England 4-0
11/12th Place
England bt Netherlands 4-1
Semi-finals
Germany bt Croatia 4-0; Hungary bt Russia 4-0
3rd/4th Place
Croatia bt Russia 4-0
Final
Hungary bt Germany 4-2
Final Standings: 1. Hungary; 2. Germany; 3. Croatia; 4. Russia; 11. England; 33. Wales; 35. Ireland; 36. Scotland

Men's World Cup
Yangzhou, China   Oct 12-15
No British players participated.
Semi-finals
Kim Tae-soo bt Jean-Michel Saive 21-13, 21-13, 21-15
Ma Lin bt Wang Liqin 21-17, 21-14, 21-14
3rd/4th Place
Wang Liqin bt Jean-Micel Saive 19-21, 21-16, 21-13
Final
Ma Lin bt Kim Tae-soo 21-10, 21-13, 21-9

Women's World Cup
Phnom Penh, Cambodia   Jan 28-30
Same format as men's World Cup. No British players
Semi-finals
Wang Nan bt Sun Jin 21-14, 21-17, 23-21
Li Ju bt Chen Jing 21-19, 21-17, 21-14
3rd/4th Place
Sun Jin bt Chen Jing 21-14, 17-21, 21-14, 21-15
Final
Li Ju bt Wang Nan 21-10, 20-22, 21-17, 21-16

Europe Top 12
Alassio, Italy   Feb 4-6

Men
Semi-finals
Werner Schlager AUT bt Jean-Philip Gatien FRA 19-21, 21-11, 16-21, 22-20, 23-21
Yang Min ITA bt Jörg Rosskopf GER 23-21, 21-16, 13-21, 19-21, 21-19
Final
Werner Schlager bt Yang Min 21-19, 21-17, 21-15

Women
Semi-finals
Mihaela Steff ROM bt Jie Schöpp GER 14-21, 21-17, 21-19, 17-21, 21-19
Qianhong Gotsch GER bt Ni Xia Lian LUX 18-21, 21-17, 21-6, 21-19
Final
Qianhong Gotsch bt Mihaela Steff 21-19, 21-16, 21-12

ITTF Pro Tour Grand Finals
Sydney   Jan 13-16

Men's Singles Final
Kong Linghui bt Liu Guozheng 21-18, 21-11, 21-16

Men's Doubles Final
Ma Lin/Kong Linghui bt Patrick Chila/J-P Gatien 21-12, 21-18, 12-21, 21-13

Women's Singles Final
Chen Jing bt Li Ju 21-11, 13-21, 21-18, 6-21, 21-16

Women's Doubles Final
Li Ju/Wang Nan bt Sun Jin/Yang Ying 21-9, 21-12, 19-21, 21-18

Commonwealth Championships
February 11-17, Singapore

Men's Singles
Quarter-finals
Johnny Huang CAN bt Alex Perry ENG 21-15 21-12 21-13
Duan Yong Jun SIN bt Kurt Liu CAN 21-10 21-13 21-7
Chetan Baboor IND bt Toriola Segun NGR 20-22 21-13 21-6 21-12
Matthew Syed ENG bt Sen Yew Fai SIN 21-16 21-12 21-8
Semi-finals
Duan bt Huang 21-16 13-21 11-21 21-8 21-19
Syed bt Baboor 21-19 19-21 21-16 21-14
Finals
Syed bt Duan 13-21 21-16 21-8 21-19

Women's Singles
Quarter-finals
Li Jia Wei SIN bt Lay Jian Fang AUS walkover
Li Chunli NZL bt Sun Linan SIN 19-21 21-12 21-11 21-12
Zhang Xue Ling SIN bt Miao Miao AUS 22-20 23-21
Jing Jun Jong SIN bt Yao Lin Jing MAS 21-14 24-22 21-17
Semi-finals
Li SIN bt Li NZL 21-17 14-21 21-17 21-18
Jing SIN bt Zhang SIN 21-17 21-19 21-10
Final
Li bt Jing 15-21 20-22 21-11 21-14 21-19

World Rankings
As at 14 Dec, 2000

MEN

1	Wang Liqin	CHN	2159
2	Kong Linghui	CHN	2137
3	Ma Lin	CHN	2040
4	Liu Guoliang	CHN	2038
5	Liu Guozheng	CHN	2036
6	Chiang Peng-Lung	CHN	2033
7	Vladimir Samsonov	BLR	2007
8	Werner Schlager	AUT	1998
9	Zoran Primorac	CRO	1975
10	Kim Taek Soo	KOR	1954
11	Jan-Ove Waldner	SWE	1945
12	Jorgen Persson	SWE	1925
13	Jörg Rosskopf	GER	1851
14	Jean-Michel Saive	BEL	1830
15	Peter Karlsson	SWE	1753
16	Christophe Legout	FRA	1730
17	Petr Korbel	CZE	1729
18	Kalinikos Kreanga	GRE	1715
19	Seiko Iseki	JPN	1703
20	Damien Eloi	FRA	1701
45	Matthew Syed	ENG	1443
78	Carl Prean	ENG	1329
132	Alex Perry	ENG	1086
167	Terry Young	ENG	1015

WOMEN

1	Wang Nan	CHN	2340
2	Li Ju	CHN	2220
3	Sun Jin	CHN	2096
4	Chen Jing	TPE	2088
5	Yang Ying	CHN	1983
6	Zhang Yining	CHN	1941
7	Tamara Boros	CRO	1940
8	Ryu Ji Hye	KOR	1938
9	Qianhong Gotsch	GER	1914
10	Chire Koyama	JPN	1889
11	Mihaela Steff	ROM	1887
12	Jing Jun Hong	SIN	1801
13	Lin Ling	CHN	1800
14	Jing Tian-Zorner	GER	1792
14	Ni Xia Lian	LUX	1792
16	Li Nan	CHN	1782
17	Krisztina Toth	HUN	1764
18	Kim Moo Kyo	KOR	1712
19	An Konishi	JPN	1711
20	Csilla Batorfi	HUN	1705
170	Nicola Deaton	ENG	1039
171	Helen Lower	ENG	1036
191	Bethen Daunton	WAL	985
233	Linda Radford	ENG	909

Tennis

I t was a record that Roy Emerson, as good as he was, should never have held. The Australian was not even the best player of *his* time, let alone all-time. The best player of his age was Rod Laver, but he ran away to the circus and during the six seasons of his absence Emerson racked up 10 of his 12 Grand Slam wins. Laver's record was shiveringly good: even without those six years he still won 11 Slams. The Rockhampton Rocket would have taken the record beyond even Pete Sampras' reach had he hung around. But he didn't.

Sam and Georgia Sampras were over for the grand occasion, a rare visit for the folks who hadn't come over before as they figured their son was doing just fine without them. Sampras didn't let them down; he never lets anyone down on grass. Red clay is another matter. In all the time he's closed down on seven titles at Wimbledon, he has never once looked like winning at Roland Garros.

Pat Rafter had the ominous task of facing Sampras on the great day and, in an unseemly gesture, actually won the first set. He was soon more respectful though, losing the second, third and fourth set to give Sampras his 13th Slam. It was only to be expected; in 64 single matches at Wimbledon since he first played in 1989, the American has won 59 of them. He has only been beaten once in south-west London since 1992.

His epoch-making victory, though, was an island for oldies in a sea of youth. Venus Williams broke her duck at Wimbledon and followed up immediately with a second success at Flushing Meadows, and won the Olympic title too; Gustavo Kuerten continued his rising profile at Paris, where he is now approaching folk-hero status; and Sampras found himself at the wrong end of a pummelling by the young Russian Marat Safin in the US Open. Sampras didn't even get close. Agassi, approaching oldie status, also played a lesser role, his only success early-season at Melbourne. Family illnesses curtailed his season, though, not form.

Tim Henman spent the year chasing one of the lesser records; that of defeats in ATP finals without ever winning one. He was doing really well, taking his tally to seven, before he ruined the sequence with a win at Vienna. To make matters worse, he went and won again, at Brighton. Seasiders were shocked, they'd seen nothing like this since the Albion almost beat Manchester United in the 1983 Cup Final. It wasn't all port and lemons for Tim though. He played in the Davis Cup match at Wimbledon against Ecuador when a man ranked 959th in the world sealed a remarkable victory for the visitors. If only Sampras were British. He'd show them how to win on grass.

Grand Slams

Pete Sampras USA	**13**
Roy Emerson AUS	12
Bjorn Borg SWE	11
Rod Laver AUS	11
Bill Tilden USA	10
Ivan Lendl CZE/USA	8
Ken Rosewall AUS	8
Jimmy Connors USA	8
Andre Agassi USA	7
Henri Cochet FRA	7
John McEnroe USA	7
John Newcombe AUS	7
René Lacoste FRA	7
W A Larned USA	7
R D Sears USA	7
Mats Wilander SWE	7

Tennis Earners 2000

As compiled for
ACE Magazine

Women

1 **Anna Kournikova**   **£7.2m**
Prize Money: £650,000; Endorsements, etc : £6.55m

2 **Martina Hingis**   **£6.5m**
Prize Money: £2.3m; Endorsements etc: £4.2m

3 **Venus Williams**   **£4.1m**
Prize Money: £1.4m; Endorsements etc: £2.7m

4 **Serena Williams**   **£4.0m**
Prize Money: £700,000; Endorsements etc: £3.3m

5 **Lindsay Davenport**   **£3.75m**
Prize Money: £1.65m; Endorsements etc £2.1m

6 **Monica Seles**   **£3.0m**
Prize Money: £750,000; Endorsements etc: £2.25m

7 **Mary Pierce**   **£1.8m**
Prize Money: £800,000; Endorsements etc: £1m

8 **Jennifer Capriati**   **£975,000**
Prize Money: £325,000; Endorsements etc: £650,000

9 **Arantxa Sanchez Vicario**   **£950,000**
Prize Money: £550,000; Endorsements: £400,000

10 **Conchita Martinez**   **£820,000**
Prize Money: £720,000; Endorsements etc: £100,000

Men

1 **Andre Agassi**   **£11.75m**
Prize Money: £1.25m; Endorsements etc: £10.5m

2 **Gustavo Kuerten**   **£8.7m**
Prize Money: £3.1m; Endorsements etc: £5.6m

3 **Pete Sampras**   **£7.0m**
Prize Money: £1.5m; Endorsements etc: £5.5m

4 **Marat Safin**   **£4.1m**
Prize Money: £2.35m; Endorsements etc: £1.75m

4 **Michael Chang**   **£4.1m**
Prize Money: £300,000; Endorsements etc: £3.8m

6 **Pat Rafter**   **£3.5m**
Prize Money: £550,000; Endorsements etc: £2.95m

7 **Yevgeny Kafelnikov**   **£3.4m**
Prize Money: £2.5m; Endorsements etc: £900,000

8 **Lleyton Hewitt**   **£3.0m**
Prize Money: £1.2m; Endorsements etc: £1.8m

9 **Tim Henman**   **£2.8m**
Prize Money: £700,000; Endorsements etc: £2.1m

10 **Mark Philippoussis**   **£2.5m**
Prize Money: £600,000; Endorsements etc: £1.9m

The Championships

Wimbledon June 26-July 9

Men's Singles

Round 1

Selected results

Vince Spadea USA bt Greg Rusedski GBR (14)
6-3 6-7 6-3 6-7 9-7
Tim Henman GBR (8) bt Paradorn Srichaphan THA
5-7 6-3 6-1 6-3
Justin Gimelstob USA bt Barry Cowan GBR
6-3 6-4 6-7 6-3
Slava Dosedel CZE bt Nicolas Lapentti ECU (16)
6-3 6-2 0-6 6-1
Jan-Michael Gambill USA bt Lleyton Hewitt AUS (7)
6-3 6-2 7-5
Daniel Nestor CAN bt Miles MacLagan GBR
4-6 7-6 6-2 6-4
Martin Lee GBR bt Juan Antonio Marin CRC 6-2 6-4 7-6
Pat Rafter AUS (12) bt Jamie Delgado GBR 6-3 7-6 6-1
Tommy Haas GER bt Nicolas Kiefer GER (13)
5-7 6-4 6-2 6-3
Arvind Parmar GBR bt Andre Sa BRA 6-7 6-3 4-6 6-2 6-3

Women's Singles

Round 1

Selected results

Tina Pisnik SLO bt Hannah Collin GBR 6-1 7-5
Louise Latimer GBR bt Holly Parkinson USA 3-6 6-3 6-4
Anke Huber GER (11) bt Jo Ward GBR 7-5 6-2
Kristie Boogert NED bt Julie Halard-Decugis FRA (14)
7-6 0-6 6-1
Cara Black ZIM bt Sam Smith GBR 6-2 6-2
Amy Frazier USA bt Lorna Woodroffe GBR 6-4 7-6
Olga Barabanschikova BLR bt Barbara Schett AUT (15)
6-2 6-2
Anna Kournikova RUS bt Sandrine Testud 7-5 5-7 6-4
Natasha Zvereva BLR bt Julie Pullin GBR 6-4 6-3
Kim Clijsters BEL bt Nathalie Tauziat FRA 6-3 3-6 6-2
Gala Leon Garcia ESP bt Amelie Mauresmo FRA (13)
4-6 6-3 7-5
Magui Serna ESP bt Karen Cross GBR 6-3 6-4
Lucie Ahl GBR bt Barbara Schwartz AUT 6-3 6-0
Jennifer Capriati USA bt Dominique Van Roost BEL (16)
6-2 6-4

Men's Doubles

Final

T Woodbridge/M Woodforde AUS bt
P Haarhuis/S Stolle NED/AUS 6-3 6-4 6-1

Women's Doubles

Final

S Williams/V Williams USA (8) bt
J Halard-Decugis/A Sugiyama FRA/JPN 6-3 6-2

Mixed Doubles

Final

D Johnson/K Po USA bt
L Hewitt/K Clijsters AUS/BEL 6-4 7-6

Boys Doubles

Final

D Coene/K Vliegen BEL (7) bt
Andrew Banks/Ben Riby GBR 6-3 1-6 6-3

"The people treat you bad there and, for the outsider, there is practically no motivation to play there. Maybe other guys see it as the greatest tournament in the world - not me. The surface is bad and there's much more history at Roland Garros. Here [in Paris] they treat you like gods. At Wimbledon they seem to maintain the traditions - but for what?

"Let's have Wimbledon without tennis players. What would happen? Nothing. You would have a snobbish English club with their own rules and their own traditions. It's simply not right. They make exceptions for some players - the rest they treat like dirt. I think by the time I finish my career nothing will have changed at Wimbledon"

Andrei Medvedev, before being invited for tea with Tim Phillips, chairman of the All-England Club.

"I never thought that anyone at Wimbledon would do that for me. I didn't think anyone cared"

Andrei Medvedev, after having had tea with Tim Phillips, chairman of the All-England Club.

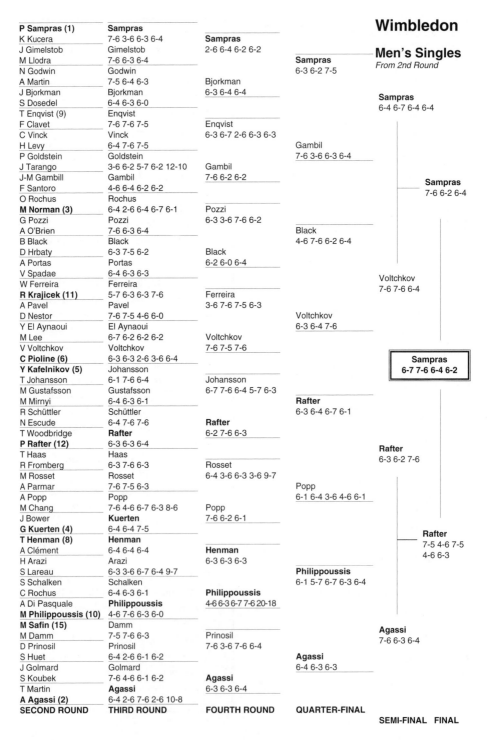

Wimbledon

Men's Singles
From 2nd Round

SECOND ROUND

P Sampras (1)
K Kucera
J Gimelstob
M Llodra
N Godwin
A Martin
J Bjorkman
S Dosedel
T Enqvist (9)
F Clavet
C Vinck
H Levy
P Goldstein
J Tarango
J-M Gambill
F Santoro
O Rochus
M Norman (3)
G Pozzi
A O'Brien
B Black
D Hrbaty
A Portas
V Spadae
W Ferreira
R Krajicek (11)
A Pavel
D Nestor
Y El Aynaoui
M Lee
V Voltchkov
C Pioline (6)
Y Kafelnikov (5)
T Johansson
M Gustafsson
M Mirnyi
R Schüttler
N Escude
T Woodbridge
P Rafter (12)
T Haas
R Fromberg
M Rosset
A Parmar
A Popp
M Chang
J Bower
G Kuerten (4)
T Henman (8)
A Clément
H Arazi
S Lareau
S Schalken
C Rochus
A Di Pasquale
M Philippoussis (10)
M Safin (15)
M Damm
D Prinosil
S Huet
J Golmard
S Koubek
T Martin
A Agassi (2)

THIRD ROUND

Sampras 7-6 3-6 6-3 6-4
Gimelstob 7-6 6-3 6-4
Godwin 7-5 6-4 6-3
Bjorkman 6-4 6-3 6-0
Enqvist 7-6 7-6 7-5
Vinck 6-4 7-6 7-5
Goldstein 3-6 6-2 5-7 6-2 12-10
Gambil 4-6 6-4 6-2 6-2
Rochus 6-4 2-6 6-4 6-7 6-1
Pozzi 7-6 6-3 6-4
Black 6-3 7-5 6-2
Portas 6-4 6-3 6-3
Ferreira 5-7 6-3 6-3 7-6
Pavel 7-6 7-5 4-6 6-0
El Aynaoui 6-7 6-2 6-2 6-2
Voltchkov 6-3 6-3 2-6 3-6 6-4
Johansson 6-1 7-6 6-4
Gustafsson 6-4 6-3 6-1
Schüttler 6-4 7-6 7-6
Rafter 6-3 6-3 6-4
Haas 6-3 7-6 6-3
Rosset 7-6 7-5 6-3
Popp 7-6 4-6 6-7 6-3 8-6
Kuerten 6-4 6-4 7-5
Henman 6-4 6-4 6-4
Arazi 6-3 3-6 6-7 6-4 9-7
Schalken 6-4 6-3 6-1
Philippoussis 4-6 7-6 6-3 6-0
Damm 7-5 7-6 6-3
Prinosil 6-4 2-6 6-1 6-2
Golmard 7-6 4-6 6-1 6-2
Agassi 6-4 2-6 7-6 2-6 10-8

FOURTH ROUND

Sampras 2-6 6-4 6-2 6-2
Bjorkman 6-3 6-4 6-4
Enqvist 6-3 6-7 2-6 6-3 6-3
Gambil 7-6 6-2 6-2
Pozzi 6-3 3-6 7-6 6-2
Black 6-2 6-0 6-4
Ferreira 3-6 7-6 7-5 6-3
Voltchkov 7-6 7-5 7-6
Johansson 6-7 7-6 6-4 5-7 6-3
Rafter 6-2 7-6 6-3
Rosset 6-4 3-6 6-3 3-6 9-7
Popp 7-6 6-2 6-1
Henman 6-3 6-3 6-3
Philippoussis 4-6 6-3 6-7 7-6 20-18
Prinosil 7-6 3-6 7-6 6-4
Agassi 6-3 6-3 6-4

QUARTER-FINAL

Sampras 6-3 6-2 7-5
Gambil 7-6 3-6 6-3 6-4
Black 4-6 7-6 6-2 6-4
Voltchkov 6-3 6-4 7-6
Rafter 6-3 6-4 6-7 6-1
Popp 6-1 6-4 3-6 4-6 6-1
Philippoussis 6-1 5-7 6-7 6-3 6-4
Agassi 6-4 6-3 6-3

SEMI-FINAL

Sampras 6-4 6-7 6-4 6-4
Voltchkov 7-6 7-6 6-4
Rafter 6-3 6-2 7-6
Agassi 7-6 6-3 6-4

Sampras 7-6 6-2 6-4
Rafter 7-5 4-6 7-5 4-6 6-3

FINAL

Sampras 6-7 7-6 6-4 6-2

Wimbledon
Women's Singles
From 2nd Round

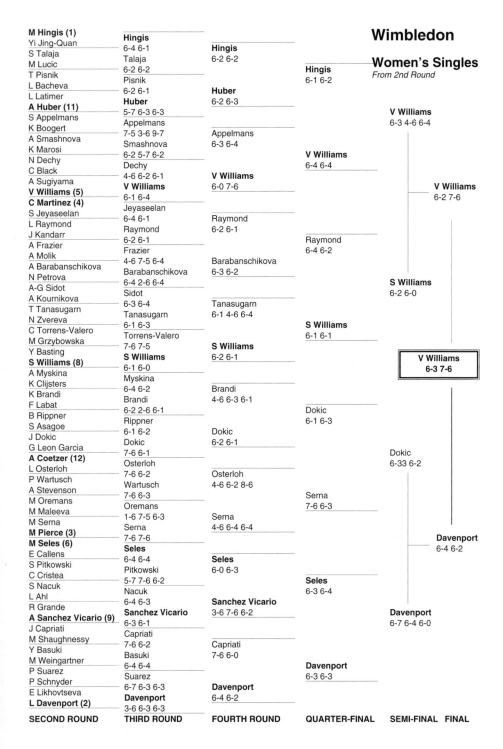

SECOND ROUND

- M Hingis (1)
- Yi Jing-Quan
- S Talaja
- M Lucic
- T Pisnik
- L Bacheva
- L Latimer
- A Huber (11)
- S Appelmans
- K Boogert
- A Smashnova
- K Marosi
- N Dechy
- C Black
- A Sugiyama
- V Williams (5)
- C Martinez (4)
- S Jeyaseelan
- L Raymond
- J Kandarr
- A Frazier
- A Molik
- A Barabanschikova
- N Petrova
- A-G Sidot
- A Kournikova
- T Tanasugarn
- N Zvereva
- C Torrens-Valero
- M Grzybowska
- Y Basting
- S Williams (8)
- A Myskina
- K Clijsters
- K Brandi
- F Labat
- B Rippner
- S Asagoe
- J Dokic
- G Leon Garcia
- A Coetzer (12)
- L Osterloh
- P Wartusch
- A Stevenson
- M Oremans
- M Maleeva
- M Serna
- M Pierce (3)
- M Seles (6)
- E Callens
- S Pitkowski
- C Cristea
- S Nacuk
- L Ahl
- R Grande
- A Sanchez Vicario (9)
- J Capriati
- M Shaughnessy
- Y Basuki
- M Weingartner
- P Suarez
- P Schnyder
- E Likhovtseva
- L Davenport (2)

THIRD ROUND

- Hingis 6-4 6-1
- Talaja 6-2 6-2
- Pisnik 6-2 6-1
- Huber 5-7 6-3 6-3
- Appelmans 7-5 3-6 9-7
- Smashnova 6-2 5-7 6-2
- Dechy 4-6 6-2 6-1
- V Williams 6-1 6-4
- Jeyaseelan 6-4 6-1
- Raymond 6-2 6-1
- Frazier 4-6 7-5 6-4
- Barabanschikova 6-4 2-6 6-4
- Sidot 6-3 6-4
- Tanasugarn 6-1 6-3
- Torrens-Valero 7-6 7-5
- S Williams 6-1 6-0
- Myskina 6-4 6-2
- Brandi 6-2 2-6 6-1
- Rippner 6-1 6-2
- Dokic 7-6 6-1
- Osterloh 7-6 6-2
- Wartusch 7-6 6-3
- Oremans 1-6 7-5 6-3
- Serna 7-6 7-6
- Seles 6-4 6-4
- Pitkowski 5-7 7-6 6-2
- Nacuk 6-4 6-3
- Sanchez Vicario 6-3 6-1
- Capriati 7-6 6-2
- Basuki 6-4 6-4
- Suarez 6-7 6-3 6-3
- Davenport 3-6 6-3 6-3

FOURTH ROUND

- Hingis 6-2 6-2
- Huber 6-2 6-3
- Appelmans 6-3 6-4
- V Williams 6-0 7-6
- Raymond 6-2 6-1
- Barabanschikova 6-3 6-2
- Tanasugarn 6-1 4-6 6-4
- S Williams 6-2 6-1
- Brandi 4-6 6-3 6-1
- Dokic 6-2 6-1
- Osterloh 4-6 6-2 8-6
- Serna 4-6 6-4 6-4
- Seles 6-0 6-3
- Sanchez Vicario 3-6 7-6 6-2
- Capriati 7-6 6-0
- Davenport 6-4 6-2

QUARTER-FINAL

- Hingis 6-1 6-2
- V Williams 6-4 6-4
- Raymond 6-4 6-2
- S Williams 6-1 6-1
- Dokic 6-1 6-3
- Serna 7-6 6-3
- Seles 6-3 6-4
- Davenport 6-3 6-3

SEMI-FINAL

- V Williams 6-3 4-6 6-4
- S Williams 6-2 6-0
- Dokic 6-33 6-2
- Davenport 6-7 6-4 6-0

FINAL

- V Williams 6-2 7-6
- Davenport 6-4 6-2

Champion: V Williams 6-3 7-6

Australian Open

Men's Singles
From 2nd round

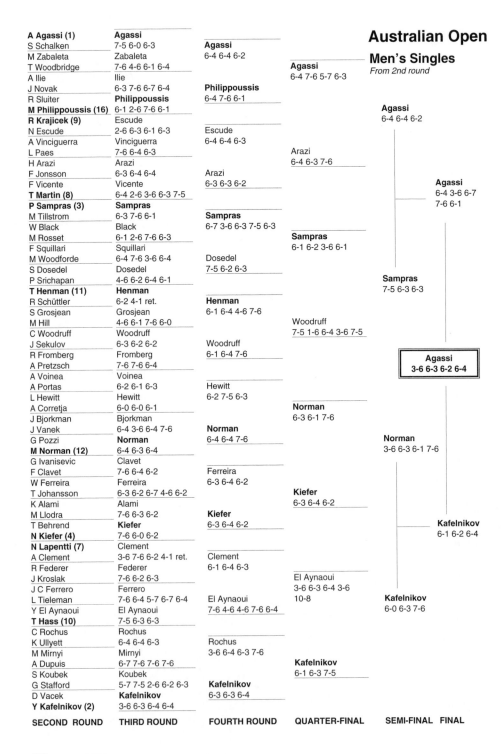

SECOND ROUND	THIRD ROUND	FOURTH ROUND	QUARTER-FINAL	SEMI-FINAL	FINAL

SECOND ROUND

- A Agassi (1)
- S Schalken
- M Zabaleta
- T Woodbridge
- A Ilie
- J Novak
- R Sluiter
- M Philippoussis (16)
- R Krajicek (9)
- N Escude
- A Vinciguerra
- L Paes
- H Arazi
- F Jonsson
- F Vicente
- T Martin (8)
- P Sampras (3)
- M Tillstrom
- W Black
- M Rosset
- F Squillari
- M Woodforde
- S Dosedel
- P Srichapan
- T Henman (11)
- R Schüttler
- S Grosjean
- M Hill
- C Woodruff
- J Sekulov
- R Fromberg
- A Pretzsch
- A Voinea
- A Portas
- L Hewitt
- A Corretja
- J Bjorkman
- J Vanek
- G Pozzi
- M Norman (12)
- G Ivanisevic
- F Clavet
- W Ferreira
- T Johansson
- K Alami
- M Llodra
- T Behrend
- N Kiefer (4)
- N Lapentti (7)
- A Clement
- R Federer
- J Kroslak
- J C Ferrero
- L Tieleman
- Y El Aynaoui
- T Hass (10)
- C Rochus
- K Ullyett
- M Mirnyi
- A Dupuis
- S Koubek
- G Stafford
- D Vacek
- Y Kafelnikov (2)

THIRD ROUND

- Agassi — 7-5 6-0 6-3
- Zabaleta
- Ilie — 7-6 4-6 6-1 6-4
- Philippoussis — 6-3 7-6 6-7 6-4
- Philippoussis — 6-1 2-6 7-6 6-1
- Escude
- Vinciguerra — 2-6 6-3 6-1 6-3
- Arazi — 7-6 6-4 6-3
- Vicente — 6-3 6-4 6-4
- Sampras — 6-4 2-6 3-6 6-3 7-5
- Black — 6-3 7-6 6-1
- Squillari — 6-1 2-6 7-6 6-3
- Dosedel — 6-4 7-6 3-6 6-4
- Henman — 4-6 6-2 6-4 6-1
- Grosjean — 6-2 4-1 ret.
- Woodruff — 4-6 6-1 7-6 6-0
- Fromberg — 6-3 6-2 6-2
- Voinea — 7-6 7-6 6-4
- Hewitt — 6-2 6-1 6-3
- Bjorkman — 6-0 6-0 6-1
- Norman — 6-4 3-6 6-4 7-6
- Clavet — 6-4 6-3 6-4
- Ferreira — 7-6 6-4 6-2
- Alami — 6-3 6-2 6-7 4-6 6-2
- Kiefer — 7-6 6-3 6-2
- Clement — 7-6 6-0 6-2
- Federer — 3-6 7-6 6-2 4-1 ret.
- Ferrero — 7-6 6-2 6-3
- El Aynaoui — 7-6 6-4 5-7 6-7 6-4
- Rochus — 7-5 6-3 6-3
- Mirnyi — 6-4 6-4 6-3
- Koubek — 6-7 7-6 7-6 7-6
- Kafelnikov — 5-7 7-5 2-6 6-2 6-3
- (Kafelnikov — 3-6 6-3 6-4 6-4)

FOURTH ROUND

- Agassi — 6-4 6-4 6-2
- Philippoussis — 6-4 7-6 6-1
- Escude — 6-4 6-4 6-3
- Arazi — 6-3 6-3 6-2
- Sampras — 6-7 3-6 6-3 7-5 6-3
- Dosedel — 7-5 6-2 6-3
- Henman — 6-1 6-4 4-6 7-6
- Woodruff — 6-1 6-4 7-6
- Hewitt — 6-2 7-5 6-3
- Norman — 6-4 6-4 7-6
- Ferreira — 6-3 6-4 6-2
- Kiefer — 6-3 6-4 6-2
- Clement — 6-1 6-4 6-3
- El Aynaoui — 7-6 4-6 4-6 7-6 6-4
- Rochus — 3-6 6-4 6-3 7-6
- Kafelnikov — 6-3 6-3 6-4

QUARTER-FINAL

- Agassi — 6-4 7-6 5-7 6-3
- Arazi — 6-4 6-3 7-6
- Sampras — 6-1 6-2 3-6 6-1
- Woodruff — 7-5 1-6 6-4 3-6 7-5
- Norman — 6-3 6-1 7-6
- Kiefer — 6-3 6-4 6-2
- El Aynaoui — 3-6 6-3 6-4 3-6 10-8
- Kafelnikov — 6-1 6-3 7-5

SEMI-FINAL

- Agassi — 6-4 6-4 6-2
- Sampras — 7-5 6-3 6-3
- Norman — 3-6 6-3 6-1 7-6
- Kafelnikov — 6-0 6-3 7-6

FINAL-stage

- Agassi — 6-4 3-6 6-7 7-6 6-1
- Kafelnikov — 6-1 6-2 6-4

FINAL

- Agassi — 3-6 6-3 6-2 6-4

Australian Open
Women's Singles
From 2nd round

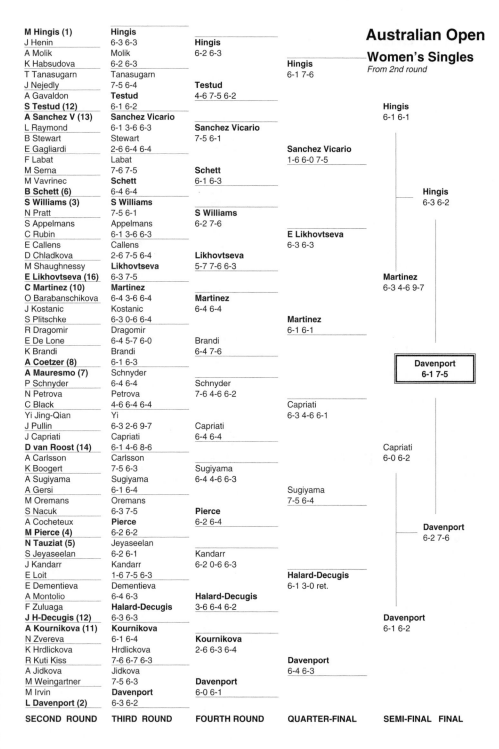

SECOND ROUND	THIRD ROUND	FOURTH ROUND	QUARTER-FINAL	SEMI-FINAL	FINAL
M Hingis (1)	Hingis 6-3 6-3				
J Henin		Hingis 6-2 6-3			
A Molik	Molik 6-2 6-3		Hingis 6-1 7-6		
K Habsudova					
T Tanasugarn	Tanasugarn 7-5 6-4			Hingis 6-1 6-1	
J Nejedly		Testud 4-6 7-5 6-2			
A Gavaldon	Testud 6-1 6-2				
S Testud (12)			Sanchez Vicario 1-6 6-0 7-5		
A Sanchez V (13)	Sanchez Vicario 6-1 3-6 6-3				
L Raymond		Sanchez Vicario 7-5 6-1			
B Stewart	Stewart 2-6 6-4 6-4				Hingis 6-3 6-2
E Gagliardi					
F Labat	Labat 7-6 7-5		Schett 6-1 6-3		
M Serna		Schett 6-1 6-3			
M Vavrinec	Schett 6-4 6-4				
B Schett (6)				E Likhovtseva 6-3 6-3	
S Williams (3)	S Williams 7-5 6-1				
N Pratt		S Williams 6-2 7-6			
S Appelmans	Appelmans 6-1 3-6 6-3		E Likhovtseva 6-3 6-3		
C Rubin					
E Callens	Callens 2-6 7-5 6-4				
D Chladkova		Likhovtseva 5-7 7-6 6-3			
M Shaughnessy	Likhovtseva 6-3 7-5				Martinez 6-3 4-6 9-7
E Likhovtseva (16)					
C Martinez (10)	Martinez 6-4 3-6 6-4		Martinez 6-4 6-4		
O Barabanschikova		Martinez 6-4 6-4			
J Kostanic	Kostanic 6-3 0-6 6-4			Martinez 6-1 6-1	
S Plitschke					
R Dragomir	Dragomir 6-4 5-7 6-0				
E De Lone		Brandi 6-4 7-6			
K Brandi	Brandi 6-1 6-3				
A Coetzer (8)					Davenport 6-1 7-5
A Mauresmo (7)	Schnyder 6-4 6-4				
P Schnyder		Schnyder 7-6 4-6 6-2			
N Petrova	Petrova 4-6 6-4 6-4		Capriati 6-3 4-6 6-1		
C Black					
Yi Jing-Qian	Yi 6-3 2-6 9-7			Capriati 6-0 6-2	
J Pullin		Capriati 6-4 6-4			
J Capriati	Capriati 6-1 4-6 8-6				
D van Roost (14)					Davenport 6-2 7-6
A Carlsson	Carlsson 7-5 6-3				
K Boogert		Sugiyama 6-4 4-6 6-3			
A Sugiyama	Sugiyama 6-1 6-4		Sugiyama 7-5 6-4		
A Gersi					
M Oremans	Oremans 6-3 7-5				
S Nacuk		Pierce 6-2 6-4			
A Cocheteux	Pierce 6-2 6-2				
M Pierce (4)				Halard-Decugis 6-1 3-0 ret.	
N Tauziat (5)	Jeyaseelan 6-2 6-1				
S Jeyaseelan		Kandarr 6-2 0-6 6-3			
J Kandarr	Kandarr 1-6 7-5 6-3		Halard-Decugis 3-6 6-4 6-2		
E Loit					Davenport 6-1 6-2
E Dementieva	Dementieva 6-4 6-3				
A Montolio		Halard-Decugis 6-3 6-3			
F Zuluaga	Halard-Decugis 6-3 6-3				
J H-Decugis (12)				Davenport 6-4 6-3	
A Kournikova (11)	Kournikova 6-1 6-4				
N Zvereva		Kournikova 2-6 6-3 6-4			
K Hrdlickova	Hrdlickova 7-6 6-7 6-3		Davenport 6-4 6-3		
R Kuti Kiss					
A Jidkova	Jidkova 7-5 6-3				
M Weingartner		Davenport 6-0 6-1			
M Irvin	Davenport 6-3 6-2				
L Davenport (2)					

Australian Open
Melbourne   Jan 17-30

Men's Singles
Selected results from round 1
Tim Henman GBR (11) bt Jerome Golmard FRA 6-7 6-3 7-6 7-6
Marc Rosset SUI bt Jamie Delgado GBR 7-6 6-3 7-6
Paradorn Srichaphan THA bt Karol Kucera SVK (14) 6-2 6-4 3-6 6-3
Richard Fromberg AUS bt Thomas Enqvist SWE (6) 6-4 7-6 4-6 3-6 10-8
Albert Portas ESP bt Gustavo Kuerten BRA (5) 4-6 4-6 6-4 7-6 6-4
Goran Ivanisevic CRO bt Cedric Pioline FRA (13) 6-4 2-6 7-5 1-6 9-7
Younes El Aynaoui MAR bt Arvind Parmar GBR 6-7 7-6 1-6 6-3 6-1
Cristophe Rochus BEL bt Albert Costa ESP (15) 6-3 6-7 6-4 6-3

Women's Singles
Selected results from round 1
Julie Pullin GBR bt Jane Chi USA 6-1 6-3
Kristie Boogert NED bt Anke Huber GER (15) 6-4 6-4

Men's Doubles
Final
E Ferreira/R Leach RSA/USA (5) bt W Black/A Kratzmann ZIM/AUS (8) 6-4 3-6 6-3 3-6 18-16

Women's Doubles
Final
L Raymond/R Stubbs USA/AUS (1) bt M Hingis/M Pierce FRA/SUI (3) 6-4 5-7 6-4

Mixed Doubles
Final
J Palmer/R Stubbs USA/AUS (3) bt T Woodbridge/A Sanchez-Vicario AUS/ESP (4) 7-5 7-6

French Open
Paris   May 29-June 11

Men's Singles
Selected results from round 1
Tim Henman GBR (13) bt Vince Spadea USA 7-5 7-5 6-4
Slava Dosedel CZE bt Greg Rusedski GBR 6-3 7-6 7-6
Mark Philippoussis AUS bt Pete Sampras USA 4-6 7-5 7-6 4-6 8-6
Jan-Michael Gambill USA bt Nicolas Kiefer GER (8) 6-3 7-5 6-1

Women's Singles
Selected result from round 1
Meghann Shaughnessy USA bt Julie Halard-Decugis FRA (12) 7-5 6-4
Fabiola Zuluaga COL bt Jennifer Capriati USA (15) 6-3 7-5
Dominique Van Roost BEL bt Lindsay Davenport USA (2) 6-7 6-4 6-3

Men's Doubles
Final
T Woodbridge/M Woodforde AUS (2) bt P Haarhuis/S Stolle NED/AUS (3) 7-6 6-4

Women's Doubles
Final
M Hingis/M Pierce SUI/FRA bt V Ruano-Pascual/P Suarez ARG (10) 6-2 6-4

Mixed Doubles
Final
D Adams/M De Swardt RSA (12) bt T Woodbridge/R Stubbs AUS (1) 6-3 3-6 6-3

US Open
New York   Aug 28-Sep 10

Men's Singles
Selected results from round 1
Tim Henman GBR (11) bt Fernando Vicente ESP 6-3 6-3 6-4
Greg Rusedski GBR bt Magnus Gustafsson SWE 6-1 6-2 6-4
Jens Knippschild GER bt Barry Cowan GBR 6-4 6-3 6-3
Tommy Haas GER bt Jamie Delgado GBR 6-3 6-1 6-1
Wayne Arthurs AUS bt Gustavo Kuerten AUS 4-6 6-3 7-6 7-6

Women's Singles
Selected results from round 1
Miriam Oremans NED bt Julie Halard-Decugis FRA (16) 6-3 6-4

Men's Doubles
Final
L Hewitt/M Mirnyi AUS/BLR bt E Ferreira/R Leach RSA/USA (4) 6-4 5-7 7-6

Women's Doubles
Final
J Halard-Decugis/A Sugiyama FRA/JPN (2) bt C Black/E Likhovtseva ZIM/RUS (10) 6-0 1-6 6-1

Mixed Doubles
Final
J Palmer/A Sanchez-Vicario USA/ESP (2) bt M Mirnyi/A Kournikova BLR/RUS (4) 6-4 6-3

Boys Doubles
Final
Lee Childs/James Nelson GBR (1) bt T Davis/R Ginepri USA 6-2 6-4

"Basically, the Davis Cup captain just sits on the court, pours them a drink and gives them a banana to eat."
David Lloyd's definition of the job of Davis Cup captain.

"I want to go as far away from this place as possible. And I won't be watching the championships on television. I know I can do well at Wimbledon and this is why it hurts more"
Greg Rusedski after his first-round defeat at Wimbledon by Vince Spadea.

"I'm not going religious, but I needed a lot of help from upstairs"
Pete Sampras, going religious after winning Wimbledon.

"I play for history. That is my motivation"
Pete Sampras.

"How about moving it to the summer?"
Pat Cash on how to improve Wimbledon.

"It's not often I get carwaxed like that. It was like looking at me when I was 19"
Pete Sampras after losing to Marat Safin in the US Open final.

"I thought 'Oh my God' people had to pay to see this match. I kept looking at the clock hoping we would at least be out there for an hour"
Martina Hingis, who lost the first set to Lindsay Davenport in the Australian final in 18 minutes. She eventually lasted an hour and five minutes before Davenport won.

"I go to bed at night and dream I have won a Grand Slam and wake up and it's a nightmare. Now I have done it, I don't have to wake up any more"
Venus Williams, after winning Wimbledon.

"Nobody in Ecuador thought we could win and in the end we needed a miracle. That miracle was Giovanni"
Raul Viver, Ecuador coach, after Giovanni Lapentti, Nicolas' younger brother and 959th ranked player in the world, sealed Ecuador's Davis Cup victory over Britain.

TO GET TO THE NUMBER ONE SEEDING
YOU KEEP FIGHTING UNLESS IT'S BROKEN OR BLEEDING
Sign at the Rick Macci Tennis Academy in Florida, where the Williams sisters learned their craft.

French Open
Men's Singles
From 2nd round

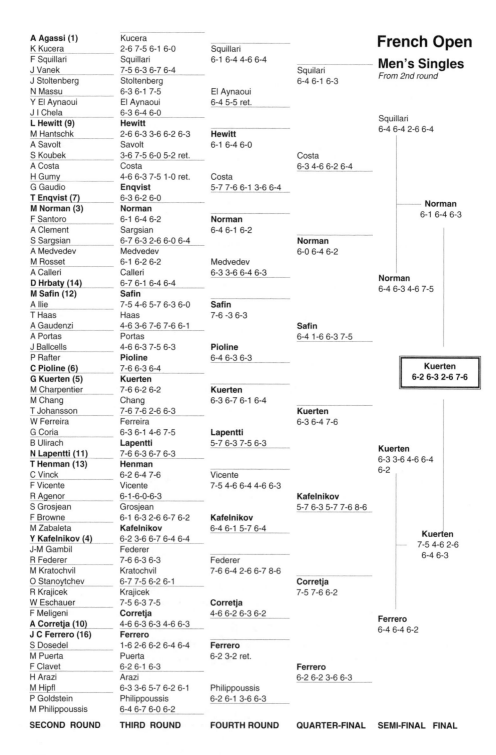

SECOND ROUND

- **A Agassi (1)**
- K Kucera
- F Squillari
- J Vanek
- J Stoltenberg
- N Massu
- Y El Aynaoui
- J I Chela
- **L Hewitt (9)**
- M Hantschk
- A Savolt
- S Koubek
- A Costa
- H Gumy
- G Gaudio
- **T Enqvist (7)**
- **M Norman (3)**
- F Santoro
- A Clement
- S Sargsian
- A Medvedev
- M Rosset
- A Calleri
- **D Hrbaty (14)**
- **M Safin (12)**
- A Ilie
- T Haas
- A Gaudenzi
- A Portas
- J Ballcells
- P Rafter
- **C Pioline (6)**
- **G Kuerten (5)**
- M Charpentier
- M Chang
- T Johansson
- W Ferreira
- G Coria
- B Ulirach
- **N Lapentti (11)**
- **T Henman (13)**
- C Vinck
- F Vicente
- R Agenor
- S Grosjean
- F Browne
- M Zabaleta
- **Y Kafelnikov (4)**
- J-M Gambil
- R Federer
- M Kratochvil
- O Stanoytchev
- R Krajicek
- W Eschauer
- F Meligeni
- **A Corretja (10)**
- **J C Ferrero (16)**
- S Dosedel
- M Puerta
- F Clavet
- H Arazi
- M Hipfl
- P Goldstein
- M Philippoussis

THIRD ROUND

- Kucera — 2-6 7-5 6-1 6-0
- Squillari — 7-5 6-3 6-7 6-4
- Stoltenberg — 6-3 6-1 7-5
- El Aynaoui — 6-3 6-4 6-0
- Hewitt — 2-6 6-3 3-6 6-2 6-3
- Savolt — 3-6 7-5 6-0 5-2 ret.
- Costa — 4-6 6-3 7-5 1-0 ret.
- **Enqvist** — 6-3 6-2 6-0
- Norman — 6-1 6-4 6-2
- Sargsian — 6-7 6-3 2-6 6-0 6-4
- Medvedev — 6-1 6-2 6-2
- Calleri — 6-7 6-1 6-4 6-4
- **Safin** — 7-5 4-6 5-7 6-3 6-0
- Haas
- Portas — 4-6 3-6 7-6 7-6 6-1
- **Pioline** — 4-6 6-3 7-5 6-3
- Kuerten — 7-6 6-3 6-4
- Chang — 7-6 6-2 6-2
- Ferreira — 7-6 7-6 2-6 6-3
- **Lapentti** — 6-3 6-1 4-6 7-5
- Henman — 7-6 6-3 6-7 6-3
- Vicente — 6-2 6-4 7-6
- Grosjean — 6-1-6-0-6-3
- **Kafelnikov** — 6-1 6-3 2-6 6-7 6-2
- Federer — 6-2 3-6 6-7 6-4 6-4
- Kratochvil — 7-6 6-3 6-3
- Krajicek — 6-7 7-5 6-2 6-1
- **Corretja** — 7-5 6-3 7-5
- Ferrero — 4-6 6-3 6-3 4-6 6-3
- Puerta — 1-6 2-6 6-2 6-4 6-4
- Arazi — 6-2 6-1 6-3
- **Philippoussis** — 6-3 3-6 5-7 6-2 6-1
- — 6-4 6-7 6-0 6-2

FOURTH ROUND

- Squillari — 6-1 6-4 4-6 6-4
- El Aynaoui — 6-4 5-5 ret.
- Hewitt — 6-1 6-4 6-0
- Costa — 5-7 7-6 6-1 3-6 6-4
- Norman — 6-4 6-1 6-2
- Medvedev — 6-3 3-6 6-4 6-3
- Safin — 7-6 -3 6-3
- Pioline — 6-4 6-3 6-3
- Kuerten — 6-3 6-7 6-1 6-4
- Lapentti — 5-7 6-3 7-5 6-3
- Vicente — 7-5 4-6 6-4 4-6 6-3
- Kafelnikov — 6-4 6-1 5-7 6-4
- Federer — 7-6 6-4 2-6 6-7 8-6
- Corretja — 4-6 6-2 6-3 6-2
- Ferrero — 6-2 3-2 ret.
- Philippoussis — 6-2 6-1 3-6 6-3

QUARTER-FINAL

- Squilari — 6-4 6-1 6-3
- Costa — 6-3 4-6 6-2 6-4
- Norman — 6-0 6-4 6-2
- Safin — 6-4 1-6 6-3 7-5
- Kuerten — 6-3 6-4 7-6
- Kafelnikov — 5-7 6-3 5-7 7-6 8-6
- Corretja — 7-5 7-6 6-2
- Ferrero — 6-2 6-2 3-6 6-3

SEMI-FINAL

- Squillari — 6-4 6-4 2-6 6-4
- Norman — 6-4 6-3 4-6 7-5
- Kuerten — 6-3 3-6 4-6 6-4 6-2
- Ferrero — 6-4 6-4 6-2

FINAL

- Norman — 6-1 6-4 6-3
- Kuerten — 7-5 4-6 2-6 6-4 6-3

Kuerten
6-2 6-3 2-6 7-6

French Open
Women's Singles
From 2nd round

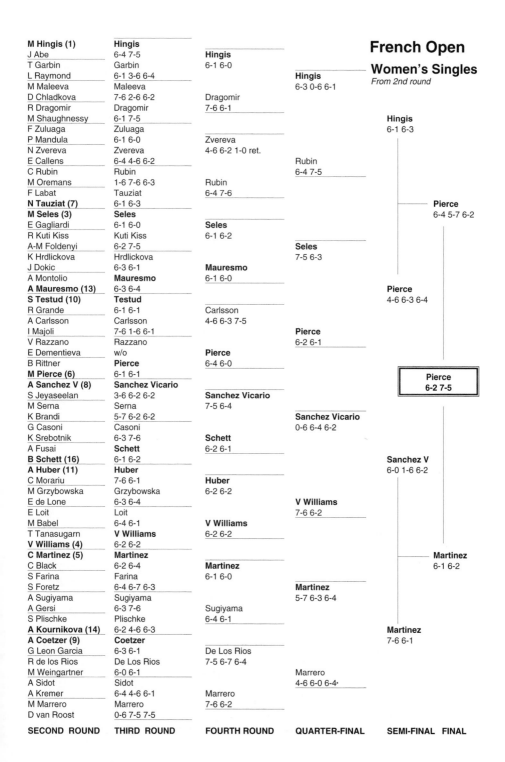

SECOND ROUND	THIRD ROUND	FOURTH ROUND	QUARTER-FINAL	SEMI-FINAL	FINAL
M Hingis (1)	Hingis				
J Abe	6-4 7-5	Hingis			
T Garbin	Garbin	6-1 6-0			
L Raymond	6-1 3-6 6-4		Hingis		
M Maleeva	Maleeva		6-3 0-6 6-1		
D Chladkova	7-6 2-6 6-2	Dragomir			
R Dragomir	Dragomir	7-6 6-1			
M Shaughnessy	6-1 7-5			Hingis	
F Zuluaga	Zuluaga			6-1 6-3	
P Mandula	6-1 6-0	Zvereva			
N Zvereva	Zvereva	4-6 6-2 1-0 ret.			
E Callens	6-4 4-6 6-2		Rubin		
C Rubin	Rubin		6-4 7-5		
M Oremans	1-6 7-6 6-3	Rubin			
F Labat	Tauziat	6-4 7-6			
N Tauziat (7)	6-1 6-3				Pierce
M Seles (3)	Seles				6-4 5-7 6-2
E Gagliardi	6-1 6-0	Seles			
R Kuti Kiss	Kuti Kiss	6-1 6-2			
A-M Foldenyi	6-2 7-5		Seles		
K Hrdlickova	Hrdlickova		7-5 6-3		
J Dokic	6-3 6-1	Mauresmo			
A Montolio	Mauresmo	6-1 6-0			
A Mauresmo (13)	6-3 6-4			Pierce	
S Testud (10)	Testud			4-6 6-3 6-4	
R Grande	6-1 6-1	Carlsson			
A Carlsson	Carlsson	4-6 6-3 7-5			
I Majoli	7-6 1-6 6-1		Pierce		
V Razzano	Razzano		6-2 6-1		
E Dementieva	w/o	Pierce			
B Rittner	Pierce	6-4 6-0			
M Pierce (6)	6-1 6-1				**Pierce**
A Sanchez V (8)	Sanchez Vicario				**6-2 7-5**
S Jeyaseelan	3-6 6-2 6-2	Sanchez Vicario			
M Serna	Serna	7-5 6-4			
K Brandi	5-7 6-2 6-2		Sanchez Vicario		
G Casoni	Casoni		0-6 6-4 6-2		
K Srebotnik	6-3 7-6	Schett			
A Fusai	Schett	6-2 6-1			
B Schett (16)	6-1 6-2			Sanchez V	
A Huber (11)	Huber			6-0 1-6 6-2	
C Morariu	7-6 6-1	Huber			
M Grzybowska	Grzybowska	6-2 6-2			
E de Lone	6-3 6-4		V Williams		
E Loit	Loit		7-6 6-2		
M Babel	6-4 6-1	V Williams			
T Tanasugarn	V Williams	6-2 6-2			
V Williams (4)	6-2 6-2				Martinez
C Martinez (5)	Martinez				6-1 6-2
C Black	6-2 6-4	Martinez			
S Farina	Farina	6-1 6-0			
S Foretz	6-4 6-7 6-3		Martinez		
A Sugiyama	Sugiyama		5-7 6-3 6-4		
A Gersi	6-3 7-6	Sugiyama			
S Plischke	Plischke	6-4 6-1			
A Kournikova (14)	6-2 4-6 6-3			Martinez	
A Coetzer (9)	Coetzer			7-6 6-1	
G Leon Garcia	6-3 6-1	De Los Rios			
R de los Rios	De Los Rios	7-5 6-7 6-4			
M Weingartner	6-0 6-1		Marrero		
A Sidot	Sidot		4-6 6-0 6-4·		
A Kremer	6-4 4-6 6-1	Marrero			
M Marrero	Marrero	7-6 6-2			
D van Roost	0-6 7-5 7-5				

US Open
Men's Singles
From 2nd round

SECOND ROUND

- A Agassi (1)
- A Clement
- H Arazi
- W Ferreira
- A Pavel
- A de Pasquale
- J Golmard
- N Lapentti (16)
- L Hewitt (9)
- J Boutter
- J Novak
- B Black
- M Rios
- J Knippschild
- C Woodruff
- T Enqvist (7)
- P Sampras (4)
- J Gimelstob
- A Calleri
- P Kralert
- R Schüttler
- T Haas
- Lee Hyung-Taik
- F Squillari (13)
- T Henman (11)
- F Gonzalez
- R Krajicek
- A Sa
- D Hrbaty
- K Alami
- A Popp
- Y Kafelnikov (5)
- M Safin (6)
- G Pozzi
- S Grosjean
- S Koubek
- R Federer
- D Nestor
- H Gumy
- J C Ferrero (12)
- N Kiefer (14)
- J Bjorkman
- S Schalken
- A Voinea
- M Mirnyi
- A Costa
- C Saulnier
- M Norman (3)
- A Corretja (8)
- M Rosset
- C Moya
- S Dosedel
- T Martin
- M Chang
- G Rusedski
- C Pioline (10)
- Philippoussis (15)
- J-M Gambil
- T Johansson
- G Blanco
- R Fromberg
- X Malisse
- J Stoltenberg
- W Arthurs

THIRD ROUND

- Clement 6-3 6-2 6-4
- Arazi 6-3 6-3 6-7 6-3
- Pavel 6-6-1 6-3 6-4
- Golmard 7-6 6-0 2-6 4-6 7-6
- Hewitt 7-6 6-4 6-4
- Novak 2-6 6-3 7-5 7-6
- Rios 4-6 6-4 6-4 7-5
- Enqvist 6-3 6-2 6-2
- Sampras 6-3 6-1 6-3
- Calleri 7-5 6-4 6-3
- Schüttler 7-6 6-2 6-4
- Lee 7-6 7-5 6-2
- Henman 6-3 6-4 6-2
- Krajicek 6-4 6-4 6-1
- Hrbaty 6-3 6-4 6-3
- Kafelnikov 6-7 6-4 6-4 6-4
- Safin 6-3 3-6 6-3 3-6 6-4
- Grosjean 6-2 6-2 4-6 6-2
- Federer 6-1 7-6 6-1
- Ferrero 1-6 6-3 6-7 6-2 6-3
- Kiefer 6-1 6-4 6-3
- Schalken 6-2 6-3 6-1
- Mirnyi 6-4 6-1 6-4
- Norman 6-3 6-4 6-3
- Corretja 6-3 7-6 6-3
- Moya 6-3 4-6 7-5 6-2
- Martin 6-4 6-2 6-4
- Pioline 6-7 3-6 6-4 7-6 6-3
- Gambil 6-4 6-4 6-4
- Johansson 6-4 7-6 6-2
- Fromberg 7-6 4-6 6-3 7-6
- Arthurs 2-6 7-6 6-4 6-4

FOURTH ROUND

- Clement 4-6 6-2 6-3 4-6 1-0 ret.
- Pavel 6-2 4-1 ret.
- Hewitt 6-3 6-3 6-3
- Enqvist 7-5 7-5 6-3
- Sampras 7-6 7-6 6-3
- Lee 6-2 3-6 6-4 6-4
- Krajicek 6-4 3-6 6-4 7-5 7-5
- Hrbaty 6-4 7-6 6-1
- Safin 6-4 7-6 1-6 3-6 7-6
- Ferrero 7-5 7-6 1-6 7-6
- Kiefer 7-5 6-3 6-4
- Norman 3-6 4-6 7-6 6-4 7-6
- Moya 7-6 6-3 4-6
- Martin 7-6 6-3 6-2
- Johansson 3-6 6-3 7-6 7-6
- Fromberg 7-6 1-6 6-3 3-6 6-3

QUARTER-FINAL

- Clement 3-6 6-2 6-1 7-6
- Hewitt 6-3 6-2 6-4
- Sampras 7-6 6-2 6-4
- Krajicek 7-6 6-4 6-1
- Safin 6-1 6-2 6-2
- Kiefer 6-2 6-7 6-1 6-3
- Martin 6-7 6-7 6-1 7-6 6-2
- Johansson 6-4 6-7 6-3 6-4

SEMI-FINAL

- Hewitt 6-2 6-4 6-3
- Sampras 7-6 6-4 7-6
- Sampras 4-6 7-6 6-4 6-2
- Safin 7-5 4-6 7-6 6-3
- Safin 6-3 7-6 7-6
- Martin 6-4 6-4 3-6 7-5

FINAL

- Safin 6-4 6-3 6-3

SECOND ROUND   THIRD ROUND   FOURTH ROUND   QUARTER-FINAL   SEMI-FINAL   FINAL

US Open
Women's Singles
From 2nd round

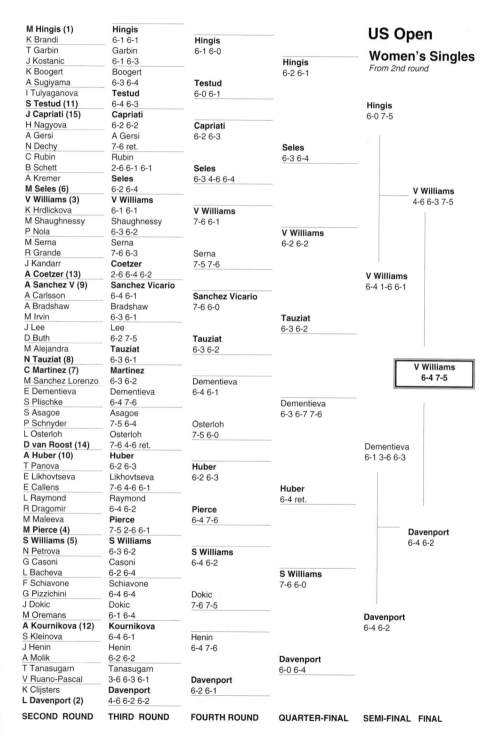

SECOND ROUND	THIRD ROUND	FOURTH ROUND	QUARTER-FINAL	SEMI-FINAL	FINAL

M Hingis (1)
K Brandi — Hingis 6-1 6-1
T Garbin — Garbin 6-1 6-3
J Kostanic — Boogert
K Boogert
A Sugiyama — Testud 6-3 6-4
I Tulyaganova
S Testud (11) — Testud 6-4 6-3

Hingis 6-1 6-0
Testud 6-0 6-1

Hingis 6-2 6-1

J Capriati (15) — Capriati 6-2 6-2
H Nagyova
A Gersi — A Gersi 7-6 ret.
N Dechy
C Rubin — Rubin 2-6 6-1 6-1
B Schett
A Kremer — Seles 6-2 6-4
M Seles (6)

Capriati 6-2 6-3
Seles 6-3 4-6 6-4

Seles 6-3 6-4

Hingis 6-0 7-5

V Williams (3) — V Williams 6-1 6-1
K Hrdlickova
M Shaughnessy — Shaughnessy 6-3 6-2
P Nola
M Serna — Serna 7-6 6-3
R Grande
J Kandarr — Coetzer 2-6 6-4 6-2
A Coetzer (13)

V Williams 7-6 6-1
Serna 7-5 7-6

V Williams 6-2 6-2

A Sanchez V (9) — Sanchez Vicario 6-4 6-1
A Carlsson
A Bradshaw — Bradshaw 6-3 6-1
M Irvin
J Lee — Lee 6-2 7-5
D Buth
M Alejandra — Tauziat 6-3 6-1
N Tauziat (8)

Sanchez Vicario 7-6 6-0
Tauziat 6-3 6-2

V Williams 6-4 1-6 6-1

V Williams 4-6 6-3 7-5

C Martinez (7) — Martinez 6-3 6-2
M Sanchez Lorenzo
E Dementieva — Dementieva 6-4 7-6
S Plischke
S Asagoe — Asagoe 7-5 6-4
P Schnyder
L Osterloh — Osterloh 7-6 4-6 ret.
D van Roost (14)

Dementieva 6-4 6-1
Osterloh 7-5 6-0

Tauziat 6-3 6-2

A Huber (10) — Huber 6-2 6-3
T Panova
E Likhovtseva — Likhovtseva 7-6 4-6 6-1
E Callens
L Raymond — Raymond 6-4 6-2
R Dragomir
M Maleeva — Pierce 7-5 2-6 6-1
M Pierce (4)

Huber 6-2 6-3
Pierce 6-4 7-6

Dementieva 6-3 6-7 7-6

V Williams 6-4 7-5

Dementieva 6-1 3-6 6-3

S Williams (5) — S Williams 6-3 6-2
N Petrova
G Casoni — Casoni 6-2 6-4
L Bacheva
F Schiavone — Schiavone 6-4 6-4
G Pizzichini
J Dokic — Dokic 6-1 6-4
M Oremans

S Williams 6-4 6-2
Dokic 7-6 7-5

Huber 6-4 ret.

A Kournikova (12) — Kournikova 6-4 6-1
S Kleinova
J Henin — Henin 6-2 6-2
A Molik
T Tanasugarn — Tanasugarn 3-6 6-3 6-1
V Ruano-Pascal
K Clijsters — Davenport 4-6 6-2 6-2
L Davenport (2)

Henin 6-4 7-6
Davenport 6-2 6-1

S Williams 7-6 6-0

Davenport 6-0 6-4

Davenport 6-4 6-2

Davenport 6-4 6-2

V Williams 6-4 7-5

339

ATP Tour 2000

Date	Tournament	Singles Final		Doubles Final		Prize Money (US$)
Jan 3 Jan 9	Qatar Mobile Open Qatar (H)	**Santoro** Schuttler	3-6 7-5 3-0 ret	**Knowles/Mirnyi** O'Brien/Palmer	6-3 6-4	$1,000,000
Jan 3 Jan 9	Goldflake Open Chennai (H)	**Golmard** Hantschk	6-3 6-7 6-3	**Boutter/Rochus** Panja/Prahlad	7-5 6-1	$450,000
Jan 3 Jan 9	AAPT Championships Adelaide (H)	**Hewitt** Enqvist	3-6 6-3 6-2	**Woodbridge/Woodforde** Hewitt/Stolle	6-4 6-2	$350,000
Jan 10 Jan 16	Heineken Open Auckland (H)	**Norman** Chang	3-6 6-3 7-5	**E Ferreira/Leach** Delaitre/Tarango	7-5 6-4	$350,000
Jan 10 Jan 16	adidas International Sydney (H)	**Hewitt** Stoltenberg	6-3 7-6	**Woodbridge/Woodforde** Hewitt/Stolle	7-5 6-4	$350,000
Jan 17 Jan 30	**Australian Open** Melbourne (H)	**Agassi** Kafelnikov	3-6 6-3 6-2 6-4	**E Ferreira/Leach** W Black/Kratzmann	6-4 3-6 6-3 3-6 18-16	$3,539,387
Feb 7 Feb 13	Duty Free Dubai Open Dubai (H)	**Kiefer** Ferrero	7-5 4-6 6-3	**Novak/Rikl** Koenig/Tramacchi	6-2 7-5	$1,000,000
Feb 7 Feb 13	Open 13 de Marseille Marseille (CI)	**Rosset** Federer	2-6 6-3 7-6	**Aspelin/Landsberg** Carrasco/Velasco	7-6 6-4	$500,000
Feb 7 Feb 13	Sybase Open San Jose, CA (CI)	**Philippoussis** Tillstrom	7-5 4-6 6-3	**Gambill/Humphries** Arnold/Taino	6-1 6-4	$375,000
Feb 14 Feb 20	Kroger/St Jude Internat'l Memphis, TN (HI)	**Larsson** B Black	6-2 1-6 6-3	**Gimelstob/Lareau** Grabb/Reneberg	6-2 6-4	$800,000
Feb 14 Feb 20	ABN Amro World Rotterdam (CI)	**Pioline** Henman	6-7 6-4 7-6	**Adams/De Jager** Henman/Kafelnikov	5-7 6-2 6-3	$850,000
Feb 21 Feb 27	AXA Cup London (CI)	**Rosset** Kafelnikov	6-4 6-4	**Adams/De Jager** Gambill/Humphries	6-3 6-7 7-6	$800,000
Feb 21 Feb 27	Abierto Mexicano Mexico City (CL)	**Chela** Puerta	6-4 7-6	**B Black/Johnson** Eltis/Rodriguez	6-3 7-5	$800,000
Feb 28 Mar 5	Copenhagen Open Denmark (CI)	**Vinciguerra** Larsson	6-3 7-6	**Damm/Prinosil** Bjorkman/Lareau	6-1 5-7 7-5	$375,000
Feb 28 Mar 5	Citrix Tennis Champs Delray Beach, FL (H)	**Koubek** Calatrava	6-1 4-6 6-4	**MacPhie/Zimonjic** Eagle/Florent	7-5 6-4	$350,000
Feb 28 Mar 5	Chevrolet Cup Santiago (CL)	**Kuerten** Puerta	7-6 6-3	**Kuerten/Prieto** Bale/Norval	6-3 6-4	$375,000
Mar 6 Mar 12	Cervaza Club Open Bogota (CL)	**Puerta** El Aynaoui	6-4 7-6	**Albano/Arnold** Balcells/Hadad	7-6 1-6 6-2	$375,000
Mar 6 Mar 12	Franklin Templeton Scottsdale, AZ (H)	**Hewitt** Henman	6-4 7-6	**Palmer/Reneberg** Galbraith/MacPherson	6-3 7-5	$375,000
Mar 13 Mar 19	Newsweek Champions Cup, Indian Wells CA (H)	**Corretja** Enqvist	6-4 6-4 6-3	**Palmer/O'Brien** Haarhuis/Stolle	6-4 7-6	$2,950,000
Mar 23 Apr 2	The Ericsson Open Miami, FL (H)	**Sampras** Kuerten	6-1 6-7 7-6 7-6	**Woodbridge/Woodforde** Damm/Hrbaty	6-3 6-4	$3,200,000

Dates	Tournament (Location)	Singles	Score	Doubles	Score	Prize
Apr 10 Apr 16	Galleryfurniture.com Challenge, Atlanta (CL)	**Ilie** Stoltenberg	6-3 7-5	**E Ferreira/Leach** Gimelstob/Knowles	6-3 6-4	$375,000
Apr 10 Apr 16	Grand Prix Hassan II Casablanca (CL)	**Vicente** Grosjean	6-4 4-6 7-6	**Clement/Grosjean** Burgsmuller/Painter	7-6 6-2	$350,000
Apr 10 Apr 16	Estoril Open Estoril (CL)	**Moya** Clavet	6-3 6-2	**Johnson/Norval** Adams/Eagle	6-4 7-5	$625,000
Apr 17 Apr 23	Monte Carlo Open Monaco (CL)	**Pioline** Hrbaty	6-4 7-6	**W Ferreira/Kafelnikov** Haarhuis/Stolle	6-3 2-6 6-1	$2,950,000
Apr 24 Apr 30	Open Seat Godo 2000 Barcelona (CL)	**Safin** Ferrero	6-3 6-3 6-4	**Kulti/Tillstrom** Haarhuis/Stolle	6-2 6-7 7-6	$1,000,000
May 1 May 7	Mallorca Open Mallorca (CL)	**Safin** Tillstrom	6-4 6-3	**Llodra/Nargiso** Martin/Vicente	7-6 7-6	$500,000
May 1 May 7	BMW Open Munich (CL)	**Squillari** Haas	6-4 6-4	**Adams/De Jager** Mirnyi/Zimonjic	6-4 6-4	$375,000
May 1 May 7	US Men's Clay Court Champs, Orlando (CL)	**Gonzalez** Massu	6-2 6-3	**Paes/Siemerink** Gimelstob/Lareau	6-3 6-4	$350,000
May 8 May 14	Italian Open Rome (CL)	**Norman** Kuerten	6-3 4-6 6-4 6-4	**Damm/Hrbaty** W Ferreira/Kafelnikov	6-4 4-6 6-3	$2,950,000
May 15 May 21	German Open Hamburg (CL)	**Kuerten** Safin	6-4 5-7 6-4 5-7 7-6	**Woodbridge/Woodforde** Arthurs/Stolle	6-7 6-4 6-3	$2,950,000
May 22 May 28	Peugeot World Team Düsseldorf (CL)	**Slovakia 3** Russia 0	*(Hrbaty/Kucera/Kroslak) (Kafelnikov/Safin)*			$1,900,000
May 21 May 28	Raiffeisen Grand Prix St Polton, Austria (CL)	**Pavel** Ilie	7-5 3-6 6-2	**Bhupathi/Kratzmann** Gaudenzi/Nargiso	7-6 6-7 6-4	$425,000
May 29 Jun 11	**French Open** Paris (CL)	**Kuerten** Norman	6-2 6-3 2-6 7-6	**Woodbridge/Woodforde** Haarhuis/Stolle	7-6 6-4	$4,526,942
June 12 June 18	Gerry Weber Open St Polton, Austria (CL)	**Prinosil** Krajicek	6-3 6-2	**Kulti/Tillstrom** Bhupathi/Prinosil	w/o	$1,000,000
Jun 12 Jun 18	Stella Artois Champs London (G)	**Hewitt** Sampras	6-4 6-4	**Woodbridge/Woodforde** Stark/Taino	6-7 6-3 7-6	$800,000
Jun 19 Jun 25	Heineken Trophy 's-Hertogenbosch (G)	**Rafter** Escude	6-1 6-3	**Damm/Suk** Haarhuis/Stolle	6-4 6-7 7-6	$400,000
Jun 19 Jun 25	The Nottingham Open Nottingham (G)	**Grosjean** B Black	7-6 6-3	**Johnson/Norval** E Ferreira/Leach	1-6 6-4 6-3	$375,000
Jun 14 Jun 20	Heineken Trophy Rosmalen, Ned (G)	**Rafter** Pavel	3-6 7-6 6-4	E Ferreira/Rikl Paes/Siemerink	Doubles final cancelled - rain	$500,000
Jun 14 Jun 20	Nottingham Open Nottingham (G)	**Pioline** Ullyett	6-3 7-5	**Galbraith/Gimelstob** Barnard/Haygarth	5-7 7-5 6-3	$350,000
Jun 21 Jul 4	**The Championships** Wimbledon (G)	**Sampras** Rafter	6-7 7-6 6-4 6-2	**Woodbridge/Woodforde** Haarhuis/Stolle	6-3 6-4 6-1	$5,614,685
Jul 5 Jul 11	Wideyes Swedish Open Bastad (CL)	**Norman** Vinciguerra	6-1 7-6	**Kulti/Tillstrom** Gaudenzi/Nargiso	4-6 6-2 6-3	$375,000
Jul 5 Jul 11	UBS Swiss Open Gstaad (CL)	**Corretja** Puerta	6-1 6-3	**Novak/Rikl** Golmard/Kohlmann	3-6 6-3 6-4	$600,000

Dates	Tournament	Singles Winner / Runner-up	Score	Doubles Winner / Runner-up	Score	Prize
Jul 5 Jul 11	Miller Lite Champs Rhode Island (G)	**Wessels** Knippschild	7-6 6-3	**Erlich/Levy** Spencer/Sprengelmeyer	7-6 7-5	$375,000
Jul 17 Jul 23	Mercedes Cup Stuttgart (CL)	**Squillari** Gaudio	6-2 3-6 4-6 6-4 6-2	**Novak/Rikl** Arnold/Johnson	5-7 6-2 6-3	$1,000,000
Jul 17 Jul 23	Energis Dutch Open Amsterdam (CL)	**Gustafsson** Sluiter	6-7 6-3 7-6 6-1	**Roitman/Schneiter** Kempes/Van Scheppingen	4-6 6-4 6-1	$400,000
Jul 17 Jul 23	Croatia Open Umag (CL)	**Rios** Puerta	7-6 4-6 6-3	**Lopez-Moron/Portas** Ljubicic/Zovko	6-1 7-6	$400,000
Jul 24 Jul 30	Generali Open Kitzbuhel, Austria (CL)	**Corretja** Alvarez	6-3 6-1 3-0 ret	**Albano/Suk** Eagle/Florent	6-3 3-6 6-3	$800,000
Jul 24 Jul 30	Mercedes-Benz Cup Los Angeles, CA (H)	**Chang** Gambill	6-7 6-3 ret	**Kilderry/Stolle** Gambill/Humphries	w/o	$375,000
Jul 24 Jul 30	San Marino Int San Marino (CL)	**Calatrava** Brugera	7-6 1-6 6-4	**Cibulec/Friedl** Etlis/Waite	7-6 7-5	$350,000
Jul 31 Aug 6	Masters Canada Toronto (H)	**Safin** Levy	6-2 6-3	**Lareau/Nestor** Eagle/Florent	6-3 7-6	$2,950,000
Aug 7 Aug 13	Masters Cincinnati Cincinnati (H)	**Enqvist** Henman	7-6 6-4	**Woodbridge/Woodforde** E Ferreira/Leach	7-6 6-4	$2,950,000
Aug 14 Aug 20	RCA Championships Indianapolis (H)	**Kuerten** Safin	3-6 7-6 7-6	**Hewitt/Stolle** Bjorkman/Mirnyi	6-2 3-6 6-3	$800,000
Aug 14 Aug 20	Legg Mason Classic Washington DC (H)	**Corretja** Agassi	6-2 6-3	**Agassi/Sargsian** O'Brien/Palmer	7-5 6-1	$800,000
Aug 21 Aug 27	Waldbaum's Hamlet Cup Long Island (H)	**Norman** Enqvist	6-3 5-7 7-5	**Stark/Ullyett** Gambill/Humphries	6-4 6-4	$375,000
Aug 28 Sep 10	**US Open** Flushing Meadow (H)	**Safin** Sampras	6-4 6-3 6-3	**Hewitt/Mirnyi** E Ferreira/Leach	6-4 5-7 7-6	$6,257,000
Sep 11 Sep 17	Gelsor Open Bucharest (CL)	**Balcells** Hantschk	6-4 3-6 7-6	**Martin/Ran** Bowen/Hood	7-6 6-1	$375,000
Sep 11 Sep 17	President's Cup Tashkent (H)	**Safin** Sanguinetti	6-3 6-4	**Gimelstob/Humphries** Barnard/Koenig	6-3 6-2	$525,000
Sep 19 Sep 28	Sydney Olympics Sydney (H)	**Kafelnikov RUS** Haas GER	7-6 3-6 6-2 4-6 6-3	**Corretja/Costa ESP** Adams/De Jager RSA	2-6 6-4 6-3	
Sep 25 Oct 1	Campionati di Sicilia Sicily (CL)	**Rochus** Nargiso	7-6 6-1	**Carbonnel/Garcial** Albano/Goellner	w/o	$375,000
Oct 2 Oct 8	Salem Open Hong Kong (H)	**Kiefer** Philippoussis	7-6 2-6 6-2	**W Black/Ullyett** Hrbaty/Prinosil	6-1 6-2	$375,000
Oct 9 Oct 15	Japan Open Tokyo (H)	**Schalken** Lapentti	6-4 3-6 6-1	**Bhupathi/Paes** Hill/Tarango	6-4 6-7 6-3	$800,000
Oct 9 Oct 15	CA Tennis Trophy Vienna (HI)	**Henman** Haas	6-4 6-4 6-4	**Kafelnikov/Zimonjic** Novak/Rikl	6-4 6-4	$800,000
Oct 16 Oct 22	Heineken Open Shanghai (CI)	**Norman** Schalken	6-4 4-6 6-3	**Haarhuis/Schalken** Pala/Vizner	6-2 3-6 6-4	$375,000
Oct 16 Oct 22	adidas Open Toulouse (CI)	**Corretja** Moya	6-3 6-2	**Boutter/Moya** Johnson/Norval	7-6 4-6 7-6	$400,000

Oct 23	Davidoff Swiss Indoors	**Enqvist**	6-2 4-6 7-6	**Johnson/Norval**	7-6 4-6 7-6	$1,000,000
Oct 29	Basel (CI)	Federer	1-6 6-1	Federer/Hrbaty		
Oct 23	Kremlin Cup 2000	**Kafelnikov**	6-2 7-5	**Bjorkman/Prinosil**	6-2 6-3	$1,000,000
Oct 29	Vienna (CI)	Prinosil		Novak/Rikl		
Oct 30	Masters Series Stuttgart	**W Ferreira**	7-6 3-6 6-7	**Novak/Rikl**	3-6 6-3 6-4	$2,950,000
Nov 5	Stuttgart (CI)	Hewitt	7-6 6-2	Johnson/Norval		
Nov 4	British Championships*	**Childs**	4-6 6-3 6-4	**Delgado/Lee**	6-3 3-6 6-3	
Nov 12	Telford (HI)	Hilton		Davidson/Freelove		
Nov 6	Grand Prix de Lyon	**Clement**	7-6 7-6	**Haarhuis/Stolle**	6-1 6-7 7-6	$800,000
Nov 12	Lyon (CI)	Rafter		Ljubicic/Waite		
Nov 6	St Petersburg Open	**Safin**	2-6 6-4 6-4	**Nestor/Ullyett**	7-6 7-5	$800,000
Nov 12	St Petersburg (CI)	Hrbaty		Shimada/Wakefield		
Nov 13	Masters Paris	**Safin**	3-6 7-6 3-6	**Kulti/Mirnyi**	6-4 7-5	$2,950,000
Nov 19	Paris (CI)	Philippoussis	7-6	Haarhuis/Nestor		
Nov 20	The Samsung Open	**Henman**	6-2 6-2	**Hill/Tarango**	6-3 7-5	$400,000
Nov 26	Brighton (CI)	Hrbaty		Goldstein/Thomas		
Nov 20	Scania Stockholm Open	**Johansson**	6-2 6-4	**Knowles/Nestor**	6-3 6-2	$800,000
Nov 26	Stockholm (CI)	Kafelnikov		Pala/Vizner		
Nov 23	Masters Cup	**Kuerten**	6-4 6-4 6-4			$3,700,000
Nov 28	Lisbon (HI)	Agassi				
Dec 8	Davis Cup	**Spain 3**	*(Costa/Ferrero/Balcells/Corretja)*			
Dec 10	Barcelona (CLI)	Australia 1	*(Hewitt/Rafter/Stolle/Woodforde)*			
Dec 11	ATP Doubles Champ's			**Johnson/Norval**	7-6 6-3 6-4	$750,000
Dec 17	Bangalore (H)			Bhupathi/Paes		

*Legend: H = Hard; CL = Clay; G = Grass; C = Carpet; I = Indoors   * Not ATP Tour event*

2000 ATP Champions Race

The Champions Race is based on performances in ATP tour events in the calendar year. This differs from the ATP Entry system which is a 12-month rolling system and is used to determine seedings for ATP events.

1	Gustavo Kuerten BRA	839
2	Marat Safin RUS	824
3	Pete Sampras USA	677
4	Magnus Norman SWE	622
5	Yevgeny Kafelnikov RUS	587
6	Andre Agassi USA	553
7	Lleyton Hewitt AUS	525
8	Alex Corretja ESP	495
9	Thomas Enqvist SWE	442
10	Tim Henman GBR	404
64	Greg Rusedski GBR	115
139	Jamie Delgado GBR	26
145	Arvind Parmar GBR	23
159	Barry Cowan GBR	19
184	Martin Lee GBR	11
257	Lee Childs GBR	3
270	Oliver Freelove GBR	2
301	Miles MacLagan GBR	1
306	Luke Milligan GBR	1

2000 Ranking Lists

Men
Entry List Final Standings

1	Gustavo Kuerten	BRA	4195
2	Marat Safin	RUS	4120
3	Pete Sampras	USA	3385
4	Magnus Norman	SWE	3110
5	Yevgeny Kafelnikov	RUS	2935
6	Andre Agassi	USA	2765
7	Lleyton Hewitt	AUS	2625
8	Alex Corretja	ESP	2475
9	Thomas Enqvist	SWE	2210
10	Tim Henman	GBR	2020
11	Mark Philippoussis	AUS	1865
12	Juan Carlos Ferrero	ESP	1840
13	Wayne Ferreira	RSA	1770
14	Franco Squillari	ARG	1598
15	Patrick Rafter	AUS	1535
16	Cedric Pioline	FRA	1520
17	Dominik Hrbaty	SVK	1395
18	Arnaud Clement	FRA	1360
19	Sebastien Grosjean	FRA	1325
20	Nicolas Kiefer	GER	1265
21	Mariano Puerta	ARG	1235
22	Sjeng Schalken	NED	1163
23	Tommy Haas	GER	1145
24	Nicolas Lapentti	ECU	1130
25	Younes El Aynaoui	MAR	1115
69	Greg Rusedski	GBR	575

Women
Final Standings

1	Martina Hingis	SUI	6180
2	Lindsay Davenport	USA	5022
3	Venus Williams	USA	3694
4	Monica Seles	USA	3255
5	Conchita Martinez	ESP	2795
6	Serena Williams	USA	2306
7	Mary Pierce	FRA	2162
8	Anna Kournikova	RUS	2158
9	Arantxa Sanchez-Vicario	ESP	2132
10	Nathalie Tauziat	FRA	1963
11	Amanda Coetzer	RSA	1798
12	Elena Dementieva	RUS	1774
13	Chandra Rubin	USA	1760
14	Jennifer Capriati	USA	1664
15	Julie Halard-Decugis	FRA	1436
16	Amelie Mauresmo	FRA	1426
17	Sandrine Testud	FRA	1414
18	Kim Clijsters	BEL	1398
19	Anke Huber	GER	1370
20	Amy Frazier	USA	1255
21	Elena Likhovtseva	RUS	1216
22	Magdalena Maleeva	BUL	1108
23	Barbara Schett	AUT	1065
24	Patty Schnyder	SUI	1056
25	Jelena Dokic	AUS	1054
111	Louise Latimer	GBR	296

2000 Prize Money

Men
Final Standings

		$
1	Gustavo Kuerten	4,701,610
2	Yevgeny Kafelnikov	3,755,599
3	Marat Safin	3,524,959
4	Thomas Enqvist	2,381,060
5	Pete Sampras	2,254,598
6	Andre Agassi	1,884,443
7	Magnus Norman	1,846,269
8	Lleyton Hewitt	1,642,572
9	Alex Corretja	1,530,062
10	Wayne Ferreira	1,237,864
11	Dominik Hrbaty	1,195,760
12	Nicolas Lapentti	1,126,305
13	Tim Henman	1,057,823
14	Cedric Pioline	888,789
15	Mark Philippoussis	839,567
16	Patrick Rafter	814,586
17	Juan Carlos Ferrero	812,636
18	Jiri Novak CZE	776,933
19	Max Mirnyi BLR	760,933
20	Franco Squillari	754,458
21	Arnaud Clement	671,815
22	Todd Woodbridge AUS	662,871
23	Sébastien Grosjean	655,280
24	Fabrice Santoro FRA	652,131
25	Mark Woodforde AUS	649,410

Women
Final Standings

		$
1	Martina Hingis	3,457,049
2	Lindsay Davenport	2,444,734
3	Venus Williams	2,074,150
4	Mary Pierce	1,208,018
5	Monica Seles	1,208,018
6	Conchita Martinez	1,067,930
7	Serena Williams	1,026,818
8	Anna Kournikova	984,930
9	Julie Halard-Decugis	879,570
10	Arantxa Sanchez-Vicario	819,689
11	Nathalie Tauziat	761,211
12	Al Sugiyama JPN	729,635
13	Elena Dementieva	613,627
14	Amanda Coetzer	593,357
15	Lisa Raymond USA	560,474
16	Sandrine Testud	547,384
17	Elena Likhovtseva	536,014
18	Chandra Rubin	528,020
19	Jennifer Capriati	488,861
20	Barbara Schett	470,987
21	Anke Huber	447,441
22	Jelena Dokic	429,880
23	Kim Clijsters	418,503
24	Amelie Mauresmo	365,074
25	Dominique Van Roost BEL	351,854

WTA Tour 2000

Date	Tournament	Singles Final		Doubles Final		Prize Money
Jan 3 Jan 9	Australian Hardcourt Gold Coast (HO)	**Talaja** Martinez	6-0 0-6 6-4	**Halard-Decugis/Kournikova** Appelmans/Grande	6-3 6-0	$180,000
Jan 3 Jan 9	ABS Bank Classic Auckland (HO)	**Kremer** Black	6-4 6-4	**Black/Fusai** Schwartz/Wartusch	3-6 6-3 6-4	$112,500
Jan 10 Jan 16	adidas International Sydney (HO)	**Mauresmo** Davenport	7-6 6-4	**Halard-Decugis/Sugiyama** Hingis/Pierce	6-0 6-3	$420,000
Jan 10 Jan 16	Tasmanian International Hobart (HO)	**Clijsters** Rubin	2-6 6-2 6-2	**Grande/Loit** Clijsters/Molik	6-2 2-6 6-3	$112,500
Jan 17 Jan 30	**Australian Open** Melbourne (HO)	**Davenport** Hingis	6-1 7-5	**Raymond/Stubbs** Hingis/Pierce	6-4 5-7 6-4	$3,539,387
Jan 31 Feb 6	Pan Pacific Open Tokyo (CI)	**Hingis** Testud	6-3 7-5	**Hingis/Pierce** Fusai/Tauziat	6-4 6-1	$1,050,000
Feb 7 Feb 13	Open Gaz de France Paris (HI)	**Tauziat** S Williams	7-5 6-2	**Halard-Decugis/Testud** Carlsson/Loit	3-6 6-3 6-4	$520,000
Feb 7 Feb 13	Copa Colsanitas Bogota, Colombia (CL)	**Wartusch** Garbin	4-6 6-1 6-4	**Montalvo/Suarez** Kuti Kis/Mandula	6-4 6-2	$142,500
Feb 14 Feb 20	Brazil Ladies Open Sao Paolo (CL)	**Kuti Kis** Suarez	4-6 6-4 7-5	**Montalvo/Suarez** Husrova/Labat	5-7 6-4 6-3	$142,500
Feb 14 Feb 20	Faber Grand Prix Hannover (HI)	**S Williams** Chladkova	6-1 6-1	**Carlsson/Zvereva** Farina/Habsudova	6-3 6-4	$520,000
Feb 21 Feb 27	IGA Superthrift Classic Oklahoma City (HO)	**Seles** Dechy	6-1 7-6	**Morariu/Po** Tanasugarn/Tatarkova	6-4 4-6 6-2	$1,300,000
Feb 28 Mar 5	State Farm Classic Scottsdale (HO)	Hingis Davenport	cancelled due to rain			$1,300,000
Mar 6 Mar 19	Newsweek Champions Cup, Indian Wells (HO)	**Davenport** Hingis	4-6 6-4 6-0	**Davenport/Morariu** Kournikova/Zvereva	6-2 6-3	$1,050,000
Mar 20 Apr 9	Ericsson Open Key Biscane FL (HO)	**Hingis** Davenport	6-3 6-2	**Halard-Decugis/Sugiyama** Arendt/Bollegraf	4-6 7-5 6-4	$1,950,000
Apr 10 Apr 16	Bausch & Lomb Amelia Island (HO)	**Seles** Martinez	6-3 6-2	**Hantuchova/Rampre** Osterloh/Washington	7-5 6-2	$142,500
Apr 10 Apr 16	Estoril Open Estoril (CL)	**Huber** Dechy	6-2 1-6 7-5	**Krizan/Srebotnik** Hopmans/Torrens-Valero	6-0 7-6	$180,000
Apr 17 Apr 23	Westel Budapest Open Budapest (CL)	**Garbin** Boogert	6-2 7-6	**Bacheva/Torrens-Valero** Kostanic/Nacuk	6-0 6-2	$142,500
Apr 17 Apr 23	Family Circle Cup Hilton Head (CL)	**Pierce** Sanchez-V	6-1 6-0	**Ruano-Pascual/Suarez** Martinez/Tarabini	7-5 6-3	$180,000
May 1 May 7	Betty Barclay Cup Hamburg (CL)	**Hingis** Sanchez-V	6-3 6-3	**Kournikova/Zvereva** Arendt/Bollegraf	6-7 6-2 6-4	$520,000
May 1 May 7	Croatian Open Bol (CL)	**Pisnik** Mauresmo	7-6 7-6	**Halard-Decugis/Morariu** Krizan/Srebotnik	6-2 6-2	$142,500

Dates	Tournament	Singles	Score	Doubles	Score	Prize
May 8 May 14	Warsaw Cup Poland (CL)	**Nagyova** Hopmans	2-6 6-4 7-5	**Garbin/Husarova** Tulyaganova/Zaporozhanova	6-3 6-1	$112,500
May 8 May 14	German Open Berlin (CL)	**Martinez** Coetzer	6-1 6-2	**Martinez/Sanchez-Vicario** Coetzer/Morariu	3-6 6-2 7-6	$1,050,000
May 15 May 21	Italian Open Rome (CL)	**Seles** Mauresmo	6-2 7-6	**Raymond/Stubbs** Sanchez-Vicario/Serna	6-3 4-6 6-3	$1,050,000
May 15 May 21	Mexx Sport Open Antwerp (CL)	**Coetzer** Torrens-Valero	4-6 6-2 6-3	**Appelmans/Clijsters** Hopkins/Rampre	6-1 6-1	$112,500
May 22 May 28	Strasbourg International Strasbourg (CL)	Talaja Kuti Kis	**cancelled**			$190,000
May 22 May 28	Madrid Open Madrid (CL)	**Leon Garcia** Zuluaga	6-1 6-3	**Raymond/Stubbs** Leon Garcia/S Lorenzo	6-1 6-3	$180,000
May 29 Jun 11	**French Open** Paris (CL)	**Pierce** Martinez	6-2 7-5	**Hingis/Pierce** Ruano Pascual/Suarez	6-2 6-4	$5,159,915
Jun 12 Jun 18	DFS Classic Birmingham (G)	**Raymond** Tanasugarn	6-2 6-7 6-4	**McQuillan/McShea** Black/Selyutina	6-3 7-6	$180,000
Jun 12 Jun 18	Tashkent Open Uzbekistan (HO)	**Tulyaganova** Schiavone	6-3 2-6 6-3	**Li Na/Li Ting** Tulyaganona/Zaporozhanova	3-6 6-3 6-4	$112,500
Jun 19 Jun 25	Direct Line Champ's Eastbourne (G)	**Halard-Decugis** Van Roost	7-6 6-4	**Sugiyama/Tauziat** Raymond/Stubbs	2-6 6-3 7-6	$520,000
Jun 14 July 20	Heineken Trophy 's-Hertogenbosch (G)	**Hingis** Dragomir	6-2 3-0 ret	**De Lone/Pratt** Barclay/Habsudova	7-6 4-3 ret	$180,000
Jun 26 July 9	**The Championships** Wimbledon (G)	**V Williams** Davenport	6-3 7-6	**S Williams/V Williams** Halard-Decugis/Sugiyama	6-3 6-2	$5,614,685
July 10 July 16	Torneo Internazionale Palermo (CL)	**Nagyova** Nola	6-3 7-5	**Farina/Grande** Dragomir/Ruano Pascual	6-4 0-6 7-6	$142,500
July 10 July 16	Uniqa Grand Prix Porschach, Austria (CL)	**Schett** Schnyder	5-7 6-4 6-4	**Montalvo/Suarez** Schett/Schnyder	7-6 6-1	$180,000
July 17 July 23	Idea Prokom Open Sopot, Poland (CL)	**Huber** Leon Garcia	7-6 6-3	**Ruano Pascual/Suarez** Carlsson/Grande	7-5 6-1	$142,500
July 17 July 23	Sanex Trophy (CL) Knokke-Heist, Belgium	**Smashnova** Van Roost	6-2 7-5	**Casoni/Tulyaganova** Barclay/Dyrberg	2-6 6-4 6-4	$112,500
July 24 July 30	Bank of the West Classic Stanford (HO)	**V Williams** Davenport	6-1 6-4	**Rubin/Testud** Black/Frazier	6-4 6-4	$520,000
July 31 Aug 6	Acura Classic San Diego (HO)	**V Williams** Seles	6-0 6-7 6-3	**Raymond/Stubbs** Davenport/Kournikova	4-6 6-3 7-6	$520,000
Aug 7 Aug 13	estyle.com Classic Los Angeles (HO)	**S Williams** Davenport	4-6 6-4 7-6	**Callens/Van Roost** Po/Sidot	6-2 7-5	$520,000
Aug 14 Aug 20	du Maurier Open Toronto (HO)	**Hingis** S Williams	0-6 6-3 3-0 ret	**Hingis/Tauziat** Halard-Decugis/Sugiyama	6-3 3-6 6-4	$1,050,000
Aug 21 Aug 27	Pilot Pen International New Haven (HO)	**V Williams** Seles	6-2 6-4	**Halard-Decugis/Sugiyama** Ruano Pascual/Suarez	6-4 5-7 6-2	$520,000
Aug 28 Sep 10	**US Open** Flushing Meadow (HO)	**V Williams** Davenport	6-4 7-5	**Halard-Decugis/Sugiyama** Black/Likhovtseva	6-0 1-6 6-1	$6,257,000

Date	Tournament	Singles		Doubles		Prize
Sep 19 Sep 28	Sydney Olympics Sydney (HO)	**V Williams USA** 6-2 6-4 Dementieva RUS		**V Williams/S Williams USA** 6-1 6-1 Boogert/Oremans NED		
Sep 25 Sep 31	Seat Open Luxembourg (CI)	**Capriati** Maleeva	4-6 6-1 6-4	**Fusai/Tauziat** Bacheva/Torrens-Valero	6-3 7-6	$180,000
Oct 2 Oct 8	Toyota Princess' Cup Tokyo (HI)	**S Williams** J Halard-Decugis	7-5 6-1	**Halard-Decugis/Sugiyama** 6-0 6-2 Miyagi/Suarez		$520,000
Oct 2 Oct 8	Porsche Grand Prix Filderstadt (HI)	**Hingis** Clijsters	6-0 6-3	**Hingis/Kournikova** Sanchez-Vicario/Schett	6-4 6-2	$520,000
Oct 9 Oct 15	Japan Open Tokyo (HI)	**Halard-Decugis** 5-7 7-5 6-4 Frazier		**Halard-Decugis/Morariu** Krizan/Srebotnik	6-1 6-2	$142,500
Oct 9 Oct 15	Swisscom Challenge Zurich (HI)	**Hingis** Davenport	6-4 4-6 7-5	**Hingis/Kournikova** Po/Sidot	6-3 6-4	$1,050,000
Oct 16 Oct 22	Generali Open Linz (HI)	**Davenport** V Williams	6-4 3-6 6-2	**Mauresmo/Rubin** Sugiyama/Tauziat	6-4 6-4	$520,000
Oct 16 Oct 22	Heineken Open Shanghai (CI)	**Shaughnessy** 7-6 7-5 Tulyaganova		**Osterloh/Tanasugarn** Grande/Shaughnessy	7-5 6-1	$1,050,000
Oct 25 Oct 31	Generali Open Linz (CI)	**Pierce** Testud	7-6 6-1	**Spirlea/Vis** Krizan/Neiland	6-4 6-3	$520,000
Oct 23 Oct 29	Ladies Kremlin Cup Moscow (HI)	**Hingis** Kournikova	6-3 6-1	**Halard-Decugis/Sugiyama** Hingis/Kournikova		$520,000
Oct 23 Oct 29	Eurotel Slovak Indoor Bratislava (HI)	**Bedanova** Oremans	6-1 5-7 6-3	**Habsudova/Hantuchova** Mandula/Wartusch	w/o	$520,000
Oct 30 Nov 5	Sparkassen Cup Leipzig (HI)	**Clijsters** Likhovtseva	7-6 4-6 6-4	**Sanchez-Vicario/Sidot** 6-7 7-5 6-3 Clijsters/Courtois		$112,500
Oct 30 Nov 5	Challenge Bell Quebec (HI)	**Rubin** Capriati	6-4 6-2	**Pratt/Shaughnessy** Callens/Po	6-3 6-4	$520,000
Nov 6 Nov 12	Advanta Championships Philadelphia (HO)	**Davenport** Hingis	7-6 6-4	**Hingis/Kournikova** Raymond/Stubbs	6-2 7-5	$520,000
Nov 6 Nov 12	Wismilak International Kuala Lumpur (HI)	**Nagyova** Majoli	6-4 6-2	**Nagyova/Plischke** Horn/Webb	6-4 7-6	$520,000
Nov 13 Nov 19	Volvo Women's Open Pattaya City (HO)	**Kremer** Panova	6-1 6-4	**Basuki/Vis** Krizan/Srebotnik	6-3 6-3	$520,000
Nov 13 Nov 29	Chase Championships New York (CI)	**Seles** Dementieva	6-1 7-6	**Hingis/Kournikova** Arendt/Bollegraf	6-2 6-3	$2,000,000

Legend: HO = Hard Outdoors; CL = Clay; G = Grass; HI = Hard Indoors; CI = Carpet Indoors

Davis Cup by NEC

World Group First Round
Ostrava   Feb 4-6
Czech Republic bt Great Britain 4-1
Slava Dosedel lost to Tim Henman
7-6 (7-4) 7-5 1-6 5-7 3-6
Jiri Novak beat Jamie Delgado
6-4 7-6 (7-4) 6-3
Novak/David Rikl beat Neil Broad/Henman
6-4 6-2 6-2
Novak bt Henman
6-4 6-2 6-2
Bohdan Ulihrach bt Delgado
5-7 7-5 6-4

World Group Qualifying
Wimbledon   July 14-16
Great Britain lost to Ecuador 2-3
G Rusedski lost to N Lapentti 3-6 7-6 (7-3) 5-7 6-4 5-7
TIm Henman bt Luis Adrian Morejon 6-2 6-1 6-4
Henman/A Parmar lost to G Lapentti/N Lapentti
3-6 5-7 3-6
Henman bt N Lapentti 6-1 6-4 6-4
Parmar lost to G Lapentti 6-4 6-3 1-6 3-6 3-6

World Group - other matches
First Round
Feb 4-6
Zimbabwe lost to USA 2-3
Spain bt Italy 4-1
Russia bt Belgium 4-1
Slovakia bt Austria 3-2
Brazil bt France 4-1
Germany bt Netherlands 4-1
Switzerland lost to Australia 2-3

Quarter-finals
Apr 7-9
USA bt Czech Republic 3-2
Spain bt Russia 4-1
Brazil bt Slovakia 4-1
Australia bt Germany 3-2

Semi-finals
July 14-16
Australia bt Brazil 5-0
P Rafter bt G Kuerten; L Hewitt bt F Meligeni
S Stolle/M Woodforde bt Kuerten/J Oncins
Hewitt bt A Sa; Rafter bt Meligeni

July 21-23
Spain bt USA 5-0
A Costa bt T Martin; A Corretja bt J-M Gambill
J Balcells/Corretja bt Martin/C Woodruff
JC Ferrero bt V Spadea; Balcells bt Gambill

Final
Barcelona   Dec 8-10
Spain bt Australia 3-1
A Costa lost to L Hewitt 1-6 6-2 4-6 4-6; JC Ferrero bt P Rafter 6-7 (4-7) 7-6 (7-2) 6-2 3-1 ret; J Balcells/A Corretja bt S Stolle/M Woodforde 6-4 6-4 6-4; Ferrero bt Hewitt 6-2 7-6 (7-5) 4-6 6-4; Rafter v Corretja not played

Fed Cup

Final
Las Vegas Nov 27-28
United States bt Spain 5-0
L Davenport bt A Sanchez-Vicario; M Seles bt C Martinez; L Davenport bt C Martinez 6-1 6-2; J Capriati bt A Sanchez-Vicario 6-1 1-0 ret; Capriati/Raymond bt Serna/Ruano-Pascual 4-6 6-4 6-2

Triathlon

S imon Lessing's words were to prove prophetic "You can't win every time," he said, after coming second at the 1999 world championships. Having waited so long for Triathlon at the Olympics, Lessing was perhaps past his prime when the moment came and he failed to win there as well.

All the talk before Sydney was of Lessing. For Great Britain he was to be the first favourite of the games, the best possible chance of an early gold medal. But the ominous signs were there. Lessing had dropped out of the World Cup race at Lausanne in August, which should have constituted his Olympic warm-up, and though he had taken his 1999 world championship defeat by Dimitry Gaag philosophically, he had lost nevertheless.

Jason Queally had already trumped Lessing to Great Britain's first gold of the games, when the former South African lined up for Sunday's race. Lessing and Australia's Craig Walton did much of the work, particularly during the cycle leg, but work alone does not win prizes, and Lessing was well off the pace in the run, usually his strongest element.

Runners win prizes and Canadian Simon Whitfield broke away to take the title by 80 metres from the German Stephan Vukovic. The Czech, Jan Rehula, only took the bronze, but his ecstasy was such you could have believed that he had won the Sydney Lottery too. Lessing came ninth and Tim Don, the second Briton home, was four seconds back in tenth. For Lessing it was a massive disappointment, for Don, by contrast, it was cause for some celebration. The 1998 world junior champion was in only his second season at senior level and the referee's son can only get better.

Britain's third representative, Andrew Johns, was struck down with an illness that sapped his strength before the event. It was a shame because he had won both the European Championships and the Lausanne World Cup race in the months preceding the Games and looked to be peaking at the right time.

For the Australians, the triathlon was about the only misery suffered by the nation all that fortnight. Their first man home was Miles Stewart in sixth and the women, threatening a clean sweep of the medals, came away with just the one - Michellie Jones's silver. She was accompanied on the podium by the Swiss pair of Magali Messmer, who won bronze and Brigitte McMahon who made history by winning the first Olympic medal in the sport. The British women had no luck. Both Sian Brice and Michelle Dillon (and one of the favourites, Carol Montgomery of Canada) were eliminated through crashes on the cycle stage and Steph Forrester came just 15th.

Bike crashes apart, the Sydney races passed off smoothly. The same cannot be said for the world championships, held in Perth in April. Something was noticeably wrong when the times for the women's run came through. The winner, Nicole Hackett, was one of a number of women who had broken the men's world record for 10,000m. Well, they would have done, except the course was 2km short, the runners directed through only four laps instead of five. Officials at first tried to deny it, which made them look even more ridiculous.

World Championships

Perth, Australia   April 30
1.5km swim, 40km bike, 10km run (women ran only 8k)

Men

1	Olivier Marceau	FRA	1:51:40
2	Peter Robertson	AUS	1:51:54
3	Craig Walton	AUS	1:51:58
14	Andrew Johns	GBR	1:52:36

Women

1	Nicole Hackett	AUS	1:54:43
2	Carole Montgomery	CAN	1:54:50
3	Michellie Jones	AUS	1:55:25
30	Sian Brice	GBR	1:57:29

Junior Men

1	Frederic Belaubre	FRA	1:57:32
2	Leonid Ivanov	RUS	1:57:57
3	Dimitriv Smurov	KZK	1:58:30
32	Eliot Chalifour	GBR	2:06:13

Junior Women

1	Anneliese Heard	GBR	2:10:06
2	Melanie Mitchell	AUS	2:11:28
3	Nicola Spirig	SUI	2:12:19
12	Catherine Hare	GBR	2:16:30
13	Kerrie Cloke	GBR	2:16:43
15	Lesley Paterson	GBR	2:18:27

Long Distance World Championships

Nice, France   June 18
4km swim, 120km bike, 30km run

Men

1	Peter Sandvang	DEN	6:22:01
2	Cyrille Neveu	FRA	6:23:17
3	Francois Chabaud	FRA	6:26:49

Women

1	Isabelle Mouthon	FRA	7:04:48
2	Natascha Badmann	SUI	7:05:44
3	Daniella Locarno	ITA	7:11:43
7	Helen Purdy	GBR	7:23:03

Winter World Championships

Jaca, Spain   Mar 4
10km run, 30km cross-country ski, 10km run

Men

1	Nicolas Lebrun	FRA	2:12:30
2	Christoph Mauch	SUI	2:14:57
3	Juan Apilluelo	ESP	2:15:47

Women

1	Karin Möbes	SUI	2:42:39
2	Gabi Pauli	GER	2:43:38
3	Sigrid Lang	GER	2:45:54

World Rankings

Men

As at March 17 2001

1	Hamish Carter	NZL	1532
2	Dimitry Gaag	KZK	1520
3	Chris Hill	AUS	1254
4	Andrew Johns	GBR	1157
5	Greg Bennett	AUS	1018
6	Gilberto Gonzalez	VEN	877
7	Craig Walton	AUS	850
8	Chris McCormack	AUS	848
9	Simon Lessing	GBR	844
10	Jan Rehula	CZE	808
11	Shane Reed	NZL	804
12	Miles Stewart	AUS	693
13	Simon Whitfield	CAN	631
14	Greg Welch	AUS	624
15	Vladimir Polikarpenko	UKR	604
16	Martin Krnavek	CZE	601
17	Reto Hug	SUI	595
18	Jamie Hunt	NZL	585
19	Craig Watson	NZL	543
19	Olivier Marceau	FRA	543
23	Tim Don	GBR	470
30	Marc Jenkins	GBR	424
73	Richard Allen	GBR	243
96=	Stuart Hayes	GBR	173
99=	Richard Stannard	GBR	166
107	Craig Ball	GBR	150
128=	Craig Twigg	GBR	116
131=	Spencer Smith	GBR	115

Women

1	Michellie Jones	AUS	1858
2	Emma Carney	AUS	1328
3	Loretta Harrop	AUS	1283
4	Barbara Lindquist	USA	1232
5	Steph Forrester	GBR	1062
6	Siri Lindley	USA	1009
7	Rina Hill	NZL	971
8	Jackie Gallagher	AUS	969
9	Magali Messmer	SUI	924
10	Nicole Hackett	AUS	864
11	Isabelle Mouthon	FRA	777
11	Haruna Hosoya	JPN	777
13	Carole Montgomery	CAN	771
14	Jennifer Guttierrez	USA	701
15	Sharon Donnelly	CAN	699
16	Mieke Suys	BEL	689
17	Joanne King	AUS	686
18	Anja Dittmer	GER	647
19	Sian Brice	GBR	644
20	Marie Overbye	DEN	608
26	Michelle Dillon	GBR	538
48	Leanda Cave	GBR	332
58	Annaliese Heard	GBR	269
70=	Julie Dibens	GBR	196
75=	Heather Williams	GBR	185
113	Annie Emmerson	GBR	92

World Cup
Round 1
Rio de Janeiro, Brazil   *Mar 26*
Men

1	Dimitry Gaag	KZK	1:44:30
2	Simon Whitfield	CAN	1:44:55
3	Andry Glushchenko	UKR	1:44:57
20	Marc Jenkins	GBR	1:48:18
25	Richard Allen	GBR	1:48:42
26	Richard Stannard	GBR	1:48:49

Women

1	Carol Montgomery	CAN	1:57:37
2	Steph Forrester	GBR	1:58:42
3	Carla Moreno	BRA	1:59:00
4	Sian Brice	GBR	1:59:09
19	Heather Williams	GBR	2:03:08

Round 2
Big Island, Hawaii   *Apri 1*
Men

1	Hamish Carter	NZL	1:51:58
2	Rob Barel	NED	1:53:06
3	Levi Maxwell	AUS	1:53:42
10	Andrew Johns	GBR	1:54:21

Women

1	Michellie Jones	AUS	2:02:04
2	Anja Dittmer	GER	2:02:42
3	Joanna Zeiger	USA	2:02:52
26	Heather Williams	GBR	2:08:19

Round 3
Ihigaki, Japan   *April 9*
Men

1	Courtney Atkinson	AUS	1:48:06
2	Johannes Enzenhofer	AUT	1:48:15
3	Takumi Obara	JPN	1:48:18
7	Craig Ball	GBR	1:48:43
19	Richard Allen	GBR	1:50:25
25	Richard Stannard	GBR	1:51:35

Women

1	Rina Hill	AUS	2:01:40
2	Haruna Hosoya	JPN	2:02:26
3	Akiko Hirao	JPN	2:02:29
4	Steph Forrester	GBR	2:02:34

Round 4
Sydney, Australia   *April 16*
Men

1	Peter Robertson	AUS	1:49:32
2	Stefan Vuckovic	GER	1:49:58
3	Volodymyr Polikarpenko	UKR	1:50:09

Women

1	Michellie Jones	AUS	2:02:30
2	Bridgit McMahon	SUI	2:02:40
3	Magali Messmer	SUI	2:02:45

Round 5
Toronto   *July 8*
Men

1	Simon Lessing	GBR	1:46:41
2	Gilberto Gonzalez	VEN	1:46:56
3	Dimitry Gaag	KAZ	1:47:02

Women

1	Carol Montgomery	CAN	1:56:20
2	Sharon Donnelly	CAN	1:57:37
3	Jennifer Gutierrez	USA	1:57:42

Round 6
Tokyo   *July 16*
Men

1	Chris Hill	AUS	1:48:23
2	Miles Stewart	AUS	1:48:57
3	Kris Gemmel	NZL	1:49:34

Women

1	Rina Hill	NZL	2:03:03
2	Yulie Koumegawa	JPN	2:03:18
3	Pilar Hidalgo	ESP	2:03:32

Round 7
Corner Brook, Newfoundland   *July 30*
Men

1	Craig Walton	AUS	1:55:54
2	Simon Whitfield	CAN	1:56:06
3	Gilberto Gonzalez	VEN	1:56:14
12	Marc Jenkins	GBR	2:00:09
17	Craig Ball	GBR	2:04:49

Women

1	Barb Lindquist	USA	2:10:56
2	Joanna Zeiger	USA	2:12:32
3	Marie Overbye	DEN	2:12:42
7	Michelle Dillon	GBR	2:15:25

Round 8
Tizaujvaros, Hungary   *Aug 6*
Men

1	Martin Krnavek	CZE	1:45:29
2	Shane Reed	NZL	1:46:04
3	Csaba Kuttor	HUN	1:46:10
12	Richard Stannard	GBR	1:49:05

Women

1	Loretta Harrop	AUS	1:54:42
2	Siri Lindley	USA	1:55:18
3	Steph Forrester	GBR	1:56:53
13	Heather Williams	GBR	1:59:32
17	Annaliese Heard	GBR	2:01:12
18	Michelle Dillon	GBR	2:01:24

Round 9
Lausanne   *Aug 12*
Men

1	Andrew Johns	GBR	1:52:36
2	Hamish Carter	NZL	1:52:40
3	Craig Watson	NZL	1:52.45
23	Richard Stannard	GBR	1:59:58
27	Stuart Hayes	GBR	2:01:18

Women

1	Siri Lindley	USA	2:05:23
2	Brigitte McMahon	SUI	2:05:58
3	Michellie Jones	AUS	2:06:33

Round 10
Cancun, Mexico   *Nov 5*
Men

1	Oscar Galindez	ARG	1:44:12
2	Matthew Reed	NZL	1:44:52
3	Hector Llanos	ESP	1:45:00
16	Richard Stannard	GBR	1:46:49

Women

1	Siri Lindley	USA	1:57:52
2	Ana Burgos	ESP	1:58:35
3	Pilar Hildago	ESP	2:00:21

World Cup Final Standings

Men

1. Dimitry Gaag KZK; 2. Hamish Carter NZL;
3. Simon Whitfield CAN; 15. Andrew Johns GBR

Women

1. Michellie Jones AUS; 2. Carole Montgomery CAN;
3. Siri Lindley USA; 6. Steph Forrester GBR

European Championships

Stein, Netherlands   July 8

Men

1	Andrew Johns	GBR	1:54:31
2	Reto Hug	SUI	1:54:35
3	Erik van der Linden	NED	1:54:40
6	Tim Don	GBR	1:54:55
8	Richard Allen	GBR	1:55:19
22	Marc Jenkins	GBR	1:56:56
24	Richard Stannard	GBR	1:57:12

Women

1	Kathleen Smet	BEL	2:06:49
2	Magali Messmer	SUI	2:07:23
3	Julie Dibens	GBR	2:08:54
5	Sian Brice	GBR	2:09:21
9	Michelle Dillon	GBR	2:10:52
14	Anneliese Heard	GBR	2:11:33
22	Annie Emmerson	GBR	2:16:11
30	Heather Williams	GBR	2:30:52

Hawaii Ironman

Kona, Hawaii   Oct 14
2.4m swim, 112m bike, 26.2m run

Men

1	Peter Reid	CAN	8:21:00
2	Tim DeBoom	USA	8:23:09

Women

1	Natascha Badmann	SUI	9:26:16
2	Lori Bowden	CAN	9:29:04

The London Triathlon

Docklands

Men

1	Simon Lessing	GBR	1:50:35
2	Stuart Hayes	GBR	1:53:44
3	Richard Stannard	GBR	1:55:05

Women

1	Leanda Cave	GBR	2:03:44
2	Henrietta Freeman	GBR	2:05:12
3	Annie Emmerson	GBR	2:12:05

Duathlon

World Championship

Calais, France   Oct 8
10km run, 40km cycle, 5km run

Men

1	Benny Vansteelant	BEL	1:46:05
2	Yann Million	FRA	1:47:11
3	Huub Maas	NED	1:47:40
30	Paul Lowe	GBR	1:52:05
32	Wayne Smith	GBR	1:52:53

Women

1	Steph Forrester	GBR	2:02:02
2	Siri Lindley	USA	2:02:04
3	Christane Soeder	GER	2:02:14
4	Fiona Lothian	GBR	2:02:21
11	Helen Purdy	GBR	2:07:04

World Long Distance Championship

Pretoria, South Africa   Nov 12

Men

1	Benny Vansteelant	BEL	2:32:38
2	Felix Martinez	ESP	2:36:14
3	Marino Vanhoenacker	BEL	2:36:51
24	Wayne Smith	GBR	2:53:54

Women

1	Edwige Pitel	FRA	2:53:00
2	Dolorita Fuchs-Gerber	SUI	2:55:45
3	Irma Heeren	NED	2:56:15

Volleyball

Men's World League 2000

		Pts	Matches W	L	Sets W	L	Ratio	Points W	L	Ratio
Pool A										
1	Yugoslavia	21	9	3	32	15	2.133	1116	1013	1.102
2	Italy	20	8	4	28	23	1.217	1159	1128	1.027
3	Argentina	16	4	8	23	28	0.821	1136	1171	0.987
4	Canada	15	3	9	15	32	0.469	1007	1126	0.894
Pool B										
1	Russia	21	9	3	31	14	2.214	1073	987	1.087
2	France	19	7	5	24	21	1.143	1027	1040	0.988
3	Cuba	17	5	7	21	24	0.875	1074	1063	1.010
4	Netherlands	15	3	9	13	30	0.433	944	1028	0.918
Pool C										
1	USA	22	10	2	31	15	2.067	1104	999	1.105
2	Brazil	20	8	4	28	16	1.750	1048	969	1.082
3	Poland	17	5	7	21	24	0.875	1020	1036	0.985
4	Spain	13	1	11	9	34	0.265	871	1039	0.838
Final Six										
1	Italy	9	4	1	13	8	1.625	459	452	1.015
2	Russia	8	3	2	13	7	1.857	452	413	1.094
3	Yugoslavia	8	3	2	11	8	1.375	440	403	1.092
4	Brazil	7	2	3	8	11	0.727	404	420	0.962
5	Netherlands	7	2	3	7	12	0.583	409	435	0.940
6	USA	6	1	4	8	14	0.571	474	515	0.920

Third-fourth place play-off
Brazil bt Yugoslavia 3-0 (25-19 25-21 25-21)

Final
Italy bt Russia 3-2 (25-22 18-25 20-25 25-21 15-13)

Women's World Grand Prix 2000

Preliminary Round

		Pts	Matches W	L	Sets W	L	Ratio	Points W	L	Ratio
1	Cuba	18	9	0	27	4	6.750	746	607	1.229
2	Russia	17	8	1	24	10	2.400	770	675	1.141
3	Brazil	16	7	2	23	8	2.875	744	658	1.131
4	China	13	4	5	18	17	1.059	777	756	1.028
5	USA	13	4	5	15	19	0.789	745	775	0.961
6	Korea	12	3	6	15	20	0.750	753	772	0.975
7	Italy	10	1	8	6	26	0.231	631	753	0.838
8	Japan	9	0	9	3	27	0.111	574	744	0.772

Classification matches fifth-eighth
USA bt Japan 3-0
Korea bt Italy 3-1
Seventh-eighth place match
Italy bt Japan 3-1

5th-6th place match
Korea bt USA 3-0
Classification matches first-fourth
Russia bt Brazil 3-0
Cuba bt China 3-1

Third-fourth place play-off
Brazil bt China 3-1

Final
Cuba bt Russia 3-1
21-25 25-15 25-23 25-21

Weightlifting

European Championships
Sofia   *Apr 22-30*

*The scores shown in kgs are for snatch/clean & jerk,
followed by the total. Where totals are equal, higher
ranking is given to the lifter with the lighter body weight*

Men

56kg
1	Halil Mutlu TUR	135/165	300.0
2	Ivan Ivanov BUL	125/157.5	282.5
3	Adrian Jugau ROM	125/157.5	282.5

62kg
1	Nikolay Penchalov CRO	147.5/177.5	325.0
2	Sevdalin Minchev BUL	145/177.5	322.5
3	Naim Suleymanoglu TUR	140/170	310.0

69kg
1	Sergei Lavrenov BLR	150/187.5	337.5
2	Georgi Markov BUL	152.5/185	337.5
3	Yasin Arslan TUR	150/175	325.0

77kg
1	Zlatan Vanev BUL	165/207.5	372.5
2	Plamen Jeliazkov BUL	162.5/202.5	365.0
3	Ilirian Suli ALB	165/195	360.0
15	Stewart Cruickshank GBR	130/160	290.0

85kg
1	George Asanidze GEO	180/210	390.0
2	Georgi Gardev BUL	175/210	385.0
3	Iouri Mishkovets RUS	170/205	375.0

94kg
1	Szymon Kolecki POL	180/232.5	412.5
2	Vadim Vacarcuic MDA	170/225	395.0
3	Bunyami Sudas TUR	175/217.5	392.5
13	Anthony Arthur GBR	150/180	330.0
14	Andrew Callard GBR	140/185	325.0

105kg
1	Metin Kadir BUL	185/230	415.0
2	Robert Dolega POL	182.5/227.5	410.0
3	Evgeny Shichliannikov RUS	185/225	410.0
12	Thomas Yule GBR	165/197.5	362.5
18	Karl Grant GBR	150/190	340.0

+105kg
1	Ashot Danielyan ARM	205/252.5	457.5
2	Ronny Weller GER	205/250	455.0
3	Viktors Scerbatis LAT	200/245	445.0
13	Giles Greenwood GBR	165/200	365.0

Women

48kg
1	Donka Mincheva BUL	85/102.5	187.5
2	Eva Giganti ITA	75/95	170.0
3	Olena Zinovyeva UKR	75/95	170.0

53kg
1	Izabela Rifatova BUL	82.5/105	187.5
2	Estafania Juan ESP	80/102.5	182.5
3	Siyka Stoeva BUL	82.5/95	177.5

58kg
1	Neli Jankova BUL	87.5/115	202.5
2	Aleksandra Klejnmowska	87.5/110	197.5
3	Natalya Skakun UKR	85/110	195.0
6	Michaela Breeze GBR	82.5/105	187.5
13	Heather Allison GBR	65/80	145.0

63kg
1	Valentina Popova RUS	102.5/125	227.5
2	Josefa Perez ESP	85/105	190.0
3	Veronika Buranova CZE	80/102.5	182.5

69kg
1	Milena Trendafilova BUL	105/127.5	232.5
2	Daniela Kerkelova BUL	100/127.5	227.5
3	Irina Kasimova RUS	97.5/125	222.5
9	Suzanne Blackburn GBR	70/87.5	157.5

75kg
1	Svetlana Habirova RUS	107.5/132.5	240.0
2	Venera Mannanova RUS	107.5/125	232.5
3	Beata Prei POL	97.5/130	227.5
13	Rachael Clark GBR	85/102.5	187.5

+75kg
1	Vita Rudenok UKR	112.5/137.5	250.0
2	Monique Riesterer GER	110/135	245.0
3	Albina Khomich RUS	110/127.5	237.5

Wrestling

The story goes that when Aleksandr Karelin had a fridge delivered to his block of flats he carried it up the stairs to the eighth floor because there was no lift. The true story is that Karelin only carried the fridge up because he thought it might get damaged if he threw it up. Yes, Karelin is strong. So strong that folk in Siberia are convinced that he is the strongest man in the world; so strong that he did not lose a fight for 17 years; so strong that when he was beaten in the Olympic final even his opponent said much the same. "It was like pushing against a horse," said Rulon Gardner, omitting to mention that it was a shire horse with a loaded dray coming full pelt at him down a steep hill that he was likening it to.

Yet it happened. For all that, Karelin lost. Juan Antonio Samaranch was ready (as he had been for Redgrave), Russia was ready, the wrestling world was ready, and Karelin lost. The moment of his defeat was so innocuous, that it hardly merited a whisper from the packed hall. True, only 10 at most of the 4,000 would have had the faintest inkling of the significance when Karelin lost his grip on the farmer's boy from Nebraska in the second period. The broken handhold counted as a point to the American and Karelin was behind in a competition for the first time in anyone's memory. Karelin now had to make the pace, had to attempt to throw his arms around the 54-inch frame of the 29-year-old and lever him off the ground for the famed and feared reverse body lift that Gardner and the American team were expecting.

Karelin heaved and hauled and the fridge would have gone tumbling all the way down the eight flights of stairs, but Gardner was more mobile than the fridge. Not much more, but enough. He kept his centre of gravity as low as possible; drifted back perhaps to the days at school when he was taunted for his weight (doing him fine now); to the days on the farm humping 100lbs of hay that built muscle upon that fat; to the nights with coaches Dan Chandler, Steve Fraser and Rob Hermann studying videos of the Siberian Bear and laying the seeds for this moment. And when it was over and the gold medal round his neck, the bulbous American said that he, "Didn't know how big a deal it was." But he was kidding himself. In Siberia, where the temperature drops to minus-50 celsius and the permafrost crunches underfoot when you run, Gardner is a magician. The man who beat the strongest man on Earth can only be the strongest man on Earth.

The Life and Times of

Aleksandr Karelin

Born
September 19th 1967
Novosibirsk, Siberia
(1,750 miles east of Moscow)

Weight at Birth
15lbs

Weight at 33-years-old
290lb

Wrestling Good Times
Thirteen European Titles
Nine World Titles
Three Olympic Titles

Wrestling Bad Times
Losing to Fellow Russian
Igor Rostorotsky in 1987
(His only other senior defeat)

Interests
Poetry, Ballet, Politics,
Siberia, Milk and Fridges

Freestyle

European Championships
Budapest   *Apr 6-9*

Men
54kg
1	Alexander Zacharuk	UKR
2	Leonid Tchoutchounov	RUS
3	Ivan Dyorev	BUL

58kg
1	Mourad Ramazanov	RUS
2	Arif Kama	TUR
3	Evgeny Buslowich	UKR

63kg
1	Mourat Umakhanov	RUS
2	Sergey Smal	BLR
3	Serafim Barzakov	BUL
14	John Melling	GBR

69kg
1	Emzari Bedeneishvili	GEO
2	Sergey Demtchenko	BLR
3	Nicolai Paslari	BUL

76kg
1	Bouvaisa Saitiev	RUS
2	Adem Bereket	TUR
3	Gurami Michedlidse	GEO
19	Thomas Coppola	GBR

85kg
1	Adam Saitiev	RUS
2	Beibulat Musaev	BLR
3	Gabor Kapuvari	HUN
18	Joseph Luigi Bianco	GBR

97kg
1	Sagid Murtasaliev	RUS
2	Arawat Sabejew	GER
3	Vadim Tasoev	UKR

130kg
1	Marek Garmulewicz	POL
2	David Musulbes	RUS
3	Sven Thiele	GER

Greco-Roman

European Championships
Moscow   *April 14-16*

Men
54kg
1	Marian Sandu	ROM
2	Boris Ambartsoumov	RUS
3	Alfred Ter-Mkrtchyan	GER

58kg
1	Istvan Majoros	HUN
2	Armen Nazaryan	BUL
3	Rifat Yildiz	GER

63kg
1	Warterez Samurgashev	RUS
2	Beat Motzer	SUI
3	Vitali Shuk	BLR

69kg
1	Alexei Glushov	RUS
2	Csaba Hirbik	HUN
3	Movses Karapetyan	ARM

76kg
1	Viatcheslav Makarenko	BLR
2	David Manukyan	UKR
3	Mourat Kardanov	RUS

85kg
1	Martin Lidberg	SWE
2	Andrey Batura	BLR
3	Alexander Menshikov	RUS

97kg
1	Sergey Lishtvan	BLR
2	Georgi Koguashvili	RUS
3	Mehmet Oezal	TUR

130kg
1	Alexander Karelin	RUS
2	Sergey Mureiko	BUL
3	Bardos Mihaly Deak	HUN

Extras

Aussie Rules

Grand Final
Melbourne CG   Sep 2
Essendon 19:21 **135**
Melbourne 11:9   **75**

Gaelic Football

All-Ireland Final
Croke Park   Sep 24
Kerry 0:14 (14)   Galway 0:14 (14)

Replay
Croke Park   Oct 7
Kerry 0:17 (17)   Galway 1:10 (13)

Greyhound Racing

Derby Final 480m
Wimbledon   June 2
1 (2) Rapid Ranger   7/4F   -
2 (3) Rackenthall Jet   7/1   3½
3 (4) Greefield Deal   14/1   2
4 (1) Deerfield Sunset   2/1   Nk
5 (5) Smoking Bullet   8/1   6¾
6 (6) Farloe Club   3/1   2¼
Time: 28.71; Trainer: C Lister

Grand National
Wimbledon   Mar 28
1 (5) Tuttles Minister   7/2   -
2 (6) Catunda Leonardo 13/8F   Sh
3 (3) Apple Rambler   16/1   Nk
4 (2) Lenson Eddie   9/2   2¼
5 (1) Silbury Willow   7/1   3½
6 (4) Kennyswell Smoke   3/1   5½
Time: 28.36; Trainer: T Foster

Handball

Euro Championships
Men
Zagreb, Croatia Jan 30
Sweden 32   Russia 31
Women
Bucharest, Romania, Dec 17
Hungary 32   Ukraine 30

Hurling

All-Ireland Final
Croke Park   Sep 10
Kilkenny 5:15   Offaly 1:14

Karate

World Championships
Munich, Germany   Oct 12-15
Men's Kata
Team
1. Japan; 2. France; 3. Spain
Individual
1. Michael Millon FRA

Men's Kumite
Team
1. France; 2. Germany; 3. England
Individual
-60kg: 1. Cecil Boulesnane FRA
-55kg: 1. Lazaar Boskovic GER
-70kg: 1. Gustaff Lefevre CRO
-75kg: 1. Ivan Leal Reglero ESP
-80kg: 1. Daniel Sabanovic NED
+80kg: 1. M Aly Ndiaye SEN
Open: 1. Christophe Pinna FRA

Women's Kata
Team
1.France; 2. Japan; 3. Italy
Individual
1. Atsuko Wakai JPN

Women's Kumite
Team
1. France; 2. Spain; 3. Japan
Individual
-53kg: 1. Hiromi Hasama JPN
-60kg: 1. Alexandra Witteborn GER
+70kg: 1. Natsu Yamaguchi JPN
Open: 1. Yildiz Aras TUR

Polo

Gold Cup
Geebung 13   Black Bears 8

Racquets

British Open
Men's Singles
James Male bt Peter Brake 5-1

Men's Doubles
Male/Hue-Williams bt
Barker/Robinson 4-2

Real Tennis

World Championship
Men's Singles
Robert Fahey AUS
bt Wayne Davies GBR
7-0

Shooting

European Shotgun Championships
Montecatini, Italy   July 3-9
Men
Double Trap
1. Vassili Mossin RUS 178
4. Richard Faulds GBR 173
15. Charles Dean GBR
24. John Bellamy GBR
Skeet
1. Pietro Genga ITA 147
26= Drew Harvey &
Philip Musson GBR
32. John Davison GBR
Trap
1 Joao Rebelo POR 141
12= Peter Boden & Kevin Gill GBR

Women
Double Trap
1. Susanne Kiermayer GER 136
17. Anita North GBR
19. Bernadette Mallinson GBR
Skeet
1. Maarit Lepomaki FIN 93
10. Pinky Le Grelle GBR
11. Elena Little GBR
15. Susan Bramley GBR
Trap
1. Anne Focan BEL 91
12. Anita North GBR
25=. Lesley Goddard & Sarah
Gibbins GBR

Taekwondo

Euro Championships
Patra, Greece   May 4-7
Men
-54kg: Juan Antonio Ramos ESP
-58kg: Michalis Mouroutsos GRE
-62kg: Erol Denk GER
-67kg: Gerogios Ionas GRE
-72kg: Acharki Aziz GER
-78kg: Ayclin Bekir TUR
-84kg: Faissal Ebnosalib GER
+84kg: Bahri Tanrikucu TUR

Women
-47kg: Aseneio Belen ESP
-51kg: Svetlana Noskova RUS
-55kg: Tosun Hamide Bikcin TUR
-59kg: Virginia Lourens NED
-63kg: Tasbakan Aysenir TUR
-67kg: E Nazarova RUS
-72kg: Elli Mistakidou GRE
+72kg: M Konyahina RUS

Water Skiing

World Cup
Final Standings
British only shown in top 10
Men's Jump
1 Freddy Krueger USA 625
2 Jaret Llewellyn CAN 580
3 Wade Cox USA 490
7 Jason Steels GBR 215
Men's Slalom
1 Andy Mapple GBR 600
2 Chris Parrish USA 490
3 Wade Cox USA 455
5 Jodi Fisher GBR 316
7 Matthew Southam GBR 203
9 Glenn Campbell GBR 180

Women's Jump
1 Toni Neville AUS 725
2 Emma Sheers AUS 685
3 Britta Grebe-Llewellyn AUT 485
5 Sarah Gatty Saunt GBR 245
Women's Slalom
1 Kristi Overton-Johnson USA 800
2 Toni Neville AUS 560
3 Karen Truelove USA 425
6 Sarah Gatty Saunt GBR 299

Euro Championships
Moscow, Russia   Aug 4-8
Team
1. Belarus 978.8; 2. France 866.6;
3. Italy 786.7; 4. Great Britain 634.0
Men
Final Overall
1 Oleg Deviatovski BLR 2385.2
2 Thomas Asher GBR 2252.8
3 Patrizio Buzzots ITA 222.5
9 Jason Seels GBR 1960.4

Jump
1 Christopher Duverger FRA 60.8m
2 Markus Vouk AUT 59.7m
3 Jason Seels GBR 59.6m
Slalom
1 Glenn Campbell GBR 5@10.75m
2 William Asher GBR 3@10.75m
3 Patrice Martin FRA 3@10.75m
10 Jason Seels GBR 2.5@14.25m
Tricks
1 Nicolas Le Forestier FRA 10990
2 Aleksei Zernosek BLR 9560
3 Oleg Deviatovski BLR 9530
5 Thomas Asher GBR 9010

Women
Final Overall
1 Anais Amade FRA 2414.8
2 Marina Mosti ITA 2373.5
3 Sarah Gatty Saunt GBR 2356.0
Jump
1 Britta Grebe Llewellyn AUT 49.1m
2 Angeliki Andriopoulou GRE 47.8m
3 Marina Mosti ITA 47.4m
9 Sarah Gatty Saunt GBR 44.2m
Slalom
1 Geraldine Jamin FRA 2.5@11.25m
2 Sarah G Saunt GBR 4.5@12.0m
3 Irene Reinstaller ITA 2.5@11.25m
Tricks
1 Frederique Savin FRA 6820
2 Marina Basinskaya BLR 6750
3 Marina Mosti ITA 6480
8 Sarah Gatty Saunt GBR 5810

World Cableski Championships
Piestany   Sept 1-3
Team
1. Belarus; 2. Germany
3. Austria; 6. Great Britain
Men
Overall
1 Alexei Zernossek BLR
2 Andreas Pape GER
3 Michael Madar GER
Slalom
1 Alois Krenn AUT 2@11.25m
2 Alexander Graw GER 2@12m
3 Marc-Andre Meier GER 5@13m
Tricks
1 Alexei Zernossek BLR 9040
2 Jouri Rykter BLR 8210
3 Maksim Semavine BLR 7150
Jump
1 Manfred Hintringer AUT 54.1m
2 Daniel Resl CZE 52.5m
3 Jochen Luers GER 52.2m
Women
Overall
1 Julia Meier-Gromyko BLR
2 Irina Turets BLR
3 Olga Pavlova BLR
8 Lisa Adams GBR

Slalom
1 Lisa Adams GBR 1@10.25m
2 Irina Turets BLR 4@12m
3 Julia Meier-Gromyko BLR 4@12m
Tricks
1 Julia Meier-Gromyko BLR 6890
2 Irina Turets BLR 6820
3 Tatjana Avdonina BLR 6770
Jump
1 Britta Grebe-Llewellyn AUT 40.6m
2 Julia Meier-Gromyko BLR 40.3m
3 Olga Pavlova BLR 37.5m

World Barefoot Championships
Fergus Falls, Minnesota Aug 22-27
Team
1 USA 8717.30
2 Australia7622.34
3 South Africa 6515.90
9 Great Britain 4425.14
    Small/Meehan/Wilsdon
Overall
1 Ron Scarpa USA 2897
2 Keith St Onge USA 2853
3 Lane "Dawg" Bowers USA 2811
9 David Small GBR 2314
Jump
1 Massimiliano Colosio ITA 25.60m
2 Brett Sands AUS 25.40m
3 Lane Bowers USA 25.2m
Slalom
1 Jason Lee USA
2 Keith St Onge USA
3 Jon Kretchman USA
Tricks
1 Ron Scarpa USA 6480
2 Lane Bowers USA 6690
3 Keith St Onge USA 6490
Women
Overall
1 Nadine De Villiers RSA 3000
2 Rachel George USA 2321
3 Gizella Halasz AUS 2318
Jump
1 Nadine De Villiers RSA 18.60m
2 Rachel George USA 13m
3 Elisa Valerio ITA 12.40m
Slalom
1 Nadine De Villiers RSA
2 Rachel George USA
3 Gizella Halasz AUS
Tricks
1 Nadine De Villiers RSA 2650
2 Gizella Halasz AUS 2220
3 Rachel George USA 2080

The Archive

A sport by sport listing of past champions and records

AMERICAN FOOTBALL

SUPER BOWL

Season		Winner	Runner-up	Score	Venue	Attendance	MVP	Team-Pos
I	15.1.67	Green Bay	Kansas City	35-10	Los Angeles	61,946	Bart Starr (GB-QB)	
II	14.1.68	Green Bay	Oakland	33-14	Miami	75,546	Bart Starr (GB-QB)	
III	12.1.69	New York Jets	Baltimore	16-7	Miami	75,389	Joe Namath (NY-QB)	
IV	11.1.70	Kansas City	Minnesota	23-7	New Orleans	80,582	Len Dawson (KC-QB)	
V	17.1.71	Baltimore	Dallas	16-13	Miami	79,204	Chuck Howley (D-LB)	
VI	16.1.72	Dallas	Miami	24-3	New Orleans	81,023	Roger Staubach (D-QB)	
VII	14.1.73	Miami	Washington	14-7	Los Angeles	90,182	Jake Scott (M-S)	
VIII	31.1.74	Miami	Minnesota	24-7	Houston	71,882	Larry Csonka (M-RB)	
IX	12.1.75	Pittsburgh	Minnesota	16-6	New Orleans	80,997	Franco Harris (P-RB)	
X	18.1.76	Pittsburgh	Dallas	21-7	Miami	80,187	Lynn Swann (P-WR)	
XI	9.1.77	Oakland	Minnesota	32-14	Pasadena	103,438	Fred Biletnikoff (O-WR)	
XII	15.1.78	Dallas	Denver	27-10	New Orleans	75,583	White & Martin (D-DT/DE)	
XIII	21.1.79	Pittsburgh	Dallas	35-31	Miami	79,484	Terry Bradshaw (P-QB)	
XIV	20.1.80	Pittsburgh	Los Angeles	31-19	Pasadena	103,985	Terry Bradshaw (P-QB)	
XV	25.1.81	Oakland	Philadelphia	27-10	New Orleans	76,135	Jim Plunkett (O-QB)	
XVI	24.1.82	San Francisco	Cincinnati	26-21	Pontiac	81,270	Joe Montana (SF-QB)	
XVII	30.1.83	Washington	Miami	27-17	Pasadena	103,667	John Riggins (W-RB)	
XVIII	22.1.84	LA Raiders	Washington	38-9	Tampa	72,920	Marcus Allen (LA-RB)	
XIX	20.1.85	San Francisco	Miami	38-16	Stanford	84,059	Joe Montana (SF-QB)	
XX	26.1.86	Chicago	New England	46-10	New Orleans	73,818	Richard Dent (CH-DE)	
XXI	25.1.87	New York Gts	Denver	39-20	Pasadena	101,063	Phil Simms (NY-QB)	
XXII	13.1.88	Washington	Denver	42-10	San Diego	73,302	Doug Williams (W-QB)	
XXIII	22.1.89	San Francisco	Cincinnati	20-16	Miami	75,129	Jerry Rice (SF-WR)	
XXIV	28.1.90	San Francisco	Denver	55-10	New Orleans	72,919	Joe Montana (SF-QB)	
XXV	27.1.91	New York Gts	Buffalo	20-19	Tampa	73,813	Ottis Anderson (NY-RB)	
XXVI	26.1.92	Washington	Buffalo	37-24	Minneapolis	63,130	Mark Rypien (W-QB)	
XXVII	31.1.93	Dallas	Buffalo	52-17	Pasadena	98,374	Troy Aikman (D-QB)	
XXVIII	30.1.94	Dallas	Buffalo	30-13	Atlanta	72,817	Emmitt Smith (D-RB)	
XXIX	29.1.95	San Francisco	San Diego	49-28	Miami	74,107	Steve Young (S-QB)	
XXX	28.1.96	Dallas	Pittsburgh	27-17	Arizona	76,347	Larry Brown (D-CB)	
XXXI	26.1.97	Green Bay	New England	35-21	New Orleans	72,301	Desmond Howard (GB-WR)	
XXXII	25.1.98	Denver	Green Bay	31-24	San Diego	68,912	Terrell Davis (D-RB)	
XXXIII	31.1.99	Denver	Atlanta	34-19	Miami	74,803	John Elway (D-QB)	
XXXIV	30.1.00	St Louis	Tennessee	23-16	Atlanta	72,625	Kurt Warner (S-QB)	

WORLD BOWL

1991	London Monarchs 21	Barcelona Dragons 0	Wembley Stadium, London
1992	Sacramento Surge 21	Orlando Thunder 17	Olympic Stadium, Montreal
1995	Frankfurt Galaxy 26	Amsterdam Admirals 22	Olympic Stadium, Amsterdam
1996	Scottish Claymores 32	Frankfurt Galaxy 27	Murrayfield, Edinburgh
1997	Barcelona Dragons 38	Rhein Fire 24	Olympic Stadium, Barcelona
1998	Rhein Fire 34	Frankfurt Galaxy 10	Waldstadion, Frankfurt
1999	Frankfurt Galaxy 38	Barcelona Dragons 24	Rheinstadion, Dusseldorf
2000	Rhein Fire 13	Scottish Claymores 10	Waldstadion, Frankfurt

ANGLING

WORLD FRESHWATER CHAMPIONS

Year	Individual	Team
1957	Mandelli ITA	Italy
1958	Garroit BEL	Belgium
1959	Robert Tesse FRA	France
1960	Robert Tesse FRA	Belgium
1961	Ramon Legogue FRA	East Germany
1962	Raimondo Tedasco ITA	Italy
1963	William Lane ENG	France
1964	Joseph Fontanet FRA	France
1965	Robert Tesse FRA	Romania
1966	Henri Guiheneuf FRA	France
1967	Jacques Isenbaert BEL	Belgium
1968	Gunter Grebenstein FRG	France
1969	Robin Harris ENG	Netherlands
1970	Marcel Van den Eynde BEL	Belgium
1971	Dino Bassi ITA	Italy
1972	Hubert Levels HOL	France
1973	Pierre Michiels BEL	Belgium
1974	Aribert Richter FRG	France
1975	Ian Heaps ENG	France
1976	Dino Bassi ITA	Italy
1977	Jean Mainil BEL	Luxembourg
1978	Jean-Pierre Fourgeat FRA	France
1979	Gerard Heulard FRA	France
1980	Wolf-Rudiger Kremkus FRG	West Germany
1981	Dave Thomas ENG	France
1982	Kevin Ashurst ENG	Netherlands
1983	Wolf-Rudiger Kremkus FRG	Belgium
1984	Bobby Smithers IRE	Luxembourg
1985	Dave Roper ENG	England
1986	Lud Wever HOL	Italy
1987	Clive Branson WAL	England
1988	Jean-Pierre Fougeat FRA	England
1989	Tom Pickering ENG	Wales
1990	Bob Nudd ENG	France
1991	Bob Nudd ENG	England
1992	David Wesson AUS	Italy
1993	Mario Barros POR	Italy
1994	Bob Nudd ENG	England
1995	Paul Jean FRA	France
1996	Alan Scotthorne ENG	Italy
1997	Alan Scotthorne ENG	Italy
1998	Alan Scotthorne ENG	England
1999	Bob Nudd ENG	Spain
2000	Jacopo Falsini ITA	Italy

NATIONAL LEAGUE CHAMPIONS

The National League began in 1906, results from 1960

Year	Individual	Team
1960	K Smith	King's Lynn
1961	J Blakey	Coventry
1962	V Baker	Lincoln
1963	R Sims	Northampton N
1964	C Burch	Kidderminster
1965	D Burr	Rugby
1966	R Jarvis	Boston
1967	E Townsin	Derby Railway
1968	D Groom	Leighton Buzz
1969	R Else	Stoke
1970	B Lakey	Cambridge
1971	R Harris	Leicester
1972	P Coles	Birmingham
1973	A Wright	Grimsby
1974	P Anderson	Leicester
1975	M Hoad-Reddick	Birmingham
1976	N Wells	Birmingham
1977	R Foster	Coventry
1978	D Harris	Coleshill
1979	M Cullen	Barnsley
1980	P Burrell	Notts
1981	D Steer	Essex
1982	A Mayer	Rotherham
1983	D Howl	Notts
1984	C Gregg	Coleshill
1985	B Oliver	ABC
1986	M Stabler	I Walton, Staffs
1987	J Robinson	Nottingham
1988	S Hall	Redditch
1989	B Wickens	Reading
1990	S Cheetham	Trevs
1991	P Hargreaves	I Walton
1992	K Gregory	Nottingham
1993	S Canty	Liverpool
1994	S Ellis	Highfield
1995	S Tyler	Barnsley
1996	R Mitchell	Scunthorpe
1997	A Whiteley	Barnsley
1998	M Runacres	Southport
1999	G Frith	Redditch
2000	T Flannery	Daiwa Gordon League

WORLD FLY FISHING CHAMPIONS

Year	Individual	Team
1981	C Wittkamp HOL	Netherlands
1982	Viktor Diez ESP	Italy
1983	S Fernandez ESP	Italy
1984	Tony Pawson ENG	Italy
1985	Leslaw Frasik POL	Poland
1986	Slivoj Svoboda TCH	Italy
1987	Brian Leadbetter ENG	England
1988	John Pawson ENG	England
1989	Wladislaw Trzebuinia POL	Poland
1990	Franciszek Szajnik POL	Czechoslovakia
1991	Brian Leadbetter ENG	New Zealand
1992	Pierluigi Coccito ITA	Italy
1993	Russell Owen WAL	England
1994	Pascal Cognard FRA	Czech Republic
1995	Jeremy Herrmann ENG	England
1996	Pierluigi Coccito ITA	Czech Republic
1997	Pascal Cognard FRA	France
1998	Tomas Starychfojtu CZE	Czech Republic
1999	Ross Stewart AUS	Australia
2000	Pascal Cognard FRA	France

ARCHERY

TARGET WORLD CHAMPIONS (OLYMPIC)

Year	Men's Individual	Women's Individual	Men's Team	Women's Team
1931	Michael Sawicki POL	Janina Kurkowska POL	France	Poland
1932	Laurent Reth BEL	Janina Kurkowska POL	Poland	Poland
1933	Don Mackenzie USA	Janina Kurkowska POL	Belgium	Poland
1934	Henry Kjellson SWE	Janina Kurkowska POL	Sweden	Poland
1935	Adrien Van Kolen BEL	Ina Catani SWE	Czechoslovakia	Great Britain
1936	Emil Heilborn SWE	Janina Kurkowska POL	Czechoslovakia	Poland
1937	Georges DeRons BEL	Ingo Simon GBR	Poland	Great Britain
1938	Frantisek Hadas TCH	Nora Weston Martyr GBR	Czechoslovakia	Poland
1939	Roger Beday FRA	Janina Kurkowska POL	France	Poland
1946	Einar Tang-Holbek DEN	Nilla de Wharton Burr GBR	Denmark	Great Britain
1947	Hans Deutgen SWE	Janina Kurkowska POL	Czechoslovakia	Denmark
1948	Hans Deutgen SWE	Nilla de Wharton Burr GBR	Sweden	Czechoslovakia
1949	Hans Deutgen SWE	Barbara Waterhouse GBR	Czechoslovakia	Great Britain
1950	Hans Deutgen SWE	Jean Lee USA	Denmark	Finland
1952	Stellan Andersson SWE	Jean Lee USA	Sweden	USA
1953	Bror Lundgren SWE	Jean Richards USA	Sweden	Finland
1955	Nils Andersson SWE	Katarzyna Wisniowska POL	Sweden	Great Britain
1957	Oziek Smathers USA	Carole Meinhart USA	USA	USA
1958	Stig Thysell SWE	Sigrid Johansson SWE	Finland	USA
1959	James Caspers USA	Ann Weber Hoyt USA	USA	USA
1961	Joe Thornton USA	Nancy Vonderheide USA	USA	USA
1963	Charles Sandin USA	Victoria Cook USA	USA	USA
1965	Matti Haikonen FIN	Maire Lindholm FIN	USA	USA
1967	Ray Rogers USA	Maria Maczynska POL	USA	Poland
1969	Hardy Ward USA	Dorothy Lidstone CAN	USA	Soviet Union
1971	John Williams USA	Emma Gapchenko URS	USA	Poland
1973	Viktor Sidoruk URS	Linda Myers USA	USA	Soviet Union
1975	Darrell Pace USA	Zebiniso Rustamova URS	USA	Soviet Union
1977	Richard McKinney USA	Luann Ryon USA	USA	USA
1979	Darrell Pace USA	Kim Jin-Ho KOR	USA	Korea
1981	Kyosti Laasonen FIN	Natalya Butuzova URS	USA	Soviet Union
1983	Richard McKinney USA	Kim Jin-Ho KOR	USA	Korea
1985	Richard McKinney USA	Irina Soldatova URS	Korea	Soviet Union
1987	Vladimir Echeev URS	Ma Xiaojun CHN	West Germany	Soviet Union
1989	Stanislaw Zabrodsky URS	Kim Soo-Nyung KOR	Korea	Korea
1991	Simon Fairweather AUS	Kim Soo-Nyung KOR	Korea	Korea
1993	Park Kyung-Mo KOR	K Hyo-Jung KOR	France	Korea
1995	Lee Kyung-Chul KOR	Natalya Valeeva MLD	Korea	Korea
1997	Kim Kyung-Ho KOR	Kim Du-Ri KOR	Korea	Korea
1999	Hong Sung-Chil KOR	Lee Fon-Kung KOR	Italy	Italy

INDOOR WORLD CHAMPIONS

Year	Men's Olympic Team	Men's Compound Team	Women's Olympic Team	Women's Compound Team
1991	Sebastian Flute FRA -	Joe Asay USA -	Natalya Valeeva -	Lucia Panico ITA -
1993	Gennady Mitrofanov RUS -	Kirk Ethridge USA -	Jennifer O'Donnell USA	Inga Low USA
1995	Magnus Pettersson SWE USA	Michael Hendrikse USA USA	Natalya Valeeva MLD Ukraine	Glenda Penaz USA USA
1997	Chung Jae-Hun KOR Korea	Dee Wilde USA Sweden	Tetyana Muntyan UKR Germany	Valerie Fabre FRA USA
1999	Magnus Pettersson SWE Australia	James Butts USA USA	Natalia Valeeva ITA France	Ashley Kamuf USA France

ASSOCIATION FOOTBALL

WORLD CUP FINALS

Year	Winners	Runners-up	Venue	Attendance
1930	**Uruguay** 4	Argentina 2	Montevideo, Uruguay	90,000
	Dorado, Cea, Iriarte, Castro	*Peucelle, Stabile*		
1934	**Italy** 2	Czechoslovakia 1 *	Rome, Italy	55,000
	Orsi, Schiavio	*Puc*		
1938	**Italy** 4	Hungary 2	Paris, France	50,000
	Colaussi (2), Piola (2)	*Titkos, Sarosi*		
1950	**Uruguay** 2	Brazil 1 **	Rio de Janeiro, Brazil	199,854
	Schiaffino, Ghiggia	*Friaca*		
1954	**West Germany** 3	Hungary 2	Berne, Switzerland	55,000
	Morlock, Rahn (2)	*Puskas, Czibor*		
1958	**Brazil** 5	Sweden 2	Stockholm, Sweden	49,737
	Vava (2), Pele (2), Zagalo	*Liedholm, Simonsson*		
1962	**Brazil** 3	Czechoslovakia 1	Santiago, Chile	69,068
	Amarildo, Zito, Vava	*Masopust*		
1966	**England** 4	West Germany 2 *	London, England	93,000
	Hurst (3), Peters	*Haller, Weber*		
1970	**Brazil** 4	Italy 1	Mexico City, Mexico	110,000
	Pele, Gerson,	*Boninsegna*		
	Jairzinho, Carlos Alberto			
1974	**West Germany** 2	Holland 1	Munich, West Germany	77,833
	Breitner (pen), Müller	*Neeskens (pen)*		
1978	**Argentina** 3	Holland 1 *	Buenos Aires, Argentina	77,000
	Kempes (2), Bertoni	*Nanninga*		
1982	**Italy** 3	West Germany 1	Madrid, Spain	92,000
	Rossi, Tardelli, Altobelli	*Breitner*		
1986	**Argentina** 3	West Germany 2	Mexico City, Mexico	114,580
	Brown, Valdano,	*Rummenigge, Völler*		
	Burruchaga			
1990	**West Germany** 1	Argentina 0	Rome, Italy	73,603
	Brehme (pen)			
1994	**Brazil** 0	Italy 0 *	Los Angeles, USA	94,194
	Brazil won 3-2 on penalties			
1998	**France** 3	Brazil 0	Paris, France	75,000
	Zidane 2, Petit			

ASSOCIATION FOOTBALL

EUROPEAN CHAMPIONSHIP FINALS

1960	**Soviet Union** 2	Yugoslavia 1 *	Paris, France	17,966
	Metreveli, Ponedelnik	*Galic*		
1964	**Spain** 2	Soviet Union 1	Madrid, Spain	105,000
	Pereda, Marcellino	*Khusainov*		
1968	**Italy** 1	Yugoslavia 1 *	Rome, Italy	85,000
	Domenghini	*Dzajic*		
Replay	**Italy** 2	Yugoslavia 0	Rome, Italy	50,000
	Riva, Anastasi			
1972	**West Germany** 3	Soviet Union 0	Brussels, Belgium	43,437
	G Müller (2), Wimmer			
1976	**Czechoslovakia** 2	West Germany 2 *	Belgrade, Yugoslavia	45,000
	Svehlik, Dobias	*D Muller, Holzenbein*		
	(Czechoslovakia won 5-4 on penalties)			
1980	**West Germany** 2	Belgium 1	Rome, Italy	47,864
	Hrubesch (2)	*Van der Eycken*		
1984	**France** 2	Spain 0	Paris, France	47,000
	Platini, Bellone			
1988	**Holland** 2	Soviet Union 0	Munich, Germany	72,308
	Gullit, Van Basten			
1992	**Denmark** 2	Germany 0	Gothenburg, Sweden	37,800
	Jensen, Vilfort			
1996	**Germany** 2	Czech Republic 1***	London, England	76,000
	Bierhoff (2)	*Berger (pen)*		
2000	**France** 2	Italy 1***	Rotterdam, Netherlands	50,000
	Wiltord, Trezeguet	*Delvecchio*		

*after extra time   **deciding match of final pool   ***after sudden death extra time (Golden Goal)

EUROPEAN CHAMPIONS CUP

Year	Winner	Runner-up
1956	**Real Madrid** 4	Reims 3
1957	**Real Madrid** 2	Florentina 0
1958	**Real Madrid** 3	AC Milan 2 *(aet)*
1959	**Real Madrid** 2	Reims 0
1960	**Real Madrid** 7	Eintracht Frankfurt 3
1961	**Benfica** 3	Barcelona 2
1962	**Benfica** 5	Real Madrid 3
1963	**AC Milan** 2	Benfica 1
1964	**Internazionale** 3	Real Madrid 1
1965	**Internazionale** 1	Benfica 0
1966	**Real Madrid** 2	Partizan Belgrade 1
1967	**Celtic** 2	Internazionale 1
1968	**Manchester Utd** 4	Benfica 1 *(aet)*
1969	**AC Milan** 4	Ajax 1
1970	**Feyenoord** 2	Celtic 1 *(aet)*
1971	**Ajax** 2	Panathinaikos 0
1972	**Ajax** 2	Internazionale 0
1973	**Ajax** 1	Juventus 0
1974	Bayern Munich 1	Atletico Madrid 1
	Bayern Munich 4	Atletico Madrid 0
1975	**Bayern Munich** 2	Leeds Utd 0
1976	**Bayern Munich** 1	St Etienne 0
1977	**Liverpool** 3	B Moenchengladbach 1
1978	**Liverpool** 1	FC Brugge 0
1979	**Nottingham Forest** 1	Malmo 0
1980	**Nottingham Forest** 1	Hamburg 0
1981	**Liverpool** 1	Real Madrid 0
1982	**Aston Villa** 1	Bayern Munich 0
1983	**Hamburg** 1	Juventus 0
1984	**Liverpool** 1	Roma 1
	(aet: Liverpool won 4-2 on penalties)	
1985	**Juventus** 1	Liverpool 0
1986	**Steaua Bucharest** 0	Barcelona 0
	(aet: Steaua won 2-0 on penalties)	
1987	**Porto** 2	Bayern Munich 1
1988	**PSV Eindhoven** 0	Benfica 0
	(aet: PSV won 6-5 on penalties)	
1989	**AC Milan** 4	Steaua Bucharest 0
1990	**AC Milan** 1	Benfica 0
1991	**Red Star Belgrade** 0	Marseille 0
	(aet: Red Star won 5-3 on penalties)	
1992	**Barcelona** 1	Sampdoria 0 *(aet)*
1993	Marseille* 1	**AC Milan** 0
1994	**AC Milan** 4	Barcelona 0
1995	**Ajax** 1	AC Milan 0
1996	**Juventus** 1	Ajax 1
	(aet: Juventus won 4-2 on penalties)	
1997	**Borussia Dortmund** 3	Juventus 1
1998	**Real Madrid** 1	Juventus 0
1999	**Manchester Utd** 2	Bayern Munich 1
2000	**Real Madrid** 3	Valencia 0

* subsequently stripped of title

ASSOCIATION FOOTBALL

INTER-CITIES FAIRS CUP

Year	Winners	Score	Runners-up
1958	**Barcelona**	2-2 6-0	London
1960	**Barcelona**	0-0 4-1	Birmingham City
1961	**Roma**	2-2 2-0	Birmingham City
1962	**Valencia**	6-2 1-1	Barcelona
1963	**Valencia**	1-2 2-0	Dynamo Zagreb
1964	**Zaragoza**	2-1*	Valencia
1965	**Ferencvaros**	1-0*	Juventus
1966	**Barcelona**	0-1 4-2	Zaragoza
1967	**Dynamo Zagreb**	2-0 0-0	Leeds United
1968	**Leeds United**	1-0 0-0	Ferencvaros
1969	**Newcastle United**	3-0 2-3	Ujpest Dozsa
1970	**Arsenal**	1-3 3-0	Anderlecht
1971	**Leeds United**	2-2 1-1	Juventus

Over one leg only

UEFA CUP

Year	Winners	Score	Runners-up
1972	**Tottenham H**	2-1 1-1	Wolverhampton
1973	**Liverpool**	3-0 0-2	M'gladbach
1974	**Feyenoord**	2-0 2-2	Tottenham H
1975	**M'gladbach**	1-0 1-1	Twente E
1976	**Liverpool**	3-2 1-1	F C Brugge
1977	**Juventus**	1-0 1-2*	Athletic Bilbao
1978	**PSV Eindhoven**	3-0 0-0	Bastia
1979	**M'gladbach**	1-0 1-1	Red Star B
1980	**E'tracht Frankfurt**	1-0 2-3*	M'gladbach
1981	**Ipswich Town**	3-0 2-4	AZ 67 Alkmaar
1982	**IFK Gothenburg**	1-0 3-0	SV Hamburg
1983	**Anderlecht**	1-0 1-1	Benfica
1984	**Tottenham H**	1-1 1-1**	Anderlecht
1985	**Real Madrid**	3-0 0-1	Videoton
1986	**Real Madrid**	5-1 0-2	Cologne
1987	**IFK Gothenburg**	1-0 1-1	Dundee Utd
1988	**Bayer Leverkusen**	0-3 3-0**	Espanyol
1989	**Napoli**	2-1 3-3	VFB Stuttgart
1990	**Juventus**	3-1 0-0	Fiorentina
1991	**Internazionale**	2-0 0-1	AS Roma
1992	**Ajax**	2-2 0-0*	Torino
1993	**Juventus**	3-1 3-0	B Dortmund
1994	**Internazionale**	1-0 1-0	Salzburg
1995	**Parma**	1-0 1-1	Juventus
1996	**Bayern Munich**	2-0 3-1	Bordeaux
1997	**Schalke**	1-0 0-1**	Internazionale
1998	**Internazionale**	3-0	Lazio
1999	**Parma**	3-0	Marseille
2000	**Galatasaray**	0-0**	Arsenal

From 1998, the final over one leg only
* won on away goals ** won on penalties

EUROPEAN CUP WINNERS' CUP

Year	Winners	Runner-up
1961	**Fiorentina** 2	Rangers 0 *(1st Leg)*
	Fiorentina 2	Rangers 1 *(2nd Leg)*
1962	Atletico Madrid 1	Fiorentina 1
	Atletico Madrid 3	Fiorentina 0
1963	**Tottenham H** 5	Atletico Madrid I
1964	Sporting Lisbon 3	MTK Budapest 3 *(aet)*
	Sporting Lisbon 1	MTK Budapest 0
1965	**West Ham Utd** 2	Munich 1860 0
1966	**B Dortmund** 2	Liverpool 1 *(aet)*
1967	**Bayern Munich** 1	Rangers 0 *(aet)*
1968	**AC Milan** 2	Hamburg 0
1969	**Slovan Bratislava** 3	Barcelona 2
1970	**Manchester City** 2	Gornik Zabrze 1
1971	Chelsea 1	Real Madrid 1 (aet)
	Chelsea 2	Real Madrid 1 (aet)
1972	**Rangers** 3	Dynamo Moscow 2
1973	**AC Milan** 1	Leeds Utd 0
1974	**Magdeburg** 2	AC Milan 0
1975	**Dynamo Kiev** 3	Ferencvaros 0
1976	**Anderlecht** 4	West Ham U 2
1977	**Hamburg** 2	Anderlecht 0
1978	**Anderlecht** 4	Austria/WAC 0
1979	**Barcelona** 4	Fort. Dusseldorf 3 *(aet)*
1980	**Valencia** 0	Arsenal 0
	(aet: Valencia won 5-4 on penalties)	
1981	**Dynamo Tblisi** 2	Carl Zeiss Jena 1
1982	**Barcelona** 2	Standard Liege 1
1983	**Aberdeen** 2	Real Madrid 1 *(aet)*
1984	**Juventus** 2	Porto 1
1985	**Everton** 3	Rapid Vienna 1
1986	**Dynamo Kiev** 3	Atletico Madrid 0
1987	**Ajax** 1	Lokomotiv Leipzig 0
1988	**Mechelen** 1	Ajax 0
1989	**Barcelona** 2	Sampdoria 0
1990	**Sampdoria** 2	Anderlecht 0
1991	**Manchester Utd** 2	Barcelona 1
1992	**Werder Bremen** 2	Monaco 0
1993	**Parma** 3	Antwerp 1
1994	**Arsenal** 1	Parma 0
1995	**Real Zaragoza** 2	Arsenal 1
1996	**PSG** 1	Rapid Vienna 0
1997	**Barcelona** 1	Paris St Germain 0
1998	**Chelsea** 1	Vfb Stuttgart 0
1999	**Lazio** 2	Mallorca 1

Competition terminated 1999 to make way for expanded Champions League and UEFA Cup.

DIVISION 1

	Winners	Pts	Runners-up	Pts
1888-89	Preston NE	40	Aston Villa	29
1889-90	Preston NE	33	Everton	31
1890-91	Everton	29	Preston NE	27
1891-92	Sunderland	42	Preston NE	37
1892-93	Sunderland	48	Preston NE	37
1893-94	Aston Villa	44	Sunderland	38
1894-95	Sunderland	47	Everton	42
1895-96	Aston Villa	45	Derby County	41
1896-97	Aston Villa	47	Sheffield Utd	36
1897-98	Sheffield Utd	42	Sunderland	37
1898 99	Aston Villa	45	Liverpool	43
1899-00	Aston Villa	50	Sheffield Utd	48
1900-01	Liverpool	45	Sunderland	43
1901-02	Sunderland	44	Everton	41
1902-03	Sheffield Wed	42	Aston Villa	41
1903-04	Sheffield Wed	47	Man City	44
1904-05	Newcastle Utd	48	Everton	47
1905-06	Liverpool	51	Preston NE	47
1906-07	Newcastle Utd	51	Bristol City	48
1907-08	Man Utd	52	Aston Villa	43
1908-09	Newcastle Utd	53	Everton	46
1909-10	Aston Villa	53	Liverpool	48
1910-11	Man Utd	52	Aston Villa	51
1911-12	Blackburn Rvrs	49	Everton	46
1912-13	Sunderland	54	Aston Villa	50
1913.14	Blackburn Rvrs	51	Aston Villa	44
1914-15	Everton	46	Oldham Athletic	45
1919-20	West Brom Alb	60	Burnley	51
1920-21	Burnley	59	Man City	54
1921-22	Liverpool	57	Tottenham	51
1922-23	Liverpool	60	Sunderland	54
1923-24	Huddersfield T	57	Cardiff City	57
1924-25	Huddersfield T	58	West Brom Alb	56
1925-26	Huddersfield T	57	Arsenal	52
1926-27	Newcastle Utd	56	Huddersfield T	51
1927-28	Everton	53	Huddersfield T	51
1928-29	Sheffield Wed	52	Leicester City	51
1929-30	Sheffield Wed	60	Derby County	50
1930-31	Arsenal	66	Aston Villa	59
1931-32	Everton	56	Arsenal	54
1932 33	Arsenal	58	Aston Villa	54
1933-34	Arsenal	59	Huddersfield T	56
1934-35	Arsenal	58	Sunderland	54
1935-36	Sunderland	56	Derby County	48
1936-37	Man City	57	Charlton Ath	54
1937-38	Arsenal	52	Wolverhampton	51
1938-39	Everton	59	Wolverhampton	55
1946-47	Liverpool	57	Man Utd	56
1947-48	Arsenal	59	Man Utd	52
1948-49	Portsmouth	58	Man Utd	53
1949-50	Portsmouth	53	Wolverhampton	53
1950-51	Tottenham H	60	Man Utd	56
1951-52	Man Utd	57	Tottenham H	53
1952-53	Arsenal	54	Preston NE	54
1953 54	Wolverhampton	57	West Brom Alb	53
1954-55	Chelsea	52	Wolverhampton	48
1955-56	Man Utd	60	Blackpool	49
1956-57	Man Utd	64	Tottenham	56
1957-58	Wolverhampton	64	Preston NE	59
1958-59	Wolverhampton	61	Man Utd	55
1959-60	Burnley	55	Wolverhampton	54
1960-61	Tottenham H	66	Sheffield Wed	58
1961-62	Ipswich Town	56	Burnley	53
1962-63	Everton	61	Tottenham	55
1963-64	Liverpool	57	Man Utd	53
1964-65	Man Utd	61	Leeds United	61
1965-66	Liverpool	61	Leeds United	55
1966-67	Man Utd	60	Nottingham F	56
1967-68	Man City	58	Man Utd	56
1968 69	Leeds Utd	67	Liverpool	61
1969-70	Everton	66	Leeds Utd	57
1970-71	Arsenal	65	Leeds Utd	64
1971-72	Derby County	58	Leeds Utd	57
1972-73	Liverpool	60	Arsenal	57
1973-74	Leeds Utd	62	Liverpool	57
1974-75	Derby County	53	Liverpool	51
1975-76	Liverpool	60	QPR	59
1976-77	Liverpool	57	Man City	56
1977-78	Nottingham F	64	Liverpool	57
1978-79	Liverpool	68	Nottingham F	60
1979-80	Liverpool	60	Man Utd	58
1980-81	Aston Villa	60	Ipswich Town	56
1981-82	Liverpool	87	Ipswich Town	83
1982-83	Liverpool	82	Watford	71
1983-84	Liverpool	80	Southampton	77
1984-85	Everton	90	Liverpool	77
1985-86	Liverpool	88	Everton	86
1986-87	Everton	86	Liverpool	77
1987-88	Liverpool	90	Man Utd	81
1988-89	Arsenal	76	Liverpool	76
1989-90	Liverpool	79	Aston Villa	70
1990-91	Arsenal	83	Liverpool	76
1991-92	Leeds Utd	82	Man Utd	78

PREMIER LEAGUE

	Winners	Pts	Runners-up	Pts
1992-93	Man Utd	84	Aston Villa	74
1993-94	Man Utd	92	Blackburn Rvrs	84
1994-95	Blackburn	89	Man Utd	88
1995-96	Man Utd	82	Newcastle Utd	78
1996-97	Man Utd	75	Newcastle Utd	68
1997-98	Arsenal	78	Man Utd	77
1998-99	Man Utd	79	Arsenal	78
1999-00	Man Utd	91	Arsenal	73

ASSOCIATION FOOTBALL

FA CUP

Scorers from first Wembley final (1923) onwards

Year	Winners	Runners-up
1872	**Wanderers** 1	Royal Engineers 0
1873	**Wanderers** 2	Oxford University 0
1874	**Oxford University** 2	Royal Engineers 0
1875	Royal Engineers 1	Old Etonians 1*
	Royal Engineers 2	Old Etonians 0
1876	Wanderers 1	Old Etonians 1
	Wanderers 3	Old Etonians 0
1877	**Wanderers** 2	Oxford University 1*
1878	**Wanderers** 3	Royal Engineers 1
1879	**Old Etonians** 1	Clapham Rovers 0
1880	**Clapham Rovers** 1	Oxford University 0
1881	**Old Carthusians** 3	Old Etonians 0
1882	**Old Etonians** 1	Blackburn Rovers 0
1883	**Blackburn Olympic** 2	Old Etonians 1*
1884	**Blackburn Rovers** 2	Queen's Park 1
1885	**Blackburn Rovers** 2	Queen's Park 0
1886	Blackburn Rovers 0	WBA 0
	Blackburn Rovers 2	WBA 0
1887	**Aston Villa** 2	WBA 0
1888	**WBA** 2	Preston North End 1
1889	**Preston North End** 3	Wolverhampton Wdrs 0
1890	**Blackburn Rovers** 6	Sheffield Wednesday 1
1891	**Blackburn Rovers** 3	Notts County 1
1892	**WBA** 3	Aston Villa 0
1893	**Wolv'hampton W** 1	Everton 0
1894	**Notts County** 4	Bolton Wanderers 1
1895	**Aston Villa** 1	WBA 0
1896	**Sheffield Wed** 2	Wolverhampton Wdrs 1
1897	**Aston Villa** 3	Everton 2
1898	**Nottingham Forest** 3	Derby County 1
1899	**Sheffield United** 4	Derby County 1
1900	**Bury** 4	Southampton 0
1901	Tottenham Hotspur 2	Sheffield United 2
	Tottenham Hotspur 3	Sheffield United 1
1902	Sheffield United 1	Southampton 1
	Sheffield United 2	Southampton 1
1903	**Bury** 6	Derby County 0
1904	**Manchester City** 1	Bolton Wanderers 0
1905	**Aston Villa** 2	Newcastle United 0
1906	**Everton** 1	Newcastle United 0
1907	**Sheffield Wed** 2	Everton 1
1908	**Wolv'hampton W** 3	Newcastle United 1
1909	**Manchester United** 1	Bristol City 0
1910	Newcastle United 1	Barnsley 1
	Newcastle United 2	Barnsley 0
1911	Bradford City 0	Newcastle United 0
	Bradford City 1	Newcastle United 0
1912	Barnsley 0	WBA 0
	Barnsley 1	WBA 0*
1913	**Aston Villa** 1	Sunderland 0
1914	**Burnley** 1	Liverpool 0
1915	**Sheffield United** 3	Chelsea 0
1920	**Aston Villa** 1	Huddersfield Town 0*
1921	**Tottenham Hotspur** 1	Wolverhampton Wdrs 0
1922	**Huddersfield Town** 1	Preston North End 0
1923	**Bolton Wanderers** 2	West Ham United 0
	Jack, JR Smith	
1924	**Newcastle United** 2	Aston Villa 0
	Harris, Seymour	
1925	**Sheffield United** 1	Cardiff City 0
	Tunstall	
1926	**Bolton Wanderers** 1	Manchester City 0
	Jack	
1927	**Cardiff City** 1	Arsenal 0
	Ferguson	
1928	**Blackburn Rovers** 3	Huddersfield Town 1
	Roscamp (2), McLean	*Jackson*
1929	**Bolton Wanderers** 2	Portsmouth 0
	Butler, Blackmore	
1930	**Arsenal** 2	Huddersfield Town 0
	James, Lambert	
1931	**WBA** 2	Birmingham City 1
	WG Richardson (2)	*Bradford*
1932	**Newcastle United** 2	Arsenal 1
	Allen (2)	*John*
1933	**Everton** 3	Manchester City 0
	Stein, Dean, Dunn	
1934	**Manchester City** 2	Portsmouth 1
	Tilson (2)	*Rutherford*
1935	**Sheffield Wed** 4	WBA 2
	Rimmer (2), Hooper,	*Boyes, Sandford*
	Palethorpe	
1936	**Arsenal** 1	Sheffield United 0
	Drake	
1937	**Sunderland** 3	Preston North End 1
	Gurney, Carter	*F O'Donnell*
	Burbanks	
1938	**Preston North End** 1	Huddersfield Town 0*
	Mutch (pen)	
1939	**Portsmouth** 4	Wolverhampton Wdrs 1
	Parker (2), Barlow,	*Dorsett*
	Anderson	
1946	**Derby County** 4	Charlton Athletic 1*
	Stamps (2), Doherty,	*H Turner*
	H Turner (og)	
1947	**Charlton Athletic** 1	Burnley 0*
	Duffy	
1948	**Manchester United** 4	Blackpool 2
	Rowley (2), Pearson,	*Shimwell (pen),*
	Mortensen	
	Anderson,	
1949	**Wolv'hampton W** 3	Leicester City 1
	Pye (2), Smyth	*Griffiths*
1950	**Arsenal** 2	Liverpool 0
	Lewis (2)	
1951	**Newcastle United** 2	Blackpool 0
	Milburn (2)	
1952	**Newcastle United** 1	Arsenal 0
	G Robledo	
1953	**Blackpool** 4	Bolton Wanderers 3
	Mortensen (3), Perry	*Lofthouse, Moir, Bell*
1954	**WBA** 3	Preston North End 2
	Allen (2,1 pen)	*Morrison, Wayman*
	Griffin	
1955	**Newcastle United** 3	Manchester City 1
	Milburn, Mitchell,	*Johnstone*
	Hannah	

1956	**Manchester City** 3	Birmingham City 1
	Hayes, Dyson,	*Kinsey*
	Johnstone	
1957	**Aston Villa** 2	Manchester United 1
	McParland (2)	*Taylor*
1958	**Bolton Wanderers** 2	Manchester United 0
	Lofthouse (2)	
1959	**Nottingham Forest** 2	Luton Town 1
	Dwight, Wilson	*Pacey*
1960	**Wolv'hampton Wdrs** 3	Blackburn Rovers 0
	McGrath (og), Deeley (2)	
1961	**Tottenham Hotspur** 2	Leicester City 0
	Smith, Dyson	
1962	**Tottenham Hotspur** 3	Burnley 1
	Greaves, Smith,	*Robson*
	Blanchflower (pen)	
1963	**Manchester United** 3	Leicester City 1
	Herd (2), Law	*Keyworth*
1964	**West Ham United** 3	Preston North End 2
	Sissons, Hurst, Boyce	*Holden, Dawson*
1965	**Liverpool** 2	Leeds United 1*
	Hunt, St John	*Bremner*
1966	**Everton** 3	Sheffield Wednesday 2
	Trebilcock (2), Temple	*McCalliog, Ford*
1967	**Tottenham Hotspur** 2	Chelsea 1
	Robertson, Saul	*Tambling*
1968	**WBA** 1	Everton 0*
	Astle	
1969	**Manchester City** 1	Leicester City 0
	Young	
1970	**Chelsea** 2	Leeds United 2*
	Houseman,	*Charlton, Jones*
	Hutchinson	
	Chelsea 2	Leeds United 1*
	Osgood, Webb	*Jones*
1971	**Arsenal** 2	Liverpool 1*
	Kelly, George	*Heighway*
1972	**Leeds United** 1	Arsenal 0
	Clarke	
1973	**Sunderland** 1	Leeds United 0
	Porterfield	
1974	**Liverpool** 3	Newcastle United 0
	Keegan (2), Heighway	
1975	**West Ham United** 2	Fulham 0
	A Taylor (2)	
1976	**Southampton** 1	Manchester United 0
	Stokes	
1977	**Manchester United** 2	Liverpool 1
	Pearson, J Greenhoff	*Case*
1978	**Ipswich Town** 1	Arsenal 0
	Osborne	
1979	**Arsenal** 3	Manchester United 2
	Talbot, Stapleton,	*McQueen, McIlroy*
	Sunderland	
1980	**West Ham United** 1	Arsenal 0
	Brooking	
1981	Tottenham Hotspur 1	Manchester City 1*
	Hutchison (og)	*Hutchison*
	Tottenham Hotspur 3	Manchester City 2
	Villa (2), Crooks	*Mackenzie,*
		Reeves (pen)
1982	Tottenham Hotspur 1	QPR 1*
	Hoddle	*Fenwick*
	Tottenham Hotspur 1	QPR 0
	Hoddle (pen)	
1983	Manchester United 2	Brighton & Hove Alb 2*
	Stapleton, Wilkins	*Smith, Stevens*
	Manchester United 4	Brighton & Hove Alb 0
	Robson (2), Whiteside,	
	Muhren (pen)	
1984	**Everton** 2	Watford 0
	Sharp, Gray	
1985	**Manchester United** 1	Everton 0*
	Whiteside	
1986	**Liverpool** 3	Everton 1
	Rush (2), Johnston	*Lineker*
1987	**Coventry City** 3	Tottenham Hotspur 2*
	Bennett, Houchen,	*C Allen, Mabbutt*
	Mabbutt (og)	
1988	**Wimbledon** 1	Liverpool 0
	Sanchez	
1989	**Liverpool** 3	Everton 2*
	Aldridge, Rush (2)	*McCall (2)*
1990	**Manchester United** 3	Crystal Palace 3*
	Pemberton (og),	*O'Reilly, I Wright (2)*
	Hughes (2)	
Rply	**Manchester United** 1	Crystal Palace 0
	Martin	
1991	**Tottenham Hotspur** 2	Nottingham Forest 1*
	Stewart, Walker (og)	*Pearce*
1992	**Liverpool** 2	Sunderland 0
	Thomas, Rush	
1993	Arsenal 1	Sheffield Wednesday 1*
	Wright	*Hirst*
Rply	**Arsenal** 2	Sheffield Wednesday 1*
	Wright, Linighan	*Waddle*
1994	**Manchester United** 4	Chelsea 0
	Cantona (2 (2 pens)	
	Hughes, McClair	
1995	**Everton** 1	Manchester United 0
	Rideout	
1996	**Manchester United** 1	Liverpool 0
	Cantona	
1997	**Chelsea** 2	Middlesbrough0
	Di Matteo, Newton	
1998	**Arsenal** 2	Newcastle 0
	Overmars, Anelka	
1999	**Manchester United** 2	Newcastle 0
	Sheringham, Scholes	
2000	**Chelsea** 1	Aston Villa 0
	Di Matteo	

* after extra time

ASSOCIATION FOOTBALL

LEAGUE CUP
Played as a two-leg final until 1966

1961	**Aston Villa**	0-2 3-0	Rotherham Utd
1962	**Norwich City**	3-0 1-0	Rochdale
1963	**Birmingham City**	3-1 0-0	Aston Villa
1964	**Leicester City**	1-1 3-2	Stoke City
1965	**Chelsea**	3-2 0-0	Leicester City
1966	**WBA**	1-2 4-1	West Ham United

1967 **QPR** 3   WBA 2
1968 **Leeds United** 1   Arsenal 0
1969 **Swindon Town** 3   Arsenal 1*
1970 **Manchester City** 2   WBA 1*
1971 **Tottenham Hotspur** 2 Aston Villa 0
1972 **Stoke City** 2   Chelsea 1
1973 **Tottenham Hotspur** 2 Norwich City 0
1974 **Wolverhampton W** 2 Manchester City 1
1975 **Aston Villa** 1   Norwich City 0
1976 **Manchester City** 2 Newcastle Utd 1*
1977 Aston Villa 1   Everton1*
     Aston Villa 3   Everton 2*
1978 Nottingham Forest 0 Liverpool 0*
     Nottingham Forest 1 Liverpool 0*
1979 **Nottingham Forest** 3 Southampton 2
1980 **Wolverhampton W** 1 Nottingham Forest 0
1981 Liverpool 1   West Ham Utd 1*
     Liverpool 2   West Ham Utd 1

MILK CUP
1982 **Liverpool** 3   Tottenham Hotspur 1*
1983 **Liverpool** 2   Manchester Utd 1*
1984 Liverpool 0   Everton 0*
     Liverpool 1   Everton 0
1985 **Norwich City** 1   Sunderland 0
1986 **Oxford Utd** 3   QPR 0

LITTLEWOODS CUP
1987 **Arsenal** 2   Liverpool 1
1988 **Luton Town** 3   Arsenal 2
1989 **Nottingham Forest** 3 Luton Town 1
1990 **Nottingham Forest** 1 Oldham Athletic 0

RUMBELOWS LEAGUE CUP
1991 **Sheffield Wed** 1   Manchester Utd 0
1992 **Manchester Utd** 1   Nottingham Forest 0

COCA-COLA CUP
1993 **Arsenal** 2   Sheffield Wed 1
1994 **Aston Villa** 3   Manchester Utd 1
1995 **Liverpool** 2   Bolton Wanderers 1
1996 **Aston Villa** 3   Leeds Utd 0
1997 Leicester City 1   Middlesbrough 1*
     Leicester City 1   Middlesbrough 0*
1998 **Chelsea** 2   Middlesbrough 0

WORTHINGTON CUP
1999 **Tottenham H** 1   Leicester City 0
2000 **Leicester City** 2   Tranmere Rovers 1
* After extra time

ASSOCIATION FOOTBALL

SCOTTISH LEAGUE

	Winners	Runner-up
1890-91	Dumbarton/Rangers	
1891-92	Dumbarton	Celtic
1892-93	Celtic	Rangers
1893-94	Celtic	Hearts
1894-95	Hearts	Celtic
1895-96	Celtic	Rangers
1896-97	Hearts	Hibernian
1897-98	Celtic	Rangers
1898-99	Rangers	Hearts
1899-00	Rangers	Celtic
1900-01	Rangers	Celtic
1901-02	Rangers	Celtic
1902-03	Hibernian	Dundee
1903-04	Third Lanark	Hearts
1904-05	Celtic	Rangers
1905-06	Celtic	Hearts
1906-07	Celtic	Dundee
1907-08	Celtic	Falkirk
1908-09	Celtic	Dundee
1909-10	Celtic	Falkirk
1910-11	Rangers	Aberdeen
1911-12	Rangers	Celtic
1912-13	Rangers	Celtic
1913-14	Celtic	Rangers
1914-15	Celtic	Hearts
1915-16	Celtic	Rangers
1916-17	Celtic	Morton
1917-18	Rangers	Celtic
1918-19	Celtic	Rangers
1919-20	Rangers	Celtic
1920-21	Rangers	Celtic
1921-22	Celtic	Rangers
1922-23	Rangers	Airdrieonians
1923-24	Rangers	Airdrieonians
1924-25	Rangers	Airdrieonians
1925-26	Celtic	Airdrieonians
1926-27	Rangers	Motherwell
1927-28	Rangers	Celtic
1928-29	Rangers	Celtic
1929-30	Rangers	Motherwell
1930-31	Rangers	Celtic
1931-32	Motherwell	Rangers
1932-33	Rangers	Motherwell
1933-34	Rangers	Motherwell
1934-35	Rangers	Celtic
1935-36	Celtic	Rangers
1936-37	Rangers	Aberdeen
1937-38	Celtic	Hearts
1938-39	Rangers	Celtic
1946-47	Rangers	Hibernian
1947-48	Hibernian	Rangers
1948-49	Rangers	Dundee
1949-50	Rangers	Hibernian
1950-51	Hibernian	Rangers
1951-52	Hibernian	Rangers
1952-53	Rangers	Hibernian
1953-54	Celtic	Hearts
1954-55	Aberdeen	Celtic
1955-56	Rangers	Aberdeen
1956-57	Rangers	Hearts
1957-58	Hearts	Rangers
1958-59	Rangers	Hearts
1959-60	Hearts	Kilmarnock
1960-61	Rangers	Kilmarnock
1961-62	Dundee	Rangers
1962-63	Rangers	Kilmarnock
1963-64	Rangers	Kilmarnock
1964-65	Kilmarnock	Hearts
1965-66	Celtic	Rangers
1966-67	Celtic	Rangers
1967-68	Celtic	Rangers
1968-69	Celtic	Rangers
1969-70	Celtic	Rangers
1970-71	Celtic	Aberdeen
1971-72	Celtic	Aberdeen
1972-73	Celtic	Rangers
1973-74	Celtic	Hibernian
1974-75	Rangers	Hibernian
1975-76	Rangers	Celtic
1976-77	Celtic	Rangers
1977-78	Rangers	Aberdeen
1978-79	Celtic	Rangers
1979-80	Aberdeen	Celtic
1980-81	Celtic	Aberdeen
1981-82	Celtic	Aberdeen
1982-83	Dundee Utd	Celtic
1983-84	Aberdeen	Celtic
1984-85	Aberdeen	Celtic
1985-86	Celtic	Hearts
1986-87	Rangers	Celtic
1987-88	Celtic	Hearts
1988-89	Rangers	Aberdeen
1989-90	Rangers	Aberdeen
1990-91	Rangers	Aberdeen
1991-92	Rangers	Hearts
1992-93	Rangers	Aberdeen
1993-94	Rangers	Aberdeen
1994-95	Rangers	Motherwell
1995-96	Rangers	Celtic
1996-97	Rangers	Celtic
1997-98	Celtic	Rangers
1998-99	Rangers	Celtic
1999-00	Rangers	Celtic

SCOTTISH FA CUP

1874	**Queen's Park** 2	Clydesdale 0	
1875	**Queen's Park** 3	Renton 0	
1876	Queen's Park 1	Third Lanark 1	
	Queen's Park 2	Third Lanark 0	
1877	Vale of Leven 0	Rangers 0	
	Vale of Leven 1	Rangers 1	
	Vale of Leven 3	Rangers 2	
1878	**Vale of Leven** 1	Third Lanark 0	
1879	**Vale of Leven** 1	Rangers 1	

Leven awarded Cup, Rangers refused replay

1880	**Queen's Park** 3	Thornlibank 0	
1881	Queen's Park 2	Dumbarton 1	

Abandoned due to pitch invasion

	Queen's Park 3	Dumbarton 1	
1882	Queen's Park 2	Dumbarton 2	
	Queen's Park 4	Dumbarton 1	
1883	Dumbarton 2	Vale of Leven 2	
	Dumbarton 2	Vale of Leven 1	
1884	**Queen's Park**		

Queen's Park awarded Cup as Vale of Leven did not appear

1885	Renton 0	Vale of Leven 0	
	Renton 3	Vale of Leven 1	
1886	**Queen's Park** 3	Renton 1	
1887	**Hibernian** 2	Dumbarton 1	
1888	**Renton** 6	Cambuslang 1	
1889	Third Lanark 3	Celtic 1	

Abandoned due to snowstorm

	Third Lanark 2	Celtic 1	
1890	Queen's Park 1	Vale of Leven 1	
	Queen's Park 2	Vale of Leven 1	
1891	**Hearts** 1	Dumbarton 0	
1892	Celtic 1	Queen's Park 0	

Abandoned due to pitch invasion

1892	**Celtic** 1	Queen's Park 0	
1893	Queen's Park 0	Celtic 1	

Abandoned due to frost

	Queen's Park 2	Celtic 1	
1894	**Rangers** 3	Celtic 1	
1895	**St Bernard's** 2	Renton 1	
1896	**Hearts** 3	Hibernian 1	
1897	**Rangers** 5	Dumbarton 1	
1898	**Rangers** 2	Kilmarnock 0	
1899	**Rangers** 2	Rangers 0	
1900	**Celtic** 4	Queen's Park 3	
1901	**Hearts** 4	Celtic 3	
1902	**Hibernian** 1	Celtic 0	
1903	Rangers 1	Hearts 1	
	Rangers 0	Hearts 0	
	Rangers 2	Hearts 0	
1904	**Celtic** 3	Rangers 2	
1905	Third Lanark 0	Rangers 0	
	Third Lanark 3	Rangers 0	
1906	**Hearts** 1	Third Lanark 0	
1907	**Celtic** 3	Hearts 0	
1908	**Celtic** 5	St Mirren 1	
1909	Celtic 2	Rangers 2	
	Celtic 1	Rangers 1	

Cup not awarded, riot

1910	Dundee 2	Clyde 2	
	Dundee 0	Clyde 0	
	Dundee 2	Clyde 1	
1911	Celtic 0	Hamilton Academicals 0	
	Celtic 2	Hamilton Academicals 0	
1912	**Celtic** 2	Clyde 0	
1913	**Falkirk** 2	Raith Rovers 0	
1914	Celtic 0	Hibernian 0	
	Celtic 4	Hibernian 1	
1920	**Kilmarnock** 3	Albion Rovers 2	
1921	**Partick Thistle** 1	Rangers 0	
1922	**Morton** 1	Rangers 0	
1923	**Celtic** 1	Hibernian 0	
1924	**Airdrieonians** 2	Hibernian 0	
1925	**Celtic** 2	Dundee 1	
1926	**St Mirren** 2	Celtic 0	
1927	**Celtic** 3	East Fife 1	
1928	**Rangers** 4	Celtic 0	
1929	**Kilmarnock** 2	Rangers 0	
1930	Rangers 0	Partick Thistle 0	
	Rangers 2	Partick Thistle 1	
1931	Celtic 2	Motherwell 2	
	Celtic 4	Motherwell 2	
1932	Rangers 1	Kilmarnock 1	
	Rangers 3	Kilmarnock 0	
1933	**Celtic** 1	Motherwell 0	
1934	**Rangers** 5	St Mirren 0	
1935	**Ranger** 2	Hamilton Academicals 1	
1936	**Rangers** 1	Third Lanark 0	
1937	**Celtic** 2	Aberdeen 1	
1938	East Fife 1	Kilmarnock 1	
	East Fife 4	Kilmarnock 2	
1939	**Clyde** 4	Motherwell 0	
1947	**Aberdeen** 2	Hibernian 1	
1948	Rangers 1	Morton 1	
	Rangers 1	Morton 0	
1949	**Rangers** 4	Clyde 1	
1950	**Rangers** 3	East Fife 0	
1951	**Celtic** 1	Motherwell 0	
1952	**Motherwell** 4	Dundee 0	
1953	Rangers 1	Aberdeen 1	
	Rangers 1	Aberdeen 0	
1954	**Celtic** 2	Aberdeen 1	
1955	Clyde 1	Celtic 1	
	Clyde 1	Celtic 0	
1956	**Hearts** 3	Celtic 1	
1957	Falkirk 1	Kilmarnock 1	
	Falkirk 2	Kilmarnock 1	
1958	**Clyde** 1	Hibernian 0	
1959	**St Mirren** 3	Aberdeen 1	
1960	**Rangers** 2	Kilmarnock 0	
1961	Dunfermline 0	Celtic 0	
	Dunfermline 2	Celtic 0	
1962	**Rangers** 2	St Mirren 0	
1963	Rangers 1	Celtic 1	
	Rangers 3	Celtic 0	
1964	**Rangers** 3	Dundee 1	
1965	**Celtic** 3	Dunfermline 2	
1966	**Rangers** 0	Celtic 0	
	Rangers 1	Celtic 0	

ASSOCIATION FOOTBALL

Year	Winner		Runner-up	
1967	Celtic	2	Aberdeen	0
1968	Dunfermline	3	Hearts	1
1969	Celtic	4	Rangers	1
1970	Aberdeen	3	Celtic	1
1971	Celtic	1	Rangers	1
	Celtic	2	Rangers	1
1972	Celtic	6	Hibernian	1
1973	Rangers	3	Celtic	2
1974	Celtic	3	Dundee United	0
1975	Celtic	3	Airdrieonians	1
1976	Rangers	3	Hearts	1
1977	Celtic	1	Rangers	0
1978	Rangers	2	Aberdeen	1
1979	Rangers	0	Hibernian	0
	Rangers	0	Hibernian	0
	Rangers	3	Hibernian	2
1980	Celtic	1	Rangers	0*
1981	Rangers	0	Dundee United	0
	Rangers	4	Dundee United	1
1982	Aberdeen	4	Rangers	1*
1983	Aberdeen	1	Rangers	0*
1984	Aberdeen	2	Celtic	1*
1985	Celtic	2	Dundee United	1
1986	Aberdeen	3	Hearts	0
1987	St Mirren	1	Dundee United	0*
1988	Celtic	2	Dundee United	1
1989	Celtic	1	Rangers	0
1990	Aberdeen	0	Celtic	0

Aberdeen won 9-8 on penalties

Year	Winner		Runner-up	
1991	Motherwell	4	Dundee United	3*
1992	Rangers	2	Airdrieonians	1
1993	Rangers	2	Aberdeen	1
1994	Dundee United	1	Rangers	0
1995	Celtic	1	Airdrieonians	0
1996	Rangers	5	Hearts	1
1997	Kilmarnock	1	Falkirk	0
1998	Hearts	2	Rangers	1
1999	Rangers	1	Celtic	0
2000	Rangers	4	Aberdeen	0

* After extra time

SCOTTISH LEAGUE CUP

Year	Winners		Runners-up	
1946-47	Rangers	4	Aberdeen	0
1947-48	East Fife	0	Falkirk	0*
Replay	East Fife	4	Falkirk	1
1948-49	Rangers	2	Raith Rovers	0
1949-50	East Fife	3	Dunfermline A	0
1950-51	Motherwell	3	Hibernian	0
1951-52	Dundee	3	Rangers	2
1952-53	Dundee	2	Kilmarnock	0
1953-54	East Fife	3	Partick Thistle	2
1954-55	Hearts	4	Motherwell	2
1955-56	Aberdeen	2	St Mirren	1
1956-57	Celtic	0	Partick Thistle	0*
Replay	Celtic	3	Partick Thistle	0
1957-58	Celtic	7	Rangers	1
1958-59	Hearts	5	Partick Thistle	1
1969-60	Hearts	2	Third Lanark	1
1960-61	Rangers	2	Kilmarnock	0
1961-62	Rangers	1	Hearts	1*
Replay	Rangers	3	Hearts	1
1962-63	Hearts	1	Kilmarnock	0
1963-64	Rangers	5	Morton	0
1966-45	Rangers	2	Celtic	1
1965-66	Celtic	2	Rangers	1
1966-67	Celtic	1	Rangers	0
1967-68	Celtic	5	Dundee	3
1968-69	Celtic	6	Hibernian	2
1969-70	Celtic	1	St.Johnstone	0
1970-71	Rangers	1	Celtic	0
1971-72	Partick Thistle	4	Celtic	1
1972-73	Hibernian	2	Celtic	1
1973-74	Dundee	1	Celtic	0
1974-75	Celtic	6	Hibernian	3
1975-76	Rangers	1	Celtic	0
1976-77	Aberdeen	2	Celtic	1
1977-78	Rangers	2	Celtic	1
1978-79	Rangers	2	Aberdeen	1
1979-80	Dundee United	0	Aberdeen	0
	Dundee United	3	Aberdeen	0**
1980-81	Dundee United	3	Dundee	0**
1981-82	Rangers	2	Dundee United	1
1982-83	Celtic	2	Rangers	1
1983-84	Rangers	3	Celtic	2*
1984-85	Rangers	1	Dundee United	0
1985-86	Aberdeen	3	Hibernian	0
1986-87	Rangers	2	Celtic	1
1987-88	Rangers	3	Aberdeen	3*

Rangers won 5-3 on penalties

Year	Winners		Runners-up	
1988-89	Rangers	3	Aberdeen	2
1989-90	Aberdeen	2	Rangers	1*
1990-91	Rangers	2	Celtic	1*
1991-92	Hibernian	2	Dunfermline	0
1992-93	Rangers	2	Aberdeen	1
1993-94	Rangers	2	Hibernian	1
1994-95	Raith Rovers	2	Celtic	2

Raith won 6-5 on penalties

Year	Winners		Runners-up	
1995-96	Aberdeen	2	Dundee	0
1996-97	Stranraer	1	St Johnstone	0
1997-98	Celtic	3	Dundee United	0
1998-99	Rangers	2	St Johnstone	1
1999-00	Celtic	2	Aberdeen	0

* after extra time ** Played at Dens Park, Dundee

ATHLETICS

WORLD RECORDS
Men

100m	9.79 (+0.1)	Maurice Greene	USA	Athens	June 16, 1999
200m	19.32 (+0.4)	Michael Johnson	USA	Atlanta	August 1, 1996
400m	43.18	Michael Johnson	USA	Seville	August 26, 1999
800m	1:41.11	Wilson Kipketer	DEN	Cologne	August 24, 1997
1000m	2:11.96	Noah Ngeny	KEN	Rieti	September 5, 1999
1500m	3:26.00	Hicham El Guerrouj	MAR	Rome	July 14, 1998
1 Mile	3:43.13	Hicham El Guerrouj	MAR	Rome	July 7, 1999
2000m	4:44.79	Hicham El Guerrouj	MAR	Berlin	September 8, 1999
3000m	7:20.67	Daniel Komen	KEN	Rieti	September 1, 1996
5000m	12:39.36	Haile Gebrselassie	ETH	Helsinki	June 12, 1998
10,000m	26:22.75	Haile Gebrselassie	ETH	Hengelo	June 1, 1998
Marathon	2:05:42	Khalid Khannouchi	MAR	Chicago	October 24, 1999
3000msc	7:55.72	Bernard Barmasai	KEN	Cologne	August 24, 1997
110mh	12.91 (+0.5)	Colin Jackson	GBR	Stuttgart	August 20, 1993
400mh	46.78	Kevin Young	USA	Barcelona	August 6, 1992
High Jump	2.45m	Javier Sotomayor	CUB	Salamanca	July 27, 1993
Pole Vault	6.14m A	Sergey Bubka	UKR	Sestriere	July 31, 1994
Long Jump	8.95m (+0.3)	Mike Powell	USA	Tokyo	August 30, 1991
Triple Jump	18.29m (+1.3)	Jonathan Edwards	GBR	Gothenburg	August 7, 1995
Shot	23.12m	Randy Barnes	USA	Los Angeles	May 20, 1990
Discus	74.08m	Jürgen Schult	GER	Neubrandenburg	June 6, 1986
Hammer	86.74m	Yury Sedykh	URS	Stuttgart	August 30, 1986
Javelin	98.48m	Jan Zelezny	CZE	Jena	May 25, 1996
Decathlon	8994	Tomas Dvorak	CZE	Prague	July 3-4, 1999
4x100m	37.40	United States		Barcelona/Stuttgart	8.8.92/21.8.93
4x400m	2:54.20	United States (Young/Pettigrew/Washington/Johnson) New York			July 22, 1998
20km Walk	1:17:25	Bernardo Segura	MEX	Bergen	May 7, 1994
50km Walk	3:40:57	Thierry Toutain	FRA	Héricourt	September 29, 1996

Women

100m	10.49 (0.0)	Florence Griffith-Joyner	USA	Seoul	July 16, 1988
200m	21.34 (+1.3)	Florence Griffith-Joyner	USA	Seoul	September 29, 1988
400m	47.60	Marita Koch	GDR	Canberra	October 6, 1985
800m	1:53.28	Jarmila Kratochvilova	TCH	Munich	July 26, 1983
1000m	2:28.98	Svetlana Masterkova	RUS	Brussels	August 23, 1996
1500m	3:50.46	Qu Yunxia	CHN	Beijing	September 11, 1993
1 Mile	4:12.56	Svetlana Masterkova	RUS	Zürich	August 14, 1996
2000m	5:25:36	Sonia O'Sullivan	IRL	Edinburgh	July 8, 1994
3000m	8:06.11	Wang Junxia	CHN	Beijing	September 13, 1993
5000m	14:28.09	Jiang Bo	CHN	Shanghai	October 23, 1997
10,000m	29:31.78	Wang Junxia	CHN	Beijing	September 8, 1993
Marathon	2:20:43	Tegla Loroupe	KEN	Berlin	September 26, 1999
3000msc	9:40.20	Cristina Iloc-Casandra	ROM	Reims	August 30, 2000
100mh	12.21 (+0.7)	Yordanka Donkova	BUL	Stara Zagora	August 20, 1988
400mh	52.61	Kim Batten	USA	Gothenburg	August 11, 1995
High Jump	2.09m	Stefka Kostadinova	BUL	Rome	August 30, 1987
Pole Vault	4.63m	Stacy Dragila	USA	Sacramento	July 23, 2000
Long Jump	7.52m (+1.4)	Galina Chistyakova	URS	Leningrad	June 11, 1988
Triple Jump	15.50m	Inessa Kravets	UKR	Gothenburg	August 10, 1994
Shot	22.63m	Natalya Lisovskaya	URS	Moscow	June 6, 1987
Discus	76.80m	Gabriele Reinsch	GER	Neubrandenburg	July 9, 1988
Hammer	76.07m	Michaela Melinte	ROM	Rüdlingen	August 29, 1999
Javelin	69.48m	Trine Solberg-Hattestad	NOR	Oslo	July 28, 2000
Heptathlon	7291	Jackie Joyner-Kersee	USA	Seoul	September 24, 1988
4x100m	41.37	East Germany		Canberra	October 6, 1985
4x400m	3:15.17	Soviet Union		Seoul	October 1, 1988
20km Walk	1:35:23	Kristina Saltanovic	LTU	Kaunas	August 3, 2000

A = Record set at altitude

ATHLETICS

BRITISH RECORDS
Men

100m	9.87	Linford Christie	Stuttgart	August 15, 1993
200m	19.87 A*	John Regis	Sestriere	July 31, 1994
300m	31.56	Doug Walker	Gateshead	July 19, 1998
400m	44.36	Iwan Thomas	Birmingham	July 13, 1997
600m	1:14.95	Steve Heard	Haringey	July 14, 1991
800m	1:41.73 **	Sebastian Coe	Florence	June 10, 1981
1000m	2:12.18	Sebastian Coe	Oslo	July 11, 1981
1500m	3:29.67	Steve Cram	Nice	July 16, 1985
1 Mile	3:46.32	Steve Cram	Oslo	July 27, 1985
2000m	4:51.39	Steve Cram	Budapest	August 4, 1985
3000m	7:32.79	Dave Moorcroft	Crystal Palace	July 17, 1982
2 Miles	8:13.51	Steve Ovett	Crystal Palace	September 15, 1978
5000m	13:00.41	Dave Moorcroft	Oslo	July 7, 1982
10,000m	27:18.14	Jon Brown	Brussels	August 28, 1998
20,000m	57:28.7	Carl Thackery	La Flèche	March 31, 1990
1 Hour	20,855m	Carl Thackery	La Flèche	March 31, 1990
Half-marathon	60:09	Paul Evans	Marrakesh	January 15, 1995
25,000m	1:15:22.6	Ron Hill	Bolton	July 21, 1965
30,000m	1:31:30.4	Jim Alder	Crystal Palace	September 5, 1970
Marathon	2:07:13	Steve Jones	Chicago	October 20, 1985
2000msc	5:19.86	Mark Rowland	Crystal Palace	August 28, 1988
3000msc	8:07.96	Mark Rowland	Seoul	September 30, 1988
110mh	12.91 (+0.5)	Colin Jackson	Stuttgart	August 20, 1993
200mh	22.63	Colin Jackson	Cardiff	June 1, 1991
400mh	47.82	Kriss Akabusi	Barcelona	August 6, 1992
High Jump	2.37m	Steve Smith	Seoul	September 20, 1992
	2.37m	Steve Smith	Stuttgart	August 22, 1993
Pole Vault	5.80m	Nick Buckfield	Haniá	May 27, 1998
Long Jump	8.23m	Lynn Davies	Berne	June 30, 1968
Triple Jump	18.29m (+1.3)	Jonathan Edwards	Gothenburg	August 7, 1995
Shot	21.68m	Geoff Capes	Cwmbran	May 18, 1980
Discus	66.64m	Perris Wilkins	Edgbaston	June 6, 1998
Hammer	77.54m	Martin Girvan	Wolverhampton	May 12, 1994
Javelin	91.46m	Steve Backley	Auckland	January 25, 1992
Decathlon	8847	Daley Thompson	Los Angeles	August 9, 1994
20km Walk	1:22:03	Ian McCombie	Seoul	April 27, 1988
50km Walk	3:51:37	Chris Maddocks	Burrator	October 28, 1990
4x100m	37.73	Great Britain	Seville	August 29, 1999
		Gardener/Campbell/Devonish/Chambers		
4x200m	1:21.29	Great Britain	Birmingham	June 23, 1989
4x400m	2:56.60	Great Britain	Atlanta	August 3, 1996
		Thomas/Baulch/Richardson/Black		
4x800m	7:03.89 WR	Great Britain	Crystal Palace	August 30, 1982
		Elliot/Cook/Cram/Coe		
4x1500m	14:56.8	Great Britain	Bourges	June 23, 1979
4x1 Mile	16:21.1	British Milers' Club Team	Oxford	July 10, 1993

* A=Record set at altitude
** Time taken from photo-electric cell

ATHLETICS

BRITISH RECORDS
Women

100m	11.10	Kathy Cook	Rome	September 5, 1981
200m	22.10	Kathy Cook	Los Angeles	August 9, 1984
300m	35.46	Kathy Cook	Crystal Palace	August 18, 1984
400m	49.43	Kathy Cook	Los Angeles	August 6, 1984
600m	1:26.18	Diane Modahl	Crystal Palace	August 22, 1987
800m	1:56.21	Kelly Holmes	Monaco	September 9, 1995
1000m	2:32.55	Kelly Holmes	Leeds	June 15, 1995
1500m	3:58.07	Kelly Holmes	Sheffield	June 29, 1997
1 Mile	4:17.57	Zola Budd	Zurich	August 21, 1985
2000m	5:26.93	Yvonne Murray	Edinburgh	July 8, 1994
3000m	8:27.40	Paula Radcliffe	Zurich	August 11, 1999
5000m	14:43.54	Paula Radcliffe	Crystal Palace	August 7, 1999
10,000m	30:26.97	Paula Radcliffe	Sydney	September 30, 2000
20,000m	1:15:46	Carolyn Hunter-Rowe	Barry	March 6, 1994
1 Hour	16,364m	Alison Fletcher	Bromley	September 3, 1997
Half-marathon	1:07:07	Paula Radcliffe	South Shields	October 22, 2000
Marathon	2:25:56	Veronique Marot	London	April 23, 1989
3000msc	10:08.11	Tara Krzywicki	Stretford	September 5, 2000
100mh	12.80	Angie Thorp	Atlanta	July 31, 1996
400mh	52.74	Sally Gunnell	Stuttgart	August 19, 1993
High Jump	1.95m	Diana Davies	Oslo	June 26, 1982
Pole Vault	4.35m	Janine Whitlock	Prague	June 5, 2000
Long Jump	6.90m	Beverly Kinch	Helsinki	August 14, 1983
Triple Jump	15.15m	Ashia Hansen	Fukuoka	September 13, 1997
Shot	19.36m	Judy Oakes	Gateshead	August 14, 1988
Discus	67.48m	Meg Ritchie	Walnut	April 26, 1981
Hammer	67.44m	Lorraine Shaw	Gateshead	July 15, 2000
Javelin	59.50m	Karen Martin	Cosford	July 14, 1999
Heptathlon	6831	Denise Lewis	Talence	July 30, 2000
5000m Walk	22:01.53	Lisa Kehler	Birmingham	July 26, 1998
10km Walk	45:18.8	Vicky Lupton	Watford	September 2, 1995
20km Walk	1:56:59	Cath Reader	Loughborough	October 21,1995
4x100m	42.43	Great Britain	Moscow	August 1, 1980
		Oakes/Cook/Callender/Lannaman		
4x200m	1:31.57	Great Britain	Crystal Palace	August 20, 1977
4x400m	3:22.01	Great Britain	Atlanta	August 3, 1996
		Hansen/Smith/Gunnell/Keough		
4x800m	8:19.9	Great Britain	Sheffield	June 5, 1992

ATHLETICS

WORLD CHAMPIONSHIPS
1983 Helsinki; 1987 Rome;
1991 Tokyo; 1993 Stuttgart; 1995
Gothenburg; 1997 Athens

Men
100m
1983 **Carl Lewis** USA
1987 **Carl Lewis** USA*
1991 **Carl Lewis** USA
1993 **Linford Christie** GBR
1995 **Donovan Bailey** CAN
1997 **Maurice Greene** USA
1999 **Maurice Greene** USA
Won by Ben Johnson, later
stripped of title for drug-taking

200m
1983 **Calvin Smith** USA
1987 **Calvin Smith** USA
1991 **Michael Johnson** USA
1993 **Frankie Fredericks** NAM
1995 **Michael Johnson** USA
1997 **Ato Boldon** TRI
1999 **Maurice Greene** USA

400m
1983 **Bert Cameron** JAM
1987 **Thomas Schonlebe** GDR
1991 **Antonio Pettigrew** USA
1993 **Michael Johnson** USA
1995 **Michael Johnson** USA
1997 **Michael Johnson** USA
1999 **Michael Johnson** USA

800m
1983 **Willi Wulbeck** FRG
1987 **Billy Konchellah** KEN
1991 **Billy Konchellah** KEN
1993 **Paul Ruto** KEN
1995 **Wilson Kipketer** DEN
1997 **Wilson Kipketer** DEN
1999 **Wilson Kipketer** DEN

1500m
1983 **Steve Cram** GBR
1987 **Abdi Bile** SOM
1991 **Noureddine Morceli** ALG
1993 **Noureddine Morceli** ALG
1995 **Noureddine Morceli** ALG
1997 **Hicham El Guerrouj** MAR
1999 **Hicham El Guerrouj** MAR

5000m
1983 **Eamonn Coghlan** IRE
1987 **Said Aouita** MAR
1991 **Yobes Ondieki** KEN
1993 **Ismael Kirui** KEN
1995 **Ismael Kirui** KEN
1997 **Daniel Komen** KEN
1999 **Salah Hissou** MAR

10,000m
1983 **Alberto Cova** ITA
1987 **Paul Kipkoech** KEN
1991 **Moses Tanui** KEN
1993 **Haile Gebrselassie** ETH
1995 **Haile Gebrselassie** ETH
1997 **Haile Gebrselassie** ETH
1999 **Haile Gebrselassie** ETH

Marathon
1983 **Rob de Castella** AUS
1987 **Douglas Wakiihuri** KEN
1991 **Hiromi Taniguchi** JPN
1993 **Mark Plaatjes** USA
1995 **Martin Fiz** ESP
1997 **Abel Antón** ESP
1999 **Abel Antón** ESP

3000m Steeplechase
1983 **Patriz Ilg** FRG
1987 **Francesco Panetta** ITA
1991 **Moses Kiptanui** KEN
1993 **Moses Kiptanui** KEN
1995 **Moses Kiptanui** KEN
1997 **Wilson Kipketer Boit** KEN
1999 **Christopher Koskei** KEN

110m Hurdles
1983 **Greg Foster** USA
1987 **Greg Foster** USA
1991 **Greg Foster** USA
1993 **Colin Jackson** GBR
1995 **Allen Johnson** USA
1997 **Allen Johnson** USA
1999 **Colin Jackson** GBR

400m Hurdles
1983 **Edwin Moses** USA
1987 **Edwin Moses** USA
1991 **Samuel Matete** ZAM
1993 **Kevin Young** USA
1995 **Derrick Adkins** USA
1997 **Stéphane Diagana** FRA
1999 **Fabrizio Mori** ITA

High Jump
1983 **Genn Avdeyenko** URS
1987 **Patrik Sjoberg** SWE
1991 **Charles Austin** USA
1993 **Javier Sotomayor** CUB
1995 **Troy Kemp** BAH
1997 **Javier Sotomayor** CUB
1999 **Vyacheslav Voronin** RUS

Pole Vault
1983 **Sergey Bubka** URS
1987 **Sergey Bubka** URS
1991 **Sergey Bubka** URS
1993 **Sergey Bubka** UKR
1995 **Sergey Bubka** UKR
1997 **Sergey Bubka** UKR
1999 **Maksim Tarasov** RUS

Long Jump
1983 **Carl Lewis** USA
1987 **Carl Lewis** USA
1991 **Mike Powell** USA
1993 **Mike Powell** USA
1995 **Ivan Pedroso** CUB
1997 **Ivan Pedroso** CUB
1999 **Ivan Pedroso** CUB

Triple Jump
1983 **Zdzislaw Hoffmann** POL
1987 **Khristo Markov** BUL
1991 **Kenny Harrison** USA
1993 **Mike Conley** USA
1995 **Jonathan Edwards** GBR
1997 **Yoelbi Quesada** CUB
1999 **Charles Friedek** GER

Shot
1983 **Edward Sarul** POL
1987 **Werner Günthör** SUI
1991 **Werner Günthör** SUI
1993 **Werner Günthör** SUI
1995 **John Godina** USA
1997 **John Godina** USA
1999 **CJ Hunter** USA

Discus
1983 **Imrich Bugar** TCH
1987 **Jürgen Schult** GDR
1991 **Lars Riedel** GER
1993 **Lars Riedel** GER
1995 **Lars Riedel** GER
1997 **Lars Riedel** GER
1999 **Anthony Washington** USA

Hammer
1983 **Sergey Litvinov** URS
1987 **Sergey Litvinov** URS
1991 **Yuriy Sedykh** URS
1993 **Andrey Abduvalyev** TJK
1995 **Andrey Abduvalyev** TJK
1997 **Heinz Weis** GER
1999 **Karsten Kobs** GER

Javelin
1983 **Detlef Michel** GDR
1987 **Seppo Räty** FIN
1991 **Kimmo Kinnunen** FIN
1993 **Jan Zelezny** CZE
1995 **Jan Zelezny** CZE
1997 **Marius Corbett** RSA
1999 **Aki Parviainen** FIN

Decathlon
1983 **Daley Thompson** GBR
1987 **Torsten Voss** GDR
1991 **Dan O'Brien** USA
1993 **Dan O'Brien** USA
1995 **Dan O'Brien** USA
1997 **Tomás Dvorák** CZE
1999 **Tomás Dvorák** CZE

20km Walk
1983 **Ernesto Canto** MEX
1987 **Maurizio Damilano** ITA
1991 **Maurizio Damilano** ITA
1993 **Valentin Massana** ITA
1995 **Michele Didoni** ITA
1997 **Daniel Garcia** MEX
1999 **Ilya Markov** RUS

ATHLETICS

50km Walk
1983 **Ronald Weigel** GDR
1987 **Hartwig Gauder** GDR
1991 **Aleksandr Potashov** URS
1993 **Jesús Angel Garcia** ESP
1995 **Valentin Kononen** FIN
1997 **Robert Korzeniowski** POL
1999 **German Skurygin** RUS

4x100m Relay
1983 **USA**
1987 **USA**
1991 **USA**
1993 **USA**
1995 **Canada**
1997 **Canada**
1999 **USA**

4x400m Relay
1983 **Soviet Union**
1987 **USA**
1991 **Great Britain**
1993 **USA**
1995 **USA**
1997 **USA**
1999 **USA**

Women

100m
1983 **Marlies Gohr** GDR
1987 **Silke Gladisch** GDR
1991 **Katrin Krabbe** GER
1993 **Gail Devers** USA
1995 **Gwen Torrence** USA
1997 **Marion Jones** USA
1999 **Marion Jones** USA

200m
1983 **Marita Koch** GDR
1987 **Silke Gladisch** GDR
1991 **Katrin Krabbe** GER
1993 **Merlene Ottey** JAM
1995 **Merlene Ottey*** JAM
1997 **Zhanna Pintusevich** UKR
1999 **Inger Miller** USA
Gwen Torrence finished first, but was disqualified for running out of her lane

400m
1983 **Jarmila Kratochvilova** TCH
1987 **Olga Bryzgina** URS
1991 **Marie-José Pérec** FRA
1993 **Jearl Miles** USA
1995 **Marie-José Pérec** FRA
1997 **Cathy Freeman** AUS
1999 **Cathy Freeman** AUS

800m
1983 **Jarmila Kratochvilova** TCH
1987 **Sigrun Wodars** GDR
1991 **Lilia Nurutdinova** URS
1993 **Maria Mutola** MOZ
1995 **Ana Quirot** CUB
1997 **Ana Quirot** CUB
1999 **Ludmila Formanova** CZE

1500m
1983 **Mary Decker** USA
1987 **Tatyana Samolenko** URS
1991 **Hassiba Boulmerka** ALG
1993 **Liu Dong** CHN
1995 **Hassiba Boulmerka** ALG
1997 **Carla Sacramento** POR
1999 **Svetlana Masterkova** RUS

3000m*
1983 **Mary Decker** USA
1987 **Tatyana Samolenko** URS
1991 **Tatyana Dorovskikh**** URS
1993 **Qu Yunxia** CHN
* Superseded by the 5000m
** née Samolenko

5000m
1995 **Sonia O'Sullivan** IRL
1997 **Gabriela Szabo** ROM
1999 **Gabriela Szabo** ROM

10,000m
1987 **Ingrid Kristiansen** NOR
1991 **Liz McColgan** GBR
1993 **Wang Junxia** CHN
1995 **Fernanda Ribeiro** POR
1997 **Sally Barsosio** KEN
1999 **Gete Wami** ETH

Marathon
1983 **Grete Waitz** NOR
1987 **Rosa Mota** POR
1991 **Wanda Panfil** POL
1993 **Junko Asari** JPN
1995 **Manuela Machado** POR
1997 **Hiromi Suzuki** JPN
1999 **Yong Song-ock** PRK

100m Hurdles
1983 **Bettine Jahn** GDR
1987 **Ginka Zagorcheva** BUL
1991 **Ludmila Narozhilenko** URS
1993 **Gail Devers** USA
1995 **Gail Devers** USA
1997 **Ludmila Engquist**** SWE
1999 **Gail Devers** USA
** née Narozhilenko

400m hurdles
1983 **Yekaterina Fesenko** URS
1987 **Sabine Busch** GDR
1991 **Tatyana Ledovskaya** URS
1993 **Sally Gunnell** GBR
1995 **Kim Batten** USA
1997 **Nezha Bidouane** MAR
1999 **Daimi Pernia** CUB

High Jump
1983 **Tamara Bykova** URS
1987 **Stefka Kostadinova** BUL
1991 **Heike Henkel** GER
1993 **Ioamnet Quintero** CUB
1995 **Stefka Kostadinova** BUL
1997 **Hanne Haugland** NOR
1999 **Inga Babakova** UKR

Pole Vault
1999 **Stacy Dragila** USA

Long Jump
1983 **Heike Daute** GDR
1987 **Jackie Joyner-Kersee** USA
1991 **Jackie Joyner-Kersee** USA
1993 **Heike Drechsler** GER
1995 **Fiona May** ITA
1997 **Lyudmila Galkina** RUS
1999 **Niurka Montalvo** ESP

Triple Jump
1993 **Ana Biryukova** RUS
1995 **Inessa Kravets** UKR
1997 **Sárka Kaspárková** CZE
1999 **Paraskevi Tsiamita** GRE

Shot
1983 **Helena Fibingerova** TCH
1987 **Natalya Lisovskaya** URS
1991 **Zhihong Huang** CHN
1993 **Zhihong Huang** CHN
1995 **Astrid Kumbernuss** GER
1997 **Astrid Kumbernuss** GER
1999 **Astrid Kumbernuss** GER

Discus
1983 **Martina Opitz** GDR
1987 **Martina Hellmann*** GDR
1991 **Tsvet. Khristova** BUL
1993 **Olga Burova** RUS
1995 **Ellina Svereva** BLR
1997 **Beatrice Faumuina** NZL
1999 **Franka Dietzsch** GER
* née Opitz

Hammer
1999 **Michaela Melinte** ROM

Javelin
1983 **Tiina Lillak** FIN
1987 **Fatima Whitbread** GBR
1991 **Xu Demei** CHN
1993 **Trine Hattestad** NOR
1995 **Natalya Shikolenko** BLR
1997 **Trine Hattestad** NOR
1999 **Mirela Manjani-Tzelili** GRE

Heptathlon
1983 **Ramona Neubert** GDR
1987 **Jackie Joyner-Kersee** USA
1991 **Sabine Braun** GER
1993 **Jackie Joyner-Kersee** USA
1995 **Ghada Shouaa** SYR
1997 **Sabine Braun** GER
1999 **Eunice Barber** FRA

10km Walk
1987 **Irina Strakhova** URS
1991 **Alina Ivanova** URS
1993 **Sari Essayah** FIN
1995 **Irina Stankina** RUS
1997 **Annarita Sidoti** ITA

20km Walk
1999 **Liu Hongyu** CHN

ATHLETICS

WORLD CHAMPIONSHIPS (Cont)

4x100m Relay
1983 East Germany
1987 USA
1991 Jamaica
1993 Russia
1995 USA
1997 USA
1999 Bahamas

4x400m Relay
1983 East Germany
1987 East Germany
1991 Soviet Union
1993 USA
1995 USA
1997 Germany
1999 Russia

WORLD CROSS-COUNTRY CHAMPIONS

From 1998, the championships also incorporated a short race (over 4km for both men and women). The results are given with the traditional races first, the short races below.

Year	Men	Women
1973	Pekka Paivarinto FIN	Paola Cacchi ITA
1974	Eric de Beck BEL	Paola Cacchi ITA
1975	Ian Stewart SCO	Julie Brown USA
1976	Carlos Lopes POR	Carmen Valero ESP
1977	Leon Schots BEL	Carmen Valero ESP
1978	John Treacy IRL	Grete Waitz NOR
1979	John Treacy IRL	Grete Waitz NOR
1980	Craig Virgin USA	Grete Waitz NOR
1981	Craig Virgin USA	Grete Waitz NOR
1982	Mohamed Kedir ETH	Maricica Puica ROM
1983	Bekele Debele ETH	Grete Waitz NOR
1984	Carlos Lopes POR	Maricica Puica ROM
1985	Carlos Lopes POR	Zola Budd ENG
1986	John Ngugi KEN	Zola Budd ENG
1987	John Ngugi KEN	Annette Sergent FRA
1988	John Ngugi KEN	Ingrid Kristiansen NOR
1989	John Ngugi KEN	Annette Sergent FRA
1990	Khalid Skah MAR	Lynn Jennings USA
1991	Khalid Skah MAR	Lynn Jennings USA
1992	John Ngugi KEN	Lynn Jennings USA
1993	William Sigei KEN	Albertina Dias POR
1994	William Sigei KEN	Helen Chepngeno KEN
1995	Paul Tergat KEN	Derartu Tulu ETH
1996	Paul Tergat KEN	Gete Wami ETH
1997	Paul Tergat KEN	Derartu Tulu ETH
1998	Paul Tergat KEN	Sonia O'Sullivan IRL
	John Kibowen KEN	Sonia O'Sullivan IRL
1999	Paul Tergat KEN	Gete Wami ETH
	Benjamin Limo KEN	Jackline Maranga KEN
2000	Mohammed Mourhit BEL	Derartu Tulu ETH
	John Kibowen KEN	Kutre Dulecha ETH

BOSTON MARATHON

The oldest of the major marathons, Boston was first run in 1897 although at just under 40km. It was run over the full distance for the first time in 1927

1975	Bill Rogers USA	Liane Winger FRG
1976	Jack Fultz USA	Kim Merritt USA
1977	Jerome Drayton CAN	Miki Gorman USA
1978	Bill Rogers USA	Gayle Barron USA
1979	Bill Rogers USA	Joan Benoit USA
1980	Bill Rodgers USA	Jacqui Gareau CAN
1981	Toshihiko Seko JPN	Allison Roe NZL
1982	Alberto Salazar USA	Charlotte Teske FRG
1983	Greg Meyer USA	Joan Benoit USA
1984	Geoff Smith GBR	Lorraine Moller NZL
1985	Geoff Smith GBR	Lisa Weidenbach USA
1986	Rob de Castella AUS	Ingrid Kristiansen NOR
1987	Toshihiko Seko JPN	Rosa Mota POR
1988	Ibrahim Hussein KEN	Rosa Mota POR
1989	Abebe Mekonnen ETH	I Kristiansen NOR
1990	Gelindo Bordin ITA	Rosa Mota POR
1991	Ibrahim Hussein KEN	Wanda Panfil POL
1992	Ibrahim Hussein KEN	Olga Markova RUS
1993	Cosmas N'Deti KEN	Olga Markova RUS
1994	Cosmas N'Deti KEN	Uta Pippig GER
1995	Cosmas N'Deti KEN	Uta Pippig GER
1996	Moses Tanui KEN	Uta Pippig GER
1997	Lameck Aguta KEN	Fatuma Roba ETH
1998	Moses Tanui KEN	Fatuma Roba ETH
1999	Joseph Chebet KEN	Fatuma Roba ETH
2000	Elijah Lagat KEN	CatherineNderebaKEN

LONDON MARATHON

Year	Men	Women
1981	Dick Beardsley USA* & Inge Simonsen NOR*	Joyce Smith GBR
1982	Hugh Jones GBR	Joyce Smith GBR
1983	Mike Gratton GBR	Grete Waitz NOR
1984	Charlie Spedding GBR	Ingrid Kristiansen NOR
1985	Steve Jones GBR	I Kristiansen NOR
1986	Toshihiko Seko JPN	Grete Waitz NOR
1987	Hiromi Taniguchi JPN	I Kristiansen NOR
1988	H Jorgensen DEN	I Kristiansen NOR
1989	Doug Wakiihuri KEN	Veronique Marot GBR
1990	Allister Hutton GBR	Wanda Panfil POL
1991	Yakov Tolstikov URS	Rosa Mota POR
1992	Antonio Pinto POR	Katrin Dörre GER
1993	Eamonn Martin GBR	Katrin Dörre GER
1994	Dionicio Ceron MEX	Katrin Dörre GER
1995	Dionicio Ceron MEX	Malgorzata Sobanska POL
1996	Dionicio Ceron MEX	Liz McColgan GBR
1997	Antonio Pinto POR	Joyce Chepchumba KEN
1998	Abel Anton ESP	Catherine McKiernan IRL
1999	Abdel El Mouaziz MAR	Joyce Chepchumba KEN
2000	Antonio Pinto POR	Tegla Loroupe KEN

ATHLETICS

NEW YORK MARATHON

Year	Men	Women
1976	Bill Rodgers USA	Miki Gorman USA
1977	Bill Rodgers USA	Miki Gorman USA
1978	Bill Rodgers USA	Grete Waitz NOR
1979	Bill Rodgers USA	Grete Waitz NOR
1980	Alberto Salazar USA	Grete Waitz NOR
1981	Alberto Salazar USA	Allison Roe NZL**
1982	Alberto Salazar USA	Grete Waitz NOR
1983	Rod Dixon NZL	Grete Waitz NOR
1984	Orlando Pizzolato ITA	Grete Waitz NOR
1985	Orlando Pizzolato ITA	Grete Waitz NOR
1986	Gianni Poli ITA	Grete Waitz NOR
1987	Ibrahim Hussein KEN	Priscilla Welch GBR
1988	Steve Jones GBR	Grete Waitz NOR
1989	Juma Ikangaa TAN	Ingrid Kristiansen NOR
1990	Doug Wakiihuri KEN	Wanda Panfil POL
1991	Salvador Garcia MEX	Liz McColgan GBR
1992	Willie Mtolo RSA	Lisa Ondieki AUS
1993	Andres Espinoza MEX	Uta Pippig GER
1994	German Silva MEX	Tecla Lorupe KEN
1995	German Silva MEX	Tecla Lorupe KEN
1996	Giacomo Leone ITA	Anuta Catuna ROM
1997	John Kagwe KEN	F Rochat-Moser SUI
1998	John Kagwe KEN	Franca Fiacconi ITA
1999	Joseph Chebet KEN	Adriana Fernandez MEX
2000	Abdel El Mouaziz MAR	Ludmila Petrova RUS

* Dead-heated
** The course used in 1981-1983 was found to be 155m short and the world bests of Salazar and Roe were invalidated

BADMINTON

WORLD CHAMPIONS

MEN'S SINGLES
1977 **Flemming Delfs** DEN
1980 **Rudy Hartono** INA
1983 **Icuk Sugiarto** INA
1985 **Hang Jian** CHN
1987 **Yang Yang** CHN
1989 **Yang Yang** CHN
1991 **Zhao Jianhua** CHN
1993 **Joko Suprianto** INA
1995 **Heryanto Arbi** INA
1997 **Peter Rasmussen** DEN
1999 **Sun Jun** CHN

WOMEN'S SINGLES
1977 **Lene Köppen** DEN
1980 **Wiharjo Verawaty** INA
1983 **Li Lingwei** CHN
1985 **Han Aiping** CHN
1987 **Han Aiping** CHN
1989 **Li Lingwei** CHN
1991 **Tang Jiuhong** CHN
1993 **Susi Susanti** INA
1995 **Ye Zhaoying** CHN
1997 **Ye Zhaoying** CHN
1999 **Camilla Martin** DEN

MEN'S DOUBLES
1977 **Wahjudi/Tjun** INA
1980 **Chandra/Christian** INA
1983 **Fladberg/Hellerdie** DEN
1985 **Park Joo-Bong/Kim Moon-Soo** KOR
1987 **Li Yongbo/Tian Bingye** CHN
1989 **Li Yongbo/Tian Bingye** CHN
1991 **Park Joo-Bong/Kim Moon-Soo** KOR
1993 **Subagja/Gunawan** INA
1995 **Mainaky/Subagja** INA
1997 **Sigit/Wijaya** INA
1999 **Ha/Kim** KOR

WOMEN'S DOUBLES
1977 **Tuganoo/Vero** JPN
1980 **Perry/Webster** GBR
1983 **Lin Ying/Wu Dixie** CHN
1985 **Han Aiping/Li Lingwei** CHN
1987 **Lin Ying/Guan Weizhen** CHN
1989 **Lin Ying/Guan Weizhen** CHN
1991 **Gan Weizhen/Nong Qunha** CHN
1993 **Nong Qunha/Zhou Lei** CHN
1995 **Gil/Jang** KOR
1997 **Ge/Gu** CHN
1999 **Ge/Gu** CHN

MIXED DOUBLES
1977 **Stovgaard/Köppen** DEN
1980 **Christian/Wogoeno** INA
1983 **Kihlström/Perry** SWE/GBR
1985 **Park Joo-bong/Yoo Sang-hee** KOR
1987 **Wang Pengrin/Shi Fagying** CHN
1989 **Park Joo-Bong/Chung Myung-Hee** KOR
1991 **Park Joo-Bong/Chung Myung-Hee** KOR
1993 **Lund/Bengtsson** DEN/SWE
1995 **Lund/Thomsen** DEN

1997 **Liu/Ge** CHN
1999 **Kim/Ra** KOR

SUDIRMAN CUP (Team)
1989 **Indonesia**
1991 **Korea**
1993 **Korea**
1995, 97 & 99 **China**

THOMAS CUP (Men's Team)
1949, 52 & 55 **Malaya**
1958, 61 & 64 **Indonesia**
1967 **Malaysia**
1970, 73, 76 & 79 **Indonesia**
1982 **China**
1984 **Indonesia**
1986, 88 & 90 **China**
1992 **Malaysia**
1994, 96, 98 & 2000 **Indonesia**

UBER CUP (Women's Team)
1957, 59 & 63 **United States**
1966,69 & 73 **Japan**
1975 **Indonesia**
1978 & 81 **Japan**
1981 **Japan**
1984, 86, 88, 90 & 92 **China**
1994 **Indonesia**
1996 **Indonesia**
98 & 2000 **China**

EUROPEAN CHAMPIONS

MEN'S SINGLES
1976 **Flemming Delfs** DEN
1978 **Flemming Delfs** DEN
1980 **Flemming Delfs** DEN
1982 **Jens Peter Nierhoff** DEN
1984 **Morten Frost** DEN
1986 **Morten Frost** DEN
1988 **Darren Hall** ENG
1990 **Steve Baddeley** ENG
1992 **Paul-Eric Høyer-Larsen** DEN
1994 **Paul-Eric Høyer-Larsen** DEN
1996 **Paul-Eric Høyer-Larsen** DEN
1998 **Peter Gade Christensen** DEN
2000 **Peter Gade Christensen** DEN

WOMEN'S SINGLES
1978 **Lene Köppen** DEN
1980 **Liselotte Blumer** SWE
1982 **Lene Köppen** DEN
1984 **Helen Troke** ENG
1986 **Helen Troke** ENG
1988 **Kirsten Larsen** DEN
1990 **Pernille Nedergaard** DEN
1992 **Pernille Nedergaard** DEN
1994 **Lim Xiaoqing** SWE
1996 **Camilla Martin** DEN
1998 **Camilla Martin** DEN
2000 **Camilla Martin** DEN

BASEBALL

	Winners	Runners-up	Score
1903	Boston Red Sox (AL)	Pittsburgh Pirates (NL)	5-3
1904	*No Series*		
1905	New York Giants (NL)	Philadelphia Athletics (AL)	4-1
1906	Chicago White Sox (AL)	Chicago Cubs (NL)	4-2
1907	Chicago Cubs (NL)	Detroit Tigers (AL)	4-0 with 1 tie
1908	Chicago Cubs (NL)	Detroit Tigers (AL)	4-1
1909	Pittsburgh Pirates (NL)	Detroit Tigers (AL)	4-3
1910	Philadelphia Athletics (AL)	Chicago Cubs (NL)	4-1
1911	Philadelphia Athletics (AL)	New York Giants (NL)	4-2
1912	Boston Red Sox (AL)	New York Giants (NL)	4-3 with 1 tie
1913	Philadelphia Athletics	New York Giants (NL)	4-1
1914	Boston Braves (NL)	Philadelphia Athletics (AL)	4-0
1915	Boston Red Sox (AL)	Philadelphia Phillies (NL)	4-1
1916	Boston Red Sox (AL)	Brooklyn Dodgers (NL)	4-1
1917	Chicago White Sox (AL)	New York Giants (NL)	4-2
1918	Boston Red Sox (AL)	Chicago Cubs (NL)	4-2
1919	Cincinnati Reds (NL)	Chicago White Sox (AL)	5-3
1920	Cleveland Indians (AL)	Brooklyn Dodgers (NL)	5-2
1921	New York Giants (NL)	New York Yankees (AL)	5-3
1922	New York Giants (NL)	New York Yankees (AL)	4-0 with 1 tie
1923	New York Yankees (AL)	New York Giants (NL)	4-2
1924	Washington Senators (AL)	New York Giants (NL)	4-3
1925	Pittsburgh Pirates (NL)	Washington Senators (AL)	4-3
1926	St Louis Cardinals (NL)	New York Yankees (AL)	4-3
1927	New York Yankees (AL)	Pittsburgh Pirates (NL)	4-0
1928	New York Yankees (AL)	St Louis Cardinals (NL)	4-0
1929	Philadelphia Athletics (AL)	Chicago Cubs (NL)	4-1
1930	Philadelphia Athletics (AL)	St Louis Cardinals (NL)	4-2
1931	St Louis Cardinals (NL)	Philadelphia Athletics (AL)	4-3
1932	New York Yankees (AL)	Chicago Cubs (NL)	4-0
1933	New York Giants (NL)	Washington Senators (AL)	4-1
1934	St Louis Cardinals (NL)	Detroit Tigers (AL)	4-3
1935	Detroit Tigers (AL)	Chicago Cubs (NL)	4-2
1936	New York Yankees (AL)	New York Giants (NL)	4-2
1937	New York Yankees (AL)	New York Giants (NL)	4-1
1938	New York Yankees (AL)	Chicago Cubs (NL)	4-0
1939	New York Yankees (AL)	Cincinnati Reds (NL)	4-0
1940	Cincinnati Reds (NL)	Detroit Tigers (AL)	4-3
1941	New York Yankees (AL)	Brooklyn Dodgers (NL)	4-1
1942	St Louis Cardinals (NL)	New York Yankees (AL)	4-1
1943	New York Yankees (AL)	St Louis Cardinals (NL)	4-1
1944	St Louis Cardinals (NL)	St Louis Browns (AL)	4-2
1945	Detroit Tigers (AL)	Chicago Cubs (NL)	4-3
1946	St Louis Cardinals (NL)	Boston Red Sox (AL)	4-3
1947	New York Yankees (AL)	Brooklyn Dodgers (NL)	4-3
1948	Cleveland Indians (AL)	Boston Braves (NL)	4-2
1949	New York Yankees (AL)	Brooklyn Dodgers (NL)	4-1
1950	New York Yankees (AL)	Philadelphia Phillies (NL)	4-0
1951	New York Yankees (AL)	New York Giants (NL)	4-2
1952	New York Yankees (AL)	Brooklyn Dodgers (NL)	4-3
1953	New York Yankees (AL)	Brooklyn Dodgers (NL)	4-2
1954	New York Giants (NL)	Cleveland Indians (AL)	4-0
1955	Brooklyn Dodgers (NL)	New York Yankees (AL)	4-3
1956	New York Yankees (AL)	Brooklyn Dodgers (NL)	4-3
1957	Milwaukee Braves (NL)	New York Yankees (AL)	4-3
1958	New York Yankees (AL)	Milwaukee Braves (NL)	4-3
1959	Los Angeles Dodgers (NL)	Chicago White Sox (ZAL)	4-2
1960	Pittsburgh Pirates (NL)	New York Yankees (AL)	4-3
1961	New York Yankees (AL)	Cincinnati Reds (NL)	4-1

BASEBALL

	Winners	Runners-up	Score
1962	**New York Yankees (AL)**	San Francisco Giants (NL)	4-3
1963	**Los Angeles Dodgers (NL)**	New York Yankees (AL)	4-0
1964	**St Louis Cardinals (NL)**	New York Yankees (AL)	4-3
1965	**Los Angeles Dodgers (NL)**	Minnesota Twins (AL)	4-3
1966	**Baltimore Orioles (AL)**	Los Angeles Dodgers (NL)	4-0
1967	**St Louis Cardinals (NL)**	Boston Red Sox (AL)	4-3
1968	**Detroit Tigers (AL)**	St Louis Cardinals (NL)	4-3
1969	**New York Mets (NL)**	Baltimore Orioles (AL)	4-1
1970	**Baltimore Orioles (AL)**	Cincinnati Reds (NL)	4-1
1971	**Pittsburgh Pirates (NL)**	Baltimore Orioles (AL)	4-3
1972	**Oakland Athletics (AL)**	Cincinnati Reds (NL)	4-3
1973	**Oakland Athletics (AL)**	New York Mets (NL)	4-3
1974	**Oakland Athletics (AL)**	Los Angeles Dodgers (NL)	4-1
1975	**Cincinnati Reds (NL)**	Boston Red Sox (AL)	4-3
1976	**Cincinnati Reds (NL)**	New York Yankees (AL)	4-0
1977	**New York Yankees (AL)**	Los Angeles Dodgers (NL)	4-2
1978	**New York Yankees (AL)**	Los Angeles Dodgers (NL)	4-2
1979	**Pittsburgh Pirates (NL)**	Baltimore Orioles (AL)	4-3
1980	**Philadelphia Phillies (NL)**	Kansas City Royals (AL)	4-2
1981	**Los Angeles Dodgers (NL)**	New York Yankees (AL)	4-2
1982	**St Louis Cardinals (NL)**	Milwaukee Brewers (AL)	4-3
1983	**Baltimore Orioles (AL)**	Philadelphia Phillies (NL)	4-1
1984	**Detroit Tigers (AL)**	San Diego Padres (NL)	4-1
1985	**Kansas City Royals (AL)**	St Louis Cardinals (NL)	4-3
1986	**New York Mets (NL)**	Boston Red Sox (AL)	4-3
1987	**Minnesota Twins (AL)**	St Louis Cardinals (NL)	4-3
1988	**Los Angeles Dodgers (NL)**	Oakland Athletics (AL)	4-1
1989	**Oakland Athletics (AL)**	San Francisco Giants (NL)	4-0
1990	**Cincinnati Reds (NL)**	Oakland Athletics (AL)	4-0
1991	**Minnesota Twins (AL)**	Atlanta Braves (NL)	4-3
1992	**Toronto Blue Jays (AL)**	Atlanta Braves (NL)	4-2
1993	**Toronto Blue Jays (AL)**	Philadelphia Phillies (NL)	4-2
1994	No Series		
1995	**Atlanta Braves (NL)**	Cleveland Indians (AL)	4-2
1996	**New York Yankees (AL)**	Atlanta Braves (NL)	4-2
1997	**Florida Marlins (NL)**	Cleveland Indians (AL)	4-3
1998	**New York Yankees (AL)**	San Diego Padres (NL)	4-0
1999	**New York Yankees (AL)**	Atlanta Braves (NL)	4-0
2000	**New York Yankees (AL)**	New York Mets (NL)	4-1

Baseball Briefing

Subscriptions:

Trevor Kendall, 2 Drury Close, Waltham, Grimsby DN37 0XP

BASKETBALL

NATIONAL (EBBA) CUP WINNERS

Year	Winners	Runner-up	Score
1936	Hoylake YMCA	London Polytechnic	32-21
1937	Hoylake YMCA	Latter Day Saints	23-17
1938	Catford Saints	Rochdale Greys	61-47
1939	Catford Saints	Rochdale Greys	53-41
1940	Birmingham Inst	Central YMCA	35-30
1947	Carpathians	Birmingham D'bran	48-25
1948	Latter Day Saints	Latvian Society	39-30
1949	Latter Day Saints	Birmingham D'bran	44-35
1950	Latter Day Saints	USAF Burtonwood	43-32
1951	Birmingham D'bran	London Polytechnic	34-33
1952	London Poly	Birmingham D'bran	40-29
1953	London Poly	Birmingham D'bran	55-46
1954	London Poly	Nottingham YMCA	98-53
1955	London Poly	Birmingham D'bran	58-54
1957	Central YMCA	London Polytechnic	63-51
1958	Central YMCA	East Ham	48-40
1959	Aspley OB	Birmingham D'bran	58-39
1960	Central YMCA	London Polytechnic	95-62
1961	London University	Central YMCA	68-59
1962	Central YMCA	RAE Eagles	87-47
1963	Central YMCA	London University	70-69
1964	Central YMCA	London University	78-56
1965	Aldershot Warriors	Oxford University	79-63
1966	Oxford University	Aldershot Warriors	91-70
1967	Central YMCA	Vauxhall Motors	64-62
1968	Oxford University	Aldershot Warriors	61-59
1969	Central YMCA	Aldershot Warriors	70-62
1970	Liverpool Police	Oxford University	73-67
1971	Manchester Uni	Sutton	88-81
1972	Avenue (Leyton)	Cambridge	58-66
1973	London Latvian SK	Sutton	70-69
1974	Sutton & C Palace	Embassy All Stars	120-100
1975	Embassy All Stars	Sutton & C Palace	82-81
1976	Crystal Palace	Embassy All Stars	108-88
1977	Crystal Palace	Embassy All Stars	91-90
1978	Crystal Palace	Coventry	89-87
1979	Doncaster	Crystal Palace	73-71
1980	Crystal Palace	Doncaster	97-67
1981	Crystal Palace	Doncaster	91-74
1982	Solent	Doncaster	127-91
1983	Solent	Birmingham	98-97
1984	Solent	Leicester	86-67
1985	Kingston	Manchester United	103-98
1986	Kingston	Solent	113-82
1987	Kingston	Portsmouth	95-87
1988	Kingston	Portsmouth	90-84
1989	Bracknell	Manchester	87-75
1990	Kingston	Sunderland	103-78
1991	Sunderland	Leicester	88-81
1992	Kingston	Thames Valley	90-71
1993	Guildford	Worthing	82-72
1994	Worthing	Thames Valley	92-83
1995	Sheffield Sharks	Thames Valley	89-66
1996	London Towers	Sheffield Sharks	70-58
1997	Leopards	Sheffield Sharks	87-79
1998	Thames Valley	Leicester Tigers	82-78
1999	Sheffield Sharks	Leopards	67-65
2000	Sheffield Sharks	Manchester Giants	89-80

LEAGUE CHAMPIONS - MEN

Year	Winners	Runners-up
1972-73	Avenue (Leyton)	Liverpool
1973-74	Crystal Palace	Islington
1974-75	Islington	Crystal Palace
1975-76	Crystal Palace	Islington
1976-77	Crystal Palace	Manchester
1977-78	Crystal Palace	Milton Keynes
1978-79	Doncaster	Crystal Palace
1979-80	Crystal Palace	Doncaster
1980-81	Birmingham	Crystal Palace
1981-82	Crystal Palace	Solent
1982-83	Crystal Palace	Sunderland
1983-84	Solent	Crystal Palace
1984-85	Kingston	Manchester United
1985-86	Manchester United	Kingston
1986-87	Portsmouth	Kingston
1987-88	Portsmouth	Kingston
1988-89	Glasgow	Livingston
1989-90	Kingston	Sunderland
1990-91	Kingston	Sunderland
1991-92	Kingston	Thames Valley
1992-93	Worthing	Thames Valley
1993-94	Thames Valley	Worthing
1994-95	Sheffield Sharks	Thames Valley
1995-96	London Towers	Sheffield
1996-97	Leopards	London Towers
1997-98	Gtr London Leopards	Birmingham Bullets
1998-99	Sheffield Sharks	Manchester Giants
1999-00	Manchester Giants	Birmingham Bullets

LEAGUE CHAMPIONS - WOMEN

Year	Winners	Runners-up
1975-76	Tigers (Herts)	Cleveland E
1976-77	Tigers (Herts)	Southgate
1977-78	Cleveland E	Tigers (Herts)
1978-79	Cleveland E	Tigers (Herts)
1979-80	Tigers	Cleveland E
1980-81	Southgate	Crystal Palace
1981-82	Southgate	Northampton
1982-83	Southgate	Northampton
1983-84	Northampton	Nottingham
1984-85	Northampton	Crystal Palace
1985-86	Crystal Palace	Northampton
1986-87	Northampton	Crystal Palace
1987-88	Northampton	Stockport
1988-89	Northampton	London YMCA
1989-90	Northampton	Sheffield
1990-91	Sheffield	London YMCA
1991-92	Sheffield	Thames Valley
1992-93	Sheffield	Northampton
1993-94	Sheffield	Northampton
1994-95	Sheffield	Barking & Dagenham
1995-96	Sheffield Hatters	Birmingham
1996-97	Sheffield Hatters	Thames Valley Ladies
1997-98	Sheffield Hatters	Thames Valley Ladies
1998-99	Sheffield Hatters	Rhondda Rebels
1999-00	Sheffield Hatters	Spelthorne Acers

BASKETBALL

NATIONAL LEAGUE

1938	Goodyears
1939	Firestones
1940	Firestones
1941	Oshkosh
1942	Oshkosh
1943	Fort Wayne Pistons
1944	Fort Wayne Pistons
1945	Fort Wayne Pistons
1946	Rochester Royals
1947	Chicago Stags
1948	Minneapolis Lakers
1949	Anderson Packers

NBA

1947	Philadelphia Warriors
1948	Baltimore Bullets
1949	Minneapolis Lakers
1950	Minneapolis Lakers
1951	Rochester Royals
1952	Minneapolis Lakers
1953	Minneapolis Lakers
1954	Minneapolis Lakers
1955	Syracuse Nationals
1956	Philadelphia Warriors
1957	Boston Celtics
1958	St Louis Hawks
1959	Boston Celtics
1960	Boston Celtics
1961	Boston Celtics
1962	Boston Celtics
1963	Boston Celtics
1964	Boston Celtics
1965	Boston Celtics
1966	Boston Celtics
1967	Philadelphia 76ers
1968	Boston Celtics
1969	Boston Celtics
1970	New York Knicks
1971	Milwaukee Bucks
1972	Los Angeles Lakers
1973	New York Knicks
1974	Boston Celtics
1975	Golden State Warriors
1976	Boston Celtics
1977	Portland Trail Blazers
1978	Washington Bullets
1979	Seattle Supersonics
1980	Los Angeles Lakers
1981	Boston Celtics
1982	Los Angeles Lakers
1983	Philadelphia 76ers
1984	Boston Celtics
1985	Los Angeles Lakers
1986	Boston Celtics
1987	Los Angeles Lakers
1988	Los Angeles Lakers
1989	Detroit Pistons
1990	Detroit Pistons
1991	Chicago Bulls
1992	Chicago Bulls
1993	Chicago Bulls
1994	Houston Rockets
1995	Houston Rockets
1996-98	Chicago Bulls
1999	San Antonio Spurs
2000	Los Angeles Lakers

NBA LEADING SCORERS

1950	George Mikan (Mn)	1865
1951	George Mikan (Mn)	1932
1952	Paul Arizin (Ph)	1674
1953	Neil Johnston (Ph)	1564
1954	Neil Johnston (Ph)	1759
1955	Neil Johnston (Ph)	1631
1956	Bob Pettit (St L)	1849
1957	Paul Arizin (Ph)	1817
1958	George Yardley (Dt)	2001
1959	Bob Pettit (St L)	2105
1960	Wilt Chamberlain (Ph)	2707
1961	Wilt Chamberlain (Ph)	3033
1962	Wilt Chamberlain (Ph)	4029
1963	Wilt Chamberlain (SF)	3586
1964	Wilt Chamberlain (SF)	2948
1965	Wilt Chamberlain (SF/Ph)	2534
1966	Wilt Chamberlain (Ph)	2649
1967	Rick Barry (SF)	2775
1968	Dave Bing (Dt)	2142
1969	Elvin Hayes (SD)	2327
1970	Jerry West (LA)	2309
1971	Lew Alcindor (Ml) *	2596
1972	Kareem Abdul-Jabbar (Ml)	2822
1973	Nate Archibald (KC/Om)	2719
1974	Bob McAdoo (Bf)	2261
1975	Bob McAdoo (Bf)	2831
1976	Bob McAdoo (Bf)	2427
1977	Pete Maravich (NO)	2273
1978	George Gervin (SA)	2232
1979	George Gervin (SA)	2365
1980	George Gervin (SA)	2585
1981	Adrian Dantley (Ut)	2452
1982	George Gervin (SA)	2551
1983	Alex English (Dn)	2326
1984	Adrian Dantley (Ut)	2418
1985	Bernard King (NY)	1809
1986	Dominique Wilkins (At)	2366
1987	Michael Jordan (Ch)	3041
1988	Michael Jordan (Ch)	2868
1989	Michael Jordan (Ch)	2633
1990	Michael Jordan (Ch)	2753
1991	Michael Jordan (Ch)	2580
1992	Michael Jordan (Ch)	2404
1993	Michael Jordan (Ch)	2541
1994	David Robinson (SA)	2383
1995	Shaquille O'Neal (Orl)	2315
1996	Michael Jordan (Ch)	2491
1997	Michael Jordan (Ch)	2431
1998	Michael Jordan (Ch)	2357
1999	Shaquille O'Neal (LA) **	1289
2000	Shaquille O'Neal (LA)	2344

took name of Kareem Abdul-Jabbar

*** season latestarting through players' strike*

BILLIARDS

WORLD CHAMPIONS
English unless otherwise stated

1870 William Cook
1870 John Roberts jnr
1870 Joseph Bennett
1871 John Roberts jnr
1871 William Cook
1875 John Roberts jnr
1880 Joseph Bennett
1885 John Roberts jnr
1889 Charles Dawson
1901 H W Stevenson
1901 Charles Dawson
1901 H W Stevenson
1903 Charles Dawson
1908 Melbourne Inman
1909 H W Stevenson
1910 H W Stevenson
1911 H W Stevenson
1912 Melbourne Inman
1913 Melbourne Inman
1914 Melbourne Inman
1919 Melbourne Inman
1920 Willie Smith
1921 Tom Newman
1922 Tom Newman
1923 Willie Smith
1924 Tom Newman
1925 Tom Newman
1926 Tom Newman
1927 Tom Newman
1928 Joe Davis
1929 Joe Davis
1930 Joe Davis
1932 Joe Davis
1933 Walter Lindrum AUS
1934 Walter Lindrum AUS
1951 Clark McConachy NZL
1968 Rex Williams
1971 Leslie Driffield
1971 Rex Williams
1980 Fred Davis
1982 Rex Williams
1983 Rex Williams
1984 Mark Wildman
1985 Ray Edmonds
1986 Robbie Foldvari AUS
1987 Norman Dagley
1988 Norman Dagley
1989 Mike Russell
1991 Mike Russell
1992 Geet Sethi IND
1993 Geet Sethi IND
1994 Peter Gilchrist
1995 Geet Sethi IND
1996 Mike Russell
1998 Geet Sethi IND

BOBSLEIGH

BOBSLEIGH

Year	Two-man	Four-man
1930	*No event*	Italy
1931	Killian/Huber GER	Germany
1933	Papana/Hubert ROM	*No event*
1934	Frim/Dumitrescu ROM	Germany
1935	Capadrutt/Diener SUI	Germany
1937	McEnvoy/Black GBR	Great Britain
1938	Fischer/Thielacke GER	Great Britain
1939	Lundnen/Kuffer BEL	Switzerland
1947	Feierabend/Waser SUI	Switzerland
1949	Endrich/Waller SUI	USA
1950	Feierabend/Waser SUI	USA
1951	Osterl/Nieberl FRG	W Germany
1953	Endrich/Stoeckli SUI	USA
1954	Scheibmeier/Zambelli ITA	Switzerland
1955	Feierabend/Warburton SUI	Switzerland
1957	Monti/Alvera ITA	Switzerland
1958	Monti/Alvera ITA	W Germany
1959	Monti/Alvera ITA	USA
1961	Monti/Siorpaes ITA	Italy
1962	Ruatti/De Lorenzo ITA	W Germany
1963	Monti/Siorpaes ITA	Italy
1965	Nash/Dixon GBR	Canada
1966	Monti/Siorpaes ITA	*
1967	Thaler/Durnthaler AUT	**
1969	de Zordo/Frassinelli ITA	W Germany
1970	Floth/Bader FRG	Italy
1971	Gaspari/Armano ITA	Switzerland
1973	Zimmerer/Utzshneider FRG	Switzerland
1974	Zimmerer/Utzshneider FRG	W Germany
1975	Alvera/Perruquet ITA	Switzerland
1977	Hiltebrand/Meier SUI	E Germany
1978	Schärer/Benz SUI	E Germany
1979	Schärer/Benz SUI	W Germany
1981	Germeshausen/Gerhardt GDR	E Germany
1982	Schärer/Benz SUI	Switzerland
1983	Pichler/Leuthold SUI	Switzerland
1985	Hoppe/Schauerhammer GDR	E Germany
1986	Hoppe/Schauerhammer GDR	Switzerland
1987	Pichler/Poltera SUI	Switzerland
1989	Hoppe/Musiol GDR	Switzerland
1990	Weder/Gerber SUI	Switzerland
1991	Lochner/Zimmermann GER	Germany
1993	Langen/Joechel GER	Switzerland
1995	Langen/Hampel GER	Germany
1996	Langen/Zimmermann GER	Germany
1997	Götschi/Acklin SUI	Germany
1999	Huber/Ranzi ITA	France
2000	Langen/Zimmerman SUI	Germany

* Not decided due to fatal accident
** Not decided due to thaw

LUGE

	Men	Women
1955	Anton Salvesen NOR	Karla Kienzl AUT
1956	-	Maria Isser AUT
1957	Hans Schaller FRG	M Semczyszak POL
1958	Jerzy Wojnar POL	-
1959	Herbert Thaler AUT	Elly Lieber AUT
1960	Helmuth Berndt FRG	Maria Isser AUT
1961	Jerzy Wojnar POL	Elisab. Nagele SUI
1962	Thomas Kohler GDR	Ilse Geisler GDR
1963	Fritz Nachmann FRG	Ilse Geisler GDR
1965	Hans Plenk FRG	O Enderlein GDR
1967	Thomas Kohler GDR	O Enderlein GDR
1969	Josef Feistmantl AUT	Petra Tierlich GDR
1970	Josef Fendt FRG	Barbara Piecha POL
1971	Karl Brunner ITA	E Demleitner FRG
1973	Hans Rinn GDR	M Schumann GDR
1974	Josef Fendt FRG	M Schumann GDR
1975	Wolfram Fiedler GDR	M Schumann GDR
1977	Hans Rinn GDR	M Schumann GDR
1978	Paul Hildgartner ITA	Vera Sosulya URS
1979	Detlef Gunther GDR	Mel Sollmann GDR
1981	Sergey Danilin URS	Mel Sollmann GDR
1983	Miroslav Zajonc CAN	Steffi Martin GDR
1985	Michael Walter GDR	Steffi Martin GDR
1987	Markus Prock AUT	C Schmidt GDR
1989	Georg Hackl FRG	Susi Erdmann GDR
1990	Georg Hackl FRG	G Kohlisch GDR
1991	Arnold Huber ITA	Susi Erdmann GDR
1993	Wendel Suckow USA	G Weissensteiner ITA
1995	Armin Zöggeler ITA	Gabi Kohlisch GER
1996	Markus Prock AUT	Jana Bode GER
1997	Georg Hackl GER	Susi Erdmann GER
1999	Armin Zöggeler ITA	S Wiedermann GER
2000	Jens Müller GER	Sylke Otto GER

MEN'S TWO-SEATER

1955	Hans Krausner/Herbert Thaler AUT
1957	Josef Strillinger/Fritz Nachmann FRG
1958	Josef Strillinger/Fritz Nachmann FRG
1960	Reinhold Frosch/Ewald Walch AUT
1961	Roman Pichler/Raimondo Prinoth ITA
1962	Giovanni Graber/Gianp'lo Ambrosi ITA
1963	Ryszard Pedrak/Lucjan Kudzia POL
1965	Wolfgang Scheidel/Thomas Kohler GDR
1967	Klaus Bonsack/Thomas Kohler GDR
1969	Manfred Schmid/Ewald Walch AUT
1970	Manfred Schmid/Ewald Walch AUT
1971	Paul Hildgartner/Walter Plaikner ITA
1973	Horst Hornlein/Reinhard Bredow GDR
1974	Bernd Hann/Ulrich Hann GDR
1975	Bernd Hann/Ulrich Hann GDR
1977	Hans Rinn/Norbert Hahn GDR
1978	Dainis Bremse/Aigars Krikis URS
1979	Hans Brandner/Balthasar Schwarm FRG
1981	Bernd Hann/Ulrich Hann GDR
1983	Jorg Hoffmann/Jochen Pietzsch GDR
1985	Jorg Hoffmann/Jochen Pietzsch GDR
1987	Jorg Hoffmann/Jochen Pietzsch GDR
1989	Stefan Krausse/Jan Behrendt GDR
1990	Hansjorg Raffl/Norbert Huber ITA
1991	Stefan Krausse/Jan Behrendt GER
1993	Stefan Krausse/Jan Behrendt GER
1995	Stefan Krausse/Jan Behrendt GER
1996	Tobias Schiegl/Markus Schiegl AUT
1997	Tobias Schiegl/Markus Schiegl AUT
1999	Patric Leitner/Alexander Reisch GER
2000	Patric Leitner/Alexander Reisch GER

BOWLS

World Outdoor Championships - Men

	Singles	Pairs	Triples	Fours	Team
1966	David Bryant ENG	Kelly/Palm AUS	Australia	New Zealand	Australia
1972	Malwyn Evans WAL	Delgado/Liddell HKG	United States	England	Scotland
1976	Doug Watson RSA	Watson/Moseley RSA	South Africa	South Africa	South Africa
1980	David Bryant ENG	Sandercock/Reuben RSA	England	Hong Kong	England
1984	Peter Belliss NZL	Adrain/Arculli SCO/USA	Ireland	England	Scotland
1988	David Bryant ENG	Brassey/Belliss NZL	New Zealand	Ireland	England
1992	Tony Allcock ENG	Corsie/Marshall SCO	Israel	Scotland	Scotland
1996	Tony Allcock ENG	Henry/Allen IRE	Scotland	England	Scotland
2000	Jeremy Henry IRE	Sneddon/Marshall SCO	New Zealand	Wales	Australia

World Outdoor Championships - Women

	Singles	Pairs	Triples	Fours	Team
1969	Gladys Doyle PNG	McDonald/Cridlan RSA	South Africa	South Africa	South Africa
1973	Elsie Wilkie NZL	Lucas/Jenkinson AUS	New Zealand	New Zealand	New Zealand
1977	Elsie Wilke NZL	Wong/Chok HKG	Wales	Australia	Australia
1981	Norma Shaw ENG	Bell/Allely IRE	Hong Kong	England	England
1985	Merle Richardson AUS	Richardson/Craig AUS	Australia	Scotland	Australia
1988	Janet Ackland WAL	Johnston/Nolan IRE	Australia	Australia	England
1992	Margaret Johnston IRE	Johnston/Nolan IRE	Scotland	Scotland	Scotland
1996	Carmelita Anderson NSL	Johnston/Nolan IRE	South Africa	Australia	South Africa
2000	Margaret Johnston IRE	Letham/Lindores SCO	New Zealand	New Zealand	England

World Indoor Championships - Men

	Singles	Pairs		Singles	Pairs
1979	David Bryant ENG	No event	1990	John Price WAL	Bryant/Allcock ENG
1980	David Bryant ENG	No event	1991	Richard Corsie SCO	Bryant/Allcock ENG
1981	David Bryant ENG	No event	1992	Ian Schuback AUS	Bryant/Allcock ENG
1982	John Watson SCO	No event	1993	Richard Corsie SCO	Smith/Thomson ENG
1983	Bob Sutherland SCO	No event	1994	Andy Thomson ENG	Curtis/Schuback AUS
1984	Jim Baker IRE	No event	1995	Andy Thomson ENG	Marshall/Corsie SCO
1985	Terry Sullivan WAL	No event	1996	David Gourlay jnr SCO	Kirkow/Schubank AUS
1986	Tony Allcock ENG	Bryant/Allcock ENG	1997	Hugh Duff SCO	King/Allcock ENG
1987	Tony Allcock ENG	Bryant/Allcock ENG	1998	Paul Foster SCO	Corsie/Robertson SCO
1988	Hugh Duff SCO	Schuback/Yates AUS	1999	Alex Marshall SCO	Rees/Price WAL
1989	Richard Corsie SCO	Bryant/Allcock ENG	2000	Robert Weale WAL	Gourlay/Marshall SCO

English Bowling Association Championships
First competition 1905 - results from 1985 only

	Singles	Pairs	Triples	Fours
1985	Roy Keating Devon	Haxby Road Yorks	Clevedon Somerset	Aldershot Essex
1986	Wynne Richards Surrey	Owton Lodge Durham	Poole Park Dorset	Stony Stratford Bucks
1987	David Holt Lancs	Bolton Lancs	Worcester County	Aylesbury Tn Bucks
1988	Richard Bray Cornwall	Leicester	Belgrave Leics	Summertown Oxon
1989	John Ottaway Norfolk	Essex County	Southbourne Sussex	Blackheath & G Kent
1990	Tony Allcock Gloucs	Wymondham D Norfolk	Cheltenham Gloucs	Bath Avon
1991	Tony Allcock Gloucs	Wigton Cumbria	Wigton Cumbria	Wokingham Berks
1992	Stephen Farish Cumbria	Blackheath & G Kent	Chandos Pk Bucks	Bournemouth Hants
1993	John Wickham Devon	Erdington Ct Warwicks	Preston Sussex	Reading Berks
1994	Kevin Morley Notts	Pontelan North'berland	Torquay Devon	Cheltenham Gloucs
1995	John Leeman Durham	Swindon W Wiltshire	Cheltenham Gloucs	Hollingbury Pk Sussex
1996	John Ottaway Norfolk	Bank Ho Hotel Worcs	Brit Cellophane S'erset	March Cons Cambs B
1997	Richard Brittan Warwick B	Dorchester Dorset	Wigton Cumbria	Swindon West Wilts
1998	Grant Burgess	Stoke Stafford	Bolton Lancs	Banbury Boro Oxon
1999	Nicky Brett Hunts	Northampton	Hampshire	Buckinghamshire
2000	John Ottaway Norfolk	Cumbria	Northumberland	Lancashire

BOXING

WORLD CHAMPIONS - UNDISPUTED

HEAVYWEIGHT
1882 John L Sullivan USA
1892 James J Corbett USA
1897 Bob Fitzsimmons GBR
1899 James J Jeffries USA
1905 Marvin Hart USA
1906 Tommy Burns CAN
1908 Jack Johnson USA
1915 Jess Willard USA
1919 Jack Dempsey USA
1926 Gene Tunney USA
1930 Max Schmeling GER
1932 Jack Sharkey USA
1933 Primo Carnera ITA
1934 Max Baer USA
1935 James J Braddock USA
1937 Joe Louis USA
1949 Ezzard Charles USA
1951 Jersey Joe Walcott USA
1952 Rocky Marciano USA
1956 Floyd Patterson USA
1959 Ingemar Johansson SWE
1960 Floyd Patterson USA
1962 Sonny Liston USA
1964 Cassius Clay USA
1970 Joe Frazier USA
1973 George Foreman USA
1974 Muhammed Ali USA
1978 Leon Spinks USA
1987 Mike Tyson USA
1999 Lennox Lewis GBR

CRUISERWEIGHT
1988 Evander Holyfield USA

LIGHT HEAVYWEIGHT
1903 Jack Root AUT
1903 George Gardner IRL
1903 Bob Fitzsimmons GBR
1905 Jack O'Brien USA
1912 Jack Dillon USA
1916 Battling Levinsky USA
1920 Georges Carpentier FRA
1922 Battling Siki SEN
1923 Mike McTigue IRL
1925 Paul Berlenbach USA
1926 Jack Delaney CAN
1927 Jim Slattery USA
1927 Tommy Loughran USA
1930 Jim Slattery USA
1930 Maxie Rosenbloom USA
1934 Bob Olin USA
1935 John Henry Lewis USA
1939 Melio Bettina USA
1939 Billy Conn USA
1941 Anton Christoforidis GRE
1941 Gus Lesnevich USA
1948 Freddie Mills GBR

1950 Joey Maxim USA
1952 Archie Moore USA
1962 Harold Johnson USA
1963 Willie Pastrano USA
1965 José Torres PUR
1966 Dick Tiger NGR
1968 Bob Foster USA
1983 Michael Spinks USA
1999 Roy Jones USA

MIDDLEWEIGHT
1891 Jack Dempsey IRL
1891 Bob Fitzsimmons GBR
1898 Tommy Ryan USA
1907 Stanley Ketchel USA
1908 Billy Papke USA
1908 Stanley Ketchel USA
1910 Billy Papke USA
1911 Cyclone Thompson USA
1913 Frank Klaus USA
1913 George Chip USA
1914 Al McCoy USA
1917 Mike O'Dowd USA
1920 Johnny Wilson USA
1923 Harry Greb USA
1926 Tiger Flowers USA
1926 Mickey Walker USA
1931 Gorilla Jones USA
1932 Marcel Thil FRA
1941 Tony Zale USA
1947 Rocky Graziano USA
1948 Tony Zale USA
1948 Marcel Cerdan ALG
1949 Jake la Motta USA
1951 Sugar Ray Robinson USA
1951 Randolph Turpin GBR
1951 Sugar Ray Robinson USA
1953 Carl 'Bobo' Olsen HAW
1955 Sugar Ray Robinson USA
1957 Gene Fullmer USA
1957 Sugar Ray Robinson USA
1957 Carmen Basilio USA
1958 Sugar Ray Robinson USA
1960 Paul Pender USA
1961 Terry Downes GBR
1962 Paul Pender USA
1963 Dick Tiger NGR
1963 Joey Giardello USA
1965 Dick Tiger NGR
1966 Emile Griffith USA
1968 Nino Benvenuti ITA
1970 Carlos Monzon ARG
1976 Carlos Monzon ARG
1977 Rodrigo Valdez COL
1978 Hugo Corro ARG
1979 Vito Antuofermo ITA
1980 Alan Minter GBR
1980 Marvin Hagler USA

JUNIOR MIDDLEWEIGHT
1962 Denny Moyer USA
1963 Ralph Dupas USA
1963 Sandro Massinghi ITA
1965 Nino Benvenuti ITA
1966 Kim Ki-soo KOR
1968 Sandro Massinghi ITA
1969 Freddie Little USA
1970 Carmelo Bossi ITA
1971 Koichi Wajima JPN
1974 Oscar Albarado USA
1975 Koichi Wajima JPN

WELTERWEIGHT
1892 Billy Smith CAN
1894 Tommy Ryan USA
1896 Charles 'Kid' McCoy USA
1898 Mysterious Billy Smith
1900 Rube Ferns USA
1900 Matty Matthews USA
1901 Rube Ferns USA
1901 Joe Walcott BAR
1904 Dixie Kid USA
1905 Joe Walcott BAR
1906 Honey Mellody USA
1907 Mike 'Twin' Sullivan USA
1915 Ted Kid Lewis GBR
1916 Jack Britton USA
1917 Ted Kid Lewis GBR
1919 Jack Britton USA
1922 Micky Walker USA
1926 Pete Latzo USA
1927 Joe Dundee ITA
1929 Jackie Fields USA
1930 Jack Thompson USA
1930 Tommy Freeman USA
1931 Jack Thompson USA
1931 Lou Broulliard CAN
1932 Jackie Fields USA
1933 Young Corbett III ITA
1933 Jimmy McLarnin IRL
1934 Barney Ross USA
1934 Jimmy McLarnin IRL
1935 Barney Ross USA
1938 Henry Armstrong USA
1940 Fritzie Zivic USA
1941 Freddie Cochrane USA
1946 Marty Servo USA
1946 Sugar Ray Robinson USA
1951 Johnny Bratton USA
1951 Kid Gavilan CUB
1954 Johnny Saxton USA
1955 Tony de Marco USA
1955 Carmen Basilio USA
1956 Johnny Saxton USA
1956 Carmen Basilio USA
1958 Virgil Atkins USA
1958 Don Jordon DOM
1960 Benny Kid Paret CUB
1961 Emile Griffith USA

BOXING

1961 Benny Kid Paret CUB
1962 Emile Griffith USA
1963 Louis Rodriguez CUB
1963 Emile Griffith USA
1966 Curtis Cokes USA
1969 Jose Napoles CUB
1970 Billy Backus USA
1971 Jose Napoles CUB
1981 Sugar Ray Leonard USA
1985 Don Curry USA
1986 Lloyd Honeyghan GBR

JUNIOR WELTERWEIGHT
1922 Pinky Mitchell USA
1926 Mushy Callahan USA
1930 Jackie Kid Berg GBR
1931 Tony Canzoneri USA
1932 Johnny Jaddick USA
1933 Battling Shaw MEX
1933 Tony Canzoneri USA
1933 Barney Ross USA
1946 Tippy Larkin USA
1959 Carlos Ortiz PUR
1960 Duilio Loi ITA
1962 Eddie Perkins USA
1962 Duilio Loi ITA
1963 Roberto Cruz PHI
1963 Eddie Perkins USA
1965 Carlos Hernandez VEN
1966 Sandro Lopopolo ITA
1967 Paul Fujii USA

LIGHTWEIGHT
1896 George Lavigne USA
1899 Frank Erne SUI
1902 Joe Gans USA
1908 Battling Nelson DEN
1910 Ad Wolgast USA
1912 Willie Ritchie USA
1914 Freddie Welsh GBR
1917 Benny Leonard USA
1925 Jimmy Goodrich USA
1925 Rocky Kansas USA
1926 Sammy Mandell USA
1930 Al Singer USA
1930 Tony Canzoneri USA
1933 Barney Ross USA
1935 Tony Canzoneri USA
1936 Lou Ambers USA
1938 Henry Armstrong USA
1939 Lou Ambers USA
1940 Lew Jenkins USA
1941 Sammy Angott USA
1942 Beau Jack USA
1943 Bob Montgomery USA
1943 Sammy Angott USA
1944 Juan Zurita MEX
1945 Ike Williams USA
1951 Jimmy Carter USA
1952 Lauro Salas MEX

1952 Jimmy Carter USA
1954 Paddy de Marco USA
1954 Jimmy Carter USA
1955 Wallace Bud Smith USA
1956 Joe Brown USA
1962 Carlos Ortiz PUR
1965 Ismael Laguna PAN
1965 Carlos Ortiz PUR
1968 Carlos Teo Cruz DOM
1969 Mando Ramos USA
1970 Ismael Laguna PAN
1978 Roberto Duran PAN

JUNIOR LIGHTWEIGHT
1921 Johnny Dundee ITA
1923 Jack Bernstein USA
1923 Johnny Dundee ITA
1924 Kid Sullivan USA
1925 Mike Ballerino USA
1925 Tod Morgan USA
1929 Benny Bass USA
1931 Kid Chocolate CUB
1933 Frankie Klick USA
1959 Harold Gomes USA
1960 Flash Elorde PHI
1967 Yoshiaki Numata JPN
1967 Hiroshi Kobayashi JPN

FEATHERWEIGHT
1892 George Dixon CAN
1897 Solly Smith USA
1898 Dave Sullivan IRL
1898 George Dixon CAN
1900 Terry McGovern USA
1901 Young Corbett USA
1904 Abe Attell USA
1912 Johnny Kilbane USA
1923 Eugene Criqui FRA
1923 Johnny Dundee ITA
1925 Louis Kid Kaplan USA
1927 Benny Bass USA
1928 Tony Canzoneri USA
1928 Andre Routis FRA
1929 Battling Battalino USA
1933 Freddie Miller USA
1936 Petey Sarron USA
1937 Henry Armstrong USA
1938 Joey Archibald USA
1946 Willie Pep USA
1948 Sandy Saddler USA
1949 Willie Pep USA
1950 Sandy Sadler USA
1957 Hogan Kid Bassey NGR
1959 Davey Moore USA
1963 Sugar Ramos CUB
1964 Vicente Saldivar MEX

JUNIOR FEATHERWEIGHT
1922 Jack Kid Wolfe USA
1923 Carl Duane USA

BANTAMWEIGHT
1890 George Dixon CAN
1899 Terry McGovern USA
1901 Harry Forbes USA
1903 Frankie Neil USA
1904 Joe Bowker GBR
1905 Jimmy Walsh USA
1910 Johnny Coulon CAN
1914 Kid Williams DEN
1917 Pete Herman USA
1920 Joe Lynch USA
1921 Pete Herman USA
1921 Johnny Buff USA
1922 Joe Lynch USA
1924 Abe Goldstein USA
1924 Eddie Martin USA
1925 Charley Rosenberg USA
1929 Al Brown PAN
1936 Tony Marino USA
1936 Sixto Escobar PUR
1937 Harry Jeffra USA
1938 Sixto Escobar PUR
1940 Lou Salica USA
1942 Manuel Ortiz USA
1947 Harold Dade USA
1947 Manuel Ortiz USA
1950 Vic Toweel RSA
1952 Jimmy Carruthers AUS
1954 Robert Cohen ALG
1956 Mario D'Agata ITA
1957 Alphonse Halimi ALG
1959 Joe Becerra MEX
1962 Eder Jofre BRA
1965 Fighting Harada JPN
1968 Lionel Rose AUS
1969 Ruben Olivares MEX
1970 Chucho Castillo MEX
1971 Ruben Olivares MEX
1972 Rafael Herrera MEX
1972 Enrique Pinder PAN

FLYWEIGHT
1916 Jimmy Wilde GBR
1923 Pancho Villa PHI
1925 Fidel La Barba USA
1937 Benny Lynch GBR
1938 Peter Kane GBR
1943 Jackie Paterson GBR
1948 Rinty Monaghan GBR
1950 Terry Allen GBR
1950 Dado Marino HAW
1952 Yoshio Shirai JPN
1954 Pascual Perez ARG
1960 Pone Kingpetch THA
1962 Fighting Harada JPN
1963 Pone Kingpetch THA
1963 Hiroyuki Ebihara JPN
1964 Pone Kingpetch THA
1965 Salvatore Burruni ITA

BOXING

WORLD CHAMPIONS
- DISPUTED
HEAVYWEIGHT
WBA
1958 Virgil Atkins USA
1965 Ernie Terrell USA
1968 Jimmy Ellis USA
1978 Muhammad Ali USA
1979 John Tate USA
1980 Mike Weaver USA
1982 Mike Dokes USA
1983 Gerrie Coetzee RSA
1984 Greg Page USA
1985 Tony Tubbs USA
1986 Tim Witherspoon USA
1986 James Smith USA
1987 Mike Tyson USA
1990 J 'Buster' Douglas USA
1990 Evander Holyfield USA
1992 Riddick Bowe USA
1993 Evander Holyfield USA
1994 Michael Moorer USA
1994 George Foreman USA
1995 Bruce Seldon USA
1996 Mike Tyson USA
1996 Evander Holyfield USA
1999 Lennox Lewis GBR
2000 Evander Holyfield USA
WBC
1978 Ken Norton USA
1978 Larry Holmes USA
1984 Tim Witherspoon USA
1984 Pinklon Thomas USA
1986 Trevor Berbick JAM
1989 Mike Tyson USA
1990 J 'Buster' Douglas USA
1990 Evander Holyfield USA
1992 Riddick Bowe USA
1992 Lennox Lewis GBR
1994 Oliver McCall USA
1995 Frank Bruno GBR
1996 Mike Tyson USA
1997 Lennox Lewis GBR
IBF
1984 Larry Holmes USA
1985 Michael Spinks USA
1987 Tony Tucker USA
1989 J 'Buster' Douglas USA
1990 Evander Holyfield USA
1992 Riddick Bowe USA
1993 Evander Holyfield USA
1994 Michael Moorer USA
1994 George Foreman USA
1995 Francois Botha* RSA
1996 Michael Moorer USA
1997 Evander Holyfield USA
1999 Lennox Lewis GBR
Stripped of title - tested positive

WBO
1989 Francesco Damiani ITA
1991 Ray Mercer USA
1992 Michael Moorer USA
1993 Tommy Morrison USA
1993 Michael Bentt USA
1994 Herbie Hide GBR
1995 Riddick Bowe USA
1996 Henry Akinwande GBR
1997 Herbie Hide GBR
1999 Vitali Klitshko UKR

CRUISERWEIGHT
WBA
1982 Ossie Ocasio PUR
1984 Piet Crous RSA
1985 Dwight Muh'd Qawi USA
1986 Evander Holyfield USA
1989 Taoufik Belbouli FRA
1989 Robert Daniels USA
1991 Bobby Cruz USA
1993 Orlin Norris USA
1995 Nate Miller USA
1997 Fabrice Tiozzo FRA
2000 Virgil Hill USA
WBC
1979 Marvin Camel USA
1980 Carlos de Leon PUR
1982 S T Gordon USA
1983 Carlos de Leon PUR
1985 Alfonso Ratliff USA
1985 Bernard Benton USA
1986 Carlos de Leon PUR
1988 Evander Holyfield USA
1989 Carlos de Leon PUR
1990 Massimiliano Duran ITA
1991 Anaclet Wamba FRA
1996 Marcelo Dominguez ARG
1998 Juan Carlos Gomez CUB
IBF
1983 Marvin Camel USA
1984 Lee Roy Murphy USA
1986 Rickey Parkey USA
1987 Evander Holyfield USA
1989 Glenn McCrory GBR
1990 Jeff Lampkin USA
1991 James Warring USA
1992 Alfred Cole USA
1996 Adolpho Washington USA
1997 Uriah Grant JAM
1997 Imamu Mayfield USA
1998 Arthur Williams USA
1999 Vassily Jirov USA
WBO
1989 Richard Pultz USA
1990 Magne Havna NOR
1992 Tyrone Booze USA
1993 Markus Bott GER
1993 Nestor Giovannini ITA
1995 D Michalczewski GER

1995 Ralf Rocchigiani GER
1997 Carl Thompson GBR
1999 Johnny Nelson GBR

LIGHT-HEAVYWEIGHT
WBA
1971 Vicente Rondon VEN
1974 Victor Galindez ARG
1978 Mike Rossman USA
1979 Victor Galindez ARG
1979 Marvin Johnson USA
1980 Eddie Mustafa Mh'd USA
1981 Michael Spinks USA
1986 Marvin Johnson USA
1987 Leslie Stewart JAM
1987 Virgil Hill USA
1991 Thomas Hearns USA
1992 Iran Barkley USA
1992 Virgil Hill USA
1997 D Michalczewski GER
1997 Louis Del Valle USA
1998 Roy Jones USA
WBC
1974 John Conteh GBR
1977 Miguel Cuello ARG
1978 Mate Parlov YUG
1978 Marvin Johnson USA
1979 Matthew Saad Mh'd USA
1981 Dwight Muh'd Qawi USA
1985 JB Williamson USA
1986 Dennis Andries GBR
1987 Thomas Hearns USA
1988 Donny Lalonde CAN
1988 Sugar Ray Leonard USA
1989 Dennis Andries GBR
1989 Jeff Harding AUS
1990 Dennis Andries GBR
1991 Jeff Harding AUS
1994 Mike McCallum JAM
1995 Fabrice Tiozzo FRA
1996 Roy Jones USA
1997 Montell Griffin USA
1997 Roy Jones USA
1998 Graciano Rocchigiani ITA
1999 Roy Jones USA
IBF
1985 Slobodan Kacar YUG
1986 Bobby Czyz USA
1987 P Charles Williams USA
1993 Henry Maske GER
1996 Virgil Hill USA
1997 D Michalczewski GER
1997 William Guthrie USA
1998 Reggie Johnson USA
1999 Roy Jones USA
WBO
1988 Michael Moorer USA
1991 Leeonzer Barber USA
1995 D Michalczewski GER

BOXING

SUPER-MIDDLEWEIGHT
WBA
1984 Park Chong-Pal KOR
1988 F Obelmejias VEN
1989 Baek In-Chul KOR
1990 Christophe Tiozo FRA
1991 Victor Cordoba PAN
1992 Michael Nunn USA
1994 Steve Little USA
1994 Frank Liles USA
1999 Byron Mitchell USA
2000 Bruno Girard FRA
WBC
1988 Sugar Ray Leonard USA
1990 Mauro Galvano ITA
1992 Nigel Benn GBR
1996 Sugarboy Malinga RSA
1996 Vincenzo Nardiello ITA
1996 Robin Reid GBR
1997 Sugarboy Malinga RSA
1998 Richie Woodhall GBR
1999 Marcus Beyer GER
2000 Glenn Catley GBR
2000 Dingaan Thobela RSA
IBF
1984 Murray Sutherland CAN
1988 Grac Rocchigiani FRG
1990 Lindell Holmes USA
1991 Darrin van Horn USA
1992 Iran Barkley USA
1993 James Toney USA
1994 Roy Jones USA
1997 Charles Brewer USA
1998 Sven Ottke GER
WBO
1988 Thomas Hearns USA
1991 Chris Eubank GBR
1995 Steve Collins IRL
1997 Joe Calzaghe GBR

MIDDLEWEIGHT
WBA
1987 Sambu Kalambay ZAI
1989 Mike McCallum USA
1992 Reggie Johnson USA
1994 John D Jackson USA
1994 Jorge Castro ARG
1995 Shinji Takehara JPN
1996 William Joppy USA
1997 Julio Cesar Green DOM
1998 William Joppy USA
WBC
1974 Rodrigo Valdez COL
1987 Sugar Ray Leonard USA
1987 Thomas Hearns USA
1988 Iran Barkley USA
1989 Roberto Duran PAN
1990 Julian Jackson USA
1993 Gerald McClellan USA
1995 Julian Jackson USA
1995 Quincy Taylor USA

1996 Keith Holmes USA
1998 Hassine Cherifi FRA
1999 Keith Holmes USA
IBF
1987 Frank Tate USA
1988 Michael Nunn USA
1991 James Toney USA
1993 Roy Jones USA
1994 Bernard Hopkins USA
1998 Robbie Allen USA
1999 Bernard Hopkins USA
WBO
1989 Doug De Witt USA
1990 Nigel Benn GBR
1990 Chris Eubank GBR
1991 Gerald McClellan USA
1993 Chris Pyatt GBR
1994 Steve Collins IRL
1995 Lonnie Bradley USA
1997 Otis Grant CAN
1999 Armand Krajne SVK

SUPER-WELTERWEIGHT
WBA
1975 Yuh Jae-Do KOR
1976 Koichi Wajima JPN
1976 Jose Duran ESP
1976 Angel Castellini ARG
1977 Eddie Gazo NCA
1978 Masashi Kudo JPN
1979 Ayube Kalule UGA
1981 Sugar Ray Leonard USA
1981 Tadashi Mihara JPN
1982 Davey Moore USA
1983 Roberto Duran PAN
1984 Mike McCallum JAM
1988 Julian Jackson USA
1991 Gilbert Dele FRA
1991 Vinny Pazienza USA
1992 Cesar Vasquez ARG
1992 Vinny Pazienza USA
1992 Julio Cesar Vasquez ARG
1995 Pernell Whitaker USA
1995 Carl Daniels USA
1995 Julio C'r Vasquez ARG
1996 Laurent Boudouani FRA
1999 David Reid USA
2000 Felix Trinidad PUR
WBC
1975 Miguel de Oliviera BRA
1975 Elisha Obed BAH
1976 Eckhard Dagge FRG
1977 Rocky Mattioli ITA
1979 Maurice Hope GBR
1981 Wilfred Benitez USA
1982 Thomas Hearns USA
1986 Duane Thomas USA
1987 Lupe Aquino MEX
1988 Gianfranco Rosi ITA
1988 Don Curry USA
1989 Rene Jacquot FRA

1989 John Mugabi UGA
1990 Terry Norris USA
1993 Simon Brown JAM
1994 Terry Norris USA
1995 Luis Santana DOM
1995 Terry Norris USA
1997 Keith Mullings USA
1999 Javier Castillejo ESP
IBF
1984 Mark Medal USA
1984 Carlos Santos PUR
1986 Buster Drayton USA
1987 Matthew Hilton CAN
1988 Robert Hines USA
1989 Darrin Van Horn USA
1989 Gianfranco Rosi ITA
1994 Vincent Pettway USA
1996 Terry Norris USA
1997 Raul Marquez USA
1997 Luis Ramon Campas MEX
1999 Fernando Vargas USA
2000 Felix Trinidad PUR
WBO
1988 John David Jackson USA
1993 Verno Phillips USA
1995 Gianfranco Rosi ITA
1995 Paul Jones GBR
1996 Bronko McKart USA
1996 Ronald Wright USA
1998 Harry Simon NAM

WELTERWEIGHT
WBA
1975 Angel Espada PUR
1976 Pipino Cuevas MEX
1980 Thomas Hearns USA
1983 Don Curry USA
1987 Mark Breland USA
1987 Marlon Starling USA
1988 Tomas Molinares COL
1989 Mark Breland USA
1990 Aaron Davis USA
1991 Meldrick Taylor USA
1992 Crisanto Espana VEN
1994 Ike Quartey GHA
1998 James Page USA
WBC
1975 John H Stracey GBR
1976 Carlos Palomino MEX
1979 Wilfred Benitez USA
1979 Sugar Ray Leonard USA
1980 Roberto Duran PAN
1980 Sugar Ray Leonard USA
1983 Milton McCrory USA
1987 Lloyd Honeyghan GBR
1987 Jorge Vaca MEX
1988 Lloyd Honeyghan GBR
1989 Marlon Starling USA
1990 Maurice Blocker USA
1991 Simon Brown JAM
1991 Buddy McGirt USA

BOXING

1993 Pernell Whitaker USA
1997 Oscar De La Hoya USA
1999 Felix Trinidad PUR
    Vacant
2000 Shane Moseley USA

IBF
1984 Don Curry USA
1987 Lloyd Honeyghan GBR
1988 Simon Brown JAM
1991 Buddy McGirt USA
1992 Felix Trinidad PUR
    Vacant

WBO
1989 Genaro Leon MEX
1989 Manning Galloway USA
1993 Gert Bo Jacobsen DEN
1993 Eamonn Loughran IRL
1996 Jose Luis Lopez MEX
1996 Michael Loewe ROM
1998 Ahmed Katajev RUS

SUPER-LIGHTWEIGHT
WBA
1968 Nicolino Loche ARG
1972 Alfonso Frazer PAN
1972 Antonio Cervantes COL
1976 Wilfred Benitez USA
1977 Antonio Cervantes COL
1980 Aaron Pryor USA
1984 Johnny Bumphus USA
1984 Gene Hatcher USA
1985 Ubaldo Sacco ARG
1986 Patrizio Oliva ITA
1987 Juan Martin Coggi ARG
1990 Loreto Garza USA
1991 Edwin Rosario PUR
1992 Morris East PHI
1993 Juan Martin Coggi ARG
1994 Frankie Randall USA
1996 Juan Martin Coggi ARG
1996 Frankie Randall USA
1997 Khalid Rahilou FRA
1998 Sharmba Mitchell USA

WBC
1968 Pedro Adigue PHI
1970 Bruno Acari ITA
1974 Perico Fernandez ESP
1975 Saensak MuangsurinTHA
1976 Miguel Velasquez ESP
1976 Saensak MuangsurinTHA
1978 Kim Sang-Hyun KOR
1980 Saoul Mamby USA
1982 Leroy Haley USA
1983 Bruce Curry USA
1984 Billy Costello USA
1985 Lonnie Smith USA
1986 Tsuyoshi Hamada JAP
1986 Rene Arredondo MEX
1987 Rene Arredondo MEX
1988 Roger Mayweather USA

1989 Julio Cesar Chavez MEX
1994 Frankie Randall USA
1994 Julio Cesar Chavez MEX
1996 Oscar De La Hoya USA
1998 *Vacant*
1999 Kostya Tszyu AUS

IBF
1983 Aaron Pryor USA
1986 Gary Hinton USA
1986 Joe Louis Manley USA
1987 Terry Marsh GBR
1988 James Buddy McGirtUSA
1988 Meldrick Taylor USA
1990 Julio Cesar Chavez MEX
1991 Rafael Pineda COL
1992 Pernell Whitaker USA
1993 Charles Murray USA
1994 Jake Rodriguez USA
1995 Konstantin Tszyu RUS
1997 Vince Phillips USA
1999 Terron Millett USA
2000 Zab Judah USA

WBO
1989 Hector Camacho PUR
1991 Greg Haugen USA
1991 Hector Camacho PUR
1992 Carlos Gonzalez MEX
1993 Zack Padilla USA
1994 Sammy Fuentes PUR
1996 Giovanni Parisi ITA
1998 Carlos Gonzalez MEX
1999 Randall Bailey USA

LIGHTWEIGHT
WBA
1970 Ken Buchanan GBR
1972 Roberto Duran PAN
1979 Ernesto Espana VEN
1980 Hilmer Kenty USA
1981 Sean O'Grady USA
1981 Claude Noel TRI
1981 Arturo Frias USA
1982 Ray Mancini USA
1984 Livingstone BrambleUSA
1986 Edwin Rosario PUR
1987 Julio Cesar Chavez MEX
1989 Edwin Rosario PUR
1990 Juan Nazario PUR
1990 Pernell Whitaker USA
1992 Joey Gamache USA
1992 Tony Lopez USA
1993 Dingaan Thobela RSA
1993 Orzoubek Nazarov RUS
1998 Jean Baptiste Mendy FRA
1999 Julien Lorcy FRA
1999 Stefano Zoff ITA
1999 Gilbert Serrano VEN
2000 Takanori Hatekeyama JPN

WBC
1971 Pedro Carrasco ESP

1972 Mando Ramos USA
1972 Chango Carmona MEX
1972 Rodolfo Gonzalez MEX
1974 Guts Ishimatsu JPN
1976 Esteban de Jesus PUR
1979 Jim Watt GBR
1981 Alexis Arguello NCA
1983 Edwin Rosario PUR
1984 Jose Luis Ramirez MEX
1985 Hector Camacho PUR
1987 Jose Luis Ramirez MEX
1988 Julio Cesar Chavez MEX
1989 Pernell Whitaker USA
1992 Miguel Gonzalez MEX
1996 Jean-B Mendy FRA
1997 Steve Johnson USA
1998 Cesar Bazan MEX
1999 Stevie Johnson USA
2000 Jose Luis Castillo MEX

IBF
1984 Charlie Brown USA
1984 Harry Arroyo USA
1985 Jimmy Paul USA
1986 Greg Haugen USA
1987 Vinny Pazienza USA
1988 Greg Haugen USA
1989 Pernell Whitaker USA
1992 Tracy Spann USA
1993 Freddie Pendleton USA
1994 Rafael Ruelas USA
1995 Phillip Holliday RSA
1997 Shane Mosley USA
1999 Paul Spadafora USA

WBO
1989 Amancio Castro COL
1989 Mauricio Aceves MEX
1990 Dingaan Thobela RSA
1992 Giovanni Parisi ITA
1994 Oscar De La Hoya USA
1996 Artur Grigorjan UZB

SUPER-FEATHERWEIGHT
WBA
1971 Alfredo Marcano VEN
1972 Ben Villaflor PHI
1973 Kuniaki Shibata JPN
1973 Ben Villaflor PHI
1976 Sam Serrano PUR
1980 Yasutsune Uehara JPN
1981 Sam Serrano PUR
1983 Roger Mayweather USA
1984 Rocky Lockridge USA
1985 Wilfredo Gomez PUR
1986 Alfredo Layne PAN
1986 Brian Mitchell RSA
1991 Joey Gamache USA
1991 Genaro Hernandez USA
1995 Choi Yong-Soo KOR
1998 Takanori Hatekayama JPN
1999 Lavka Sim MGL

1999 Jong Kwon-baek KOR
2000 Joel Casamayor USA

WBC
1969 Rene Barrientos PHI
1970 Yoshiaki Numata JPN
1971 Ricardo Arredondo MEX
1974 Kuniaki Shibata JPN
1975 Alfredo Escalera PUR
1978 Alexis Arguello NCA
1980 Rafael Limon MEX
1981 Cornelius Edwards UGA
1981 Rolando Navarette PHI
1982 Rafael Limon MEX
1982 Bobby Chacon USA
1983 Hector Camacho PUR
1984 Julio Cesar Chavez MEX
1988 Azumah Nelson GHA
1994 Jesse James Leija MEX
1995 Gabe Ruelas USA
1995 Azumah Nelson GHA
1997 Genaro Hernandez USA
1998 Floyd Mayweather USA

IBF
1984 Yuh Hwan-Kil KOR
1985 Lester Ellis AUS
1985 Barry Michael AUS
1987 Rocky Lockridge USA
1988 Tony Lopez USA
1989 Juan Molina PUR
1990 Tony Lopez USA
1991 Brian Mitchell RSA
1993 John John Molina PUR
1995 Eddie Hopson USA
1995 Tracy Patterson USA
1995 Arturo Gatti CAN
1998 Roberto Garcia USA
1999 Diego Corrales USA
2000 Steve Forbes USA

WBO
1989 Juan Molina PUR
1989 Kamel Bou Ali TUN
1992 Jimmy Bredhal DEN
1994 Oscar De La Hoya USA
1994 Regilio Tuur NED
1998 Marco A Barrera MEX
1999 Anatoly Alexandrov KZK
1999 Acelino Freitas BRA

FEATHERWEIGHT
WBA
1968 Raul Rojas USA
1968 Shozo Saijyo JPN
1971 Antonio Gomez VEN
1972 Ernesto Marcel PAN
1974 Ruben Olivares MEX
1974 Alexis Arguello NCA
1977 Rafael Ortega PAN
1977 Cecilio Lastra ESP
1978 Eusebio Pedroza PAN
1985 Barry McGuigan IRL

1986 Steve Cruz USA
1987 Toni Esparragoza VEN
1991 ParkYoung-Kyun KOR
1992 Wilfredo Vazquez COL
1992 Park Young-Kyun KOR
1993 Eloy Rojas VEN
1996 Wilfredo Vazquez COL
1998 Fred Norwood USA
1998 Antonio Cermeno VEN
1999 Freddie Norwood USA
2000 Derrick Gainer USA

WBC
1968 Howard Winstone GBR
1968 Jose Legra CUB
1969 Johnny Famechon FRA
1970 Vicente Saldivar MEX
1970 Kuniaki Shibata JPN
1972 Clemente Sanchez MEX
1972 Jose Legra CUB
1973 Eder Jofre BRA
1974 Bobby Chacon USA
1975 Ruben Olivares MEX
1975 David Kotey GHA
1976 Danny Lopez USA
1980 Salvador Sanchez MEX
1982 Juan Laporte PUR
1984 Wilfredo Gomez PUR
1984 Azumah Nelson GHA
1988 Jeff Fenech AUS
1990 Marcos Villasana MEX
1991 Paul Hodkinson GBR
1993 Gregorio Vargas MEX
1993 Kevin Kelley USA
1995 Alejandro Gonzalez MEX
1995 Manuel Medina MEX
1995 Luisito Espinosa PHI
1999 Naseem Hamed GBR
2000 Guty Espadas MEX

IBF
1984 Oh Min-Keum KOR
1985 Chung Ki-Young KOR
1986 Antonio Rivera PUR
1988 Calvin Grove USA
1988 Jorge Paez MEX
1991 Troy Dorsey USA
1991 Manuel Medina MEX
1993 Tom Johnson USA
1997 Naseem Hamed GBR
1997 Hector Lizarraga MEX
1998 Manuel Medina MEX
1999 Cesar Soto MEX
1999 Paul Ingle GBR
2000 Mbulelo Botile RSA

WBO
1989 Maurizio Stecca ITA
1989 Louie Espinoza USA
1990 Jorge Paez MEX
1991 Maurizio Stecca ITA
1992 Colin McMillan GBR

1992 Ruben Palacio COL
1993 Steve Robinson GBR
1995 Naseem Hamed GBR

SUPER BANTAMWEIGHT
WBA
1977 Hong Soo-Hwan KOR
1978 Ricardo Cardona COL
1980 Leo Randolph USA
1980 Sergio Palma ARG
1982 Leo Cruz DOM
1984 Loris Stecca ITA
1984 Victor Callejas PUR
1987 Louis Espinoza USA
1987 Julio Gervacio DOM
1988 Bernardo Pinango VEN
1988 Juan Jose Estrada MEX
1989 Jesus Salud USA
1990 Luis Mendoza COL
1991 Raul Perez MEX
1992 Wilfredo Vasquez PUR
1995 Antonio Cermeno VEN
1998 Enrique Sanchez MEX
1998 Carlos Barreto VEN
1999 Nestor Garza MEX
2000 Clarence Adams USA

WBC
1976 Rigoberto Riasco PAN
1976 Royal Kobayashi JPN
1976 Yum Dong-Kyun KOR
1977 Wilfredo Gomez PUR
1983 Jaime Garza USA
1984 Juan Meza MEX
1985 Lupe Pintor MEX
1986 Samart Payakarun THA
1987 Jeff Fenech AUS
1988 Daniel Zaragoza MEX
1990 Paul Banke USA
1990 Pedro Decima ARG
1991 Kiyoshi Hatanaka JPN
1991 Daniel Zaragoza MEX
1992 Thierry Jacob FRA
1992 Tracy Patterson USA
1994 Hector A Sanchez DOM
1995 Daniel Zaragoza MEX
1997 Erik Morales MEX
2000 Willie Jorin USA

IBF
1983 Bobby Berna PHI
1984 Suh Seung-Il KOR
1985 Kim Ji-Won KOR
1987 Lee Seung-Hoon KOR
1988 Jose Sanabria VEN
1989 Fabrice Benichou FRA
1990 Welcome Ncita RSA
1992 Kennedy McKinney USA
1994 Vuyani Bungu RSA
1999 Benedict Ledwaba RSA

WBO
1989 Kenny Mitchell USA

BOXING

1989 **Valerio Nati** ITA
1990 **Orlando Fernandez** PUR
1991 **Jesse Benevides** USA
1992 **Duke McKenzie** GBR
1993 **Daniel Jimenez** PUR
1995 **Marco A Barrera** MEX
1996 **Junior Jones** USA
1997 **Kennedy McKinney** USA
1998 *Vacant*
1999 **Marco A Barrera** MEX

BANTAMWEIGHT
WBA

1973 **Romeo Anaya** MEX
1973 **Arnold Taylor** RSA
1974 **Hong Soo-Hwan** KOR
1975 **Alfonso Zamora** MEX
1977 **Jorge Lujan** PAN
1980 **Julian Solis** PUR
1980 **Jeff Chandler** USA
1984 **Richard Sandoval** USA
1986 **Gaby Canizales** USA
1986 **Bernardo Pinango** VEN
1987 **Takuya Muguruma** JPN
1987 **Park Chang-Young** KOR
1987 **Wilfredo Vasquez** PUR
1988 **Khaokor Galaxy** THA
1988 **Moon Sung-Kil** KOR
1989 **Khaokor Galaxy** THA
1989 **Luisito Espinosa** PHI
1991 **Israel Contreras** VEN
1992 **Eddie Cook** USA
1992 **Jorge Julio** COL
1993 **Junior Jones** USA
1994 **John M Johnson** USA
1994 **Doarung Petroleum** THA
1995 **Veeraphol Sahaprom** THA
1996 **Nana Konadu** THA
1996 **Daorung C Siriwat** THA
1998 **Nana Konadu** THA
1998 **Johnny Tapia** USA
1999 **Paulie Ayala** USA

WBC

1973 **Rafael Herrera** MEX
1974 **Rodolfo Martinez** MEX
1976 **Carlos Zarate** MEX
1979 **Lupe Pintor** MEX
1983 **Alberto Davila** USA
1985 **Daniel Zaragoza** MEX
1985 **Miguel Lora** COL
1988 **Raul Perez** MEX
1991 **Greg Richardson** USA
1991 **Joichiro Tatsuyoshi** JPN
1992 **Victor Rabanales** MEX
1993 **Byun Jong-Il** KOR
1993 **Yasuei Yakushiji** JPN
1995 **Wayne McCullough** IRL
1996 **Siri Singmanassak** THA
1997 **Joichiro Tatsuyoshi** JPN
1999 **Veeraphol Sahaprom** THA

IBF

1984 **Satoshi Shingaki** JPN
1985 **Jeff Fenech** AUS
1987 **Kelvin Seabrooks** USA
1988 **Orlando Canizales** USA
1995 **Harold Maestre** COL
1995 **Mbulelo Botile** RSA
1997 **Tim Austin** USA

WBO

1989 **Israel Contreras** VEN
1991 **Gaby Canizales** USA
1991 **Duke McKenzie** GBR
1992 **Rafael Del Valle** PUR
1994 **Alfred Kotey** GHA
1995 **Daniel Jimenez** PUR
1996 **Robbie Regan** WAL
1997 *Vacant*
1999 **Jorge E Julio** COL

SUPER FLYWEIGHT
WBA

1981 **Gustavo Ballas** ARG
1981 **Rafael Pedroza** PAN
1982 **Jiro Watanabe** JPN
1984 **Khaosai Galaxy** THA
1992 **Katsuya Onizuka** GBR
1994 **Hyung Chui-Lee** KOR
1995 **Alimi Goitea** VEN
1996 **Yokthai Sit-Oar** THA
1997 **Satoshi Iida** JPN
1999 **Jesus Rojas** VEN
1999 **Hideki Todaka** JPN
2000 **Leo Gomez** VEN

WBC

1980 **Rafael Orono** VEN
1981 **Kim Chul-Ho** KOR
1982 **Rafael Orono** VEN
1983 **Payao Poontarat** THA
1984 **Jiro Watanabe** JPN
1986 **Gilberto Roman** MEX
1987 **Santos Laciar** ARG
1987 **Jesus Rojas** COL
1988 **Gilberto Roman** MEX
1989 **Nana Yaw Konadu** GHA
1990 **Moon Sung-Kil** KOR
1993 **Jose Luis Bueno** MEX
1994 **Hiroshi Kawashima** JPN
1996 **Gerry Penalosa** PHI
1998 **Cho In-Joo** KOR
2000 **Masanori Tokuyama** JPN

IBF

1983 **Chun Joo-Do** KOR
1985 **Ellyas Pical** INA
1986 **Cesar Polanco** DOM
1986 **Chang Tae-Il** KOR
1987 **Ellyas Pical** INA
1989 **Juan Polo Perez** COL
1990 **Robert Quiroga** USA
1993 **Julio Cesar Borboa** MEX
1994 **Harold Grey** USA

1995 **Carlos Salazar** ARG
1996 **Harold Grey** USA
1996 **Danny Romero** USA
1997 **Johnny Tapia** USA
1999 **Mark Johnson** USA
2000 **Felix Machado** VEN

WBO

1989 **Jose Ruiz** PUR
1992 **Johnny Bredhal** DEN
1994 **Johnny Tapia** USA
1999 **Victor Godoy** ARG
1999 **Diego Morales** MEX

FLYWEIGHT
WBA

1966 **Horacio Accavallo** ARG
1969 **Hiroyuki Ebihara** JPN
1969 **Bernabe Villacampo** PHI
1970 **B Chartvanchai** THA
1970 **Masao Ohba** JPN
1973 **Chartchai Chionoi** THA
1974 **Susumu Hanagata** JPN
1975 **Erbito Salavarria** PHI
1976 **Alfonso Lopez** PAN
1976 **Guty Espadas** MEX
1978 **Betulio Gonzalez** VEN
1979 **Luis Ibarra** PAN
1980 **Kim Tae-Shik** KOR
1980 **Shoji Oguma** JPN
1980 **Peter Mathebula** RSA
1981 **Santos Laciar** ARG
1981 **Luis Ibarra** PAN
1981 **Juan Herrera** MEX
1982 **Santos Laciar** ARG
1985 **Hilario Zapata** PAN
1987 **Fidel Bassa** COL
1989 **Jesus Rojas** VEN
1990 **Lee Yul-Woo** KOR
1990 **Yukihito Tamakama** JPN
1991 **Elvis Alvarez** COL
1991 **Kim Yong-Kang** KOR
1992 **Aqueles Guzman** VEN
1992 **David Griman** VEN
1994 **Saensor Ploenchit** THA
1996 **Jose Bonilla** VEN
1998 **Hugo Soto** ARG
1998 **Mauricio Pastrana** COL
1999 **Leo Gamez** VEN
2000 **Sornpichai**
Kratchingdaeng THA

WBC

1966 **Walter McGowan** GBR
1966 **Chartchai Chionoi** THA
1969 **Efren Torres** MEX
1970 **Chartchai Chionoi** THA
1970 **Erbito Salavarria** PHI
1972 **Venice Borkorsor** THA
1973 **Betulio Gonzalez** VEN
1974 **Shoji Oguma** JPN
1975 **Miguel Canto** MEX

BOXING

1979 **Park Chan-Hee** KOR
1981 **Antonio Avelar** MEX
1982 **Prudencio Cardona** COL
1982 **Freddie Castillo** MEX
1982 **Eleoncio Mercedes** DOM
1983 **Charlie Magri** GBR
1983 **Frank Cedeno** PHI
1984 **Koji Kobayashi** JPN
1984 **Gabriel Bernal** MEX
1984 **Sot Chitalada** THA
1988 **Kim Yong-Kang** KOR
1989 **Sot Chitalda** THA
1991 **M Kittikasem** THA
1992 **Yuri Arbachakov** RUS
1997 **Chatchai Sasakul** THA
1998 **Manny Pacquio** PHI
1999 **Medgoen Singsurat** THA
2000 **Malcolm Tunacao** PHI

IBF
1983 **Kwon Soon-Chun** KOR
1985 **Chung Chong-Kwan** KOR
1986 **Chung Bi-Won** KOR
1986 **Shin Hi-Sup** KOR
1987 **Dodie Penalosa** PHI
1987 **Choi Chang-Ho** KOR
1988 **Rolando Bohol** PHI
1988 **Duke McKenzie** GBR
1989 **Dave McAuley** GBR
1992 **Rodolfo Blanco** COL
1992 **P Sitbangprachan** THA
1994 **Francisco Tejedor** COL
1995 **Danny Romero** USA
1996 **Mark Johnson** USA
1999 **Irene Pacheco** COL

WBO
1989 **Elvis Alvarez** COL
1990 **Isidro Perez** MEX
1992 **Pat Clinton** GBR
1993 **Jake Matlala** RSA
1995 **Alberto Jimenez** MEX
1996 **Carlos Salazar** ARG
1998 **Ruben Sanchez** MEX
1999 **Isidro Garcia** USA

LIGHT FLYWEIGHT
WBA
1975 **Jaime Rios** PAN
1976 **Juan Jose Guzman** DOM
1976 **Yoko Gushiken** JPN
1981 **Pedro Flores** MEX
1981 **Kim Hwan-Jin** KOR
1981 **Katsuo Takashiki** JPN
1983 **Lupe Madera** MEX
1984 **Francisco Quiroz** DOM
1985 **Joey Olivo** USA
1985 **Yuh Myung-Woo** KOR
1992 **Hiroki Ioka** JPN
1992 **Yuh Myung-Woo** KOR
1993 **Leo Gamez** VEN
1995 **Hiyong Choi** KOR

1996 **Carlos Murillo** PAN
1996 **Keiji Yamaguchi** JPN
1996 **Pichit Chor Siriwat** THA
2000 **Beibis Mendoza** COL

WBC
1975 **Franco Udella** ITA
1975 **Luis Estaba** VEN
1978 **Freddie Castillo** MEX
1978 **Netrnoi Vorasingh** THA
1978 **Kim Sung-Kun** KOR
1980 **Shigeo Nakajima** JPN
1980 **Hilario Zapata** PAN
1982 **Amado Ursua** MEX
1982 **Tadashi Tomori** JPN
1982 **Hilario Zapata** PAN
1983 **Chang Jung-Koo** KOR
1988 **German Torres** MEX
1989 **Lee Yul-Woo** KOR
1989 **Humberto Gonzalez** MEX
1990 **Rolando Pascua** PHI
1991 **Melchor Cob Castro** MEX
1991 **Humberto Gonzalez** MEX
1993 **Michael Carbajal** USA
1994 **Humberto Gonzalez** MEX
1995 **Saman Sorjaturong** THA
1999 **Choi Yo-sam** KOR

IBF
1983 **Dodie Penalosa** PHI
1986 **Choi Chong-Hwan** KOR
1988 **Tacy Macalos** PHI
1989 **M Kittikasem** THA
1990 **Michael Carbajal** USA
1991 **Welcome Ncita** RSA
1992 **Michael Carbajal** USA
1994 **Humberto Gonzalez** MEX
1995 **Saman Sorjaturong** THA
1996 **Michael Carbajal** USA
1997 **Mauricio Pastrana** COL
1998 *Vacant*
1999 **Will Grigsby** USA
1999 **Ricardo Lopez** MEX

WBO
1989 **Jose de Jesus** PUR
1993 **Josue Camacho** PUR
1994 **Michael Carbajal** USA
1994 **Paul Weir** GBR
1995 **Jake Matlala** RSA
1997 **Jesus Chong** MEX
1997 **Melchor Cob Castro** MEX
1998 **Juan Cordoba** ARG

STRAWWEIGHT
WBA
1988 **Leo Gamez** DOM
1989 **Kim Bong-Jun** KOR
1991 **Choi Hi-Yong** KOR
1992 **Hideyuki Ohashi** JPN
1993 **Chana Porpaoin** THA
1995 **Rosendo Alvarez** NCA
1998 **Ricardo Lopez** MEX

1999 **Noel Arambulet** VEN
2000 **Joma Gamboa** PHI
2000 **Keitaro Hoshino** JPN
WBC
1987 **Lee Kyung-Yung** KOR
1988 **Hiroki Ioka** JPN
1988 **Napa Kiatwanchai** THA
1989 **Choi Jeum-Hwan** KOR
1990 **Hideyuki Ohashi** JPN
1990 **Ricardo Lopez** MEX
2000 **Jose Antonio Aguirre** MEX
IBF
1988 **Sam Sithnaruepol** THA
1989 **Nico Thomas** INA
1989 **Eric Chavez** PHI
1990 **F Lookmingkwan** THA
1992 **Manuel Melchor** PHI
1992 **Ratanopol Sorvorapin** THA
1998 **Zolani Lepethelo** RSA
WBO
1989 **Rafael Torres** DOM
1993 **Paul Weir** GBR
1993 **Alex Sanchez** PUR
1997 **Ricardo Lopez** MEX
1998 **Kermin Guardia** COL

BOXING

WORLD AMATEUR CHAMPIONS

SUPER-HEAVYWEIGHT (+91kg)
1982 Tyrell Biggs USA
1983 Tyrell Biggs USA
1986 Teofilio Stevenson CUB
1989 Roberto Baladao CUB
1991 Roberto Baladao CUB
1993 Roberto Baladao CUB
1995 Aleksey Lezin RUS
1997 George Kandelaki GEO
1999 Siren Samil TUR

HEAVYWEIGHT (-91KG)
1974 Teofilio Stevenson CUB
1978 Teofilio Stevenson CUB
1982 Aleksandr Lagubkin URS
1983 Willie De Witt CAN
1986 Felix Savon CUB
1989 Felix Savon CUB
1993 Felix Savon CUB
1995 Felix Savon CUB
1997 Felix Savon CUB
1999 Michael Bennett USA

LIGHT-HEAVYWEIGHT (-81kg)
1974 Mate Parlov YUG
1978 Sixto Soria CUB
1982 Pablo Romero CUB
1983 Pablo Romero CUB
1986 Pablo Romero CUB
1989 Henry Maske GDR
1991 Torsten May GER
1993 Ramon Garbey CUB
1995 Antonio Tarver USA
1997 Aleksandr Labziak RUS
1999 Michael Simms USA

MIDDLEWEIGHT (-75kg)
1974 Rufat Riskiyev URS
1978 Jose Gomez CUB
1982 Bernando Comas CUB
1983 Bernando Comas CUB
1986 Darin Allen USA
1989 Andrey Kurnyavka URS
1991 Tommaso Russo ITS
1993 Ariel Hernandez CUB
1995 Ariel Hernandez CUB
1997 Zsolt Erdei HUN
1999 Utkirbeck Haydarov UZB

LIGHT-MIDDLEWEIGHT (-71kg)
1974 Rolando Garbey CUB
1978 Viktor Savchenko URS
1982 Aleksandr Koshkin URS
1983 Shawn O'Sullivan CAN
1986 Angel Espinosa CUB
1989 Israel Akopkokhyan URS
1991 Juan Lemus CUB
1993 Francisc Vastag ROM

1995 Francisc Vastag ROM
1997 Alfredo Duvergel CUB
1999 Marin Simion ROM

WELTERWEIGHT (-67kg)
1974 Emilio Correa CUB
1978 Valery Rachkov URS
1982 Mark Breland USA
1983 Mark Breland USA
1986 Kenneth Gould USA
1989 Francisc Vastag ROM
1991 Juan Hernandez CUB
1993 Juan Hernandez CUB
1995 Juan Hernandez CUB
1997 Oleg Saitov RUS
1999 Juan Hernandez CUB

LIGHT-WELTERWEIGHT (-63.5kg)
1974 Ayub Kalule UGA
1978 Valery Lvov URS
1982 Carlos Garcia CUB
1983 Carlos Garcia CUB
1986 Vasily Shishov URS
1989 Igor Ruzhnikov URS
1991 Konstantin Tszyu URS
1993 Hector Vinent CUB
1995 Hector Vinent CUB
1997 Dorel Simion ROM
1999 Mahammat Abdullaev UZB

LIGHTWEIGHT (-60kg)
1974 Vasily Solomin URS
1978 Andeh Davidson NGR
1982 Angel Herrera CUB
1983 Pernell Whitaker USA
1986 Adolfo Horta CUB
1989 Julio Gonzalez CUB
1991 Marco Rudolph GER
1993 Damian Austin CUB
1995 Leonard Doroftei ROM
1997 Aleksandr Maletin RUS
1999 Mario Kindelan CUB

FEATHERWEIGHT (-57kg)
1974 Howard Davis USA
1978 Angel Herrera CUB
1982 Adolfo Horta CUB
1983 Adolfo Horta CUB
1986 Kelcie Banks USA
1989 Airat Khamatov URS
1991 Kirkor KIrkorov BUL
1993 Serafim Todorov BUL
1995 Serafim Todorov BUL
1997 Istvan Kovacs HUN
1999 Ricardo Juarez USA

BANTAMWEIGHT (-54kg)
1974 Wilfredo Gomez PUR
1978 Adolfo Horta CUB
1982 Floyd Favors USA
1983 Floyd Favors USA
1986 Moon Sung-Kil KOR
1989 Enrique Carrion CUB
1991 Serafim Todorov BUL
1993 Alexander Hristov BUL
1995 Raimkul Malachbekov RUS
1997 Raimkul Malachbekov RUS
1999 Raicu Crinu ROM

FLYWEIGHT (-51kg)
1974 Douglas Rodriguez CUB
1978 Henryk Srednicki POL
1982 Yury Aleksandrov URS
1983 Steve McCrory USA
1986 Pedro Reyes CUB
1989 Yury Arbachakov URS
1991 Istvan Kovacs HUN
1993 Waldemar Font CUB
1995 Zoltan Lunke GER
1997 Manuel Mantilla CUB
1999 Bulat Jumadilov KZK

LIGHT-FLYWEIGHT (-48kg)
1974 Jorge Hernandez CUB
1978 Stephen Muchoki KEN
1982 Ismail Mustafov BUL
1983 Rafael Saiz CUB
1986 Juan Torres CUB
1989 Eric Griffin USA
1991 Eric Griffin USA
1993 Nshan Muntjian ARM
1995 Daniel Petrov BUL
1997 Maikro Romero CUB
1999 Brian Viloria USA

CANOEING

SPRINT
Annually except Olympic years

Men
K1 200
1994 Sergey Kalesnik BLR
1995 Piotr Markiewicz POL
1997 Vince Fehervari HUN
1998 Michael Kolganov ISR
1999 Michael Kolganov ISR

K1 500
1989 Martin Hunter AUS
1990 Sergey Kalesnik URS
1991 Renn Crichlow CAN
1993 Mikko Kolehmainen FIN
1994 Zsombor Borhi HUN
1995 Piotr Markiewicz POL
1997 Botond Storcz HUN
1998 Akos Vereckei HUN
1999 Akos Vereckei HUN

K1 1000
1989 Zsolt Gyulay HUN
1990 Knut Holmann NOR
1991 Knut Holmann NOR
1993 Knut Holmann NOR
1994 Clint Robinson AUS
1995 Knut Holmann NOR
1997 Botond Storcz HUN
1998 Lutz Liwowski GER
1999 Lutz Liwowski GER

K2 200
1994 Friemuth/Wysocki GER
1995 Bonomi/Scarpa ITA
1997 Fehervari/Hegedus HUN
1998 Fehervari/Hegedus HUN
1999 Fehervari/Hegedus HUN

K2 500
1989 Bluhm/Gutsche GDR
1990 Kalesnik/Tishchenko URS
1991 Roman/Sánchez ESP
1993 Bluhm/Gutsche GER
1994 Bluhm/Gutsche GER
1995 Bonomi/Scarpa ITA
1997 Trim/Collins AUS
1998 Riszdorfer/Baca SVK
1999 Twardowski/Wysocki POL

K2 1000
1989 Bluhm/Gutsche GDR
1990 Bluhm/Gutsche GDR
1991 Bluhm/Gutsche GDR
1993 Bluhm/Gutsche GER
1994 Staal/Nielsen DEN
1995 Rossi/Scarpa ITA
1997 Rossi/Negri ITA
1998 Rossi/Negri ITA
1999 Riszdorfer/Baca SVK

K4 200
1994 Russia
1995 Hungary
1997 Russia
1998 Hungary
1999 Hungary

K4 500
1989 Soviet Union
1990 Soviet Union
1991 Germany
1993 Russia
1994 Russia
1995 Russia
1997 Hungary
1998 Germany
1999 Germany

K4 1000
1989 Hungary
1990 Hungary
1991 Hungary
1993 Germany
1994 Russia
1995 Germany
1997 Germany
1998 Germany
1999 Hungary

C1 200
1994 Nikolay Buhalov BUL
1995 Nikolay Buhalov BUL
1997 Bela Belicza HUN
1998 Martin Doktor CZE
1999 Maxim Opalev RUS

C1 500
1989 Mikhail Slivinsky URS
1990 Mikhail Slivinsky URS
1991 Mikhail Slivinsky URS
1993 Nikolay Buhalov BUL
1994 Nikolay Buhalov BUL
1995 Nikolay Buhalov BUL
1997 Martin Doktor CZE
1998 Maxim Opalev RUS
1999 Maxim Opalev RUS

C1 1000
1989 Ivan Klementyev URS
1990 Ivan Klementyev URS
1991 Ivan Klementyev EUN
1993 Ivan Klementyev RUS
1994 Ivan Klementyev RUS
1995 Imre Pulai HUN
1997 Andreas Dittmer GER
1998 Steve Giles CAN
1999 Maxim Opalev RUS

C2 200
1994 Masojkov/Dovgalionok BLR
1995 Kolonics/Horváth HUN

K4 200
1997 Zereske/Gille GER
1998 Zereske/Gille GER
1999 Fomitchev/Artemida RUS

C2 500
1989 Zhuravsky/Reneysky URS
1990 Zhuravsky/Reneysky URS
1991 Paliza/Szabó HUN
1993 Kolonics/Horváth HUN
1994 Andreiev/Obreja ROM
1995 Kolonics/Horváth HUN
1997 Kolonics/Horváth HUN
1998 Kolonics/Horváth HUN
1999 Jedraszko/Baraszkiewicz POL

C2 1000
1989 Fredriksen/Nielsson DEN
1990 Papke/Spelly GDR
1991 Papke/Spelly GER
1993 Nielsson/Fredericksen DEN
1994 Dittmer/Kirchbach GER
1995 Kolonics/Horváth HUN
1997 Kirchbach/Roder GER
1998 Kovalev/Kostoglod RUS
1999 Kovalev/Kostoglod RUS

C4 200
1994 Russia
1995 Hungary
1997 Belarus
1998 Czech Republic
1999 Hungary

C4 500
1989 Soviet Union
1990 Soviet Union
1991 Soviet Union
1993 Hungary
1994 Hungary
1995 Hungary
1997 Hungary
1998 Hungary
1999 Russia

C4 1000
1989 Soviet Union
1990 Soviet Union
1991 Soviet Union
1993 Hungary
1994 Hungary
1995 Romania
1997 Romania
1998 Hungary
1999 Russia

CANOEING

SPRINT

Women

K1 200
1994 Rita Koban HUN
1995 Rita Koban HUN
1997 Caroline Brunet CAN
1998 Caroline Brunet CAN
1999 Caroline Brunet CAN

K1 500
1989 Katrin Borchert GDR
1990 Josefa Idem FRG
1991 Katrin Borchert GER
1993 Birgit Schmidt GER
1994 Birgit Schmidt GER
1995 Rita Koban HUN
1997 Caroline Brunet CAN
1998 Caroline Brunet CAN
1999 Caroline Brunet CAN

K1 1000
1997 Caroline Brunet CAN
1998 Josefa Idem ITA
1999 Caroline Brunet CAN

K2 200
1994 Koban/Laky HUN
1995 Kennedy/Gibeau CAN
1997 Fischer/Schuck GER
1998 Gibeau/Furneaux CAN
1999 Aramburu/Manchon ESP

K2 500
1989 Nothnagel/Singer GDR
1990 Portwich/Von Seck GDR
1991 Portwich/Von Seck GER
1993 Olsson/Andersson SWE
1994 Urbanczyk/Hajcel POL
1995 Portwich/Schuck GER
1997 Fischer/Schuck GER
1998 Borchert/Wood AUS
1999 Sokolowska/Pastuszka POL

K2 1000
1997 Fischer/Bednar GER
1998 Wood/Bochert AUS
1999 Wood/Bochert AUS

K4 200
1994 Hungary
1995 Canada
1997 Germany
1998 Hungary
1999 Hungary

K4 500
1989 East Germany
1990 East Germany
1991 East Germany
1993 East Germany

1995 East Germany
1997 Germany
1998 Germany
1999 Hungary

SLALOM

(Held since 1949, alternate years, full list for men's K1, others from varying dates)

Men

K1
1949 Othmar Eiterer AUT
1951 Hans Frühwirth AUT
1953 Walter Kirschnaum FRG
1955 Sigi Holzhauer FRG
1957 Manfred Vogt GDR
1959 Paul Farrant GBR
1961 Eberhard Gläser GDR
1963 Jürgen Bremer GDR
1965 Kurt Presslmayr AUT
1967 Jürgen Bremer GDR
1969 Claude Peschier FRA
1971 Siegbert Horn GDB
1973 Norbert Sattler AUT
1975 Siegbert Horn GDR
1977 Albert Venn GBR
1979 Peter Fauster AUT
1981 Richard Fox GBR
1983 Richard Fox GBR
1985 Richard Fox GBR
1987 Tony Prijon GER
1989 Richard Fox GBR
1991 Shaun Pearce GBR
1993 Richard Fox GBR
1995 Oliver Fix GER
1997 Thomas Becker GER
1999 David Ford CAN

K1 Team
1979 Great Britain
1981 Great Britain
1983 Great Britain
1985 Great Britain
1987 Great Britain
1989 Yugoslavia
1991 France
1993 Great Britain
1995 Germany
1997 Great Britain
1999 Germany

C1
1979 Jon Lugbill USA
1981 Jon Lugbill USA
1983 Jon Lugbill USA
1985 David Hearn USA
1987 Jon Lugbill USA
1989 Jon Lugbill USA
1991 Martin Lang GER
1993 Martin Lang GER

1995 David Hearn USA
1997 Michal Martikan SVK
1999 Emmanuel Brugvin FRA

C1 Team
1979 USA
1981 USA
1983 USA
1985 USA
1987 USA
1989 USA
1991 USA
1993 Slovenia
1995 Germany
1997 Slovakia
1999 Poland

C2
1979 Welsnik/Czupryna GER
1981 Garvis/Garvis USA
1983 Haller/Haller USA
1985 Küppers/Impelmann FRG
1987 Calori/Calori FRA
1989 Hemmer/Loose FRG
1991 Adisson/Forgues FRA
1993 Simek/Rohan CZE
1995 Kolomanski/Staniszewski POL
1997 Adisson/Forgues FRA
1999 Jiras/Mader CZE

C2 Team
1989 France
1991 France
1993 Czech Republic
1995 Czech Republic
1997 France
1999 Czech Republic

Women

K1
1979 Cathy Hearn USA
1981 Ulrike Deppe FRG
1983 Liz Sharman GBR
1985 Margit Messelhauser FRG
1987 Liz Sharman GBR
1989 Myriam Jerusalmi FRA
1991 Elisabeth Micheler GER
1993 Myriam Jerusalmi FRA
1995 Lynn Simpson GBR
1997 Brigitte Guibal FRA
1999 Stepanka Hilgertova CZE

K1 Team
1989 France
1991 France
1993 France
1995 Germany
1997 France
1999 Germany

ENGLAND v AUSTRALIA

	W	L	D
1876-77	1	1	0
1878-79	0	1	0
1880	1	0	0
1881-82	0	2	2
1882	0	1	0
1882-83	2	2	0
1884	1	0	2
1884-85	3	2	0
1886	3	0	0
1886-87	2	0	0
1887-88	1	0	0
1888	2	1	0
1890	2	0	0
1891-92	1	2	0
1893	1	0	2
1894-95	3	2	0
1896	2	1	0
1897-98	1	4	0
1899	0	1	4
1901-02	1	4	0
1902	1	2	2
1903-04	3	2	0
1905	2	0	3
1907-08	1	4	0
1909	1	2	2
1911-12	4	1	0
1912	1	0	2
1920-21	0	5	0
1921	0	3	2
1924-25	1	4	0
1926	1	0	4
1928-29	4	1	0
1930	1	2	2
1932-33	4	1	0
1934	1	2	2
1936-37	2	3	0
1938	1	1	2
1946-47	0	3	2
1948	0	4	1
1950-51	1	4	0
1953	1	0	4
1954-55	3	1	1
1956	2	1	2
1958-59	0	4	1
1961	1	2	2
1962-63	1	1	3
1964	0	1	4
1965-66	1	1	3
1968	1	1	3
1970-71	2	0	4
1972	2	2	1
1974-75	1	4	1
1975	0	1	3
1976-77	0	1	0
1977	3	0	2
1978-79	5	1	0
1979-80	0	3	0
1980	0	0	1
1981	3	1	2
1982-83	1	2	2
1985	3	1	2
1986-87	2	1	2
1987-88	0	0	1
1989	0	4	2
1990-91	0	3	2
1993	1	4	1
1994-95	1	3	1
1997	2	3	1
1998-99	1	3	1
Total	93	117	86

ENGLAND v S AFRICA

	W	L	D
1888-89	2	0	0
1891-92	1	0	0
1895-96	3	0	0
1898-99	2	0	0
1905-06	1	4	0
1907	1	0	2
1909-10	2	3	0
1912	3	0	0
1913-14	4	0	1
1922-23	2	1	2
1924	3	0	2
1927-28	2	2	1
1929	2	0	3
1930-31	0	1	4
1935	0	1	4
1938-39	1	0	4
1947	3	0	2
1948-49	2	0	3
1951	3	1	1
1955	3	2	0
1956-57	2	2	1
1960	3	0	2
1964-65	1	0	4
1965	0	1	2
1994	1	1	1
1995-96	0	1	4
1998	2	1	2
1999-2000	1	2	2
Total	50	23	47

ENGLAND v W INDIES

	W	L	D
1928	3	0	0
1929-30	1	1	2
1933	2	0	1
1934-35	1	2	1
1939	1	0	2
1947-48	0	2	2
1950	1	3	0
1953-54	2	2	1
1957	3	0	2
1959-60	1	0	4

CRICKET

1963	1	3	1
1966	1	3	1
1967-68	1	0	4
1969	2	0	1
1973	0	2	1
1973-74	1	1	3
1976	0	3	2
1980	0	1	4
1980-81	0	2	2
1984	0	5	0
1985-86	0	5	0
1988	0	4	1
1989-90	1	2	1
1991	2	2	1
1993-94	1	3	1
1997-98*	1	3	2
2000	3	1	1
Total	31	52	43

* Draws include one Test abandoned

ENGLAND v NEW ZEALAND

	W	L	D
1929-30	1	0	3
1931	1	0	2
1932-33	0	0	2
1937	1	0	2
1946-47	0	0	1
1949	0	0	4
1950-51	1	0	1
1954-55	2	0	0
1958	4	0	1
1958-59	1	0	1
1962-63	3	0	0
1965	3	0	0
1965-66	0	0	3
1969	2	0	1
1970-71	1	0	1
1973	2	0	1
1974-75	1	0	1
1977-78	1	1	1
1978	3	0	0
1983	3	1	0
1983-84	0	1	2
1986	0	1	2
1987-88	0	0	3
1990	1	0	2
1994	1	0	2
1996-97	2	0	1
1999	1	2	1
Total	37	6	39

ENGLAND v SRI LANKA

	W	L	D
1981-82	1	0	0
1984	0	0	1
1988	1	0	0
1991	1	0	0
1992-93	0	1	0

1998	0	1	0
Total	3	2	1

ENGLAND v INDIA

	W	L	D
1932	1	0	0
1933-34	2	0	1
1936	2	0	1
1946	1	0	2
1951-52	1	1	3
1952	3	0	1
1959	5	0	0
1961-62	0	2	3
1963-64	0	0	5
1967	3	0	0
1971	0	1	2
1972-73	1	2	2
1974	3	0	0
1976-77	3	1	1
1979	1	0	3
1979-80	1	0	0
1981-82	0	1	5
1982	1	0	2
1984-85	2	1	2
1986	0	2	1
1990	1	0	2
1992-93	0	3	0
1996	1	0	2
Total	32	14	38

ENGLAND v PAKISTAN

	W	L	D
1954	1	1	2
1961-62	1	0	2
1962	4	0	1
1967	2	0	1
1968-69	0	0	3
1971	1	0	2
1972-73	0	0	3
1974	0	0	3
1977-78	0	0	3
1978	2	0	1
1982	2	1	0
1983-84	0	1	2
1987	0	1	4
1987-88	0	1	2
1992	1	2	2
1996	0	2	1
2000-01	1	0	2
Total	15	9	34

ENGLAND v ZIMBABWE

	W	L	D
1996-97	0	0	2
2000	1	0	1
Total	1	0	3

CRICKET

WORLD CUP

1975 West Indies
1979 West Indies
1983 India
1987 Australia
1992 Pakistan
1995 Sri Lanka
1999 Australia

COUNTY CHAMPIONSHIP

1864 Surrey
1865 Nottinghamshire
1866 Middlesex
1867 Yorkshire
1868 Nottinghamshire
1869 Nottinghamshire &
      Yorkshire *(shared)*
1870 Yorkshire
1871 Nottinghamshire
1872 Nottinghamshire
1873 Gloucestershire &
      Nottinghamshire
      (shared)
1874 Gloucestershire
1875 Nottinghamshire
1876 Gloucestershire
1877 Gloucestershire
1878 *Undecided*
1879 Lancashire &
      Nottinghamshire
      (shared)
1880 Nottinghamshire
1881 Lancashire
1882 Lancashire &
      Nottinghamshire
      (shared)
1883 Nottinghamshire
1884 Nottinghamshire
1885 Nottinghamshire
1886 Nottinghamshire
1887 Surrey
1888 Surrey
1889 Lancashire,
      Nottinghamshire &
      Surrey *(shared)*
1890 Surrey
1891 Surrey
1892 Surrey
1893 Yorkshire
1894 Surrey
1895 Surrey
1896 Yorkshire
1897 Lancashire
1898 Yorkshire
1899 Surrey
1900 Yorkshire

1901 Yorkshire
1902 Yorkshire
1903 Middlesex
1904 Lancashire
1905 Yorkshire
1906 Kent
1907 Nottinghamshire
1908 Yorkshire
1909 Kent
1910 Kent
1911 Warwickshire
1912 Yorkshire
1913 Kent
1914 Surrey
1915-1918 *Not held*
1919 Yorkshire
1920 Middlesex
1921 Middlesex
1922 Yorkshire
1923 Yorkshire
1924 Yorkshire
1925 Yorkshire
1926 Lancashire
1927 Lancashire
1928 Lancashire
1929 Nottinghamshire
1930 Lancashire
1931 Yorkshire
1932 Yorkshire
1933 Yorkshire
1934 Lancashire
1935 Yorkshire
1936 Derbyshire
1937 Yorkshire
1938 Yorkshire
1939 Yorkshire
1940-1945 *Not held*
1946 Yorkshire
1947 Middlesex
1948 Glamorgan
1949 Middlesex &
      Yorkshire *(shared)*
1950 Lancashire & Surrey
      (shared)
1951 Warwickshire
1952 Surrey
1953 Surrey
1954 Surrey
1955 Surrey
1956 Surrey
1957 Surrey
1958 Surrey
1959 Yorkshire
1960 Yorkshire
1961 Hampshire
1962 Yorkshire
1963 Yorkshire
1964 Worcestershire
1965 Worcestershire

1966 Yorkshire
1967 Yorkshire
1968 Yorkshire
1969 Glamorgan
1970 Kent
1971 Surrey
1972 Warwickshire
1973 Hampshire
1974 Worcestershire
1975 Leicestershire
1976 Middlesex
1977 Kent &
      Middlesex *(shared)*
1978 Kent
1979 Essex
1980 Middlesex
1981 Nottinghamshire
1982 Middlesex
1983 Essex
1984 Essex
1985 Middlesex
1986 Essex
1987 Nottinghamshire
1988 Worcestershire
1989 Worcestershire
1990 Middlesex
1991 Essex
1992 Essex
1993 Middlesex
1994 Warwickshire
1995 Warwickshire
1996 Leicestershire
1997 Glamorgan
1998 Leicestershire
1999 Surrey
2000 Surrey*;
Northamptonshire
*Since 2000, championship split
into two divisions*

CRICKET

NATWEST TROPHY
(Gillette Cup 1963-80)

1963 **Sussex** beat Worcestershire by 14 runs
1964 **Sussex** beat Warwickshire by 8 wkts
1965 **Yorkshire** beat Surrey by 175 runs
1966 **Warwickshire** beat Worcestershire by 5 wkts
1967 **Kent** beat Somerset by 32 runs
1968 **Warwickshire** beat Sussex by 4 wkts
1969 **Yorkshire** beat Derbyshire by 69 runs
1970 **Lancashire** beat Sussex by 6 wkts
1971 **Lancashire** beat Kent by 24 runs
1972 **Lancashire** beat Warwickshire by 4 wkts
1973 **Gloucestershire** beat Sussex by 40 runs
1974 **Kent** beat Lancashire by 4 wkts
1975 **Lancashire** beat Middlesex by 7 wkts
1976 **Northants** beat Lancashire by 4 wkts
1977 **Middlesex** beat Glamorgan by 5 wkts
1978 **Sussex** beat Somerset by 5 wkts
1979 **Somerset** beat Northamptonshire by 45 runs
1980 **Middlesex** beat Surrey by 7 wkts
1981 **Derbyshire** beat Northants fewer wkts lost (scores level)
1982 **Surrey** beat Warwickshire by 9 wkts
1983 **Somerset** beat Kent by 24 runs
1984 **Middlesex** beat Kent by 4 wkts
1985 **Essex** beat Nottinghamshire by 1 run
1986 **Sussex** beat Lancashire by 7 wkts
1987 **Nottinghamshire** beat Northants by 3 wkts
1988 **Middlesex** beat Worcestershire by 3 wkts
1989 **Warwickshire** beat Middlesex by 4 wkts
1990 **Lancashire** beat Northamptonshire by 7 wkts
1991 **Hampshire** beat Surrey by 4 wkts
1992 **Northants** beat Leicestershire by 8 wkts
1993 **Warwickshire** beat Sussex by 5 wkts
1994 **Worcestershire** beat Warwickshire by 8 wkts
1995 **Warwickshire** beat Northants by 4 wkts
1996 **Lancashire** beat Essex by 129 runs
1997 **Essex** beat Warwickshire by 9 wkts
1998 **Essex** beat Leicester by 192 runs
1999 **Gloucestershire** beat Somerset by 50 runs
2000 **Gloucestershire** beat Warwickshire by 22 runs on the Duckworth/Lewis method

BENSON & HEDGES CUP

1972 **Leicestershire** beat Yorkshire by 5 wkts
1973 **Kent** beat Worcestershire by 39 runs
1974 **Surrey** beat Leicestershire by 27 runs
1975 **Leicestershire** beat Middlesex by 5 wkts
1976 **Kent** beat Worcestershire by 43 runs
1977 **Gloucestershire** beat Kent by 64 runs
1978 **Kent** beat Derbyshire by 6 wkts
1979 **Essex** beat Surrey by 35 runs
1980 **Northants** beat Essex by 6 runs
1981 **Somerset** beat Surrey by 7 wkts
1982 **Somerset** beat Nottinghamshire by 9 wkts
1983 **Middlesex** beat Essex by 4 runs
1984 **Lancashire** beat Warwickshire by 6 wkts
1985 **Leicestershire** beat Essex by 5 wkts
1986 **Middlesex** beat Kent by 2 runs

1987 **Yorkshire** beat Northants fewer wkts lost (scores level)
1988 **Hampshire** beat Derbyshire by 7 wkts
1989 **Nottinghamshire** beat Essex by 3 wkts
1990 **Lancashire** beat Worcestershire by 69 runs
1991 **Worcestershire** beat Lancashire by 65 runs
1992 **Hampshire** beat Kent by 41 runs
1993 **Derbyshire** beat Lancashire by 6 runs
1994 **Warwickshire** beat Worcestershire by 6 wkts
1995 **Lancashire** beat Kent by 35 runs
1996 **Lancashire** beat Northants by 31 runs
1997 **Surrey** beat Kent by 8 wkts
1998 **Lancashire** beat Derby by 9 wkts
1999 **Gloucestershire** beat Yorkshire by 124 runs
2000 **Gloucestershire** beat Glamorgan by 7 wkts

AXA LIFE LEAGUE
*(John Player League 1969-86,
Refuge Assurance League 1987-91,
no sponsor 1992)*

1969 **Lancashire**
1970 **Lancashire**
1971 **Worcestershire**
1972 **Kent**
1973 **Kent**
1974 **Leicestershire**
1975 **Hampshire**
1976 **Kent**
1977 **Leicestershire**
1978 **Hampshire**
1979 **Somerset**
1980 **Warwickshire**
1981 **Essex**
1982 **Sussex**
1983 **Yorkshire**
1984 **Essex**
1985 **Essex**
1986 **Hampshire**
1987 **Worcestershire**
1988 **Worcestershire**
1989 **Lancashire**
1990 **Derbyshire**
1991 **Nottinghamshire**
1992 **Middlesex**
1993 **Glamorgan**
1994 **Warwickshire**
1995 **Kent**
1996 **Surrey**
1997 **Warwickshire**
1998 **Lancashire**

CGU NATIONAL LEAGUE

	Division One	Division Two
1999	**Lancashire Lightning**	Sussex
2000	**Gloucestershire Gladiators**	Surrey

CURLING

WORLD CHAMPIONSHIPS

	Men	Venue	Women	Venue
1959	Canada	Falkirk & Edinburgh	-	-
1960	Canada	Falkirk & Edinburgh	-	-
1961	Canada	Ayr, Kirkaldy, Perth & Edinburgh	-	-
1962	Canada	Falkirk & Edinburgh	-	-
1963	Canada	Perth, Scotland	-	-
1964	Canada	Calgary, Canada	-	-
1965	USA	Perth	-	-
1966	Canada	Vancouver, Canada	-	-
1967	Scotland	Perth	-	-
1968	Canada	Pointe Claire, Canada	-	-
1969	Canada	Perth	-	-
1970	Canada	Uttica, USA	-	-
1971	Canada	Megeve, France	-	-
1972	Canada	Regina, Canada	-	-
1973	Sweden	Regina	-	-
1974	USA	Berne, Switzerland	-	-
1975	Switzerland	Perth	-	-
1976	USA	Duluth, USA	-	-
1977	Sweden	Karlstad, Sweden	-	-
1978	USA	Winnipeg, Canada	-	-
1979	Norway	Berne	Switzerland	Perth
1980	Canada	Moncton, Canada	Canada	Perth
1981	Switzerland	London, Canada	Sweden	Perth
1982	Canada	Garmisch, Germany	Denmark	Geneva, Switzerland
1983	Canada	Regina	Switzerland	Moose Jaw, Canada
1984	Norway	Duluth	Canada	Perth
1985	Canada	Glasgow, Scotland	Canada	Jonkoping, Sweden
1986	Canada	Toronto, Canada	Canada	Kelowna, Canada
1987	Canada	Vancouver	Canada	Chicago, USA
1988	Norway	Lausanne, Switzerland	Germany	Glasgow
1989	Canada	Milwaukie, USA	Canada	Milwaukie*
1990	Canada	Vasteras, Sweden	Norway	Vasteras, Sweden
1991	Scotland	Winnipeg	Norway	Winnipeg
1992	Switzerland	Garmisch	Sweden	Garmisch
1993	Canada	Geneva	Canada	Geneva
1994	Canada	Obertsdorf	Canada	Obertsdorf
1995	Canada	Brandon	Sweden	Brandon
1996	Canada	Hamilton	Canada	Hamilton
1997	Sweden	Berne	Canada	Berne
1998	Canada	Kamloops, Canada	Sweden	Kamloops
1999	Scotland	St John, Canada	Sweden	St John
2000	Canada	Braehead, Glasgow	Canada	Braehead

* Championships played together for the first time

World Champions

Men

Track - men's amateur races ceased in 1992, professional races in 1992, to be replaced by Open events, which are listed first. Amateur and pro records follow.

SPRINT
1993 Gary Neiwand AUS
1994 Martin Nothstein USA
1995 Darryn Hill AUS
1996 Florian Rousseau FRA
1997 Florian Rousseau FRA
1998 Florian Rousseau FRA
1999 Laurent Gane FRA
2000 Jan Van Eijden GER

INDIVIDUAL PURSUIT
1993 Graeme Obree GBR
1994 Chris Boardman GBR
1995 Graeme Obree GBR
1996 Chris Boardman GBR
1997 Philippe Ermenault FRA
1998 Philippe Ermenault FRA
1999 Robert Bartko GER
2000 Jens Lehmann GER

TEAM PURSUIT
1993 Australia
1994 Germany
1995 Australia
1996 Italy
1997 Italy
1998 Ukraine
1999 Germany
2000 Germany

POINTS RACE
1993 Etienne de Wilde BEL
1994 Bruno Risi SUI
1995 Silvio Martinello ITA
1996 Juan Llaneras ESP
1997 Silvio Martinello ITA
1998 Juan Llaneras ESP
1999 Bruno Risi SUI
2000 Juan Llaneras ESP

KEIRIN
1993 Gary Neiwand AUS
1994 Martin Nothstein USA
1995 Frédéric Magne FRA
1996 Martin Nothstein USA
1997 Frédéric Magne FRA
1998 Jens Fiedler GER
1999 Jens Fiedler GER
2000 Frédéric Magne FRA

KILOMETRE TIME TRIAL
1993 Florain Rousseau FRA
1994 Florian Rousseau FRA
1995 Shane Kelly AUS
1996 Shane Kelly AUS

1997 Shane Kelly AUS
1998 Arnaud Tournant FRA
1999 Arnaud Tournant FRA
2000 Arnaud Tournant FRA

MADISON
1995 Martinello/Villa ITA
1996 Martinello/Villa ITA
1997 Alzamora/Llaneras ESP
1998 De Wilde/Gilmour BEL
1999 Galvez/Llaneras ESP
2000 Steinwag/Weispfennig GER

OLYMPIC SPRINT
1995 Germany
1996 Australia
1997 France
1998 France
1999 France
2000 France

INDIVIDUAL TIME TRIAL
1994 Chris Boardman GBR
1995 Miguel Induráin ESP
1996 Alex Zülle SUI
1997 Laurent Jalabert FRA
1998 Abraham Olano ESP
1999 Jan Ullrich GER
2000 Sergey Gontchar UKR

ROAD RACE
1994 Luc Leblanc FRA
1995 Abraham Olano ESP
1996 Johan Museeuw BEL
1997 Laurent Brochard FRA
1998 Oscar Camenzind SUI
1999 Oscar Freire ESP
2000 Romans Vainsteins LAT

MOTOR PACED
1993 Jens Veggerby DEN
1994 Carsten Podlesch GER

TANDEM
1993 Paris/Chiappa ITA
1994 Colas/Magné FRA

AMATEUR SPRINT
First held 1893
1970 Daniel Morelon FRA
1971 Daniel Morelon FRA
1973 Daniel Morelon FRA
1974 Anton Tkac TCH
1975 Daniel Morelon FRA
1977 Hans-J Geschke GDR
1978 Anton Tkac TCH
1979 Lutz Hesslich GDR
1981 Sergey Kopylov URS
1982 Sergey Kopylov URS
1983 Lutz Hesslich GDR
1985 Lutz Hesslich GDR
1986 Michael Hubner GDR
1987 Lutz Hesslich GDR

1989 Bill Huck GDR
1989 Bill Huck GDR
1991 Jens Fiedler GER

AMATEUR 1 KM TIME TRIAL
First held 1966
1970 Niels Fredborg DEN
1971 Eduard Rapp URS
1973 Janusz Kierzkowski POL
1974 Eduard Rapp URS
1975 Klaus Gronke GDR
1977-9 &1981 Lothar ThomsGDR
1982 Fredy Schmidtke FRG
1983 Sergey Kopylov URS
1985 Jens Glucklich GDR
1986 Maik Malchow GDR
1987 Martin Vinnicombe AUS
1989 Jens Glucklich GDR
1990 Alex Kirichenko URS
1991 Jose Manuel Moreno ESP

AMATEUR 4KM PURSUIT
First held 1946
1970 Xavier Kurmann SUI
1971 Martin-E Rodriguez COL
1973 Knut Knudsen NOR
1974 Hans Lutz FRG
1975 Thomas Huschke GDR
1977 Norbert Durpisch GDR
1978 Detlef Macha GDR
1979 Nikolai Makarov URS
1981 Detlef Macha GDR
1982 Detlef Macha GDR
1983 Viktor Kupovets URS
1985 Vyacheslav Yekimov URS
1986 Vyacheslav Yekimov URS
1987 Gintautas Umaras URS
1989 Vyacheslav Yekimov URS
1990 Evgeni Berzin URS
1991 Jens Lehmann GER

AMATEUR 4KM TEAM PURSUIT
First held 1962
1970 West Germany
1971 Italy
1973-5West Germany
1977-9 & 1981 East Germany
1982 Soviet Union
1983 West Germany
1985 Italy
1986 Czechoslovakia
1987 Soviet Union
1989 East Germany
1990 Soviet Union
1991 Germany

AMATEUR MOTOR-PACED
100km - 1893-1914; 1hr - 1958-71; 50km - 1970 - 1992
1970 Cees Stam NED
1971-3 Horst Gnas FRG
1974 Jean Breuer FRG

CYCLING

1975	Gaby Minneboo NED		Frank Weber FRG		1987	Italy
1976	Gaby Minneboo NED	1985	Vitezlav Voboril		1989	East Germany
1977	Gaby Minneboo NED		Roman Rehousek TCH		1991	Italy
1978	Rainer Podlesch GDR	1986	Vitezlav Voboril		1993	Italy
1979	Matthe Pronk NED		Roman Rehousek TCH		1994	Italy
1980	Gaby Minneboo NED	1987	Fabrice Colas			

1981 Matthe Pronk NED
1982 Gaby Minneboo NED
1983 Rainer Podlesch GDR
1984 Jan de Nijs NED
1985 Roberto Dotti ITA
1986 Mario Gentili ITA
1987 Mario Gentili ITA
1988 Vincenzo Colamartino ITA
1989 Roland Konigshofer AUT
1990 Roland Konigshofer AUT
1991 Roland Konigshofer AUT
1992 Carsten Podlesch GER

AMATEUR 50KM POINTS
1976 Walter Baumgartner SUI
1977 Constant Tourne BEL
1978 Noel de Jonckheere BEL
1979 Jiri Slama TCH
1980 Gary Sutton AUS
1981 Lutz Haueisen GDR
1982 Hans-Joachim Pohl GDR
1983 Michael Marcussen DEN
1985 Martin Penc TCH
1986 Dan Frost DEN
1987 Marat Ganeeyev URS
1989 Marat Satybyidiev URS
1990 Stephen McGlede AUS
1991 Bruno Risi SUI

AMATEUR TANDEM SPRINT
First held 1966
1970 Jorgen Barth
     Rainer Muller FRG
1971 Jurgen Geschke
     Werner Otto GDR
1973 Vladimir Vackar
     Miroslav Vymazal TCH
1974 Vladimir Vackar
     Miroslav Vymazal TCH
1976 Benedykt Kocot
     Janusz Kotlinski POL
1977 Vladimir Vackar
     Miroslav Vymazal TCH
1978 Vladimir Vackar
     Miroslav Vymazal TCH
1979 Yave Cahard
     Frank Depine FRA
1980 Van Kucirek
     Pavel Martinek TCH
1981 Van Kucirek
     Pavel Martinek TCH
1982 Van Kucirek
     Pavel Martinek TCH
1983 Philippe Vernet
     Frank Depine FRA
1984 Jorgen Greil

1987 Fabrice Colas
     Frederic Magne FRA
1988 Fabrice Colas
     Frederic Magne FRA
1989 Fabrice Colas
     Frederic Magne FRA
1990 Gianiuca Capitano
     Federico Paris ITA
1991 Eyk Pokorny
     Emanuel Raasch GER
1992 Gianiuca Capitano
     Federico Paris ITA

AMATEUR ROAD RACE
1970 Jorgen Schmidt DEN
1971 Regis Ovion FRA
1973 Ryszard Szurkowski POL
1974 Janusz Kowalski POL
1975 Andre Gevers NED
1977 Claudio Corti ITA
1978 Gilbert Glaus SUI
1979 Gianni Giacomini ITA
1981 Andrey Vedernikov URS
1982 Bernd Drogan GDR
1983 Uwe Raab GDR
1985 Lech Piasecki POL
1986 Uwe Ampler GDR
1987 Richard Vivien FRA
1989 Joachim Halupczok POL
1990 Mirko Gualdi ITA
1991 Viktor Ryaksinskiy URS
1993 Jan Ullrich GER
1994 Alex Pederson DEN
1995 Danny Nellison NED

AMATEUR TEAM TIME TRIAL
1962 Italy
1963 France
1964 Italy
1965 Italy
1966 Denmark
1967 Sweden
1968 Sweden
1969 Sweden
1970 Soviet Union
1971 Belgium
1973 Poland
1974 Sweden
1975 Poland
1977 Soviet Union
1978 Netherlands
1979 East Germany
1981 East Germany
1982 Netherlands
1983 Soviet Union
1985 Soviet Union
1986 Netherlands

PROFESSIONAL SPRINT
1970 Gordon Johnson AUS
1971 Leijin Loevesijn NED
1972 Robert van Lancker BEL
1973 Robert van Lancker BEL
1974 Peder Pedersen DEN
1975 John Nicnholon AUS
1976 John Nicnholon AUS
1977 Koichi Nakano JPN
1978 Koichi Nakano JPN
1979 Koichi Nakano JPN
1980 Koichi Nakano JPN
1981 Koichi Nakano JPN
1982 Koichi Nakano JPN
1983 Koichi Nakano JPN
1984 Koichi Nakano JPN
1985 Koichi Nakano JPN
1986 Koichi Nakano JPN
1987 Noboyuki Tawara JPN
1988 Stephen Pate AUS
1989 Claudio Golinelli ITA
1990 Michael Hubner GDR
1991 Carey Hall AUS*
1992 Michael Hubner GER
failed a drugs test title left vacant

PROFESSIONAL 5KM PURSUIT
First held in 1939
1970 Hugh Porter GBR
1971 Dirk Baert BEL
1972 Hugh Porter GBR
1973 Hugh Porter GBR
1974 Roy Schuiten NED
1975 Roy Schuiten NED
1976 Francesco Moser ITA
1977 Gregor Braun FRG
1978 Gregor Braun FRG
1979 Bert Osterbosch NED
1980 Tony Doyle GBR
1981 Alain Bondue FRA
1982 Alain Bondue FRA
1983 Steele Bishop AUS
1984 Hans-Henrik Oersted DEN
1985 Hans-Henrik Oersted DEN
1986 Tony Doyle GBR
1987 Hans-Henrik Oersted DEN
1988 Lech Piasecki POL
1989 Colin Sturgess GBR
1990 Vyacheslav Yekimov URS
1991 Francis Moreau FRA
1992 Mike McCarthy USA

PROFESSIONAL POINTS PACE
1980 Stan Tourne BEL
1981 Urs Freuler SUI
1982 Urs Freuler SUI

CYCLING

1983	Urs Freuler SUI
1984	Urs Freuler SUI
1985	Urs Freuler SUI
1986	Urs Freuler SUI
1987	Urs Freuler SUI
1988	Daniel Wyder SUI
1989	Urs Freuler SUI
1990	Laurent Blondl FRA
1991	Vyacheslav Yekimov URS
1992	Bruno Risi SUI

PROFESSIONAL KEIRIN

1980	Danny Clark AUS
1981	Danny Clark AUS
1982	Gordon Singleton Can
1983	Urs Freuler SUI
1984	Robert Dill-Bundi SUI
1985	Urs Freuler SUI
1986	Michel Vaarten BEL
1987	Harurni Honda Jap
1988	Claudio Golinelli ITA*
1989	Claudio Golinelli ITA
1990	Michael Hubner GDR
1991	Michael Hubner GER
1992	Michael Hubner GER

*failed drugs test title left vacant

PRO MOTOR PACED

First held 1895

1970	Ehrenfried Rudolph FRG
1971	Theo Verschueren BEL
1972	Theo Verschueren BEL
1973	Cees Stam NED
1974	Cees Stam NED
1975	Dieter Kemper FRG
1976	Wilfried Peffgen FRG
1977	Cees Stam NED
1978	Wilfried Peffgen FRG
1979	Martin Venix NED
1980	Wilfried Peffgen FRG
1981	Rene Kos NED
1982	Martin Venix NED
1983	Bruno Vicini ITA
1984	Horst Schotz FRG
1985	Bruno Vicini ITA
1986	Bruno Vicini ITA
1987	Max Hurtzler SUI
1988	Danny Clark AUS
1989	Giovanni Renosto ITA
1990	Walter Brugna ITA
1991	Danny Clark AUS
1992	Peter Steiger SUI

PROFESSIONAL ROAD RACE

First held 1927

1970	Jean-Pierre Monsere BEL
1971	Eddy Merckx BEL
1972	Marino Basso ITA
1973	Felice Gimondi ITA
1974	Eddy Merckx BEL
1975	Hennie Kuiper NED
1976	Freddy Maertens BEL

1977	Francesco Moser ITA
1978	Gerrie Knetemann NED
1979	Jan Raas NED
1980	Bernard Hinault FRA
1981	Freddy Maertens BEL
1982	Giuseppe Saronni ITA
1983	Greg LeMond USA
1984	Claude Criquielion BEL
1985	Joop Zoetemelk NED
1986	Moreno Argentin ITA
1987	Stephen Roche IRE
1988	Maurizio Fondriest ITA
1989	Greg LeMond USA
1990	Rudy Dhaenens BEL
1991	Gianni Bugno ITA
1992	Gianni Bugno ITA
1993	Lance Armstrong USA
1994	Luc Leblanc FRA
1995	Abraham Olano ESP
1996	Johan Museeuw BEL

Women

SPRINT

First held 1958

1969	Galina Tsareva URS
1970	Galina Tsareva URS
1971	Galina Tsareva URS
1972	Galina Yermolayeva URS
1973	Sheila Young USA
1974	Tamara Piltsikova URS
1975	Sue Novarra USA
1976	Sheila Young USA
1977	Galina Tsareva URS
1978	Galina Tsareva URS
1979	Galina Tsareva URS
1980	Sue Reber-Novarra USA
1981	Sheila Ochowitz-Young USA
1982	Connee Paraskevin USA
1983	Connee Paraskevin USA
1984	Connee Paraskevin USA
1985	Isabelle Nicoloso FRA
1986	C Rothenburger GDR
1987	Erika Salumyae URS
1989	Erika Salumyae URS
1990	C Young-Paraskevin USA
1991	Ingrid Haringa NED
1993	Tanya Dubnikoff CAN
1994	Galina Enioukina RUS
1995	Félicia Ballanger FRA
1996	Félicia Ballanger FRA
1997	Félicia Ballanger FRA
1998	Félicia Ballanger FRA
1999	Félicia Ballanger FRA
2000	Natalia Markovnichenko BLR

3KM PURSUIT

1970-74	Tamara Garkushina URS
1975	K van Oosten-Hage NED

1976	K van Oosten-Hage NED
1977	Vera Kuznetsova URS
1978	K van Oosten-Hage NED
1979	K van Oosten-Hage NED
1980	Nadezhda Kibardina URS
1981	Nadezhda Kibardina URS
1982	Rebecca Twigg USA
1983	Connie Carpenter USA
1984	Rebecca Twigg USA
1985	Rebecca Twigg USA
1986	Jeannie Longo FRA
1987	Rebecca Twigg USA
1988	Jeannie Longo FRA
1989	Jeannie Longo FRA
1990	L van Moorsel NED
1991	Petra Rossner GER
1993	Rebecca Twigg USA
1994	Marion Clignet FRA
1995	Rebecca Twigg USA
1996	Marion Clignet FRA
1997	Judith Arndt GER
1998	Lucy T Sharman AUS
1999	Marion Clignet FRA
2000	Yvonne McGregor GBR

500M TIME TRIAL

1995-99	Félicia Ballanger FRA
2000	Natalia Markovnichenko BLR

30KM POINTS

1987	Sally Hodge GBR
	demonstration event
1989	Jeannie Longo FRA
1990	Karen Nedliday NZL
1991-94	Ingrid Haringa NED
1995	Svet. Samokhvalova RUS
1996	S Samokhvalova RUS
1997	Natalia Karimova RUS
1998	Feodora Ruano ESP
1999	Marion Clignet FRA
2000	Marion Clignet FRA

ROAD RACE

First held 1958

1970 & 71	Anna Konkina URS
1971	Anna Konkina URS
1972	Genevieve Gambillon FRA
1973	Nicole Vandenbroeck BEL
1974	Genevieve Gambillon FRA
1975	Trijntje Fopma NED
1976	K van Oosten-Hage NED
1977	Josiane Bost FRA
1978	Beate Habetz FRG
1979	Petra de Bruin NED
1980	Beth Heiden USA
1981	Ute Enzenauer FRG
1982	Mandy Jones GBR
1983	Marianne Berglund SWE
1985	Jeannie Longo FRA
1986	Jeannie Longo FRA
1987	Jeannie Longo FRA

CYCLING

1989 Jeannie Longo FRA
1990 Catherine Marsal FRA
1991 L van Moorsel NED
1993 L Van Moorsel NED
1994 Monica Valvik NOR
1995 Jeannie Longo FRA
1996 Barbara Heeb SUI
1997 A Cappellotto ITA
1998 Diana Ziluite LTU
1999 Edita Pucinskaite LTU
2000 Zinaida Stahurskaia BLR

INDIVIDUAL TIME TRIAL
1994 Karen Kurreck USA
1995 Jeannie Longo FRA
1996 Jeannie Longo FRA
1997 Jeannie Longo FRA
1998 Leontien van Moorsel NED
1999 L Zijlaard-van Moorsel NED
2000 Mari Holden USA

WOMEN'S 50 KM TEAM TRIAL
1987 Soviet Union
1988 Italy
1989 Soviet Union
1990 Netherlands
1991 France
1992 USA
1993 Russia
1994 Russia

Grands Tours
TOUR DE FRANCE
1903 Maurice Garin FRA
1904 Henri Cornet FRA
1905 Louis Trousselier FRA
1906 Rene Pottier FRA
1907 Lucien Petit-Breton FRA
1908 Lucien Petit-Breton FRA
1909 Francois Faber LUX
1910 Octave Lapize FRA
1911 Gustave Garrigou FRA
1912 Odile Defraye BEL
1913 Philippe Thys BEL
1914 Philippe Thys BEL
1919 Firmin Lambot BEL
1920 Philippe Thys BEL
1921 Leon Scieur BEL
1922 Firmin Lambot BEL
1923 Henri Pelissier FRA
1924 Ottavio Bottecchia ITA
1925 Ottavio Bottecchia ITA
1926 Lucien Buysse BEL
1927 Nicholas Frantz LUX
1928 Nicholas Frantz LUX
1929 Maurice De Waele BEL
1930 Andre Leducq FRA
1931 Antonin Magne FRA
1932 Andre Leducq FRA
1933 Georges Speicher FRA

1934 Antonin Magne FRA
1935 Romain Maes BEL
1936 Sylvere Maes BEL
1937 Roger Lapebie FRA
1938 Gino Bartali ITA
1939 Sylvere Maes BEL
1947 Jean Robic FRA
1948 Gino Bartali ITA
1949 Fausto Coppi ITA
1950 Ferdinand Kubler SUI
1951 Hugo Koblet SUI
1952 Fausto Coppi ITA
1953 Louison Bobet FRA
1954 Louison Bobet FRA
1955 Louison Bobet FRA
1956 Roger Walkowiak FRA
1957 Jacques Anquetil FRA
1958 Charly Gaul LUX
1959 Federico Bahamontes ESP
1960 Gastone Nencini ITA
1961 Jacques Anquetil FRA
1962 Jacques Anquetil FRA
1963 Jacques Anquetil FRA
1964 Jacques Anquetil FRA
1965 Felice Gimondi ITA
1966 Lucien Aimar FRA
1967 Roger Pingeon FRA
1968 Jan Janssen HOL
1969 Eddy Merckx BEL
1970 Eddy Merckx BEL
1971 Eddy Merckx BEL
1972 Eddy Merckx BEL
1973 Luis Ocana ESP
1974 Eddy Merckx BEL
1975 Bernard Thevenet FRA
1976 Lucien van Impe BEL
1977 Bernard Thevenet FRA
1978 Bernard Hinault FRA
1979 Bernard Hinault FRA
1980 Joop Zoetemelk HOL
1981 Bernard Hinault FRA
1982 Bernard Hinault FRA
1983 Laurent Fignon FRA
1984 Laurent Fignon FRA
1985 Bernard Hinault FRA
1986 Greg LeMond USA
1987 Stephen Roche IRE
1988 Pedro Delgado ESP
1989 Greg LeMond USA
1989 Greg LeMond USA
1991 Miguel Induráin ESP
1992 Miguel Induráin ESP
1993 Miguel Induráin ESP
1994 Miguel Induráin ESP
1995 Miguel Induráin ESP
1996 Bjarne Riis DEN
1997 Jan Ullrich GER
1998 Marco Pantani ITA
1999 Lance Armstrong USA

2000 Lance Armstrong USA

GIRO d'ITALIA
First held 1909
1980 Bernard Hinault FRA
1981 Giovani Battaglin ITA
1982 Bernard Hinault FRA
1983 Guiseppe Saronni ITA
1984 Francesco Moser ITA
1985 Bernard Hinault FRA
1986 Roberto Visentini ITA
1987 Stephen Roche IRE
1988 Andy Hampsten USA
1989 Laurent Fignon FRA
1990 Gianni Bugno ITA
1991 Franco Chioccioli ITA
1992 Miguel Induráin ESP
1993 Miguel Induráin ESP
1994 Evgeny Berzin RUS
1995 Tony Rominger SUI
1996 Pavel Tonkov RUS
1997 Ivan Gotti ITA
1998 Marco Pantani ITA
1999 Ivan Gotti ITA
2000 Stefano Garzelli ITA

VUELTA DE ESPANA
First held 1935
1980 Faustino Ruperez ESP
1981 Giovanni Battaglin ITA
1982 Marino Lejaretta ESP
1983 Bernhard Hinault FRA
1984 Eric Caritoux FRA
1985 Pedro Delgado ESP
1986 Alvaro Pino ESP
1987 Luis Herrera COL
1988 Sean Kelly IRL
1989 Pedro Delgado ESP
1990 Marco Giovanetti ITA
1991 Melchior Mauri ESP
1992 Tony Rominger SUI
1993 Tony Rominger SUI
1994 Tony Rominger SUI
1995 Laurent Jalabert FRA
1996 Alex Zulle SUI
1997 Alex Zulle SUI
1998 Abraham Olano ESP
1999 Jan Ullrich GER
2000 Roberto Heras ESP

DARTS

WORLD PROFESSIONAL CHAMPIONS

Year	Winner	Runner-up	Score
1978	Leighton Rees	John Lowe	11-7
1979	John Lowe	Leighton Rees	5-0
1980	Eric Bristow	Bobby George	5-3
1981	Eric Bristow	John Lowe	5-3
1982	Jocky Wilson	John Lowe	5-3
1983	Keith Deller	Eric Bristow	6-5
1984	Eric Bristow	Dave Whitcombe	7-1
1985	Eric Bristow	John Lowe	6-2
1986	Eric Bristow	Dave Whitcombe	6-0
1987	John Lowe	Eric Bristow	6-4
1988	Bob Anderson	John Lowe	6-4
1989	Jocky Wilson	Eric Bristow	6-4
1990	Phil Taylor	Eric Bristow	6-1
1991	Dennis Priestley	Eric Bristow	6-0
1992	Phil Taylor	Mike Gregory	6-5
1993	John Lowe	Alan Warriner	6-3
1994*	John Part	Bobby George	6-0
	Dennis Priestley	Phil Taylor	6-1
1995	Richie Burnett	Raymond Barneveld	6-3
	Phil Taylor	Rod Harrington	6-2
1996	Steve Beaton	Richie Burnett	6-3
	Phil Taylor	Dennis Priestley	6-4
1997	Les Wallace	Marshall James	6-3
	Phil Taylor	Dennis Priestley	6-3
1998	Ray Barneveld	Richie Burnett	6-5
	Phil Taylor	Dennis Priestley	6-0
1999	Ray Barneveld	Ronnie Baxter	6-5
	Phil Taylor	Peter Manley	6-2
2000	Ted Hankey	Ronnie Baxter	6-0
	Phil Taylor	Dennis Priestley	7-3

BDO version is given first, WDC version second

WORLD MASTERS

Year	Winner	
1974	Cliff Inglis	ENG
1975	Alan Evans	WAL
1976	John Lowe	ENG
1977	Eric Bristow	ENG
1978	Ronnie Davis	ENG
1979	Eric Bristow	ENG
1980	John Lowe	ENG
1981	Eric Bristow	ENG
1982	Dave Whitcombe	ENG
1983	Eric Bristow	ENG
1984	Eric Bristow	ENG
1985	Dave Whitcombe	ENG
1986	Bob Anderson	ENG
1987	Bob Anderson	ENG
1988	Bob Anderson	ENG
1989	Peter Evison	ENG
1990	Phil Taylor	ENG
1991	Rod Harrington	ENG
1992	Dennis Priestley	ENG
1993	Steve Beaton	ENG
1994	Richie Burnett	ENG

NEWS OF THE WORLD

Competition terminated when paper withdrew its support in 1991. (British unless stated)

Year	Winner
1948	Harry Leadbetter
1949	Jack Boyce
1950	Dixie Newberry
1951	Harry Perryman
1952	Tommy Gibbons
1953	Jimmy Carr
1954	Oliver James
1955	Tom Reddington
1956	Trevor Peachey
1957	Alwyn Mullins
1958	Tommy Gibbons
1959	Albert Welch
1960	Tom Reddington
1961	Alec Adamson
1962	Eddie Brown
1963	Robbie Rumney
1964	Tom Barrett
1965	Tom Barrett
1966	Wilf Ellis
1967	Wally Seaton
1968	Bill Duddy
1969	Barry Twomlow
1970	Henry Barney
1971	Dennis Filkins
1972	Brian Netherton
1973	Ivor Hodgkinson
1974	Peter Chapman
1975	Derek White
1976	Bill Lennard
1977	Mick Norris
1978	Stefan Lord SWE
1979	Bobby George
1980	Stefan Lord SWE
1981	John Lowe
1982	Roy Morgan
1983	Eric Bristow
1984	Eric Bristow
1985	Dave Lee
1986	Bobby George
1987	Mike Gregory
1988	Mike Gregory
1989	Dave Whitcombe
1990	Paul Cook

EQUESTRIANISM

JUMPING

WORLD CHAMPIONSHIP - MEN

Year	Rider		Horse
1953	Francisco Goyoago	ESP	Quorum
1954	Hans Gunter Winkler	FRG	Halla
1955	Hans Gunter Winkler	FRG	Halla
1956	Raimondo d'Inzeo	ITA	Merano
1960	Raimondo d'Inzeo	ITA	Gowran Girl
1966	P Jonqueres d'Oriola	FRA	Pomone B
1970	David Broome	GBR	Beethoven
1974	Hartwig Steenken	FRG	Simona
1978	Gerd Wilffang	FRG	Roman
1982	Norbert Koof	FRG	Fire II
1986	Gail Greenhough	CAN	Mr T
1990	Eric Navet	FRA	Quito de Baussy
1994	Franke Sloothaak	GER	San Patrignano Weihaiwej
1998	Rodrigo Pessoa	BRA	Gandini Lianos

WORLD CHAMPIONSHIP - WOMEN

1965	Marion Coakes	GBR	Stroller
1970	Janou Lefebvre	FRA	Rocket
1974	Janou Tissot (née Lefebvre)	FRA	Rocket

VOLVO WORLD CUP

1979	Hugo Simon	AUT	Gladstone
1980	Conrad Homfeld	USA	Balbuco
1981	Michael Matz	USA	Jet Run
1982	Melanie Smith	USA	Calypso
1983	Norman Dello Joio	USA	I Love You
1984	Mario Deslauriers	CAN	Aramis
1985	Conrad Homfeld	USA	Abdullah
1986	Leslie Burr-Lenehan	USA	McLain
1987	Katharine Burdsall	USA	The Natural
1988	Ian Millar	CAN	Big Ben
1989	Ian Millar	CAN	Big Ben
1990	John Whitaker	GBR	Milton
1991	John Whitaker	GBR	Milton
1992	Thomas Fruhmann	AUT	Bockmann's Genius
1993	Ludger Beerbaum	GER	Almox Ratina Z
1994	Jos Lansink	HOL	Bollvorm's Libero H
1995	Nick Skelton	GBR	Midnight Madness
1996	Hugo Simon	AUT	E T FRH
1997	Hugo Simon	AUT	E T FRH
1998	Jos Lansink	NED	Nissan Calvaro Z
1999	Rodrigo Pessoa	BRA	Baloubet du Roi
2000	Rodrigo Pessoa	BRA	Baloubet du Roi

THREE-DAY EVENTING

WORLD CHAMPIONSHIPS - INDIVIDUAL

1966	Carlos Moratorio	ARG	Chalon
1970	Mary Gordon-Watson	GBR	Cornishman V
1974	Bruce Davidson	USA	Irish Cap
1978	Bruce Davidson	USA	Might Tango
1982	Lucinda Green	GBR	Regal Realm
1986	Virginia Leng	GBR	Priceless
1990	Blyth Tait	NZL	Messiah
1994	Vaughan Jefferis	NZL	Bounce
1998	Blyth Tait	NZL	Ready Teddy

BADMINTON HORSE TRIALS

Year	Rider		Horse
1949	John Shedden	GBR	Golden Willow
1950	Tony Collings	GBR	Remus
1951	Hans Schwarzenbach	SUI	Vae Victus
1952	Mark Darley	IRE	Emily Little
1953	Lawrence Rook	GBR	Starlight
1954	Margaret Hough	GBR	Bambi
1955	Frank Weldon	GBR	Kilbarry
1956	Frank Weldon	GBR	Kilbarry
1957	Sheila Willcox	GBR	High and Mighty
1958	Sheila Willcox	GBR	High and Mighty
1959	Sheila Waddington (née Willcox)	GBR	Airs and Graces
1960	Bill Roycroft	AUS	Our Solo
1961	Lawrence Morgan	AUS	Salad Days
1962	A Drummond-Hay	GBR	Merely-a-Monarch
1963	Susan Fleet	GBR	Gladiator
1964	James Templer	GBR	M'Lord Connolly
1965	Eddie Boylan	IRE	Durlas Eile
1966	*Not held*		
1967	Celia Ross-Taylor	GBR	Jonathan
1968	Jane Bullen	GBR	Our Nobby
1969	Richard Walker	GBR	Pasha
1970	Richard Meade	GBR	The Poacher
1971	Mark Phillips	GBR	Great Ovation
1972	Mark Phillips	GBR	Great Ovation
1973	Lucinda Prior-Palmer	GBR	Be Fair
1974	Mark Phillips	GBR	Columbus
1975	*Cancelled after dressage*		
1976	Lucinda Prior-Palmer	GBR	Wideawake
1977	Lucinda Prior-Palmer	GBR	George
1978	Jane Holderness-Roddam (née Bullen)	GBR	Warrior
1979	Lucinda Prior-Palmer	GBR	Killaire
1980	Mark Todd	NZL	Southern Comfort
1981	Mark Phillips	NZL	Lincoln
1982	Richard Meade	GBR	Speculator lil
1983	Lucinda Green (née Prior-Palmer)	GBR	Regal Realm
1984	Lucinda Green	GBR	Beagle Bay
1985	Virginia Holgate	GBR	Priceless
1986	Ian Stark	GBR	Sir Wattie
1987	*Not held*		
1988	Ian Stark	GBR	Sir Wattie
1989	Virginia Leng (née Holgate)	GBR	Master Craftsman
1990	Nicola McIrvine	GBR	Middle Road
1991	Rodney Powell	GBR	The Irishman
1992	Mary Thompson	GBR	King William
1993	Virginia Leng	GBR	Welton Houdini
1994	Mark Todd	NZL	Horton Point
1995	Bruce Davidson	USA	Eagle Lion
1996	Mark Todd	NZL	Bertie Blunt
1997	David O'Connor	USA	Custom Made
1998	Chris Bartle	GBR	Word Perfect II
1999	Ian Stark	GBR	Jaybee
2000	Mary King	GBR	Star Appeal

FENCING

World Champions

MEN'S FOIL		MEN'S EPEE	MEN'S SABRE
1921	-	Lucien Gaudin FRA	-
1922	-	Raoul Herde NOR	Adrianus de Jong HOL
1923	-	Wouter Brouwer HOL	Adrianus de Jong HOL
1925	-	-	János Garay HUN
1926	Giorgio Chiavacci ITA	Georges Tainturier FRA	Sándor Gambos HUN
1927	Oreste Puliti ITA	Georges Buchard FRA	Sándor Gambos HUN
1929	Oreste Puliti ITA	Philippe Cattiau FRA	Gyula Glykais HUN
1930	Giulio Gaudini ITA	Philippe Cattiau FRA	György Piller HUN
1931	Rene Lemoine FRA	Georges Buchard FRA	György Piller HUN
1933	Gioacch'o Guaragna ITA	Georges Buchard FRA	Endre Kabos HUN
1934	Giulio Gaudini ITA	Pál Dunay HUN	Endre Kabos HUN
1935	shared by four men	Hans Drakenberg SWE	Aladár Gerevich HUN
1937	Gustavo Marzi ITA	Bernard Schmetz FRA	Pál Kovács HUN
1938	Gioacch'o Guaragna ITA	Michel Pécheux FRA	Aldo Montano ITA
1947	Christian d'Oriola FRA	Edouard Artigas FRA	Aldo Montano ITA
1949	Christian d'Oriola FRA	Dario Mangiarotti ITA	Gastone Daré FRA
1950	Renzo Nostino ITA	Mogens Luchow DEN	Jean Levavasseur FRA
1951	Manlio Di Rosa ITA	Edoardo Mangiarotti ITA	Aladar Gerevich HUN
1953	Christian d'Oriola FRA	Jozsef Sakovics HUN	Pál Kovács HUN
1954	Christian d'Oriola FRA	Edoardo Mangiarotti ITA	Rudolf Kárpáti HUN
1955	Jozsef Gyuricza HUN	Giorgio Anglesio ITA	Aladár Gerevich HUN
1957	Mihaly Fülöp HUN	Armand Mouyal FRA	Jerzy Pawlowski POL
1958	Giancarlo Bergamini ITA	Bill Hoskyns GBR	Yakov Rylsky URS
1959	Allan Jay GBR	Bruno Khabarov URS	Rudolf Kárpáti HUN
1961	Ryszard Parulski POL	Jack Guittet FRA	Yakov Rylsky URS
1962	German Sveshnikov URS	Istvan Kausz HUN	Zoltan Horvath HUN
1963	Jean-Cl'de Magnan FRA	Roland Losert AUT	Yakov Rylsky URS
1965	Jean-Cl'de Magnan FRA	Zoltan Nemere HUN	Jerzy Pawlowski POL
1966	German Sveshnikov URS	Aleksey Nikanchikov URS	Jerzy Pawlowski POL
1967	Viktor Putyatin URS	Aleksey Nikanchikov URS	Mark Rakita URS
1969	Friedrich Wessel FRG	Bogdan Andrzejewski POL	Viktor Sidiak URS
1970	Friedrich Wessel FRG	Aleksey Nikanchikov URS	Tibor Pézsa HUN
1971	Vasiliy Stankovich URS	Grigoriy Kriss URS	Michele Maffei ITA
1973	Christian Noël FRA	Rolf Edling SWE	Mario Aldo Monttano ITA
1974	Aleks'dr Romankov URS	Rolf Edling SWE	Mario Aldo Monttano ITA
1975	Christian Noël FRA	Alexander Pusch FRG	Vladimir Nazlimov URS
1977	Aleks'dr Romankov URS	Johan Harmenberg SWE	Pál Gerevich HUN
1978	Didier Flament FRA	Alexander Pusch FRG	Viktor Krovopuskov URS
1979	Aleks'dr Romankov URS	Philippe Riboud FRA	Vladimir Nazlimov URS
1981	Vladimir Smirnov URS	Zoltan Szekely HUN	Mariusz Wodke POL
1982	Aleks'dr Romankov URS	Jenö Pap HUN	Viktor Krovopuskov URS
1983	Aleks'dr Romankov URS	Ellmar Bormann FRG	Vasiliy Etropolski BUL
1985	Mauro Numa ITA	Philippe Boisse FRA	Gyorgy Nebald HUN
1986	Andrea Borella ITA	Philippe Riboud FRA	Sergey Mindirgassov URS
1987	Mathias Gey FRG	Volker Fischer FRG	Jean François Lamour FRA
1989	Alexander Koch FRG	Manuel Pereira ESP	Grigoriy Kirienko URS
1990	Philippe Omnès FRA	Thomas Gerull FRG	György Nébald HUN
1991	Ingo Weissenborn GER	Andrey Shuvalov URS	Grigory Kirienko URS
1993	Alexander Koch GER	Pavel Kolobkov RUS	Grigory Kirienko RUS
1994	Rolando Tuckers CUB	Pavel Kolobkov RUS	Felix Becker GER
1995	Dmitri Chevtchenko RUS	Eric Srecki RUS	Grigory Kirienko RUS
1997	Sergey Golubitsky UKR	Eric Srecki FRA	Stanislaw Pozdniakov RUS
1998	Sergey Golubitsky UKR	Hugues Obry FRA	Luigi Tarantino ITA
1999	Sergey Golubitsky UKR	Arnd Schmitt GER	Damien Touya FRA

FENCING

World Champions

WOMEN'S FOIL

1929	Helene Mayer	GER
1930	Jenny Addam	BEL
1931	Helene Mayer	GER
1933	Gwen Nelligan	GBR
1934	Ilona Elek	HUN
1935	Ilona Elek	HUN
1937	Helene Mayer	GER
1938	Marie Sediva	CZE
1947	Ellen Müller-Preiss	AUT
1949	Ellen Müller-Preiss	AUT
1950	Ellen Müller-Preiss	AUT
	Renée Garilhe	FRA
	Title shared	
1951	Ilona Elek	HUN
1953	Irene Camber	ITA
1954	Karen Lachman	DEN
1955	Lidia Domolki	HUN
1957	Aleksandra Zabelina	URS
1958	Valentina Kiselyeva	URS ITA
1959	Yelina Yefimova	URS
1961	Heidi Schmid	FRG
1962	Olga Szabo-Orban	ROM
1963	Ildiko Rejto	HUN
1965	Galina Gorokhova	URS
1966	Tatyana Samusenko	URS
1967	Aleksandra Zabelina	URS
1969	Yelena Novikova	URS
1970	Galina Gorokhova	URS
1971	Marie-Chantal Demaille	FRA
1973	Valentina Nikonova	URS
1974	Ildiko Bobis	HUN
1975	Ecaterina Stahl	ROM
1977	Valentina Sidorova	URS
1978	Valentina Sidorova	URS
1979	Cornelia Hanisch	FRG
1981	Cornelia Hanisch	FRG
1982	Naila Giliazova	URS
1983	Dorina Vaccaroni	ITA
1985	Cornelia Hanisch	FRG
1986	Anja Fichtel	GER
1987	Elisabeta Tufan	ROM
1989	Olga Velichko	URS
1990	Anja Fichtel	GER
1991	Giovanna Trillini	ITA
1993	Fracesca Bortolozzi	ITA
1994	Reka Szabo-Lazar	ROM
1995	Laura Badea	ROM
1997	Giovanna Trillini	ITA
1998	Sabine Bau	GER
1999	Valentina Vazzali	ITA

WOMEN'S EPEE

1989	Anja Straub	SUI
1990	Taime Chappe	CUB
1991	Marianne Horvath	HUN
1991	Marianne Horvath	HUN
1993	Oksana Yermakova	EST
1994	Laura Chiesa	ITA
1995	Joanna Jakimiuk	POL
1997	Miraide Garcia	CUB
1998	Laura Flessel	FRA
1999	Laura Flessel-Colovic	FRA

WOMEN'S SABRE

1999	Elena Jemaeva	AZE

FENCING

World Champions

	Men			Women		
	Team Foil	*Team Epee*	*Team Sabre*	*Team Foil*	*Team Epee*	*Team Sabre*
1929	Italy	-	-	-	-	-
1930	Italy	Belgium	Hungary	-	-	-
1931	Italy	Italy	Hungary	-	-	-
1932	-	-	-	Denmark	-	-
1933	Italy	Italy	Hungary	Hungary	-	-
1934	Italy	France	Hungary	Hungary	-	-
1935	Italy	France	Hungary	Hungary	-	-
1936	-	-	-	West Germany	-	-
1937	Italy	Italy	Hungary	Hungary	-	-
1938	Italy	France	Italy	-	-	-
1947	France	France	Italy	Denmark	-	-
1948	-	-	-	Denmark	-	-
1949	Italy	Italy	Italy	-	-	-
1950	Italy	Italy	Italy	France	-	-
1951	France	France	Hungary	France	-	-
1952	-	-	-	Hungary	-	-
1953	France	Italy	Hungary	Hungary	-	-
1954	Italy	Italy	Hungary	Hungary	-	-
1955	Italy	Italy	Hungary	Hungary	-	-
1956	-	-	-	Soviet Union	-	-
1957	Hungary	Italy	Hungary	Italy	-	-
1958	France	Italy	Hungary	Soviet Union	-	-
1959	Soviet Union	Hungary	Poland	Hungary	-	-
1961	Soviet Union	Soviet Union	Poland	Soviet Union	-	-
1962	Soviet Union	France	Poland	Hungary	-	-
1963	Soviet Union	Poland	Poland	Soviet Union	-	-
1965	Soviet Union	France	Soviet Union	Soviet Union	-	-
1966	Soviet Union	France	Hungary	Soviet Union	-	-
1967	Romania	Soviet Union	Soviet Union	Hungary	-	-
1969	Soviet Union	Soviet Union	Soviet Union	Romania	-	-
1970	Soviet Union	Hungary	Soviet Union	Soviet Union	-	-
1971	France	Hungary	Soviet Union	Soviet Union	-	-
1973	Soviet Union	West Germany	Hungary	Hungary	-	-
1974	Soviet Union	Sweden	Soviet Union	Soviet Union	-	-
1975	France	Sweden	Soviet Union	Soviet Union	-	-
1977	West Germany	Sweden	Soviet Union	Soviet Union	-	-
1978	Poland	Hungary	Hungary	Soviet Union	-	-
1979	Soviet Union	Soviet Union	Soviet Union	Soviet Union	-	-
1981	Soviet Union	Soviet Union	Hungary	Soviet Union	-	-
1982	Soviet Union	France	Hungary	Italy	-	-
1983	West Germany	France	Soviet Union	Italy	-	-
1985	Italy	West Germany	Soviet Union	West Germany	-	-
1986	Italy	West Germany	Soviet Union	Soviet Union	-	-
1987	West Germany	Soviet Union	Soviet Union	Hungary	-	-
1989	Soviet Union	Italy	Soviet Union	West Germany	Hungary	-
1990	Italy	Italy	Soviet Union	Italy	West Germany	-
1991	Cuba	Soviet Union	Hungary	Italy	Hungary	-
1993	Germany	Italy	Hungary	Germany	Hungary	-
1994	Italy	France	Russia	Romania	Spain	-
1995	Cuba	Germany	Italy	Italy	Hungary	-
1997	France	Cuba	France	Italy	Hungary	-
1998	Poland	Hungary	Hungary	Italy	France	-
1999	France	Germany	France	Germany	Hungary	Italy

GOLF

THE OPEN

Year	Winner		Score	Venue
1860	Willie Park Snr	GBR	174	Prestwick
1861	Tom Morris Snr	GBR	163	Prestwick
1862	Tom Morris Snr	GBR	163	Prestwick
1863	Willie Park Snr	GBR	168	Prestwick
1864	Tom Morris Snr	GBR	167	Prestwick
1865	Andrew Strath	GBR	162	Prestwick
1866	Willie Park Snr	GBR	169	Prestwick
1867	Tom Morris Snr	GBR	170	Prestwick
1868	Tom Morris Jnr	GBR	157	Prestwick
1869	Tom Morris Jnr	GBR	154	Prestwick
1870	Tom Morris Jnr	GBR	149	Prestwick
1872	Tom Morris Jnr	GBR	166	Prestwick
1873	Tom Kidd	GBR	179	St Andrews
1874	Mungo Park	GBR	159	Musselburgh
1875	Willie Park Snr	GBR	166	Prestwick
1876	Bob Martin	GBR	176	St Andrews
1877	Jamie Anderson	GBR	160	Musselburgh
1878	Jamie Anderson	GBR	157	Prestwick
1880	Jamie Anderson	GBR	169	St Andrews
1880	Robert Ferguson	GBR	162	Musselburgh
1881	Robert Ferguson	GBR	170	Prestwick
1882	Robert Ferguson	GBR	171	St Andrews
1883	Willie Fernie	GBR	158*	Musselburgh
1884	Jack Simpson	GBR	160	Prestwick
1885	Bob Martin	GBR	171	St Andrews
1886	David Brown	GBR	157	Musselburgh
1887	Willie Park Jnr	GBR	161	Prestwick
1888	Jack Burns	GBR	171	St Andrews
1889	Willie Park Jnr	GBR	155*	Musselburgh
1890	John Ball *(am)*	GBR	164	Prestwick
1891	Hugh Kirkaldy	GBR	166	St Andrews
1892	Harold Hilton *(am)*	GBR	305	Muirfield
1893	Will Auchterlonie	GBR	322	Prestwick
1894	John H Taylor	GBR	326	Sandwich
1895	John H Taylor	GBR	322	St Andrews
1896	Harry Vardon	GBR	316*	Muirfield
1897	Harold Hilton *(am)*	GBR	314	Hoylake
1898	Harry Vardon	GBR	307	Prestwick
1899	Harry Vardon	GBR	310	Sandwich
1900	John H Taylor	GBR	309	St Andrews
1901	James Braid	GBR	309	Muirfield
1902	Sandy Herd	GBR	307	Hoylake
1903	Harry Vardon	GBR	300	Prestwick
1904	Jack White	GBR	296	Sandwich
1905	James Braid	GBR	318	St Andrews
1906	James Braid	GBR	300	Muirfield
1907	Arnaud Massy	FRA	312	Hoylake
1908	James Braid	GBR	291	Prestwick
1909	John H Taylor	GBR	295	Deal
1910	James Braid	GBR	299	St Andrews
1911	Harry Vardon	GBR	303	Sandwich
1912	Edward Ray	GBR	295	Muirfield
1913	John H Taylor	GBR	304	Hoylake
1914	Harry Vardon	GBR	306	Prestwick
1920	George Duncan	GBR	303	Deal
1921	Jock Hutchinson	USA	296*	St Andrews
1922	Walter Hagen	USA	300	Sandwich
1923	Arthur Havers	GBR	295	Troon
1924	Walter Hagen	USA	301	Hoylake
1925	Jim Barnes	USA	300	Prestwick
1926	Bobby Jones *(am)*	USA	291	Royal Lytham
1927	Bobby Jones *(am)*	USA	285	St Andrews
1928	Walter Hagen	USA	292	Sandwich
1929	Walter Hagen	USA	292	Muirfield
1930	Bobby Jones *(am)*	USA	291	Hoylake
1931	Tommy Armour	USA	296	Carnoustie
1932	Gene Sarazen	USA	283	Prince's
1933	Densmore Shute	USA	292*	St Andrews
1934	Henry Cotton	GBR	283	Sandwich
1935	Alfred Perry	GBR	283	Muirfield
1936	Alfred Padgham	GBR	287	Hoylake
1937	Henry Cotton	GBR	290	Carnoustie
1938	Reg Whitcombe	GBR	295	Sandwich
1939	Dick Burton	GBR	290	St Andrews
1946	Sam Snead	USA	290	St Andrews
1947	Fred Daly	GBR	293	Hoylake
1948	Henry Cotton	GBR	284	Muirfield
1949	Bobby Locke	RSA	283*	Sandwich
1950	Bobby Locke	RSA	279	Troon
1951	Max Faulkner	GBR	285	Portrush
1952	Bobby Locke	RSA	287	Royal Lytham
1953	Ben Hogan	USA	282	Carnoustie
1954	Peter Thomson	AUS	283	Royal Birkdale
1955	Peter Thomson	AUS	281	St Andrews
1956	Peter Thomson	AUS	286	Hoylake
1957	Bobby Locke	RSA	279	St Andrews
1958	Peter Thomson	AUS	278*	Royal Lytham
1959	Gary Player	RSA	284	Muirfield
1960	Kel Nagle	AUS	278	St.Andrews
1961	Arnold Palmer	USA	284	Royal Birkdale
1962	Arnold Palmer	USA	276	Troon
1963	Bob Charles	NZL	277*	Royal Lytham
1964	Tony Lema	USA	279	St Andrews
1965	Peter Thomson	AUS	285	Royal Birkdale
1966	Jack Nicklaus	USA	282	Muirfield
1967	Rob. de Vicenzo	ARG	278	Hoylake
1968	Gary Player	RSA	289	Carnoustie
1969	Tony Jacklin	GBR	280	Royal Lytham
1970	Jack Nicklaus	USA	283*	St Andrews
1971	Lee Trevino	USA	278	Royal Birkdale
1972	Lee Trevino	USA	278	Muirfield
1973	Tom Weiskopf	USA	276	Troon
1974	Gary Player	RSA	282	Royal Lytham
1975	Tom Watson	USA	279*	Carnoustie
1976	Johnny Miller	USA	279	Royal Birkdale
1977	Tom Watson	USA	268	Turnberry
1978	Jack Nicklaus	USA	281	St Andrews
1979	Seve Ballesteros	ESP	283	Royal Lytham
1980	Tom Watson	USA	271	Muirfield
1981	Bill Rogers	USA	276	Sandwich
1982	Tom Watson	USA	284	Troon
1983	Tom Watson	USA	275	Royal Birkdale
1984	Seve Ballesteros	ESP	276	St Andrews
1985	Sandy Lyle	GBR	282	Sandwich
1986	Greg Norman	AUS	280	Turnberry
1987	Nick Faldo	GBR	279	Muirfield
1988	Seve Ballesteros	ESP	273	Royal Lytham
1989	Mark Calcavecchia	USA	275*	Troon
1990	Nick Faldo	GBR	270	St Andrews
1991	Ian Baker-Finch	AUS	272	Royal Birkdale

GOLF

THE OPEN

1992	Nick Faldo GBR	272	Muirfield
1993	Greg Norman AUS	267	Sandwich
1994	Nick Price ZIM	268	Turnberry
1995	John Daly USA	282*	St Andrews
1996	Tom Lehman USA	271	Royal Lytham
1997	Justin Leonard USA	272	Royal Troon
1998	Mark O'Meara USA	280*	Birkdale
1999	Paul Lawrie GBR	290*	Carnoustie
2000	Tiger Woods USA	269	St Andrews

US OPEN

Year	Winner (USA unless stated)	Score	Venue
1895	Horace Rawlins	173	Newport
1896	James Foulis	152	Shinnecock Hs
1897	Joe Lloyd	162	Chicago
1898	Willie Smith	315	Baltimore
1900	Harry Vardon GBR	313	Chicago
1901	Willie Anderson	331*	Myopia Hunt
1902	Laurie Auchterlonie	307	Garden City
1903	Willie Anderson	307*	Baltusrol
1904	Willie Anderson	303	Glen View
1905	Willie Anderson	314	Myopia Hunt
1906	Alex Smith	295	Onwentsia
1907	Alex Ross	302	Philadelphia
1908	Fred McLeod	322*	Myopia Hunt
1909	George Sargent	290	Englewood
1910	Alex Smith	298*	Philadelphia
1911	John McDermott	307*	Chicago
1912	John McDermott	294	Buffalo
1913	Francis Ouimet (am)	304*	Brookline
1914	Walter Hagen	290	Midlothian
1915	Jerome Travers (am)	297	Baltusrol
1916	Charles Evans Jnr (am)	286	Minikahda
1919	Walter Hagen	301*	Brae Burn
1920	Edward Ray GBR	295	Inverness
1921	Jim Barnes	289	Columbia
1922	Gene Sarazen	288	Skokie
1923	Bobby Jones (am)	296*	Inwood
1924	Cyril Walker	297	Oakland Hills
1925	Willie Macfarlane	291*	Worcester
1926	Bobby Jones (am)	293	Scioto
1927	Tommy Armour	301 *	Oakmont
1928	Johnny Farrell	294*	Olympia Flds
1929	Bobby Jones (am)	294*	Winged Foot
1930	Bobby Jones (am)	287	Interlachen
1931	Billy Burke	292*	Inverness
1932	Gene Sarazen	286	Fresh Meadow
1933	Johnny Goodman (am)	287	North Shore
1934	Olin Dutra	293	Merion
1935	Sam Parks Jnr	299	Oakmont
1936	Tony Manero	282	Baltusrol
1937	Ralph Guldahl	281	Oakland Hills
1938	Ralph Guldahl	284	Cherry Hills
1939	Byron Nelson	284*	Philadelphia
1940	Lawson Little	287*	Canterbury
1941	Craig Wood	284	Colonial
1946	Lloyd Mangrum	284*	Canterbury
1947	Lew Worsham	282*	St Louis
1948	Ben Hogan	276	Riviera
1949	Cary Middlecoff	286	Medinah
1950	Ben Hogan	287*	Merion
1951	Ben Hogan	287	Oakland Hills
1952	Julius Boros	281	Northwood
1953	Ben Hogan	283	Oakmont
1954	Ed Furgol	284	Baltusrol
1955	Jack Fleck	287*	Olympic
1956	Cary Middlecoff	281	Oak Hill
1957	Dick Mayer	282*	Inverness
1958	Tommy Bolt	283	Southern Hills
1959	Billy Casper	282	Winged Foot
1960	Arnold Palmer	280	Cherry Hills
1961	Gene Littler	281	Oakland Hills
1962	Jack Nicklaus	283*	Oakmont
1963	Julius Boros	293*	Brookline
1964	Ken Venturi	278	Congressional
1965	Gary Player RSA	282*	Bellerive
1966	Billy Casper	278*	Olympic
1967	Jack Nicklaus	275	Baltusrol
1968	Lee Trevino	275	Oak Hill
1969	Orville Moody	281	Champions
1970	Tony Jacklin GBR	281	Hazeltine
1971	Lee Trevino	280*	Merion
1972	Jack Nicklaus	290	Pebble Beach
1973	Johnny Miller	279	Oakmont
1974	Hale Irwin	287*	Winged Foot
1975	Lou Graham	287	Medinah
1976	Jerry Pate	277	Atlanta
1977	Hubert Green	278	Southern Hills
1978	Andy North	285	Cherry Hills
1979	Hale Irwin	284	Inverness
1980	Jack Nicklaus	272	Baltusrol
1981	David Graham AUS	273	Merion
1982	Tom Watson	282	Pebble Beach
1983	Larry Nelson	280	Oakmont
1984	Fuzzy Zoeller	276*	Winged Foot
1985	Andy North	279	Oakland Hills
1986	Raymond Floyd	279	Shinnecock Hls
1987	Scott Simpson	277	Olympic Club
1988	Curtis Strange	278	Brookline
1989	Curtis Strange	278	Oak Hill
1990	Hale Irwin	280*	Medinah
1991	Payne Stewart	282*	Hazeltine
1992	Tom Kite	285	Monterey
1993	Lee Janzen	272	Baltusrol
1994	Ernie Els RSA	279	Oakmont
1995	Corey Pavin	280	Shinnecock Hls
1996	Steve Jones	278	Oakland Hills
1997	Ernie Els RSA	280	Congressional
1998	Lee Janzen	280	Olympic Club
1999	Payne Stewart	279	Pinehurst
2000	Tiger Woods	272	Pebble Beach

* after play off

GOLF

US MASTERS
(US unless stated)

Year	Winners	Score
1934	Horton Smith	284
1935	Gene Sarazen	282*
1936	Horton Smith	285
1937	Byron Nelson	283
1938	Henry Picard	285
1939	Ralph Guldahl	279
1940	Jimmy Demaret	280
1941	Craig Wood	280
1942	Byron Nelson	280*
1946	Herman Keiser	282
1947	Jimmy Demaret	281
1948	Claude Harmon	279
1949	Sam Snead	282
1950	Jimmy Demaret	283
1951	Ben Hogan	280
1952	Sam Snead	286
1953	Ben Hogan	274
1954	Sam Snead	289*
1955	Cary Middlecoff	279
1956	Jack Burke Jnr	289
1957	Doug Ford	282
1958	Arnold Palmer	284
1959	Art Wall Jnr	284
1960	Arnold Palmer	282*
1961	Gary Player RSA	280
1962	Arnold Palmer	280*
1963	Jack Nicklaus	286
1964	Arnold Palmer	276
1965	Jack Nicklaus	271
1966	Jack Nicklaus	288*
1967	Gay Brewer	280
1968	Bob Goalby	277
1969	George Archer	281
1970	Billy Casper	279*
1971	Charles Coody	279
1972	Jack Nicklaus	286
1973	Tommy Aaron	283
1974	Gary Player RSA	278
1975	Jack Nicklaus	276
1976	Raymond Floyd	271
1977	Tom Watson	276
1978	Gary Player RSA	277
1979	Fuzzy Zoeller	280*
1980	S Ballesteros ESP	275
1981	Tom Watson	280
1982	Craig Stadler	284*
1983	S Ballesteros ESP	280
1984	Ben Crenshaw	277
1985	Bernh. Langer FRG	282
1986	Jack Nicklaus	279
1987	Larry Mize	285*
1988	Sandy Lyle GBR	281
1989	Nick Faldo GBR	283*
1990	Nick Faldo GBR	278*
1991	Ian Woosnam GBR	277
1992	Fred Couples	275
1993	Bernh. Langer GER	277
1994	J-M Olazábal ESP	279
1995	Ben Crenshaw	274
1996	Nick Faldo GBR	276
1997	Tiger Woods	270
1998	Mark O'Meara	279
1999	J-M Olazábal ESP	280
2000	Vijay Singh FIJ	278

US PGA

Year	Winner	Score
1916	Jim Barnes	1 up
1919	Jim Barnes	6 & 5
1920	Jock Hutchison	1 up
1921	Walter Hagen	3 & 2
1922	Gene Sarazen	4 & 3
1923	Gene Sarazen	38th
1924	Walter Hagen	2 up
1925	Walter Hagen	6 & 5
1926	Walter Hagen	5 & 3
1927	Walter Hagen	1 up
1928	Leo Diegel	6 & 5
1929	Leo Diegel	6 & 4
1930	Tommy Armour	1 up
1931	Tom Creavy	2 & 1
1932	Olin Dutra	4 & 3
1933	Gene Sarazen	5 & 4
1934	Paul Runyan	38th
1935	Johnny Revolta	5 & 4
1936	Densmore Shute	3 & 2
1937	Densmore Shute	37th
1938	Paul Runyan	8 & 7
1939	Henry Picard	37th
1940	Byron Nelson	1 up
1941	Vic Ghezi	38th
1942	Sam Snead	2 & 1
1944	Bob Hamilton	1 up
1945	Byron Nelson	4 & 3
1946	Ben Hogan	6 & 4
1947	Jim Ferrier	2 & 1
1948	Ben Hogan	7 & 6
1949	Sam Snead	3 & 2
1950	Chandler Harper	4 & 3
1951	Sam Snead	7 & 6
1952	Jim Turnesa	1 up
1953	Walter Burkemo	2 & 1
1954	Chick Harbert	4 & 3
1955	Doug Ford	4 & 3
1956	Jack Burke	3 & 2
1957	Lionel Hebert	2 & 1
1958	Dow Finsterwald	276
1959	Bob Rosburg	277
1960	Jay Hebert	281
1961	Jerry Barber	277*
1962	Gary Player RSA	278
1963	Jack Nicklaus	279
1964	Bobby Nichols	271
1965	Dave Marr	280
1966	Al Geiberger	280
1967	Don January	281*
1968	Julius Boros	281
1969	Raymond Floyd	276
1970	Dave Stockton	279
1971	Jack Nicklaus	281
1972	Gary Player RSA	281
1973	Jack Nicklaus	277
1974	Lee Trevino	276
1975	Jack Nicklaus	276
1976	Dave Stockton	281
1977	Lanny Wadkins	282*
1978	John Mahaffey	276*
1979	David Graham AUS	272*
1980	Jack Nicklaus	274
1981	Larry Nelson	273
1982	Raymond Floyd	272
1983	Hal Sutton	274
1984	Lee Trevino	273
1985	Hubert Green	278
1986	Bob Tway	276
1987	Larry Nelson	287*
1988	Jeff Sluman	272
1989	Payne Stewart	276
1990	Wayne Grady AUS	282
1991	John Daly	276
1992	Nick Price ZIM	278
1993	Paul Azinger	272
1994	Nick Price ZIM	269
1995	Steve Elkington AUS	267
1996	Mark Brooks	277*
1997	Davis Love III	269
1998	Vijay Singh	271
1999	Tiger Woods	277
2000	Tiger Woods	270*

* after play off

GOLF

WORLD MATCHPLAY

Year	Winner	Runner-up	Score
1964	**Arnold Palmer** USA	Neil Coles ENG	2&1
1965	**Gary Player** RSA	Peter Thomson AUS	3&2
1966	**Gary Player** RSA	Jack Nicklaus USA	6&4
1967	**Arnold Palmer** USA	Peter Thomson AUS	1 up
1968	**Gary Player** RSA	Bob Charles NZL	1 up
1969	**Bob Charles** NZL	Gene Littler USA	37th
1970	**Jack Nicklaus** USA	Lee Trevino USA	2&1
1971	**Gary Player** RSA	Jack Nicklaus USA	5&4
1972	**Tom Weiskopf** USA	Lee Trevino USA	4&3
1973	**Gary Player** RSA	G Marsh AUS	40th
1974	**Hale Irwin** USA	Gary Player RSA	3&1
1975	**Hale Irwin** USA	Al Geiberger USA	4&2
1976	**David Graham** AUS	Hale Irwin USA	38th
1977	**Graham Marsh** AUS	Ray Floyd USA	5&3
1978	**Isao Aoki** JPN	Simon Owen NZL	3&2
1979	**Bill Rogers** USA	Isao Aoki JPN	1 up
1980	**Greg Norman** AUS	Sandy Lyle SCO	1 up
1981	**S Ballesteros** ESP	Ben Crenshaw USA	1 up
1982	**S Ballesteros** ESP	Sandy Lyle SCO	37th
1983	**Greg Norman** AUS	Nick Faldo ENG	3&2
1984	**S Ballesteros** ESP	B Langer FRG	2&1
1985	**S Ballesteros** ESP	B Langer FRG	6&5
1986	**Greg Norman** AUS	Sandy Lyle SCO	2&1
1987	**Ian Woosnam** WAL	Sandy Lyle SCO	1 up
1988	**Sandy Lyle** SCO	Nick Faldo ENG	2&1
1989	**Nick Faldo** ENG	Ian Woosnam WAL	1 up
1990	**Ian Woosnam** WAL	Mark McNulty ZIM	4&2
1991	**S Ballesteros** ESP	Nick Price ZIM	3&2
1992	**Nick Faldo** ENG	Jeff Sluman USA	8&7
1993	**Corey Pavin** USA	Nick Faldo ENG	1 up
1994	**Ernie Els** RSA	C Montgomerie SCO	4&2
1995	**Ernie Els** RSA	Steve Elkington AUS	3&1
1996	**Ernie Els** RSA	Vijay Singh FIJ	3&2
1997	**Vijay Singh** FIJ	Ernie Els RSA	1 hole
1998	**Mark O'Meara** USA	Tiger Woods USA	1 hole
1999	**C Montgomerie** SCO	Mark O'Meara USA	3&2
2000	**Lee Westwood** ENG	C Montgomerie SCO	38th

WORLD CUP OF GOLF

1953	**Argentina** (de Vicenzo & Cerda)	287
1954	**Australia** (Thomson & Nagle)	556
1955	**USA** (Furgol & Harbert)	560
1956	**USA** (Hogan & Snead)	567
1957	**Japan** (Nakamura & Ono)	557
1958	**Ireland** (Bradshaw & O'Connor)	579
1959	**Australia** (Nagle & Thomson)	563
1960	**USA** (Palmer & Snead)	565
1961	**USA** (Demaret & Snead)	560
1962	**USA** (Palmer & Snead)	557
1963	**USA** (Nicklaus & Palmer)	482
1964	**USA** (Nicklaus & Palmer)	554
1965	**South Africa** (Henning & Player)	571
1966	**USA** (Nicklaus & Palmer)	548
1967	**USA** (Nicklaus & Palmer)	557
1968	**Canada** (Balding & Knudson)	569
1969	**USA** (Moody & Trevino)	552
1970	**Australia** (Devin & Graham)	544
1971	**USA** (Nicklaus & Trevino)	555
1972	**Taiwan** (Hsieh & Lu)	438
1973	**USA** (Miller & Nicklaus)	558
1974	**South Africa** (Cole & Hayes)	554
1975	**USA** (Graham & Miller)	554
1976	**Spain** (Ballesteros & Pinero)	574
1977	**Spain** (Ballesteros & Garrido)	591
1978	**USA** (Mahaffey & North)	564
1979	**USA** (Mahaffey & Irwin)	575
1980	**Canada** (Halidorson & Nelford)	572
1982	**Spain** (Canizares & Pinero)	563
1983	**USA** (Caldwell & Cook)	565
1984	**Spain** (Canizares & Rivero)	414
1985	**Canada** (Halidorson & Barr)	559
1987	**Wales** (Woosnam & Llewellyn)	574
1988	**USA** (Crenshaw & McCumber)	560
1989	**Australia** (Fowler & Grady)	278
1990	**Germany** (Langer & Giedeon)	556
1991	**Sweden** (Forsbrand & Johansson)	563
1992	**USA** (Couples & Love III)	548
1993	**USA** (Couples & Love III)	556
1994	**USA** (Couples & Love III)	536
1995	**USA** (Couples & Love III)	543
1996	**South Africa** (Els & Westner)	547
1997	**Ireland** (Harrington & McGinley)	545
1998	**England** (Faldo & Carter)	568
1999	**USA** (Woods/O'Meara)	545

RYDER CUP

1927	Worcester, Massachusetts	USA	9.5-2.5
1929	Moortown, Yorkshire	GBR	7-5
1931	Scioto, Ohio	USA	9-3
1933	Southport & Ainsdale, Lancs	GBR	6.5-5.5
1935	Ridgewood, New Jersey	USA	9-3
1937	Southport & Ainsdale, Lancs	USA	8-4
1947	Portland, Oregon	USA	11-1
1949	Ganton, Yorkshire	USA	7-5
1951	Pinehurst, North Carolina	USA	9.5-2.5
1953	Wentworth, Surrey	USA	6.5-5.5
1955	Thunderbird G&CC, C'fornia	USA	8-4
1957	Lindrick, Yorkshire	GBR	7.5-4.5
1959	Eldorado CC, California	USA	8.5-3.5
1961	Royal Lytham, Lancs	USA	14.5-9.5
1963	Atlanta, Georgia	USA	23-9
1965	Royal Birkdale, Lancs	USA	19.5-12.5
1967	Houston, Texas	USA	23.5-8.5
1969	Royal Birkdale, Lancs	Drawn	16-16
1971	St Louis, Missouri	USA	18.5-13.5
1973	Muirfield, Scotland	USA	19-13
1975	Laurel Valley, Pennsylvania	USA	21-11
1977	Royal Lytham, Lancs	USA	12.5-7.5
1979	Greenbrier, West Virginia	USA	17-11
1981	Walton Heath, Surrey	USA	I8.5-9.5
1983	PGA National, Florida	USA	14.5-13.5
1985	The Belfry, Sutton Coldfield	Europe	16.5-11.5
1987	Muirfield Village, Ohio	Europe	15-13
1989	The Belfry, Sutton Coldfield	Drawn	14-14
1991	Kiawah Island, S Carolina	USA	14.5-13.5
1993	The Belfry, Sutton Coldfield	USA	15-13
1995	Oak Hill CC, Rochester, NY	Europe	14-5-13.5
1997	Valderrama, Spain	Europe	14.5-13.5
1999	Brookline, Massachusets	USA	14.5-13.5

GYMNASTICS

ARTISTIC

Men

ALL-AROUND
1983 Dmitri Bilozerchev URS
1985 Yuri Korolev URS
1987 Dmitri Bilozerchev URS
1989 Igor Korobchinski URS
1991 Grigori Misutin URS
1993 Vitali Scherbo BLR
1994 Ivan Ivankov BLR
1995 Li Xiaoshuang CHN
1997 Ivan Ivankov BLR
1999 Nikolay Krukov RUS

FLOOR
1983 Tong Fei CHN
1985 Tong Fei CHN
1987 Lou Yun CHN
1989 Igor Korobchinski URS
1991 Igor Korobchinski URS
1993 Grigori Misutin URS
1994 Vitali Scherbo BLR
1995 Vitali Scherbo BLR
1996 Vitali Scherbo BLR
1997 Alexei Nemov RUS
1999 Alexei Nemov RUS

POMMEL HORSE
1983 Dmitri Bilozerchev URS
1985 Valentin Mogilni URS
1987 Dmitri Bilozerchev URS
     Borkai HUN
1989 Valentin Mogilni URS
1991 Valeri Belenki URS
1993 Pae Gil-Su KOR
1994 Marius Urzica ROM
1995 Li Donhgua SUI
1996 Pae Gil-Su KOR
1997 Valeri Belenki GER
1999 Alexei Nemov RUS

RINGS
1983 Dmitri Bilozerchev URS
     Koji Gushiken JPN
1985 Li Ning CHN/Korolev URS
1987 Yuri Korolev URS
1989 Andreas Aguilar FRA
1991 Grigori Misutin URS
1993 Yuri Chechi ITA
1994 Yuri Chechi ITA
1995 Yuri Chechi ITA
1996 Yuri Chechi ITA
1997 Yuri Chechi ITA
1999 Dong Zhen CHN

VAULT
1983 Artur Akopian URS
1985 Tong Fei CHN
1987 S Kroll GDR/Lou Yun CHN
1989 Jörg Behrendt GDR
1991 Yu Ok-Yul KOR
1993 Vitaly Scherbo BLR

1994 Vitaly Scherbo BLR
1995 Alexei Nemov RUS
     Grigori Misutin RUS
1996 Alexei Nemov RUS
1997 Sergei Fedorchenko KZK
1999 Li Xiaoping CHN

PARALLEL BARS
1983 Artemov URS/Lou CHN
1985 Kroll GDR/Mogilni URS
1987 Vladimir Artemov URS
1989 Li Jing CHN/Artemov URS
1991 Li Jing CHN
1993 Vitali Scherbo BLR
1994 Liping Huang CHN
1995 Vitali Scherbo BLR
1996 Rustam Cahripov UKR
1997 Zhang Jinjing CHN
1999 Lee Joo-Hyung KOR

HIGH BAR
1983 Dmitri Bilozerchev URS
1985 Tong Fei CHN
1987 Dmitri Bilozerchev URS
1989 Li Chunyang CHN
1991 Li Chunyang CHN
     Ralf Büchner GER
1993 Sergei Charkov RUS
1994 Vitali Scherbo BLR
1995 Andreas Wecker GER
1996 Jesus Carballo ESP
1997 Jani Tanskanen FIN
1999 Jesus Caballo ESP

TEAM
1983 China
1985, 87, 89 & 91 Soviet Union
1993 *no competition*
1994 & 95 China
1996 *no competition*
1997 & 99 China

Women

ALL-AROUND
1983 Natalia Yurchenko URS
1985 Oksana Omelianchik URS
     Yelena Sushnova URS
1987 Aurelia Dobre ROM
1989 S'lana Boguinskaya URS
1991 Kim Zmeskal USA
1993 Shannon Miller USA
1994 Shannon Miller USA
1995 Lilia Podkopayeva UKR
1997 Svetlana Khorkina RUS
1999 Maria Olaru ROM

VAULT
1983 Boriana Stoyanova BUL
1985 Yelena Sushnova URS
1987 Yelena Sushnova URS
1989 Olessia Dudnik URS
1991 Lavinia Milosovici ROM

1993 Yelena Puskin BLR
1994 Gina Gogean ROM
1995 Lilia Podkopayeva UKR
     Simona Amanar ROM
1996 Gina Gogean ROM
1997 Simona Amanar ROM
1999 E Zamolodchikova RUS

ASYMMETRIC BARS
1983 Maxi Gnauck GDR
1985 Gabriela Fahnrich GDR
1987 Daniela Silivas ROM
     D Thümmler GDR
1989 Fan Di CHN
     Daniela Silivas ROM
1991 Kim Gwang-suk KOR
1993 Shannon Miller USA
1994 Li Luo CHN
1995 Svetlana Khorkina RUS
1996 Svetlana Khorkina RUS
     Yelena Piskun BLR
1997 Svetlana Khorkina RUS
1999 Svetlana Khorkina RUS

BEAM
1983 Olga Mostepanova URS
1985 Daniela Silivas ROM
1987 Aurelia Dobre ROM
1989 Daniela Silivas ROM
1991 S'lana Boguinskaya URS
1993 Lavinia Milosovici ROM
1994 Shannon Miller USA
1995 Mo Huilan CHN
1996 Dina Kochetkova RUS
1997 Gina Gogean ROM
1999 Ling Jie CHN

FLOOR
1983 Ekaterina Szabo ROM
1985 Oksana Omelianchik URS
1987 Yelena Sushnova URS
     Daniela Silivas ROM
1989 Daniela Silivas ROM
     S'lana Boguinskaya URS
1991 Bontas ROM
     Chusovitina URS
1993 Shannon Miller USA
1994 Dina Kochetkova RUS
1995 Gina Gogean ROM
1996 Gina Gogean ROM
     Kui Yuanyuan CHN
1997 Gina Gogean ROM
1999 Andreea Raducan ROM

TEAM
1983 & 85 Soviet Union
1987 Romania
1989 & 91 Soviet Union
1993 *no competition*
1994 & 95 Romania
1996 *no competition*
1997 & 99 Romania

HOCKEY

WORLD CUP

Men		Women	
1971	Pakistan	1974	Netherlands
1973	Netherlands	1976	West Germany
1975	India	1978	Netherlands
1978	Pakistan	1981	West Germany
1982	Pakistan	1983	Netherlands
1986	Australia	1986	Netherlands
1990	Netherlands	1990	Netherlands
1994	Pakistan	1994	Australia
1998	Netherlands	1998	Australia

EUROPEAN CUP

Men		Women
1970	West Germany	-
1974	Spain	-
1978	West Germany	-
1983	Netherlands	Netherlands (1984)
1987	Netherlands	Netherlands
1991	Germany	England
1995	Germany	Netherlands
1999	Germany	Netherlands

CHAMPIONS TROPHY

Men		Women
1978	Pakistan	-
1980	Pakistan	-
1981	Netherlands	-
1982	Netherlands	-
1983	Australia	-
1984	Australia	-
1985	Australia	-
1986	West Germany	-
1987	West Germany	Netherlands
1988	West Germany	-
1989	Australia	South Korea
1990	Australia	-
1991	Germany	Australia
1992	Germany	-
1993	Australia	Australia
1994	Pakistan	-
1995	Germany	Australia
1996	Netherlands	-
1997	Germany	Australia
1998	Netherlands	-
1999	Australia	Australia
2000	Netherlands	Netherlands

EUROPEAN CLUB CHAMPIONS CUP

MEN

1969-70	Club Egara de Terasa ESP
1971-75	Frankfurt 1880 FRG
1976-78	Southgate ENG
1979	Klein Zwitserland NED
1980	Slough ENG
1981	Klein Zwitserland NED
1982-83	Dynamo Alma-Ata URS
1984	TG 1846 Frankental FRG
1985	Atletico Terrasa ESP
1986	Kampong, Utrecht NED
1987	Bloemendaal NED
1988-95	Uhlenhorst Mülheim FRG
1996	SV Kampong NED
1997	HGC Wasenaar NED
1998	Athletic Terrassa ESP
1999	's-Hertogenbosch NED
2000	Club an der Alster GER

WOMEN

1974	Harvestehuder, Hamburg FRG
1976-82	Amsterdam NED
1983-87	HGC Wassenaar NED
1988-90	Amsterdam NED
1991	HGC Wassenaar NED
1992	Amsterdam NED
1993	Russelsheimer GER
1994	HGC Wassenaar NED
1995-96	S V Kampong NED
1997	Berliner GER
1998	Russelsheimer GER
1999	Rott Weiss GER
2000	's Hertogenbosch NED

NATIONAL LEAGUE

Men		Women
1989	Southgate	-
1990	Hounslow	Slough
1991	Havant	Slough
1992	Havant	Slough
1993	Hounslow	Ipswich
1994	Havant	Leicester
1995	Teddington	Slough
1996	Cannock	Hightown
1997	Reading	Slough
1998-9	Cannock	Slough
2000	Canterbury	Hightown

NATIONAL CUP

1972-3	Hounslow	-
1974-5	Southgate	-
1976	Nottingham	-
1977	Slough	-
1978	Guildford	-
1979	Slough	Chelmsford
1980	Slough	Norton
1981	Slough	Sutton Coldfield
1982	Southgate	Slough
1983	Neston	Slough
1984	East Grinstead	Sheffield
1985	Southgate	Ipswich
1986	Southgate	Slough
1987	Southgate	Ealing
1988	Southgate	Ealing
1989	Hounslow	Ealing
1990	Havant	Sutton Coldfield
1991	Hounslow	Sutton Coldfield
1992	Hounslow	Hightown
1993	Hounslow	Leicester
1994	Teddington	Slough
1995	Guildford	Hightown
1996	Reading	Ipswich
1997	Teddington	Hightown
1998	Cannock	Clifton
1999	Reading	Slough
2000	Reading	Clifton

THE DERBY

* filly

Year	Winner	Jockey
1780	Diomed	Sam Arnull
1781	Young Eclipse	Charles Hindley
1782	Assassin	Sam Arnull
1783	Saltram	Charles Hindley
1784	Sergeant	Sam Arnull
1785	Aimwell	Charles Hindley
1786	Noble	J White
1787	Sir Peter Teazle	Sam Arnull
1788	Sir Thomas	William South
1789	Skyscraper	Sam Chifney
1790	Rhadamanthus	John Arnull
1791	Eager	Matt Stephenson
1792	John Bull	Frank Buckle
1793	Waxy	Bill Clift
1794	Daedalus	Frank Buckle
1795	Spread Eagle	Anthony Wheatley
1796	Didelot	John Arnull
1797	(unnamed colt)	John Singleton
1798	Sir Harry	Sam Arnull
1799	Archduke	John Arnull
1800	Champion	Bill Clift
1801	Eleanor*	John Saunders
1802	Tyrant	Frank Buckle
1803	Ditto	Bill Clift
1804	Hannibal	Bill Arnull
1805	Cardinal Beaufort	Denni Fitzpatrick
1806	Paris	John Shepherd
1807	Election	John Arnull
1808	Pan	Frank Collinson
1809	Pope	Tom Goodison
1810	Whalebone	Bill Clift
1811	Phantom	Frank Buckle
1812	Octavius	Bill Arnull
1813	Smolensko	Tom Goodison
1814	Blucher	Bill Arnull
1815	Whisker	Tom Goodison
1816	Prince Leopold	Will Wheatley
1817	Azor	Jem Robinson
1818	Sam	Sam Chifney jr
1819	Tiresias	Bill Clift
1820	Sailor	Sam Chifney jr
1821	Gustavus	Sam Day
1822	Moses	Tom Goodison
1823	Emilius	Frank Buckle
1824	Cedric	Jem Robinson
1825	Middleton	Jem Robinson
1826	Lapdog	George Dockeray
1827	Mameluke	Jem Robinson
1828	Cadland	Jem Robinson
1829	Frederick	John Forth
1830	Priam	Sam Day
1831	Spaniel	WillWheatley
1832	St Giles	Bill Scott
1833	Dangerous	Jem Chapple
1834	Plenipotentiary	Patrick Conolly
1835	Mundig	Bill Scott
1836	Bay Middleton	Jem Robinson
1837	Phosphorus	George Edwards
1838	Amato	Jim Chapple
1839	Bloomsbury	Sim Templeman
1840	Little Wonder	William MacDonald
1841	Coronation	Patrick Conolly
1842	Attila	Bill Scott
1843	Cotherstone	Bill Scott
1844	Orlando	Nat Flatman
1845	Merry Monarch	Foster Bell
1846	Pyrrhus the First	Sam Day
1847	Cossack	Sim Templeman
1848	Surplice	Sim Templeman
1849	The Flying Dutchman	Charlie Marlow
1850	Voltigeur	Job Marson
1851	Teddington	Job Marson
1852	Daniel O'Rourke	Frank Butler
1853	West Australian	Frank Butler
1854	Andover	Alfred Day
1855	Wild Dayrell	Robert Sherwood
1856	Ellington	Tom Aldcroft
1857	Blink Bonny*	Jack Charlton
1858	Beadsman	John Wells
1859	Musjid	John Wells
1860	Thormanby	Harry Custance
1861	Kettledrum	Ralph Bullock
1862	Caractacus	John Parsons
1863	Macaroni	Tom Challoner
1864	Blair Athol	Jim Snowden
1865	Gladiateur	Harry Grimshaw
1866	Lord Lyon	Harry Custance
1867	Hermit	John Daley
1868	Blue Gown	John Wells
1869	Pretender	John Osborne
1870	Kingcraft	Tom French
1871	Favonius	Tom French
1872	Cremorne	Charlie Maidment
1873	Doncaster	Fred Webb
1874	George Freder'k	Harry Custance
1875	Galopin	Jack Morris
1876	Kisber	Charlie Maidment
1877	Silvio	Fred Archer
1878	Sefton	Harry Constable
1879	Sir Bevys	George Fordham
1880	Bend Or	Fred Archer
1881	Iroquois	Fred Archer
1882	Shotover*	Tom Cannon
1883	St Blaise	Charlie Wood
1884	St Gatien	Charlie Wood
	Harvester *d/h*	Sam Loates
1885	Melton	Fred Archer
1886	Ormonde	Fred Archer
1887	Merry Hampton	Jack Watts
1888	Ayrshire	Fred Barrett
1889	Donovan	Tommy Loates
1890	Sainfoin	Jack Watts
1891	Common	George Barrett
1892	Sir Hugo	Fred Allsopp
1893	Isinglass	Tommy Loates
1894	Ladas	Jack Watts
1895	Sir Visto	Sam Loates

HORSE RACING

Year	Winner	Jockey		Year	Winner	Jockey
1896	Persimmon	Jack Watts		1956	Lavandin	Rae Johnstone
1897	Galtee More	Charlie Wood		1957	Crepello	Lester Piggott
1898	Jeddah	Otto Madden		1958	Hard Ridden	Charlie Smirke
1899	Flying Fox	Morny Cannon		1959	Parthia	Harry Carr
1900	Diamond Jubilee	Herbert Jones		1960	St Paddy	Lester Piggott
1901	Volodyovski	Lester Reiff		1961	Psidium	Roger Poincelet
1902	Ard Patrick	Skeets Martin		1962	Larkspur	Neville Sellwood
1903	Rock Sand	Danny Maher		1963	Relko	Yves St-Martin
1904	St Amant	Kempton Cannon		1964	Santa Claus	Scobie Breasley
1905	Cicero	Danny Maher		1965	Sea Bird II	Pat Glennon
1906	Spearmint	Danny Maher		1966	Charlottown	Scobie Breasley
1907	Orby	Johnny Reiff		1967	Royal Palace	George Moore
1908	Signorinetta*	Billy Bullock		1968	Sir Ivor	Lester Piggott
1909	Minoru	Herbert Jones		1969	Blakeney	Ernie Johnson
1910	Lemberg	Bernard Dillon		1970	Nijinsky	Lester Piggott
1911	Sunstar	George Stern		1971	Mill Reef	Geoff Lewis
1912	Tagalie*	Johnny Reiff		1972	Roberto	Lester Piggott
1913	Aboyeur	Edwin Piper		1973	Morston	Eddie Hide
1914	Durbar II	Matt MacGee		1974	Snow Knight	Brian Taylor
1915	Pommern	Steve Donoghue		1975	Grundy	Pat Eddery
1916	Fifinella*	Joe Childs		1976	Empery	Lester Piggott
1917	Gay Crusader	Steve Donaghue		1977	The Minstrel	Lester Piggott
1918	Gainsborough	Joe Childs		1978	Shirley Heights	Greville Starkey
1919	Grand Parade	Fred Templeman		1979	Troy	Willie Carson
1920	Spion Kop	Frank O'Neill		1980	Henbit	Willie Carson
1921	Humorist	Steve Donoghue		1981	Shergar	Walter Swinburn
1922	Captain Cuttle	Steve Donoghue		1982	Golden Fleece	Pat Eddery
1923	Papyrus	Steve Donoghue		1983	Teenoso	Lester Piggott
1924	Sansovino	Tommy Weston		1984	Secreto	Christy Roche
1925	Manna	Steve Donoghue		1985	Slip Anchor	Steve Cauthen
1926	Coronach	Joe Childs		1986	Shahrastani	Walter Swinburn
1927	Call Boy	Charlie Elliott		1987	Reference Point	Steve Cauthen
1928	Fellstead	Harry Wragg		1988	Kahyasi	Ray Cochrane
1929	Trigo	Joe Marshall		1989	Nashwan	Willie Carson
1930	Blenheim	Harry Wragg		1990	Quest For Fame	Pat Eddery
1931	Cameronian	Freddie Fox		1991	Generous	Alan Munro
1932	April the Fifth	Fred Lane		1992	Dr Devious	John Reid
1933	Hyperion	Tommy Weston		1993	Commander in Chief	Mick Kinane
1934	Windsor Lad	Charlie Smirke		1994	Erhaab	Willie Carson
1935	Bahram	Freddie Fox		1995	Lammtarra	Water Swinburn
1936	Mahmoud	Charlie Smirke		1996	Shaamit	Michael Hills
1937	Mid-day Sun	Michael Beary		1997	Benny The Dip	Willie Ryan
1938	Bois Roussel	Charlie Elliott		1998	High-Rise	Olivier Peslier
1939	Blue Peter	Eph Smith		1999	Oath	Kieren Fallon
1940	Pont l'Eveque	Sam Wragg		2000	Sinndar	Johnny Murtagh
1941	Owen Tudor	Billy Nevett				
1942	Watling Street	Harry Wragg				

1000 GUINEAS
(since 1950)

Year	Winner	Jockey
1943	Straight Deal	Tommy Carey
1944	Ocean Swell	Billy Nevett
1945	Dante	Billy Nevett
1946	Airborne	Tommy Lowrey
1947	Pearl Diver	George Bridgland
1948	My Love	Rae Johnstone
1949	Nimbus	Charlie Elliott
1950	Galcador	Rae Johnstone
1951	Arctic Prince	Charlie Spares
1952	Tulyar	Charlie Smirke
1953	Pinza	Gordon Richards
1954	Never Say Die	Lester Piggott
1955	Phil Drake	Freddie Palmer

Year	Winner	Jockey
1950	Camaree	Rae Johnstone
1951	Belle Of All	Gordon Richards
1952	Zabara	Ken Gethin
1953	Happy Laughter	Manny Mercer
1954	Festoon	Scobie Beasley
1955	Meld	Harry Carr
1956	Honeylight	Edgar Britt
1957	Rose Royal II	Charlie Smirke
1958	Bella Paola	Serge Boullenger
1959	Petite Etoile	Doug Smith
1960	Never Too Late	Roger Poincelet
1961	Sweet Solera	Bill Rickaby

Year	Winner	Jockey
1962	Abermaid	Bill Williamson
1963	Hula Dancer	Roger Poincelet
1964	Pourparler	Garnie Bougoure
1965	Night Off	Bill Williamson
1966	Glad Rags	Paul Cook
1967	Fleet	George Moore
1968	Caergwrle	Sandy Barclay
1969	Full Dress II	Ron Hutchinson
1970	Humble Duty	Lester Piggott
1971	Altesse Royale	Yves St-Martin
1972	Waterloo	Eddie Hide
1973	Mysterious	Geoff Lewis
1974	Highclere	Joe Mercer
1975	Nocturnal Spree	Johnny Roe
1976	Flying Water	Yves St-Martin
1977	Mrs McArdy	Eddie Hide
1978	Enstone Spark	Ernie Johnson
1979	One in a Million	Joe Mercer
1980	Quick As Lightning	Brian Rouse
1981	Fairy Footsteps	Lester Piggott
1982	On The House	John Reid
1983	Ma Biche	Freddie Head
1984	Pebbles	Philip Robinson
1985	Oh So Sharp	Steve Cauthen
1986	Midway Lady	Ray Cochrane
1987	Miesque	Freddie Head
1988	Ravinella	George Moore
1989	Musical Bliss	Walter Swinburn
1990	Salsabil	Willie Carson
1991	Shadayid	Willie Carson
1992	Hatoof	Walter Swinburn
1993	Sayyedati	Walter Swinburn
1994	Las Meninas	John Reid
1995	Harayir	Richard Hills
1996	Bosra Sham	Pat Eddery
1997	Sleepytime	Kieren Fallon
1998	Cape Verdi	Frankie Dettori
1999	Wince	Kieren Fallon
2000	Lahan	Richard Hills

2000 GUINEAS

(since 1950)

Year	Winner	Jockey
1950	Palestine	Charlie Smirke
1951	Ki Ming	Charlie Elliott
1952	Thunderhead II	Roger Poincelet
1953	Nearula	Edgar Britt
1954	Darius	Manny Mercer
1955	Our Babu	Doug Smith
1956	Gilles De Retz	Frank Barlow
1957	Crepello	Lester Piggott
1958	Pall Mall	Doug Smith
1959	Taboun	George Moore
1960	Martial	Ron Hutchinson
1961	Rockavon	Norman Stirk
1962	Privy Councillor	Bill Rickaby
1963	Only For Life	Jimmy Lindley
1964	Baldric II	Bill Pyers
1965	Niksar	Duncan Keith
1966	Kashmir II	Jimmy Lindley
1967	Royal Palace	George Moore
1968	Sir Ivor	Lester Piggott
1969	Right Tack	Geoff Lewis
1970	Nijinsky	Lester Piggott
1971	Brigadier Gerard	Joe Mercer
1972	High Top	Willie Carson
1973	Mon Fils	Frankie Durr
1974	Nonoalco	Yves St-Martin
1975	Bolkonski	Gianfranco Dettori
1976	Wollow	Gianfranco Dettori
1977	Nebbiolo	Gabriel Curran
1978	Roland Gardens	Frankie Durr
1979	Tap On Wood	Steve Cauthen
1980	Known Fact	Willie Carson
1981	To-Agori-Mou	Greville Starkey
1982	Zino	Freddie Head
1983	Lomond	Pat Eddery
1984	El Gran Senor	Pat Eddery
1985	Shadeed	Lester Piggott
1986	Dancing Brave	Greville Starkey
1987	Don't Forget Me	Willie Carson
1988	Doyoun	Walter Swinburn
1989	Nashwan	Willie Carson
1990	Tirol	Mick Kinane
1991	Mystiko	Michael Roberts
1992	Rodrigo de Triano	Lester Piggott
1993	Zafonic	Pat Eddery
1994	Mister Baileys	Jason Weaver
1995	Pennekamp	Thierry Jarnet
1996	Mark Of Esteem	Frankie Dettori
1997	Entrepreneur	Mick Kinane
1998	King Of Kings	Mick Kinane
1999	Island Sands	Frankie Dettori
2000	King's Best	Kieren Fallon

THE OAKS

(Since 1950)

Year	Winner	Jockey
1950	Asmena	Rae Johnstone
1951	Neasham Belle	Stan Clayton
1952	Frieze	Edgar Britt
1953	Ambiguity	Joe Mercer
1954	Sun Cap	Rae Johnstone
1955	Meld	Harry Carr
1956	Sicarelle	Freddie Palmer
1957	Carrozza	Lester Piggott
1958	Bella Paola	Max Garcia
1959	Petite Etoile	Lester Piggott
1960	Never Too Late	Roger Poincelet
1961	Sweet Solera	Bill Rickaby
1962	Monade	Yves St-Martin
1963	Noblesse	Garnie Bougoure
1964	Homeward Bound	Greville Starkey
1965	Long Look	Jack Purtell
1966	Valoris	Lester Piggott
1967	Pia	Eddie Hide
1968	La Lagune	Gerard Thiboeuf
1969	Sleeping Partner	John Gorton
1970	Lupe	Sandy Barclay
1971	Altesse Royale	Geoff Lewis
1972	Ginevra	Tony Murray

HORSE RACING

1973	Mysterious	Geoff Lewis	1976	Crow	Yves St-Martin
1974	Polygamy	Pat Eddery	1977	Dunfermline*	Willie Carson
1975	Juliette Marny	Lester Piggott	1978	Julio Mariner	Eddie Hide
1976	Pawneese	Yves St-Martin	1979	Son of Love	Alain Lequeux
1977	Dunfermline	Willie Carson	1980	Light Cavalry	Joe Mercer
1978	Fair Salinia	Greville Starkey	1981	Cut Above	Joe Mercer
1979	Scintillate	Pat Eddery	1982	Touching Wood	Paul Cook
1980	Bireme	Willie Carson	1983	Sun Princess*	Willie Carson
1981	Blue Wind	Lester Piggott	1984	Commanche Run	Lester Piggott
1982	Time Charter	Billy Newnes	1985	Oh So Sharp*	Steve Cauthen
1983	Sun Princess	Willie Carson	1986	Moon Madness	Pat Eddery
1984	Circus Plume	Lester Piggott	1987	Reference Point	Steve Cauthen
1985	Oh So Sharp	Steve Cauthen	1988	Minster Son	Willie Carson
1986	Midway Lady	Ray Cochrane	1989	Michelozo	Steve Cauthen
1987	Unite	Walter Swinburn	1990	Snurge	Richard Quinn
1988	Diminuendo	Steve Cauthen	1991	Toulon	Pat Eddery
1989*Snow Bride		Steve Cauthen	1992	User Friendly*	George Duffield
1990	Salsabil	Willie Carson	1993	Bob's Return	Philip Robinson
1991	Jet Ski Lady	Christy Roche	1994	Moonax	Pat Eddery
1992	User Friendly	George Duffield	1995	Classic Cliche	Frankie Dettori
1993	Intrepidity	Michael Roberts	1996	Shantou	Frankie Dettori
1994	Balanchine	Frankie Dettori	1997	Silver Patriarch	Pat Eddery
1995	Moonshell	Frankie Dettori	1998	Nedawi	John Reid
1996	Lady Carla	Pat Eddery	1999	Mutafaweq	Frankie Dettori
1997	Reams Of Verse	Kieren Fallon	2000	Millenary	Richard Quinn
1998	Shahtoush	Mick Kinane			
1999	Ramruna	Kieren Fallon			
2000	Love Divine	Richard Quinn			

Aliysa (Walter Swinburn) won, but was disq after a drugs test

ST LEGER
(since 1950)

Year	Winner	Jockey
1950	Scratch II	Rae Johnstone
1951	Talma II	Rae Johnstone
1952	Tulyar	Charlie Smirke
1953	Premonition	Eph Smith
1954	Never Say Die	Charlie Smirke
1955	Meld*	Harry Carr
1956	Cambremer	Freddie Palmer
1957	Ballymoss	Tommy Burns
1958	Alcide	Harry Carr
1959	Cantelo*	Eddie Hide
1960	St Paddy	Lester Piggott
1961	Aurelius	Lester Piggott
1962	Hethersett	Harry Carr
1963	Ragusa	Garnie Bougoure
1964	Indiana	Jimmy Lindley
1965	Provoke	Joe Mercer
1966	Sodium	Frankie Durr
1967	Ribocco	Lester Piggott
1968	Ribero	Lester Piggott
1969	Intermezo	Ron Hutchinson
1970	Nijinsky	Lester Piggott
1971	Athens Wood	Lester Piggott
1972	Boucher	Lester Piggott
1973	Peleid	Frankie Durr
1974	Bustino	Joe Mercer
1975	Bruni	Tony Murray

HORSE RACING

GRAND NATIONAL

Year	Winnner	Jockey
1836	The Duke	N/A
1837	The Duke	Mr Potts*
1838	Sir William	T Oliver
1839	Lottery	J Mason
1840	Jerry	Bretherton†
1841	Charity	H Powell
1842	Gay Lad	T Oliver
1843	Vanguard	T Oliver
1844	Discount	Crickmere
1845	Cureall	B Loft
1846	Pioneer	W Taylor
1847	Matthew	D Wynne
1848	Chandler	J Little*
1849	Peter Simple	Cunn'ham
1850	Abd-el-Kader	C Green
1851	Abd-el-Kader	T Abbott
1852	Miss Mowbray	Goodman†
1853	Peter Simple	T Oliver
1854	Bourton	J Tasker
1855	Wanderer	J Hanlon
1856	Freetrader	G Stevens
1857	Emigrant	C Boyce
1858	Little Charley	W Archer
1859	Half Caste	C Green
1860	Anatis	Pickernell*
1861	Jealousy	J Kendall
1862	Huntsman	Lamplugh
1863	Emblem	G Stevens
1864	Emblematic	G Stevens
1865	Alcibiade	Coventry*
1866	Salamander	Goodman†
1867	Cortolvin	J Page
1868	The Lamb	G Ede*
1869	The Colonel	G Stevens
1870	The Colonel	G Stevens
1871	The Lamb	Pickernell*
1872	Casse Tete	J Page
1873	Disturbance	Rich'dson*
1874	Reugny	Rich'dson*
1875	Pathfinder	Pickernell*
1876	Regal	J Cannon
1877	Austerlitz	F Hobson*
1878	Shifnal	J Jones
1879	The Liberator	G More*
1880	Empress	T Beasley*
1881	Woodbrook	T Beasley*
1882	Seaman	Manners*
1883	Zoedone	G Kinsky*
1884	Voluptuary	T Wilson*
1885	Roquefort	T Wilson*
1886	Old Joe	T Skelton
1887	Gamecock	B Daniels
1888	Playfair	Mawson
1889	Frigate	T Beasley*
1890	Ilex	Night'gall
1891	Come Away	H Beasley*
1892	Father O'Flynn	R Owen*
1893	Cloister	B Dollery
1894	Why Not	Night'gall
1895	Wild Man from Borneo	J Widger*
1896	The Soarer	Campbell*
1897	Manifesto	Kavanagh
1898	Drogheda	J Gourley
1899	Manifesto	Will'mson
1900	Ambush II	Anthony
1901	Grudon	Night'gall
1902	Shannon Lass	D Read
1903	Drumcree	Woodland
1904	Moifaa	A Birch
1905	Kirkland	T Mason
1906	Ascetic's Silver	Hastings*
1907	Eremon	A Newey
1908	Rubio	H Bletsoe
1909	Lutteurill	Parfrement
1910	Jenkinstown	Chadwick
1911	Glenside	Anthony*
1912	Jerry M	E Piggott
1913	Covertcoat	Woodland
1914	Sunloch	W Smith
1915	Ally Sloper	J Anthony*
1916	Vermouth	J Reardon
1917	Ballymacad	T Driscoll
1918	Poethlyn	E Piggott
1919	Poethlyn	E Piggott
1920	Troytown	J Anthony*
1921	Shaun Spadah	D Rees
1922	Music Hall	B Rees
1923	Sergeant Murphy	T Bennett*
1924	Master Robert	B Trudgill
1925	Double Chance	J Wilson*
1926	Jack Horner	Watkinson
1927	Sprig	T Leader
1928	Tipperary Tim	B Dutton*
1929	Gregalach	B Everett
1930	Shaun Goilin	Cullinan
1931	Grakle	B Lyall
1932	Forbra	J Hamey
1933	Kellsboro' Jack	Williams
1934	Golden Miller	G Wilson
1935	Reynoldstown	F Furlong*
1936	Reynoldstown	F Walwyn*
1937	Royal Mail	Williams
1938	Battleship	B Hobbs
1939	Workman	T Hyde
1940	Bogskar	M Jones
1946	Lovely Cottage	B Petre*
1947	Caughoo	Dempsey
1948	Sheila's Cottage	Thompson
1949	Russian Hero	McMorrow
1950	Freebooter	J Power
1951	Nickel Coin	J Bullock
1952	Teal	Thompson
1953	Early Mist	B Marshall
1954	Royal Tan	B Marshall
1955	Quare Times	P Taaffe
1956	E.S.B.	D Dick
1957	Sundew	F Winter
1958	Mr. What	Freeman
1959	Oxo	Scudamore
1960	Merryman II	G Scott
1961	Nicolaus Silver	B Beasley
1962	Kilmore	F Winter
1963	Ayala	P Buckley
1964	Team Spirit	Robinson
1965	Jay Trump	T Smith*
1966	Anglo	T Norman
1967	Foinavon	Buck'ham
1968	Red Alligator	B Fletcher
1969	Highland Wedding	E Harty
1970	Gay Trip	P Taaffe
1971	Specify	J Cook
1972	Well To Do	G Thorner
1973	Red Rum	B Fletcher
1974	Red Rum	B Fletcher
1975	L'Escargot	Carberry
1976	Rag Trade	J Burke
1977	Red Rum	T Stack
1978	Lucius	B Davies
1979	Rubstic	M Barnes
1980	Ben Nevis	Fenwick*
1981	Aldaniti	Champion
1982	Grittar	Saunders*
1983	Corbiere	B De Haan
1984	Hallo Dandy	Doughty
1985	Last Suspect	H Davies
1986	West Tip	Dunwoody
1987	Maori Venture	S Knight
1988	Rhyme'N Reason	B Powell
1989	Little Polveir	J Frost
1990	Mr Frisk	Armytage*
1991	Seagram	N Hawke
1992	Party Politics	Llewellyn
1993	Not Run**	
1994	Miinnehoma	Dunwoody
1995	Royal Athlete	J Titley
1996	Rough Quest	Fitzgerald
1997	Lord Gyllene	A Dobbin
1998	Earth Summit	Llewellyn
1999	Bobbyjo	P Carberry
2000	Papillon	R Walsh

* amateur jockey
** false start, but many continued to race. Esha Ness won; the race subsequently declared void.

423

ICE HOCKEY

WORLD CHAMPIONS

Year	Winner	Runner-up
1920	Canada	USA
1924	Canada	USA
1928	Canada	Sweden
1930	Canada	Germany
1931	Canada	USA
1932	Canada	USA
1933	USA	Canada
1934	Canada	USA
1935	Canada	Switzerland
1936	Great Britain	Canada
1937	Canada	Gt Britain
1938	Canada	Gt Britain
1939	Canada	USA
1947	Czechoslov'a	Sweden
1948	Canada	Czech'kia
1949	Czechoslov'a	Canada
1950	Canada	USA
1951	Canada	Sweden
1952	Canada	USA
1953	Sweden	WGermany
1954	Soviet Union	Canada
1955	Canada	USSR
1956	Soviet Union	USA
1957	Sweden	USSR
1958	Canada	USSR
1959	Canada	USSR
1960	USA	Canada
1961	Canada	Czech'kia
1962	Sweden	Canada
1963	Soviet Union	Sweden
1964	Soviet Union	Sweden
1965	Soviet Union	Czech'kia
1966	Soviet Union	Czech'kia
1967	Soviet Union	Sweden
1968	Soviet Union	Czech'kia
1969	Soviet Union	Sweden
1970	Soviet Union	Sweden
1971	Soviet Union	Czech'kia
1972	Czechoslov'a	USSR
1973	Soviet Union	Sweden
1974	Soviet Union	Czech'kia
1975	Soviet Union	Czech'kia
1976	Czechoslov'a	USSR
1977	Czechoslov'a	Sweden
1978	Soviet Union	Czech'kia
1979	Soviet Union	Czech'kia
1981	Soviet Union	Sweden
1982	Soviet Union	Czech'kia
1983	Soviet Union	Czech'kia
1985	Czechoslov'a	Canada
1986	Soviet Union	Sweden
1987	Sweden	USSR
1989	Soviet Union	Canada
1990	Soviet Union	Sweden
1991	Sweden	Canada
1992	Sweden	Finland
1993	Russia	Sweden
1994	Canada	Finland
1995	Finland	Sweden
1996	Czech Rep	Canada
1997	Canada	Sweden
1998	Sweden	Finland
1999	Czech Rep	Finland
2000	Czech Rep	Slovakia

STANLEY CUP

Year	Winner
1939-40	New York Rangers
1940-41	Boston Bruins
1941-42	Toronto Maple Leafs
1942-43	Detroit Red Wings
1943-44	Montreal Canadiens
1944-45	Toronto Maple Leafs
1945-46	Montreal Canadiens
1946-47	Toronto Maple Leafs
1947-48	Toronto Maple Leafs
1948-49	Toronto Maple Leafs
1949-50	Detroit Red Wings
1950-51	Toronto Maple Leafs
1951-52	Detroit Red Wings
1952-53	Montreal Canadiens
1953-54	Detroit Red Wings
1954-55	Detroit Red Wings
1955-56	Montreal Canadiens
1956-57	Montreal Canadiens
1957-58	Montreal Canadiens
1958-59	Montreal Canadiens
1959-60	Montreal Canadiens
1960-61	Chicago Blackhawks
1961-62	Toronto Maple Leafs
1962-63	Toronto Maple Leafs
1963-64	Toronto Maple Leafs
1964-65	Montreal Canadiens
1965-66	Montreal Canadiens
1966-67	Toronto Maple Leafs
1967-68	Montreal Canadiens
1968-69	Montreal Canadiens
1969-70	Boston Bruins
1970-71	Montreal Canadiens
1971-72	Boston Bruins
1972-73	Montreal Canadiens
1973-74	Philadelphia Flyers
1974-75	Philadelphia Flyers
1975-76	Montreal Canadiens
1976-77	Montreal Canadiens
1977-78	Montreal Canadiens
1978-79	Montreal Canadiens
1979-80	New York Islanders
1980-81	New York Islanders
1981-82	New York Islanders
1982-83	New York Islanders
1983-84	Edmonton Oilers
1984-85	Edmonton Oilers
1985-86	Montreal Canadiens
1986-87	Edmonton Oilers
1987-88	Edmonton Oilers
1988-89	Calgary Flames
1989-90	Edmonton Oilers
1990-91	Pittsburgh Penguins
1991-92	Pittsburgh Penguins
1992-93	Montreal Canadiens
1993-94	New York Rangers
1994-95	New Jersey Devils
1995-96	Colorado Avalanche
1996-97	Detroit Red Wings
1997-98	Detroit Red Wings
1998-99	Dallas Stars
1999-2000	New Jersey Devils

ICE SKATING

WORLD CHAMPIONS

	Men	Women	Pairs	Ice Dancing
1886	G Fuchs GER	-	-	-
1887	G Hügel AUT	-	-	-
1898	H Grenander SWE	-	-	-
1899	G Hügel AUT	-	-	-
1900	G Hügel AUT	-	-	-
1901-05	U Salchow SWE	-	-	-
1906	G Fuchs GER	M Syers GBR	-	-
1907	U Salchow SWE	M Syers GBR	-	-
1908	U Salchow SWE	L Kronberger HUN	Hübler/Berger GER	-
1909	U Salchow SWE	L Kronberger HUN	Johnson/Johnson	-
1910	U Salchow SWE	L Kronberger HUN	Hübler/Burger GER	-
1911	U Salchow SWE	L Kronberger HUN	Eilers/Jakobsson FIN	-
1912	F Kachler AUT	O M Horvath HUN	Johnson/Johnson	-
1913	F Kachler AUT	O M Horvath HUN	Englemann/Mejstrick AUT	-
1914	G Sandahl SWE	O M Horvath HUN	Eilers/Jakobsson FIN	-
1922	G Grafstrom SWE	H Planck AUT	Engelmann/Berger AUT	-
1923	F Kachler AUT	H Planck AUT	Jakobsson/Jakobsson FIN	-
1924	G Grafstrom SWE	H Planck AUT	Englenmann/Berger AUT	-
1925	W Böckl AUT	H Jaross AUT	Jaross/Wrede AUT	-
1926	W Böckl AUT	H Jaross AUT	Joly/Brunet FRA	-
1927	W Böckl AUT	S Henie NOR	Jaross/Wrede AUT	-
1928	W Böckl AUT	S Henie NOR	Joly/Brunet FRA	-
1929	G Grafstrom SWE	S Henie NOR	Scholz/Kaiser AUT	-
1930	K Schäfer AUT	S Henie NOR	A Brunet/P Brunet FRA	-
1931	K Schäfer AUT	S Henie NOR	Rotter/Szollas HUN	-
1932	K Schäfer AUT	S Henie NOR	A Brunet/P Brunet FRA	-
1933	K Schäfer AUT	S Henie NOR	Rotter/Szollas HUN	-
1934	K Schäfer AUT	S Henie NOR	Rotter/Szollas HUN	-
1935	K Schäfer AUT	S Henie NOR	Rotter/Szollas HUN	-
1936	K Schäfer AUT	S Henie NOR	Herber/Baier GER	-
1937	F Kaspar AUT	C Colledge GBR	Herber/Baier GER	-
1938	F Kaspar AUT	M Taylor GBR	Herber/Baier GER	-
1939	G Sharp GBR	M Taylor GBR	Herber/Baier GER	-
1947	H Gerschwiler SUI	B Ann Scott CAN	Lannoy/Baugniet BEL	-
1948	R Button USA	B Ann Scott CAN	Lannoy/Baugniet BEL	-
1949	R Button USA	A Vrzanova TCH	Kekesy/Kiraly HUN	-
1950	R Button USA	A Vrzanova TCH	K Kennedy/P Kennedy USA	-
1951	R Button USA	J Altwegg GBR	R Falk/P Falk FRG	-
1952	R Button USA	J du Bief FRA	R Falk/P Falk FRG	Westwood/Demmy GBR
1953	H A Jenkins USA	T Albright USA	J Nicks/J Nicks GBR	Westwood/Demmy GBR
1954	H A Jenkins USA	G Busch FRG	Dafoe/Bowden CAN	Westwood/Demmy GBR
1955	H A Jenkins USA	T Albright USA	Dafoe/Bowden CAN	Westwood/Demmy GBR
1956	H A Jenkins USA	C Heiss USA	Schwarz/Oppelt AUT	Weight/Thomas GBR
1957	D Jenkins USA	C Heiss USA	Wagner/Paul CAN	Markham/Jones GBR
1958	D Jenkins USA	C Heiss USA	Wagner/Paul CAN	Markham/Jones GBR
1959	D Jenkins USA	C Heiss USA	Wagner/Paul CAN	Denny/Jones GBR
1960	A Giletti FRA	C Heiss USA	Wagner/Paul CAN	Denny/Jones GBR
1962	D Jackson CAN	S Dijkstra NED	Jelinek/Jelinek CAN	Romanova/Roman TCH
1963	D McPherson CAN	S Dijkstra NED	Kilius/Bäumler FRG	Romanova/Roman TCH
1964	Schnelidorfer FRG	S Dijkstra NED	Kilius/Bäumler FRG	Romanova/Roman TCH
1965	A Calmat FRA	P Burka CAN	Belousova/Protopopov URS	Romanova/Roman TCH
1966	E Danzer AUT	P Fleming USA	Belousova/Protopopov URS	Towler/Ford GBR
1967	E Danzer AUT	P Fleming USA	Belousova/Protopopov URS	Towler/Ford GBR
1968	E Danzer AUT	P Fleming USA	Belousova/Protopopov URS	Towler/Ford GBR
1969	T Wood USA	G Seyfert GDR	Rodnina/Ulanov URS	Towler/Ford GBR
1970	T Wood USA	G Seyfert GDR	Rodnina/Ulanov URS	Pakhomova/Gorshkov URS
1971	O Nepela TCH	B Schuba AUT	Rodnina/Ulanov URS	Pakhomova/Gorshkov URS
1972	O Nepela TCH	B Schuba AUT	Rodnina/Ulanov URS	Pakhomova/Gorshkov URS
1973	O Nepela TCH	K Magnussen CAN	Rodnina/Zaitsev URS	Pakhomova/Gorshkov URS

ICE SKATING

1974	J Hoffmann GDR	C Errath GDR	Rodnina/Zaitsev URS	Pakhomova/Gorshkov URS
1975	S Volkov URS	D De Leeuw NED	Rodnina/Zaitsev URS	Moiseyeva/Minenkov URS
1976	J Curry GBR	D Hamill USA	Rodnina/Zaitsev URS	Pakhomova/Gorshkov URS
1977	V Kovalyev URS	L Fratianne USA	Rodnina/Zaitsev URS	Moiseyeva/Minenkov URS
1978	C Tickner USA	A Potzsch GDR	Rodnina/Zaitsev URS	Linichuk/Karponosov URS
1979	V Kovalyev URS	L Fratianne USA	Babilonia/Gardner USA	Linichuk/Karponosov URS
1980	J Hoffmann GDR	A Potzsch GDR	Tcherkasova/Shakrai URS	Regoczy/Sallay HUN
1981	S Hamilton USA	D Biellmann SUI	Vorobyeva/Lissovsky URS	Torvill/Dean GBR
1982	S Hamilton USA	E Zayak USA	Baess/Theirbach GDR	Torvill/Dean GBR
1983	S Hamilton USA	R Sumners USA	Valova/Vasilyev URS	Torvill/Dean GBR
1984	S Hamilton USA	K Witt GDR	Underhill/Martini CAN	Torvill/Dean GBR
1985	A Fadeyev URS	K Witt GDR	Valova/Vasilyev URS	Bestiaminova/Bukin URS
1986	B Boitano USA	D Thomas USA	Gordyeva/Grinkov URS	Bestiaminova/Bukin URS
1987	B Orser CAN	K Witt GDR	Gordyeva/Grinkov URS	Bestiaminova/Bukin URS
1988	B Boitano USA	K Witt GDR	Valova/Vasilyev URS	Bestiaminova/Bukin URS
1989	K Browning CAN	M Ito JPN	Gordyeva/Grinkov URS	Klimova/Ponomarenko URS
1990	K Browning CAN	J Trenary USA	Gordyeva/Grinkov URS	Klimova/Ponomarenko URS
1991	K Browning CAN	K Yamaguchi JPN	Mishkutienok/Dmitryev CIS	I & P Duchesnay FRA
1992	V Petrenko UKR	K Yamaguchi JPN	Mishkutienok/Dmitryev CIS	Klimova/Ponomar'ko URS
1993	K Browning CAN	O Baiul UKR	Brasseur/Eisler CAN	Usova/Zhulin RUS
1994	Elvis Stojko CAN	Y Sato JPN	Shishkova/Naumov RUS	Gritschuk/Platov RUS
1995	Elvis Stojko CAN	Lu Chen CHN	Kovarikova/Novotny TCH	Gritschuk/Platov RUS
1996	Todd Eldredge USA	Michelle Kwan USA	Eltsova/Bouchkov RUS	Gritschuk/Platov RUS
1997	Elvis Stojko CAN	Tara Lipinski USA	Wötzel/Steuer GER	Gritschuk/Platov RUS
1998	Alexei Yagudin RUS	Michelle Kwan USA	Bereznaya/Sikhuralidze RUS	Krylova/Ovsyannikov RUS
1999	Alexei Yagudin RUS	M Butyrskaya RUS	Bereznaya/Sikhuralidze RUS	Krylova/Ovsyannikov RUS
2000	Alexei Yagudin RUS	Michelle Kwan USA	Petrova/Tikhonov RUS	Anissina/Peizerat FRA

BRITISH CHAMPIONS (FROM 1972)

1972	J Curry	M McLean	McCafferty/Taylforth	Green/Watts
1973	J Curry	J Scott	Sessions/Harrison	Green/Watts
1974	J Curry	G Keddie	McCafferty/Taylforth	Green/Watts
1975	J Curry	K Richardson	Taylforth/Taylforth	Green/Watts
1976	R Cousins	K Richardson	Lindsey/Beckwith	Thompson/Maxwell
1977	R Cousins	K Richardson	Lindsey/Beckwith	Thompson/Maxwell
1978	R Cousins	D Cottrill	Garland/Daw	Torvill/Dean
1979	R Cousins	K Richardson	Garland/Daw	Torvill/Dean
1980	C Howarth	K Wood	Garland/Daw	Torvill/Dean
1981	M Pepperday	D Cottrill	Garland/Jenkins	Torvill/Dean
1982	M Pepperday	K Wood	Garland/Jenkins	Torvill/Dean
1983	M Pepperday	S A Jackson	Garland/Jenkins	Torvill/Dean
1984	S Pickavance	S A Jackson	Cushley/Cushley	Barber/Slater
1985	S Pickavance	J Conway	Peake/Naylor	Jones/Askham
1986	P Robinson	J Conway	Peake/Naylor	Jones/Askham
1987	P Robinson	J Conway	Peake/Naylor	Jones/Askham
1988	C Newberry	J Conway	Peake/Naylor	Jones/Askham
1989	S Cousins	E Murdoch	Peake/Naylor	Burton/Place
1990	S Cousins	J Conway	Peake/Naylor	Hall/Bloomfield
1991	S Cousins	J Conway	Pritchard/Briggs	Bruce/Place
1992	S Cousins	C von Saher	Pearce/Shorten	Humphreys/Lanning
1993	S Cousins	S Main	Mednick/Briggs	Torvill/Dean
1994	S Cousins	J Arrowsmith	Rogers/Aldred	Fitzgerald/Kyle
1995	S Cousins	S Main	Rogers/Aldred	Humphreys/Askew
1996	N Wilson	J Arrowsmith	Rogers/Aldred	Humphreys/Askew
1997	S Cousins	J. Arrowsmith	Polulischenko/Seabrook	Clements/Shortland
1998	C Shorten	S Main	Polulischenko/Seabrook	Clements/Shortland
1999	N Wilson	T Sear	Kemp/Thomas	Keeble/Zalewski
2000	A Street	Z Jones	Sfikas/Seabrook	Humphreys/Baranov

JUDO

WORLD CHAMPIONS

Men

-60kg
1979	Thierry Ray	FRA
1981	Yasuhiko Moriwaki	JPN
1983	Khazret Tletseri	URS
1985	Shinji Hosokawa	JPN
1987	Kim Jae-yup	KOR
1989	Amiran Totikashvilli	URS
1991	Tadanori Koshino	JPN
1993	Ryuki Sonoda	JPN
1995	Nikolai Ojeguine	RUS
1997	Tadahiro Nomura	JPN
1999	Manuolo Poulet	CUB

-65
1979	Nikolay Soludukhin	URS
1981	Katsu. Kashiwazaki	JPN
1983	Nikolay Soludukhin	URS
1985	Yuri Sokolov	URS
1987	Yosuke Yamamoto	JPN
1989	Drago Becanovic	YUG
1991	Udo Quellmalz	GER
1993	Yukimasa Nakamura	JPN
1995	Udo Quellmalz	GER
1997	Kim Hyuk	KOR

-66kg
1999	Larbi Benbouaoud	FRA

-71kg
1979	Kyoto Katsuki	JPN
1981	Park Chong-hak	KOR
1983	Hidetoshi Nakanishi	JPN
1985	Ahn Byeong-kuen	KOR
1987	Mike Swain	USA
1989	Toshihiko Koga	JPN
1991	Toshihiko Koga	JPN
1993	Hoon Chung	KOR
1995	Daisuke Hideshima	JPN
1997	Kenzo Nakamura	JPN

-73kg
1999	Jimmy Pedro	USA

-78kg
1979	Shozo Fujii	JPN
1981	Neil Adams	GBR
1983	Nobutoshi Hikage	JPN
1985	Nobutoshi Hikage	JPN
1987	Hirotaka Okada	JPN
1989	Kim Byung-ju	KOR
1991	Daniel Lascau	GER
1993	Ki-Young Chun	KOR
1995	Toshihiko Toga	JPN
1997	Cho In-chul	KOR

-81kg
1999	Graeme Randall	GBR

-86kg
1979	Detlef Ultsch	GDR
1981	Bern'd Tchoullouyan	FRA
1983	Detlef Ultsch	GDR
1985	Peter Seisenbacher	AUT
1987	Fabien Canu	FRA
1989	Fabien Canu	FRA
1991	Hirotaka Okada	JPN
1993	Yoshio Nakamura	JPN
1995	Jeon Ki-Young	KOR
1997	Jeon Ki-Young	KOR

-90kg
1999	Hidehiko Yoshida	JPN

-95kg
1979	Tengiz Khubuluri	URS
1981	Tengiz Khubuluri	URS
1983	Valeriy Divisenko	URS
1985	Hitoshi Sugai	JPN
1987	Hitoshi Sugai	JPN
1989	Koba Kurtanidze	URS
1991	Stephane Traineau	FRA
1993	Antal Kovacs	HUN
1995	Pawel Nastula	POL
1997	Pawel Nastula	POL

-100kg
1999	Kosei Inoue	JPN

+95kg
1979	Yasuhiro Yamashita	JPN
1981	Yasuhiro Yamashita	JPN
1983	Yasuhiro Yamashita	JPN
1985	Cho Yong-chul	KOR
1987	Grigory Vertichev	URS
1989	Naoya Ogawa	JPN
1991	Sergey Kosorotov	RUS
1993	David Douillet	FRA
1995	David Douillet	FRA
1997	David Douillet	FRA

+100kg
1999	Shinichi Shinohara	JPN

Open
1979	Sumio Endo	JPN
1981	Yasuhiro Yamashita	JPN
1983	Hitoshi Saito	JPN
1985	Yoshimi Masaki	JPN
1987	Naoya Ogawa	JPN
1989	Naoya Ogawa	JPN
1991	Naoya Ogawa	JPN
1993	Rafael Kubacki	POL
1995	David Douillet	FRA
1997	Rafael Kubacki	POL
1999	Shinichi Shinohara	JPN

JUDO

Women

-48kg
1980   Jane Bridge GBR
1982   Karen Briggs GBR
1984   Karen Briggs GBR
1986   Karen Briggs GBR
1987   Zhangyun Li CHN
1989   Karen Briggs GBR
1991   Cécile Nowak FRA
1993   Ryoko Tamura JPN
1995   Ryoko Tamura JPN
1997   Ryoko Tamura JPN
1999   Ryoko Tamura JPN

-52kg
1980   Edith Hrovat AUT
1982   Loretta Doyle GBR
1984   Kaori Yamaguchi JPN
1986   Dominique Brun FRA
1987   Sharon Rendle GBR
1989   Sharon Rendle GBR
1991   Alessandra Giungi ITA
1993   Rodriguez Verdecia CUB
1995   Marie-Claire Restoux FRA
1997   Marie-Claire Restoux FRA
1999   Noriko Narasaki JPN

-56kg
1980   Gerda Winklbauer AUT
1982   Beatrice Rodriguez FRA
1984   Ann-Maria Burns USA
1986   Ann Hughes GBR
1987   Catherine Arnaud FRA
1989   Catherine Arnaud FRA
1991   Miriam Blasco ESP
1993   Nicola Fairbrother GBR
1995   Driulis Gonzalez CUB
1997   Isabel Fernandez ESP
1999   Driulis Gonzalez CUB

-61 kg
1980   Anita Staps HOL
1982   Martine Rothier FRA
1984   Natasha Hernandez VEN
1986   Diane Bell GBR
1987   Diane Bell GBR
1989   Catherine Fleury FRA
1991   Fraucke Eickoff GER
1993   Gella Vandecaveye BEL
1995   Jung Sung-Sook KOR
1997   S Vandenhende FRA
1999   Kaiko Maeda JPN

-66kg
1980   Edith Simon AUT
1982   Brigitte Deydier FRA
1984   Brigitte Deydier FRA
1986   Brigitte Deydier FRA
1987   Alexandra Schreiber FRG
1989   Emanuela Pierantozzi ITA
1991   Emanuela Pierantozzi ITA
1993   Cho Min-Sun KOR
1995   Cho Min-Sun KOR
1997   Kate Howey GBR
1999   Sibelius Veranes CUB

-72kg
1980   Jocelyne Triadou FRA
1982   Barbara Classen FRG
1984   Ingrid Berghmans BEL
1986   Irene de Kok HOL
1987   Irene de Kok HOL
1989   Ingrid Berghmans BEL
1991   Kim Mi-jung KOR
1993   Chunhui Leng CHN
1995   Castellana Luna CUB
1997   Noriko Anno JPN
1999   Noriko Anno JPN

+72kg
1980   Margarita de Cal ITA
1982   Natalina Lupino FRA
1984   Maria-Teresa Motta ITA
1986   Gao Fengliang CHN
1987   Gao Fengliang CHN
1989   Gao Fengliang CHN
1991   Moon Ji-yoon KOR
1993   Johanna Hagn GER
1995   Angelique Seriese BEL
1997   Christine Cicot FRA
1999   Beate Maksymov POL

Open
1980   Ingrid Berghmans BEL
1982   Ingrid Berghmans BEL
1984   Ingrid Berghmans BEL
1986   Ingrid Berghmans BEL
1987   Gao Fengliang CHN
1989   Estella Rodriguez CUB
1991   Zhuang Xiaoyan CHN
1993   Beata Maksymow POL
1995   M Van Der Lee NED
1997   Daina Beltran CUB
1999   Daina Beltran CUB

MODERN PENTATHLON

World Champions

Men

Year	Individual	Team
1949	Tage Bjurefelt SWE	Sweden
1950	Lars Hall SWE	Sweden
1951	Lars Hall SWE	Sweden
1953	Gábor Benedek HUN	Sweden
1954	Björn Thofelt SWE	Hungary
1955	Konstantin Salnikov URS	Hungary
1957	Igor Novikov URS	Soviet Union
1958	Igor Novikov URS	Soviet Union
1959	Igor Novikov URS	Soviet Union
1961	Igor Novikov URS	Soviet Union
1962	Eduards Dobnikov URS	Soviet Union
1963	András Balczó HUN	Hungary
1965	András Balczó HUN	Hungary
1966	András Balczó HUN	Hungary
1967	András Balczó HUN	Hungary
1969	András Balczó HUN	Soviet Union
1970	Peter Kelemen HUN	Hungary
1971	Boris Onischenko URS	Soviet Union
1973	Pavel Lednev URS	Soviet Union
1974	Pavel Lednev URS	Soviet Union
1975	Pavel Lednev URS	Hungary
1977	Janusz Pyciak-Peciak POL	Poland
1978	Pavel Lednev URS	Poland
1979	Robert Nieman USA	USA
1981	Janusz Pyciak-Peciak POL	Poland
1982	Daniele Masala ITA	Soviet Union
1983	Anatoly Starostin URS	Soviet Union
1985	Attila Mizsér HUN	Soviet Union
1986	Carlo Massullo ITA	Italy
1987	Joël Bouzou FRA	Hungary
1989	László Fábián HUN	Hungary
1990	Gianluca Tiberti ITA	Soviet Union
1991	Arkadiusz Skrzypaszek POL	Unified Team
1993	Richard Phelps GBR	Hungary
1994	Dmitri Svatkovsky RUS	France
1995	Dmitri Svatkovsky RUS	Italy
1997	Sebastien Deleigne FRA	Hungary
1998	Sebastien Deleigne FRA	Mexico
1999	Gabor Balogh HUN	Hungary
2000	Andrejus Zadneprovskis LTU	USA

Women

Year	Individual	Team
1981	Anne Ahlgren SWE	Great Britain
1982	Wendy Norman GBR	Great Britain
1983	Lynn Chernobrywy CAN	Great Britain
1984	Svetlana Yakovleva URS	Soviet Union
1985	Barbara Kotowska POL	Poland
1986	Irina Kiselyeva URS	Soviet Union
1987	Irina Kiselyeva URS	Soviet Union
1988	Dorata Idzi POL	Poland
1989	Lori Norwood USA	Poland
1990	Eva Fjellerup DEN	Poland
1991	Eva Fjellerup DEN	Poland
1992	Iwona Kowalewska POL	Poland
1993	Eva Fjellerup DEN	Italy
1994	Eva Fjellerup DEN	Italy
1995	Kerstin Danielsson SWE	Hungary
1996	Janna Dolgacheva BLR	Russia
1997	Elizaveta Suvorova RUS	Italy
1998	Anna Sulima POL	Poland
1999	Zsuszanna Voros HUN	Russia
2000	Pernille Svarre DEN	Poland

MOTOR CYCLING

Grand Prix

125cc	250cc	500cc
1949 Nello Pagani ITA	Bruno Ruffo ITA	Leslie Graham GBR
1950 Bruno Ruffo ITA	Dario Ambrosini ITA	Umberto Masetti ITA
1951 Carlo Ubbiali ITA	Bruno Ruffo ITA	Geoff Duke GBR
1952 Cecil Sandford GBR	Enrico Lorenzetti ITA	Umberto Masetti ITA
1953 Werner Haas FRG	Werner Haas FRG	Geoff Duke GBR
1954 Rupert Hollaus AUT	Werner Haas FRG	Geoff Duke GBR
1955 Carlo Ubbiali ITA	Herman Muller FRG	Geoff Duke GBR
1956 Carlo Ubbiali ITA	Carlo Ubbiali ITA	John Surtees GBR
1957 Tarquinio Provini ITA	Cecil Sandford GBR	Libero Liberati ITA
1958 Carlo Ubbiali ITA	Tarquinio Provini ITA	John Surtees GBR
1959 Carlo Ubbiali ITA	Carlo Ubbiali ITA	John Surtees GBR
1960 Carlo Ubbiali ITA	Carlo Ubbiali ITA	John Surtees GBR
1961 Tom Phillis AUS	Mike Hailwood GBR	Gary Hocking ZIM
1962 Luigi Taveri SUI	Jim Redman ZIM	Mike Hailwood GBR
1963 Hugh Anderson NZL	Jim Redman ZIM	Mike Hailwood GBR
1964 Luigi Taveri SUI	Phil Read GBR	Mike Hailwood GBR
1965 Hugh Anderson NZL	Phil Read GBR	Mike Hailwood GBR
1966 Luigi Taveri SUI	Mike Hailwood GBR	Giacomo Agostini ITA
1967 Bill Ivy GBR	Mike Hailwood GBR	Giacomo Agostini ITA
1968 Phil Read GBR	Phil Read GBR	Giacomo Agostini ITA
1969 Dave Simmonds GBR	Kel Caruthers AUS	Giacomo Agostini ITA
1970 Dieter Braun FRG	Rod Gould GBR	Giacomo Agostini ITA
1971 Angel Nieto ESP	Phil Read GBR	Giacomo Agostini ITA
1972 Angel Nieto ESP	Jarno Saarinen FIN	Giacomo Agostini ITA
1973 Kent Andersson SWE	Dieter Braun FRG	Phil Read GBR
1974 Kent Andersson SWE	Walter Villa ITA	Phil Read GBR
1975 Paolo Pileri ITA	Walter Villa ITA	Giacomo Agostini ITA
1976 Pier-Paolo Bianchi ITA	Walter Villa ITA	Barry Sheene GBR
1977 Pier-Paolo Bianchi ITA	Mario Lega ITA	Barry Sheene GBR
1978 Eugenio Lazzarini ITA	Kork Ballington RSA	Kenny Roberts USA
1979 Angel Nieto ESP	Kork Ballington RSA	Kenny Roberts USA
1980 Pir-Paolo Bianchi ITA	Anton Mang FRG	Kenny Roberts USA
1981 Angel Nieto ESP	Anton Mang FRG	Marco Lucchinelli ITA
1982 Angel Nieto ESP	Jean-Louis Tournadre FRA	Franco Uncini ITA
1983 Angel Nieto ESP	Carlos Lavado VEN	Freddie Spencer USA
1984 Angel Nieto ESP	Christian Sarron FRA	Eddie Lawson USA
1985 Fausto Gresini ITA	Freddie Spencer USA	Freddie Spencer USA
1986 Luca Cadalora ITA	Carlos Lavado VEN	Eddie Lawson USA
1987 Fausto Gresini ITA	Anton Mang FRG	Wayne Gardner AUS
1988 Jorge Martinez ESP	Sito Pons ESP	Eddie Lawson USA
1989 Alex Criville ESP	Sito Pons ESP	Eddie Lawson USA
1990 Loris Capirossi ITA	John Kocinski USA	Wayne Rainey USA
1991 Loris Capirossi ITA	Luca Cadalora ITA	Wayne Rainey USA
1992 Alessandro Gramigni ITA	Luca Cadalora ITA	Wayne Rainey USA
1993 Dirk Raudies GER	Loris Capirossi ITA	Kevin Schwantz USA
1994 Kazuto Sakata JPN	Massimiliano Biaggi ITA	Michael Doohan AUS
1995 Haruchika Aoki JPN	Massimiliano Biaggi ITA	Michael Doohan AUS
1996 Haruchika Aoki JPN	Massimiliano Biaggi ITA	Michael Doohan AUS
1997 Valentino Rossi ITA	Massimiliano Biaggi ITA	Michael Doohan AUS
1998 Kazuto Sakata JPN	Loris Capirossi ITA	Michael Doohan AUS
1999 Emilio Alzamora ESP	Valentino Rossi ITA	Alex Criville ESP
2000 Roberto Locatelli ITA	Olivier Jacque FRA	Kenny Roberts Jr USA

MOTOR CYCLING

Superbikes

World Champions

1988 **Fred Merkel** USA
1989 **Fred Merkel** USA
1990 **Raymond Roche** FRA
1991 **Doug Polen** USA
1992 **Doug Polen** USA
1993 **Scott Russell** USA
1994 **Carl Fogarty** GBR
1995 **Carl Fogarty** GBR
1996 **Troy Corser** AUS
1997 **John Kocinski** USA
1998 **Carl Fogarty** GBR
1999 **Carl Fogarty** GBR
2000 **Colin Edwards** USA

Race Wins

59	Carl Fogarty
27	Doug Polen
23	Raymond Roche
21	Troy Corser
16	Giancarlo Falappa
15	Colin Edwards
14	Pierfrancesco Chili
	Scott Russell
	John Kocinski
13	Aaron Slight
12	Noriuki Haga
11	Stephane Mertens
10	Fabrizio Pirovano

Wins in a Season

17	Doug Polen 1991
13	Carl Fogarty 1995
11	Carl Fogarty 1993
	Carl Fogarty 1999
10	Carl Fogarty 1994
9	Scott Russell 1994
	John Kocinski 1997
8	Raymond Roche 1990

Manufacturers

1988 **Honda**
1989 **Honda**
1990 **Honda**
1991 **Ducati**
1992 **Ducati**
1993 **Ducati**
1994 **Ducati**
1995 **Ducati**
1996 **Ducati**
1997 **Honda**
1998 **Ducati**
1999 **Ducati**
2000 **Ducati**

MOTOR RACING

FORMULA 1 CHAMPIONS

Year	Winning Driver	Car	Runner up	Winning Constructor
1950	Giuseppe Farina ITA	Alfa Romeo	Juan Manuel Fangio ARG	-
1951	Juan Manuel Fangio ARG	Alfa Romeo	Alberto Ascari ITA	-
1952	Alberto Ascari ITA	Ferrari	Giuseppe Farina ITA	-
1953	Alberto Ascari ITA	Ferrari	Juan Manuel Fangio ARG	-
1954	Juan Manuel Fangio ARG	Maserati/Mercedes	Jose Gonzalez ARG	-
1955	Juan Manuel Fangio ARG	Mercedes-Benz	Stirling Moss GBR	-
1956	Juan Manuel Fangio ARG	Lancia-Ferrari	Stirling Moss GBR	-
1957	Juan Manuel Fangio ARG	Maserati	Stirling Moss GBR	-
1958	Mike Hawthorn GBR	Ferrari	Stirling Moss GBR	Vanwall
1959	Jack Brabham AUS	Cooper-Climax	Tony Brooks GBR	Cooper-Climax
1960	Jack Brabham AUS	Cooper-Climax	Bruce McLaren NZL	Cooper-Climax
1961	Phil Hill USA	Ferrari	Wolfgang von Trips FRG	Ferrari
1962	Graham Hill GBR	BRM	Jim Clark GBR	BRM
1963	Jim Clark GBR	Lotus-Climax	Graham Hill GBR	Lotus-Climax
1964	John Surtees GBR	Ferrari	Graham Hill GBR	Ferrari
1965	Jim Clark GBR	Lotus-Climax	Graham Hill GBR	Lotus-Climax
1966	Jack Brabham AUS	Brabham-Repco	John Surtees GBR	Brabham-Repco
1967	Denny Hulme NZL	Brabham-Repco	Jack Brabham AUS	Brabham-Repco
1968	Graham Hill GBR	Lotus-Ford	Jackie Stewart GBR	Lotus-Ford
1969	Jackie Stewart GBR	Matra-Ford	Jacky Ickx BEL	Matra-Ford
1970	Jochen Rindt AUT	Lotus-Ford	Jacky Ickx BEL	Lotus-Ford
1971	Jackie Stewart GBR	Tyrrell-Ford	Ronnie Peterson SWE	Tyrrell-Ford
1972	Emerson Fittipaldi BRA	Lotus-Ford	Jackie Stewart GBR	Lotus-Ford
1973	Jackie Stewart GBR	Tyrrell-Ford	Emerson Fittipaldi BRA	Lotus-Ford
1974	Emerson Fittipaldi BRA	McLaren-Ford	Clay Regazzoni SUI	McLaren-Ford
1975	Niki Lauda AUT	Ferrari	Emerson Fittipaldi BRA	Ferrari
1976	James Hunt GBR	McLaren-Ford	Niki Lauda AUT	Ferrari
1977	Niki Lauda AUT	Ferrari	Jody Scheckter RSA	Ferrari
1978	Mario Andretti USA	Lotus-Ford	Ronnic Peterson SWE	Lotus-Ford
1979	Jody Scheckter RSA	Ferrari	Gilles Villeneuve CAN	Ferrari
1980	Alan Jones AUS	Williams-Ford	Nelson Piquet BRA	Williams-Ford
1981	Nelson Piquet BRA	Brabham-Ford	Carlos Reutemann ARG	Williams-Ford
1982	Keke Rosberg FIN	Williams-Ford	Pironi FRA and Watson GBR	Ferrari
1983	Nelson Piquet BRA	Brabham-BMW	Alain Prost FRA	Ferrari
1984	Niki Lauda AUT	McLaren-TAG	Alain Prost FRA	McLaren-TAG
1985	Alain Prost FRA	McLaren-TAG	Michele Alboreto ITA	McLaren-TAG
1986	Alain Prost FRA	McLaren-TAG	Nigel Mansell GBR	Williams-Honda
1987	Nelson Piquet BRA	Williams-Honda	Nigel Mansell GBR	Williams-Honda
1988	Ayrton Senna BRA	McLaren-Honda	Alain Prost FRA	McLaren-Honda
1989	Alain Prost FRA	McLaren-Honda	Ayrton Senna BRA	McLaren-Honda
1990	Ayrton Senna BRA	McLaren-Honda	Alain Prost FRA	McLaren-Honda
1991	Ayrton Senna BRA	McLaren-Honda	Nigel Mansell GBR	McLaren-Honda
1992	Nigel Mansell GBR	Williams-Renault	Ricardo Patrese ITA	Williams-Renault
1993	Alain Prost FRA	Williams-Renault	Ayrton Senna BRA	Williams-Renault
1994	Michael Schumacher GER	Benetton-Ford	Damon Hill GBR	Williams-Renault
1995	Michael Schumacher GER	Benetton-Renault	Damon Hill GBR	Benetton-Renault
1996	Damon Hill GBR	Williams-Renault	Jacques Villeneuve CAN	Williams-Renault
1997	Jacques Villeneuve CAN	Williams-Renault	Heinz-Harald Frentzen GER	Williams-Renault
1998	Mika Hakkinen FIN	McLaren-Mercedes	Michael Schumacher GER	McLaren-Mercedes
1999	Mika Hakkinen FIN	McLaren-Mercedes	Eddie Irvine GBR	Ferrari
2000	Michael Schumacher GER	Ferrari	Mika Hakkinen FIN	Ferrari

MOTOR RACING

INDY CAR CHAMPIONS

(USA unless stated)

Year	Winner
AAA	
1950	Henry Banks
1951	Tony Bettenhausen
1952	Chuck Stevenson
1953	Sam Hanks
1954	Jimmy Bryan
1955	Bob Sweikert
USAC	
1956	Jimmy Bryan
1957	Jimmy Bryan
1958	Tony Bettenhausen
1959	Rodger Ward
1960	AJ Foyt Jnr
1961	AJ Foyt Jnr
1962	Rodger Ward
1963	AJ Foyt Jnr
1964	AJ Foyt Jnr
1965	Mario Andretti
1966	Mario Andretti
1967	AJ Foyt Jnr
1968	Bobby Unser
1969	Mario Andretti
1970	Al Unser
1971	Joe Leonard
1972	Joe Leonard
1973	Roger McCluskey
1974	Bobby Unser
1975	AJ Foyt Jnr
1976	Gordon Johncock
1977	Tom Sneva
1978	Tom Sneva
1979	AJ Foyt Jnr
CART	
1979	Rick Mears
1980	Johnny Rutherford
1981	Rick Mears
1982	Rick Mears
1983	Al Unser
1984	Mario Andretti
1985	Al Unser
1986	Bobby Rahal
1987	Bobby Rahal
1988	Danny Sullivan
1989	Emerson Fittipaldi BRA
1990	Al Unser Jnr
1991	Michael Andretti
IndyCar	
1992	Bobby Rahal
1993	Nigel Mansell GBR
1994	Paul Tracy CAN
1995	Jacques Villeneuve CAN
PPG Cart	
1996	Jimmy Vasser
1997	Alex Zanardi ITA
1998	Alex Zanardi ITA
1999	Juan Montoya BRA
2000	Gil de Ferran BRA

LE MANS

Year	Drivers	Car
1949	Chinetti ITA/Selsdon GBR	Ferrari
1950	Rosier/Rosier FRA	Talbot-Lago
1951	Walker/Whitehead GBR	Jaguar
1952	Lang/Riess FRG	Mercedes-Benz
1953	Rolt/Hamilton GBR	Jaguar
1954	Gonzalez ARG/Trintignant FRA	Ferrari
1955	Hawthorn/Bueb GBR	Jaguar
1956	Flockhart/Sanderson GBR	Jaguar
1957	Flockhart/Bueb GBR	Jaguar
1958	Gendebien BEL/Hill USA	Ferrari
1959	Shelby/Salvadori GBR	Aston Martin
1960	Gendebien/Frere BEL	Ferrari
1961	Gendebien BEL/Hill USA	Ferrari
1962	Gendebien/Hill	Ferrari
1963	Scarfiotti/Bandini ITA	Ferrari
1964	Guichet FRA/Vaccarella ITA	Ferrari
1965	Rindt AUT/Gregory USA	Ferrari
1966	Amon/McLaren NZL	Ford
1967	Gurney/Foyt USA	Ford
1968	Rodriguez MEX/Bianchi BEL	Ford
1969	Ickx BEL/Oliver GBR	Ford
1970	Herrmann FRG/Attwood GBR	Porsche
1971	Marko AUT/van Lennep HOL	Porsche
1972	Pescarolo FRA/Hill GBR	Matra-Simca
1973	Pescarolo/Larrousse FRA	Matra-Simca
1974	Pescarolo/Larrousse FRA	Matra-Simca
1975	Ickx BEL/Bell GBR	Mirage-Ford
1976	Ickx BEL/van Lennep HOL	Porsche
1977	Ickx BEL/Barth FRG/Haywood USA	Porsche
1978	Jaussaud/Pironi FRA	Renault Alpine
1979	Ludwig FRG/Whittington USA/ Whittington USA	Porsche
1980	Jaussaud/Rondeau FRA	Rondeau-Ford
1981	Ickx BEL/Bell GBR	Porsche
1982	Ickx BEL/Bell GBR	Porsche
1983	Schuppan/Haywood/Holbert	Porsche
1984	Ludwig FRG/Pescarolo FRA	Porsche
1985	Ludwig/Winter FRG/Barillo ITA	Porsche
1986	Stuck FRG/Bell GBR/Holbert USA	Porsche
1987	Stuck/Bell/Holbert	Porsche
1988	Lammers HOL/Dumfries GBR/ Wallace GBR	Jaguar
1989	Mass/Reuter FRG/Dickens SWE	Mercedes
1990	Nielsen DEN/Brundle GBR/Cobb USA	Jaguar
1991	Herbert GBR/Gachot BEL/ Wendler GER	Mazda
1992	Warwick/Blundell GBR/Dalmas FRA	Peugeot
1993	Bouchut/Helary FRA	Peugeot
1994	Dalmas FRA/Haywood USA/ Baldi ITA	Porsche
1995	Dalmas FRA/Lehto FIN	McLaren
1996	Jones/Reuter/Wurtz	Porsche
1996	Jones/Reuter/Wurtz	Porsche
1997	Alboreto/Johansson/Kristensen	Joest
1998	McNish/Ortelli/Aiello	Porsche AG
1999	Martini/Dalmas/Winkelhock	BMW
2000	Biela/Kristensen/Pirro	Audi

MOTOR RACING

World Rally Champions

There was no drivers championship until 1977

1968	-	Ford
1969	-	Ford
1970	-	Porsche
1971	-	Alpine-Renault
1972	-	Lancia
1973	-	Alpine-Renault
1974	-	Lancia
1975	-	Lancia
1976	-	Lancia
1977	Sandro Munari ITA	Fiat
1978	Markku Alen FIN	Fiat
1979	Bjorn Waldgard SWE	Ford
1980	Walter Rohrl FRG	Fiat
1981	Ari Vatanen FIN	Talbot
1982	Timo Salanen FIN	Audi
1983	Hannu Mikkola FIN	Lancia
1984	Stig Blomqvist SWE	Audi
1985	Timo Salanen FIN	Peugeot
1986	Juha Kankkunen FIN	Peugeot
1987	Juha Kankkunen FIN	Lancia
1988	Mikki Biasion ITA	Lancia
1989	Mikki Biasion ITA	Lancia
1990	Carlos Sainz ESP	Lancia
1991	Juha Kankkunen FIN	Lancia
1992	Carlos Sainz ESP	Lancia
1993	Juha Kankkunen FIN	Toyota
1994	Didier Auriol FRA	Toyota
1995	Colin McRae GBR	Subaru
1996	Tommi Makinen FIN	Subaru
1997	Tommi Makinen FIN	Subaru
1998	Tommi Makinen FIN	Subaru
1999	Tommi Makinen FIN	Subaru
2000	Marcus Gronholm FIN	Peugeot

NETBALL

World Champions

1963	Australia
1967	Australia
1971	New Zealand
1975	Australia
1979*	Australia
	New Zealand
	Trinidad
1983	Australia
1987	New Zealand
1991	Australia
1995	Australia
1999	Australia

* Title shared

ROWING

WORLD CHAMPIONS
Olympic year championships not included

Men

SINGLE SCULLS
1962 **Vyacheslav Ivanov** URS
1966 **Don Spero** USA
1970 **Alberto Demiddi** ARG
1974 **Wolfgang Honig** GDR
1975 **Peter-Michael.Kolbe** FRG
1977 **Joachim Dreifke** GDR
1978 **Peter-Michael Kolbe** FRG
1979 **Pertti Karppinen** FIN
1981 **Rodiger Reiche** GDR
1982 **Rodiger Reiche** GDR
1983 **Peter-Michael Kolbe** FRG
1985 **Pertti Karppinen** FIN
1986 **Peter-Michael Kolbe** FRG
1987 **Thomas Lange** GDR
1989 **Thomas Lange** GDR
1990 **Juri Jaanson** URS
1991 **Thomas Lange** GER
1993 **Derek Porter** CAN
1994 **Andre Willms** GER
1995 **Iztok Cop** SLO
1997 **James Kovan** USA
1998 **Rob Waddell** NZL
1999 **Rob Waddell** NZL

DOUBLE SCULLS
1962 **René Duhamel/Bernard Monnereau** FRA
1966 **Melchior Borgin/Martin Studach** SUI
1970 **Jorgen Engelbrech/Niels Secher** DEN
1974 **Christof Kreuziger/Hans-Ulrich Schmied** GDR
1975 **Alf Hansen/Frank Hansen** NOR
1977 **Chris Baillieu/Michael Hart** GBR
1978 **Alf Hansen/Frank Hansen** NOR
1979 **Alf Hansen/Frank Hansen** NOR
1981 **Klaus Kroppelien/Joachim Dreifke** GDR
1982 **Alf Hansen/Rolf Thorsen** NOR
1983 **Thomas Lange/Uwe Heppner** GDR
1985 **Thomas Lange/Uwe Heppner** GDR
1986 **Alberto Belgori/Igor Pescialli** ITA
1987 **Vasil Radeyev/Danatyl Yordanov** BUL
1989 **Lars Bjøness/Rol Bent Thorsen** NOR
1990 **Christophe Zerbst/Arnold Jonke** AUT
1991 **Henk-Jan Zwolle/Nicolaas Rienks** NED
1993 **Yves Lamargue/Samuel Barathay** FRA
1994 **Lars Bjøness/Rol Bent Thorsen** NOR
1995 **Christiansen/Halabo-Hansen** DEN
1997 **Stephan Volkert/Andreas Hajek** GER
1998 **Stephan Volkert/Andreas Hajek** GER
1999 **Luka Spik/Iztok Cop** SLO

QUAD SCULLS
1974 **East Germany**
1975 **East Germany**
1977 **East Germany**
1978 **East Germany**
1979 **East Germany**
1981 **East Germany**

1982 **East Germany**
1983 **West Germany**
1985 **Canada**
1986 **Soviet Union**
1987 **Soviet Union**
1989 **Romania**
1990 **Soviet Union**
1991 **Soviet Union**
1993 **Germany**
1994 **Italy**
1995 **Italy**
1997 **Italy**
1998 **Italy**
1999 **Germany**

COXLESS PAIR
1962 **Dieter Bender/Gunther Zumkeller** FRG
1966 **Peter Gorny/Werner Klatt** GDR
1970 **Peter Gorny/Werner Klatt** GDR
1974 **Bernd Landvoig/Jorg Landvoig** GDR
1975 **Bernd Landvoig/Jorg Landvoigt** GDR
1977 **Vitaliy Yeliseyev/Aleksandr Kulagin** URS
1978 **Bernd Landvoig/Jörg Landvoigt** GDR
1979 **Bernd Landvoig/Jörg Landvoigt** GDR
1981 **Yuriy Pimenov/Nikolay Pimenov** URS
1982 **Magnus Grepperud/Sverre Loken** NOR
1983 **Carl Ertel/Ulf Sauerbrey** GDR
1985 **Nikolay Pimenov/Yury Pimenov** URS
1986 **Nikolay Pimenov/Yury Pimenov** URS
1987 **Andrew Holmes/Steven Redgrave** GBR
1989 **Thomas Jung/Uwe Kellner** GDR
1990 **Thomas Jung/Uwe Kellner** GDR
1991 **Steven Redgrave/Matthew Pinsent** GBR
1993 **Steven Redgrave/Matthew Pinsent** GBR
1994 **Steven Redgrave/Matthew Pinsent** GBR
1995 **Steven Redgrave/Matthew Pinsent** GBR
1997 **Michel Andrieux/J-Christophe Rolland** FRA
1998 **Robert Sens/Detlewf Kirchoff** GER
1999 **Drew Ginn/James Tompkins** AUS

COXED PAIR
1962 **West Germany**
1966 **Netherlands**
1970 **Romania**
1974 **Soviet Union**
1975 **East Germany**
1977 **Bulgaria**
1978 **East Germany**
1979 **East Germany**
1981 **Italy**
1982 **Italy**
1983 **East Germany**
1985 **Italy**
1986 **Great Britain**
1987 **Italy**
1989 **Italy**
1990 **Italy**
1991 **Italy**
1993 **Great Britain**
1994 **Croatia**
1995 **Italy**

ROWING

1997	USA
1998	Australia
1999	USA

COXLESS FOUR
1962	West Germany
1966	East Germany
1970	East Germany
1974	East Germany
1975	East Germany
1977	East Germany
1978	Soviet Union
1979	East Germany
1981	Soviet Union
1982	Switzerland
1983	West Germany
1985	West Germany
1986	USA
1987	East Germany
1989	East Germany
1990	Australia
1991	Australia
1993	France
1994	Italy
1995	Italy
1997	Great Britain
1998	Great Britain
1999	Great Britain

COXED FOUR
1962	West Germany
1966	East Germany
1970	West Germany
1974	East Germany
1975	Soviet Union
1977	East Germany
1978	East Germany
1979	East Germany
1981	East Germany
1982	East Germany
1983	New Zealand
1985	Soviet Union
1986	East Germany
1987	East Germany
1989	Romania
1990	East Germany
1991	Germany
1993	Romania
1994	Romania
1995	USA
1997	France
1998	Australia
1999	USA

EIGHTS
1962	West Germany
1966	West Germany
1970	East Germany
1974	USA
1975	East Germany
1977	East Germany
1981	Soviet Union

1982	New Zealand
1983	New Zealand
1985	Soviet Union
1986	Australia
1987	USA
1989	West Germany
1990	West Germany
1991	Germany
1993	Germany
1994	USA
1995	Germany
1997	USA
1998	USA
1999	USA

LIGHTWEIGHT SINGLE SCULLS
1974	William Belden USA
1975	Reto Wyss SUI
1977	Reto Wyss SUI
1978	José Antonio Montosa ESP
1979	William Belden USA
1981	Scott Roop USA
1982	Raimund Haberl AUT
1983	Bjarne Eltang DEN
1985	Ruggero Verroca ITA
1986	Peter Antonie AUS
1987	Willem Van Belleghem BEL
1989	Frans Goebel NED
1990	Frans Goebel NED
1991	Niall O'Toole IRL
1993	Peter Haining GBR
1994	Peter Haining GBR
1995	Peter Haining GBR
1997	Karsten Nielsen DEN
1998	Stefano Basalini ITA
1999	Karsten Nielsen DEN

LIGHTWEIGHT DOUBLE SCULLS
1978	Bornick/Gilje NOR
1979	Bornick/Gilje NOR
1981	Esposito/Verroca ITA
1982	Esposito/Verroca ITA
1983	Esposito/Verroca ITA
1985	Crispon/Renault FRA
1986	Smith/Whitwell GBR
1987	Gandola/Calabrese ITA
1989	Schmölzer/Rantasa AUT
1990	Peterson/Dreher USA
1991	Von Warburg/Buchheit GER
1993	Lynagh/ Hick AUS
1994	Esposito/Crispi ITA
1995	Geir/Geir SUI
1997	Kucharski/Sycz POL
1998	Kucharski/Sycz POL
1999	Krispi/Pettinari ITA

LIGHTWEIGHT QUAD SCULLS
1989	West Germany
1990	Italy
1991	Australia
1993	-
1994	Austria

ROWING

1995 Austria
1997 Italy
1998 Italy
1999 Italy

LWT COXLESS PAIR
1993 Spain
1994 Italy
1995 Italy
1997 Switzerland
1998 France
1999 Italy

LWT COXLESS FOURS
1974 Australia
1975 France
1977 France
1978 Switzerland
1979 Great Britain
1981 Australia
1982 Italy
1983 Spain
1985 West Germany
1986 Italy
1987 West Germany
1989 West Germany
1990 West Germany
1991 Great Britain
1993 USA
1994 Denmark
1995 Italy
1997 Italy
1998 Denmark
1999 Denmark

LWT EIGHTS
1974 USA
1975 West Germany
1977 Great Britain
1978 Great Britain
1979 Spain
1981 Denmark
1982 Italy
1983 Spain
1985 Italy
1986 Italy
1987 Italy
1989 Italy
1990 Italy
1991 Italy
1993 Canada
1994 Great Britain
1995 Denmark
1997 Australia
1998 Germany
1999 USA

Women

SINGLE SCULLS
1974, 75 & 77 **Christine Scheiblich** GDR
1978 **Christine Hann** *(nee Scheiblich)* GDR
1979 **Sandra Toma** ROM
1981 **Sandra Toma** ROM
1982 **Irina Fettisova** URS
1983 **Jutta Hampe** GDR
1985 **Cornelia Linse** GDR
1986 **Jutta Hampe** GDR
1987 **Magdalena Georgeyeva** BUL
1989 **Elisabeta Lipa** ROM
1990 **Birgit Peter** GDR
1991 **Silken Laumann** CAN
1993 **Jana Thieme** GER
1994 **Trine Hansen** DEN
1995 **Maria Brandin** SWE
1997 **Ekaterina Khodotovich** BLR
1998 **Irina Fedotova** RUS
1999 **Ekaterina Karsten** BLR

DOUBLE SCULLS
1974 **Yelena Antonova/Galina Yermoleyeva** URS
1975 **Yelena Antonova/Galina Yermoleyeva** URS
1977 **Anke Borchmann/Roswietha Zobelt** GDR
1978 **Svetla Otzetova/Zdravka Yordanova** BUL
1979 **Cornelia Linse/Heidi Westphal** GDR
1981 **M Kokarevitha/Antonina Makhina** URS
1982 **Yelena Braticko/Antonina Makhina** URS
1983 **Jutta Scheck/Martina Schroter** GDR
1985 **Sylvia Schurabe/Martina Schroter** GDR
1986 **Sylvia Schurabe/Beate Schramm** GDR
1987 **Steska Madina/Violeta Ninova** BUL
1989 **Jana Sorgers/Beate Schramm** GDR
1990 **Kathrin Boron/Beate Schramm** GDR
1991 **Kathrin Boron/Beate Schramm** GER
1993 **Philippa Baker/Brennda Lawson** NZL
1994 **Philippa Baker/Brenda Lawson** NZL
1995 **Marnie McBean/Kathleen Heddle** CAN
1997 **Boron/Molle** GER
1998 **Jana Thieme/Katrin Boron** GER
1999 **Jana Thieme/Katrin Boron** GER

QUAD SCULLS
1974 East Germany
1975 East Germany
1977 East Germany
1978 Bulgaria
1979 East Germany
1981 Soviet Union
1982 Soviet Union
1983 East Germany
1985 East Germany
1986 East Germany
1987 East Germany
1989 East Germany
1990 East Germany
1991 Germany
1993 China
1994 Germany
1995 Germany

ROWING

1997 Germany
1998 Germany
1999 Germany

COXLESS PAIRS
1974 Marilena Ghita/Cornelia Neascu ROM
1975 Sabine Dahne/Angelika Noack GDR
1977 Sabine Dahne/Angelika Noack GDR
1978 Cornelia Bugel/Ute Steindorf GDR
1979 Cornelia Bugel/Ute Steindorf GDR
1981 Sigrid Anders/Iris Rudolph GDR
1982 Silvia Frohlich/Marita Sandig GDR
1983 Silvia Frohlich/Marita Sandig GDR
1985 Rodica Arba/Elena Florea ROM
1986 Rodica Arba/Olga Homeghi ROM
1987 Rodica Arba/Olga Homeghi ROM
1989 Kathrin Haaker/Judith Zeidler GDR
1990 Stefanie Werremeier/Ingeburg Althoff FRG
1991 Marnie McBean/Kathleen Heddle CAN
1993 Christine Gosse/Helene Cortin FRA
1994 Christine Gosse/Helene Cortin FRA
1995 Megan Still/Kate Slatter AUS
1997 Emma Robinson/Alison Korn CAN
1998 Emma Robinson/Alison Korn CAN
1999 Emma Robinson/Theresa Luke CAN

COXED FOUR
Discontinued since 1987
1974 East Germany
1975 East Germany
1977 East Germany
1978 East Germany
1979 Soviet Union
1981 Soviet Union
1982 Soviet Union
1983 Soviet Union
1985 East Germany
1986 Romania
1987 Romania

COXLESS FOUR
1986 USA
1989 East Germany
1990 Romania
1991 Canada
1993 China
1994 Netherlands
1995 USA
1997 Great Britain
1998 Ukraine
1999 Belarus

EIGHTS
1974 East Germany
1975 East Germany
1977 East Germany
1978 Soviet Union
1979 Soviet Union
1981 Soviet Union
1983 Soviet Union
1985 Soviet Union
1986 Soviet Union
1987 Soviet Union

1989 Romania
1990 Romania
1991 Canada
1993 Romania
1994 Germany
1995 USA
1997 Romania
1998 Romania
1999 Romania

LIGHTWEIGHT SINGLE SCULLS
1985 Adair Ferguson AUS
1986 Maria Sava ROM
1987 M Georgieva BUL
1989 Kris Karlson USA
1990 Mette Jenson DEN
1991 Philippa Baker NZL
1993 Michelle Darvill CAN
1994 Constanta Pipota ROM
1995 Regina Joyce AUS
1997 Sarah Garner USA
1998 Pia Vogel SUI
1999 Pia Vogel SUI

LIGHTWEIGHT DOUBLE SCULLS
1985 Lin Clark/Beryl Crockford GBR
1986 Chris Ernst/Cary Beth Sands USA
1987 Stefka Madina/Violeta Ninova BUL
1989 Cary Beth Sands/Kris Karlson USA
1990 Ulla Jensen/Regitze Siggaard DEN
1991 Christiane Weber/Claudia Waldi GER
1993 Collen Miller/Wendy Wiebe CAN
1994 Collen Miller/Wendy Wiebe CAN
1995 Collen Miller/Wendy Wiebe CAN
1997 Michelle Darvill/Angelika Brand GER
1998 Christine Collins/Sarah Garner USA
1999 Constanta Burcica/Camelia Macovicuic ROM

RUGBY LEAGUE

WORLD CUP

	Winner	Venue
1954	Great Britain	France
1957	Australia	Australia
1960	Great Britain	England
1968	Australia	Aus/Nzl
1970	Australia	England
1972	Great Britain	France
1975*	Australia	Worldwide
1977	Australia	Aus/Nzl
1988	Australia	N Zealand
1992	Australia	England
1995	Australia	Eng/Wal
2000	Australia	UK/Irl/Fra

World Chps played home & away

WORLD CLUB

1997	Brisbane Broncos
1999	Melbourne Storm

LEAGUE CHAMPIONS

1973-74	Salford
1974-75	St. Helens
1975-76	Salford
1976-77	Featherstone Rovers
1977-78	Widnes
1978-79	Hull Kingston Rovers
1979-80	Bradford Northern
1980-81	Bradford Northern
1981-82	Leigh
1982-83	Hull
1983-84	Hull Kingston Rovers
1984-85	Hull Kingston Rovers
1985-86	Halifax
1986-87	Wigan
1987-88	Widnes
1988-89	Widnes
1989-90	Wigan
1990-91	Wigan
1991-92	Wigan
1992-93	Wigan
1993-94	Wigan
1994-95	Wigan
1995-96	Wigan

SUPER LEAGUE

1996	St. Helens Saints
1997	Bradford Bulls
1998	Wigan Warriors
1999	Bradford Bulls
2000	Wigan Warriors

PREMIERSHIP TROPHY

1975	Leeds
1976	St. Helens
1977	St. Helens
1978	Bradford Northern
1979	Leeds
1980	Widnes
1981	Hull Kingston Rovers
1982	Widnes
1983	Widnes

1984	Hull Kingston Rovers
1985	St. Helens
1986	Warrington
1987	Wigan
1988	Widnes
1989	Widnes
1990	Widnes
1991	Hull
1992	Wigan
1993	St. Helens
1994	Wigan
1995	Wigan
1996	Wigan
1996	Wigan
1997	Wigan Warriors

GRAND FINAL

1998	Wigan Warriors
1999	St Helens
2000	St Helens

CHALLENGE CUP

1897	Batley
1899	Oldham
1900	Swinton
1901	Batley
1902	Broughton Rangers
1903	Halifax
1904	Halifax
1905	Warrington
1906	Bradford
1907	Warrington
1908	Hunslet
1909	Wakefield Trinity
1910	Leeds
1911	Broughton Rangers
1912	Dewsbury
1913	Huddersfield
1914	Hull
1915	Huddersfield
1920	Huddersfield
1921	Leigh
1922	Rochdale Hornets
1923	Leeds
1924	Wigan
1925	Oldham
1926	Swinton
1927	Oldham
1928	Swinton
1929	Wigan
1930	Widnes
1931	Halifax
1932	Leeds
1933	Huddersfield
1934	Hunslet
1935	Castleford
1936	Leeds
1937	Widnes
1938	Salford
1939	Halifax
1941	Leeds

1942	Leeds
1943	Dewsbury
1944	Bradford Northern
1945	Huddersfield
1946	Wakefield Trinity
1947	Bradford Northern
1948	Wigan
1949	Bradford Northern
1950	Warrington
1951	Wigan
1952	Workington Town
1953	Huddersfield
1954	Warrington
1955	Barrow
1956	St. Helens
1957	Leeds
1958	Wigan
1959	Wigan
1960	Wakefield Trinity
1961	St. Helens
1962	Wakefield Trinity
1963	Wakefield Trinity
1964	Widnes
1965	Wigan
1966	St. Helens
1967	Featherstone Rovers
1968	Leeds
1969	Castleford
1970	Castleford
1971	Leigh
1972	St. Helens
1973	Featherstone Rovers
1974	Warrington
1975	Widnes
1976	St. Helens
1977	Leeds
1978	Leeds
1979	Widnes
1980	Hull Kingston Rovers
1981	Widnes
1982	Hull
1983	Featherstone Rovers
1984	Widnes
1985	Wigan
1986	Castleford
1987	Halifax
1988	Wigan
1989	Wigan
1990	Wigan
1991	Wigan
1992	Wigan
1993	Wigan
1994	Wigan
1995	Wigan
1996	St. Helens
1997	St. Helens
1998	Sheffield Eagles
1999	Leeds Rhinos
2000	Bradford Bulls

RUGBY UNION

WORLD CUP

1987 *Melbourne Cricket Ground*
New Zealand 29   France 9
1991 *Twickenham*
Australia 12   England 6
1995 *Ellis Park, Johannesburg*
South Africa 15   New Zealand 12 *aet*
1999 *Millennium Stadium, Cardiff*
Australia 35   France 12

Lions v South Africa

1910 **Lions** 10 **South Africa** 14
    Lions 8 **South Africa** 3
    Lions 5 **South Africa** 21
1924 **Lions** 3 **South Africa** 7
    Lions 0 **South Africa** 17
    Lions 3 **South Africa** 3
1938 **Lions** 12 **South Africa** 26
    Lions 3 **South Africa** 19
    Lions 21 **South Africa** 16
1955 **Lions** 23 **South Africa** 22
    Lions 9 **South Africa** 25
    Lions 9 **South Africa** 6
    Lions 8 **South Africa** 22
1962 **Lions** 3 **South Africa** 3
    Lions 0 **South Africa** 3
    Lions 3 **South Africa** 8
    Lions 14 **South Africa** 34
1968 **Lions** 20 **South Africa** 25
    Lions 6 **South Africa** 6
    Lions 6 **South Africa** 11
    Lions 6 **South Africa** 19
1974 **Lions** 12 **South Africa** 3
    Lions 28 **South Africa** 9
    Lions 26 **South Africa** 9
    Lions 13 **South Africa** 13
1980 **Lions** 22 **South Africa** 26
    Lions 19 **South Africa** 26
    Lions 10 **South Africa** 12
    Lions 17 **South Africa** 13
1997 **Lions** 25 **South Africa** 16
    Lions 18 **South Africa** 15
    Lions 16 **South Africa** 35

Lions v New Zealand

1930 **Lions** 6 **New Zealand** 3
    Lions 10 **New Zealand** 13
    Lions 10 **New Zealand** 15
    Lions 8 **New Zealand** 22
1950 **Lions** 9 **New Zealand** 9
    Lions 0 **New Zealand** 8
    Lions 3 **New Zealand** 6
    Lions 8 **New Zealand** 11
1959 **Lions** 17 **New Zealand** 18
    Lions 8 **New Zealand** 11
    Lions 8 **New Zealand** 22
    Lions 9 **New Zealand** 6
1966 **Lions** 3 **New Zealand** 20
    Lions 12 **New Zealand** 16
    Lions 6 **New Zealand** 19
    Lions 11 **New Zealand** 24

1971 **Lions** 9 **New Zealand** 3
    Lions 12 **New Zealand** 22
    Lions 13 **New Zealand** 3
    Lions 14 **New Zealand** 14
1977 **Lions** 12 **New Zealand** 16
    Lions 13 **New Zealand** 9
    Lions 7 **New Zealand** 19
    Lions 9 **New Zealand** 10
1983 **Lions** 12 **New Zealand** 16
    Lions 0 **New Zealand** 9
    Lions 8 **New Zealand** 15
    Lions 6 **New Zealand** 38
1993 **Lions** 18 **New Zealand** 20
    Lions 20 **New Zealand** 7
    Lions 13 **New Zealand** 30

Lions v Australia

1930 **Lions** 5 **Australia** 6
1950 **Lions** 19 **Australia** 6
    Lions 24 **Australia** 3
1959 **Lions** 17 **Australia** 6
    Lions 24 **Australia** 3
1966 **Lions** 11 **Australia** 8
    Lions 31 **Australia** 0
1989 **Lions** 12 **Australia** 30
    Lions 19 **Australia** 12
    Lions 19 **Australia** 18

FOUR / FIVE / SIX NATIONS

1883 **England**
1884 **England**
1886 **England & Scotland**
1887 **Scotland**
1890 **England & Scotland**
1891 **Scotland**
1892 **England**
1893 **Wales**
1894 **Ireland**
1895 **Scotland**
1896 **Ireland**
1899 **Ireland**
1900 **Wales**
1901 **Scotland**
1902 **Wales**
1903 **Scotland**
1904 **Scotland**
1905 **Wales**
1906 **Ireland & Wales**
1907 **Scotland**
1908 **Wales**
1909 **Wales**
1910 **England**
1911 **Wales**
1912 **England & Ireland**
1913 **England**
1914 **England**
1920 **England Wales & Scotland**
1921 **England**
1922 **Wales**
1923 **England**
1924 **England**

RUGBY UNION

FIVE NATIONS (cont)

1925 Scotland
1926 Scotland & Ireland
1927 Scotland & Ireland
1928 England
1929 Scotland
1930 England
1931 Wales
1932 England Ireland & Wales
1933 Scotland
1934 England
1935 Ireland
1936 Wales
1937 England
1938 Scotland
1939 England Ireland & Wales
1947 Wales & England
1948 Ireland
1949 Ireland
1950 Wales
1951 Ireland
1952 Wales
1953 England
1954 England Wales & France
1955 Wales & France
1956 Wales
1958 England
1959 France
1960 France & England
1961 France
1962 France
1963 England
1964 Scotland & Wales
1965 Wales
1966 Wales
1967 France
1968 France
1969 Wales
1970 Wales & France
1971 Wales
1973 *Five way tie*
1974 Ireland
1975 Wales
1976 Wales
1977 France
1978 Wales
1979 Wales
1980 England
1981 France
1982 Ireland
1983 France & Ireland
1984 Scotland
1985 Ireland
1986 France & Scotland
1987 France
1988 Wales & France
1989 France
1990 Scotland
1991 England
1992 England

1993 France
1994 Wales
1995 England
1996 England
1997 France
1998 France
1999 Scotland
2000 England

EUROPEAN CUP

1996-97 Brive
1997-98 Bath
1998-99 Bath
1999-2000 Northampton

ENGLISH LEAGUE CHAMPIONS

1987-88 Leicester
1988-89 Bath
1989-90 Wasps
1990-91 Bath
1991-92 Bath
1992-93 Bath
1993-94 Bath
1994-95 Leicester
1995-96 Bath
1996-97 Wasps
1997-98 Newcastle
1998-99 Leicester
1999-2000 Leicester

WELSH LEAGUE CHAMPIONS

1990-91 Neath
1991-92 Swansea
1992-93 Llanelli
1993-94 Swansea
1994-95 Cardiff
1995-96 Neath
1996-97 Pontypridd
1997-98 Swansea
1998-99 Llanelli

WELSH / SCOTTISH LEAGUE

1999-2000 Cardiff

RUGBY UNION

SCOTTISH LEAGUE CHAMPIONS

1973-74	Hawick
1974-75	Hawick
1975-76	Hawick
1976-77	Hawick
1977-78	Hawick
1978-79	Heriots FP
1979-80	Gala
1981-82	Hawick
1982-83	Gala
1983-84	Hawick
1984-85	Hawick
1985-86	Hawick
1986-87	Hawick
1987-88	Kelso
1988-89	Kelso
1989-90	Melrose
1990-91	Boroughmuir
1991-92	Melrose
1992-93	Melrose
1993-94	Melrose
1994-95	Stirling County
1995-96	Melrose
1996-97	Melrose
1997-98	Watsonians
1998-99	Heriots FP
1999-00	Heriots FP

ALL-IRELAND LEAGUE CHAMPIONS

1990-91	Cork Constitution
1991-92	Garryowen
1992-93	Young Munster
1993-94	Garryowen
1994-95	Shannon
1995-96	Shannon
1996-97	Shannon
1997-98	Shannon
1998-99	Garryowen
1999-00	St Mary's

PILKINGTON CUP

	Winner	Runner-up
1972	Gloucester 17	Moseley 6
1973	Coventry 27	Bristol 15
1974	Coventry 26	London Scottish 6
1975	Bedford 28	Rosslyn Park 12
1976	Gosforth 23	Rosslyn Park 14
1977	Gosforth 27	Waterloo 11
1978	Gloucester 6	Leicester 3
1979	Leicester 15	Moseley 12
1980	Leicester 21	London Irish 9
1981	Leicester 22	Gosforth 15
1982	Gloucester & Moseley Shared 12-12 aet	
1983	Bristol 28	Leicester 22
1984	Bath 10	Bristol 9
1985	Bath 24	London Welsh 15
1986	Bath 25	Wasps 17
1987	Bath 19	Wasps 12
1988	Harlequins 28	Bristol 22
1989	Bath 10	Leicester 6
1990	Bath 48	Gloucester 6
1991	Harlequins 25	Northampton 13 aet
1992	Bath 15	Harlequins 12 aet
1993	Leicester 23	Harlequins 16
1994	Bath 21	Leicester 9
1995	Bath 36	Wasps 16
1996	Bath 16	Leicester 15
1997	Leicester 9	Sale 3
1998	Saracens 48	Wasps 18
1999	Wasps 29	Newcastle 19
2000	Wasps 31	Northampton 23

SWALEC CUP

1972	Neath 15	Llanelli 9
1973	Llanelli 30	Cardiff 7
1974	Llanelli 12	Aberavon 10
1975	Llanelli 15	Aberavon 6
1976	Llanelli 15	Swansea 4
1977	Newport 16	Cardiff 15
1978	Swansea 13	Newport 9
1979	Bridgend 18	Pontypridd 12
1980	Bridgend 15	Swansea 9
1981	Cardiff 14	Bridgend 6
1982	Cardiff 12*	Bridgend 12
1983	Pontypool 18	Swansea 6
1984	Cardiff 24	Neath 19
1985	Llanelli 15	Cardiff 14
1986	Cardiff 28	Newport 21
1987	Cardiff 16	Swansea 15 aet
1988	Llanelli 28	Neath 13
1989	Neath 14	Llanelli 13
1990	Neath 16	Bridgend 10
1991	Llanelli 24	Pontypool 9
1992	Llanelli 16	Swansea 7
1993	Llanelli 21	Neath 18
1994	Cardiff 15	Llanelli 8
1995	Swansea 17	Pontypridd 12
1996	Pontypridd 29	Neath 22
1997	Cardiff 33	Swansea 26
1998	Llanelli 19	Ebbw Vale 12
1999	Swansea 37	Llanelli 10
2000	Llanelli 22	Swansea 12

* won on most tries

RUGBY UNION

COUNTY CHAMPIONSHIP

	Winners	Runners-up
1889	**Yorkshire**	
1890	**Yorkshire**	
1891	**Lancashire**	
1892	**Yorkshire**	
1893	**Yorkshire**	
1894	**Yorkshire**	
1895	**Yorkshire**	
1896	**Yorkshire**	Surrey
1897	**Kent**	Cumberland
1898	**Northumberland**	Midlands
1899	**Devon**	Northumberland
1900	**Durham**	Devon
1901	**Devon**	Durham
1902	**Durham**	Gloucestershire
1903	**Durham**	Kent
1904	**Kent**	Durham
1905	**Durham**	Middlesex
1906	**Devon**	Durham
1907	**Devon & Durham** *(shared)*	
1908	**Cornwall**	Durham
1909	**Durham**	Cornwall
1910	**Gloucestershire**	Yorkshire
1911	**Devon**	Yorkshire
1912	**Devon**	Northumberland
1913	**Gloucestershire**	Cumberland
1914	**Midlands**	Durham
1920	**Gloucestershire**	Yorkshire
1921	**Gloucestershire** 31	Leicestershire 4
1922	**Gloucestershire** 19	North Midlands 0
1923	**Somerset** 8	Leicestershire 6
1924	**Cumberland** 14	Kent 3
1925	**Leicestershire** 14	Gloucestershire 6
1926	**Yorkshire** 15	Hampshire 14
1927	**Kent** 22	Leicestershire 12
1928	**Yorkshire** 12	Cornwall 8
1929	**Middlesex** 9	Lancashire 8
	(after 8-8 draw)	
1930	**Gloucestershire** 13	Lancashire 7
1931	**Gloucestershire** 10	Warwickshire 9
1932	**Gloucestershire** 9	Durham 3
1933	**Hampshire** 18	Lancashire 7
1934	**East Midlands** 10	Gloucestershire 0
1935	**Lancashire** 14	Somerset 0
1936	**Hampshire** 13	Northumberland 6
1937	**Gloucestershire** 5	East Midlands 0
1938	**Lancashire** 24	Surrey 12
1939	**Warwickshire** 8	Somerset 3
1947	**Lancashire** 14	Gloucestershire 3
	(after 8-8 draw)	
1948	**Lancashire** 5	Eastern Counties 0
1949	**Lancashire** 9	Gloucestershire 3
1950	**Cheshire** 5	East Midlands 0
1951	**East Midlands** 10	Middlesex 0
1952	**Middlesex** 9	Lancashire 6
1953	**Yorkshire** 11	East Midlands 3
1954	**Middlesex** 24	Lancashire 6
1955	**Lancashire** 14	Middlesex 8
1956	**Middlesex** 13	Devon 9
1957	**Devon** 12	Yorkshire 3
1958	**Warwickshire** 16	Cornwall 8
1959	**Warwickshire** 14	Gloucestershire 9
1960	**Warwickshire** 9	Surrey 6
1961	**Cheshire** 5	Devon 3
	(after 0-0 draw)	
1962	**Warwickshire** 11	Hampshire 6
1963	**Warwickshire** 13	Yorkshire 10
1964	**Warwickshire** 8	Lancashire 6
1965	**Warwickshire** 15	Durham 9
1966	**Middlesex** 6	Lancashire 0
1967	**Surrey & Durham**	
	(shared after 14-14 & 0-0 draws)	
1968	**Middlesex** 9	Warwickshire 6
1969	**Lancashire** 11	Cornwall 9
1970	**Staffordshire** 11	Gloucestershire 9
1971	**Surrey** 1 4	Gloucestershire 3
1972	**Gloucestershire** 11	Warwickshire 6
1973	**Lancashire** 17	Gloucestershire 12
1974	**Gloucestershire** 22	Lancashire 12
1975	**Gloucestershire** 13	Eastern Counties 9
1976	**Gloucestershire** 24	Middlesex 9
1977	**Lancashire** 17	Middlesex 6
1978	**North Midlands** 10	Gloucestershire 7
1979	**Middlesex** 1 9	Northumberland 6
1980	**Lancashire** 21	Gloucestershire 15
1981	**Northumberland** 15	Gloucestershire 6
1982	**Lancashire** 7	North Midlands 3
1983	**Gloucestershire** 19	Yorkshire 7
1984	**Gloucestershire** 36	Somerset 1 8
1985	**Middlesex** 12	Notts, Lincs, Derbys 9
1986	**Warwickshire** 16	Kent 6
1987	**Yorkshire** 22	Middlesex 11
1988	**Lancashire** 23	Warwickshire 18
1989	**Durham** 13	Cornwall 9
1990	**Lancashire** 32	Middlesex 9
1991	**Cornwall** 29	Yorkshire 20
1992	**Lancashire** 9	Cornwall 6
1993	**Lancashire** 9	Yorkshire 6
1994	**Yorkshire** 26	Durham 3
1995	**Northumberland** 9	Warwickshire 15
1996	**Gloucestershire** 17	Warwickshire 13
1997	**Cumbria** 21	Somerset 13
1998	**Cheshire** 21	Cornwall 14
1999	**Cornwall** 24	Gloucestershire 15
2000	**Yorkshire** 16	Devon 9

SAILING

America's Cup Winners

Year	Winning boat (skipper)	Score	Challenger
1870	**Magic** (Andrew Comstock)	-	Cambria GBR
1871	**Columbia** (Nelson Comstoek)	4-1	Livonia GBR
	Sappho (Sam Greenwood)		
1876	**Madeleine** (Josephus Williams)	2-0	Countess Dufferin CAN
1881	**Mischief** (Nathaniel Clock)	2-0	Atalanta CAN
1885	**Puritan** (Aubrey Crocker)	2-0	Genesta GBR
1886	**Mayflower** (Martin Stone)	2-0	Galatea GBR
1887	**Volunteer** (Henry Haff)	2-0	Thistle GBR
1893	**Vigilant** (William Hansen)	3-0	Valkyrie II GBR
1895	**Defender** (Henry Haff)	3-0	Valkyrie lil GBR
1899	**Columbia** (James Barr)	3-0	Shamrock GBR
1901	**Columbia** (James Barr)	3-0	Shamrock II GBR
1903	**Reliance** (James Barr)	3-0	Shamrock lil GBR
1920	**Resolute** (Charles Adams)	3-2	Shamrock IV GBR
1930	**Enterprise** (Harold Vanderbilt)	4-0	Shamrock V GBR
1934	**Rainbow** (Harold Vanderbilt)	4-2	Endeavour GBR
1937	**Ranger** (Harold Vanderbilt)	4-0	Endeavour II GBR
1958	**Columbia** (Briggs Cunningham)	4-0	Sceptre GBR
1962	**Weatherly** (Emil MosbacherJr)	4-1	Gretel AUS
1964	**Constellation** (Bob Bavier Jr)	4-0	Sovereign GBR
1967	**Intrepid** (Emil Mosbacher Jr)	4-0	Dame Pattie AUS
1970	**Intrepid** (Bill Ficker)	4-1	Gretel II AUS
1974	**Courageous** (Ted Hood)	4-0	Southern Cross AUS
1977	**Courageous** (Ted Turner)	4-0	Australia AUS
1980	**Freedom** (Dennis Conner)	4-1	Australia AUS
1983	**Australia II** (John Bertrand)	4-3	Liberty USA
1987	**Stars & Stripes** (Dennis Conner)	4-0	Kookaburra lil AUS
1988	**Stars & Stripes** (Dennis Conner)	2-0	New Zealand NZL
1992	**America 3** (Bill Koch)	4-1	Il Moro di Venezia ITA
1995	**Black Magic I** (Russell Coutts)	5-0	Young America USA
2000	**Team New Zealand** (Coutts)	5-0	Prada ITA

All winning boats from USA, except Australia II in 1983 and Black Magic I (New Zealand) in 1995

Admiral's Cup Winners

Year	Winner	Year	Winner
1957	Great Britain	1979	Australia
1959	Great Britain	1981	Great Britain
1961	USA	1983	West Germany
1963	Great Britain	1985	West Germany
1965	Great Britain	1987	New Zealand
1967	Australia	1989	Great Britain
1969	USA	1991	France
1971	Great Britain	1993	Germany
1973	West Germany	1995	Italy
1975	Great Britain	1997	USA
1977	Great Britain	1999	Netherlands

SKIING

World Champions
There is no World Championship in Olympic years.

MEN'S DOWNHILL
1950 Zeno Colo ITA
1954 Christian Pravda AUT
1958 Toni Sailer AUT
1962 Karl Schranz AUT
1966 Jean-Claude Killy FRA
1970 Bernard Russi SUI
1974 David Zwilling AUT
1978 Josef Walcher AUT
1982 Harti Weirather AUT
1985 Pirmin Zurbriggen SUI
1987 Peter Müller SUI
1989 Hansjörg Tauscher FRG
1991 Franz Heinzer SUI
1993 Urs Lehmann SUI
1996 Patrick Ortlieb AUT
1997 Bruno Kernan SUI
1999 Hermann Maier AUT

MEN'S SUPER G
1987 Pirmin Zurbriggen SUI
1989 Martin Hangl SUI
1991 Stefan Eberharter AUT
1993 *race cancelled*
1996 Atle Skaardal NOR
1997 Atle Skaardal NOR
1999 Hermann Maier AUT

MEN'S GIANT SLALOM
1950 Zeno Colo ITA
1954 Stein Eriksen NOR
1958 Toni Sailer AUT
1962 Egon Zimmermann AUT
1966 Guy Périllat FRA
1970 Karl Schranz AUT
1974 Gustavo Thoeni ITA
1978 Ingemar Stenmark SWE
1982 Steve Mahre USA
1985 Markus Wasmaier FRG
1987 Pirmin Zurbriggen SUI
1989 Rudolf Nierlich AUT
1991 Rudolf Nierlich AUT
1993 Kjetil Andre Aamodt NOR
1996 Alberto Tomba ITA
1997 Michael von Grünigen SUI
1999 Lasse Kjus NOR

MEN'S SLALOM
1950 Georges Schneider SUI
1954 Stein Eriksen NOR
1958 Josef Rieder AUT
1962 Charles Bozon FRA
1966 Carlo Senoner ITA
1970 Jean-Noël Augert FRA
1974 Gustavo Thoeni ITA
1978 Ingemar Stenmark SWE
1982 Ingemar Stenmark SWE
1985 Jonas Nilsson SWE
1987 Frank Wörndl FRG
1989 Rudolf Nierlich AUT
1991 Marc GirardelliAUT
1993 Kjetil Andre Aamodt NOR
1996 Alberto Tomba ITA
1997 Tom Stiansen NOR
1999 Kalle Palander FIN

MEN'S COMBINED
1954 Stein Eriksen NOR
1958 Toni Sailer AUT
1962 Karl Schranz AUT
1966 Jean-Claude Killy FRA
1970 Bill Kidd USA
1974 Franz Klammer AUT
1978 Andreas Wenzel LIE
1982 Michel Vion FRA
1985 Pirmin Zurbriggen SUI
1987 Marc Girardelli LUX
1989 Marc Girardelli LUX
1991 Stefan Eberharter AUT
1993 Lasse Kjus NOR
1996 Marc Girardelli LUX
1997 Kjetil Andre Aamodt NOR
1999 Kjetil Andre Aamodt NOR

WOMEN'S DOWNHILL
1950 Trude B-Jochum AUT
1954 Ida Schöpfer SUI
1958 Lucille Wheeler CAN
1962 Christl Haas AUT
1966 Marielle Goitschel FRA
1970 Annerösli Zyrd SUI
1974 Annemarie Moser-Pröll AUT
1978 Annemarie M-Pröll AUT
1982 Gerry Sorensen CAN
1985 Michela Figini SUI
1987 Maria Walliser SUI
1989 Maria Walliser SUI
1991 Petra Kronberger AUT
1993 Kate Pace CAN
1996 Picabo Street USA
1997 Hilary Lindh USA
1999 Renate Goetschl AUT

WOMEN'S SUPER G
1987 Maria Walliser FRG
1989 Ulrike Maier AUT
1991 Ulrike Maier AUT
1993 Katja Seizinger GER
1996 Isolde Kostner ITA
1997 Isolde Kostner ITA
1999 Alex Meissnitzer AUT

WOMEN'S GIANT SLALOM
1950 Dagmar Rom AUT
1954 Lucienne Schmitt FRA
1958 Lucille Wheeler CAN
1962 Marinne Jahn AUT
1966 Marielle Goitschel FRA
1970 Betsy Clifford CAN
1974 Fabienne Serrat FRA
1978 Maria Epple FRG
1982 Erika Hess SUI
1985 Diann Roffe USA
1987 Vreni Schneider SUI
1989 Vreni Schneider SUI
1991 Pernilla Wiberg SWE
1993 Carole Merle FRA
1996 Deborah Compagnoni ITA
1997 Deborah Compagnoni ITA
1999 Alex Meissnitzer AUT

WOMEN'S SLALOM
1950 Dagmar Rom AUT
1954 Trude Klecker AUT
1958 Inger Björnbakken NOR
1962 Marinne Jahn AUT
1966 Annie Famose FRA
1970 Ingrid Lafforgue FRA
1974 Hanni Wenzel LIE
1978 Lea Sölkner AUT
1982 Erika Hess SUI
1985 Perrine Pelen FRA
1987 Erika Hess SUI
1989 Mateja Svet YUG
1991 Vreni Schneider SUI
1993 Karin Buder AUT
1996 Pernilla Wiberg SWE
1997 Deborah Compagnoni ITA
1999 Zali Steggal AUS

WOMEN'S COMBINED
1954 Ida Schöpfer SUI
1958 Frieda Dänzer SUI
1962 Marielle Goitschel FRA
1966 Marielle Goitschel FRA
1970 Michele Jacot FRA
1974 Fabienne Serrat FRA
1978 Annemarie M-Pröll AUT
1982 Erika Hess SUI
1985 Erika Hess SUI
1987 Erika Hess SUI
1989 Tamara McKinney USA
1991 Chantal Bournissen SUI
1993 Miriam Vogt GER
1996 Pernilla Wiberg SWE
1997 Renate Goetschl AUT
1999 Pernilla Wiberg SWE

World Cup winners
From 1980 onwards

MEN'S OVERALL
1967 Jean-Claude Killy FRA
1968 Jean-Claude Killy FRA
1969 Karl Schranz AUT
1970 Karl Schranz AUT
1971 Gustavo Thoeni ITA
1972 Gustavo Thoeni ITA
1973 Gustavo Thoeni ITA
1974 Piero Gros ITA
1975 Gustavo Thoeni ITA

SKIING

1976 Ingemar Stenmark SWE	**MEN'S SUPER G**	1974 Gustavo Thoeni ITA
1977 Ingemar Stenmark SWE	1986 Markus Wasmeier FRG	1975 Ingemar Stenmark SWE
1978 Ingemar Stenmark SWE	1987 Pirmin Zurbriggen SUI	1976 Ingemar Stenmark SWE
1979 Ingemar Stenmark SWE	1988 Pirmin Zurbriggen SUI	1977 Ingemar Stenmark SWE
1980 Andreas Wenzel LIE	1989 Pirmin Zurbriggen SUI	1978 Ingemar Stenmark SWE
1981 Phil Mahre USA	1990 Pirmin Zurbriggen SUI	1979 Ingemar Stenmark SWE
1982 Phil Mahre USA	1991 Franz Heinzer SUI	1980 Ingemar Stenmark SWE
1983 Phil Mahre USA	1992 Paul Accola SUI	1981 Ingemar Stenmark SWE
1984 Pirmin Zurbriggen SUI	1993 Kjetil Andre Aamodt NOR	1982 Phil Mahre USA
1985 Marc Girardelli LUX	1994 Jan Einar Thorsen NOR	1983 Ingemar Stenmark SWE
1986 Marc Girardelli LUX	1995 Peter Runggaldier ITA	1984 Marc Girardelli LUX
1987 Pirmin Zurbriggen SUI	1996 Atle Skaardal NOR	1985 Marc Girardelli LUX
1988 Pirmin Zurbriggen SUI	1997 Luc Alphand FRA	1986 Rok Petrovic YUG
1989 Marc Girardelli LUX	1998 Hermann Maier AUT	1987 Bojan Krizaj YUG
1990 Pirmin Zurbriggen SUI	1999 Hermann Maier AUT	1988 Alberto Tomba ITA
1991 Marc Girardelli LUX	2000 Hermann Maier AUT	1989 Armin Bittner FRG
1992 Paul Accola SUI		1990 Armin Bittner FRG
1993 Marc Girardelli LUX	**MEN'S GIANT SLALOM**	1991 Marc Girardelli LUX
1994 Kjetil Andre Aamodt NOR	1967 Jean-Claude Killy FRA	1992 Alberto Tomba ITA
1995 Alberto Tomba ITA	1968 Jean-Claude Killy FRA	1993 Tomas Fogdoe SWE
1996 Lasse Kjus NOR	1969 Karl Schranz AUT	1994 Alberto Tomba ITA
1997 Luc Alphand FRA	1970 Gustavo Thoeni ITA	1995 Alberto Tomba ITA
1998 Hermann Maier AUT	1971 Thoeni/Russel ITA/FRA	1996 Sébastien Amiez FRA
1999 Lasse Kjus NOR	1972 Gustavo Thoeni ITA	1997 Thomas Sykora AUT
2000 Hermann Maier AUT	1973 Hans Hinterseer AUT	1998 Thomas Sykora AUT
	1974 Piero Gros ITA	1999 T Stangassinger AUT
MEN'S DOWNHILL	1975 Ingemar Stenmark SWE	2000 Kjetil Andre Aamodt NOR
1967 Jean-Claude Killy FRA	1976 Ingemar Stenmark SWE	
1968 Gerhard Nenning AUT	1977 Heini Hemmi SUI	**WOMEN'S OVERALL**
1969 Karl Schranz AUT	1978 Ingemar Stenmark SWE	1967 Nancy Greene USA
1970 Schranz/Cordin both AUT	1979 Ingemar Stenmark SWE	1968 Nancy Greene USA
1971 Bernhard Russi SUI	1980 Ingemar Stenmark SWE	1969 Gertrud Gabl AUT
1972 Bernhard Russi SUI	1981 Ingemar Stenmark SWE	1970 Michele Jacot FRA
1973 Roland Collombin SUI	1982 Phil Mahre USA	1971 Annemarie Moser-Pröll
1974 Roland Collombin SUI	1983 Phil Mahre USA	AUT
1975 Franz Klammer AUT	1984 Ingemar Stenmark SWE	1972 Annemarie Moser-Pröll
1976 Franz Klammer AUT	1985 Marc Girardelli LUX	1973 Annemarie Moser-Pröll
1977 Franz Klammer AUT	1986 Joel Gaspoz SUI	1974 Annemarie Moser-Pröll
1978 Franz Klammer AUT	1987 Pirmin Zurbriggen SUI	1975 Annemarie Moser-Pröll
1979 Peter Muller SUI	1988 Alberto Tomba ITA	1976 Rosi Mittermaier FRG
1980 Peter Muller SUI	1989 Ole Christ'n Furuseth NOR	1977 Lise-Marie Morerod SUI
1981 Harti Weirather AUT	1990 Ole Christ'n Furuseth NOR	1978 Hanni Wenzel LIE
1982 Podborski/Muller CAN/SUI	1991 Alberto Tomba ITA	1979 Annemarie Moser-Pröll
1983 Franz Klammer AUT	1992 Alberto Tomba ITA	1980 Hanni Wenzel LIE
1984 Urs Raber SUI	1993 Kjetil Andre Aamodt NOR	1981 Marie-Therese Nadig SUI
1985 Helmut Hohlfehner AUT	1994 Christian Mayer AUT	1982 Erika Hess SUI
1986 Peter Wirnsberger AUT	1995 Alberto Tomba ITA	1983 Tamara McKinney USA
1987 Pirmin Zurbriggen SUI	1996 Michael von Grünigen SUI	1984 Erika Hess SUI
1988 Pirmin Zurbriggen SUI	1997 Michael von Grünigen SUI	1985 Michela Figini SUI
1989 Marc Girardelli LUX	1998 Hermann Maier AUT	1986 Maria Walliser SUI
1990 Helmut Hohlfehner AUT	1999 Michael von Grünigen SUI	1987 Maria Walliser SUI
1991 Franz Heinzer SUI	2000 Hermann Maier AUT	1988 Michela Figini SUI
1992 Franz Heinzer SUI		1989 Vreni Schneider SUI
1993 Franz Heinzer SUI	**MEN'S SLALOM**	1990 Petra Kronberger AUT
1994 Marc Girardelli LUX	1967 Jean-Claude Killy FRA	1991 Petra Kronberger AUT
1995 Luc Alphand FRA	1968 Domeng Giovanoli SUI	1992 Petra Kronberger AUT
1996 Luc Alphand FRA	1969 Augert/Matt/Penz/Russel	1993 Anita Wachter AUT
1997 Luc Alphand FRA	1970 Russel/Penz both FRA	1994 Vreni Schneider SUI
1998 Andreas Schifferer AUT	1971 Jean-Noel Augert FRA	1995 Vreni Schneider SUI
1999 Lasse Kjus NOR	1972 Jean-Noel Augert FRA	1996 Katja Seizinger GER
2000 Hermann Maier AUT	1973 Gustavo Thoeni ITA	1997 Pernilla Wiberg SWE

446

SKIING

1998 Katja Seizinger GER	1970 Michelle Jacot FRA	1990 Vreni Schneider SUI
1999 Alex Meissnitzer AUT	Francoise Macchi FRA	1991 Petra Kronberger AUT
2000 Renate Götschl AUT	1971 Annemarie Moser-Pröll	1992 Vreni Schneider SUI
	1972 Annemarie Moser-Pröll	1993 Vreni Schneider SUI
WOMEN'S DOWNHILL	1973 Monica Kaserer AUT	1994 Vreni Schneider SUI
1967 Marielle Goitschel FRA	1974 Hani Wenzel LIE	1995 Vreni Schneider SUI
1968 Isabelle Mir FRA &	1975 Annemarie Moser-Pröll	1996 Elfi Eder AUT
Olga Pall AUT	1976 Lise-Marie Morerod SWE	1997 Pernilla Wiberg SWE
1969 Wiltrud Drexel AUT	1977 Lise-Marie Morerod SWE	1998 Ylva Nowén SWE
1970 Isabelle Mir FRA	1978 Lise-Marie Morerod SWE	1999 Sabine Egger AUT
1971 Annemarie Moser-Pröll	1979 Christa Kinshoffer FRG	2000 Michael Dorfmeister AUT
1972 Annemarie Moser-Pröll	1980 Hanni Wenzel LIE	
1973 Annemarie Moser-Pröll	1981 Tamara McKinney USA	
1974 Annemarie Moser-Pröll	1982 Irene Epple FRG	
1975 Annemarie Moser-Pröll	1983 Tamara McKinney USA	
1976 Brigitte H-Totschnig AUT	1984 Erika Hess SUI	
1977 Brigitte H-Totschnig AUT	1985 Michela Figini SUI &	
1978 Annemarie Moser-Pröll	Marina Kiehl FRG	
1979 Annemarie Moser-Pröll	1986 Vreni Schneider SUI	
1980 Marie-Therese Nadig SUI	1987 Maria Walliser SUI &	
1981 Marie-Therese Nadig SUI	Vreni Schneider SUI	
1982 C Gros-Gaudenier FRA	1988 Mateja Svet YUG	
1983 Doris De Agostini SUI	1989 Vreni Schneider SUI	
1984 Maria Walliser SUI	1990 Anita Wachter AUT	
1985 Michela Figini SUI	1991 Vreni Schneider SUI	
1986 Maria Walliser SUI	1992 Carole Merle FRA	
1987 Michela Figini SUI	1993 Carole Merle FRA	
1988 Michela Figini SUI	1994 Anita Wachter AUT	
1989 Michela Figini SUI	1995 Vreni Schneider SUI	
1990 K Gütensohn-Knopl FRG	1996 Martina Ertl GER	
1991 Chantal Bournissen SUI	1997 Deborah Compagnoni ITA	
1992 Katja Seizinger GER	1998 Martina Ertl GER	
1993 Katja Seizinger GER	1999 Alex Meissnitzer AUT	
1994 Katja Seizinger GER	2000 Michaela Dorfmeister AUT	
1995 Picabo Street USA		
1996 Picabo Street USA	**WOMEN'S SLALOM**	
1997 Renate Götschl AUT	1967 Marielle Goitschel FRA &	
1998 Katja Seizinger GER	Annie Famose FRA	
1999 Renate Götschl AUT	1968 Marielle Goitschel FRA	
2000 Regina Haeusl GER	1969 Gertrud Gabl AUT	
	1970 Ingrid Laforgue FRA	
WOMEN'S SUPER G	1971 Britt Laforgue FRA &	
1986 Marina Kiehl FRG	Betsy Clifford CAN	
1987 Maria Walliser SUI	1972 Britt Laforgue FRA	
1988 Michela Figini SUI	1973 Patricia Emonet FRA	
1989 Carole Merle FRA	1974 Christa Zechmeister FRG	
1990 Carole Merle FRA	1975 Lise-Marie Morerod SWE	
1991 Carole Merle FRA	1976 Rosi Mittermaier GER	
1992 Carole Merle FRA	1977 Lise-Marie Morerod SWE	
1993 Carole Merle FRA	1978 Hanni Wenzel LIE	
1994 Katja Seizinger GER	1979 Regina Sackl AUT	
1995 Katja Seizinger GER	1980 Perrine Pelen FRA	
1996 Katja Seizinger GER	1981 Erika Hess SUI	
1997 Hilde Gerg GER	1982 Erika Hess SUI	
1998 Katja Seizinger GER	1983 Erika Hess SUI	
1999 Alex Meissnitzer AUT	1984 Tamara McKinney USA	
2000 Renate Götschl AUT	1985 Erika Hess SUI	
	1986 Roswitha Steiner AUT	
WOMEN'S GIANT SLALOM	1987 C Schmidhauser SUI	
1967 Nancy Greene USA	1988 Roswitha Steiner AUT	
1968 Nancy Greene USA	1989 Vreni Schneider SUI	
1969 Marilyn Cochran USA		

SNOOKER

WORLD CHAMPIONS

The World Championship took place up to 1952 when a disagreement caused the professional players to organise their own match-play tournament which ended in 1957. The World Championship was not staged again until 1964 when it was revived on a challenge basis. In 1969 it adopted the knockout format.

All winners British unless otherwise stated

Year	Winner	Score	Runner-up
1927	**Joe Davis**	20-11	Tom Dennis
1928	**Joe Davis**	16-13	Fred Lawrence
1929	**Joe Davis**	19-14	Tom Dennis
1930	**Joe Davis**	25-12	Tom Dennis
1931	**Joe Davis**	25-21	Tom Dennis
1932	**Joe Davis**	30-19	Clark McConachy NZL
1933	**Joe Davis**	25-18	Willie Smith
1934	**Joe Davis**	25-23	Tom Newman
1935	**Joe Davis**	25-20	Willie Smith
1936	**Joe Davis**	34-27	Horace Lindrum AUS
1937	**Joe Davis**	32-29	Horace Lindrum AUS
1938	**Joe Davis**	37-24	Sidney Smith
1939	**Joe Davis**	43-30	Sidney Smith
1940	**Joe Davis**	37-36	Fred Davis
1946	**Joe Davis**	78-67	Horace Lindrum AUS
1947	**W Donaldson**	82-63	Fred Davis
1948	**Fred Davis**	84-61	Walter Donaldson
1949	**Fred Davis**	80-65	Walter Donaldson
1950	**W Donaldson**	51-46	Fred Davis
1951	**Fred Davis**	58-39	Walter Donaldson
1952	**Horace Lindrum AUS**	94-49	Clark McConachy NZL

Professional Match-Play Championship

Year	Winner	Score	Runner-up
1952	**Fred Davis**	38-35	Walter Donaldson
1953	**Fred Davis**	37-34	Walter Donaldson
1954	**Fred Davis**	39-21	Walter Donaldson
1955	**Fred Davis**	37-34	John Pulman
1956	**Fred Davis**	38-35	John Pulman
1957	**John Pulman**	39-34	Jackie Rea

Challenge Matches

Year	Winner	Score	Runner-up
1964	**John Pulman**	19-16	Fred Davis
1964	**John Pulman**	40-33	Rex Williams
1965	**John Pulman**	37-36	Fred Davis
1965	**John Pulman**	25-22	Rex Williams
1965	**John Pulman**	39-12	F van Rensburg RSA
1966	**John Pulman**	5-2	Fred Davis
1968	**John Pulman**	39-34	Eddie Charlton AUS

Knock-out

Year	Winner	Score	Runner-up
1969	**John Spencer**	37-34	Gary Owen
1970	**Ray Reardon**	37-33	John Pulman
1971*	**John Spencer**	37-29	Warren Simpson AUS
1972	**Alex Higgins**	37-32	John Spencer
1973	**Ray Reardon**	38-32	Eddie Charlton AUS
1974	**Ray Reardon**	22-12	Graham Miles
1975	**Ray Reardon**	31-30	Eddie Charlton AUS
1976	**Ray Reardon**	27-16	Alex Higgins
1977	**John Spencer**	25-21	Cliff Thorburn CAN
1978	**Ray Reardon**	25-18	Perrie Mans RSA
1979	**Terry Griffiths**	24-16	Dennis Taylor
1980	**Cliff Thorburn CAN**	18-16	Alex Higgins
1981	**Steve Davis**	18-12	Doug Mountjoy
1982	**Alex Higgins**	18-15	Ray Reardon
1983	**Steve Davis**	18-6	Cliff Thorburn CAN
1984	**Steve Davis**	18-16	Jimmy White
1985	**Dennis Taylor**	18-17	Steve Davis
1986	**Joe Johnson**	18-12	Steve Davis
1987	**Steve Davis**	18-14	Joe Johnson
1988	**Steve Davis**	18-11	Terry Griffiths
1989	**Steve Davis**	18-3	John Parrott
1990	**Stephen Hendry**	18-12	Jimmy White
1991	**John Parrott**	18-11	Jimmy White
1992	**Stephen Hendry**	18-14	Jimmy White
1993	**Stephen Hendry**	18-5	Jimmy White
1994	**Stephen Hendry**	18-17	Jimmy White
1995	**Stephen Hendry**	18-9	Nigel Bond
1996	**Stephen Hendry**	18-12	Peter Ebdon
1997	**Ken Doherty**	18-12	Stephen Hendry
1998	**John Higgins**	18-12	Ken Doherty
1999	**Stephen Hendry**	18-11	Mark Williams
2000	**Mark Williams**	18-16	Matthew Stevens

* Played November 1970

SQUASH

WORLD AMATEUR CHAMPIONSHIP

1967	**Geoff Hunt** AUS
1969	**Geoff Hunt** AUS
1971	**Geoff Hunt** AUS
1973	**Cameron Nancarrow** AUS
1976	**Kevin Shawcross** AUS
1977	**Maqsood Ahmed** PAK
1979	**Jahangir Khan** PAK
1981	**Steve Bowditch** AUS
1983	**Jahangir Khan** PAK
1985	**Jahangir Khan** PAK

The World Amateur was gradually replaced by the World Open as Squash became more professional

WORLD OPEN
Men

1976	**Geoff Hunt** AUS
1977	**Geoff Hunt** AUS
1979	**Geoff Hunt** AUS
1980	**Geoff Hunt** AUS
1981	**Jahangir Khan** PAK
1982	**Jahangir Khan** PAK
1983	**Jahangir Khan** PAK
1984	**Jahangir Khan** PAK
1985	**Jahangir Khan** PAK
1986	**Ross Norman** NZL
1987	**Jansher Khan** PAK
1988	**Jahangir Khan** PAK
1989	**Jansher Khan** PAK
1990	**Jansher Khan** PAK
1991	**Rodney Martin** AUS
1992	**Jansher Khan** PAK
1993	**Jansher Khan** PAK
1994	**Jansher Khan** PAK
1995	**Jansher Khan** PAK
1996	**Jansher Khan** PAK
1997	**Rodney Eyles** AUS
1998	**Jonathon Power** CAN
1999	**Peter Nicol** GBR

BRITISH OPEN
Men

1930	**Don Butcher** GBR
1931	**Don Butcher** GBR
1932	**Abdelfattah Amr Bey** EGY
1933	**Abdelfattah Amr Bey** EGY
1934	**Abdelfattah Amr Bey** EGY
1935	**Abdelfattah Amr Bey** EGY
1936	**Abdelfattah Amr Bey** EGY
1937	**Abdelfattah Amr Bey** EGY
1938	**James Dear** GBR
1946	**Mahmoud Karim** EGY
1947	**Mahmoud Karim** EGY
1948	**Mahmoud Karim** EGY
1949	**Mahmoud Karim** EGY
1950	**Hashim Khan** PAK
1951	**Hashim Khan** PAK
1952	**Hashim Khan** PAK
1953	**Hashim Khan** PAK
1954	**Hashim Khan** PAK
1955	**Hashim Khan** PAK
1956	**Roshan Khan** PAK
1957	**Hashim Khan** PAK
1958	**Azam Khan** PAK
1959	**Azam Khan** PAK
1960	**Azam Khan** PAK
1961	**Azam Khan** PAK
1962	**Mohibullah Khan** PAK
1963	**Abdel. Abou Taleb** EGY
1964	**Abdelfattah Abou Taleb**
1965	**Abdelfattah Abou Taleb**
1966	**Abdelfattah Abou Taleb**
1967	**Jonah Barrington** GBR
1968	**Jonah Barrington** GBR
1969	**Geoff Hunt** AUS
1970	**Jonah Barrington** GBR
1971	**Jonah Barrington** GBR
1972	**Jonah Barrington** GBR
1973	**Jonah Barrington** GBR
1974	**Geoff Hunt** AUS
1975	**Qamar Zaman** PAK
1976	**Geoff Hunt** AUS
1977	**Geoff Hunt** AUS
1978	**Geoff Hunt** AUS
1979	**Geoff Hunt** AUS
1980	**Geoff Hunt** AUS
1981	**Geoff Hunt** AUS
1982	**Jahangir Khan** PAK
1983	**Jahangir Khan** PAK
1984	**Jahangir Khan** PAK
1985	**Jahangir Khan** PAK
1986	**Jahangir Khan** PAK
1987	**Jahangir Khan** PAK
1988	**Jahangir Khan** PAK
1989	**Jahangir Khan** PAK
1990	**Jahangir Khan** PAK
1991	**Jahangir Khan** PAK
1992	**Jansher Khan** PAK
1993	**Jansher Khan** PAK
1994	**Jansher Khan** PAK
1995	**Jansher Khan** PAK
1996	**Jansher Khan** PAK
1997	**Jansher Khan** PAK
1998	**Peter Nicol** GBR
1999	**Jonathon Power** CAN
2000	**David Evans** WAL

SQUASH

WORLD OPEN

Women

1976	Heather McKay	AUS
1979	Heather McKay	AUS
1981	Rhonda Thorne	AUS
1983	Vicki Cardwell	AUS
1985	Susan Devoy	NZL
1987	Susan Devoy	NZL
1989	Martine Le Moignan	GBR
1990	Susan Devoy	NZL
1991	Susan Devoy	NZL
1992	Susan Devoy	NZL
1993	Michelle Martin	AUS
1994	Michelle Martin	AUS
1995	Michelle Martin	AUS
1996	Sarah Fitz-Gerald	AUS
1997	Sarah Fitz-Gerald	AUS
1998	Sarah Fitz-Gerald	AUS
1999	Cassie Campion	GBR
2000	Carol Owens	AUS

BRITISH OPEN

Women

1922	Joyce Cave	GBR
1922	Sylvia Huntsman	GBR
1923	Nancy Cave	GBR
1924	Joyce Cave	GBR
1925	Cecily Fenwick	GBR
1926	Cecily Fenwick	GBR
1928	Joyce Cave	GBR
1929	Nancy Cave	GBR
1930	Nancy Cave	GBR
1931	Cecily Fenwick	GBR
1932	Susan Noel	GBR
1933	Susan Noel	GBR
1934	Susan Noel	GBR
1934	Margot Lumb	GBR
1935	Margot Lumb	GBR
1936	Margot Lumb	GBR
1937	Margot Lumb	GBR
1938	Margot Lumb	GBR
1939	Margot Lumb	GBR
1947	Joan Curry	GBR
1948	Joan Curry	GBR
1949	Joan Curry	GBR
1950	Janet Morgan	GBR
1951	Janet Morgan	GBR
1952	Janet Morgan	GBR
1953	Janet Morgan	GBR
1954	Janet Morgan	GBR
1955	Janet Morgan	GBR
1956	Janet Morgan	GBR
1957	Janet Morgan	GBR
1958	Janet Morgan	GBR
1959	Janet Morgan	GBR
1960	Sheila Macintosh	GBR
1961	Fran Marshall	GBR
1962	Heather Blundell	AUS
1963	Heather Blundell	AUS
1964	Heather Blundell	AUS
1965	Heather Blundell	AUS
1966	Heather McKay	AUS
1967	Heather McKay	AUS
1968	Heather McKay	AUS
1969	Heather McKay	AUS
1970	Heather McKay	AUS
1971	Heather McKay	AUS
1972	Heather McKay	AUS
1973	Heather McKay	AUS
1974	Heather McKay	AUS
1975	Heather McKay	AUS
1976	Heather McKay	AUS
1977	Heather McKay	AUS
1978	Susan Newman	AUS
1979	Barbara Wall	AUS
1980	Vicki Hoffman	AUS
1981	Vicki Hoffman	AUS
1982	Vicki Cardwell	AUS
1983	Vicki Cardwell	AUS
1984	Susan Devoy	NZL
1985	Susan Devoy	NZL
1986	Susan Devoy	NZL
1987	Susan Devoy	NZL
1988	Susan Devoy	NZL
1989	Susan Devoy	NZL
1990	Susan Devoy	NZL
1991	Lisa Opie	GBR
1992	Susan Devoy	NZL
1993	Michelle Martin	AUS
1994	Michelle Martin	AUS
1995	Michelle Martin	AUS
1996	Michelle Martin	AUS
1997	Michelle Martin	AUS
1998	Michelle Martin	AUS
1999	Leilani Joyce	NZL
2000	Leilani Joyce	NZL

SPEED SKATING

SHORT TRACK WORLD CHAMPIONS

Year Venue	Men	Women
1976 Champaign	**Alan Rattray** USA	**Celeste Chlapaty** USA
1977 Grenoble	**Gaetan Boucher** CAN	**Brenda Webster** CAN
1978 Solihull	**James Lynch** AUS	**Sarah Doctor** USA
1979 Quebec	**Hiroshi Toda** JPN	**Sylvie Daigle** CAN
1980 Milan	**Gaetan Boucher** CAN	**Miyoshi Kato** JPN
1981 Meudon	**Benoit Baril** CAN	**Miyoshi Kato** JPN
1982 Moncton	**Guy Daignault** CAN	**Maryse Perreault** CAN
1983 Tokyo	**Louis Grenier** CAN	**Sylvie Daigle** CAN
1984 Peterborough	**Guy Daignault** CAN	**Mariko Kinoshita** JPN
1985 Amsterdam	**Toshinobu Kawai** JPN	**Eiko Shishii** JPN
1986 Chamonix	**Tatsuyoshi Ishihara** JPN	**Bonnie Blair** USA
1987 Montreal	**Toshinobu Kawai** JPN/**Michel Daignault** CAN	**Eiko Shishii** JPN
1988 St Louis	**Peter van de Velde** NED	**Sylvie Daigle** CAN
1989 Solihull	**Michel Daignault** CAN	**Sylvie Daigle** CAN
1990 Amsterdam	**Lee Joon-Ho** KOR	**Sylvie Daigle** CAN
1991 Sydney	**Wilf O'Reilly** GBR	**Nathalie Lambert** CAN
1992 Denver	**Kim Ki-Hoon** KOR	**Kim So-Hee** KOR
1993 Beijing	**Marc Gagnon** CAN	**Nathalie Lambert** CAN
1994 Guildford	**Marc Gagnon** CAN	**Nathalie Lambert** CAN
1995 Gjøvik	**Chae Ji-hoon** KOR	**Chun Lee-Kyung** KOR
1996 The Hague	**Marc Gagnon** CAN	**Chun Lee-Kyung** KOR
1997 Nagano	**Kim Dong-sung** KOR	**Chun Lee-Kyung** KOR/**Yang Yang** CHN
1998 Vienna	**Marc Gagnon** CAN	**Yang A Yang** CHN
1999 Sofia	**Li Jiajun** CHN	**Yang A Yang** CHN
2000 Sheffield	**Rioung Min** KOR	**Yang A Yang** CHN

BRITISH CHAMPIONS
Abbreviations: ALD=Aldwych, ALT=Altrincham, MOH=Mohawks, NOT=Nottingham

Year Venue	Men	Women
1981 Streatham	not held	**Lisa Harrold** NOT
1982 Birmingham	**Gary Rudd** ALD	**Lisa Harrold** NOT
1983 Nottingham	**Wilf O'Reilly** MOH/**Gary Rudd** ALD	**Caron New** MOH
1984 Peterborough	**Wilf O'Reilly** MOH	**Amanda Worth** NOT
1985 Richmond	**Wilf O'Reilly** MOH	**Nicola Bell** NOT
1986 Peterborough	**Wilf O'Reilly** MOH	**Nicola Bell** NOT
1987 Solihull	**Wilf O'Reilly** MOH	**Amanda Worth** NOT
1988 Richmond	**Wilf O'Reilly** MOH	**Caron New** MOH
1989 Richmond	**Wilf O'Reilly** MOH	**Alyson Birch** ALT
1990 Humberside	**Staurt Horsepool** NOT	**Alyson Birch** ALT
1991 Richmond	**Wilf O'Reilly** MOH	**Debbie Palmer** ALD
1992 Humberside	**Matthew Jasper** NOT	**Debbie Palmer** ALD
1993 Humberside	**Nicky Gooch** ALD	**Debbie Palmer** ALD
1994 Humberside	**Nicky Gooch** ALD	**Debbie Palmer** ALD
1995 Guildford	**Matthew Jasper** NOT	**Debbie Palmer** ALD
1996 Guildford	**Nicky Gooch** ALD	**Debbie Palmer** ALD
1997 Guildford	**Nicky Gooch** ALD	**Debbie Palmer** ALD
1998 Guildford	**Nicky Gooch** ALD	**Debbie Palmer** ALD

WORLD CHAMPIONS

Men

50m Freestyle
1986 Tom Jager USA
1991 Tom Jager USA
1994 Alexander Popov RUS
1998 Bill Pilczuk USA

100m Freestyle
1973 Jim Montgomery USA
1975 Andrew Coan USA
1978 David McCagg USA
1982 Jorg Woithe GDR
1986 Matt Biondi USA
1991 Matt Biondi USA
1994 Alexander Popov RUS
1998 Alexander Popov RUS

200m Freestyle
1973 Jim Montgomery USA
1975 Tim Shaw USA
1978 William Forrester USA
1982 Michael Gross FRG
1986 Michael Gross FRG
1991 Giorgio Lamberti ITA
1994 Antti Kasvio FIN
1998 Michael Klim AUS

400m Freestyle
1973 Rick DeMont USA
1975 Tim Shaw USA
1978 Vladimir Salnikov URS
1982 Vladimir Salnikov URS
1986 Rainer Henkel FRG
1991 Jörg Hoffmann GER
1994 Kieren Perkins AUS
1998 Ian Thorpe AUS

1500m Freestyle
1973 Steve Holland AUS
1975 Tim Shaw USA
1978 Vladimir Salnikov URS
1982 Vladimir Salnikov URS
1986 Rainer Henkel FRG
1991 Jörg Hoffmann GER
1994 Kieren Perkins AUS
1998 Grant Hackett AUS

100m Backstroke
1973 Roland Matthes GDR
1975 Roland Matthes GDR
1978 Robert Jackson USA
1982 Dirk Richter GDR
1986 Igor Polyanski URS
1991 Jeff Rouse USA
1994 Martin Lopez-Zubero ESP
1998 Lenny Krayzelburg USA

200m Backstroke
1973 Roland Matthes GDR
1975 Zoltan Verraszto HUN
1978 Jesse Vassallo USA
1982 Rick Carey USA
1986 Igor Polyanski URS
1991 Martin Zubero ESP
1994 Vladimir Selkov RUS
1998 Lenny Krayzelburg USA

100m Breaststroke
1973 John Hencken USA
1975 David Wilkie GBR
1978 Walter Kusch GDR
1982 Steve Lundquist USA
1986 Victor Davis CAN
1991 Norbert Rosza HUN
1994 Norbert Rosza HUN
1998 Fred Deburghgraeve BEL

200m Breaststroke
1973 David Wilkie GBR
1975 David Wilkie GBR
1978 Nick Nevid USA
1982 Victor Davis CAN
1986 Josef Szabó HUN
1991 Mike Barrowman USA
1994 Norbert Rosza HUN
1998 Kurt Grote USA

100m Butterfly
1973 Bruce Robertson CAN
1975 Greg Jagenburg USA
1978 Joe Bottom USA
1982 Matt Gribble USA
1986 Pablo Morales USA
1991 Anthony Nesty SUR
1994 Rafal Szukala POL
1998 Michael Klim AUS

200m Butterfly
1973 Robin Backhaus USA
1975 William Forrester USA
1978 Mike Bruner USA
1982 Michael Gross FRG
1986 Michael Gross FRG
1991 Melvin Stewart USA
1994 Denis Pankratov RUS
1998 Denis Silantiev RUS

200m Individual Medley
1973 Gunnar Larsson SWE
1975 András Hargitay HUN
1978 Graham Smith CAN
1982 Alexsei Sidorenko URS
1986 Tamás Darnyi HUN
1991 Tamás Darnyi HUN
1994 Jani Sievinen FIN
1998 Marcel Wouda NED

400m Individual Medley
1973 András Hargitay HUN
1975 András Hargitay HUN
1978 Jesse Vassallo USA
1982 Ricardo Prado BRA
1986 Tamás Darnyi HUN
1991 Tamás Darnyi HUN
1994 Tom Dolan USA
1998 Tom Dolan USA

4x100m Freestyle Relay
1973 United States
1975 United States
1978 United States
1982 United States
1986 United States
1991 United States
1994 United States
1998 United States

4x200m Freestyle Relay
1973 United States
1975 West Germany
1978 United States
1982 United States
1986 East Germany
1991 Germany
1994 Sweden
1998 Australia

4x100m Medley Relay
1973 United States
1975 United States
1978 United States
1982 United States
1986 United States
1991 United States
1994 United States
1998 Australia

1m Springboard
1991 Edwin Jongejans NED
1994 Evan Stewart ZIM
1998 Zhuocheng Yu CHN

3m Springboard
1973 Phil Boggs USA
1975 Phil Boggs USA
1978 Phil Boggs USA
1982 Greg Louganis USA
1986 Greg Louganis USA
1991 Kent Ferguson USA
1994 Zhuocheng Yu CHN
1998 Dmitri Sautin RUS

10m Platform
1973 Klaus Dibiasi ITA
1975 Klaus Dibiasi ITA
1978 Greg Louganis USA
1982 Greg Louganis USA
1986 Greg Louganis USA
1991 Sun Shuwei CHN
1994 Dmitri Sautin RUS
1998 Dmitri Sautin RUS

3m Springboard Synchro
1998 Xu/Yu CHN

Platform Synchro
1998 Shuwei Sn/Liang Tian CHN

SWIMMING

Water Polo
1973 Hungary
1975 Soviet Union
1978 Italy
1982 Soviet Union
1986 Yugoslavia
1991 Yugoslavia
1994 Italy
1998 Spain

Women

50m Freestyle
1986 Tamara Costache ROM
1991 Zuang Yong CHN
1994 Jingyi Le CHN
1998 Amy Van Dyken USA

100m Freestyle
1973 Kornelia Ender GDR
1975 Kornelia Ender GDR
1978 Barbara Krause GDR
1982 Birgit Meineke GDR
1986 Kristin Otto GDR
1991 Nicole Haislett USA
1994 Jingyi Le CHN
1998 Jenny Thompson USA

200m Freestyle
1973 Keena Rothhammer USA
1975 Shirley Babashoff USA
1978 Cynthia Woodhead USA
1982 A Verstappen NED
1986 Heike Friedrich GDR
1991 Hayley Lewis AUS
1994 F van Almsick GER
1998 Claudia Poll CRC

400m Freestyle
1973 Heather Greenwood USA
1975 Shirley Babashoff USA
1978 Tracey Wickham AUS
1982 Carmela Schmidt GDR
1986 Heike Friedrich GDR
1991 Janet Evans USA
1994 Aihua Yang CHN
1998 Yan Chen CHN

800m Freestyle
1973 Novella Calligaris ITA
1975 Jenny Tunrall AUS
1978 Tracey Wickham AUS
1982 Kim Lineham USA
1986 Astrid Strauss GDR
1991 Janet Evans USA
1994 Janet Evans USA
1998 Brooke Bennett USA

100m Backstroke
1973 Ulrike Richter GDR
1975 Ulrike Richter GDR
1978 Linda Jezek USA
1982 Kristin Otto GDR
1986 Betsy Mitchell USA
1991 Krisztina Egerszegi HUN
1994 Cihong He CHN
1998 Lea Maurer USA

200m Backstroke
1973 Melissa Belote USA
1975 Birgit Treiber GDR
1978 Linda Jezek USA
1982 Cornelia Sirch GDR
1986 Cornelia Sirch GDR
1991 Krisztina Egerszegi HUN
1994 Cihong He CHN
1998 Roxanna Maracineanu FRA

100m Breaststroke
1973 Renate Vogel GDR
1975 Hannelore Anke GDR
1978 Yulia Bogdanova URS
1982 Ute Geweniger GDR
1986 Sylvia Gerasch GDR
1991 Linley Frame AUS
1994 Samantha Riley AUS
1998 Kristy Kowal USA

200m Breaststroke
1973 Renate Vogel GDR
1975 Hannelore Anke GDR
1978 Lina Kachushite URS
1982 Svetlana Varganova URS
1986 Silke Horner GDR
1991 Yelena Volkova URS
1994 Samantha Riley AUS
1998 Agnes Kovacs HUN

100m Butterfly
1973 Kornelia Ender GDR
1975 Kornelia Ender GDR
1978 M Pennington USA
1982 Mary Meagher USA
1986 Kornelia Gressler GDR
1991 Qian Hong CHN
1994 Limin Liu CHN
1998 Jenny Thompson USA

200m Butterfly
1973 Rosemarie Kother GDR
1975 Rosemarie Kother GDR
1978 Tracy Caulkins USA
1982 Ines Geissler GDR
1986 Mary Meagher USA
1991 Summer Sanders USA
1994 Limin Liu CHN
1998 Susan O'Neill AUS

200m Individual Medley
1973 Angela Hubner GDR
1975 Kathy Heddy USA
1978 Tracy Caulkins USA
1982 Petra Schneider GDR
1986 Kristin Otto GDR
1991 Lin Li CHN
1994 Lu Bin CHN
1998 Yanyan Wu CHN

400m Individual Medley
1973 Gudrun Wegner GDR
1975 Ulrike Tauber GDR
1978 Tracy Caulkins USA
1982 Petra Schneider GDR
1986 Kathleen Nord GDR
1991 Lin Li CHN
1994 Guohong Dai CHN
1998 Yan Chen CHN

4x100m Freestyle Relay
1973 & 75 East Germany
1978 United States
1982 East Germany
1986 East Germany
1991 United States
1994 China
1998 United States

4x200m Freestyle Relay
1986 East Germany
1991 Germany
1994 China
1998 Germany

4x100m Medley Relay
1973 & 75 East Germany
1978 United States
1982 East Germany
1986 East Germany
1991 United States
1994 China
1998 United States

1m Springboard
1991 Gao Min CHN
1994 Lixia Chen CHN
1998 Irina Lashko RUS

3m Springboard
1973 Christine Kohler GDR
1975 Irina Kalinina URS
1978 Irina Kalinina URS
1982 Megan Neyer USA
1986 Gao Min CHN
1991 Gao Min CHN
1994 Shuping Tan CHN
1998 Yulia Pakhalina RUS

10m Platform Diving
1973 Ulrike Knape SWE
1975 Janet Ely USA
1978 Irina Kalinina URS
1982 Wendy Wyland USA
1986 Lin Chen CHN
1991 Fu Mingxia CHN
1994 Fu Mingxia CHN
1998 Olena Zhupyna UKR

3m Springboard Synchro
1998 Lashko/Pakhalina RUS

10m Platfrom Synchro
1998 Zhupyna/Serbina UKR

SWIMMING

Synchronised Swimming

Solo
1973 **Teresa Anderson** USA
1975 **Gail Buzonas** USA
1978 **Helen Vandenburg** CAN
1982 **Tracie Ruiz** USA
1986 **Carolyn Waldo** CAN
1991 **Sylvie Frechette** CAN
1994 **Becky Dyroen Lance** USA
1998 **Olga Sedakova** RUS

Duet
1973 **Anderson/Johnson** USA
1975 **Curren/Norrish** USA
1978 **Calkins/Vandenburg** CAN
1982 **Hambrook/Kryczka** CAN
1986 **Cameron/Waldo** CAN
1991 **Josephson/Josephson**USA
1994 **Lancer/Sidduth** USA
1998 **Sedakova/Brousnikina** RUS

Team
1973 **United States**
1975 **United States**
1978 **United States**
1982 **Canada**
1986 **Canada**
1991 **United States**
1994 **United States**
1998 **Russia**

Water Polo
1986 **Australia**
1991 **Netherlands**
1994 **Hungary**
1998 **Italy**

TABLE TENNIS

WORLD CHAMPIONS

Men's Singles
1926	Roland Jacobi HUN
1928	Zoltan Mechlovits HUN
1929	Fred Perry GBR
1930	Viktor Barna HUN
1931	Miklos Szabados HUN
1932	Viktor Barna HUN
1933	Viktor Barna HUN
1934	Viktor Barna HUN
1935	Viktor Barna HUN
1936	Stanislav Kolar TCH
1937	Richard Bergmann AUT
1938	Bohumil Vana TCH
1939	Richard Bergmann AUT
1947	Bohumil Vana TCH
1948	Richard Bergmann GBR
1949	Johnny Leach GBR
1950	Richard Bergmann GBR
1951	Johnny Leach GBR
1952	Hiroji Satoh JPN
1953	Ferenc Sidó HUN
1954	Ichiro Ogimura JPN
1955	Toshiaki Tanaka JPN
1956	Ichiro Ogimura JPN
1957	Toshiaki Tanaka JPN
1959	Jung Kuo-tuan CHN
1961	Chuang Tse-tung CHN
1963	Chuang Tse-tung CHN
1965	Chuang Tse-tung CHN
1967	Nobuhiko Hasegawa JPN
1969	Shigeo Ito JPN
1971	Stellan Bengtsson SWE
1973	Hsi En-ting CHN
1975	Istvan Jonyer HUN
1977	Mitsuru Kohno JPN
1979	Seiji Ono JPN
1981	Guo Yuehua CHN
1983	Guo Yuehua CHN
1985	Jiang Jialiang CHN
1987	Jiang Jialiang CHN
1989	Jan-Ove Waldner SWE
1991	Jorgen Persson SWE
1993	J-Philippe Gatien FRA
1995	Kong Linghui CHN
1997	Jan-Ove Waldner SWE
1999	Liu Goulilang CHN

Men's Team 1975 on
1975	China
1977	China
1979	Hungary
1981	China
1983	China
1985	China
1987	China
1989	Sweden
1991	Sweden
1993	Sweden
1995	China

1997	China
1999	China

Men's Doubles 1969 on
1969	Alser/Johansson SWE
1971	Jonyer/Klampar HUN
1973	Bengtsson/Johansson SWE
1975	Gergely/Jonyer HUN
1977	Li/Liang CHN
1979	Surbek/Stipancic YUG
1981	Cai/Li CHN
1983	Surbeh/Kalinic YUG
1985	Applegren/Carlsson SWE
1987	Chen/Wei CHN
1989	Rosskopf/Fetzner FRG
1991	Karlsson/von Scheele SWE
1993	Wang/Lu CHN
1995	Wang/Lu CHN
1997	Kong/Liu CHN
1999	Kong/Liu CHN

Women's Singles
1926	Maria Mednyanszky HUN
1928	Maria Mednyanszky
1929	Maria Mednyanszky
1930	Maria Mednyanszky
1931	Maria Mednyanszky
1932	Anna Sipos HUN
1933	Anna Sipos HUN
1934	Marie Kettnerova TCH
1935	Marie Kettnerova TCH
1936	Ruth Aarons USA
1937	Ruth Aarons USA and Trudi Pritzi AUT*
1938	Trudi Pritzi AUT
1939	Vlasta Depetrisova TCH
1947	Gizi Farkas HUN
1948	Gizi Farkas HUN
1949	Gizi Farkas HUN
1950	Angelica Rozeanu ROM
1951	Angelica Rozeanu ROM
1952	Angelica Rozeanu ROM
1953	Angelica Rozeanu ROM
1954	Angelica Rozeanu ROM
1955	Angelica Rozeanu ROM
1956	Tomi Okawa JPN
1957	Fujie Eguchi JPN
1959	Kimiyo Matsuzaki JPN
1961	Chiu Chunghui CHN
1963	Kimiyo Matsuzaki JPN
1965	Naoko Fukazu JPN
1967	Sachiko Morisawa JPN
1969	Toshiko Kowada JPN
1971	Lin Huiching CHN
1973	Hu Yu-lan CHN
1975	Pak Yung-sun KOR
1977	Pak Yung-sun KOR
1979	Ge Xinai CHN
1981	Tong Ling CHN
1983	Cao Yanhua CHN

1985	Cao Yanhua CHN
1987	He Zhili CHN
1989	Qiao Hong CHN
1991	Deng Yaping CHN
1993	Hyun Jung Hwa CHN
1995	Deng Yaping CHN
1997	Deng Yaping CHN
1999	Wang Nan CHN

Finalists. Title was left vacant

Women's Team 1977 on
1977	China
1979	China
1981	China
1983	China
1985	China
1987	China
1989	China
1991	Korea
1993	China
1995	China
1997	China
1999	China

Women's Doubles 1969 on
1969	Grinberg/Rudnova URS
1971	Cheng/Lin CHN
1973	Alexandru ROM/Hamada JPN
1975	Alexandru/Takashima
1977	Pak/Yang CHN
1979	Zhang/Zhang CHN
1981	Zhang/Cao CHN
1983	Shen/Dai CHN
1985	Dai/Geng CHN
1987	Yang/Hyun KOR
1989	Qiao/Deng CHN
1991	Chen/Gao CHN
1993	Liu/Qiao CHN
1995	Deng/Lui CHN
1997	Deng/Yang CHN
1999	Wang/Li CHN

Mixed Doubles 1965 on
1965	Kimura/Seki JPN
1967	Hasegawa/Yamanaka JPN
1969	Hasegawa/Kono JPN
1971	Chang/Lin CHN
1973	Liang/Li CHN
1975	Gomozkov/Ferdman URS
1977	Secretin/Bergeret FRA
1979	Liang/Ge CHN
1981	Xie/Huang CHN
1983	Guo/Ni CHN
1985	Cai/Cao CHN
1987	Hui/Geng CHN
1989	Yoo/Hyun KOR
1991	Wang/Liu CHN
1993	Wang/Liu CHN
1995	Wang/Liu CHN
1997	Liu/Wang CHN
1999	Ma/Zhang CHN

TENNIS

WIMBLEDON

Men's Singles

1877 Spencer Gore GBR
1878 Frank Hadow GBR
1879 Rev John Hartley GBR
1880 Rev John Hartley GBR
1881 William Renshaw GBR
1882 William Renshaw GBR
1883 William Renshaw GBR
1884 William Renshaw GBR
1885 William Renshaw GBR
1886 William Renshaw GBR
1887 Herbert Lawford GBR
1888 Ernest Renshaw GBR
1889 William Renshaw GBR
1890 Willoughby Hamilton GBR
1891 Wilfred Baddeley GBR
1892 Wilfred Baddeley GBR
1893 Joshua Pim GBR
1894 Joshua Pim GBR
1895 Wilfred Baddeley GBR
1896 Harold Mahoney GBR
1897 Reginald Doherty GBR
1898 Reginald Doherty GBR
1899 Reginald Doherty GBR
1900 Reginald Doherty GBR
1901 Arthur Gore GBR
1902 Lawrence Doherty GBR
1903 Lawrence Doherty GBR
1904 Lawrence Doherty GBR
1905 Lawrence Doherty GBR
1906 Lawrence Doherty GBR
1907 Norman Brookes AUS
1908 Arthur Gore GBR
1909 Arthur Gore GBR
1910 Tony Wilding NZL
1911 Tony Wilding NZL
1912 Tony Wilding NZL
1913 Tony Wilding NZL
1914 Norman Brookes AUS
1919 Gerald Patterson AUS
1920 Bill Tilden USA
1921 Bill Tilden USA
1922 Gerald Patterson AUS
1923 William Johnston USA
1924 Jean Borotra FRA
1925 Rene Lacoste FRA
1926 Jean Borotra FRA
1927 Henri Cochet FRA
1928 Rene Lacoste FRA
1929 Henri Cochet FRA
1930 Bill Tilden USA
1931 Sidney Wood USA
1932 Ellsworth Vines USA
1933 Jack Crawford AUS
1934 Fred Perry GBR
1935 Fred Perry GBR
1936 Fred Perry GBR
1937 Donald Budge USA
1938 Donald Budge USA

1939 Bobby Riggs USA
1946 Yvon Petra FRA
1947 Jack Kramer USA
1948 Bob Falkenburg USA
1949 Ted Schroeder USA
1950 Budge Patty USA
1951 Dick Savitt USA
1952 Frank Sedgman AUS
1953 Vic Seixas USA
1954 Jaroslav Drobny EGY
1955 Tony Trabert USA
1956 Lew Hoad AUS
1957 Lew Hoad AUS
1958 Ashley Cooper AUS
1959 Alex Olmedo USA
1960 Neale Fraser AUS
1961 Rod Laver AUS
1962 Rod Laver AUS
1963 Chuck McKinley USA
1964 Roy Emerson AUS
1965 Roy Emerson AUS
1966 Manuel Santana ESP
1967 John Newcombe AUS
1968 Rod Laver AUS
1969 Rod Laver AUS
1970 John Newcombe AUS
1971 John Newcombe AUS
1972 Stan Smith USA
1973 Jan Kodes TCH
1974 Jimmy Connors USA
1975 Arthur Ashe USA
1976 Bjorn Borg SWE
1977 Bjorn Borg SWE
1978 Bjorn Borg SWE
1979 Bjorn Borg SWE
1980 Bjorn Borg SWE
1981 John McEnroe USA
1982 Jimmy Connors USA
1983 John McEnroe USA
1984 John McEnroe USA
1985 Boris Becker FRG
1986 Boris Becker FRG
1987 Pat Cash AUS
1988 Stefan Edberg SWE
1989 Boris Becker FRG
1990 Stefan Edberg SWE
1991 Michael Stich GER
1992 Andre Agassi USA
1993 Pete Sampras USA
1994 Pete Sampras USA
1995 Pete Sampras USA
1996 Richard Krajicek NED
1997 Pete Sampras USA
1998 Pete Sampras USA
1999 Pete Sampras USA
2000 Pete Sampras USA

Women's Singles

1884 Maud Watson GBR
1885 Maud Watson GBR
1886 Blanche Bingley GBR
1887 Lottie Dod GBR
1888 Lottie Dod GBR
1889 Blanche Hillyard GBR
1890 Helene Rice GBR
1891 Lottie Dod GBR
1892 Lottie Dod GBR
1893 Lottie Dod GBR
1894 Blanche Hillyard GBR
1895 Charlotte Cooper GBR
1896 Charlotte Cooper GBR
1897 Blanche Hillyard GBR
1898 Charlotte Cooper GBR
1899 Blanche Hillyard GBR
1900 Blanche Hillyard GBR
1901 Charlotte Sterry GBR
1902 Muriel Robb GBR
1903 Dorothea Douglass GBR
1904 Dorothea Douglass GBR
1905 May Sutton USA
1906 Dorothea Douglass GBR
1907 May Sutton USA
1908 Charlotte Sterry GBR
1909 Dora Boothby GBR
1910 D Lambert Chambers GBR
1911 D Lambert Chambers GBR
1912 Ethel Larcombe GBR
1913 D Lambert Chambers GBR
1914 D Lambert Chambers GBR
1919 Suzanne Lenglen FRA
1920 Suzanne Lenglen FRA
1921 Suzanne Lenglen FRA
1922 Suzanne Lenglen FRA
1923 Suzanne Lenglen FRA
1924 Kathleen McKane GBR
1925 Suzanne Lenglen FRA
1926 Kathleen Godfree GBR
1927 Helen Wills USA
1928 Helen Wills USA
1929 Helen Wills USA
1930 Helen Wills Moody USA
1931 Cilly Aussem GER
1932 Helen Wills Moody USA
1933 Helen Wills Moody USA
1934 Dorothy Round GBR
1935 Helen Wills Moody USA
1936 Helen Jacobs USA
1937 Dorothy Round GBR
1938 Helen Wills Moody USA
1939 Alice Marble USA
1946 Pauline Betz USA
1947 Margaret Osborne USA
1948 Louise Brough USA
1949 Louise Brough USA
1950 Louise Brough USA
1951 Doris Hart USA
1952 Maureen Connolly USA

TENNIS

1953 **Maureen Connolly** USA
1954 **Maureen Connolly** USA
1955 **Louise Brough** USA
1956 **Shirley Fry** USA
1957 **Althea Gibson** USA
1958 **Althea Gibson** USA
1959 **Maria Bueno** BRA
1960 **Maria Bueno** BRA
1961 **Angela Mortimer** GBR
1962 **Karen Susman** USA
1963 **Margaret Smith** AUS
1964 **Maria Bueno** BRA
1965 **Margaret Smith** AUS
1966 **Billie Jean King** USA
1967 **Billie Jean King** USA
1968 **Billie Jean King** USA
1969 **Ann Jones** GBR
1970 **Margaret Court** AUS
1971 **Evonne Goolagong** AUS
1972 **Billie Jean King** USA
1973 **Billie Jean King** USA
1974 **Chris Evert** USA
1975 **Billy Jean King** USA
1976 **Chris Evert** USA
1977 **Virginia Wade** GBR
1978 **Martina Navratilova** TCH
1979 **Martina Navratilova** TCH
1980 **Evonne Cawley** AUS
1981 **Chris Evert Lloyd** USA
1982 **Martina Navratilova** USA
1983 **Martina Navratilova** USA
1984 **Martina Navratilova** USA
1985 **Martina Navratilova** USA
1986 **Martina Navratilova** USA
1987 **Martina Navratilova** USA
1988 **Steffi Graf** FRG
1989 **Steffi Graf** FRG
1990 **Martina Navratilova** USA
1991 **Steffi Graf** GER
1992 **Steffi Graf** GER
1993 **Steffi Graf** GER
1994 **Conchita Martinez** ESP
1995 **Steffi Graf** GER
1996 **Steffi Graf** GER
1997 **Martina Hingis** SUI
1998 **Jana Novotna** CZE
1999 **Lindsay Davenport** USA
2000 **Venus Williams** USA

Men's Doubles

1879 **Erskine/Lawford** GBR
1880 **E & W Renshaw** GBR
1881 **E & W Renshaw** GBR
1882 **Hartley/Richardson** GBR
1883 **Grinstead/WElldon** GBR
1884 **E & W Renshaw** GBR
1885 **E & W Renshaw** GBR
1886 **E & W Renshaw** GBR
1887 **Bowes-Lyon/Wilberforce** GBR
1888 **E & W Renshaw** GBR
1889 **E & W Renshaw** GBR
1890 **Pim/Stoker** GBR
1891 **H & W Baddeley** GBR
1892 **Barlow/Lewis** GBR
1893 **Pim/Stoker** GBR
1894 **H & W Baddeley** GBR
1895 **H & W Baddeley** GBR
1896 **H & W Baddeley** GBR
1897 **L & R Doherty** GBR
1898 **L & R Doherty** GBR
1899 **L & R Doherty** GBR
1900 **L & R Doherty** GBR
1901 **L & R Doherty** GBR
1902 **Risely/Smith** GBR
1903 **L & R Doherty** GBR
1904 **L & R Doherty** GBR
1905 **L & R Doherty** GBR
1906 **Risely/Smith** GBR
1907 **Brookes/Wilding** AUS/NZL
1908 **Ritchie/Wilding** GBR/NZL
1909 **Gore/Barrett** GBR
1910 **Ritchie/Wilding** GBR/NZL
1911 **Decugis/Gobert** GBR
1912 **Dixon/Barrett** GBR
1913 **Dixon/Barrett** GBR
1914 **Brookes/Wilding** AUS/NZL
1919 **Wood/Thomas** AUS
1920 **Garland/Williams** USA
1921 **Lycett/Woosnam** GBR
1922 **Anderson/Lycett** AUS/GBR
1923 **Godfree/Lycett** GBR
1924 **Hunter/Richards** USA
1925 **Borotra/Lacoste** FRA
1926 **Brugnon/Cochet** FRA
1927 **Hunter/Tilden** USA
1928 **Brugnon/Cochet** FRA
1929 **Allison/Van Ryn** USA
1930 **Allison/Van Ryn** USA
1931 **Lott/Van Ryn** USA
1932 **Borotra/Brugnon** FRA
1933 **Borotra/Brugnon** FRA
1934 **Lott/Stoefen** USA
1935 **Crawford/Quist** AUS
1936 **Hughes/Tuckey** GBR
1937 **Budge/Mako** USA
1938 **Budge/Mako** USA
1939 **Cooke/Riggs** USA
1946 **Brown/Kramer** USA
1947 **Falkenburg/Kramer** USA
1948 **Bromwich/Sedgman** AUS
1949 **Gonzales/Parker** USA
1950 **Bromwich/Quist** AUS
1951 **McGregor/Sedgman** AUS
1952 **McGregor/Sedgman** AUS
1953 **Hoad/Rosewall** AUS
1954 **Hartwig/Rose** AUS
1955 **Hartwig/Hoad** AUS
1956 **Hoad/Rosewall** AUS
1957 **Mulloy/Patty** USA
1958 **Davidson/Schmidt** SWE
1959 **Emerson/Fraser** AUS
1960 **Osuna/Ralston** USA
1961 **Emerson/Fraser** AUS
1962 **Hewitt/Stolle** AUS
1963 **Osuna/Palafox** MEX
1964 **Hewitt/Stolle** AUS
1965 **Newcombe/Roche** AUS
1966 **Fletcher/Newcombe** AUS
1967 **Hewitt/McMillan** SAF
1968 **Newcombe/Roche** AUS
1969 **Newcombe/Roche** AUS
1970 **Newcombe/Roche** AUS
1971 **Emerson/Laver** AUS
1972 **Hewitt/McMillan** SAF
1973 **Connors/Nastase** USA
1974 **Newcombe/Roche** AUS
1975 **Gerulaitis/Mayer** USA
1976 **Gotffried/Ramirez** USA/MEX
1977 **Case/Masters** AUS
1978 **Hewitt /McMillan** SAF
1979 **Fleming/McEnroe** USA
1980 **McNamara/McNamee** AUS
1981 **Fleming/McEnroe** USA
1982 **McNamara/McNamee** AUS
1983 **Fleming/McEnroe** USA
1984 **Fleming/McEnroe** USA
1985 **Gunthardt/Taróczy** SUI/HUN
1986 **Nystrom/Wilander** SWE
1987 **Flach/Seguso** USA
1988 **Flach/Seguso** USA
1989 **Fitzgerald/Jarryd** AUS/SWE
1990 **Leach/Pugh** USA
1991 **Fitzgerald/Jarryd** AUS/SWE
1992 **McEnroe/Stich** AUS/SWE
1993 **Woodbridge/Woodforde** AUS
1994 **Woodbridge/Woodforde**
1995 **Woodbridge/Woodforde**
1996 **Woodbridge/Woodforde**
1997 **Woodbridge/Woodforde**
1998 **Eltingh/Haarhuis** NED
1999 **Bhupati/Paes** IND
2000 **Woodbridge/Woodforde**

Women's Doubles

1913 **McNair/Boothby** GBR
1914 **Morton/Ryan** USA
1919 **Lenglen/Ryan** FRA/USA
1920 **Lenglen/Ryan** FRA/USA
1921 **Lenglen/Ryan** FRA/USA
1922 **Lenglen/Ryan** FRA/USA
1923 **Lenglen/Ryan** FRA/USA
1924 **Wightman/Wills** USA
1925 **Lenglen/Ryan** FRA/USA
1926 **Browne/Ryan** USA
1927 **Wills/Ryan** USA

1928 Saunders/Watson GBR
1929 Mitchell/Watson GBR
1930 Wills Moody/Ryan USA
1931 Barron/Mudford GBR
1932 Metaxa/Sigart FRA/BEL
1933 Mathieu/Ryan FRA/USA
1934 Mathieu/Ryan FRA/USA
1935 James/Stammers GBR
1936 James/Stammers GBR
1937 Mathieu/Yorke FRA/GBR
1938 Fabyan/Marble USA
1939 Fabyan/Marble USA
1946 Brough/Osborne USA
1947 Hart/Todd USA
1948 Brough/Du Pont USA
1949 Brough/Du Pont USA
1950 Brough/Du Pont USA
1951 Fry/Hart USA
1952 Fry/Hart USA
1953 Fry/Hart USA
1954 Brough/Du Pont USA
1955 Mortimer/Shilcock GBR
1956 Buxton/Gibson GBR/USA
1957 Gibson/Hard USA
1958 Bueno/Gibson BRA/USA
1959 Arth/Hard USA
1960 Bueno/Hard BRA/USA
1961 Hantze/Moffitt USA
1962 Moffit/Susman USA
1963 Bueno/Hard BRA/USA
1964 Smith/Turner AUS
1965 Bueno/Moffitt BRA/USA
1966 Bueno/Richey BRA/USA
1967 Casals/King USA
1968 Casals/King USA
1969 Court/Tegart AUS
1970 Casals/King USA
1971 Casals/King USA
1972 King/Stove USA/NED
1973 Casals/King USA
1974 Goolagong/Michel AUS/USA
1975 Kiyomura/S'matsu JPN
1976 Evert/Navratilova USA/TCH
1977 Cawley/Russell AUS/USA
1978 Reid/Turnbull USA
1979 King/Navratilova USA/TCH
1980 Jordan/Smith USA
1981 Navratilova/Shriver USA
1982 Navratilova/Shriver USA
1983 Navratilova/Shriver USA
1984 Navratilova/Shriver USA
1985 Jordan/Smylie USA/AUS
1986 Navratilova/Shriver USA
1987 K-Kilsch/Sukova FRG/TCH
1988 Graf/Sabatini FRG/ARG
1989 Novotna/Sukova TCH
1990 Novotna/Sukova TCH
1991 Savchenko/Zvereva URS
1992 Fernandez/Zvereva

USA/BLR
1993 Fernandez/Zvereva
1994 Fernandez/Zvereva
1995 Novotna/Sanchez Vicario CZE/ESP
1996 Hingis /Sukova SUI/CZE
1997 Fernandez /Zvereva USA/BLR
1998 Hingis/Novotna SUI/CZE
1999 Davenport/Morariu USA
2000 V Williams/S Williams USA

Mixed Doubles *since 1950*
1950 Sturgess/Brough RSA/USA
1951 Sedgman/Hart AUS/USA
1952 Sedgman/Hart AUS/USA
1953 Seixas/Hart USA
1954 Seixas/Hart USA
1955 Seixas/Hart USA
1956 Seixas/Fry USA
1957 Rose/Hard AUS/USA
1958 Howe/Coghlan AUS
1959 Laver/Hard AUS/USA
1960 Laver/Hard AUS/USA
1961 Stolle/Turner AUS
1962 Fraser/Du Pont AUS/USA
1963 Fletcher/Smith AUS
1964 Stolle/Turner AUS
1965 Fletcher/Smith AUS
1966 Fletcher/Smith AUS
1967 Davidson/King AUS/USA
1968 Fletcher/Court AUS/USA
1969 Stolle/Jones AUS/GBR
1970 Nastase/Casals ROM/USA
1971 Davidson/King AUS/USA
1972 Nastase/Casals ROM/USA
1973 Davidson/King AUS/USA
1975 Riessen/Court USA/AUS
1976 Roche/Durr AUS/FRA
1977 Hewitt/Stevens RSA
1978 McMillan/Stove RSA/NED
1979 Hewitt/Stevens RSA
1980 Austin/Austin USA
1981 McMillan/Stove RSA/NED
1982 Curren/Smith RSA/USA
1983 Lloyd/Turnbull GBR/AUS
1984 Lloyd/Turnbull GBR/AUS
1985 McNamee/N'lova AUS/USA
1986 Flach/Jordan USA
1987 Bates/Durie GBR
1988 Stewart/Garrison USA
1989 Pugh/Novotna USA/CZE
1990 Leach/Garrison USA
1991 Fitzgerald/Smylie AUS
1992 Suk/Savchenko CZE/LAT
1993 Woodforde/Navratilova AUS/USA
1994 Woodbridge/Sukova AUS/CZE
1995 Stark/Navratilova USA
1996 Suk/Sukova CZE

1997 Suk/Sukova CZE
1998 Mirnyi/Williams BLR/USA
1999 Paes/Raymond IND/USA
2000 Johnson/Po USA

US OPEN
Men's Singles
(First played 1881)
1946 Jack Kramer USA
1947 Jack Kramer USA
1948 Ricardo Gonzales USA
1949 Ricardo Gonzales USA
1950 Arthur Larsen USA
1951 Frank Sedgman USA
1952 Frank Sedgman USA
1953 Tony Trabert USA
1954 Vic Seixas USA
1955 Tony Trabert USA
1956 Ken Rosewall AUS
1957 Malcolm Anderson AUS
1958 Ashley Cooper AUS
1959 Neale Fraser AUS
1960 Neale Fraser AUS
1961 Roy Emerson AUS
1962 Rod Laver AUS
1963 Raphael Osuna MEX
1964 Roy Emerson AUS
1965 Manuel Santana ESP
1966 Fred Stolle AUS
1967 John Newcombe AUS
1968 Arthur Ashe USA
Open Arthur Ashe USA
1969 Stan Smith USA
Open Rod Laver AUS
1970 Ken Rosewall AUS
1971 Stan Smith USA
1972 Ilie Nastase ROM
1973 John Newcombe AUS
1974 Jimmy Connors USA
1975 Manuel Orantes ESP
1976 Jimmy Connors USA
1977 Guillermo Vilas ARG
1978 Jimmy Connors USA
1979 John McEnroe USA
1980 John McEnroe USA
1981 John McEnroe USA
1982 Jimmy Connors USA
1983 Jimmy Connors USA
1984 John McEnroe USA
1985 Ivan Lendl TCH
1986 Ivan Lendl TCH
1987 Ivan Lendl TCH
1988 Mats Wilander SWE
1989 Boris Becker FRG
1990 Pete Sampras USA
1991 Stefan Edberg SWE
1992 Stefan Edberg SWE
1993 Pete Sampras USA
1994 Andre Agassi USA
1995 Pete Sampras USA

TENNIS

1996	Pete Sampras USA	1997	Martina Hingis SUI	1983	Yannick Noah FRA
1997	Pat Rafter AUS	1998	Lindsay Davenport USA	1984	Ivan Lendl TCH
1998	Pat Rafter AUS	1999	Serena Williams USA	1985	Mats Wilander SWE
1999	Andre Agassi USA	2000	Venus Williams USA	1986	Ivan Lendl TCH
2000	Marat Safin RUS			1987	Ivan Lendl TCH

Women's Singles
(First played 1887)

FRENCH OPEN

Men's Singles

1946	Pauline Betz USA	1925	Rene Lacoste FRA	1988	Mats Wilander SWE
1947	Louise Brough USA	1926	Henri Cochet FRA	1989	Michael Chang USA
1948	Margaret Du Pont USA	1927	Rene Lacoste FRA	1990	Andres Gomez ECU
1949	Margaret Du Pont USA	1928	Henri Cochet FRA	1991	Jim Courier USA
1950	Margaret Du Pont USA	1929	Rene Lacoste FRA	1992	Jim Courier USA
1951	Maureen Connolly USA	1930	Henri Cochet FRA	1993	Sergi Bruguera ESP
1952	Maureen Connolly USA	1931	Jean Borotra FRA	1994	Sergi Bruguera ESP
1953	Maureen Connolly USA	1932	Henri Cochet FRA	1995	Thomas Muster AUT
1954	Doris Hart USA	1933	Jack Crawford AUS	1996	Yevgeny Kafelnikov RUS
1955	Doris Hart USA	1934	Gottfried Von Cramm GER	1997	Gustavo Kuerten BRA
1956	Shirley Fry USA	1935	Fred Perry GBR	1998	Carlos Moya ESP
1957	Althea Gibson USA	1936	Gottfried Von Cramm	1999	Andre Agassi USA
1958	Althea Gibson USA	1937	Henner Henkel GER	2000	Gustavo Kuerten BRA
1959	Maria Bueno BRA	1938	Donald Budge USA		
1960	Darlene Hard USA	1939	Donald McNeill USA		**Women's Singles**
1961	Darlene Hard USA	1946	Marcel Bernard FRA	1925	Suzanne Lenglen FRA
1962	Margaret Smith AUS	1947	Jozsef Asboth HUN	1926	Suzanne Lenglen FRA
1963	Maria Bueno BRA	1948	Frank Parker USA	1927	Kea Bouman NED
1964	Maria Bueno BRA	1949	Frank Parker USA	1928	Helen Wills Moody FRA
1965	Margaret Smith AUS	1950	Budge Patty USA	1929	Helen Wills Moody FRA
1966	Maria Bueno BRA	1951	Jaroslav Drobny EGY	1930	Helen Wills Moody USA
1967	Billie Jean King USA	1952	Jaroslav Drobny EGY	1931	Cilly Aussem GER
1968	Margaret Court AUS	1953	Ken Rosewall AUS	1932	Helen Moody USA
Open	Virginia Wade GBR	1954	Tony Trabert USA	1933	Margaret Scriven GBR
1969	Margaret Court AUS	1955	Tony Trabert USA	1934	Margaret Scriven GBR
Open	Margaret Court AUS	1956	Lew Hoad AUS	1935	Hilde Sperling GER
1970	Margaret Court AUS	1957	Sven Davidson SWE	1936	Hilde Sperling GER
1971	Billie Jean King USA	1958	Mervyn Rose AUS	1937	Hilde Sperling GER
1972	Billie Jean King USA	1959	Nicola Pietrangeli ITA	1938	Simone Mathieu FRA
1973	Margaret Court AUS	1960	Nicola Pietrangeli ITA	1939	Simone Mathieu FRA
1974	Billie Jean King USA	1961	Manuel Santana ESP	1946	Margaret Osborne USA
1975	Chris Evert USA	1962	Rod Laver AUS	1947	Pat Todd USA
1976	Chris Evert USA	1963	Roy Emerson AUS	1948	Nelly Landry FRA
1977	Chris Evert USA	1964	Manuel Santana ESP	1949	Margaret Du Pont USA
1978	Chris Evert USA	1965	Fred Stolle AUS	1950	Doris Hart USA
1979	Tracy Austin USA	1966	Tony Roche AUS	1951	Shirley Fry USA
1980	Chris Evert Lloyd USA	1967	Roy Emerson AUS	1952	Doris Hart USA
1981	Tracy Austin USA	1968	Ken Rosewall AUS	1953	Maureen Connolly USA
1982	Chris Evert Lloyd USA	1969	Rod Laver AUS	1954	Maureen Connolly USA
1983	Martina Navratilova USA	1970	Jan Kodes TCH	1955	Angela Mortimer GBR
1983	Martina Navratilova USA	1971	Jan Kodes TCH	1956	Althea Gibson USA
1985	Hanna Mandlikova TCH	1972	Andres Gimeno ESP	1957	Shirley Bloomer GBR
1986	Martina Navratilova USA	1973	Ilie Nastase ROM	1958	Zsuzsi Kormoczy HUN
1987	Martina Navratilova USA	1974	Bjorn Borg SWE	1959	Christine Truman GBR
1988	Steffi Graf FRG	1975	Bjorn Borg SWE	1960	Darlene Hard USA
1989	Steffi Graf FRG	1976	Adriano Panatta ITA	1961	Ann Haydon GBR
1990	Gabriela Sabatini ARG	1977	Guillermo Vilas ARG	1962	Margaret Smith AUS
1991	Monica Seles YUG	1978	Bjorn Borg SWE	1963	Lesley Turner AUS
1992	Monica Seles YUG	1979	Bjorn Borg SWE	1964	Margaret Smith AUS
1993	Steffi Graf GER	1980	Bjorn Borg SWE	1965	Lesley Turner AUS
1994	Aranxta Sanchez ESP	1981	Bjorn Borg SWE	1966	Ann Jones GBR
1995	Steffi Graf GER	1982	Mats Wilander SWE	1967	Françoise Durr FRA
1996	Steffi Graf GER			1968	Nancy Richey USA
				1969	Margaret Court AUS
				1970	Margaret Court AUS
				1971	Evonne Goolagong AUS

TENNIS

1972 Billie Jean King USA	1974 Jimmy Connors USA	1977* Evonne Cawley AUS
1973 Margaret Court AUS	1975 John Newcombe AUS	1978* Christine O'Neill AUS
1974 Chris Evert USA	1976 Mark Edmondson AUS	1979* Barbara Jordan USA
1975 Chris Evert USA	1977 Roscoe Tanner USA	1980* Hana Mandlikova TCH
1976 Sue Barker GBR	1977* Vitas Gerulaitis USA	1981* Martina Navratilova USA
1977 Mimi Jausovec YUG	1978* Guillermo Vilas ARG	1982* Chris Evert Lloyd USA
1978 Virginia Ruzici ROM	1979* Guillermo Vilas ARG	1983* Martina Navratilova USA
1979 Chris Evert Lloyd USA	1980* Brian Teacher USA	1984* Chris Evert Lloyd USA
1980 Chris Evert Lloyd USA	1981* Johan Kriek RSA	1985* Martina Navratilova USA
1981 Hana Mandlikova TCH	1982* Johan Kriek RSA	1987 Hana Mandlikova TCH
1982 Martina Navratilova USA	1983* Mats Wilander SWE	1988 Steffi Graf FRG
1983 Chris Evert Lloyd USA	1984* Mats Wilander SWE	1989 Steffi Graf FRG
1984 Martina Navratilova USA	1985* Stefan Edberg SWE	1990 Steffi Graf FRG
1985 Chris Evert Lloyd USA	1987 Stefan Edberg SWE	1991 Monica Seles YUG
1986 Chris Evert Lloyd USA	1988 Mats Wilander SWE	1992 Monica Seles YUG
1987 Steffi Graf FRG	1989 Ivan Lendl TCH	1993 Monica Seles YUG
1988 Steffi Graf FRG	1990 Ivan Lendl TCH	1994 Steffi Graf GER
1989 Arantxa Sanchez V ESP	1991 Boris Becker GER	1995 Mary Pierce FRA
1990 Monica Seles YUG	1992 Jim Courier USA	1996 Monica Seles USA
1991 Monica Seles YUG	1993 Jim Courier USA	1997 Martina Hingis SUI
1992 Monica Seles YUG	1994 Pete Sampras USA	1998 Martina Hingis SUI
1993 Steffi Graf GER	1995 Andre Agassi USA	1999 Martina Hingis SUI
1994 Aranxta Sanchez V ESP	1996 Boris Becker USA	2000 Lindsay Davenport USA
1995 Steffi Graf GER	1997 Pete Sampras USA	*Championships held in December
1996 Steffi Graf GER	1998 Petr Korda CZE	
1997 Iva Majoli CRO	1999 Yevgeny Kafelnikov RUS	
1998 Arantxa Sanchez V ESP	2000 Andre Agassi USA	
1999 Steffi Graf GER		
2000 Mary Pierce FRA		

AUSTRALIAN OPEN

Women's singles

	1946 Nancye Bolton AUS
	1947 Nancye Bolton AUS
	1948 Nancye Bolton AUS

Men's Singles

1946 John Bromwich AUS	1949 Doris Hart USA
1947 Dinny Pails AUS	1950 Louise Brough USA
1948 Adrian Quist AUS	1951 Nancye Bolton AUS
1949 Frank Sedgman AUS	1952 Thelma Long AUS
1950 Frank Sedgman AUS	1953 Maureen Connolly USA
1951 Dick Savitt USA	1954 Thelma Long AUS
1952 Ken McGregor AUS	1955 Beryl Penrose AUS
1953 Ken Rosewall AUS	1956 Mary Carter AUS
1954 Mervyn Rose AUS	1957 Shirley Fry USA
1955 Ken Rosewall AUS	1958 Angela Mortimer GBR
1956 Lew Hoad AUS	1959 Mary Reitano AUS
1957 Ashley Cooper AUS	1960 Margaret Smith AUS
1958 Ashley Cooper AUS	1961 Margaret Smith AUS
1959 Alex Olmedo USA	1962 Margaret Smith AUS
1960 Rod Laver AUS	1963 Margaret Smith AUS
1961 Roy Emerson AUS	1964 Margaret Smith AUS
1962 Rod Laver AUS	1965 Margaret Smith AUS
1963 Roy Emerson AUS	1966 Margaret Smith AUS
1964 Roy Emerson AUS	1967 Nancy Richey USA
1965 Roy Emerson AUS	1968 Billie Jean King USA
1966 Roy Emerson AUS	1969 Margaret Court AUS
1967 Roy Emerson AUS	1970 Margaret Court AUS
1968 Bill Bowrey AUS	1971 Margaret Court AUS
1969 Rod Laver AUS	1972 Virginia Wade GBR
1970 Arthur Ashe USA	1973 Margaret Court AUS
1971 Ken Rosewall AUS	1974 Evonne Goolagong AUS
1972 Ken Rosewall AUS	1975 Evonne Goolagong AUS
1973 John Newcombe AUS	1976 Evonne Cawley AUS
	1977 Kerry Reid AUS

TENNIS

DAVIS CUP

1900	USA 3	British Isles 0
1902	USA 3	British Isles 2
1903	British Isles 4	USA 1
1904	British Isles 5	Belgium 0
1905	British Isles 5	USA 0
1906	British Isles 5	Great Britain 0
1907	Australasia 3	British Isles 2
1908	Australasia 3	USA 2
1909	Australasia 5	USA 0
1911	Australasia 5	USA 0
1912	British Isles 3	Australasia 2
1913	USA 3	British Isles 2
1914	Australasia 3	USA 2
1919	Australasia 4	British Isles 1
1920	USA 5	Australasia 0
1921	USA 5	Japan 0
1922	USA 4	Australasia 1
1923	USA 4	Australasia 1
1924	USA 5	Australasia 0
1925	USA 5	France 0
1926	USA 4	France 1
1927	France 3	USA 2
1928	France 4	USA 1
1929	France 3	USA 2
1930	France 4	USA 1
1931	France 3	Great Britain 2
1932	France 3	USA 2
1933	Great Britain 3	France 2
1934	Great Britain 4	USA 1
1935	Great Britain 5	USA 0
1936	Great Britain 3	France 2
1937	USA 4	Great Britain 1
1938	USA 3	Australia 2
1939	Australia 3	USA 2
1946	USA 5	Australia 0
1947	USA 4	Australia 1
1948	USA 5	Australia 0
1949	USA 4	Australia 1
1950	Australia 4	USA 1
1951	Australia 3	USA 2
1952	Australia 4	USA 1
1953	Australia 3	USA 2
1954	United Staes 3	Australia 2
1955	Australia 5	USA 0
1956	Australia 5	USA 0
1957	Australia 3	USA 2
1958	USA 3	Australia 2
1959	Australia 3	USA 2
1960	Australia 4	Italy 1
1961	Australia 5	Italy 0
1962	Australia 5	Mexico 0
1963	USA 3	Australia 2
1964	Australia 3	USA 2
1965	Australia 4	Spain 1
1966	Australia 4	India 1
1967	Australia 4	Spain 1
1968	USA 4	Australia 1
1969	USA 5	Romania 0
1970	USA 5	West Germany 0
1971	USA 3	Romania 2
1972	USA 3	Romania 2
1973	Australia 5	USA 0
1974	South Africa beat India by walkover	
1975	Sweden 3	Czechoslovakia 2
1976	Italy 4	Chile 1
1977	Australia 3	Italy 1
1978	USA 4	Great Britain 1
1979	USA 5	Italy 0
1980	Czechoslovakia 4	Italy 1
1981	USA 3	Argentina 1
1982	USA 4	France 1
1983	Australia 3	Sweden 2
1984	Sweden 4	USA 1
1985	Sweden 3	West Germany 2
1986	Australia 3	Sweden 2
1987	Sweden 5	India 0
1988	West Germany 4	Sweden 1
1989	West Germany 3	Sweden 2
1990	USA 3	Australia 2
1991	France 3	USA 1
1992	USA 3	Switzerland 1
1993	Germany 4	Australia 1
1994	Sweden 4	Russia 1
1995	USA 3	Russia 2
1996	France 3	Sweden 2
1997	Sweden 5	USA 0
1998	Sweden 4	Italy 1
1999	Australia 3	France 2
2000	Spain 3	Australia 1

KB FED CUP

The Federation Cup began in 1963. In 1995, the Cup became the Fed Cup and adopted a similar format to the Davis Cup

1963　*Queen's, London*
USA 2 Australia 1

1964　*Germantown CC, Philadelphia*
Australia 2 USA 1

1965　*Kooyong Tennis Club, Melbourne*
Australia 2 USA 1

1966　*Press Sporting Club, Turin*
USA 3 Germany 0

1967　*Blau Weiss Club, Berlin*
USA 2 Great Britain 0

1968　*Stade Roland Garros, Paris*
Australia 3 Netherlands 0

1969　*Athens Tennis Club*
USA 2 Australia 1

1970　*Freiburg Tennis Club*
Australia 3 Germany 0

1971　*Perth, Australia*
Australia 3 Great Britain 0

1972　*Ellis Park, Johannesburg*
South Africa 2 Great Britain 1

1973　*Bad Homberg, Germany*
Australia 3 South Africa 0

1974　*Tennis Club of Naples*
Australia 2 USA 1

1975　*Aixoise CC, France*
Czechoslovakia 3 Australia 0

1976　*The Spectrum, Philadelphia*
USA 2 Australia 1

1977　*Devonshire Park, Eastbourne*
USA 2 Australia 1

1978　*Kooyong Stadium, Melbourne*
USA 2 Australia 1

1979　*RSHE de Campo, Madrid*
USA 3 Australia 0

1980　*Rot-Weiss TC, Berlin*
USA 3 Australia 0

1981　*Tamagawa-en RC, Tokyo*
USA 3 Great Britain 0

1982　*Decathlon Club, Santa Clara, CA*
USA 3 West Germany 0

1983　*Albisguetli TC, Zurich*
Czechoslovakia 2 West Germany 1

1984　*Esporte Clube Pinheiros, Sao Paulo*
Czechoslovakia 2 Australia 1

1985　*Nagoya Green TC, Japan*
Czechoslovakia 2 USA 1

1986　*Stvanice Stadium, Prague*
USA 3 Czechoslovakia 0

1987　*Hollyburn CC, Vancouver*
West Germany 2 USA 1

1988　*Flinders Park, Melbourne*
Czechoslovakia 2 Soviet Union 1

1989　*Ariake TC, Tokyo*
USA 3 Spain 0

1990　*Peachtree World of Tennis, Atlanta*
USA 2 Soviet Union 1

1991　*City of Nottingham TC*
Spain 2 USA 1

1992　*Waldstadion, Frankfurt*
Germany 2 Spain 1

1993　*Waldstadion, Frankfurt*
Spain 3 Australia 0

1994　*Waldstadion, Frankfurt*
Spain 3 USA 0

1995　*Club Tenis de Valencia*
Spain 3 USA 2

1996　*Atlantic City Convention Centre*
USA 3 Spain 0

1997　*Brabanthallen, 's-Hertogenbosch*
France 4 Netherlands 1

1998　*Geneva*
Spain 3 Switzerland 2

1999　*Stanford University, California*
USA 4 Russia 1

2000　*Las Vegas*
USA 5 Spain 0

TRIATHLON

TRIATHLON
Men
1989 Mark Allen USA
1990 Greg Welch AUS
1991 Miles Stewart AUS
1992 Simon Lessing GBR
1993 Spencer Smith GBR
1994 Spencer Smith GBR
1995 Simon Lessing GBR
1996 Simon Lessing GBR
1997 Chris McCormack AUS
1998 Simon Lessing GBR
1999 Dimitry Gaag KZK
2000 Olivier Marceau FRA
Women
1989 Erin Baker NZL
1990 Karen Smyers USA
1991 Joanne Ritchie CAN
1992 Michellie Jones AUS
1993 Michellie Jones AUS
1994 Emma Carney AUS
1995 Karen Smyers USA
1996 Jackie Gallagher AUS
1997 Emma Carney AUS
1998 Joanne King AUS
1999 Loretta Harrop AUS
2000 Nicole Hackett AUS

LONG DISTANCE TRIATHLON
Men
1994 Rob Barel NED
1995 Simon Lessing GBR
1996 Greg Welch AUS
1997-98 Luc Van Lierde BEL
1999 Peter Sandvang DEN
2000 Peter Sandvang DEN
Women
1994 Isabelle Mouthon FRA
1995 Jenny Rose NZL
1996 Karen Smyers USA
1997 Ines Estedt GER
1998 Rina Hill AUS
1999 Suzanne Nielsen DEN
2000 Isabelle Mouthon FRA

DUATHLON
Men
From 1993 on
1993 Greg Welch AUS
1994 Norman Stadler GER
1995 Oscar Galindez ARG
1996 Andrew Noble AUS
1997 Jonathon Hall AUS
1998-99 Yann Million FRA
2000 Benny Vansteelant BEL
Women
1993 Carol Montgomery CAN
1994 Irma Heeren NED
1995 Natascha Badman SUI
1996 Jackie Gallagher AUS
1997-98 Irma Heeren NED

VOLLEYBALL

Indoor World Champions

	Men	Women
1949	Soviet Union	-
1952	Soviet Union	Soviet Union
1956	Czechoslovakia	Soviet Union
1960	Soviet Union	Soviet Union
1962	Soviet Union	Japan
1966	Czechoslovakia	Japan
1970	East Germany	Soviet Union
1974	Poland	Japan
1978	Soviet Union	Cuba
1982	Soviet Union	China
1986	USA	China
1990	Italy	Soviet Union
1994	Italy	Cuba
1998	Italy	Cuba

World Cup Winners

	Men	Women
1965	Soviet Union	-
1969	East Germany	-
1973	-	Soviet Union
1977	Soviet Union	Japan
1981	Soviet Union	China
1985	USA	China
1989	Cuba	Cuba
1991	Unified Team	Cuba
1995	Italy	Cuba
1999	Cuba	Russia

Obituary

Betty Archdale (cricketer)   In 1934, Archdale led the first tour to Australia and New Zealand by an England women's cricket team. Following hot on the heels of "Bodyline" the tour was a success and well supported. After the war Archdale settled in Australia becoming an outspoken headmistress and in her later years one of Australia's 100 living treasures. She was one of the first ten women awarded honorary MCC membership. Archdale died aged 92.

Martin Aldridge (footballer)   Aldridge played for five League clubs and was on-loan at non-league Rushden & Diamonds from Blackpool when he was killed in a car crash aged 25.

Major Derek Allhausen (skier and show jumper)   Allhausen competed in the 1948 Winter Olympics as a skier, but it was in the Summer Olympics twenty years later, that he had his finest sporting hour. Allhausen was the captain of the Great Britain three-day event team that won gold in Mexico. He was also member of European championship winning teams in 1957, 1967 and 1969. Allhausen retired in 1970 after a broken leg, but his horse, Laurieston was ridden to individual and team success at the Munich Olympics in 1972 by Richard Meade. Major Allhausen died aged 86.

George Armstrong (footballer)   The much-loved winger made 621 appearances for the Arsenal first team, and was a member of the 1970-71 team which won the Double. Known as Geordie, from his Durham background, he played his first match for Arsenal in 1961 and was with the club for 16 years before moving on to Leicester City. Armstrong finished his playing career at Stockport, then coached in Kuwait, at Aston Villa and Fulham, before coming full cycle, when George Graham signed him to help with the coaching back at Arsenal. As reverse team coach, Armstrong was successful in nurturing young talent, including Ray Parlour, who was one of his protegés. It was while he was overseeing training in November at the club's Hertforshire ground that Armstrong collapsed and died. He was 56.

Bunny Austin (tennis player)   During the heyday of British tennis in the 1930's, Austin and Fred Perry were the star acts. Together they formed the basis of the of the Great Britain team that won the Davis Cup in 1933 and defended it for the three years. Individually Austin reached the final of Wimbledon twice, in 1932 and 1938, losing to Ellsworth Vines and Donald Budge. He appeared in one other Grand Slam final, at Roland Garros in 1937, losing to Henner Henkel of Germany. Austin set a new trend by becoming the first man to wear shorts on Centre Court, but his activities during the war led to him to be banished from the All England Club. When war broke out, Austin went to work with Moral Rearmament in America. He served with the US Army from 1943-45, but on returning to England in 1962, he was refused membership of the All England Club, his application rejected because of unpaid subscriptions. However, it was generally believed that it was due to his work with MRA. At the age of 77 he was finally given membership and as recently as July was involved in a Wimbledon parade of champions. Austin, who remains the last British man to reach the Wimbledon men's singles final, died on his 94th birthday.

Chris Balderstone (cricketer, footballer and umpire)   A successful dual sportsman, Balderstone won two Test caps for England, against the West Indies in 1976, and played League football. In 1975, the all-rounder had been a member of Leicestershire's county championship winning side and in September played for the county during the day, and a league game for Doncaster Rovers in the evening, resuming his innings the next morning and going on to make a century. Balderstone became an umpire after his retirement and stood in two one-day internationals. He died, aged 59.

James Burridge (racehorse owner) Burridge, the breeder of Desert Orchid, died aged 78. Desert Orchid followed the coffin at the funeral.

Phil Carrick (cricketer)   Carrick captained Yorkshire to victory in the 1987 Benson and Hedges Cup and scored 9,994 runs and took more than 1,000 wickets in first-class cricket. Carrick died of leukaemia aged 47.

Lord Colin Cowdrey (cricketer)   Born in India on Christmas Eve 1932, Colin Cowdrey was christened Michael Colin giving him the initials MCC. He began playing for Kent, his only professional county, as a 17-year-old. In four years he had progressed to captain of his county and was selected for the Ashes tour to Australia in 1953-54. In 1957, Cowdrey and Peter May set a Test record for the fourth wicket of 411 against the West Indies, a record that still exists. Two years later Cowdrey captained England for the first time. He captained by example and in 1963 defied a broken wrist to bat against the West Indies and save the game. His time as Kent captain coincided with a successful era for the county. In 1967 Kent won the Gillette Cup and in 1970 the county championship for the first time since 1913. His greatest achievement as England captain was in 1968 when he led his side to victory in the West Indies. Although Cowdrey retired from Tests in 1971, he was persuaded to come out of retirement in 1975, at the age of 42, to face the Australians with Lillee and Thompson at the height of their powers. His Test in that series was his 114th and last. In total, he scored 7,624 Test runs, a record at the time, at an average of 44.06. He retired from first class cricket in 1976, with 42,719 runs and 107 centuries. After his retirement, Cowdrey was President of the MCC as well as ICC chairman. In 1972 he was awarded the CBE, in 1992 a knighthood and in 1996 made Lord Cowdrey of Tonbridge. After a stroke in July, Cowdrey, a gentleman of cricket, died in his sleep aged 67.

Robin Duchesne (sailing administrator) For 14 years, Duchesne was secretary-general of the Royal Yachting Association. He died, aged 63, in April.

Joey Dunlop   (motor cycle racer) Northern Ireland motor cycle racer, killed during a race in Estonia aged 48. *See Motor Cycling section.*

Frankie Durr (jockey and trainer)   Durr twice rode the winner of the 2,000 Guineas and the St Leger, and would have accumulated more than his 2,000 career winners if he had ridden in evening meetings, which he often shunned to spend time with his family. Durr later became a trainer. He died, in January, aged 73.

Benny Fenton (footballer and manager) A forward who spent most of his playing career with Charlton, Fenton, like his brother Ted, later moved into management, his best years coming at Millwall from 1966-74. He died in July, aged 81.

Stan Flashman (football owner)   The self styled "King of the Ticket Touts" was also the chairman of Barnet Football Club. He took over the club in 1985 and led them into the Football League six years later. Flashman died aged 69.

Bernard Gadney (rugby union player) Gadney as the oldest surviving England rugby union international. He won 14 caps at scrum-half between 1932 and 1938, eight of which were as captain. As captain he won the Triple Crown in 1934 and led England's victory over New Zealand in 1936. Gadney died in hospital aged 91.

Peter Keenan (boxer)   The Scottish bantamweight Keenan won British, European and Commonwealth titles, but came up short in his world title bout with South African Vic Toweel in 1952. After retirement Keenan became a promoter and was instrumental in bringing Sonny Liston and Muhammad Ali to Britain. Keenan died in July aged 71.

Chris Lander (journalist)   Lander was a respected cricket writer for the Mirror and the Sun and was Ian Botham's ghost writer, joining the cricketer for his walk from John O'Groats to Lands End. Lander died of cancer aged 59.

Trevor Leggett (judo player and teacher) In the post-war years, almost all the British internationals were coached by Leggett, who became the wellspring of British judo in its formative years. One of the most accomplished exponents of the craft in Britain, Leggett spent many years in Japan, including two years internment during the war. Leggett was also head of the BBC's Japanese service for 24 years, until 1970, and was awarded the Order of the Sacred Treasure by the Japanese government in 1984. Leggett died in August, aged 85.

Cliff Lloyd (footballer and administrator) Lloyd played as a fullback for Fulham, but it was not as a footballer that he put his mark on the game. As secretary of the Professional Footballers' Association, a job which he held for 28 years, Lloyd was a key figure during the association's ground-breaking period. when, with Jimmy Hill as chairman, the PFA won the abolition of the maximum wage, and freedom for players at the end of their contracts. Lloyd dien in January, aged 84.

Willie Maddren (footballer)   Maddren, a stalwart player for Middlesbrough and a former manager at Ayresome Park, died aged 49, after suffering from Motor Neurone Disease for five years. Maddren helped to raise more than £200,000 for research into the illness before his death.

Wilf Mannion (footballer)   Mannion, on more than one occasion voted Middlesbrough's greatest all-time player, was one of many England names whose prime years were taken by World War II. Known as "The Golden Boy" both for his blond hair and his ball skills, Mannion did not make his England debut until he was 28. He eventually played 26 times, scoring 11 goals, including a hat-trick on his debut against Northern Ireland. He also scored in England's first game in the World Cup finals, against Chile in 1950. Throughout his career, he never enjoyed an easy relationship with the Middlesbrough officials, the club preventing him from touring South Africa with England in 1938 and ten years later rejecting his request for a move. Celtic had offered £30,000, a record, but because of the contract signed for him by his parents when he was a minor, he could not leave. He refused to play for five months, but with an ill wife and young child, he had to give in. After leaving

Middlesbrough in 1954 he struggled with a series of menial jobs, eventually granted a testimonial by Middlesbrough in 1983. In 1999, he was voted one of the Football League's greatest 100 players. Mannion died in April aged 81.

John McPhail (footballer) McPhail was a former Celtic captain who scored the winning goal in the 1951 Scottish Cup final. McPhail, who was capped five times by Scotland, died after a short illness aged 76.

Sir Stanley Matthews (football) Matthews was the son of a professional boxer, but chose a different path signing for Stoke City football club, his hometown team, at the age of 14. He won his first England cap in 1934, just two years after turning professional. Matthews would win 57 caps in total, invariably on the right wing, and played in the 1950 and 1954 World Cups. In his domestic career, Matthews played 700 games for just two clubs, Stoke and Blackpool, with whom he won the 1953 FA Cup final at the age of 38. The final became known as 'The Matthews Final', although the man himself gave the credit to teammate Stan Mortensen, who had scored a hat-trick for Blackpool. Matthews rejoined Stoke in 1961 with the club near the foot of the Second Division. Gates rose from 9,000 to 36,000 and the club were promoted the following year. Matthews became the first footballer to be knighted in 1964 and ended his career in 1965 at the age of 50. He was known as "the wizard of dribble". In retirement, he spent a spell as the general manager of Port Vale and during that time - in 1968 - the club were expelled from the Football League for contravening League regulations. Matthews resigned from his position, although the club were later re-instated. Matthews died, aged 85.

James Riddell (skier) Riddell was vice-captain of the Great Britain ski team in the 1936 Winter Olympics. Riddell, who avoided giving a Nazi salute at the games, died aged 90

Trevor Radford (jockey) Radford had not ridden for 46 years when he re-applied for an amateur jockeys' licence in 1999. Radford, whose earlier rides had been as an apprentice at Epsom in 1953, was 64 when the Jockey Club approved his application. In August, in his sixth race since his comeback, his mount Landican Lane fell. Radford got to his feet, but feeling unwell was later rushed to hospital, where he died.

Jeff Rowland (handball) One of the founding members of the British Handball Association and a member of the British team that played in the Olympic qualification tournament in 1972, Rowland died of cancer aged 59.

Helen Tomkinson (skier) Tomkinson competed in the 1936 Winter Olympics and four world championships before the war curtailed heer career. In the post-war years, she managed the British women's ski team at four Olympic Games. Tomkinson died in April, aged 86.

Len Shackleton (footballer) Shackleton was best known for his scoring exploits at Sunderland - 101 goals in 348 games. However, before he played at Roker Park, Shackleton played for Bradford Park Avenue and Newcastle, for whom he scored six goals on his debut in a 13-0 win over Newport County. Shackleton fell out with the Newcastle board and moved to Wearside for £30,000. His autobiography 'Clown Prince of Soccer' included the famous chapter called 'The Average Director's Knowledge of Football', followed by a blank page. Despite his considerable ability, Shackleton was awarded only five England caps. He suffered a heart-attack in August, and died in November aged 78.

Auriol Sinclair (racehorse trainer) Sinclair was one of the first women to own a training licence. Arguably her best horse was Arctic Actress who was favourite for the 1969 Grand National, but was withdrawn after breaking a blood vessel in the Welsh National. Sinclair died aged 81.

Brian Statham (cricketer) Statham was the England new-ball partner of 'Fiery' Fred Trueman and had the magnificent Test record of 252 wickets at an average 24.84 from his 70 matches. A Lancashire stalwart, he took 2,260 wickets in his first-class career which lasted for 18 years. He was a big man but also a true gentleman of cricket and proved the ideal foil for the explosive Trueman, and Frank Tyson before him. One of the 1955 Wisden cricketers of the year, Statham, who had been suffering from leukaemia, died in June just six days short of his 70th birthday.

E W Swanton (journalist/broadcaster) Ernest "Jim" Swanton was a respected author, broadcaster and journalist for the Daily Telegraph. Swanton started his career on the London Evening Standard in 1926. During the war he was held prisoner in Singapore for three years and post-war he was the Telegraph's rugby, cricket and football correspondent, although cricket was always his first love. He also became a renowned BBC broadcaster and wrote more than 20 books. He died, aged 92.

Norman Wainwright (swimming) The youngest of four sons, whose father William managed the local swimming pool in Hanley, Wainwright went on to become one of Britain's best pre-war swimmers. He captured 21 national titles, won two

European and two Commonwealth gold medals and represented his country in three Olympic Games, the last in 1948 when he was 34. Wainwright died in May, aged 85.

Jack Walker (football owner) Walker pumped a huge amount of his personal fortune, made in the steel industry, into Blackburn Rovers. His investment was rewarded with the 1995 Premier League title. Walker died aged 71.

Bob Weighill (rugby administrator) An England international, Weighill went on to become the secretary of the RFU for 12 years until 1986. Weighill died in October, aged 80

Simon Wigg (speedway rider) Wigg, a former long track world champion, retired at the end of the 1998 season and died in November, at the age of 40, after a long illness.

Howard Winstone (boxer) A Commonwealth amateur champion, Winstone was three times frustrated in his bid to become a world professional champion by the Mexican Vincente Saldivar. Winstone eventually won the WBC version of the bantamweight title, but was already past his best. Winstone died in September, aged 61.

Overseas

Gino Bartali (Italy, cyclist) Bartali won three Giros d'Italia - in 1936, 1937 and 1946 and two Tours de France in 1938 and 1948. His 1948 victory helped calm political tensions in Italy and his battles with another great Italian cyclist, Fausto Coppi, made cycling hugely popular in Italy after the war. Bartali died aged 85.

Tertius Bosch (South Africa, cricket) Bosch played his one and only Test match for South Africa in 1992 in Bridgetown, against the West Indies in what was the South African's first Test match since their return from sporting exile. Bosch died after contracting a virus in February aged 33.

Shay Brennan (Ireland, footballer) Brennan, capped 19 times by Ireland, was best known as a member of Manchester United's 1968 European Cup winning team. Brennan died whilst playing golf in June aged 63.

Donald Budge (USA, tennis) Donald Budge was the first tennis player to complete the Grand Slam, winning all the four major tournaments in 1938. Although his elevation to the best player in the world owed something to Fred Perry's decision to turn professional in 1936. Budge was in imperious form in his golden year, losing only one set as he captured the four Grand Slam titles. Budge's father had emigrated to America from Scotland, having played football for Rangers and Budge was brought up with sport being a huge part of family life. However he only took up tennis seriously at 17. Budge, who won six grand slam titles in all, died aged 84.

Mae Faggs Starr (USA, athlete) Faggs Starr competed in three Olympic Games, the highspot coming in 1952 when she was a member of the American 100m relay squad, which won gold. Faggs Starr died in January. She was 67.

Roy Fredericks (Guyana, cricket) Fredericks was a member of the West Indies side that one the first World Cup in 1975, but was best remembered for a 71-ball century against the Lillee-Thompson attack in Australia in 1975-76. He died of cancer aged 58.

Alexander Klimenko (Ukraine, athlete) The 1994 European shot put champion was killed in a drive-by shooting in Kiev in March. He was 29.

Tom Landry (USA, american football) Landry coached the Dallas Cowboys from their inception in 1960, up until 1988. During that time they reached five Super Bowls, winning two. Landry died in February aged 75.

Sandra Schmirler (Canada, curling) Known as Schmirler the curler, Schmirler was the skip of the Canadian team that won the women's curling gold medal at the Nagano Olympics. Schmirler died in March aged 36.

Sandra Scmitt (Austrian, freestyle skier) Schmitt won the dual moguls title at the freestyle world championships in Switzerland in 1999. The 19-year-old died in November, one of 155 people killed in a fire which broke out on a funicular train in Kitzsteinhorn.

Bruno Schutz (Germany, racing trainer) In his training career, Schutz send out 2,207 winners from his stable in Cologne. Schutz, whose son Andreas is currently Germany top trainer, died in June, aged 60.

Karsten Solheim (Norway, golf equipment designer) Solheim invented the Ping putter and gave his name to the women's equivalent of the Ryder Cup which started in 1990. Solheim died aged 88.

Russ Thomas (New Zealand, rugby administrator) Thomas, who managed the All Blacks during the eighties, was instrumental in the organisation of the first rugby union World Cup in 1987. He died in February, aged 73.

Emil Zatopek (Czech Republic, athletics) Zatopek recorded what is still seen as the finest set of distance results ever at the 1952 Olympics in Helsinki. In the space of eight days, Zatopek, born in 1922 in Koprivnice, won the 5,000m, 10,000m and the Marathon. Such a feat has never been repeated before or since. In 1948, Zatopek had won the 10,000m at the London Olympics and took silver in the 5,000m. From 1948 to 1954 he won 38 consecutive 10,000m races and set 18 world records, retiring in 1958. Ten years later, his country Czechoslovakia was invaded by the Soviet Union. Zatopek spoke out against it and had his Communist Party membership withdrawn and was expelled from the army. He later worked for the Ministry of Sport until his retirement in 1982 after which he lived just outside Prague with his wife Dana, who won the 1952 javelin Olympic title. Zatopek died in November aged 78.

2001 Calendar of Events

January

1	Athletics	City of Rome Marathon
1-5	Ice Hockey	World Under-20 Chp *Moscow*
1-3	Darts	PDC World Cps *Purfleet, Surrey*
1	Sailing	The Race *Barcelona*
1-7	Tennis	ATP Tour Event *Adelaide*
1-7	Tennis	Gold Flake Open, ATP *Chennai, India*
1-7	Tennis	Qatar Mobil Open, ATP *Doha*
1-7	Tennis	Hopman Cup *Perth, Australia*
1-7	Tennis	WTA Tour Event *Gold Coast, Australia*
1-7	Tennis	WTA Tour Event *Auckland, New Zealand*
2-6	Cricket	Australia v W Indies 5th Test, *Sydney*
2	Cricket	NZ v Zimbabwe, 1-Day *Taupo*
2	Cricket	S Africa v S Lanka 2nd Test, *Cape Town*
3-7	Golf	WGC-Match Play *Victoria, Australia*
4	Cricket	NZ v Zimbabwe, 1-Day *Wellington*
6	Football	Scottish Cup, 2nd round
6	Football	FA Cup, 3rd round
6-14	Darts	BDO World Chps *Frimley Green, Surrey*
6	Motor Cycling	Indoor Trial World Chp *Sheffield*
6	Rugby Union	Tetley Bitter Cup, s-finals
6-7	Skiing	World Cup, men, GS, SL *Les Arcs, France*
6-7	Skiing	World Cup, women, GS, SL *Maribor, Slovenia*
7	Cricket	NZ v Zimbabwe, 1-Day *Auckland*
7	Cycling	Cyclo-cross World Cup *Zeddam, Netherlands*
8-14	Tennis	Heineken Open, ATP Tour *Auckland*
8-14	Tennis	adidas Int, ATP & WTA *Sydney*

8-14	Tennis	WTA Tour Events *Hobart & Canberra*
9	Cricket	S Africa v S Lanka, 1-Day *Paarl*
9	Skiing	World Cup, men, GS *Adelboden, Switzerland*
10	Football	Worthington Cup, s-f, 1st leg
11	Cricket	Australia v W I, 1-day *Melbourne*
11	Cricket	S Africa v S Lanka, 1-day *Cape Town*
11-14	Golf	Tucson Open *Arizona, USA*
11-14	Golf	Mercedes Championship *Hawaii*
11	Motor Cycling	Indoor Trial World Chp *Dubai*
11-14	Table Tennis	Kenshoen Grand Finals *Yokohama*
12-14	Rugby Union	Heineken Cup, 5th round
12	Skiing	World Cup, women, DH *Haus Im Ennstal, Austria*
12-14	Spd Skating	European L Track Chps *Baselga di Pine, Italy*
13	Cricket	W I v Zimbabwe, 1-day *Brisbane*
13-14	Cycling	British Cyclo-cross Chps *Sutton Park, Birmingham*
13	Motor Cycling	Indoor Trial World Chp *Koblenz, Germany*
13	Skiing	World Cup, men, DH *Wengen, Switzerland*
13	Skiing	World Cup, women, SG *Haus Im Ennstal, Austria*
13-21	Snooker	Nations Cup *The Hexagon, Reading*
13-14	Swimming	World Cup 6 *Imperia, Italy*
14	Cricket	Australia v W I, 1-day *Brisbane*
14	Cricket	S Africa v S Lanka, 1-day *Bloemfontein*
14	Horse Racing	Ladbroke Hurdle *Leopardstown*
14	Skiing	World Cup, men, SL, C *Wengen, Switzerland*
14	Skiing	World Cup, women, SL, C *Flachau, Austria*
14-21	Skiing	World Freestyle Chps *Whistler, Canada*

15-28	Tennis	Australian Open *Melbourne*
16-21	Bobsleigh	European Chps, men *Königssee, Germany*
17	Cricket	Australia v W I, 1-day *Sydney*
17	Cricket	S Africa v S Lanka, 1-day *Johannesburg*
17-18	Swimming	World Cup 7, *Sheffield*
18-21	Golf	Sony Open in Hawaii
18-21	Golf	South African PGA *Houghton GC, Jo'burg*
19-21	Hockey	European Nations Cup *Ind, A Div, men, Lucerne*
19-21	Hockey	European Nations Cup *Ind, B Div, men, Vienna*
19-20	Motor Racing	Monte Carlo Rally
19-21	Rugby Union	Heineken Cup, 6th rd
19-20	Skiing	World Cup, men, SG, DH *Kitzbühel, Austria*
19-20	Skiing	World Cup, women, DH, SG *Cortina d'Ampezzo, Italy*
19-21	Spd Skating	European S Track Chps *The Hague, Netherlands*
20	Athletics	Fila Int Cross-country *Belfast*
20	Basketball	BBL All Star Game *T'west Arena, Newcastle*
20-24	Cricket	S Africa v S L, 3rd Test *Centurion Park*
20-Feb 4	Handball	Men's World Chps, *France*
20-21	Spd Skating	World Sprint L Track Chps *Inzell, Germany*
20-21	Swimming	World Cup 8, *Berlin*
21	Cricket	Aus v Zimbabwe, 1-day *Sydney*
21-28	Ice Skating	European Championships *Bratislava, Slovakia*
21	Motor Cycling	Indoor Trial World Chp *Turin, Italy*
21	Skiing	World Cup, men, SL, C *Kitzbühel, Austria*
21	Skiing	World Cup, women, GS *Cortina d'Ampezzo, Italy*
22-28	Snowboarding	World Championships *Madonna, Italy*
23	Cricket	W I v Zimbabwe, 1-day *Sydney*
23	Skiing	World Cup, men, SL *Schladming, Austria*
24	Football	Worth'ton Cup, s-f, 2nd lgs
24	Basketball	European Chps, s-f rd Croatia v England
24-Feb 4	Bobsleigh	World Chps, men *St Moritz, Switzerland*
24-28	Snooker	Welsh Open, *Cardiff*
24-25	Swimming	World Cup 9, *Stockholm*
25	Cricket	W I v Zimbabwe, 1-day *Adelaide*
25-28	Golf	South African Open *East London GC*
25-28	Golf	Phoenix Open, *Arizona*
26	Athletics	Int Indoor Mtg, *Halle*
26	Cricket	Australia v W I, 1-day *Adelaide*
26	Rugby League	World Club Challenge St Helens v Brisbane *Bolton*
26-28	Rugby Union	Heineken Cup, q-fs
26-28	Rugby Union	World Cup Sevens *Mar del Plata, Argentina*
26	Skiing	World Cup, women, GS *Ofterschwang, Germany*
27	Football	Scottish Cup, 3rd round
27	Football	FA Cup, 4th round
27-28	Athletics	British Indoor Chps *Birmingham*
27	Athletics	International Indoor Mtg *Karlsruhe, Germany*
27	Basketball	European Chps, s-f rd *England v Hungary*
27	Fencing	Corble Cup, A grade men's sabre, *London*
27-28	Judo	Russian 'Super A', *Moscow*
27	Motor Cycling	Indoor Trial World Chp *Geneva, Switzerland*
27-28	Skiing	World Cup, men, DH, SG *Garmisch, Germany*
27	Skiing	World Cup, women, SL *Ofterschwang, Germany*
27-28	Swimming	World Cup 10, *Paris*
28	Am Football	Superbowl XXXV *Tampa, Florida*
28	Cricket	Aus v Zimbabwe, 1-day *Sydney*
28-30	Hockey	European Nations Cup Ind, A Div, women, *Vienna*
28-30	Hockey	European Nations Cup Ind, B Div, women, *Lievin*
28-Feb 10	Skiing	World Championships *St Anton, Austria*
29-Feb 4	Tennis	ATP Tour Event, *Milan*
29-Feb 4	Tennis	Colombia Open, ATP Tour
29-Feb 4	Tennis	WTA Tour Event, *Tokyo*
30	Cricket	Aus v Zimbabwe, 1-day *Hobart*
31-Feb 3	Bobsleigh	World Cup, women, *Nagano*
31	Cricket	NZ v S Lanka, 1-day *Napier*

February

1-2	Swimming	World Cup
Sheffield
1-4	Golf	Heineken Classic
Perth, Australia
1-4	Golf	Pebble Beach Pro-Am
California
2	Athletics	Millrose Games
New York
2	Cricket	W I v Zimbabwe, 1-day
Perth, Australia
3	Cricket	NZ v S Lanka, 1-day
Wellington
3-4	Cycling	World Cyclo-cross Chps
Tabor, Czech Republic
3	Rugby Union	Italy v Ireland, Six Nations
Rome
3	Rugby Union	Wales v England, Six Ntns
Cardiff
3-9	Squash	Tournament of Chpns, men
Central Station, New York
4	Football	Scottish League Cup, s-fs
4	Athletics	Sparkassan Cup - Indoors
Stuttgart
4	Athletics	Valencia Marathon
4	Athletics	Int Cross-country
Vilamoura, Portugal
4	Cricket	Aus v Zimbabwe, 1-day
Perth, Australia
4	Horse Racing	Hennessey Gold Cup
Leopardstown
4	Motor Cycling	Indoor Trial World Chp
Barcelona
4	Rugby Union	Six Nations
France v Scotland
4-11	Snooker	The Masters
Wembley CC
5-9	Bobsleigh	World Chps, women
Calgary, Canada
5-11	Tennis	Davis Cup, 1st round
5-11	Tennis	WTA Tour Event, Paris
6-11	Bobsleigh	World Skeleton Chps
Calgary, Canada
6-8	Bowls	Australia v England
Sydney
6	Cricket	NZ v Sri Lanka, 1-day
Auckland
6-11	Table Tennis	English Open
Chatham, Kent
7	Cricket	1-day Tournament, Final 1
Sydney
8	Cricket	NZ v Sri Lanka, 1-day
Hamilton

8-11	Golf	Buick International
LaJolla, California
8-11	Golf	Greg Norman Holden Int
The Lakes GC, Sydney
8-11	Ice Hockey	Olympic Qual Trnmt, women
Engelberg, Switzerland
8-11	Ice Hockey	Olympic Qual Trnmt, Grp A
men, Oslo, Norway
8-11	Ice Hockey	Olympic Qual Trnmt, Grp B
men, Klagenfurt, Austria
8-14	Ice Hockey	Euro Youth Olympic Winter
Days, Vuokatti, Finland
9	Cricket	1-day Tournament, Final 2
Melbourne
9-11	Motor Racing	Swedish Rally
10	Horse Racing	Tote Gold Trophy, Newbury
10	Motor Cycling	Indoor Trial World Chp
Lisbon, Portugal
10-11	Judo	Paris 'Super A' Tournament
10-17	Sailing	Tornado World Chp
Richards Bay, South Africa
10-11	Spd Skating	World Long Track Chps
Budapest, Hungary
11	Athletics	Sparkassen Cup - Indoors
Dortmund, Germany
11	Athletics	International Indoor Match
WAL-ENG-NIR, Cardiff
11	Cricket	1-day Tournament, Final 3
Melbourne
11	Cricket	NZ v Sri Lanka, 1-day
Christchurch
12-18	Tennis	ATP Tour Event, Marseille
12-18	Tennis	ATP Tour Event
Copenhagen
12-18	Tennis	ATP Tour Event, Chile
12-18	Tennis	WTA Tour Event, Nice
12-18	Tennis	WTA Tour Event, Doha
13	Football	Champions League, Grp C
B Munich v S Moscow
O. Lyonnais v Arsenal
		Champions League, Grp D
Leeds Utd v Anderlecht
Real Madrid v Lazio
14	Football	Wales v Mexico, friendly
Cardiff
14	Football	Champions League Grp A
Sturm Graz v Panathinaikos
Valencia v Man Utd
		Champions League Grp B
Galatasaray v Deportivo
AC Milan v PSG
14	Football	World Cup Qualifiers
Belgium v San Marino, Gp 6
Portugal v Andorra, Gp 2

15	Football	Ticket sales for the 2002 FIFA World Cup begin
15	Football	UEFA Cup 4th rd, 1st leg Porto v Nantes Roma v Liverpool AEK Athens v Barcelona Stuttgart v Celta Vigo Alaves v Inter Rayo Vallecano v Bordeaux PSV Einhoven v Parma Sl Prague v Kaiserslautern
15	Athletics	Global Galan - Indoors *Stockholm*
15-18	Golf	Bob Hope Classic *La Quinta, Indian Wells*
15-18	Golf	Carlsberg Malaysian Open *Saujana G & CC*
16	Athletics	Sydney Track Classic
16-18	Hockey	European Club Chp, A Div *men, Wettingen, Switzerland*
16	Motor Cycling	Ind Trial World Chp, *Vienna*
16-18	Skiing	World Cup, men, GS, SL x 2 *Shiga Kogen, Japan*
16-17	Skiing	World Cup, women, SG x 2 SL, *Garmisch, Germany*
16-25	Skiing	World Nordic Chps *Lahti, Finland*
16-18	Swimming	British GP, *Leeds*
17	Football	Scottish Cup, 4th round
17	Football	FA Cup, 5th round
17	Cricket	NZ v Pakistan, 1-day *Auckland*
17	Motor Cycling	Indoor Trial World Chp *Paris*
17	Rugby Union	Six Nations Ireland v France England v Italy Scotland v Wales
18	Athletics	Norwich Union Indoor GP Birmingham
19-25	Tennis	ATP Event, Buenos Aires
19-25	Tennis	ATP Championship Series *Rotterdam*
19-25	Tennis	ATP Championship Series *Memphis*
19-25	Tennis	WTA Tour Event, *Dubai*
19-25	Tennis	WTA Tour Event *Oklahoma*
20	Football	Champions League Grp A Panathinaikos v Sturm Graz Man Utd v Valencia Champions League Grp B Deportivo v Galatasaray PSG v AC Milan
20	Cricket	NZ v Pakistan, 1-day *Napier*

21	Football	Champions League Grp C Spartak Moscow v B Munich Arsenal v O Lyonnais Champions League Grp D Lazio v Real Madrid Anderlecht v Leeds Utd
22	Football	UEFA Cup 4th rd, 2nd leg Nantes v Porto Liverpool v Roma Barcelona v AEK Athens Celta Vigo v Stuttgart Inter v Alaves Bordeaux v Rayo Vallecano Parma v PSV Einhoven Kaiserslautern v Sl Prague
22	Cricket	NZ v Pakistan, 1-day *Wellington*
22-26	Cricket	S Lanka v England, 1st Test *Galle*
22-25	Golf	Singapore Masters
22-25	Golf	Nissan Open *Pacific Palisades, California*
23	Athletics	Flanders Indoor, *Ghent*
23-25	Hockey	European Club Chp, A Div women, *Les Ponts de Cé*
23-25	Luge	World Championships *Calgary, Canada*
23-25	Motor Racing	Cyprus Rally
24-25	Judo	Munich 'Super A' Trnmnt
24	Rugby Union	Tetley Bitter Cup Final *Twickenham*
24-25	Skiing	World Cup, men, DH, SG *Snow Basin, Utah*
24-25	Skiing	World Cup, women, DH, SG *Lenzerheide, Switzerland*
25	Football	Worthington Cup Final *Milennium Stdm, Cardiff*
25	Athletics	Meeting Gaz de France (Indoors), *Lievin*
25	Cricket	NZ v Pakistan, 1-day *Christchurch*
26-Mar 4	Skiing	World Disability Chps *Snow Basin, Utah*
26-Mar 4	Tennis	ATP Championship Series *Acapulco, Mexico*
26-Mar 4	Tennis	ATP Chp Series, *Dubai*
26-Mar 4	Tennis	ATP Tour Event *San Jose, USA*
26-Mar 4	Tennis	WTA Tour Event *Scottsdale, Arizona*
28	Football	Ireland v Denmark, friendly *Dublin*
28	Football	England v Spain, friendly *Villa Park*
28	Cricket	NZ v Pakistan, 1-day *Dunedin*

March

1	Athletics	Melbourne Track Classic
1-4	Golf	Dubai Desert Classic
1-4	Golf	Genuity Championship *Miami, Florida*
4	Motor Racing	Australian GP *Albert Park, Melbourne*
3	Athletics	Int Indoor Match FRA-GBR-GER-ITA, *Vittel*
3	Boxing	Naseem Hamed v Marco Antonio Barrera
3	Fencing	City of Glasgow, A grade men's epée
3	Motor Cycling	Indoor Trial World Chp *Bremen, Germany*
3	Rowing	Women's Eights Head *River Thames*
3	Rugby Union	Six Nations Italy v France England v Scotland Wales v Ireland
3	Skiing	World Cup, men, DH, SG *Kvitfjell, Norway*
4	Cycling	World Cycle Speedway Chps *Adelaide*
5-11	Tennis	ATP Tour Event *Scottsdale, USA*
5-11	Tennis	ATP Tour Event *Delary Beach, USA*
5-18	Tennis	WTA Tour Event *Indian Wells, USA*
6	Football	Champions League Grp C Arsenal v Spartak Moscow O Lyonnais v B Munich
		Champions League Grp D Real Madrid v Leeds Utd Lazio v Anderlecht
6-11	Bobsleigh	World Cup Finals, men *Lake Placid, USA*
7	Football	Champions League Grp A Sturm Graz v Valencia Panathinaikos v Man Utd
		Champions League Grp B Deportivo v PSG Galatasaray v AC Milan,
7-11	Badminton	Yonex All England *NIA, Birmingham*
7-11	Cricket	Sri Lanka v England 2nd Test, *Kandy*
7-11	Skiing	World Cup Final *Are, Sweden*
8	Football	UEFA Cup Quarter-finals
8-11	Archery	World Ski Archery Chps *Kubalonka, Poland*
8-11	Golf	Qatar Masters
8-11	Golf	Honda Classic *Coral Springs, Florida*
8-11	Squash	Irish Open, men *Dublin*
8-12	Cricket	New Zealand v Pakistan 1st Test, *Auckland*
9-11	Athletics	World Indoor Chps *Lisbon, Portugal*
9-13	Cricket	WI v South Africa, 1st Test *Georgetown, Guyana*
9-11	Motor Racing	Rally of Portugal
9-11	Spd Skating	World Long Track Chps, *single dist, Salt Lake City*
10	Football	Scottish Cup, quarter-finals
10	Football	FA Cup, quarter-finals
10	Cycling	World Cup, women *Canberra*
10-18	Snooker	Asian Masters, *Bangkok*
11-18	Cycling	Paris-Nice
11	Motor Cycling	Motocross World Chps *Bellpuig, Spain*
11	Motor Cycling	Superbike World Chp, rd 1 *Valencia*
11	Motor Racing	Monterray Grand Prix CART series
12-18	Tennis	Newsweek Champion Cup *Indian Wells, USA*
13-18	Archery	World Indoor Target Chps *Castellanza, Italy*
13	Football	Champions League Grp A Man Utd v Sturm Graz Valencia v Panathinaikos
		Champions League Grp B AC Milan v Deportivo PSG v Galatasaray
13-15	Horse Racing	Cheltenham Festival
14	Football	Champions League Grp C Bayern Munich v Arsenal Sp Moscow v O Lyonnais
		Champions League Grp D Leeds Utd v Lazio Anderlecht v Real Madrid
15	Football	UEFA Cup Quarter-finals
15-19	Cricket	NZ v Pakistan, 2nd Test *Hamilton*
15-19	Cricket	SL v England, 3rd Test *Colombo*
15-18	Golf	Turespaña Masters
15-18	Golf	Bay Hill Invitational *Orlando, Florida*
16-18	Diving	Grand Prix, *Manchester*
17-21	Cricket	WI v S Africa, 2nd Test *Port of Spain, Trinidad*

17	**Motor Cycling**	Indoor Trial World Chp *Madrid*
17	**Rowing**	Head of the River *River Thames*
17	**Rugby Union**	Six Nations France v Wales Scotland v Italy
18	**Football**	Scottish CIS Cup Final
18	**Cycling**	World Cup, women *Hamilton, New Zealand*
18-25	**Ice Skating**	World Championships *Vancouver, Canada*
18	**Motor Cycling**	Motocross World Chps *Valkenswaard, Netherlands*
18	**Motor Racing**	Malaysian GP *Kuala Lumpur*
19-Apr 1	**Tennis**	Ericsson Open *Miami*
22-25	**Golf**	Nabisco Chp, LPGA *Rancho Mirage, California*
22-25	**Golf**	THE PLAYERS Chp *Ponte Vedra Beach, Fla*
22-25	**Golf**	Madeira Island Open
22	**Horse Racing**	Flat Season Starts *Doncaster*
23	**Cricket**	S Lanka v England, 1-day *Premedasa*
23-25	**Motor Racing**	Rally Catalunya
23-25	**Swimming**	British GP, *Glasgow*
24	**Football**	World Cup Qualifiers: England v Finland, Gp 9 *Anfield, Liverpool* Germany v Albania, Gp 9 Croatia v Latvia, Gp 6 Scotland v Belgium, Gp 6 Bosnia v Austria, Gp 7 Spain v Liechtenst'n, Gp 7 Yugoslavia v Switzer'd, Gp 1 Russia v Slovenia, Grp 1 Luxemb'rg v Faroes, Gp 1 Andorra v Netherlands, Gp 2 Cyprus v Ireland, Gp 2 Bulgaria v Iceland, Gp 3 N Ireland v Czech R, Gp 3
24	**Football**	Malta v Denmark, Gp 3 Sweden v Macedonia, Gp 4 Turkey v Slovakia, Gp 4 Azerbaijan v Moldova, Gp 4 Ukraine v Belarus, Gp 5 Norway v Poland, Gp 5 Armenia v Wales, Gp 5 Hungary v Lithuania, Gp 5 Romania v Italy, Gp 5
24-25	**Athletics**	World Cross-country Chps *Dublin*
24	**Basketball**	Uni-ball Trophy Final
24	**Cycling**	Primavera Rosa, W Cup women

24	**Cycling**	Milan-San Remo, W Cup
24	**Horse Racing**	Dubai World Cup *Nad Al Sheba*
24-25	**Motor Cycling**	Trial World Championship Guernsey
24	**Rowing**	The Boat Race, *R Thames*
24	**Rugby Union**	Six Nations Ireland v England
24	**Spd Skating**	World S Track Team Chps *Nobeyama, Japan*
25	**Cricket**	S Lanka v England, 1-day *Premedasa*
25	**Hockey**	EHL Cup Finals
25	**Motor Racing**	Rio 200, CART series
25-31	**Squash**	Al Ahram Masters, men World GP Finals, women *Egypt*
25	**Horse Racing**	Irish Flat Season starts *The Curragh*
27-31	**Cricket**	NZ v Pakistan, 3rd Test *Christchurch*
27	**Cricket**	S Lanka v England, 1-day *Colombo*
27-Apr 1	**Snooker**	Irish Masters *Goffs Complex, Co Kildare*
28	**Football**	World Cup Qualifiers Albania v England, Gp 9 Greece v Germany, Gp 9 Scotland v S Marino, Gp 6 Liechtenstein v Bosnia, Gp 7 Austria v Israel, Gp 7 Russia v Faroes, Gp 1 Switzerland v Luxb'g, Gp 1 Slovenia v Yugoslavia, Gp 1 Portugal v Netherlands, Gp 2 Cyprus v Estonia, Gp 2 Andorra v Ireland, Gp 2 Czech R v Denmark, Gp 3 Bulgaria v N Ireland, Gp 3 Moldova v Sweden, Gp 4 Slovakia v Azerbaijan, Gp 4 Macedonia v Turkey, Gp 4 Poland v Armenia, Gp 5 Wales v Ukraine, Gp 5 Belarus v Norway, Gp 5 Georgia v Romania, Gp 5 Italy v Lithuania, Gp 5
28-Apr 1	**Badminton**	Grand Prix Finals
29-Apr 2	**Cricket**	WI v S Africa, 3rd Test *Bridgetown, Barbados*
29-Apr 1	**Golf**	BellSouth Classic *Duluth, Georgia*
30-Apr 1	**Spd Skating**	World Short Track Chps *Seoul*
31-Apr 8	**Curling**	World Championships *Lausanne, Switzerland*
31-Apr 1	**Ice Hockey**	Superleague play-offs semi-finals & final

April

Date	Sport	Event
1	Cycling	Archer International GP *High Wycombe*
1	Fencing	Ipswich Cup, A grade *women's epée*
1	Motor Cycling	Superbike World Chp, rd 2 *Kyalami, South Africa*
1	Motor Cycling	Motocross World Chps *Belo Horizonte, Brazil*
1	Motor Racing	Brazilian GP *Interlagos, Sao Paulo*
1	Rowing	Women's Boat Race *River Thames*
2-8	Ice Hockey	World Chp, women *Plymouth/Rochester, USA*
2-8	Tennis	Davis Cup, 2nd round
2-8	Tennis	WTA Tour Event, *Porto*
3-4	Football	Champions League q-f, 1st leg
5	Football	UEFA Cup s-f, 1st leg
5-8	Golf	The Masters *Augusta National, Georgia*
6-10	Cricket	WI v South Africa, 4th Test *St Johns, Antigua*
7	Athletics	European 10,000m Challenge *Barakaldo, Spain*
7	Horse Racing	Grand National, *Aintree*
7	Rugby Union	Six Nations Scotland v Ireland England v France
8	Football	FA Cup, semi-finals
8	Cycling	Tour of Flanders, W Cup, men
8	Motor Cycling	Japanese GP, *Suzuka*
8	Motor Racing	Toyota Grand Prix, CART *Long Beach, California*
8	Rugby Union	Six Nations Italy v Wales
8-15	Snooker	Scottish Open, *Aberdeen*
9-15	Tennis	ATP/WTA Tour Event *Estoril, Portugal*
9-15	Tennis	ATP Tour Event *Casablanca*
9-15	Tennis	WTA Tour Event *Amelia Island, USA*
10-15	Swimming	World Championship Trials *Manchester*
11	Basketball	Korac Cup Final, 1st leg Ronchetti Cup Final, 1st leg
12-16	Equestrianism	World Cup Final, jumping *Gothenberg, Sweden*
12-15	Golf	Worldcom Classic *Hilton Head, S Carolina*
12-15	Golf	Moroccan Open
13-16	Hockey	European Cup Winners' Cup
13-20	Table Tennis	Commonwealth Chps *New Dehli, India*
14	Football	Scottish Cup, Semi-finals
14	Athletics	Balmoral Road Races
14	Basketball	BBL Chp, round 1 *Skydome Arena, Coventry*
15	Cycling	Paris-Roubaix, World Cup
15	Motor Cycling	Motocross World Chps *Broadford, Australia*
15	Motor Racing	San Marino GP *Imola, Bologna*
15	Triathlon	World Cup 1 *Gamagori, Japan*
15-21	Ice Hockey	World Chp, Div 1 Gp B, men (includes GB), *Ljubljana*
16	Basketball	BBL Chp, quarter-finals *Skydome Arena, Coventry*
16	Horse Racing	Irish Grand National *Fairyhouse, Ireland*
16-22	Tennis	Monte Carlo Open ATP Masters Series
16-22	Tennis	WTA Tour Event *Charleston*
16-22	Tennis	WTA Tour Event, *Budapest*
17-18	Football	Champions League q-f, leg 2
17	Basketball	Saporta Cup *Varsovie, Poland*
17	Basketball	Ronchetti Cup Final, 2nd leg Korac Cup Final, 2nd leg
18	Basketball	End of NBA Regular Season
18	Cycling	Le Fleche Walloon, W Cup women, *Belgium*
19	Football	UEFA Cup Semi-finals
19-22	Golf	Algarve Portuguese Open
19-22	Wrestling	European Freestyle Chp *Varsovie, Poland*
19-23	Cricket	WI v South Africa, 5th Test *Kingston, Jamaica*
20-23	Cricket	First county chp matches
21	Basketball	BBL Chp, semi-finals *Skydome Arena, Coventry*
21	Horse Racing	Scottish Grand National *Ayr*
21-22	Judo	British Open Chps *NIA, Birmingham*
21-22	Motor Cycling	Trial World Championships *St Joan Abadesses, Spain*
21-23	Sailing	Yngling European Chp *Lake Garda, Italy*
21-May 7	Snooker	World Championships *Crucible Theatre, Sheffield*
22	Athletics	Flora London Marathon

22	Athletics	Rotterdam Marathon
22	Cycling	Liège-Bastogne-Liège, W Cup
22	Hockey	Premiership Finals
22	Motor Cycling	South African GP, *Welkom*
22	Motor Cycling	Superbike World Chp, rd 3 *Phillip Island, Australia*
22	Triathlon	World Cup 2 *Ishigaki, Japan*
23-May 6	Table Tennis	World Championships *Osaka, Japan*
23-29	Tennis	ATP Championship Series *Barcelona*
23-29	Tennis	ATP Tour Event, *Atlanta*
24-27	Horse Racing	Punchestown Festival
24-29	Weightlifting	European Championships *Trencin, Slovakia*
25	Football	World Cup Qualifiers Latvia v San Marino, Gp 6 Yugoslavia v Russia, Gp 1 Netherlands v Cyprus, Gp 2 Ireland v Andorra, Gp 2 Malta v Iceland, Gp 3
25	Football	Poland v Scotland, Friendly *Bydgoszcz, Poland*
26-29	Golf	Open de España, *Girona*
26-29	Golf	Greater Greensboro *Greensboro, North Carolina*
27-28	Rowing	World Cup *Princeton, New Jersey*
27-29	Swimming	British GP, *Bath*
28	Cricket	WI v South Africa, 1-day *Kingston, Jamaica*
28	Cycling	Amstel Gold, World Cup *Netherlands*
28	Horse Racing	Whitbread Gold Cup *Sandown*
28-May 13	Ice Hockey	World Championship, men *Cologne, Hanover & Nurb'g*
28-29	Motor Cycling	Trial World Chp *Paços de Ferreira, Portugal*
28	Triathlon	World Cup 3 *St Petersburg, USA*
29	Motor Cycling	Motocross World Chps *Genk, Belgium*
29	Motor Cycling	Superbike World Chp, rd 4 *Sugo, Japan*
29	Motor Racing	Texas 600, CART series *Fort Worth, Texas*
29	Motor Racing	Spanish GP, *Barcelona*
30-May 6	Tennis	ATP Tour Event, *Munich*
30-May 6	Tennis	ATP Tour Event, *Mallorca*
30-May 6	Tennis	WTA Tour Event, *Hamburg*
30-May 6	Tennis	WTA Tour Event

May

1	Cricket	The Trophy, round 1
1-2	Football	Champions League s-f, leg 1
2	Cricket	WI v South Africa, 1-day *St Johns, Antigua*
3-6	Golf	Classic of New Orleans *English Turn G & CC*
3-6	Golf	Open de France *Lyon GC*
4-6	Motor Racing	Rally Argentina
5-6	Football	Nationwide League last League matches
5	Basketball	BBL Championship Final *Wembley Arena*
5	Cricket	WI v South Africa, 1-day *Grenada*
5	Horse Racing	2000 Guineas *Newmarket*
5	Horse Racing	Kentucky Derby *Churchill Downs*
5-6	Gymnastics	European Sports Acro Chps *Faro, Portugal*
6	Athletics	Grand Prix Brasil *Rio*
6	Cricket	WI v South Africa, 1-day *Grenada*
6	Horse Racing	1000 Guineas *Newmarket*
6	Motor Cycling	Spanish GP *Jerez*
6	Motor Racing	Bosch Grand Prix, CART *Nazareth Speedway, Penn*
7	Football	AXA Women's FA Cup Final
7-13	Tennis	Italian Open, ATP Masters *Rome*
7-13	Tennis	German Open, WTA Tour *Berlin*
7-13	Tennis	WTA Tour Event, *Warsaw*
8-9	Football	Champions League s-f, leg 2
9	Cricket	WI v South Africa, 1-day *Bridgetown, Barbados*
10-13	Golf	Byron Nelson Classic *Irving, Texas*
10-13	Golf	International Open *The De Vere Belfry, Wishaw*
11-13	Basketball	European Cup Superleague *Final Four, Bercy, Paris*
12	Football	FA Cup Final *Millennium Stadium*
12	Athletics	Japan Grand Prix *Osaka, Japan*
12	Cricket	WI v South Africa, 1-day *Port of Spain, Trinidad*

12	**Rugby Union**	Zurich Championship Final *Twickenham*
12-16	**Sailing**	49er European Chp *Brest, France*
13	**Football**	Nationwide League play-offs semi-finals, 1st leg
13	**Motor Cycling**	Superbike World Chp, rd 5 *Monza, Italy*
13	**Motor Cycling**	Motocross World Chps *Teutschenthal, Germany*
13	**Motor Racing**	Austrian GP, *Spielberg*
13	**Triathlon**	World Cup 4, *Rennes, France*
14-20	**Tennis**	German Open, ATP Masters *Hamburg*
14-20	**Tennis**	Italian Open, WTA, *Rome*
14-20	**Tennis**	WTA Tour Event, *Antwerp*
15	**Cricket**	The Trophy, round 2
16	**Football**	UEFA Cup Final *Dortmund, Germany*
16	**Cricket**	WI v South Africa, 1-day *Arnos Vale*
17-21	**Cricket**	England v Pakistan, 1st Test *Lord's*
17-20	**Golf**	Mastercard Colonial *Fort Worth, Texas*
17-20	**Golf**	Open TPC of Europe *St Leon Rot, Heidelberg*
17-20	**Golf**	Italian Ladies' Open *Poggio dei Medici, Tuscany*
17-20	**Wrestling**	European Greco-Roman Chp *Antalya, Turkey*
18-20	**Judo**	European Championships *Paris*
19	**Football**	Premier League final matches
19-June 10	**Cycling**	Giro d'Italia
19-20	**Gymnastics**	European Artistic Team Chps *Riesa, Germany*
19	**Horse Racing**	Juddmonte Lockinge Stakes *Newbury*
19-20	**Motor Cycling**	Trial World Championship *Mons, Belgium*
19	**Motor Racing**	Firestone 500, CART *Twin Ring Motegi, Japan*
20	**Athletics**	Oregon Track Classic *Portland, Oregon*
20	**Motor Cycling**	French GP, *Le Mans*
20-27	**Tennis**	ATP World Team Chps
21-27	**Tennis**	ATP Tour Event *St Pölten, Austria*
21-27	**Tennis**	WTA Tour Event, *Strasbourg*
21-27	**Tennis**	WTA Tour Event, *Madrid*
22-23	**Cricket**	Super Cup, quarter-final
23	**Football**	Champions League Final *Milan*

23-26	**Multi-Events**	East Asian Games *Osaka, Japan*
24-27	**Golf**	Kemper Insurance Open *Potomac, Maryland*
24-27	**Golf**	German Ladies Open *Treudelberg GCC, Hamburg*
25	**Cricket**	Super Cup, semi-final
25-28	**Golf**	Volvo PGA Championship *Wentworth Club, Surrey*
25-27	**Swimming**	Speedo Super GP Final *Manchester*
26	**Football**	Scottish Cup Final
26	**Football**	Nationwide Div 3 Play-off Final
26-27	**Athletics**	International Multi-Events Mtg *Gotzis, Austria*
26	**Athletics**	Great Wall Marathon *China*
26-27	**Canoeing**	Slalom World Cup *Gournois, Switzerland*
26	**Horse Racing**	Irish 2000 Guineas *The Curragh*
27	**Football**	Nationwide Div 2 Play-off Final
27	**Athletics**	Prefontaine Classic *Eugene, USA*
27	**Cricket**	The Trophy, round 3
27	**Horse Racing**	Irish 1000 Guineas *The Curragh*
27	**Motor Cycling**	Superbike World Chp, rd 6 *Donington Park*
27	**Motor Cycling**	Motocross World Chps *Spa-Francorchamps, Belgium*
27	**Motor Racing**	Monaco GP
28	**Football**	Nationwide Div 1 Play-off Final
28-Jun 2	**Badminton**	Sudirman Cup *Seville, Spain*
28-Jun 2	**Multi-Events**	Games for theSmall States of Europe, *San Marino*
28-Jun 10	**Tennis**	French Open *Roland Garros, Paris*
30-Jun 10	**Football**	FIFA Confederations Cup *Japan/Korea*
31-Jun 3	**Canoeing**	Wildwater European Chps *Valsesia, Italy*
31-Jun 4	**Cricket**	England v Pakistan, 2nd Test *Old Trafford*
31-Jun 3	**Golf**	Chandler's British Masters *Woburn, Milton Keynes*
31-Jun 3	**Golf**	Memorial Tournament *Dublin, Ohio*
31-Jun 3	**Golf**	US Women's Open *Pine Needles Lodge & GC North Carolina*
31-Jun 3	**Table Tennis**	World Club Chp, men *China*

June

1-3	Motor Racing	Acropolis Rally *Greece*
1-4	Hockey	European Club Chp
2	Football	World Cup Qualifiers Greece v Albania, Gp 9 Finland v Germany, Gp 9 Croatia v San Marino, Gp 6 Belgium v Latvia, Gp 6 Spain v Bosnia, Gp 7 Liechtenstein v Israel, Gp 7 Russia v Yugoslavia, Gp 1 Faroes v Switzerland, Gp 1 Slovenia v Luxemb'g, Gp 1 Ireland v Portugal, Gp 2 Estonia v Netherlands, Gp 2 Iceland v Malta, Gp 3 N Ireland v Bulgaria, Gp 3 Denmark v Czech R, Gp 3 Turkey v Azerbaijan, Gp 4 Macedonia v Moldova, Gp 4 Sweden v Slovakia, Gp 4 Armenia v Belarus, Gp 5 Wales v Poland, Gp 5 Ukraine v Norway, Gp 5 Romania v Hungary, Gp 5 Georgia v Italy, Gp 5
2	Athletics	AAI Games *Bangor, Ireland*
3-10	Boxing	World Amateur Chps *Belfast*
2-3	Canoeing	Slalom World Cup *Merano, Italy*
2	Cycling	World Cup, women *Montreal*
2	Greyhounds	Greyhound Derby *Wimbledon*
2-3	Motor Cycling	Trial World Championship *Twin Ring Motegi, Japan*
3-10	Badminton	World Championships *Seville, Spain*
3-6	Equestrianism	Badminton Horse Trials *Gloucestershire*
3	Horse Racing	Prix du Jockey Club (French Derby) *Chantilly*
3	Motor Cycling	Italian GP *Mugello*
3	Motor Racing	Miller Lite 225, CART *West Allis, Wisconsin, USA*
3	Triathlon	World Cup 5 *Marseille*
5	Cricket	Australia v Middlesex, 1-day *Lord's*
6	Football	World Cup Qualifiers Greece v England, Gp 9 Albania v Germany, Gp 9 Latvia v Croatia, Gp 6
6	Football	World Cup Qualifiers San Marino v Belgium, Gp 6 Iceland v Bulgaria, Gp 6 Denmark v Malta, Gp 3 Israel v Spain, Gp 7 Switzerland v Slovenia, Gp 1 Luxembourg v Russia, Gp 1 Faroes v Yugoslavia, Gp 1 Estonia v Ireland, Gp 2 Czech R v N Ireland, Gp 3 Turkey v Macedonia, Gp 4 Sweden v Moldova, Gp 4 Azerbaijan v Slovakia, Gp 4 Norway v Belarus, Gp 5 Ukraine v Wales, Gp 5 Armenia v Poland, Gp 5 Lithuania v Romania, Gp 5 Hungary v Georgia, Gp 5
6-10	Squash	British Open *Birmingham*
6-9	Table Tennis	China Open (ITTF Pro Tour)
7	Cricket	Australia v Northants, 1-day
7	Cricket	England v Pakistan, 1-day Tournament, *Edgbaston*
7-10	Equestrianism	Bramham Horse Trials *West Yorkshire*
7-10	Golf	FedEx St Jude Classic *Memphis, Tennessee*
7-10	Golf	English Open *Forest of Arden Hotel*
7-10	Golf	French Ladies' Open *Arras GC, Anzin St Aubin*
8	Athletics	Meeting Sevilla 2001
8-10	Gymnastics	European Rhythmic Chps *Geneva*
8	Horse Racing	Vodafone Oaks *Epsom*
9-10	Athletics	International Decathlon *Arles, France*
9-10	Canoeing	Slalom World Cup *Tacen, Slovenia*
9	Cricket	Australia v Pakistan, 1-day tournament, *Cardiff*
9	Horse Racing	Vodafone Derby *Epsom*
9	Motor Cycling	Speedway World Chp GP *Cardiff*
9-10	Motor Cycling	Trial World Championship *Goldendale, Washington*
9	Rugby Union	Lions v Western Australia *Perth, Australia*
10	Athletics	Women's 10km, *Dublin*
10	Athletics	Bedfordshire Int Games *Bedford*
10	Cricket	England v Australia, 1-day tournament, *Bristol*

10	Cycling	First Union Liberty Classic W Cup, women *Philadelphia*
10	Horse Racing	Prix de Diane *Chantilly*
10	Motor Cycling	Superbike World Chp, rd 7 *Lausitzring, Germany*
10	Motor Cycling	Motocross World Chps *Kärtenring, Austria*
10	Motor Racing	Canadian GP *Montreal*
11	Athletics	Athens GP
11	Cricket	The Trophy, round 4
11-17	Tennis	Stella Artois, ATP Tour *Queen's Club, London*
11-17	Tennis	Gerry Weber Open, ATP *Halle, Germany*
11-17	Tennis	DFS Classic *Birmingham*
11-17	Tennis	WTA Tour Event *Tashkent, Uzbekistan*
12	Cricket	England v Pakistan, 1-day tournament, *Lord's*
12	Rugby Union	Lions v Queensland President's XV, *Townsville*
13-16	Golf	Evian Masters, women *Evian-les-Bains, France*
14	Athletics	Ericsson GP *Helsinki*
14	Cricket	England v Australia, 1-day tournament, *Old Trafford*
14	Cricket	Super Cup Final *Lord's*
14-17	Golf	US Open *Southern Hills CC, Tulsa*
14-16	Rowing	World Cup, *Seville*
16	Cricket	Pakistan v Australia, 1-day tournament, *Durham*
16	Rugby Union	Lions v Queensland Reds *Brisbane*
16	Rugby Union	South Africa v France *Ellis Park, Johannesburg*
17-July 7	Football	World Youth Chp *Argentina*
17	Athletics	Meeting de Geants du Nord *Lille, France*
17	Cricket	England v Pakistan, 1-day tournament, *Headingley*
17	Motor Cycling	Catalan GP *Barcelona*
June 17	Motor Cycling	Speedway World Chp Overseas Final, *Poole*
17	Motor Racing	Tenneco Grand Prix, CART *Belle Isle, Detroit*
18-22	Squash	Super Series Final, men *London*

18-24	Tennis	ATP/WTA Tour Event 's-Hertogenbosch, Ned
18-24	Tennis	Nottingham Open, ATP
18-23	Tennis	Direct Line Tournament *Eastbourne*
19	Cricket	Australia v Pakistan, 1-day tournament, *Trent Bridge*
19-22	Horse Racing	Royal Ascot
19	Rugby Union	Lions v Australia 'A' *Gosford, NSW*
21	Cricket	England v Australia, 1-day tournament, *The Oval*
21-24	Golf	Compaq European GP *Slaley Hall, Northumberland*
21-24	Golf	Buick Classic *Harrison, NY*
21-24	Golf	McDonald's LPGA *Evian-les-Bains, France*
21-24	Triathlon	European Championships *Carlsbad, Czech Republic*
22-July 1	Air Sports	World Air Games *Granada, Spain*
22-23	Athletics	European Cup, 2nd League Group A, *Riga, Latvia*
23-24	Athletics	European Cup, Super League, *Bremen, Germany*
22-23	Multi-Sports	Pacific Rim Chps *Los Angeles*
23-24	Athletics	European Cup, 1st League Group A, *Vaasa, Finland*
23-24	Athletics	European Cup, 1st League Group B, *Budapest*
23	Cricket	Final, 1-day tournament *Lord's*
23-24	Cycling	International Grand Prix *Meadowbank*
23-24	Rowing	Women's Henley
23	Rugby Union	Lions v NSW Watarahs *Sydney*
23	Rugby Union	South Africa v France *King's Park, Durban*
24	Motor Cycling	Motocross World Chps *Arsago Seprio, Italy*
24	Motor Cycling	Superbike World Chp, rd 8 *Misano, San Marino*
24	Motor Racing	G I Joe's 200, CART *Portland Raceway, Oregon*
24	Motor Racing	European GP *Nurburgring, Germany*
25-27	Cricket	MCC v Australia *Arundel, West Sussex*
25-July 8	Tennis	The Open Championships *Wimbledon*
26	Rugby Union	Lions v NSW Country *Coff Harbour, Australia*

27-July 1	Equestrianism	European Chps, jumping *Arnhem, Netherlands*
28-July 1	Golf	Greater Hartford Open *Cromwell, Connecticut*
28-July 1	Golf	Murphy's Irish Open *Fota Island, Cork*
29	Athletics	Golden Gala, Golden L *Rome*
29-July 1	Cricket	Essex v Australia *Chelmsford*
29-July 1	Rowing	World Cup, *Vienna*
29-July 6	Sailing	Star European Chp *Kalovig, Denmark*
30-July 1	Cycling	European M Bike Chps *Italy*
30-July 1	Motor Cycling	Trial World Championship *Foppolo, Italy*
30	Motor Cycling	Dutch GP *Assen, Netherlands*
30	Rugby Union	Lions v Australia *Brisbane*
30	Rugby Union	South Africa v Italy
30	Rugby Union	New Zealand v France
30-July 7	Sailing	Europe Class World Chp *Vilamoura, Portugal*

July

1-2	Athletics	Euro Cup, Combined Events *Oulu, Finland*
1	Horse Racing	Budweiser Irish Derby *The Curragh*
1	Motor Cycling	Motocross World Chps *Uddevalla, Sweden*
1	Motor Racing	French GP *Magny Cours*
1	Motor Racing	The Marconi GP, CART *Cleveland, Ohio*
2-6	Bowls	British Isles Chps *Belfast*
3-8	Fencing	European Championships *Koblenz, Germany*
3	Rugby Union	Lions v ACT Brumbies *Canberra*
4	Athletics	Athletissima 2001 *Lausanne*
4-8	Rowing	Henley Regatta
5-9	Cricket	England v Australia, 1st Test *Edgbaston*
5-8	Golf	Advil Western Open *Illinois, USA*
5-8	Golf	Smurfit European Open *The K Club, Dublin*
6	Athletics	Meeting Gaz de France *Golden League, St Denis*

6-8	Golf	Kellogg's Ladies Masters *Mottram Hall GC, Cheshire*
6	Motor Cycling	British GP *Donington Park*
7	Athletics	Cork City Games
7	Horse Racing	Eclipse Stakes *Sandown Park*
7	Rugby Union	Lions v Australia *Melbourne*
7	Triathlon	World Cup 7, *Toronto*
7-8	Cycling	International Grand Prix *Cardiff*
7-8	Motor Cycling	Trial World Championship *Troisfontaines, France*
7-29	Cycling	Tour de France
8	Motor Cycling	Superbike World Chp, rd 9 *Laguna Seca, California*
8-13	Athletics	NatWest Island Games *Douglas, IOM*
9	Athletics	Nikaia, *Nice*
9-18	Sailing	470 European Chp *Dun Laoghaire, Ireland*
9-15	Tennis	ATP Tour Event *Bastad, Sweden*
9-15	Tennis	ATP Tour Event *Gstaad, Switzerland*
9-15	Tennis	ATP Tour Event *Newport, Rhode Is, USA*
9-15	Tennis	WTA Tour Event *Klagenfurt, Germany*
9-15	Tennis	WTA Tour Event *Palermo, Italy*
10-12	Horse Racing	July Cup Meeting *Newmarket*
11	Football	Champions League, 1st qualifying round, 1st leg
12-15	Athletics	World Youth Chps *Debrecen, Hungary*
12-15	Golf	Greater Milwaukee Open *Wisconsin, USA*
12-15	Golf	Loch Lomond Invitational
12-14	Golf	Austrian Ladies' Open *Murhoff*
13	Athletics	Bislett Games, Golden L *Oslo, Norway*
13-15	Athletics	World Chps Trials *Birmingham*
13-16	Cricket	Somerset v Australia *Taunton*
13-15	Motor Racing	Safari Rally, *Kenya*
13-15	Rowing	World Cup Final, *Munich*
14-15	Canoeing	European Marathon Chps *Gyor, Hungary*
14-15	Motor Cycling	Trial World Championship *Sant Julia, Andorra*

14	**Rugby Union**	Lions v Australia *Sydney*
15	**Horse Racing**	Kildangan Stud Irish Oaks *The Curragh*
15	**Motor Cycling**	Motocross World Chps *Ernée, France*
15	**Motor Racing**	Molson Indy, CART series *Toronto*
15	**Motor Racing**	British GP *Silverstone*
15-21	**Sailing**	Yngling World Chp *Newport, Rhode Is*
16-22	**Mod Pentathlon**	World Championships *Millfield, Somerset*
16-26	**Multi-Events**	Maccabiah Games *Israel*
16-28	**Sailing**	Admiral's Cup *Cowes, Isle of Wight*
16-22	**Tennis**	ATP Championship Series Stuttgart
16-22	**Tennis**	Croatian Open, ATP Tour Event, Umag
16-22	**Tennis**	ATP Tour Event Amsterdam
16-22	**Tennis**	WTA Tour Event *Sopot, Poland*
16-22	**Tennis**	WTA Tour Event *Knokke-Heist, Belgium*
17	**Athletics**	DN Galan *Stockholm*
17-29	**Hockey**	World Cup Qualifer, men *Edinburgh*
17-29	**Swimming**	World Championships *Fukuoka, Japan*
18	**Football**	Champions League, 1st qualifying round, 2nd leg
19-23	**Cricket**	England v Australia, 2nd Test *Lord's*
19-22	**Golf**	Open Golf Championship *Royal Lytham & St Annes*
19-22	**Golf**	B C Open *Endicott, New York*
19-24	**Multi-Events**	Francophone Games *Ottawa & Hull, Canada*
20	**Athletics**	Herculis Zepter, Golden L *Monte Carlo*
21	**Rugby Union**	South Africa v New Zealand *Cape Town*
21	**Triathlon**	World Championships *Edmonton, Canada*
22-Aug 1	**Disab Sport**	Deaf World Games *Rome*
22	**Motor Cycling**	German GP *Sachsenring*
22	**Motor Racing**	Michigan 500, CART *Brooklyn, Michigan, USA*
22-27	**Multi-Events**	European Yth Olympic Days *Murcia, Spain*
23-29	**Tennis**	ATP Tour Event *San Marino*
23-29	**Tennis**	ATP Tour Event, *L Angeles*
23-29	**Tennis**	ATP Championship Series *Kitzbühel, Austria*
23-29	**Tennis**	WTA Tour Event *Stanford, USA*
23-29	**Tennis**	WTA Tour Event *Casablanca, Morocco*
24-25	**Cricket**	The Trophy, quarter-final
25-28	**Archery**	European Grand Prix Final *St Petersburg, Russia*
25	**Football**	Champions League, 2nd qualifying round, 1st leg
25-29	**Equestrianism**	Royal International Show *Hickstead*
26-29	**Golf**	John Deere Classic *Silvis, Illinois, USA*
26-29	**Golf**	TNT Dutch Open *Noordwijk, Netherlands*
26-29	**Golf**	Championship of Europe, women, *Royal Porthcawl*
26-28	**Gymnastics**	World Trampoline Chps *Odense, Denmark*
26-29	**Judo**	World Championships *Munich, Germany*
27	**Athletics**	Norwich Union British GP *Crystal Palace*
27-29	**Cycling**	World BMX Chps *Louisville, Kentucky*
28-30	**Cricket**	Hampshire v Australia *West End, Southampton*
28	**Horse Racing**	K George VI & Q Elizabeth Diamond Stakes, *Ascot*
28-Aug 4	**Orienteering**	World Championships *Tampere, Finland*
29	**Motor Cycling**	Superbike World Chp, rd 10 *Brands Hatch*
29	**Motor Racing**	German GP *Hockenheim, Germany*
29	**Motor Racing**	Target Grand Prix, CART *Cicero, Illinois*
29	**Triathlon**	World Cup 8 *Corner Brook, Canada*
30-Aug 12	**Football**	FIFA World Club Chp *Spain*
30-Aug 8	**Sailing**	Laser World Chps, *Cork*
30-Aug 5	**Tennis**	du Maurier Int, ATP Masters *Montreal, Canada*
30-Aug 5	**Tennis**	WTA Tour Event *San Diego, USA*
30-Aug 5	**Tennis**	WTA Tour Event *Basle, Switzerland*
31-Aug 4	**Horse Racing**	Goodwood Meeting

August

1	**Athletics**	DN Galan, GPI *Stockholm*
1	**Football**	Champions League, 2nd qualifying round, 2nd leg
1-5	**Canoeing**	European Canoe Polo Chps
		Bydgoxzcz, Poland
2-6	**Cricket**	England v Australia, 3rd Test *Trent Bridge*
2-5	**Golf**	The International *Castle Pines GC, Colorado*
2-5	**Golf**	Volvo Scandinavian Masters *Barseback G & CC, Sweden*
2-5	**Golf**	Weetabix Women's Open *Sunningdale GC, Berkshire*
2-12	**Sailing**	Star World Championships *Medemblik, Netherlands*
3-12	**Athletics**	World Championships *Edmonton, Canada*
3	**Cycling**	Trophée International, World Cup, women, *France*
4-5	**Canoeing**	Slalom World Cup *Troja, Prague, Czech Rep*
4-5	**Equestrianism**	Gatcombe Pk Horse Trials
4-11	**Sailing**	Cowes Week *Isle of Wight*
4-11	**Sailing**	Mistral European Chps *Marseille*
5	**Motor Cycling**	Motocross World Chps *Namur, Belgium*
5	**Triathlon**	World Chps, Long Distance *Frederica, Denmark*
6-12	**Tennis**	ATP Chp, ATP Masters *Cincinnati, USA*
6-12	**Tennis**	WTA Tour Event *Los Angeles*
7-8	**Football**	Champions League, 3rd qualifying round, 1st leg
8-10	**Cricket**	Sussex v Australia, *Hove*
9-12	**Golf**	The Wales Open, *Newport*
9-12	**Golf**	New Albany Golf Classic *Ohio*
9-12	**Golf**	Buick Open *Grand Blanc, Missouri*
9-12	**Golf**	Compaq Ladies' Open *Osterakers GC, Sweden*
10-12	**Equestrianism**	European Dressage Chp *Verden, Germany*
11-12	**Canoeing**	Slalom World Cup *Augsburg, Germany*
11-12	**Cricket**	The Trophy, semi-final
11	**Cycling**	San Sebastian Classic *World Cup, men*
11	**Cycling**	International Track Meeting *Manchester*
11-12	**Mod Pentathlon**	World Cup Final
11	**Rugby Union**	New Zealand v Australia *Dunedin*
12	**Horse Racing**	Phoenix Stakes *Leopardstown*
12	**Motor Cycling**	Motocross World Chps *Roggenburg, Switzerland*
12	**Motor Racing**	Miller Lite 200, CART *Lexington, Ohio, USA*
12	**Triathlon**	World Cup 9 *Yamaguichi, Japan*
13-19	**Tennis**	RCA Championship, ATP *Indianapolis, USA*
13-19	**Tennis**	Legg Mason Classic, ATP *Washington, USA*
13-19	**Tennis**	WTA Tour Event *Montreal, Canada*
15	**Football**	World Cup Qualifiers Yugoslavia v Faroes, Gp 1 Estonia v Cyprus, Gp 2
15-19	**Equestrianism**	World Driving Pairs Chp *Riesenbeck, Germany*
16-20	**Cricket**	England v Australia, 4th Test *Headingley*
16-19	**Golf**	West of Ireland Open
16-19	**Golf**	US PGA Championship *Atlanta AC, Georgia*
16-26	**Multi-Events**	World Games, *Akita, Japan*
17	**Athletics**	Weltklasse, Golden League *Zurich, Switzerland*
17-26	**Sailing**	Laser European Chps *Puck Bay, Poland*
17-19	**Table Tennis**	Women's World Cup
18	**Horse Racing**	Arlington Million *Arlington Heights, Illinois*
18-26	**Rowing**	World Championships *Lucerne, Switzerland*
18	**Rugby Union**	Australia v South Africa
18-25	**Sailing**	Tornado European Chp *Silvaplana, Switzerland*
18	**Triathlon**	World Cup 10 *Tiszaujvaros, Hungary*
19	**Athletics**	Norwich Union Classic *Gateshead*
19	**Cycling**	HEW-Cyclassics Cup, World Cup, men, *Hamburg*
19-26	**Hockey**	Champions Trophy, women *Amstelveen, Netherlands*
19	**Motor Cycling**	World Long Track Chp Final 2, *Kent*
19	**Motor Cycling**	Motocross World Chps *Gaildorf, Germany*

19	**Motor Racing**	Motorola 220, CART *Elkhart Lake, Wisconsin*
19	**Motor Racing**	Hungarian GP *Hungaroring, Budapest*
19-Sep 1	**Bowls**	EBA National Chps *Worthing*
20-26	**Golf**	Reno-Tahoe Open *Montreux G & CC, Nevada*
20-26	**Tennis**	ATP Tour Event, *Long Island*
20-25	**Tennis**	WTA Tour Event *New Haven, USA*
21-22	**Football**	Champions League, 3rd qualifying round, 2nd leg
21-23	**Horse Racing**	York Ebor Meeting
22-26	**Canoeing**	World Flatwater Chps *Poznan, Poland*
22-Sep 1	**Multi-Events**	Universiade, *Beijing*
23-27	**Cricket**	England v Australia, 5th Test *The Oval*
23-26	**Equestrianism**	Hickstead Derby
23-26	**Golf**	Scottish PGA Championship *Gleneagles Hotel*
23-26	**Golf**	WGC - NEC Invitational *Firestone CC, Akron, Ohio*
24	**Football**	European Super Cup *Stade Louis II, Monaco*
24	**Athletics**	Memorial Van Damme, Golden League, *Brussels*
24-26	**Golf**	Irish Ladies' Open *Faithlegg GC, Waterford*
24-26	**Motor Racing**	Rally of Finland
24-26	**Volleyball**	World Grand Prix Final *Macau*
25	**Rugby Union**	New Zealand v South Africa *Eden Park, Auckland*
25	**Triathlon**	World Cup 11 *Lausanne, Switzerland*
26	**Cycling**	Zurich Chp, World Cup, men
26	**Motor Cycling**	Czech Republic GP *Brno, Czech Republic*
27-Sep 9	**Tennis**	US Open *Flushing Meadow, New York*
29	**Cricket**	The 2002 Trophy, round 1
29-Sep 7	**Sailing**	Mistral World Chps *Athens, Greece*
30-Sept 2	**Equestrianism**	Burghley Horse Trials
30-Sep 2	**Golf**	BMW Open, *Munich*
30-Sep 2	**Golf**	Air Canada Chps *Surrey, British Columbia*
31	**Athletics**	ISTAF 2001, Golden League *Berlin*
31-Sep 2	**Golf**	Mexx Sport Ladies' Open *Netherlands*

September

1	**Athletics**	ISTAF 2000, Golden League *Berlin*
1	**Football**	World Cup Qualifiers Germany v England, Gp 9 Albania v Finland, Gp 9 Scotland v Croatia, Gp 6 Bosnia v Israel, Gp 7 Spain v Austria, Gp 7 Switzerland v Yugoslavia, Gp 1 Slovenia v Russia, Gp 1 Faroes v Luxembourg, Gp 1 Andorra v Portugal, Gp 2 Ireland v Netherlands, Gp 2 Iceland v Czech Rep, Gp 3 Malta v Bulgaria, Gp 3 Denmark v N Ireland, Gp 3 Macedonia v Sweden, Gp 4 Moldova v Azerbaijan, Gp 4 Slovakia v Turkey, Gp 4 Belarus v Ukraine, Gp 5 Wales v Armenia, Gp 5 Poland v Norway, Gp 5 Georgia v Hungary, Gp 5 Lithuania v Italy, Gp 5
1	**Cricket**	The Trophy, Final, *Lord's*
1	**Rugby Union**	Australia v New Zealand Stadium Australia, Sydney
1-2	**Canoeing**	World Marathon Chps *Stockton-on-Tess*
1-2	**Motor Cycling**	Trial World Championship *Nepomuk, Czech Republic*
2	**Horse Racing**	Moyglare Stud Stakes *The Curragh, Ireland*
2	**Motor Cycling**	Superbike World Chp, rd 11 *Oschersleben, Germany*
2	**Motor Cycling**	Motocross World Chps *Lierop, Netherlands*
2	**Motor Racing**	Belgian GP *Spa Francorchamps*
2	**Motor Racing**	Indy Vancouver, CART *Vancouver, British Columbia*
3-9	**Cycling**	Tour of Britain
4-7	**Multi-Events**	Goodwill Games *Brisbane, Australia*
5	**Football**	World Cup Qualifier England v Albania, Gp 9 Finland v Greece, Gp 9 San Marino v Croatia, Gp 6 Belgium v Scotland, Gp 6 Liechtenstein v Spain, Gp 7 Austria v Bosnia, Gp 7 Yugoslavia v Slovenia, Gp 1 Luxemb'g v Switzerland, Gp 1 Faroes v Russia, Gp 1 Netherlands v Estonia, Gp 2 Cyprus v Portugal, Gp 2 Czech Republic v Malta, Gp 3

5	**Football**	World Cup Qualifiers Bulgaria v Denmark, Gp 3 N Ireland v Iceland, Gp 3 Turkey v Sweden, Gp 4 Slovakia v Moldova, Gp 4 Azerbaijan v Macedonia, Gp 4 Ukraine v Armenia, Gp 5 Belarus v Poland, Gp 5 Norway v Wales, Gp 5 Georgia v Lithuania, Gp 5 Hungary v Romania, Gp 5
6-9	**Equestrianism**	Blenheim Horse Trials
6-9	**Golf**	Omega European Masters *Crans-sur-Sierre, Switzerland*
6-9	**Golf**	Bell Canadian Open *Royal Montreal GC, Quebec*
7-9	**Golf**	Int Ladies' Matchplay *Scotland*
8-9	**Canoeing**	Slalom World Cup *Waussau*
8	**Horse Racing**	Stanley Leisure Sprint Cup *Haydock*
8	**Horse Racing**	Irish Champion Stakes *Leopardstown*
8-16	**Cycling**	World Mountain Bike Chps *Vail, Colorado, USA*
8-16	**Sailing**	470 World Championships *Koper, Slovenia*
8-16	**Volleyball**	European Chps, men *Ostrava, Czech Republic*
8-17	**Multi-Sports**	South East Asia Games *Kuala Lumpur, Malaysia*
8-30	**Cycling**	Vuelta a Espana
9	**Athletics**	IAAF Grand Prix Final *Melbourne, Australia*
9	**Cycling**	Swiss GP, World Cup, women *Switzerland*
9	**Horse Racing**	Prix du Moulin *Longchamp, France*
9	**Motor Cycling**	Portuguese GP *Estoril*
9	**Motor Cycling**	Superbike World Chp, rd 12 *Assen, Netherlands*
10-16	**Tennis**	ATP Tour Event *Bucharest, Romania*
10-16	**Tennis**	President's Cup, ATP *Tashkent, Uzbekistan*
10-16	**Tennis**	WTA Tour Event *Hawaii, USA*
10-16	**Tennis**	WTA Tour Event *Sao Paulo, Brazil*
11-12	**Football**	Champions League, Gp Stage
11-14	**Multi-Events**	Mediterranean Games *Tunis*
11-16	**Triathlon**	World Duathlon Chps *Rimini, Italy*
12-15	**Cricket**	Final County Chp matches
13	**Football**	UEFA Cup, 1st round, 1st leg
13-16	**Golf**	WGC-American Express Chp *St Louis, Missouri*
13-16	**Golf**	Tampa Bay Classic *Palm Harbour, Florida*
13-16	**Golf**	Scottish Ladies' Open
14-24	**Sailing**	49er World Championships *Malcesine, Italy*
15	**Athletics**	Super Track & Field Meet *Yokohama, Japan*
15	**Horse Racing**	St Leger, *Doncaster*
15	**Horse Racing**	Irish St Leger *The Curragh*
15	**Motor Racing**	German 500, CART series *Lausitz, Germany*
15-22	**Bowls**	European Championships *St Helier, Jersey*
16	**Athletics**	BUPA Great North Run *Newcastle-South Shields*
16	**Cycling**	Tour of Rotterdam, W Cup women
16	**Horse Racing**	Prix Vermeille *Longchamp*
16	**Motor Cycling**	Motocross World Chps *Misano, Italy*
16	**Motor Racing**	Italian GP *Monza, Milan*
16	**Rugby League**	Super League regular season ends
16	**Horse Racing**	National Stakes *The Curragh, Ireland*
16-22	**Archery**	World Target Championships *Beijing*
17-22	**Tennis**	WTA Tour Event *Tokyo*
17-22	**Tennis**	WTA Tour Event *Quebec*
17-23	**Tennis**	ATP Tour Event *Shanghai, China*
17-23	**Tennis**	Davis Cup, 3rd round
18-19	**Football**	Champions League, Gp Stage
18-Oct 1	**Hockey**	World Cup Qualifer, women *Amiens/Abbeville, France*
20-23	**Canoeing**	World Slalom Championships *Ocoee River, Georgia, USA*
20-23	**Golf**	Marconi Pennsylvania Classic *Ligonier, Pennsylvania*
20-23	**Golf**	Trophée Lancôme, *Paris*
21-23	**Motor Racing**	Rally New Zealand
21-29	**Sailing**	Finn Gold Cup *Marblehead, Massachusetts*
21-23	**Squash**	European Club Chps *Rennes, France*

22	Horse Racing	Ayr Gold Cup
22	Motor Racing	Rockingham 500, CART *Rockingham Motor Speedway, Corby, Northants*
22-30	Volleyball	European Championships women, *Ostrava, Czech Rep*
23	Horse Racing	Prix de la Salamandre *Longchamp*
23	Motor Cycling	Valencian GP
23	Triathlon	World Cup 12, *Athens*
24-30	Tennis	ATP Tour Event, *Hong Kong*
24-30	Tennis	ATP Tour Event, *Palermo*
24-30	Tennis	WTA Tour Event, *Leipzig*
24-30	Tennis	WTA Tour Event, *Bali*
25-26	Football	Champions League, Gp Stage
25-29	Wrestling	World Championships *New York*
26-30	Cycling	World Track Championships *Anvers, Antwerp, Belgium*
27-30	Golf	Texas Open at La Cantera *San Antonio, Texas*
28	Football	UEFA Cup, 1st round, 2nd leg
28-30	Golf	The Ryder Cup *The De Vere Belfry, Wishaw*
29	Athletics	European 100km Chp *Winschoten, Netherlands*
29	Australian Rules	Grand Final, *Melbourne*
29	Horse Racing	Fillies' Mile, *Ascot*
29	Horse Racing	Queen Elizabeth II Stakes *Ascot*
29	Triathlon	World Cup 13, *Palermo*
30	Motor Cycling	Superbike World Chp, rd 14 *Imola, Italy*
30	Motor Racing	USA GP *Indy, Indianapolis*

October

1	Horse Racing	Prix de l'Arc de Triomphe *Longchamp*
1-7	Tennis	ATP/WTA Tour Event *Moscow*
1-7	Tennis	ATP/WTA Chp Series *Tokyo*
2	Horse Racing	Cheveley Park Stakes *Newmarket*
4-7	Golf	Linde German Masters *Gut Lärchenhof, Cologne*
4-7	Golf	Michelob Championship *Williamsburg, Virginia*
4-13	Weightlifting	World Championships *Nauru*
5-7	Motor Racing	San Remo Rally

6	Football	Germany v Finland, Gp 9 England v Greece, Gp 9 Croatia v Belgium, Gp 6 Scotland v Latvia, Gp 6 Yugoslavia v L'bourg, Gp 1 Russia v Switzerland, Gp 1 Slovenia v Faroes, Gp 1 Netherlands v Andorra, Gp 2 Portugal v Estonia, Gp 2 Ireland v Cyprus, Gp 2 Czech Rep v Bulgaria, Gp 3 Denmark v Iceland, Gp 3 Malta v N Ireland, Gp 3 Wales v Belarus, Gp 5 Armenia v Norway, Gp 5 Poland v Ukraine, Gp 5 Italy v Hungary, Gp 5 Romania v Georgia, Gp 5
6	Triathlon	Hawaii Ironman Triathlon
7	Football	World Cup Qualifiers Israel v Austria, Gp 7 Bosnia v Liechtenstein, Gp 7 Macedonia v Slovakia, Gp 4 Moldova v Turkey, Grp 4 Sweden v Azerbaijan, Gp 4
7	Athletics	World Half-marathon Chps *Bristol*
7	Cycling	Paris-Tours, W Cup, men
7	Horse Racing	Prix de l'Arc de Triomphe *Longchamp*
7	Motor Cycling	Pacific GP *Motegi, Japan*
7	Motor Racing	Texaco/Havoline GP, CART *Houston, Texas*
8-14	Tennis	ATP Chp Series, *Lyon*
8-14	Tennis	ATP Chp Series, *Vienna*
8-14	Tennis	WTA Tour Event *Filderstadt, Germany*
8-14	Tennis	WTA Tour Event, *Shanghai*
9-14	Cycling	World Road Racing Chps *Lisbon, Portugal*
9-14	Squash	Women's World Open *Melbourne*
11-14	Equestrianism	European Chps, eventing *Pau, France*
11-14	Golf	Belgacom Open *Knokke Heist, Belgium*
11-14	Golf	Invensys Classic *Las Vegas, USA*
13	Rugby League	Super League Grand Final *Old Trafford*
14	Motor Cycling	Australian GP *Phillip Island*
14	Motor Racing	Honda Grand Prix, CART *Laguna Seca, California*
14	Motor Racing	Japanese GP, *Suzuka*
14	Triathlon	World Cup 14, *Sydney*

15-20	Squash	World Men's Chps *Melbourne*
15-21	Tennis	Eurocard Open, ATP Master Series, *Stuttgart*
15-21	Tennis	WTA Tour Event *Zurich*
15-21	Tennis	WTA Tour Event *Bratislava, Slovakia*
16-17	Football	Champions League, Gp Stage
16-Nov 1	Fencing	World Championships *Nimes, France*
18-21	Golf	National Car Rental Classic *Lake Buena Vista, Florida*
18-21	Golf	The Links Championship *St Andrews*
19-21	Motor Racing	Corsica Rally
20	Cycling	Tour of Lombardy, W Cup
20-29	Gymnastics	World Rhythmic Chps *Vienna*
20	Horse Racing	Dubai Champion Stakes *Newmarket*
20	Horse Racing	Darley Dewhurst Stakes *Newmarket*
20-21	Judo	European Team Chps *Manchester*
21	Motor Cycling	Malaysian GP, *Sepang*
22-27	Squash	World Men's Team Chps *Melbourne*
22-28	Tennis	ATP Tour Event *St Petersburg, Russia*
22-28	Tennis	ATP Tour Event, *Basle*
22-28	Tennis	ATP Tour Event, *Stockholm*
22-27	Tennis	WTA Tour Event *Linz, Austria*
22-27	Tennis	WTA Tour Event, *Luxemb'g*
23-24	Football	Champions League, Gp Stage
25	Football	UEFA Cup, 2nd rd, 1st leg
25-28	Golf	Calloway Gardens Resort *Pine Mountain, Georgia*
25-28	Golf	BBVA Masters de Madrid
27	Horse Racing	Racing Post Tophy *Doncaster*
27	Horse Racing	Breeders' Cup Raceday *Belmont Park, New York*
28-Nov 4	Gymnastics	World Artistic Chps *Ghent, Belgium*
28	Motor Racing	Honda Indy 300, CART *Gold Coast, Queensland*
28	Triathlon	World Cup 15, *Rio*
29-Nov 4	Tennis	Open de Paris, *ATP Master Series*
29-Nov 4	Tennis	WTA Tour Chp, *Munich*
29-Nov 4	Tennis	WTA Tour Event, *K Lumpur*

November

1-4	Golf	Italian Open *Is Molas GC, Sardinia*
1-4	Golf	THE TOUR Championship *Houston, Texas*
1-4	Golf	S Farm Bureau Classic *Madison, Mississippi*
2-4	Motor Racing	Rally Australia
3-11	Hockey	Champions Trophy, men *Lahore, Pakistan*
4	Motor Cycling	Rio GP
4	Motor Racing	Marlboro 500, CART *California Spdway, Fontana*
4	Triathlon	World Cup 16, *Cancun*
5-11	Tennis	ATP World Doubles Chps
5-11	Tennis	WTA Tour Event, *Thailand*
6	Horse Racing	Melbourne Cup, *Flemington*
6-7	Football	Champions League, Gp Stage
8	Football	UEFA Cup, 2nd rd, 2nd leg
8-11	Golf	Volvo Masters, *Jerez*
8-11	Table Tennis	Men's World Cup
10	Rugby Union	England v Australia *Twickenham*
12-18	Tennis	Tennis Masters Cup *Lisbon, Portugal*
15-18	Golf	WGC - EMC World Cup *Gotemba, Japan*
17	Rugby Union	England v Romania *Twickenham*
20-21	Football	Champions League, Gp Stage
22	Football	UEFA Cup, 3rd rd, 1st leg
23-25	Motor Racing	Rally of Great Britain
24	Rugby Union	England v South Africa T*wickenham*
25	Horse Racing	Japan Cup, *Tokyo*
26-Dec 1	Tennis	Davis Cup Final

December

1	Horse Racing	Hennessey G Cup, *Newbury*
1-2	Horse Racing	Fairyhouse Meeting
4-5	Football	Champions League, Gp Stage
6	Football	UEFA Cup, 3rd rd, 2nd leg
8-9	Athletics	European X-country Chps *Thun, Switzerland*
13-16	Swimming	European Short Course Chps, *Antwerp*
19-23	Equestrianism	Olympia Showjumping
Dec 26	Horse Racing	King George VI Chase *Kempton*
Dec 27	Horse Racing	Welsh National, *Chepstow*

Federations

AMERICAN FOOTBALL
World League of American Football
99 Kings Road
London SW3 4PA
Tel: 0207 225 3070
Website: www.nfleurope.com

NFL (USA)
Tel: 001 212 450 2000
Website: www.nfl.com

ANGLING
National Federation of Anglers
Halliday House, Egginton Junction
Nr Hilton, Derbyshire DE65 6GU
Tel: 01283 734735
Website: www.the-nfa.org.uk/

ARCHERY
Grand National Archery Society
Lilleshall National Sports Centre
Newport, Shropshire TF10 9AT
Tel: 01952 677888
Website: www.gnas.org

International Federation (FITA)
Tel: 0041 21 6143050
Website: www.archery.org

ASSOCIATION FOOTBALL
The Football Association
16 Lancaster Gate
London W2 3LW
Tel: 0207 262 4542
Website: www.the-fa.org

International Federation (FIFA)
Tel: 0041 1 384 9595
Website: www.fifa.com

European Federation (UEFA)
Tel: 0041 2 299 4444
Website: www.uefa.com

The Football League
Unit 5, Edward VII Quay
Navigation Way
Preston, Lancs PR2 2YF
Tel: 01772 325800

Website:
Nationwide:
www.football.nationwide.co.uk

Football Association of Wales
3 Westgate Street, Cardiff CF1 1JF
Tel: 02920 372325
Website: www.faw.org.uk

Scottish Football Association
6 Park Gardens
Glasgow G3 7YE
Tel: 0141 332 6372
Website: www.scottishfa.co.uk

N Ireland Association
20 Windsor Avenue,
Belfast BT9 6EG
Tel: 02890 669458
Websote: www.irishfa.com

Women's Football Association
16 Lancaster Gate
London W2 3LW
Tel: 0207 262 4542

ATHLETICS
UK Athletics
10 Harbourne Road
Edgbaston
Birmingham B15 3AA
Tel: 0121 456 5098
Website: www.ukathletics.org/

International Federation (IAAF)
Tel: 00377 93 10 88 88
Website: www.iaaf.org

BADMINTON
Badminton Association of England
National Badminton Centre
Bradwell Road
Loughton Lodge
Milton Keynes MK8 9LA
Tel: 01908 268400

International Badminton Federation
Tel: 01242 221030
Website: www.intbadfed.org

BASEBALL
Baseball Softball UK
Ariel House
74a Charlotte Street
London W1P 1LR
Tel: 0207 453 7055
website: www.baseballsoftballuk.com

International Baseball Association
Tel: 0041 21 318 8240
Website: www.baseball.ch

Major League (USA)
Tel: 001 212 931 7800
Website:
www.majorleaguebaseball.com

BASKETBALL
English Basketball Association
48 Bradford Road, Stanningley
Leeds LS28 6DF
Tel: 0113 236 1166

British Basketball League
The Lodge, Castle Bromwich Hall
Chester Road,
Birmingham, B36 9DE
Tel: 01217491355
Website: www.bbl.org.uk

National Basketball Association (USA)
Tel: 001 212 407 8000
Website: www.nba.com

BILLIARDS AND SNOOKER
World Snooker
2 Ground Floor, Albert House
111-117 Victoria Street,
Bristol BS1 6AX
Tel: 0117 317 8200
Website: www.worldsnooker.com/

BOBSLEIGH
British Bobsleigh Association
Albany House
5 New Street
Salisbury SP1 2PH
Tel: 01722 340014
Website: www.british-bobsleigh.com

International Federation (FIBT)
Via Piranesi, 44/B
I20137 Milan, Italy
Tel: 0039 02 757 3319
Website: www.bobsleigh.com

BOWLS
English Bowling Association
Lyndhurst Road
Worthing BN11 2AZ
Tel: 01903 820222

World Bowls Board
Tel: 01903 247468

BOXING
Amateur Boxing Association
Crystal Palace Sports Centre
London SE19 2BB
Tel: 0208 778 0251

British Boxing Board of Control
Jack Petersen House
52A Borough High Street
London SE1 1XW
Tel: 0207 403 5879

CANOEING
British Canoe Union
John Dudderidge House
Adbolton Lane, West Bridgford
Nottingham NG2 5AS
Tel: 0115 982 1100
Website: www.bcu.org.uk

International Canoe Fed (FIC)
Tel: 0036 1 363 4832
Website: www.canoeicf.com

CRICKET
England and Wales Cricket Board
Lord's Cricket Ground
St John's Wood, London NW8 8QN
Tel: 0207 432 1200
Website: www.lords.org
General website (Cricinfo):
www-aus.cricket.org

CROQUET
The Croquet Association
Hurlingham Club, Ranelagh
Gardens, London SW6 3PR
Tel: 0207 736 3148
Website: www.croquet.org.uk

World Croquet Federation
Tel: 01270 820296
Website: www.worldcroquet.u-
net.com

CURLING
English Curling Association
Tel: 01923 825004

Royal Caledonian (Scottish Ass)
Tel: 0131 333 3003

World Curling Federation
81 Great King Street
Edinburgh EH3 6RN
Tel: 0131 556 4884
Website: www.curling.org

CYCLING
British Cycling Federation
Stewart Street
Manchester M11 4DQ
Tel: 0161 230 2301
Website: www.bcf.uk.com

International Cycling Union (UCI)
Tel: 00 41 21 622 0580
Website: www.uci.ch

DARTS
British Darts Organisation
2 Pages Lane, Muswell Hill
London N10 1PS
Tel: 0208 883 5055

PDC
1133 Hessle Road\
Kingston upon Hull, HU4 6SB
Tel: 01482 575400
Website: www.planetdarts.co.uk

EQUESTRIAN
British Equestrian Federation
British Equestrian Centre
Stoneleigh Park, Kenilworth
Warwickshire CV8 2LR
Tel: 02476 698871
Website: www.bef.co.uk

International Federation (FEI)
Tel: 0041 21 312 5656
Website: www.horsesport.org

FENCING
Amateur Fencing Association
1 Barons Gate, 33 Rothschild Rd
London W4 5HT
Tel: 0208 742 3032
Website: www.britishfencing.com

International Federation (FIE)
Tel: 0041 21 320 3115
Website:www.fie.ch

GOLF
European Golf Tour
Wentworth Drive, Virginia Water
Surrey GU25 4LX
Tel: 01344 842881
Website: www.europeantour.com

Women's European Tour
The Tytherington Club
Dorchester Way, Tytherington
Macclesfield SK10 2JP
Tel: 01625 611444
Website: www.ladieseuropeantour
.com

US PGA Tour
Tel: 001 904 285 3700
Website: www.pgatour.com

US LPGA Tour
Tel: 001 904 274 6200
Website: www.lpga.com

GREYHOUND RACING
National Greyhound Racing Club
Twyman House, 16 Bonny Street
London NW1 9QD
Tel: 0207 267 9256
Website: www.thedogs.co.uk

GYMNASTICS
**British Amateur Gymnastics
Association**
Ford Hall
Lilleshall National Sports Centre
Newport TF10 9NB
Tel: 01952 820330
Website: www.baga.co.uk

International Federation (FIG)
Tel: 0041 32 494 6410
Website: www.fig-gymnastics.com

HANDBALL
**International Handball
Association**
Tel: 0041 61 228 9040

British Handball Federation
Tel: 01706 229354
Website: www.englandhandball.com

HANG GLIDING
Hang Gliding and Paragliding
The Old School Room
Loughborough Road
Leicester LE4 5PJ
Tel: 0116 261 1322

HOCKEY
National Hockey Foundation
The Stadium, Silbury Boulevard
Milton Keynes MK9 1NR
Tel: 01908 246800
Website: www.hockeyonline.co.uk

International Federation (FIH)
Tel: 00 32 2 219 4537
Website:www.fihockey.org

HORSE RACING
British Horse Racing Board
42 Portman Square
London W1H 0EN
Tel: 0207 396 0011
Website: www.bhb.co.uk/bhb/

ICE HOCKEY
British Ice Hockey Association
The Galleries of Justice
Shire Hall, The Lace Market
Nottingham NG1 1HN
Tel: 0115 915 9204
Website: icehockeyuk.co.uk

International Federation (IIHF)
Website: www.iihf.com

National Hockey League (NHL)
Tel: 001 212 789 2000
Website: www.nhl.com

ICE SKATING
National Ice Skating Assoc of UK
Lower Parliament Street
Nottingham NG1 1LA
Tel: 0115 853 3100
Website: www.iceskating.org.uk

International Skating Union (ISU)
Tel: 0041 21 612 6666
Website:www.isu.org

JUDO
British Judo Association
7A Rutland Street
Leicester LE1 1RB
Tel: 0116 255 9669
Fax: 0116 255 9660
Website: www.britishjudo.org.uk

International Judo Federation
Tel: 0082 2 3398 1017
Website: ww.ijf.org

KARATE
English Karate Governing Body
Tel: 0208 599 0711
Website: www.ekgb.org.uk

World Karate Federation (WFK)
Tel: 00 30 1 271 7564
Website: www.wkf.net

LACROSSE
English Lacrosse Association
PO Box 2041, Reading RG4 7GU
Tel: 0161 834 4582
Website: www.englishlacrosse.co.uk

LUGE
International Federation (FIL)
Tel: 0049 86 526 6960
Website: www.fil-luge.org

MODERN PENTATHLON
Modern Pentathlon Assoc of GB
Pentathlon House
1 Mount Pleasant, Tadley
Hampshire RG26 4JH
Tel: 0118 981 7181

International Union of Modern Pentathlon
Tel: 00377 97 77 85 55
Website: www.pentathlon.org

MOTOR CYCLING
Auto-Cycle Union
ACU House, Wood Street, Rugby
Warwickshire CV21 2YX
Tel: 01788 540519

International Federation (FIM)
Tel: 0041 22 950 9500
Website:www.fim.com

MOTOR SPORTS
RAC Motor Sports Association
Motor Sports House
Riverside Park
Colnbrook, Slough SL3 OHG
Tel: 01753 681736

International Federation (FIA)
Tel: 00 33 1 43 12 44 66
Website:www.fia.com

NETBALL
All England Netball Association
Netball House
9 Paynes Park, Hitchin SG5 1EH
Tel: 01462 442344
Website: www.england-netball.co.uk

International Netball Fed (INF)
Tel: 0121 446 4451
Website: www.netball.org

OLYMPIC GAMES
International Olympic Committee
Chateau de Vidy
1007 Lausanne
Switzerland
Tel: 00 41 21 621 6111
Website: www.olympic.org

ORIENTEERING
British Orienteering Federation
Riversdale
Dale Road North, Darley Dale,
Matlock DE4 2HX
Tel: 01629 734042
Web: www.cix.co.uk/~bof/index.html

International Orienteering Federation (IOF)
Tel: 00358 9 348 13112
Website:www.orienteering.org

POLO
Hurlingham Polo Association
Manor Farm, Little Coxwell
Faringdon
Oxford SN7 7LW
Tel: 01367 242828
Website: www.hpa-polo.co.uk

REAL TENNIS AND RACKETS
Tennis and Rackets Association
c/o The Queens Club
Palliser Road
West Kensington
London W14 9EQ
Tel: 0207 386 3447
Website: www.real-tennis.com

ROWING
Amateur Rowing Association
The Priory, 6 Lower Mall
Hammersmith
London W6 9DJ
Tel: 0208 741 5314
Website: www.ara-rowing.org

International Federation (FISA)
Tel: 0041 21 617 8373
Website:www.fisa.org

RUGBY LEAGUE
The Rugby Football League
Red Hall, Red Hall Lane
Leeds LS71 8NB
Tel: 0113 232 9111
Website: www.rfl.co.uk

RUGBY UNION
The Rugby Football Union
Rugby Road
Twickenham, Middx TW1 1DZ
Tel: 0208 892 8161
Website: www.rfu.com

Irish Rugby Football Union
62 Lansdowne Road
Ballsbridge
Dublin
Tel: 00 3531 668 4601
Website: www.irfu.ie

Scottish Rugby Union
7/9 Roseburn Street
Edinburgh EH12 5PJ
Tel: 0131 3372346
Website: www.sru.org.uk

Welsh Rugby Union
PO Box 22, Cardiff CF1 1JL
Tel: 02920 390111
Website: www.wru.com

International Rugby Board (IRFB)
Tel: 00353 1 662 5444
Website: www.irfb.org

SAILING
Royal Yachting Association
RYA House, Romsey Road
Eastleigh
Hants SO50 9YA
Tel: 01703 629962
Website:www.rya.org.uk

International Federation (ISAF)
Tel: 01703 635111
Website: www.sailing.org

SHOOTING
National Rifle Association
Bisley Camp
Brookwood
Woking, Surrey GU24 0PB
Tel: 01483 797777
Website: www.bssc.org.uk

International Federation (ISSF)
Website: www.issf-shooting.org

SKIING
British Ski Federation
Hillend
Biggar Road
Midlothian EH10 7ER
Tel: 0131 445 7676
Web: www.complete-skier/skier/bssf

International Federation (FIS)
Tel: 00 41 33 244 6161
Website: www.fis-ski.com

SNOOKER
See Billiards

SPEEDWAY
British Speedway Promoters Association
Website: www.british-speedway.co.uk

SQUASH
Squash Rackets Association
PO Box 52
Manchester M12 5FF
Tel: 0161 231 4499
Website: www.squash.co.uk

World Squash Federation
Tel: 01424 429245
Website: www.worldsquash.org

SWIMMING
Amateur Swimming Association
Harold Fern House
Derby Square, Loughborough
Leics LE11 5AL
Tel: 01509 618700
Website: www.britishswimming.org

International Federation (FINA)
Tel: 0041 21 310 4710
Website: www.fina.org

TABLE TENNIS
English Table Tennis Association
Queensbury House
Havelock Road
Hastings TN34 1HF
Tel: 01424 722525
Website: www.etta.co.uk

International Table Tennis Federation
Tel: 00 41 21 340 7090
Website: www.ittf.com

TENNIS
Lawn Tennis Association
The Queens Club
Barons Court
West Kensington
London W14 9EG
Tel: 0207 381 7000
Website: www.lta.org.uk

International Tennis Federation
Tel: 0208 878 6464
Website: www.itftennis.com

International Men's Tennis (ATP)
Tel: 00377 93 50 44 77
Website: www.atptour.com

International Women's Tennis (WTA)
Tel: 001 203 978 1702
Website: www.wtatour.com

TENPIN BOWLING
British Tenpin Bowling Association
114 Balfour Road
Ilford
Essex IG1 4JD
Tel: 0208 478 1745
Website: www.gotenpin.co.uk

TRAMPOLINING
See Gymnastics

TRIATHLON
British Triathlon Association
PO Box 26
Ashby de la Zouche
Leicester LE65 2ZR
Tel: 01530 414234
Website: www.britishtriathlon.org

International Triathlon Union
Website: www.triathlon.org

VOLLEYBALL
English Volleyball Association
27 South Road, West Bridgford
Nottingham NG2 7AG
Tel: 0115 981 6324
Website: www.volleyballengland.org

International Federation
Tel: 00 41 21 345 3535
Website: www.fivb.ch

WATER SKIING
British Water Ski Federation
390 City Road
London EC1V 2QA
Tel: 0207 833 2855
Website: www.britishwaterski.co.uk

International Waterski Federation
Tel: 00 39 051 615 5015
Website: www.iwsf.com

WEIGHTLIFTING
British Amateur Weightlifters Association
131 Hurst Street
Oxford
OX4 1HE
Tel: 01865 790096
Website: www.bawla.com

International Weightlifting Federation
Tel: 00 36 1 353 0530
Website: www.iwf.net

WRESTLING
British Amateur Wrestling Association
41 Great Clowes Street
Salford
Greater Manchester M7 9RQ
Tel: 0161 832 9209
Website: www.homeusers.prestel.co.uk/bawa

International Federation (FILA)
Website: www.fila-wrestling.org

British World Champions

ARCHERY, FIELD
Women's Barebow: **Patricia Lovell**

ATHLETICS, OUTDOOR
110m Hurdles: **Colin Jackson**
Half-marathon: **Paula Radcliffe**
Cross-country, Long course: **Paula Radcliffe**

ATHLETICS, INDOOR
Men's 400m: **Daniel Caines**

BILLIARDS
Women: **Emma Bonney**

BOWLS, INDOORS
Men's Singles: **Robert Weale**
Men's Pairs: **Scotland** (Gourlay/Marshall)
Women's Singles: **Caroline McAllister**

BOWLS, OUTDOORS
Men's Singles: **Jeremy Henry**
Men's Pairs: **Scotland** (Sneddon/Marshall)
Men's Fours: **Wales** (Williams/Rees/Weale/
Thomas)
Women's Singles: **Margaret Johnston**
Women's Pairs: **Scotland**
(Letham/Lindores)

BOXING, PROFESSIONAL
WBO, Cruiserweight: **Johnny Nelson**
WBO, Supermiddleweight: **Joe Calzaghe**

CANOE POLO
Men's Team: **Great Britain**

CANOE SAILING
Men: **Leslie Noble**

CYCLING
Women's 3000m Pursuit: **Yvonne
McGregor**

CROQUET
Men's Individual: **Robert Fulford**

DARTS
PDC: **Phil Taylor**
BDO: **John Walton**

JUDO
Men's Under 81kg: **Graeme Randall**

MOTOR CYCLING
Speedway: **Mark Loram**
Trials: **Dougie Lampkin**
Sidecar: **Steve Webster/Paul Woodhead**

ORIENTEERING
Women's Short Distance: **Yvette Baker**

PARAGLIDING
Individual: **John Pendry**

RACKETS
Men's Singles: **James Male**
Men's Doubles: **Male/Hue-Williams**

REAL TENNIS
Women: **Penny Lumley**

ROWING
Men's Coxless Four: **Great Britain**
(Cracknell/Redgrave/Coode/Pinsent)
Men's Coxed Four: **Great Britain** (Smith/
Williams/Garbett/Dunn/Potts)
Men's Lwt Coxless Pair: **Great Britain**
(Myers/Taylor)

RUGBY LEAGUE
World Club Champions: **St Helens**

SHOOTING
World Sporting: **George Digweed**

SNOOKER
Men: **Ronnie O'Sullivan**
Women: **Lisa Quick**

SQUASH
Men's Individual: **Peter Nicol**

SWIMMING
Men's 50m Free, S-C: **Mark Foster**
Men's 50m Fly, S-C: **Mark Foster**
Men's 200m Fly, S-C: **James Hickman**
Women's 4 x 200m Free: **Great Britain**
(Sheppard/Huddart/Pickering/Rolph)

TRIATHLON
Duathlon: **Steph Forrester**

TUG-OF-WAR, OUTDOOR
Men's 560kg Club: **Sandhurst**
Men's 640kg club: **Felton Eccles**
Men's 720kg club: **St Patricks**

TUG-OF-WAR, OUTDOOR
Men's 560kg: **England;** Men's 640kg:
Scotland; Men's 680kg: **England**

WATER-SKIING
Men's Slalom: **Andy Mapple**
Women's Cableski Slalom: **Lisa Adams**

Sports Internet Directory

The sports internet directory (SID) is a selection of key sites, categorised alphabetically. We have also listed in a separate box, the sites which are our favourites, which best meet the requirements of ease of access, are constantly updated and offer reliable information. The nature of the internet means that we can offer no guarantee that the sites will still be as good next week as they were last. Some sites, like that of the International Cycling Fed (UCI) changed overnight from being extremely useful to inaccessible. Where sites have caused recent problems for us - repeatedly crashing the machine is the most frustrating - then we have starred the **website address**. For information, the research for this directory was done on an iMac (500), using an ADSL connection.

Air Sports

International Federation
www.fai.org

UK Federation
www.skygod.demon.co.uk

Others
www.paragliding.net

American Football

National Football League (NFL)
www.nfl.com

Arizona Cardinals	www.azcardinals.com
Atlanta Falcons	www.atlantafalcons.com
Baltimore Ravens	www.baltimoreravens.com
Buffalo Bills	www.buffalobills.com
Carolina Panthers	www.cpanthers.com
Chicago Bears	www.chicagobears.com
Cincinnati Bengals	www.bengals.com
Cleveland Browns	www.clevelandbrowns.com
Dallas Cowboys	www.dallascowboys.com
Denver Broncos	www.denverbroncos.com
Detroit Lions	www.detroitlions.com
Green Bay Packers	www.packers.com
Houston Texans	www.houstontexans.com
Indianapolis Colts	www.colts.com
Jacksonville Jaguars	www.jaguarsnfl.com
Kansas City Chiefs	www.kcchiefs.com
Miami Dolphins	www.miamidolphins.com
Minnesota Vikings	www.vikings.com
New England Patriots	www.patriots.com
New Orleans Saints	www.neworleanssaints.com
New York Giants	www.giants.com
New York Jets	www.newyorkjets.com
Oakland Raiders	www.raiders.com
Philadelphia Eagles	www.eaglesnet.com
Pittsburgh Steelers	www.pittsburghsteelers.com
San Diego Chargers	www.chargers.com
San Francisco 49ers	www.sf49ers.com
Seattle Seahawks	www.seahawks.com
St Louis Rams	www.stlouisrams.com
Tampa Bay Buccaneers	www.buccaneers.com
Tennessee Titans	www.titansonline.com
Washington Redskins	www.redskins.com

American Football (cont)

Superbowl
www.superbowl.com

NFL Europe
www.nfleurope.com

Amsterdam Admirals	www.admirals.nl
Barcelona Dragons	www.dragons.es
Berlin Thunder	www.berlin-thunder.de
Frankfurt Galaxy	www.frankfurt-galaxy.com
Rhein Fire	www.rhein-fire.de
Scottish Claymores	www.claymores.co.uk

Women's Pro Football
www.womensprofootball.com

College Football (NCAA)
www.ncaafootball.net

American Sports

Fox Sports
www.foxsports.com

ESPN
www.espn.go.com

CBS
www.sportsline.com

Angling

Federation of Fly Fishers
www.fedflyfishers.org

National Fed of Anglers
www.the-nfa.org.uk

Scottish Angling
www.dholt.demon.co.uk/index.ht

Angling News
www.angling-news.co.uk/

Archery

International Target Federation (FITA)
www.archery.org

International Field Archery Association (IFAA)
w.archery-ifaa.org

European and Mediterranean Archery Union
www.emau.com

The Grand National Archery Society (UK)
www.gnas.org

English Field Archery
www.fieldarcher.com

Association Football

International Federation (FIFA)
www.fifa.com

European Federation (UEFA)
www.uefa.com

National Federations

England	www.the-fa.org
Scotland	www.scottishfa.co.uk
Wales	www.faw.org.uk
Northern Ireland	www.irishfa.com
Ireland	www.fai.ie

World Cup 2002
www.fifaworldcup.com

English Premiership

Arsenal	www.arsenal.com
Aston Villa	www.avfc.co.uk
Blackburn Rovers	www.rovers.co.uk
Bolton Wanderers	www.bwfc.co.uk
Charlton Athletic	www.cafc.co.uk
Chelsea	www.chelseafc.co.uk
Derby County	www.dcfc.co.uk
Everton	www.evertonfc.com
Fulham	www.fulhamfc.co.uk
Ipswich Town	www.itfc.co.uk
Leeds United	www.lufc.com
Leicester City	www.lcfc.co.uk
Liverpool	www.liverpoolfc.tv
Manchester United	www.manutd.com
Middlesbrough	www.mfc.co.uk
Newcastle United	www.nufc.co.uk
Southampton	www.saintsfc.co.uk
Sunderland	www.safc.com
Tottenham Hotspur	www.spurs.co.uk
West Ham United	www.westhamunited.co.uk

English Division 1

Barnsley	www.barnsleyfc.co.uk
Birmingham City	www.bcfc.com
Bradford City	www.bradfordcityfc.co.uk
Burnley	www.burnleyfootballclub.com
Coventry City	www.ccfc.co.uk
Crewe Alexandra	www.crewealexfc.co.uk
Crystal Palace	www.cpfc.co.uk
Gillingham	www.gillinghamfootballclub.com
Grimsby Town	www.gtfc.co.uk
Manchester City	www.mcfc.co.uk
Millwall	www.millwallfc.co.uk
Norwich City	www.canaries.co.uk

SID Five-Star Sites

www.racingpost.com

The Racing Post's site is a wonderfully comprehensive horse racing form and news guide.

www.cricinfo.com

Fabulously comprehensive site, our only caveat that sometimes it has proved difficult to download on a Mac.

www.cyclingnews.com

Organised by date, so easier to find recent cycling events. Everything is there somewhere, though.

www.stevegtennis.com

The site they tried to ban. For men's tennis, Steve G's site is far more accessible than the mazy ATP site.

www.europark.com

Motor Cycling is not well-served, so the Japanese-inspired site gives valuable archive details.

Nottingham Forest	www.nottinghamforest.co.uk
Portsmouth	www.portsmouthfc.co.uk
Preston North End	www.pnefc.net
Rotherham United	www.themillers.co.uk
Sheffield United	www.sufc.co.uk
Sheffield Wednesday	www.swfc.co.uk
Stockport County	www.stockportcounty.com
Walsall	www.saddlers.co.uk
Watford	www.watfordfc.com
West Bromwich Albion	www.wba.co.uk
Wimbledon	www.wimbledon-fc.co.uk
Wolverhampton W	www.wolves.co.uk

English Division 2

Blackpool	www.blackpoolfc.co.uk
Bournemouth	www.afcb.co.uk
Brentford	www.brentfordfc.co.uk
Brighton & Hove Albion	www.seagulls.co.uk
Bristol City	www.bcfc.co.uk
Bury	buryfc.co.uk
Cambridge United	www.cambridgeunited.com
Cardiff City	www.cardiffcityfc.co.uk
Chesterfield	www.chesterfield-fc.co.uk
Colchester United	www.colchesterunited.net
Huddersfield Town	www.htafc.com
Northampton Town	www.ntfc.co.uk
Notts County	www.nottscountyfc.co.uk
Oldham Athletic	www.oldhamathletic.co.uk
Peterborough United	www.theposh.com
Port Vale	www.port-vale.co.uk
Queen's Park Rangers	www.qpr.co.uk
Reading	www.readingfc.co.uk
Stoke City	www.stokecityfc.co.uk
Swindon Town	www.swindonfc.co.uk
Tranmere Rovers	www.tranmererovers.co.uk
Wigan Athletic	www.wiganlatics.co.uk
Wrexham	www.wrexhamafc.co.uk
Wycombe Wanderers	www.wycombewanderers.co.uk

English Division 3

Bristol Rovers	www.bristolrovers.co.uk
Carlisle United	www.carlisleunited.co.uk
Cheltenham Town	www.the-robins.co.uk
Darlington	www.darlingtonfc.net
Exeter City	www.exetercityfc.co.uk
Halifax Town	www.halifaxafc.net
Hartlepool United	www.hartlepoolunited.co.uk
Hull City	www.hullcityafc.net
Kidderminster Harriers	www.harriers.co.uk
Leyton Orient	leytonorient.com
Lincoln City	www.redimps.com
Luton Town	www.lutontown.co.uk
Macclesfield Town	www.mtfc.co.uk
Mansfield Town	www.mansfieldtown.net
Oxford United	www.oufc.co.uk
Plymouth Argyle	www.pafc.co.uk
Rochdale	www.rochdaleafc.co.uk
Rushden & Diamonds	www.thediamondsfc.com
Scunthorpe United	www.scunthorpe-united.co.uk
Shrewsbury Town	www.shrewsburytown.co.uk
Southend United	www.southendunited.co.uk
Swansea City	www.swansfc.co.uk
Torquay United	www.torquayunited.com
York City	www.ycfc.net

Scottish Premiership
www.scotprem.com

Aberdeen	www.afc.co.uk
Celtic	www.celticfc.co.uk
Dundee	www.dundeefc.co.uk
DundeeUnited	www.dundeeunitedfc.co.uk
Dunfermline	www.dunfermline-athletic.com
Hearts	www.heartsfc.co.uk
Hibernian	www.hibs.co.uk
Kilmarnock	www.kilmarnockfc.co.uk
Livingstone	www.livingstonefc.co.uk
Motherwell	www.motherwellfc.co.uk
Rangers	www.rangers.co.uk
St Johnstone	www.stjohnstonefc.co.uk

Other Sites

www.teamtalk.com
www.fourfourtwo.com
www.football365.com
www.worldsoccer.com
www.soccernet.com
www.planetfootball.com
www.soccerbase.com

Athletics

International Federation (IAAF)
www.iaaf.org

European Athletic Association (EAA)
www.eaa-athletics.ch

UK Athletics
www.ukathletics.org

Other Federations

Amsterdam Admirals	www.admirals.nl
Athletics Australian	www.athletics.org.au
Athletics Canadian	www.athleticscanada.com
French Federation	www.athle.org
German Federation	www.dlv-sport.de
US Track & Field	www.ustaf.org

Track Events (Golden League)

Golden Gala-Rome	www.goldengala.it/
Gaz de France-Paris	www.gazdefrance.com
Bislett Games-Oslo	www.bislettgames.com
Herculis-Monaco	www.herculis.com
Weltklasse-Zurich	www.weltklasse.ch
Van Damme-Brussels	www.memorialvandamme.be
ISTAF - Berlin	www.istaf.de

Road Running

Marathon Assoc	www.aims-association.org
London Marathon	www.london-marathon.co.uk
Rotterdam Marathon	www.rotterdammarathon.nl
Berlin Marathon	www.berlin-marathon.com
New York Marathon	www.nyrrc.org
Boston Marathon	www.bostonmarathon.org

Magazines

Track and Field News	www.trackandfieldnews.com
Runners' World	www.runnersworld.com
Running Stats	www.runningstats.com

Australian Rules Football

International AF Confederation
www.iafc.org.au

Australian Football League
www.afl.com.au

British ARF League
www.barfl.co.uk

Badminton

International Federation (IBF)
www.intbadfed.org

European Badminton Union (EBU)
www.eurobadminton.org/

National Federations
England   www.baofe.co.uk
Wales   www.welshbadminton.net
Scotland   www.scotbadminton.demon.co.uk

General Badminton Site
www.worldbadminton.net

Baseball

Major League Baseball
www.mlb.com

International Baseball Association
www.baseball.ch

British Baseball
www.baseballsoftballuk.com

Basketball

National Basketball Association (NBA)
www.nba.org

Women's NBA
www.wnba.com

International Basketball Federation (FIBA)
www.fiba.com

British Basketball League (BBL)
www.bbl.org.uk

English Basketball
www.basketballengland.org.uk/

Other Sites
www.britball.co.uk
www.btinternet.com/~wordsworth.ma/homepage.htm

Biathlon

International Biathlon Union
www.ibu.at

Bobsleigh/Luge

International Bobsleigh Federation (FIBT)
www.bobsleigh.com

International Luge Federation
www.fil-luge.org

British Bobsleigh Association
british-bobsleigh.com

British Luge Association
www.gbla.org.uk

General Sites
www.bobsledder.com
www.luge.com

Bowls

English Bowling Association
www.bowlsengland.com

British Crown Green Bowling Association
www.bowls.org

General Site
www.bowlsclubs.co.uk

Boxing

World Boxing Council
www.wbcboxing.com

International Boxing Federation
www.ibf-usba-boxing.com

World Boxing Organisation
www.wbo-int.com/

World Boxing Association
www.wbaonline.com

International Amateur Boxing Association
www.aiba.net/

Other Sites
www.usatoday.com/sports/boxing/news.htm
www.sportsline.com/u/boxing/
www.ipcress.com/box
www2.xtdl.com/~brasslet/index.html
www.secondsout.com
www.boxing.clara.net
www.boxing-records.com
www.amateur-boxing.com
www.femboxer.com

Canoeing

International Canoe Federation
www.canoeicf.com

British Canoe Union
www.bcu.org.uk

Irish Canoe Union
www.irishcanoeunion.com

Precision (slalom newspaper)
www.canoekayak.com

Cricket

Cricinfo has established a near-monopoly in internet cricket, and is generally the best route to the various authorites, be it the ECB or the ICC

Cricinfo
www.cricinfo.com

Wisden
www.wisden.co.uk

Channel 4
www.cricket4.com

Other Sites
www.criclive.com
www.cricketline.com

Croquet

World Croquet Federation
www.worldcroquet.u-net.com

The Croquet Association
www.croquet.org.uk

Curling

There was no active website for the International Curling Association when the directory was compiled

Scottish Federation
www.scotcurl.co.uk

Canadian Federation
www.curling.ca

Cycling

International Cycling Union (UCI)
www.uci.ch

British Cycling Federation (BCF)
www.bcf.uk.com

Tour de France
www.letour.fr

Other Sites
www.cyclingnews.com
www.cyclingteams.com
www.cycling4all.com
www.descent-world.co.uk
www.bmxtra.com/news.htm

Darts

International Darts Players Association
www.idpa.net/

Professional Darts Corporation
www.planetdarts.co.uk

Equestrianism

International Federation (FEI)
www.horsesport.org

British Equestrian Federation
www.bef.co.uk

British Show Jumping Association
www.bsja.co.uk

British Dressage
www.britishdressage.co.uk

Events

Olympia	www.olympia-show-jumping co.uk
Badminton	www.badminton-horse.co.uk
Burghley	www.burghley.co.uk

Statistics Site
www.bcm.nl

General Site
www.equestrian.co.uk

Fencing

International Federation (FIE)
www.fie.ch

British Fencing Assocation
www.BritishFencing.com

Gaelic Sports

Gaelic Athletic Association
www.gaa.ie

Golf

US Men's Golf Tour
www.pgatour.com

European Men's Golf Tour
www.europeantour.com

US Women's Tour
www.lpga.com

European Women's Tour
www.ladieseuropeantour.com

English Golf Union (amateur)
www.englishgolfunion.org

US Golf Association (amateur)
www.usga.org

General Site
www.golf.com

Greyhound Racing

British Greyhound Racing Board
www.thedogs.co.uk

Magazine
www.greyhoundmonthly.com

Stud Directory
www.fredsharpe.freeserve.co.uk

Gymnastics

International Federation (FIG)
www.fig-gymnastics.com

European Gymnastics Union
www.gymnastics-ueg.org

British Gymnastics
www.baga.co.uk

US Gymnastics
www.usa-gymnastics.org

World Championship Site (Ghent)
www.worldchampgym2001.com

General Sites
www.gymmedia.com
www.gymn-forum.com

Rhythmic Gymnastics
rsg.net

Trampolining
www.tramp-net.com

Handball

European Federation (EHF)
www.eurohandball.com

England Handball Association
www.englandhandball.com

Hockey

International Federation (FIH)
www.fihockey.org

English Hockey Association (EHA)
www.hockeyonline.co.uk

Australian Hockey
www.hockey.org.au

German Hockey
www.german-fieldhockey.de

General Site
www.fieldhockey.com

Horse Racing

British Horseracing Board
www.bhb.co.uk

Weatherbys
www.weatherbys-group.com

USA Jockey Club
www.jockeyclub.com

Breeders Cup
www.breederscup.com

Irish Racing
www.irish-racing.com

French Racing
www.france-galop.fr

Racecourses

Aintree	www.aintree.co.uk
Ascot	www.ascot.co.uk
Cheltenham	www.cheltenham.co.uk
Epsom	www.epsomderby.co.uk
Goodwood	www.goodwood.co.uk
Newbury	www.newbury-racecourse.co.uk
Newmarket	www.newmarketracecourses.co.uk
Sandown	www.sandown.co.uk
York	www.yorkraceourse.co.uk

General Sites
www.racingpost.co.uk
www.racenews.co.uk
www.racemeetings.co.uk

Ice Hockey

International Ice Hockey Federation (IIHF)
www.iihf.com

US National Hockey League
www.nhl.com

UK Ice Hockey (IHUK)
www.icehockeyuk.co.uk

English Ice Hockey Association
www.eiha.co.uk

General Site
www.azhockey.com

Ice Skating

International Federation (ISU)
www.isu.org

British Federation (NISA)
www.iceskating.org.uk

US Federation
www.usfsa.org

Judo

International Federation (IJF)
www.ijf.org

British Federation (BJF)
www.britishjudo.org.uk

Scottish Federation
www.scotjudo.org

Karate

International Federation
www.wkf.net

European Federation
www.eku.com

English Federation
www.ekgb.org.uk

Modern Pentathlon

International Federation (UIMP)
www.pentathlon.org

British Federation
www.mpagb.easynet.co.uk

Motor Cycling

International Federation
www.fim.ch

British Federation (ACU)
www.acu.org.uk

World Superbikes
www.motonline.com

Grand Prix Racing
www.motograndprix.com

Sidecar Racing
www.sidecarworld.com

Speedway
www.speedwaygp.com

General Site
www.europark.com

Motor Racing

International Federation
www.fia.com

Formula 1
www.f1-online.com
www.formula1.com

Rallying
www.rally-live.com

US Championship Series (CART)
www.cart.com

Le Mans
www.club-arnage.com

Netball

International Federation (IFNA)
www.netball.org

All-England Assocation
www.england-netball.co.uk

New Zealand Association
www.netballnz.co.nz

Australian Association
www.netball.asn.au

Orienteering

International Federation
www.orienteering.org

British Federation
ww.cix.co.uk/bof

Polo

Hurlingham
www.hpa-polo.co.uk

US Association
www.uspolo.org

Rackets

General Site
www.rackets.co.uk

Real Tennis

General Site
www.real-tennis.com

Rowing

International Federation (FISA)
www.worldrowing.com

British Federation (ARA)
www.ara-rowing.org

The Boat Race
www.theboatrace.org

Henley Regatta
henley.rowing.org.uk

General Site
users.ox.ac.uk/~quarrell/

Rugby League

National Rugby League - Australia
www.nrl.com.au

British Amateur Rugby League
www.barla.org.uk

General Sites
www.planetrugbyleague.co.uk
rleague.com

Rugby Union

International Federation
www.irfb.com

National Governing Bodies

RFU (England)	www.rfu.com
Argentina	www.uar.com.ar
Australia	www.rugby.com.au
France	www.ffr.fr
Ireland	www.irfu.ie
Italy	www.federazioneitalianarugby.it
New Zealand	www.nzrugby.co.nz
Scotland	www.sru.org.uk
South Africa	www.sarugby.net
Wales	www.wru.co.uk

Six Nations
www.sixnationsweb.com

General Sites
www.planet-rugby.com
www.scrum.com

Sailing

International Federation (ISAF)
www.sailing.org

Royal Yachting Association
www.rya.org.uk

Americas Cup
www.americascup.org

Cowes Week
www.cowesweek.co.uk

Shooting

International Federation
www.issf-shooting.org

British Small-Bore (NSRA)
www.nsra.co.uk

British Clay Pigeon (CPSA)
www.cpsa

Skiing

InternationalFederation (FIS)
www.fis-ski.com

British Skiing
www.britski.org

World Cup
www.irisco.net

Snowboarding
www.mountainzone.com/Snowboard

Snooker

World Snooker
www.worldsnooker.com

General Sites
www.snookernet.com
www.110sport.com/snooker/

Squash

International Federation
www.squash.org

Women's Squash (wispa)
www.wispa.net

Men's Squash (PSA)
www.pas-squash.org

Swimming

International Federation (FINA)
www.fina.org

British Federation
www.britishswimming.org

US Federation
www.usa-swimming.org

Australian Federation
www.ausswim.telstra.com.au

British Diving
www.diving-gbdf.com

General Sites
www.swimnews.com
www.swiminfo.com

Table Tennis

International Federation
www.ittf.com

European Federation
www.ettu.org

English Federation
www.etta.co.uk

Taekwondo

International Federation
www.itf-taekwondo.com

Tennis

International Federation (ITF)
www.itftennis.com

Men's Tennis (ATP)
www.atptennis.com
www.stevegtennis.com

Women's Tennis (WTA)
www.sanexwta.com
www.acemantennis.com

Lawn Tennis Association
www.lta.org.uk

Events

Wimbledon	www.wimbledon.org
Australian Open	www.ausopen.org
French Open	www.frenchopen.org
US Open	www.usopen.org
Davis Cup	www.daviscup.org
ATP Masters Series	www.masters-series.com

Triathlon

International Federation (ITU)
www.triathlon.org

European Federation (ETU)
www.etu.org

British Federation (BTA)
www.britishtriathlon.co.uk

General Site
www.triathlonlive.com

Volleyball

International Federation
www.fivb.ch

Weightlifting

International Federation
www.iwf.net

European Federation
www.tradecenter.sm/ewf/

British Federation
www.weights.demon.co.uk

Archive Site
www.iat.uni-leipzig.de/weight.htm

Wrestling

International Federation
www.fila-wrestling.org

British Federation
www.homeusers.prestel.co.uk/bawa

Newspapers

The Guardian: www.guardianunlimited.co.uk

Daily Telegraph: www.telegraph.co.uk

The Times: www.thetimes.co.uk

The Independent: www.independent.co.uk

New York Times: www.nytimes.com

LA Times: www.lattimes.com

USA Today: www.usatoday.com

Sydney Morning Herald: www.smh.com.au

L'Equipe: www.lequipe.fr

Abbreviations

TIMES

Where a time is shown, hours minutes and seconds are separated by a colon. A full point is used only as a decimal point for parts of a second. eg 3 hours 23 minutes and 7.5 seconds is shown as 3:23:7.50

In cycling events, the time for each rider is shown as the difference between themselves and the winner, using either @ or + sign.

st   same time

OTHERS

WR	World Record
ER	European Record
BR	British Record
J	Junior
w/o	Walk over
ret	Retired
aet	After extra time

COUNTRIES

AFG	Afghanistan		ENG	England
AHO	Netherlands Antilles		ERI	Eritrea
ALB	Albania		ESA	El Salvador
ALG	Algeria		ESP	Spain
AND	Andorra		EST	Estonia
ANG	Anguilla		ETH	Ethiopia
ANO	Angola		FIJ	Fiji
ANT	Antigua and Barbuda		FIN	Finland
ARG	Argentina		FKI	Falkland Islands
ARM	Armenia		FRA	France
ARU	Aruba		FRO	Faeroe Islands
ASA	American Samoa		FSM	Federated States of Micronesia
AUS	Australia			
AUT	Austria		GAB	Gabon
AZE	Azerbaijan		GAM	The Gambia
BAH	Bahamas		GBR	Great Britain and NI
BAN	Bangladesh		GBS	Guinea-Bissau
BAR	Barbados		GEO	Georgia
BDI	Burundi		GER	Germany
BEL	Belgium		GHA	Ghana
BEN	Benin		GIB	Gibraltar
BER	Bermuda		GRE	Greece
BHU	Bhutan		GRN	Grenada
BIH	Bosnia-Herzegovina		GUA	Guatemala
BIZ	Belize		GUE	Guernsey
BLR	Belarus		GUI	Guinea
BOL	Bolivia		GUM	Guam
BOT	Botswana		GUY	Guyana
BRA	Brazil		HAI	Haiti
BRN	Bahrain		HKG	Hong Kong
BRU	Brunei		HON	Honduras
BUL	Bulgaria		HUN	Hungary
BUR	Burkina Faso		INA	Indonesia
CAF	Central African Republic		IND	India
CAM	Cambodia		IOM	Isle of Man
CAN	Canada		IRL	Ireland
CAY	Cayman Islands		IRI	Iran
CGO	Congo		IRQ	Iraq
CHI	Chile		ISL	Iceland
CHN	People's Rep of China		ISR	Israel
CIV	Cote d'Ivoire		ISV	US Virgin Islands
CKI	Cook Islands		ITA	Italy
CMR	Cameroon		IVB	British Virgin Islands
COD	D R of Congo		JAM	Jamaica
COL	Colombia		JER	Jersey
COM	Comoros		JOR	Jordan
CPV	Cape Verde		JPN	Japan
CRC	Costa Rica		KEN	Kenya
CRO	Croatia		KGZ	Kyrgyzstan
CUB	Cuba		KIR	Kiribati
CYP	Cyprus		KOR	Korea
CZE	Czech Republic		KSA	Saudi Arabia
DEN	Denmark		KUW	Kuwait
DJI	Djibouti		KZK	Kazakhstan
DMN	Dominica		LAO	Laos
DOM	Dominican Republic		LAT	Latvia
ECU	Equador		LBA	Libya
EGY	Egypt		LBR	Liberia

LES	Lesotho	OMA	Oman	SUR	Surinam
LIE	Liechenstein	PAK	Pakistan	SVK	Slovak Republic
LTU	Lithuania	PLW	Palau	SWE	Sweden
LUX	Luxemburg	PAN	Panama	SWZ	Swaziland
MAC	Macedonia	PAR	Paraguay	SYR	Syria
MAD	Madagascar	PER	Peru	TAN	Tanzania
MAR	Morocco	PHI	Philippines	TCI	Turks and Caikos Islands
MAS	Malaysia	PNG	Papua New Guinea	TGA	Tonga
MAW	Malawi	POL	Poland	THA	Thailand
MDA	Moldova	POR	Portugal	TJK	Tadjikistan
MDV	Maldives	PRK	North Korea	TKM	Turkmenistan
MEX	Mexico	PUR	Puerto Rico	TOG	Togo
MKD	FYR of Macedonia	QAT	Qatar	TPE	Taiwan (Chinese Taipei)
MLI	Mali	ROM	Romania	TRI	Trinidad & Tobago
MLT	Malta	RSA	South Africa	TUN	Tunisia
MGL	Mongolia	RUS	Russia	TUR	Turkey
MNT	Montserrat	RWA	Rwanda	TUV	Tuvalu
MON	Monaco	SAM	Samoa	UAE	United Arab Emirates
MOZ	Mozambique	SCO	Scotland	UGA	Uganda
MRI	Mauritius	SEN	Senegal	UKR	Ukraine
MTN	Mauritania	SEY	Seychelles	URU	Uruguay
MYA	Myanmar	SIN	Singapore	USA	United States
NAM	Namibia	SKN	St Kitts and Nevis	UZB	Uzbekistan
NAU	Nauru	SLE	Sierra Leone	VAN	Vanuatu
NCA	Nicaragua	SLO	Slovenia	VIE	Vietnam
NED	Netherlands	SMR	San Marino	VEN	Venezuela
NEP	Nepal	SOL	Solomon Islands	VIN	St Vincent and the
NFI	Norfolk Islands	SOM	Somalia		Grenadines
NGR	Nigeria	SRI	Sri Lanka	WAL	Wales
NIG	Niger	STH	St Helena	YUG	Yugoslavia
NIR	Northern Ireland	STL	St Lucia	ZAM	Zambia
NOR	Norway	STP	Sao Tome and Principe	YEM	Yemen
NIU	Niue	SUD	Sudan	ZIM	Zimbabwe
NZL	New Zealand	SUI	Switzerland		